Kerrie M
Kurt Van
Samuel Erskine
Steve Buchanan

with Anders Bengtsson
Jakob Gottlieb Svendsen
Kathleen Wilson
Kenneth van Surksum
Oskar Landman
Patrik Sundqvist
Peter Quagliariello

System Center 2012 Service Manager

UNLEASHED

SAMS | 800 East 96th Street, Indianapolis, Indiana 46240 USA

System Center 2012 Service Manager Unleashed

ISBN-13: 978-0-672-33707-9
ISBN-10: 0-672-33707-X

Library of Congress Control Number: 2014936271

Printed in the United States of America

First Printing September 2014

Trademarks

All terms mentioned in this book that are known to be trademarks or service marks have been appropriately capitalized. Sams Publishing cannot attest to the accuracy of this information. Use of a term in this book should not be regarded as affecting the validity of any trademark or service mark.

Warning and Disclaimer

Every effort has been made to make this book as complete and as accurate as possible, but no warranty or fitness is implied. The information provided is on an "as is" basis. The author and the publisher shall have neither liability nor responsibility to any person or entity with respect to any loss or damages arising from the information contained in this book.

Special Sales

For information about buying this title in bulk quantities, or for special sales opportunities (which may include electronic versions; custom cover designs; and content particular to your business, training goals, marketing focus, or branding interests), please contact our corporate sales department at corpsales@pearsoned.com or (800) 382-3419.

For government sales inquiries, please contact governmentsales@pearsoned.com.

For questions about sales outside the U.S., please contact international@pearsoned.com.

Editor-in-Chief
Greg Wiegand

Acquistions Editor
Joan Murray

Development Editor
Mark Renfrow

Managing Editor
Kristy Hart

Senior Project Editor
Lori Lyons

Copy Editor
Geneil Breeze

Indexer
Tim Wright

Proofreader
Kathy Ruiz

Technical Editor
Anders Ravnholt

Editorial Assistant
Cindy Teeters

Cover Designer
Mark Shirar

Senior Compositor
Gloria Schurick

Contents at a Glance

Table of Contents

Part V   Beyond Service Manager

20   Management Packs   629

About the Authors

Kerrie Meyler, MVP, is the lead author of numerous System Center books in the Unleashed series, including *System Center 2012 Operations Manager Unleashed* (2013), *System Center 2012 Orchestrator Unleashed* (2013), *System Center 2012 Configuration Manager Unleashed* (2012) and *System Center 2012 R2 Configuration Manager Unleashed Supplement* (2014). She is an independent consultant with more than 17 years of Information Technology experience. Kerrie was responsible for evangelizing SMS while a Sr. Technology Specialist at Microsoft, and has presented on System Center technologies at TechEd and MMS.

Kurt Van Hoecke, MVP, managing consultant at inovativ Belgium, focuses on the System Center product suite, including Service Manager, Configuration Manager, and Orchestrator. Kurt is a coauthor to *System Center 2012 Orchestrator Unleashed* (2013) and contributor to *System Center Service Manager 2010 Unleashed* (2011). Kurt has been working with Service Manager beginning with the beta versions and has a number of Service Manager deployments to his credit.

Samuel Erskine, MCT, MCTS, is an independent IT consultant specializing in Service Manager and Configuration Manager. He was the lead author of *Microsoft System Center 2012 Service Manager Cookbook* (Packt, 2012) and *Microsoft System Center 2012 Orchestrator Cookbook* (Packt, 2013), and was a contributing author to *System Center 2012 Configuration Manager Unleashed* (2012) With more than 18 years of IT experience, Samuel focuses on providing training and consultancy services in the United Kingdom and other locations and blogs at www.itprocessed.com.

Steve Buchanan, MVP, MCITP, MCSE, is a regional solution lead with Concurrency. Steve has worked in IT for 14 years with a focus on systems management. He coauthored *Microsoft System Center Data Protection Manager 2012 SP1* (Packt, 2013) and authored *Microsoft System Center Data Protection Manager 2010* (Packt, 2011). Steve enjoys blogging about his adventures in systems management and cloud technologies at www.buchatech.com.

About the Contributors

Anders Bengtsson is a Microsoft senior premier field engineer, focusing on System Center and Microsoft Cloud OS. His projects include building dynamic data centers and automated self-service solutions. Anders has written a number of System Center training courses and workshops, including the Service Manager and Operations Manager advanced courses for Microsoft Learning. Prior to joining Microsoft, Anders was a Microsoft MVP from 2007-2010 for his work in the System Center community, including more than 10,000 posts in news groups and forums. He has presented at numerous Microsoft conferences and events, including TechDays, MMS, and TechEd, and coauthored *System Center 2012 Orchestrator Unleashed* (2013) and *System Center Service Manager 2010 Unleashed* (2011).

Jakob Gottlieb Svendsen, MVP, is a senior consultant, trainer, and chief developer at Coretech A/S, a System Center Gold Partner and member of the System Center Alliance. Since starting at Coretech in 2007, he has focused on scripting and development, primarily developing tools, extensions, and scripts for System Center. His primary product focus is Orchestrator & Windows Azure Pack/Service Management Automation. He has presented at TechEd and is a member of the TechNet Influencers team. Jakob has authored several System Center courses for Coretech and blogs at http://blog.coretech.dk/jgs.

Kathleen Wilson is an Architect at Microsoft in the Worldwide Datacenter Center of Excellence Team, focusing on developing solutions for cloud management, operations, and support. Previously in Microsoft Consulting Services, Kathleen focused on Service Manager, Service Management, and Private Cloud, and has worked with Service Manager since 2009. Kathleen received her first ITIL certification in 1998 and is an ITIL v3 Expert. She is a coauthor of *Microsoft System Center: Optimizing Service Manager* (Microsoft Press, 2013) and coauthored the Service Manager 2010 and Service Manager 2012 courses for Microsoft Learning.

Kenneth van Surksum, MCT and previous MVP, is a trainer and System Center consultant at insight24, a company based in the Netherlands. With over 10 years of experience, Kenneth has worked with Service Manager from its launch in 2010. Kenneth was a contributing author to *System Center 2012 Configuration Manager Unleashed* (2012) and *System Center 2012 R2 Configuration Manager Unleashed Supplement* (2014), and coauthored *Mastering Windows 7 Deployment* (Sybex, 2011). He blogs at http://www.vansurksum.com and is chief editor for several websites about virtualization and cloud computing, http://www.virtualization.info and http://www.cloudcomputing.info.

Oskar Landman, a consultant at inovativ in The Netherlands and previous MVP, has more than 10 years of IT consulting experience. Oskar focuses on Service Manager, Operations Manager, and Orchestrator, delivering System Center solutions to large enterprise customers combining these products. Oskar is also one of the founders of www.authoringfriday.com, a blog focusing on advanced extensions and customizations for Service Manager, Operations Manager, and Orchestrator. Oskar was a contributing author to *System Center 2012 Operations Manager Unleashed* (2013) and *System Center Service Manager 2010 Unleashed* (2011).

Patrik Sundqvist, CTO and co-founder of Gridpro and previous MVP, works as a solutions architect and developer focusing on self-service and process automation and has spent the last 10 years building process automation solutions on top of Microsoft's products. Patrik has worked with Service Manager since its early betas and coauthored *System Center Service Manager 2010 Unleashed* (2011).

Peter Quagliariello is a consultant with Acceleres, a Microsoft Silver Partner for Management and Virtualization. He has worked with Service Manager since its release in 2010 and led numerous Service Manager implementation and optimization projects for clients. Peter has been ITIL-certified since 1998 and is a contributor to Microsoft Operations Framework (MOF). His consulting career also includes many IT service management assessment and implementation projects.

Dedication

In memory of Jack Meltzer, who was always a guiding light.

Dad, you are deeply missed. Rest in peace.

Acknowledgments

Writing a book is an all-encompassing and time-consuming project, and this book certainly meets that description. The authors and contributors would like to offer their sincere appreciation to all those who helped with *System Center 2012 Service Manager Unleashed*. This includes ClearPointe Technology for dedicating lab resources, John Joyner for his assistance with the lab, Ranganathan Srikanth, Anshuman Nangia, and Anders Ravnholt of Microsoft, Raymond Chou, Nate Lasnoski, and Pete Zerger.

We would also like to thank our spouses and significant others for their patience and understanding during the many hours spent on this book.

Thanks also go to the staff at Pearson, in particular to Neil Rowe, who worked with us since *Microsoft Operations Manager 2005 Unleashed* (Sams, 2006), Joan Murray, Lori Lyons, Loretta Yates, and Cindy Teeters.

We Want to Hear from You!

As the reader of this book, *you* are our most important critic and commentator. We value your opinion and want to know what we're doing right, what we could do better, what areas you'd like to see us publish in, and any other words of wisdom you're willing to pass our way.

We welcome your comments. You can email or write to let us know what you did or didn't like about this book—as well as what we can do to make our books better.

Please note that we cannot help you with technical problems related to the topic of this book.

When you write, please be sure to include this book's title and author as well as your name and email address. We will carefully review your comments and share them with the author and editors who worked on the book.

Email: consumer@samspublishing.com

Mail: Sams Publishing
          ATTN: Reader Feedback
          800 East 96th Street
          Indianapolis, IN 46240 USA

Reader Services

Visit our website and register this book at informit.com/register for convenient access to any updates, downloads, or errata that might be available for this book.

Foreword

Service Manager is a vision—an addition to System Center built to be "the most customizable and extensible product in the System Center suite." The growth of this System Center component, its impact on customers, and third-party integration since its release, are astounding. This growth has driven the birth of a community that is deeply entrenched and passionate about Service Manager. They have been a catalyst for the solution, its growth, and the proprietors of Service Manager. Twitter, blogging, eBooks, online videos, and presentations have fed to form user groups and social champions that drive feedback directly to Microsoft.

Service Manager is a complex component with unique capabilities that drive adoption of processes, proven simply by you reading this book. Directions, best practices, and knowledge from MVPs, social leaders, and Microsoft are all scribed in the pages to follow. Each dedicated their time to grow the understanding and delivery of this versatile platform.

Service management is a critical component of today's cloud, and the clouds of the future for private and hybrid scenarios. The cloud's automation is the key component for consumers of technology, from small to the largest enterprise. Service Manager is the glue of these vast systems, providing configuration, incident, change, and problem management. Integration with the entire System Center suite enables you to obtain a more flexible workflow engine with Orchestrator, Operations Manager, and Configuration Manager to catalog your assets, track requests, route alerting, automated resolution and tasks, and broadens capabilities from simple service request fulfillment to connecting complex processes in public clouds such as Windows Azure or other service providers.

The focus of this book is to help you, the IT professional, use this platform to be plugged into the process and armed with getting your Service Manager implementation underway. Before getting started with Service Manager's platform, a key thing to remember is it's not just about this software. The fact is, it's about service management, understanding the services your organization provides, and how to measure. Are you are managing risk? Operating efficiently? How are costs impacting the business?

Kathleen Wilson, one of the contributors to this book, said it best: "Service Manager requires you to understand your process and how people in IT interact with each other; just because you can customize and script it does not mean it's useful. Service Manager is about people and process first."

Take the time to realize you don't just install Service Manager because you own it, but to transform your organization; giving it the visibility, integration, and extensible platform to be successful.

The coauthors and contributors to this book will guide you through the key components you need to be successful. They have been awarded our most esteemed recognitions for their contributions. We leave you in the best hands as you take this journey forward.

See you out there!

Christian Booth, former Sr. Program Manager: Windows Server / System Center and Global Program Lead, MVP System Center: Cloud and Datacenter, Microsoft Corporation

Srikanth Ranganathan, Principal Lead Program Manager: Windows Server / System Center, Microsoft Corporation

Introduction

System Center 2012 Service Manager builds on Microsoft's Service Manager 2010 release, adding enhanced authoring capabilities, release management, service request fulfillment, chargeback, a new self-service portal, and integration with System Center Orchestrator for increased automation capabilities. Service Manager's level of integration with the Information Technology Infrastructure Library (ITIL) and Microsoft Operations Framework (MOF) is unique among the System Center components.

Service Manager provides built-in processes based on industry best practices and is a departure from other System Center components in that it is not fundamentally a technology management tool, but a work management tool. To make the most of Service Manager requires understanding the work it is intended to manage: the work associated with managing Information Technology (IT) services. Service Manager is also infinitely customizable. Its essence is a customizable platform with solutions on top.

Service Manager is unique for other reasons—the fact that it touches so many different types of individuals in an organization, and because of its high level of integration with other System Center components through connectors and its centralized data warehouse. By unifying knowledge across System Center, Service Manager helps IT align to business needs while lowering time to resolution.

A Toolset That Delivers IT as a Service

Service Manager 2012 provides a toolset to standardize service delivery; integrate people, process, and knowledge; and standardize data center processes.

Service Manager helps standardize service delivery by

- ▶ **Enabling self-service for application owners and end users:** Service Manager's service catalog provides application owners and end users access to standardized service offerings that span applications and infrastructure. Role-based policies enable application owners to make their requests, which are fulfilled automatically by Service Manager. Templates and workflows help you easily author and publish service offerings that align with your own business processes.

- ▶ **Enabling self-service requests for private cloud infrastructure:** You can provision and allocate infrastructure requests to internal IT business units based on their requirements, submitted through the self-service portal, and specify service level agreements (SLAs) with different tiers of availability for infrastructure resources. Costs for storage, network, and compute resources can be tracked and charged to internal cost centers.

- ▶ **Delivering self-service business intelligence:** Service Manager makes self-service reporting simple and easy to use through dashboards. Its data warehouse offers a comprehensive view of your enterprise by pulling data from multiple data sources, including other System Center components and Active Directory. Integration with

Microsoft Office helps enhance your ability to customize operational and business service reports.

Service Manager integrates people, processes, and knowledge across enterprise infrastructure and applications by

▶ **Enabling compliance and standardization:** The Service Manager configuration management database (CMDB) captures relationships across infrastructure and applications and facilitates continued compliance.

▶ **Standardizing data center processes:** Processes are standardized using workflows built around industry best practices.

▶ **Using connectors:** Connectors import data automatically from Active Directory and other System Center components. In addition, the Orchestrator connector supports fulfilling service requests through process automation capabilities such as runbook execution, while the Virtual Machine Manager connector imports library data including virtual machine and service templates into the CMDB, enabling users to request service offerings through the self-service portal.

▶ **Enabling management of your private cloud:** Service Manager tracks configuration items such as virtual machine templates, application service templates, virtual machines, physical hosts, and application services to help you manage a private cloud.

Service Manager standardizes data center processes with best practice workflows by

▶ **Providing process workflows built on industry best practices:** Workflows exist for incident management, problem management, service level agreement (SLA) management, and service request fulfillment. These help you deliver predictable operational SLAs for your data center application and infrastructure services.

▶ **Offering closed-loop change and release management:** This management is integrated into the service request fulfillment process, helping mitigate risks arising from high-impact changes that could span multiple application and infrastructure components.

About This Book

System Center 2012 Service Manager Unleashed focuses on the core capabilities of Service Manager 2012: its relationship to MOF and ITIL, integration with other System Center components, design, planning, installation, how it works, and extensibilities. Because of the high level of integration with ITIL, a number of chapters focus on process.

This book is divided into six sections:

Part I, "Service Manager Overview and Concepts," introduces service management and Service Manager, discussing its history, concepts, relationship to MOF and ITIL, and architectural design. These topics are discussed in Chapter 1, "Service Management Basics"; Chapter 2, "Service Manager History and Terminology"; Chapter 3, "MOF, ITIL, and System Center"; and Chapter 4, "Looking Inside System Center 2012 Service Manager."

Part II, "**Planning and Installation**," steps through design, planning, and installation. Chapter 5, "Planning and Designing System Center 2012 Service Manager," discusses envisioning and planning for Service Manager 2012, delving into physical design topologies and including licensing considerations. Chapter 6, "Installing and Upgrading to System Center 2012 Service Manager," steps through the installation process.

Part III, "**Service Manager Operations**," focuses on Service Manager operations and processes in your environment. This includes Chapter 7, "Using Service Manager"; Chapter 8, "Working with Connectors"; Chapter 9, "Business Services"; Chapter 10, "Service Manager Service Catalog"; Chapter 11, "Incident Management"; Chapter 12, "Automation and Chargeback"; Chapter 13, "Problem Management"; Chapter 14, "Change Request and Configuration Management"; and Chapter 15, "Release Management."

Part IV, "**Administering Service Manager**," includes Chapter 16, "Managing Notifications"; Chapter 17, "Service Manager Security"; and Chapter 18, "Maintenance, Backup, and Recovery." These chapters discuss those key functionalities and their use in Service Manager. Chapter 19, "Managing Service Manager Performance," is a must-read for Service Manager administrators in shops of all sizes.

Part V, "**Beyond Service Manager**," looks at going beyond the box. Service Manager is extremely customizable and extensible with no two installations using it the same way. This section includes Chapter 20, "Management Packs"; Chapter 21, "Data Warehouse and Reporting"; Chapter 22, "Customizing Service Manager"; and Chapter 23, "Advanced Customization Scenarios." Chapter 24, "Using PowerShell," explores the power of PowerShell and shows what can be done beyond the Service Manager console.

Part VI, "**Appendixes**," includes three appendixes. Appendix A, "User Role Profiles Supplement," includes tables on user role profile classes and relationship permissions and mapping user file profiles with ITIL/MOF roles. Appendix B, "Reference URLs," incorporates useful references you can access for further information, and Appendix C, "Available Online," is a guide to supplementary resources offered with the book that you can download from Pearson's website at http://www.informit.com/store/system-center-2012-service-manager-unleashed-9780133744194.

Fast Track: A Quick Look at What's New

Many chapters in this book include a "Fast Track" section. Fast Track is an aid to Service Manager 2010 administrators who are familiar with *System Center Service Manager 2010 Unleashed*. This section provides a quick overview of what has changed from the previous version. Some features have major enhancements, some relatively few, and some are completely new. Chapters covering new features and topics such as design and installation do not include a Fast Track.

Disclaimers and Fine Print

As always, there are several disclaimers. The information provided is probably outdated the moment the book goes to print. In addition, the moment Microsoft considers code development on any product complete, it begins working on a service pack or future release; as the authors continue to work with the product, it is likely yet another one or two wrinkles will be discovered! The authors and contributors of *System Center 2012 Service Manager Unleashed* have made every attempt to present information that is accurate and current as known at the time. Updates and corrections will be provided on the InformIT website at http://www.informit.com/store/system-center-2012-service-manager-unleashed-9780133744194.

Thank you for purchasing *System Center 2012 Service Manager Unleashed*. The authors hope it is worth your while.

PART I

Service Manager Overview and Concepts

IN THIS PART

Service Management Basics

System Center 2012 Service Manager is an integrated platform for automating and adapting information technology service management (ITSM) best practices, such as those found in the Information Technology Infrastructure Library (ITIL) and Microsoft Operations Framework (MOF), to your organization's requirements. Service Manager provides built-in processes for Incident Management, Problem Management, Change Management, Service Request Fulfillment, Release Management, Knowledge Management, and Configuration Management. It includes a service catalog, dashboards, and reporting.

As an ITSM solution, Service Manager uses its configuration management database (CMDB) and process integration to help deliver IT as a service. Service Manager automatically connects knowledge and information from System Center Orchestrator, System Center Virtual Machine Manager (VMM), System Center Operations Manager, System Center Configuration Manager, and Active Directory (AD) Domain Services. Service Manager provides the following capabilities to deliver integration, efficiency, and business alignment for your Information Technology (IT) services:

▶ **Integrating process and knowledge across System Center:** Through its integration capabilities with other System Center components, Service Manager provides an integrated service management platform. This helps reduce downtime and improve the quality of services in the data center.

▶ **Providing an accurate and relevant knowledge base:** Knowledge base information resides in the CMDB; this contains product and user knowledge that enables IT analysts to quickly identify and resolve incidents. The knowledge base also assists end users, who can use the self-service portal (SSP) to search for information to help solve issues. Organizations can create and manage their own knowledge base articles and make this information accessible to IT analysts and end users.

▶ **Lowering costs and improving responsiveness:** As IT organizations increasingly must become more efficient and do more with less, Service Manager's capabilities can help improve end user satisfaction. Service Manager improves end user satisfaction in two ways:

  ▶ By enabling self-service for end users

  ▶ By implementing ITIL process and standards such as Incident Management, Problem Management, and Knowledge Management

These increase the service team's responsiveness to end users and lower costs by facilitating better standards within IT.

▶ **Improving business alignment:** Service Manager helps your organization align with its business goals and adapt to new requirements through its configuration management, compliance, risk management, reporting, and analysis capabilities.

▶ **Delivering immediate value with built-in process management packs:** Included with Service Manager are core process management packs for Incident Management, Problem Management, Service Request Fulfillment, Change Management, Release Management, Configuration Management, and Knowledge Management.

▶ **Automating processes:** Service Manager helps automate repetitive, simple, and manual processes through integration with System Center Orchestrator. Examples of automation with Orchestrator include creating user accounts, resetting passwords, creating databases, provisioning virtual machines, and more.

▶ **Offering IT as a Service (ITaaS):** Through its service catalog, Service Manager can meet ITIL Service Request Fulfillment functionality. This enables IT departments to offer an effective and efficient means for handling service requests from end users. The service catalog consists of service offerings and request offerings published via the SSP.

This chapter introduces System Center Service Manager. Various abbreviations include SCSM, SM, and Service Manager; this book uses the nomenclature of Service Manager. Service Manager provides user-centric support, enables data center management efficiency, and enables you to align to your organization's business goals and adapt to ever-changing business requirements.

Ten Reasons to Use Service Manager

Why should you use Service Manager 2012 in the first place? How does this make your daily life easier? Although this book covers the features and benefits of Service Manager in detail, it definitely helps to have some quick ideas to illustrate why Service Manager is worth a look!

Consider ten compelling reasons why you might want to use Service Manager:

1. Your support desk is overwhelmed with manually entering user requests...24/7 while end users are demanding self-service and cloud services.

2. You realize service desk management would be much simpler if you had visibility and information for all your systems on a single console.

3. You discover email is down when upper management calls the service desk. Although this mechanism is effective in getting your attention, it is stress inducing and not particularly proactive.

4. You would be more productive if you weren't dealing with user issues all day...and night. And during lunch and vacation.

5. The bulk of your department's budget pays for teams of contractors to manage user support and the service desk when self-service and automation could cut down on this and relieve IT to focus on more strategic tasks.

6. You're tired of going through each of your servers looking for reports you need on your client, server, physical, and virtual environments.

7. Your system admins are patching and updating production systems during business hours, often bringing down servers in the process.

8. By the time you update your user documentation, everything has changed and you have to start all over again!

9. You can't stay on top of adapting to your organization's business needs when you're not sure of your current capabilities.

10. You don't have the time to write down all the troubleshooting information that is in your brain, and your boss is concerned you might be hit by a truck (or want to take that vacation). This probably is not the best way to support end users.

While somewhat tongue-in-cheek, these topics represent real problems for many IT managers and support staff. If you are one of these individuals, you owe to it yourself to explore how you can leverage Service Manager to solve many of these common issues. These pain points are common to almost all users of Microsoft technologies to some degree, and Service Manager holds solutions for all of them.

However, perhaps the most important reason for using Service Manager is the peace of mind it can bring, knowing that you have complete visibility and control of your IT systems. The productivity this can bring to your organization is a tremendous benefit as well.

The Problem with Today's Systems

With increasing operational requirements unaccompanied by linear growth in IT staffing levels, organizations must continually find ways to streamline administration through tools and automation. Today's IT systems are prone to a number of problems from the perspective of service management, including

- ▶ System unavailability
- ▶ Configuration "shift and drift"
- ▶ System isolation
- ▶ Lack of historical information
- ▶ Not enough expertise
- ▶ Missing incidents and information
- ▶ Lack of process consistency
- ▶ Not meeting service level expectations

This list should not be surprising, as these problems manifest themselves in all IT shops with varying degrees of severity. In fact, Forrester Research estimates that 82% of larger shops are pursuing service management, and 67% plan to increase Windows management. The next sections look at the issues.

Why Do Systems Go Down?

Let's start with examining reasons why systems go down. Figure 1.1 illustrates reasons for system outages, based on the authors' personal experiences and observations, and the following list describes some of these reasons.

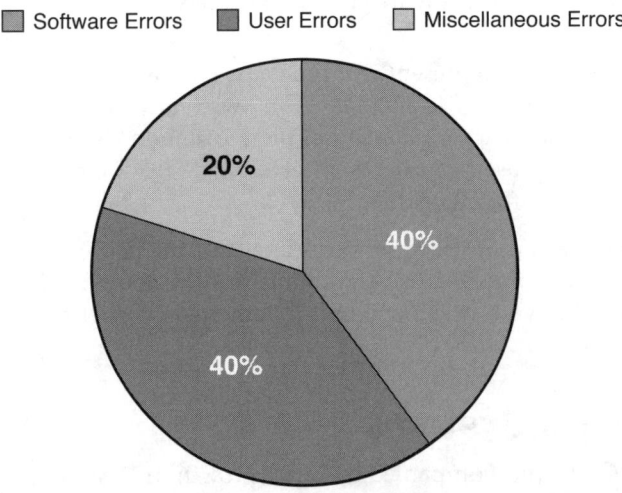

Causes of System Outages

◼ Software Errors   ◼ User Errors   ◻ Miscellaneous Errors

FIGURE 1.1   Causes of system outages.

▶ **Software errors:** Software is responsible for somewhat less than half the errors. These errors include software coding errors, software integration errors, data corruption, and such.

▶ **User errors:** End users and operators cause a little less than half the errors. This includes incorrectly configuring systems, failing to catch warning messages that turn into errors, accidents, unplugging the power cord, and so on.

▶ **Miscellaneous errors:** This last category is fairly small. Causes of problems include disk crashes, power outages, viruses, natural disasters, and so on.

As Figure 1.1 demonstrates, the vast majority of failures are due to software level errors and user errors. It is surprising to note that hardware failures account for only a small percentage of problems, which is a tribute to modern systems such as Redundant Array of Independent Disks (RAID), clustering, and other mechanisms deployed to provide server and application redundancy.

The numbers show that to reduce system downtime, which affects user satisfaction and productivity, you need to attack the software and user error components of the equation. That is where you get the most "bang for the buck."

Configuration "Shift and Drift"

Even IT organizations with well-defined and documented change management policies can have procedures that fall short of perfection. Unplanned and unwanted changes frequently find their way into production, sometimes as an unintended side effect of an approved, scheduled change.

You may be familiar with an old philosophical saying: If a tree falls in a forest and no one is around to hear it, does it make a sound?

Here's the change management equivalent: If a change is made on a system and no one is around to hear it, does identifying it make a difference?

The answer to this question absolutely is "yes"; every change to a system can potentially affect its functionality or security, or that system's adherence to corporate or regulatory compliance.

As an example, adding a feature to a web application component may affect the application binaries by potentially overwriting files or settings that were replaced with a critical security patch. Or perhaps the engineer implementing the change sees a setting he thinks is misconfigured and decides to just "fix" it while already working on the system. In an e-commerce scenario, where sensitive customer data is involved, this could have potentially devastating consequences, not to mention that troubleshooting something you don't know has changed is like looking for the proverbial needle in a haystack.

At the end of the day, your management platform must incorporate a strong element of baseline configuration monitoring and enforcement to ensure configuration standards are implemented and maintained with the required consistency.

System Isolation

Microsoft Windows Server and the applications running run on it expose a wealth of information with event logs, performance counters, and application-specific logs. However, this data is isolated and typically server-centric—making it difficult to determine what and where a problem really is. To get a handle on your systems, you need to take actions to prevent the situation shown in Figure 1.2, where you have multiple islands of information.

Places where you find isolated information include data and statistics stored in various databases, event logs, and performance counters. In addition, consultants, engineers, and subject matter experts have information locked up in their heads or written down on whiteboards and paper napkins. Other areas include undocumented changes, undocumented service requests, incidents that are similar but not shown as related to each other to help determine the root cause of problems, and decentralized asset information.

Each of these is as much an island of information as the statistics and data stored on any computer.

FIGURE 1.2   Multiple islands of information.

Although system information is captured in various ways, it is typically lost over time, and the information is not centralized or reviewed regularly. Most application information is also server-centric, typically stored on the server and specific to the server where that application resides. There is no built-in, system-wide, cross-system view of critical information.

Incidents, problems, service requests, and change requests are recurring events throughout IT. Some organizations have this data within separate systems, without a single point of visibility. When data is stored on separate systems, it is isolated, and comprehensive reporting becomes difficult. This is also true for servers, IIS websites, SQL instances, and other objects; data regarding these systems are not typically stored in a central location to enable good asset management inventory. As cloud scenarios continue to be adopted, tracking these assets becomes complex if they are not managed centrally. Islands of information, where data is stranded on any given island, make it difficult to get to needed information in a timely or effective manner. Not having that information can make managing user satisfaction a difficult endeavor.

System Center can help to alleviate these islands of information. Operations Manager can track monitoring information in a single place. You can bring Operations Manager alert data into Service Manager to populate incidents and problems as well as be a starting point for change requests. Monitored objects from Operations Manager and information from Configuration Manager can also be brought into Service Manager to populate the CMDB. Service Manager's CMDB and data warehouse have the ability to alleviate these islands of information and bring them into a single point for reporting.

Lack of Historical Information

Sometimes you may capture information about problems, but are unable to look back in time to see whether this is an isolated instance or part of a recurring pattern. An incident can be a one-time blip or can indicate an underlying issue; not having a historical context makes it difficult to understand the significance of any particular incident. Consider the following example:

A company retains a consultant to determine why a database application has performance problems. To prove there is an issue, the in-house IT staff points out that users are complaining about performance but the memory and CPU on the database server are only 50% utilized. By itself, this does not say what the problem might be. It could be that memory and the CPU are normally 65% utilized and the problem is really a network utilization problem, which in turn is reducing the load on the other resources. The problem could be that the application is poorly written. A historical context could provide useful information.

As an expert, the consultant would develop a hypothesis and test it, which takes time and costs money. Rather than trying to solve a problem, many IT shops just throw more hardware at it—only to find that this does not necessarily improve performance. Utilizing historical records could show that system utilization actually dropped at the same time that users started complaining and the problem is actually elsewhere.

Lack of Expertise

Do you lack the in-house expertise needed to support users calling the service desk? Is your documentation inadequate and you don't have the knowledge to keep it current? Do you pay an arm and a leg to have contractors manage user support and expectations?

If the expertise you need is not available for those areas needing attention, you can incur additional costs and even potential downtime. This can translate to loss of user productivity, system outages, and ultimately higher operational costs if emergency measures are required to resolve problems.

Missing Incidents and Information

Sometimes problems are detected by what occurred elsewhere. The information reported to operations and change management systems can affect system availability and user satisfaction. If that information is not available to the service desk, it might as well be an isolated island of information.

One of the primary tasks of the service desk team is incident detection and recording. A complete service management solution must be able to capture information occurring throughout the data center, generating trouble tickets as appropriate, managing user expectations as necessary, and providing efficient and responsive support for end users. The CMDB must provide the information required for analysts to resolve issues quickly. Without the capability to incorporate information throughout the IT organization, the service desk is severely handicapped in the quality of support it can provide to its customers.

Reported incidents can also disappear from sight by not being assigned to an owner. A service management solution must be able to track information from the time it enters the system until the problem is resolved and the issue closed.

Lack of Process Consistency

Many IT organizations are unorganized in terms of identifying and resolving problems. Using standard procedures and a methodology helps to minimize risk and solve issues faster.

A *methodology* is a framework of processes and procedures used by those who work in a discipline. You can look at a methodology as a structured process that defines the who, what, where, when, and why of your operations, and the procedures to use when defining problems, solutions, and courses of action.

When employing a standard set of processes, it is important to ensure that the framework adopted adheres to accepted industry standards or best practices. Employing a standard set of processes also considers business requirements, to ensure continuity between expectations and the services delivered by the IT organization. Consistent use of a repeatable and measurable set of practices allows organizations to quantify their progress more accurately to facilitate adjustment of processes as necessary to improve future results. The most effective IT organizations build an element of self-examination into their service management strategy to ensure processes can be incrementally improved or modified to meet the changing needs of the business.

With IT's continually increased role in running successful business operations, having a structured and standard way to define IT operations that are aligned to the needs of the business is critical to meet the expectations of business stakeholders. This alignment results in improved business relationships, where business units engage IT as a partner in developing and delivering innovations to drive business results.

Not Meeting Service Level Expectations

Customer satisfaction is all about perception. Customer satisfaction is not necessarily about objective quality of service; it is how your customer (the end user and the business) sees that quality. There will be times that your users see the service as much better than it is, and also times when that service is perceived as much worse than it is in reality—usually due to bad communication, or from isolated cases that have high visibility.

Keeping your end users satisfied is about providing excellent services, but it is also about managing their expectations about what excellent services actually are.

```
End User Satisfaction = Perception - Expectation
```

The expectation part of this equation is managed by your service level agreements and how well you meet them. The goal of service level management is ensuring that the agreed level of IT services are provided, and that any future services will be delivered as agreed upon. A service level agreement (SLA) is just a document; service level management—the process that creates that document—helps IT and the business you are supporting to understand each other.

If you have not established expectations, you will not be able to satisfy your end users as to the quality of the service IT is providing, and you will not be perceived as a valuable part of the business.

What It's All About

It can be intimidating when you consider the fact that the problems described to this point could happen even in an ostensibly "managed" environment. However, these examples serve to illustrate that the very processes used for service management must themselves be reviewed periodically and updated, so they might accommodate changes in tools and technologies employed from the desktop to the data center. By not correlating data across systems, being aware of potential issues, maintaining a history of past performance and problems, and so on, IT shops open themselves up to putting out fires and fighting time bombs that could be prevented by using a more systematic approach to service management, which is described in the next section.

Service Management Defined

IT is responsible for providing the technology resources required to support the objectives of the organization it serves. These comprise applications, file and print resources, communication and collaboration resources, networks, servers, desktops, and mobile devices. To those paying for and using these capabilities, these are far more significant than raw hardware and software components. IT consumers require that these resources be matched to organizational demands, predictable and available, stable and secure, reliable and cost effective; and they need someone to call for help when needed.

Delivering these capabilities in a stable, secure, predictable, and affordable manner requires much more than providing hardware and software. Those technology components are wrapped in planning, design, operating, and support practices that enable them to deliver exactly what consumers expect, and at a reasonable cost. Organizing IT as services is intended to optimize the value of IT—by providing an ongoing means of matching technology capability to functional, performance, and financial requirements.

IT service management is the concept of organizing and presenting information technology capabilities to business customers and users as a set of services. Think of it as a wrapper for the raw technology components, providing the ways and means to deliver technology as services. IT service management centers on the customer's perspective of IT's contribution to the business, an approach distinctly different from technology-centered approaches to IT management.

In practice, IT service management is implemented as a series of specialized processes that work together to deliver and support IT services. These processes are technology-agnostic and share strategies and objectives with other process improvement disciplines such as Total Quality Management (TQM), Six Sigma, and Capability Maturity Model Integration (CMMI). IT service management processes aim to enhance the efficiency and effectiveness of fundamental IT work, and emphasize alignment of that work with business needs for functionality, performance, and cost.

The Importance of Service Management to IT

Service management has not always been a key discipline for IT. IT has historically focused on designing and delivering optimal technical solutions that did not necessarily align optimally with business needs. This context was narrow and inward looking. As IT became a more vital contributor to business results, there was greater emphasis on organizing it in ways that closely matched its solutions to business requirements. This broadened the context, as IT looked outward to position its capability within relevant business requirements.

This broad, business-oriented context is one of the chief reasons IT service management is important. Service management positions IT in a business context, featuring mechanisms to match what IT does to what the business demands, both at the time of design and on an ongoing basis. These mechanisms exist within various IT service management processes.

Key Concepts in IT Service Management

To obtain a good grasp of IT service management fundamentals, you should understand several key IT service management concepts:

▶ IT service management focuses on managing IT as a set of business-facing IT services. This packages IT capability into services that ideally are easy for users to understand and consume, with straightforward measures of quality and cost.

▶ The IT organization is positioned as the service provider, responsible for delivering IT services in accordance with agreed standards for quality and cost.

▶ The business is the consumer, responsible for articulating requirements and funding IT services. It contains two constituents: customers who pay for the IT services, and users who utilize them in their work.

Evolution of the CMDB

A configuration management database is a repository of information related to all the components of an information system. Configuration management itself focuses on establishing and maintaining consistency of a system or product's performance and its functional and physical attributes with its requirements, design, and operational information throughout its life cycle. A CMDB contains configuration item (CI) information and is used to understand CI relationships and track their configuration. Configuration management can assist in maintaining asset management data for configuration items.

The term CMDB stems from ITIL v2 (in ITIL v3 it is known as a configuration management system or CMS), where it represents the authorized configuration of the significant components of the IT environment. The CMDB is a fundamental component of the ITIL framework's configuration management process. CMDB implementations often involve federation, the inclusion of data into the CMDB from other sources. Information in a CMDB is typically used for planning, identification, control, monitoring, and verification.

The Service Manager CMDB is a database containing details of configuration items and details of the important relationships between those configuration items. These relationships capture, record, and provide output about the status, urgency, historical changes, and the impact of data between CIs.

Service Manager orchestrates and unifies knowledge across System Center by using its CMDB and process integration to connect knowledge and information from Orchestrator, Virtual Machine Manager, Operations Manager, Configuration Manager, and Active Directory Domain Services.

Strategies for Service Management

Microsoft utilizes a multifaceted approach to IT service management. This strategy includes advancements in the following areas:

▶ Adoption of a model-based management strategy (a component of the Dynamic Systems Initiative, discussed in "Microsoft's Dynamic Systems Initiative," the next section of this chapter) to implement synthetic transaction technology. Service Manager 2012 is intended to deliver a service-based set of scenarios, enabling you to define models of services to deliver to end users using a *service map*—a combination of Operation Manager's distributed application functionality with Service Manager business services.

▶ Using an Infrastructure Optimization (IO) model as a framework for aligning IT with business needs, and as a standard for expressing an organization's maturity in service management. The "Optimizing Your Infrastructure" section discusses the IO model further. The IO model describes your IT infrastructure in terms of cost, security risk, and operational agility.

▶ Building complete management solutions on this infrastructure, either through making them available in the operating system or by using Service Manager, Operations Manager, Configuration Manager, and other System Center components.

Microsoft's Dynamic Systems Initiative

A large percentage of IT departments' budgets and resources typically focuses on mundane maintenance tasks such as applying software patches or monitoring the health of a network, without leaving the staff with the time or energy to focus on more exhilarating (and more productive) strategic initiatives.

The Dynamic Systems Initiative, or DSI, is a Microsoft and industry strategy intended to enhance the Windows platform, delivering a coordinated set of solutions that simplify and automate how businesses design, deploy, and operate their distributed systems. Using DSI helps IT and developers create operationally aware platforms. By designing systems that are more manageable and automating operations, organizations can reduce costs and proactively address their priorities.

DSI is about building software that enables knowledge of an IT system to be created, modified, transferred, and operated on throughout the life cycle of that system. It is a commitment from Microsoft and its partners to help IT teams capture and use knowledge to design systems that are more manageable and to automate operations, which in turn reduces costs and gives organizations additional time to focus proactively on what is most important. By innovating across applications, development tools, the platform, and management solutions, DSI results in

▶ Increased productivity and reduced costs across all aspects of IT

▶ Increased responsiveness to changing business needs

▶ Reduced time and effort required to develop, deploy, and manage applications

Microsoft positions DSI as the connector of the entire system and service life cycles.

Microsoft Product Integration

DSI focuses on automating data center operational jobs and reducing associated labor through self-managing systems. Following are several examples where Microsoft products and tools integrate with DSI:

▶ Operations Manager uses the application knowledge captured in management packs to simplify identifying issues and their root causes, facilitating resolution and restoring services or preventing potential outages, and providing intelligent management at the system level.

▶ Configuration Manager employs model-based configuration baseline templates in its Desired Configuration Management feature to automate identification of undesired shifts in system configurations.

▶ Service Manager uses model-based management packs. You can easily add new models describing your own configuration items or work items to track their life cycle. Each data model is stored in one or more management packs that make up the model.

▶ Visual Studio is a model-based development tool that leverages SML (Service Modeling Language), enabling operations managers and application architects to collaborate early in the development phase and ensure applications are modeled with operational requirements in mind.

▶ Windows Server Update Services (WSUS) enable greater and more efficient administrative control through modeling technology that enables downstream systems to construct accurate models representing their current state, available updates, and installed software.

SDM AND SML: WHAT'S THE DIFFERENCE?

Microsoft originally used the System Definition Model (SDM) as its standard schema with DSI. SDM was a proprietary specification put forward by Microsoft. The company later decided to implement SML, which is an industry-wide published specification used in heterogeneous environments. Using SML helps DSI adoption by incorporating a standard that Microsoft's partners can understand and apply across mixed platforms. Service Modeling Language is discussed later in the section "The Role of Service Modeling Language in IT Operations."

End-to-end automation could include update management, availability and performance monitoring, change and configuration management, and rich reporting services. Microsoft's System Center is a single offering of integrated management tools and solutions that help you manage your client devices, data centers, and private/public cloud environments. System Center provides the tools and knowledge to manage physical and virtual resources, services, applications, monitoring, data protection, configuration, and automation effectively within your IT infrastructure, thus helping to ease operations, reduce troubleshooting time, and improve planning capabilities.

The Importance of DSI

There are three architectural elements behind the DSI initiative:

▶ That developers have tools (such as Visual Studio) to design applications in a way that makes them easier for administrators to manage after those applications are in production

▶ That Microsoft products can be secured and updated in a uniform way

▶ That Microsoft server applications are optimized for management, to take advantage of System Center

DSI represents a departure from the traditional approach to systems management. DSI focuses on designing for operations from the application development stage, rather than a more customary operations perspective that concentrates on automating task-based processes. This strategy highlights the fact that Microsoft's Dynamic Systems Initiative is about building software that enables knowledge of an IT system to be created, modified, transferred, and used throughout the life cycle of a system. DSI's core principles of knowledge, models, and the life cycle are key in addressing the challenges of complexity and manageability faced by IT organizations. By capturing knowledge and incorporating health models, DSI can facilitate easier troubleshooting and maintenance, and thus lower TCO.

The Role of Service Modeling Language in IT Operations

A key underlying component of DSI is the XML-based (eXtensible Markup Language) SML specification. SML is a standard developed by several leading information technology companies that defines a consistent way for infrastructure and application architects to define how applications, infrastructure, and services are modeled in a consistent way.

SML facilitates modeling systems from a development, deployment, and support perspective with modular, reusable building blocks that eliminate the need to reinvent the wheel when describing and defining a new service. This results in systems that are easier to develop, implement, manage, and maintain, resulting in reduced total cost ownership (TCO) to the organization. SML is a core technology that will continue to play a prominent role in future products developed to support the ongoing objectives of DSI.

NOTE: SML RESOURCES ON THE WEB

For more information on Service Modeling Language, view the latest draft of the SML standard at http://www.w3.org/TR/sml/. For additional technical information on SML from Microsoft, see http://technet.microsoft.com/en-us/library/bb725986.aspx.

MOF and ITIL

Microsoft Operations Framework and the Information Technology Infrastructure Library are two prominent service management frameworks that define many concepts and practices central to Service Manager. These frameworks and their most relevant components are described in greater detail in Chapter 3, "MOF, ITIL, and System Center."

Introducing ITIL

Originally developed in the 1980s by the British government, ITIL has become the de facto standard for IT service management. ITIL was eventually released publicly and is published as a set of books with content collaboratively developed by a consortium of industry experts. ITIL takes a life cycle approach to IT service management, providing technology-agnostic, descriptive guidance on IT service management processes and functions. ITIL has spawned an industry of consultancy and training services, and features a multilevel certification scheme for individual IT professionals.

Introducing MOF

MOF is Microsoft's adaptation of ITIL and extends ITIL's technology-neutral best practices with more prescriptive guidance, aimed at Microsoft-centered environments. Like ITIL, MOF takes a life cycle approach to IT service management and derives guidance from the real world experiences of Microsoft professionals. Unlike ITIL, MOF is at no charge, and it extends generic process guidance with management reviews, companion guides, and job aids. A single certification is available.

COBIT: A Framework for IT Governance and Control

Control Objectives for Information and related Technology (COBIT) is an IT governance framework and toolset developed by ISACA, the Information Systems Audit and Control Association. COBIT enables managers to bridge the gap between control requirements, technical issues, and business risks; it provides an end-to-end business view of the governance of enterprise IT that reflects the central role of information and technology in creating value for enterprises. COBIT was first released in 1996 and is now at version 5, released in 2011. Service Manager, which is the focal point in System Center for IT compliance, implements IT governance and compliance.

Total Quality Management: TQM

TQM's goal is to continuously improve the quality of products and processes. It functions on the premise that the quality of the products and processes is the responsibility of everyone involved with the creation or consumption of the products or services offered by the organization. TQM capitalizes on the involvement of management, workforce, suppliers, and even customers, to meet or exceed customer expectations.

Six Sigma

Six Sigma is a business management strategy, originally developed by Motorola, that seeks to identify and remove the causes of defects and errors in manufacturing and business processes. Six Sigma process improvement originated from Motorola's drive toward reducing defects by minimizing variation in processes through metrics measurement. Applications of the Six Sigma project execution methodology have since expanded to incorporate practices common in TQM and supply chain management; this includes customer satisfaction and developing closer supplier relationships.

CMMI

CMMI is a process improvement approach providing organizations with the essential elements of effective processes. It can be used to guide process improvement—across a project, a division, or an entire organization—thus helping to integrate traditionally separate organizational functions, set process improvement goals and priorities, provide guidance for a quality processes, and provide a point of reference for appraising current processes. Benefits you can realize from CMMI include

▶ Linking your organization's activities to your business objectives

▶ Increasing your visibility into your organization's activities, helping ensure your service or product meets the customer's expectations

▶ Learning from new areas of best practice, such as measurement and risk

Business Process Management

Business process management (BPM) is a management approach focused on aligning all aspects of an organization with the wants and needs of clients. It is a holistic management approach, promoting business effectiveness and efficiency while striving for innovation, flexibility, and integration with technology. BPM attempts to improve processes continuously and can be considered a process optimization process. It is argued that BPM enables organizations to be more efficient, effective, and capable of change than with a functionally focused, traditional hierarchical management approach. BPM can help organizations gain higher customer satisfaction, product quality, delivery speed, and time-to-market speed.

Service Management Mastery: ISO/IEC 20000

You can think of ITIL and ITSM as providing a framework for IT to rethink the ways in which it contributes to and aligns with the organization. ISO/IEC 20000, which is the first international standard for IT service management, institutionalizes these processes. ISO/IEC 20000 helps companies to align IT services and business strategy, and create a formal framework for continual service improvement, and provides benchmarks for comparison to best practices.

ISO/IEC 20000 was developed to reflect the best-practice guidance contained within ITIL. The standard also supports other IT service management frameworks and approaches, including MOF, COBIT, CMMI, and Six Sigma. ISO/IEC 20000 includes the design, transition, delivery, and improvement of services that fulfill service requirements and provide value for the customer and the service provider.

ISO/IEC 20000 provides organizational or corporate certification for organizations that effectively adopt and implement its code of practice.

Optimizing Your Infrastructure

According to Microsoft, analysts estimate that more than 70% of the typical IT budget is spent on infrastructure—managing servers, operating systems, storage, and networking. Add to that the challenge of refreshing and managing desktop and mobile devices, and there's not much left over for anything else. Microsoft describes an Infrastructure Optimization model that categorizes the state of one's IT infrastructure, describing the impacts on cost, security risks, and the ability to respond to changes. Using the model shown in Figure 1.3, you can identify where your organization is and where you want to be:

▶ **Basic:** Reactionary, with much time spent fighting fires

▶ **Standardized:** Gaining control

▶ **Rationalized:** Enabling the business

▶ **Dynamic:** Being a strategic asset

Although most organizations are somewhere between the basic and standardized levels in this model, typically one would prefer to be a strategic asset rather than fighting fires. Once you know where you are in the model, you can use best practices from ITIL and guidance from MOF to develop a plan to progress to a higher level. The IO model describes the technologies and steps organizations can take to move forward, whereas MOF explains the people and processes required to improve that infrastructure. Similar to ITSM, the IO model is a combination of people, processes, and technology.

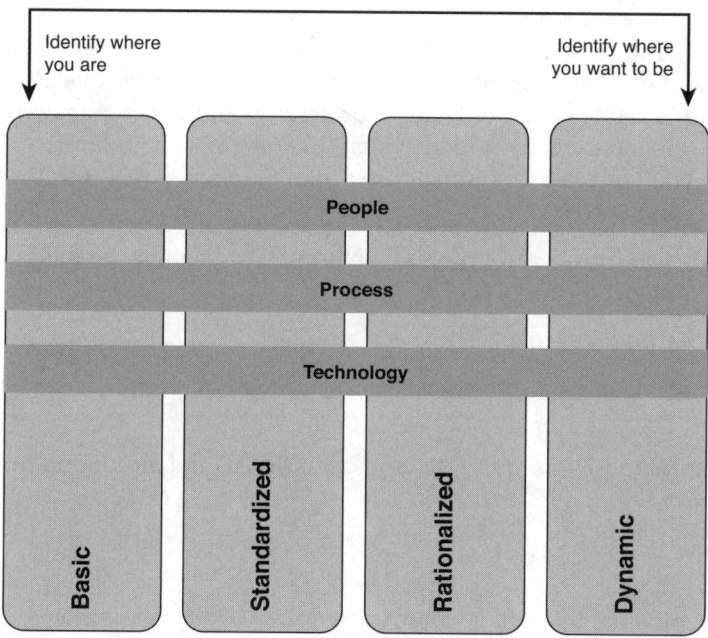

FIGURE 1.3   The Infrastructure Optimization model.

More information about Infrastructure Optimization is available at http://www.microsoft.com/technet/infrastructure.

NOTE: ABOUT THE IO MODEL

Not all IT shops will want or need to be dynamic. Some will choose, for all the right business reasons, to be less than dynamic! The IO model includes a three-part goal:

▶ Communicate that there are levels

▶ Target the desired levels

▶ Provide reference on how to get to the desired levels

Realize that infrastructure optimization can be by application or by function, rather than a single ranking for the entire IT department.

Items that factor into an IT organization's adoption of the IO model include cost, ability, and whether the organization fits into the business model as a cost center versus being an asset, along with a commitment to move from being reactive to proactive.

From Fighting Fires to Gaining Control

At the Basic level, your infrastructure is hard to control and expensive to manage. Processes are manual, IT policies and standards are either nonexistent or not enforced, and you don't have the tools and resources (or time and energy) to determine the overall health of your applications and IT services. Not only are your desktop and server management costs out of control, but you are in reactive mode when it comes to security threats and user support. In addition, you tend to use manual rather than automated methods for applying software deployments and patches.

Does this sound familiar? If you can gain control of your environment, you may be more effective at work! Here are some steps to consider:

▶ Develop standards, policies, and controls.

▶ Alleviate security risks by developing a security approach throughout your IT organization.

▶ Adopt best practices, such as those found in ITIL, and operational guidance found in the MOF.

▶ Build IT to become a strategic asset.

If you can achieve operational nirvana, this will go a long way toward your job satisfaction and IT becoming a constructive part of your business.

From Gaining Control to Enabling the Business

A standardized infrastructure introduces control by using standards and policies to manage desktops and servers. These standards control how you introduce machines into your network. As an example, using Directory Services will manage resources, security policies, and access to resources. Shops at the Standardized level realize the value of basic standards and some policies, but still tend to be reactive. Although you now have a managed IT infrastructure and are inventorying your hardware and software assets and starting to manage licenses, your patches, software deployments, and desktop services are not yet automated. Security-wise, the perimeter is now under control, although internal security may still be a bit loose. Service management becomes a recognized concept, and your organization is taking steps to implement it.

To move from a standardized state to the Rationalized level, you need to gain more control over your infrastructure and implement proactive policies and procedures. You might also begin to look at implementing service management. At this stage, IT can also move more toward becoming a business asset and ally, rather than a burden.

From Enabling the Business to Becoming a Strategic Asset

At the Rationalized level, you have achieved firm control of desktop and service management costs. Processes and policies are in place and beginning to play a large role in supporting and expanding the business. Security is now proactive, and you are responding to threats and challenges in a rapid and controlled manner.

Using technologies such as lite-touch and zero-touch operating system deployment helps you to minimize costs, deployment time, and technical challenges for software rollouts. Because your inventory is now under control, you have minimized the number of images to manage, and desktop management is now largely automated. You also are purchasing only the software licenses and new computers the business requires, giving you a handle on costs. Security is now proactive with policies and control in place for desktops, servers, firewalls, and extranets. You have implemented service management in several areas and are taking steps to implement it more broadly across IT.

Mission Accomplished: IT as a Strategic Asset

At the Dynamic level, your infrastructure is helping run the business efficiently and stay ahead of competitors. Your costs are now fully controlled. You have also achieved integration between users and data, desktops and servers, and the different departments and functions throughout your organization.

Your IT processes are automated and often incorporated into the technology itself, allowing IT to be aligned and managed according to business needs. New technology investments yield specific, rapid, and measurable business benefits. Measurement is good—it helps you justify the next round of investments!

Using self-provisioning software and quarantine-like systems to ensure patch management and compliance with security policies allows you to automate your processes, which in turn improves reliability, lowers costs, and increases your service levels. Service management is implemented for all critical services with service level agreements and operational reviews.

According to IDC research (October 2006), very few organizations achieve the Dynamic level of the Infrastructure Optimization model—due to the lack of availability of a single toolset from a single vendor to meet all requirements. Through execution on its vision in DSI, Microsoft aims to change this. To read more on this study, visit http://download. microsoft.com/download/a/4/4/a4474b0c-57d8-41a2-afe6-32037fa93ea6/IDC_ windesktop_IO_whitepaper.pdf.

TIP: MICROSOFT INFRASTRUCTURE OPTIMIZATION HELPS REDUCE COSTS

The April 21, 2009, issue of *Biztech* magazine includes an article by Russell Smith about Microsoft's Infrastructure Optimization model. Russell makes the following points:

▶ While dynamic or fully automated systems that are strategic assets to a company sometimes seem like a far-off dream, infrastructure optimization models and products can help get you closer to making IT a valuable business asset.

▶ Microsoft's Infrastructure Optimization is based on Gartner's Infrastructure Maturity model and provides a simple structure to evaluate the efficiency of core IT services, business productivity, and application platforms.

▶ Though the ultimate goal is to make IT a business enabler across all three areas, you need to concentrate on standardizing core services: moving your organization from a basic infrastructure (in which most IT tasks are carried out manually) to a managed infrastructure with some automation and knowledge capture.

For additional information and the complete article, see http://www.biztechmagazine. com/article.asp?item_id=569.

Bridging the Service Management Gap

System Center 2012 Service Manager is Microsoft's software tool for solving service management issues and is a key component in Microsoft's management strategy and System Center. Service Manager is a comprehensive service management solution that uses its CMDB to collect information not only related to incident management, problem management, change requests and configuration management, and release management, but to consolidate information from other System Center components including Operations Manager, Configuration Manager, and Virtual Machine Manager. As discussed at the beginning of this chapter, Service Manager now incorporates the following benefits:

▶ **Integrates processes and knowledge across System Center:** In terms of integration and knowledge for System Center, consider Service Manager, the CMDB, and its connectors, as the glue for System Center. Microsoft provides connectors for Active Directory, Exchange, Configuration Manager, Operations Manager, Virtual Machine Manager, and Orchestrator to bring data into the CMDB from these other System Center components. Once data from these connectors are in Service Manager, IT departments have the necessary information available to work with in one place. Other System Center components such as Data Protection Manager and some other non-System Center products can also have their data brought into Service Manager's CMDB using Orchestrator or CSV files.

▶ **Provides an accurate and relevant knowledge base:** Knowledge management in Service Manager utilizes an internal and external repository. The service desk team creates internal knowledge base articles; external knowledge base articles simply are web links to external resources such as knowledge base articles on the Internet or technical articles that can be used to solve a problem.

Knowledge–based articles can be linked to configuration items, incidents, problems, and change requests. Linking knowledge base articles to items in Service Manager ensures that the service desk has accurate and relevant information to understand and solve problems. End users can search and view knowledge base articles within the self-service portal, enabling them to view solutions that can resolve their problems on their own before opening a new incident. Figure 1.4 shows an example of a knowledge base article and a configuration item that has been linked to the knowledge base article.

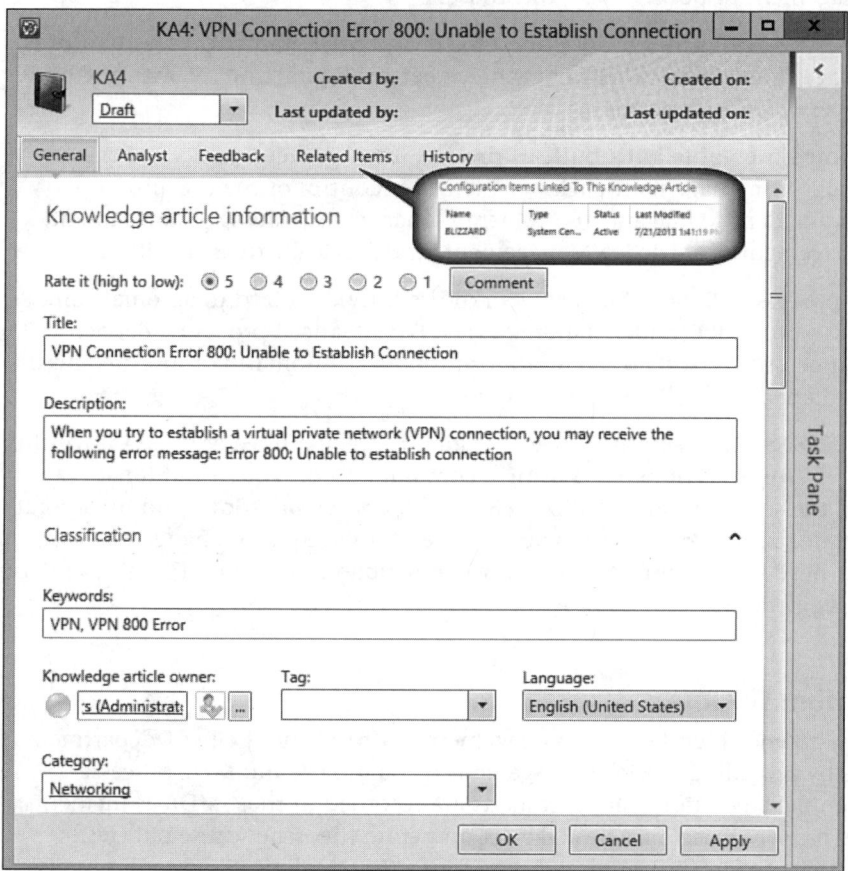

FIGURE 1.4   Knowledge base article in Service Manager.

▶ **Lowers costs and provides improved responsiveness:** Service Manager can help run IT services more efficiently, monitor responses, and meet metrics defined within its SLAs, leading to improved customer satisfaction. This can be accomplished using the features and functionality within Service Manager to accomplish the following:

    ▶ Integrating with Operations Manager and Configuration Manager

    ▶ Tracking all items and alerts that arise as configuration items and incidents

▶ Using templates, workflows, and escalations to route incidents to the correct teams immediately

▶ Improving time to resolution through knowledge management

▶ Reducing the risks of changes through change and release management

Ultimately, organizations will experience lower operational costs and improved service management responsiveness to end users.

▶ **Improves business alignment:** Adoption of ITIL and MOF frameworks, as part of a Service Manager implementation, help achieve better alignment of IT with the business objectives of the organization.

▶ **Delivers immediate value with built-in process management packs:** Service Manager's built-in management packs enable better control of the organization's processes for Incident Management, Problem Management, Change Management, Release Management, Knowledge Management, and Service Request Fulfillment.

▶ **Automates processes:** Service Manager workflows can be utilized to automate and adapt processes into MOF and ITIL frameworks. For advanced processes, Service Manager can be used to surface Orchestrator runbooks, automating those advanced processes and enabling self-service automation.

▶ **Enables IT as a Service:** Service Manager enables IT to be offered as a service within organizations. This is accomplished using a combination of request fulfillment, automation, and the service catalog. Utilizing Service Manager workflows and incorporating Orchestrator runbooks can automate many end user requests, change requests, or tasks that need to be completed to resolve an incident, freeing up IT staff to focus on more strategic needs.

Delivering System Uptime

Service Manager is an end-to-end service management platform that helps IT departments reduce downtime by providing service management through ITIL and MOF processes. Consider this example: Operations Manager alerts are recorded in the CMDB as incidents and routed to the proper IT personnel to take action before the issues cause outages. These alerts are also stored in the data warehouse for further analytical and reporting use. Tracking Operations Manager alerts can also assist with identifying bottlenecks, performance issues, health trends, and resource needs, in turn enabling IT to use proactive rather than reactive Problem Management to ensure service level agreements and service availability are met.

Addressing Configuration "Shift and Drift"

Service Manager's change management and configuration management functionality assist in addressing shift and drift through enforcing configuration and compliance requirements, utilizing the Change Management processes within Service Manager and detection of noncompliant configurations through the Configuration Manager connector.

Consolidating Information

Service Manager consolidates information throughout System Center by pulling information into the CMDB. Data is moved into the data warehouse for long-term storage, available for analysis, dashboards, and reporting use. Information generated directly in Service Manager such as incidents, problems, changes, activities, and service requests are first stored in the CMDB and then moved to the data warehouse. Examples of information contained in the CMDB are users and printers from Active Directory, computers from Configuration Manager, alerts and objects from Operations Manager, and virtual servers from Virtual Machine Manager. Other types of information contained in the CMDB include business services, environments (production or development), computers, users, software, printers, software updates, and other objects. Figure 1.5 shows examples of configuration item types within Service Manager.

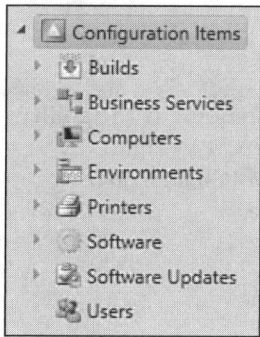

FIGURE 1.5   Configuration items within the CMDB.

Providing Historical Information

The data warehouse in Service Manager serves as a resource for historical data, not only regarding activity in IT but also for configuration items. The data warehouse lets you view the information it contains quickly and efficiently, presenting that data in ways that make it easy to view, print, or publish. Service Manager also provides historical information through Change Management processes. Figure 1.6 shows an example of reports found in the Service Manager data warehouse by default. Notice there are different reporting categories—such as Change Management, Incident Management, and Configuration Management. These reports show information that is important for metrics and measuring IT service management performance. These reports are just the tip of the iceberg when it comes to the reporting, dashboard, and analytical capabilities found within Service Manager.

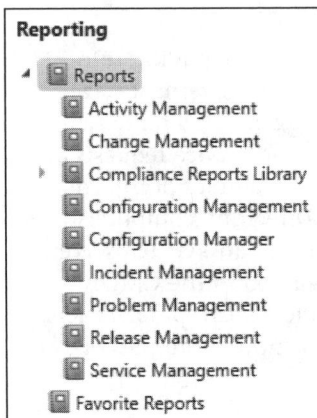

FIGURE 1.6   Reports in the Service Manager data warehouse.

An example of further analytical capability found within the data warehouse is the ability to analyze your service management data in Excel PowerPivot. The report in Figure 1.7 is an example of active versus resolved incidents, represented in a PivotChart made with Excel PowerPivot using a cube in the Service Manager data warehouse.

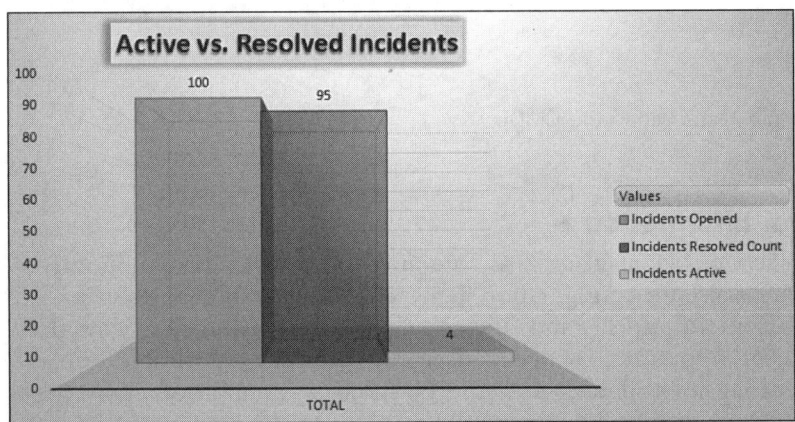

FIGURE 1.7   PivotChart in Excel from Service Manager data warehouse data.

Delivering Expertise

Service Manager delivers expertise to your IT teams through the MOF and ITIL frameworks upon which it was built, helping IT teams to start using ITIL processes. Utilizing ITIL processes such as Incident Management presents a consistent way of handling incidents that in turn helps improve end user satisfaction, incorporating Change Management improves tracking of changes within your environment and reduces risk, and using Knowledge Management helps document solutions to problems and enables you to resolve problems faster.

Utilizing Incident Management and Change Management helps processes be consistent, providing documentation even with personnel turnover. These help to lower your operational cost and reduce the time needed to find solutions to resolve issues. In addition, all incidents, change management information, and knowledge base articles are stored in the CMDB and the data warehouse for historical purposes.

Addressing Missing Incidents and Information

All incidents, problems, and changes can be tracked in Service Manager. Data from other systems can be brought into Service Manager's CMDB through connectors and tracked as asset information. One example of information flowing from another system into Service Manager is System Center Operations Manager, which monitors your infrastructure and generates alerts. While Operations Manager can track and address these alerts, the effort to resolve those alerts is not tracked. Bringing alerts from Operations Manager into Service Manager enables the alert to be made into an incident; the effort it takes to resolve each issue is tracked and prioritized, along with any changes that need to be made to resolve the incident.

Providing Process Consistency

Utilizing Service Manager's change management, templates, workflows, and automation capabilities assists in providing improved visibility and accountability, and reduces operational risk. The activities and approval matrix within Service Manager's change management feature help IT departments to build dynamic yet controlled processes around changes in infrastructure such as updates, releases, and tracking.

Meeting Service Level Agreements

Service Manager can help IT departments to progress from being reactive to proactive, from being cost centers to service providers exceeding service level agreements, and move to a true ITaaS model. Moving to an ITaaS model utilizing System Center components can help IT departments become strategic and be prepared to move toward cloud-based services. One of the many ways Service Manager can help IT move to an ITaaS model is by offering out-of-the-box service level objective (SLO) tracking and metrics as well as chargeback. Figure 1.8 shows an example of priority calculations within Service Manager. Priority calculations help track the urgency and impact of incidents being a part of SLO and metric tracking.

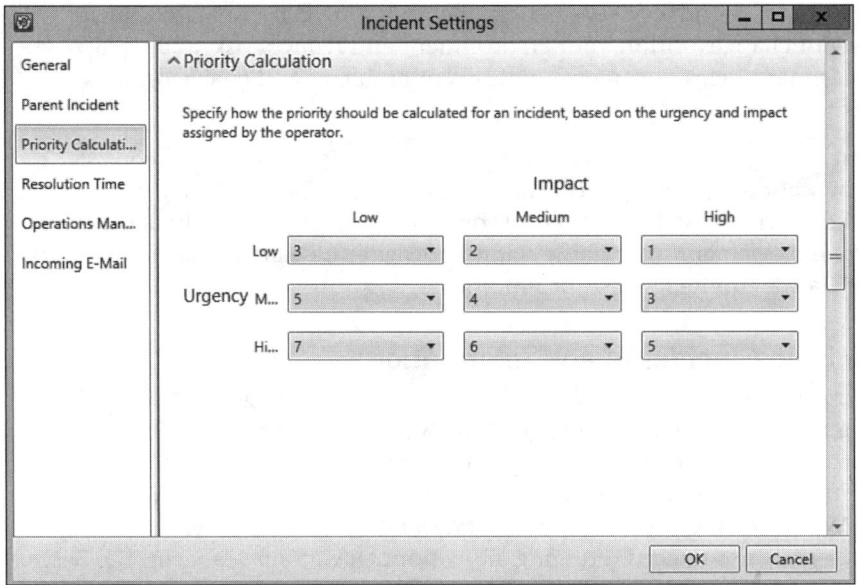

FIGURE 1.8   Priority calculation in incident settings.

Overview of Microsoft System Center

Microsoft first announced System Center in 2003 at the Microsoft Management Summit (MMS), where it was envisioned as a future solution to provide customers of all sizes with complete application and system management. (See http://www.microsoft.com/presspass/press/2003/mar03/03-18mssystemcenterpr.mspx for the original press release.) The first phase was anticipated to include Microsoft Operations Manager (MOM) 2004—later released as MOM 2005—and Systems Management Server (SMS) 2003.

WHAT IS SYSTEM CENTER?

System Center is a brand name for Microsoft's systems management tools and as such has new components added over time. System Center represents a means to integrate system management tools and technologies to help you with systems operations, service management, troubleshooting, and planning.

Different from the releases of Microsoft Office (another Microsoft product), Microsoft initially released System Center in "waves"; the components were not released simultaneously. The first wave initially included SMS 2003, MOM 2005, and System Center Data Protection Manager 2006; 2006 additions included System Center Reporting Manager 2006 and System Center Capacity Planner 2006.

The second wave included Operations Manager 2007, Configuration Manager 2007, System Center Essentials 2007, Virtual Machine Manager 2007, and new releases of Data Protection Manager and Capacity Planner. Next released were System Center Essentials 2007, updates to Virtual Machine Manager (version 2008) Operations Manager 2007 R2, Configuration Manager 2007 R2 and R3, Data Protection Manager 2010, and Service Manager 2010. Think of these as rounding out the second wave.

Microsoft has also widened System Center with its acquisitions of Opalis (rebranded for System Center 2012 as Orchestrator) and AVIcode (integrated into Operations Manager as application performance monitoring or APM). With System Center 2012, Microsoft has moved from the wave approach and now releases the various components at once as a single product. System Center 2012 also includes the first version of a common installer.

The components of System Center 2012 at its release include Service Manager, Operations Manager, Configuration Manager, Endpoint Protection, Data Protection Manager, Orchestrator, Virtual Machine Manager, App Controller, and Advisor. System Center Advisor, previously licensed separately, is now available as a free download, offering a configuration-monitoring cloud service for a number of Microsoft products including SQL Server, Windows Server, SharePoint, Exchange, Lync, and Virtual Machine Manager. System Center 2012 brings substantial new capabilities to all areas of the System Center space, including Service Manager. Microsoft's System Center 2012 cloud and data center solutions provide a common management toolset for your private and public cloud applications and services to help you deliver ITaaS to your business. For further information on what's new in System Center 2012 and its Service Manager component, see Chapter 2, "Service Manager History and Terminology."

System Center builds on Microsoft's DSI, introduced in the "Microsoft's Dynamic Systems Initiative" section earlier in the chapter, which is designed to deliver simplicity, automation, and flexibility in the data center across the IT environment. Microsoft System Center components share the following DSI-based characteristics:

▶ Ease of use and deployment

▶ Based on industry and customer knowledge

▶ Scalability (both up to the largest enterprises and down to the smallest organizations)

Figure 1.9 illustrates the relationship between the System Center components and MOF.

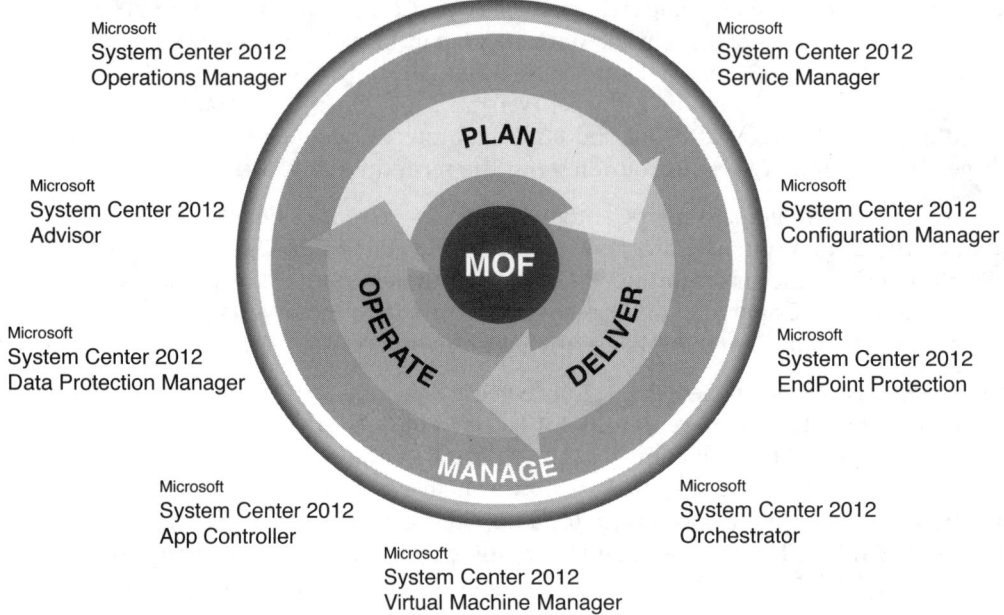

FIGURE 1.9   MOF with System Center components.

Reporting and Trend Analysis

The data gathered by the System Center components is collected in self-maintaining data warehouses, enabling numerous reports to be viewable. By using the SQL Server Reporting Services (SSRS) engine, reports can also be exported to a Report Server file share; using the Web Archive format retains links, and reports can be scheduled and emailed, enabling users to open these reports without accessing a console. The Service Manager data warehouse is installed in a management group separate from the other Service Manager components and includes individual data marts for Operations Manager and Configuration Manager. The data warehouse enables IT professionals and management access to business intelligence (BI) around the IT infrastructure without needing to be SQL or business intelligence experts. The data warehouse comes with pre-built data cubes and the ability to surface the data in PowerPivot or SharePoint's Performance Point. Gartner Group considers Microsoft as a leader in the BI market, as shown in its Magic Quadrant for Business Intelligence, displayed in Figure 1.10.

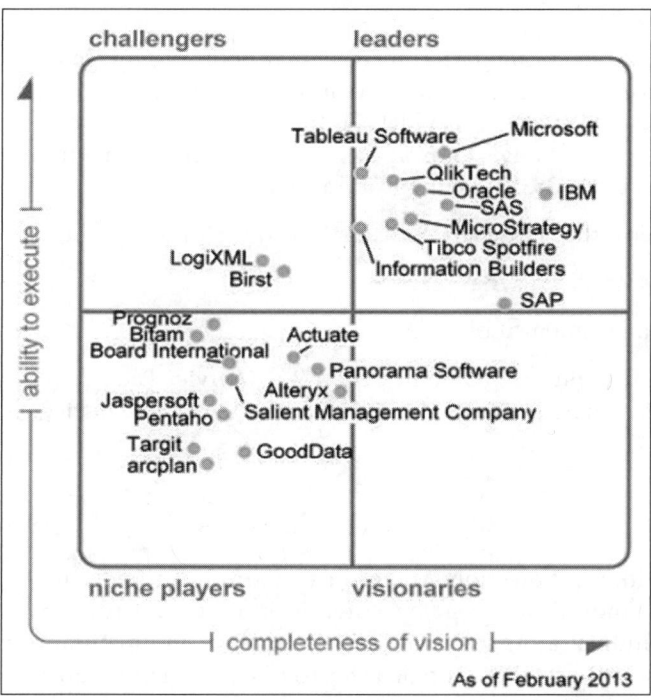

FIGURE 1.10   Magic Quadrant for Business Intelligence (Gartner Group, February 2013).

Operations Management

System Center 2012 Operations Manager provides the monitoring component of delivering ITaaS, helping you to manage your data center and cloud environments by

▶ Delivering flexible and cost effective enterprise-class monitoring and diagnostics while reducing the total cost of ownership by leveraging commodity hardware, configurations, and heterogeneous environments

▶ Helping to ensure the availability of business-critical applications and services through market-leading .NET and JEE application performance monitoring and diagnostics

▶ Providing a comprehensive view of data centers, and public and private clouds

System Center 2012 Operations Manager also adds extensively to those network monitoring capabilities available with Operations Manager 2007 R2 by incorporating EMC Smarts technology.

Enterprise Client Management

Microsoft's current release of its flagship configuration management tool, System Center 2012 Configuration Manager, delivers the functionality to detect "shift and drift" in system configurations. Configuration Manager consolidates information about clients and servers, hardware, and software into a single console for centralized management and control. Configuration Manager includes the following features:

▶ Increasing the quality of service that IT departments deliver to their business units.

▶ Reducing the operational cost to deliver that service.

▶ Delivering a best-of-breed management tool.

▶ Using the Intune Connector introduced in System Center 2012 Service Pack (SP) 1, Configuration Manager integrates with Windows Intune for mobile device management.

Endpoint Protection

Previously known as Forefront Endpoint Protection, Microsoft's enterprise antimalware product had its name changed and moved into System Center. Its integration with Configuration Manager enables administrators to better deploy, monitor, and maintain antimalware software and updates, and provides a single infrastructure for client management and security.

Configuration Manager integration enables System Center 2012 Endpoint Protection to provide a single infrastructure for deploying and managing endpoint protection. You have a single view into the compliance and security of client systems through antimalware, patching, inventory, and usage information.

Service Management

Using Service Manager implements a single point of contact for all service requests, knowledge, and workflow. System Center 2012 Service Manager incorporates processes such as Incident Management, Problem Management, Change Management, and Release Management.

Service Manager's CMDB includes data from Active Directory and Configuration Manager, Operations Manager, Virtual Machine Manager, and Orchestrator through its connectors, enabling it to consolidate information throughout System Center. Some examples follow:

▶ When Operations Manager detects a condition that requires human intervention and tracking for resolution, Service Manager can fill this gap. Without Service Manager, one would need to create a ticket or incident in a service desk application. Now, within System Center, Operations Manager can hand off Incident Management to Service Manager.

▶ The Orchestrator connector enables runbooks to be exposed to end users through Service Manager's service catalog and then be initiated from Service Manager. For example, a new hire request offering could be published to the SSP, a department manager could complete this form, and Service Manager would start an Orchestrator runbook that creates the new hire's user account in Active Directory.

Protecting Data

System Center 2012 Data Protection Manager is Microsoft's enterprise disk-based backup solution for continuous data protection supporting Windows servers and Microsoft workloads such as SQL Server, Exchange, SharePoint, and Hyper-V—as well as Windows desktops and laptops. Data Protection Manager provides block-level backup as changes occur, utilizing Microsoft's Virtual Disk Service and Shadow Copy technologies.

This version of Data Protection Manager includes a number of enhancements over the previous version, including

▶ Centralized management

▶ Centralized monitoring

▶ Remote administration

▶ Remote recovery

▶ Role-based management

▶ Remote corrective actions

▶ Scoped troubleshooting

▶ Push to resume backups

▶ SLA-based alerting

▶ Consolidated alerts

▶ Alert categorization

▶ PowerShell

▶ Cloud backup to Azure

Data Protection Manager 2012 includes the ability for roaming laptops to get centrally managed policies around desktop protection. It also provides native site-to-site replication for disaster recovery to another Data Protection Manager server. Data Protection Manager includes centrally managed system state and bare metal recovery.

Virtual Machine Management

Virtual Machine Manager is Microsoft's management platform for heterogeneous virtualization infrastructures. Virtual Machine Manager provides centralized management of virtual machines across several popular hypervisors, specifically Windows Server 2008

R2, 2012, and 2012 R2 Hyper-V, VMware ESXi, and Citrix XenServer implementations. It enables increased utilization of physical servers, centralized management of a virtual infrastructure, delegation of administration in distributed environments, and rapid provisioning of new virtual machines by system administrators and users via a self-service portal.

System Center 2012 Virtual Machine Manager includes the ability to build both Hyper-V hosts and host clusters as it moves from being a virtual management solution to a private cloud solution in terms of management and provisioning. This provisioning involves deploying services using service templates in addition to simply configuring storage and networking.

Virtual Machine Manager enables you to

▶ Deliver flexible and cost-effective IaaS. You can pool and dynamically allocate virtualized data center resources (compute, network, and storage) enabling a self-service infrastructure, with flexible role-based delegation and access control.

▶ Apply cloud principles to provisioning and servicing your data center applications with techniques such as service modeling, service configuration, and image-based management. You can also state-separate your applications and services from the underlying infrastructure using server application virtualization. This results in a "service-centric" approach to management where you manage the application or service life cycle and not just data center infrastructure or virtual machines.

▶ Optimize your existing investments by managing multihypervisor environments such as Hyper-V, Citrix XenServer, and VMware using a single pane of glass.

▶ Dynamically optimize your data center resources based on workload demands, while ensuring reliable service delivery with features like high availability.

▶ Achieve best-of-breed virtualization-management for Microsoft workloads such as Exchange and SharePoint.

Deploy and Manage in the Cloud

System Center 2012 App Controller is a self-service portal built on Silverlight, allowing IT managers to more easily deploy and manage applications in cloud infrastructures. App Controller provides a single console for managing multiple private and public clouds while provisioning virtual machines and services to individual business units. Using App Controller with Virtual Machine Manager, data center administrators are able to provision not only virtual machine operating system (OS) deployments but also, leveraging Server App-V, deploy and manage down to the application level, minimizing the number of virtual hard disk (VHD) templates necessary to maintain.

Orchestration and Automation

System Center 2012 Orchestrator is based on Opalis Integration Server (OIS), acquired by Microsoft in December 2009. It provides an automation platform for orchestrating and integrating IT tools to drive down the cost of one's data center operations while improving the reliability of IT processes. Orchestrator enables organizations to automate best practices, such as those found in MOF and ITIL, by using workflow processes that coordinate System Center and other management tools to automate incident response, change and compliance, and service life cycle management processes.

The IT process automation software reduces operational costs and improves IT efficiency by delivering services faster and with fewer errors. Orchestrator replaces manual, resource-intensive, and potentially error-prone activities with standardized, automated processes. This component can orchestrate tasks between Configuration Manager, Operations Manager, Service Manager, Virtual Machine Manager, Data Protection Manager, Active Directory, Windows Azure, and third-party management tools. This positions it to automate any IT process across a heterogeneous environment, providing full solutions for incident management, change and configuration management, and provisioning and service management.

Cloud-Based Configuration Monitoring

System Center Advisor promises to offer configuration-monitoring cloud service for Microsoft Windows Server, SQL Server, Exchange, Lync, Virtual Machine Manager, and SharePoint deployments. Microsoft servers in the Advisor cloud analyze the uploaded data, and then provide feedback to the customer in the Advisor console in the form of alerts about detected configuration issues. System Center Advisor's mission statement is to be a proactive tool to help Microsoft customers avoid configuration problems, reduce downtime, improve performance, and resolve issues faster. Its web-based console is written with Silverlight and is similar to the look and feel of the Microsoft Intune console, Microsoft's cloud-based management service for PCs and other devices.

The Value Proposition of Service Manager

IT organizations must provide efficient and effective services while contending with pressures to reduce operating costs, ensure compliance, and add business value. Service Manager orchestrates people, process, and technology across the Microsoft platform. By integrating information, knowledge, processes, activities, and workflows, System Center Service Manager reduces the cost and improves the quality of IT services.

The value of Service Manager lies in these areas:

- ▶ Delivering efficient and responsive support through the self-service portal for provisioning, self-help and managing requests

- ▶ Optimizing processes and ensuring their use through templates that guide IT analysts through best practices for change and incident management

- ▶ Reducing resolution times by cutting across organizational silos, ensuring that the right information from incident, problem, change, or asset records is accessible through a single pane

- ▶ Extending the value of the Microsoft platform by connecting the processes and activities among System Center components, and using reporting as a driver for key performance indicators (KPIs)

Summary

This chapter introduced you to service management. You learned that service management is a process that touches many areas within ITIL and MOF, such as incident/problem management, change/release management, configuration management, asset management, request fulfillment, automation, dashboards, and reporting. It discussed the functionality delivered in Service Manager that you can leverage to meet these challenges more easily and effectively.

Microsoft's management approach, which incorporates the processes and software tools of MOF and DSI, is a strategy or blueprint intended to build automation and knowledge into data center operations. Microsoft's investment in DSI includes building systems designed for operations, developing an operationally aware platform, and establishing a commitment to intelligent management software.

Service Manager drives integration, efficiency, and IT business alignment. Together with Operations Manager, Configuration Manager, Virtual Machine Manager, Orchestrator, and the other System Center components, Service Manager is a critical component in Microsoft's approach to system management that can increase your organization's agility in delivering on its service commitments to the business.

The next chapter looks at the technology and terminology used by this component, and looks at its features, including changes in System Center 2012 and Service Manager.

Service Manager History and Terminology

From a functional point of view, System Center Service Manager can be seen as a software solution that supports the processes defined in the Microsoft Operations Framework (MOF) and Information Technology Infrastructure Library (ITIL). MOF is Microsoft's practical interpretation of the ITIL standard containing best practices for Information Technology (IT) service management. Chapter 3, "MOF, ITIL, and System Center," discusses MOF and ITIL and how these relate to System Center.

From a technical point of view, System Center Service Manager is a workflow management system, similar to System Center Operations Manager and System Center Orchestrator, where Microsoft has implemented its MOF processes as workflows within the software. Customers are able to extend the workflow management system with their own custom business processes as necessary, as Service Manager supports extensions through customized management packs.

This chapter looks at the history of Service Manager. It discusses the development of the product that led to Service Manager 2010 and changes in the 2012 and 2012 R2 versions. It also discusses terminology used by this System Center component.

The History of Service Manager

In 2006, Microsoft began developing a new product with the codename "Service Desk." The goal of Service Desk was to provide the functionality to support MOF processes in conjunction with the technology provided by other IT management products offered by Microsoft. Microsoft planned for a first release of Service Desk around the second half of 2008.

While developing and testing Service Desk, which was based on Office SharePoint Server 2007 Enterprise in combination with SQL Server 2005, Microsoft concluded that the product did not meet performance and scalability requirements. The decision was made in early 2008 to delay release until 2010. Microsoft also decided to use System Center Operations Manager as a basis for the product, now known as Service Manager. At its annual Microsoft Management Summit (MMS) in April 2010, Microsoft announced the availability of System Center Service Manager 2010, which was the first release of the product.

Evidence that Service Manager was designed on top of Operations Manager technology still exists in this System Center component. As an example, consider the name of the event log that contains Service Manager-specific information; this is still called Operations Manager.

Service Manager 2010

Service Manager became generally available in June 2010. The first release provided functionality around Incident Management, Problem Management, and Change Management. Service Manager included a configuration management database (CMDB) automatically populated through the use of connectors extracting information from Active Directory, System Center Configuration Manager, and System Center Operations Manager. Service Manager 2010 used a self-service portal website allowing end users to create new incidents and change requests and view their status from a web page. It incorporated an analyst portal for managing change requests; allowing IT analysts to view and approve review activities, view and complete manual activities, and view change requests.

NOTE: MATURITY OF SERVICE MANAGER 2010

Service Manager 2010 was clearly a version 1 product, meaning it did not necessarily include all the features and functionality you might find in a more mature IT service management product. Microsoft did not provide all of the processes defined in MOF, and implementing many of the commonly used customizations required directly editing XML in management packs.

For an overview of the functionality provided at that time, the authors recommend the following two articles:

▶ "System Center Service Manager 2010: An Integrated Platform for IT Service Management," written by the Service Manager product team. This can be found at: http://blogs.technet.com/b/systemcenter/archive/2010/04/23/system-center-service-manager-2010-an-integrated-platform-for-it-service-management.aspx.

▶ "Getting Started with System Center Service Manager 2010," written by John Savill from Windows IT Pro, available at http://windowsitpro.com/system-center/getting-started-system-center-service-manager-2010.

In December 2010, Microsoft released Service Pack (SP) 1 for System Center Service Manager 2010, containing more than 500 bug fixes, additional language support, and support for using SQL Server 2008 R2 as a database platform. The service pack did not include any new functionality.

Service Manager 2012

The next version of Service Manager was initially planned as a Release 2 (R2) for Service Manager 2010. However, Microsoft decided to rename this to Service Manager 2012 to align the naming and release cycle with the other System Center components.

Service Manager 2012 adds Service Request Fulfillment and Release Management as new functionality, and enhances existing functionality by including parent incidents as an option for Incident Management, the ability to change the visual perspective for activity workflows, and the capability to integrate Service Manager with System Center Orchestrator, allowing Orchestrator runbooks to be leveraged by the service request fulfillment functionality.

Service Manager 2012 SP 1

Microsoft released System Center 2012 SP 1 shortly after the release of Windows Server 2012, primarily to support installation of System Center on the new operating system. Updates to Service Manager include support for Windows Server 2012 and Windows 8, improved Operations Manager integration by pre-installing the monitoring agent, and a new chargeback feature for tracking utilization of VMM resources. The release also brought support for SQL 2012 with AlwaysOn as an availability topology.

Microsoft discusses what's new in System Center 2012 SP 1 Service Manager at http://technet.microsoft.com/en-us/library/jj614408.aspx.

Service Manager 2012 R2

The System Center 2012 R2 release focuses on delivering advanced capabilities for managing a private cloud platform and delivering new end user computing integrations for managing multidevice environments. For Service Manager, the R2 release includes minor bug fixes that address various stability and performance needs. Support is added to install Service Manager on Windows Server 2012 R2 and Windows 8.1.

Microsoft discusses what's new in System Center 2012 R2 Service Manager at http://technet.microsoft.com/en-us/library/dn299380.aspx.

To resolve issues for the product in between releasing service packs, Microsoft also provides so-called update rollups (URs). Update rollups are released for System Center and consist of several updates for the individual components. To find the latest UR for System Center, http://social.technet.microsoft.com/wiki/contents/articles/4226.list-of-build-numbers-for-system-center-service-manager.aspx provides a complete overview of build numbers and update releases.

Going forward, Microsoft is focusing on the following:

▶ Continuing to update and develop Service Manager, reiterated on February 18, 2014, in the blog post at http://blogs.technet.com/b/servicemanager/archive/2014/02/18/system-center-service-manager-a-phoenix-in-its-own-right.aspx.

▶ Beginning with System Center 2012 Update Rollup 2, Service Manager and the other System Center components are in a quarterly update rollup cycle. This should further improve functionality, stability, and performance.

Service Manager Terminology

This book uses some specific terminology related to System Center Service Manager. The remainder of this chapter briefly discusses this terminology from a technical and functional point of view. Understanding the terminology is essential for further understanding the concepts covered in the upcoming chapters of this book.

Technical Terminology

The next sections describe the terminology used from a technological point of view, covering the terminology of the infrastructure components that make up a Service Manager environment.

Management Groups

A management group is a basic unit of functionality and contains at a minimum a Service Manager management server and a Service Manager database. A management group in Service Manager must have a unique name, which is case sensitive and cannot be changed after it is created. Microsoft does not support using the same management group name for Operations Manager and Service Manager management groups.

A Service Manager implementation must contain at least one management group but could contain more. It contains an operational management group that includes the CMDB and workflow server. It could optionally contain a data warehouse management group for reporting purposes, containing one data warehouse management server and several data warehouse databases.

More information regarding management groups can be found in Chapter 4, "Looking Inside System Center 2012 Service Manager."

Service Manager Management Server

The Service Manager management server provides the core Service Manager functionality. The first installed Service Manager management server is responsible for security access and updating and running workflows. It also provides console access and serves as a target for programming using the software development kit (SDK), and interacts with the Service Manager database. A management group could contain several Service Manager management servers, enabling additional Service Manager administrative consoles to access the Service Manager environment. Having more than one Service Manager management server in a management group allows for scale-out scenarios, providing additional capacity and performance for Service Manager.

Service Manager Database

The Service Manager database contains the data actively used by the Service Manager management server. Data in this operational database can be divided into configuration items, work items, and knowledge items; these make up the CMDB functionality. Settings related to the technical configuration of Service Manager are also stored in this database.

Configuration, Work, and Knowledge Items

Active configuration items are stored within the operational database. These configuration items are either imported using one of the Service Manager connectors or any other automatic mechanism, or are defined manually. Examples of configuration items include computers, software, software updates, users, and groups.

Work items refer to specific items leveraging one of the Service Manager-provided functionalities. Examples include a created incident, change request, or service request.

Knowledge items contain technical documentation supporting work items. Knowledge can help end users and IT personnel to answer common questions, and understand and solve incidents and problems.

Within the Service Manager database, configuration items, work items, and knowledge items can have a relationship with each other. Work items can be related to one or more configuration items or knowledge items. On a configuration item, you can also see work items that reference that configuration item. This allows you to see which incidents are active for a specific computer, and also allows you to see which business services are impacted by a specific problem. Figure 2.1 shows the relationship between configuration items, work items, and knowledge items.

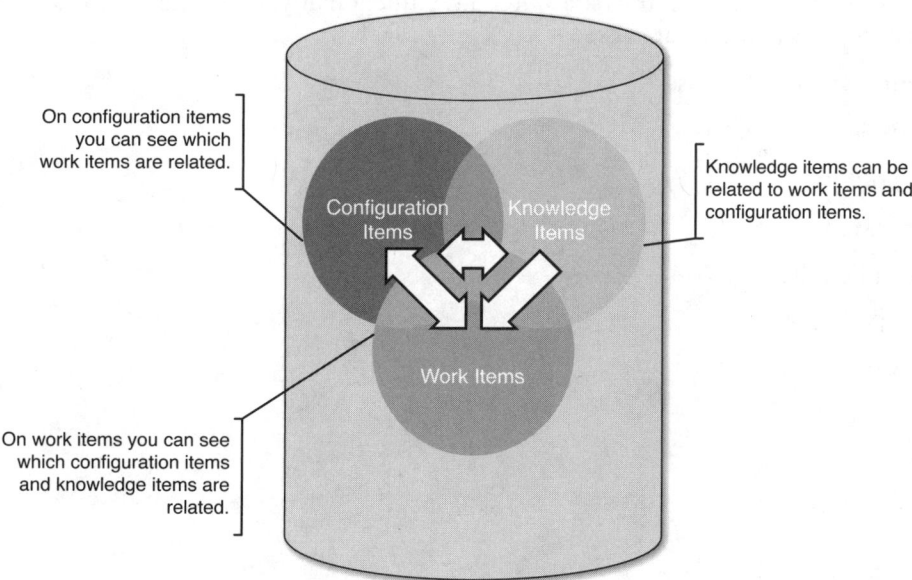

FIGURE 2.1   The Service Manager database contains configuration items, work items, and knowledge items.

Service Manager automatically grooms nonactive items from the Service Manager database; the schedule depends on the type of item. Grooming nonactive items from the Service Manager database keeps the database clean and optimizes its performance.

The Service Manager data warehouse provides historical data, including data that is groomed from the Service Manager database.

Data Warehouse Management Server

The data warehouse management server is responsible for moving data to the data warehouse databases and performing transform, load, and cube processing. The data warehouse management server and its associated databases comprise a data warehouse management group; a Service Manager implementation can have only one data warehouse management group.

You can register one or several Service Manager management groups with one data warehouse management group.

Grooming and registering with the data warehouse is discussed in Chapter 21, "Data Warehouse and Reporting."

Data Warehouse Databases

The following databases make up the data warehouse functionality, and Figure 2.2 shows the relationships among these databases.

- ▶ Reporting Services databases

- ▶ Analysis Services databases

- ▶ DWRepository

- ▶ DWDataMart

- ▶ DWStagingAndConfig

- ▶ CMDWDataMart

- ▶ OMDWDataMart

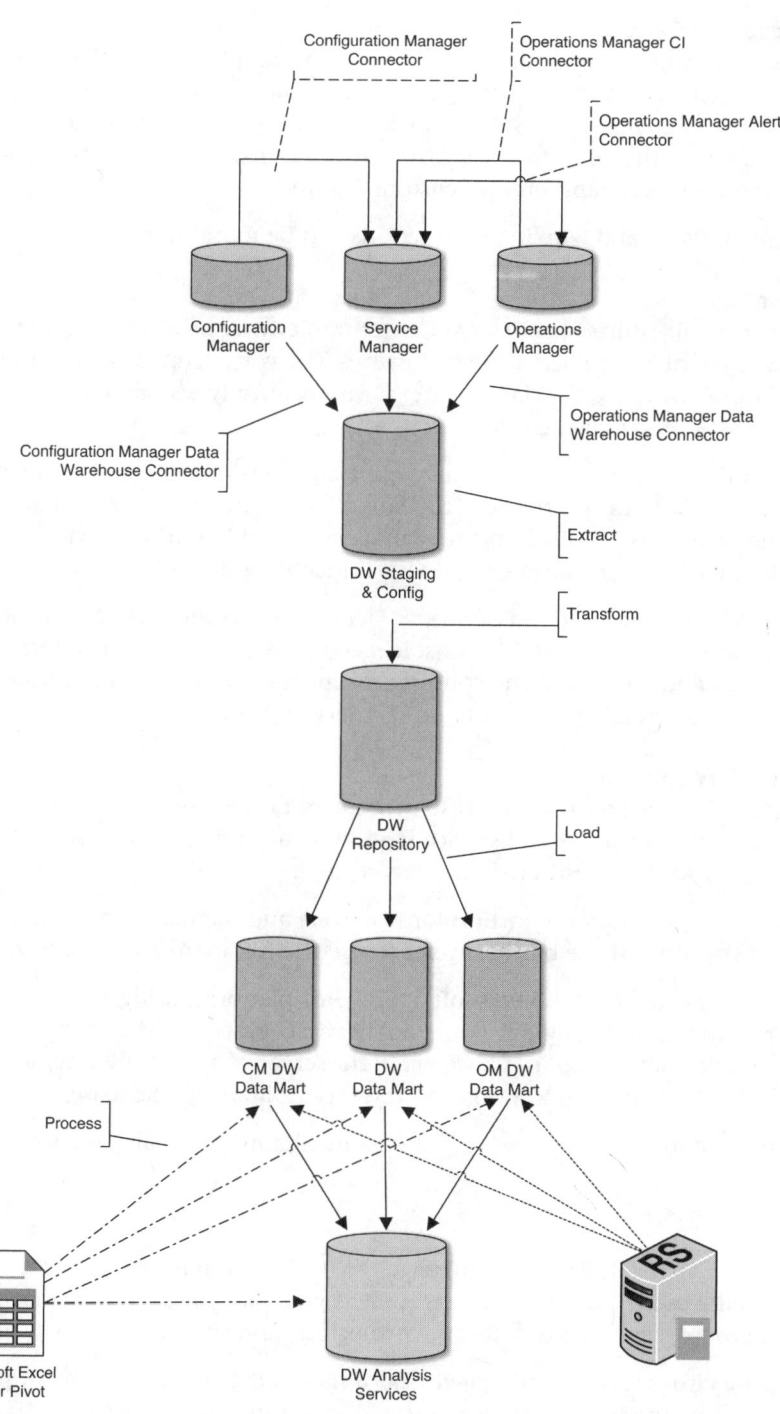

FIGURE 2.2   The Service Manager data warehouse dataflow.

Service Manager Reporting Server

The Service Manager reporting server utilizes SQL Server Reporting Services (SSRS), which is used by Service Manager to publish reports. The reports published by Service Manager can be run from the Service Manager console or the SSRS website. Service Manager provides some reports out of the box; these are installed when installing the data warehouse feature. You can also create and publish custom reports.

More information about using and working with reports can be found in Chapter 21.

Service Manager Console

The Service Manager console utilizes the System Center framework, providing a common look and feel across different System Center components. The console incorporates the look and feel of Microsoft Outlook, making it easier for users already acquainted with Outlook to adopt the Service Manager console.

The console is the administrative interface for managing all facets of the Service Manager infrastructure. It is used to administer the Service Manager infrastructure and work with Service Manager. The console is installed on the management server during Service Manager installation and can be installed on individual machines as well.

Access to the Service Manager console can be scoped depending on the security role of the user starting the console. By scoping the console, Service Manager administrators can limit what a user can do and see within the console. For more information about how to configure security in Service Manager see Chapter 17, "Service Manager Security."

Service Manager Self-Service Portal

The Service Manager self-service portal is a website where end users can interact with Service Manager by creating incidents and service requests. The end user can also view the status of incidents and service requests after they are created.

The self-service portal also provides interaction for reviewers and manual activity implementers, reducing the need for those business roles to use the full management console.

The self-service portal is hosted on the Microsoft SharePoint platform, using the SharePoint web parts functionality and providing applications based on Microsoft Silverlight. The self-service portal also uses a web content server, which is the interface between the Microsoft Silverlight applications and the Service Manager database.

Information on using the self-service portal is included in Chapter 7, "Using Service Manager."

Management Packs

Management packs are eXtensible Markup Language (XML) files containing definitions that define not only data models but also objects such as views for the Service Manager console, workflows, groups, queues, tasks, forms, connectors, and so on.

Management packs are either sealed or unsealed. *Sealed* means that the management pack is read-only and cannot be modified. *Unsealed* means that the management pack is writable, allowing changes to be stored. Management packs can also be bundled into so-called management pack bundles.

All customizations (also referred to as *authoring*) made after installing Service Manager are also stored in management packs. For example, if you want to modify the incident form, you would save your modification from the Service Manager Authoring Tool in a management pack and then import it into Service Manager.

Management packs are discussed in Chapter 20, "Management Packs." Authoring is covered in Chapter 22, "Customizing Service Manager," and Chapter 23, "Advanced Customization Scenarios."

Forms

Work items in Service Manager are created using one of the predefined forms. When an incident resolver wants to log a new incident, he opens a form that asks for details about the incident (see Figure 2.3). Forms for all work items are available out of the box and can be extended using authoring if needed. Within a form, you can supply custom information in a text field, or choose from a list of options using a drop-down list.

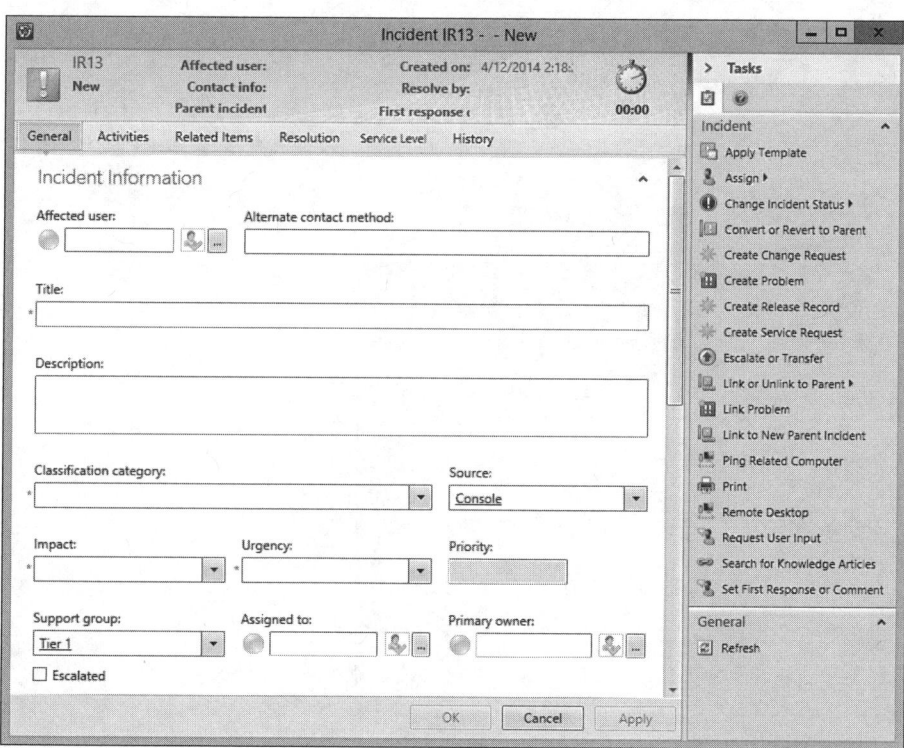

FIGURE 2.3   Default incident form.

Templates

Templates can be used to prefill forms used in Service Manager. Using templates makes it possible to create predefined forms. Microsoft provides many templates out of the box; using the templates lets you provide the default behavior of work items, making it easier for those individuals who are creating the work item, since much of the information needed is already prefilled.

Lists

Lists can be used to provision drop-down lists used within forms (see Figure 2.4). Lists are provided as part of the Service Manager installation and can be modified or extended using custom values.

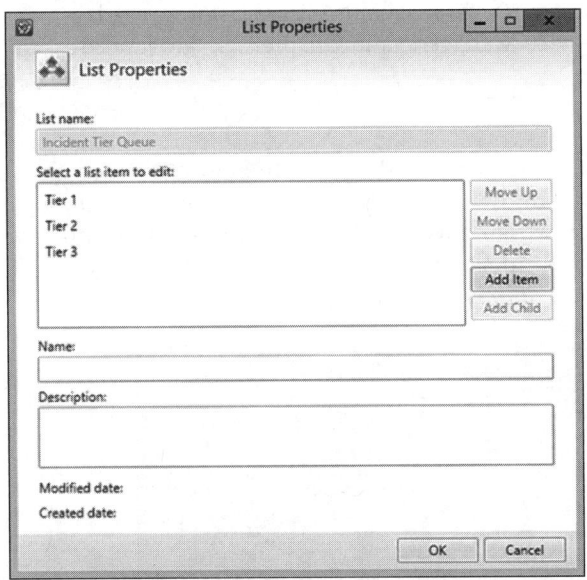

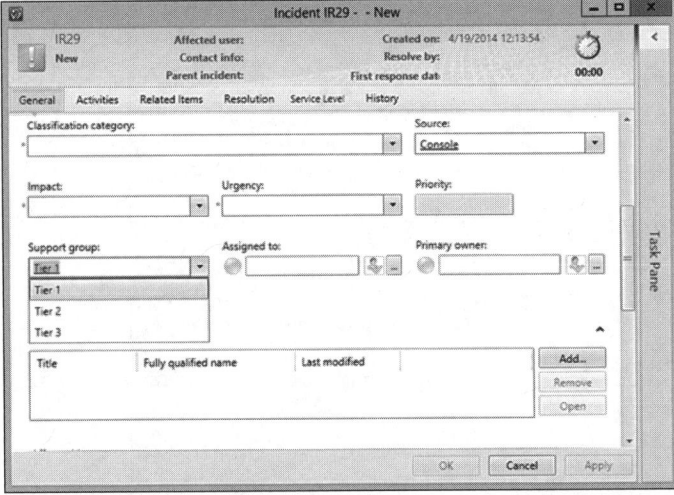

FIGURE 2.4   Default Incident Tier Queue list and corresponding Support group drop-down list in incident form.

Queues

The name "queue" is actually badly chosen by Microsoft, because Incident Management terminology usually refers to a queue as an incident queue, which is the queue where incidents reside belonging to a support group.

However, in the context of Service Manager, queues are used to group work items based on several criteria. To make things even more complex, criteria could be each incident assigned to a support group.

Queues must be created when you want to leverage service level management functionality. If you create a service level objective (SLO), you must supply a queue for the service level. For example, if you want to define an SLO for Tier 1 you should create a queue containing all the incidents for Tier 1.

Another reason for using queues is to give users different rights depending on the queue the work item is part of. For example, you could create an Incident Resolver role that is scoped to incidents that are part of the Tier 1 queue. This means that if an incident is assigned to Support Group Tier 1, the user has the rights of an incident resolver. You could then make that same user a Read-Only operator for the incidents in the other queues, giving that user the right to see incidents but not modify them.

Views

Views contain views of the Service Manager database based on certain criteria. Service Manager comes with many predefined views, and you can create additional views when needed. Figure 2.5 shows the default views provided for Incident Management. If you create an extra incident support group, you could create a corresponding incident view that displays all the incidents dispatched to this group.

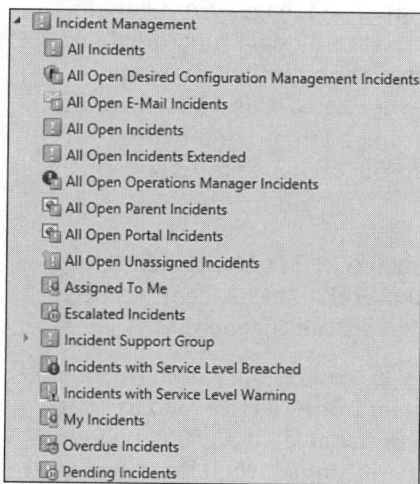

FIGURE 2.5   Default Incident Management views.

Groups

You can create two types of groups within Service Manager:

- ▶ Configuration item groups
- ▶ Catalog item groups

Configuration item groups can be used to group similar configuration items together. A Service Manager administrator could create a group of all the SQL servers, giving a certain Service Manager role the ability to log incidents for those configuration items only.

Catalog item groups are used with Service Request Fulfillment; catalog item groups allow grouping of catalog items together. For example, the Service Manager administrator could decide to make different request offerings and service offerings available, depending on the department to which the end user belongs.

Groups can have static or dynamic members based on certain criteria; they can also be nested. More information about catalog groups can be found in Chapter 10, "Service Manager Service Catalog."

Tasks

Tasks allow you to execute certain actions based on the selected context. For example, when you create a computer object, the Tasks pane of the console shows only the actions you can perform for that configuration item, such as creating a change request for the selected configuration item. Tasks available per process are further explained in Chapters 11 through 15, covering the IT service management processes supported by Service Manager.

Connectors

Connectors are used to transfer data into Service Manager. Out of the box, Service Manager contains connectors for Active Directory, Operations Manager, Configuration Manager, Orchestrator, and Virtual Machine Manager. To transfer data from other systems, Service Manager provides CSV-import capabilities through the CSV connector. Connectors are discussed in Chapter 8, "Working with Connectors." Microsoft also provides an Exchange connector, but rather than importing configuration items, this connector allows Service Manager to interact with Microsoft Exchange to receive emails.

Notification

Notification provides the ability to send out emails from Service Manager to involved individuals. A notification can be used to notify an end user that an incident has been created, or to notify a reviewer that a new review activity is awaiting approval.

Notifications can be sent by creating subscriptions or by extending the workflows in Service Manager. The notifications are translated into rules in the Service Manager database; these are evaluated each time an object is created or updated, at a predefined interval, or when a relationship object is added or deleted (for example, when the assigned user is added to an incident). Notifications are discussed in Chapter 16, "Managing Notifications."

Notification Channels

Notification channels are used by the notification functionality provided by Service Manager. By default Service Manager contains only an email notification channel, which can be configured by specifying a Simple Mail Transfer Protocol (SMTP) server.

Email Templates

Email templates are used when sending notifications from Service Manager. An email template contains a message subject and a message body, which can either be in plain text or HTML. Within email templates, you could define dynamic fields (variables) that are filled in at time of sending the notification, comparable with mail merge functionality provided by Microsoft Word.

Subscriptions

Subscriptions can be used to specify when a notification must be sent. Subscriptions have extended capabilities when it comes to notifications; this includes sending to static recipients and creating recurring notifications. As an example, you could send a reminder notification every 24 hours to a reviewer asking him to approve or deny a review activity.

Runbooks

Runbooks contain an overview of the runbooks imported using the System Center Orchestrator connector. Runbooks can be used from runbook automation activities, which can be triggered from different work items.

Functional Terminology

The next sections describe the terminology used from a functional point of view; these cover the terminology of the components used when working with Service Manager.

Announcements

Announcements provide a method for communicating brief messages with end users via the self-service portal. These could be used, for example, to announce maintenance taking place, or to communicate about currently known issues.

Displaying announcements is not enabled in the self-service portal by default, but this functionality can be added by adding a portal announcement page in SharePoint. Announcements can be created using the Service Manager console or the self-service portal. See Chapter 7 for information.

Automation and Chargeback

Automation is about using control systems to minimize or reduce human intervention. Chargeback is a mechanism used by Information Technology (IT) departments to allocate and/or bill costs associated with departmental usage. Chapter 12, "Automation and Chargeback," provides detail about these concepts, which leverage other System Center components such as System Center Virtual Machine Manager, System Center Operations Manager, and System Center Orchestrator.

Terminology Related to Work Items

Service Manager supports several IT service management processes out of the box. How these processes supported by Service Manager interact with MOF and ITIL is described in Chapter 3. The supported processes follow:

- ▶ Incident Management

- ▶ Problem Management

- ▶ Service Request Fulfillment

- ▶ Change Management

- ▶ Configuration Management

- ▶ Release Management

Incident Management

The purpose of Incident Management is to deal with incidents, unplanned interruptions in IT service, or degradation in IT service quality. Incident Management as a process is described in Chapter 3. Incident Management within Service Manager from a technical point of view is covered in Chapter 11, "Incident Management."

Problem Management

The intent of Problem Management is to deal with unknown causes of one or more incidents. A problem provides a structured way to find the root cause of the incidents and to relate existing incidents and change requests so the root cause can be solved. Chapter 3 covers the Problem Management process in more detail, and Chapter 13, "Problem Management," discusses how to set up Problem Management in Service Manager.

Service Request Fulfillment

The purpose of Service Request Fulfillment is to deal with service requests, which are predefined requests that can be requested from an IT service provider. The Service Request Fulfillment process is detailed in Chapter 3. Chapter 10 describes how to set up Service Request Fulfillment within Service Manager.

Service Request Fulfillment uses a service catalog in which service offerings are displayed. Service offerings can contain one or more request offerings. Service offerings are user-facing catalog items that describe an IT service and contain a set of specific services users can request. A request offering is a user-facing process that creates a service request or incident.

Change Management

Change Management provides standardized methods and procedures for introducing changes to IT services. This is accomplished by creating change requests, which consist of a series of activities necessary to complete the change. Change Management as a process is described in Chapter 3. Setting up Change Management is discussed in Chapter 14, "Change Request and Configuration Management."

Release Management

Release Management is the process of building, testing, and deploying releases into a managed environment. This is done by creating release requests. Release Management as a process is discussed in Chapter 3. Chapter 15, "Release Management," discusses setting up Release Management in Service Manager.

Activity Management

Activity Management is actually not an IT service management process. Activities can be created within the processes, however, and Microsoft made the decision to consolidate all of these activities into one node within the Service Manager console. Activities contain action items for users or a group of users; this could be something that needs to be reviewed or something that needs to be done. There are several types of activities; a list follows.

▶ **Manual activities:** A manual activity describes something that someone needs to do.

▶ **Review activities:** These describe something that someone needs to review.

▶ **Parallel activities:** These describe more activities that can be executed in parallel.

▶ **Sequential activities:** These describe more activities that must be executed in a sequential order.

▶ **Dependent activities:** These describe additional activities that are dependent on each other.

Service Level Management

Service level management in Service Manager provides the ability to associate and monitor service level targets for incidents and service requests. Service level management consists of a calendar, the definition of what you want to measure, and the service level objective, where you specify threshold values for Warning or Breached. Chapter 11 discusses service level management in detail.

Terminology Related to Configuration Items

This section describes the terminology used within configuration items. Configuration items are normally imported using one of the connectors provided with Service Manager. It is possible though to use other methods such as Orchestrator, PowerShell, or any other programmatic method to import configuration items into the Service Manager database (CMDB).

Computers

These contain all the computer objects that are imported using one of the connectors or custom-created CIs using the `Computer` class.

Printers

Printers contain all the published printers in Active Directory imported using the AD connector or any custom method.

Software

Software contains all the software imported from the Configuration Manager connector. The software displayed is gathered by Configuration Manager using its inventory functionality.

Software Updates

Software updates contain the software updates imported using the Configuration Manager connector, leveraging the information coming from the software update functionality.

Users

Users contain both users and groups imported using the Active Directory connector.

Business Services

Business services are imported from Operations Manager, where they are known as distributed applications. Chapter 9, "Business Services," discusses business services and how you could use them in Service Manager.

Builds

Builds are used within the Release Management process and represent a version or build of a specific type of software, program, operating system image, and more.

Environments

Environments are also used within the Release Management process and are used to describe which environments are available in your environment. A build can reside in one or more environments. Examples of environments include Development, Test, Acceptance, and Production.

Terminology Related to Knowledge Items

Knowledge items consist of knowledge articles, which are forms that contain knowledge information. Knowledge articles can be filled with external knowledge imported from a URL or with company-specific information. The articles can be extended with keywords, making them easier to find, and rated to give them higher ranking in the search functionality within Service Manager. Knowledge articles can also be related to configuration items and work items, and can be viewed from both the Service Manager console and the self-service portal. Information about creating knowledge articles can be found in Chapter 7.

Summary

This chapter discussed the history of Service Manager and how it evolved to its current version. The chapter also discussed terminology from a technical point of view, covering configuration items, work items, and knowledge items, and how they relate to each other. It also covered functional terminology, defining the concepts that you may encounter when working with Service Manager.

MOF, ITIL, and System Center

Service Manager is a departure from other System Center components in that it is not fundamentally a technology management tool, but a work management tool. To make the most of Service Manager requires understanding the work it is intended to manage: the work associated with managing Information Technology (IT) services.

As outlined in Chapter 1, "Service Management Basics," IT service management best practices are described in a number of established process frameworks. Service Manager derives its processes from two of those frameworks, Microsoft Operations Framework (MOF) and the IT Infrastructure Library (ITIL). This chapter provides a primer on the MOF and ITIL processes available in System Center 2012 Service Manager. It discusses the IT service management concepts and processes central to Service Manager, and can be used as an introductory resource for those IT professionals with limited IT service management experience needing to apply these concepts and processes using Service Manager. Process sections outline the process purpose, roles, and basic activities, and describe how the processes relate to one another and how their effectiveness is measured. It is specifically intended to provide context for Chapters 9 through 15 in this book that describe specific Service Manager functionality.

About ITIL

The IT Infrastructure Library, first developed by the British government in the 1980s, was intended to improve the quality of that government's IT service provisioning. ITIL was later released publicly in the interest of providing a framework of good practice for IT service provisioning.

At its core, ITIL is a set of books centering on a collection of IT management processes and functions.

ITIL has been collaboratively developed by IT professionals worldwide. This approach taps the subject matter expertise and real-world experience of the developers to produce guidance that is high quality, pragmatic, and relevant. ITIL underwent a significant revision in 2007, which introduced an integrated service life cycle approach to IT service management. Intended to emphasize the business value of IT services, it addressed service management challenges brought about by technology advancements such as virtualization and operational trends such as outsourcing. Figure 3.1 illustrates the areas of ITIL.

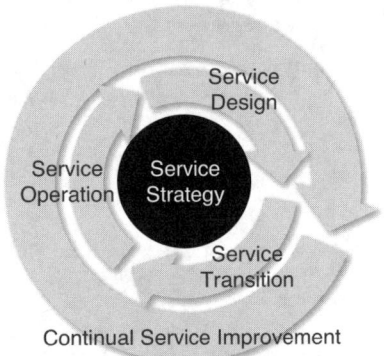

FIGURE 3.1   The IT Infrastructure Library.

The core of ITIL is comprised of five volumes, each corresponding to a step in the service life cycle:

- ▶ **Service Strategy:** This volume covers the identification of market opportunities for which services could be developed to meet a requirement on the part of internal or external customers. Key areas are service portfolio management and financial management.

- ▶ **Service Design:** This focuses on the work required to develop the service strategy into a comprehensive design for delivering and supporting the service. Key areas are availability management, capacity management, continuity management, and security management.

- ▶ **Service Transition:** The Service Transition volume centers on deploying the service design to production to create a new service or modify an existing one. Key areas are change management, release management, configuration management, and service knowledge management.

- ▶ **Service Operation:** This volume outlines the activities necessary to operate the services in accordance with agreed functional requirements and service levels. Key areas are incident management, problem management, and request fulfillment.

- ▶ **Continual Service Improvement:** The Continual Service Improvement volume presents techniques for improving the quality and business value of IT services. Key areas are service reporting, service measurement, and service level management.

The ITIL ecosystem is mature; it includes a certification scheme supported by accredited training as well as a range of independent consulting services and software tools. ITIL best practice is also the basis for ISO/IEC 20000, the international service management standard. This allows ITIL adopter organizations to be certified as compliant with service management best practices.

ITIL is intended to apply broadly regardless of the underpinning technology. It was designed with the intention of being adapted by commercial IT product and service companies to complement their offerings with consistent process guidance.

ITIL remains the property of the British government and is recognized as the most comprehensive publicly available and widely adopted guidance on IT service management.

3

About MOF

MOF is an ITIL adaptation originating in the late 1990s as a resource for Microsoft customers to help enhance the reliability, stability, and security of their Microsoft-based environments. MOF was developed to extend ITIL's descriptive operations guidance and provide more prescriptive guidance specific to Microsoft technologies. Similar to ITIL, MOF takes a life cycle-based approach to organizing guidance on how to implement reliable and cost-effective IT services based on Microsoft technologies. This life cycle now includes the former Microsoft Solutions Framework (MSF), thereby incorporating guidance on solution development into MOF.

Illustrated in Figure 3.2, the MOF life cycle is based on three phases underpinned by a layer of core practices and principles. Each of these components contains a collection of related service management functions (SMFs), which define activities and roles. They also feature management reviews, which are internal controls to ensure ongoing business-IT alignment, capture organizational learning, and highlight improvement opportunities.

▶ **Plan phase:** The Plan phase focuses on aligning IT service strategy to support business needs. Key areas are policy, financial management, and reliability.

▶ **Deliver phase:** This phase outlines practices to ensure IT services are developed and deployed so they are matched to business requirements and ready for operations. Key areas are planning, building, deploying, and stabilizing service-based solutions.

▶ **Operate phase:** The Operate phase covers maintaining and supporting IT services so they reliably and efficiently meet the needs of the business. Key areas are operations, service monitoring, customer service, and problem management.

▶ **Manage layer:** This layer integrates and coordinates work throughout the three life cycle phases with emphasis on maximizing business value and minimizing risk. Key areas are governance, risk, compliance, change, and configuration.

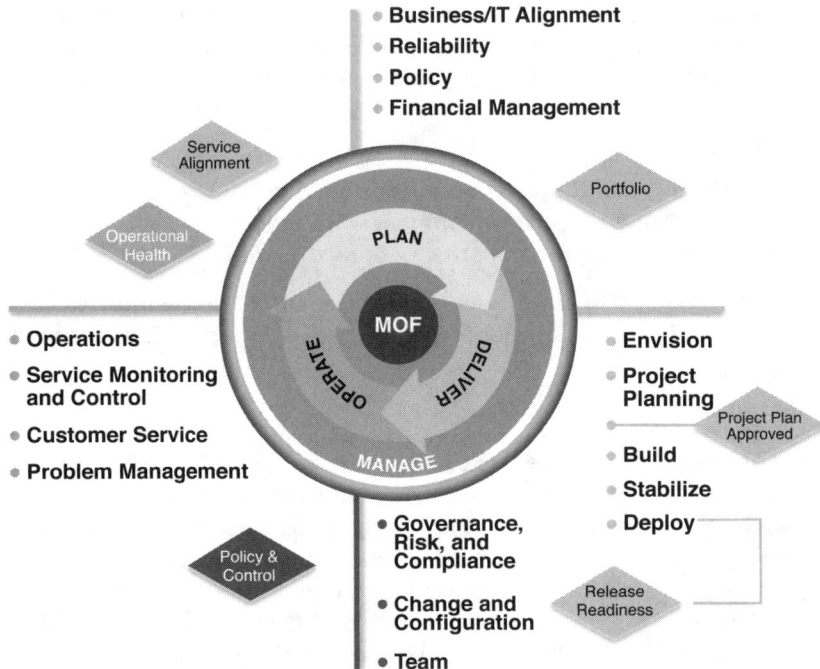

FIGURE 3.2   Microsoft Operations Framework.

Currently at version 4.0, MOF is comprised of a series of free downloadable whitepapers and job aids. Some of these resources feature general process guidance that is applicable to both Microsoft and non-Microsoft environments, while many resources provide guidance specific Microsoft technologies. MOF's content reflects the experience of Microsoft's field professionals, customers, partners, and internal IT groups.

MOF, ITIL, and the Cloud

Cloud computing and the new IT service paradigms it poses are reflected in MOF and ITIL. Microsoft has continued to evolve MOF and to apply MOF principles and practices to specific Microsoft technologies, publishing content outlining the applicability of service management principles to the private cloud and MOF-based guides for various cloud component technologies. The most recent revision of ITIL, published in 2011, addresses cloud computing, predominantly in the Service Strategy book.

When considering IT service management's applicability to any computing model, it is important to focus on the principles that underpin IT service management. Many of these principles are essentially timeless, making them equally relevant to cloud computing and the mainframe-computing era. The processes covered in this chapter are as equally relevant to traditional enterprise computing as they are to the cloud. Enterprise or cloud issues need to be fixed, changes implemented, requests fulfilled, and configurations managed. While the approaches may vary, the objectives are consistent:

▶ IT service management has been applied to traditional enterprise computing for many years, with the intent of keeping a relatively static catalog of IT services predictable, secure, cost efficient, and matched to business needs. Cycles in traditional enterprise environments can be long with reasonable opportunity to plan and adapt as needs change.

▶ Cloud services are often on-demand and offered through self-service so consumers can easily select the service they want when they want it, increasingly from multiple device platforms. This variability means cloud services must be highly elastic, scaling rapidly and automatically as demand changes. Cloud services are usually underpinned by pools of physical and virtual resources shared among consumers, with individual consumption measured to provide accurate charging. These environments require IT service management practices that reflect limited opportunities for planning and adaptation.

Consider how change management is executed in both traditional enterprise and cloud environments: Change is common in both environments, so change management is an essential process with common objectives of making changes efficiently, consistently, and with limited service disruption. However, the process itself might vary between the two environments as might the definition of a change. The traditional enterprise environment may feature an established rhythm with defined change approval cycles and deployment. Contrast this with cloud environments, where speed and responsiveness dictate a more fluid rhythm, with highly flexible approval and deployment cycles.

The virtualization and automation technologies prevalent in cloud computing heavily influence the means in which IT service management is applied. These technologies make it easier to respond more rapidly and efficiently to demand changes and service disruptions. While these technologies play an important role in enterprise computing, they are even more vital to the success of cloud environments.

> **TIP: FOR MORE INFORMATION ON MOF OR ITIL**
>
> This chapter is merely a primer on a small set of guidance found in both ITIL and MOF. Those interested in additional information regarding ITIL should visit http://www.itil-officialsite.com. For details on MOF, visit http://www.microsoft.com/mof.

Applying IT Service Management

The topic of applying IT service management could easily fill a book itself. Because it is process-based, applying IT service management typically involves process improvement initiatives that can comprise procedural changes, terminology changes, role changes, and metric changes. While this book is about software, software is only part of the picture of effective IT service management implementation. The changes associated with IT service management initiatives often require people to work differently and sometimes require them to think differently, which may represent the greatest challenges to success. Quality and productivity require coordination between technology, processes, and people.

Approaching IT Service Management Initiatives

There is no precise formula for implementing IT service management in an IT organization. As noted in the previous section, IT service management is implemented as a set of individual process improvement initiatives. These initiatives generally follow a standard approach, which involves

- ▶ Establishing measurable objectives for the process
- ▶ Determining gaps in the existing process that prevent it from achieving the established objectives
- ▶ Developing action plans to close those gaps
- ▶ Implementing action plans
- ▶ Monitoring of objectives and adjustment to processes as needed

The time and effort associated with an individual process improvement initiative varies based on the size of the organization, the size of the gaps identified, and the resources applied. The following are some guiding principles for IT service management implementation and are broadly applicable to any related initiative:

- ▶ **Begin with the end in mind:** Like any improvement initiative, a clear picture of the desired end state keeps work on track. An IT organization pursuing an IT service management initiative should be able to articulate the benefits expected from the overall initiative, along with the benefits expected from the adoption of or improvements to individual processes. Ideally, these will be measurable (such as reduction in total incidents, reduction in failed changes), which can be tracked over time as an indicator of success. Keep in mind that IT service management provides the means to achieving desired results and does not represent an end in itself.

- ▶ **Define scope carefully:** As noted in the "Applying IT Service Management" section, these initiatives typically demand cultural change in addition to technical change, and most organizations can only deal with so much change at one time. It is important to have a realistic sense of how much change an organization can deal with at once and to organize IT service management initiatives based on that limit. For example, a small IT organization may not be in a good position to absorb changes to more than one process at a time effectively. In this case, it is probably better to focus on a single process at a time and move to the next process only when the current process reaches a predefined level of quality.

- ▶ **Think beyond the tool:** IT service management improvement initiatives frequently center on the adoption of a new software tool such as System Center Service Manager, but IT service management should not be thought of as merely a software project. The effectiveness of any IT service management software tool depends in part on how well the tool fits the organization, how well the tool is configured to meet the organization's specific needs, and how consistently the organization utilizes the tool.

▶ **Don't expect results without the right resources:** Like any project or program an organization undertakes, success depends on adequate resourcing throughout its lifespan. An IT service management initiative probably won't be able to attain and sustain success if the right resources are not devoted at the right times and in the right measures. It is important that individuals within the IT organization provide ownership of selected process-based projects; these owners should possess a clear picture of success for that process.

▶ **Take a long view:** IT service management initiatives typically get plenty of attention when something new is implemented, but that attention often declines with time as processes mature and resources are needed for new projects. While this is natural, care must be taken to ensure that the initial investment in IT service management improvements is sustained over time by applying adequate ongoing attention. This means continually measuring results and responding with adjustments needed to meet defined objectives.

MOF and ITIL Processes Supported by Service Manager

Table 3.1 outlines the IT service management processes supported by Service Manager and provides guidance on where information on those processes can be found in both MOF and ITIL.

TABLE 3.1   Service Manager Processes in MOF and ITIL

Service Manager Process	MOF SMF	ITIL Process
Incident Management	Customer Service	Incident Management
Service Request Fulfillment	Customer Service	Request Fulfillment
Problem Management	Problem	Problem Management
Change Management	Change and Configuration	Change Management
Release Management	Change and Configuration / Deploy	Release and Deployment Management
Configuration Management	Change and Configuration	Service Asset and Configuration Management

IT Service Management Processes in Service Manager

The following sections summarize the Service Manager-supported processes. Table 3.2 lists the subsections contained in each section.

TABLE 3.2   IT Service Management Processes in Service Manager

Subsection	Contents
Process purpose	Summarizes the key outcomes and value proposition
Common roles	Highlights the typical roles within the process
Essential activities	Outlines the fundamental work performed to achieve the purpose
Relationships to other processes	Describes how the process relates to the other processes supported by Service Manager
How to measure	Presents common metrics

About Incident Management

An *incident* is an unplanned interruption in IT service or degradation in IT service quality or a potential disruption or degradation. Examples of incidents follow:

▶ The outage of a major business application

▶ A failed hard disk in a RAID array

▶ Data missing in a report

▶ The inability of a single end user to print normally

As these examples indicate, incidents vary in scale and severity. Incidents might affect only one user or an entire enterprise, and their resulting business impact might be small or significant. Incidents with the greatest business impact are termed *major incidents*.

The Purpose of Incident Management

The purpose of Incident Management is to deal with incidents by restoring normal service operation as quickly as possible. By doing so, Incident Management helps minimize adverse effects and supports delivery of services in line with customer expectations.

Effective Incident Management contributes to high service availability and provides valuable data about IT service delivery and usage. For example, incident data can help IT service managers identify underperforming IT components, highlight gaps in user knowledge, and uncover unmet user requirements.

Common Roles in Incident Management

The common roles in Incident Management follow:

▶ The *affected user* is the end user experiencing an interruption in an IT service or degradation in service quality.

▶ *Analysts* are the individual IT staff members responsible for recording, investigating, diagnosing, and resolving incidents.

▶ The *primary owner* of an incident is an analyst who monitors incident progress throughout its life cycle.

▶ *Support groups* are the specialist IT workgroups in which analysts work, with the service desk being the principle support group in the process.

Essential Process Activities within Incident Management

Figure 3.3 illustrates the activities essential to the Incident Management process; these are described in this section. Incident Management begins with the detection of an interruption to normal service; this is recorded as an incident. Initial support is provided and classification applied to codify the nature and priority of the incident. The incident is investigated and diagnosed and an appropriate resolution is implemented so that normal service can be recovered, after which the incident is closed.

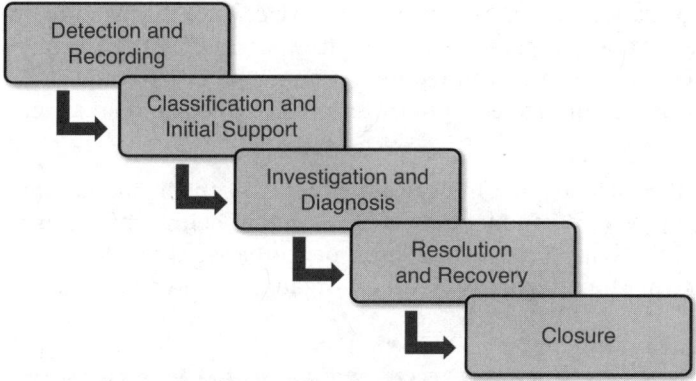

FIGURE 3.3   Incident Management process activities.

▶ **Detection and recording:** The Incident Management process begins when a request for help is received from an affected user by the service desk or an alert is received based on an event in a monitoring tool such as Operations Manager. The receipt of this help request or alert is the detection of the incident.

When an incident is detected, a unique record of this contact is created with relevant details about the user and the reported issue or event. This record might be created manually by an analyst or created automatically if submission occurs through mail, a self-service resource, or if the monitoring tool is configured to automatically generate an incident record.

Information typically recorded at this point includes

▶ Date and time created

▶ User affected by the incident (where applicable) including contact information

▶ A brief summary of the reported issue or event

▶ The source of the incident (e.g., phone, email, Operations Manager alert)

NOTE: AUTOMATED INCIDENT RECORDING IN SERVICE MANAGER

Service Manager supports automated recording of incidents from email through the Exchange connector, automated recording of incidents from Operations Manager alerts through the Operations Manager Alert connector, and automated recording of incidents based on noncompliant configuration items through the Configuration Manager connector. Service Manager connectors are discussed in Chapter 8, "Working with Connectors."

▶ **Classification and initial support:** Upon recording of the incident, the analyst can classify the incident and provide initial support. This includes confirming that this is indeed a disruption or degradation in service, prioritizing the incident, and assigning it to a support group and/or analyst for resolution.

If this is a request for information, an existing feature or service, or a new feature or service, it is categorized as a service request after which it is handled by the Service Request Fulfillment process. If what has been reported is an actual or potential service failure, it is confirmed as an incident, prioritization is applied, and an assignment made.

A category is assigned to the incident that indicates the nature of the incident. The category may indicate the type of component affected (examples being email, printing, business application), the symptom (such as error, performance issue, damage), or a combination of the two. The category is useful for organizing and analyzing incidents in reports.

NOTE: INCIDENT CATEGORIZATION IN SERVICE MANAGER

Service Manager 2012 provides a configurable, hierarchical list for incident categorization.

Prioritization of an incident involves determining its impact and urgency, the product of which indicates the incident's overall importance.

▶ *Impact* indicates the overall business impact of the incident; this is typically determined by the number of users affected and the business process(es) affected. A single user unable to print is likely a low impact incident while an entire department unable to utilize a business-critical application is a likely high impact incident.

▶ *Urgency* indicates the speed with which resolution is required and like impact, business impact is the key criterion. Incidents with high business impact are generally classified with high urgency, while incidents with low business impact are generally classified with low urgency.

NOTE: INCIDENT PRIORITIZATION IN SERVICE MANAGER

Service Manager features a configurable priority matrix based on impact and urgency values.

The incident is assigned to the support group and/or analyst best equipped to resolve it. In some cases, analysts within the service desk may be equipped to resolve the incident; in other cases, the incident may be immediately escalated to analysts in a specialist support group. An incident may be assigned to several support groups and/or analysts throughout its life cycle.

NOTE: SERVICE LEVEL OBJECTIVES IN SERVICE MANAGER

Service level objectives (SLOs) for response, assignment, and resolution can be applied to incidents in Service Manager. SLOs feature configurable calendars and time-based metrics that can be applied based on a range of criteria such as incident priority, support group, category, or source.

In some cases, it might be desirable to assign a primary owner to the incident. This analyst remains assigned to the incident until it is resolved and ensures that the incident progresses promptly and efficiently toward resolution.

If the incident is the result of an outage or other large-scale service disruption, it may be appropriate to relate the incident to a single parent incident. This parent incident is effectively the master incident for the disruption to which many child incidents can be linked to coordinate diagnosis and resolution and to better indicate scope.

NOTE: PARENT/CHILD INCIDENTS IN SERVICE MANAGER

Service Manager provides the ability to identify individual incidents as parent incidents to which multiple child incidents can be linked to synchronize status and automate resolution or reactivation.

▶ **Investigation and diagnosis:** Resolving an incident begins with the assigned analyst reviewing the data recorded about the incident through this point in the process. Some investigation may be required to confirm the data gathered or collect additional relevant information. Investigation may also include reviewing knowledge base articles to determine whether a solution already exists, reviewing problem records to determine whether the incident is the result of a known error, and reviewing active changes to determine whether this is a planned interruption.

Diagnosis of the incident may determine that the incident needs reassignment to a different support group or analyst should additional knowledge, troubleshooting resources, or permissions are necessary for resolution. In these cases, the incident is escalated or transferred to the appropriate support group or analyst.

Throughout this activity, the analysts involved will document their work in the incident record. This provides a clear record of the steps taken to investigate and diagnose the incident. It is also important to keep the affected user(s) informed and set expectations about when resolution will occur.

NOTE: LOGGING ANALYST ACTIONS IN SERVICE MANAGER

Service Manager features an incident action log in which analyst comments can be recorded throughout the duration of the incident.

▶ **Resolution and recovery:** Investigation and diagnosis ideally culminate in prompt identification of an appropriate fix or workaround. A *fix* indicates a permanent repair for the root cause of the incident, while a *workaround* indicates a temporary solution to restore normal service with continued chance of incident recurrence.

Depending on the nature of the incident and the identified fix or workaround, resolution may be straightforward and immediate, or could be complex. A simple and immediate resolution may involve installing a patch on a desktop or unlocking a user account. A more complex and less immediate resolution may necessitate application of a service pack to an application environment to fix a bug or the procurement of new hardware to replace a failed component; either may involve engaging the Change Management process for authorization and scheduling.

Again, work in this step is documented in the incident record as this ensures a full accounting of the resolution with communication to the affected user(s) as needed. Resolution is categorized, capturing the nature of the resolution (e.g., resolved on first contact, resolved by a vendor, knowledge transfer provided) to aid in trending where and how incidents are resolved.

▶ **Closure:** After the fix or workaround is applied, the analyst confirms with the affected user(s) that normal service has been restored. Depending on the nature of the incident and the impacted service, confirmation of resolution may be immediate (confirming an account is unlocked) or may require some time (confirming a weekly process runs as expected).

The incident record is not closed until resolution is confirmed and data in the incident record is complete. As the incident is now a historic record of the event, accurate codification is essential to provide useful reporting.

NOTE: RESOLUTION AND CLOSURE IN SERVICE MANAGER

Service Manager features distinct Resolved and Closed statuses, which must occur in order so that incidents are always resolved and then closed.

Other Service Manager-Supported Processes Relating to Incident Management

Table 3.3 outlines the relationship between Incident Management and other Service Manager-supported processes.

TABLE 3.3   How Incident Management Relates to Other Processes

Incident Management Provides	Incident Management Receives
To Problem Management:	**From Problem Management:**
Incident data may indicate the presence of an underlying problem or may indicate the effectiveness of a problem solution.	Incident Management relies on data about problems and known errors during investigation and diagnosis.
To Configuration Management:	**From Configuration Management:**
Incident data may highlight faulty configuration items.	Configuration data may be used in investigation and diagnosis.
To Change Management:	**From Change Management:**
Incident data may highlight partial or complete failures in changes.	Incidents may require Change Management for application of complex fixes.

How to Measure Incident Management

Table 3.4 presents metrics useful in managing the Incident Management process and measuring its effectiveness.

TABLE 3.4   Incident Management Metrics

Metrics	Purpose
Count of incidents created	Indicate overall volume and provide control measures
Count of incidents resolved	
Count of incidents active	
Count of incidents on hold	
Percentage of incidents within service level objective	Indicates timeliness of key portions of the process (time to assign, time to respond, time to resolution)
	May suggest need for process improvement, additional staffing, or changes in SLO targets
Percentage of major incidents	Indicates overall volume of highly critical incidents
Percentage of incidents by resolution category	Indicates how and where incidents were resolved (such as first contact, tier 2, trained end user)
	Indicates the effectiveness of various support tiers
	Highlights opportunities to train users and prevent related incidents
Percentage of incidents by support group	Indicates the groups responsible for creating or resolving incidents

The data in Table 3.4 may be organized and filtered as follows:

▶ By analyst to establish individual workload and assess individual performance

▶ By support group to establish team workload

▶ By priority to establish ratios and trends in incident criticality

▶ By source to highlight where incidents originate

About Service Request Fulfillment

A service request is a general term that represents of range of requests made by an IT service provider. The scope of service requests range from requests for an established service, a new service, or for information. Examples of service requests follow:

▶ A request for access to a shared folder

▶ A request for a new report

▶ A request for help in utilizing an application

▶ A request for a new device

▶ A proposal for a new application feature

▶ A request for information about how to obtain a new device

The Purpose of Service Request Fulfillment

Service Request Fulfillment provides a mechanism to handle requests for standard services with an established fulfillment model or requests for information. The objective of Service Request Fulfillment is to provide users with prompt, convenient, and centralized access to standard services and information, and to fulfill requests efficiently and consistently. Centralizing and standardizing the process of requesting, approving, and fulfilling service requests reduces effort and turnaround, ensuring consistent application of policies and fulfillment procedures.

Common Roles in Service Request Fulfillment

The common roles in Service Request Fulfillment follow:

▶ The *affected user* is the end user requesting service or information.

▶ *Owners* are IT staff members with overall responsibility for fulfillment of service requests.

▶ *Reviewers* approve or reject service requests; they may reside inside or outside the IT organization depending on the nature of the request.

▶ *Activity implementers* are IT staff members that carry out fulfillment activities within overall service requests.

▶ *Support groups* are the specialist IT workgroups in which analysts work, with the service desk being the principle support group in the process.

Essential Activities within Service Request Fulfillment

Figure 3.4 shows the activities essential to the Service Request Fulfillment process. Service Request Fulfillment begins with receipt of a request that is recorded and appropriately classified for the proper fulfillment model to be applied. When necessary, appropriate approval is obtained and the request is fulfilled. Satisfactory completion of the request is confirmed before the request is ultimately closed.

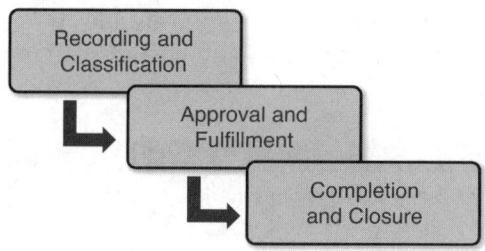

FIGURE 3.4   Service Request Fulfillment process activities.

▶ **Recording and classification:** Service Request Fulfillment begins with receipt of a user request for information, fulfillment of an existing service, or provision of new service.

Upon receipt, a unique record of this contact is created with relevant details about the user and the request. This record may be created automatically if a user submits the help request through email or a self-service resource.

Classification involves determining the appropriate fulfillment procedure based on the request. The fulfillment procedure for a service request includes any approvals and fulfillment actions required to complete the request. Ideally, these fulfillment models reside in templates within the service management tool so they are easy to reference and apply.

Self-service resources such as portals or intranet sites can provide a convenient menu of requests to end users. These resources can gather relevant details for a specific request and channel it through the appropriate fulfillment model.

NOTE: SELF-SERVICE AND THE SERVICE CATALOG IN SERVICE MANAGER

Service Manager features a configurable, SharePoint-based self-service portal with Silverlight web parts that enables end users to submit service requests and incidents, monitor the status of those items, and add comments. Integral to the self-service portal is the service catalog, a tool for configuring and organizing portal content. The service catalog packages incident and service request templates into request offerings with descriptive information and prompts. Request offerings can be grouped into customized service offerings and service offerings into customized categories.

Some requests may fall outside the scope of the Service Request Fulfillment process and may actually be requests for changes that should be handled through Change Management. For example, a request for enablement of new application functionality may have operational implications above the level of approval granted within established Service Request Fulfillment models.

▶ **Approval and fulfillment:** Request approval varies and is typically based on factors including cost and security. Some requests may be preapproved and not require case-by-case approval, while other requests may require one or more approvals. Ideally, approvals should be automated by the service management tool and documented in the service request record.

NOTE: SERVICE REQUEST APPROVAL IN SERVICE MANAGER

Service Manager provides specialized activities that facilitate and document approvals for service requests.

Fulfillment activities also vary based on the nature of the request. The service desk may complete simple requests, while other requests may require work by specialist groups or vendors, and some requests may require some combination of the three. Some fulfillment activities may be automated such as adding a user to an Active Directory group or granting access to a folder. All fulfillment work should be documented appropriately in the service request record.

▶ **Completion and closure:** The overall service request is complete after all fulfillment activities are complete. At this point, the request owner contacts the requester to confirm the service request has been fulfilled successfully and there are no outstanding items or issues with the outcome. The record then can be closed and the completion status classified.

How Other Processes Relate to Service Request Fulfillment

Table 3.5 outlines the relationship between Service Request Fulfillment and other Service Manager-supported processes.

TABLE 3.5   How Service Request Fulfillment Relates to Other Processes

Service Request Fulfillment Provides	Service Request Fulfillment Receives
To Change Management:	**From Incident Management:**
Some requests initiated through Service Request Fulfillment may actually be changes due to risk or scale and should be processed through Change Management.	Some end user requests initially recorded as incidents may truly be service requests and therefore need to be converted.

How to Measure Service Request Fulfillment

Table 3.6 presents metrics useful in managing the Service Request Fulfillment process and measuring its effectiveness.

TABLE 3.6   Service Request Fulfillment Management Metrics

Metrics	Purpose
Count of service requests created Count of service requests completed Count of service requests active Count of service requests on hold	Indicate overall volume and provide control measures
Average time to complete service requests	Helps identify the overall time required to fulfill service requests, which can be useful in setting SLOs
Percentage of unsuccessful (failed, partially implemented) service requests	Indicates the success or failure of service requests Helps highlight failure patterns

The data in Table 3.6 may be organized and filtered as follows:

- ▶ By analyst to establish individual workload and assess individual performance
- ▶ By support group to establish team workload
- ▶ By priority to establish ratios and trends in service request importance
- ▶ By source to highlight where service requests originate

About Problem Management

A problem is the unknown cause of one or more incidents. Problem Management involves managing the life cycle of problems, which includes recording incident and operations data about a problem with an IT service or system, researching the root cause, and developing workarounds or fixes. Examples of problems follow:

- ▶ Repeated performance issues on a server
- ▶ An outage to a business application affecting many users
- ▶ A confirmed bug in an application

The Purpose of Problem Management

The objective of Problem Management is to prevent incidents from occurring and to minimize the impact of unpreventable incidents. Consider this example to understand the ways in which Problem Management provides value:

An application develops periodic performance issues, causing incidents to be generated by many users experiencing service degradation. A problem is raised and a resource assigned to investigate the root cause of the performance issues. Initially, a workaround is identified that quickly and temporarily restores normal service for affected users. Eventually, a solution is identified that permanently fixes the root cause, eliminating the performance issues and the subsequent incidents.

Common Roles in Problem Management

The *problem analyst* is the principal role for Problem Management. Problem analysts are the individual IT staff members assigned to investigate problems.

Essential Activities within Problem Management

Figure 3.5 illustrates the activities essential to the Problem Management process; descriptions follow.

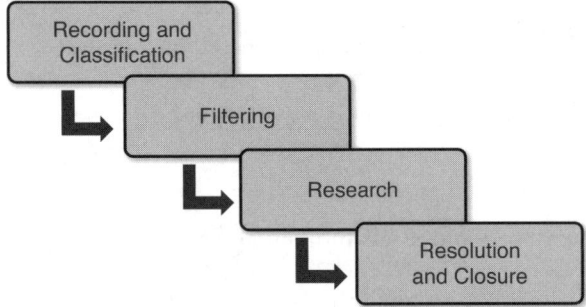

FIGURE 3.5   Problem Management process activities.

▶ **Recording and classification:** When a problem is identified or suspected, a check is made of existing problem and known error records to determine whether this is an existing problem or a new one. If new, a record is created that captures details about the problem's symptoms. Where applicable, existing incident records are linked to the problem record to indicate that the incidents are related to the problem.

Classification involves assigning a category and priority to the problem. The problem category indicates the nature of the problem (e.g., hardware, software, network) so that active problems can be better organized and past problems better analyzed.

Problem priority is handled similarly to incident priority in that a numeric priority value is derived from assignment of impact and urgency values.

▶ *Impact* indicates the overall business impact of the problem, typically a function of the number and nature of existing or potential incidents caused by it.

▶ *Urgency* indicates the speed with which resolution is required.

Priority is important in Problem Management since organizations typically have more problems than problem analysts can manage at one time. Therefore, problem analysts must focus effort on the highest priority problems.

▶ **Filtering:** The problem should be filtered to determine whether further work on the problem is justified. Data gathered about the problem is reviewed to establish an overall justification for devoting time and effort to investigation and resolution. The time, effort, and resources needed to research the problem are considered, as are the time, effort, and resources needed for resolution (if it is possible to envision resolution at this point).

If the overall investment in problem resolution exceeds the impact of any resulting incidents, the problem generally should not be pursued. In these cases, it may be better to live with the problem than to resolve it.

The outcome of filtering is a prioritized list of problems that warrant investigation and possibly resolution. In cases where the resolution is unable to be determined at this point in the process, further filtering may occur after the determined resolution since the resolution may not warrant the investment.

▶ **Research:** Researching a problem involves reproducing the problem to determine the underlying root cause. This may involve creating or utilizing a non-production environment to study symptoms and gather additional data about the problem's behavior.

Root cause analysis techniques are important to effective Problem Management and are applied in this step of the process. Several good root cause analysis techniques can be used in problem research, including

> ▶ Fishbone diagrams
>
> ▶ Fault tree analysis
>
> ▶ Pain value analysis
>
> ▶ Pareto analysis
>
> ▶ Kepner and Tregoe

Determination of a problem's root cause may be an iterative process, so further filtering may be necessary between iterations to justify continued research.

Research may produce a workaround or a fix for the problem. A workaround is a temporary means of restoring normal service operation for related incidents and may be identified before a fix. If so, the workaround is documented and published as a knowledge article so it can be applied during Incident Management while a fix is pursued.

Research may also yield the identification of a permanent fix to a problem. Identifying a fix triggers further filtering to ensure the fix can be justified; some problems may require a complex fix involving upgrades to infrastructure or applications—these may not be justifiable when compared to the impact of incidents resulting from the problem.

When a temporary workaround or permanent fix is identified, the problem is flagged as a known error. Known errors may be consulted during incident management to determine the availability of a workaround or fix for a specific incident.

NOTE: KNOWN ERRORS AND WORKAROUNDS IN SERVICE MANAGER

Service Manager allows problems to be identified as known errors with a checkbox and provides a specialized text box to capture workarounds.

▶ **Resolution and closure:** In cases where the fix is justified, it is implemented using the appropriate process. Some larger problem fixes require engaging the Change Management process to ensure appropriate authorization, testing, and implementation scheduling, while smaller fixes may be implemented independently.

The problem record is closed after all work is completed on the problem.

How Other Processes Relate to Problem Management

Table 3.7 outlines the relationship between Problem Management and other Service Manager-supported processes.

TABLE 3.7   How Problem Management Relates to Other Processes

Problem Management Provides	Problem Management Receives
To Incident Management:	**From Incident Management:**
The resolution of a problem may resolve related incidents.	Recurring incidents may generate a problem.
To Change Management:	**From Change Management:**
The resolution of a problem may necessitate a change.	A successfully completed change may resolve a problem.
	From Configuration Management:
	Configuration items with recurring incidents may indicate a problem.

How to Measure Problem Management

Table 3.8 presents metrics useful in managing the Problem Management process and measuring its effectiveness.

TABLE 3.8   Problem Management Metrics

Metrics	Purpose
Count of problems created	Indicate overall volume and provide control measures
Count of problems active	
Count of problems resolved	
Count of problems on hold	

Metrics	Purpose
Known errors as a percentage of all problems	Highlights the effectiveness of problem diagnosis and the ability to generate workarounds or fixes
Percent reduction in incidents	May suggest areas where problem management is proactively reducing instances of service degradation
Average time to resolution	Helpful in estimating resolution time for future problems and in determining whether additional resources are required

The data in Table 3.8 may be organized and filtered as follows:

▶ By analyst to establish individual workload and assess individual performance

▶ By priority to highlight the most important problems

▶ By category to expose trends in the type of problems arising

▶ By source to highlight where problems most commonly originate

About Change Management

A change is the addition, modification, or removal of a component of an IT service. Examples of changes follow:

▶ The addition of a new feature to a business application

▶ The replacement of a failing hardware component on a physical server

▶ The decommissioning of a server

▶ The modification of a process

The Purpose of Change Management

Change Management provides standardized methods and procedures for introducing changes to IT services. These standards enable prompt and efficient disposition of changes, including authorization, development, testing, scheduling, and implementation. This standardization also reduces the risk of adverse effects from changes. Finally, Change Management ensures that changes are documented appropriately including the work planned, the work performed, and the resulting changes to affected configuration items.

Common Roles in Change Management

Common roles in Change Management follow:

▶ The *requester* is the individual who initiates the change request.

▶ The *owner* is the individual with overall responsibility for successful implementation of the change.

▶ *Reviewers* approve or reject change requests.

▶ *Implementers* are responsible for implementation of the change (a single change might require multiple implementers depending on complexity).

Essential Process Activities within Change Management

Figure 3.6 shows the activities essential to the Change Management process; these are described in this section. The process begins with the initiation of a request for change, classified based on scope, complexity, and risk. The request flows through the appropriate approval path, and after it is approved, it is scheduled for release. The change is developed and testing is performed to minimize risk of business disruption. After the change is deemed ready, it is released to the target environment where it is subsequently stabilized and validated as complete. A review commensurate with the scale of the change is conducted to record lessons learned.

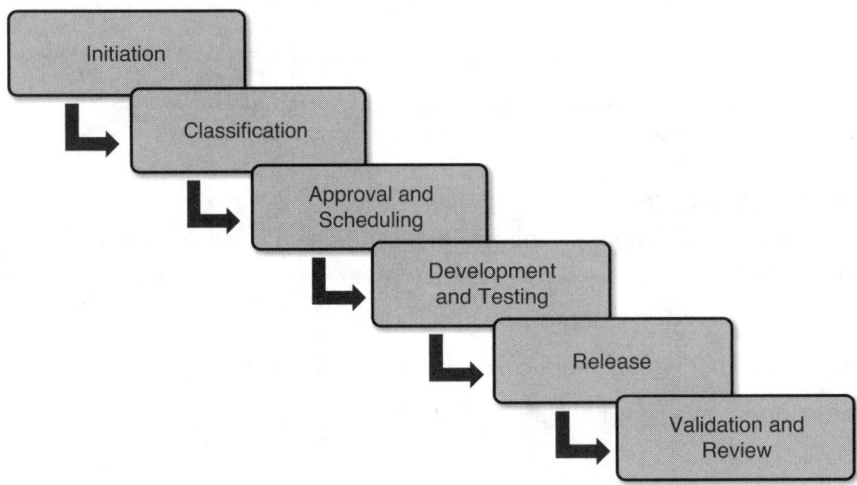

FIGURE 3.6   Change Management process activities.

▶ **Initiation:** Change Management begins with the initiation of a change request, the formal record of the change. The change request is the central record of the change and is updated continually throughout the Change Management life cycle. The change request describes the change in as much detail as possible, including at a minimum:

   ▶ Requester

   ▶ Description of the change

   ▶ Reason for the change

   ▶ The configuration items to be changed

   ▶ The risk associated with the change

At this point, the change is screened to ensure that the information provided is clear and complete before moving further in the process. If it is not, the requester must provide any additional information or clarification necessary.

▶ **Classification:** Classifying a change involves categorizing and prioritizing the change based on the data provided in the change request. The output of this step greatly influences the course of the change through the rest of the Change Management process.

Change categorization takes into account the resources required for the change (human and financial), the risk associated with the change, and experience with the change (or with similar changes). Change categories vary by organization, with typical categories described in Table 3.9.

TABLE 3.9   Change Categories

Category	Resources	Risk	Experience
Standard	Limited	Low	High
Minor	Moderate	Medium	Moderate
Major	Significant	High	Varies
Emergency	Varies	Varies	Varies

▶ *Standard changes* are small, low risk changes that require limited resources and carry low risk of adverse effects with predictable outcomes. These are considered routine because they are made with regularity and therefore have well known and proven successful procedures. Standard changes might include rebooting nonproduction servers or applying security patches to noncritical systems.

▶ *Minor changes* are larger, less common, and riskier than standard changes, usually affecting a larger portion of the organization. Their scope is often limited to a single functional area and single IT workgroup. Minor changes require greater care and consideration than standard changes, including case-by-case review and approval. Minor changes might include granting users administrative privileges to production resources or making a production network upgrade that requires downtime.

▶ *Major changes* carry the highest risk and cost and usually affect a large portion of the organization and/or a critical business function. They are often cross-functional, involving multiple IT workgroups. As a result, major changes require broad approval and a high degree of rigor to minimize business impact. Major changes might include a SQL Server upgrade on a production cluster or moving a group of critical servers to a new data center.

▶ *Emergency changes* require rapid processing because of a business need to implement the change quickly. This means emergency changes may not have the customary or desired amount of planning and testing. Emergency changes are often the result of major incidents where the risk associated with the change is outweighed by the adverse effect of the incident. Emergency changes might include deploying a patch to remediate a significant vulnerability or to fix a functional issue in a critical application.

NOTE: CHANGE REQUEST CATEGORIZATION IN SERVICE MANAGER

Service Manager change request templates have change categories built-in.

▶ **Approval and scheduling:** The approval path and approving body for a change is based on the category. Having predefined approval paths and approving bodies enables efficient and risk-appropriate assessment of proposed changes within the environment.

NOTE: CHANGE REQUEST APPROVAL AND SCHEDULING IN SERVICE MANAGER

Service Manager features specialized review activities for recording approvals for change requests. Service Manager also provides overall start and end date properties as well as downtime start and end dates for change scheduling.

Standard and minor changes have the most straightforward approval paths because they carry the lowest impact and risk. Changes categorized as standard changes are typically reviewed and approved once and are considered preapproved thereafter. Every minor change typically is reviewed and approved, though the approval body may be a single manager if the scope of change is limited to a single functional area.

Major changes are usually reviewed and approved by a team of representatives called a change advisory board (CAB). CAB members represent a cross section of IT workgroups and may include business representatives to ensure a business perspective. Risk and impact are carefully assessed for major changes, considering the significant downside if the change is not completely successful. Policies dictate requirements for majority or unanimous approval and individual votes are captured in the change request.

Emergency changes are reviewed and approved by an emergency CAB whose members have the authority needed to fast-track change approval. Because of the urgency of emergency changes, approval may sometimes occur after the fact.

Deployment is scheduled after changes are approved, other than standard changes where deployment can be scheduled promptly after classification. Organizations maintaining established change windows typically schedule all but emergency changes within those windows. Other organizations schedule changes at times when business impact is lowest and the recovery time adequate should there be a need to roll back. Major changes may necessitate a phased schedule, depending on complexity.

A forward schedule of change might be used to publish the change deployment schedule. The forward schedule of change is the central reference for change deployment schedules.

▶ **Development and testing:** Like approval and scheduling, change category drives development and testing practices. Business, operational, and technical requirements, use cases, and affected configuration elements factor into change development and testing plans and procedures. The aim is to establish that a change is fully ready for production implementation, with the lowest possible risk of adverse business impact.

NOTE: ORGANIZING WORK WITHIN CHANGE REQUESTS IN SERVICE MANAGER

Service Manager change requests contain configurable activities that are used to organize and assign work (e.g., development, testing, release, and so on) within the overall change.

The relative simplicity of standard and minor changes means that development and testing require limited time, effort, and resources. A standard change always follows the predefined procedures for that change, while minor changes may require more specialized but still straightforward development and testing procedures.

The complexity of major changes might make development and testing more time, effort, and resource-intensive. These changes may demand specialized lab environments, extensive testing and perhaps pilot deployments, and end user feedback.

Emergency changes often afford less time for development and testing than is desired. The scope of these activities may be less than optimal and driven mainly by the time available. In the case of an emergency, the risk of operating without the change may be greater than the risk of abbreviating development and testing.

No changes can move into production without confirmation that all testing is complete, all implementation activities are assigned, all necessary communication to affected groups has occurred, and all operations and support teams are prepared. The decision about the readiness of a change for release is another variable based on category.

▶ **Release:** The work of releasing a change into the production environment includes not only the implementation activities, but also stabilization of the change during its early life cycle, confirmation of acceptance, transfer of responsibility to relevant operations and support teams, and updates to relevant documentation.

▶ **Validation and review:** Validation of a change confirms its success or failure in both business and technical terms. For standard and minor changes, this might be a quick and simple matter of verifying expected functionality. For major changes, this might require a period of monitoring to verify that the change meets all intended business and technical objectives.

Formal post-implementation review (PIR) of a change assesses and documents the results. This is often reserved for major changes, and reviews the change in technical, business, schedule, and budget terms to determine the degree of success or failure and to identify any lessons learned that could be applied to future changes.

How Other Processes Relate to Change Management

Table 3.10 outlines the relationship between Change Management and other Service Manager-supported processes.

TABLE 3.10   How Change Management Relates to Other Processes

Change Management Provides	Change Management Receives
To Incident Management:	**From Incident Management:**
Changes may inadvertently cause new incidents.	Changes may be necessary to resolve some incidents.
To Problem Management:	**From Problem Management:**
A change request may resolve a problem.	Implementation of solutions to problems may require changes.
To Configuration Management:	
Changes require updates to affected configuration items (CIs).	**From Configuration Management:**
	Assessment of proposed changes relies on configuration data.
To Release Management:	**From Release Management:**
Related changes to be bundled into a single overall release.	Deployment of changes may occur through a release.

How to Measure Change Management

Table 3.11 presents metrics useful in managing the Change Management process and measuring its effectiveness.

TABLE 3.11   Change Management Metrics

Metrics	Purpose
Count of changes created	Indicate overall volume and provide control measures
Count of changes completed	
Count of changes in progress	
Count of incidents resulting from changes	Highlights potential quality problems in the change management process
Emergency changes as a percentage of all changes	Highlights the degree to which changes fall outside the established approval and deployment mechanisms
Average time to completion	The average time required to complete changes
Unauthorized changes as a percentage of all changes	Helps determine where changes circumvent the process

Metrics	Purpose
Failed changes as a percentage of all changes	Provides an opportunity to look for trends that may improve the success rate of changes

This data may be organized and filtered as follows:

▶ By analyst to establish individual workload and assess individual performance

▶ By category to establish ratios and trends in change scope

▶ By risk to identify ratios and trends in risk profiles

About Release Management

Release Management is the process of building, testing, and deploying releases into a managed environment. Releases are packages of related assets and service components, examples of which include

▶ A major business application upgrade

▶ A desktop operating system deployment

▶ Rollout of a new mobile device class

Release Management is the coordination point between the development teams building releases and the operations teams responsible for the release in the production environment.

The Purpose of Release Management

Releases are often complex, and Release Management addresses that complexity with standard methods and deliverables that

▶ Provide a consistent implementation approach for releases

▶ Ensure the readiness of release packages and the managed environment into which they will be deployed

▶ Enable release traceability and auditability

Through these methods and deliverables, Release Management ensures that releases achieve their intended objectives with minimal impact to production services.

Common Roles in Release Management

The most consistent role in Release Management is that of the *release manager*. This individual is responsible for the overall release and coordinating the various resources needed for successful deployment. A release may be thought of as a project, and the release manager is similar to a project manager.

Other resources likely participate in a release as coordinated by the release manager. Resources are required to build, test, and deploy the release as well as to periodically review status to determine whether the release is ready to proceed to the next step.

Essential Process Activities within Release Management

Figure 3.7 shows the activities essential to the Release Management process; these are described in this section. Release Management begins with the development of a plan and a design for the release. After authorization of those plans, the release is built and tested, and a final review undertaken to confirm the readiness of the release for deployment. The release is deployed to the target environment.

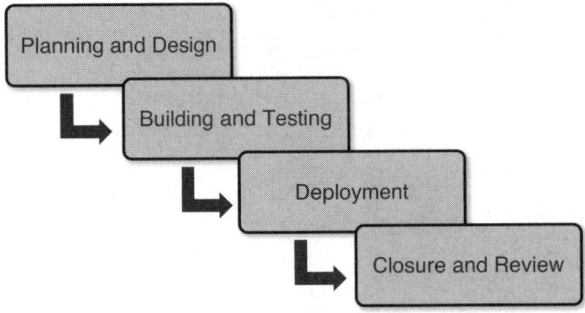

FIGURE 3.7   Release Management process activities.

▶ **Planning and design:** Release Management begins with development of a release plan that outlines the following information:

   ▶ The scope and content of the release

   ▶ The resources who build, test, and deploy the release

   ▶ The technologies available to build, test, and deploy the release

   ▶ The affected business and IT organization(s) and stakeholders

   ▶ The associated risks

   ▶ The authorization points through which the release will pass including pass/fail criteria

Design of the release takes into account various components of the managed environment and formulates a specific approach to the release to building, testing, and deploying the release. These components include the organizations, support and operations processes, and configuration items affected by the release. This work also establishes priorities and dependencies (e.g., installation of prerequisite software components, training of support analysts), which suggest a specific sequence of deployment activities.

Build and test plans are developed that define the build activities and testing methods to be employed for the release. If pilots are to be part of the release, corresponding plans are also developed. Finally, any new managed environments are identified that are required for build and test.

Deployment plans consider the logistic and financial aspects of moving the release into the managed environment. These plans define the means of deployment and consider the physical locations involved in the release, schedule requirements and dependencies, stakeholder communications, knowledge transfer, contractual or license requirements, and overall success criteria for deployment.

NOTE: RELEASE DOCUMENTATION IN SERVICE MANAGER

Release documentation can be uploaded to a Service Manager release record in Rich Text Format (RTF) or as an attached file.

The first authorization point occurs at the end of planning and design. This authorization point examines the plans and designs developed for the release to ensure they meet or exceed the established pass/fail criteria before moving into building and testing the release.

▶ **Building and testing:** Releases are built and tested with a combination of processes, tools, and technologies required to deploy the release successfully into the managed environment without adverse impact to other systems or services. This work includes deployment of any new environments needed to facilitate build and test activities.

Building involves development of the components of the release package and development of the deployment process itself. Building also includes producing build documents, used to

- ▶ Record details of any new managed environments
- ▶ Ensure release components can be built in a reproducible manner
- ▶ Capture information essential to the teams responsible for ongoing support and operations

Testing activities vary widely depending on the nature of the release, available human and technical resources, and organizational testing standards. The objective is to ensure

- ▶ Individual components meet established requirements and quality criteria.
- ▶ Release packages will be successful in the target environments.
- ▶ The people who will support and operate the release are prepared.
- ▶ The overall service will meet service level performance targets and business needs.

For some releases, pilots may be desirable as a means to validate the release package and release process (for example, deployment of a new desktop operating system). Pilot plans should include success criteria for the pilot, since the pilot represents another authorization point in the overall process.

The authorization point at the end of building and testing is the release readiness review. This checkpoint evaluates the release to determine whether the release package is ready, the target environment is ready, and the teams involved with and impacted by the release are ready. This is the final checkpoint before deployment.

▶ **Deployment:** After confirmation that the release is ready, the release is deployed to the managed environment. In cases where the release is being piloted, the pilot is the first step in deployment and helps uncover any aspects of the release not ready for full deployment. Pilot results determine the need for additional building or testing and may suggest adjustments to the deployment process.

NOTE: RELEASE DEPLOYMENT IN SERVICE MANAGER

Release deployment in Service Manager is handled by linking deployment activities within individual changes to deployment activities in the related release. Detailed data about scheduling can be managed in the release record, including downtime details.

The full deployment follows the deployment plan, focused on moving the release packages into the managed environment according to the designed release process. In addition, communications to stakeholders are made, training and knowledge transfer for support and operations teams occurs, any configuration items no longer needed are decommissioned, and final documentation is published including technical documents, continuity plans, service level agreements (SLAs), and contracts.

The final authorization point for the release involves verifying the deployment was successful. Upon completion of deployment activities, the following are confirmed:

▶ The new capability deployed is performing as expected based on defined criteria.

▶ The resources responsible for supporting and operating the new capability are adequately prepared.

▶ All relevant documentation is up-to-date.

When the release is verified as successful, the release can move into an early life support mode during which the release is stabilized. The deployment team remains involved with the release as issues and gaps are identified and remediated, and until the support and operations teams can manage with full independence.

▶ **Closure and review:** Closing a release involves wrapping up any open issues and capturing lessons learned that can benefit future releases. Anything still outstanding at the end of early life support is transitioned to the appropriate group or individual so it can be addressed. The post-implementation review assesses the overall release to judge the success of the existing process and identify potential improvements to benefit future releases.

How to Measure Release Management

Table 3.12 presents metrics useful in managing the Release Management process and measuring its effectiveness.

TABLE 3.12   Release Management Metrics

Metrics	Purpose
Count of releases created Count of releases active Count of releases completed	Indicate overall volume and provide control measures
Customer/user satisfaction with new capability	Ensures that the benefits expected by those funding and those using newly released capability are being achieved and if not, why
Count of release-related incidents	Helps identify various issues in the standard release process or specific to a given release package, which may require immediate attention (bugs) or may warrant process changes (policy or procedure gaps)

About Configuration Management

Configuration Management identifies and controls selected components of a service or a system configuration. Configuration Management also identifies the relationships between these components that provide a logical model of services and systems.

A component under the control of Configuration Management is termed a configuration item or CI. Here are examples of common configuration items:

▶ Desktop computers

▶ Servers

▶ Network devices

▶ Applications

▶ Documentation

Data about CIs is commonly stored in a configuration management database (CMDB). The CMDB is the definitive information repository for CIs, and typically contains data about CI technical specifications, ownership, and relationships.

The Purpose of Configuration Management

Configuration Management protects the integrity of services and systems by defining, documenting, and controlling their configurations. Configuration Management ensures that only authorized and known configurations are present within the environment.

Configuration Management underpins many other IT service management processes by supplying an accurate map of the environment. Accurate CI information improves the efficiency and effectiveness of other processes:

▶ Incidents can be resolved faster because analysts have easy access to data about affected CIs.

▶ The root cause of problems can be determined more efficiently because analysts can easily search and analyze CI data.

▶ Changes can be assessed and deployed with lower risk of failure because relationships between CIs are easily referenced.

Basic Activities within Configuration Management

Figure 3.8 shows the activities essential to the Configuration Management process; these are described in this section. Configuration Management begins with planning to determine the right level of management needed for configuration items in the environment. Key details of the CIs are identified and control mechanisms applied to ensure data matches the physical environment. The history of the CI is accounted for based on status and periodic audits undertaken to verify accuracy of CI data.

NOTE: CONFIGURATION MANAGEMENT AUTOMATION

Once a largely manual process, Configuration Management now is frequently automated with software tools such as System Center Configuration Manager that automate CI inventory. With the right tools, CI data can be automatically populated into a CMDB and kept up to date as changes occur. It is usually still necessary to manually enter and maintain data about some nondiscoverable CIs, but these cases are more frequently the exception rather than the rule.

Automated CI inventory has greatly improved the accuracy and efficiency of Configuration Management. Because of automation, some of the work described in this section is less relevant.

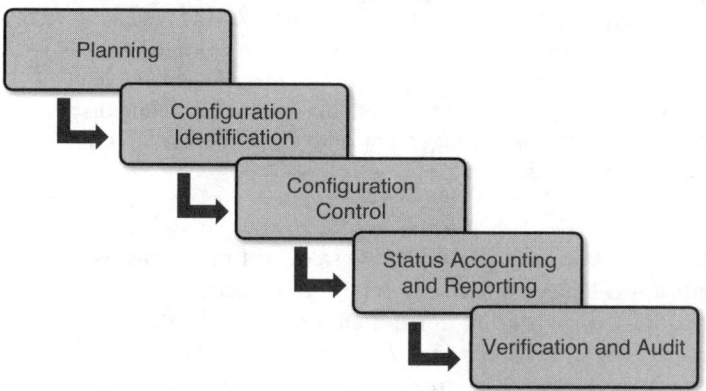

FIGURE 3.8   Configuration Management process activities.

▶ **Planning:** The managers responsible for Configuration Management determine the appropriate level of management required for the CIs within the environment. This is based on factors including the size and complexity of the environment and the frequency and nature of change.

▶ **Configuration identification:** Configuration identification selects key details about CIs including naming conventions, attributes, ownership, and relationships. These details support the manageability and traceability of CIs.

  ▶ *Naming conventions* define standards for naming CIs.

  ▶ *Attributes* are technical specifications for the CI (device manufacturer, software version, amount of RAM, and so on) that are necessary to support other processes such as Incident Management, Problem Management, or Change Management.

  ▶ *Ownership* establishes the groups and individuals responsible for CIs. CI owners might play a role in approving changes or resolving problems affecting their CIs.

  ▶ *Relationships* establish dependencies among CIs. The relationships between CIs are established so that dependencies can be clearly identified when assessing change impact or troubleshooting incidents and problems.

CI relationships within complex systems or services are often best illustrated graphically. A service map is a communication tool that displays an IT service's constituent CIs and their relationships to better convey dependencies.

NOTE: BUSINESS SERVICES IN SERVICE MANAGER

Service Manager enables service mapping through a specialized CI called a *business service*. Business services feature groups of related CIs organized hierarchically to illustrate dependent relationships, and can be created both manually and by importing distributed application groups created in Operations Manager. For additional information on business services, see Chapter 9, "Business Services."

▶ **Configuration control:** Configuration control provides control mechanisms over CIs while maintaining an up-to-date and accurate record of CI attributes, location, ownership, and relationships. Configuration control covers configuration attributes such as licenses, versions, access, and source media to ensure that CI data maintained in the CMDB reflects the physical environment.

▶ **Status accounting and reporting:** Configuration items generally progress through multiple states during their life cycle. A configuration item might begin in a development state, move to a production or in service state, and eventually move to a decommissioned or out of service state. Status accounting defines each of these states and ensures they are applied appropriately to individual configuration items. Status reporting tracks the history of CI state changes as a CI moves through its lifecycle.

▶ **Verification and audit:** Periodic audits ensure conformity between CMDB data and actual configuration items. The availability of automated discovery tools has reduced the need for large scale auditing of configuration items to maintain an accurate CMDB, so verification and audit are often reserved for nondiscoverable configuration items.

How to Measure Configuration Management

Table 3.13 presents metrics useful in managing the Configuration Management process and measuring its effectiveness.

TABLE 3.13   Configuration Management Metrics

Metrics	Purpose
Top CIs affected by incidents	Highlights the CIs most frequently involved in service disruption
	May lead to the identification of problems
Top CIs changed	Highlights the CIs most frequently changed
	Suggests areas in the environment that may be at greater risk of service disruption

Summary

System Center Service Manager organizes the work associated with managing IT services and provides built-in functionality that supports several key IT service management processes. These processes are derived from MOF and ITIL, two prominent and related best practice process frameworks for managing IT services, which include

- ▶ Incident Management for addressing disruptions in normal service
- ▶ Service Request Fulfillment for handling routine requests
- ▶ Problem Management for remediating the root causes of repetitive incidents
- ▶ Change Management for introducing change with low risk to service disruption
- ▶ Release Management for bundling related changes into low risk release packages
- ▶ Configuration Management for maintaining a map of the environment's configuration that supports other processes

Service Manager is slightly different than its companion tools in System Center because it focuses on managing work, not technology. As such, using Service Manager effectively requires some knowledge of the processes discussed in this chapter. For further information about any of these processes, you can reference the MOF and ITIL source materials, available at http://www.itil-officialsite.com and http://www.microsoft.com/mof.

CHAPTER 4

Looking Inside System Center 2012 Service Manager

System Center 2012 Service Manager is the second major version of Service Manager. This System Center component completes Microsoft's approach to operations and the service management life cycle. Chapter 3, "MOF, ITIL, and System Center," discusses how Service Manager supports the Information Technology Infrastructure Library (ITIL) areas of incident, service request, problem, knowledge, change, and release management. This chapter looks at how Service Manager works by presenting an architectural overview and discussing its features.

If you are new to Service Manager but familiar with the architecture of System Center Operations Manager, you may recognize many similarities in Service Manager's architecture, as Service Manager was built using the Operations Manager platform. In fact, while Operations Manager, Service Manager, and Virtual Machine Manager (VMM) were originally developed using separate code platforms, Microsoft made a strategic decision in 2008 to unify the product platforms. Going forward, each component can benefit from the development of the other components. This decision has provided value to both Microsoft and its customers in several areas:

▶ Speeding up the product development cycle by utilizing common functionality, enabling each component to provide additional features more quickly.

▶ Reusing code that has already been tested and proven in other components, giving higher quality to new features in components reusing that code.

▶ Customers familiar with one of the components (Operations Manager as an example) feel at home and have less of a learning curve when administering or using one of the other components, such as Service Manager or VMM.

Architectural Overview

Service Manager is often referred to as an integrated platform for Information Technology service management (ITSM), where *integrated* refers to Service Manager's leveraging the capabilities of other System Center components. This is accomplished by using connectors that can dynamically import and maintain information updated in the Service Manager database (also known as the Service Manager configuration management database, or CMDB).

Figure 4.1 presents an overview of the Service Manager architecture. The main component is the CMDB (titled SM DB in the graphic). The CMDB tracks configuration items as computers and work items such as incidents, and how these items relate to each other through their life cycle.

Above the Database Layer (shown in the Platform Infrastructure section of Figure 4.1) is the Data Access Layer. This layer is a set of assemblies that understand how to communicate with the database. Using these assemblies for read/write operations against the database ensures consistency of the database data. Responsible for securing access to the Data Access Layer is a Windows Communication Foundation (WCF) service, hosted in the System Center Data Access Service, and a set of assemblies that consumes the WCF service and simplifies the communication with the service. When using the Service Manager software development kit (SDK) to develop your own solutions, you would reference these assemblies and use the methods and classes that they provide.

TIP: THE SERVICE MANAGER SDK AND MORE INFORMATION ON CONNECTORS

For information on getting started with the Service Manager SDK, see http://msdn. microsoft.com/en-us/library/hh964679.aspx. Service Manager uses connectors to integrate information from Active Directory, Operations Manager, Orchestrator, Virtual Machine Manager, and Configuration Manager. For information on these connectors, see the "Service Manager Connectors" section later in this chapter and Chapter 8, "Working with Connectors."

Service Manager 2012 uses three Windows services:

▶ System Center Data Access Service (DAS)

▶ Microsoft Monitoring Agent

▶ System Center Management Configuration

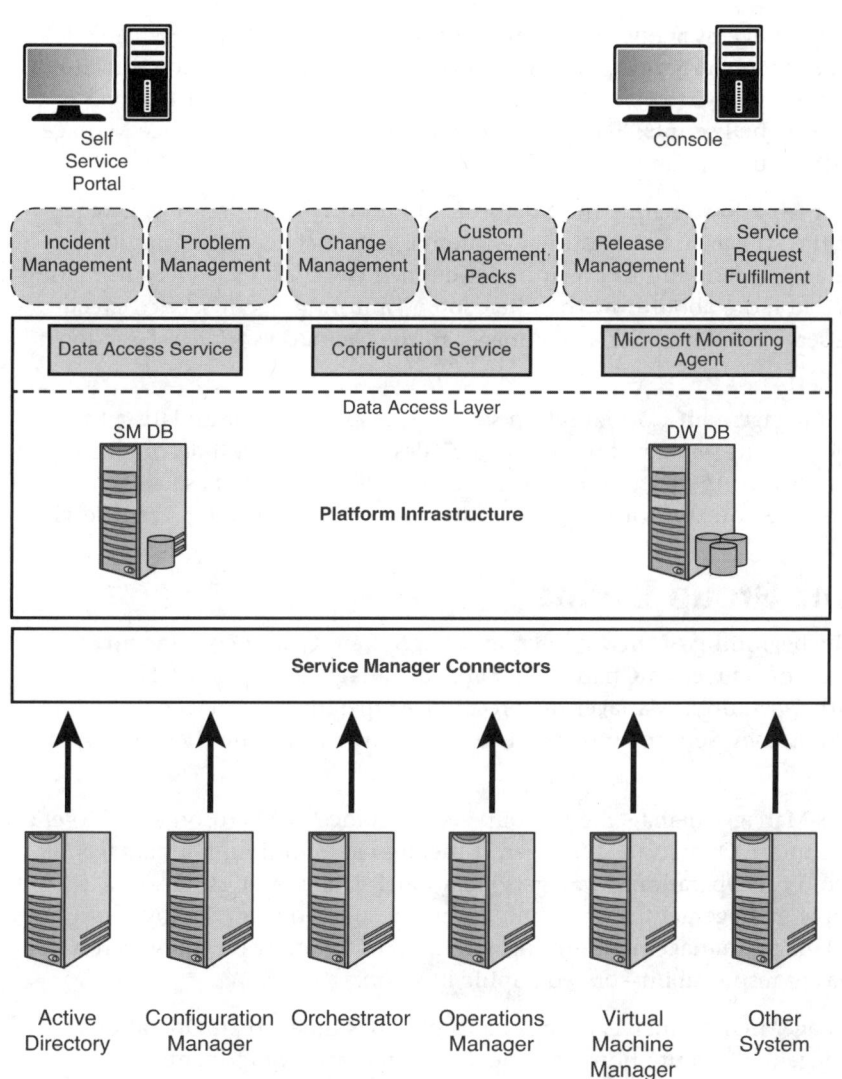

FIGURE 4.1   Architectural overview of Service Manager 2012.

NOTE: ABOUT SERVICE NAMES

In Service Manager 2010, the Microsoft Monitoring Agent service was named System Center Management. If you look at the service properties, you can see that it is still executing the same executable as in Service Manager 2010 (HealthService.exe).

The System Center Data Access Service component provides data access to Service Manager for clients such as the Service Manager console. Other clients include workflows, the Service Manager self-service portal, Orchestrator runbooks, and third-party developed solutions such as PowerShell scripts. Even the internal workflows within Service Manager use the DAS to read and manipulate data in the CMDB.

The Service Manager workflow engine, the Microsoft Monitoring Agent service, is what makes the product tick; this is used to automate internal jobs such as calculating target resolution time for an incident and to execute user-defined workflows such as automating a change request. Read more about how the Microsoft Monitoring Agent service executes workflows and the services used by Service Manager in the "Windows Services" section later in this chapter.

The System Center Management Configuration service is responsible for updating the Microsoft Monitoring Agent services if workflows or rules are modified. It accomplishes this by reading workflow configuration data in the Service Manager database and then passing instructions based on this information to the Microsoft Monitoring Agent service.

Management Group Defined

As mentioned at the beginning of this chapter, another System Center component is Operations Manager, introduced in Chapter 1, "Service Management Basics." Those readers familiar with Operations Manager may recognize Operations Manager also uses those service names used by Service Manager. The same is true regarding the concept of a management group.

▶ An Operations Manager management group is an instance of Microsoft's end-to-end monitoring solution, Operations Manager. It includes at a minimum a management server and the Operations Manager operational database. It can also include agents, multiple management servers, and a web console. You can deploy multiple Operations Manager management groups within your organization; these can be based on areas of responsibility or geographic location.

▶ A Service Manager management group is conceptually similar to an Operations Manager management group; however, the data warehouse components are deployed in their own management group. The data warehouse solution delivered with Service Manager is ultimately intended as the data warehouse for multiple System Center components. For this reason, it is not bound to a specific Service Manager installation (or Service Manager management group); rather, you can configure multiple Service Manager installations to work with the same data warehouse.

NOTE: ABOUT MANAGEMENT GROUP NAMES

Management group names must be unique. Do not use the same management group name when deploying a Service Manager management group and a Service Manager data warehouse management group. Furthermore, do not use the management group name you are using for your Operations Manager installation. Note that management group names are also case-sensitive.

A Service Manager implementation consists of two management groups when the data warehouse feature is utilized:

- A management group for Service Manager

- A management group for the data warehouse feature

The management group for Service Manager must include a management server and a database, the Service Manager database. It can include multiple management servers and consoles as necessary. The management group for the data warehouse includes the data warehouse management server and the data warehouse databases.

You connect these management groups to each other through an internal connector.

TIP: ABOUT REGISTERING TO THE DATA WAREHOUSE

The internal connector used within Service Manager is not visible in the Service Manager console, except from the Connect to data warehouse page of the console. Should you need to remove a connector, you can use the "unregister" feature on the Connect to a data warehouse page.

Most organizations, regardless of size, deploy a Service Manager environment that includes one management group for Service Manager and one for the data warehouse; this is analogous to a single Active Directory (AD) forest or a single Exchange organization.

Very large organizations may choose to deploy multiple Service Manager management groups to distribute the workload and administration responsibilities. You might also deploy multiple Service Manager environments when there are multiple internal Information Technology (IT) organizations or you have a need for test environments.

As the Service Manager data warehouse is built using the same platform as the rest of Service Manager, which means the data warehouse management server and Service Manager management server share the same Windows services, you cannot host all Service Manager roles on the same machine. These three services, the System Center Data Access Service, System Center Management Configuration, and Microsoft Monitoring Agent, are discussed in the "Windows Services" section later in the chapter.

Service Manager Server Features

Six main features comprise Service Manager 2012. Some are optional, while in some enterprise scenarios you might need to deploy multiple instances of some features—for example, management servers.

The Service Manager 2012 features follow:

▶ Service Manager management server

▶ Service Manager database

▶ Data warehouse management server

▶ Data warehouse database

▶ Service Manager console

▶ Self-service portal

> **NOTE: ACTIVE DIRECTORY REQUIREMENT FOR SERVER FEATURES**
>
> All computers hosting any Service Manager features must be members of a domain.

Using a Minimum Installation

If your organization does not require reporting capabilities, you can create a minimum installation by installing Service Manager on a single computer hosting both the Service Manager management server and the Service Manager database. Figure 4.2 shows an example of a minimum installation of Service Manager 2012.

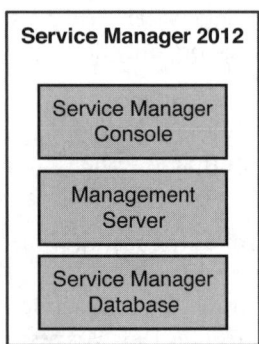

FIGURE 4.2   Minimum installation of Service Manager 2012 on a single physical server.

Adding Reporting Capabilities

Installing reporting services requires two management groups, one for Service Manager, and one for the data warehouse; you then connect them to each other. As both management groups use the same features from the common System Center platform (services being an example mentioned in the previous section), you are not able to install all features on a single server.

Figure 4.3 shows a Service Manager 2012 installation including the data warehouse and reporting features. This installation is based on two servers; these can be two physical servers or a single physical server running two virtual guest systems. Large organizations typically scale out Service Manager features over multiple servers, such as separating the data warehouse and reporting features between one server for the data warehouse databases and a second server for SQL Server Reporting Services (SSRS), which would include the data warehouse management server.

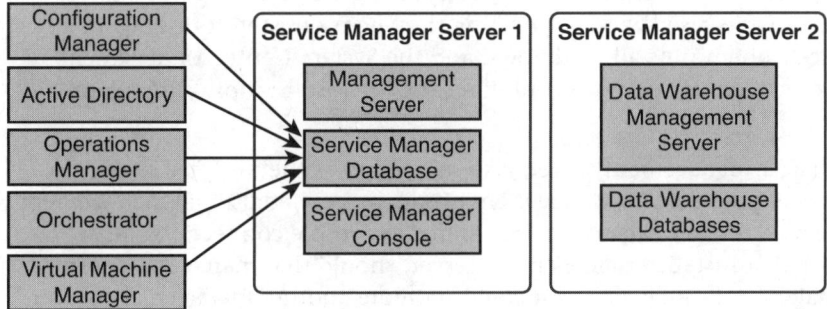

FIGURE 4.3   Minimum installation of Service Manager 2012 when including the data warehouse feature.

Service Manager uses connectors to populate the Service Manager database with configuration items from external systems. Out of the box, Service Manager 2012 includes seven connectors:

▶ Active Directory connector

▶ Configuration Manager connector

▶ Operations Manager Alert connector

▶ Operations Manager CI connector

▶ Orchestrator Runbook connector

▶ Virtual Machine Manager CI connector

▶ CSV connector

An additional connector for Exchange is available as a separate download at http://www.microsoft.com/en-us/download/details.aspx?id=38791. These connectors are discussed in the "Service Manager Connectors" section later in this chapter.

NOTE: MINIMIZING SQL SERVER

You can minimize the number of SQL servers required by sharing a single SQL Server installation (properly sized) between your data warehouse databases and the Service Manager database.

The next sections discuss the different server features.

Service Manager Management Server

The Service Manager management server is where the primary software portion of Service Manager is installed and running. The Service Manager console connects to this server role. This server is also the server hosting the Microsoft Monitoring Agent service (HealthService), which runs all workflows, and the System Center Management Configuration service, which updates and configures the Microsoft Monitoring Agent service.

The first Service Manager management server, also referred to as the *workflow server*, handles all workflows in your Service Manager environment. Any additional management servers deployed are used to load balance Service Manager console connections. As workflows run only on the first installed management server, should that management server fail—say due to a major hardware issue—you could promote another management server to run workflows.

Service Manager Database (ServiceManager)

The ServiceManager database contains all configuration and operating data for the management group and the Service Manager installation. This database is also the Service Manager 2012 implementation of the CMDB. The CMDB contains Service Manager configuration items such as computers and printers. It also contains all work items, including objects such as incidents and change requests.

Data Warehouse Management Server

The data warehouse management server controls the workflow processes associated with the data warehouse. There are four main processes:

▶ DWMaintenance

▶ Management pack synchronization

▶ Extract, transform, and load

▶ Cube processing

These workflows, also known as jobs, transfer data from the CMDB database to the data warehouse database. These jobs are described in Table 4.1 and discussed further in Chapter 21, "Data Warehouse and Reporting."

TABLE 4.1   Workflows that Populate the DWDataMart Database

Process	Workflow Description
DWMaintenance	This job performs maintenance on the data warehouse, such as indexing and updating statistics. It starts automatically after the MPSyncJob finishes and runs every hour.
MPSyncJob	This job synchronizes management packs from the data source (typically the CMDB). The management packs define the structure and content of the data warehouse. It runs every hour.
Extract	The Extract job retrieves data from the Service Manager database. It queries the Service Manager database for the delta data from its last run and writes this new data into the DWStagingAndConfig database in the data warehouse. There are two extract jobs in Service Manager: ▶ A job for the Service Manager management group ▶ A job for the data warehouse management group This job runs every 5 minutes.
Transform	This job takes the raw data from the staging area and does any cleansing, reformatting, and aggregation required to get it into the final format for reporting. This transformed data is written into the DWRepository database. It runs every 30 minutes.
Load	The Load job queries the data from the DWRepository database and inserts it into the DWDataMart database. The DWDataMart is the database used for all end user reporting needs. This runs every hour.
Cube processing	Cube processing is divided into two tasks, dimension processing and partition processing. These jobs load the data from the data mart into the cubes for browsing. They run every 24 hours.

Data Warehouse Database

Service Manager uses the data warehouse for long-term storage of data, such as incidents. It is used as the data source for reports, as old data is groomed from the Service Manager database on a recurring interval to maintain performance and keep the CMDB at a manageable size.

The data warehouse is a logical database; it actually consists of three databases with different roles:

▶ DWStagingAndConfig

▶ DWRepository

▶ DWDataMart

The extract job populates the DWStagingAndConfig database with data, which is transformed into a correct format in the DWRepository database; the load process then transfers the data to content for the DWDataMart database. You can also find a DWASDatabase database on your SQL Server; this is used by SQL Server Analysis Services (SSAS) and stores Microsoft online analytical processing (OLAP) cubes.

There could be two additional databases: OMDWDataMart and CMDWDataMart. These databases store data from Operations Manager (OM) and Configuration Manager (CM).

Data is automatically transferred from the ServiceManager database to the DWDataMart database with a 5–60 minute latency delay. The process responsible for populating the data mart with data is divided into six parts; these jobs were previously listed in Table 4.1.

The primary reason for three different databases is that it helps organizations more easily optimize their hardware environments. In high volume environments, you would want to place the DWStagingAndConfig and DWRepository databases on hardware optimized for read and write I/O, whereas you should optimize the DWDataMart for read I/O only. Using separate databases enables organizations to segregate the DWDataMart to a different server and drive from DWStagingAndConfig and DWRepository. The DWStagingAndConfig and DWRepository databases must be located on the same server.

> **NOTE: THE LENGTH OF TIME IT TAKES FOR DATA TO APPEAR IN REPORTS**
>
> The jobs listed in Table 4.1 work together to populate the data mart, which is where reports are run. You can also use the cubes to browse information. Each job runs independently of each other:
>
> ▶ The Extract job runs every 5 minutes.
>
> ▶ The Transform job runs every 30 minutes.
>
> ▶ The Load job runs every 60 minutes.
>
> In a normally operating Service Manager 2012 environment, it takes approximately two hours before you would see the data in the reports. Cubes are processed every 24 hours.

Service Manager Console

The Service Manager 2012 console is used by all different user roles that work with this component. The console is automatically installed when you install a Service Manager 2012 management server. It could also be installed on other computers, such as a service desk operator's workstation. The console experience is controlled by role-based security, which provides each security role with a common set of views, tasks, templates, and objects. The console is discussed in detail in Chapter 7, "Using Service Manager." Role-based security is discussed in Chapter 17, "Service Manager Security."

There is also an Authoring Tool, sometimes called the Authoring console. The Authoring Tool is used to author management packs and customize the product. For additional information about the Service Manager Authoring Tool, see Chapter 20, "Management Packs," and Chapter 22, "Customizing Service Manager."

Self-Service Portal (SSP)

The end user portion of the SSP enables users to report incidents, search knowledge articles, and request services. End users can also follow the status of their tickets (incidents or service requests). The SSP is a web portal providing self-service for end users, say, to request new software or a new virtual machine. The portal can also be used by reviewers to work with review tasks, such as reviewing and approving change requests or service requests. Engineers can also use the portal to view and complete manual activities.

The SSP is driven by a service catalog that defines offerings available in the portal. The service catalog allows an administrator to easily define a new form, associate it with a work item template (incident or service request), and publish it on the portal.

TIP: MORE ABOUT SELF-SERVICE PORTAL

Chapter 10, "Service Manager Service Catalog," discusses using the service catalog to easily create new offerings for the SSP in Service Manager.

Windows Services

Computers running Service Manager features also host particular Windows services in specific configurations depending on their functions. The next sections describe services that exist when Service Manager features are deployed.

System Center Data Access Service (OMSDK)

The System Center Data Access Service (OMSDK), also referred to as the SDK service, can be considered the core service for Service Manager. This service is installed on all management servers. All data flowing to and from the database is transported via the System Center Data Access Service. Between the System Center Data Access Service and the database is a layer known as the Data Access Layer (DAL), previously shown in Figure 4.1.

The DAL is a set of dynamic link libraries (DLLs) used internally in the platform. The DAL is transparent to Service Manager users. The DAL uses ADO.NET to communicate with the database, with a default communication port of 1433. ADO.NET is a set of software components you can use to access data and data services. The System Center Data Access Service account is configured as the Service Manager account while installing Service Manager.

You can verify the account being used by looking at the Properties page of the System Center Data Access Service in services.msc, the Windows services application. Figure 4.4 shows the portion of this application displaying the services used by Service Manager 2012. Clicking on a particular service and selecting the Log On tab identifies the account being used.

System Center Data Access Service	Microsoft S...	Running	Automatic	ODYSSEY\SM_MSAA
System Center Management Configuration	System Cen...	Running	Automatic	ODYSSEY\SM_MSAA
Microsoft Monitoring Agent	The Monito...	Running	Automatic	Local System

FIGURE 4.4   Configuration of account settings for Service Manager services.

Your management servers also list a service named Microsoft Monitoring Agent APM. Service Manager has a built-in Operations Manager agent. The Operations Manager agent includes the Microsoft Monitoring Agent APM service. This service is used for deep application monitoring and is disabled until it is started from Operations Manager.

The System Center Data Access Service is a Windows service with a Windows communication foundation interface that exposes all programmatic web service application program interfaces (APIs) for the Service Manager platform. WCF is a framework for building service-oriented applications. You can use this framework to send data as asynchronous messages from one endpoint to another.

All communication with the ServiceManager database is through the System Center Data Access Service, which authenticates and authorizes users using Authorization Manager. Authorization Manager (AzMan) is a role-based security architecture for Windows. Additional information on AzMan is available at http://msdn.microsoft.com/en-us/library/bb897401.aspx.

Figure 4.5 shows the SDK service components.

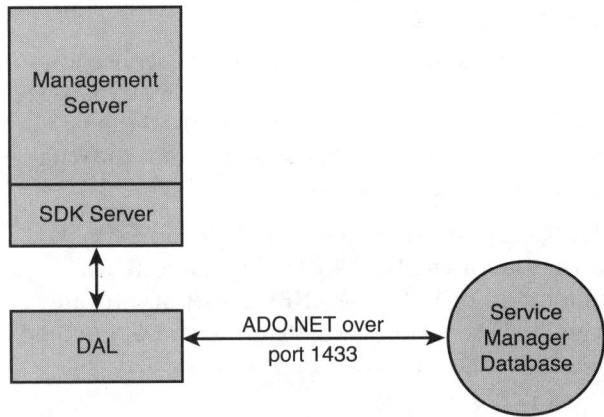

FIGURE 4.5   SDK service components.

Microsoft Monitoring Agent (HealthService)

The Microsoft Monitoring Agent service provides a general execution environment for modules. Different modules form different workflows, enabling workflows such as database grooming, incident workflows, and report deployment. A typical workflow contains a source model, a condition module, and an action module:

▶ The *data source module* defines the condition that triggers the workflow to run.

▶ The *condition module* is an optional module.

▶ The *write action module* defines the workflow actions.

The functionality of this service is primarily defined by the management packs you install. The health service is extended by installing new management packs and updating existing ones. Future versions of these management packs containing new functionality provide updates to the agent health services as the management server pushes out the required updates. Management packs are discussed in the "Modeling and Management Pack Schema" section of this chapter.

The Microsoft Monitoring Agent service does not run the workflows directly. Instead, it starts an instance of healthservice.exe that runs the workflows. You may occasionally see a large number of healthservice.exe instances running at your management server; this is normal. The Microsoft Monitoring Agent service runs each workflow separately from each other to ensure they cannot interrupt one another. Another benefit of running in isolated instances is that each instance can use different credentials and be monitored individually by the management server. If one workflow is hanging or using an unusual amount of hardware resources, it can be terminated without interrupting another workflow. Figure 4.6 shows the Service Manager 2012 workflow.

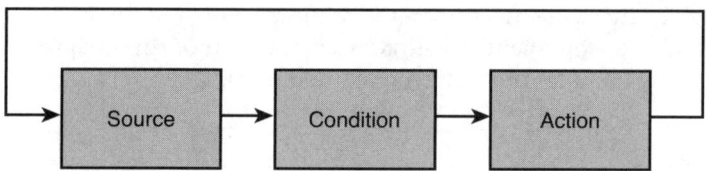

FIGURE 4.6   The Service Manager 2012 workflow.

System Center Management Configuration (OMCFG)

The OMCFG service manages the relationships and running configuration of the Service Manager 2012 environment. This service is responsible for providing the configuration to each health service (Microsoft Monitoring Agent service). It sends sensitive data as part of the data used to configure the health service. The sensitive data is stored and maintained by the ServiceManager database. The SDK API prevents the Microsoft Monitoring Agent service from viewing the data and forces the data to be passed to the System Center Data Access Service in an encrypted form that uses the public key of the target health service. In this process, the DAS acts as an intermediary for delivering the encrypted configuration from the database to the target health service on a management server.

The configuration that a Microsoft Monitoring Agent service receives consists of workflows. These workflows can be tasks, discoveries, and rules. Each workflow is built up from a number of modules. The most common workflow in Service Manager 2012 is a rule. Examples of rules are management pack synchronization to the data warehouse, connectors, and notification workflows. For information about notification workflows, see Chapter 16, "Managing Notifications."

Service Manager Workflow

As mentioned in the "Architectural Overview" section of this chapter, workflows in Service Manager are what make this System Center component tick. Whether Service Manager is sending out a notification email or calculating the target resolution time of an incident, it is performed by Service Manager workflows. You could also add custom workflows to Service Manager to automate any type of internal or even external process. Regardless if you want to guard your business rules when it comes to change management or provision a new Active Directory user automatically, these processes can be automated by using the workflow engine in Service Manager.

NOTE: AUTOMATION OF IT PROCESSES USING WORKFLOW ENGINE

Since System Center Orchestrator is deeply integrated into Service Manager 2012, it is often the preferred engine for automating external processes and sometimes even internal processes. Service Manager 2010 used the internal workflow engine to automate both internal and external processes since Orchestrator wasn't part of the picture. Orchestrator simplifies automation and integration with other systems; this is its core focus.

Service Manager workflows are not the same as Windows Workflow Foundation workflows. To recap the "Microsoft Monitoring Agent (HealthService)" section of this chapter, a typical Service Manager workflow includes the following components:

▶ Data source module

▶ Condition module (optional)

▶ Write action module

A Windows Workflow Foundation workflow differs as it would typically be executed by the write action module if an event occurs in the data source module that fulfills the condition in the condition module. The write action does not necessarily need to execute a Windows Workflows Foundation workflow; it could execute a number of different things including PowerShell scripts/commands; the action taken depends on which write action module is being used.

As discussed in the upcoming "Data Modeling" section of the chapter, adding a new workflow to Service Manager consists of importing a management pack (which has a workflow defined), along with deploying necessary files (such as assembly files containing Windows Workflow Foundation workflows).

When a new workflow definition is imported into Service Manager, the System Center Configuration service picks up information about the new workflow (through the Data Access Layer) and passes instructions over to the Microsoft Monitoring Agent service. The Microsoft Monitoring Agent service spawns a new MonitoringHost process that uses the defined subscription to listen for matching events (let's say a new Incident created), which fulfills the defined criteria ("Incident classification equals Printing Problem," in this example).

When the MonitoringHost receives an event matching the criteria it submits the defined task to the System Center Data Access Service, which uses the Data Access Layer to store the task submission in the ServiceManager database JobStatus table.

The System Center Management Configuration service picks up a new task request (based on the JobStatus data) via the Data Access Layer, which hands over the task request to the Microsoft Monitoring Agent service.

The Microsoft Monitoring Agent service spawns a new MonitoringHost process to execute the task. After executing defined write actions, the task executes a Windows Workflow Foundation module, which calls the System Center Data Access Service to update the Service Manager database (JobStatus table) via the Data Access Layer. See Figure 4.7 for an illustration of how the Service Manager platform makes use of a workflow definition.

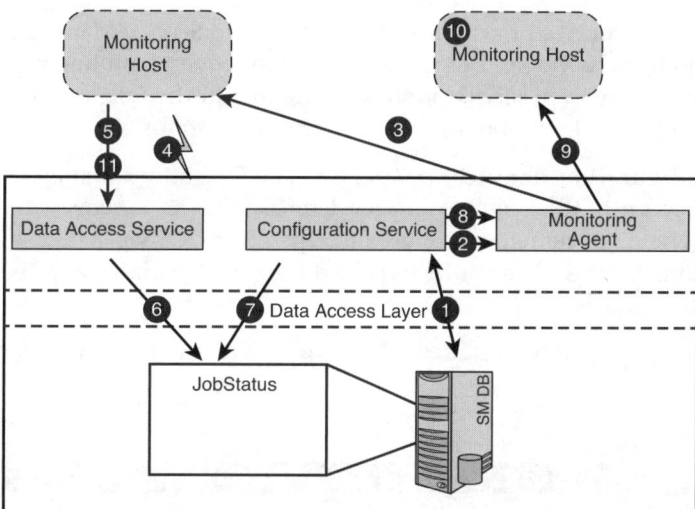

❶ Configuration Service retrieves information about new management pack.
❷ Configuration Service passes workflow information to Monitoring Agent.
❸ Monitoring Agent spawns a new Monitoring Host.
❹ An event is received.
❺ Monitoring Host passes task submission to Data Access Service.
❻ Data Access Service stores the information in JobStatus.
❼ Configuration Service picks up a new task request.
❽ Configuration Service hands over task instructions to Monitoring Agent.
❾ Monitoring Agent spawns a new Monitoring Host.
❿ Monitoring Host executes the task.
⓫ Monitoring Host executes workflow that updates JobStatus – "Completed".

FIGURE 4.7   Workflow communications.

Service Manager Connectors

Using connectors for the initial load of data to the CMDB provides a jumpstart for setting up the Service Manager database. After the initial load, the connectors run periodically and update the CMDB with changes from each source system. This functionality gives Service Manager what has been called a dynamic CMDB, as it is a CMDB that is updated automatically. The following are the connectors provided out of the box:

▶ **Active Directory connector:** Use the Active Directory connector to import information about users, groups, printers, and computers.

▶ **Configuration Manager connector:** Use the Configuration Manager connector to import hardware and software information from Configuration Manager.

▶ **Operations Manager Alert connector:** This connector registers incidents in Service Manager based on alerts in Operations Manager.

▶ **Virtual Machine Manager connector:** Use the Virtual Machine Manager connector to import virtual environment information including virtual machine information.

▶ **Orchestrator connector:** This connector synchronizes runbooks to Service Manager. Runbooks can be triggered by activities and used for automated request fulfillment triggered by a service request. The web service address configured in the Orchestrator runbook connector is used to invoke runbooks and query runbook status.

▶ **Operations Manager configuration item (CI) connector:** The Operations Manager CI connector imports objects into the Service Manager database that are discovered by Operations Manager. The management packs used in Operations Manager that contain the class definitions for the CIs must be imported into Service Manager prior to importing the associated objects.

▶ **CSV connector:** Use a comma separated value (CSV) file to import any type of object defined in the CMDB.

CAUTION: DELETING A CONNECTOR

Deleting a connector deletes all objects owned by that connector from the CMDB. Therefore, should you need to shut down a connector for any reason, it is best to disable the connector rather than delete it. Deleting a connector deletes all objects where the connector is the only currently existing discovery source (source being connectors, users, or another registered source that has created or updated an object).

A supported connector for Exchange, developed by the Service Manager product team, was released in mid-2013. The connector enables deeper integration with Exchange, allowing end users to create, update, resolve, or close incidents, and more. For information on the Exchange connector, see http://www.microsoft.com/en-us/download/details.aspx?id=38791.

In addition to the Orchestrator connector, there is a System Center Service Manager integration pack (IP) that makes it easy to do CRUD (create, read, update, and delete) operations in the CMDB from Orchestrator. The IP helps customers integrate Service Manager with those systems not covered by out-of-the-box connectors. Information about Orchestrator is available at http://technet.microsoft.com/en-us/library/hh237242.aspx and *System Center 2012 Orchestrator Unleashed* (Sams, 2013).

Connectors, including the Exchange connector and the Orchestrator connector, are discussed in Chapter 8.

Modeling and Management Pack Schema

The core of the Service Manager architecture is the highly modular database, the Service Manager database (CMDB). The term "modular" is appropriate as you can create your own models or extend existing describing objects that you want to track during their lifetime. The next sections introduce data modeling and the management pack schema.

Data Modeling

Service Manager 2012 lets you easily add new models describing your own configuration items or work items to track their life cycle. A data model in the CMDB consists of class types, properties, and relationships (which describe how objects relate to each other).

Each data model is stored in one or more management packs that together make up the model. When you import management packs (through the System Center Data Access Service) into Service Manager using the console or PowerShell, the Service Manager Data Access Layer reads the content of the management pack and creates a representation of the data model within the database. The data model is populated in the database as follows:

▶ A new class type in the management pack results in a new table in the Service Manager database.

▶ A column is added to the table for each property defined in the class type in the management pack.

▶ For each relationship defined between class types in a management pack, a relationship entry is added to the table that represents the relationship and its constraints.

▶ For each object of a given class type (for example, a `Windows Computer`) added to the Service Manager database, a line would be added in a matching table, created when importing the management pack into the Service Manager database.

If you delete a management pack in Service Manager using the console or another method, this would result in deletion of the associated database objects such as tables and relationship entries.

The fact that everything is stored in management packs provides you with a simple process for transferring models between different environments; it is as simple as exporting and importing the management pack from one management group to another, such as from a test environment to a production environment.

TIP: MORE ABOUT MANAGEMENT PACKS

Management packs can be seen as eXtensible Markup Language (XML) files containing definitions that define not only data models but also objects such as views for the Service Manager console, workflows, groups, queues, tasks, connectors, and so on. Chapter 22 and Chapter 23 provide additional detail on this topic and information on how to define these objects.

When defining a new data model for Service Manager 2012, you define class types and properties and define how the classes relate to each other. Defined classes are used (and should be reused) to define specialized models using inheritance. Figure 4.8 provides an example of inheritance, displaying the `Microsoft.Windows.Computer` class type as a specialized type of a `System.ConfigItem`, which is a specialized type of `System.Entity`. Each new specialized type can add new properties that are unique for that specialized type but inherit the common properties from parent class types. The figure also shows an example of how `System.User` relates to `System.ConfigItem`. This effectively means that all class types that derive from the `System.ConfigItem` can be related to a `System.User` object using the `System.ConfigItem.OwnedByUser` relationship.

Chapters 22 and 23 describe in more detail how to create your own data models and implement them in the Service Manager CMDB.

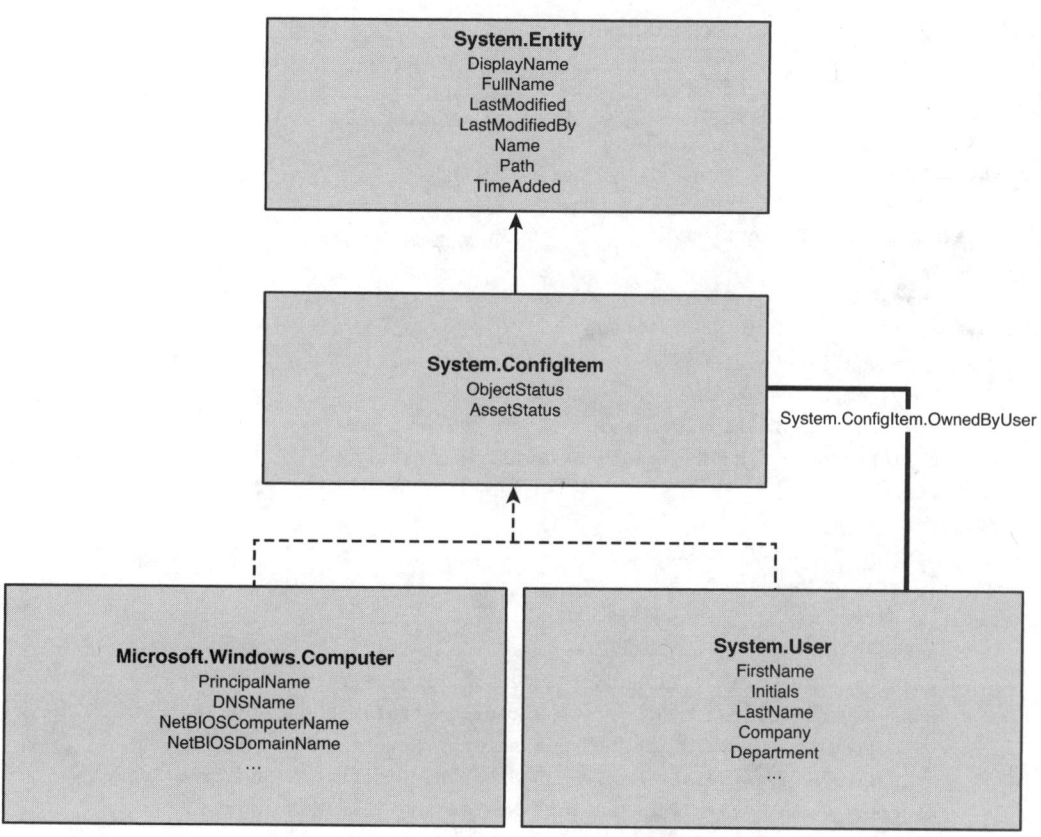

FIGURE 4.8   Data model inheritance and relationships example.

Management Pack Schema

The modeling schema for Service Manager comes from Operations Manager, the first version of which was 1.0. Service Manager 2010 used version 1.1; this extended the schema with features such as class extensions and categories and included all the functionality and experience previously acquired by Operations Manager 2007. Service Manager 2012 uses an updated version, 2.0, of the management pack schema. The schema is named System Center Common Schema; for more information about the schema update see Microsoft TechNet at http://technet.microsoft.com/en-us/library/hh524231.aspx.

Listing 4.1 is a code example that demonstrates a management pack based on common management pack schema, which contains a class type definition for a simple configuration item. The class type has a base class defined and the attribute "Extension" equals "false," which means this defines a new type of object that can be stored in the CMDB. Had there been a class type attribute saying "Extension" equals "true," this would just have extended the class type declared as Base with the new properties defined.

LISTING 4.1   Management Pack Example

```
<ManagementPack SchemaVersion="2.0" ContentReadable="true"
xmlns:xsd="http://www.w3.org/2001/XMLSchema">
<Manifest>
  <Identity>
    <ID>Oddysey.CI</ID>
    <Version>1.0.0.0</Version>
  </Identity>
        <Name>Odyssey Configuration Items</Name>
  <References>
    <Reference Alias="System">
      <ID>System.Library</ID>
      <Version>7.0.5826.216</Version>
      <PublicKeyToken>31bf3856ad364e35</PublicKeyToken>
    </Reference>
  </References>
</Manifest>
<TypeDefinitions>
  <EntityTypes>
    <ClassTypes>
      <ClassType ID="Odyssey.CI.Phone" Accessibility="Public" Abstract="false"
        Base="System!System.ConfigItem" Extension="false">
        <Property ID="SerialNumber" Type="string" Key="true"
          CaseSensitive="false" MaxLength="256" MinLength="0" Required="true" />
        <Property ID="Make" Type="string" MaxLength="256" MinLength="0"
          Required="false" />
        <Property ID="Model" Type="string" MaxLength="256" MinLength="0"
          Required="false" />
        <Property ID="PurchaseDate" Type="datetime" Required="true" />
      </ClassType>
    </ClassTypes>
  </EntityTypes>
    </TypeDefinitions>
  </ManagementPack>
```

The modular schema primarily used by the Service Manager database is also used
in the DWStagingAndConfig database in the data warehouse. The purpose of the
DWStagingAndConfig database is to store configuration information for the data warehouse and act as a temporary place to stage the data moving from the ServiceManager
database into the other parts of the data warehouse (DWRepository and DWDataMart).

NOTE: MANAGEMENT PACK SCHEMA VERSION 2.0

Management packs written for System Center Service Manager 2012 can take advantage of the new version of the management pack schema (version 2.0), although you can still import older management packs (version 1.0 and 1.1) into Service Manager. This makes it possible to import older management packs from your Operations Manager 2007 and Service Manager 2010 environments that already contain data model definitions.

Service Manager Console

Daily work is performed in the Service Manager 2012 console, regardless of your role in the Service Manager environment. Your access to the console is controlled by security roles configured by Service Manager administrators. If you are a service desk analyst, you might only need to see those incidents assigned to you or your team. If you are the service desk manager, you might need to see all active incidents for all levels of support and need to run reports to make sure the unit is working as expected. Additional information on security in Service Manager is available in Chapter17.

The layout of the Service Manager console is similar to other System Center components, the intent being to provide a quicker learning curve. The console is divided into a number of areas and workspaces, as displayed in Figure 4.9.

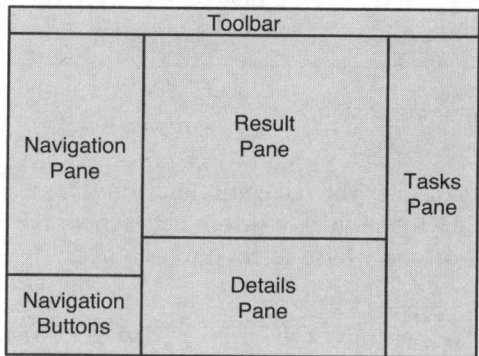

FIGURE 4.9   Layout of the Service Manager 2012 console.

Figure 4.10 shows the Work Items -> All Incidents folder of the Service Manager console. This shows all open incidents.

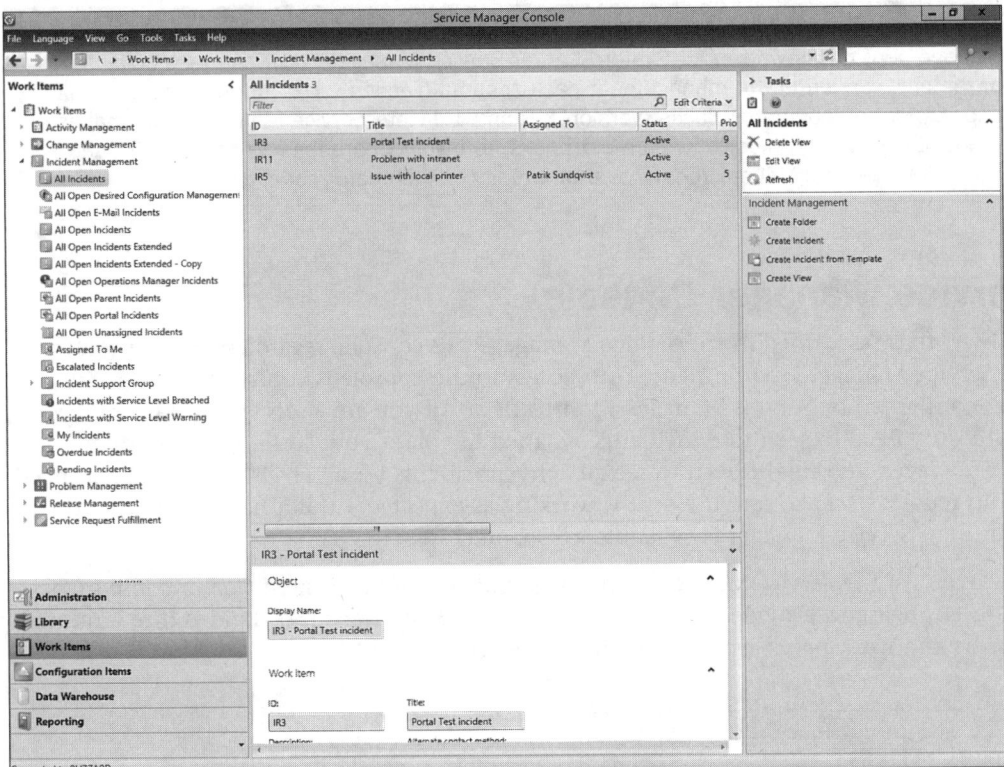

FIGURE 4.10   The Service Manager 2012 console after installation.

Figure 4.11 displays the navigation sections of the console. The navigation buttons (Wunderbars) in the bottom left side of the console let you quickly switch between workspaces. Following is a quick introduction to each workspace (also referred to as a *space* or *node*):

▶ **Administration:** Enables configuring high-level settings of the Service Manager 2012 management group. Examples of tasks that can be carried out in this workspace are configuring notifications, working with management packs, working with accounts, and configuring connectors. Only administrators have access to this workspace.

▶ **Library:** This workspace enables working with templates, tasks, queues, groups, knowledge, and lists. In general, this is where you configure values to be shared between objects in the other workspaces. As an example, you could create templates here to use in change requests or incidents. You also manage your groups and queues here, which you can use with security roles.

▶ **Work Items:** This is where you create work items and work with work items such as change requests, incidents, problems, and service requests and release records, new types added in Service Manager 2012. You can scope down this workspace using different security roles to fit your organization's requirements.

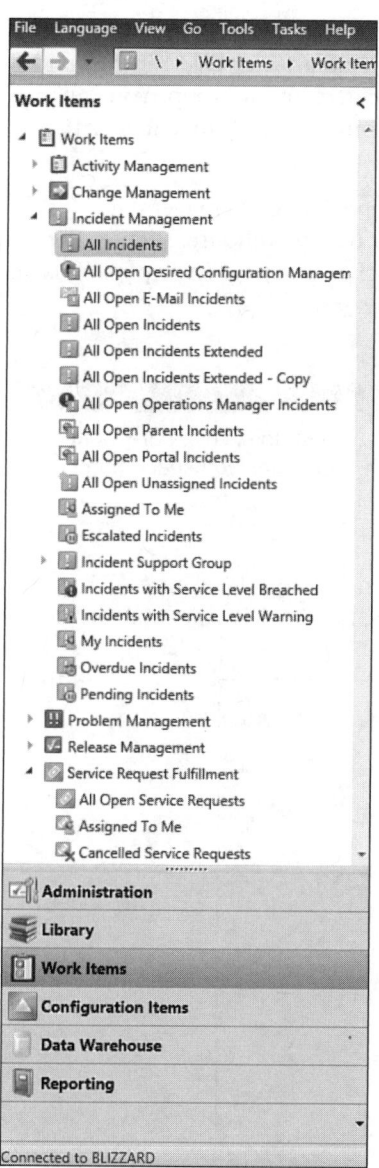

FIGURE 4.11   The Navigation pane and Navigation buttons of the Service Manager 2012 console.

▶ **Configuration Items:** Use this workspace to view all your configuration items. This is where you can see all computers; you can open the Properties page of a specific computer to see how many CPUs it has. You can extend Service Manager 2012 with more CI classes, such as one for projects; these additional classes would be suitable to show in this workspace.

► **Data Warehouse:** This workspace is visible if you have installed the Service Manager data warehouse. In this workspace, you can work with data warehouse settings and configure high-level settings of the data warehouse management group. You can also reach your analysis libraries or connect Excel to one of the OLAP cubes with a simple click of a console task. This feature is optional.

► **Reporting:** This workspace is visible if you installed the Service Manager data warehouse. It enables you to run reports against your data warehouse, such as the number of incidents last week or the most common change category. Reporting is an optional feature. Reporting utilizes the SSRS engine.

NOTE: EXTENDING THE CONSOLE

You can extend the console with additional workspaces. As an example, third-party solutions around asset management extend the console with an additional workspace named IT Asset Management.

The Result and Details panes of the console are displayed in Figure 4.12. Figure 4.13 focuses on the Tasks pane, which is on the right side of the Service Manager console.

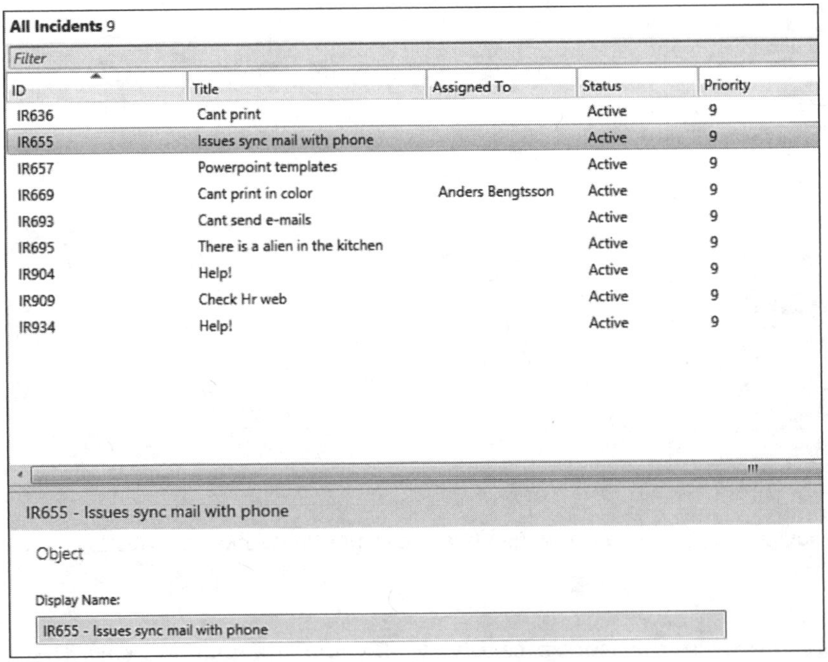

ID	Title	Assigned To	Status	Priority
IR636	Cant print		Active	9
IR655	Issues sync mail with phone		Active	9
IR657	Powerpoint templates		Active	9
IR669	Cant print in color	Anders Bengtsson	Active	9
IR693	Cant send e-mails		Active	9
IR695	There is a alien in the kitchen		Active	9
IR904	Help!		Active	9
IR909	Check Hr web		Active	9
IR934	Help!		Active	9

All Incidents 9

Filter

IR655 - Issues sync mail with phone

Object

Display Name:

IR655 - Issues sync mail with phone

FIGURE 4.12   The Result and Details panes of the Service Manager 2012 console.

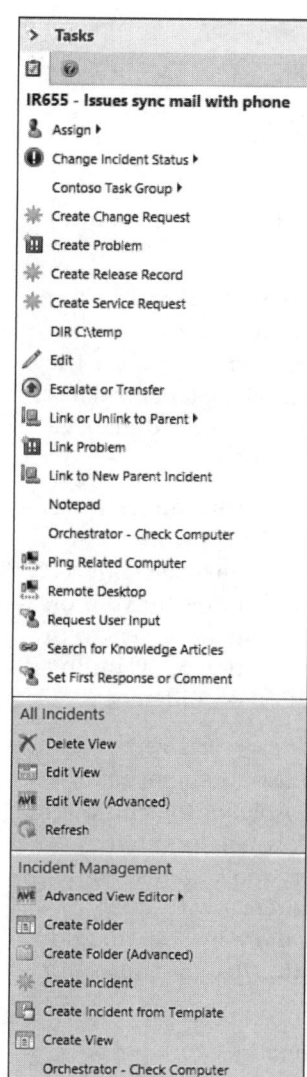

FIGURE 4.13   The Tasks pane of the Service Manager 2012 console.

Content of the Tasks pane is dynamic; it changes based on the type of work item selected and what view is selected in which folder of the Navigation pane. The Tasks pane shown in Figure 4.13 includes a number of custom tasks, for example, DIR C:\temp and Contoso Task Group. Creating custom tasks is an effective way to speed up manual tasks. The example Task pane also includes a task named Advanced View Editor, which is an unsupported tool available at TechNet Gallery. The Advanced View Editor tool can be used to configure views in the console; additional information is at http://gallery.technet.microsoft.com/Advanced-View-Editor-20-377353f5.

Communications

Service Manager 2012 uses a variety of network ports that are optimized for security and performance. Communication with the databases, the Service Manager database and the data warehouse database, is by standard SQL client/server protocols, specifically OLE DB (Object Linking and Embedding Database).

For communications between servers and the console, the primary transmission control protocol (TCP) port used by Service Manager 2012 is 5724.

The initial Service Manager management server hosts data access, workflow services, and authorization services. This management server executes workflows and sends notifications. If this server is unavailable, most features of Service Manager are inaccessible. The management server depends completely on its connection to the Service Manager database to function. If the Service Manager database goes offline, the consoles and management servers are not functional.

Both the Service Manager database and a management server must be continuously available to provide uninterrupted continuity of management functions. This requirement makes clustering the Service Manager database and load balancing the management server top considerations when designing a highly available management solution for your organization. For management servers, you can deploy additional management servers to the same Service Manager management group to provide failover. See Chapter 5, "Planning and Designing System Center 2012 Service Manager," for information on different topologies.

Table 4.2 lists communications paths and ports, but it does not illustrate the need for RPC/DCOM communication between the management server, console, or the end user workstation. Depending on how you work, you might need to allow network traffic to workstations for service desk operators to run tasks and recovery tools against end user workstations. In addition, if you use Excel or other tools to interact with Analysis Services, you need to check its communication requirements. For more information on firewall requirements when working with Analysis Services, see http://technet.microsoft.com/en-us/library/ms174937.aspx.

Note that new extensions to Service Manager may require additional network ports.

TABLE 4.2   Communication Paths and Ports

From Feature	Port Number and Direction	To Feature
Service Manager console	5724 >	Service Manager management server
Service Manager console	5724 >	Data warehouse management server
Service Manager management server	1433 >	Remote Service Manager database
Service Manager management server	5724 >	Data warehouse server

From Feature	Port Number and Direction	To Feature
Service Manager management server	5724 >	Operations Manager 2007 Alert and CI connector
Service Manager management server	389 >	Active Directory connector
Service Manager management server	1433 >	Configuration Manager 2007 CI connector
Service Manager management server	RPC dynamic ports >	Configuration Manager 2007 software provisioning connector
Data warehouse server	1433 >	Remote data warehouse database server
SSRS server	1433 >	Remote data warehouse database server
Data warehouse server	1433 >	Remote Service Manager database server
Web browser	443 >	Self-service portal
Self-service portal	1433 >	Service Manager database
Web browser	80 >	SSRS

Fast Track

System Center 2012 Service Manager offers many improvements and new features. On the infrastructure side, Service Manager 2012 includes a new self-service portal powered by a service catalog and support for new and improved connectors, and Orchestrator is now the preferred engine between infrastructure components in the data center. In terms of work items, Service Manager 2012 adds support for service requests and release management. The combination of the self-service portal, service catalog, support for service requests, and the Orchestrator connector provide you with a first-class automation platform. In addition, the data warehouse is improved with the addition of OLAP cubes.

Summary

This chapter provided a look inside Service Manager 2012 from a general overview down to macro perspectives. It first described how Service Manager features are deployed in a minimum installation of two machines, and then discussed an installation including multiple machines and adding the data warehouse feature. The chapter presented a first look at management packs and workflow and introduced the Service Manager 2012 console and portal. It also looked at the ports used between component features and the different Windows services used by Service Manager 2012.

With this background, you are now ready for the following chapters, which delve deeper into the features and capabilities of Service Manager 2012.

PART II

Planning and Installation

IN THIS PART

CHAPTER 5

Planning and Designing System Center 2012 Service Manager

The preceding chapters discuss and introduce System Center 2012 Service Manager. This chapter provides the information necessary for planning and designing your deployment of this System Center component. Planning focuses on determining how and what Service Manager is intended for in your organization. Design captures those specifications for what you are building and why, enabling you to build, test, and ultimately deploy your solution. Information Technology (IT) projects often fail because of mixed expectations and result in finger pointing. You can avoid these problems by creating a high-level design document, using it to drive decisions and establish expectations with the stakeholders and sponsors in your organization.

Service Manager installation and deployment is straightforward once you configure the prerequisites required for its deployment. This chapter discusses and provides contextual information for two areas:

▶ How you plan to use Service Manager in your specific environment

▶ The type of deployment configurations to use based on available resources

Determining these two pillars of planning and design are the objectives of this chapter. The chapter begins with the usage perspective and concludes with supported and available deployment scenarios.

Planning to Use Service Manager

Business challenges (pains) and business enablers (gains) typically drive deployment of any IT product or service. Understanding the pains and gains Service Manager addresses is critical to your planning activities. Simply looking at the minimum hardware and software requirements for this System Center component does not answer the pain/gain question. Following is a list of scenarios that can drive an organization to turn to Service Manager:

▶ Replacing an existing IT service management (ITSM) toolset due to cost

▶ Replacing an existing ITSM toolset due to scalability issues

▶ Using other System Center components and owning server licenses for Service Manager

▶ Taking a journey to the private cloud using System Center

▶ Insourcing an outsourced service desk

This list gives examples of adoption drivers for Service Manager and provides a planning baseline. The planning baseline is the concept of determining where you want to go, and more importantly, establishing a criterion that tells you when you get there.

Establishing and Optimizing the Business Requirements

As part of your initial planning for Service Manager, you should establish the business requirements for its deployment. This typically takes the form of a vision statement. Examples of a vision statement for Service Manager follow:

▶ The organization plans to improve customer satisfaction by 70% through efficient management of the incident management life cycle process.

▶ The organization intends to reduce unplanned outages due to unauthorized changes and provide end users with the means to request services that do not require management authorization.

These examples relate to incident management, service request fulfillment, and change management processes; these are business objectives that Service Manager addresses and provides a means to achieve.

Having established the business drivers, the next step is to optimize these objectives and requirements using a scoping document.

Scoping the Service Manager Deployment Objectives

A scoping document drives the planning activity to avoid plans that are overly ambitious and not aligned to available resources. These resources fall into the following categories:

▶ Budget available for the deployment

▶ Technical resource expertise

▶ Time line to deliver

▶ Governance and organizational procedures in place to support the objectives

▶ Senior management support

This list is by no means conclusive and can be expanded based on your specific environment. It highlights some of the business areas that, if not planned for, could introduce risk and ultimate failure in achieving your objectives with Service Manager.

Using the two examples discussed in the previous section, "Establishing and Optimizing the Business Requirements," a high-level scope could be as illustrated in Table 5.1.

TABLE 5.1   Scoping Business Objectives for a Service Manager Deployment

Vision Statement	Scope
Improve customer satisfaction by 70% through efficient management of the Incident Management life cycle process.	The initial phase of the deployment is limited to internal infrastructure Incident Management. Business applications supported by external and third-party processes are implemented in Phase 2 of the deployment.
Reduce unplanned outages due to unauthorized change.	Phase 1 implements Change Management for IT-controlled business services infrastructure; these are later extended to business services under the control of the Application Support team. Existing change processes are maintained until Phase 2 of the project.
Provide end users with the means to request services that do not require authorization from management.	Deploy the self-service solution using Service Request Fulfillment. Initial available services do not require authorization. Phase 2 extends this capability to service requests requiring authorization.

The scope categories act as drivers for those work tasks necessary to understand your current environment and validate assumptions. The vision is typically driven by senior stakeholders, who may not have a true understanding of the current environment or the challenges faced by those tasked with deploying a tool such as System Center Service Manager. Scoping your objectives enables your implementation to meet the organization's goals.

The scope should act as your blueprint for conversations with the overall deployment team. A typical Service Manager deployment team includes but is not limited to the following:

▶ Sponsor and main management stakeholders

▶ Project manager(s)

▶ Affected business unit leaders

▶ Technical IT staff

▶ External consultancy firm (optional)

The output of the scope should be aligned to a RACI model (Responsible, Accountable, Consulted, and Informed). This tool can be used to match up roles and responsibilities with processes. It defines who is responsible for the specific scope area, accountable for the success of the scope area, consulted for the requirements of the scope area, and who needs to be informed. Table 5.2 lists elements of a generic framework for aligning scope outputs to the RACI model.

TABLE 5.2   Example of the RACI Model Applied to Scope Outputs

Scope	Sponsor	Business Unit	Technical Team	Users
Output 1	I	A/R/C	R/C	I
Output 2	I	A/R/C	R/C	I
Output 3	I	A/R/C	R/C	I
Output 4	R/I	A/R/C	R/C	I

Assessing and Capturing the Current Environment

After completing initial scoping activities, you must plan to assess and document the current environment for a Service Manager deployment. The assessment is usually performed using information-gathering techniques. Use the most appropriate of these techniques to gather the required information:

▶ Interviews

▶ Workshops

▶ Surveys

▶ Reviews of existing procedural standard operating documentation

The goal is to gather and document information on the following areas, planning for the tasks identified in each area:

▶ **Geographical factors**

  ▶ Identify end users and their locations

  ▶ Document language requirements

  ▶ Identify and document time zones in scope

▶ **Organizational structure**

  ▶ Identify organizational hierarchy (business units and ITSM teams)

  ▶ Determine administrative policies and procedures

  ▶ Discuss and capture the overall business strategic direction

- ▶ **Network topology**
    - ▶ Source or create a network topology diagram of your environment
    - ▶ Document available network bandwidth and usage patterns
- ▶ **Security considerations**
    - ▶ Document organizational policies and procedures
    - ▶ Identify and document operating system security rules and policies
    - ▶ Identify and document SQL Server security
    - ▶ Identify and document network security
    - ▶ Identify and document Internet Information Services (IIS) security
- ▶ **Active Directory structure and domain models**
    - ▶ Document domain model in use
    - ▶ Capture Active Directory forest information
    - ▶ Identify and document organizational units and relevant mandatory group policies
    - ▶ Agree to and document service account compliance rules
- ▶ **ITSM processes, frameworks, and compliance standards**
    - ▶ Capture alignment to the Information Technology Infrastructure Library (ITIL)
    - ▶ Document any enforced audit and industry standards
    - ▶ Document Asset Management processes and procedures
    - ▶ Document Configuration Management processes and procedures
    - ▶ Document Change and Release Management processes and procedures
    - ▶ Document Incident Management, Problem Management, and Service Request Fulfillment processes and procedures
- ▶ **System management tools in use**
    - ▶ Record the list of System Center components in use
    - ▶ Document non-Microsoft toolsets and their scope of management
    - ▶ Document integrations in place
    - ▶ Document internally developed tools and utilities used to support ITSM

Plan to capture and document the actual mode of operation versus what is supposed to happen. The accuracy of your assessment can significantly reduce the risk of invalid assumptions that could derail a Service Manager deployment. You need to understand what Service Manager can deliver to your existing processes versus what is not achievable.

REAL WORLD: ASSESSMENT SPECIFIC TO YOUR ENVIRONMENT

The information provided in this chapter is based on real-world experiences of the authors. Realize that not every aspect applies to your organization; you can add or remove what is or is not relevant.

Assessing and capturing the environment specific to the objectives of a Service Manager deployment is a continual process. Use the process as an initial baseline, updating the appropriate information as your environment changes. Aligning your assessment to an existing change management process can assist in keeping the information gathered as accurate as possible.

Creating the Deployment Plan

A recommended practice for any IT product deployment is to document the steps from project inception to implementation. This sequence of steps is known as a *deployment plan*. Successful Service Manager deployments require that you have a deployment plan to deliver on the identified and agreed upon scope. A deployment typically consists of the following phases:

▶ Planning and design phase

▶ Build and configuration phase

▶ Pilot phase

▶ Production rollout phase

These are discussed in the following sections. You may have heard of similar types of practices envisioned in the Microsoft Solutions Framework (MSF), whose phases are Envision, Plan, Develop, Stabilize, and Deploy. MSF is now incorporated into the Microsoft Operations Framework (MOF), discussed in Chapter 3, "MOF, ITIL, and System Center." These are standard deployment practices, regardless of the framework.

Planning and Design

The planning and design phase involves identifying and capturing those requirements specific to the build and configuration phase. The output of this phase is usually a functional specification document, a high-level design document, and a low-level design document. The functional specification is a high-level description of what must be achieved and provides a technical blueprint of the environment architecture, the high-level design document discusses the overall technical requirements but in an abstract form, and the low-level design captures detailed information about each functional area. Functional areas include but are not limited to operating system standards, security requirements, and fault tolerance. These documents serve as your blueprint and provide a clear scope for the project. There typically are changes to the scope of any IT deployment project; you should incorporate these into the functional specifications with good project management change control practices to avoid scope creep.

Build and Configuration Phase

The build and configuration phase follows sign-off of the design and functional specifications. The activities in this phase typically include

▶ Operating system provisioning on a physical or virtual server

▶ Installation of Service Manager prerequisites and infrastructure dependency configurations (such as required firewall ports)

▶ Installation of Service Manager server roles as agreed in the design documents

▶ Post-installation configuration according to the project deliverables, captured in the functional specifications

The configuration aspect is a continual process during and after your Service Manager deployment. Post-deployment updates are driven by additional functional requirements and updates by Microsoft to System Center Service Manager. In this phase, you should plan for at least a test (sometimes known as preproduction or staging) and a production environment. (An additional development environment is strongly recommended by the authors.) The test environment should be a prototype of production but does not need to scale to the same load requirements.

REAL WORLD: DEVELOPMENT ENVIRONMENT VERSUS TEST ENVIRONMENT

Service Manager has many moving parts that you can configure in a variety of ways to achieve the desired outcome. A real world approach is to have three environments (development, test, and production). The development environment provides a safe area for configuration testing and experimentation. The test environment should reflect the production environment configuration and serve to validate your changes before implementing in production.

This approach has great value and minimal investments (you can build the development environment using workstation class host hardware). Most modern workstation hosts have virtualization capabilities and provide an excellent low cost platform for your development builds, enabling you to easily add or remove what is or is not relevant.

Performing a Pilot

The pilot phase is where you validate the configuration with controlled load and access. This phase involves providing access to Service Manager for controlled scenario tests. Plan to create a test case document based on the functional specification document. The test case document should map to the original agreed upon business objectives, and its output must provide validation as to whether those objectives are achieved. The authors recommend utilizing a test environment for the pilot. You can use the following steps for your production rollout:

1. Test the functional specification in the test environment.

2. Adjust the test environment configuration and retest if required.

3. Update configuration documentation and export configuration settings where supported.

4. Import validated test settings into production and manually update those settings where exports are not supported.

The pilot phase provides your best opportunity to validate assumptions and the intended use of Service Manager. Plan to have a spectrum of testers from end users to managers for each process category.

The authors recommend using a table listing functional tests and the expected outcomes of each test. Table 5.3 provides an example of functional areas and tests you can perform.

TABLE 5.3   Examples of Pilot Phase Functional Tests

Functional Area or Process	Pilot Test
Notification channel	Telnet test without email client
Active Directory connector	New users synchronized
	Updated existing user properties
Incident Management	Assign default support group on creation of incidents
Incident Management	SLO changes when impact and urgency are modified to reflect new priority
Service Request Fulfillment	Review activity and manual activity flow as expected

Production Rollout

Installing Service Manager into a production environment is the first step in your production rollout phase. This phase includes but is not limited to the following, described in the following sections:

▶ Implementation planning

▶ Communication and training

▶ Activation of agreed upon functional processes

▶ Continual adjustment to production based on feedback

Implementation Planning

Service Manager deployment is no different in principle from any technology-related deployment. The success or failure of most technology deployments can be traced back to the overall quality of planning. The implementation plan should ensure that the rollout minimizes the impact to ongoing business activities. For example, plan to go live on the last working day of the week, as this allows time for regression to a known working state. You should also plan to have an agreed upon live date (a point of no return) and initial functionality activation list.

Communication and Training

You must plan to communicate to all users at all levels of the business. A successfully validated approach is ensuring the project has strong leadership and support from the highest level of the organization's management team. Plan to train all users with direct and indirect access to the various features of Service Manager. The training plan must also include the underpinning processes implemented by Service Manager (for example, ITIL and MOF). A cost-effective approach is "training the trainer"; you train key users of Service Manager, who in turn create and deliver organization-specific training in house.

Activation of Agreed Functional Processes

Service Manager's modular framework allows you to phase activating functional processes in production. There is no value in having a big bang approach to your production rollout. Two reasons that enable a safe phased rollout follow:

▶ System Center Service Manager can coexist with other tools and products providing a side-by-side experience even in production.

▶ The class-based separation of ITIL processes provides a platform for modular activation of functional areas. Organizations often start with a base configuration management database (CMDB) and Incident Management. You can configure other processes in the Service Manager but delay their use in production.

Continual Adjustment to Production Based on Feedback

Deployment into production is not a static process. Service Manager is continually evolving and so is your environment. You should plan for this changing state of Service Manager and your IT environments. These changes include business objectives, incremental and major updates to the component, and process optimization.

The objective is to plan for change from the beginning of the rollout, as change is inevitable. The value of upfront planning is it reduces risk and enables a positive culture that embraces change. The quality of this feedback and improvement loop is enhanced when all levels of users provide input. Avoid focusing exclusively on component updates like hot-fixes and service packs; a change such as the sentence structure on the user portal could have a large positive impact on the quality of incidents raised by users.

One of the core outputs of the deployment plan is how Service Manager infrastructure changes are managed with minimal risk to the standard operating state of your environment.

Review and Sign-Off of the Deployment Plan

The final planning task is review and sign-off of the actual deployment plan. Service Manager often changes how people work, and it introduces new infrastructure components. Sign-off underpins the entire planning and deployment strategy, which is illustrated in Figure 5.1.

In typical Service Manager deployments, the review and sign-off is performed by technical peers for the technology aspects, and by the management team accountable for the project deliverables. Sign-off effectively baselines all documentation and provides the delivery team with an authoritative scope reference.

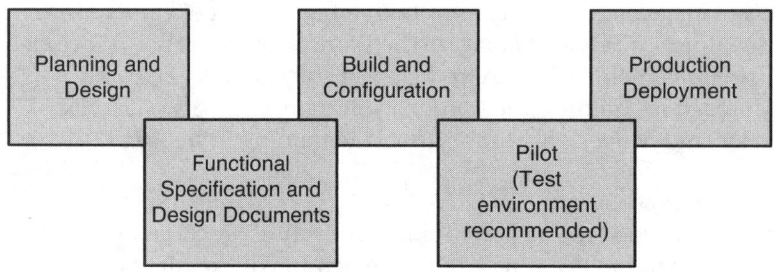

FIGURE 5.1   Planning and deployment strategy.

Planning to Deploy Service Manager

The "Planning to Use Service Manager" section discussed how you plan to use Service Manager in your specific environment. This section focuses on the type of deployment configurations to use based on available resources. It begins with the core areas you must plan for in a deployment of System Center Service Manager and concludes with examples of common deployment scenarios.

Planning for Licensing

Do you have the correct licenses and enough of those licenses for your planned deployment? The answer is *it depends*! In many large enterprises, software licensing is well-managed and has a dedicated team. That said, the authors recommend you check and validate licensing requirements prior to deploying Service Manager.

Licensing of Microsoft software can be a confusing field of expertise. This section includes a simplified primer for the specific licenses you require for Service Manager. A full and current source of information for System Center licensing is available at http://www. microsoft.com/licensing/about-licensing/SystemCenter2012.aspx.

> **NOTE: LICENSING CAN CHANGE**
>
> The System Center licensing model explained here is valid as of mid-2014 and may be changed at any time.

To determine licensing costs, realize that there are two different types of management licenses (MLs) available:

▶ **System Center 2012 Standard ML:** Used for lightly virtualized or nonvirtualized environments

▶ **System Center 2012 Datacenter ML:** Used for highly virtualized environments

The only difference between the two editions is the number of operating system environments (OSEs) that you can manage per license. Datacenter allows an unlimited number of OSEs per license; Standard allows managing up to two OSEs per license.

The licensing model can be simplified further by separating it into server management licenses and client management licenses.

Server Management License

A server management license (SML) is required to perform a management action on a server operating system environment. An example would be software deployment using System Center Configuration Manager, including the site server.

SMLs are physical processor-based, with each license covering up to two physical processors. Both the Standard and Datacenter product editions include rights to run each SML associated with System Center, plus a run-time instance of SQL Server Standard edition when utilized by the SQL engine used by a System Center component. In a high availability environment, you may determine SQL Server Enterprise edition is a better fit.

Client Management License

You cannot purchase SMLs just by MLs alone. There is a Client Management Suite, which is an additional licensing suite for customers wanting to utilize additional functionality. This includes Service Manager, Operations Manager, Data Protection Manager, and Orchestrator licenses for machines managed by those System Center components. These licenses can be bundled with Software Assurance; each Microsoft product license covered by Software Assurance can be upgraded to the most recent version of that product for no additional cost. Additional information on Software Assurance for Microsoft's server and cloud platform is available at http://www.microsoft.com/licensing/software-assurance/by-product.aspx#tab=3.

A client management license (CML) is necessary when performing a management action on a client operating system. An example is an application deployment to a client OSE.

Service Manager, unlike some other System Center 2012 components, is not agent-based. Instead, licensing is based on the number of users, clients, and servers being managed and stored within the CMDB. This difference requires you to perform the server and client management license count using the configuration items (CIs) you manage in the CMDB. Figure 5.2 provides a visual representation of the steps you take to evaluate and count license requirements for Service Manager.

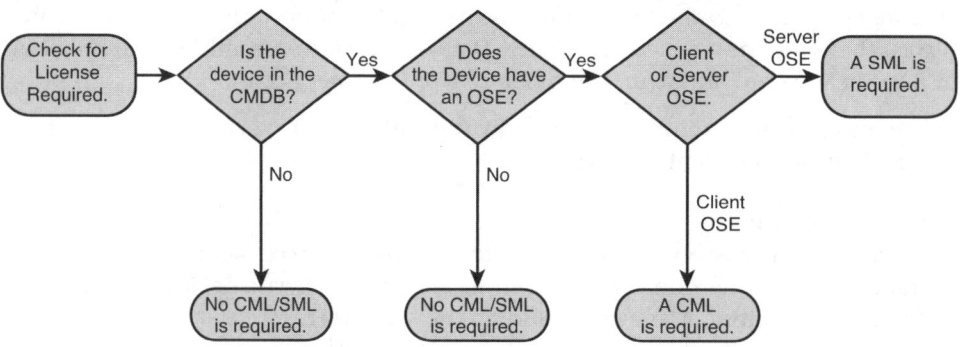

FIGURE 5.2   Evaluating device license requirements.

NOTE: WHEN A CLIENT MANAGEMENT LICENSE IS NECESSARY

A client management license must be assigned to a device for each OSE managed by Service Manager, except for OSEs on devices functioning only as network infrastructure devices (Open Systems Interconnection [OSI] Layer 3 or below).

An OSE is all or part of an operating system instance, or all or part of a virtual (or other emulated) operating system instance that enables separate machine identity (primary computer name or similar unique identifier) or separate administrative rights, and instances of any applications configured to run on the operating system instance of parts previously identified.

OSEs can be physical or virtual:

▶ A physical OSE is configured to run directly on a physical hardware system.

▶ A virtual OSE is configured to run on a virtual (or otherwise emulated) hardware system.

A physical hardware system can have either or both of the following: one physical OSE and one or more virtual OSEs.

An additional option for client operating systems is licensing by number of users. The per user license option provides entitlement to manage devices owned by users.

The authors recommend you discuss your organization-specific licensing options with a Microsoft reseller or a member of the Microsoft account team assigned to your organization.

CAUTION: ABOUT SERVICE MANAGER TRIAL VERSIONS

Do not plan to install Service Manager in evaluation mode if you intend to later use it in production. The evaluation edition cannot be converted to a full edition; it must be reinstalled. This applies even when the installation is within the 180-day evaluation period.

Common Design Scenarios

A System Center Service Manager design is based on a number of mandatory rules and optional choices specific to the placement of the infrastructure servers for your Service Manager deployment. Chapter 4, "Looking Inside System Center 2012 Service Manager," discusses the architecture and servers required for a Service Manager deployment. The baseline of any Service Manager design must comply with these rules, summarized in Table 5.4.

TABLE 5.4   Service Manager Infrastructure Server Combinations

Infrastructure Server	Coexistence Rules
Service Manager management server	Can coexist with the Service Manager and data warehouse database servers. Cannot be combined with the Service Manager data warehouse management server or the self-service portal server.
Service Manager database server	Can coexist with the Service Manager data warehouse database server.
Service Manager data warehouse management server	Can coexist with the Service Manager data warehouse database server.
	Cannot be combined with the Service Manager management server or the self-service portal server.
Service Manager data warehouse database server	Can coexist with the Service Manager database server.
Service Manager self-service portal server	Can be combined with the Service Manager management server (however, this is not recommended for performance reasons).

Background and latest information supporting the information summarized in Table 5.4 can be found at http://technet.microsoft.com/en-us/library/hh519675.aspx.

Figure 5.3 illustrates a simplified logical view of System Center 2012 Service Manager.

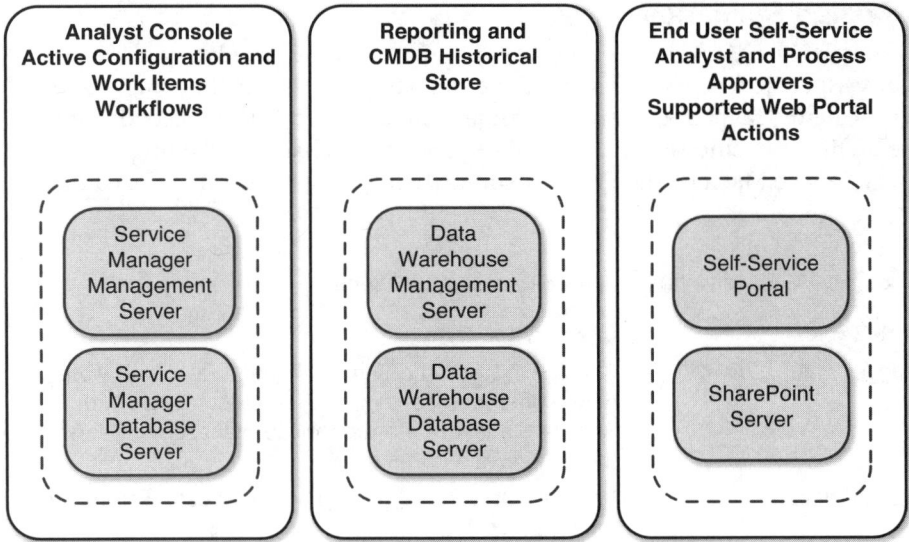

FIGURE 5.3   Logical view of Service Manager features.

Having established the rules and supported configurations for Service Manager features, you must determine which to deploy. The features illustrated in Figure 5.3 that you have to or may want to deploy are

▶ **Service Manager management server:** This is the only mandatory feature in a Service Manager environment. The feature enables the System Center Service Manager component-supported ITSM processes, and its installation includes the Service Manager CMDB. This feature must be deployed with a supported database server, which can be co-located on the same server. There are no reporting, historical, or end user self-service capabilities if this is the only feature deployed.

▶ **Data warehouse management server:** This is an optional feature. It enables the retention of historical CMDB data and provides comprehensive reporting capabilities. This feature must be deployed with a supported database server and can be co-located on the same server.

▶ **Self-service portal:** This is an optional feature. It enables self-service capabilities for

   ▶ **End users:** Web-enabled capability to create and track incidents and service requests.

   ▶ **Analyst and Process Approvers:** Web-enabled capability to approve review activities and to complete manual activities. These activities are typically associated with service requests and change requests. Being web-based, it reduces the users to whom you must deploy the console to perform approvals or complete manual activities.

In addition, all users with access to the self-service portal can view and search for published knowledge base articles. For additional information regarding the self-service portal, see Chapter 7, "Using Service Manager."

Those features you decide to deploy are driven by the goals and objectives of the project. The "Creating the Deployment Plan" section earlier in this chapter discussed how to plan, agree, and obtain sign-off on these scope objectives. As an example, if the project scope states users must have self-service capabilities, you must deploy the self-service portal feature. Additionally, if the business scope states you must retain data and provide reporting capabilities, a data warehouse feature is required.

After establishing Service Manager feature requirements, proceed to the best configuration you can deploy, based on infrastructure resources and budget for the project. The next two sections of the chapter discuss two common deployment scenarios, leveraging these three available features. The three-server and five-server configurations could be considered base configurations. You can reconfigure each scenario type with fewer (in the case of the five-server scenario) or more servers by combining features or further separating performance-related parts of a feature.

Three-Server Scenario Design
The three-server design is the simplest configuration for a Service Manager deployment. This design incorporates all three features illustrated in Figure 5.3. Its objective is to use the least amount of servers (physical or virtual) to deploy an environment providing all the functionality of System Center Service Manager. The design, illustrated in Figure 5.4, also achieves a clear separation of features. The design follows:

▶ **Server 1:** Service Manager self-service portal server, with a local dedicated installation of Microsoft SharePoint

▶ **Server 2:** Service Manager management server with a local dedicated installation of Microsoft SQL Server

▶ **Server 3:** Service Manager data warehouse management server with a local dedicated installation of Microsoft SQL Server

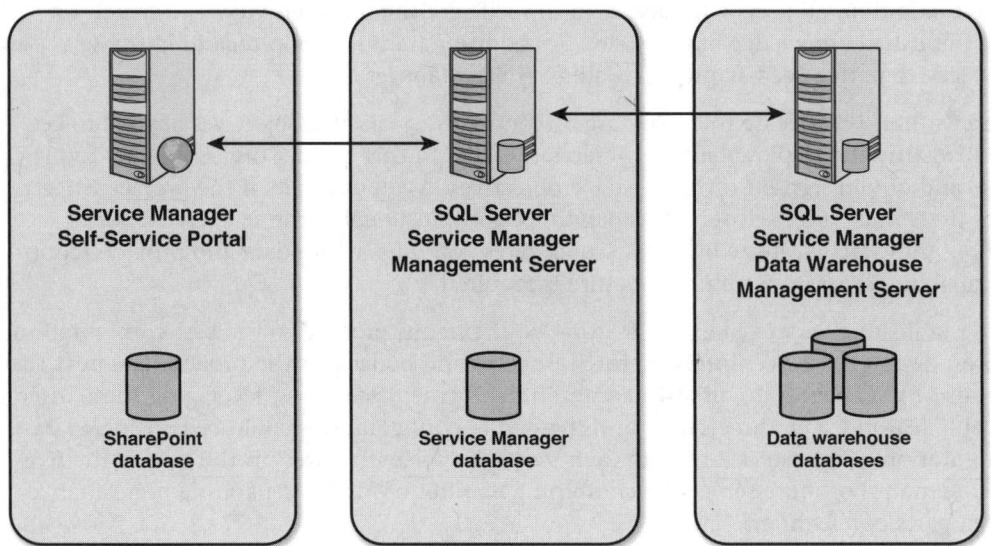

FIGURE 5.4   Deploying all Service Manager features using three servers.

NOTE: SELF-SERVICE PORTAL OPERATING SYSTEM

Microsoft supports installing the self-service portal on the Service Manager management server. SharePoint 2010 is the only supported version for the portal. Microsoft supports SharePoint 2010 Service Pack (SP) 2 on a management server running Windows Server 2012 or Windows Server 2012 R2. If using an earlier version of SharePoint 2010, the Service Manager management server must be running Windows Server 2008 R2.

The three-server deployment scenario is commonly used in small organizations and test environments, as it is designed for smaller deployments.

Five-Server Scenario Design

The five-server design, shown in Figure 5.5, is a common scaled-out configuration for Service Manager deployments. This design incorporates the three features but offloads the Microsoft SQL Server components to dedicated servers for the two management servers. There are a number of advantages to this deployment design, primarily performance related. The design follows:

▶ **Server 1:** Service Manager management server

▶ **Server 2:** Microsoft SQL Server dedicated to the Service Manager management server

▶ **Server 3:** Service Manager data warehouse management server

▶ **Server 4:** Microsoft SQL Server dedicated to the Service Manager data warehouse management server

▶ **Server 5:** Service Manager self-service server with a local installation of Microsoft SharePoint

This design is typically used by medium- to enterprise-sized organizations' implementations of System Center 2012 Service Manager. The design gains performance and scalability advantages. Performance gains are achieved when appropriate resources are assigned to meet the demands of the target environment.

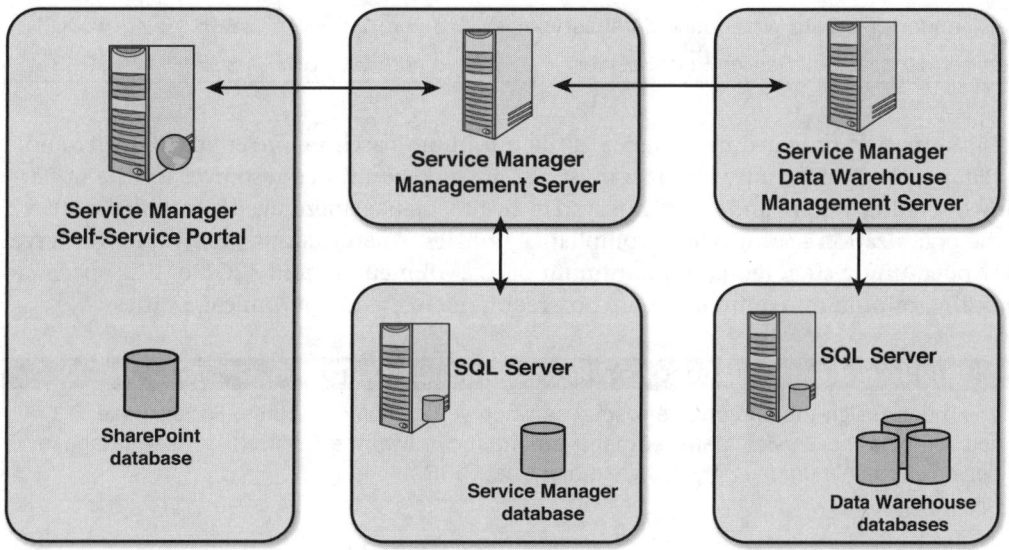

FIGURE 5.5   Deploying all Service Manager features with five servers.

The next sections of the chapter delve deeper into planning for actual capacity, network considerations, security, availability, fault tolerance, and resilience of the environment regardless of the scenario type.

Capacity Planning

How much is enough? Again, the answer is *it depends*. In addition, you must make the appropriate investment. Capacity planning for Service Manager has two facets:

▶ Minimum requirements for the Service Manager components

▶ Planned workload of the Service Manager environment

Table 5.5 lists the minimum recommended requirements for the Service Manager features.

TABLE 5.5   Service Manager Features Sizing

Feature	CPU	Memory	Disk
Console	2 core 2.66GHz	2GB	10GB
Service Manager management server (console connections and workflow)	4 core 2.66GHz	8GB	10GB
Service Manager database server	8 core 2.66GHz	8GB	10GB
Service Manager Data Warehouse management server	4 core 2.66GHz	8GB	10GB
Service Manager Data Warehouse database server	8 core 2.66GHz	8GB	400GB
Service Manager Self-Service Portal server	8 core 2.66GHz	8GB	80GB

The information provided in Table 5.5 is the minimum baseline for Service Manager and its required additional software. You must also include additional resources for the under-lying operating system and operating system health management agents installed as part of the organization's security and compliance policies. As an example, the Windows Server 2012 operating system requires a minimum of 512MB memory and 32GB of disk space. Typically, minimum requirements are box requirements, and your mileage varies.

CAUTION: INCREASE RESOURCES WHEN COMBINING FEATURES

You must assign the appropriate resources when you combine features. For example, if you combine the Service Manager management server with the Service Manager database server, the minimum memory assigned must be 16GB.

The second part of capacity planning and scaling is the planned workload. Microsoft provides a sizing helper (available as part of the Service Manager job aids) online at http://go.microsoft.com/fwlink/p/?LinkID=232378. The sizer is also discussed in Chapter 19, "Managing Service Manager Performance."

The SM2012_Sizer.xls spreadsheet, included with the Service Manager job aids, automatically calculates server resources required including database sizes. The calculation uses the values you enter for the matrix requested, such as the number of computers in the CMDB.

A workload assessment requires understanding the current operating environment. This would include, for example, the number of incidents raised per week, and the planned number of analysts that would concurrently connect to Service Manager.

The authors recommend performing a baseline exercise to determine the capacity requirements for your environment. This exercise typically requires building a prototype or test lab deployment for Service Manager. This enables you to measure the impact of workloads on all areas of capacity required to operate Service Manager. Use the following steps to gather the required data:

1. Create a list of scenarios for all areas scoped for the Service Manager deployment.

2. Create a list of the performance and capacity matrix for measuring operating system load; this could include disk and memory measurement counters.

3. Use a performance-measuring tool to capture the impact of running the scenario tests.

Use the information gathered from the baseline to calculate the actual capacity required for a full deployment.

Security and Authentication Planning

Security and authentication planning for Service Manager deployments fall into three categories:

▶ Infrastructure management server security

▶ Service accounts and system groups

▶ Administrative users and end user security

Infrastructure Management Server Security

The infrastructure management server security category requires that all servers belong to the same Active Directory domain. The Service Manager features are installed on these servers. You could also secure the self-service portal server web application using a certificate for additional security.

Service Accounts and System Groups

The next category is the service accounts and groups you are required to provide during Service Manager installation and configuration.

Table 5.6 lists security requirements for service accounts and the groups used during the deployment and operation of Service Manager. The table is extracted from the planning guide, which is part of the full Service Manager documentation. You can view and download Microsoft's documentation at http://technet.microsoft.com/en-us/library/hh495575. aspx. For additional information on security in Service Manager, see Chapter 17, "Service Manager Security."

TABLE 5.6   Important Users and Groups Required for Service Manager

Account	Permissions	Usage in Service Manager
Management group administrators (Service Manager management server)	Must be a domain group.	Added to Service Manager Administrators user role.
Service Manager services account	Must be a domain user and member of local Administrators group.	Becomes the Operational System Account. Assigned to the logon account for the System Center Data Access Service. Assigned to the logon account for the System Center Management Configuration service. Becomes member of the sdk_users and configsvc_users database roles for the Service-Manager database. If you change the credentials for these two services, make sure the new account has a SQL login in the ServiceManager database and that it is a member of the Builtin\Administrators group.
Workflow account	Must be domain user. Must have permissions to send email and must have a mailbox on the Simple Mail Transfer Protocol (SMTP) server (required for the email incident feature). Must be member of local Users security group. Must be made a member of the Service Manager Administrators user role for email notifications to function properly.	This account is used for all workflows and is made a member of the Service Manager Workflows user role.
Management group administrators (data warehouse management server)	Must be a domain group.	Added to the data warehouse administrators user role.

Account	Permissions	Usage in Service Manager
Service Manager services account (data warehouse)	Must be a domain user and member of local Administrators group on the data warehouse management server. Must be the same account used for the Service Manager management server services account.	Becomes the data warehouse system Run As account. Assigned to the ServiceManager SDK service account. Assigned to ServiceManager Config account. Becomes member of the sdk_ users and configsvc_users database roles for the DWDataMart database. Becomes member of the db_ datareader database role for the DWRepository database. Becomes member of the configsvc_users database role for the ServiceManager database.
Reporting account	Must be a domain account and member of local Administrators group.	Used by SQL Server Reporting Services (SSRS) to access the DWDataMart database to get data for reporting. Becomes member of the db_ datareader database role for the DWDataMart database. Becomes member of the report-user database role for the DWDataMart database.
Analysis Services account	Must be a domain account.	Used to communicate with data marts. Account is added as an administrator role in the Analysis Services server database (DWASDatabase) for database processing and cube reading.

You must also plan for connector accounts, which must be provided to configure the supported Service Manager connectors. Chapter 8, "Working with Connectors," discusses the Service Manager connectors in detail, including recommended practices for user accounts.

Administrative Users and End User Security

The third area is the list of groups and users used for accessing and interacting with Service Manager. Typical categories are analysts and end users. Plan to use groups for role-based security assignment. The users and groups vary by organization. You should plan to use groups created specifically for Service Manager interaction. Table 5.7 provides an example of process role security planning.

TABLE 5.7   Important Users and Groups Required for Service Manager

Active Directory Group	Process	Usage in Service Manager
SCSM_IR Analysts	Incident Management	Assign the Incident Resolver role or equivalent. Users in this group manage the investigation and resolution of incidents.
SCSM_SR Support	Service Request Fulfillment	Assign the Service Request Analyst role. First point of contact for all service requests.
SCSM_CM Managers	Change Management	Assign the Change Managers role. Responsible for managing the change schedule.
SCSM_HR Portal Users	Secure service catalog access	Role-based access to service and request offerings published to the self-service portal. Sensitive HR authorized and initiated automated processes.

You must also plan to review and adhere to your specific organization security policies and compliance standards.

CAUTION: RESTRICTING SECURITY PRACTICES

Security is necessary when appropriate, but beware of taking it to the level where it negatively affects Service Manager performance. Share Microsoft's documentation on securing Service Manager with your security teams. The security team's role is to protect the environment; however, they need the correct information from the team responsible for your Service Manager deployment.

Network Considerations

There are two areas to plan for as part of network considerations in a Service Manager deployment:

▶ System interaction with Service Manager

▶ User interaction with Service Manager

These are discussed in the following sections.

System Interaction with Service Manager

The types of network communication depend on the specific Service Manager deployment scenario you use. For example, the three-server design has no communication over the network between the management servers and their respective database servers. The five-server scenario provides the best example for discussing all the types of network communications you must plan to configure and manage.

In the five-server scenario, you must plan for fast and reliable connectivity between the management servers and their respective databases. You must also plan for connectivity and communication between each management server, as inadequate bandwidth may cause issues. As an example, the reporting node is not available in the Service Manager console if the connection between the Service Manager management server and the data warehouse management server drops due to low bandwidth.

You also want to consider the firewall ports required by Service Manager. Firewall port settings are both network and security planning considerations in a Service Manager deployment. Chapter 4 lists the ports required for Service Manager, and you may also want to check Microsoft's technical documentation at http://technet.microsoft.com/en-US/library/hh495567.aspx for any updates. You must configure firewalls appropriately to ensure that network communication is not impacted by a loss of Service Manager functionality.

TIP: NETWORK PLACEMENT OF SERVICE MANAGER SERVERS

The authors recommend placing all Service Manager infrastructure servers on the same network segment. This may involve using the same virtual LAN (VLAN) configured on the same switch. Avoid placing these servers on segments of the network already hosting high demand network bandwidth application servers.

You should plan for communication between Service Manager and its connectors. For example, Service Manager can be configured to connect to a System Center Configuration Manager site database (2007, 2012, or 2012 R2 versions). Ensuring a robust connection between Service Manager and the Configuration Manager site database can reduce delays in synchronizing the data. You should also plan for when the connectors are scheduled to run, as this would have a high impact on writes to the ServiceManager database.

User Interaction with Service Manager

A fully deployed Service Manager environment (having a management server, a data warehouse management server, and a self-service portal) has two forms of user interaction. The two types of users are Service Manager console users and Service Manager self-service portal users. Review the quality of service on network links between users and the respective Service Manager feature being accessed, and plan for available versus actual bandwidth by measuring bandwidth during peak usage.

Planning for Availability, Resilience, and Fault Tolerance

The areas of availability, resilience, and fault tolerance of any IT application are best addressed by focusing on business objectives and the associated investment. The desired business objective is to have systems that are *always on and never slow*. This can be achieved only if the business has the right resources, specifically infrastructure and supportability, which has associated costs.

Service Manager deployments can be made highly available, resilient, and fault tolerant with supportability constraints. Availability and resilience are often misunderstood. The two methods are similar in principle but not necessarily in what they achieve. How they differ follows:

▶ Availability is typically about ensuring that a particular system is accessible in the event of failure. An example would be in a disaster scenario where you could fail over to an alternative site to access the application.

▶ Resilience is usually about making access to the application resistant to failure in the first place.

Fault tolerance is the bridge between availability and resilience.

Purists may disagree with the simplified explanation offered in this chapter. The intent, however, is to provide a basis for how you achieve the objective of *always on and never slow* with a Service Manager deployment.

Available options, specific to the components of the infrastructure:

▶ **Service Manager management server:** The first server you install is automatically configured as the workflow server and also provides console connections. The options available to you are

  ▶ Install one or more secondary management servers to service console connections.

  ▶ Configure the console connections to target the secondary management servers. (Analysts can manually fail over their connections to an alternative management server in the event of failure.) You can automate the console failover process by using hardware or software-based network load balancing (NLB).

  ▶ The workflow server feature does not provide for automatic failover; you must promote one of the available secondary servers to take over the feature. This process is included in the Service Manager documentation and is discussed in Chapter 18, "Maintenance, Backup, and Recovery."

▶ **Microsoft SQL Server:** Service Manager supports the fault-tolerant features of Microsoft SQL Server. You make Service Manager available, resilient, and fault-tolerant by installing the underlying databases on a clustered SQL Server instance. The typical configuration is a two-node active/passive cluster. The SQL instance of the database is configured to fail over to the passive node to achieve fault tolerance. Clustering requires a significant financial investment.

▶ **Service Manager data warehouse management server:** The data warehouse does not provide for a secondary management server. In this case, availability, resilience, and fault tolerance involve the placement of the databases and the analysis service features. Following are options you can plan for with your deployment:

  ▶ Install the database instance on a highly available cluster. Although the data warehouse databases can be on the same instance as the ServiceManager database, this requires allocating adequate resources to avoid performance degradation.

> ▶ SSRS is not supported on a cluster, so it must be installed on a separate server. You could host the reporting services database on a clustered instance if desired.

▶ **Service Manager self-service portal server:** The self-service portal relies on Microsoft SharePoint. The free version of SharePoint does not include fault-tolerant features. You must use an enterprise version of the product that provides this functionality. The main configurable options for the self-service portal follow:

> ▶ Install additional portal servers.

> ▶ Configure NLB for all the portal servers.

Figure 5.6 shows all the options configured in a highly available and resilient configuration.

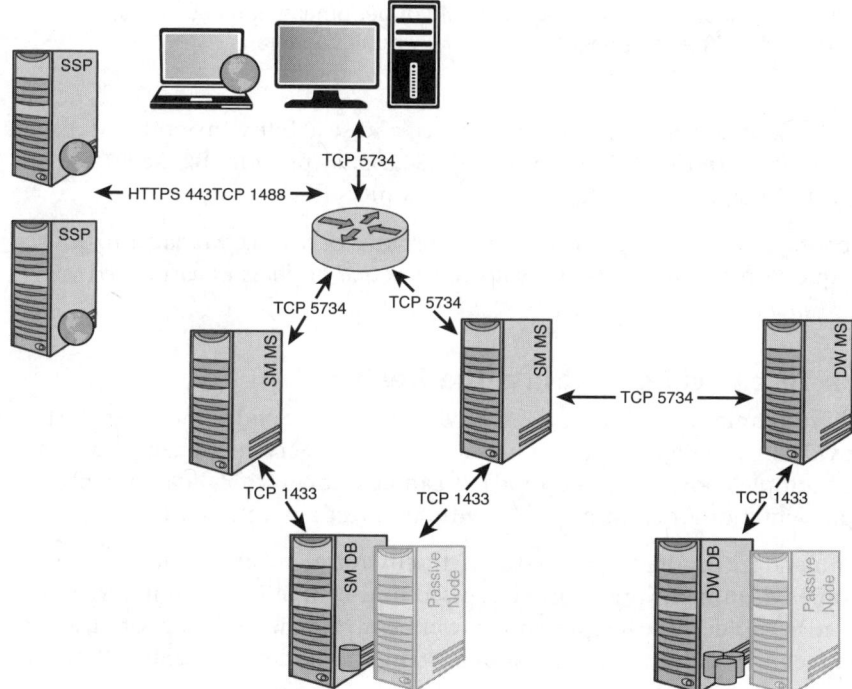

FIGURE 5.6   Highly available and resilient configuration for Service Manager.

You must also plan to implement performance-enhancing practices that improve the resilience and fault tolerance of Service Manager. Some recommended options follow:

▶ Invest in disk drive redundancy such as a redundant array of inexpensive disks (RAID).

▶ Use separate physical disks for the databases, temp files, and log files.

▶ Assign adequate memory based on tested load.

▶ Use location redundancy where appropriate and affordable. This is typically an extension of your organization's disaster recovery policy.

REAL WORLD: USING VIRTUALIZATION FOR SERVICE MANAGER SERVERS

Microsoft supports installation of Service Manager features on virtualization platforms, although you must make sure you assign appropriate resources. Disk input/output (I/O) tends to be one of the most important areas to consider. Plan to create the virtual machines on separate physical disk volumes or LUNs, and avoid overallocating virtual resources such as memory (allowed by some virtualization platforms).

Make sure you allocate the same resources as you would to a physical server. Virtualization reduces the number of physical servers but is not a reason to starve resources to critical application servers. A good practice for measuring Service Manager performance with virtualization is to use a tool capable of performing end-to-end monitoring of the virtual machines (from the host to the actual virtual machine).

Microsoft provides information to plan for performance and scalability in Service Manager at http://technet.microsoft.com/en-US/library/hh495684.aspx. Appendix B, "Reference URLs," includes a list of popular and informative community sites.

The deployment configuration should reflect the importance of Service Manager to your organization. The question you must ask is *what is the risk and business impact of Service Manager not being available?*

Incorporating a Test Environment into the Design

The authors highly recommend deploying a test environment for Service Manager. Test environments provide an excellent return on a low investment. Service Manager has many moving parts and multiple configuration options. It can be difficult to validate the design and expected implementation of ITSM processes without a test environment.

The authors recommend incorporating a development environment in addition to the test and production environments previously discussed in the "Build and Configuration Phase" section of this chapter. A development environment provides a variety of business risk reduction and technical benefits. The most important and notable benefits follow:

▶ Low investment configuration validation

▶ The use of management pack export and import processes to transfer validated configurations into the production environment

▶ A training environment for Service Manager

▶ Support for change management of the production environment

Plan to include a test environment as a mandatory criterion for your deployment. Service Manager is constantly undergoing improvements and changes. You reduce the risk of affecting business dependent services by using a test environment throughout the Service Manager life cycle.

Summary

This chapter discussed and provided guidance on planning and designing System Center Service Manager. The chapter focused on the two core areas of the planning activities: business objective planning and technical objective planning. The chapter also discussed several scenario deployments.

The next chapter provides a detailed discussion on installing and upgrading to System Center 2012 Service Manager, post-installation configuration, uninstallation, and troubleshooting installation issues.

5

CHAPTER 6

Installing and Upgrading to System Center 2012 Service Manager

Chapter 5, "Planning and Designing System Center 2012 Service Manager," discussed the activities you must perform before installing System Center 2012 Service Manager. Service Manager is simple to install and, as with the other System Center 2012 components, includes prerequisites for systems where you are installing server features. The ease of your installation is related to how well you plan and configure those prerequisites. There are a number of installation choices, which are driven by your planning activities. At a minimum, you must install the core components to deliver the base Service Manager functionality. Additionally functionalities such as reporting and self-service capabilities are provided by installing and configuring optional features on one or more servers.

A Service Manager installation consists of three core features and dependent subfeatures. The core features and additional subfeatures follow:

▶ **Service Manager management server:** This is the heart of the Service Manager installation, commonly known as the workflow management server. Its dependent subfeature is the Service Manager database, also known as the configuration management database (CMDB).

▶ **Service Manager data warehouse server:** This optional part of Service Manager is responsible for the delivery and management of reports. Its dependent subfeature is the Service Manager data warehouse database.

▶ **Self-service portal:** This is an optional component required for the self-service features of Service Manager. Its dependent subfeature is the SharePoint content and Web Server.

This chapter discusses installing a new Service Manager environment. It includes two types of configurations for a new installation—a five-server installation and three-server installation—and covers the upgrade process. These scenarios are introduced in Chapter 5. The installation uses Service Manager 2012 R2 in the odyssey.com environment. Service Manager 2012 R2 UR3 was released in July 2014; check for the most current update release.

A Service Manager installation must be performed in a specific order due to its chain of feature dependencies. The order of installation steps follows:

1. Create service account users and groups in Active Directory.

2. Install the supported operating system for all servers.

3. Install and configure prerequisites for all servers.

4. Install the supported SQL Server version on the database servers. Refer to Chapter 5 for details on SQL Server prerequisites.

5. Install and configure prerequisites by server function.

6. Install the Service Manager management server.

7. Install the data warehouse management server.

8. Install the self-service portal server.

9. Register the data warehouse management server with the Service Manager management server.

10. Apply the latest Service Manager service pack or update rollup if not slipstreamed with the media used during installation.

Pre-Installation Tasks

A successful Service Manager installation depends on the proper installation and configuration of all required prerequisites. Chapter 5 discusses those dependencies and requirements to be met prior to installation. The next sections discuss preparing for installation and installing and configuring prerequisites.

Preparing and Understanding Installation Prerequisites

The authors recommend creating an installation checklist similar to Table 6.1, based on your specific environment.

REAL WORLD: INCREMENTAL OPERATING SYSTEM AND MANAGEMENT AGENT REQUIREMENTS

Hardware requirements should consider additional requirements for the supported operating system and management agents. Minimum requirements are for the System Center Service Manager feature, which you must add to the operating system (OS) minimum requirements. Examples of management agents are antivirus and the System Center Configuration Manager agent.

TABLE 6.1   Service Manager Installation Checklist

Scenario Server	Feature Dependencies	Notes
Service Manager management server	Minimum hardware requirements scaled to your environment Supported operating system Minimum mandatory software requirements	Can be combined with the Service Manager database server in a three-server installation scenario. Typically used in development and proof of concept environments.
Service Manager database server	Minimum hardware requirements scaled to your environment Supported operating system Minimum mandatory software requirements Supported SQL Server version and minimum features	Can be combined with the Service Manager management server in a three-server installation scenario. Typically used in development and proof of concept environments. You could also use a dedicated remote shared SQL Server. The authors recommend using separate SQL instances for production deployments.
Service Manager data warehouse management server	Minimum hardware requirements scaled to your environment Supported operating system Minimum mandatory software requirements	Can be combined with the Service Manager data warehouse management server in a three-server installation scenario.
Service Manager data warehouse database server	Minimum hardware requirements scaled to your environment Supported operating system Minimum mandatory software requirements Supported SQL Server Version and minimum features	Can be combined with the Service Manager data warehouse management server in a three-server installation scenario. You could also use a dedicated remote shared SQL Server. The authors recommend using separate SQL instances for production deployments.

6

Scenario Server	Feature Dependencies	Notes
Service Manager self-service portal	Minimum hardware requirements scaled to your environment Supported operating system Minimum mandatory software requirements Supported SharePoint Server version	Can be SharePoint Foundation 2010 with the database for SharePoint installed locally as illustrated in Figure 6.1.

This chapter steps through an installation of Service Manager using two specific scenarios:

▶ A new System Center 2012 Service Manager environment based on the five-server design

▶ Performing the upgrade in an existing Service Manager 2010 three-server environment

The servers in the Odyssey.com domain used in this book with Service Manager are listed in Table 6.2, and the topology for the new and upgraded environments is displayed in Figure 6.1 and Figure 6.2, respectively.

TABLE 6.2   Odyssey Service Manager Installation Server Roles

Server Name	Service Manager Feature
Blizzard	Service Manager 2012 management server
Cyclone	Service Manager 2012 database server
Cumulus	Service Manager 2012 data warehouse management server
Monsoon	Service Manager 2012 data warehouse database server
Tsunami	Service Manager 2012 self-service portal
Whiteout	Service Manager 2010 management server and database
Tobor	Service Manager 2010 data warehouse management server and databases
Hurricane	Service Manager 2010 self-service portal

REAL WORLD: USING PHYSICAL OR VIRTUAL SERVERS

Microsoft's System Center 2012 Service Manager documentation describes three types of deployments using a mixture of physical and virtual servers, with several of the physical servers in the documentation designated as *virtualization hosts*. The authors achieve the same objective using the actual number of required Service Manager servers (physical or virtual). The official documentation maps to the three- and five-server scenarios discussed in this chapter and Chapter 5. The installation procedures in this chapter support using physical or virtual servers for the Service Manager functionality.

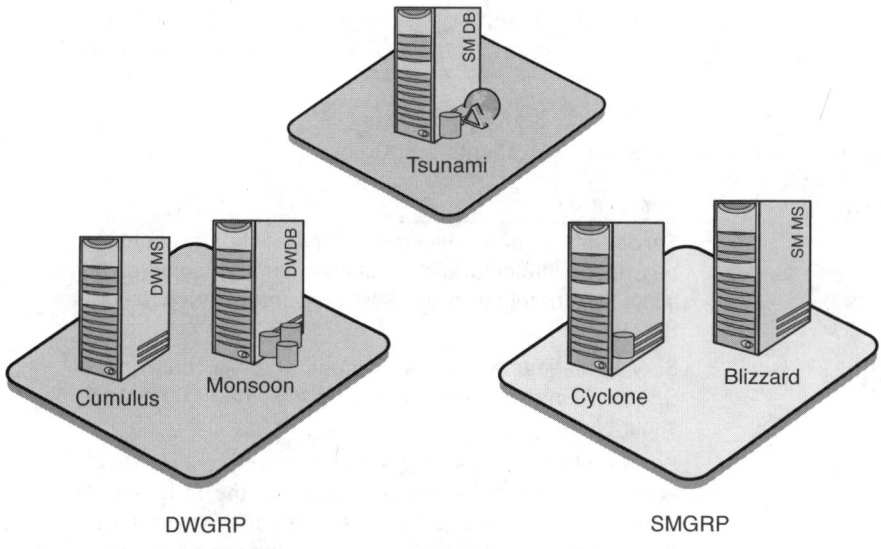

FIGURE 6.1   Service Manager 2012 Odyssey five-server topology.

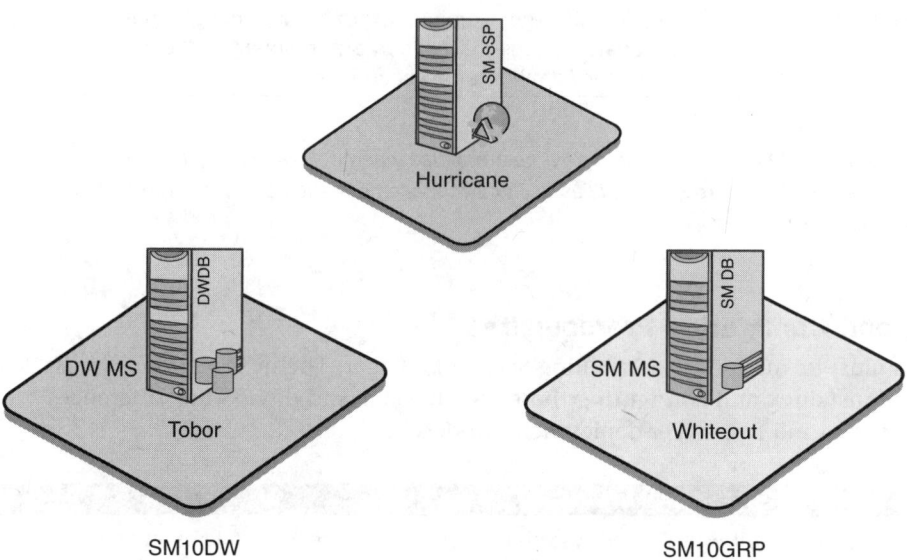

FIGURE 6.2   Service Manager 2010 Odyssey three-server topology.

You should also identify the specific Active Directory accounts and groups used during the installation and requested by the setup program. Table 6.3 lists the accounts used in the Odyssey environment.

TABLE 6.3   Service Manager Active Directory Accounts and Groups

Account or Group	Description
SM_MSAA	Service Manager management server action account. Must be a local administrator on all management servers. This account is mapped to the System Center Data Access Service.
SM_WFA	Service Manager workflow account. This account runs all Service Manager workflows and is assigned to the Workflow security role.
SM_RPT	Service Manager reporting services user account. This account is designated for connecting to the SQL Reporting Server instance as a proxy to read reports. You must specify the user account details when installing the data warehouse.
SM_AdminService_accounts*	Service Manager service accounts requiring local administrator rights on Service Manager servers. Using a group removes the need to add individual accounts to each Service Manager management server.
SCSM12 Full Admins	Service Manager Administrators group. This group is requested during installation and mapped to the Service Manager Administrators security role.

*This group is optional but recommended as a best practice when delegating accounts to a local administrators group. Using groups simplifies account management should you need to add or remove user accounts.

Installing and Configuring Prerequisites

Prerequisites must be met prior to installing Service Manager. The next sections discuss the process of installing and configuring these prerequisites and discuss the differences between the three- and five-server deployment models.

CAUTION: PREREQUISITES MAY CHANGE

Visit the official Microsoft website for System Center at http://technet.microsoft.com/en-us/library/hh519608.aspx to obtain the latest information prior to your installation.

SQL Server Requirements

The two management server components, the Service Manager management server and the Service Manager data warehouse management server, require a supported version of Microsoft SQL Server. The SQL Server installation can be co-located on the respective management server or a separate dedicated remote server. Following are the supported management server database requirements:

▶ **SQL Server version:** The following versions and editions are required and supported:

   ▶ SQL Server 2008 R2 SP 1/SP 2 Standard, Datacenter (64-bit)

   ▶ SQL Server 2012 Standard, Enterprise (64-bit)

   ▶ SQL Server 2012 SP 1 Standard, Enterprise (64-bit)

▶ **SQL Server requirements:** The required configuration for the supported editions and versions of SQL Server follows:

   ▶ **Database collation:** SQL_Latin1_General_100_CI_AS is required for multi-language support. This is not the default collation. The default limits Service Manager to English-only language support. If you plan to use Service Manager for multilanguage support you must use SQL_Latin1_General_100_CI_AS. You must use the same collation for the Service Manager and data warehouse database servers.

   ▶ **SQL Server features:** Database engine services, full text search, and management tools (optional).

   ▶ **Authentication method:** Windows authentication.

   ▶ **SQL Server instance:** The authors recommend a dedicated instance of SQL Server for the management server database.

   ▶ **SQL Server memory:** Chapter 5 discusses scaling based on the size and planned workload of your environment. In the three-server scenario where the management server and the database server are installed on the same server, you must include the minimum memory requirements for both features.

TIP: ACCOUNT TYPE FOR THE SQL SERVER SERVICE

You can configure the SQL Server service to use an Active Directory (AD) domain account or the Local System account. Microsoft's SQL Server product team recommends using a domain account as a security best practice. Using a domain account requires manually registering the Service Principle Name (SPN) for the account. Information on SPN registration is available at the http://technet.microsoft.com/en-us/library/hh427336.aspx. The SPN is automatically registered when using the Local System account.

Operating System Requirements

The Windows operating system requirements for Service Manager 2012 follow:

- **Operating system version:** One of these supported operating systems:

    - Windows Server 2008 R2 SP 1 (Standard, Enterprise, or Datacenter editions)

    - Windows Server 2012 (Standard or Datacenter editions)

- **Minimum hardware requirements:** Minimum hardware requirements are in addition to the supported hardware requirements for the operating system. Chapter 5 provides guidance on these requirements.

- **Operating system features:** .NET Framework 3.5 SP 1 or above.

Account Delegation

Add those user accounts and groups that require local administrator privileges to the servers you are using for your Service Manager deployment. Figure 6.3 shows the group membership for Odyssey, where there are two groups used to delegate local administrator rights to the Service Manager administrators and the Service Manager service accounts requiring local rights (management server action account and workflow account).

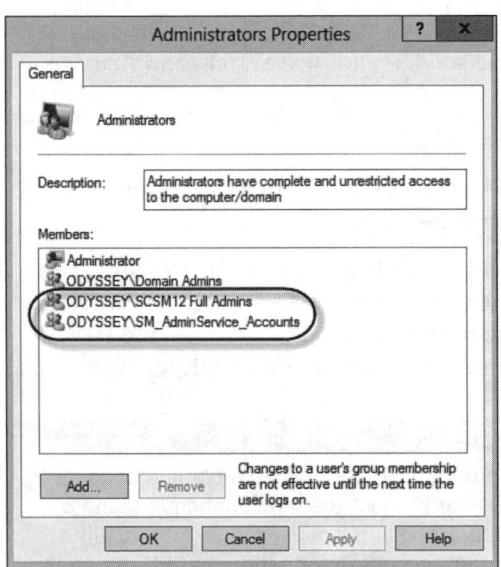

FIGURE 6.3   Service Manager Active Directory groups added to local Administrators group.

Management Server Prerequisites

Specific management server prerequisites follow:

▶ **ADO.NET Data Services Update for .NET Framework 3.5 SP 1 for Windows Server 2008 R2:** Download from the Microsoft official site. The link to the download is provided on the installation media.

▶ **SQL Server 2008 R2 Native Client or SQL Server 2012 Native Client:** Download from the Microsoft official site. The link to the download is provided on the installation media.

▶ **Microsoft Report Viewer Redistributable:** This is available on the Service Manager installation media.

You must install these additional prerequisites before beginning installation.

Five-Server Scenario Installation

The section discusses installing System Center 2012 R2 Service Manager features for the five-server deployment scenario. This includes installing the Service Manager management server, the data warehouse management server, and the web portal server. The databases are installed on separate servers from the management servers.

Installing the Service Manager Management Server

The Service Manager management server is the core mandatory feature and must be installed first with its corresponding database server feature. The following is a checklist of activities to perform before starting the installation:

1. Install a supported operating system.

2. The server must belong to the same Active Directory domain as the other Service Manager management servers and Service Manager features.

3. Install and configure the prerequisites for the Service Manager management server including a supported SQL Server installation (local or remote). In the five-server scenario, the SQL Server installation is remote.

TIP: TAKE SNAPSHOTS IN VIRTUALIZED ENVIRONMENTS

Resolving issues during installation can be challenging. This could be due to an unintended mistake such as selecting the wrong database collation. If using a virtual server, you can take milestone snapshots during your installation. Plan to take snapshots at different stages of your installation to provide for incremental rollbacks. Be sure to take the same point in time snapshots for the database servers used by the management servers.

After installing the prerequisites, install the management server. Follow these steps:

1. Log on to the server (Blizzard in this example) using a domain user account with local administration privileges and administrative rights to the SQL Server.

2. Start the installation from the System Center 2012 R2 Service Manager media splash screen. Under Install, select **Service Manager management server** (see Figure 6.4).

> **CAUTION: PRODUCT REGISTRATION DOES NOT ALLOW CONVERSION FROM EVALUATION TO PRODUCTION EDITION WITHOUT MICROSOFT SUPPORT**
>
> The product registration page asks for a valid registration key or to select the 180-day evaluation option. If you select to evaluate Service Manager, you can rerun the installation to enter a product key; however, you cannot use the existing database without contacting Microsoft for a workaround. This is the equivalent of a reinstallation, as all configuration data is lost from the evaluation edition.

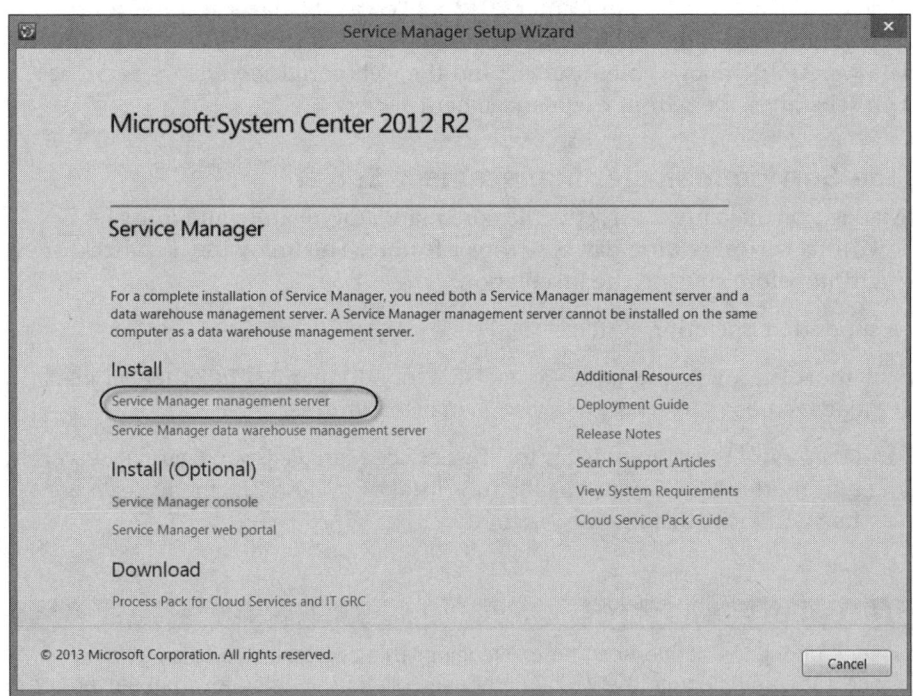

FIGURE 6.4   Start Service Manager management server installation.

3. The significant pages of the wizard to configure for installing a Service Manager management server follow:

▶ **Getting Started:** Accept or provide an alternative installation location. Figure 6.5 shows a selection using the defaults.

▶ **Configure the Service Manager database:** Type the server name (remote or local) and then select the instance and database name for the server hosting the CMDB database; this is ServiceManager by default. Provide an initial size and accept or modify the location of the data and log file folders. Figure 6.6 shows the remote server Cyclone (the remote server running SQL Server 2012 in the Odyssey lab).

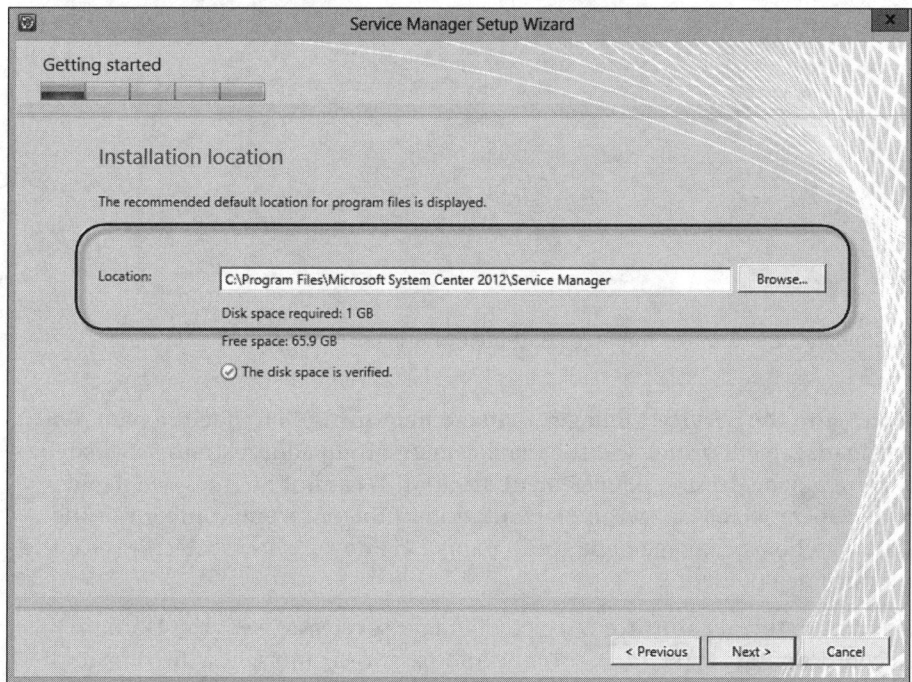

FIGURE 6.5   Default installation location.

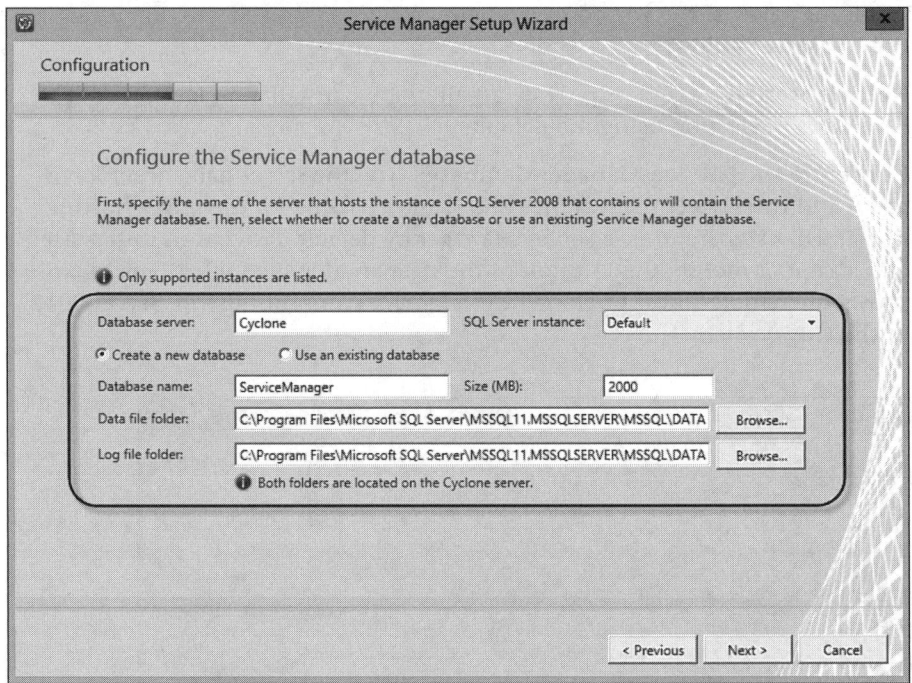

FIGURE 6.6   Configure the Service Manager database settings.

▶ **Configure the Service Manager management group:** Provide the names of the management group and the management group administrators. Specify a unique name for the management group (this cannot be the same name as an Operations Manager implementation in the same environment or the data warehouse management group name). Figure 6.7 shows selections for the Odyssey deployment.

▶ **Configure the account for Service Manager services:** Select the **Domain account** option. Type the user name and password, and select the domain from the drop-down, as shown in Figure 6.8.

▶ **Configure the Service Manager workflow account:** Select **Domain account**. Type the user name and password, and select the domain from the drop-down (see Figure 6.9).

▶ **Additional Settings configuration:** Select whether to **Help improve System Center Service Manager** and **Use Microsoft Updates to help keep your computer secure and up-to-date**.

▶ **Installation summary:** A summary page with your installation setting is displayed prior to installation. You can go back and change your selections and details.

▶ **Setup completed successfully:** This final page is shown with a successful installation. Figure 6.10 displays this page with two post-installation options: **Open the Encryption Backup or Restore Wizard after Setup closes** and **Open the Service Manager console when Setup closes**. The authors recommend selecting the first option to back up the encryption key for the management group.

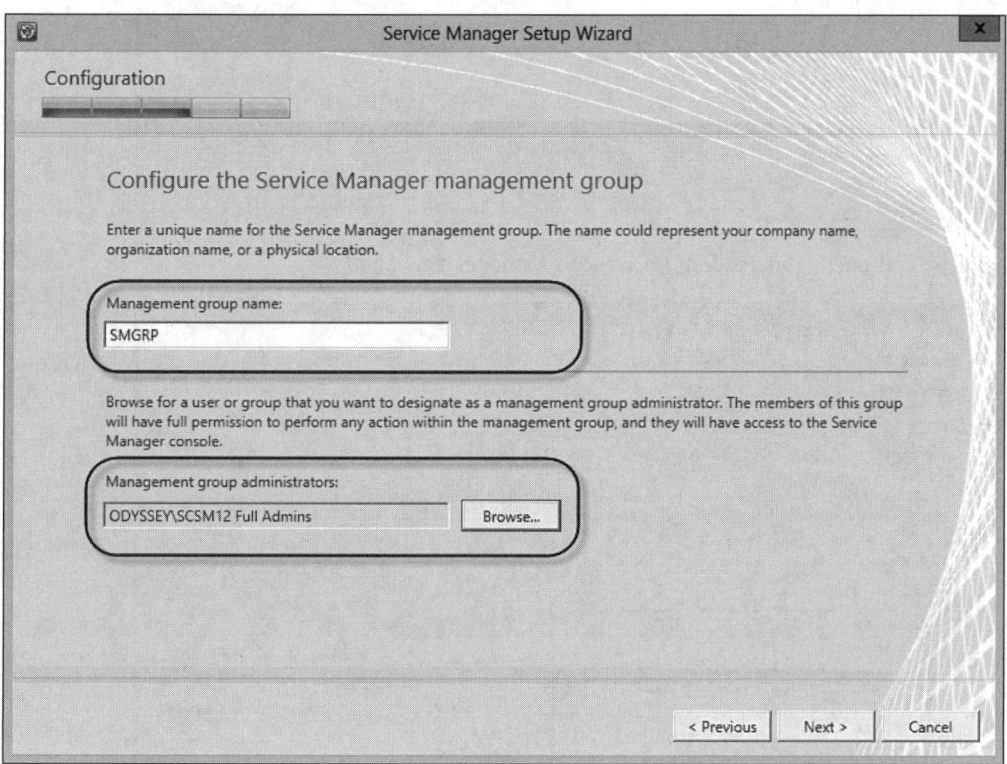

FIGURE 6.7   Specify the Service Manager management group name and administrators.

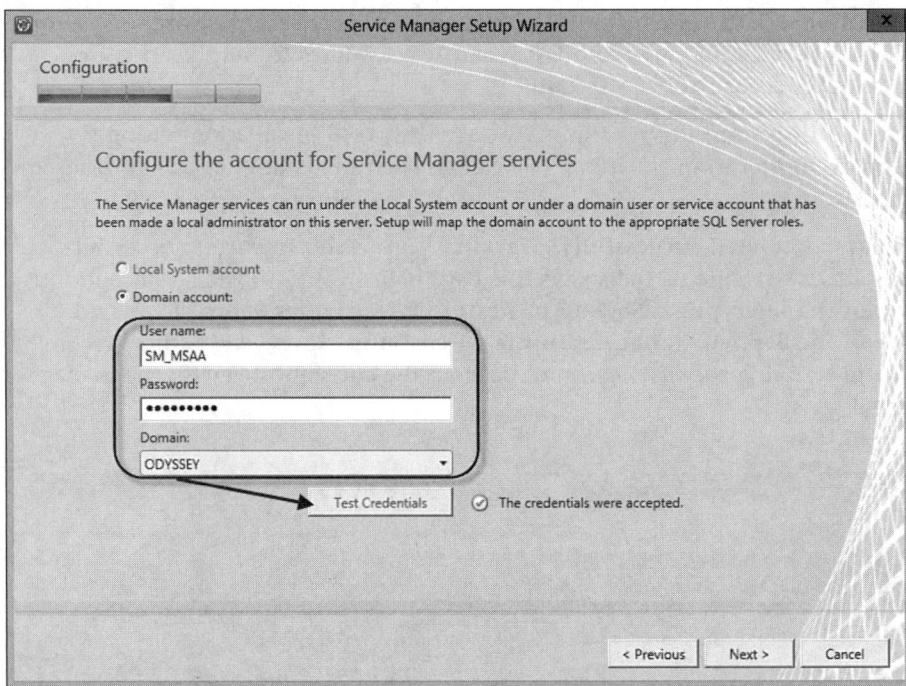

FIGURE 6.8   Specify the account for Service Manager services.

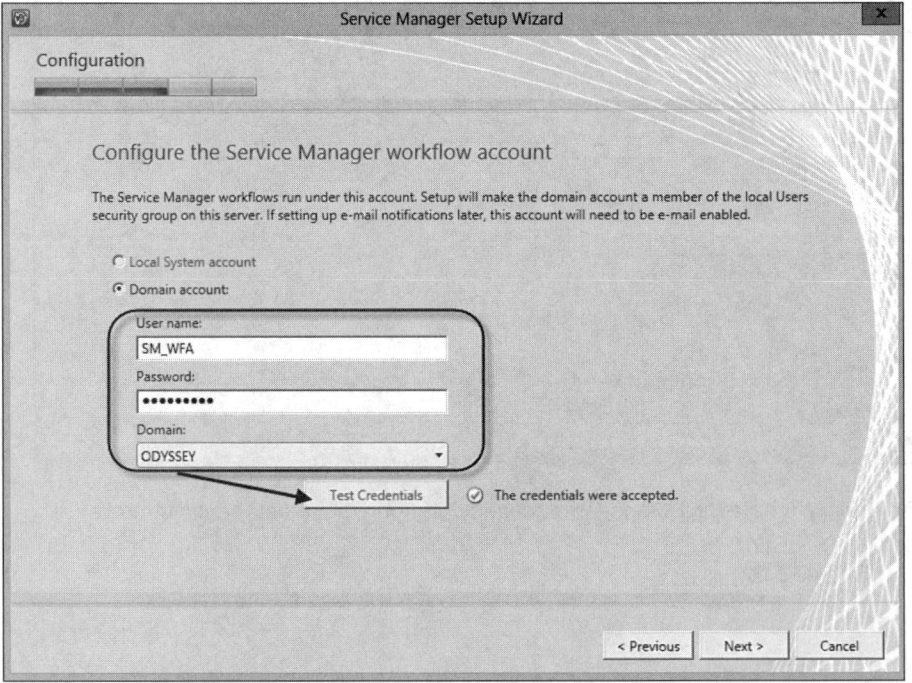

FIGURE 6.9   Specify the Service Manager workflow account.

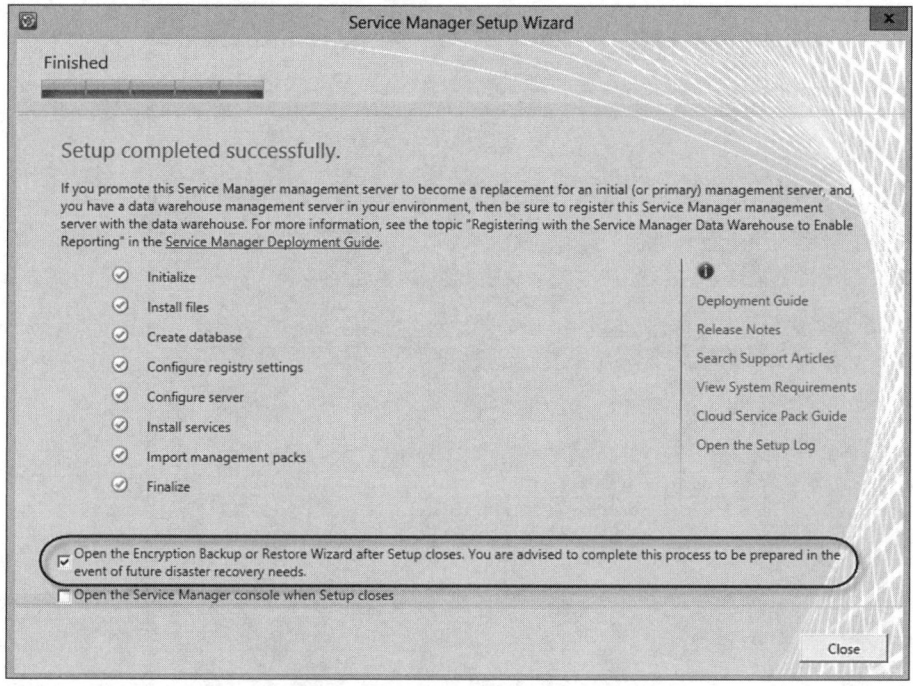

FIGURE 6.10   Service Manager installation complete.

4. Selecting the recommended option to back up the encryption key starts the Encryption Key Backup or Restore Wizard.

Select backup and provide a location for the key file. Although this location can be a local drive (shown in Figure 6.11), you should copy the file to a secure location as part of your recommended disaster recovery process for Service Manager. You must also provide a password for the encryption key file.

NOTE: BACK UP THE ENCRYPTION KEY NOW

The authors recommend you back up the encryption key and store the resulting file in a secure location. The key is required to recover the management servers. Information on recovering a Service' Manager installation is in Chapter 18, "Maintenance, Backup, and Recovery."

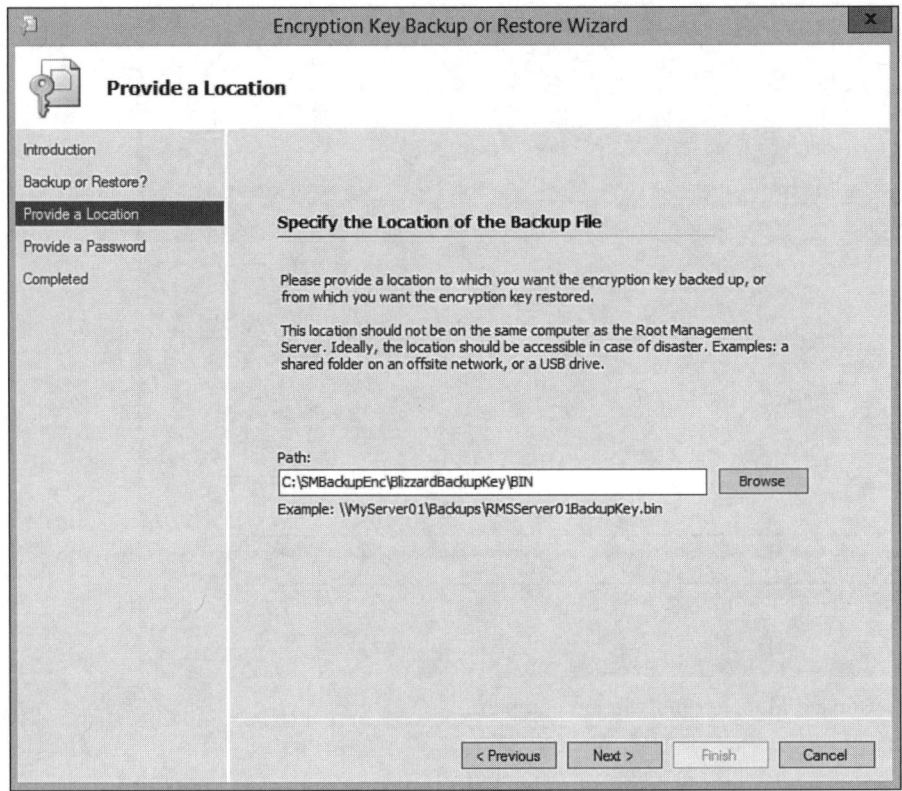

FIGURE 6.11   Specify the encryption key file details.

Installing the Service Manager Data Warehouse Management Server

The Service Manager data warehouse management server is optional but must be installed if you are using reports, in which case you must install this feature with its corresponding databases. A checklist of activities you must perform prior to installation follows:

1. Install a supported operating system.

2. The server must belong to an Active Directory domain.

3. Install and configure the prerequisites for the Service Manager data warehouse management server (see the "Management Server Prerequisites" section earlier in the chapter), including the mandatory supported SQL Server installation (local or remote). In the five-server scenario, the SQL Server installation is remote.

4. Install the SQL Server Native Client. Download the respective version of the native client using the link provided on the installation media.

When using a remote SQL Server Reporting Services (SSRS) server for the data warehouse, you must modify that remote server for the SQL reports to work properly within Service Manager. If running SSRS on the data warehouse server (not recommended by the authors), no modifications are required. To prepare a remote SSRS server, follow these steps:

1. Copy Microsoft.EnterpriseManagement.Reporting.Code.dll to the SSRS server. This file is located in the \Prerequisites folder on the Service Manager installation media. Copy the file to the \Bin folder on the SSRS server; it is in one of the following paths:

   ▶ **Default instance of SQL Server:**

   SQL Server 2008 Service Pack 1: *%ProgramFiles%*\Microsoft SQL Server\ MSRS10.MSSQLSERVER\Reporting Services\ReportServer\bin

   SQL Server 2008 R2: *%ProgramFiles%*\Microsoft SQL Server\MSRS10_50. MSSQLSERVER\Reporting Services\ReportServer\bin

   SQL Server 2012: *%ProgramFiles%*\Microsoft SQL Server\MSRS11. MSSQLSERVER\Reporting Services\ReportServer\bin

   ▶ **Non-default instance of SQL Server (named instance):** *%ProgramFiles%*\ Microsoft SQL Server\MSRS<*SQL Version Number*>.<*Instance*>\Reporting Services\ReportServer\bin

2. Update rssrvpolicy.config. To do this, go to the SSRS server and locate the file in one of the following paths:

   ▶ **Default instance of SQL Server**

   SQL Server 2008 Service Pack 1: *%ProgramFiles%*\Microsoft SQL Server\ MSRS10.MSSQLSERVER\Reporting Services\ReportServer\

   SQL Server 2008 R2: *%ProgramFiles%*\Microsoft SQL Server\MSRS10_50. MSSQLSERVER\Reporting Services\ReportServer\

   SQL Server 2012: *%ProgramFiles%*\Microsoft SQL Server\MSRS11. MSSQLSERVER\Reporting Services\ReportServer\

   ▶ **Non-default instance of SQL Server (named instance):** *%ProgramFiles%*\ Microsoft SQL Server\MSRS<*SQL Version Number* >.<*Instance*>\Reporting Services\ReportServer\

Open the rssrvpolicy.config file. You can use Notepad or an eXtended Markup Language (XML) editor such as Notepad ++, which can be downloaded from http:// notepad-plus-plus.org. Locate or search for <CodeGroup>. Add the code in bold to the existing <CodeGroup> segment.

```
<CodeGroup
    class="UnionCodeGroup"    version="1"
    PermissionSetName="FullTrust"
    Name="Microsoft System Center Service Manager Reporting Code Assembly"
    Description="Grants the SCSM Reporting Code assembly full trust
    permission.">
    <IMembershipCondition
        class="StrongNameMembershipCondition"
        version="1"
PublicKeyBlob="0024000004800000940000000602000000240000525341310004000001
000100B5FC90E7027F67871E773A8FDE8938C81DD402BA65B9201D60593E96C492651E889
CC13F1415EBB53FAC1131AE0BD333C5EE6021672D9718EA31A8AEBD0DA0072F25D87DBA6FC
90FFD598ED4DA35E44C398C454307E8E33B8426143DAEC9F596836F97C8F74750E5975C64E
2189F45DEF46B2A2B1247ADC3652BF5C308055DA9"
/>
</CodeGroup>
```

3. Save the rssrvpolicy.config file.

4. Update the rsreportserver.conf file, located in one of the following paths:

   ▶ **Default instance of SQL Server**

      SQL Server 2008 Service Pack 1: *%ProgramFiles%*\Microsoft SQL Server\
      MSRS10.MSSQLSERVER\Reporting Services\ReportServer\

      SQL Server 2008 R2: *%ProgramFiles%*\Microsoft SQL Server\MSRS10_50.
      MSSQLSERVER\Reporting Services\ReportServer\

      SQL Server 2012: *%ProgramFiles%*\Microsoft SQL Server\MSRS11.
      MSSQLSERVER\Reporting Services\ReportServer\

   ▶ **Non-default instance of SQL Server (named instance):** *%ProgramFiles%*\
      Microsoft SQL Server\MSRS<*SQL Version Number* >.<*Instance*>\Reporting
      Services\ReportServer\

   Open the rsreportserver.conf file, using Notepad or an XML editor such as Notepad
   ++. Locate or search for <Data>. Add the following extension tag after the other
   extension tags in the <Data> segment.

```
<Extension Name="SCDWMultiMartDataProcessor"
Type="Microsoft.EnterpriseManagement.Reporting.MultiMartConnection, Microsoft.
EnterpriseManagement.Reporting.Code" />
```

5. Save the rsreportserver.conf file.

With the prerequisites installed, it is time to install the data warehouse management server. Perform the following steps:

1. Log on to the server (Cumulus in this example) using a domain user account with local administrator privileges and administrative rights to the SQL Server database.

2. Start the installation from the System Center 2012 Service Manager splash screen. Under Install, select **Service Manager data warehouse management server** (see Figure 6.12).

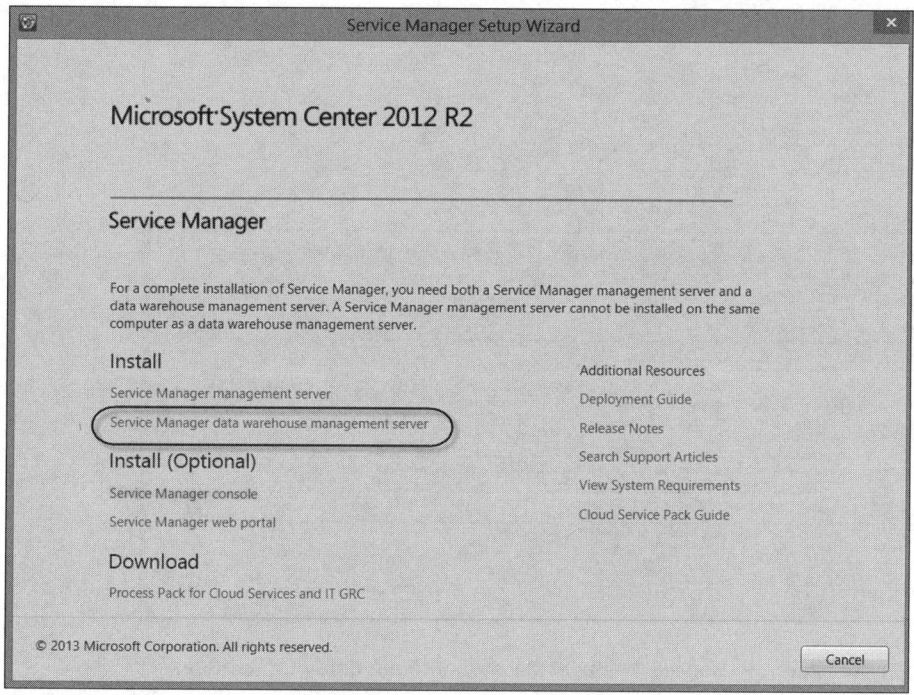

FIGURE 6.12   Start Service Manager data warehouse management server installation.

3. Following are the significant wizard pages when installing a Service Manager data warehouse management server:

▶ **Getting Started:** Accept or provide an alternative installation location.

▶ **Configure the data warehouse databases:** Provide the server name and select the instance and database name for the server hosting the data warehouse databases. There are three databases to specify. Provide an initial size and accept or modify the data and log file folder locations for each. Figure 6.13 shows the remote server Monsoon (the remote SQL Server in the Odyssey lab).

▶ **Configure the additional data warehouse datamarts:** These additional databases are optional and can only be selected during initial installation. Provide the server name; select an instance and database name for the server hosting the data warehouse databases. There are two databases to configure. Provide an initial size and accept or modify the data and log file folder locations (see Figure 6.14).

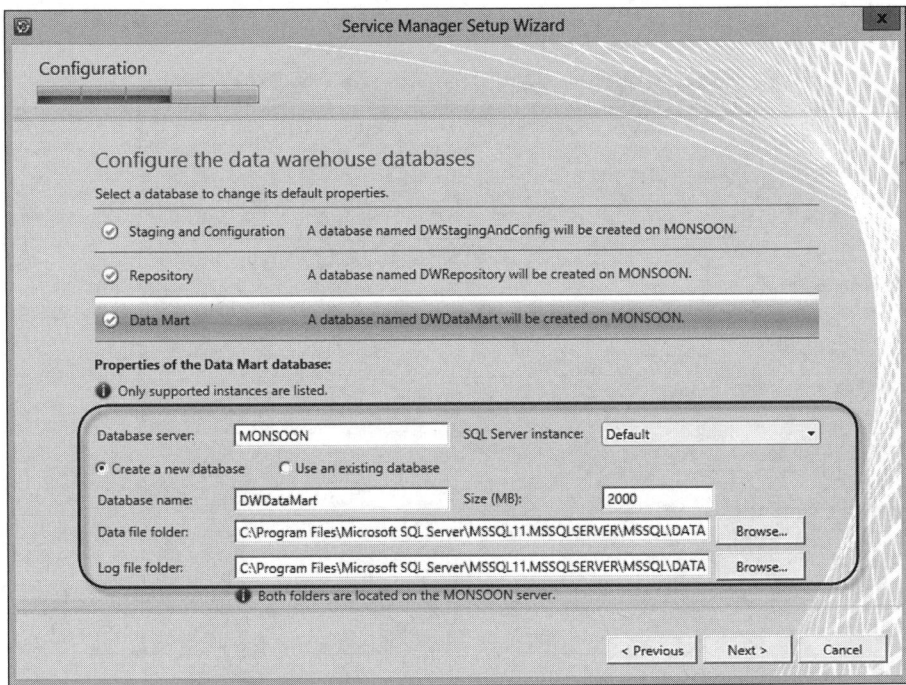

FIGURE 6.13   Configure the Service Manager data warehouse default databases.

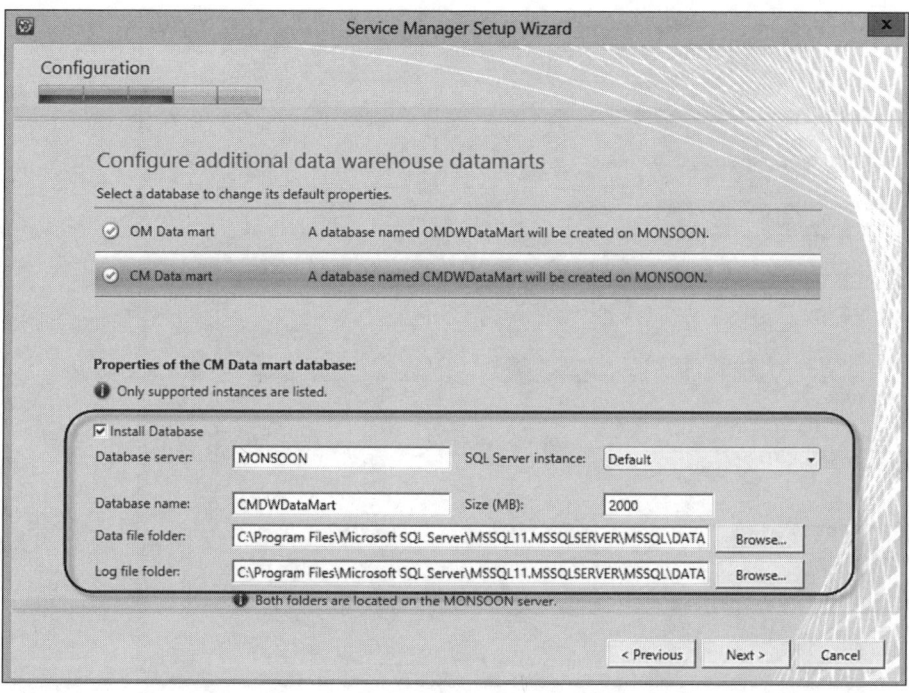

FIGURE 6.14   Configure the Service Manager data warehouse additional databases.

CAUTION: DISK SPACE FOR ADDITIONAL DATABASES

The two optional databases, OMDatamart and CMDatamart, have an undocumented space requirement. The installation automatically creates database files with a combined size of approximately 24GB. You must plan for this space requirement even if you select the 2000MB (2GB) default size in the wizard.

▶ **Configure the data warehouse management group:** There are two mandatory configuration settings, **Management group name** and **Management group administrators**. Specify a unique name for the management group (this cannot be the same name as your Operations Manager implementation or the Service Manager management server group name). Figure 6.15 shows the selections for Odyssey.

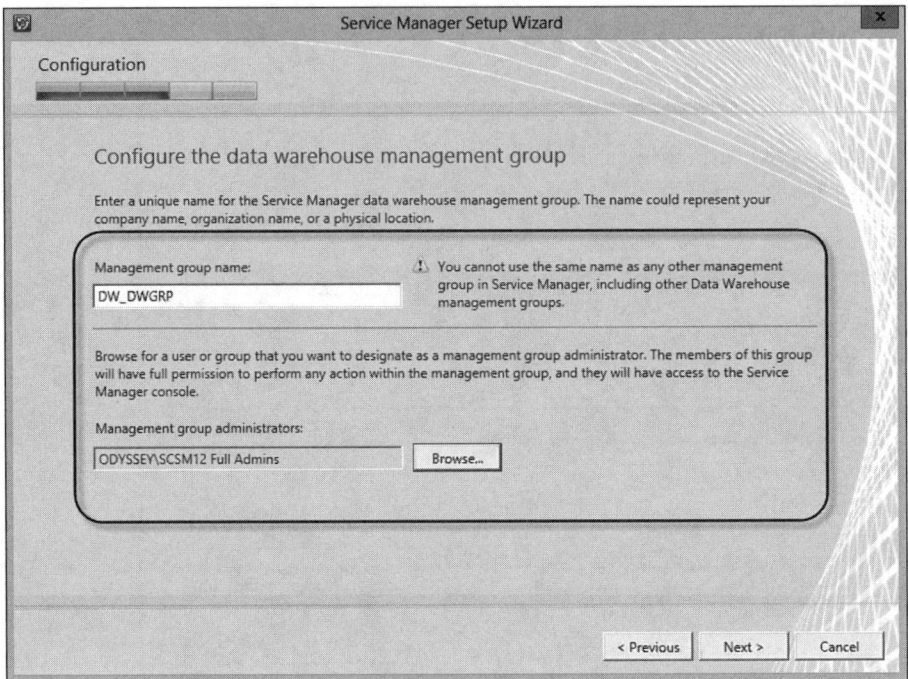

FIGURE 6.15   Specify the data warehouse management group name and administrators.

▶ **Configure the account for Service Manager services:** Select the domain account option. Type the user name and password and select the domain from the drop-down. The account specified here is the management server action account listed in Table 6.3.

▶ **Configure the reporting server for the data warehouse:** Provide the server name, instance, and database name for the server hosting SSRS for the data warehouse. Setup verifies the default web service URL. When using a remote SQL Server, you must perform the manual deployment steps listed in the deployment guide; check the box that these are complete before proceeding to the next step in the wizard. Figure 6.16 shows the Odyssey SSRS selection.

▶ **Configure the reporting account:** Type the user name and password, and select the domain for the reporting user account from the drop-down (see Figure 6.17).

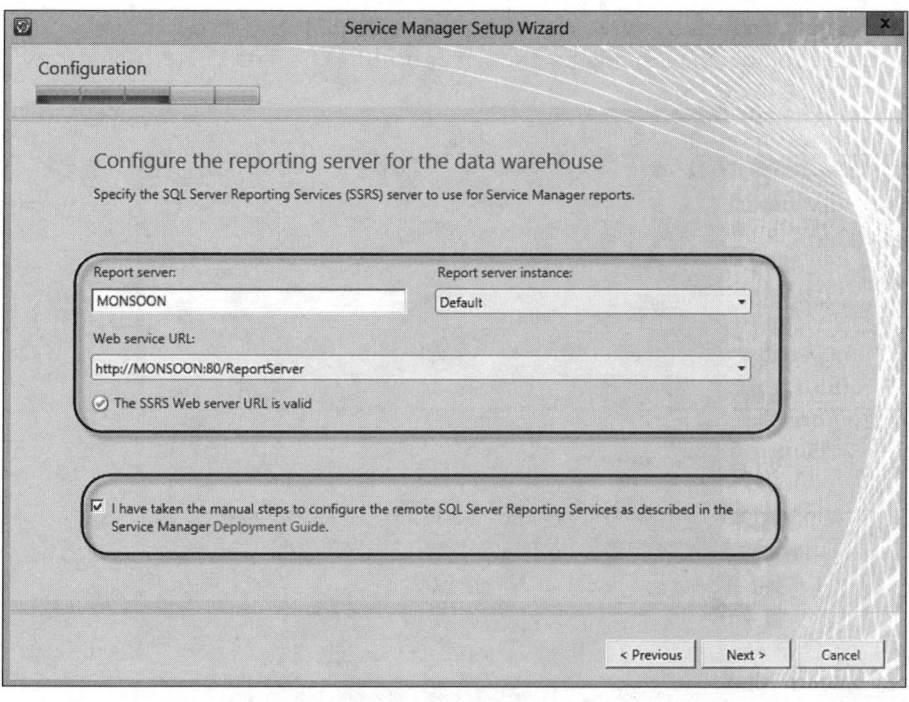

FIGURE 6.16   Reporting Services selection for the data warehouse.

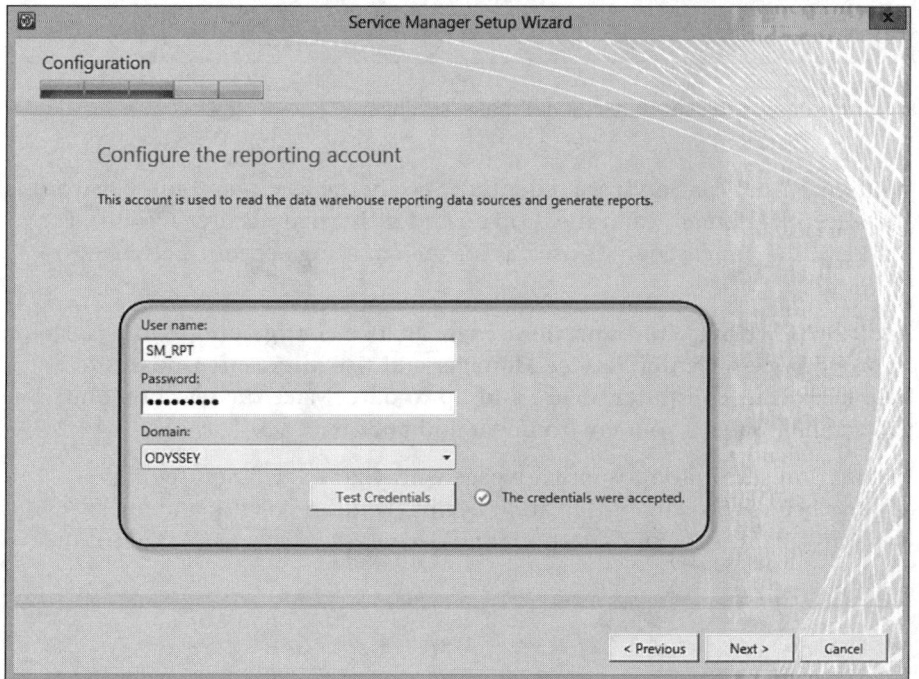

FIGURE 6.17   Specifying the account for reporting.

▶ **Configure Analysis Services for OLAP cubes:** Provide the server name, instance, and database name for the server hosting the data OLAP cube database (see Figure 6.18).

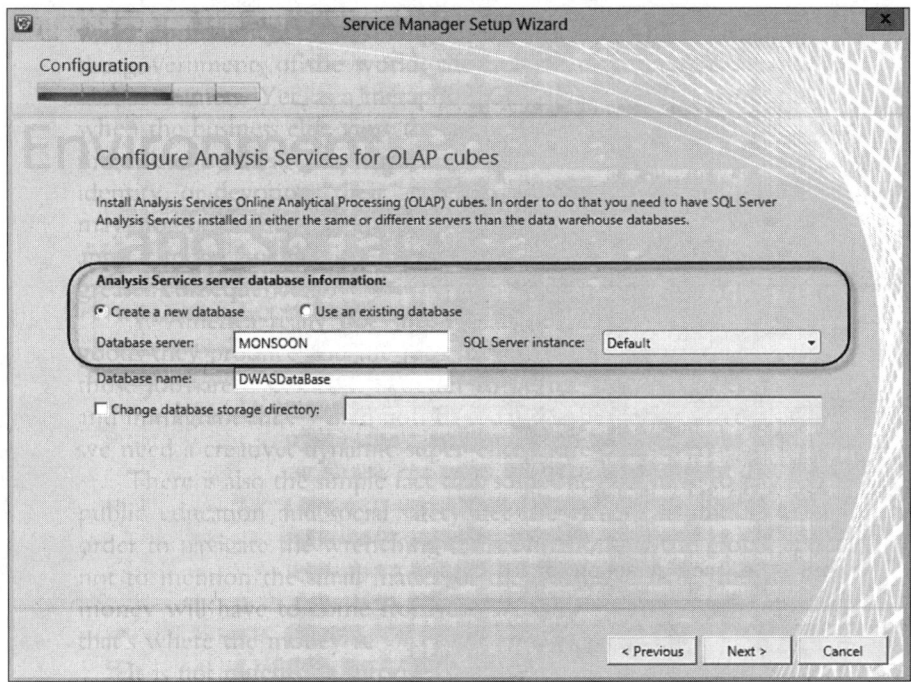

FIGURE 6.18   Configuring Analysis Services database settings.

▶ **Configure Analysis Services credential:** Specify the user name and password, and select the domain from the drop-down for the analysis user account. For Odyssey, the same account is used as for the reporting account (see Figure 6.19).

▶ **Additional Settings configuration:** There are two configuration settings; **Help improve System Center Service Manager** and **Use Microsoft Updates to help keep your computer secure and up-to-date**. Make the selection on these pages appropriate to your environment and policies.

▶ **Installation summary:** A summary page with your installation settings displays before the actual installation begins. You can go back and make any necessary changes to your selections and details.

▶ **Setup completed successfully:** This final page of the wizard is shown when installation is successful. It includes the **Open the Encryption Backup or Restore Wizard after Setup closes** option. The authors recommend backing up the encryption key for the management group.

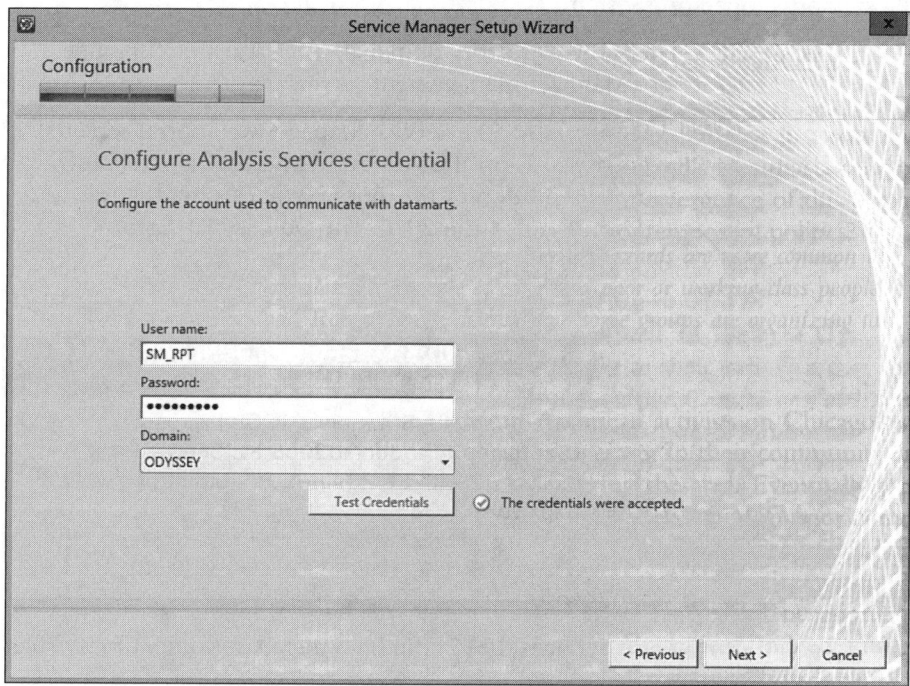

FIGURE 6.19   Providing Analysis Services service account credentials.

4. Selecting to back up the encryption key starts the Encryption Key Backup and Restore Wizard. Select the backup option and provide a location and password for the key file. If the key file is saved to a local drive, copy it to a secure location as part of your disaster recovery process for Service Manager.

Installing the Service Manager Web Portal

The Service Manager web portal is an optional component, and is installed if you require a self-service experience for your IT service management deliverables. The activities to perform prior to installation follow:

1. Install a supported operating system.

2. The server must belong to an Active Directory domain, which must be the same domain as the portal's Service Manager management server.

3. Install and configure the prerequisites for the Service Manager web portal server(s). The required number of servers depends on the version of Microsoft SharePoint being used. In the simplest implementation of this portal, you can use the free version of the product, SharePoint Foundation 2010. The Odyssey lab uses SharePoint Foundation 2010 on a single server.

> **CAUTION: SERVICE MANAGER 2012 SP 1/R2 AND SHAREPOINT FOUNDATON 2010 INSTALLATIONS**
>
> The SharePoint 2010 Foundation setup wizard installs SQL Server 2008 Express; however, Service Manager 2012 SP 1/R2 requires SQL Server 2008 R2 Service Pack (SP) 2. Download and install SQL Server 2008 R2 with SP 2, available from http://www. microsoft.com/en-us/download/details.aspx?id=30438.

The web portal server prerequisites follow:

▶ Microsoft Internet Information Services (IIS) 7; the IIS 6 metabase compatibility role service must be selected.

▶ SSL certificate for IIS (optional); a valid certificate must be installed for secure access to the portal.

▶ SQL Server 2012 Analysis Management Objects (AMO).

To install the web portal server, follow these steps:

1. Log on to the server (Tsunami in this example) using a domain user account with local administrator privileges.

2. Start the installation from the System Center 2012 Service Manager splash screen. Under Install, select **Service Manager web portal** (see Figure 6.20).

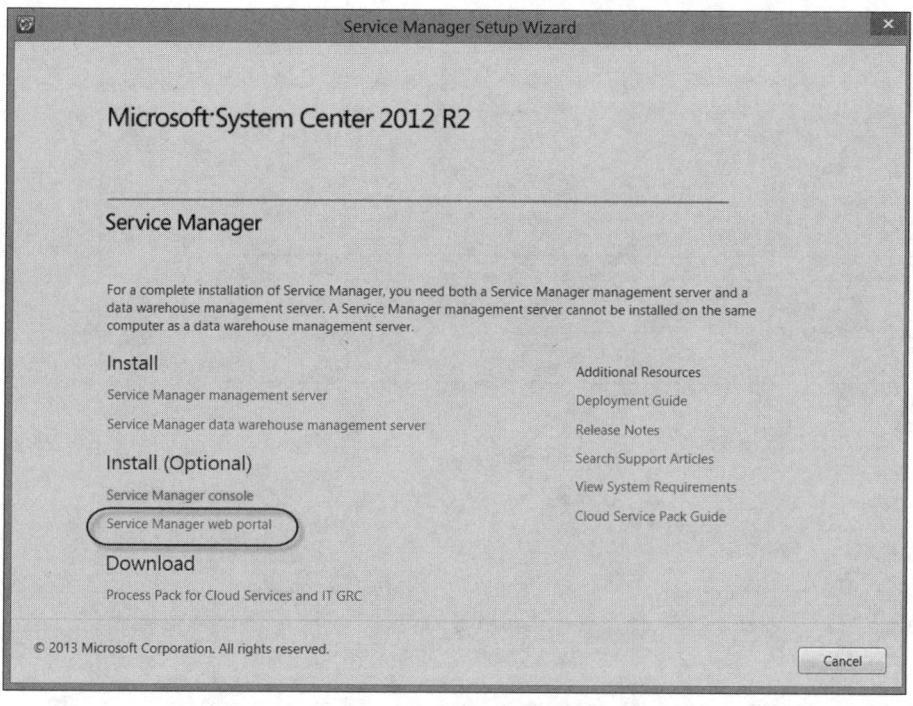

FIGURE 6.20   Initiating the Service Manager web portal installation.

3. The significant wizard pages for installing a Service Manager web portal server
   follow:

   ▶ **Getting Started:** Check **Web Content Server** and **SharePoint Web Parts**. This
      is the case when installing both portal parts on the same server. Microsoft
      supports separating the two parts, but this is dependent on your SharePoint
      installation type and Service Manager design. Figure 6.21 displays the selection
      for an installation where both parts are on the same server.

   ▶ **Installation:** Accept the default (see Figure 6.22) or provide an alternative
      installation location.

   ▶ **Configure the Service Manager Self-Service Portal name and port:** Provide
      the web content server website name and specify a port for the website; the
      default has SSL checked with port 444. Uncheck this option and specify a port
      if you have not provisioned a certificate for the server (see Figure 6.23).

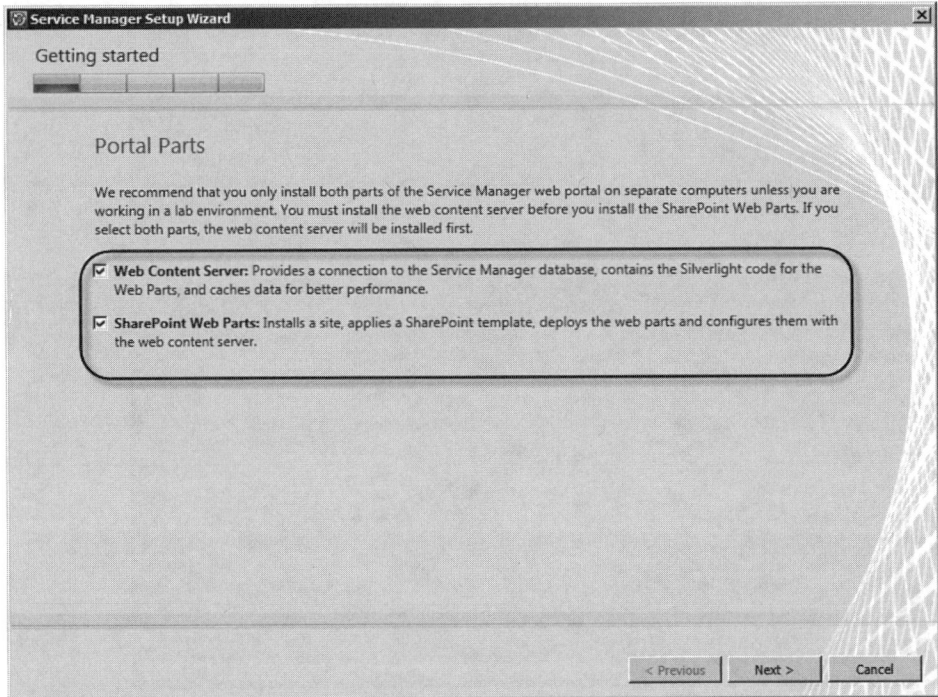

FIGURE 6.21   Portal parts selection.

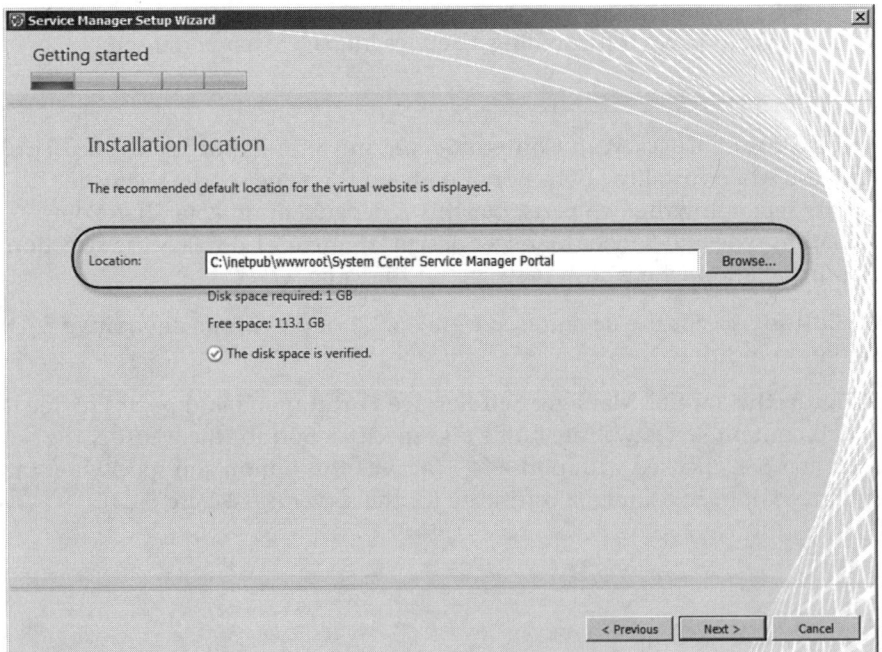

FIGURE 6.22   Self-service portal default installation folder.

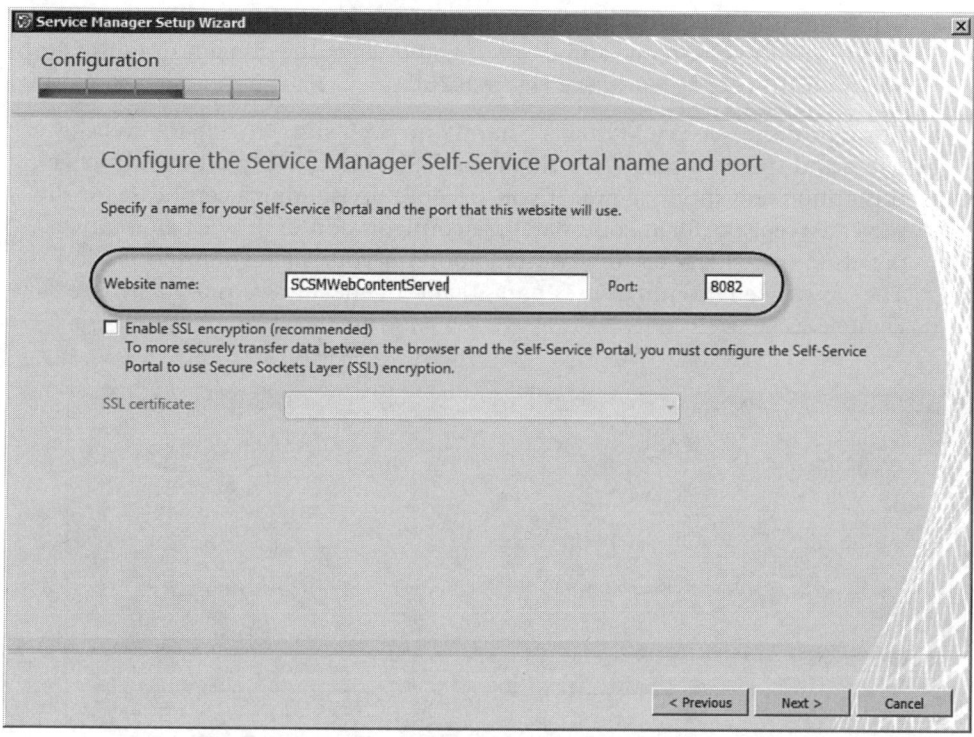

FIGURE 6.23   Web content server configuration.

▶ **Select the Service Manager database:** Specify the server name, and select the instance and database name for the server hosting the Service Manager databases (see Figure 6.24).

▶ **Configure the account for the Self-Service Portal:** Type the user name and password, and select the domain from the drop-down for the user account (see Figure 6.25). This is the account specified for the Service Manager management server (SM_MSAA).

▶ **Configure the account for the Service Manager SharePoint application pool:** Type the user name and password, and select the domain from the drop-down for the user account (see Figure 6.26).

▶ **Configure the Service Manager SharePoint web site:** Provide the website name and specify a port; the default uses SSL option with port 443. Uncheck this option and specify a port if you are not provisioning a certificate for the server. Accept the SharePoint database configuration or provide alternative details to match any custom configuration for your SharePoint installation. The Odyssey environment uses port 80 and the default website name (see Figure 6.27).

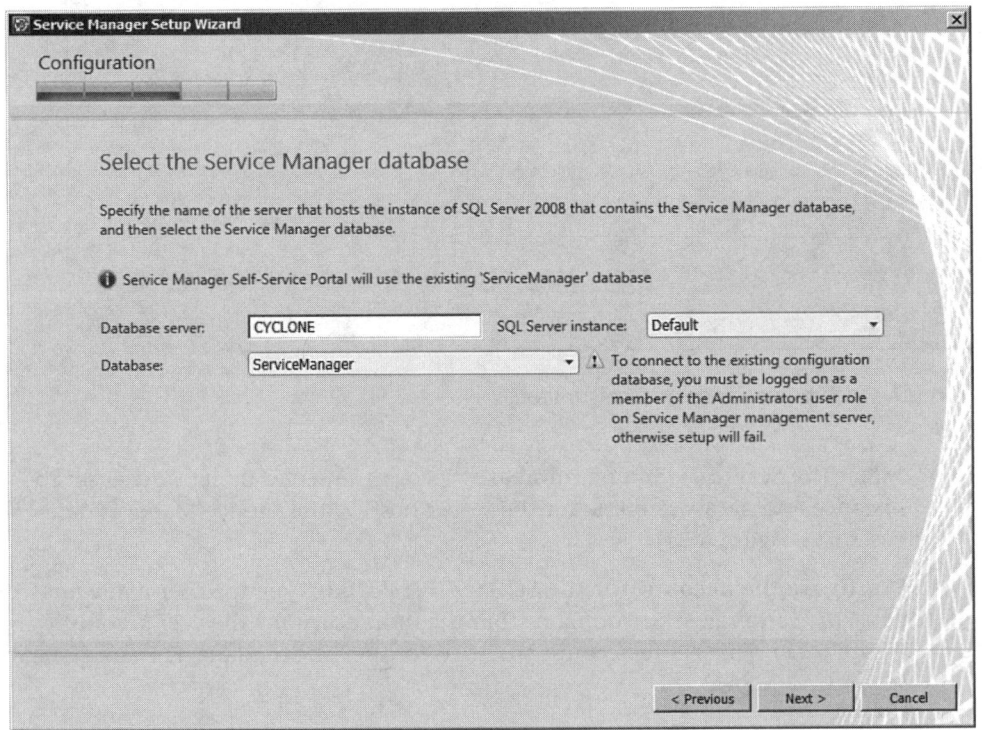

FIGURE 6.24   Server Manager database selection.

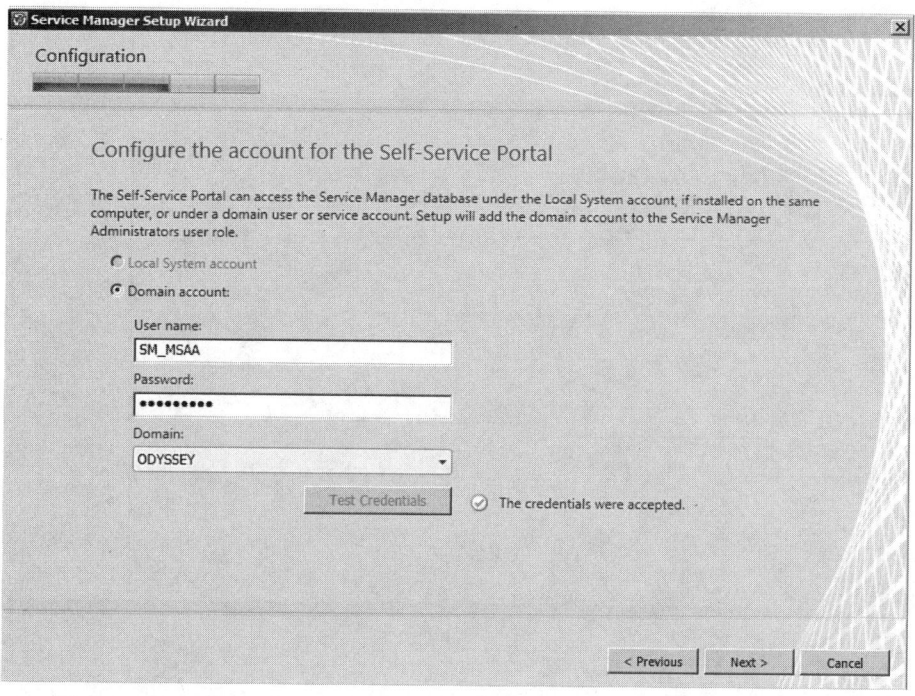

FIGURE 6.25   Configuring the self-service portal account for Service Manager database access.

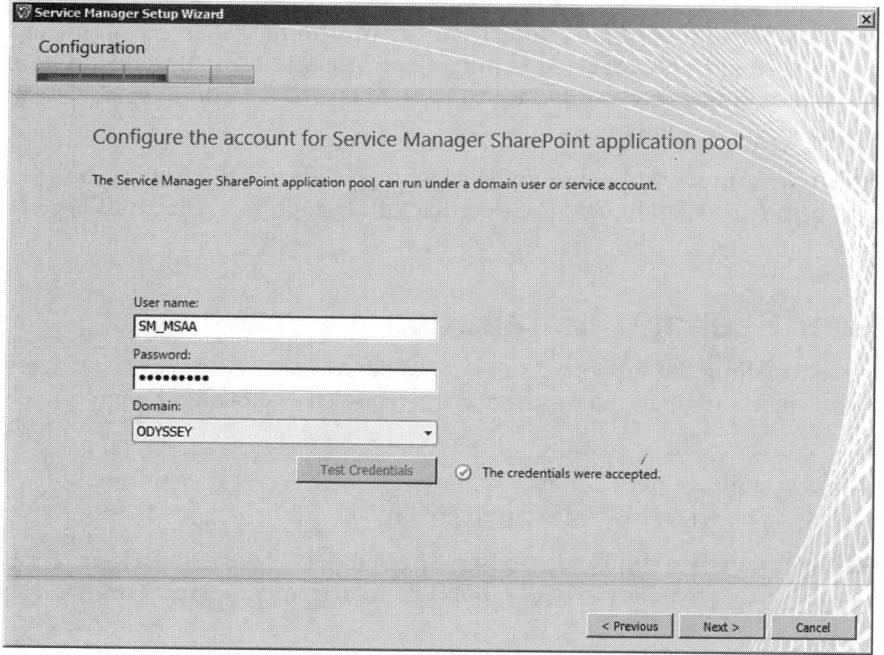

FIGURE 6.26   Specifying the SharePoint application pool account.

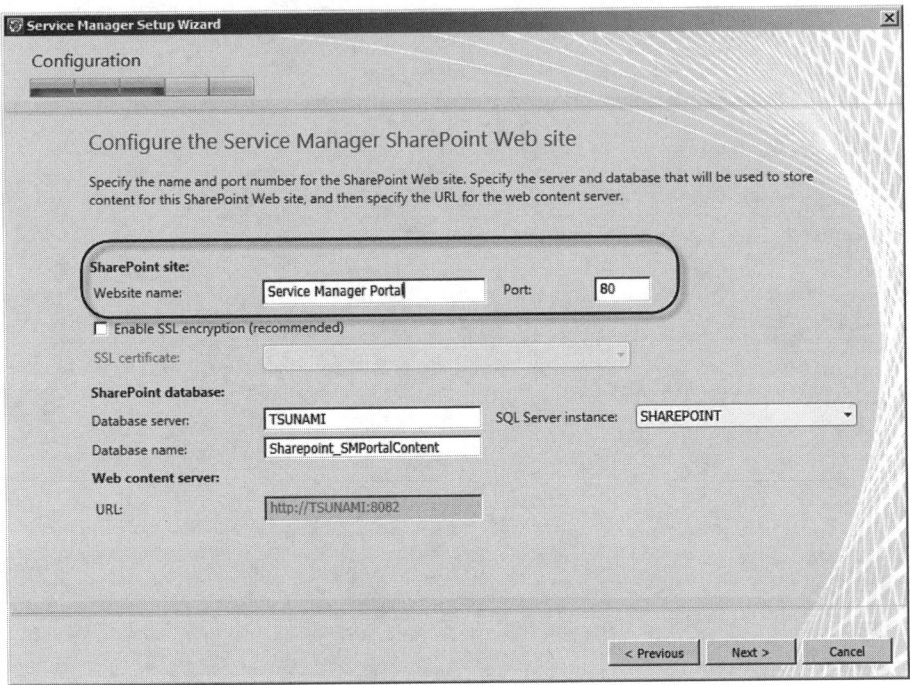

FIGURE 6.27   Self-service website configuration.

▶ **Additional Settings configuration:** There are two configuration settings, **Help improve System Center Service Manager** and **Use Microsoft Updates to help keep your computer secure and up-to-date**. Make the selection appropriate to your environment and policies.

▶ **Installation summary:** A summary page with your installation setting is shown before installation begins. Select **Back** to change your selections if necessary.

Three-Server Scenario Installation

As an alternative to installing the supported roles of System Center 2012 Service Manager on five servers, you could install all roles using three servers. The following is what differs when using three servers:

▶ **Service Manager management server database:** The SQL Server prerequisite is installed on the same server as the management server.

▶ **Service Manager data warehouse databases:** The SQL Server prerequisites are installed on the same server as the data warehouse management server. This includes the SSRS feature.

▶ **SSRS DLL and Configuration file edits:** The step to copy the DLL to the data warehouse management server and the additional edits in the SSRS configuration files is not required.

The installation steps for deploying to three servers are the same as described previously in the "Five-Server Scenario Installation" section. The differences discussed in this section should be taken into account at the relevant steps; for example, you do not need to specify a remote database server to install the Service Manager management and data warehouse management servers.

Upgrading to Service Manager 2012

System Center 2012 R2 Service Manager is the fourth release of Service Manager. Microsoft supports upgrading from the previous versions to the current version (Service Manager 2012 R2). Table 6.4 lists the minimum requirements for upgrading.

TABLE 6.4   Service Manager 2010 to 2012 R2 Upgrade Minimum Requirements

Feature or Dependency	Requirements
Service Manager management server	Must be at Service Manager 2010 SP 1 with cumulative update 3 (CU3) or higher applied.
Service Manager data warehouse management server	Must be at Service Manager 2010 SP 1 with CU3 or higher applied.
Service Manager data warehouse database server	SQL Server 2008 R2 SP 1 Analysis Services.
Service Manager console operating system	Windows XP is no longer supported. The suggested workaround for Windows XP is using Remote Desktop services application publishing.
Management servers operating system and other components	Windows Server 2008 R2 SP 1, SQL Native Client, SQL Server 2008 AMO, SQL Server 2008 Analysis Data Objects (ADO), and PowerShell 2.0.
Self-service portal	No upgrade path. You must install a new Service Manager 2012 R2 self-service portal after completing the upgrade of the other component features.

The only supported upgrade type is an in-place upgrade. This is a two-step process: You must first upgrade to the base version of System Center 2012 Service Manager (without a service pack) and then upgrade to Service Manager 2012 R2.

Performing an in-place upgrade could potentially make the upgrade high risk. Test the upgrade process in a nonproduction environment (preferably with a copy of your current Service Manager 2010 environment). You should also have a tested recovery method should you need to revert to the previous version due to upgrade issues.

The authors recommend you approach this upgrade as a project, ensuring you plan, test, resource, and manage it as a critical business application upgrade.

After preparing for the upgrade (Table 6.4 lists the minimum requirements), you are ready to install the upgradable features of Service Manager 2010. Note that the self-service portal cannot be upgraded. The upgrade must be performed in a specific order, including backup tasks. The order of upgrade tasks follows:

1. Perform a Service Manager disaster recovery test as documented by Microsoft at http://technet.microsoft.com/en-us/library/hh914226.aspx.

2. Back up the encryption key for all management servers.

3. Disable all connectors on the Service Manager 2010 management server.

4. Stop and disable all data warehouse jobs.

5. Back up all the Service Manager databases and the SSRS databases.

6. Back up custom report RDL files.

7. Back up all unsealed management packs.

8. Identify and document all customizations including independent software vendor (ISV) extensions/solutions.

9. Install and configure prerequisites by server function.

10. Upgrade the supported features to the base level of Service Manager 2012 (without Service Pack 1).

11. Upgrade the supported features to Service Manager 2012 R2.

Performing a disaster recovery test is the most important step and a critical best practice before upgrading your production environment. Remember there is no undo button for the in-place upgrade.

The next sections discuss upgrading the three supported features of Service Manager 2010. You must perform the upgrade in the following order:

1. Data warehouse management server

2. Service Manager management server

3. Service Manager consoles

Upgrading the Data Warehouse Management Server

The first server to upgrade is the data warehouse management server (if using a data warehouse). This management server must first be updated to the minimum requirements discussed earlier in the "Installing and Configuring Prerequisites" section. The prerequisites follow:

▶ Add the Analysis Services feature to the existing data warehouse database server or use an existing SQL Server 2008 R2 SP 1 Analysis Services server with the correct collation.

▶ Apply CU3 or higher for Service Manager 2010 SP 1.

▶ Install SQL Server Native Client and SQL Server 2008 AMO on the management server if the database is on a remote SQL Server.

▶ Close all Service Manager consoles connected to the Service Manager 2010 environment you plan to upgrade.

The steps to perform the data warehouse management server upgrade follow:

1. Log on to the server (Tobor in this example) using a domain user account with local administrator and Service Manager administrator role privileges.

2. Start the upgrade from the System Center 2012 Service Manager media splash screen. Under Upgrade, select **Service Manager data warehouse management server** (see Figure 6.28).

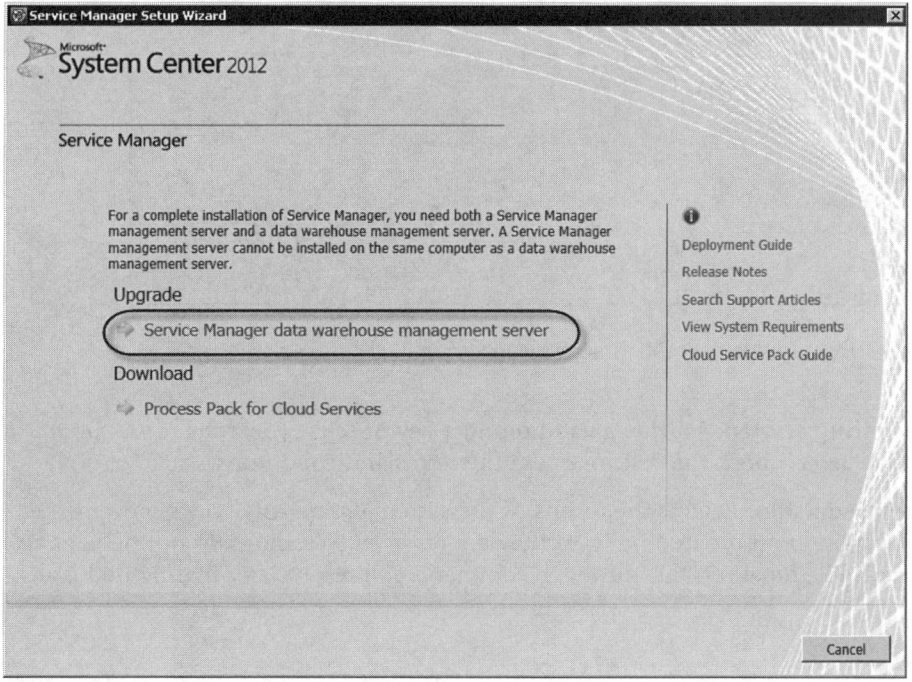

FIGURE 6.28   Initiate the Service Manager data warehouse upgrade to Service Manager 2012.

3. Following are the significant wizard pages to configure when upgrading a Service Manager 2010 data warehouse server to the 2012 version:

▶ **Prepare for upgrade:** Check the two boxes to confirm you have read the upgrade order and timing guide, and that you have also prepared for the disaster recovery scenario (see Figure 6.29).

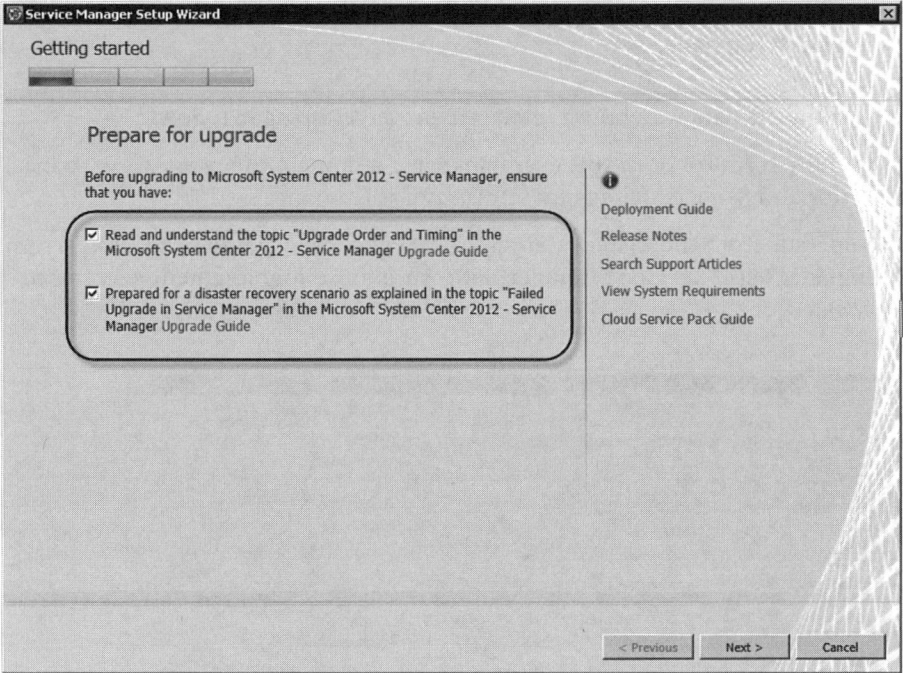

FIGURE 6.29   Upgrade documentation acknowledgement.

▶ **Getting Started:** Provide a valid product key or select the evaluation option. If you agree, check the box to accept the terms and conditions.

▶ **Prerequisites:** Review the results of the system check. Any errors prevent the upgrade from proceeding until they are resolved. Warnings do not prevent an upgrade; however, the authors recommend you resolve any highlighted issues.

▶ **Configure the additional data warehouse datamarts:** These additional databases are optional and can only be selected during the upgrade. Type the server name and select the instance and database name for the server hosting the data warehouse databases. There are two databases to configure. Provide an initial size and accept or modify the data and log file folder locations (see Figure 6.30).

▶ **Configure the reporting account:** Enter the user name and password, and select the domain for the reporting user account from the drop-down.

▶ **Configure Analysis Services for OLAP cubes:** Provide the server name, instance, and database name for the server hosting the data OLAP cube database. You can specify a different folder to place the database. Figure 6.31 shows the default values for this setting once the supported SQL Server and instance are selected, and highlights the storage option.

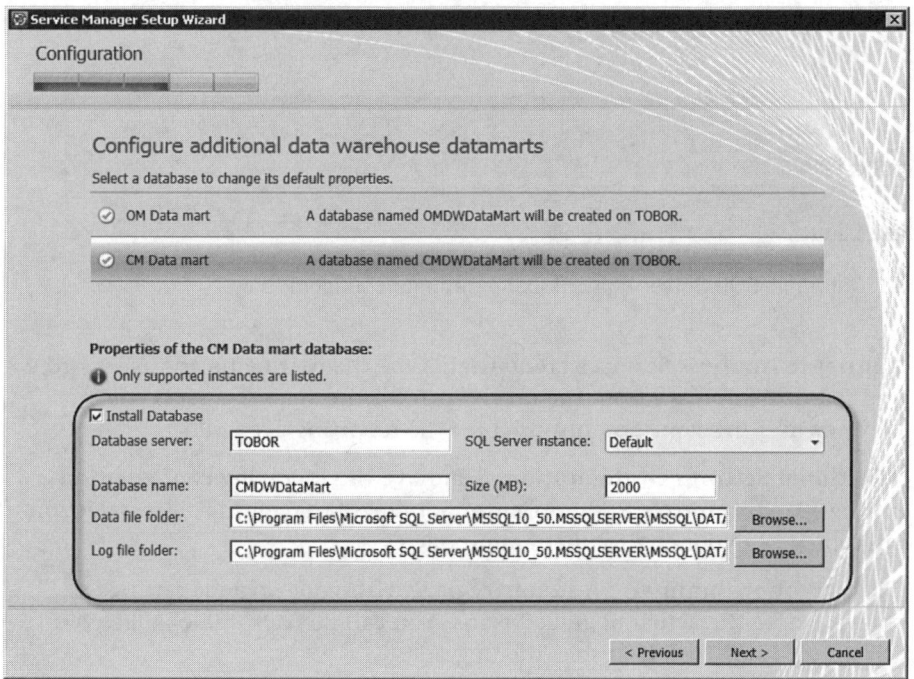

FIGURE 6.30   Additional Analysis datamart cubes.

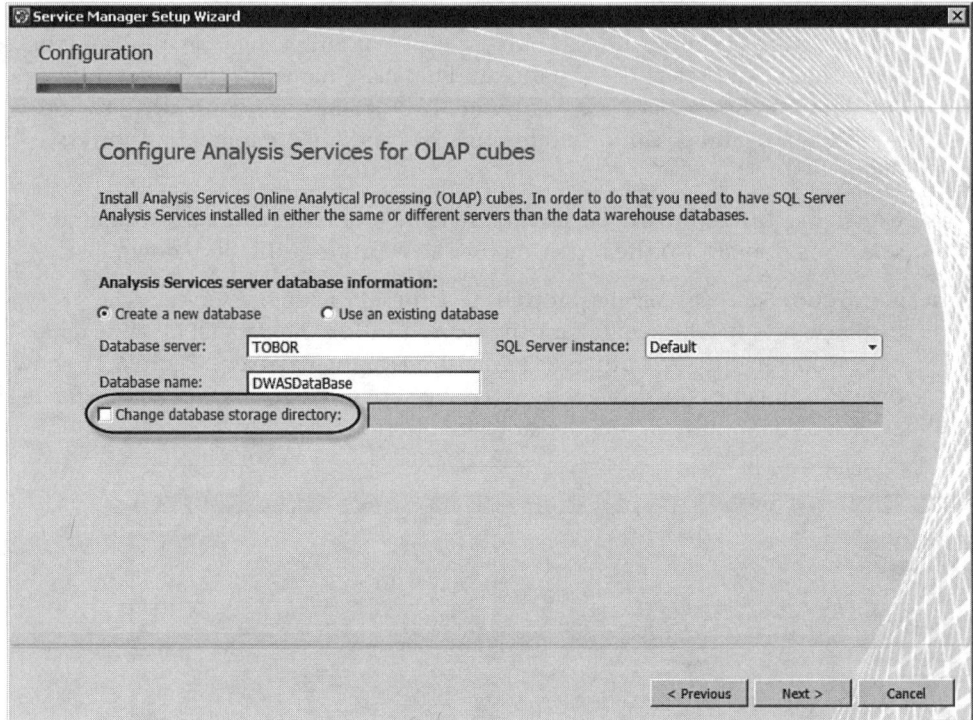

FIGURE 6.31   Datamart SQL Server and database settings configuration.

▶ **Configure Analysis Services credential:** Type the user name and password, and select the domain from the drop-down for the analysis user account. Odyssey uses the same account used for the reporting account.

▶ **Additional Settings configuration:** You have the following configuration setting—**Help improve System Center Service Manager**. Make the selection appropriate to your environment and policies.

▶ **Configuration summary:** A summary page with your upgrade settings is shown before the actual upgrade begins. You can go back and change your selections. Click **Install** to start the upgrade.

TIP: BACKUP THE ENCRYPTION KEY

After the upgrade completes successfully, Figure 6.32 displays with a check box to back up the encryption key for the data warehouse management server. You may have already made a backup prior to the upgrade; this particular option is related to the upgraded state. This is a good time to back up the Service Manager 2012 key to ensure you are ready for a full disaster recovery scenario.

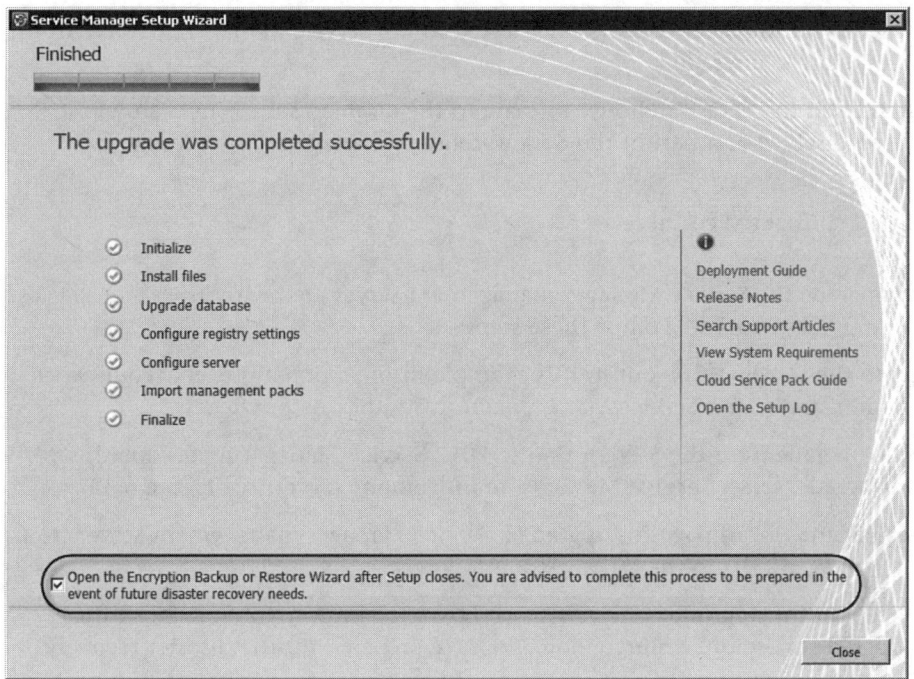

FIGURE 6.32   Upgrade completion status.

Having successfully upgraded to Service Manager 2012 RTM, upgrade again using the Service Manager 2012 R2 media. Apply CU2 for Service Manager 2012 before upgrading to R2.

Upgrading the Service Manager Management Server

After upgrading the data warehouse (if you had one), the next server to upgrade is the Service Manager management server. You must first update this management server with the prerequisite minimum requirements (see Table 6.4), as follows:

▶ Apply CU3 or higher for Service Manager 2010 SP 1.

▶ Install SQL Server Native Client and SQL Server 2008 AMO on the management server if the database is hosted on a remote SQL Server.

▶ Close all Service Manager consoles connected to the Service Manager 2010 environment you plan to upgrade.

▶ Ensure that all the data warehouse jobs are in the disabled state. These should have been disabled as a part of the data warehouse management server upgrade prerequisites.

▶ Disable all configured connectors.

The steps to upgrade the Service Manager management server are nearly the same as those of the data warehouse upgrade. Follow these steps:

1. Log on to the server (Whiteout in this example) using a domain user account with local administrator and Service Manager administrator role privileges.

2. Start the upgrade from the System Center 2012 Service Manager media splash screen. Under Upgrade, select **Service Manager management server** (see Figure 6.33).

3. The significant wizard pages to upgrade a Service Manager management server from Service Manager 2010 to the 2012 version follow:

   ▶ **Prepare for upgrade:** Check the two boxes to confirm you have read the upgrade order and timing guide and have prepared for the disaster recovery scenario.

   ▶ **Product registration:** Provide a valid product key or select the evaluation option on this page. If you agree, check the box to accept the terms and conditions.

▶ **Prerequisites:** Review the results of the system check. Errors prevent the upgrade from proceeding until resolved. Warnings do not prevent an upgrade, although you should resolve any highlighted issues.

▶ **Configuration summary:** A summary page with your upgrade setting is displayed before the actual upgrade begins. You can go back and change your selections. Click **Install** to start the upgrade.

▶ **Finished:** Figure 6.34 displays in the case of a successful upgrade. It has two post-installation options—**Open the Encryption Backup or Restore Wizard after Setup closes** and **Open the Service Manager console when Setup closes**. The authors recommend selecting the first option to back up the encryption key for the management group.

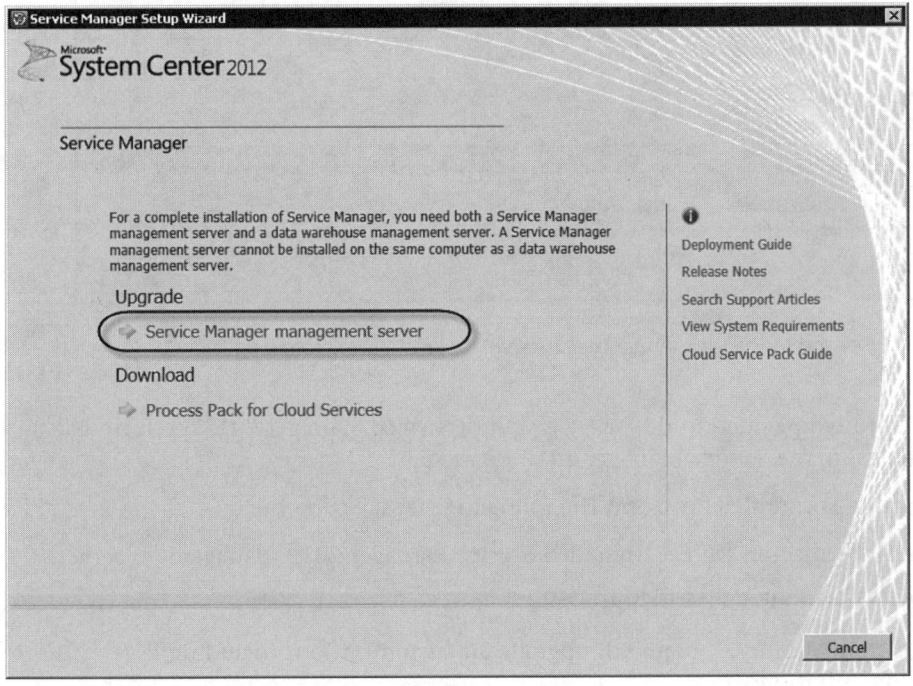

FIGURE 6.33   Initiate the Service Manager management server upgrade to Service Manager 2012 RTM.

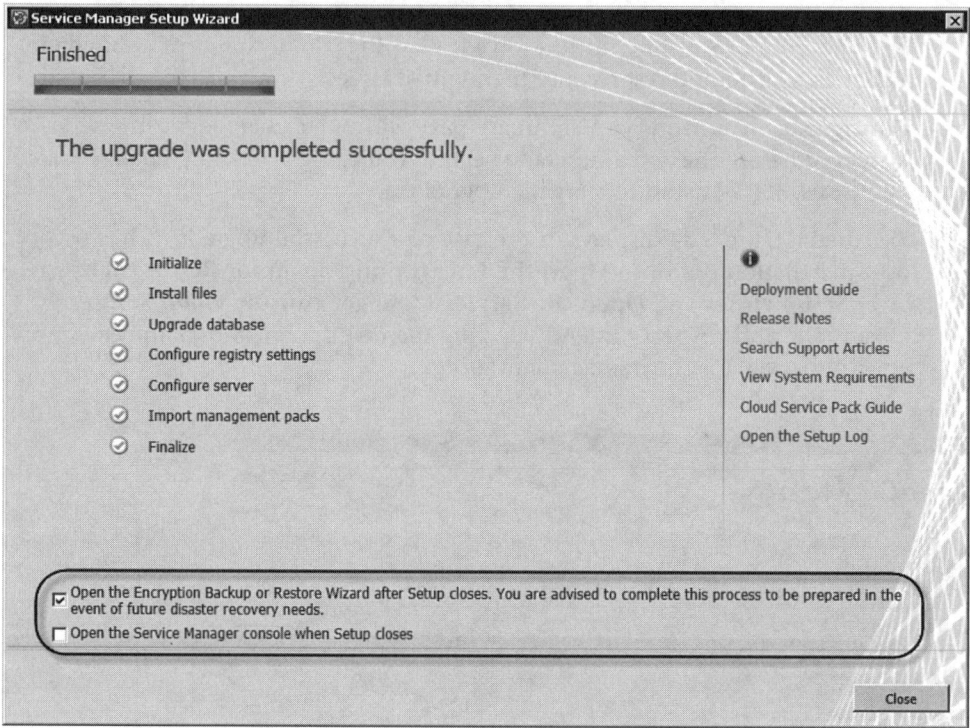

FIGURE 6.34   Service Manager management server upgrade complete page.

Having successfully upgraded to the base version of Service Manager 2012, perform the same upgrade using the Service Manager 2012 R2 media.

After the upgrade is complete, perform the following steps:

1. Enable all connectors on the upgraded Service Manager 2012 management server.

2. Enable and start all data warehouse jobs.

3. Test for compatibility; if required, upgrade all customizations including ISV extensions/solutions.

Upgrading the Service Manager Console

The final upgradable part of Service Manager 2010 is the console. You have two options:

▶ Apply CU3 or higher, upgrade to Service Manager 2012, and then upgrade to Service Manager 2012 R2.

▶ Uninstall the 2010 console and install the Service Manager 2012 R2 console.

The second option may be the simplest to implement and manage. It includes the following:

1. Uninstalling the console from the control panel applet.

2. Installing the required console prerequisites as described in Table 6.4.

3. Closing all running desktop applications and restarting the computer.

Install the System Center 2012 R2 Service Manager console by performing the following steps:

1. Log on to the computer you plan to install the console on using a domain user account with local administrator privileges.

2. Start the installation from the System Center 2012 Service Manager R2 media splash screen. Under Install (Optional), select **Service Manager console** (see Figure 6.35).

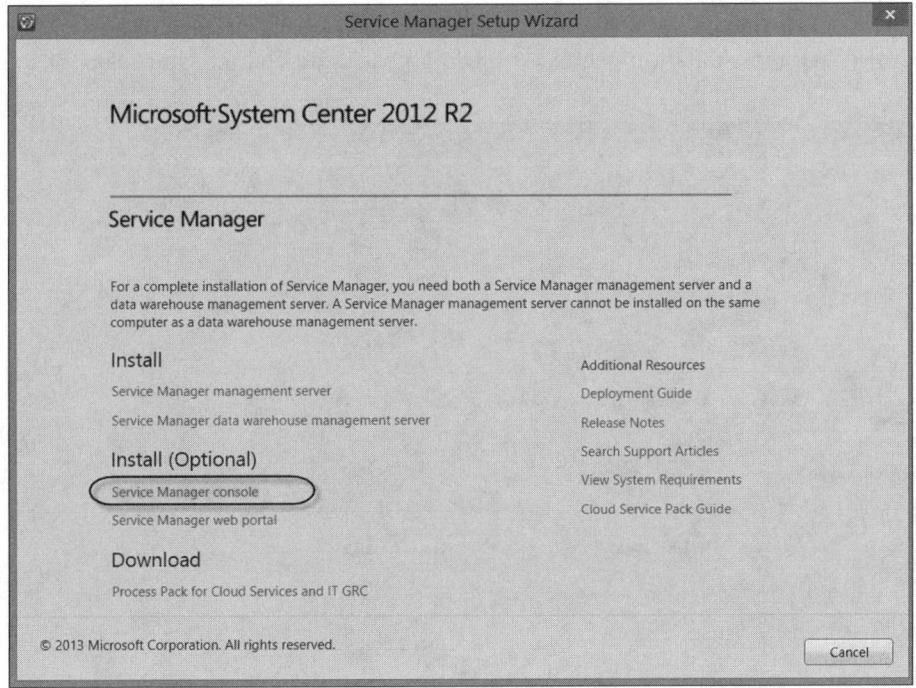

FIGURE 6.35   Start Service Manager console installation.

3. The significant wizard pages required for installing a Service Manager console follow:

> ▶ **Product registration:** Provide details for the name and organization fields. If you agree, check the box to accept the terms and conditions.

> ▶ **Installation location:** Accept the default or provide an alternative installation location.

> ▶ **Checking for requirements:** Review the results of the system check. Errors prevent the installation from proceeding until resolved. Warnings do not prevent installation, although you should resolve any highlighted issues. Figure 6.36 highlights the prerequisites the wizard tests for and their current compliance state.

> ▶ **Additional Settings configuration pages:** You have two configuration settings—**Help improve System Center Service Manager** and **Use Microsoft Updates to help keep your computer secure and up-to-date**. Make the selection on these pages appropriate to your environment and policies.

> ▶ **Installation summary:** A summary page with your installation setting is shown before installation begins. You can go back and change your selections.

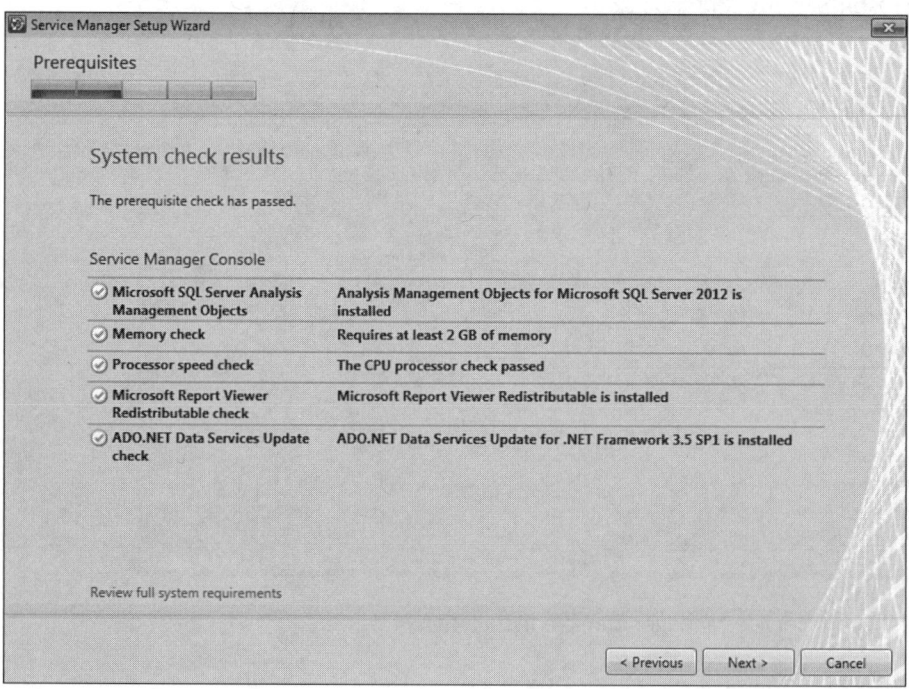

FIGURE 6.36   Service Manager console installation prerequisite check.

The final page confirms whether the installation was successful or whether you need to perform troubleshooting activities to resolve a failure. Troubleshooting options and tools are discussed in the next section.

Troubleshooting Installations and Upgrades

A Service Manager 2012 installation can present some technical challenges and issues. Table 6.5 lists troubleshooting resources, known issues, and resolutions.

TABLE 6.5   Troubleshooting Resources and Known Issues

Resource/Issue	Notes
Log file: SCSMInstall.log and SCSMSetup.log	Service Manager provides detailed logging of the installation process. The logs can be found in the folder of the installation user profile, at %*LOCALAPPDATA*%\Temp. Search for **Value 3**.
Incorrect or missing dependency component configuration	Most common troubleshooting issues are associated with missing or incorrectly configured dependencies. You must ensure you have installed and configured the required prerequisites. Plan to review the latest supported configuration information.
Firewalls	Verify that the required ports used by Service Manager during and after the installation process are configured properly on firewalls (operating system or external appliances).
User and computer account rights	Ensure the required rights have been assigned to users or computer accounts used in the installation and configuration processes.
TechNet: Search for Troubleshooting System Center 2012 - Service Manager Deployment Issues	This is the official Microsoft location for the latest information on the component.

TIP: USER FORUMS AND BLOGS

Service Manager troubleshooting information is available on various Internet user forums. Use search engines such as Bing and Google to aid with troubleshooting, as there are many community leaders discussing the most current issues and resolutions.

Recommended Post-Installation Tasks

After installing or upgrading to Service Manager 2012, there are several initial post-deployment tasks. The Administration Overview pane in the Service Manager console outlines these tasks and provides short-cut links to each relevant section of the console. Figure 6.37 shows the overview page. The post-installation tasks on this page must be performed in the appropriate order for your requirements and differ based on your situation. The following sections discuss post-installation tasks for new and upgraded environments.

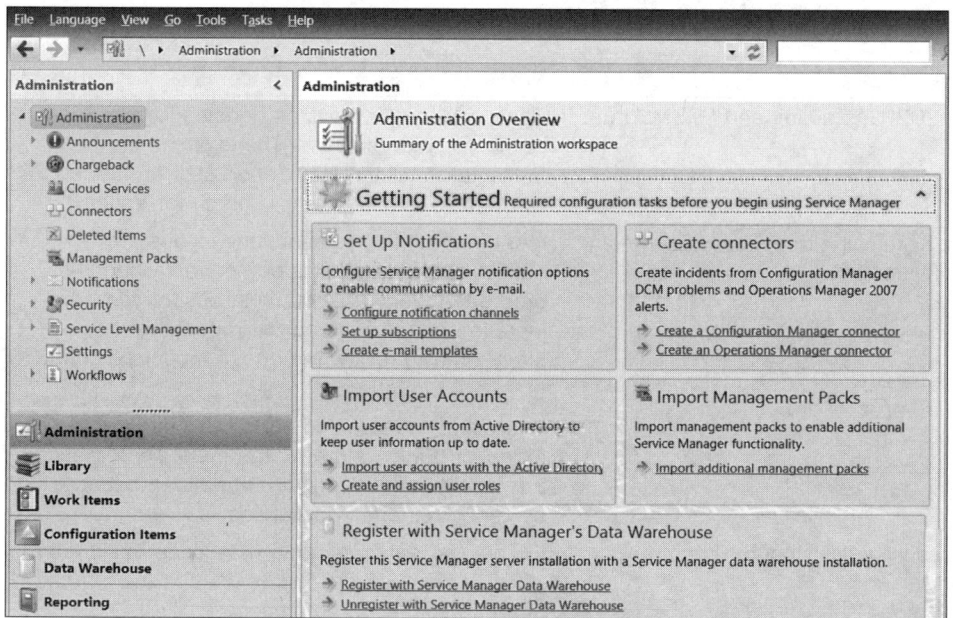

FIGURE 6.37   Administration Overview pane of the Service Manager console.

For New Installations

The three main categories of tasks follow:

▶ **Register with the Service Manager Data Warehouse:** You must register with the data warehouse if you want to use the reporting component of Service Manager. This option requires you to have a data warehouse management server installed with its required database server. The steps to register a data warehouse are discussed in Chapter 21, "Data Warehouse and Reporting."

▶ **Create Connectors:** Part of the power of Service Manager is its capability to dynamically populate the CMDB and automatically maintain configuration items. This function is managed through the connector framework; for example, the Active Directory connector populates the CMDB with user and computer information from Active Directory. Configuring connectors is discussed in Chapter 8, "Working with Connectors."

▶ **Import Management Packs:** Management packs store your personalization and customization of Service Manager. Create these management packs in the Authoring Tool and import them into Service Manager. Management packs are discussed extensively in Chapter 20, "Management Packs."

The Settings section under the Administration node in the console is often overlooked. This section allows you to configure global settings such as the prefix of incidents, incident priority calculation, and data retention. Configure these settings appropriately.

Post-Installation Tasks for Upgraded Environments

If you have upgraded to this version of Service Manager, the post-installation activities may have already been performed. Review each relevant area and update as needed. For example, the Orchestrator and Virtual Machine Manager connectors are new to Service Manager 2012 and would need to be configured.

Removing a Service Manager Installation

Removing Service Manager should be performed in the reverse order from which you installed the various features. Here is the removal order:

1. Optionally perform a complete backup of the environment.

2. Unregister the data warehouse (if you configured this option).

3. Uninstall the data warehouse management server.

4. Delete the data warehouse databases.

5. Uninstall secondary management server(s).

6. Uninstall the first Service Manager Server management server (this is the workflow management server).

7. Delete the Service Manager database.

8. Uninstall the self-service portal server(s).

9. Uninstall Service Manager console(s).

Perform the Service Manager uninstallation using the Remove option under Control Panel -> Programs and Features. Use the SQL Server management tools to delete the databases.

CAUTION: RECYCLING THE UNINSTALLED SERVERS

If you reuse the servers after removing Service Manager, you should reinstall the operating system. The removal process may leave settings in the Windows registry that could affect reinstalling Service Manager or installing another application.

Summary

This chapter discussed and provided guidance on installing and upgrading to System Center 2012 Service Manager, including installing the console, troubleshooting installation issues, and removing a Service Manager installation.

The next chapter provides a detailed discussion on the Service Manager console and the self-service portal.

PART III

Service Manager Operations

IN THIS PART

Using Service Manager

This chapter provides an overview of the Service Manager console and portal, which are used to access Service Manager to manage work items and configuration items, and to administer the tool. Different roles in an organization need access to Service Manager to perform their daily functions; the interface they choose to access Service Manager differs depending on what they are trying to do and whom they are. The following list outlines the types of roles in an organization who use Service Manager to manage their activities:

▶ Incident support analysts (service desk analysts and upper tier support)

▶ Problem managers

▶ Change managers, change initiators, change approvers

▶ Service request support analysts

▶ Release managers, release implementers, release testers, release approvers

▶ Configuration managers

▶ IT management

▶ End users

▶ Service Manager administrators

Understanding the type of access and the type of work that needs to be performed determines the role type and interface most suitable for managing work items. Many interfaces facilitate access to Service Manager; each has a specific purpose for the type of activities that one can perform. The interfaces to Service Manager are

▶ Service Manager console

▶ Service Manager Authoring Tool

▶ Service Manager self-service portal

▶ Service Manager PowerShell

▶ Service Manager reporting

Connectors in Service Manager also provide another way for data and systems to access Service Manager. Service Manager connectors, which are not an interface but provide data and interact with Service Manager, are covered in detail in Chapter 8, "Working with Connectors." For more information on PowerShell and its integration with Service Manager, see Chapter 24, "Using PowerShell." Using the Service Manager Authoring Tool is discussed in Chapter 22, "Customizing Service Manager." This chapter focuses on the Service Manager console and self-service portal access. Table 7.1 maps the different interfaces and the role types that are suited to use them.

TABLE 7.1   Service Manager Interfaces and Usage Types

Console	Role Type
Service Manager console	Change managers, change initiators, change approvers
	Service request support analysts
	Release managers, release implementers, release testers, release approvers
	Configuration managers
	Information Technology (IT) management
	Service Manager administrators
Service Manager Authoring Tool	Service Manager administrators
Service Manager portal	End users
	Service request approvers
Service Manager PowerShell console	Service Manager administrators, or anyone who would like to use PowerShell within Service Manager
Service Manager reporting	Anyone who needs access to reports and reporting

Service Manager Console Overview

The Service Manager console is where all IT users of this System Center component access the Service Manager features. The breadth and depth of what a user can do in Service Manager is determined by the type of use of Service Manager and the access granted by its security-based user roles. Access to the Service Manager console is controlled by user roles; see Chapter 17, "Service Manager Security," for additional information on user roles in Service Manager. Prior to implementing and granting access to Service Manager, consider those items users need to access in the Service Manager console, determine the minimum and maximum access you need to provide each user of Service Manager, and apply the appropriate roles.

During the planning phase of Service Manager, you need to determine the types of roles in your organization and the access required for the Service Manager console. Table 7.2 lists some considerations, and Table 7.3 describes typical console access for the roles.

TABLE 7.2   Considerations for Service Manager Console Access

Consideration	Why You Need to Know
Process management packs to be leveraged in Service Manager	Determine what roles and management packs will be available for use.
Users of Service Manager in your organization	List the organizational groups and functional groups who will be using Service Manager:
	IT management
	End users/customers
	Service desk
	Second tier support
	Third tier support
	Application support
	Change management
	Reporting analysts
	Knowledge authors/technical writers
	Configuration managers
	Problem managers
	Release managers
	Incident manager
	Service level manager
	HR
	Facilities
Access required to Service Manager console	How and what will the users of Service Manager access and use Service Manager in your organization? What access do they require:
	No access/portal only
	Access by management pack
	Advanced operators
	Administrators

TABLE 7.3   Typical Access to Service Manager

Role	Console	Portal
Administrators	Yes	Yes
Managers	Yes	Yes
End users	No	Yes
Process managers/owners	Yes	Yes
Reporting analysts	Yes	Possible
Service Manager authors	Yes	Yes

What you can see and do in the Service Manager console differs based on the role assigned to you as a user (such as a Tier 1 analyst, advanced operator, problem analyst). This chapter covers the console functionality in the Administrator role. Using the Service Manager console as an administrator, you can see six workspaces (see Figure 7.1), described in Table 7.4.

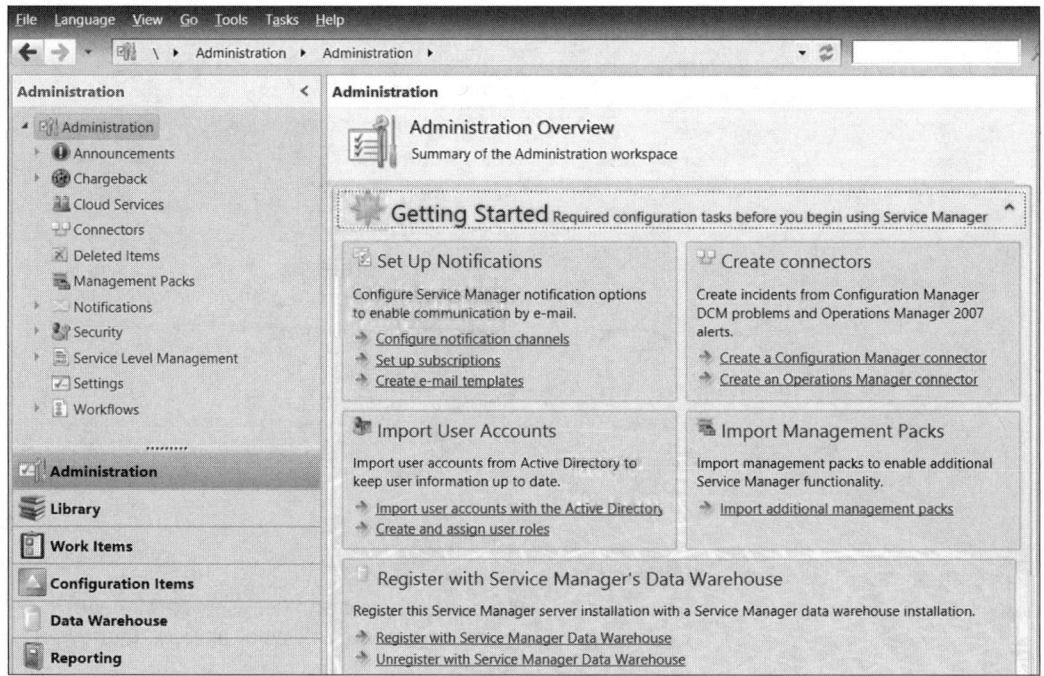

FIGURE 7.1   Administrator view of the Service Manager console.

TABLE 7.4   Service Manager Workspaces

Workspace	Use
Administration	Used by Service Manager administrators.
Library	Contains templates, queues, knowledge articles, lists, tasks, and groups. Access to these items requires elevated permissions, as modifying the content within this workspace has global impact to Service Manager.
Work items	This workspace is where all work items are created and managed in Service Manager. Work items reference incidents, problems, changes, releases, service requests, and activities.
Configuration Items	Contains all the configuration items (CIs) and CI types that are stored in the Service Manager configuration management database (CMDB).
Data Warehouse	Contains the data warehouse settings for management and administration. Access to this workspace should be limited to roles that are accountable and responsible for reporting and management of the database.
Reporting	Contains the reports for Service Manager. This only appears when the Service Manager data warehouse is installed.
Additional third-party products	When these management packs are installed, they appear as additional workspaces.

What you see in the Service Manager console depends on the security role that has been applied to you. For example, if you are assigned the End Users role in Service Manager, you are able to access only the Library, Work Items, and Configuration Items workspaces, as seen in Figure 7.2.

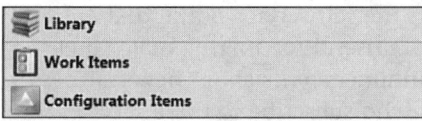

FIGURE 7.2   End user workspaces.

If you are assigned the Administrators role, you see all the items in the console and have elevated privileges that enable you to create, modify, or delete items in Service Manager.

Out of the box, Service Manager has six workspaces available. The icons appearing on the left in the Service Manager console are called the Wunderbar, or workspaces. Figure 7.3 shows the Service Manager Wunderbar (workspace). If you install third-party management packs, they also appear as workspaces in the Service Manager Wunderbar.

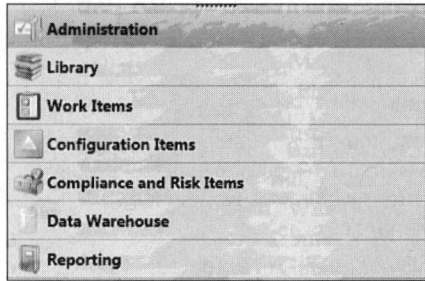

FIGURE 7.3   Compliance and Risk Items workspace added by the Governance Risk and Compliance Process management pack.

Administration of Service Manager with the Service Manager Console

The Administration workspace is used to define and configure the overall settings of Service Manager. After installation, you define the settings for how you want Service Manager to look and behave; these activities are typically performed once and are global to the application. Routine maintenance is also performed within the Administration workspace (previously shown in Figure 7.1), such as managing announcements and deleted items. The next sections outline the capabilities for each node.

Administration Workspace Node Overview

There are times when you have to create, update, or maintain your Service Manager environment. This work is performed in the Administration workspace; the next few sections cover the purpose of each node.

Announcements

You can create announcements that you can display on the self-service portal that are visible to the end users of the portal. Announcements are useful for sharing major incident issues that impact services. You can also create announcements about new features of services and policy changes that affect the end users who subscribe to these services. To show announcements on the portal page, you must create a page on the Service Manager portal, for example, to set an announcement on the portal for all IT users of Service Manager that there will be training.

First, you need to create an Announcements page on the portal. Note you need only to do this step once, when creating your first announcement. To set up an Announcements page on the self-service portal, perform the following steps:

1. Start a browser, and connect to the home page of the self-service portal, for example, http://<*WebServerName*>:82/SMPortal.

2. In the upper-left corner, click **Site Actions**, and then click **Site Settings**.

3. On the Site Settings page, in the Look and Feel area, click **Quick launch**.

4. On the Quick Launch page, click **New Navigation Link**.

5. In the Type the Web address field, type **/SMPortal/Lists/Announcements/AllItems. aspx**, and then in the description box, type **Announcements**.

6. Click **OK**, and then navigate to the home page.

Next, create an announcement. Follow these steps:

1. Start a browser, and connect to the home page of the self-service portal, for example, http://<*WebServerName*>:82/SMPortal.

2. Click **Announcements**.

3. On the Announcements—All items page, click **Add new announcement**.

4. In the Title box, type **Service Manager training session**.

5. In the Body, add additional information on when the training will occur and how to register.

6. You can set an expiration date for this announcement and select the date after the training. Then click **Save** to close the announcement.

TIP: ENABLING NON-ADMINISTRATORS TO MANAGE ANNOUNCEMENTS

The Security settings in Service Manager allow members of the Administrators, Advanced Operators, and Authors roles to create announcements. The authors recommend enabling the service desk to create announcements, as they are responsible for managing the customer's expectations.

Consideration as to whom in the service desk can create announcements should be planned, and appropriate training provided on how to manage announcements.

Connectors

One of the key features of Service Manager is the ability to bring data in from multiple sources via the connectors, enhancing the service management experience for your organization. The Service Manager CMDB is enhanced by using the Active Directory Domain Services connector, System Center Operations Manager connector, System Center Configuration Manager connector, System Center Virtual Machine Manager connector, System Center Orchestrator connector, and the Exchange connector. You can also import alerts from Operations Manager and desired configuration management (DCM) notifications for Configuration Manager to create incidents in Service Manager automatically. Alternatively, you could use a comma-separated value (CSV) connector to pull data from other sources into the Service Manager database. The CSV connector is typically used when a data source is not complete; for example, location is not populated for users in Active Directory; you can import these values into Service Manager to complete user records until Active Directory can be remediated to include location information.

TIP: DO A QUALITY CHECK OF DATA SOURCES BEFORE IMPORT

Examine the quality of data in the sources that you plan to import in Service Manager prior to running the connectors. For example, obsolete and deleted objects should be moved to a different OU in Active Directory, as these objects bloat the Service Manager database with unnecessary data and magnify that lack of management of AD objects. As Service Manager magnifies the lack of management in other System Center tools and Active Directory, the authors highly recommend that you remediate and clean up data sources prior to importing data via connectors into Service Manager.

Connectors can be manual or automatic. Table 7.5 outlines what each connector can import. For additional information, see Chapter 8.

TABLE 7.5   Service Manager Connectors

Connector	Data Imported into Service Manager
Active Directory	Computers, groups, printers, users.
Operations Manager Configuration Item (CI)	Imports Operations Manager distributed applications as business services, objects discovered by Operations Manager such as databases and websites—note you need to import these Operations Manager management packs into Service Manager.
Operations Manager Alert	This connector is a bidirectional connector that imports alerts from Operations Manager and creates incidents in Service Manager. Bidirectional connectors such as Operations Manager allow you to push and pull information to and from Service Manager.
Configuration Manager	Imports additional computer information, such as software installed, hardware inventory and links the primary user to the computer, what patches are installed.
Configuration Manager DCM	Collects noncompliance information from System Center Configuration Manager and creates an incident in Service Manager.
CSV	This connector enables data from other sources to import objects in the Service Manager database. This connector can't be scheduled but is used to augment data in the Service Manager database.
Virtual Machine Manager	You can import objects, such as virtual machine (VM) templates, service templates, and storage classifications that are created in Virtual Machine Manager (VMM) into the Service Manager database.

Connector	Data Imported into Service Manager
Exchange	The System Center Service Manager–Exchange Connector 3.0 connects Service Manager to Exchange for processing incoming emails related to activities, incidents, service requests, and change requests.
Orchestrator	This connector enables the invoking of Orchestrator runbooks from within Service Manager so that you can automate activities.

Deleted Items

Items in the Deleted Items node have been marked for deletion from the Service Manager database. If you delete an item from the Service Manager database, such as a computer, it is not deleted immediately; it is marked as pending to be deleted. Items under the Deleted Items node are those items that have been marked pending delete. The Service Manager administrator should regularly review the Deleted Items node and delete these items to ensure that the delete is completed. The Service Manager roles that can mark items for Pending Delete are the Advanced Operators and Authors, although only members of the Administrators role can actually complete the delete process.

Management Packs

The Management Packs node is where you can import new management packs into Service Manager. For example, if you want to import a System Center Operations Manager distributed application as a business service into Service Manager, you export those management packs from Operations Manager and then import them into Service Manager under this node. As with Operations Manager, management packs can be sealed or unsealed. You can also delete management packs from Service Manager, which removes the database objects and the corresponding relationship entries defined in the deleted management pack. More information on how management packs work in Service Manager is available in Chapter 20, "Management Packs."

Notifications

Notifications are important for ensuring that items in Service Manager are addressed in a timely manner. Notifications enable the delivery of alert messages when an item in Service Manager is created, resolved, or updated. To use notifications you first must configure a notification channel, which is the means to transport the message to the recipient. Areas where notifications are useful include when items are assigned to an individual or when an incident is resolved to notify the end user to close the incident. For more information on configuring notifications, see Chapter 16, "Managing Notifications."

Security

The Security workspace is where Run As accounts and user roles are defined and managed for Service Manager.

Run As accounts are used when setting up and installing Service Manager; you need to enter and define the credentials for the workflow and service accounts, for the Service

Manager connectors, for SQL Server Analysis Services (SSAS), and for SQL Server Reporting Services (SSRS). Most organizations have password security requirements; when these passwords for the Run As accounts expire, you must update the new passwords in Service Manager.

If Run As accounts user names change, they also must be changed in Service Manager. It is a best practice never to delete Run As accounts from the Service Manager console because the Service Manager management pack monitors these accounts. At regular intervals the Health service attempts to log on as the Run As accounts and raises an alert if the login fails. You should not delete Run As accounts; reuse them by changing their name or credentials. If you want to stop using a Run As account, you can change its credentials to Local System and change the name to something easy to remember, such as "Inactive."

User-based roles in Service Manager provide role-based security to the items in Service Manager and define what access they have within their assigned role. Table 7.6 lists the user roles that come with Service Manager out of the box; more information and details can be found in Chapter 17.

TABLE 7.6   Service Manager User Roles

User Role	Scope	Suggested Organizational Role to Apply
Activity Implementers	Global	IT roles responsible for implementing activities within Service Manager work items.
Administrators	Global	Service Manager Administrator.
Advanced Operators	Global	Used for power IT users, provides access to all management packs in Service Manager.
Change Initiators	Global	IT roles who initiate changes.
End Users	Global	Any end user within an organization.
Read-Only Operators	Global	Roles in an organization that need only to view items in Service Manager and not act upon them, such as management roles.
Authors	Global	Persons responsible for authoring workflows via the Authoring Tool, developer role types.
Problem Analysts	Global	Personnel responsible for managing problems.
Workflows	Global	Assigned to workflow accounts.
Incident Resolvers	Global	IT personnel who resolve incidents.
Change Managers	Global	Personnel who manage and approve changes.
Report Users	Global	Anyone who wants to view or run reports.
Release Managers	Global	Personnel responsible for creating, managing, and deploying releases.
Service Request Analysts	Global	Personnel who manage service requests; these may include HR, Facilities, and building security.

Service Level Management

Service level management in Service Manager enables the measurement of incidents and service requests. Service Manager leverages queues, which are a security boundary, that allow you to create service levels and configure notifications on warnings of when a service level is not met or is in danger of being breached.

The goal of Incident Management is to resolve the incident as quickly as possible to restore the level of service as quickly as possible. Leveraging service level management in Service Manager enables you to define the time to resolve incidents as well as create notifications when the incident is about to breach the time for resolution so that the appropriate action can be taken.

Service requests normally have a turnaround time to complete. Using service level management in Service Manager provides appropriate management and policing of the timeliness of the service requests that need to be completed.

Service Manager uses calendars, metrics, and service level objectives to create service level agreements. Measurement of operating level agreements (OLAs) and underpinning contracts (UCs) is not possible in the tool, but the resolution and completion times for incidents and service requests can be managed and measured.

Calendars in Service Manager enable you to define working days, time zones, hours, and holidays. You can have multiple calendars to cover all the different calendars, time zones, and countries for which your organization provides IT support.

Metrics are similar to service level agreements (SLAs). You need to define time metrics to measure time from start and end times for incidents and service requests so that you can measure your performance for these work items. After defining metrics, these must be associated with a service level objective (SLO). SLOs create the relationship between a queue, a calendar item, a time-based metric, and the actions that need to happen before or after you breach the service level. The authors recommend that you create the calendars and SLA metrics before creating SLOs. When working with the queues in service level management (SLM) in Service Manager, you must target work items in the same class, for example, an SLO can only apply to incident items, and you must create an SLO for service requests.

For more information on configuring service level management, see Chapter 11, "Incident Management."

Settings

In the Settings node shown in Figure 7.4, you can configure the general settings for Service Manager. These settings are set up initially after installation and rarely modified for the work items afterward.

Table 7.7 outlines what can be configured with an out of box installation of Service Manager.

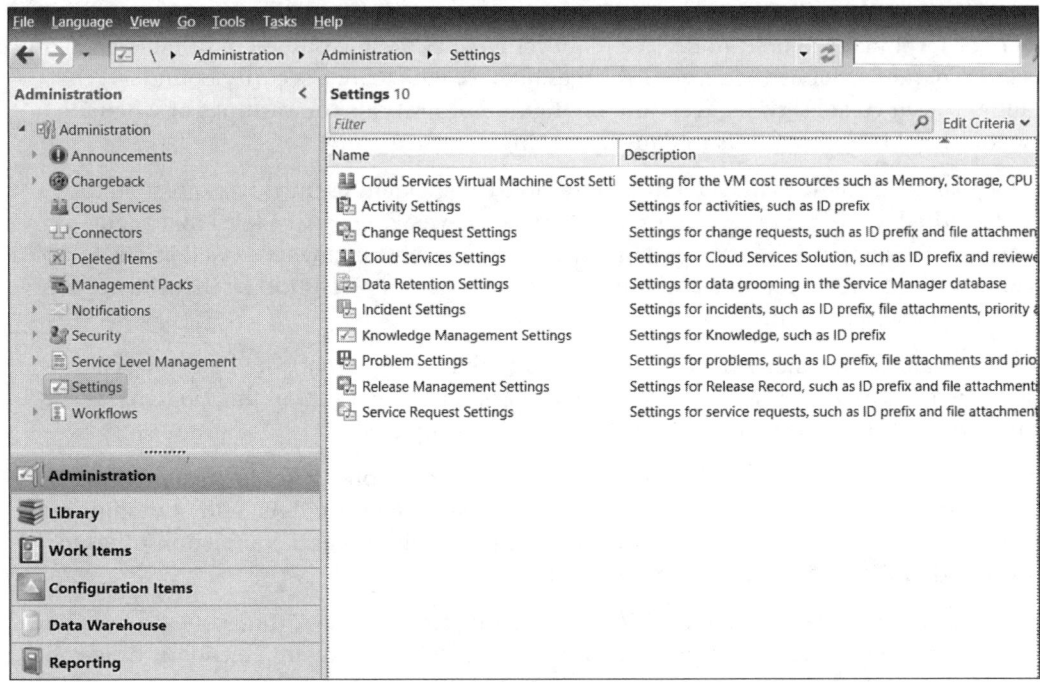

FIGURE 7.4   Settings node in the console.

TABLE 7.7   Configurable Settings in the Settings Node

Settings	What Can Be Configured
Cloud Services Virtual Machine Cost Settings	Define and set up the virtual machine cost settings for memory, storage, CPU costs per unit, miscellaneous costs, and any notes on costs for charging VMs for chargeback. For more information on chargeback, see Chapter 12, "Automation and Chargeback."
Activity Settings	You can set the prefixes for activities, manual activities, parallel activities, sequential activities, dependent activities, and runbook automation activities.
Change Request Settings	The prefix for change records, the number of files, and the size of files that can be attached to a change request.

Settings	What Can Be Configured
Cloud Services Settings	The prefixes for Tenant IDs and Cloud Resources Subscription IDs. Configure the Tenant Administrator user role, Cloud Resources Subscription user role, and setting the tenant reviewers and implementers for cloud services activities.
Data Retention Settings	Define how long closed work items (incidents, changes, service requests, release records, and problems) remain in the Service Manager database. Once removed, they remain available in the Service Manager data warehouse for reporting. You can also set the history of how long history data stays in the Service Manager database before it is removed. Use caution as these settings may cause performance issues in the Service Manager database if you let the database get too large and do not properly groom older items out to the data warehouse.
Incident Settings	The prefix for incident records, the number of files, and size of files that can be attached to an incident. Parent incident behavior: ▶ Auto resolution of child incidents ▶ Auto activation of child incidents ▶ Status of child incidents when linked to parent Priority calculation of incidents. Resolution time, based on incident priority (do not use if leveraging service level management in Service Manager). Operations Manager web URL. Incoming email, SMTP folder settings, email processing and turning on incoming email processing. Note: If using the Exchange Connector for Service Manager, do not configure these settings.
Knowledge Management Settings	The prefix for knowledge articles.
Problem Settings	The prefix for problem records, the number of files and size of files that can be attached to a problem record as well as the priority calculation for problems.
Release Management Settings	The prefix for release records, the number of files, and the size of files that can be attached to a release record.
Service Request Settings	The prefix for service requests, the number of files, and the size of files that can be attached to a service request.

Workflows

A workflow is a sequence of activities that automate a business process. Workflows can update incidents when various changes occur or create incidents from Operations Manager alerts and Configuration Manager desired configuration management connectors. For example, you can create a workflow to assign an email incident to the messaging team automatically. Workflow activities function by using templates; for the email example, a predefined incident template is applied when the incident category equals email that has predefined the support group to be the messaging team.

You can create multiple workflows for each workflow configuration; these can be enabled or disabled as needed. If a particular rule is disabled, the remaining rules still cause the workflow to run. To disable a workflow completely you must disable all the rules that call the workflow.

Figure 7.5 shows the Workflows Configuration node where you can create workflows by area.

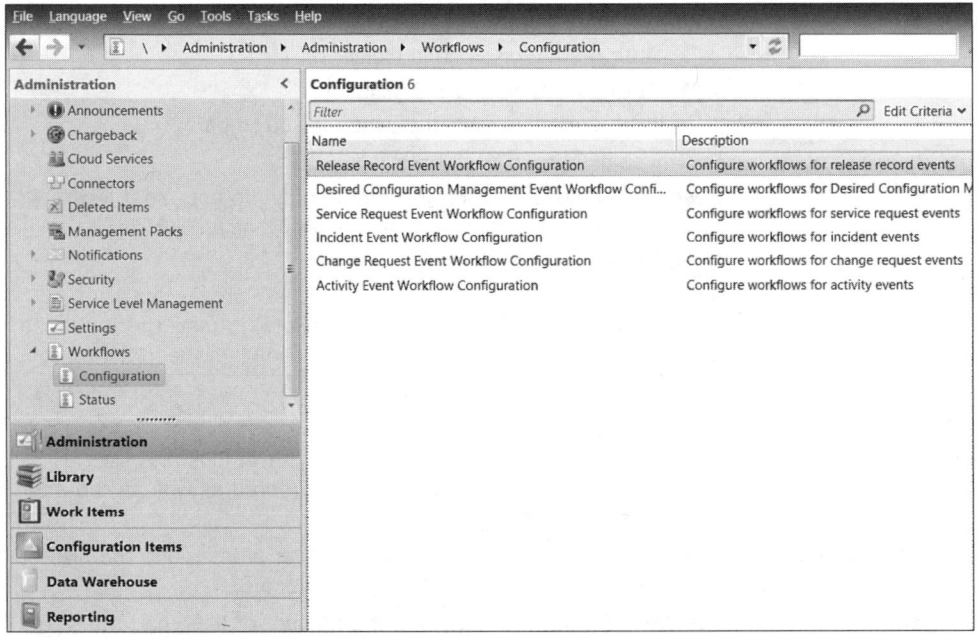

FIGURE 7.5   Workflows Configuration node.

Managing and monitoring workflows is performed in the Status area. Service Manager retains the success or failure of a workflow, and you can view the status of the workflows in the Status view. The Status view has two views available:

▶ **All Results:** This shows a view of all success and failure instances.

▶ **Errors:** This view displays only those instances when a workflow failed.

In the All Results view, you can view the log and the related object. When you view the log, you can examine the events that occurred when the workflow ran. When you view the related object, you see the form that this workflow acted on. The Errors view is limited to the most recent 250 instances. Figure 7.6 shows the Status view.

For additional information on managing workflows in Service Manager, see Chapter 16.

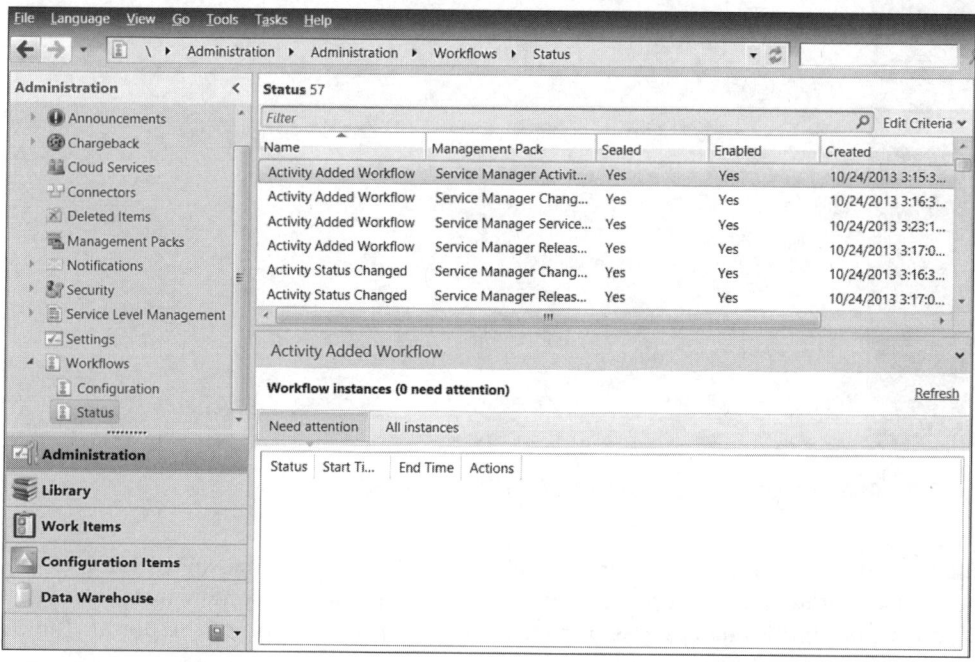

FIGURE 7.6   Status view.

Service Manager Portal Overview

The self-service portal (SSP) in Service Manager 2012 is focused on enabling end user support and self-service. End users can use the Service Manager portal to contact the service desk to create incidents and service requests. Self-service capabilities in the portal allow users to search the knowledge base, perform tasks, and view and manage their previously logged requests.

The portal is built on SharePoint and uses Silverlight for the presentation layer.

Figure 7.7 shows the out of box portal. The portal consists of three areas: the header, the left menu, and the main display area.

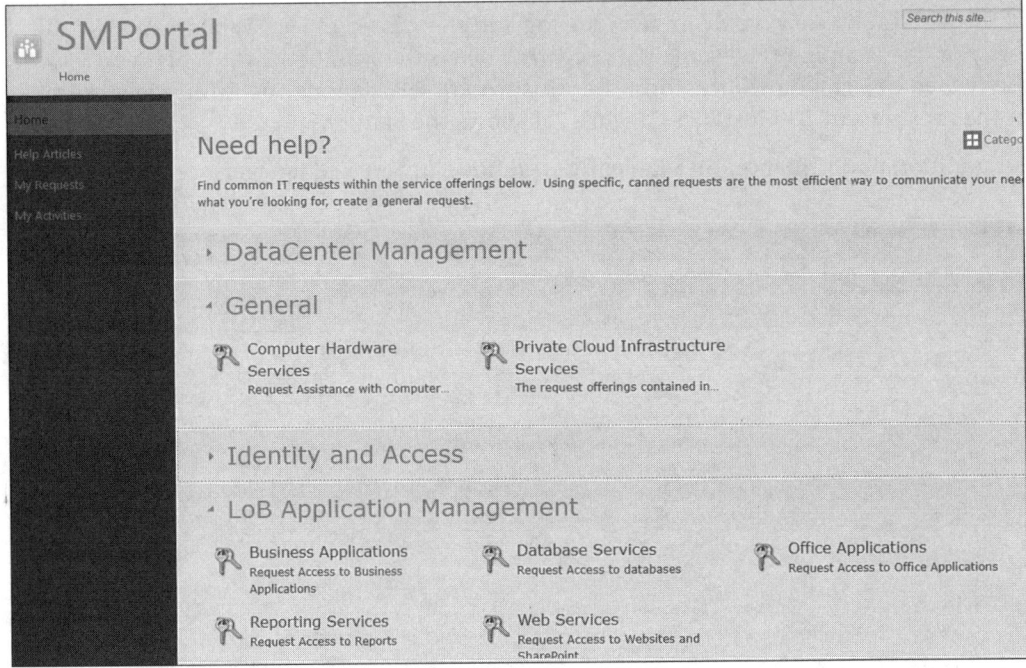

FIGURE 7.7   The Service Manager 2012 self-service portal.

The main header column uses standard SharePoint configuration. The Navigation bar on the left (see Figure 7.8) also uses SharePoint navigation controls so new items can be added to the portal; this enables ease of page changes and navigation of the portal. Table 7.8 describes the areas of the portal.

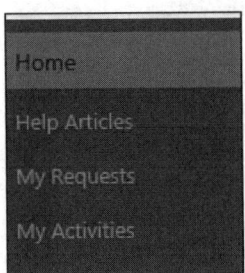

FIGURE 7.8   Navigation bar in the self-service portal.

TABLE 7.8   Portal Navigation

Area	Behavior
Home	This link takes you to the main Service Manager page.
Help Articles	This link takes you to the page where you can search all the knowledge articles.
My Requests	This link takes the logged in user to all her requests, whether open or closed. This is the history of all the requests made.
My Activities	This link takes the logged in user to all her activities, covering both manual and review activities.

Portal Main Page

The Service Manager main page (see Figure 7.9) is where the user is presented with categories that contain service offerings. These are request offerings and incident templates
grouped together to make them easy to differentiate and navigate the available options.

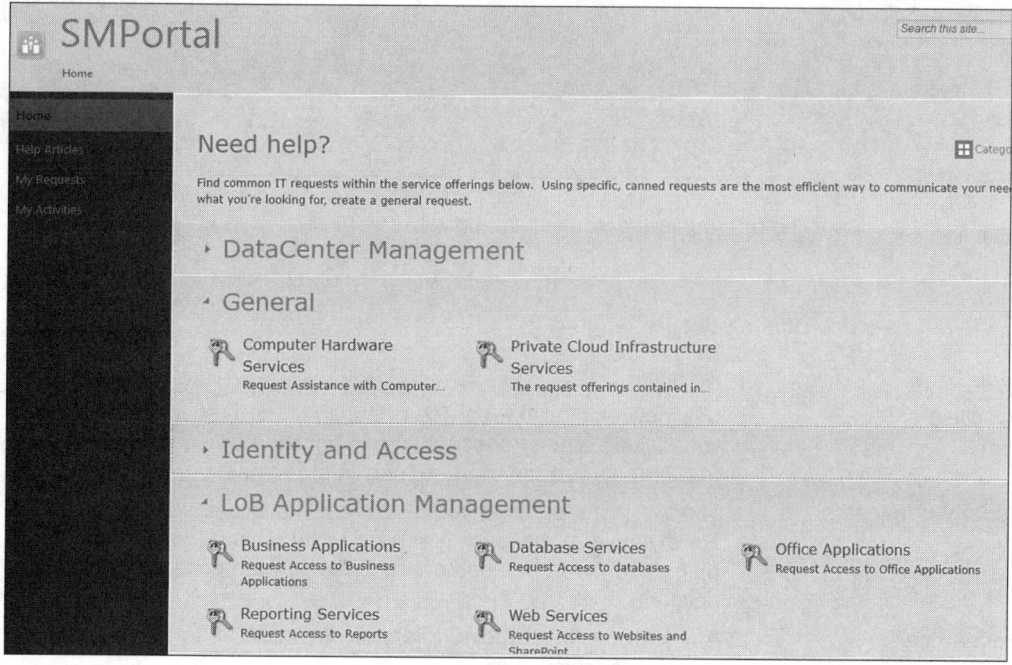

FIGURE 7.9   Main page of the self-service portal.

Service Offerings

Clicking a service offering provides the details of the service (see Figure 7.10), including the areas listed in Table 7.9.

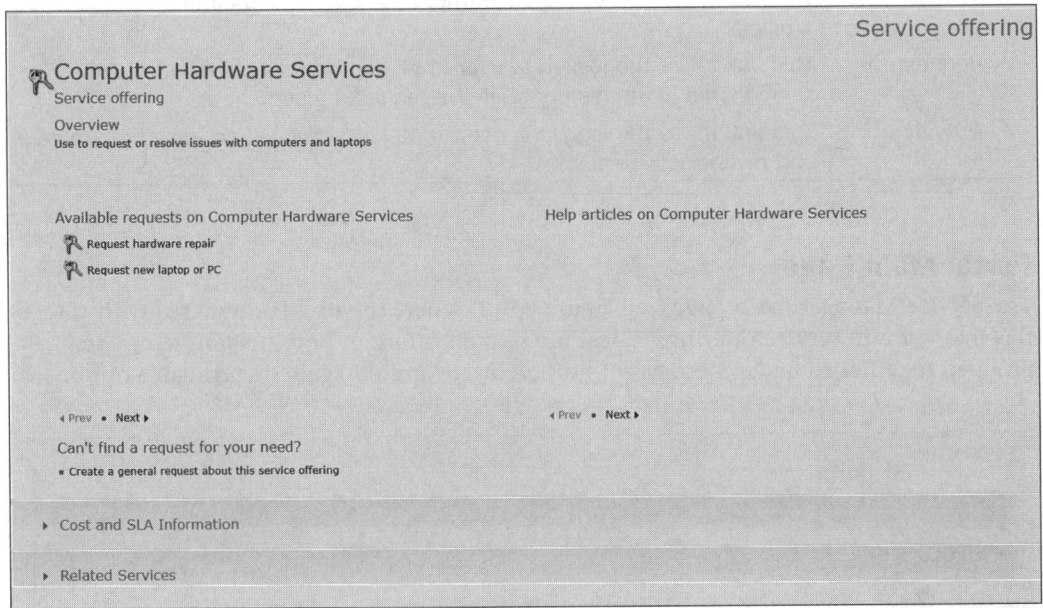

FIGURE 7.10   A service offering in the self-service portal.

TABLE 7.9   Service Offering Details

Area	Behavior
Overview	Overview of what the service offering is. The authors recommend you include a good description of what the service is, how it benefits the organization, and support information.
Available Requests	The available requests you could have for this service offering. For example, a messaging service could have offerings around distribution groups, additional storage, create account, or delete account.
Help Articles	Any relevant help articles related to this service to enable end user self-service.
Cost and SLA Information	What the cost of the service is, and what are the SLA terms for this service.
Related Services	Show the related services for this service offering. For example, a messaging service could have Lync and Exchange listed here.

Request Offerings

Request offerings are tied to Service Manager service offerings on the portal; this provides easy navigation for end users and enables end users to submit their own requests on the portal. For additional information on how to configure and use request offerings, see Chapter 12.

Knowledge Articles

Knowledge articles (displayed as Help Articles) can be leveraged in the portal to enable self-service for end users. You can search for knowledge articles by using the Search function (see Figure 7.11). The search criteria are based on keywords entered when creating the help articles, so make sure that you tag knowledge articles appropriately so end users can find them.

FIGURE 7.11   Search for knowledge article using Help Articles on the portal.

Once a knowledge article is found, the end user can click on the item's hyperlink. Service Manager stores all knowledge articles in Rich Text Format (RTF). You are prompted to open a file to view the knowledge article. Knowledge articles automatically open in Microsoft Word; you can print or search the article in Word.

My Requests

The My Requests section (see Figure 7.12) on the portal displays all the incidents and service requests created by the logged in user. It also displays incidents and service requests logged via the console. The section is broken down into two parts, a navigation part on the left side and a details section on the right. In the navigation section, the user can choose to display the requests by Type or Status. When an item is clicked in the left section, the details of that request are shown on the right. Table 7.10 lists the different areas of the details section and a description.

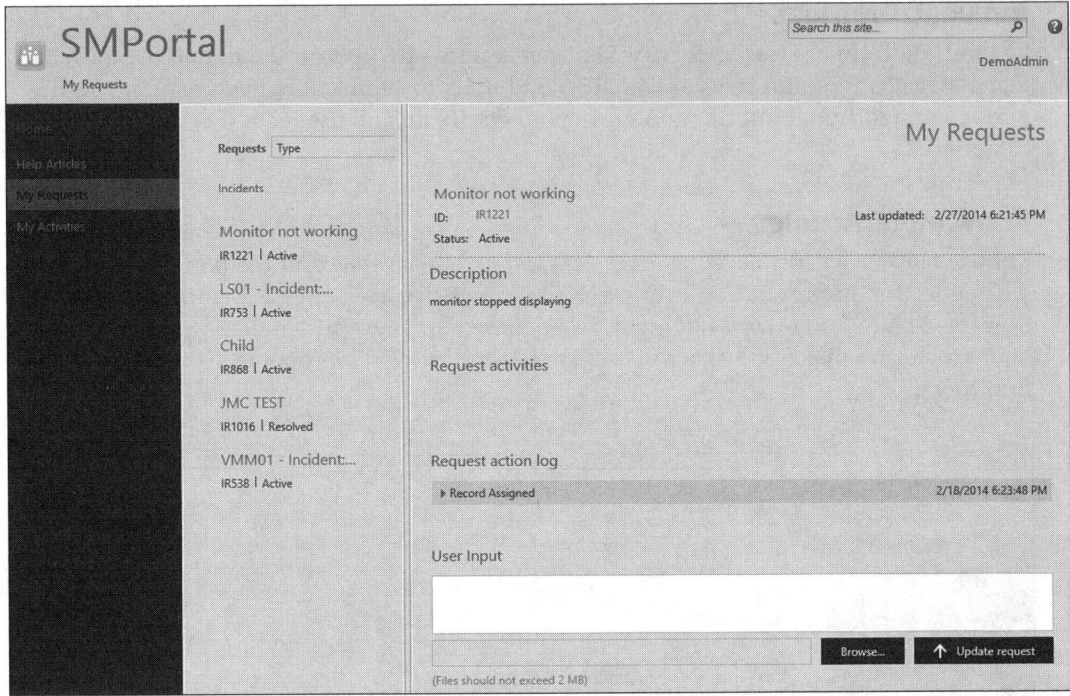

FIGURE 7.12   The My Requests section in the self-service portal.

TABLE 7.10   Areas of the Details Section

Details Section	Description
Title	This is the short title of the incident of service request.
ID	The actual incident or service request number.
Status	Displays the current status of the work item.
Last Updated	Shows the last time the work item was modified.
Description	Displays the actual description from the created work item.
Request Activities	If this work item has manual activities or review activities they are listed here.
Request Action Log	Displays the history for the work item and what was performed.
User Input	You can enter in comments in the text box or upload files to be attached to the work item.

My Activities

The My Activities section (see Figure 7.13) on the portal displays all the activities that need to be actioned by the logged in user. Activities include manual activities that need to be completed that are part of an incident, service requests, and changes that need to be actioned by the assigned IT analyst. Any approval (review) activities also appear here, and these approval activities can be actioned/approved in the portal. Figure 7.13 provides an overview of My Activities.

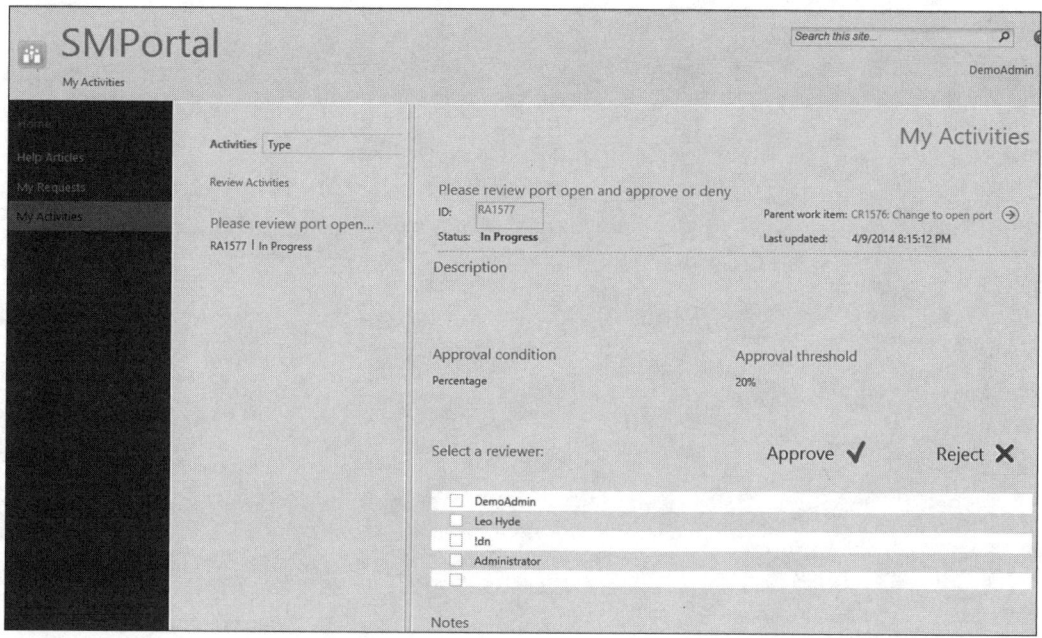

FIGURE 7.13   My Activities as displayed on the portal.

Fast Track

The largest investment in Service Manager 2012 was the creation of a new portal based on SharePoint 2010 and Silverlight. The new improved portal enables better self-service by enabling end users to create service requests, create incidents, search for knowledge, and view all requests that they have created in a single view on the portal.

Summary

This chapter provided an overview of the Service Manager console, the functionalities that can be performed from the console, and the role types necessary to use the Service Manager console. Additional information was provided about the new portal and the features that enable self-service for end users in your organization as well as sharing the capability to action approvals and view activities assigned to IT analysts. The following chapters provide you with a deeper understanding of how to manage and maintain Service Manager 2012.

Working with Connectors

System Center 2012 Service Manager is the integration component of System Center. The functionality enabling this integration is the Service Manager *connector framework*; this is the mechanism that provides connections to data sources, including but not limited to most System Center components and Microsoft Active Directory domains. This capability to connect and consume data in Service Manager differentiates and highlights a core value of this System Center component from its competitors.

Chapter 4, "Looking Inside System Center 2012 Service Manager," discusses the internal architecture of Service Manager and provides a brief introduction to the connectors used to populate its configuration management database (CMDB). The CMDB implementation in Service Manager is dynamic in nature through its capability to consume data on a schedule from the original data source. This approach is dependent on the connectors you configure and maintain for Service Manager.

This chapter discusses the connector framework, the two categories of connectors (configuration item and work item connectors), and how to create and manage the connectors created for your Service Manager deployment.

Understanding the Connector Framework

A Service Manager 2012 installation provides a platform for building your information technology service management (ITSM) processes. After installation, Service Manager is a blank slate that must be customized to meet the needs of your organization; this occurs through personalizing it to suit your requirements and needs. Service Manager at its core consists of configuration items and work items and the relationships between these items. These two categories work together (through relationships) to deliver ITSM aligned to the Information Technology Infrastructure Library (ITIL) and Microsoft Operations Framework (MOF). Two methods are supported and available for creating and managing both categories of items: manual and automatic. A third available option could be described as hybrid; this combines elements of the manual and automatic methods:

▶ **Manual:** Use the Service Manager console or PowerShell to create configuration items such as new users and computers. You also create process work items such as incidents and service requests.

▶ **Automatic:** Configure one of the following supported connectors to create work and configuration items automatically.

  ▶ Active Directory connector

  ▶ Configuration Manager connector

  ▶ Operations Manager CI connector

  ▶ Operations Manager Alert connector

  ▶ Orchestrator connector

  ▶ Virtual Manager Machine connector

▶ **Hybrid:** Microsoft provides two optional work item connectors, the CSV connector and the Exchange connector. These connectors require manual steps to set up and maintain.

These three methods write and store data in the Service Manager CMDB. Figure 8.1 illustrates a logical view of Service Manager and its connectors.

The connectors do not directly access the Service Manager database. Two approaches are used to insert data into the database: a direct connection via the software development kit (SDK), and an indirect connection using the connector framework and the SDK. These two methods depend on the connector type. Table 8.1 lists the connectors and the methods used to populate the Service Manager CMDB.

Connectors are intermediaries between the source system you are extracting information from and the model-based Service Manager database. The Service Manager database model uses terminology rooted in objected-oriented programming languages. All data is written into the database using the SDK, which understands the Service Manager model-based database and knows how to insert or extract information from the database.

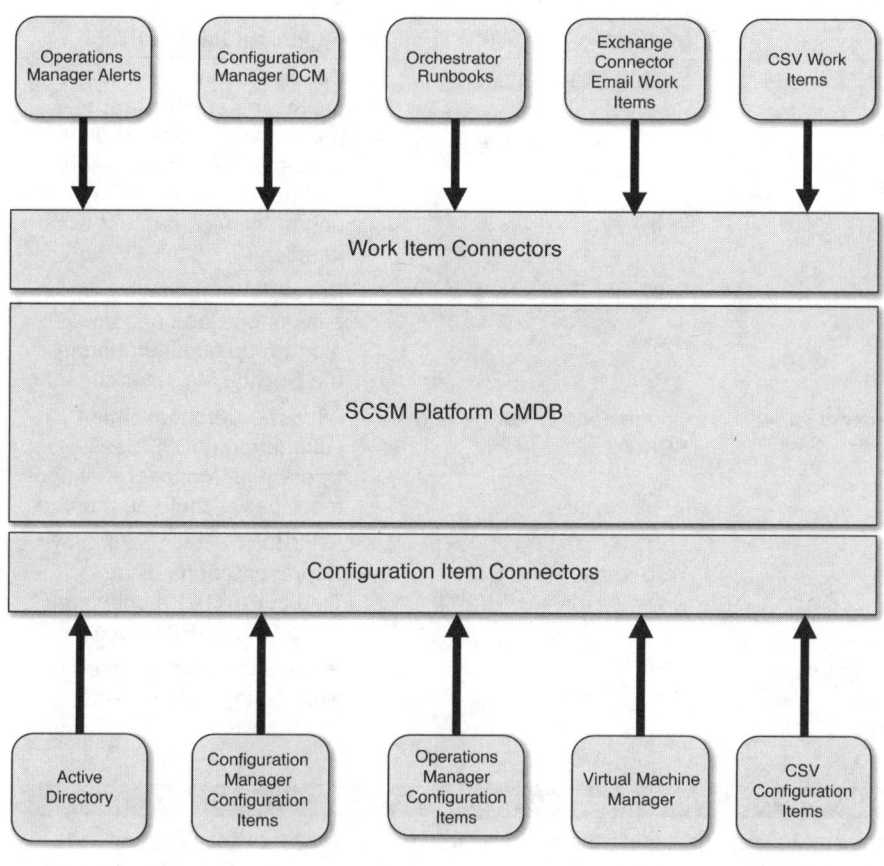

FIGURE 8.1   Logical view of connectors.

TABLE 8.1   Service Manager Connector Channels for Populating the Service Manager CMDB

Connector	Method	Additional Information
Active Directory	Connector framework and SDK	Lightweight Directory Protocol (LDAP) queries.
Configuration Manager	Connector framework and SDK	ADO.NET SQL queries for defined list of attributes.
CSV	SDK	Write to defined tables in the database. Uses eXtended Markup Language (XML) definition file and CSV data file.
DCM (Settings Management)	See Configuration Manager connector	Requires additional console configuration, and depends on the Configuration Manager connector.

Connector	Method	Additional Information
Exchange	Simple Mail Transport Protocol (SMTP)	Optional connector that processes emails sent to the Workflow user account mailbox. The emails create and update incidents or update service request work items.
Operations Manager Alert	SDK	Depends on management pack import and additional alert group configuration in the Service Manager console.
Operations Manager CI	Connector framework and SDK	Windows Communication Foundation (WCF). Uses Operations Manager management packs that you must import into Service Manager.
Orchestrator	Web service and SDK	Representational State Transfer (REST) architecture using the HTTP protocol.
Virtual Machine Manager	SDK	PowerShell cmdlets used to write configuration items.

TIP: DEMYSTIFYING THE MODEL-BASED DATABASE

Experts in Service Manager (including the authors) use terminology that may appear unusual if you are familiar with relational databases. Fundamentally the principles are the same; you have tables, views, and all the database objects provided by Microsoft SQL Server. The difference is that the Service Manager database is a representation of a class model. These classes are created as tables with columns that represent properties of the class. Instances of a class are written as values in the tables. For example, a computer is a type of the `configuration item` class, and instances of a computer are written into a specific class table in the database. The blog post at http://blogs.technet.com/b/service-manager/archive/2009/01/27/the-system-center-platform-in-service-manager-part-2-the-model-based-database.aspx introduces Service Manager's model-based database.

The next three sections in this chapter, "Configuration Item Connectors," "Work Item Connectors," and "Hybrid Service Manager Connectors," discuss the three categories of connectors.

Configuration Item Connectors

Configuration item (CI) connectors import a filtered set of objects and their properties from the source system into the Service Manager CMDB (target system). Service Manager includes CI connector wizards for the following CI connectors:

- ▶ Active Directory connector
- ▶ Configuration Manager connector
- ▶ Operations Manager CI connector
- ▶ Orchestrator connector
- ▶ Virtual Machine Manager connector

The Orchestrator connector is not strictly a CI connector as it provides process library objects (runbooks).

The connector wizards are found in the Administration node of the Service Manager console. Figure 8.2 illustrates those wizards available by default after successfully installing Service Manager 2012.

FIGURE 8.2   Service Manager connectors available by default.

Active Directory Connector

The Active Directory connector uses the Service Manager Linking Framework process to retrieve information from Active Directory.

The connector uses LDAP to retrieve a set of attributes for computers, groups, printers, and users in the domain specified for the connector. Table 8.2 lists the attributes retrieved by the Active Directory connector for a user once it is configured. The full list of attributes is available at http://technet.microsoft.com/en-us/library/gg232586.aspx.

TABLE 8.2   Connector Active Directory User Attributes

Active Directory User Attribute	Service Manager: Microsoft.AD.User Property
physicaldeliveryofficename	Office
displayname	displayname
company	Company
employeeid	Employeeid
department	Department
telephonenumber	BusinessPhone
homePhone	HomePhone
facsimileTelephoneNumber	Fax
mobile	Mobile
pager	Pager
mail	Email
givenname	FirstName
initials	Initials
sn	LastName
distinguishedname	Distinguishedname
title	Title
manager	manager
samaccountname	UserName
l	City
StreetAddress	StreetAddress
st	State
postalCode	Zip
co	Country
localeID	Locale
msRTCSIP-PrimaryUserAddress	SipAddress
objectSid	SID
Domain	Domain

The Active Directory connector retrieves information; it does not update any information at the source. This is the case even if a Service Manager administrator modifies a field in the console.

The connector process works as follows:

1. The Active Directory connector settings are read from the Service Manager database using the built-in SDK client.

2. The information retrieved from the Service Manager database specifies the LDAP query to be executed to retrieve the information from Active Directory (data provider). The Active Directory data is passed to the Linking Framework (LFx) module.

3. The LFx module writes the data into staging tables in the Service Manager database.

4. The LFx module writes the data in the staging tables into the configuration items tables using the SDK client (data consumer). The SDK client is responsible for transforming the retrieved information from Active Directory into the Service Manager class-based model.

Figure 8.3 represents the process Service Manager uses with the Active Directory connector.

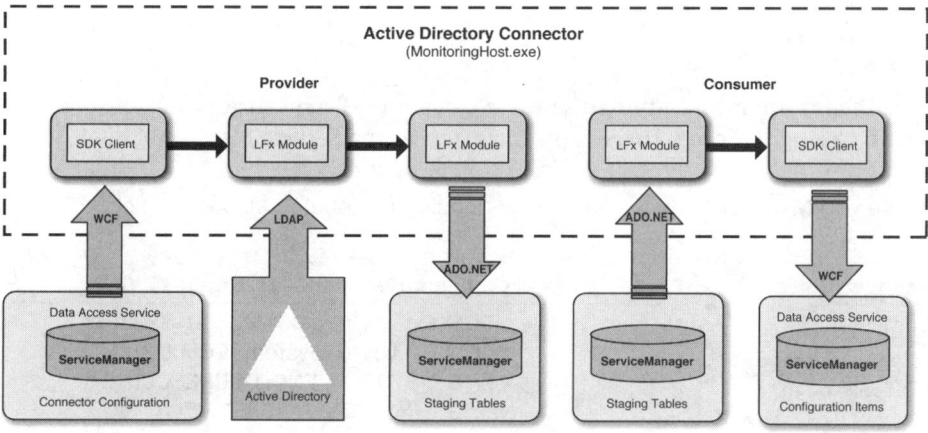

FIGURE 8.3   Active Directory connector structure.

Configuration Manager Connector

The Configuration Manager connector imports information from System Center Configuration Manager versions 2007 SP 1/R2 and 2012 RTM/SP 1/R2 into Service Manager. The Service Manager Linking Framework process is used to retrieve information from the Configuration Manager site database. The Linking Framework acts as an intermediary, transforming the data retrieved from Configuration Manager into the appropriate class model representation in the CMDB. The information available by default through the connector once the Configuration Manager connector is configured is in the following categories:

▶ Physical computer information (deployed computer)

▶ Logical computer (computer class)

▶ Operating system

▶ Logical disk

▶ Physical disk

▶ Processor

▶ Network adapter

▶ Desired Configuration Management (DCM) configuration item

▶ Noncompliance DCM configuration items

▶ Configuration Manager user information

▶ Collection information

▶ Installed software information

▶ Installed software updates information

▶ Software package

Table 8.3 lists the information imported in these categories. Each category relates to a specific view in Configuration Manager and is written to the Service Manager CMDB.

TABLE 8.3   Service Manager Connector-Retrieved Computer Attributes Mapped in Service Manager

Service Manager Class	Configuration Manager Database Views

Physical Computer:
`Microsoft.SystemCenter.`
`ConfigurationManager.`
`DeployedComputerSystem.Entity`
	SCCM.Ext.vex_GS_COMPUTER_SYSTEM SCCM.Ext.vex_R_SystemSCCM.Ext. vex_GS_SYSTEM_ENCLOSURESCCM.Ext. vex_GS_PC_BIOS

Logical Computer:
`Microsoft.Windows.ComputerSystem.`
`Entity`
	SCCM.Ext.vex_GS_COMPUTER_SYSTEM SCCM.Ext.vex_R_SystemSCCM.Ext. Vex_GS_Workstation_Status

Operating System:
`Microsoft.Windows.`
`OperatingSystemSystem.Entity`
	SCCM.Ext.vex_GS_OPERATING_SYSTEMSCCM. Ext.vex_GS_COMPUTER_SYSTEM

Logical Disk:
`Microsoft.Windows.Peripherals.`
`LogicalDiskSystem.EntityMicrosoft.`
`Windows.LogicalDeviceMicrosoft.`
`Windows.LogicalDisk`
	SCCM.Ext.vex_GS_LOGICAL_DISK

Physical Disk:
`Microsoft.Windows.Peripherals.`
`PhysicalDisk`
	SCCM.Ext.vex.GS_DISK

Service Manager Class	Configuration Manager Database Views

Processor:
 	
`System.EntityMicrosoft.Windows.`
`LogicalDeviceMicrosoft.Windows.`
`ProcessorMicrosoft.Windows.`
`Peripherals.Processor`
	SCCM.Ext.vex.GS_PROCESSOR

Network Adapter:
 	
`System.EntityMicrosoft.Windows.`
`LogicalDeviceMicrosoft.Windows.`
`NetworkAdapterMicrosoft.Windows.`
`Peripherals.NetworkAdapter`
	SCCM.Ext.vex_GS_NETWORK_ADAPTERSCCM.
	Ext.vex.GS_NETWORK_ADAPTER_CONFIGUR

Desired Configuration Management Item:
 	
`Microsoft.SystemCenter.`
`ConfigurationManager.DCM_CI`
	SCCM.Ext.vex_LocalizedCIPropertiesSCCM.
	Ext.vex_ConfigurationItems

DCM Non-Compliance Items:
 	
`Microsoft.SystemCenter.`
`ConfigurationManager.`
`DCM_NoncompliantCI`
	SCCM.Ext.vex_ConfigurationItemsSCCM.Ext.
	vex_CICurrentComplianceStatus

Configuration Manager User Information: `System.Domain.User`	SCCM_Ext.vex_GS_SYSTEM_CONSOLE_USER

Collection Information:
 	
`System.ConfigItemMicrosoft.`
`SystemCenter.ConfigurationManagergr.`
`CollectionInf`
	SCCM_Ext.vex_Collection

Installed Software Information:
 	
`System.EntitySystem.`
`SoftwareItemSystem.`
`DeviceHasSoftwareItemInstalled`
	SCCM.Ext.vex_GS_INSTALLED_SOFTWARE

Installed Software Update Information:
 	
`System.SoftwareUpdateMicrosoft.`
`Windows.SoftwareUpdate`
	SCCM.Ext.vex_
	LocalizedCategoryInstancesSCCM.
	Ext.vex_LocalizedCIPropertiesSCCM.
	Ext.vex_UpdateCIsSCCM.Ext.
	vex_UpdateComplianceStatus

Software Package:
`System.ConfigItemMicrosoft.`
`ConfigMgr.SoftwarePackage`
	SCCM_Ext.vex_Package

The specific columns of the Configuration Manager views and extended details of Table 8.3 are included in Appendix C of the Administering System Center 2012 - Service Manager documentation and are available at http://technet.microsoft.com/en-us/library/hh519741.aspx.

The connector process works as follows, and is illustrated in Figure 8.4:

1. The Configuration Manager connector settings are read from the Service Manager database using the built-in SDK client.

2. The information retrieved from the Service Manager database specifies the SQL queries using ADO.NET, which must be executed to retrieve the information from the Configuration Manager relational database (data provider). The imported data is passed to the LFx module.

3. The LFx module writes the data into staging tables in the Service Manager database.

4. The LFx module writes the data in the staging tables into the configuration items tables using the SDK client (data consumer). The SDK client is responsible for transforming the retrieved information from the Configuration Manager relational database into the Service Manager class-based model.

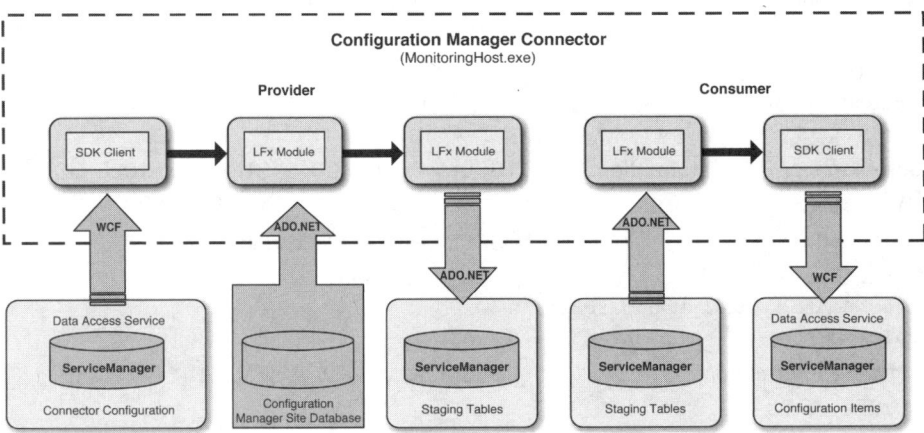

FIGURE 8.4   Configuration Manager connector structure.

Operations Manager CI Connector

The Operations Manager CI connector enables importing data from Operations Manager into the Service Manager database. The CIs imported depend on what the Operations Manager agents discover, which is dependent on the Operations Manager management packs that are imported and tuned.

The Operations Manager CI connector architecture is simpler than those connectors that rely on the Linking Framework. This is due to the common platform shared by Operation Manager and Service Manager. Both System Center components use a class-based model and share the same management pack structure. The intermediary between the two components is the Service Manager SDK. Figure 8.5 illustrates the architecture of the Operations Manager CI connector.

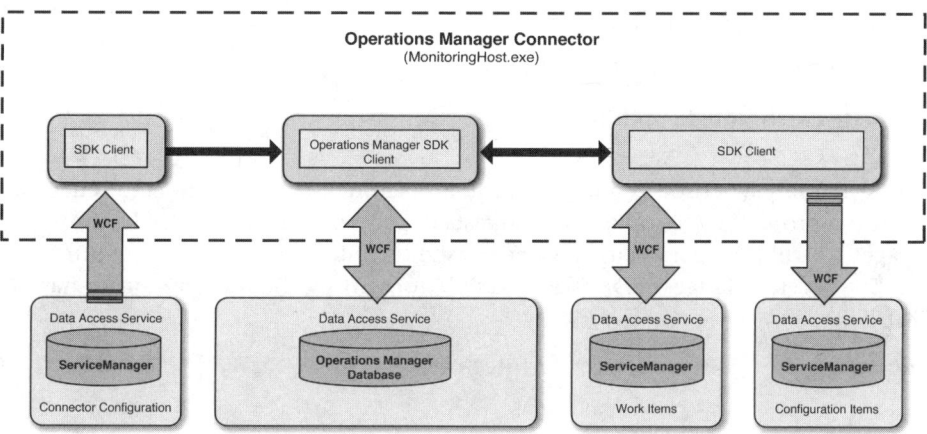

FIGURE 8.5   Operations Manager connector structure.

Virtual Machine Manager Connector

The Virtual Machine Manager connector imports data from System Center Virtual Machine Manager (VMM) into the Service Manager CMDB. The information imported by this connector follows:

- ▶ Service templates

- ▶ Virtual machine (VM) templates

- ▶ Storage classifications

- ▶ Logical networks

- ▶ Load balancers

- ▶ Load balancer VIP templates

The imported information (VMM configuration items) from the VMM database is visible in the VMM library node of the VMM console. Other CIs available from the VMM database are imported into Service Manager by the Operations Manager CI connector (this requires Operations Manager to monitor VMM, with the integration configured in VMM). The VMM connector is required because the Operations Manager CI connector depends on the Operations Manager agent discovery process. The VMM CI discovery performed by the Operations Manager agent does not include information from the VMM library node. This information is valuable should you plan to drive cloud-based service requests using Service Manager. These cloud-based service requests may fall into one or more of these types:

- ▶ Request for new virtual machines
- ▶ Additional storage requirements
- ▶ Provision of a distributed application

The library information synchronized by the Virtual Machine Manager connector enables you to present the properties these types of requests depend on, using a query to the Service Manager CMDB. The connector uses PowerShell cmdlets to retrieve the required information. The Service Manager SDK is responsible for writing the imported information into the CMDB.

Figure 8.6 illustrates the VMM connector architecture.

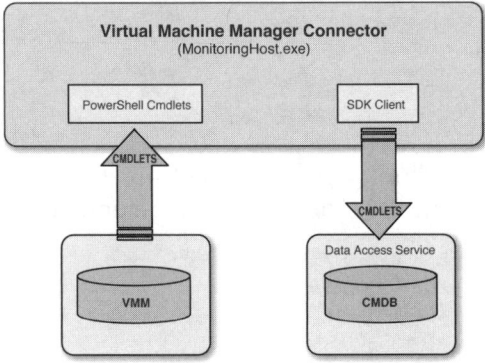

FIGURE 8.6   VMM connector architecture.

Orchestrator Connector

The Orchestrator connector enhances and expands the scope of Service Manager's process automation capabilities, which are commonly referred to as *workflows*. Orchestrator is the data center process automation component of the System Center product. Orchestrator's flexible workflow architecture enables it to integrate with other System Center components and third-party vendors. This integration leverages Orchestrator workflows, known as *runbooks*. For additional information on Orchestrator, see *System Center 2012 Orchestrator Unleashed* (Sams, 2013).

The Orchestrator connector synchronizes the runbooks selected when the connector is created. These runbooks are made available to Service Manager for use as runbook activity templates. These templates, when configured and used for activities such as service requests, allow Service Manager to execute automation tasks using Orchestrator runbooks. The connector uses the Orchestrator web service to import the runbooks into Service Manager. The connector is also responsible for triggering the runbook actions in

Orchestrator based on the runbook activity status in Service Manager. Figure 8.7 shows the Service Manager Orchestrator connector.

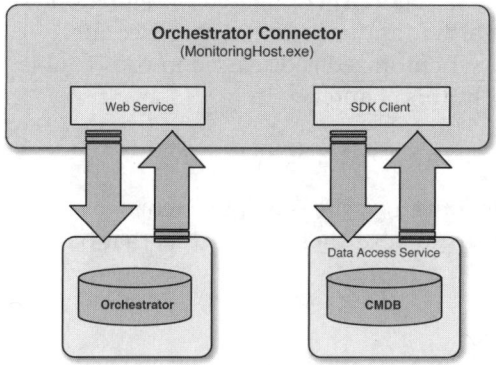

FIGURE 8.7   Orchestrator connector structure.

Work Item Connectors

This section discusses the second type of Service Manager connector, work item connectors. Service Manager has three types of work item connectors:

▶ Operations Manager Alert connector

▶ Desired Configuration Manager event workflow

▶ Hybrid connectors (CSV and Exchange connectors)

Operations Manager Alert Connector

This connector provides the ability to create incidents based on alerts raised in Operations Manager. This is the only native bidirectional connector in Service Manager. You can configure Service Manager to automatically close alerts in Operations Manager when the incident is closed or resolved in Service Manager. Conversely, the incident can be resolved in Service Manager when the alert is closed in Operations Manager. These bidirectional options are available when you create the connector.

Desired Configuration Manager Event Workflow

This is not officially classified as a Service Manager connector. The workflow is actually a subcomponent of the Configuration Manager connector and has two dependencies:

▶ Configuration Manager connector

▶ Desired Configuration Management/Settings Management

8

You must apply a Desired Configuration Management/Settings Management baseline to a collection in the Configuration Manager site. The devices in the collection report either a compliant or noncompliant state. The connector allows you to configure workflows that create incidents based on noncompliant states. You must configure Configuration Manager to synchronize this information through the Configuration Manager connector. The connector architecture and type of data synchronized is discussed in the "Configuration Item Connectors" section earlier in this chapter.

Hybrid Service Manager Connectors

This section discusses the two Microsoft hybrid connectors: the CSV and Exchange connectors. Note the term *hybrid* is used as a means to label these connectors that have manual and automation settings.

CSV Connector

The CSV connector allows you to bulk import instances of any Service Manager class or type projection into the CMDB. It can also be used to perform bulk updates of existing properties of classes. The CSV connector requires a format file and a data file.

▶ The format file must be an XML file with an .XML extension. It defines the classes or type projections properties these values represent.

▶ The data file must be a comma-separated value (CSV) file with a .CSV file extension. It contains the values to write to the Service Manager database.

The CSV connector is a special connector as it is multipurpose; it can be used to manually import configuration items and work items. If you know the class or type projection properties you need to import data to or to update, you can use the CSV connector.

Exchange Connector

The Exchange connector replaces the existing incoming email processing feature of Service Manager, which is now considered legacy as you must enable the Simple Mail Transfer Protocol (SMTP) Internet Information Services (IIS) feature on a Windows server. This process is cumbersome and is restricted to the `Incident` class. For information about the incoming mail processing feature, see http://technet.microsoft.com/en-us/library/hh519602.aspx and Chapter 11, "Incident Management."

Many organizations used the Exchange connector prior to its official release by Microsoft, as they wanted the ability to create and update work items using email. The Exchange connector is now fully supported and is the recommended option for processing emails. The Exchange connector provides the following features and capabilities using email:

▶ Creates incidents and service requests

▶ Updates incidents, problems, and the service-request action log

▶ Resolves or closes incidents

► Approves or rejects change requests

► Marks a manual activity as completed

► Adds an email file to a work item as an attachment

Creating and Working with Configuration Item Connectors

The "Understanding the Connector Framework" section earlier in the chapter discussed and provided background for importing data into the Service Manager CMDB. The next sections discuss how to configure and use these connectors.

Creating an Active Directory Connector

The steps to create an Active Directory connector follow:

1. Create or use an Active Directory user account with Read permissions to the domain you want to synchronize with the Service Manager database.

The authors recommend a dedicated Active Directory user account for each Active Directory connector you are creating. The account should be a member of only the Domain Users group.

NOTE: ABOUT CONNECTOR RUN AS ACCOUNTS

Service Manager connectors communicate with their target systems using an Active Directory user account. The specified account becomes the Run As account for the connector. This applies to all connectors discussed in this section. Refer to Chapter 17, "Service Manager Security," for additional information on Run As accounts.

---

2. Determine those objects (users, computers, and printers) you plan to synchronize with Service Manager.

This ensures you import only objects you intend to use in Service Manager. You can target organizational units (OUs) instead of the root of the domain if your Active Directory domain structure is organized to facilitate this type of filtering.

3. Create and enable the connector using the Service Manager console:

► In the Service Manager Console, navigate to **Administration -> Connectors**. Under Tasks, select **Create Connector -> Active Directory connector**, shown in Figure 8.8.

8

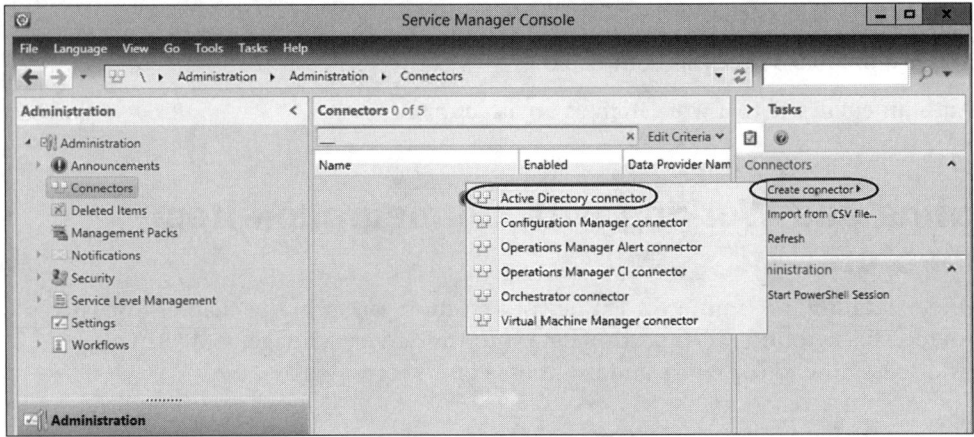

FIGURE 8.8   Initiate the Active Directory connector wizard.

▶ Click **Next** on the Before You Begin page. On the General page, give the connector a Name and optional Description (see Figure 8.9).

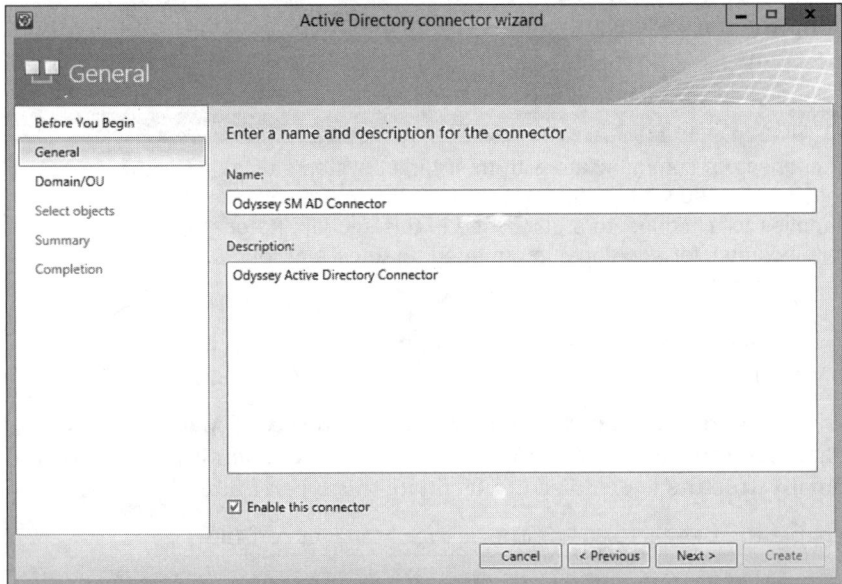

FIGURE 8.9   Enter the AD connector name and description.

▶ On the Domain/OU page, provide the required information for each section:

Server Information: Accept the default selection **Use the domain: <*management server domain*>**, or select **Let me choose the domain or OU**. The second option requires browsing to that domain or OU.

Credentials: Select **New** and enter details for the domain user account.

Test Connection: Select **Test Connection** to validate the credentials. Figure 8.10 illustrates the server information and credentials selected for the Odyssey environment.

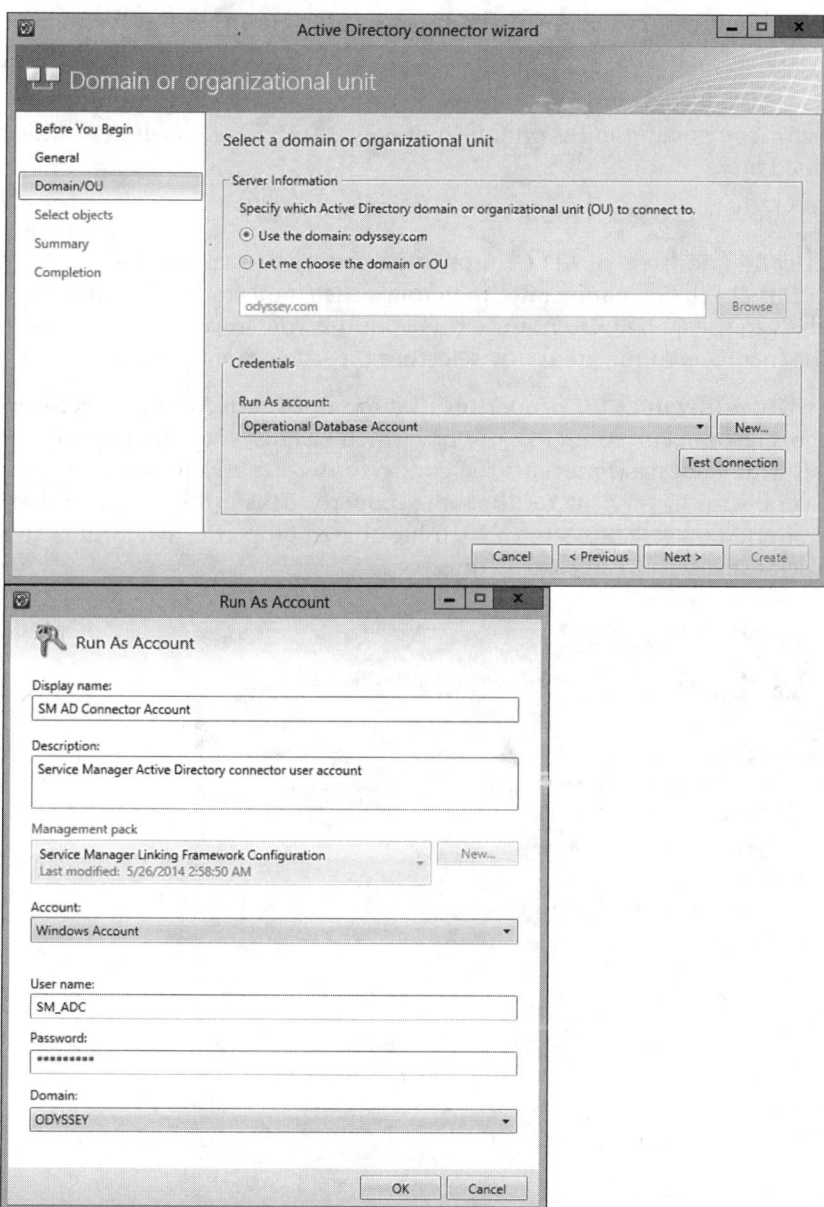

FIGURE 8.10   Target domain and credentials wizard pages.

▶ The Select objects page (see Figure 8.11) includes three configurable options:

All computers, printers, users and user groups: This is the default, which results in importing all listed objects from the target domain or OU selected (including all sub OUs).

Select individual computers, printers, users or user groups: Select the objects in which you are interested.

Provide LDAP query filters for computers, printers, users, or user groups (advanced): You could use this option to provide LDAP filters, such as to filter out disabled users.

▶ This page also has two global options:

Automatically add users of AD Groups imported by this connector: Selecting this check box enumerates the groups the connector finds and adds its members to the CMDB. Do not use this option if you are already synchronizing the members in the group (by selecting the user's domain or OU).

Do not write null values for properties that are not set in Active Directory: The authors recommend using this option, which ensures you only import properties with values and prevents the connector setting a value to null when another connector has a value for the same property. This is the case with the Configuration Manager connector, which has shared properties synchronized with those of the Active Directory connector.

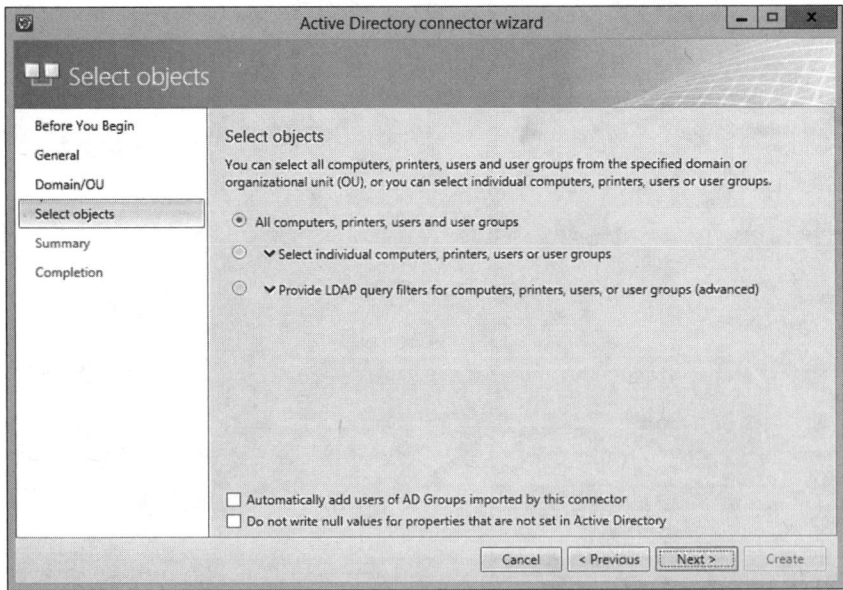

FIGURE 8.11   AD objects selection and additional filters.

▶ On the Summary page shown in Figure 8.12, review the information and click
   Create to initiate the connector creation process.

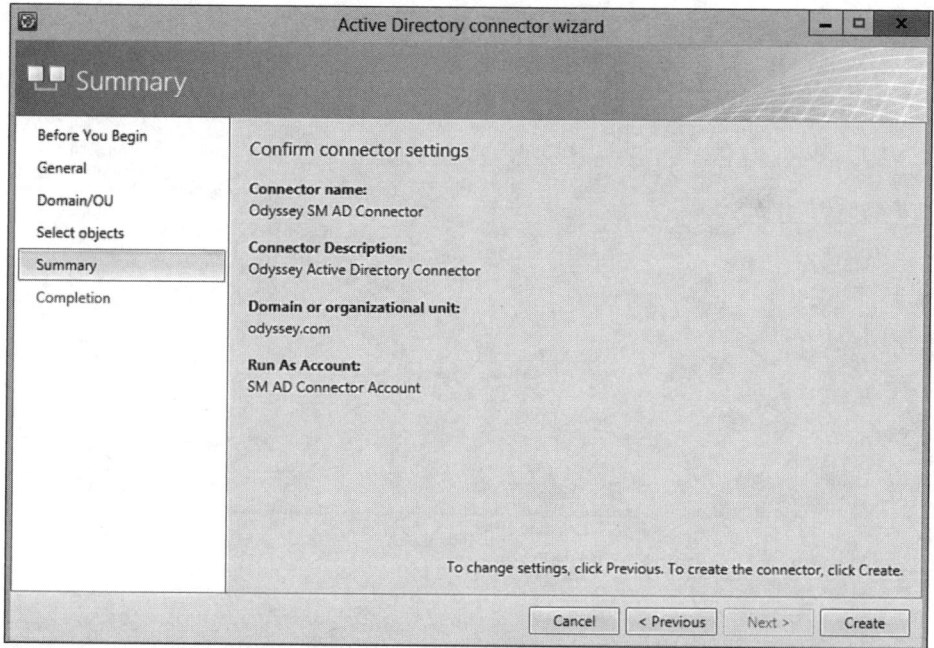

FIGURE 8.12   Active Directory connector summary page.

The Completion page does not mean synchronization is complete. You must monitor the
progress in the Service Manager console and the Service Manager event log (Operations
Manager log). The event ID to look for is 3339. Figure 8.13 shows the Service Manager
console status for the connector synchronization and an event log entry from the
Operations Manager log.

8

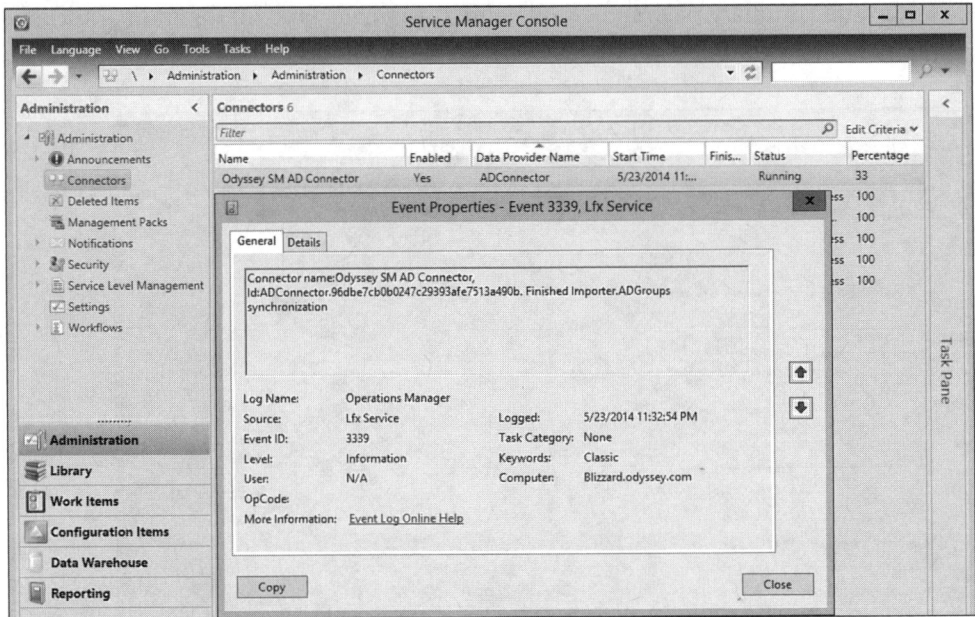

FIGURE 8.13   Monitoring the status of the AD connector.

TIP: FILTERING OUT DISABLED USERS AND COMPUTERS

Filtering options let you optimize the Active Directory connector to import only those objects you intend to use. Disabled user and computer accounts typically add no value. Using an LDAP filter, which is based on a bitwise filter, can prevent importing disabled accounts. The syntax for the bitwise filter is *attributename:ruleOID:=value*, where

▶ attributename is the Active Directory attribute name.

▶ ruleOID is a value that matches the AND and OR logical operators.

The two ruleOID operators are represented as 1.2.840.113556.1.4.803 and 1.2.840.113556.1.4.804, respectively. The value is a decimal conversion of the hexadecimal value in Active Directory. You can build a custom query in Active Directory Users and Computers (ADUC) to test your results. An example is a query that returns all disabled computers and users. The correct syntax using the bitwise rule is (UserAccountControl:1.2.840.113556.1.4.803:=2). Figure 8.14 illustrates creating a query in ADUC to test the results of the syntax.

You must create a new connector to edit these imported object properties for an existing Active Directory connector. Disable the existing connector, create a new one, wait for synchronization to complete, and delete the old connector. Figure 8.15 shows the properties of the filtered connector. Note in Service Manager you must apply the NOT operator to the filter query you use in ADUC. The NOT operator indicates to Service Manager to only import objects that are not disabled (! (UserAccountControl:1.2.840.113556.1.4.803:=2)).

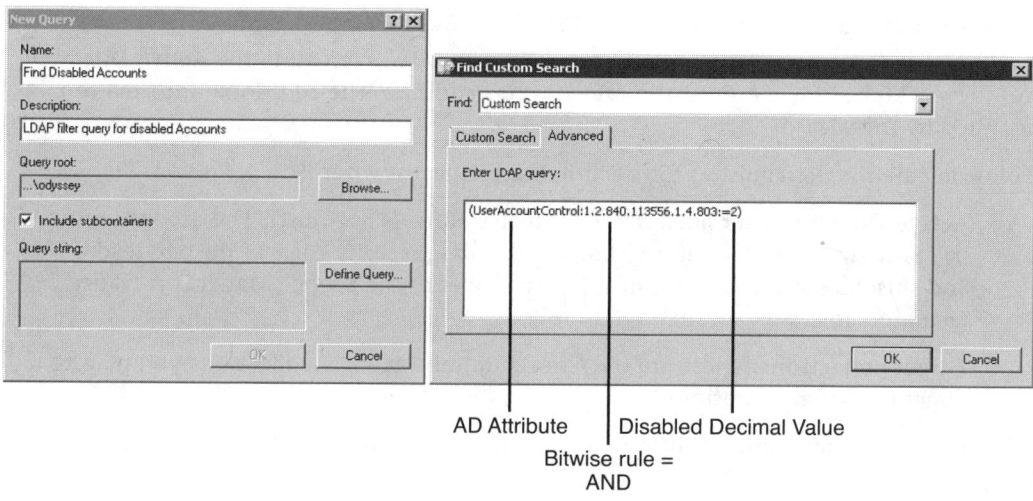

FIGURE 8.14   ADUC Saved query for disabled users and computers.

Find out more about querying Active Directory using a bitwise filter at http://support.
microsoft.com/kb/269181.

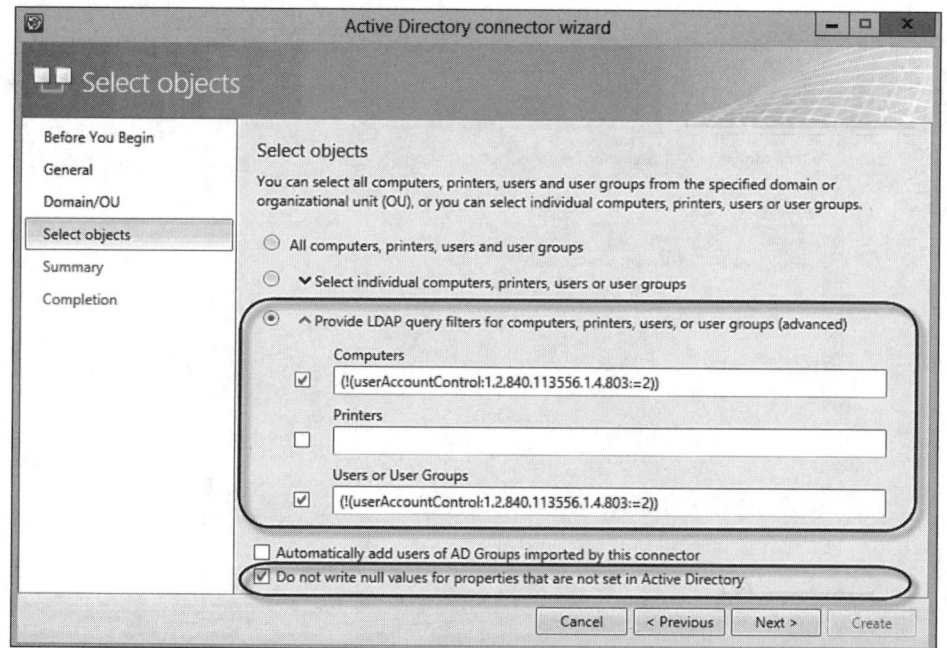

FIGURE 8.15   AD connector LDAP filtered disabled computers and user accounts.

Creating a Configuration Manager Connector

Creating the Configuration Manager connector is similar to creating the Active Directory connector. Make sure you meet the prerequisites and have the additional information required by the wizard.

Following are the prerequisites for starting the connector wizard:

▶ **Active Directory user account (Connector Run As account):** The account must be granted the Configuration Manager database security roles of db_datareader and smsdbrole_extract, and must be a member of the Service Manager Advanced Operators role.

▶ **Target collections:** These are the Configuration Manager collections you plan to target for synchronization.

▶ **Connector schedule:** Plan the schedule (day of the week and time).

The steps to create a Configuration Manager connector follow:

1. In the Service Manager console, navigate to **Administration** -> **Connectors**. In the Tasks pane, select **Create Connector** -> **Configuration Manager Connector**.

2. Click **Next** on the Before You Begin page; on the General page provide a name and description for the connector and ensure Enable is checked (see Figure 8.16).

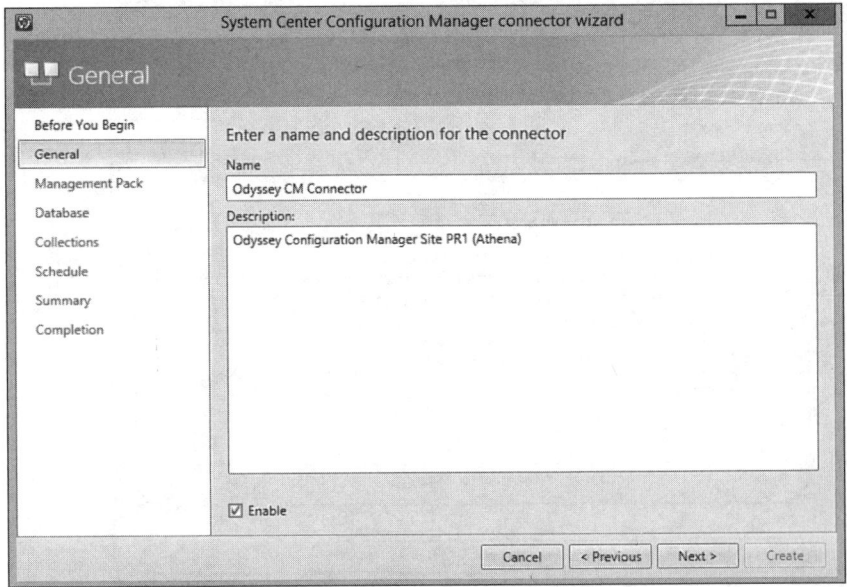

FIGURE 8.16   General page of the Configuration Manager connector wizard.

3. On the management pack selection page (see Figure 8.17), select the appropriate management pack for the version of Configuration Manager. The System Center Configuration Manager Connector Configuration management pack supports all versions of Configuration Manager 2007, and the System Center Configuration Manager Connector 2012 Configuration management pack is for version 2012 or later.

4. On the Database page, type the name of the database server, site database name, and the credentials with the appropriate delegation as discussed earlier in this section. Figure 8.18 illustrates the settings to connect to the site database for Athena in the Odyssey environment.

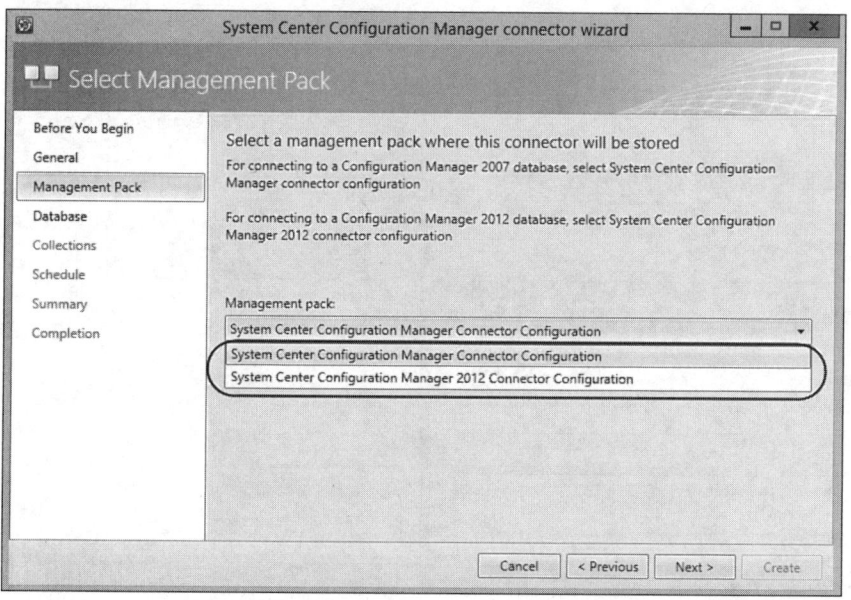

FIGURE 8.17   Selecting the management pack for the appropriate version of Configuration Manager.

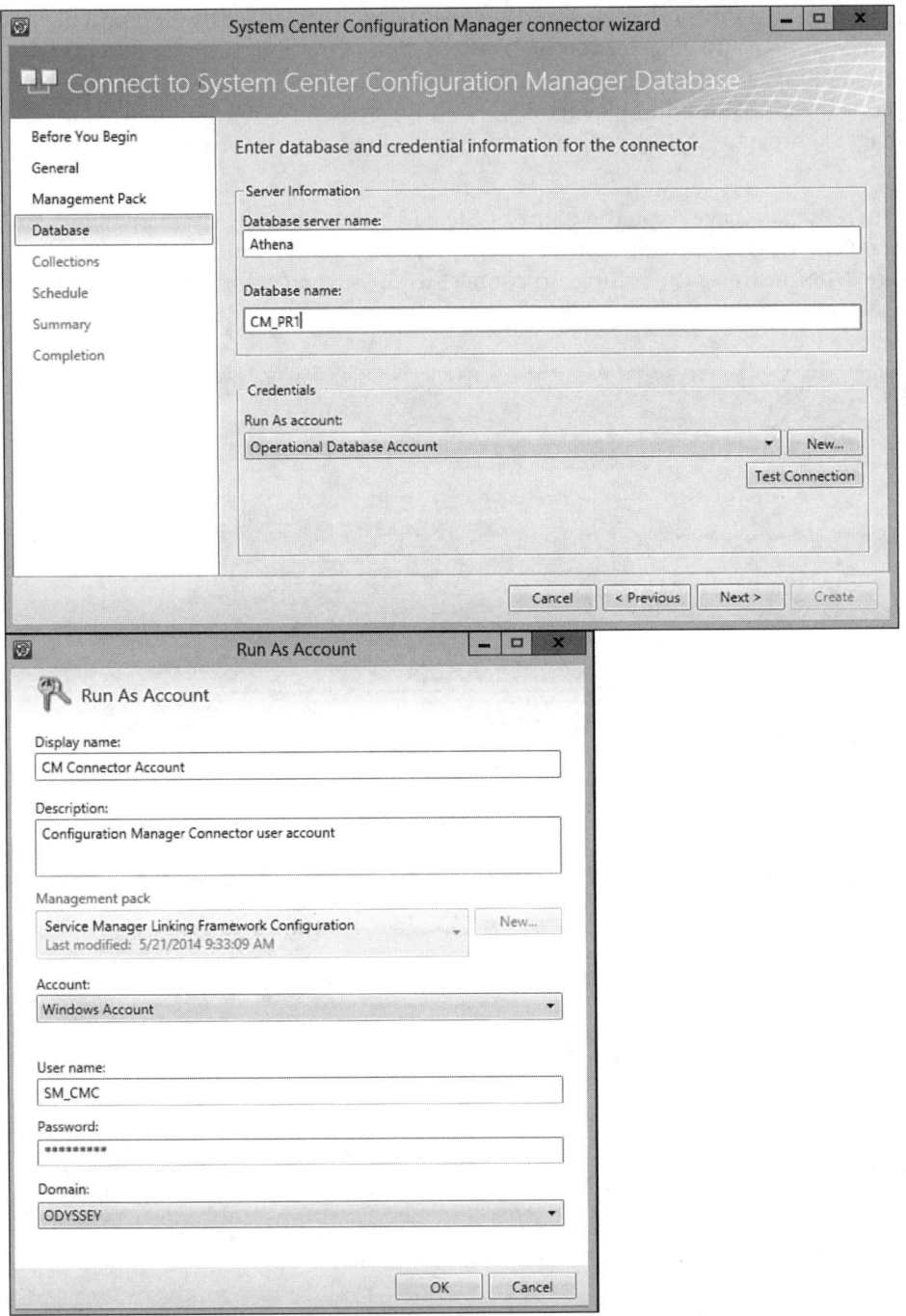

FIGURE 8.18   Configuration Manager connector database selection and configuration.

5. Select **Test Connection** to validate access to the Configuration Manager database.

6. On the next page, select the collections you plan to target. Figure 8.19 shows the collection selected for the Odyssey connector. The authors recommend checking the **Do not write null values for properties that are not set in Configuration Manager** check box. This setting ensures the connector only imports properties containing values and also prevents it from overwriting values from other connectors. (This can occur when the AD connector has a value for a computer object, but this value is not set in Configuration Manager.)

7. The last option is to set a schedule for the connector. You can run the connector daily at a specific time or on a specific day at a specific time. You could also run a manual synchronization by using the console. Figure 8.20 shows the Schedule selection page.

8. On the Summary page, click **Create** to complete creating the connector. Similar to the Active Directory connector, you must monitor the progress of the connector using the console or the Operations Manager event log (recommended by the authors).

REAL WORLD: BEWARE OF THE ALL SYSTEMS COLLECTION

The All Systems collection in a Configuration Manager site contains all computers discovered during the Configuration Manager discovery processes. This is not a good candidate for the Service Manager connector as it includes computers without agents; those computers do not have the properties imported using the connector. Plan to target a collection that has agents. Figure 8.19 targets the All Desktop and Server Clients collection, which contains all computers with an agent installed.

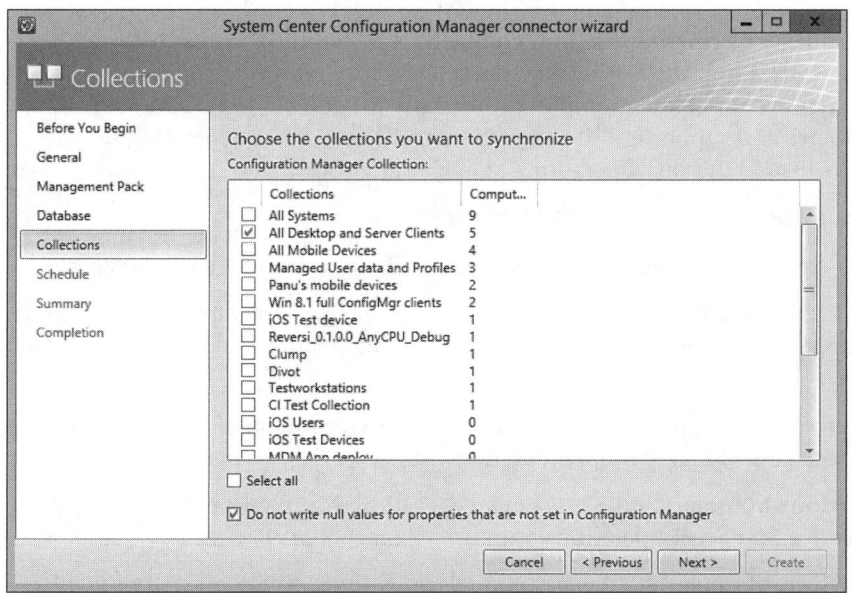

FIGURE 8.19   Configuration Manager system collection with agents installed.

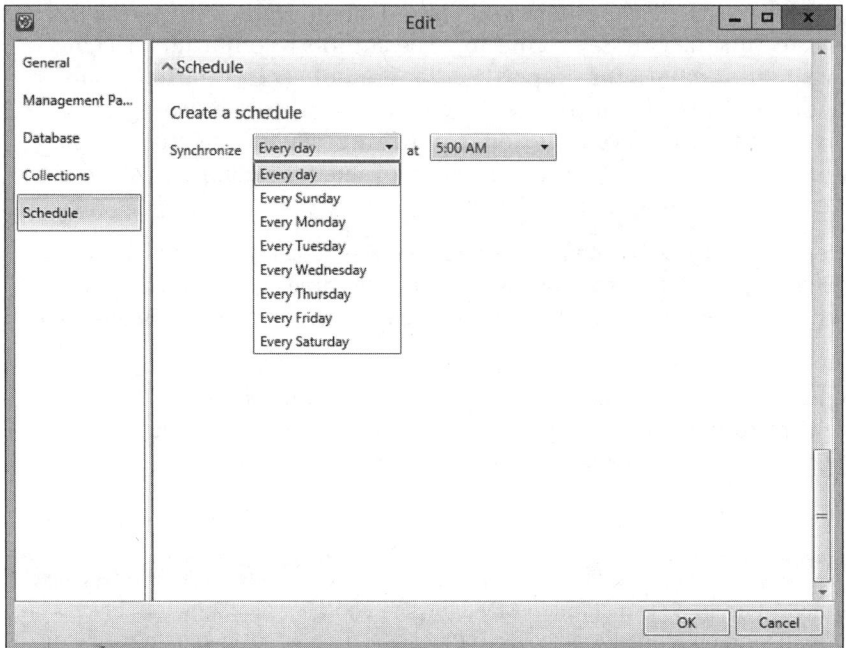

FIGURE 8.20   Selecting a schedule for the Configuration Manager connector.

Creating and Working with an Operations Manager Configuration Item Connector

The Operations Manager Configuration Item connector can import granular information about the computers imported using the Active Directory connector and/or the Configuration Manager connector. Examples of information you could import are SQL Server database names and properties, IIS properties, and much more depending on the management packs loaded in your Operations Manager environment.

Follow these steps to create the Operations Manager connector:

1. Prepare Run As account delegation in Operations Manager and Service Manager.

   The account must be a member of the Operations Manager Operator role and the Service Manager Advanced Operators role. You should create a dedicated account for this purpose.

2. Import the management packs available from the Service Manager installation folder for your Operations Manager implementation.

   ▶ **Operations Manager 2007:** *%ProgramFiles%*\Microsoft System Center 2012 R2\Service Manager\Operations Manager Management Packs

   ▶ **Operations Manager 2012:** *%ProgramFiles%*\Microsoft System Center 2012 R2\Service Manager\Operations Manager 2012 Management Packs

▶ **Operations Manager 2012 SP1:** *%ProgramFiles%*\Microsoft System Center 2012 R2\Service Manager\Operations Manager 2012 SP1 Management Packs

▶ **Operations Manager 2012 R2:** *%ProgramFiles%*\Microsoft System Center 2012 R2\Service Manager\Operations Manager 2012 R2 Management Packs

Note that part of the path to the management packs may differ if your installation was upgraded to Service Manager 2012 R2 from an earlier version.

3. Create the connector using the Service Manager console.

After completing Run As account delegation using the Operations Manager and Service Manager consoles, complete the rest of the process as follows:

1. Import the base management packs into Service Manager, depending on your version of Operations Manager:

▶ **Operations Manager 2007:** Run the installOMMPs.ps1 script from the folder specified in step 2 in the previous procedure. You must ensure the PowerShell execution policy is set appropriately. The policy is set running `Set-ExecutionPolicy Unrestricted` at an elevated PowerShell command prompt.

▶ **Operations Manager 2012/2012 SP1/2012 R2:** Use the Service Manager console to import the management packs. Navigate to **Administration -> Management Packs -> Import**. Navigate to the Management Packs location (change the file type to .mp), and select and import the management packs.

2. Create the connector as follows:

▶ In the Service Manager console, navigate to **Administration -> Connectors**. On the Tasks pane, click **Create connector -> Operations Manager CI connector**.

▶ Click **Next** to proceed to the General page; type a name for the connector and an optional description. The connector is enabled by default. Figure 8.21 shows the General page of the wizard.

▶ On the Server Details page, type the name of the Operations Manager management server and provide the credentials you plan to use according to step 2 in the previous procedure. Test the connection and click **Next**. Figure 8.22 shows the details used in the Odyssey lab.

▶ On the Management Packs page, check **Select all** and also select **Do not write null values for properties that are not set in Operations Manager**. Make sure the management pack versions match that of your Operations Manager management group.

▶ On the Schedule page, configure your preferred schedule for this connector.

▶ Review the Summary page and click **Create** to complete creating the connector.

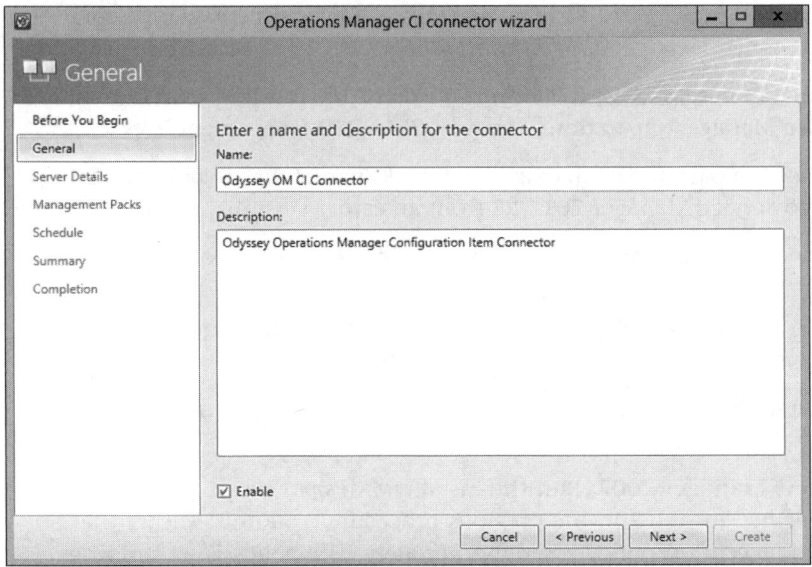

FIGURE 8.21   General page of the Operations Manager CI connector wizard.

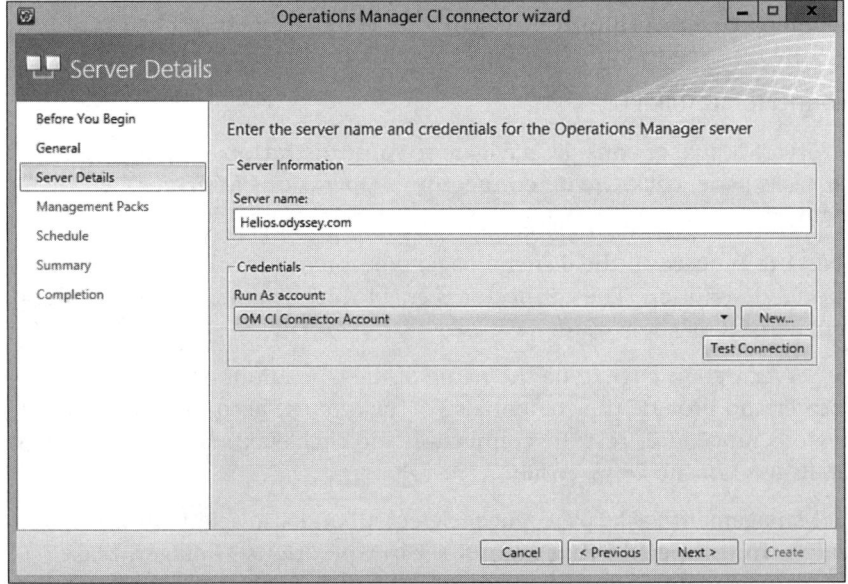

FIGURE 8.22   Operations Manager CI connector settings.

The Operations Manager CI connector enables importing additional CIs without creating additional connectors when importing from the same Operations Manager management group. There are three parts to this process:

1. Import the management packs responsible for discovering the CIs in the order of dependency. The order of import is important, as doing it incorrectly requires restarting the import wizard. You must import Management Pack A before Management Pack B if Management Pack B depends on A.

2. Make sure the class imported by the management pack is on the Allowed List.

3. Edit the connector. In the Service Manager console, navigate to **Administration -> Connectors**. Select the connector and right-click **Properties -> Management Packs**. Click **Refresh** and select the new management packs you have imported.

Using the Connector Allowed List

The Operations Manager CI connector synchronizes discovered managed objects from Operations Manager to the Service Manager CMDB. If data in your Service Manager CMDB from Operations Manager classes needs to be synchronized automatically by the Operations Manager CI connector, you should import those management packs into Service Manager. You only need to import the management pack containing the model, which are the classes, relationships, and properties.

> **TIP: IMPORTING MANAGEMENT PACKS CONTAINING CLASSES INTO SERVICE MANAGER**
>
> You can only import Operations Manager management packs that include a class definition. Attempts to import management packs without class definitions are blocked and appear with a red X in Service Manager when trying to import.

To keep the Service Manager CMDB healthy, the Operations Manager CI connector does not synchronize all classes from Operations Manager. Service Manager uses an Allowed List to control what to synchronize; only objects of classes that derive from classes in the Allowed List are synchronized.

Modifying the Connector Allowed List

The following steps describe the actions to perform to change the allowed list of classes synchronized by the Operations Manager CI connector:

1. On a Service Manager server start the Service Manager Shell.

2. In the Service Manager Shell, run `Get-SCSMAllowList`. This shows the default list of classes in the allowed list.

3. In the Service Manager Shell, run `Add-SCSMAllowListClass -Classname <class name>` to add the `<class name>` class to the Allowed List. Replace `<class name>` with the class you need to allow.

4. In the Service Manager Shell, run `Get-SCSMAllowList`. Verify the new class is in the list. Close the Service Manager Shell.

For additional information on the Allowed List, see https://blogs.technet.com/b/service-manager/archive/2010/02/26/managing-the-allowed-list-for-the-operations-manager-ci-connector-with-powershell.aspx. Start the PowerShell session from the Service Manager console to gain access to the module as indicated in Figure 8.23. See Chapter 24, "Using PowerShell," for additional information.

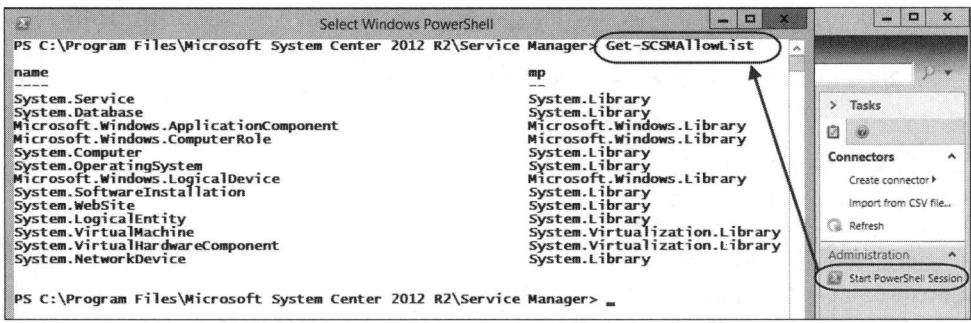

FIGURE 8.23   Using PowerShell to view the Allowed List.

TIP: LOCATION OF THE OPERATIONS MANAGER CONFIGURATION ITEMS

The only imported items automatically displayed in the Service Manager console after configuring the Operations Manager CI connector are the distributed applications you import, which are displayed under Configuration Items -> Business Services. The other properties you import, such as SQL database instances, require creating a folder under the Configuration Items node. You then create a view in this folder with the appropriate criterion to display the CIs.

Creating a Virtual Machine Manager Connector

The VMM connector builds on the Operations Manager CI connector. You must successfully create and configure the Operations Manager CI connector before creating the VMM connector. The "Creating and Working with an Operations Manager Configuration Item Connector" section discusses these steps. The authors recommend also completing the integration between Operations Manager and VMM prior to creating the Service Manager connector for VMM. Make sure the following Operations Manager management packs are imported into Service Manager:

▶ **Microsoft.Windows.InternetInformationServices.CommonLibrary:** Windows Server Internet Information Library

▶ **Microsoft.Windows.InternetInformationServices.2003:** Windows Server Internet Information Services 2003 monitoring management pack

▶ **Microsoft.Windows.InternetInformationServices.2008:** Windows Server Internet Information Services 2008 monitoring management pack. This requires two dependent management packs:

  ▶ Microsoft.Windows.Server.Library.mp

  ▶ Microsoft.Windows.Server.2008.Discovery

▶ **Microsoft.SQLServer.Library:** SQL Server Library monitoring management pack

The Service Manager official blog site provides additional information that complements the information in this chapter. VMM connector information is available at http://blogs. technet.com/b/servicemanager/archive/2012/02/09/faq-installing-all-the-prerequisite-mps-for-the-cloud-services-management-pack.aspx.

In addition to the prerequisite management packs and their dependencies, you must also import the SystemCenter.VirtualMachineManager.2012.Discovery management pack, which is located in the *%ProgramFiles%*\Microsoft System Center 2012\Virtual Machine Manager\ManagementPacks folder on the VMM management server. (The folder name may vary depending on the settings specified during VMM installation.) You also need an Active Directory user account for the connection. This account becomes the VMM connector Run As account and requires the following delegation:

▶ **VMM:** VMM Administrator role and a member of the local Administrators group on the VMM management server

▶ **Service Manager:** Member of the Service Manager Advanced Operators role

Perform the following steps to create the VMM connector:

1. Prepare Run As account delegation in VMM and Service Manager.

2. Import the management packs into Service Manager.

3. Create the connector using the Service Manager console:

  ▶ Navigate to **Administration** -> **Connectors**. Under Tasks, select **Create Connector** -> **Virtual Machine Manager Connector**.

  ▶ Click **Next** on the Before You Begin page; on the General page, provide a name for the connector, an optional description, and ensure **Enable this connector** is checked. Figure 8.24 shows the General page for the Odyssey environment.

  ▶ On the Connection page (see Figure 8.25), specify the VMM server name and click **New** to create a new Run As account using an Active Directory account with the delegation discussed earlier in this section. Click **Test Connection** to validate the properties you have configured.

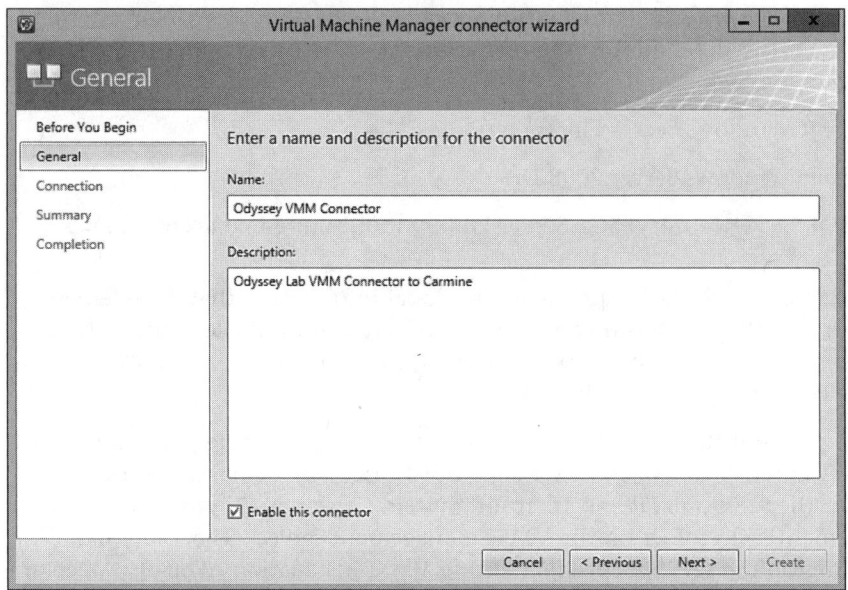

FIGURE 8.24   General page of the VMM connector wizard.

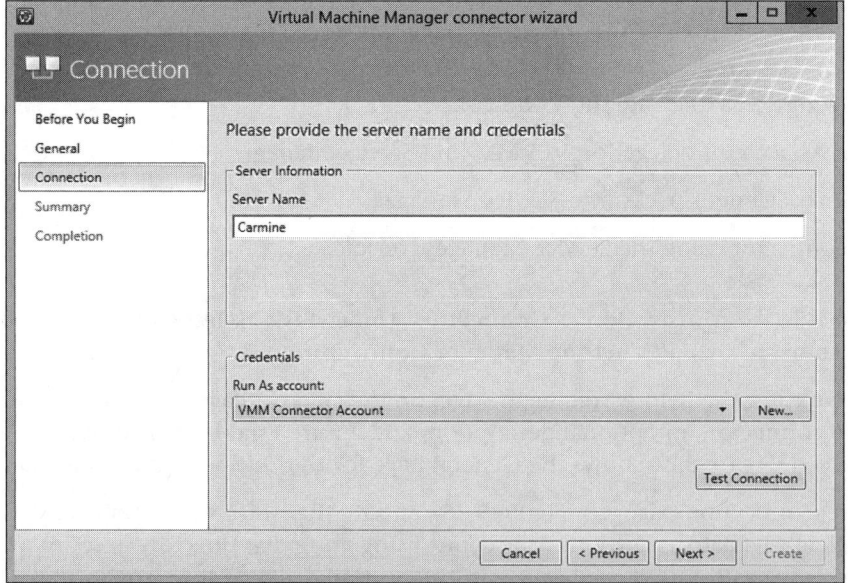

FIGURE 8.25   Odyssey VMM connector connection settings.

▶ The final page of the wizard is the Summary page, which provides details of the Operations Manager management server that this connector depends on (see Figure 8.26).

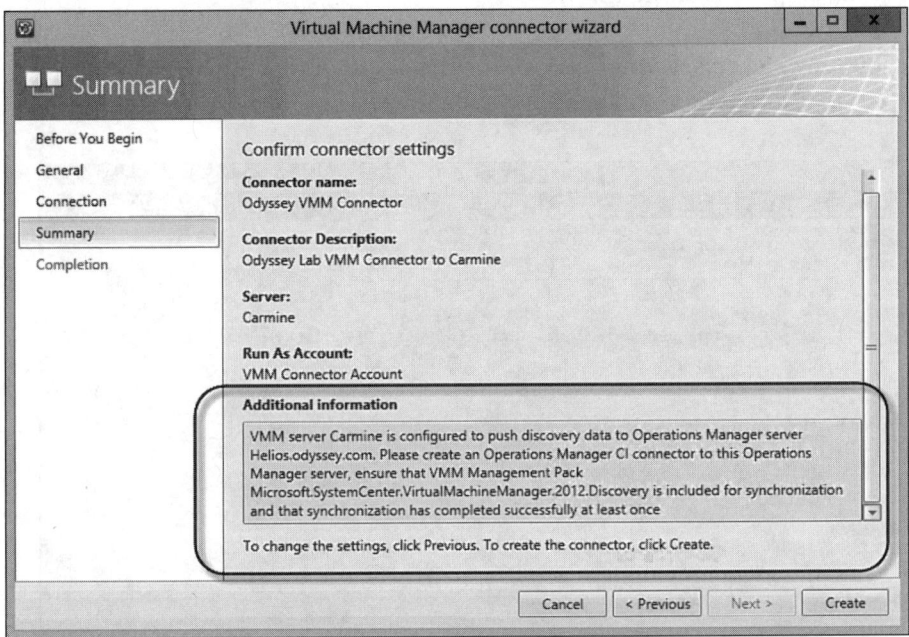

FIGURE 8.26   Summary page of the VMM connector wizard.

You can validate a successful import of the VMM CIs by creating a view in a folder in the Configuration Items node. The following steps create a folder and a view in the Service Manager console:

1. In the Service Manager console, navigate to **Configuration Items -> Tasks**, and select **Create Folder**.

2. Type a name in the Folder name field (for example, VMM connector CIs) and provide an optional description for the folder. Select an existing unsealed management pack or create a new one.

3. Select the folder you created in step 2; under Tasks, click **Create View**.

4. Type a name in the Name field and provide an optional description for the view.

5. Click the **Criteria** tab; under Search for objects of a specific class, click **Browse** and change the filter type on the right to **All basic classes**.

6. Type **template** in the search filter field and select **Virtual Machine Template**. Click **OK**.

7. Click the **Display** tab, uncheck all the default selected options and check the following options: **CPU Count**, **Display Name**, **Memory**, **Operating System Name**, **Virtual Machine Manager Server**, and **Size (GB)**.

8. Click **OK** to complete creating the view.

Figure 8.27 shows the view displaying the VMM templates imported by the VMM connector.

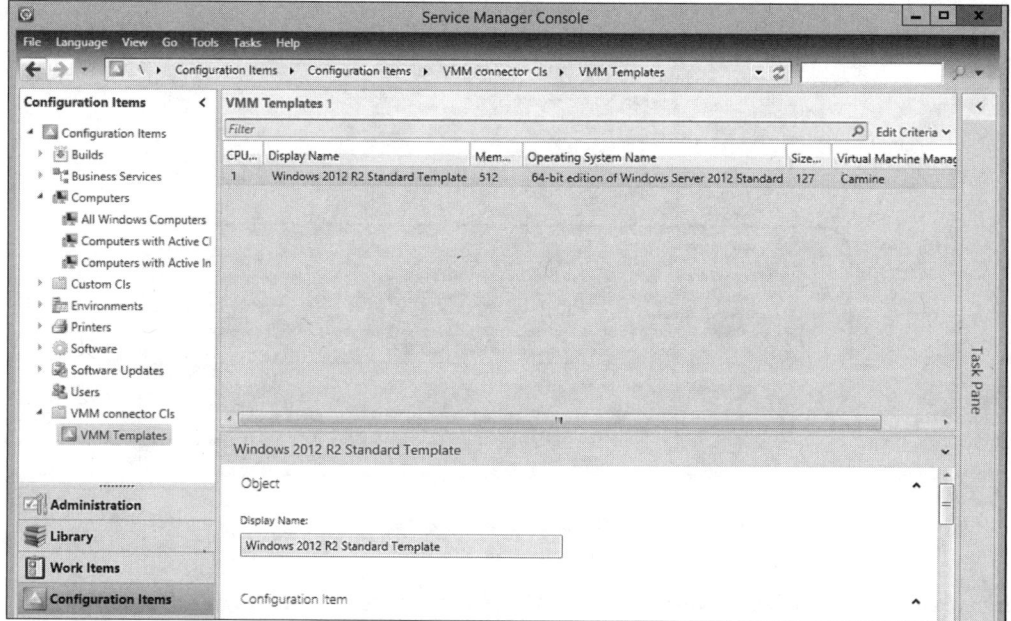

FIGURE 8.27   VMM CI view in a configuration item folder.

There is a significant amount of community and Microsoft official information discussing the connectors available in Service Manager. Appendix B, "Reference URLs," lists these sites.

Creating a CSV Connector

The CSV connector requires preparing two files prior to initiating the process in the Service Manager console. Table 8.4 provides details on the two files and the format rules for each file type.

TABLE 8.4   CSV Connector Required File Rules

File Type	Data Value File Rules
Format file	File must have an .XML extension. Create this file with an XML editor such as Notepad.exe. Match the first part of the name (before the file extension) to the first part of the name of the .CSV file. You must follow the Service Manager CSV import XML format for either a class or a type projection.
Data values file	File must have a .CSV extension. Create this file with a spreadsheet editor such as MS Excel. There must be no column heading in the file. Match the first part of the name (before the file extension) to the first part of the name of the .XML file.

Steps for creating the CSV connector files are best illustrated with two scenarios. These scenarios are based on the two CI types you can import:

▶ **Instances of a CI class:** This scenario imports a list of Windows server computers with an IP address and a domain name.

▶ **Instances of a type projection CI class:** This imports a list of supplier contacts into the CMDB. The supplier contact information is used as part of the asset management process and includes a list of users not part of the organization's Active Directory.

Importing Instances of a CI Class

The steps to follow to import the instances of a CI class are

1. Identify and document the class and the property names.

2. Construct the XML file for the class and its properties.

3. Create the CSV data file.

4. Import the data into Service Manager using the console.

Several options are available to identify the class and the properties of the CI you want to import. The simplest method for CI classes is to view SystemCenterCommonModel-SCSM1010.vsd. This file is part of the Job Aids download available at http://www.microsoft.com/en-us/download/details.aspx?id=27850.

Figure 8.28 shows the `Microsoft.Windows.Computer` class. The properties in this class are required to import instances of a Windows computer. The `PrincipalName` is a key property and mandatory when creating a CI of this type.

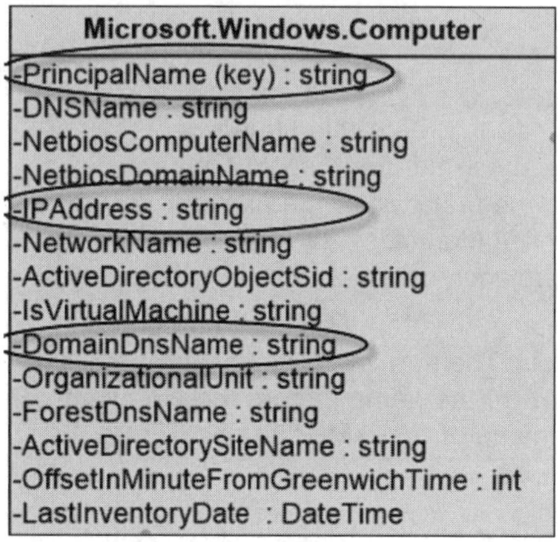

```
Microsoft.Windows.Computer
-PrincipalName (key) : string
-DNSName : string
-NetbiosComputerName : string
-NetbiosDomainName : string
-IPAddress : string
-NetworkName : string
-ActiveDirectoryObjectSid : string
-IsVirtualMachine : string
-DomainDnsName : string
-OrganizationalUnit : string
-ForestDnsName : string
-ActiveDirectorySiteName : string
-OffsetInMinuteFromGreenwichTime : int
-LastInventoryDate  : DateTime
```

FIGURE 8.28   Windows Computer class properties.

The three required properties in Figure 8.28 are `PrincipalName`, `IPAddress`, and `DomainDnsName`.

TIP: OTHER OPTION FOR IDENTIFYING CLASS PROPERTIES

Class properties are visible using the Service Manager Authoring Tool or PowerShell. Use the Class browser in the Authoring Tool to select the required class and view its properties. You can use the optional SMLets PowerShell module for additional functionality. Simply define a variable like `$CI` and pipe the output of `Get-SCSMClass` to this variable. Display the properties of the output using `$CI.PropertyCollection`. The `|` `FT` represents `Format-Table` and the properties specified after `FT` are displayed in the output. Figure 8.29 shows the output of the `Microsoft.Windows.Computer` class using PowerShell. You can use this option for all classes. See Chapter 24 for additional information on using PowerShell with Service Manager.

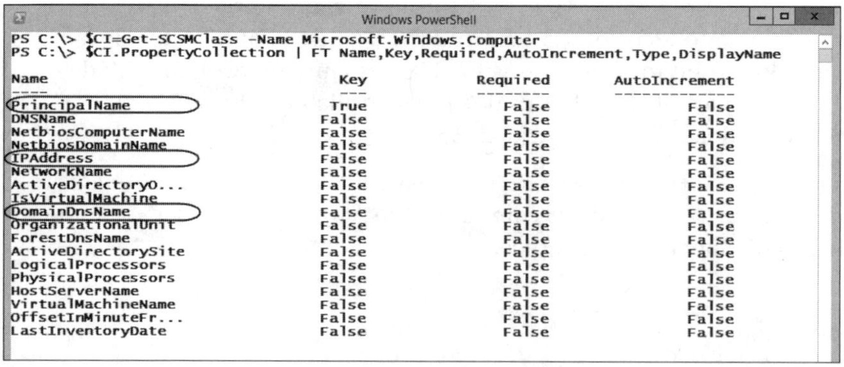

```
Windows PowerShell                                          _ □ X
PS C:\> $CI=Get-SCSMClass -Name Microsoft.Windows.Computer
PS C:\> $CI.PropertyCollection | FT Name,Key,Required,AutoIncrement,Type,DisplayName

Name                    Key         Required        AutoIncrement
----                    ---         --------        -------------
PrincipalName           True        False           False
DNSName                 False       False           False
NetbiosComputerName     False       False           False
NetbiosDomainName       False       False           False
IPAddress               False       False           False
NetworkName             False       False           False
ActiveDirectoryO...     False       False           False
IsVirtualMachine        False       False           False
DomainDnsName           False       False           False
OrganizationalUnit      False       False           False
ForestDnsName           False       False           False
ActiveDirectorySite     False       False           False
LogicalProcessors       False       False           False
PhysicalProcessors      False       False           False
HostServerName          False       False           False
VirtualMachineName      False       False           False
OffsetInMinuteFr...     False       False           False
LastInventoryDate       False       False           False
```

FIGURE 8.29   Using PowerShell to view class properties.

Use an XML editor or Notepad to create the XML format file for the three required properties. If using Notepad, you must specify All Files (*.*) as the file type when you select Save, and type the XML extension. The format file must begin and end with the `<CSVImportFormat>` tag. In the case of a class-only format, specify the class and the properties of the class. The order of the list of properties must correspond to the order of the CSV file values for the instances of the class you are importing. The XML format file content to import instances of a CI class follows:

```
<CSVImportFormat>
   <Class Type="Microsoft.Windows.Computer">
      <Property ID="PrincipalName"/>
      <Property ID="IPAddress"/>
      <Property ID="DomainDnsName"/>
   </Class>
</CSVImportFormat>
```

Save the file with a name such as Servers.xml.

The second file required must contain one or more instances of the class you are importing in a CSV file. Use Microsoft Excel or an equivalent program to create the CSV values file. You can use column headings when creating the file, if desired. After creating the file content, delete the headings and save the file in .CSV format. The order of the values (properties) must match the property ID order defined in the corresponding XML format file. Match the first part of the filename to the XML format file, such as Servers.csv. Figure 8.30 shows sample Servers.csv content.

```
ServerChp801,10.0.0.101,Odyssey.com
ServerChp802,10.0.0.102,Odyssey.com
ServerChp803,10.0.0.103,Odyssey.com
ServerChp804,10.0.0.104,Odyssey.com
```

FIGURE 8.30   Sample Servers.CSV file content.

Follow these steps to complete the import:

1. Place the .XML and .CSV files in a file system folder located on the Service Manager management server.

2. In the Service Manager console, navigate to **Administration -> Connectors**.

3. Under the Tasks pane, click **Import from CSV file**.

4. The Import Instances from CSV File wizard page opens. Browse to the file locations in which you placed the format and data files, and select **Import from CSV file** as shown in Figure 8.31.

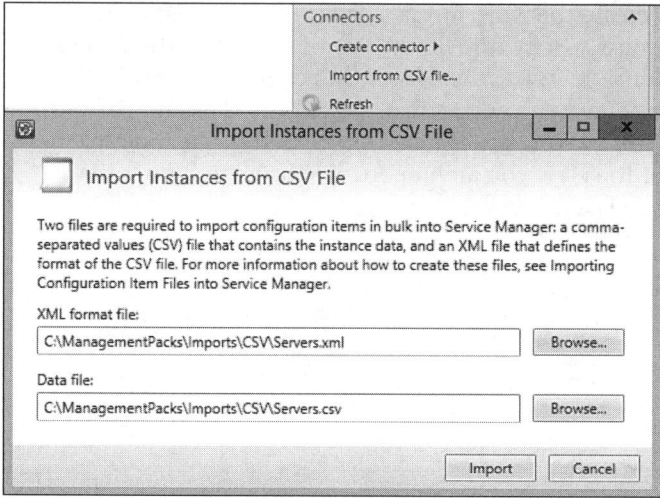

FIGURE 8.31   CSV instance import page.

5. A confirmation window opens, providing either validation of success or feedback on any errors encountered by the process.

Verify the import is successful by reviewing the Configuration Items workspace in the Service Manager console. Figure 8.32 shows the imported CIs in the console.

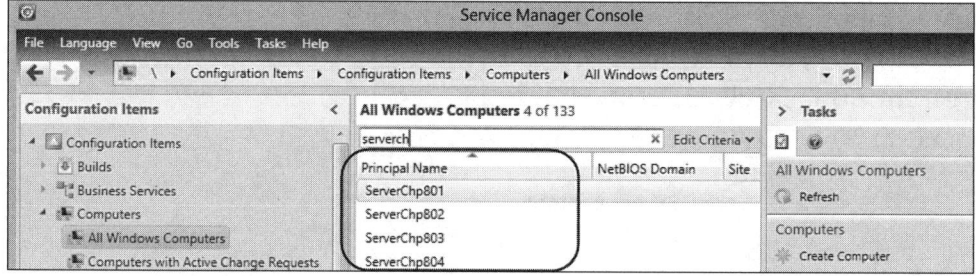

FIGURE 8.32   CSV import verification using the Service Manager console.

Importing Instances of a Type Projection CI Class

Importing instances of a CI type projection has the same steps and requirements as importing instances of a CI class, except the structure of the format file.

This scenario imports external supplier contact details into the Service Manager database. The properties the scenario requires are Domain, User Name, First Name, Last Name, Company, Business Phone, and Email address. The first two properties are required when importing user properties. The type projections and their properties using one of the options discussed are listed in Table 8.5. Type projections are discussed in Chapter 22, "Customizing Service Manager."

TABLE 8.5   Type Projection CI Properties

Class	Properties	Console Tab Display Name
System.Domain.User	Domain, UserName, FirstName, LastName, Company	General tab of the user in the Configuration Items nodeGeneral available properties.
System.Notification. EndPoint	ChannelName,TargetAddress	Notification tab. SMTP Channel and the email address.

The CSV file format remains the same as when created for a CI class. The XML format file uses a modified syntax. You must specify a type projection tag (the syntax is `<Projection Type>`) after the opening `<CSVImportFormat>` tag and provide the list of component aliases, their class, and properties as illustrated in the following XML code:

```xml
<CSVImportFormat>
  <Projection Type="System.User.Projection">
    <Seed>
      <Class Type="System.Domain.User">
        <Property ID="Domain"/>
        <Property ID="UserName"/>
        <Property ID="FirstName"/>
        <Property ID="LastName"/>
        <Property ID="Company"/>
        <Property ID="BusinessPhone"/>
      </Class>
    </Seed>
    <Component Alias="Notification">
      <Seed>
        <Class Type="System.Notification.Endpoint">
          <Property ID="Id"/>
          <Property ID="ChannelName"/>
          <Property ID="TargetAddress"/>
        </Class>
      </Seed>
    </Component>
  </Projection>
</CSVImportFormat>
```

Type projection properties must be placed in between a `<Seed>` tag. You must use the `<Class>` and `<Property>` tags to complete the type projection information in the format file. In the sample format file code for importing supplier contact information (including the contact's email address), notice that the `Component Alias=` value matches the form tab (Notification) in the Service Manager console, and the `Class Type=` value is the internal name for the type projection.

An extract of a CSV file to complement the listing for the type projection XML follows:

```
Odyssey,username1,FName1,LName1,Comp1,1111,username1_1,SMTP,username1@Odyssey.com
Odyssey,username2,FName2,LName2,Comp1,2222,username2_2,SMTP,username2@Odyssey.com
Odyssey,username3,FName3,LName3,Comp1,3333,username3_3,SMTP,username3@Odyssey.com
Odyssey,username4,FName4,LName4,Comp1,4444,username4_4,SMTP,username4@Odyssey.com
```

Creating and Working with Work Item Connectors

The "Creating and Working with Configuration Item Connectors" section discussed how to create connectors that populate configuration items in the Service Manager CMDB. Information from the CI connectors is typically available to view in the Configuration Items workspace of the Service Manager console. The next sections discuss how to configure and use work item connectors. The information from these connectors populates or updates the Work Items workspace of the console.

Creating and Working with the Operations Manager Alert Connector

Using this connector requires configurations in the Service Manager and Operations Manager consoles. The Service Manager steps are performed prior to those in Operations Manager.

First prepare the connector Active Directory user account (Run As account) in Operations Manager and Service Manager. This account must be a member of the Operations Manager Operator role and the Service Manager Advanced Operators role.

In the Service Manager console, follow these steps:

1. Navigate to **Administration** -> **Connectors**. Under Tasks, select **Create Connector** -> **Operations Manager Alert Connector**.

2. Click **Next** on the Before You Begin page; on the General page (see Figure 8.33) provide a name and description (optional) and check the Enable check box for this connector.

3. On the Server Details page, type the Operations Manager Server name. Under Credentials Run As Account, select **New** and provide the connect account information. Click **Test** to validate the connection properties. On the Alert Routing Rules page (see Figure 8.34), select **Operations Manager Incident Template**. Alert Routing is discussed in Chapter 11. You can modify these settings after the connector is created.

4. Accept the default 30 second schedule or adjust as necessary in 30-second increments. Configure the optional bidirectional setting; the options are to close alerts in Operations Manager and conversely resolve incidents in Service Manager. Figure 8.35 shows the default settings.

5. Review the Summary page and click **Create** to complete creating the connector on the Service Manager side.

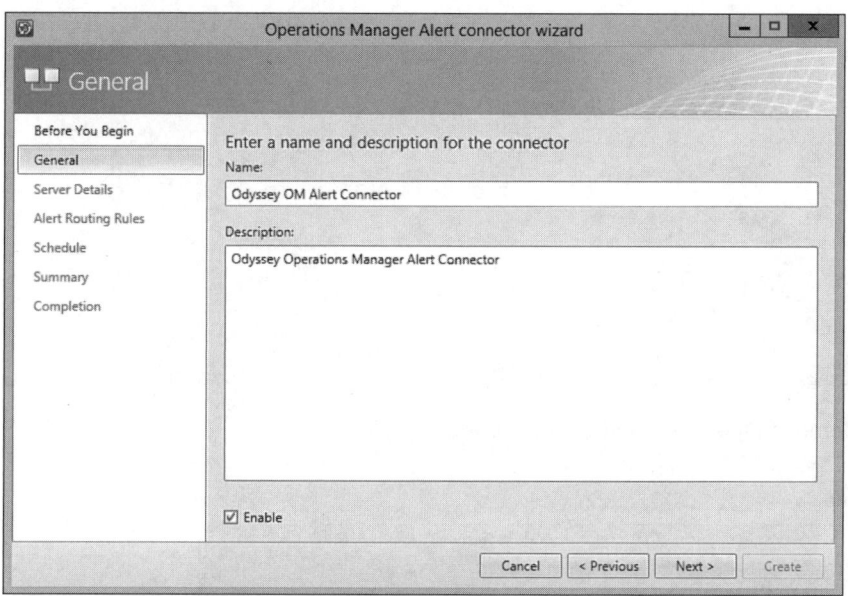

FIGURE 8.33   General page of the Operations Manager Alert connector wizard.

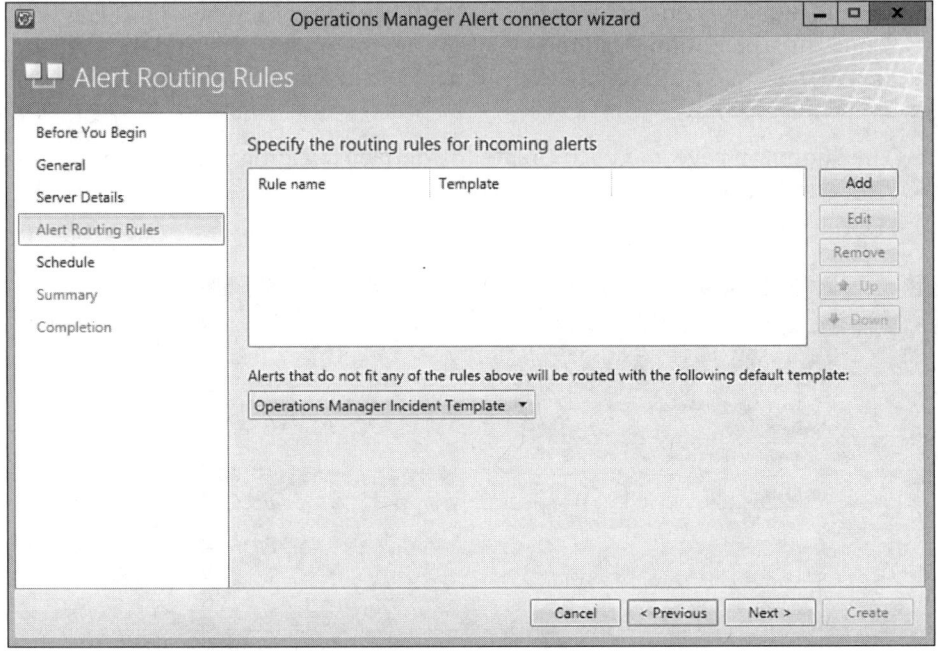

FIGURE 8.34   Operations Manager Alert connector routing rules.

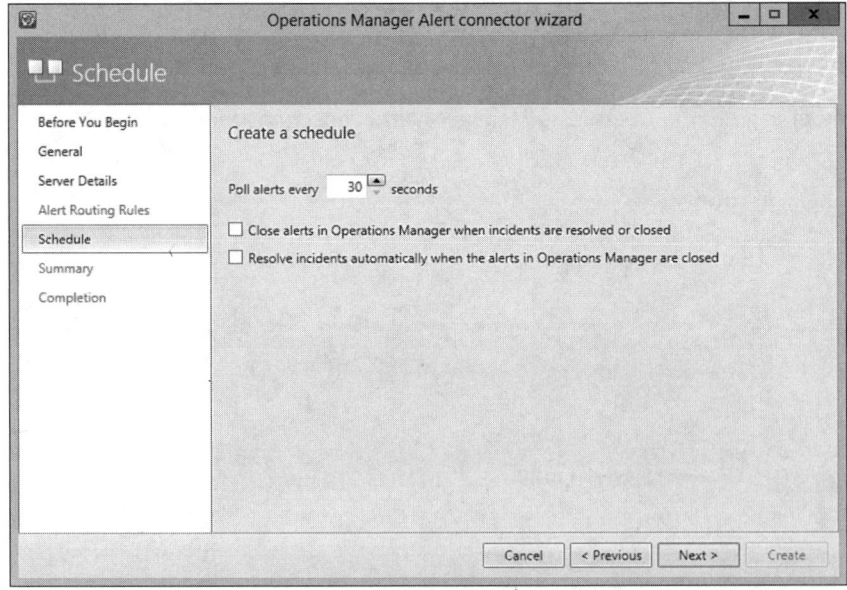

FIGURE 8.35   Operations Manager Alert connector schedule and bidirectional options.

Follow these steps to perform the second part of the configuration in the Operations Manager console:

1. Navigate to **Administration -> Product Connectors -> Internal Connectors**.

2. The Tasks pane should show the connector name you configured in the Service Manager console. Select the connector name and right-click to select **Properties**. In the Subscriptions section (see Figure 8.36), click **Add** and complete the wizard using the following information:

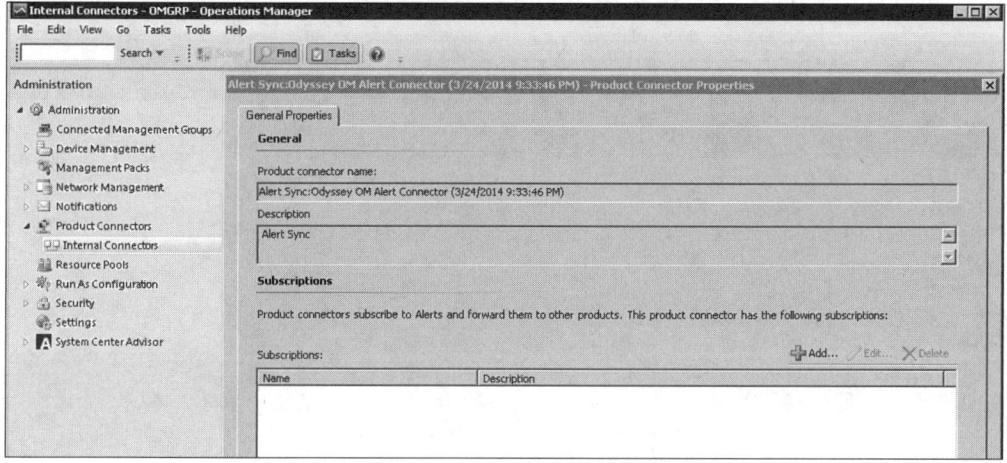

FIGURE 8.36   Operations Manager console internal connectors settings.

▶ On the General page, type a name for the subscription and click **Next**.

▶ Click **Next** on the Approvers groups page.

▶ Click **Next** on the Approve targets page.

▶ Click **OK** to complete the wizard.

You can filter the trigger for creating incidents from Operations Manager based on severity or priority of the alerts. This option requires you to tune Operations Manager appropriately. *System Center 2012 Operations Manager Unleashed* (Sams, 2013) provides information for tuning and optimizing Operations Manager.

Creating and Working with the Orchestrator Connector

The Orchestrator connector imports process workflows from System Center Orchestrator into Service Manager. The workflows are known as runbooks and when successfully imported appear in the Library workspace of the Service Manager console.

Use the Orchestrator connector to initiate supported automated processes using Service Manager. As an example, you could create an Orchestrator runbook to drive Active Directory user provisioning. The runbook for the automation, created in Orchestrator, is synchronized with Service Manager using the Orchestrator connector.

To create the Orchestrator connector in Service Manager, follow these steps.

1. In the Service Manager console, navigate to **Administration -> Connectors**. In the **Tasks** pane, select **Create connector -> Orchestrator connector**.

2. Click **Next** on the Before You Begin page. On the General page (see Figure 8.37), type a name and optional description for the connector.

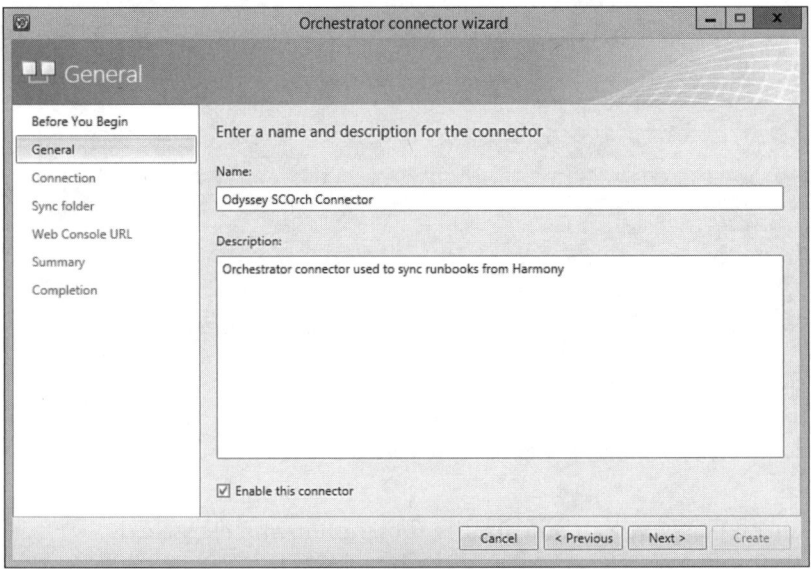

FIGURE 8.37   General page for configuring the Orchestrator connector.

3. Following are the remaining pages used to create the Orchestrator connector:

    ▶ **Connection (Server Information and Credentials):** Type the Orchestrator Web Service URL. (The default format is http://<*Orchestrator management servername*>:<*port*>/Orchestrator2012/Orchestrator.svc.)

    ▶ Select or create the credentials to connect to the Orchestrator environment. The credential (an Active Directory user account created for this purpose) is listed in the Service Manager console as a Run As account. The account must be granted the following permissions to the Runbooks node in the Orchestrator runbook designer: Read Properties, List Contents, and Publish. The permissions must also apply to all child objects.

▶ Figure 8.38 shows the settings for the Odyssey lab and creating a Run As account for this connection. Click **Test Connection** to validate the settings.

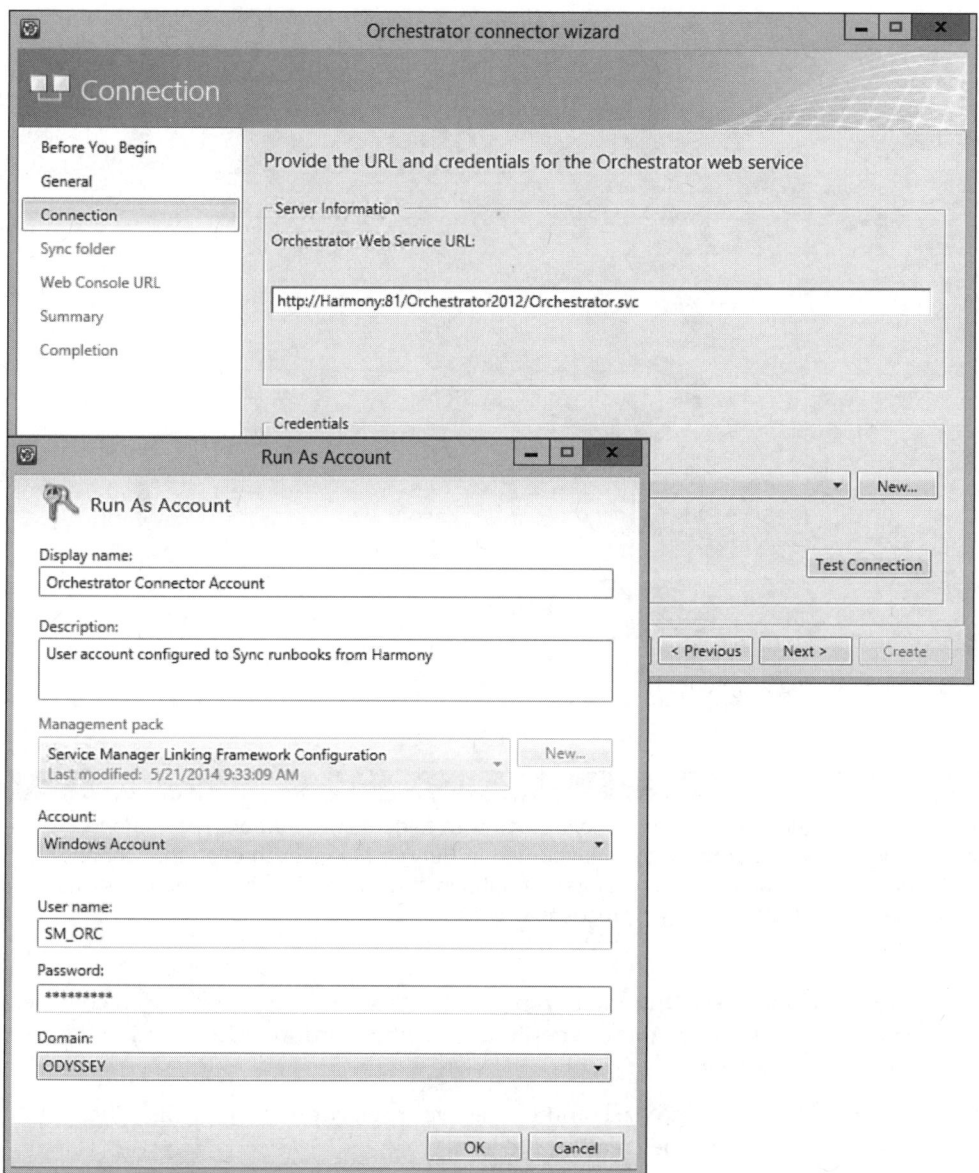

FIGURE 8.38   Connection information and Run As account configuration for the Orchestrator connector.

▶ **Sync folder:** Select the runbook folder for the connector to import and click **Next**. Figure 8.39 shows the selections for the Odyssey Orchestrator connector.

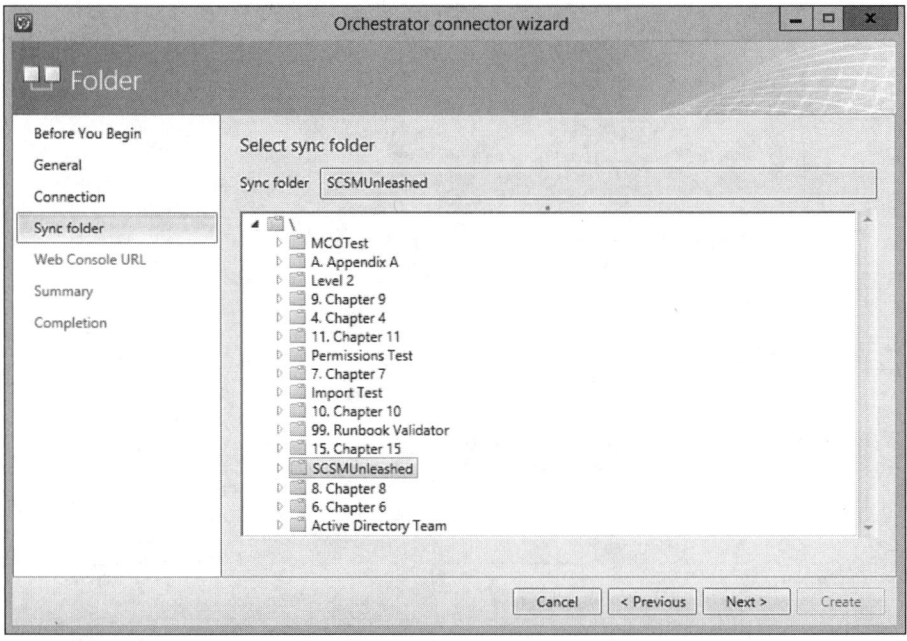

FIGURE 8.39   Selecting a sync folder.

REAL WORLD: SYNC FOLDER

Plan to organize the Orchestrator runbooks node with folders. The authors recommend creating a dedicated folder for runbooks you use in Service Manager through this connector. This provides you with security delegation options and avoids synchronizing runbooks you do not use in Service Manager processes.

▶ **Web Console URL:** Optionally type the URL for the Orchestrator web console. Specifying the URL enables hyperlinks to runbook information and job details in Service Manager.

▶ **Summary:** You can go back and change your selections and details. Click **Create** to complete the creation process.

▶ **Completion:** Click **Close** after verifying the connector was created successfully.

4. Validate the synchronization completion in the Library workspace of the Service Manager console. The runbook objects are available for selection when you create a runbook activity template. Figure 8.40 and Figure 8.41 provide examples.

Using the Orchestrator connector, you can automate the manual activities typically configured in request offerings presented in the self-service portal. This capability is discussed in Chapter 12, "Automation and Chargeback."

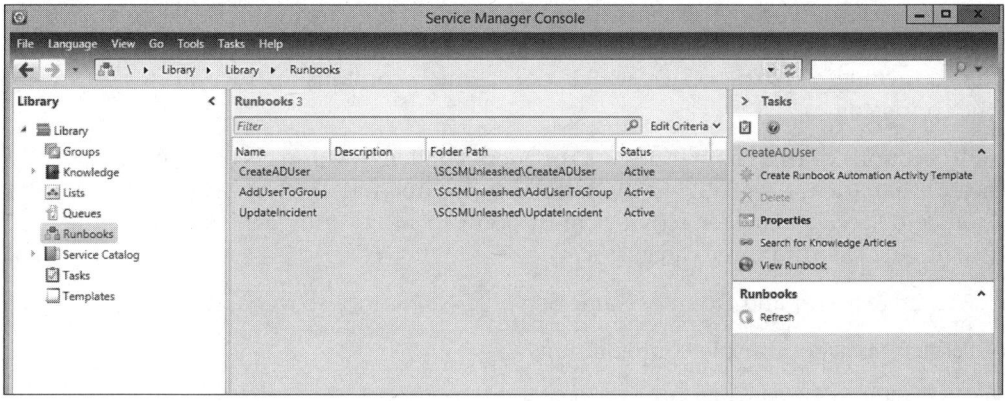

FIGURE 8.40   Runbooks in the Service Manager console.

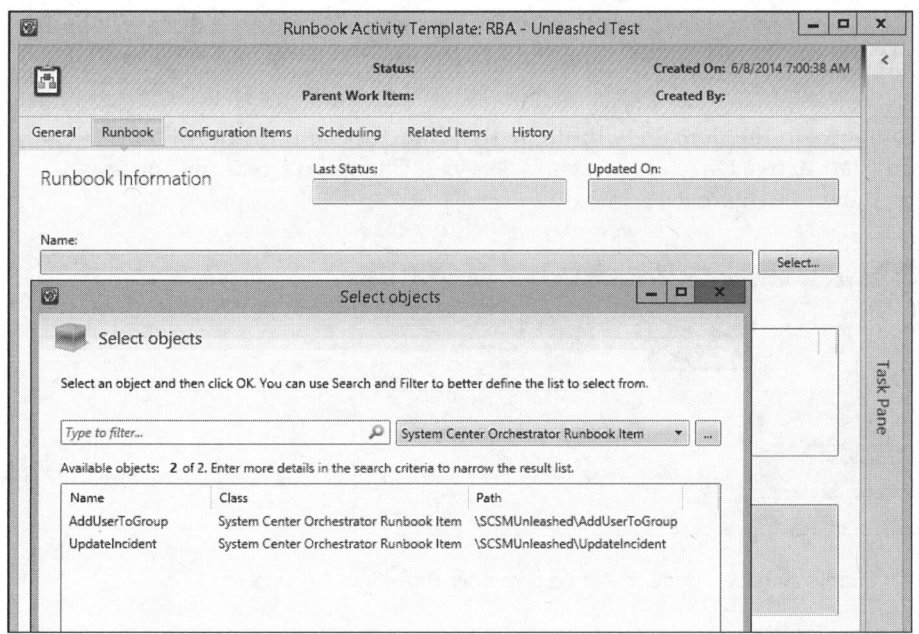

FIGURE 8.41   Runbook activity template.

Creating and Working with the Exchange Connector

The Exchange connector is supported by Microsoft but is not included with the Service Manager installation bits. You must configure the components for this connector, and then use the Create connector task to create one or more of this type of connector. Instructions for configuring this connector and required files are available at the Microsoft download site at http://www.microsoft.com/en-us/download/details.aspx?id=38791. The download includes SM2012_EC_DepGuide.docx, which contains instructions for deploying the connector.

The next sections of this chapter discuss the more challenging aspects of creating this connector that are not available in the Microsoft documentation. These additional infrastructure and Service Manager activities must occur to successfully deploy and use the connector, and fall into three categories:

▶ Exchange Server and Domain Name Server (DNS) auto discovery settings

▶ Service Manager console configurations

▶ User mailbox impersonation

Exchange Server and DNS Auto Discovery Settings

The Exchange connector requires you to provide the details of the auto discovery properties of your Exchange server deployment or DNS. You can verify the auto discovery properties of your Exchange organization using the Active Directory Sites and Services tool. Follow these steps to verify the URL setting and whether auto discovery is enabled:

1. On a computer in the domain with the Active Directory administrative tools installed, start Active Directory Sites and Services. Click **View -> Show Services Node** as shown in Figure 8.42.

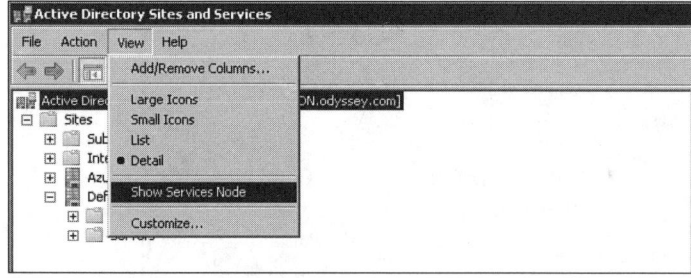

FIGURE 8.42   Enable Services node in Active Directory Sites and Services.

2. Expand **Services -> Microsoft Exchange -> <*domain*> ->Administrative Groups -> Exchange Administrative Group -> Servers -> <*Exchange server*> -> Protocols**. Select **Autodiscover** and right-click the serviceConnectionPoint object to select **Properties**.

3. Figure 8.43 shows the properties of the Exchange Server E14 in the Odyssey domain. The serviceBindingInformation should have the value of the autodiscover URL. Record this value.

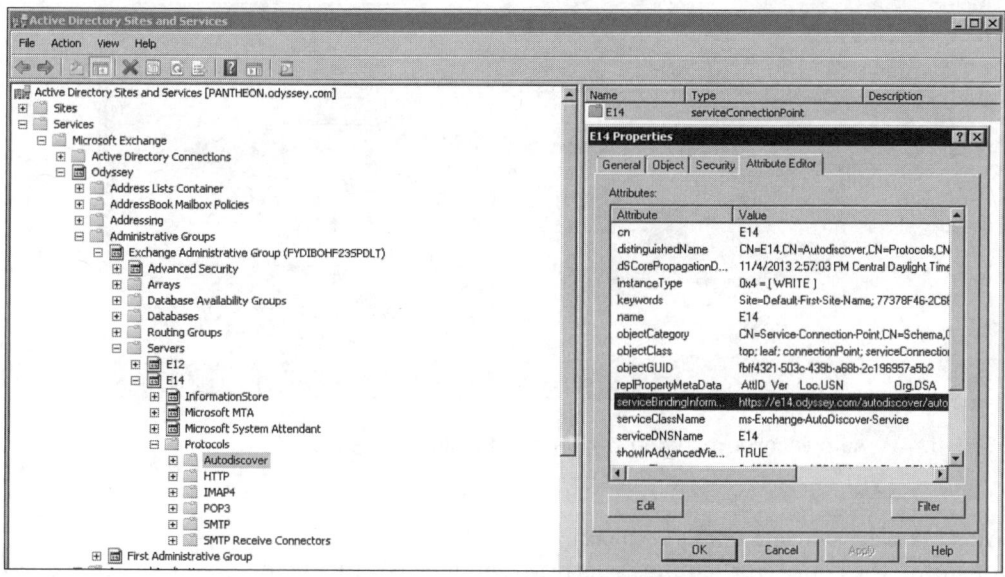

FIGURE 8.43   Autodiscover property in Active Directory Sites and Services.

The autodiscover property recorded in Active Directory Sites and Services is only one part of autodiscovery. Exchange email clients such as Outlook use this Service Connection Point (SCP) property to configure the mailbox setting. The Exchange connector requires that a DNS record is available for it to perform a similar type of configuration. The DNS record is a Service Locator (SRV) record and must exist in the forward lookup zone of the Exchange server's domain. Perform the following procedure to create the DNS record if it is not present:

1. On a domain computer with the Active Directory administration tools, start DNS. Expand **Forward Lookup Zones**. Right-click your domain name and select **Other New Records**.

2. In the Resource Record Type dialog, select **Service Location (SRV)** and click **Create Record**.

3. Provide the following property settings. Figure 8.44 shows the properties of the SRV record created in the Odyssey domain.

  ▶ **Service: _Autodiscover**

  ▶ **Protocol: _tcp**

▶ **Port number: 443**

▶ **Host offering this service: Autodiscover.*<domain>***

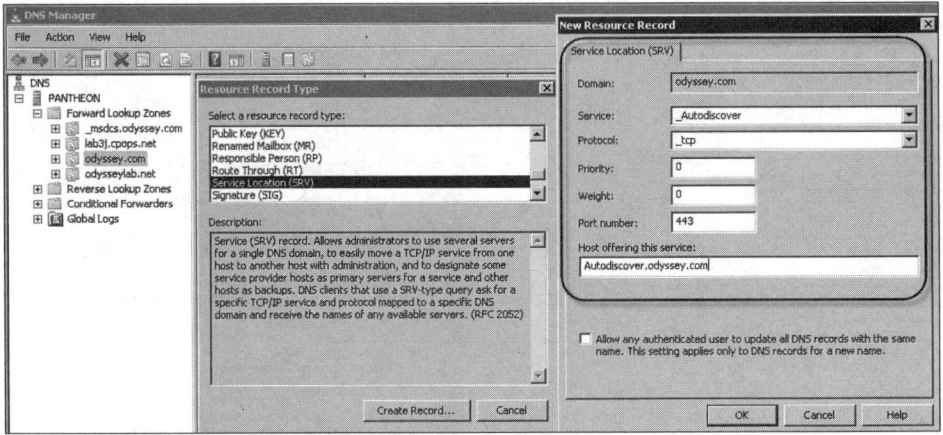

FIGURE 8.44   Autodiscover record in DNS forward lookup zone.

Service Manager Console Configurations

Configuring the connector requires selecting templates for the incident and service request classes. The authors recommend creating templates for the Exchange connector, as it provides flexibility and control over all incidents or service requests created or updated by this connector. By creating a source and classification category, you can distinguish these incidents or service requests from those created or updated by other sources.

Follow the instructions in the documentation provided as part of the download to complete configuring the Exchange connector.

User Mailbox Impersonation

Microsoft's deployment guide (SM2012_EC_DepGuide.docx), provided with the Exchange connector download, includes instructions on configuring impersonation. Impersonation is required if you need to process emails from a mailbox other than that of the Service Manager workflow user account and is configured using PowerShell. However, the PowerShell statement `New-ManagementRoleAssignment -Name:AdminImpersonateAll -Role:ApplicationImpersonation -User SCSMWorkflow` is a security and compliance risk, as it grants impersonation access to all mailboxes.

The authors recommend establishing a filter; this could be a prefix for all mailboxes the workflow account is impersonating. An example of a prefix is "SCSM." Use this string filter to create the role impersonation. The PowerShell cmdlets using this filter and a workflow user called Odyssey\SM_WFA follow:

```
New-ManagementScope -Name:ServiceManagerMailboxes -RecipientRestrictionFilter { Name
-Like *SCSM* }
```

```
New-ManagementRoleAssignment -Name:AdminImpersonateAll
-Role:ApplicationImpersonation -CustomRecipientScope:ServiceManagerMailboxes
-User:Odyssey\SM_WFA
```

This ensures only mailboxes with the filter can be impersonated.

Connector Maintenance and Troubleshooting

The Service Manager connectors generally require minimal maintenance once created and operational. There are occasions and scenarios that require you to perform adjustments to settings or troubleshoot issues relating to what is or is not synchronized. This section provides common scenarios and troubleshooting tips on Service Manager connectors.

Connector Maintenance

Maintaining connectors falls into three categories:

▶ **Out of schedule synchronization:** The connectors run continually according to the schedule selected when they were created. To perform a manual synchronization, select **Synchronize Now** in the Service Manager console.

▶ **Source environment maintenance:** You can disable connectors when the source environment from which the connector extracts information is undergoing maintenance. For example, you would disable the connector to Configuration Manager when the Configuration Manager database might temporarily contain erroneous data during planned maintenance. You can suspend and resume connector synchronization using the Enable and Disable tasks in the Service Manager console.

▶ **Updating connector settings:** After creating a connector, you can make only limited edits to its settings. To update the settings, you would need to first disable the working connector, create an updated connector, wait for successful synchronization, and then delete the old connector.

Connector Troubleshooting

Service Manager connectors can fail and require investigation to resolve the cause of the failure. Table 8.6 lists troubleshooting resources, known issues, and resolutions.

TABLE 8.6   Troubleshooting Resources and Known Connector Issues

Resource/Issue	Notes
Event Log: Operations Manager	Service Manager provides detailed logging of the connector process. The Service Manager event log (named Operations Manager) is under the Applications and Services Log. Connector issues and status can be found in the log. This should be your first point of investigation.

Resource/Issue	Notes
Incorrect or missing delegation	Most common troubleshooting issues with connectors are associated with missing or incorrect connector user delegation. Review the requirements for each connector provided in this chapter and in the Microsoft official documentation on what specific rights are required.
Source System	Make sure that the source systems from which the connectors extract information are available. A common issue is the impact of firewalls.
TechNet: Search for Troubleshooting System Center 2012 - Service Manager Deployment Issues	This is the official Microsoft location for the latest information on Service Manager.

TIP: USER FORUMS AND BLOGS

Service Manager troubleshooting information is available on various Internet user forums. Use search engines such as Bing and Google to aid with troubleshooting, as there are many community leaders discussing the most current issues and resolutions.

Summary

This chapter discussed and provided guidance on connectors you can create and work with in a Service Manager deployment. It focused on the structure and architecture of configuration item and work item connectors, and discussed creating the different types of connectors.

The next chapter discusses business services configuration items and their usage in a Service Manager deployment. Business services can be configured manually or automatically through the Operations Manager CI connector discussed in this chapter.

Business Services

Service Manager introduces business services as a virtual representation of a service from the business and user perspective, showing dependencies, responsibilities, and settings. System Center Operations Manager presents the visual representation of a service from a monitoring point of view, facilitated through its distributed application feature. Distributed applications let you define groups of components included in a service, scoping security roles, reports, and views to work with your service—regardless of the physical location of the components.

You can utilize Service Manager with Operations Manager to combine business services with distributed applications and provide a complete *service map* (introduced in Chapter 3, "MOF, ITIL, and System Center"). A service map is a logical view of a service, where Service Manager provides soft properties of this map, such as affected users and the service owner, and Operations Manager supplies the components and settings.

The combined functionality of these two System Center components provides a logical view into your business services. This chapter discusses how to create and maintain business services, and how to use them in your daily activities.

Introducing Business Services in Service Manager

Business services enable you to view and present Information Technology (IT) services from a business and user perspective. A business service or a service map is useful in almost all areas of operations management, incident management, and change management, and assists when designing new infrastructures. The business service shows the relationships defined among services and how those different services affect each other; this can assist your support team when troubleshooting. The relationship mapping can also assist in proactively defining dependencies when planning changes and in assessing risks associated with those changes. The service ownership, identified in the service map, can help with ensuring proper escalation and identifying approvers for a change against a business service.

Utilizing an organization-wide service map can show the relationships between a single server or service to other components or subservices in the organization. This assists the organization in identifying how a simple change can cause a chain reaction affecting multiple other related services, and business services as a whole.

Defining Business Services

A business service in Service Manager contains many properties and attributes; these are presented in the user interface, grouped by a number of tabs, as shown in Figure 9.1, which displays a service map. You can customize a business service to include more attributes as needed.

Figure 9.1 displays a service classified as a Web Service. Service classifications can be added by customizing the Service Classification List, located in the Service Manager console under Library -> Lists.

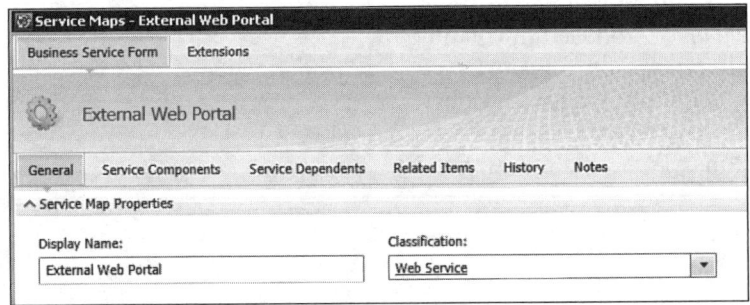

FIGURE 9.1   Tabs of a business service.

Use the Notes tab on the right of Figure 9.1 to insert notes about your service. Significant information should be defined as separate properties, such as cost center and customer information.

Service Manager manages the contents shown under the History tab (also shown in Figure 9.1); these do not require manual entry. As shown by the example in Figure 9.2, Service Manager maintains a record of all changes made to an object. If you update any property or edit a relationship of an object, that modification is recorded in the history.

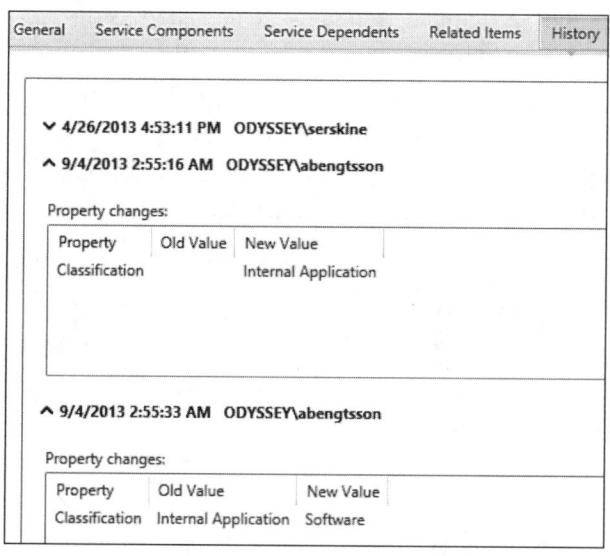

FIGURE 9.2   Displaying the history record of a business service.

Tracking changes can be useful in several ways:

▶ **To see what changed, and when it was changed:** Examples of information captured could include when extra memory was added to a computer or when an Internet Information Services (IIS) site was removed from a web farm.

▶ **To determine who made changes:** You might want to know who changed the priority of the service to Low so engineers no longer are concerned about incidents occurring during nonbusiness hours! You can also use this information to see whether a change was made in connection with a change to an object; if this is not the case, there could be an audit issues when an audit is performed against the configuration management database (CMDB).

The Related Items tab (see Figure 9.3) shows you other objects related to this business service:

▶ **Work items affecting this configuration item:** This section displays all incidents, problems, change requests, and release requests that have this business service as an affected item. These work items are related directly to the configuration item (CI). An example would be change requests about upgrading this service.

▶ **Work Items:** This section shows all work items to which this business service is related. This could be a change that has the business service as a related item, but not as the service that will be changed. An example of this would be if you were changing a router: This could affect a number of services, even if they are not the direct target for the change.

▶ **Configuration Items:** The Configuration Items section shows CIs related to the business service. Figure 9.3 shows this text box as well.

▶ **Knowledge Articles:** This section shows all knowledge articles related to the business service. Examples could include documentation or related user guides.

▶ **Attached Files:** Not displayed in Figure 9.3, this section shows all files uploaded to the business service. This might include guides in a non-knowledge article format, warranty documents, or configuration files.

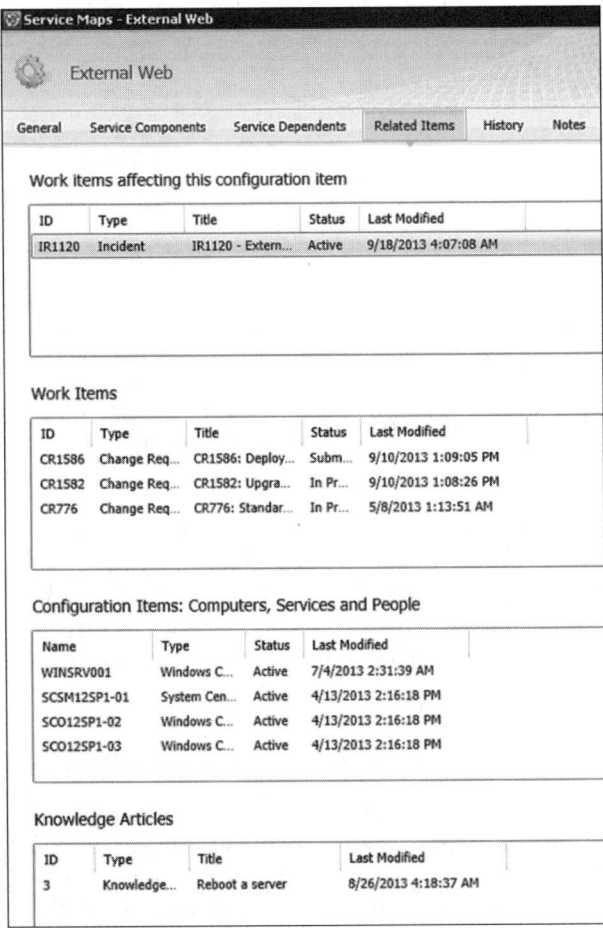

FIGURE 9.3   Viewing related items in a business service.

Characteristics of a Business Service

A significant amount of information is associated with a Service Manager business service. Tables 9.1, 9.2, and 9.3 provide information about each property of a business service object and its purpose.

TABLE 9.1 The General Tab of a Business Service

Property	Description
Display Name	The name of the service (such as External Web service).
Classification	The type of service. Examples could include internal application or storage. Use this setting to calculate the criticality of an incident or change, based on the service classification and priority. You can modify this list in the Library workspace; the list name is Service Classification.
Owned By Organization	The owner is the person or organization owning the service. For example, the Web service team.
Priority	The priority of the service. Use this setting to calculate how critical an incident or change is, based on the service classification and priority.
	This list can be modified in the Library workspace; the list name is Service Priority.
Status	Status shows the state of the service. Use this setting to calculate how to work with change requests, incidents, and problems. For example, if there is an incident reported related to this service and the service is In Maintenance, the incident will not get the priority as if the service was in service. This list is modifiable in the Library workspace; the list name is Service Status.
Availability Schedule	Availability agreements describe the availability of a service within a specified period. As an example, office hours would have 100% availability. A best practice is to determine the format you will input this value for your organization, as there is no drop-down list for this. An example could be 24/7/365, meaning 24 hours, 7 days a week, for the entire year.
Service Owner	The service owner is responsible for delivering the service within the service level. The service owner is typically the lead of the team of engineers or specialists owning the service.
Service Contacts	These are the individuals to contact regarding the service. You may decide to extend this field with information about the roles of each service contact. For example, you could specify whether the contact is a service engineer, technical specialist, or a team leader. Service contacts are the contacts for all daily questions.
Service Customers	Individual(s) who negotiates and agrees to the service level targets.
Affected Users	Persons affected when the service is not working. These individuals are using the tool as one of their primary tools.

9

TABLE 9.2   The Service Components Tab of a Business Service

Property	Description
Service Components	This field shows all components in the business service. Components can be based on a distributed application from Operations Manager.
Properties of the Selected Item	This field displays the class name and name of the selected component. On the Service Components tab, select a component and select Open to open the properties of the CI.
Related Work Items for the Selected Item	This field shows related items. For example, if a CI in the business service is added as an affected item in an incident, that incident is shown in this field.

TABLE 9.3   The Service Dependents Tab of a Business Service

Property	Description
Service Dependents	This displays all CIs on which the business service is dependent. The authors recommend adding other business services here to minimize the number of objects in the list and ensure you have a complete overview of the list of service dependents. If each component is added individually, it is difficult to see an overview of the CIs on which your business service is dependent. This list also shows whether the business services this service depends on are currently affected by an incident or change request. The drop-down menu on the right can be used to expand business services to see subcomponents; this enables you to investigate those components affected by a change request or incident.
Properties of the Selected Item	This field shows the class name and name of the selected component. Selecting **Open** displays the properties of the CI. For example, if you select a Windows computer you can see it is an instance of the `Microsoft.Windows.Computer` class, but if you view its properties, you can see all other attributes of the CI such as hardware and software.
Related Work Items for the Selected Item	This shows you related items. For example, if the CI is added as the affected item in an incident, that incident is shown in this field.

CAUTION: SELECTING OBJECTS IN SERVICE MAPS

You can select only one object at a time when working within service maps. Do not attempt to add multiple objects at the same time.

Using Operations Manager with Business Services

System Center Operations Manager, the monitoring component of System Center, is a key piece of Microsoft's cloud and datacenter management strategy. Operations Manager 2012 provides the following benefits:

- ▶ **360-degree application and service monitoring:** This capacity enables you to integrate application, client, server, and synthetic transaction monitoring into a single end-to-end solution. Service-oriented views and availability reporting allow your operations team and IT management to get the information they need to quickly identify and resolve issues that affect service levels.

- ▶ **Best of breed for Windows:** Expertise from the Microsoft product teams provides prescriptive knowledge and automated inline tasks to improve monitoring, troubleshooting, and problem resolution for more than 60 Microsoft applications and Windows Server components. Operations Manager also includes problem management and troubleshooting of client computers to accelerate identifying and resolving end user issues.

- ▶ **Single pane of glass:** Microsoft provides management packs for non-Microsoft devices such as UNIX, Linux, and J2EE application servers. Operations Manager also supports deep monitoring of network devices.

- ▶ **Increased efficiency and control of your IT environment:** Operations Manager automates routine and redundant tasks, providing intelligent reporting and monitoring to help increase efficiency and control of your environment. Its scalability can support organizations with tens of thousands of managed servers and hundreds of thousands of managed clients, using multiple management servers and connected management groups for a consolidated view of your enterprise.

Distributed Applications in Operations Manager

Distributed applications, which are one of the most powerful features of Operations Manager, enable you to view the overall monitoring state of an application, as in Figure 9.4. You can use the distributed application to show all components of a service, from the end user to the server hardware; this is also known as *end-to-end monitoring*.

Early monitoring software focused on servers and devices. This was problematic as alerts were isolated and narrow in scope. When applications and services often span multiple servers and locations, an isolated alert saying some Windows service is down simply does not provide enough information.

Distributed applications let you monitor a service from all angles. If any service component fails or is not working as needed, the entire distributed application is indicated as unhealthy. Drilling down in the distributed application lets you see the component that is the root cause. This approach enables easy identification of the failing component within the monitoring solution, which decreases troubleshooting reaction time. You can include all types of components in a distributed application, which can then be combined with a Service Manager business service to produce your service map.

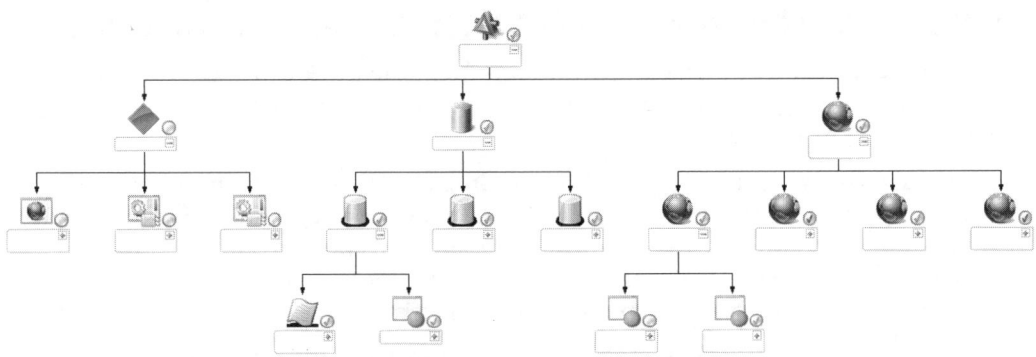

FIGURE 9.4   An Operations Manager distributed application.

A distributed application is based on a number of component groups that work in conjunction with one another. A component group is a logical group of components, similar to a folder containing files. Figure 9.4 includes component groups for applications, databases, and web servers. You can create relationships between component groups. (This relationship is for display purposes only; it does not affect health rollup or how alerts are generated.)

Objects must be discovered before they can be included in a distributed application. This is an important consideration when planning your distributed applications and service maps. If Operations Manager cannot monitor everything you need to include in the distributed application, you can create a custom class in Operations Manager or Service Manager, described later in the "Using Non-Operations Manager Components" section of this chapter. If building a business service based on a distributed application, the custom class should be built in Operations Manager.

Distributed Application Best Practices

When you are building custom distributed applications, it may be difficult to determine what to include. For example, you may want to use a distributed application for availability monitoring and run service level agreement (SLA) reports based on the application. In this case, you do not want to include every component of a service. Say your IT organization is responsible for maintaining a website, which includes a number of web servers in a web farm and a SQL Server cluster. The cluster has an active and a passive node. If you include both nodes and web servers in your distributed application and the passive SQL node has a problem, the application would show availability is affected. However, as the node is passive, its health does not affect the availability of the service! In this case, you do not want the incident to roll up and affect the availability and decrease the percentage uptime in the SLA report.

Rather, you would create two distributed applications:

▶ **An application used as a foundation for SLA monitoring:** This includes only those components that affect the availability of the service and is used for reporting uptime.

▶ **An application used by engineers:** This version includes all components. This view can be used for troubleshooting by the group that operates and maintains the application.

Building distributed applications that will be transferred to Service Manager adds another layer of complexity. Even if the transfer is complex to configure, this is often more efficient than building the business service manually in Service Manager—as attaching hundreds of configuration items to a business service is a time-consuming activity.

Service Maps as the Foundation of a Business Service

A service map is a graphical description of a service and can be used as a foundation when configuring distributed applications in Operations Manager and business services in Service Manager. There are five component categories into which you can categorize most components of a service map:

▶ **Software:** All software associated with the service, including all supporting or dependent software. For example, this could be Windows Server 2012 R2 and network software.

▶ **Hardware:** This includes all servers, network devices, and hardware devices required by the service to function. This should also take into account the model and configuration, such as an HP DL 380 G6.

▶ **Services:** These are other services required by this service to function. Services can be divided into two subcategories:

  ▶ **Upstream:** Upstream are services that provide this service with required input.

  ▶ **Downstream:** This service provides these services with input. For example, Exchange relies on downstream services such as Active Directory and backup.

▶ **Settings:** All configuration settings required by the service to work. This could include server roles such as database server or reporting server, and Internet Protocol (IP) numbers. Information about settings typically is easier to add in Service Manager than in Operations Manager.

▶ **Customers:** Information about the customer of the service; these could be the accounts payable department and geographical regions. This category is metadata that you add in Service Manager. Customer information is difficult to add in Operations Manager but can be added in Service Manager.

While some settings data can be synchronized from Operations Manager, some must be added in Service Manager; examples include Service Owner and Service Customers. You can document settings and other related items to your business service in Service Manager. You must build the other categories' components in Operations Manager prior to importing the distributed application into Service Manager.

As services change over time, you should periodically update those business services existing in Service Manager and distributed in Operations Manager to ensure they represent the real world properly. Both organizational structure and technical components may change. Organizational structure changes are generally updated in Service Manager, with technical components updated in Operations Manager. As an example, the Exchange Server team might be migrated into a messaging team, or new Exchange clusters are added to the service. These changes require updates to the distributed application and to the business service.

Maintaining business services and distributed applications requires the following:

▶ **Ownership:** An owner should be assigned to each business service and distributed application, with the responsibility for keeping them updated. The owner should have knowledge about the service. The same person could maintain both objects, or there could be multiple individuals.

▶ **Review:** There should be a regularly scheduled review of the distributed application and business service. This should occur at least on a quarterly basis. The review should also assess knowledge articles in Service Manager and verify that the monitoring in Operations Manager is carried out in an optimal manner. The authors recommend that this review be included as part of the normal change management process. If anything changes that affects the structure of the distributed application or the metadata of the business service, it should be updated in the same process. An example could be if an additional server is added to the service.

You can use the Microsoft Operations Framework (MOF) for guidance to build and maintain a service map. Building a service map is often a quick endeavor once you have gathered all the necessary information. The challenge can be getting everyone engaged in the project and ensuring that the value of a complete service map is understood. The steps to build a service map follow:

1. **Identify the team:** Building a correct service map and maintaining a business service in Service Manager requires deep knowledge about the service. This step verifies that the correct knowledge is included in the members of the project group.

2. **Define the mapping template:** This step establishes a guideline of how a service map should appear. As an example, a service map might include naming standards and software to use.

3. **Determine the appropriate level of resolution:** How many details should be included? More detailed maps are often better to use and provide more value to the organization. On the other hand, additional details make maps more complex to maintain and build.

4. **Select services for mapping:** This step helps identify which services to map. A good rule could be to start with the topmost customer facing services.

5. **Gather data and draw the service maps:** Collect all data needed, and draw the first version of the map.

6. **Establish service relationships:** Investigate and add all relationships between your service and other services to your map.

7. **Maintain the service maps:** Establish a plan to maintain and update the map.

Creating a Business Service

The example in the following sections creates a distributed application in Operations Manager and synchronizes it to Service Manager as a business service. This application, previously displayed in Figure 9.4, is called External Web and contains several databases, application components, and websites. The distributed application is built using the Operations Manager console; the management pack is then exported from Operations Manager and imported into Service Manager.

When building business services, you often use components from a number of management packs, meaning your business service depends on a number of other management packs. All dependent management packs must be imported into Service Manager as well.

Building an Operations Manager Distributed Application

The process of creating a business service begins with creating a distributed application, which is stored in an Operations Manager management pack. Distributed applications are comprised of multiple objects. These objects may be defined by different management packs, meaning they are already monitored as components of a Microsoft application or service such as SQL Server, Windows Server, or IIS, but not from the perspective of a distributed application. Adding these to a distributed application can provide an overall health view of an application that consists of distributed objects. This becomes the basis of a business service. Follow these steps to build the External Web distributed application:

1. In the Operations Manager console, navigate to **Authoring -> Distributed Application**.

2. In the Tasks pane, select **Create a New Distributed Application**.

3. On the Distributed Application Designer page, click **New** to create a new management pack.

4. On the Create a Management Pack page, input the following information and then click **Next**:

   ▶ **Name: External Web**

   ▶ **Description: Management Pack for Odyssey External Web**

5. On the Knowledge page, click **Create** to create the management pack. You have now created an unsealed management pack in which to store your distributed application. The associated monitors and rules become part of that management pack.

6. In the Distributed Application Designer page, input the following information:

   ▶ **Name: External Web**

   ▶ **Description: External Web for customers**

   ▶ **Template:** Blank (Advanced)

7. Click **OK** to open the Distributed Application Designer.

The Distributed Application Designer (see Figure 9.5) consists of a number of panes:

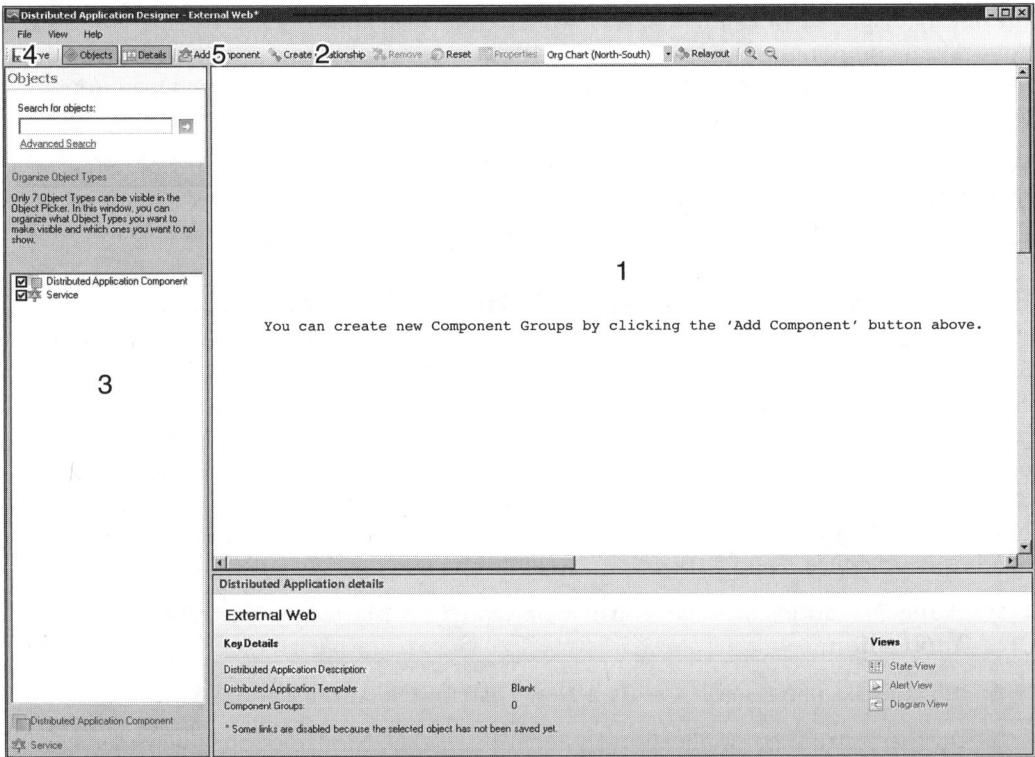

FIGURE 9.5   The panes of the Operations Manager Distributed Application Designer.

▶ The Diagram pane (1) is the Distributed Application Designer drawing board. This is where you draw your distributed application, which becomes the structure for your business service in Service Manager. You add component boxes to categorize the application components.

▶ Click **Add Component** (5) to create a component box. The example in this section requires one component for SQL databases, one for IIS websites, and one for the Windows service. The Object pane (3) shows the components you can drag and drop to your component groups.

▶ Click **Create Relationship** (2) on the toolbar to use a cursor to draw relationships describing the workflow between the component groups of your distributed application.

▶ Click **Save** (4) on the toolbar to save the distributed application to an unsealed management pack; in this case the External Web management pack.

Perform the following steps to create the distributed application:

1. In the Distributed Application Designer, select **Add Component**.

2. In the Create New Component Group dialog box, input **Databases** as the name for your component group. In the objects list, select **Configuration Item** -> **Logical Entity** -> **Application Component** -> **Database** -> **SQL Databases**, shown in Figure 9.6. Click **OK**.

3. The left side of the Distributed Application Designer, in the Object pane, now shows all databases. Because the component was configured to accept only SQL databases, you see only this type of object.

   From the object list in the Distributed Application Designer, drag and drop several databases to the Databases component group.

4. Click **Add Component**.

5. In the Create New Component Group dialog box, type **Web Servers** as the name for your component group. In the objects list, select **Configuration Item** -> **Logical Entity** -> **Application Component** -> **Web Site** -> **IIS Web Site**. Click OK.

   In the Distributed Application Designer, from the object list, drag and drop several IIS websites to the Web Servers component group.

6. Click **Add Component**.

7. In the Create New Component Group dialog box, input **Application** as the name for your component group. In the objects list select **Configuration Item** -> **Logical Entity** ->**.NET Application Component**. Click **OK**.

   In the Distributed Application Designer, from the object list, drag and drop a .NET application component to the Application Components component group.

8. Save the distributed application and close the Distributed Application Designer.

9. Now in the Operations Manager console, right-click the External Web distributed application and select **Diagram View** from the menu. A diagram view opens and shows the distributed application, as shown previously in Figure 9.4.

9

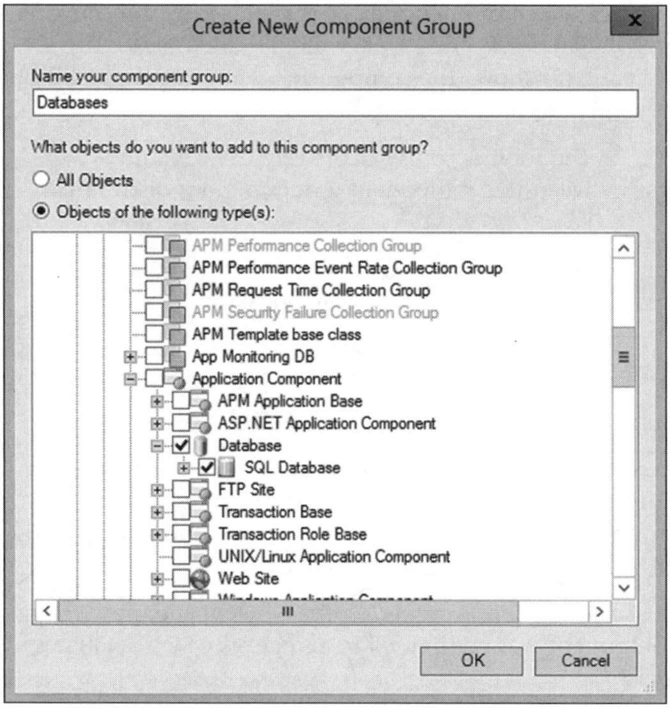

FIGURE 9.6   Class picker for a component group.

NOTE: CALCULATING THE DISTRIBUTED APPLICATION STATE

If your deployment is large, there may be a delay between the time a new distributed application is created and when its state is calculated. Until rollup configuration is calculated, the state is displayed as unmonitored (white icon).

Exporting the Operations Manager Management Pack

After creating the distributed application in Operations Manager, you must export the management pack, as Service Manager does not automatically synchronize management packs between these two System Center components. If a management pack in Operations Manager is changed, you must manually export it and import it into Service Manager. An administration workstation with both the Service Manager and Operations Manager consoles can make the process of exporting and importing management packs easier, as it removes the need to transfer files between servers and lets you perform all steps from one desktop.

To export management packs from Operations Manager, you can use the Operations Manager Shell (built on Windows PowerShell), or the Operations Manager console. You may want to use a PowerShell script if you have a large number of management packs to export or need to automate the process. The next example shows how to export the External Web management pack from the console. Follow these steps:

1. In the Operations Manager console, navigate to **Administration -> Management Packs**.

2. In the Result pane showing the list of management packs, select the **External Web** management pack. Click **Export Management Pack** from the Tasks pane.

3. In the Browse For Folder dialog box, select the target folder for the management pack. Export it to C:\MP Export\.

4. In the System Center Operations Manager pop-up window, verify that the export was successful and then click **OK**.

To achieve the same task with Operations Manager Shell, perform the following steps:

1. From the Start menu, start the Operations Manager Shell.

2. In the Operations Manager Shell, type the following command

```
get-scommanagementpack | where {$_.displayname -eq "External Web"} |
export-scommanagementpack -path "C:\MP Export"
```

NOTE: OVERWRITING A MANAGEMENT PACK FILE

If an export of the management pack exists in the export target folder, the Operations Manager Shell overwrites it. When using the Operations Manager console, a dialog box asks whether you want to overwrite the existing management pack file.

A management pack cannot be imported into Service Manager without including any management packs it depends on. The next example shows how to determine those management packs on which your management pack depends. Follow these steps:

1. In the Operations Manager console, navigate to **Administration -> Management Packs**.

2. In the Result pane of the list of management packs, select the **External Web** management pack, and then click **Properties** from the Tasks pane.

3. On the External Web page, click the Dependencies tab. This displays a list of the management packs that depend on this management pack as well as the management packs this management pack depends on, as shown in Figure 9.7.

6

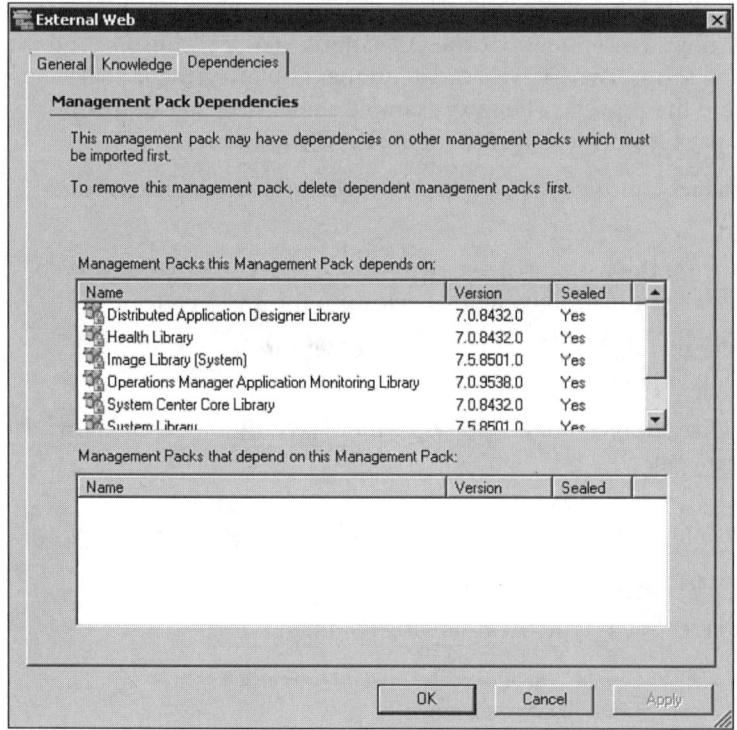

FIGURE 9.7   External Web management pack dependencies.

Importing the Management Pack into Service Manager

Next in this process is importing the External Web management pack into Service
Manager. Perform the following steps to import the management pack into Service
Manager using the Service Manager console:

1. In the Service Manager console, navigate to **Administration -> Management Packs**.

2. Select **Import** in the Tasks pane.

3. On the Select Management Packs to Import page, browse and select the management
   pack previously exported, for example, the management pack in C:\MP Export.

4. On the Import Management Packs page, click **Import**. The first time you try to
   import management packs you may receive the error message shown in Figure 9.8.
   Service Manager is telling you that there are missing management packs that this
   management pack depends on. You need to import these management packs first.

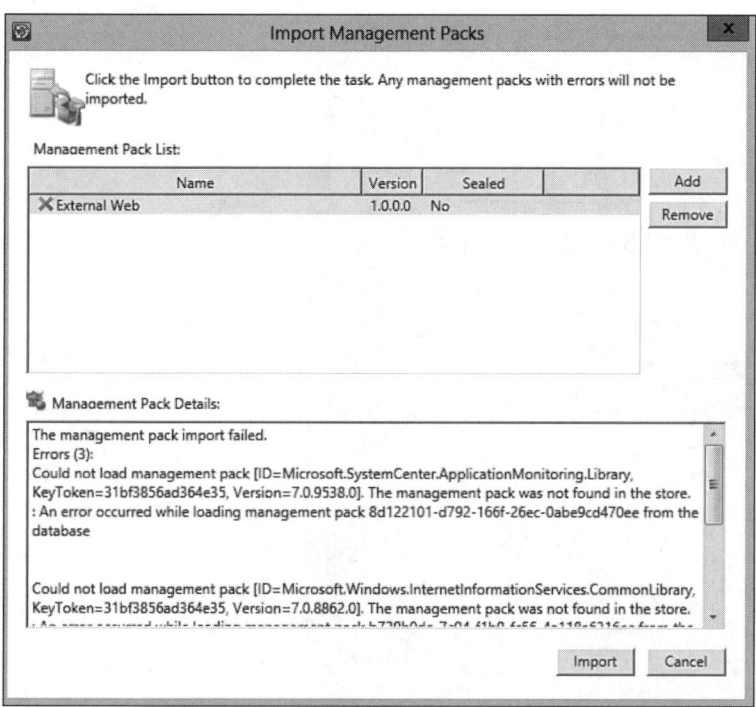

FIGURE 9.8   Error displayed when dependent management packs are not found.

TIP: IDENTIFYING THE CORRECT MANAGEMENT PACKS TO IMPORT

It might be difficult to locate the management packs to import or understand which management packs require importing. Notice in the Details section of Figure 9.8 that Service Manager displays the ID of the management pack rather than the friendly name. Figure 9.9 shows the Windows Server Internet Information Services Library management pack file, part of the IIS management pack. In the console, the management pack is displayed as Windows Service Internet Information Services Library; behind the console Service Manager and Operations Manager call it by its internal name (ID) Microsoft. Windows.InternetInformationServices.CommonLibrary.

Use the Operations Manager Shell to identify the correct management pack by typing the following command:

```
Get-SCOMManagementPack | where {$_.Name -eq "Microsoft.SystemCenter.
ApplicationMonitoring.Library"} | ft Name, Displayname
```

In some cases, you can download management packs directly from the Microsoft website, such as the SQL and IIS management packs used in this example. You can often copy core Operations Manager management packs from the Operations Manager installation folder on your management server.

9

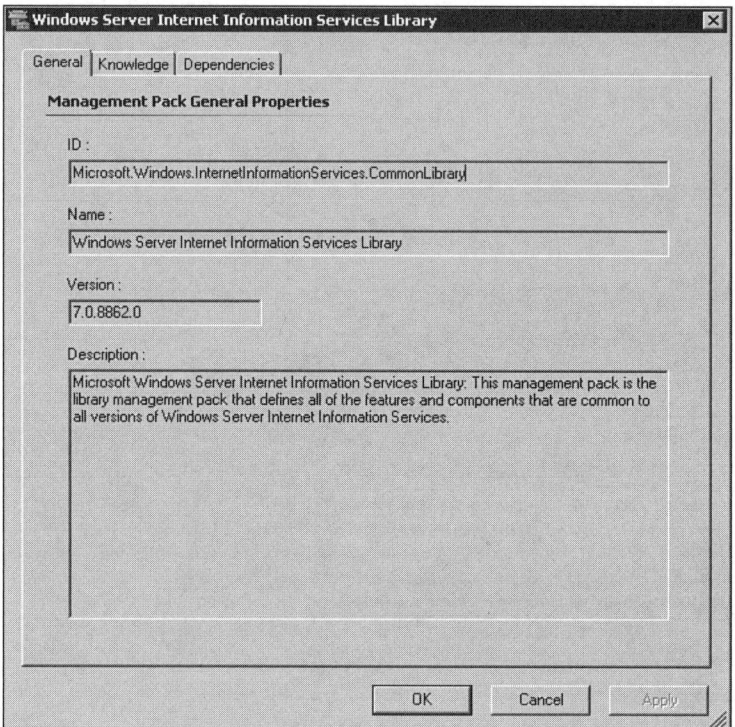

FIGURE 9.9   The management pack name (ID) and display (friendly) name.

5. After importing all dependent management packs and finally your own unsealed management pack, verify the import was successful (see Figure 9.10).

TIP: THE ROLE OF A "MODEL" MANAGEMENT PACK

The example in Figure 9.10 shows a successful import of the management pack but with some warning messages in the Management Pack Details section. A management pack authoring best practice is to store classes, combination classes, and relationship types in "model" management packs. These model management packs should be sealed so other management packs can reference to them and use resources from them, such as classes. The External Web management pack is an unsealed management pack that includes a class structure.

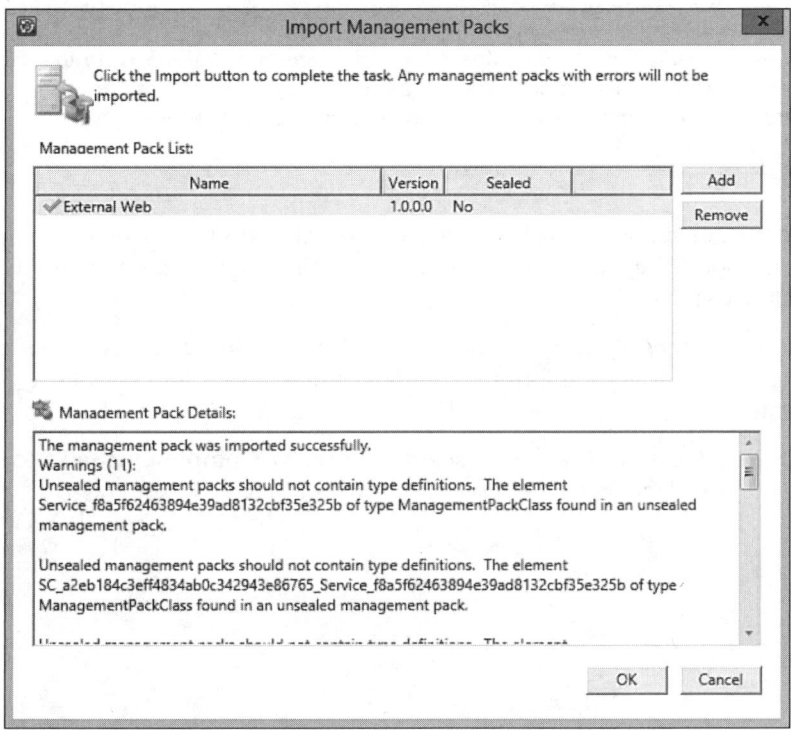

FIGURE 9.10   Successful import of a management pack into Service Manager.

Enabling Synchronization

If you open the Properties page of your new business service in Service Manager, in this example the External Web business service, you will notice no service components are displayed on the Service Components tab. There will not be any service components until you enable synchronization. The next example shows how to enable synchronization for the External Web management pack. Follow these steps:

1. In the Service Manager console, navigate to **Administration -> Connectors**.

2. In the Results pane, select the Operations Manager CI connector and click **Edit** from the Tasks pane.

3. In the Edit dialog box, select the Management Packs tab.

4. On the Management Packs tab, click **Refresh** to refresh the list of management packs to synchronize.

5. In the Management Pack list, ensure the External Web management pack is selected. Click **OK**.

6. In the Results pane, select the Operations Manager CI connector and click **Synchronize Now** from the Tasks pane.

NOTE: SYNCHRONIZING SERVICE COMPONENTS

The Operations CI connector transfers configuration items from Operations Manager to the Service Manager database (CMDB). These components are seen in your business service as service components. This connector must run successfully before your service components are listed.

7. Verify that the connector status is first Running and then changes to Finished Success. Note at this point the Operations Manager CI connector has now synchronized with Operations Manager.

8. Navigate to the Configuration Items workspace in the Service Manager console. Expand **Business Services**, select the **External Web** business service, and click **Edit** from the Tasks pane.

9. In the Service Maps - External Web window, select the **Service Components** tab and verify you see all the components of the service, as shown in Figure 9.11.

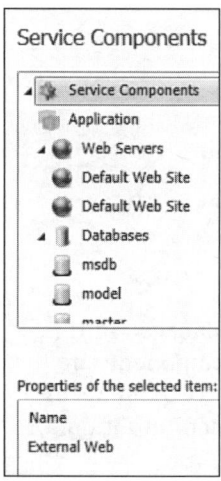

FIGURE 9.11   Service components of the External Web.

Missing Components

If any components are missing in the view, you most likely are missing a management pack or have not configured the connector to synchronize it. (You could still import the distributed application with a missing management pack, but you would be unable to synchronize all configuration items from Operations Manager.)

Once all components are in place, you can complete the remaining information for this business service, such as the service owner and affected users.

Using Non-Operations Manager Components

Some scenarios require components in your business service that do not exist in Operations Manager. There are several approaches for resolving this:

▶ **Use a third-party management pack:** Determine whether a management pack exists that you could use and import. Often a management pack exists from a Microsoft partner or the user community for unusual services and technologies.

▶ **Create a management pack containing the objects you need:** Create your own management pack containing those components. In some scenarios, the components are not actually required to be in Operations Manager to be monitored. In these cases, there is nothing to monitor; you only need the objects in Operations Manager to include them in a distributed application. The goal here is to include the components in a business service. Should you need "fake" components, you can author a management pack that discovers them based on, say, any registry key on any server. The discovery discovers instances of your custom class. Operations Manager shows the health of these fake objects as unknown and you do not notice them in the Operations Manager console.

Operations Manager 2012 has three tools for authoring a new class:

▶ **Visio Management Pack Designer:** The Visio Management Pack Designer is an add-in for Microsoft Visio 2010 used to create management packs by dragging and dropping graphical shapes. You can use this add-in to create an application model representation and standard monitoring scenarios. For more information about the Visio Management Pack Designer add-in, see http://social.technet.microsoft.com/ wiki/contents/articles/5235.visio-management-pack-designer-for-system-center-2012-operations-manager.aspx.

▶ **Visual Studio:** The Visual Studio Authoring Extensions (VSAE) enables you to use the XML code of a management pack directly. As the Visual Studio Authoring Extensions includes IntelliSense, it is not necessary to know all details of the management pack schema. The VSAE also allows multiple management pack authors to work on the same management pack project at the same time.

▶ **Operations Manager 2007 R2 Authoring console:** The Operations Manager 2007 R2 Authoring console can be used to develop management packs in a graphical user environment and supports Operations Manager 2007 R2 and 2012.

Although the Authoring console builds management packs using an older version of the management pack schema, you can use it in Operations Manager 2012 when not authoring a management pack using the 2012 schema. You cannot modify a management pack built in Operations Manager 2012 with the Operations Manager 2007 R2 Authoring console, as the schema version is higher than that supported.

6

Authoring a Management Pack

Should you require a "fake" component for your business service, this section shows how to author a simple management pack for a Telex device using the Operations Manager 2007 R2 Authoring console. This sample management pack discovers an instance of the Telex class, performing discovery based on a registry key on the management server hosting the Operations Manager root management server emulator role. The Authoring console is free for download from the Microsoft website; see http://technet.microsoft.com/en-us/library/ee957010.aspx for additional information about this console. Perform the following steps:

1. Open the Operations Manager Authoring console. Select **File -> New**.

2. On the New Management Pack page, select the **Empty Management Pack** template. Input **Odyssey** as the management pack identity. Click **Next**.

3. On the Name and Description page, input **Odyssey Telex** as the display name. Click **Create**.

4. In the Authoring console, navigate to Service Model, click **Classes**, and select **New -> Windows Local Application** from the Actions pane.

5. In the Windows Local Application page, input **Odyssey.Telex** as ID and **Odyssey Telex Discovery** as the display name. Click **Next**.

6. On the Key Properties page, click **Finish**.

7. In the Authoring console, navigate to the Health Model workspace. Click **Discoveries** and select **New -> Registry (Filtered)** from the Actions pane.

8. Input the following on the General page and click **Next**:

   ▶ **ID: Odyssey.Telex.Discovery**

   ▶ **Display Name: Odyssey Telex**

   ▶ **Target: Microsoft.SystemCenter.RootManagementServer** (This is the Operations Manager 2012 management server hosting the root management server emulator.)

9. On the Schedule page, enter **48** hours. As this discovery discovers a fake object, it does not need to run very often; once is probably sufficient. Click **Next**.

10. On the Computer page, click **Next**.

11. Click **Add** on the Registry Probe Configuration page.

12. Configure the Edit Attribute Properties window as shown in Figure 9.12, and click **OK**:

> ▶ **Object Type: Key**

> ▶ **Name: Telex**

> ▶ **Path:** HKLM**SOFTWARE**\

> ▶ **Attribute Type: Check if exists**

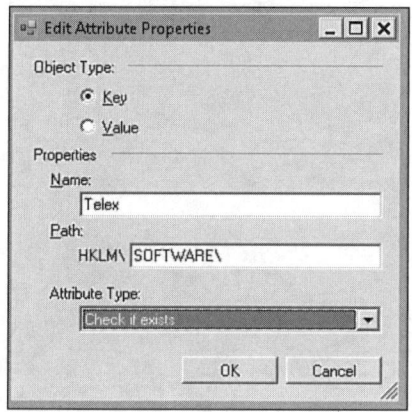

FIGURE 9.12   Attribute properties of the Odyssey Telex management pack.

13. Click **Next** on the Edit Attribute Properties page.

14. On the Expression Filter page, click **Insert**. Configure the expression filter as shown in Figure 9.13, and click **Next**:

> ▶ **Parameter Name: Values/Telex**

> ▶ **Operator: Equals**

> ▶ **Value: True**

15. On the Discovery Mapper page, select **Odyssey.Telex** as Class ID. Select **Windows Computer Display Name (Entity)** as the non-key property value. Select **Windows Computer Principal Name (Windows Computer)** as the value for the key property. Click **Finish**.

16. From the File menu, select **Save**. The management pack is saved in unsealed format as an XML file.

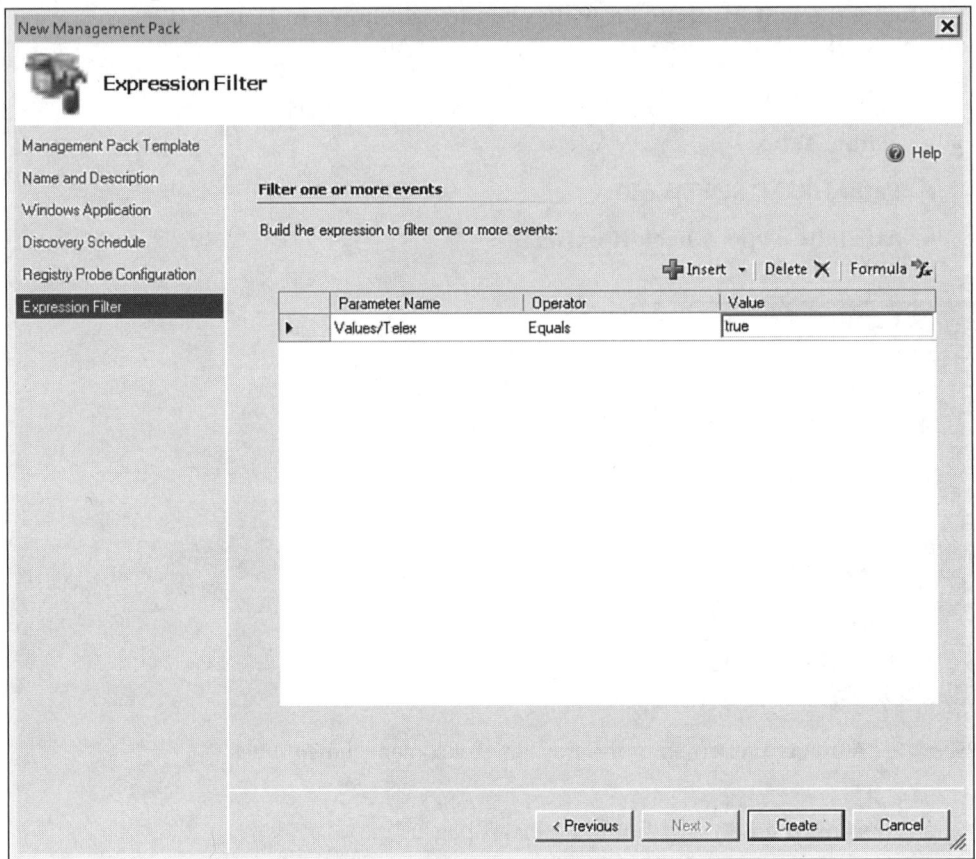

FIGURE 9.13   The expression filter in the Odyssey Telex management pack.

Importing and Using the Management Pack

The management pack created in the previous section must now be imported into Operations Manager. Open the Operations Manager console and use the Administration workspace to import the management pack. You could also import it directly from the Authoring console. To import the management pack from the Authoring console to the management group, use the Tools -> Export to Management Group option in the Authoring console.

To confirm the discovery is working, use the Discovered Inventory view in the Monitoring workspace in the Operations Manager console. This view lets you select a target class and then lists all instances and properties of that class. Figure 9.14 shows the view targeted to the Odyssey Telex class. Notice that the instance of the class has an unknown health state. This is because no monitors are rolling up to this class, so nothing can affect the health of the fake class, as shown in Figure 9.15.

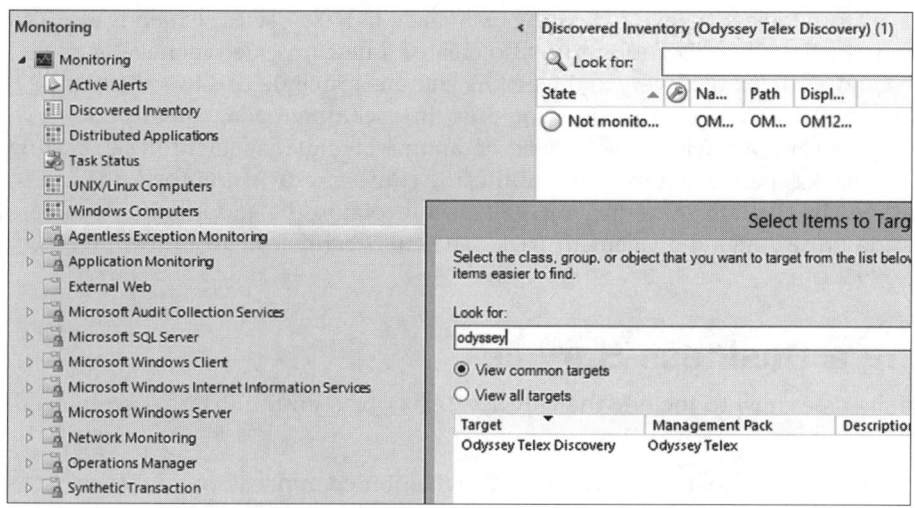

FIGURE 9.14   Use the Discovered Inventory view to see the discovery result.

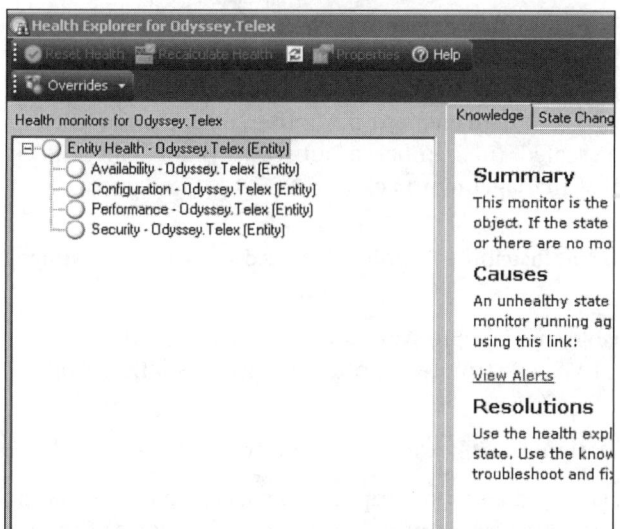

FIGURE 9.15   Health of the Odyssey Telex class, displayed in the Operations Manager Health Explorer.

To force the state of the Odyssey Telex class to be healthy, create any monitor targeting the Odyssey Telex class. Nothing needs to be monitored with this monitor; you can simply reset its health to healthy in the Operations Manager Health Explorer.

You now have a new object type in Operations Manager, Odyssey Telex, which is available for use in distributed applications. You also created a new unsealed management pack for the Odyssey Telex discovery and class. As you must include this in a distributed application in another management pack, you must first seal the management pack. (A management pack cannot reference or depend on an unsealed management pack.) Sealing a management pack is performed from the Authoring console or by using the MPSEAL tool available on the Operations Manager installation media, in the \SupportTools folder. For information on sealing a management pack, see http://technet.microsoft.com/en-us/library/bb309498.aspx.

Updating a Business Service

This section discusses how to include the Odyssey Telex object in the External Web business service.

▶ The first operation updates the External Web distributed application, and then imports the updated management pack into Service Manager. As you changed the class structure of the distributed application when you added the new Odyssey Telex object type, you must also import the management pack in Service Manager, to reflect the structure change.

▶ The second example adds the Odyssey Telex object, which is from another management pack. The Odyssey Telex management pack also must be imported into Service Manager. The Odyssey Extranet management packs including the distributed application will reference the Odyssey Telex management pack; therefore, the Odyssey Telex management pack must be sealed. (Remember, an unsealed management pack cannot reference another unsealed management pack.)

Perform the following steps to update the distributed application and import the management pack into Service Manager:

1. In the Operations Manager console, navigate to **Authoring -> Distributed Applications**. Select the External Web distributed application and click **Edit** from the Tasks pane.

2. In the Distributed Application Designer, click **Add Component**.

   In the Create New Component Group dialog box, input **Telex** as the name for your component group. In the Objects list, select **Configuration Item -> Logical Entity -> Local Application -> Windows Local Application -> Odyssey Telex**. Click **OK**.

3. From the Object list in the Distributed Application Designer, drag and drop a Telex instance to the Telex component group.

4. Save the distributed application and close the Distributed Application Designer.

5. In the Operations Manager console, right-click the External Web distributed application and select **View Diagram** from the menu. A diagram view opens and shows the distributed application, as in Figure 9.16.

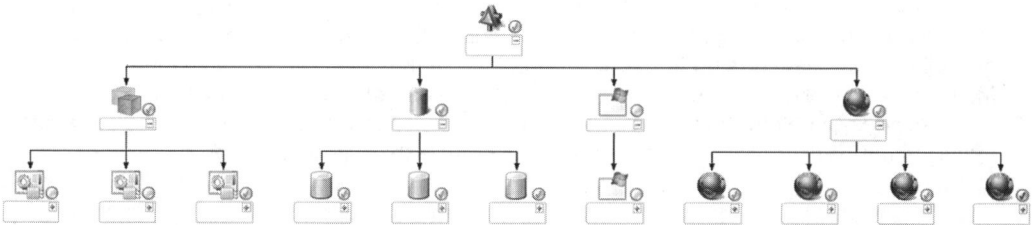

FIGURE 9.16   Components of the updated External Web.

NOTE: AUTOMATICALLY MAINTAINED DISTRIBUTED APPLICATIONS

Several Operations Manager management packs, such as the Microsoft Active Directory management pack and Microsoft Exchange management pack, include distributed applications out of the box. In these cases, the management pack automatically maintains those distributed applications.

You now must update the Service Manager side. The following steps describe the actions to perform to update Service Manager.

1. In the Operations Manager console, export the External Web management pack. This management pack must be exported into Service Manager as the structure of the service has changed. Do not forget to increment the version number of the management pack; otherwise, you cannot upgrade the management pack in Service Manager.

2. In the Service Manager console, import the sealed version of the Odyssey Telex management pack.

3. In the Service Manager console, import the updated version of the External Web management pack.

4. In the Service Manager console, verify that the Operations Manager CI connector includes the External Web management pack. Synchronize the CI connector.

5. In the Service Manager console, verify that the service map includes all new components.

NOTE: BUSINESS SERVICE MANAGEMENT PACK UPDATES

When you update a management pack in Service Manager with a new version, its customizations and configuration are retained. If you delete a management pack with a distributed application, all customization is deleted.

Say that you configure service customers on a service and upgrade the management pack containing the distributed application to version 2. All customizations are kept. However, if you delete version 1 and import version 2 of the management pack, all your customizations from version 1 such as service customers will be deleted.

There is a known issue when updating business services with a new management pack from Operations Manager: The business service is not updated in Service Manager according to the new version in the newly imported management pack from Operations Manager. This is expected to be fixed in a future release of Service Manager. The current workaround is to delete the management pack in Service Manager and import the updated management pack. This makes it a new import, rather than an upgrade of the management pack.

Automatically Mapping Operations Manager Incidents to a Business Service

Consider a scenario where alerts from Operations Manager should display as related incidents for your business service in Service Manager. Service Manager does not connect related incidents and services to each other by default. This means that when an alert on a Windows computer is included in the service components list for your service, that alert will not be related to the business service—it will be related to the Windows computer. The Service Components list shows the Windows computer with an incident work item icon next to it. Figure 9.17 displays a Windows computer in a component list with active incidents; Figure 9.18 shows a Windows computer in a component list without active incidents.

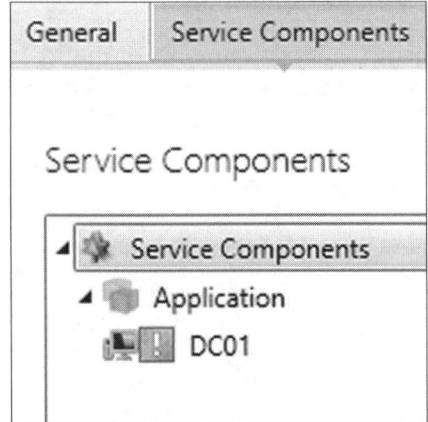

FIGURE 9.17   Windows Computer with related incident, a "!" icon before the computer.

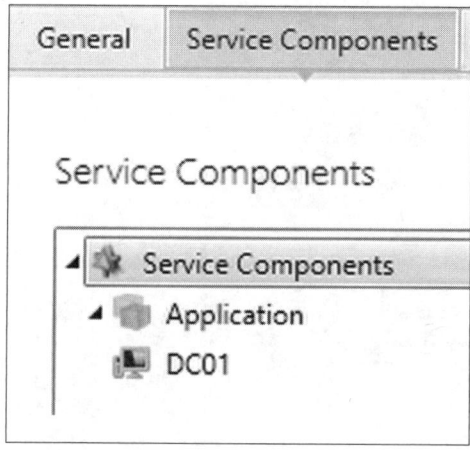

FIGURE 9.18   Windows Computer without related incidents.

For alerts to show as related to the business service, the alert must be generated having the same source as the service name. You can accomplish this using an extra dependency rollup monitor in Operations Manager. The examples in this section use the alert source of External Web.

The next procedure describes how to generate an alert when a Windows service in the External Web service changes state. While generating an alert when a Windows service stops occurs by default in Operations Manager, this procedure describes how to generate an alert as the External Web service (alert source), rather than the source as the server where the Windows service is running. This is important because when the source of the alert is the same as the business service name, the incident is automatically related to the service, as shown in Figure 9.19. Follow these steps:

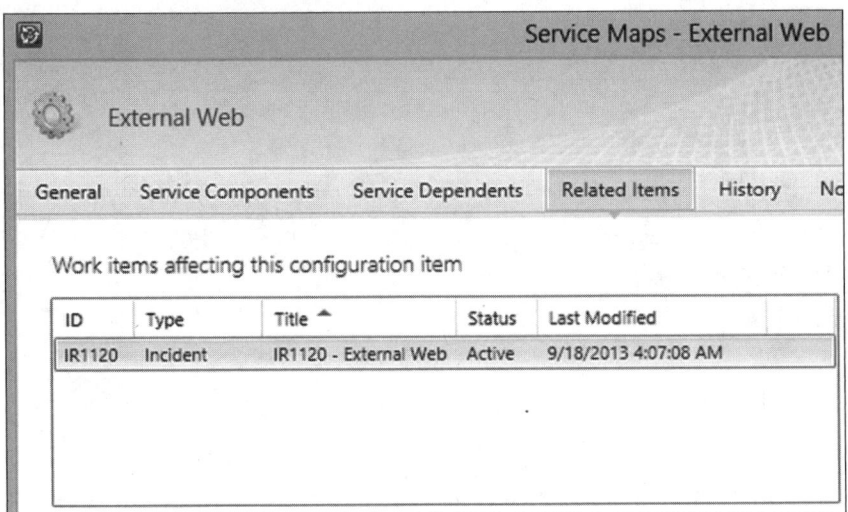

FIGURE 9.19   Operations Manager generated incident related to a business service.

1. In the Operations Manager console, navigate to **Authoring -> Monitors**.

2. Right-click **Monitors** and choose **Create a Monitor -> Dependency Rollup Monitor**. Configure the General properties page as shown in Figure 9.20 and click **Next**:

   ▶ **Name: External Web Windows Service**

   ▶ **Monitor target: Application**

   You may have multiple targets named Application; select the one in the External Web management pack.

   ▶ **Parent monitor: Availability**

   ▶ **Monitor is enabled:** Should be checked

   ▶ **Select destination management pack: External Web**

3. On the Monitor Dependency page, click **Next**.

4. Click **Next** on the Health Rollup Policy page.

5. On the Configure Alerts page, check the **Generate alerts for this monitor** check box. For the Alert Description, provide a short message stating that the Windows service is down, for example, **Telex Service down, please investigate**. Click **Create**.

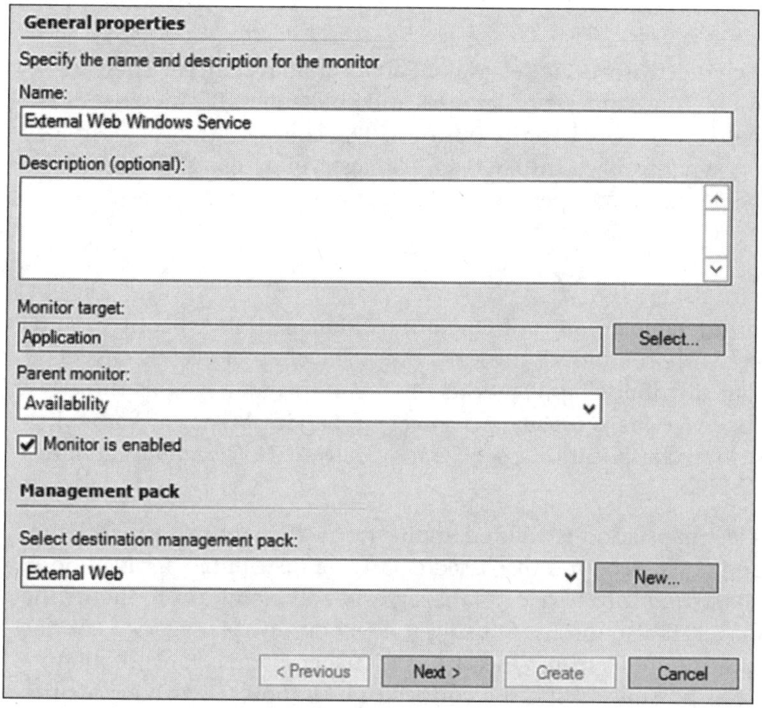

FIGURE 9.20   General properties page of the dependency rollup monitor.

Note that in this example, you still receive the original alert about the Windows service. When planning mapping between incidents and business services, it is important that you consider this to avoid multiple alerts and incidents. You can create an override to disable one of the alerts.

You could also enable one of the default aggregate rollup monitors in the External Web distributed application health model to generate an alert with the service as the alert source. A disadvantage is you cannot control the alert description.

TIP: TROUBLESHOOTING BUSINESS SERVICES

A business service includes a visual representation of your service from the business and user perspective. The business service shows your critical dependencies, settings, components, and areas of responsibility. Because a business service can show relationships between incidents and configuration items, it can assist in troubleshooting scenarios. If the issue affects multiple incidents and configuration items, you can see the relationship between these within your business service.

Fast Track

Business services have not changed since the release of Service Manager 2010. They are used the same way and provide the same set of features and challenges. Business services are used to represent the deliverables of IT to the business. The configuration of a service from Operations Manager is synchronized into Service Manager, making a single model from which changes can be managed as Operations Manager automatically detects them.

Summary

This chapter included a considerable amount of Operations Manager-related content and focused on business services and on building those services. The chapter also discussed how to plan and design your distributed applications in Operations Manager, as these are the foundation of your service maps (business services) in Service Manager. For additional information on distributed applications, see *System Center 2012 Operations Manager Unleashed* (Sams, 2013).

The chapter discussed service maps and distributed applications. It examined the different properties of a business service. The chapter discussed creating a distributed application in Operations Manager and exporting it to Service Manager, and addressing components that are not in Operations Manager. It also discussed using the Operations Manager CI connector. Synchronizing configuration items from Operations Manager is important to obtain as complete a business service as possible. Using the connector to import CIs also avoids the need for a manual process. The chapter stepped through the process of updating a service map, and looked at how to connect Operations Manager alerts with business services as related incidents.

For further information about IT services and service mapping, reference the MOF source materials, available at http://www.microsoft.com/mof and http://www.microsoft.com/en-us/download/details.aspx?id=17647.

This chapter examined the process of creating a distributed application, exporting it to Service Manager as a service map, and keeping it updated. The next chapter discusses the Service Manager service catalog, which enables IT to provide a consistent self-service experience to end users.

Service Manager Service Catalog

Part of information technology service management in the Information Technology Information Library (ITIL) framework is request fulfillment and consists of the service catalog, which can be used by Information Technology (IT) departments to provide a consistent self-service experience to end users. System Center 2012 Service Manager introduces new capabilities to System Center including a service catalog, Service Request Fulfillment, and a new self-service portal.

This chapter discusses the service catalog in general and covers all aspects of the service catalog, Service Request Fulfillment, and the self-service portal within System Center 2012 Service Manager.

Understanding the Service Catalog

The service catalog was first included in ITIL version 3 as a best practice for IT service management (ITSM). The service catalog is part of request fulfillment in the ITIL framework. Request fulfillment can be defined as a process for dealing with service requests from customers. A service request is a formal request that something be provided for or to a customer. Examples of service requests include password resets, software installations, hardware updates, and so on. Service requests differ from incidents: An incident is an issue that needs to be resolved; a service request occurs when an end user needs something and requests it.

Service requests are typically a list of business or technology services offered to the organization by IT. These services are published to the customer via the service catalog.

The service catalog can also be used to publish content to end users. The following list shows examples of types of content other than service requests that you could publish in a service catalog.

▶ Announcements

▶ Service level agreements (SLAs)

▶ Support hours

▶ Costs of services

▶ Contacts and escalation points

▶ Knowledgebase articles

▶ A place for end users to submit feedback

▶ A place to initiate incidents

The service catalog typically has two points of interaction: One for the end users and one for the service desk team. Each point of interaction has its own interface and purpose:

▶ End users utilize the interface as a front end for the items previously listed in this section. The service catalog front end in Service Manager 2012 is known as the *self-service portal* and is discussed further in the "Working in the Self-Service Portal" section later in the chapter. Figure 10.1 shows an example of a customized self-service portal.

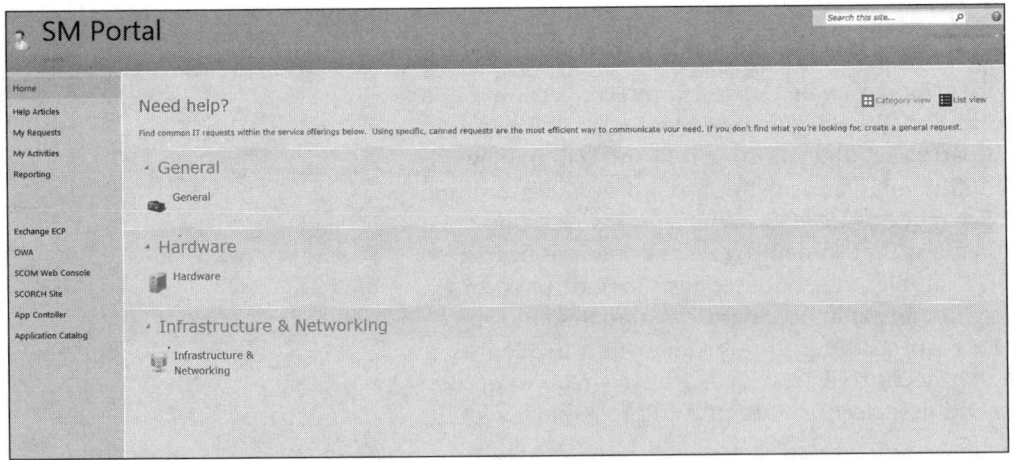

FIGURE 10.1   Customized Service Manager self-service portal.

▶ The service desk team uses the interface to manage the service catalog. This is known as the *management interface*. The management interface is used to define processes used to fulfill service requests, the forms for these requests, organization of the service requests, and the service requests themselves along with other content that may be published in the service catalog. The management aspect of the service catalog is located in the Service Manager console. Figure 10.2 shows the components of the service catalog in the Service Manager console.

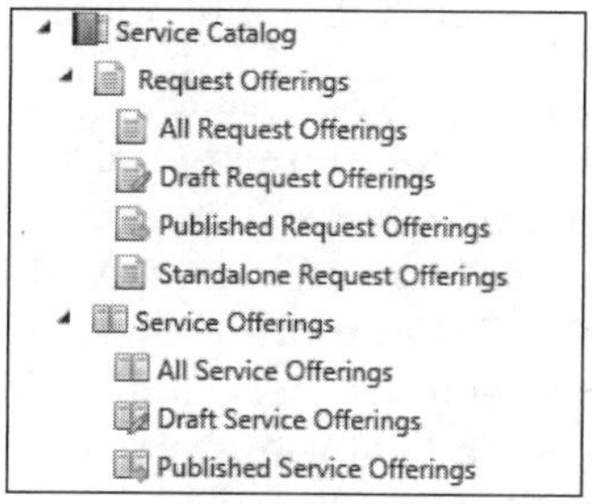

FIGURE 10.2   Service Manager service catalog menu.

NOTE: STANDALONE REQUEST OFFERINGS

Notice the Standalone Request Offerings item under the Request Offerings node in Figure 10.2. This is used for any request offerings that are not tied to a service offering. The only way these can be viewed in the self-service portal is under the List view.

The service catalog adds value to the business by providing effective and quick access to a central standardized catalog of services. It also removes the bureaucracy typically involved with requesting and receiving new or existing services.

Service Catalog Permissions

Access to items in the service catalog is granted through catalog item groups and user roles assigned to these groups. Catalog item groups are a collection of request offerings and service offerings. These can include one or more service offerings, each of which must contain at least one request offering. For example, say you have a service request offering titled Hardware and a request offering of Print Request. For an end user to see Print Request in the self-service portal, you would need to include the Print Request request offering in the Hardware service offering, which would be included in a catalog item group that the user could access through membership in a user role. The next sections discuss establishing user access to the self-service portal, creating a catalog item group, and creating a user role and associating it with a catalog item group.

10

Granting User Access to the Self-Service Portal

Users are not added directly to catalog item groups. User roles are added to Service Manager and then users are added to those user roles. Catalog groups are associated within the user roles themselves. This is how the permissions are tied together. (For additional information on security in Service Manager 2012, see Chapter 17, "Service Manager Security.")

After a user is added to a user role associated with a catalog group(s), he can access request offerings within service offerings in the self-service portal. If the user is not a member of any user roles and accesses the self-service portal, it appears blank, even if that individual has access to SharePoint itself.

SharePoint access is required but often forgotten when the service catalog and self-service portal are first set up. Without access to SharePoint, end users cannot access service and request offerings even if they have the correct permissions in Service Manager. Giving end users access to the self-service portal at the SharePoint level is easy. The authors recommend you give access to the self-service portal at the SharePoint level to all users, and control access to the service catalog via Service Manager user roles. The following example gives Authenticated Users access to view the self-service portal at the SharePoint level, addressing the access requirements. Perform the following steps:

1. Open Internet Explorer and navigate to the self-service portal as the site administrator.

2. Select **Site Actions -> Site Settings**.

3. Under Users and Permissions, select **Site Permissions**.

4. You see an information bar stating "This Web site inherits permissions from its parent. (Team Site)." Click **(Team Site)**.

5. Select **Grant Permissions**.

6. Add **Authenticated Users** and give them the permissions **Viewer (View Only)**.

7. Click **OK**.

This is all that is required for your end users to have access to the self-service portal at the SharePoint level. Service catalog permissions themselves are granted through Service Manager using catalog item groups and user roles.

Creating a Catalog Item Group

Catalog item groups are lists of catalog items used to secure access to the service catalog. They provide access to users based on user role membership. Members of this role can then see request and service offerings when they access the service catalog in the self-service portal. To create a catalog item group, follow these steps:

1. Open the Service Manager console.

2. In the Library workspace, select **Groups -> Create Catalog Group**.

3. Select **Next** on the first page, give the group a name, save it to a customized management pack, and then click **Next**.

> **NOTE: USING A CUSTOMIZED MANAGEMENT PACK**
>
> If you do not yet have a customized management pack, select **New** to create one.

4. Click **Add** on the Included Members page and select the request offerings and corresponding service offerings to be part of this catalog item group. Click **Next** when finished.

5. Leave the Dynamic members field blank and click **Next**.

6. Click **Next** on the next two pages to accept the defaults.

7. On the Summary page, click **Create** to create the group.

Creating a User Role

With the catalog item group created, the next task is to create a user role and associate it to the catalog item group. Perform the following steps:

1. In the Service Manager console, open the Administration workspace. Under Tasks, select **User Roles -> Create User Role -> End User**.

2. Give the new user role a name and optional description and click **Next**.

3. On the Management Packs page, tick the check box next to the custom management pack containing the catalog item group you created. Click **Next**.

4. On the Queues page, leave **All work items can be accessed** selected. Click **Next**.

5. On the Configuration Items page, leave the default of **All configuration items can be accessed** selected and click **Next**.

6. On the Catalog Items page, select the **Provide Access to the only the selected groups** radio button. Select the catalog item group you created and click **Next**.

7. Leave **All forms can be accessed** as the default and click **Next**.

8. On the Users page, click **Add** and select the user(s)/group(s) to add. Click **Next**.

9. Click **Create** on the Summary page to create the user role.

Chapter 17 contains additional information on creating user roles.

10

NOTE: ABOUT THE END USERS ROLE

The Service Manager End Users role is a default user role and used to access many things within Service Manager, including the self-service portal. This role is associated with the Generic Incident Request catalog group, enabling members of this role to submit generic service requests in the self-service portal. The Authenticated Users group is a member of this user role by default.

A question often asked is "Why not use this user role to give all users access to the self-service portal?" The issue is that you can only add or remove users and groups; you cannot modify associated catalog group Items. This means you cannot use this role to give access to other service and request offerings. You have two options:

► **Leave authenticated users as a member of this user role:** All users at a minimum are able to submit generic incident requests in the self-service portal.

► **Remove authenticated users from this user role:** This action requires either adding any needed users or groups to this role or controlling access to the generic incident request in the self-service portal through another user role.

Using Service Offerings

In Service Manager, service offerings are used to group request offerings. IT departments use service offerings to define the types of services offered to the business. Consider these as buckets of services at a high level that are available to the user. Table 10.1 lists examples of service and associated request offerings.

TIP: CONCEPTUALIZING SERVICE OFFERINGS

Service offerings are built from the ground up, starting with request offerings that are grouped into various containers as service offerings.

TABLE 10.1   Service Offerings with Associated Request Offerings

Service Offering	Request Offering
Cloud services	New virtual machine
	More virtual machine resources (disk, memory, and so on)
	New web application
Hardware	Computer request
	Printer request
	Smartphone request
User management	Create user account
	Modify user account
	Disable user account

The authors recommend that IT departments designate a team to determine the organization's service level management and drive their service offerings and request offerings planning from this. Once the service offerings are ready, you must create them in Service Manager and publish them to the self-service portal. End users then access the service offerings via the self-service portal to place requests.

When creating service offerings, know that request offerings must be mapped to a service offering. Follow these steps to create a service offering within Service Manager 2012:

1. In the Service Manager console, navigate to **Library** -> **Service Catalog** -> **Service Offerings**. Under Tasks, select **Create Service Offering**.

2. Click **Next** on the first page of the wizard.

3. Enter a title along with an overview and description. You can also attach a custom image by browsing to it, selecting the category for the offering, language (English by default), and be sure to select a custom management pack or create a new one. When done, click **Next**.

TIP: MODIFYING SERVICE OFFERING CATEGORY

You can modify the service offering category list if the defaults do not meet your requirements.

---

4. On the next page, add service level agreement (SLA) and cost information if necessary. Click **Next** to continue.

5. On the next page add any related services to the offering and click **Next**.

6. If you have knowledge articles that belong to this offering, add them and then click **Next**.

7. This next page is where you can add a request offering. These are covered in the next section, "About Request Offerings." Skip this for now and click **Next**.

8. Now, select whether the service offering is a draft or published. Leave this as a draft for now, you can also add an owner of this offering if you want. Click **Next** to continue.

9. On the Summary page, click **Create** to build the service offering.

REAL WORLD: LOCALIZED LANGUAGE FOR OFFERINGS

When creating service offerings and request offerings, the default language is English. You can change this to another localized language, which is useful for global implementations so that end users can view service offerings and request offerings in their own language. Note that when you change the localized language in Service Manager, SharePoint also will need language packs installed for any languages that will be used, and those must be set on the self-service portal. Figure 10.3 shows the Language selection drop-down box highlighted.

10

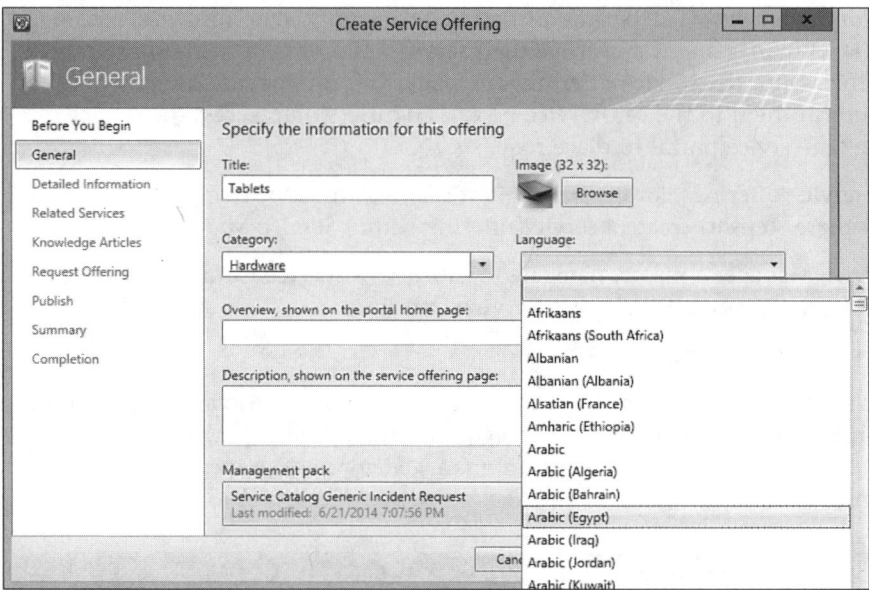

FIGURE 10.3   Select language when creating a service offering.

About Request Offerings

Request offerings are catalog items within a service catalog that are used as a service point between end users and IT departments. Request offerings are published offerings of services that end users can request from IT.

Request offerings are placed logically in groups and are tied to service offerings. The "Using Service Offerings" section earlier in the chapter showed this is a request offering of a new user account in the User Management Service Offering group. This demonstrates that end users could go to the Service Manager self-service portal to the User Management service offering, find the new user account request offering, and request setup of a new user.

Request offerings consist of a form with all the required questions and information needed to fulfill a service request. These forms are built from the Service Manager catalog and then published. You can map request offerings to service requests or to incident requests. These service requests or incident requests are templates, which you can configure to perform actions such as route or perform workflows on them after they are submitted by end users.

You can associate knowledge articles, services, and custom icons with request offerings. Request offerings are a user-friendly means for end users to be able access service requests to obtain assistance with technical issues or request services.

Using Request Offering Templates

When you create a request offering in Service Manager, you can select a template for that request offering. The template can be used around the two different request offering types of incident or service requests.

The functionality to choose between an incident and a service request provides the ability to go beyond publishing service requests on the self-service portal; it provides end users another way to initiate incidents with the service desk.

Service Manager provides default templates for service requests and incidents. You can also create your own templates to use with request offerings. Creating custom templates enables you to do things such as route certain incidents or service requests to teams or subject matter experts. As an example, if there is an incident or service request related to SharePoint, it could be routed directly to the SharePoint administrator.

In Service Manager, you should create your incident or service request templates before creating the actual request offerings. As part of creating a request offering, you select a template to be used. To create a template to be used for a request offering, perform the following steps:

1. In the Service Manager console, navigate to **Library** -> **Templates**.

2. Under Tasks, select **Create Template**.

3. Give the template a name and a description.

4. Next to the Class field, click **Browse**, select either Service Request or Incident, and click **OK**.

   ▶ If you chose **Incident**, complete any needed fields in the Incident template. You could set values in fields such as Source to Portal, set the Support Group, Impact, and Urgency to set the Priority. Figure 10.4 shows these fields.

FIGURE 10.4   Blank Incident template form.

▶ If you chose **Service Request**, complete any needed fields in the Service Request template. The fields are similar to those on the Incident template, such as Source and Support Group. Figure 10.5 shows the Service Request template form with the fields mentioned here.

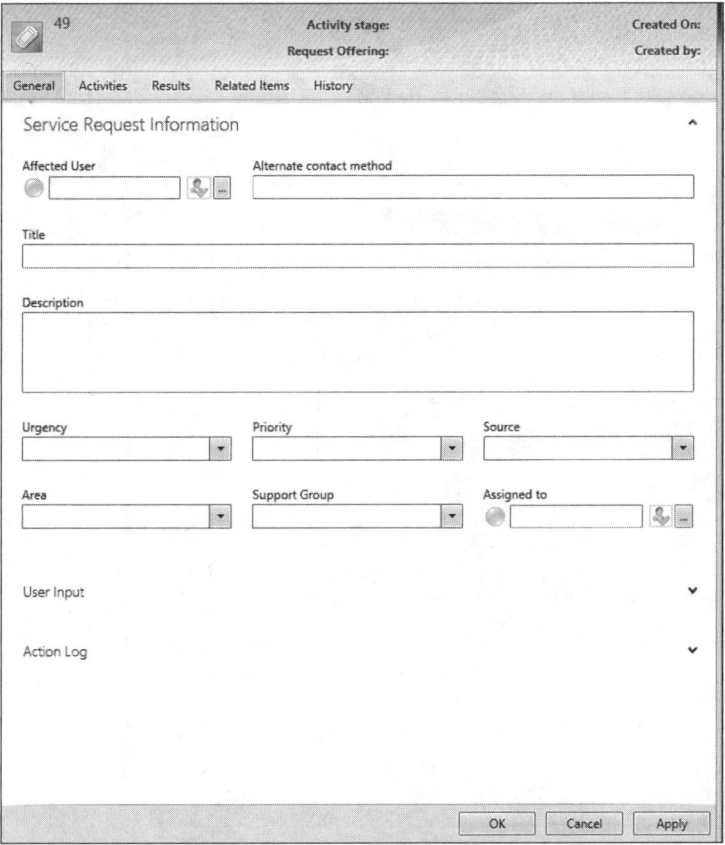

FIGURE 10.5   Blank Service Request template form.

5. After filling in the Service Request template form, click **Activities** to open the
Activities page. Click the green plus sign to add a new activity. When the Select
Template dialog box opens, choose **Default Review Activity** and click **OK**. You can
see this in Figure 10.6.

10

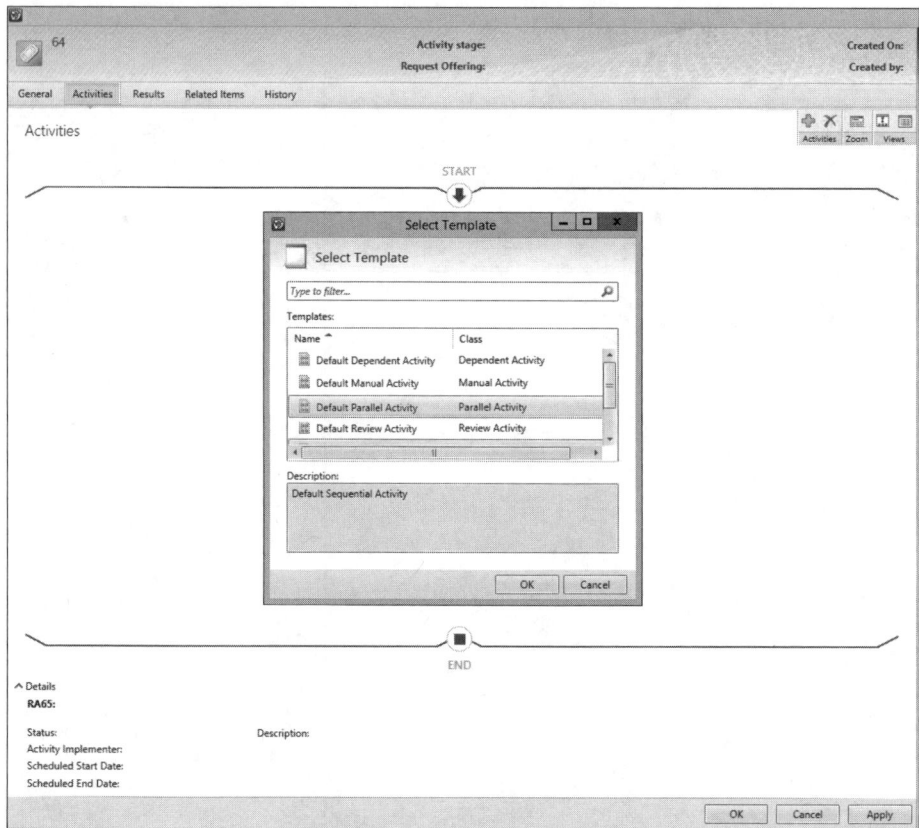

FIGURE 10.6   Activities page on the Service Request template.

6. On the Review Activity page, enter a title and description, and complete any other needed fields such as the Stage, Approval Condition, and adding Reviewers. Figure 10.7 shows the Review Activity form with the fields mentioned here populated. (Service Manager activities are discussed at http://technet.microsoft.com/en-us/library/hh832016.aspx.)

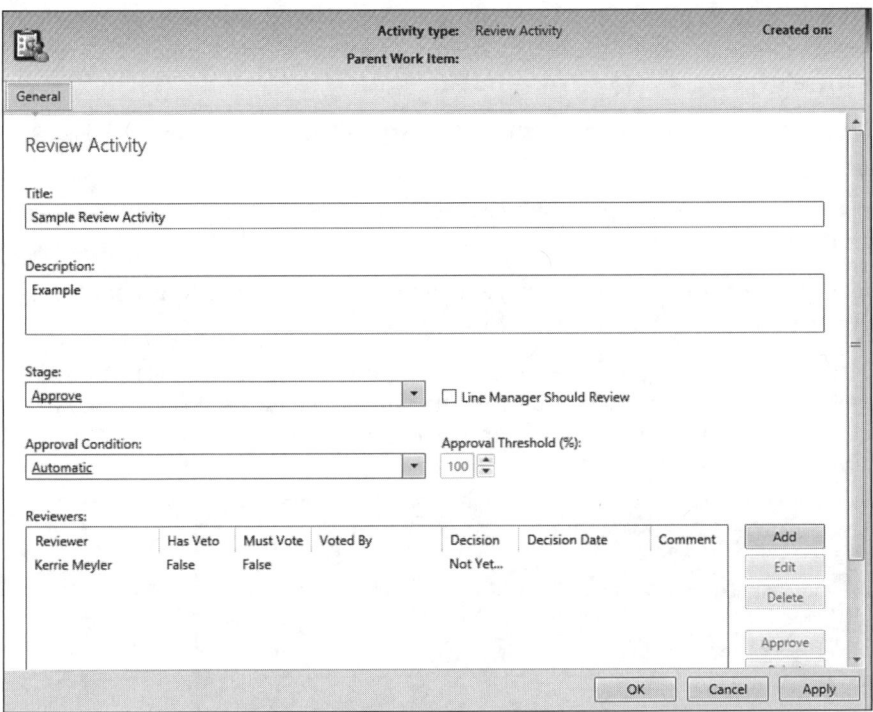

FIGURE 10.7   Review Activity template.

Setting up the Incident template requires fewer configurations than the Service Request template does. After completing the procedure in this section, you can select one of the custom templates when creating a request offering, which is discussed in the next section.

Creating a Request Offering

The previous section went over the process of creating templates for request offerings. This section discusses the process of creating a request offering. Creating a request offering includes two objectives:

▶ Creating the set of questions that appear to the end user on the offering form

▶ Mapping responses to the questions to work item classes in the CMDB for access by the service desk team

Microsoft includes an easy to use wizard for creating simple or complex offerings. Here is the process to create a request offering, along with information on the Request Offering Wizard. Follow these steps:

1. In the Service Manager console, navigate to **Library -> Service Catalog -> All Request Offerings**.

2. Under Tasks -> Request Offerings, select **Create Request Offering** to open the Create a Request Offering Wizard.

3. The first page is the Before You Begin page, which contains instructions about the Create a Request Offering Wizard. Click **Next**.

4. On the General page (see Figure 10.8), specify the Title, Image, and Description. These items are displayed to the end user in the self-service portal. Select a management pack or create a new one in which to place the request offering.

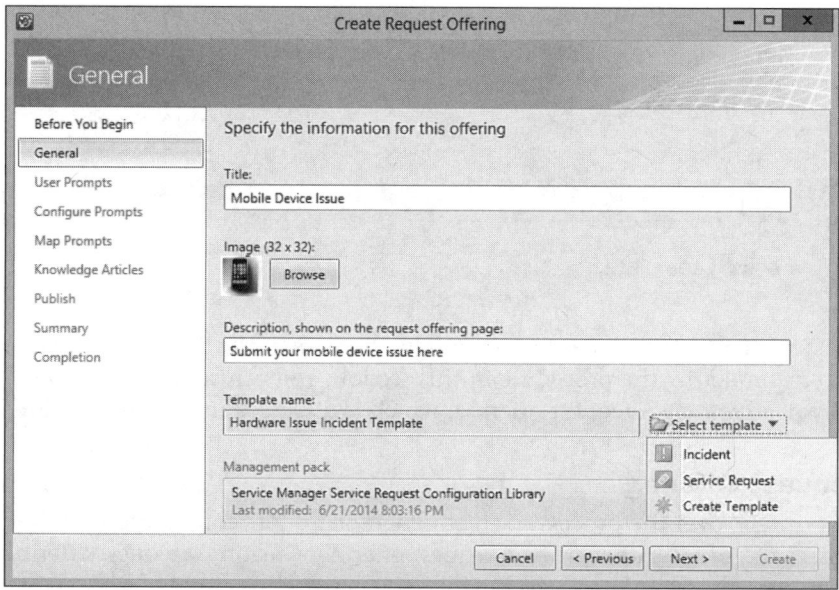

FIGURE 10.8   General page of the Request Offering Wizard.

5. Click the **Select template** drop-down in Figure 10.8. Notice this has three options for the type of template you select. The "Using Request Offering Templates" section earlier in the chapter discussed creating request offering templates. Choose an option here based on which type of request offering will be used. As an example, if

this request will allow users to request a new email account, choose **Service Request** and select the appropriate template from the list. Click **Next**.

6. The User Prompts page includes a field for form instructions. This is used to explain to the end user what is necessary to complete the form. The other fields are the actual user prompts and displayed to the end user on the request form.

7. Each user prompt is typically a question. However, as Figure 10.9 shows, some user prompts may only display text. The prompts display in the same order as listed in the wizard. Buttons to the upper right of the user prompt fields allow changes; this includes reordering using the blue arrows, using the red X to remove, and using the green plus sign to add a new user prompt. Each user prompt must have text entered for the actual question in the information text field. The Response Type specifies whether a field is required, optional, or display only, and the Prompt Type controls the field type of the question or text.

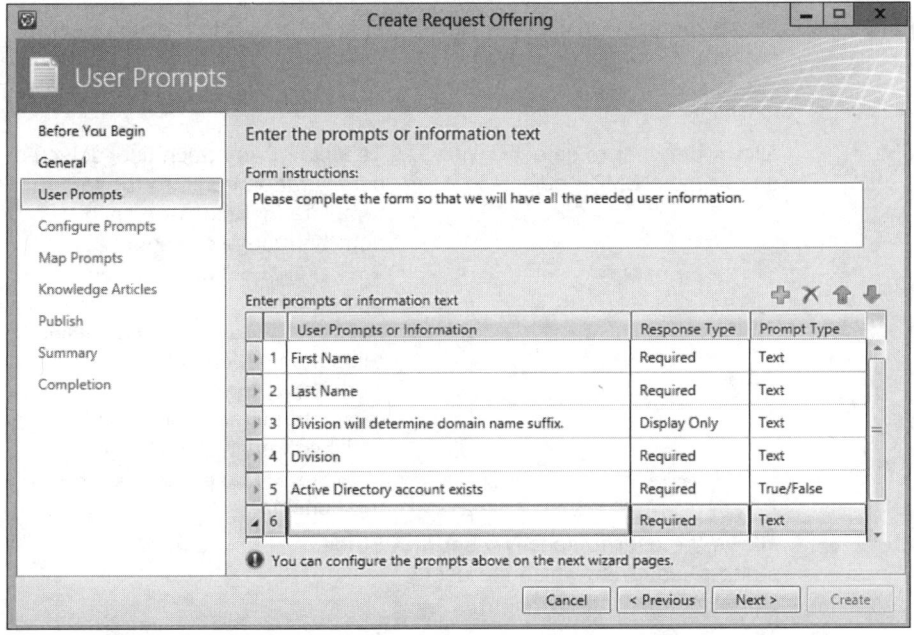

FIGURE 10.9   User Prompts page of the Request Offering Wizard.

Table 10.2 lists the controls that can be used for the prompt type.

TABLE 10.2   Prompt Type Table

Prompt Type	Description	Property Output Type
Date	Allows the user to select or view a date	Datetime
Decimal	Allows the user to input or view a numerical value containing a decimal point	Double
File Attachment	Allows the user to attach a file to the request offering	*special: Attaches the user-selected file as a `System.FileAttachment` object through the `System.WorkItemHasFileAttachment` relationship
Integer	Allows the user to input or view an integer value	Int
MP Enumeration List	Allows the user to select or view one of the child enumerations associated with a parent enumeration type	enum (*bound to a specific enum type)
Query Results	Allows the user to select or view one or more CMDB objects	*special: Can attach user-selected configuration items to the target template instance or a child activity through the `System.WorkItemAboutConfigItem` and `System.WorkItemRelatesToConfigItem` relationships; can attach work items to the target template instance or a child activity through the `System.WorkItemRelatesToWorkItem` relationship
Simple List	Allows the user to specify a set of string values from which the user can select an option	String
Text	Allows the user to enter or view text input	String
True/False	Presents a check box to the user	Bool

You can create interactive or dynamic request offering forms, depending on the user prompt type used. An example of having an interactive or dynamic user prompt on a form would be to pull a list of configuration items from the CMDB and display these on the request offering form. This allows the end user to select from a list of information rather than having to manually enter data.

Once all fields are complete on the User Prompts page, click **Next**.

8. On the Configure Prompts page, configure the properties of the user prompts types if required. For example, notice in Figure 10.10 that the Division field is highlighted and the Configure button can be clicked.

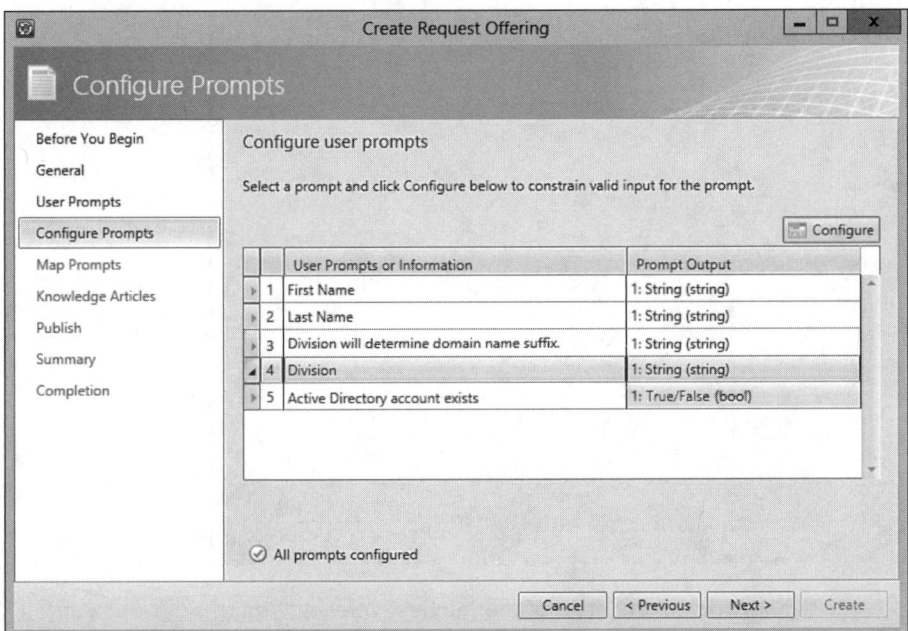

FIGURE 10.10   Configure Prompts page of the Request Offering Wizard.

9. Select **Configure** to open the Configure Text Control page (see Figure 10.11). This page contains configurable properties for the user prompt type. Make any needed changes and click **OK** to return to the Configure Prompts page. Click **Next** to continue.

10. The next page is the Map Prompts page (see Figure 10.12). This is where the user prompt types are associated with fields of a service request or an activity.

10

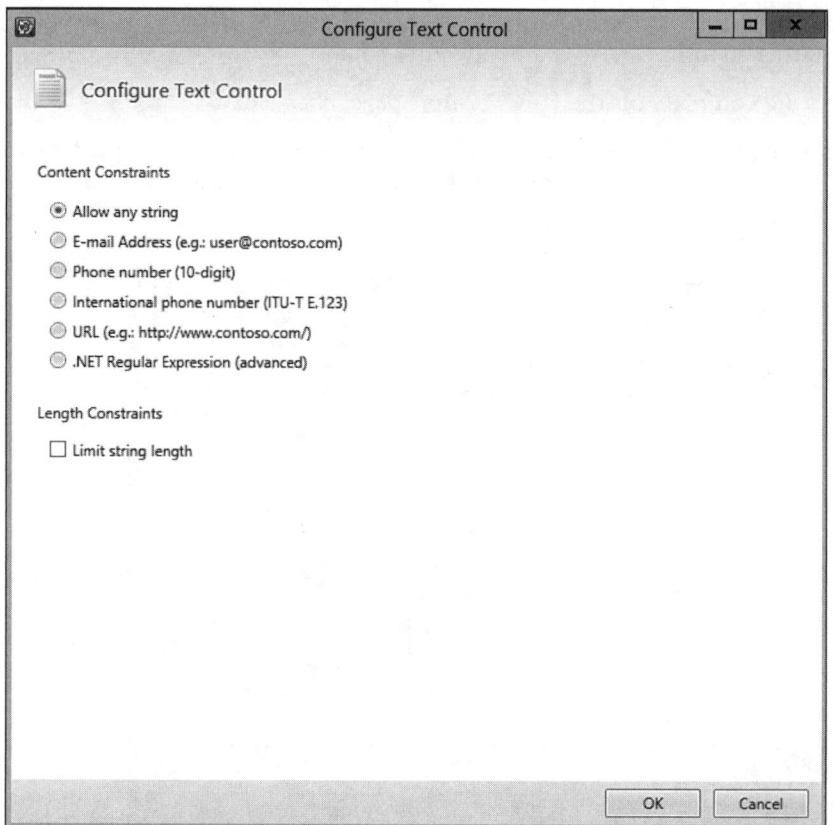

FIGURE 10.11   Configure Text Control page of the Request Offering Wizard.

All user prompt types must be associated to a field under Property before continuing. When data is submitted in the request offering prompts, it must be mapped to a property within Service Manager so the service desk can later access the incident, service request, or activity. Figure 10.12 shows you can select the service request or an activity. Notice you have properties in the grid and prompt output. You can click the drop-down, select the proper prompt output, and associate it to the property. Click **Next** after making the necessary associations.

11. On the Knowledge Articles page, you can add knowledge articles to associate with this request offering. Click **Add** as shown in Figure 10.13, select the knowledge base article you want to add, and click **Next**.

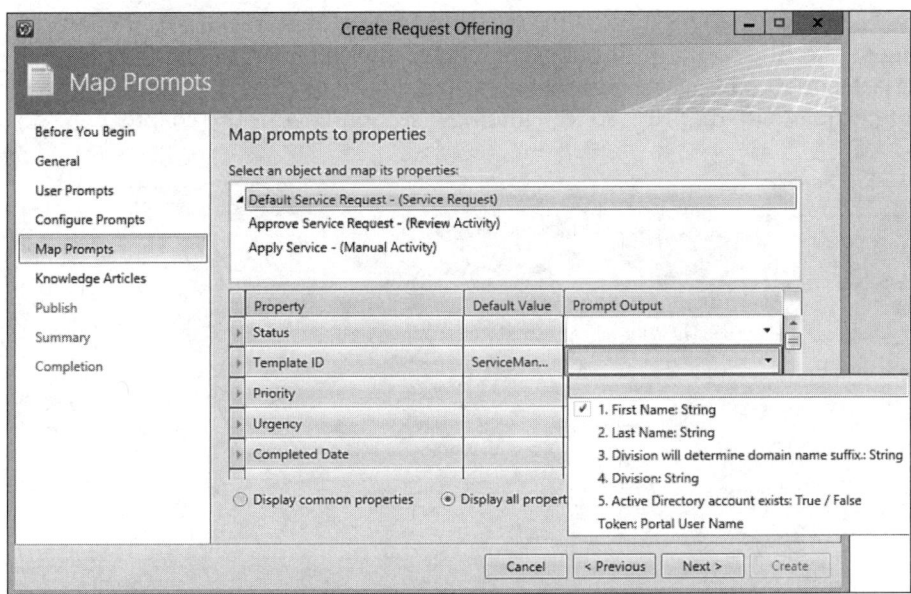

FIGURE 10.12   Map Prompts page of Request Offering Wizard.

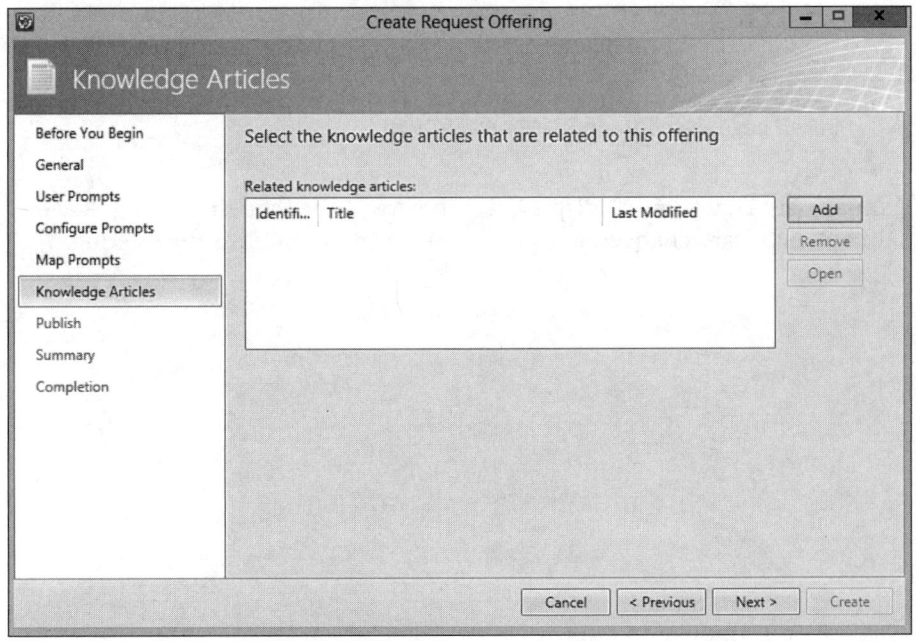

FIGURE 10.13   Knowledge Articles page of the Request Offering Wizard.

12. On the Publish page (see Figure 10.14) you can change the status of this request offering to Published. You must publish a request offering for it to display on the self-service portal. Adding a request offering to a service offering is covered in the "Adding Request Offerings to Service Offerings" section later in the chapter.

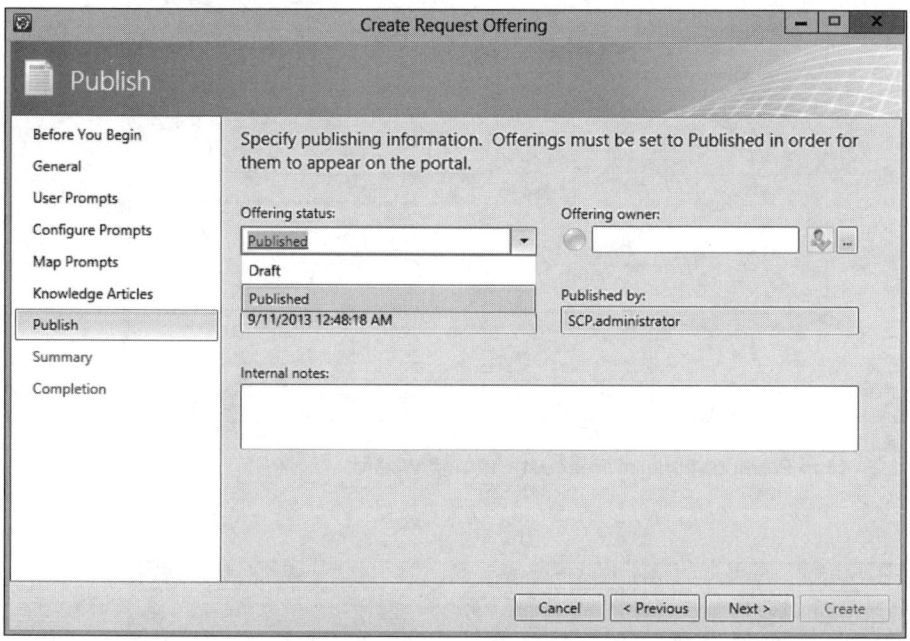

FIGURE 10.14   Publish page of the Request Offering Wizard.

13. The next page (see Figure 10.15) displays a summary of the request offering. Review and make any necessary changes, and then click **Create** to publish the offering.

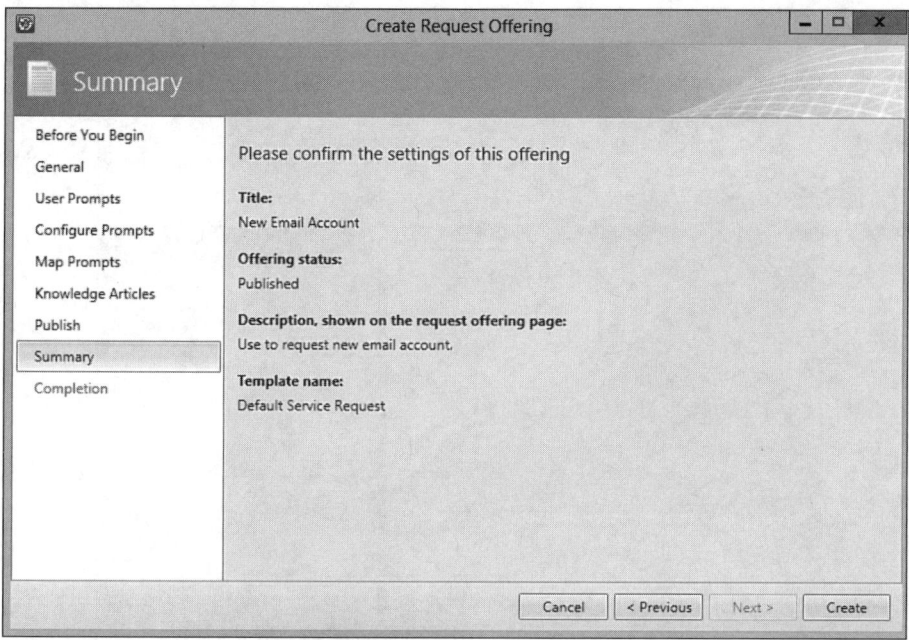

FIGURE 10.15   Summary page of the Request Offering Wizard.

Figure 10.16 and Figure 10.17 provide an example of what the request offering would look like when accessed on the self-service portal. Figure 10.16 displays the request offering after you click on it. Figure 10.17 shows the request offering form in the self-service portal.

FIGURE 10.16   Request offering on self-service portal.

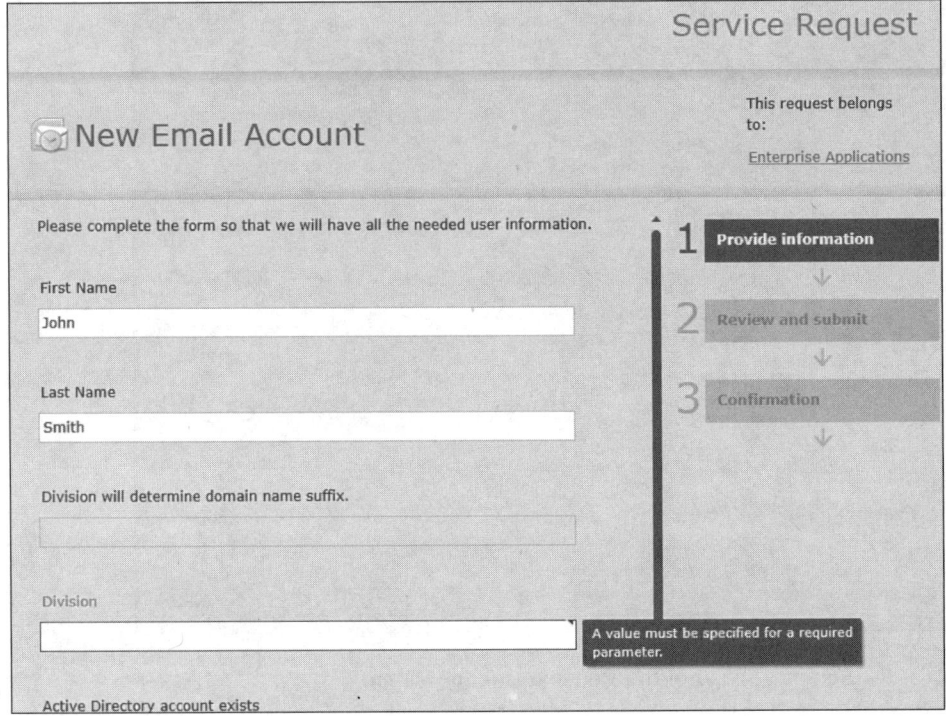

FIGURE 10.17   Additional request offering detail.

Copying Request Offerings

It may be easier to copy an existing request offering and modify it than create a new one. This functionality is available in the Service Manager service catalog. Copying may also make sense when creating a large amount of request offerings.

REAL WORLD: COPYING REQUEST OFFERINGS

The authors recommend you create a base request offering, use it as a template, and make copies of it to create the needed request offerings.

Follow these steps to copy a request offering:

1. In the Service Manager console, navigate to **Library -> Service Catalog -> Request Offerings -> All Request Offerings**.

2. Find the request offering you want to copy in the list, and click it to highlight it.

3. Under Tasks, highlight the request offering, and click **Create a Copy**.

   The Copy Request Offering dialog box opens with an option to select **Also create a copy of the template referred to in this Request Offering**. This creates a copy of the template used in the original request offering; if you do not create a copy, it will use the same template.

4. Click **OK** to create the copy of the request offering; this displays a new request offering in the list with the same name and the word "copy" prepended to it.

Adding Request Offerings to Service Offerings

Once you have your request offerings, you have two options for exposing them to end users:

▶ Leave them as standalone request offerings

▶ Associate them with service offerings

If you leave a request offering standalone, it appears in Service Manager under Request Offerings -> Standalone Request Offerings. The only way for end users to view these is with the List view in the self-service portal. Generally, Service Manager administrators use the second option.

Associating request offerings with service offerings allows you to logically group the request offerings together so end users can find them easily in the self-service portal. It also helps the service desk team keep the service catalog organized. To publish and add a request offering to a service offering, follow these steps:

1. In the Service Manager console, navigate to **Library -> Service Catalog -> All Request Offerings**.

2. Find the request offering you want to add to a service offering and select it. Under Tasks, highlight the request offering, and click **Add to Service Offering**.

3. The Select objects dialog box opens. Select the service offering you want to add to and click **Add** as shown Figure 10.18.

4. Click **OK**.

Request offerings and service offerings must be published before they are accessible on the self-service portal. The "Creating a Request Offering" section earlier in the chapter discussed publishing a request offering. This section discusses publishing a service offering. Note that when a service offering is published, it must contain at least one request offering that has also been published. Follow these steps to publish a service offering:

1. In the Service Manager console, navigate to **Library** -> **Service Catalog** -> **All Service Offerings**.

2. Locate the service offering with a published status of Draft and select it. Under Tasks, highlight the request offering, and click **Publish**.

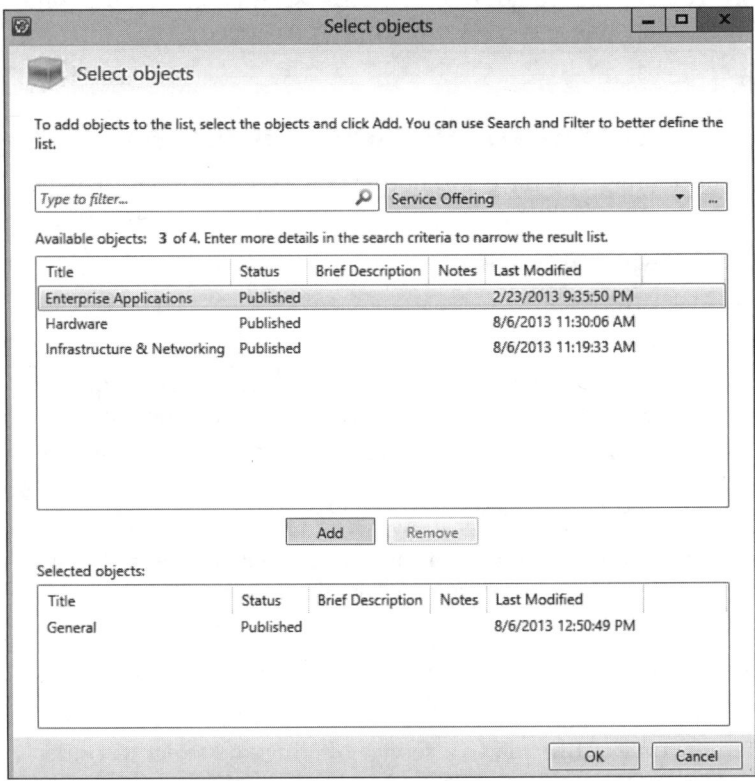

FIGURE 10.18   Select Objects dialog box.

Working in the Self-Service Portal

Service Manager 2012's self-service portal is the front-end interface for end users to access service offerings and request offerings in the service catalog. The self-service portal is a combination of SharePoint 2010 and Silverlight web parts. The platform is SharePoint 2010, with the service offerings and request offerings presented through the Silverlight web parts. There is other functionality to the self-service portal beyond the service offerings and request offerings, such as a knowledge base, the ability to access activities to approve or reject them, and communication with the service desk team.

Because the self-service portal is built on the SharePoint 2010 platform, it can be extended through other available SharePoint web parts and features to create an even more enhanced experience for your end users. Examples include adding IT announcements, password reset capabilities, creating IT calendars (forward schedule of change) so that staff knows when IT is available, adding dashboards to view IT metrics, and links to other IT related sites end users may need to access.

The previous two paragraphs provided an overview of the self-service portal; now, let's dive into information for working with request offerings in the portal. The default URL for the self-service portal is https://localhost:<port>/SMPortal. On the self-service portal home page, end users see available service offerings. Notice in Figure 10.19 there is a service offering of Hardware.

FIGURE 10.19   Self-service portal service offering.

Clicking the service offering shows related request offerings. End users can select a request offering to access its associated submission form. In this view of the portal, end users also see an overview of the service offering if one was set when the service offering was created. The bottom part shows cost and SLA information as well as any related knowledge base articles and other related service offerings. Notice in Figure 10.20 that there are two available request offerings for this Hardware service offering. This section uses the Mobile Device Issue request offering as an example.

After clicking on a request offering, the end user is presented with related knowledge base articles and a Go to request form button, shown in Figure 10.21.

Figure 10.22 shows an example of a request offering form. Each form appears different, as these are built on the back end with the fields needed for that particular request offering. This example has multiple text fields with the title required and the description optional. There is also a drop-down list of options and display-only text. Navigation at the bottom of the form is provided to go back, go to the next step, or cancel.

10

FIGURE 10.20   Available request offerings.

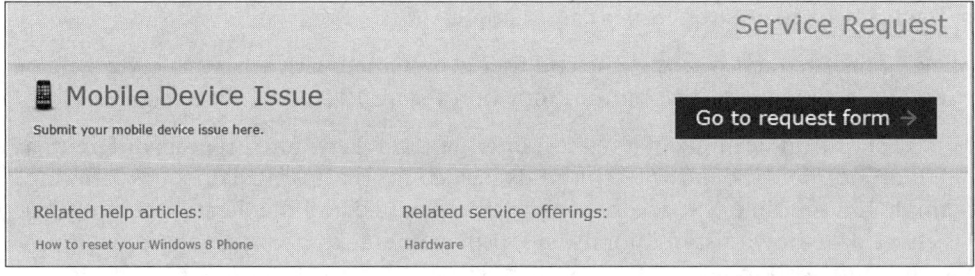

FIGURE 10.21   Accessing the service request.

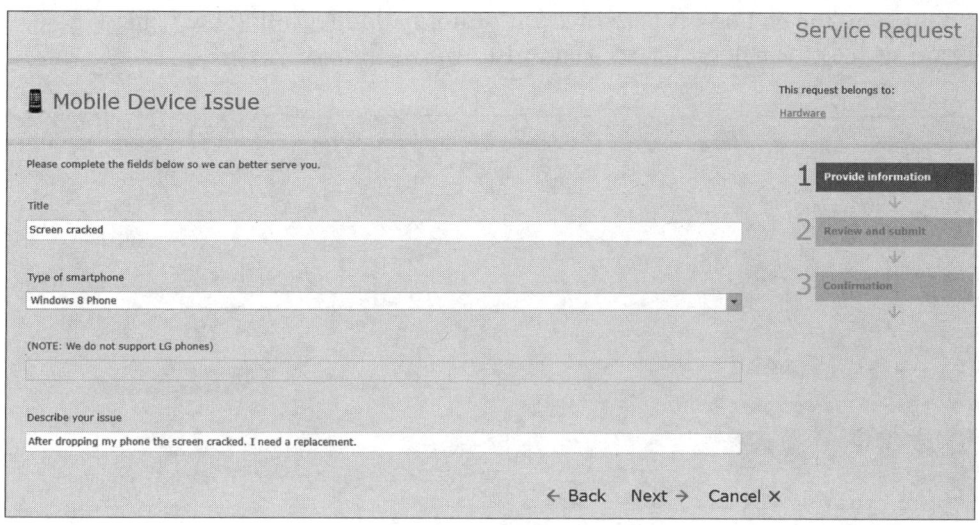

FIGURE 10.22   Request offering fields in the service request.

A summary of the request submission is displayed (see Figure 10.23) before the end user actually submits the form.

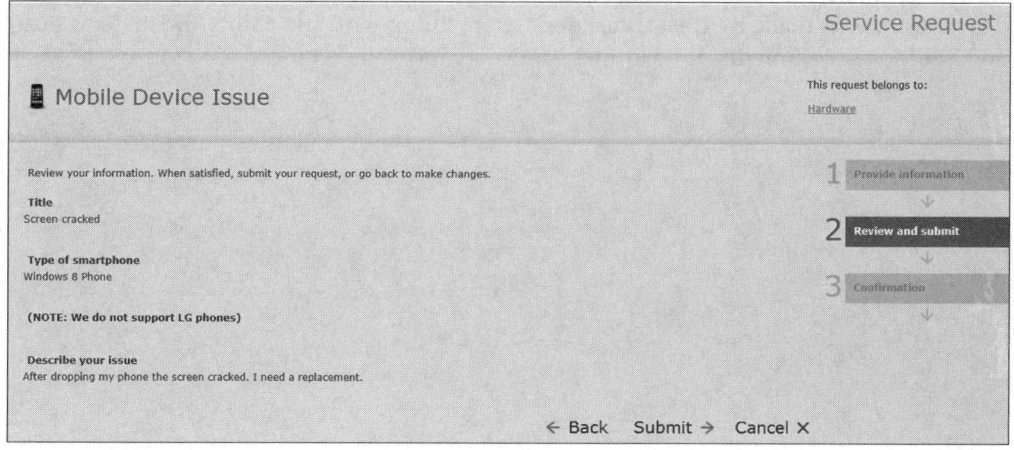

FIGURE 10.23   Request Offering summary.

10

After submission, the end user is presented with information regarding the request submission such as the request ID (see Figure 10.24).

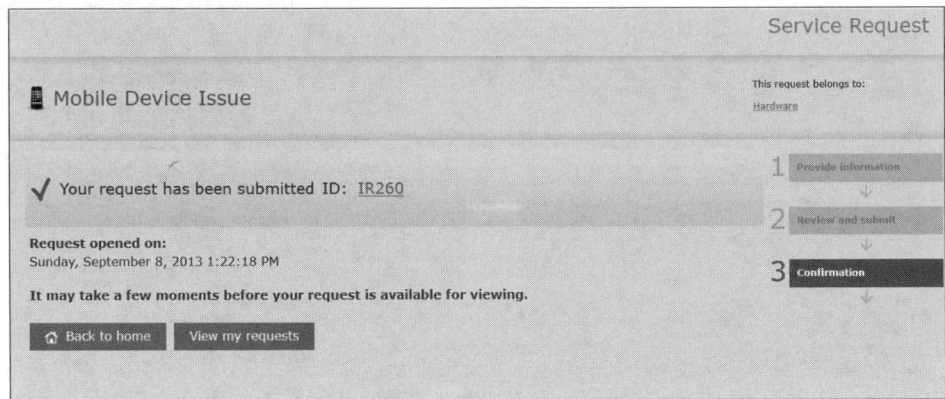

FIGURE 10.24   Service request ID for a newly submitted service request.

The left side of the self-service portal has a link titled My Requests. End users can click this to view service requests they have submitted and their status, and to update those requests. Figure 10.25 is an example of the type of information that can be viewed for submitted requests such as the status of the request, any action taken by the service desk, and any comments made by the service desk team, along with the ability for the end user to add additional comments, upload files, or even cancel the request.

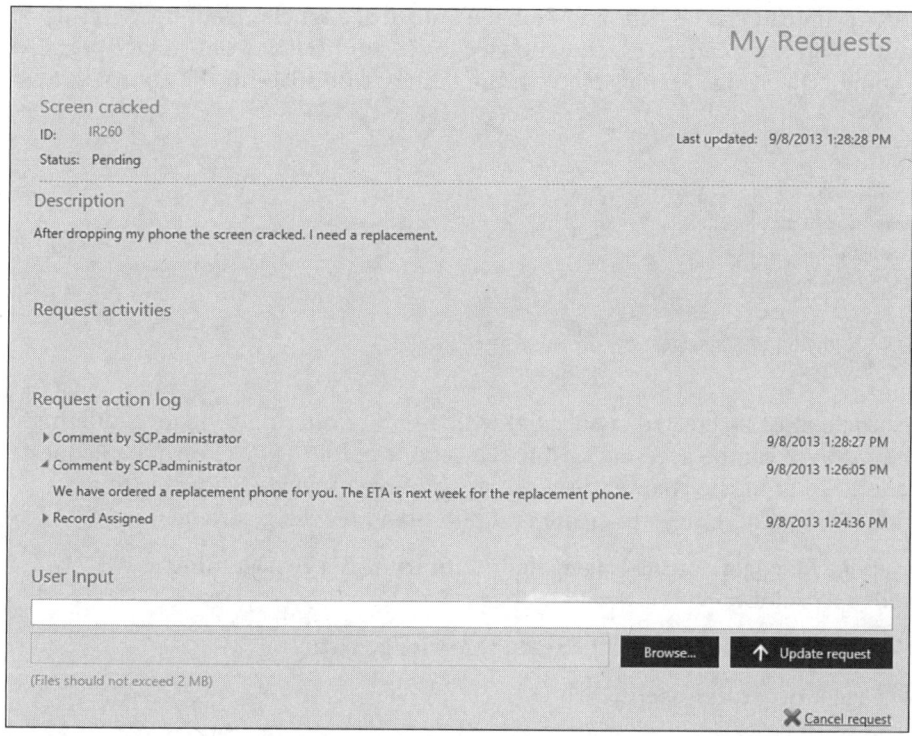

FIGURE 10.25   Updating a service request.

Using the Knowledge Base

In regards to ITIL terminology, Knowledge Management is not a part of request fulfillment and the service catalog. However, in terms of Service Manager 2012, Knowledge Management is located in the same area on the back end in the Service Manager console and the front end on the self-service portal. This section discusses Service Manager's Knowledge Management functionality.

Knowledge articles (KBs) contain resolutions to IT issues with known fixes. IT departments create and manage the knowledge articles. These give service desk staff and end users the ability to resolve IT issues on their own before opening a new incident. Knowledge articles are linked to work items within Service Manager and are associated with service offerings and/or request offerings in the service catalog. Knowledge Management within Service Manager can be found in two places:

▶ The Library workspace

▶ The self-service portal

The service desk team can create, edit, and manage knowledge articles from the Service Manager console. End users can access the knowledge articles from the self-service portal. Figure 10.26 shows Knowledge Management in the Library workspace of the console.

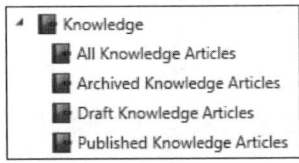

FIGURE 10.26   Knowledge Management in Service Manager.

A knowledge article must be created, associated with a service offering or request offering, and published before it can be accessed on the self-service portal. The "Creating a Request Offering" section earlier in the chapter discusses associating a knowledge article to a request offering. Follow these steps to create and publish a knowledge article:

1. In the Service Manager console, navigate to **Library -> Service Catalog -> All Knowledge Articles**.

2. Under **Tasks -> Knowledge**, select **Create Knowledge Article**.

3. A knowledge article form opens.

4. Complete the desired fields and click **OK** when done.

Figure 10.27 shows the fields on the knowledge article form:

▶ A drop-down at the top of the form can be set to Draft or Published. When this is set to Published and associated with a service offering or request offering, it is displayed on the self-service portal.

▶ Knowledge articles can be rated. This is used to gauge the usefulness of a knowledge article.

▶ Title is for the name of the knowledge article. This should be something that is easily identifiable to the end user and relates to the IT issue.

▶ Description can be used to provide an overview about what is covered in the knowledge article.

▶ The Keywords field is used to place keywords that can be used later to search for knowledge articles.

▶ You can identify the knowledge article owner.

▶ Knowledge articles can be tagged with a status, and the language can be set.

▶ A category can be set for the knowledge article. This can be used to map knowledge articles and work items such as incidents.

As an example, you could have both a knowledge article and request offering associated to the same category.

▶ Comments can be added to the knowledge article. These comments are for internal use only, so they do not display on the self-service portal.

▶ The last fields are External Content and Internal Content. External content is used to link to knowledge articles outside the organization, such as linking to a TechNet article. Internal Content is for content created by the organization's own service desk team. Text, images, and such can be entered into this field.

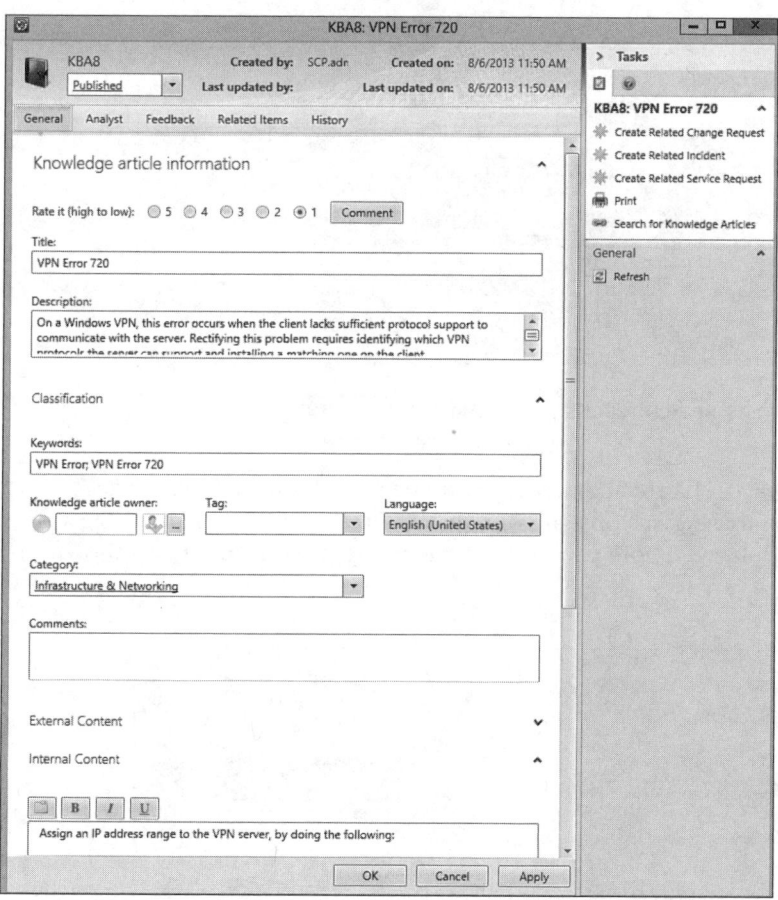

FIGURE 10.27   Service Manager knowledge article form.

Now look at the actual articles on the self-service portal. Knowledge articles are located under Help Articles in the self-service portal (see Figure 10.28).

FIGURE 10.28   Help Articles link in the self-service portal.

Clicking on Help Articles does not display them automatically. These are found or listed using a keyword search. Figure 10.29 shows that a search for **VPN** returned two knowledge articles.

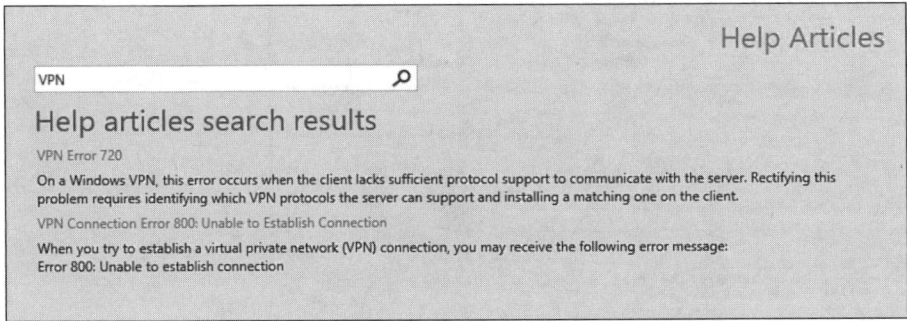

FIGURE 10.29   Help articles search results in the self-service portal.

There is an additional way to locate and access knowledge articles in the self-service portal. When navigating to a service offering or request offering, if it has knowledge articles with it, these are displayed before you go to the actual request form. This is shown in Figure 10.30.

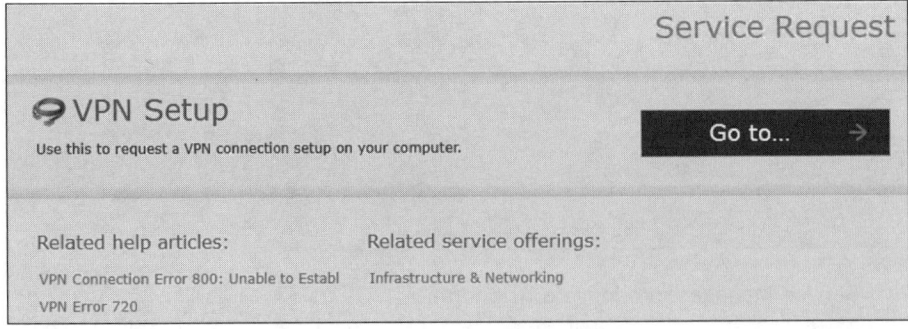

FIGURE 10.30   Help articles listed on a request form.

Knowledge articles that consist of internal content open in RTF format on the end user's local computer using either Microsoft Word or WordPad.

Fast Track

For those of you familiar with Service Manager 2010, the service catalog is a new feature in Service Manager 2012. While the previous version of this System Center component included a self-service portal, it is redesigned and has been rewritten from scratch. For additional information on the self-service portal, see Chapter 7, "Using Service Manager."

Summary

This chapter discussed what a service catalog consists of and how to plan for one. You had the opportunity to explore the service catalog within System Center 2012 Service Manager. Highlights from this chapter include topics such as working with service catalog security, working with service and request offerings, using the self-service portal, and configuring Knowledge Management.

Incident Management

Service Manager 2012 enables Incident Management by implementing and automating ticketing best practices in compliance with the Microsoft Operations Framework (MOF) and Information Technology Infrastructure Library (ITIL). By complying with these best practices, System Center Service Manager provides the building blocks to configure your own Incident Management process in accordance with industry-accepted standards.

Chapter 3, "MOF, ITIL, and System Center," explains the value of using ITIL and MOF frameworks, and provides the basis for this chapter's discussion of configuring the Incident Management process in Service Manager. This chapter examines the activities of that process to see which components in Service Manager—such as workflows or templates—can help to enable and automate Incident Management. Chapter 10, "Service Manager Service Catalog," explains how to build your service catalog in Service Manager and let users make requests using the self-service portal; the Incident Management process can utilize this functionality by enabling end users to log incidents using the self-service portal.

This chapter analyzes the Incident Management process and its configuration for service desk analysts. It also discusses how end users can utilize Service Manager.

Understanding the Incident Management Process

Planning for Incident Management in Service Manager means that the Incident Management process must be defined, agreed upon, and described—in writing—such that you, as a Service Manager administrator, can determine the steps required for implementation. The results of this analysis should include customizations and process steps that are candidates for automation. This does not need to be complicated; you could use a Visio diagram along with a description and definition of the Incident Management process in a Word document. This can be developed into a list of tasks to perform in Service Manager.

To assist with your process definition, the following list includes terms used with Incident Management (for detailed information, see Chapter 3):

▶ **Incident:** This is any event not part of the standard operation of a service. An incident causes, or may cause, an interruption or reduction in the quality of that service. Examples include a service not available or system down, or a function not working.

▶ **Service request:** A service request is an incident not considered a failure in the Information Technology (IT) infrastructure. This is a formal request for something to be provided for or to a customer. An example would be a request to reset a user's logon.

▶ **Service catalog:** The service catalog is a part of request fulfillment in the ITIL framework. It describes information about all offered IT services. This includes service offerings and request offerings. Request offerings can be defined as a process for dealing with service requests from customers.

▶ **Problem:** This is an unknown error, the underlying cause of one or more incidents.

▶ **Known error:** A known error is a problem for which a root cause and permanent fix or workaround are identified, but the fix is not yet implemented.

▶ **Workaround:** This is a temporary fix or technique eliminating the end user's reliance on the faulty service component.

You can enable your Incident Management process using different settings and functionality in Service Manager. In general, following is how the Service Manager configuration settings and functionality are split:

▶ **General Incident Management Service Manager settings:** These overall settings enable Incident Management functionality and include settings in the Incident Settings section of the Administration workspace in the console, which contains the basic settings for each process.

▶ **Enumeration (drop-down) lists in the Service Manager console and the "lists" section of the console:** These consist of a list of properties shown in drop-down lists on forms and dialog boxes. An example is Incident Classification; this contains a default set of list items you can adjust with specific values for your organization.

▶ **Incident logging entries:** An incident may be created from different entries. Incident work items can be created from the Service Manager console, from emails sent to a monitored mailbox, or using the self-service portal.

▶ **Incident Management automation:** These are template and workflow configurations for process automation.

▶ **Incident Management customization:** Customization incorporates the Authoring Tool or custom development; examples include adding or hiding fields and drop-down lists and check boxes.

▶ **Incident Management extensions:** Here you would create or acquire and implement solutions that extend Incident Management capabilities beyond what is out of the box. Third-party vendors provide add-on management packs that extend Service Manager functionality.

Incident Management in Service Manager

Incident Management manages the life cycle of all incidents, with goals of restoring services to normal as quickly as possible and minimizing business impact. Resolving incidents is a basic technical task. Providing an interface to log incidents and/or route incidents to the correct support group assists in resolving incidents and enables quick incident resolution for those organizations with well-tuned incident management processes. Service Manager orchestrates these basic tasks and provides a platform to automate the different elements in the process:

▶ Multiple sources exist for creating incident work items. Depending on the source, incident workflows could further route incidents to the correct support group. An overview of the sources to create incident work items follows:

   ▶ **Incident logging via console by the service desk:** This is the most comprehensive approach for creating incident work items. Service desk analysts can ask those questions necessary to complete the information in the work item.

   ▶ **Incidents created by end users via email or the self-service portal:** These create incident work items in Service Manager that require validation before the work items are routed, as there may not be enough information provided to resolve the incident.

   ▶ **Incidents created from Service Manager connectors, such as alerts with the Operations Manager Alert connector or Configuration Manager desired configuration management:** These incidents can be routed based on the information on the work item. While some fine-tuning may occur in Service Manager, the majority of configuration occurs at the source of the connector.

   ▶ **Other inputs, including System Center Orchestrator, the software development kit (SDK), and PowerShell:** You can use these as a source to create incident work items.

▶ Service Manager automates populating the configuration management database (CMDB) with information and keeping it current. This data is used as context for incident forms, dialog boxes, and tasks. When handling an incident, an IT support analyst can view the user's computer details and ping or remote control that computer directly from the console. This level of integration eliminates the need for a support analyst to step outside the tool to perform tasks and re-enter context data, which saves work cycles and speeds incident resolution.

▶ The Incident Management process can be automated using incident templates and workflows.

▶ Knowledge articles can help service desk analysts and end users understand and resolve incidents, and provide workarounds for those incidents without a resolution.

▶ Incident Management is linked to other management functions in Service Manager such as Change, Release, Problem, and Knowledge Management. This means you can look at an incident and see related changes, or look at a problem and see related incidents, and so on.

▶ Incident information is stored in the Service Manager data warehouse for further reporting.

Figure 11.1 illustrates an overview of Incident Management in Service Manager 2012.

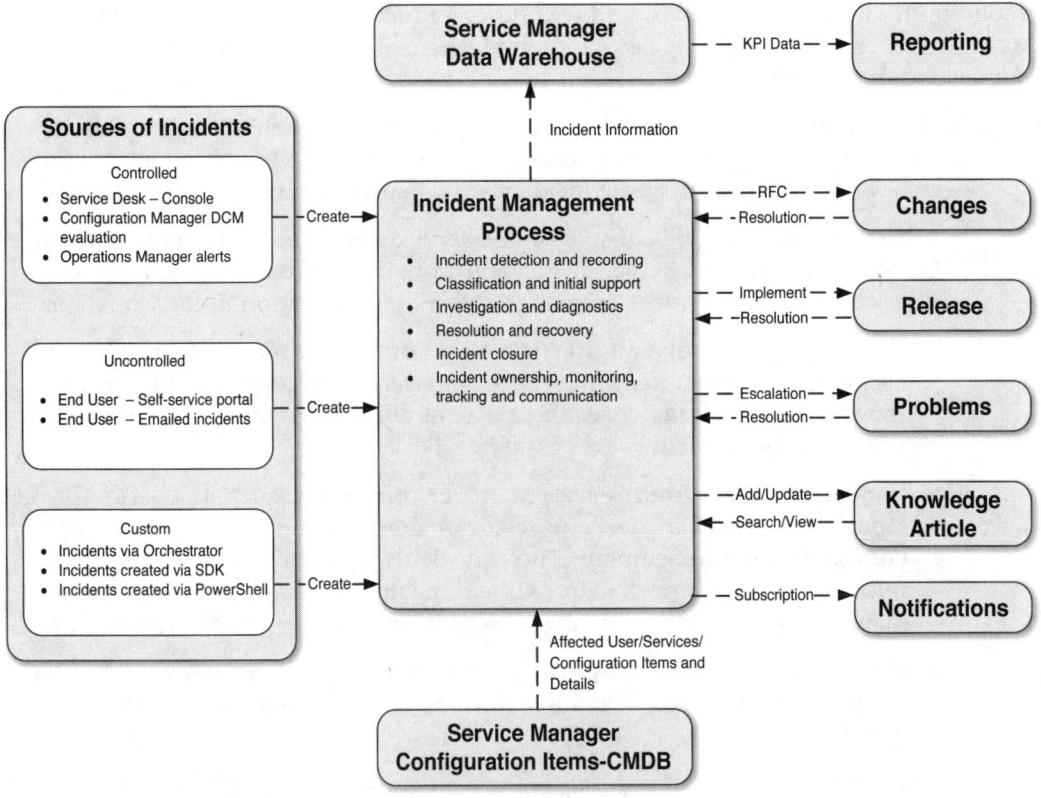

FIGURE 11.1   Incident Management in Service Manager.

The interaction between the elements shown in Figure 11.1 should become clearer as this chapter steps through the various activities. To understand the interactions and define Incident Management functionality in Service Manager, it is important to know those features that are configurable as building blocks to enable the Incident Management process.

Service Manager comes with sealed incident management packs, which enable core Incident Management functionality. The management packs contain required classes, workflows, views, forms, and reports for configuring the Incident Management process. Items customized for your environment, such as groups, queues, tasks, templates, connectors, and list items, are stored in custom unsealed management packs. These settings are applied to incident work items and are considered part of general Incident Management configuration.

TIP: MANAGEMENT PACK COMPONENTS

For information on the various components comprising a management pack, see Chapter 20, "Management Packs."

Configuring Incident Management in Service Manager occurs in different areas of the console, the primary area being the Incident Settings folder in the Administration workspace. Details regarding these settings are discussed in the "Configuring Incident Management" section of this chapter; following is an overview of those settings:

▶ **Incident Work Item Prefix:** In Service Manager, all incident numbers start with IR by default. You can change this prefix.

▶ **Incident File Attachment Policy:** Your company policy may limit the number of files you can attach to each incident to no more than ten and limit the maximum file size for each file to 2048KB. The maximum number of attached files and maximum file size settings also apply to the attached files in the Related Items tab for configuration items. Give this some consideration, as certain tickets may require a number of attachments/screenshots to resolve.

To keep storage at a reasonable size, consider establishing policies and providing training to support analysts concerning screenshot resolutions and storing commonly used documents on a support analyst SharePoint site with a link from Service Manager (this provides an added benefit of version control).

▶ **Incident Default Support Group:** Without a default support group for incidents, support personnel might have to search the All Open Incidents view to locate their incidents. These orphan incidents can be of concern, as no one picks them up and they are not resolved. Defining a default group could be a first step in your incident routing policy; this typically is set to the first-tier support group—the service desk or help desk.

▶ **Parent Incident Configuration:** Linking an incident to a parent incident lets you configure the behavior of child incidents. You can determine to not follow, automatically follow a parent's status, or let the analyst decide when a parent incident is resolved or reactivated. You can also configure the status of active child incidents.

▶ **Incident Priority Calculation:** Priorities range from 1 to 9, with 1 as the highest. Priority is based on a combination of impact and urgency. Impact and urgency settings are defined by default as High, Medium, or Low; these are determined when the incident is created.

▶ **Resolution Time:** This defines how much time it should take to resolve an incident. Resolution time is based on priority; higher-priority incidents should have resolution times.

▶ **Operations Manager Web Site:** If using Operations Manager, you can integrate its web console functionality into Service Manager incident tasks. This would enable support personnel to check Operations Manager CI health status from the Service Manager console.

Port 51908 is used by default by Operations Manager for Windows authentication with its web console. When Forms authentication is enabled, an https port (443 by default) is used for web console connectivity.

▶ **Incoming Email Support:** Configuring incoming email support enables users to send incident support requests by email. SMTP server configuration is part of the Incident Settings in the Service Manager console. Exchange connector functionality is available through importing an additional management pack. Information on the Exchange connector is available in Chapter 8, "Working with Connectors."

▶ **Notifications:** Communication is an important component of Incident Management. Affected users, support personnel, or managers might want to be notified of incidents or other changes. Service Manager lets you generate notifications for almost any type of change. Notifications are discussed in Chapter 16, "Managing Notifications."

▶ **Service Manager Incident Management Workflows:** A workflow is a sequence of activities that automates a business process, such as the Incident Management process. You can use Service Manager workflows to update incidents when various changes occur. When you create a workflow, you define when and under what circumstances it runs. As an example, a workflow can automatically change the support tier from 1 to 2 when a low priority incident is changed to a higher priority. Workflow activities apply templates and send notifications. Service Manager provides various workflows for different processes. The "Automating Incident Management" section of this chapter discusses configuring the Incident Event and Desired Configuration Management Event workflows.

Use the Library workspace of the console to configure groups, knowledge, queues, incident lists, tasks, the service catalog, and templates. A definition of these items follows:

▶ **Groups:** Groups are a collection of configuration items (CIs). These can be used to assign incident work items to a specific support team.

▶ **Service Manager Knowledge:** Knowledge articles can help service desk analysts and end users understand and resolve incidents. Knowledge can be added to the incident work item as an additional source of information to resolve the incident.

▶ **Incident Management Lists:** An incident work item is an object with a set of properties. A list represents a property of an object, and includes one or more list items. Each list item represents a possible value available for selection in the incident work item. Service Manager includes several default incident lists to use in your incident forms.

▶ **Incident Queues:** Queues group similar work items that meet specified criteria. As an example, you could group all incident work items classified as Email problems into a single queue monitored by the support desk. You can define the rights a user has to a queue, control those actions a user can perform on the content in the queue, or define service level objectives (SLOs); this is not possible for objects in a group.

▶ **Tasks:** Tasks are the actions listed to the right of the incident work item and automate repetitive actions performed by a support analyst. Analysts typically use tasks when troubleshooting user incidents. Service Manager includes tasks such as pinging a computer or creating a remote desktop connection. You can create your own tasks in the Service Manager console.

▶ **Service Catalog:** This folder consists of service offerings and request offerings. In Service Manager, service offerings are a way to group request offerings, while request offerings are catalog items within a service catalog used as a service point between end users and IT departments.

▶ **Incident Management Templates:** You could create an incident template to populate certain fields for a specified incident type. Support personnel use templates when creating incidents; these can also be used in incident workflows to automate processes. The template can prepopulate property fields in the incident work item, such as the name of the support group or assigned analyst for that work item. Following are default Incident Management templates provided by Service Manager:

> ▶ Default Incident
>
> ▶ Software Issue Incident
>
> ▶ Networking Issue
>
> ▶ Printing Issue Incident
>
> ▶ High Priority Incident
>
> ▶ Hardware Issue
>
> ▶ Operations Manager Incident

You could also use the Service Manager Authoring Tool to configure or automate Incident Management using management packs. The Authoring Tool is discussed in Chapter 20 and Chapter 22, "Customizing Service Manager."

Service Manager is integrated tightly with other System Center components such as Operations Manager, Orchestrator, Virtual Machine Manager, and Configuration Manager. This integration is implemented by configuring connectors. The "Automating Incident Management" section of this chapter discusses using information provided by the connectors. The connectors can bring automation via the following functionality in Service Manager:

▶ **Operations Manager Alert connector:** Use this connector to generate incidents automatically based on Operations Manager alerts. Support analysts can access detailed alert information through the incident work item tasks.

▶ **Configuration Manager connector:** You must create a Configuration Manager connector in Service Manager to import baselines, and workflows can be created to generate incidents automatically based on Configuration Manager desired configuration management (DCM).

▶ **Exchange connector:** The System Center Service Manager Connector for Exchange connects Service Manager to Exchange to process incoming emails. This connector is downloaded separately from the Microsoft website. The Exchange connector can be used to create and update work items, based on templates specified by an administrator.

The next section maps Incident Management process activities to Service Manager functionality.

Incident Management Process Activities

Associating Incident Management process activities with Service Manager features enables you to analyze your Incident Management process and configure the Service Manager incident environment. This provides cohesion between how you work in your processes and takes advantage of the functionality provided by the tool. The following sections assess each critical process activity and examine how you could apply Service Manager to optimize each stage. The sections highlight the elements of the Incident Management process and indicate where Service Manager can help to configure and automate that process. The "Configuring Incident Management" section of the chapter discusses configuring this functionality in Service Manager. Following are the Incident Management process steps, illustrated in Figure 11.2:

▶ **Events:** Events occur and are logged by the user. The affected user can call the service desk, send an email, or use the portal to log an incident. Connectors can monitor for events and create incident work items when an event occurs.

▶ **Incident detection and recording:** This is one of the primary jobs of support personnel and can be automated with Service Manager connectors.

▶ **Classification and initial support:** An important task for first line support is to populate the incident form, categorize it, and assign it to an appropriate queue or assignment group, should it not be resolved during the initial call.

▶ **Investigation and diagnosis:** This technical activity is part of the overall Incident Management process.

▶ **Resolution and recovery:** An incident can be resolved when the service is restored to its standard operation mode.

▶ **Incident closure:** ITIL recommends a two-step incident closure. The affected user is notified after resolution, and the incident is closed only upon confirmation within a given period of time. It is also a best practice not to reopen a closed incident, but create a new one and reference the closed incident.

▶ **Incident ownership, monitoring, tracking, and communication:** Wherever the incident is created, someone in Incident Management owns it and takes care of it. This ensures incidents do not go to an unmonitored queue.

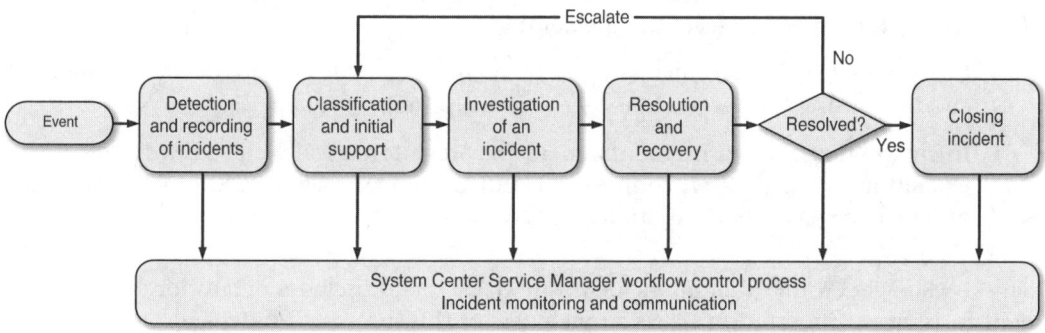

FIGURE 11.2   Activities in Incident Management.

Incident Creation

As events occur, the affected user contacts the support desk to log an incident or uses one of the self-service (email or portal) interfaces to log the incident. An event could also trigger a system for a certain action and be captured through a connector. In all cases, you want to ensure that the end user is able to request support and that the support desk can log the necessary information.

The Service Manager features involved follow:

▶ **Default incident form in the Service Manager console:** The incident management management packs provide a default incident form; this is customizable. If additional properties are configured for the `Incident` class, you can integrate them into the default form.

▶ **Self-service portal (SSP):** End users use the SSP to contact support analysts for support requests. Users can also use the portal to log service requests, search the knowledge base, and manage their requests.

▶ **Operations Manager Alert connector:** The connector automatically creates incidents based on alert subscriptions in Operations Manager.

▶ **Configuration Manager DCM compliancy incidents:** This connector automatically creates incidents based on alert subscriptions on Configuration Manager DCM CI compliancy.

▶ **Incoming email support:** This functionality enables end users to email support requests.

▶ **Incoming email support via Exchange connector:** The connector can be used to monitor Exchange mailboxes. Incoming emails can create or update incidents, with additional keywords identified to resolve or close incident work items.

Incident Detection and Recording

In a typical Incident Management process, detecting an event is related to something that occurs on an end user's system. Service Manager extends this functionality by integrating infrastructure events into the process. Event recording is dependent on the particular detection method used to create the incident:

▶ **User-related incidents:** Incidents are manually created by service desk personnel or end users using the Service Manager console, portal, or email.

▶ **Infrastructure-related incidents:** Incidents are automatically created with the Operations Manager Alert connector, Configuration Manager DCM functionality, or other sources such as Orchestrator or CSV import.

Service Manager ensures that all incidents are tracked and includes details for each incident to assist with resolution. The completeness of this information depends on the individual logging the incident or the information added to an automatically created incident work item. Given the various sources, the following list of incoming incident types includes different levels of information:

▶ **Controlled:** Incidents created by support teams must include all information necessary to resolve the incident. Support teams can be trained to work with end users to include this information and relate it to the affected configuration items.

▶ **Uncontrolled:** End user-created incidents by email or the SSP do not always include all required information and must be reviewed. The end user may need to provide additional information, or the logged work item might not even be an incident.

▶ **Automated:** Incidents automatically created by connectors include information from the source of the connector. The information included in the incident work item is hard-coded in the connector.

▶ **Custom:** This type of incoming incident is dependent on how it was created. The developer is dependent upon where the information was captured.

Uncontrolled incident work items created by end users require an additional validation step: The incident must be reviewed to determine whether it is an actual incident. For example, a user could use the SSP to log complaints; these must be filtered out of the Incident Management process.

The Service Manager items involved in this process follow:

▶ **Default incident form:** Service Manager provides a default form based on incident class properties and relationships. This form is extensible; see Chapter 22 for more information.

▶ **Service catalog:** Published request offerings in the self-service portal must include required fields that describe the event in enough detail to create incident work items. Depending on the needs of your organization, you can include additional property selections such as classification, urgency, and so on.

▶ **Incident event templates:** Templates can be utilized to achieve Incident Management flexibility. These include common settings for different types of incidents. As an example, when the service desk receives a call from a user unable to access email, the service desk operator can apply the email issue incident template and verify the appropriate information is collected from the user reporting the incident. Using templates ensures that incidents are recorded with the correct owner information, category, priority, and other related items.

Service Manager provides a set of templates to log incidents from various sources and classifications. You can use them as is or adjust them to support your own process.

▶ **Incident event workflows:** Workflows are important for detecting and recording activity. Workflows can route incidents to the correct incident queue or assign them to the correct support group. This is particularly important for incidents created automatically.

Workflows can prepopulate common settings on the incident work item and be used to route incidents. Incidents created with the portal can be routed to a dedicated queue for validation. If using the Operations Manager Alert connector, you can apply templates based on the management pack that raised the alert.

Notifications may be sent depending on the defined process and the criteria configured in workflows.

Incident Classification and Initial Support

Classification categorizes the incident by assigning a classification and priority to the work item. The initial support activity could provide a first-line resolution for incidents by checking symptoms against similar incidents or documented workarounds in knowledge articles. It is important that support analysts collect adequate information, categorize the incident properly, and provide sufficient details about the event. This information is useful when resolving the incident or for information lookups.

The incident's default support group, configured in the incident settings, is established when incident work items are created in the console. The default can be overridden by templates triggered by workflows. For example, when an incident is created from an Operations Manager alert, a different template might be applied depending on the rule specified on the connector. Assigning an incident work item consists of populating the AssignTo relationship on the form; this can be performed manually by specifying the support analyst name on the Assign to field on the form, or set using the Assign to Me or Assign to Analyst tasks. The search scope in the Assign to Analyst task can be optimized by configuring the Global Operators group in the Group folder of the Library workspace, which limits the search to analysts that are members of the Global Operators group.

Service Manager includes a default incident classification and allows you to add and remove categories, and dynamically creates different depths of classification based on the type or category. Keep in mind when creating your own incident classification that IT support and management should understand your categories, although these are usually technical.

There are three primary reasons to classify incidents:

- **Assignment and escalation:** If not solved on first call, it is an operator's task to assign the incident to a proper priority (urgency/impact), category, and support group.

- **Problem analysis:** Classifying the incident lets you easily look up similar closed incidents for documented solutions.

- **Reporting:** Reporting is important because it provides input to other information technology service management (ITSM) processes (Problem, Change, and so on) and is the primary tool of IT service managers.

When defining your own incident classification list, the authors recommend you not create too deep a classification schema.

NOTE: CLASSIFICATION LIST STRATEGY INFORMATION

There is a tradeoff regarding the levels in a classification list:

- If classification lists are not deep enough, reporting is not granular enough.
- When lists are too deep, support analysts struggle with the number of options, and the quality of ticket classification can be affected. (They end up choosing the easiest option; be particularly beware of categories such as Miscellaneous or Other.)

Striking a balance between ease of use for analysts and reporting granularity is somewhat of an art. In most cases, a two- or three-tiered classification schema should meet your needs.

The priority assigned on the incident work item is calculated based on the urgency and impact of that work item. This calculation is based on a configurable matrix. By default, mandatory fields for the incident work item are Title, Classification category, Urgency, and Impact. This is discussed further in the "Configuring Incident Management" section of this chapter.

Service Manager includes functionality to link and unlink incidents to a parent incident. Those incidents affecting the same service or with a similar description or classification can be linked to a parent. Based on the parent/child settings configured in the Administration workspace, these child incidents can be managed from their parent. A parent incident is similar to a "normal" incident work item but includes a Child Incidents tab on the incident form. You can add or remove the child incidents listed on that tab. There are two tasks for managing parent/child relationships:

▶ **Link or Unlink to Parent:** Incident work items can be linked or unlinked to an existing parent. A pop-up window opens to browse for the parent incident when executing this task. (The parent incident already exists in this scenario.)

▶ **Link to New Parent Incident:** The selected incidents are linked to a new parent incident. The parent is created, and the incidents are directly linked to the new parent incident.

TIP: CREATING A PARENT/CHILD INCIDENT OR PROBLEM WORK ITEM

You might wonder when to create a parent incident work item and link related incidents as child incidents, or to create a problem work item.

▶ Parent/child incidents are a grouping of incident work items with a related classification, description, SLO, or an event that is occurring and affecting a service. This relationship is used to manage incident work items; child incident work items follow the work item status levels of the related parent.

▶ In Problem Management, the incident work item can be related to the problem work item. The work item must follow the defined Problem Management process, which defines an approach for investigating the issue using more detailed resolution information (error descriptions, workarounds, and review notes). The Problem Management process has its own classification list and is not related to the incident service level agreement (SLA). Problem Management is discussed in Chapter 13, "Problem Management."

The Service Manager items involved in this process follow:

▶ **Incident Priority Calculation:** This is a general setting for the incident and is valid for incident work items.

▶ **Parent incident settings:** These settings define how child incidents behave with a linked parent. You can associate auto resolution and reactivation of child incidents to when the parent incident is resolved or reactivated, and define the status behavior of a child incident when linked to a parent.

▶ **Global Operators group configuration:** The Assign to Analyst search task can be scoped to this group by configuring the Global Operators group members in the Groups folder. Only members of this group are initially displayed on the selection page of the task; this can be updated by using filters.

▶ **Service Manager knowledge:** Internal knowledge is an important resource for solving incidents during the initial call. You can configure search providers such as your own SharePoint knowledge site, Microsoft TechNet, and other search engines.

▶ **Incident event templates:** Service Manager includes a number of templates for creating incident work items. Depending on your Incident Management process, you might need to create additional templates for incident work items or to use in Incident Management workflows.

▶ **Incident event workflows:** Using classifications, the correct support group can be assigned to a workflow. In addition, the calculated priority (urgency/impact settings) on the incident can trigger a workflow to assign the incident to a specialized support group. Priority settings are discussed in the "Configuring Incident Management" section of this chapter.

▶ **Operations Manager connector:** Infrastructure-related incidents are created via the Operations Manager connector. Using the connector settings in the console, you can configure alert routing rules to apply an incident template. This can automatically categorize those incidents created by the connector. The Operations Manager incident template is applied if there are no configured filters.

▶ **Desired Configuration Manager event workflows:** Configuring these workflows lets you create incidents based on Configuration Manager CI compliancy and apply a template accordingly. Category, urgency, and impact of the incident are defined by the template.

Incident Investigation and Diagnosis

Service Manager provides several sources of information for investigating incidents in the Incident Management process:

▶ The initial source is information included in the incident work item, which can be used to resolve the issue.

▶ The knowledge base can help resolve incidents. Your own documented solutions can be associated with the incident and are accessible from the incident form.

▶ Service Manager tasks can assist in finding a solution for the incident. The console provides some predefined tasks, and you can create your own tasks for actions frequently taken by the support team. As an example, you could select the incident work item and run the ping-related computer task.

▶ Business service definitions can help resolve incidents. Once an incident is created for an affected configuration item that is a member of a business service, the service reference is added to the incident work item.

▶ Service Manager announcements can be used to announce service outages.

11

Support analysts collect updated incident details and analyze all related information, particularly configuration details from the CMDB. The information to create incidents is provided by first-line support or the user, be that through the Service Manager console, SSP, or email. The analyst must ensure there is adequate information to fully investigate the issue. For those incidents created through connectors, this information is added automatically to the incident work item.

> **TIP: IMPORT OPERATIONS MANAGER MANAGEMENT PACKS FOR ADDITIONAL CLASSES**
>
> Operations Manager and Virtual Machine Manager collect information about many different types of objects, such as hard disk drives, websites, and clouds. Service Manager requires a list of class definitions for these objects; this is provided by Operations Manager management packs. To make this information available to the incident work item, import the associated Operations Manager management packs into Service Manager before configuring these connectors.

The Service Manager components involved follow:

▶ **Service Manager knowledge:** This has the same functionality as with the initial support activity. Support personnel can search for documented solutions using different search providers.

▶ **Service Manager tasks:** You can create tasks in the console and associate them with the Incident Management folder. Tasks can be configured for frequently used actions such as executables to launch from the command line while investigating an incident. Incident properties can be added as arguments to the command being executed.

▶ **Business services:** Defining business services in Service Manager provides many advantages. Examples of the benefits of defining these services include

　　▶ Enabling support personnel to see the service relationship on a configuration item.

　　▶ When investigating problems, all related information around the service (such as other open incidents or configuration items that enable the service) is available in the incident work item.

▶ **Configuration items:** CIs in Service Manager are the primary source of information. The support team loses time when this information is outdated or incomplete.

Escalating Incidents

Critical to the escalation process is being able to rapidly transfer incidents according to agreed-upon service levels. Notification workflows can notify additional support resources if necessary. Escalation can follow two paths:

- ▶ **Functional escalation (a handoff to the organizational unit or function owning the technology stream):** This is required when the incident must be escalated to those support groups better able to resolve the incident, or when the support group cannot resolve the incident within agreed-upon target times. In Service Manager, this is a reassignment of the support group with the escalated class property selection or using workflow automation.

- ▶ **Hierarchic escalation (escalation up the management chain):** This occurs when the incident requires a higher priority level. When the urgency or impact of an incident rises, its priority changes, and this can trigger a workflow.

Each resolution attempt attaches data to the incident work item to save repeating recovery procedures, which could lengthen overall resolution times. This lets Service Manager play yet another key role by automating the escalation process and pinpointing the exact source of errors.

The Service Manager features involved follow:

- ▶ **Incident event workflows:** These can be configured to automate both escalation paths. For example, the escalation property is set on the work item when the incident support group changes from first to second level support. This could also be applicable for priority changes.

- ▶ **Incident notifications:** The service desk should keep the user, incident primary owner, and assigned analysts informed of any escalations, and ensure the incident work item is updated to maintain a full history of actions. This entails configuring accurate notifications and subscriptions in Service Manager.

Incident Resolution and Recovery

An incident is resolved when the service is restored to its standard mode of operations. Any potential resolutions should be applied and tested. The specific actions to undertake and individuals involved with the recovery actions may vary, depending on the nature of the incident.

- ▶ The service desk can ask the affected user to undertake activities on his system. Incident work item information must be current to contact the affected user or apply a resolution to the affected CI.

- ▶ The service desk implementing the resolution can either centrally (say, apply a hotfix with Configuration Manager) or remotely use software to take control of the user's computer to diagnose and implement a solution.

▶ Specialized support groups may be asked to implement specific recovery actions (such as Network Support reconfiguring a router).

▶ A third-party supplier may be asked to resolve the incident.

The Service Manager features involved follow:

▶ **Incident event templates:** Service Manager includes a list of incident resolution items that you can adjust to support reporting requirements. The default incident resolution items are Auto Resolved by Problem, Cancelled, Fixed by analyst, Fixed by higher tier support, and Walk through knowledge article.

▶ **Incident notifications:** Notifications and subscriptions in Service Manager can notify the necessary individuals when closing an incident.

Closing Incidents

The support team should verify the incident is fully resolved and that the users are satisfied and agree that the incident can be closed. There is a distinction between a resolved and closed incident work item: A resolved incident work item is when the support analyst believes it is solved to the satisfaction of the user; closed is when the user confirms the incident is resolved.

A closed incident work item cannot be reopened (although you can script this in Service Manager, it is not compliant with ITIL/MOF). Rather than reopening the incident, you could always create a new incident and relate it to the closed incident. The support analyst can reopen a resolved incident work item if the problem is not resolved or the affected user does not accept the solution. The authors recommend leaving incident work items in a Resolved status for some period of time to allow the affected user to respond to the proposed solution. You would create incident closure workflows to automate closing these work items.

The Service Manager features involved follow:

▶ **Incident event workflows:** As discussed in the "Incident Management in Service Manager" section, you can create incident event workflows to automate closing incidents. As an example, if the incident is in a resolved status for two days, a workflow would automatically close the incident work item.

▶ **Incident notifications:** Notifications and subscriptions in Service Manager can notify the persons who need to close the incident.

Configuring Incident Management

The "Incident Management Process Activities" section earlier in this chapter provides an overview of the Incident Management activities from a Service Manager perspective and describes the tasks in these activities. The next sections discuss configuration options for Incident Management in Service Manager 2012.

The goal of Incident Management is to ensure users can get back to work as quickly as possible. The activities of this process should be supported by technology—not only to enable the Incident Management process, but also to enhance (automate), measure, and support the activities of that process. The configuration required for Service Manager depends on the process defined in your organization. Settings such as prefix, priority calculation, parent/child behavior, security settings, and notifications are global settings. Other settings depend on the service you want to provide to the end user. Examples follow:

▶ Service Manager can email incident requests. This provides user functionality to send an email to report an incident.

▶ Service Manager can automatically create incident work items from Operations Manager alerts and Configuration Manager DCM evaluations, which can be customized using the SDK or Orchestrator. These help integrate your infrastructure into the Incident Management process.

A process breakdown can help define those settings necessary for Service Manager. The next sections provide guidance for configuring Incident Management settings.

Incident User Roles, Groups, Queues, and Lists

The starting point of configuration is ensuring the support team can access the required work items, views, tasks, and templates. Service Manager defines a single Incident Resolvers user role with access to all incident work items, views, and so on. Defining additional user roles is important when configuring Incident Management, as these can control the console experience and tasks. Items controlled by user roles include

▶ **Access to incident work item views:** This is provided by configuring the user role with access to those views in the console.

▶ **Work items visible to the analyst:** These can be controlled by configuring queues on the user role.

▶ **Configuration items that can be viewed or related to the work item:** These are controlled by configuring Service Manager group access.

▶ **Routing incident work items:** This is provided by configuring Service Manager user roles.

You can use the Incident Resolvers user role if you do not require limited access to the incident work items in the console. This user role can access all incident work items; routing these work items can then be based on Active Directory security groups and incident queues. To limit console access, first configure the underlying features before defining user roles. For information on creating user roles in Service Manager, see Chapter 17, "Service Manager Security."

Creating Groups for Incident Management

Service Manager includes different types of groups. These include groups you can create that contain different CIs, catalog groups used to scope requests presented on the portal, and the Global Operators group. An overview of the different groups in the Groups folder of the Library workspace follows:

▶ **Service Manager groups:** These groups contain objects, typically CIs, and can be used to scope views, run reports, and scope Service Manager user roles. (Groups are for configuration items, such as computers; queues are for work items, such as incidents.) Groups can include collections of objects of the same class or different classes.

▶ **Service Manager catalog groups:** These can be created to scope requests presented on the portal for different user roles. Catalog groups include request offerings and service offerings for Service Request Management or Incident Management. You can configure user roles to list only those request items on the portal that are members of a specific catalog group. By default, the Generic Incident Request Catalog Items group provides access to generic requests on the portal.

▶ **Global Operators group:** This contains the list of analysts for your Service Manager environment. The group limits the scope of the Assign to Analyst task that is available in Incident Management and Service Request Management.

Each of these groups can be created as static, dynamic, or a combination of the two. Creating the groups is similar for all processes; only the included objects are different. More information on Service Manager catalog groups is in Chapter 10, "Service Manager Service Catalog." To create a Service Manager group, perform the following steps:

1. In the Service Manager console, navigate to **Library** -> **Groups**. Initially there are two groups in the Results pane: Generic Incident Request Catalog Items and Global Operators. To create groups for Incident Management, go to **Tasks** -> **Groups**, and select **Create Group**.

2. The Create Group wizard starts. Click **Next** on the Before You Begin page.

3. On the General page, provide a name and description for the group, such as **All Odyssey SCSM servers**. Under Management pack, ensure you have selected an unsealed management pack. Click **Next**.

4. On the Included Members page (displayed in Figure 11.3), click **Add** to select configuration items:

▶ In the Select objects dialog box (see Figure 11.4), in the right drop-down box, select a class such as `Windows Computer`.

▶ In the drop-down box on the left (with the faded text "Type to filter..."), type the search criteria to locate the object, and then click the magnifying glass or press **Enter**.

▶ Select one or more items in the Available objects list and then click **Add**. For example, all Service Manager servers can be listed in one group for further configuration of user roles, views, reporting, and so on.

▶ Verify the objects you selected in the Available objects list appear in the Selected objects list displayed in Figure 11.4, and then click **OK**.

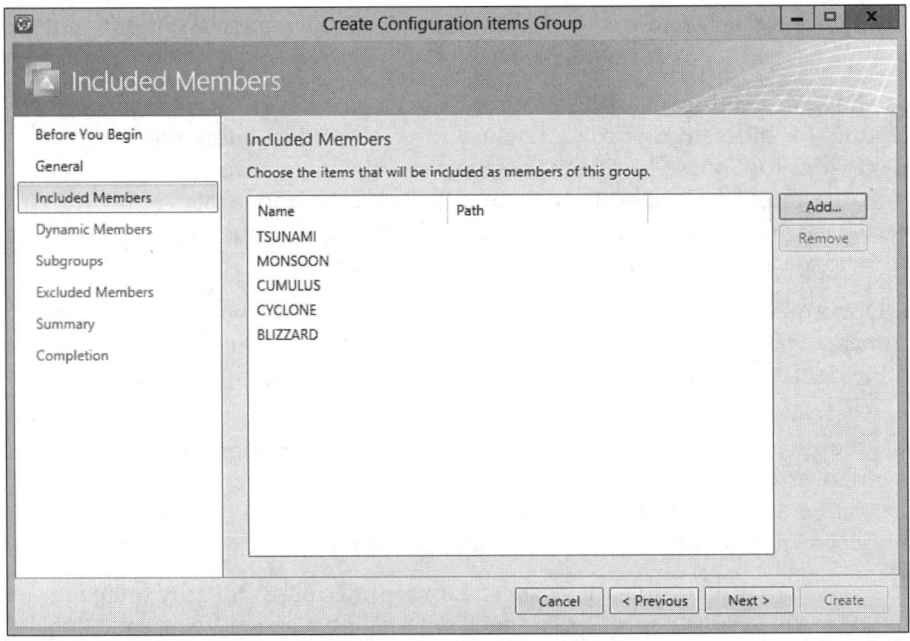

FIGURE 11.3   Included members when creating a CI group.

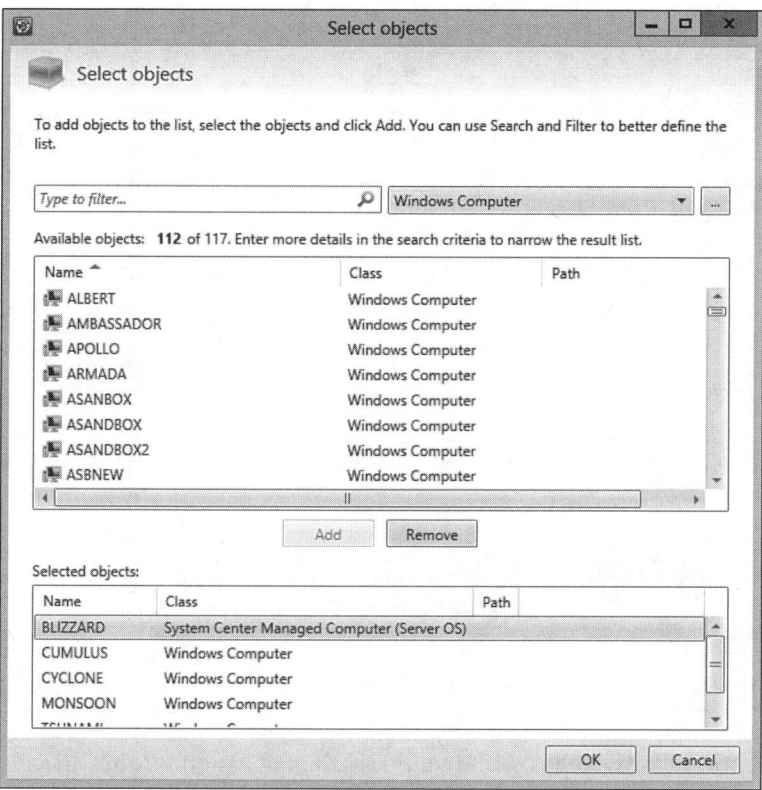

FIGURE 11.4   Group member object selection when creating a CI group.

5. Click **Next** on the Included Members page.

6. On the Dynamic Members page (see Figure 11.5), you can define a query to populate the group membership dynamically. In a dynamic group, the membership changes dynamically with changes in your environment.

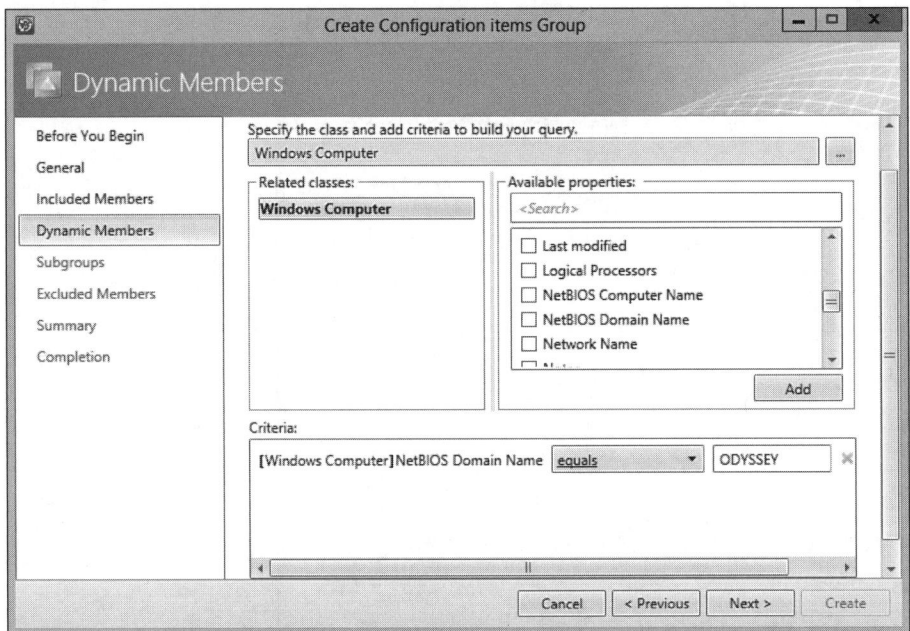

FIGURE 11.5   Adding dynamic members when creating a CI group.

> ▶ Choose the property for which to build your criteria. For example, after speci-
>   fying the `Windows Computer` class, select the NetBIOS Domain Name property,
>   and then click **Add**.

> ▶ In the related text box, enter the NetBIOS Domain Name so all the computers
>   located in that domain are included, and then click **Next**.

7. Optionally, use the Subgroups page to select subgroups of the groups you create.
   For example, if you organized your configuration items in groups and you need a
   Master – all including group, you can create a group that includes all other Incident
   Management related groups.

   On the Subgroups page, click **Modify**, and then select the specific groups you want
   as subgroups of this group. Click **OK**, and then click **Next**.

8. The Excluded Members page lets you exclude certain systems. For example, say you
   defined criteria for a dynamic membership and need to exclude certain configuration items. (This procedure is similar to step 4 with the Included Members dialog
   box.)

   On the Excluded Members dialog box, in the right drop-down box, select a class
   such as `Windows Computer`. In the left drop-down box, type the search criteria you
   want to use to locate an object, and then click the magnifying glass or press **Enter**.
   Select one or more items in the Available objects list and then click **Add**. Click **OK**,
   and then click **Next**.

9. Confirm your selections on the Summary page. Click **Create**.

10. On the Completion page, verify you receive a confirmation message that the new group was created successfully, and click **Close**.

Configuring Global Operators group membership is similar to a normal CI group. This group is created during Service Manager installation. Membership can be based on included memberships or dynamic memberships. The property page for this group includes tabs for included, dynamic, and excluded memberships. Steps 4, 6, and 8 of the previous procedure explain how to configure the different types of membership.

TIP: VALIDATE CREATION OF A SERVICE MANAGER GROUP

Validate the group is created by verifying it is in the Groups pane of the console. If necessary, press the F5 key to refresh the Service Manager console view. In the Tasks pane, under the name of the group, click **View Group Members** to confirm the configuration items are displayed in the Group Members window.

Creating an Incident Queue

The word *queue* is used differently in Service Manager than most other service management tools. Typically, a queue is a screen where you view your tickets; this is a view in Service Manager. A Service Manager queue is a container of related work items, for example, incidents. This is related to a view, or what is typically understood as a queue, but it is not the same. Service Manager 2012 includes several predefined queues. You can also create queues if your organization requires these. As an example, you can create a queue for all incident work items for the Tier 1 support team. This queue can be used to create a console view, scope the Service Manager user role, or define SLOs. Perform the following steps to create an incident queue:

1. In the Service Manager console, navigate to **Library -> Queues**. In the Tasks pane, click **Create Queue**.

2. Click **Next** on the Before You Begin page.

3. On the General page, type a name in the Queue name box, such as **All Odyssey Tier 1 incidents**.

   Next to the work item type box, click the ellipsis button (...). In the Select a Class dialog box, select a class such as **Incident**, and then click **OK**.

   In the Management pack list, select the unsealed management pack to use to store the new queue definition. Click **Next**.

4. On the Criteria page, build the criteria you want to use to filter work items for the queue, and then click **Next**. This example builds a Tier 1 incident queue, with the goal of keeping System Center Operations Manager, System Center Configuration Manager (DCM), and system-created incidents out of this queue. Figure 11.6 shows exclusions made to not include Operations Manager, Configuration Manager (DCM),

or System created incidents. Only work items meeting the specified criteria are added to that queue. Click **Next** to proceed.

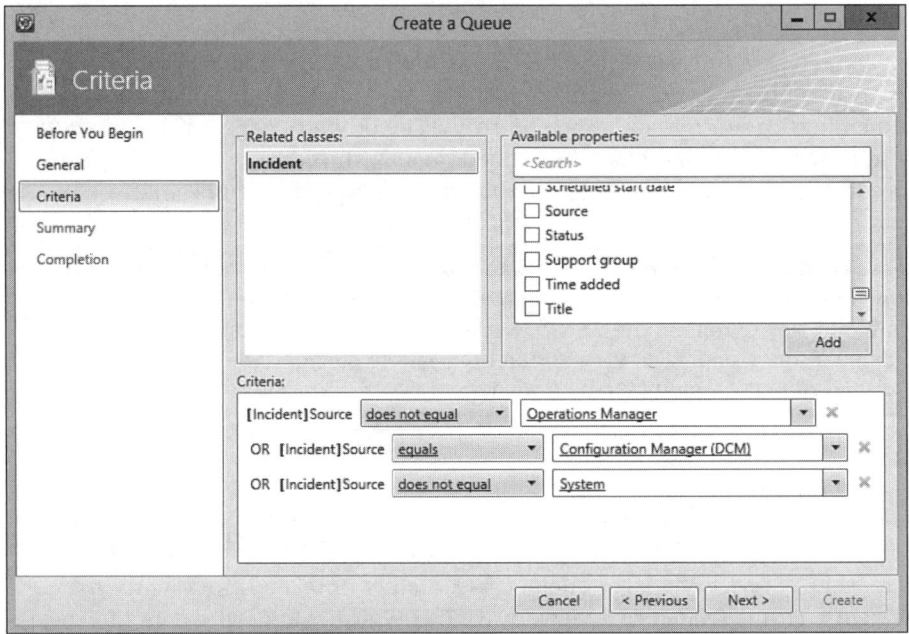

FIGURE 11.6 Creating a Tier 1 queue.

5. On the Summary page, click **Create** to create the queue.

6. On the Completion page, click **Close**.

To validate the queue was created, verify that it appears in the Queues folder of the console. In the Tasks pane, click **Properties**, and confirm that the queue appears as it was defined.

Customizing the Incident Lists Library

An incident work item includes different fields with information that can help resolve the incident. Service Manager lists represent a property of an object and include one or more list items. Each item represents a possible value for the property for the support team to select on incident forms and dialog boxes. Using lists, you can you classify different objects such as incidents, change requests, activities, or configuration items. This classification can be used to route the incident work item or with key performance indicator (KPI) reporting.

Service Manager includes several default list items for Incident Management. These default lists and list items represent a predefined list of values that can be selected by the creator of the incident work item. You can customize the Incident Lists library to reflect your organization's business practices and requirements. Table 11.1 provides an overview of the default incident lists.

TABLE 11.1   Incident Management Lists

List Name	Description	Management Pack
Incident Tier Queue	Incident Tier Queue List	Incident Management Library
Incident Status	Incident Status List	Incident Management Library
Incident Source	Incident Source List	Incident Management Library
Incident Classification	Incident Classification List	Incident Management Library
Incident Resolution	Incident Resolution List	Incident Management Library

The Classification category is required when creating an incident; you must select a list item. The default list items included for incident classification are a first level categorization; your organization may require additional levels.

For example, the Enterprise Application Problems list item may be required to create a set of child list items reflecting applications in your organization. You can use these child list items to route the incident work item to the correct support team and for reporting.

To configure the Incident Classification list for Incident Management, follow these steps:

1. In the Service Manager console, navigate to **Library** -> **Lists**. The Lists folder displays all existing lists. You can organize the information in the Results pane by clicking the column titles; this makes it easy to find the list you want to edit.

2. Select the list to which you want to add a list item (in this case, select the **Incident Classification** list). In the Tasks pane, under Incident Classification, click **Properties**.

3. In the List Properties dialog box, click **Enterprise Application Problems**, and then select **Add Child**. A new List Value list item is added. You can change the name of this new list item by clicking it and entering the new list item name in the name fields of the dialog box.

4. Select the new List Value list item. Provide a Name box and optional Description. Figure 11.7 specifies Company Web Applications as a child item of the Enterprise Application Problems list item.

5. Repeat steps 2 through 4 to create additional list items in the Incident Classification list properties. You can move list items up and down, and delete and add or create child items to build a complete list. Click **OK** to save your changes.

Because incident classification is an important part of the Incident Management process, you should be clear on the required classifications for your organization. As specified previously in the "Incident Management in Service Manager" section, routing and reporting requirements for Incident Management are the primary sources of information for building your incident classification list items.

If the list is not set up properly, the support team can lose time scrolling down the classification menu, the list becomes too complex, and incidents could end up with the incorrect incident classification. An incident classification list that reflects your organization's requirements and is known by the support team can avoid classifying incident work items as Other Problems. This is a weak classification and should be avoided, although it can be used for certain incidents if necessary.

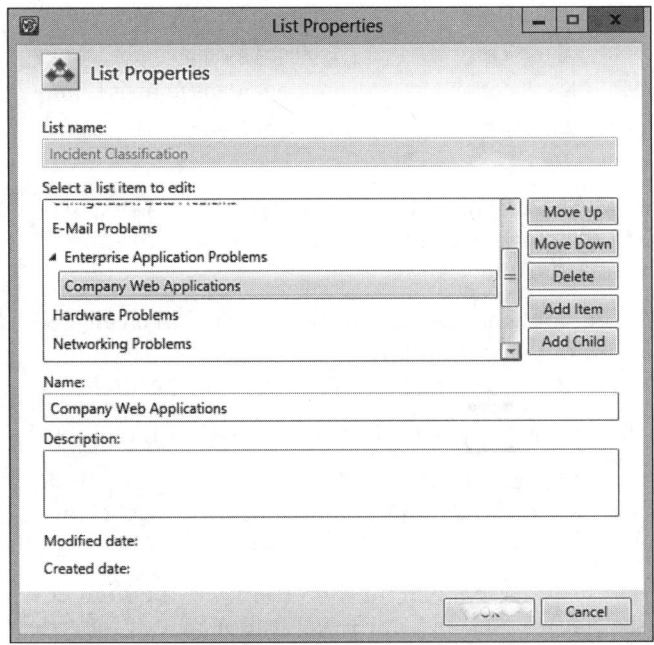

FIGURE 11.7   Edit List properties.

CAUTION: DO NOT DELETE THE DEFAULT LIST ITEMS

Do not delete the default list items included in Service Manager, as each default list item is defined by a globally unique identifier (GUID). The authors recommend changing the display names of existing items rather than deleting them.

Configuring General Incident Settings

General incident settings are scoped to all incident work items. This part of the chapter discusses customizations for Incident Management in Service Manager 2012.

Incident Management settings are configured in the Administration workspace of the console. Perform the following steps to access these settings:

1. In the Service Manager console, navigate to **Administration -> Settings**.

2. In the Settings folder, click **Incident Settings** in the Results pane.

3. In the Tasks pane, under Incident Settings, click **Properties** to open the Incident Settings dialog box.

Defining the Ticket Prefix Setting

The ticket prefix setting, displayed in Figure 11.8, is the first selection when configuring the General settings.

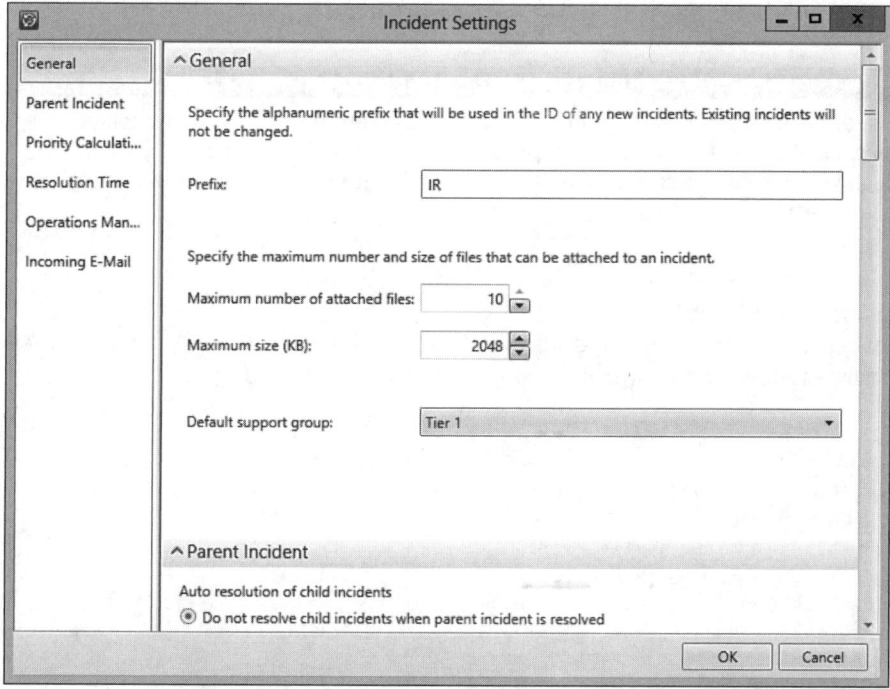

FIGURE 11.8   Specifying general incident settings.

NOTE: INCIDENT WORK ITEMS PREFIX SETTING

You can specify alphanumeric and numeric characters as a prefix for incident work items. It is best not to specify a numeric prefix to distinguish work items; this could be confusing when the number of the work item is added. The prefix specification is limited to 15 characters.

Configuring the Attached File Policy

This is discussed previously in the "Incident Management in Service Manager" section of this chapter. Note that the maximum number of attached files and maximum file size settings also apply to attached files in the Related Items tab for CIs.

Specifying the Default Support Group

Incident work items not assigned to a support group could negatively affect your KPIs. The work items end up in the overall Open Incidents queue; it may be that no one is watching this queue or these work items are handled with low priority. Service Manager lets you specify a default support group. If an incident work item is created and there is no workflow to route the work item to a support group, the incident tier queue configured as the default support group is automatically added to the work item.

TIP: ALTERNATE CONFIGURATION FOR DEFAULT SUPPORT GROUP SETTINGS

An alternative to specifying a default support group is to create a workflow that checks for unassigned incident work items and routes these work items to a dedicated support team. Although you can configure the work items assignment in other ways, it is always best to define a default support group.

Configuring Parent Incident Settings

Parent Incident settings control the child incident's behavior when linked to a parent incident. Configure the following to control child incidents (see Figure 11.9):

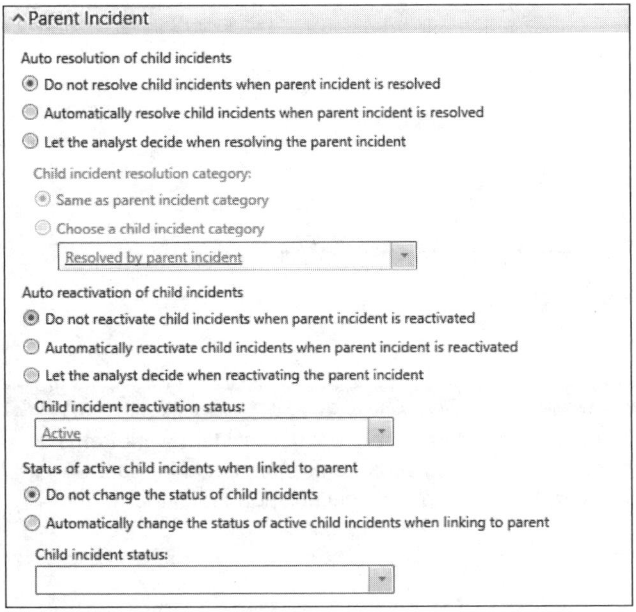

FIGURE 11.9   Customizing parent incident settings.

- ▶ Automatic resolution of linked child incidents can be configured as follows:

  - ▶ **Do not resolve child incidents when parent incident is resolved:** All child incidents must be resolved individually.

  - ▶ **Automatically resolve child incidents when parent incident is resolved:** This enables all child incidents to be resolved when the parent incident is resolved. You can specify the resolution category; this could be set to the same as the parent or selected from the resolution category list.

  - ▶ **Let the analyst decide when resolving the parent incident:** This check box is enabled on the Resolve Incident dialog, with the option to resolve child incidents when resolving the parent (faded when automatic resolution is selected). The resolution category can be the same as the parent incident or selected from the resolution category list.

- ▶ Automatic reactivation of child incidents controls the behavior of a child incident when the parent is reactivated:

  - ▶ **Do not reactivate child incidents when parent incident is reactivated:** All child incidents must be reactivated individually (if needed).

  - ▶ **Automatically reactivate child incidents when parent incident is reactivated:** With this option, all child incidents are reactivated when the parent incident is reactivated. You can also set the reactivation status and select a default status from the incident status property list.

  - ▶ **Let the analyst decide when reactivating the parent incident:** This check box is enabled on the Activate dialog, with the option to reactivate child incidents when reactivating the parent (faded when auto reactivation is selected). You can also set the reactivation status and select a default status from the incident status property list.

- ▶ Status of active child incidents when linked to a parent can be configured to change the child's status to a default. The following options are available:

  - ▶ **Do not change the status of child incidents:** All child incidents retain their status when linked to parent.

  - ▶ **Automatically change the status of active child incidents when linking to parent:** Additional settings to specify status must be specified.

Configuring Priority Calculation and Target Resolution Time for Incident Work Items

An issue's priority determines its routing, assigning, and automation. Priority in Service Manager is determined by impact and urgency. A target resolution time is associated with incident work item priority:

- ▶ **Impact of the incident:** This measures the business criticality of the incident. While this might be difficult for a service desk operator to determine, impact is usually directly proportional to a number of users influenced by the incident or the criticality of an impacted service to the business or business function.

▶ **Urgency:** This is an indicator for the time to resolve an incident. It is not a property of an event, and may vary in time for particular users or business services. (Examples would include VIP users or an event on the HR application when running payroll.)

▶ **Resolution time:** This is the time to resolve an incident. Target resolution time is the total time from when the incident work item is created until it is resolved and service restored to the user.

Impact and urgency settings (defined as High, Medium, or Low) are required input when creating the incident. You can configure the priority on an incident work item with a priority calculation table, as illustrated in Figure 11.10. Figure 11.11 illustrates the settings you could make for incident work item impact and urgency.

NOTE: ADJUSTING THE IMPACT AND URGENCY LIST ITEMS

You can adjust the impact and urgency settings of High, Medium, or Low, or define additional options using the Urgency and Impact List settings in the Lists folder of the Library node. Note that the values of these list items are applied in all work item priority matrixes.

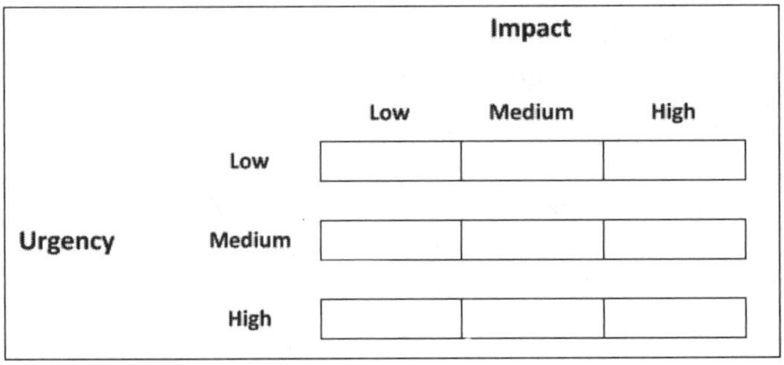

FIGURE 11.10   Priority configuration table.

Before configuring priority, you should first define the terms *impact* and *urgency* for your organization. You should raise support desk awareness regarding these definitions by educating service desk operators regularly.

Although the matrix lets you define priority levels from 1 to 9 (with corresponding resolution time), this is not mandatory. Define the priority levels based on your Incident Management process requirements. For most scenarios, a priority level configuration of four or five different levels is recommended. It is also worth considering a VIP impact category to elevate the issue's priority.

TIP: PRIORITY LEVEL CONFIGURATION FOR INCIDENT WORK ITEMS

Be aware of the following when configuring priority levels for Incident Management work items:

▶ Priority levels correspond with a target resolution time.

▶ Correct and timely handling of incident work items depends on these values.

To configure the urgency, impact, and target resolution time settings for Incident Management in the Service Manager console, follow these steps:

1. In the Administration workspace, expand **Administration -> Settings -> Incident Settings**.

2. In the Tasks pane, under Incident Settings, click **Properties**.

3. In the Incident Settings dialog box, select **Priority Calculation** on the menu to the left.

4. For each of the High, Medium, and Low settings for impact and urgency, select an incident priority value from 1–9, and then click **OK**. In this example, the priority configurations consist of five levels, as displayed in Figure 11.11.

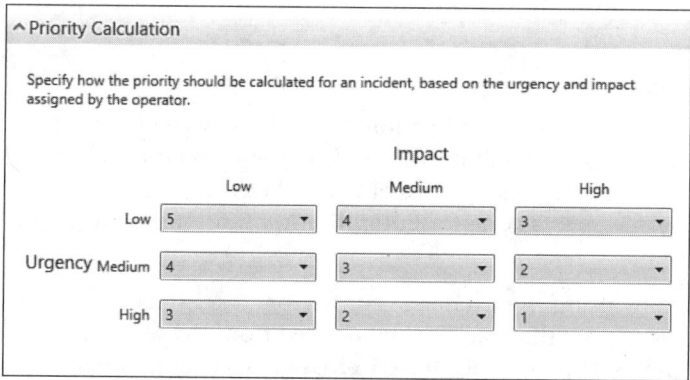

FIGURE 11.11   Priority calculation example.

5. You can set a target resolution time for each priority level you define. Select **Resolution Time** in the menu to the left of the incident settings. If you don't want to use target resolution time, check **Do not use and show legacy Target Resolution Time on Incident Form banner**. This also means no Resolved By information is specified on the incident form.

6. Should you want to configure and use target resolution time, specify the amount of time for incident resolution for each priority setting displayed in Figure 11.12.

7. Click **OK** to close the Incident Settings Wizard.

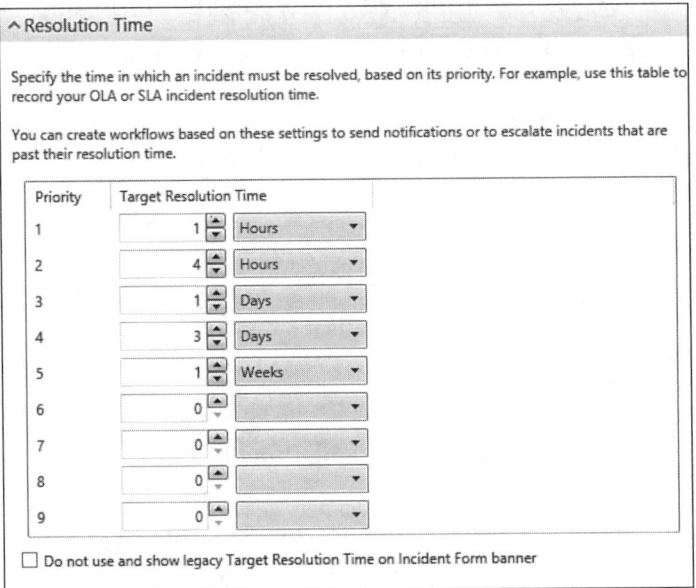

FIGURE 11.12   Target resolution time example.

Configuring Incoming Emailed Incidents

Service Manager supports emailed support requests in addition to the service desk using the console to create incidents. End users can submit incidents by sending an email to a dedicated email address; Service Manager picks up this email and creates an incident. You can use multiple email addresses, such as one for Enterprise Applications, another for hardware, and one for printer events.

This functionality can be enabled by using the Exchange connector. The Exchange connector is a separate management pack that can be downloaded from the Microsoft website and is discussed in Chapter 8. If you do not have Exchange, you could use a Simple Mail Transfer Protocol (SMTP) server for emailed incident "pickup." These are further explained in the following sections.

Providing Incoming Emailed Incidents Via SMTP Server

When an end user sends an email to log a support request, the mail server routes the message to a drop folder on the computer hosting an SMTP Server service. Service Manager monitors this share and changes the message to an incident. Service Manager parses the "From address" and attempts to match the user in the Service Manager database. If Service Manager cannot find the user in the Service Manager database, the message moves to a Badmail folder and an incident is not created.

The infrastructure required to handle incoming emailed incidents includes an existing server running the mail infrastructure or mail server supporting SMTP protocol, and a server that runs the SMTP service for Service Manager. The SMTP service role uses Internet Information Services (IIS) 6.0 SMTP services and can be installed on the server hosting the Service Manager management server feature or a separate remote server (this requires remote folder access between the SMTP server and the Service Manager server). Figure 11.13 presents an overview of mail flow.

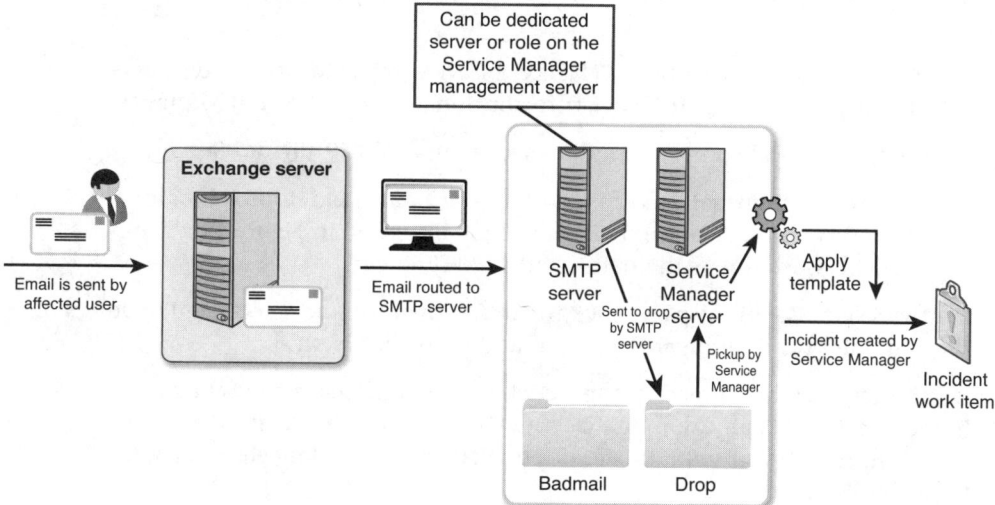

FIGURE 11.13   Emailed incidents flow.

Establishing this functionality includes the following:

▶ Configuring the mail server to route emails to the Service Manager SMTP server

▶ Configuring the Service Manager SMTP server

▶ Configuring the Inbound E-mail settings in Service Manager

These are discussed in the next sections.

Configuring the Mail Server to Route Emails

While describing the Exchange server routing configuration is beyond the scope of this book, the authors provide a walkthrough of the required configuration for your Exchange server for completeness. The goal is to define the email addresses as an accepted email domain on the server and to route emails for that domain to the SMTP server. As an example, for an Exchange mail organization you could request the following configuration:

1. In the Hub Transport configuration, create a new accepted domain such as ***.support.Odyssey.com**.

2. For this example, the SMTP connector must send all ***.support.Odyssey.com** to the SCSM SMTP server service (Smart Host).

Configuring the Service Manager SMTP Server

Service Manager uses the SMTP server to pick up routed emails from your mail environment and drop them into its mail folder. It monitors this folder and creates incidents from these emails. You can place this role on the management server if the Web Server role is installed, or use another server. Perform the following steps to configure the SMTP Server service:

1. On the computer to host the SMTP Server service, select **Start** -> **Programs** -> **Administrative Tools** -> **Internet Information Services (IIS) 6.0 Manager**.

2. Right-click the local computer node, select **New** -> **SMTP Virtual Server**.

3. In the New SMTP Virtual Server Wizard, in the Name field, type the name for the SMTP server and click **Next**. The example displayed in Figure 11.14 uses **support.Odyssey.com** as the name of the SMTP server.

4. On the Select IP Address page, click the drop-down list and select the IP address of the computer hosting the SMTP server, and then click **Next**.

5. On the Select Home Directory page, click **Browse** and select the folder for your home directory. As an example, select **C:\inetpub\mailroot** (shown in Figure 11.15). In step 8, you share this folder to enable Service Manager to pick up emails from the SMTP server.

6. On the Default Domain page, type the domain name for this virtual SMTP server (see Figure 11.16), and then click **Finish**. The domain name entered must match the domain name from step 3. Here the domain name is **support.Odyssey.com**.

7. Click **Close** to complete your changes. Navigating to the configured Home folder for the SMTP server shows a folder structure created to handle email, as illustrated in Figure 11.17.

8. Now create a share for the mail root folder. Right-click **Start** on your desktop, and then select **Explore**. In Windows Explorer, drill down to the folder that you specified as the home directory in step 5 (C:\inetpub\mailroot). If necessary, create two subfolders: **Badmail** and **Drop**.

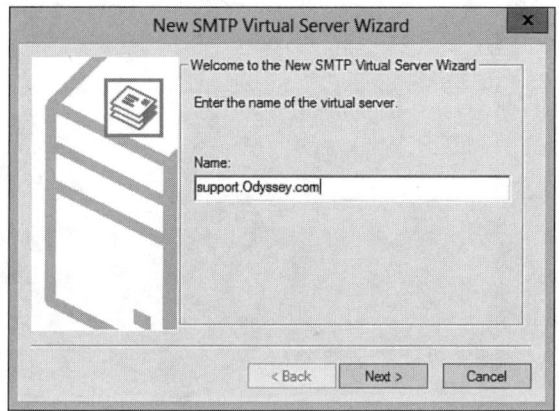

FIGURE 11.14   Naming the Service Manager SMTP server.

FIGURE 11.15   Home directory of the Service Manager SMTP server.

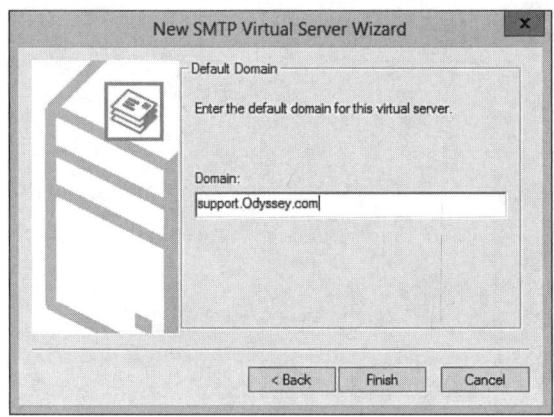

FIGURE 11.16   Specifying the SMTP server default domain.

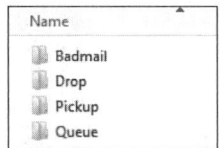

FIGURE 11.17   SMTP server folders.

9. Right-click the home folder and select **Share with -> Specific people**.

In the File Sharing dialog box, select **Find people** from the drop-down and search for the domain user specified as the Service Manager Operational System account. Click **Read/Write** and click **Share**.

Configuring the SMTP Server for Service Manager

Last in enabling support for incoming emailed incidents is to configure Service Manager with the SMTP server and drop folder specified on the SMTP server. Follow these steps:

1. In the Service Manager console, select **Administration -> Settings -> General Incident Settings**.

2. In the General Incident Settings dialog box, select **Incoming E-mail**.

In the SMTP Service drop folder location field, type the path, share, and folder for the drop folder. For this case, type *<computer_name>***mailroot****Drop** where *<computer_name>* is the name of the computer hosting the SMTP server service displayed in Figure 11.18, mailroot is the share name, and Drop is the subfolder. For this example, BLIZZARD is the SMTP server and default path to the folders.

In the SMTP Service bad folder location field, type the path, share, and folder for the bad mail folder. Type \\<***computer_name***>**mailroot****Badmail**, where <*computer_name*> is the computer hosting the SMTP Server service, mailroot is the share name, and Badmail is the subfolder.

In the Maximum number of e-mail messages to process at a time field, enter the number of emails you want Service Manager to process during an email processing cycle.

Enable **Turn on incoming e-mail processing**.

Figure 11.18 shows the Incoming E-Mail page.

3. Click **OK** to save your changes.

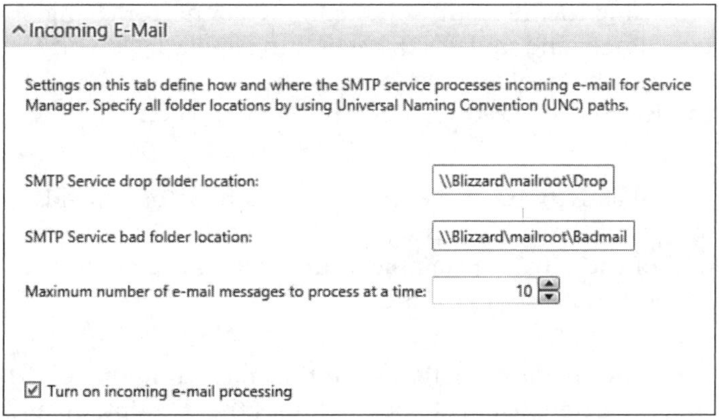

FIGURE 11.18   Incoming email sample configuration.

TIP: VERIFY THE SMTP MAIL FLOW

If Service Manager is not receiving messages and SMTP is on a remote server, try logging in with the workflow account. Open Windows Explorer, type in the UNC path (\\<*computer name*>\<*folder*>\) and verify the workflow account can access the SMTP folders.

Incoming Emailed Incidents Via the Exchange Connector

The Service Manager Exchange connector connects Service Manager to Exchange to process incoming emails related to incidents and change requests. It provides the following functionality:

▶ When a new email is sent to the monitored Exchange mailbox without a work item ID in the subject field, the Service Manager Exchange connector processes the incoming email and creates a new incident work item. The connector includes logic for new work items:

▶ If the selected incident template (a selection on the connector configuration) does not include settings for impact and urgency, those properties are set to Low.

▶ When there is no incident source specified in the template, the incident source is set to E-mail.

▶ When there is no incident status specified in the template, the incident is set to Active.

▶ When an email is sent as a reply to an email sent from Service Manager regarding an existing incident with the incident ID in the subject (such as "Subject" - [IR0012]), the connector appends the email message to the action log of the incident ID in the subject.

▶ When an email with an incident ID (example: [IR0012]) in the subject also contains the keyword for resolving or closing the incident work item; the connector changes the status of the incident accordingly and updates the action log and attaches any files. The sending user is added as the resolving or closing user, and the content of the most recent email is added to the resolution description field when the [Resolved] keyword is sent.

▶ If an email is sent with a manual activity ID in the subject, the connector appends the Notes field with the contents of the latest message body (up to 4,000 characters). If the keyword for completion of the activity (example: [Completed]) is present, the connector changes the status of the activity to Completed.

The Exchange connector populates additional information from the email content. For example, the email subject becomes the title, the email body becomes the description, and email attachments are added to the work item as file attachments.

NOTE: WORK ITEM ID MUST BE IN SQUARE BRACKETS IN SUBJECT OF EMAIL

Each message sent from Service Manager must contain the work item ID enclosed in square brackets in the subject, so when there is a reply this is in the subject to be processed by the connector. If the work item ID is not present in the subject, the connector assumes the email is for a new incident.

The connector Run As account mailbox is the mailbox accessed by the connector. The Allow Impersonation setting on the connector allows you to customize the connector so the Run As account can impersonate the credentials of the other mailbox recipient; this enables using multiple Exchange connectors that monitor different mailboxes.

Configuring Operations Manager Integration

Operations Manager can deliver added functionality to Service Manager on two levels:

▶ Automating creation of incidents from Operations Manager alerts via the Operations Manager Alert connector

▶ Using a Service Manager console task to check the health state of a configuration item

Configuring incidents from Operations Manager alerts consists of configuring the Operations Manager Alert connector in the Administration workspace of the Service Manager console and configuring the Operations Manager Web Settings under Incident Settings, also in the Administration workspace. This enables support analysts to view the information from Operations Manager by using two additional tasks in the Work Items folder:

▶ View Alert Details

▶ View CI Health State

For the Odyssey environment used in this book, HELIOS is the Operations Manager server and is specified under Incident Settings. This is shown in Figure 11.19.

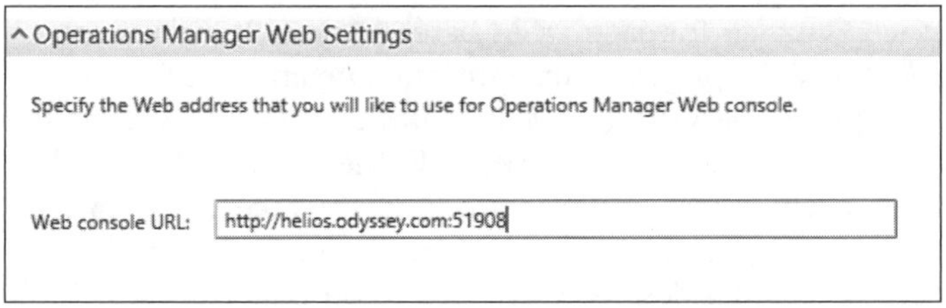

∧ Operations Manager Web Settings
Specify the Web address that you will like to use for Operations Manager Web console.
Web console URL: http://helios.odyssey.com:51908

FIGURE 11.19   Operations Manager Web Settings dialog.

You can also automate the routing and assignment of those incidents created by the connector. This is described in the "Automating Incident Management" section of this chapter.

NOTE: ENABLING AUTOMATED INCIDENT CREATION FROM OPERATIONS MANAGER ALERTS

Creating incidents from Operations Manager alerts introduces infrastructure incidents into your Incident Management process. This is completely different from when an incident is created when a user calls the support desk, which then creates an incident. As Operations Manager alerts are generated automatically, the only way to control incidents created from these alerts is to ensure the source is under control and to perform any needed alert noise management in your Operations Manager environment before enabling the connector.

You do not need to create incidents for all Operations Manager alerts. Setup of the Operations Manager connector includes two steps:

▶ Configuring your connector in Service Manager, in which you can automate incident routing (see the "Automating Incident Management" section of this chapter).

▶ Managing connector subscriptions in the Operations Manager console, where you can subscribe particular Operations Manager groups (generally associated with imported management packs). This enables you to gradually introduce infrastructure incidents into Service Manager.

You can also forward specific Operations Manager alerts to Service Manager: In the Operations Manager console, select an alert and forward it manually to Service Manager.

Configuring Configuration Manager DCM Integration

DCM consists of monitoring Configuration Manager clients to ensure they are compliant with specified values. You can monitor software versions, security settings, and software updates. Using the Configuration Manager connector, you can import configuration baselines from Configuration Manager into Service Manager, and then configure Service Manager to create incidents for each Service Manager CI reporting as noncompliant against those specified values.

Configuration consists of creating configuration baselines in Configuration Manager, and then defining a workflow in Service Manager for each DCM baseline or including them all in one workflow. The workflow lets you apply an incident template and notify the support team of noncompliant computers. Service Manager creates an incident work item for each CI that reports as noncompliant. The support desk could then be notified, or the incident work item routed to a queue where appropriate actions can be taken. This functionality helps you keep your systems compliant with defined baselines. The "Automating Incident Management" section of this chapter describes Configuration Manager DCM workflow configuration.

Automating Incident Management

Consider the categorization and assignment of an incident work item: You can create a workflow that triggers on certain criteria and apply a template to categorize the incident work item and assign it to a support group. This lets you define workflows for those processes unlikely to change often.

Different inputs of the Incident Management process can require different routing configurations of the incident work item. You can capture these requirements by creating workflows with multiple criteria. As an example, emailed incidents require you specify a template to set the support group, impact, and urgency; this information can be used in workflows. You can configure the criteria of the workflow to evaluate the source of the incident.

This part of the chapter explains and creates incident event workflows for several scenarios. There are three primary scenarios for creating a workflow:

▶ Incident event workflow for the organization's web application

▶ Automating incoming Operations Manager alerts

▶ DCM event workflow

To begin this process, you should have a clear view of what occurs in an incident event workflow. Figure 11.20 provides a graphical overview.

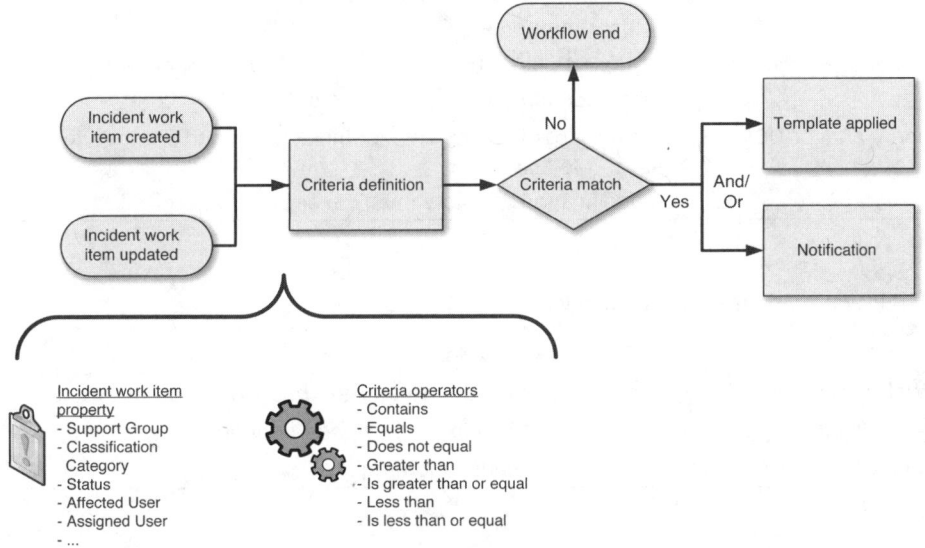

FIGURE 11.20   Overview of workflow automation.

Figure 11.20 shows the following:

1. The first trigger in an incident event workflow is an action (input) on the work item. An incident work item is created or updated.

2. The criteria definition checks the incident work item property for a particular value. Different operators can be used to evaluate this property.

3. Once there is a match, you can apply a template and/or send out a notification (action). You can create workflows only to apply templates or send out notification based on the defined criteria, or you can combine the two.

Consider what is required before these workflows can be created:

▶ The Incident Management process defines a requirement to create a template.

▶ Several other templates are required, as illustrated in Figure 11.20:

    ▶ Templates are used to automate incidents (see a list of templates in Table 11.2).

    ▶ Table 11.3 lists notification requirements. The table shows notification templates required for the different scenarios (associated workflows). Chapter 16 discusses notifications; follow the procedures in that chapter to configure the notifications required for your process. Table 11.4 lists the criteria for the workflows introduced in Table 11.3.

TABLE 11.2   Incident Automation: Templates Overview

Workflows	Template
Company Web Application	Urgency and impact incident properties must be set to High. Support group needs to be assigned – Tier2.
Operations Manager Incoming Alerts	SQL alerts need to be assigned to Tier2 support group. Classification category must be set.
Configuration Manager DCM Event	DCM events urgency, impact incident properties need to be set to Medium. Classification category must be set.

TABLE 11.3   Incident Automation: Notification Templates Overview

Workflows	Notification Template
Company Web Application	Notification to assigned support analyst.
Operations Manager Incoming Alerts	Notification to assigned support analyst.
Configuration Manager DCM Event	No notification required.

TABLE 11.4   Incident Automation: Workflow Criteria Overview

Workflows	Workflow Criteria
Company Web Application	Incident work item created. Classification category = Company Web Application. Source = Portal.
Operations Manager Incoming Alerts	Alert generated by the Operations Manager SQL management pack.
Configuration Manager DCM Event	DCM noncompliancy event from Configuration Manager.

While this section provides a single example, it shows the importance of documentation before automating the Incident Management process. This approach creates an overview of the functionality you should enable. Those individuals validating the automation process can understand the information, and you have documented the workflows for later troubleshooting.

Creating Incident Management Templates

As discussed previously in the "Incident Management in Service Manager" section of this chapter, templates can be used to configure certain work item properties or apply properties on work items that use a workflow. The next example creates an incident template for the Company Web application. Use Table 11.2 for input and defining template requirements. Perform the following steps:

1. In the Service Manager console, expand **Library -> Templates**. Select **Create Template** in the Tasks pane.

2. In the Create Template dialog box displayed in Figure 11.21, provide a name, class, and management pack.

Company Web App emailed Incidents template

Create Template

Enter a name and description for the template

Name:

Company Web App portal Incidents template

Description:

Incident template for Company Web Application

Class:

Incident   Browse...

For example, to create an incident template, select the Incident class.

Select an unsealed management pack where the template will be saved.
Management pack

Unleashed_Incident_Mgmt_Workflows   New...
Last modified: 10/27/2013 1:27:27 PM

☑ When I click OK, open the template form.

OK   Cancel

FIGURE 11.21   Creating the template.

▶ The name of the template is **Company Web App portal Incidents template**. Type a description for the incident template in the Description box.

▶ Click **Browse** to choose a class. In the Choose Class dialog box, click **Incident**, select an unsealed management pack to store the template or create a new one, and then click **OK**.

3. In the Incident Information screen (see Figure 11.22), provide the following:

▶ In the Classification category drop-down, select the category that reflects the problem to report. For this example, select **Enterprise Application Problems\ Company Web Applications** in the drop-down and set the Impact and urgency boxes to **High**.

▶ In the Support group box, select a tier. For example, if all Company Web application issues are assigned to the tier 2 support group, select Tier 2.

4. Click **OK** to save the template.

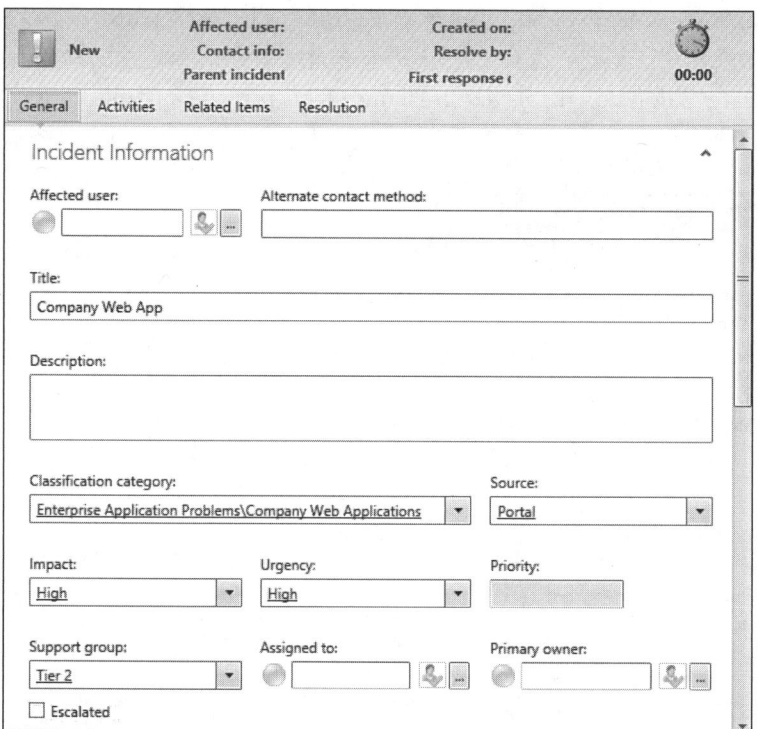

FIGURE 11.22   Specifying incident properties.

This procedure creates an incident template to use when creating templates for Operations Manager alert incident events and Configuration Manager DCM events. Table 11.2 provides an overview for creating these events, and you could use the procedure described in this section to complete creating the template. The only differences when creating these templates are the incident properties you need to select.

Creating Incident Management Workflows

A workflow is a sequence of activities that automate a process. The following procedure creates an incident event workflow for the Company Web application. Tables 11.3 and 11.4 in the "Automating Incident Management" section earlier in the chapter provide information for this process. Follow these steps:

1. In the Service Manager console, navigate to **Administration -> Workflows -> Configuration**.

2. In the Configuration pane, double-click **Incident Event Workflow Configuration**.

3. In the Configure Incident Event Workflows dialog box, click **Add**.

4. Enter the following in the Add Incident Event Workflow dialog:

▶ Click **Next** on the Before You Begin page.

▶ In the Name box on the Workflow Information page, type a name for the workflow, such as **Company Web Application event workflow**. In the Check for events list, select **When an object is created**, verify the **Enabled** check box is selected, and then click **Next**. See Figure 11.23 for details.

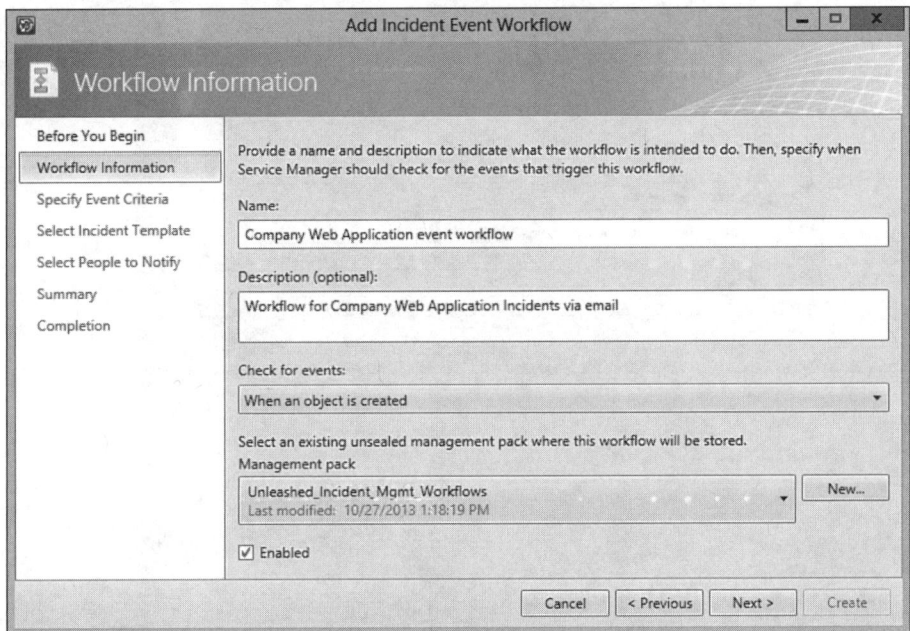

FIGURE 11.23   Workflow Information page.

▶ On the Specify Event Criteria page (see Figure 11.24), click the Changed to tab. In the Available properties list, select **Source and Incident Classification**; for each selection, click **Add**. In the Criteria box, select **equals**. In the list, select **Enterprise Application Problems\Company Web Applications** for classification and **Portal** for Source Incident properties. Click **Next**.

▶ On the Select Incident Template page (see Figure 11.25), click **Apply the following template**, and select **Company Web App Portal Incidents template**. This template sets the support group to Tier 2, Urgency to High, Impact to High, and provides a Title start text. Click **Next**.

▶ On the Select People to Notify page shown in Figure 11.26, optionally select the **Enable notification** check box, select the user to notify, and click **Next**. This example selects the default notification template.

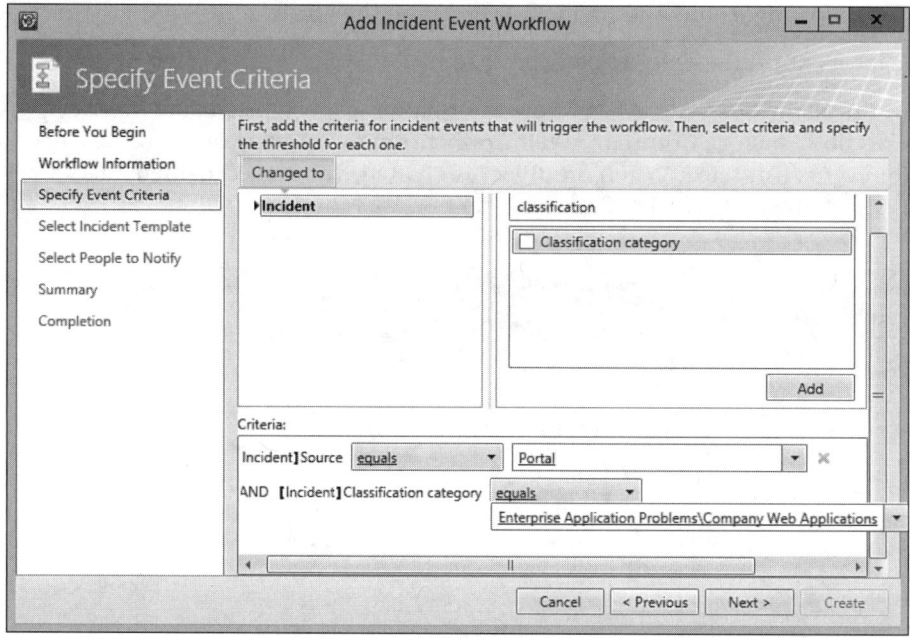

FIGURE 11.24   Specifying criteria.

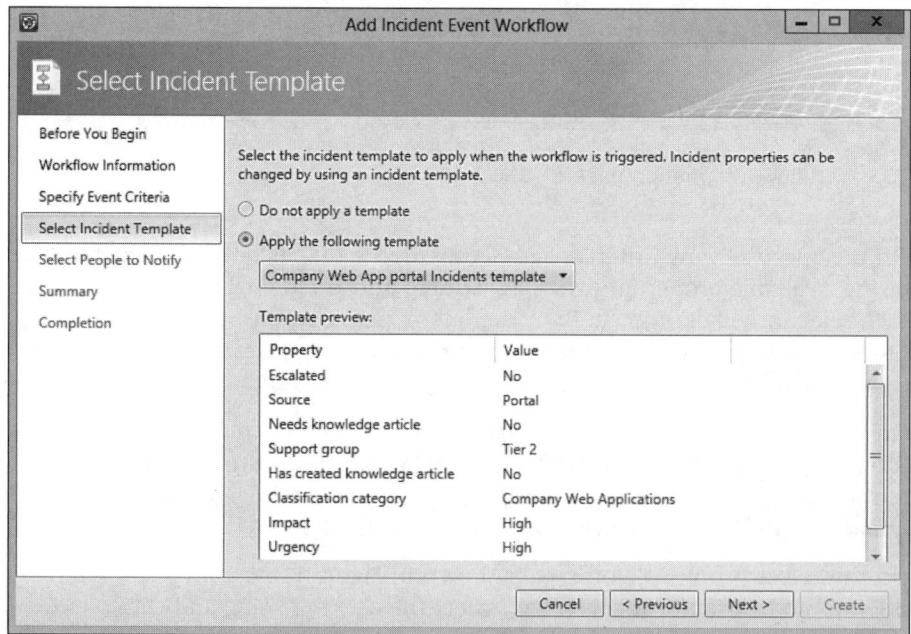

FIGURE 11.25   Selecting the incident template.

5. Review the Summary page and click **Create**. Click **Close** on the Completion page, and click **OK** in the Configure Incident Event Workflows dialog box.

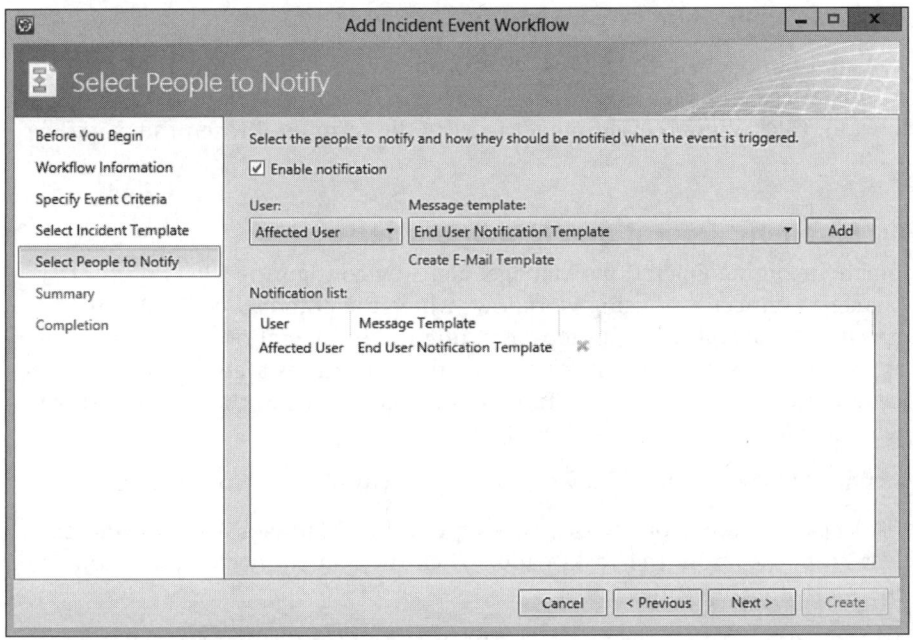

FIGURE 11.26   Specifying notifications.

A workflow is now triggered whenever an incident is created in the portal with the Company Web Application category. You can review the workflow runtime in the console, under **Administration -> Workflows -> Status**. Two views are available: one with all instances and another with the runtime instance that needs attention:

▶ The All instances view consists of all success and failure instances.

▶ The Need attention view displays only those instances when a workflow fails.

In the All instances view, you can view the log, view the related object, retry the workflow, and ignore the status instance. Watch out for the Retry and Ignore options in the Status results pane, as both options remove the workflow status instance entry.

TIP: CRITERIA DEFINITION FOR WORKFLOWS

In most cases, the authors recommend using both from and to selection criteria for updated work items. If the criteria definition is not precise enough, the workflow may be unintentionally triggered.

Perform the following steps to view workflow success and failures:

1. In the Service Manager console, navigate to **Administration -> Workflows -> Status**.

2. In the Status pane, select the workflow that you want to view (for example, **Company Web application event workflow**).

   The Need attention view in the Status results pane lets you see failing runtimes. Click **All instances** and **View log** to view the list of events that occurred when the workflow ran. Click **View related object** to view the form used when the workflow ran.

Automating Incoming Operations Manager Alerts

You can automate incoming Operations Manager alerts by configuring filters on the Operations Manager connector or using workflows where the criteria are adjusted to capture the specific alerts. Follow these steps to configure the Operations Manager connector filter to apply templates on incidents created by the Operations Manager Alert connector. The procedure uses information from Table 11.4, which specifies the requirements to configure a workflow for the SQL management pack:

1. In the Service Manager console, navigate to **Administration -> Connectors**.

2. In the Tasks pane, under Connectors, click **Operations Manager Alert Connector** and select **Properties** from the Tasks pane. When the Edit connector wizard opens, select the **Alert Routing Rules** tab.

   Click **Add** to create an alert routing rule. The alert routing rule has several options to filter specific alerts. You can define rules that filter alerts from a specific management pack, a specific computer, or a custom field specification on the alert. Based on the defined rule, you can apply a specific incident template. Click **OK** to create the routing rule.

   If you know the routing rules for your organization, you could specify multiple routing rules on the Operations Manager connector. Figure 11.27 shows an alert routing rule configuration that filters alerts raised by Operations Manager management packs that start with **Microsoft.SQLServer** and applies SQL alerts using the Operations Manager Incoming Alerts template. (This template is listed in Table 11.2 and was created previously using the procedure in the "Creating Incident Management Templates" section.)

3. Click **OK** when complete.

Notifications cannot be configured when defining an alert routing rule on the Operations Manager connector. If these are required for an incident work item created with the connector, you must to create an additional incident event workflow with a notification rule. The "Creating Incident Management Workflows" section earlier in the chapter discusses creating this additional workflow.

TIP: GENERIC APPROACH FOR FORWARDING ALERTS TO SERVICE MANAGER

Should you require a generic way to forward alerts to Service Manager, create a generic override in Operations Manager to filter on. As an example, you could set the priority field of an event in Operations Manager to High, which is a general override, to forward those alerts to Service Manager. Very few Operations Manager alerts have priority set to High.

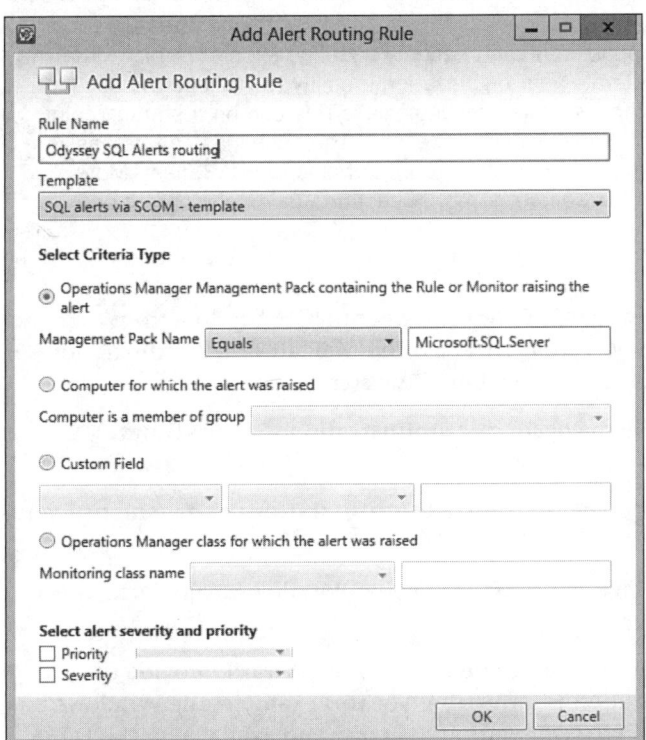

FIGURE 11.27   Operations Manager alert routing filter rule.

Creating a Desired Configuration Management Workflow

Using a DCM workflow, Service Manager automatically generates incidents when computers fall out of compliance from DCM in Configuration Manager. DCM baselines are synchronized with the Configurations Manager connector and can be selected when creating a DCM event workflow. You could create a workflow for a single baseline or select multiple baselines in a single workflow.

DCM event workflows are created in the Administration workspace of the Service Manager console. DCM baseline rules are created in the Configuration Manager console and applied to Configuration Manager collections. Before configuring a DCM event workflow, you must install the Configuration Manager connector and configure Configuration Manager DCM baselines.

TIP: MICROSOFT SECURITY COMPLIANCE MANAGER

This Solution Accelerator provides centralized security baseline management features, a baseline portfolio, customization capabilities, and security baseline export flexibility. The Compliance Manager tool can accelerate your organization's ability to manage the security and compliance process efficiently for Microsoft technologies. This can be a starting point for creating your own Configuration Manager DCM baselines. The baselines can be easily exported in a format that can be imported into Configuration Manager (CAB files). More information is available on Microsoft's website at http://technet.microsoft.com/en-us/solutionaccelerators/cc835245.aspx.

The next procedure imports the Windows 8 Enterprise Client DCM baseline from the Microsoft Security Compliance Manager tool. This baseline evaluates the Configuration Manager client for different security settings. Follow these steps:

1. In the Service Manager console, navigate to **Administration -> Workflows -> Configuration**.

2. In the Configuration pane, double-click **Desired Configuration Management Event Workflow Configuration**.

3. In the Configure Desired Configuration Management Workflows dialog box, select **Add** to create a new DCM event workflow.

4. In the Add Desired Configuration Management Workflow Wizard, provide the baseline, template, and notification information. For this example, the Windows 8 EC DCM baseline is imported in Configuration Manager and available in the DCM Event Workflow Wizard after synchronizing the connector:

   ▶ Click **Next** on the Before You Begin page. On the Workflow Information page displayed in Figure 11.28, type a name for the workflow in the Name box.

   ▶ On the Select System Center Configuration Manager Configuration Items page, select the Configuration Manager CIs you want to include in the rule, and then click **Next**. Figure 11.29 shows the Win8 Computer Security Compliance baseline synchronized in the CMDB and that all configuration items in the baseline are selected.

   ▶ On the Select Incident Template page, click **Apply the following template**; then select the template you want to apply for DCM-created incident work items. Figure 11.30 shows an example where the Configuration Manager

DCM template is applied. This template was created in the "Creating Incident Management Templates" section earlier in the chapter; the support group, urgency, and classification category are properties applied by this template. Click **Next**, and then proceed to create the DCM event workflow.

▶ On the Select People to Notify page shown in Figure 11.31, check **Enable notification**. Select the users to be notified when this rule creates an incident. For each user, specify the notification method and a template, and then click **Add**. Click **Next**.

5. On the Summary page, review your settings and click **Create**. Click **Close** on the Completion page, and click **OK** in the Configure Incident Event Workflows dialog box.

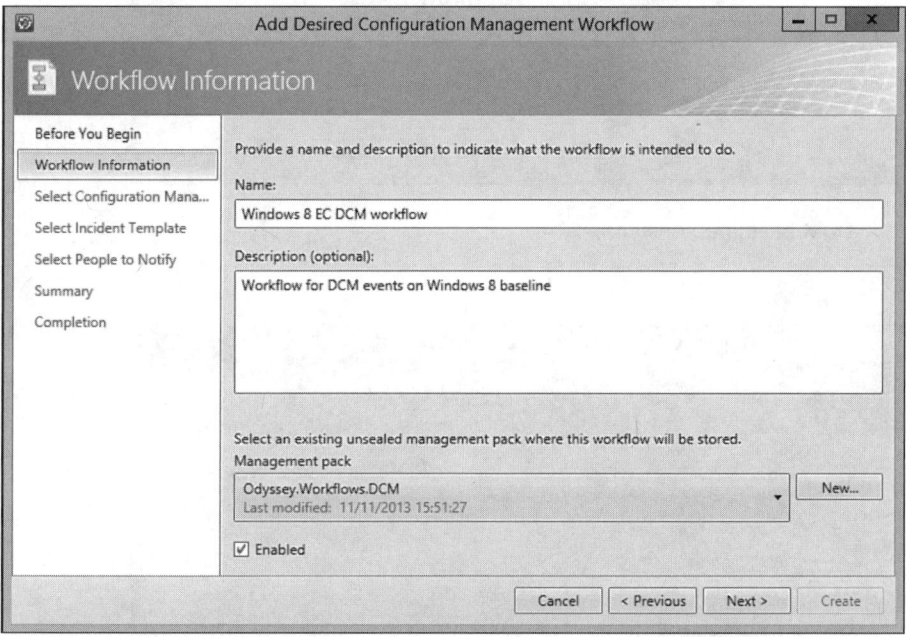

FIGURE 11.28   Overview page for the DCM workflow.

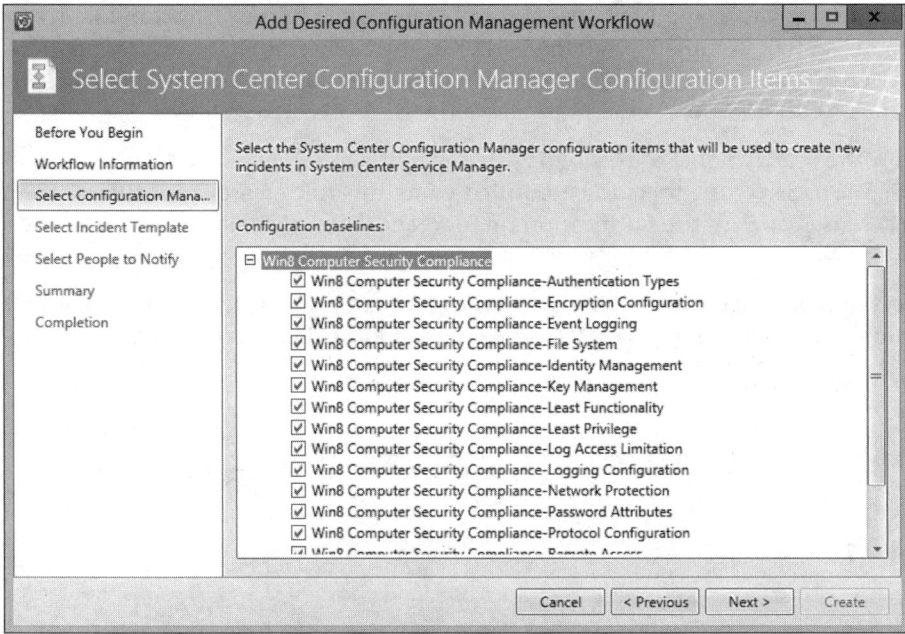

FIGURE 11.29   DCM baseline selection.

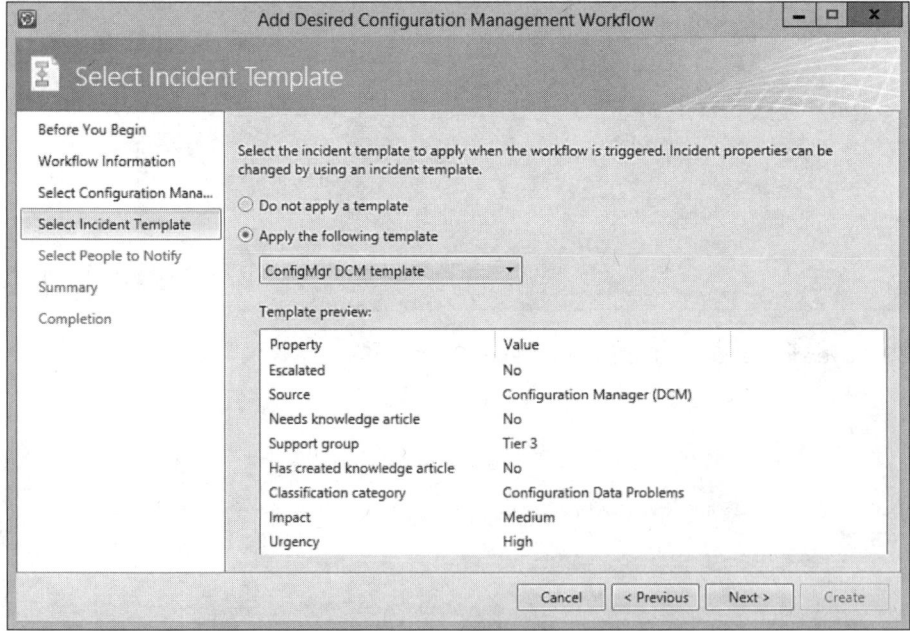

FIGURE 11.30   Template selection.

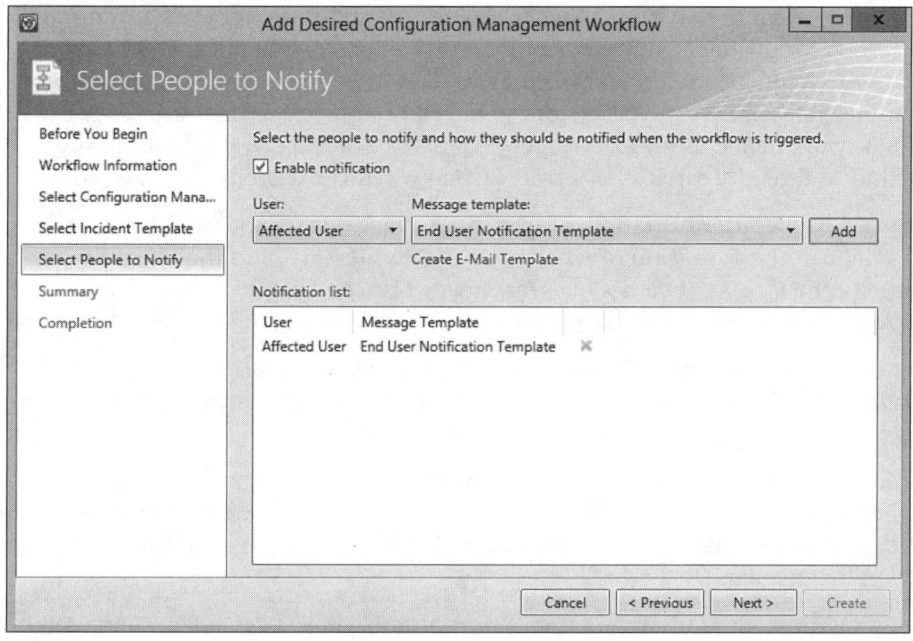

FIGURE 11.31 Specifying notification for the DCM workflow.

Service Level Management

Service level management (SLM) is part of the ITIL v3 Service Design process. Its objectives are to negotiate service level agreements with customers and to design services in accordance with the agreed service level targets. SLM processes provide a framework by which services are defined, service levels are agreed upon, and service level agreements and operational level agreements (OLAs) are developed to satisfy the agreements.

System Center in its entirety can support the SLM process. You can manage your SLA in Service Manager: Services can be defined, service offerings created, and service level objectives defined. Service performance, availability, and capacity can be monitored via Operations Manager.

NOTE: DIFFERENCE BETWEEN SLA AND SLO

There is often confusion between the usage of SLA and SLO:

▶ The SLA is the entire agreement that specifies the details around the service. The agreement defines how the service is supported, its components, times, locations, costs, performance, and the responsibilities of the involved parties.

▶ Service level objectives within an SLA describe specific key expectations for that service between a service provider and the service consumer. There are specific measurable characteristics of the SLA such as availability, throughput, frequency, response time, and quality.

Service level management in Service Manager provides the ability to associate and monitor service level targets for incidents and service requests. You can define objectives based on incident and service request timeline measurements. Say there is an agreement to respond within 30 minutes to each new incident work item. You can measure first-level response time on the new work items, set the service level status as Warning when reaching the defined deadline, and set the service level to Breached when the deadline is exceeded.

SLM is configured in the Administration workspace of the Service Manager console. It consists of a calendar, the definition of what you want to measure, and the objective—where you specify the threshold values for Warning or Breached. An overview of the building blocks for service level management follows:

▶ **Incident or service request queues:** This is the list of work items to which to apply the service level objective. Based on the criteria defined on the queue, you can differentiate work items for the service level objective.

▶ **Calendar:** The calendar is used to define work days, work hours, and holidays as a work schedule that represents the time available for analysts to resolve incidents or fulfill service requests. The calendar specified in the service level objective is the basis for measurement.

▶ **Metric:** A metric node is used to define time metrics against a calendar item. A time metric is the measurement between start and end dates for a specific date time property of the work item. Metrics could be used to measure first response date, time to resolve, first assigned date, and so on. Each date/time property of the work item can be specified as start or end dates.

▶ **Service level objective:** Service level objectives define the relationships between a queue, a calendar item, and a time metric to define the service level target. Warning and breached status level thresholds can be defined on the objective.

Warning and/or breached service level status levels can be used to trigger a notification or kick off a workflow. Figure 11.32 shows the complete flow of the SLO definition and its processing.

The Work Items workspace includes two service level specific views available for the Incident Management and Service Request Fulfillment folders, enabling management of those work items with service level warnings and breached statuses.

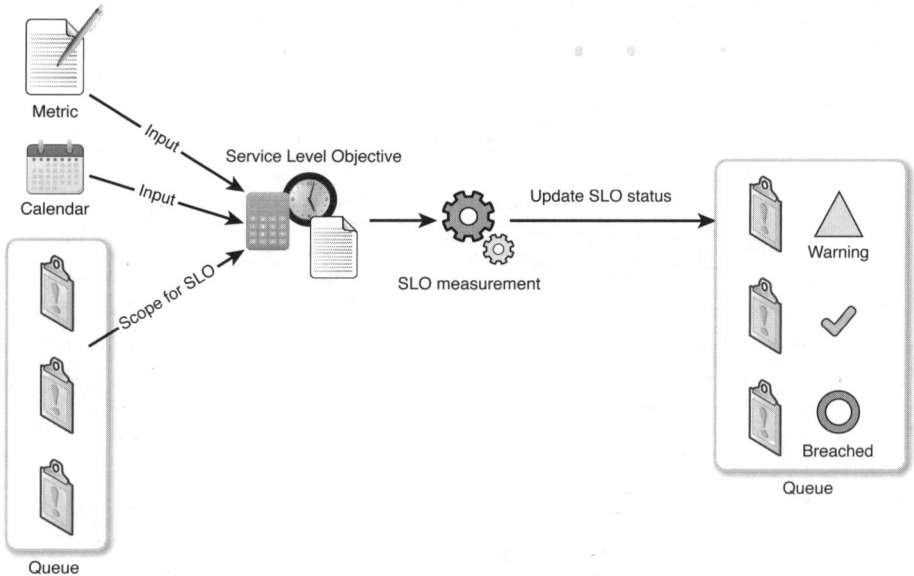

FIGURE 11.32   SLO definition and flow.

CAUTION: HIGH NUMBER OF QUEUES AND SLO DEFINITIONS IN SERVICE MANAGER

A large number of queues or SLO definitions in Service Manager can affect performance during creation and lookup. The specific number is dependent on the sizing of the servers.

The performance impact is experienced when saving the new queue or SLO definition. Additionally, lookup of these items (via default views) takes a long time and returns a "No items found" message, after which the items appear one-by-one in the view.

Normal SLO workflow execution is not affected: Work items are validated, and SLO status is set based on the measurement.

Creating a Service Level Objective Calendar Item

Calendar items are used to define work days, work hours, and holidays in System Center 2012 Service Manager. Calendar items are used as part of a service level objective, where they are measured against a time metric. Follow these steps to create a calendar item:

1. In the Service Manager console, navigate to **Administration -> Service Level Management -> Calendar**. In the Tasks pane, click **Create Calendar**.

2. In the Title box on the General page, type a title for the calendar. Figure 11.33 shows an example of **Business Hours**.

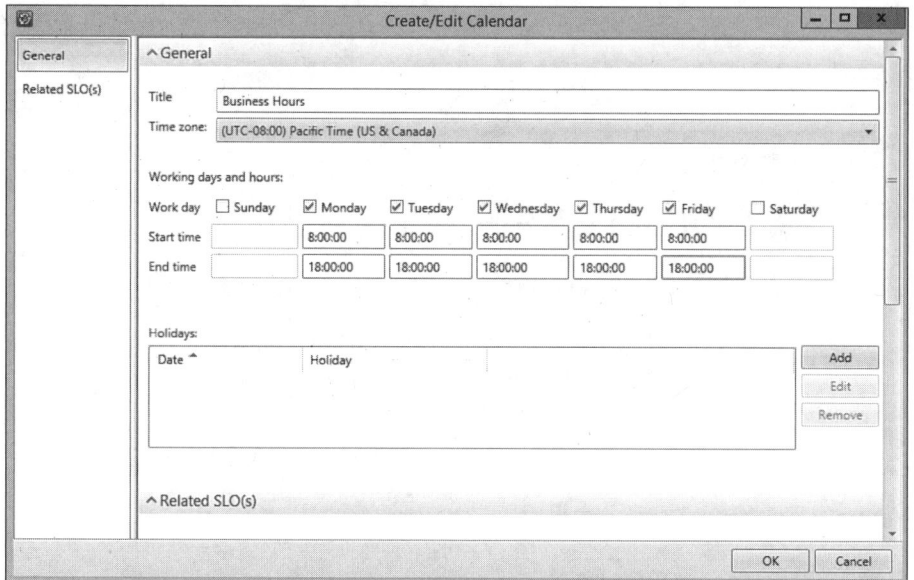

FIGURE 11.33   General page when creating a service level calendar.

3. In the **Time zone** drop down, select the time zone of your location.

4. Under **Working days and hours**, select your organization's workdays. For each selected day, enter the start and end time.

5. Under **Holidays**, click **Add** to define any holidays that your organization does not normally work. In the Add Holiday dialog box, type the name and select the date of the holiday, and then click **OK** to close the dialog box.

6. When editing calendar items, the Related SLO(s) tab provides an overview of the service level objectives that use this calendar.

7. Click **OK** to close the Create/Edit Calendar dialog box.

Creating a Service Level Objective Metric

Service Manager lets you create a service level management metric, which is analogous to SLAs, as a time metric to measure the difference between start and end times for incidents and service requests. After defining a metric, you associate it with a service level objective. If the metric is already associated with a service level objective, it appears in the Related SLO(s) area.

1. In the Service Manager console, navigate to **Administration -> Service Level Management -> Metric**. In the Tasks pane, under Metric, click **Create Metric**.

2. In the Create/Edit Metric dialog box, provide a Title for the metric. This example, shown in Figure 11.34, specifies the title **First Response date metric**.

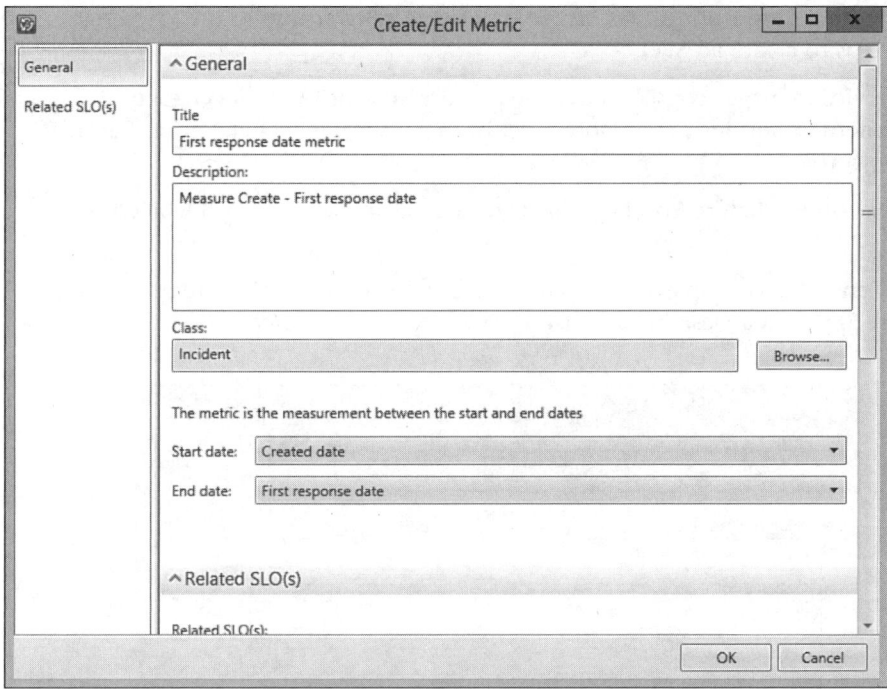

FIGURE 11.34   General page when creating a service level metric.

3. In the Description box, type a description of the metric, such as **Measure Create - First response date**.

4. In the Class section, click **Browse** to open the Select a Class dialog box. Select the `Incident` or `Service Request` class and then click **OK**. This example selects the **Incident** class.

5. Click the drop-down list next to Start date and select the item you want to use to define the date. **Created date** is selected in Figure 11.34.

6. Click the drop-down next to End date and select the item you want to use to define the end date, such as **First response date**.

7. When editing metric items, the Related SLO(s) tab gives you an overview of the service level objectives that use this metric.

8. Click **OK** to close the Create/Edit Metric dialog box.

Creating a Service Level Objective

Configuring the SLO ties it all together. The target work items where you want to apply the SLO are defined by specifying a queue. The input for the SLO measurement is the calendar and metric. Threshold values can be defined to set warning or breached statuses. Follow these steps to create an SLO:

1. In the Service Manager console, navigate to **Administration -> Service Level Management -> Service Level Objective**. In the Tasks pane, click **Create Service Level Objective**.

2. Click **Next** on the Before You Begin page of the Create Service Level Objective Wizard.

3. On the General page displayed in Figure 11.35, type a Title such as **Incident First Response SLO** and a Description for the new service level objective.

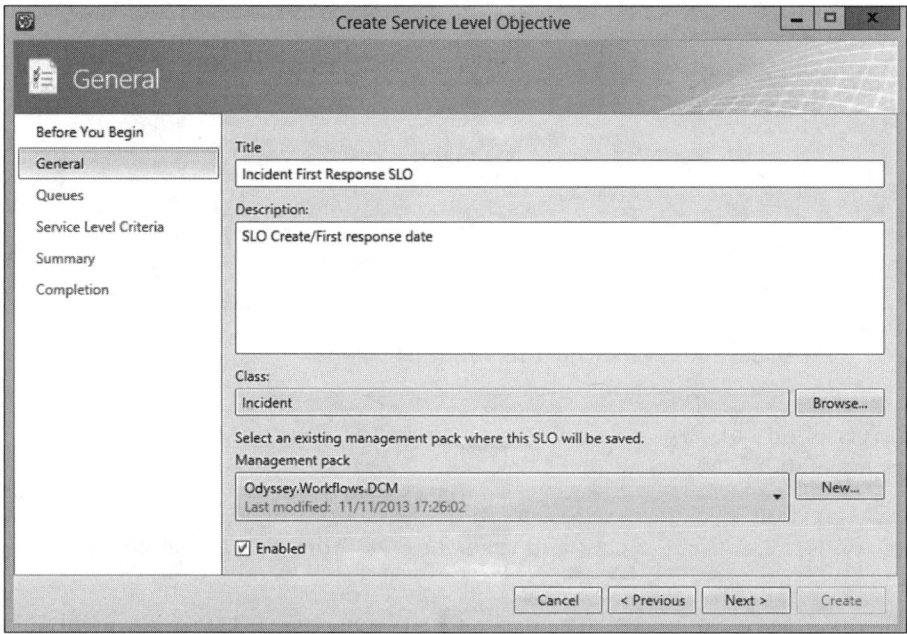

FIGURE 11.35   General page of the Create Service Level Objective Wizard.

4. Click **Browse** to the right of Class to open the Select a Class dialog box, and select the Incident or Service Request class for the type of service level objective you are creating.

5. Select a management pack or create a new one to save the configured SLO. Make sure that **Enabled** is selected, and then click **Next**.

6. On the Queues page, select the queue of work items to which you want to apply the SLO. The Incident - priority 1 queue is selected in Figure 11.36.

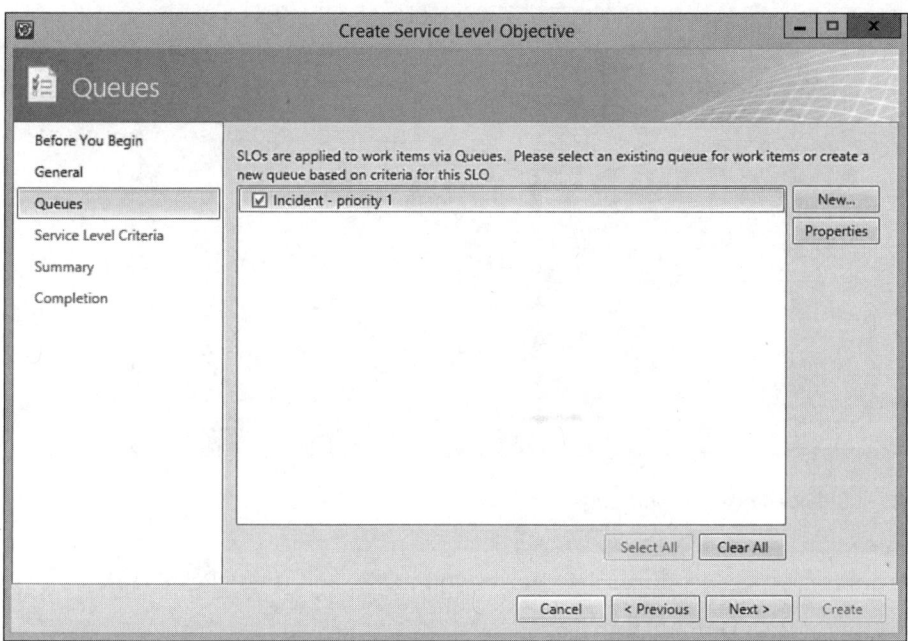

FIGURE 11.36   Service level objective queues page.

7. On the Service Level Criteria page displayed in Figure 11.37, select or create a calendar and metric, and specify the target/warning thresholds.

   For the Target threshold, specify the amount of time in hours or minutes by which the work item should be completed.

   For the Warning threshold, specify the amount of time in hours or minutes before the service level is breached, which creates a warning notification in the work item notification bar.

   Click **Next** to continue.

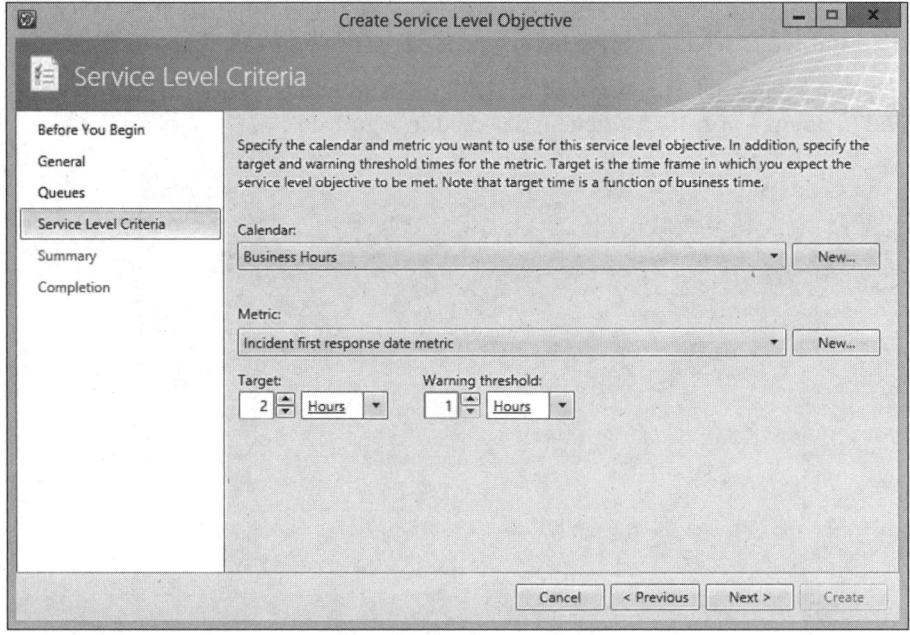

FIGURE 11.37   Service Level Criteria page.

8. On the Summary page, confirm the choices you made, and then click **Create**.

9. Click **Close** on the Completion page.

Incident Management for End Users

The previous sections of this chapter discuss configuring the Incident Management process for analysts, incident managers, or other groups involved in the process. This helps with the overall goal of resolving incidents for end users.

The end user's logged issue is more quickly resolved when the tool is used to orchestrate the process steps to solve the issue. User satisfaction can be influenced positively through proper communication during each step of the process. Service Manager includes templates, workflows, and subscriptions to optimize orchestration and communication. This is a benefit for the end user who is trying to get an issue resolved. Email interaction with work items and the self-service portal are other avenues the end user can use to take advantage of well-configured processes. This functionality closes the loop from creation of a work item, follow-up, to closure of the logged incident.

Creating Incidents

There are different avenues where an incident work item can be created. The work item could be created by a phone call where the work item is created by support staff, an emailed incident, or the self-service portal.

Incident work items created in the console can be routed directly to the correct support group. Notifications to the affected user during this process can help as the user can review issues and confirm that the support desk understands the issue.

The Exchange connector enables logging incidents by email. The connector can monitor one or more mailboxes and create new incidents from email messages. Users do not have to directly contact support individuals, as they have contact via email. As part of the communication flow, notifications can be sent to the end user when the incident is created or when the work item is routed to the correct support group.

The self-service portal enables creating incident work items by the end user. The Create Request button on the portal can be used to create incidents. The service catalog, service offerings, and request offerings can be used to optimize incident creation. Request offerings can be targeted to the Incident Management process. Incident requests can include questions required for the issue that is logged.

Incident Follow-Up

An incident's status can be used to trigger communication to the affected user or to trigger a workflow to change the incident work item. The affected user may require an update on his logged incident; typically, he would phone the service desk to obtain direct feedback on the status. Alternately, the Service Manager Exchange connector could capture follow-up emails, and the self-service portal includes an overview page of all the logged-on user's requests. This can offload work from the service desk and optimize communication with the affected user.

When using the Exchange connector, the Incident ID referenced in the subject field of the email is of significance. End users can see the incident ID and use this information when communicating with the service desk. All replies to the emailed notification are appended in the action log of the work item specified in the subject field of the email. This can trigger a workflow from which the support group of the assigned user receives notification of the updated information.

The portal provides access to details of the requests of the logged-on user. The user can consult action log items from the work item, and users can post action log items from the portal to interact with the service desk.

The affected user can always use the self-service portal to obtain the latest information regarding his request. Additional information could be posted on the portal or emailed (such as replying to the creation notification message).

Resolving and Closing Incidents

The purpose of Incident Management is to resolve issues logged by the affected user. It is all about resolving the issue; a work item can be set to Closed when the user is satisfied with the solution for a particular issue. Communicating the solution to the user can occur during an online session (such as with Windows Remote Assistance) or offline with the user being notified by email. Incident work items can be resolved from the console where the solution description can be provided by email or by the user through the self-service portal.

Fast Track

In addition to bug fixes and performance improvements from the previous version, Service Manager 2012 provides additional functionality for customizing the Incident Management process:

▶ The parent/child relationship can be configured for related work items. This is discussed in the "Configuring Parent Incident Settings" section of this chapter.

▶ SLM is tied into Incident Management and Service Request Management in Service Manager 2012. SLOs can be configured for specific services.

▶ The Exchange connector is now a Microsoft supported add-on for System Center Service Manager.

Summary

This chapter discussed Incident Management in Service Manager 2012, from describing the components to automating the process. The Service Manager console, portal functionality, and Exchange connector integration are explained from the approach of "Where can I do what?" The process breakdown described in the "Incident Management Process Activities" section of the chapter, where process activities are mapped to Service Manager Incident Management elements, should assist you in analyzing your own process and mapping it to Service Manager settings, templates, workflows, and so on. The chapter included examples to explain configuring Incident Management in Service Manager 2012. The introduction of infrastructure-related events in Incident Management was described, with examples for the Operations Manager connector and Configuration Manager DCM.

Your own Incident Management process may require additional customization of Incident Management in Service Manager. Chapter 22 includes information about extending the incident form and creating custom workflows and notifications. Reporting requirements can have an impact on customizing Incident Management; see Chapter 21, "Data Warehouse and Reporting," for additional information.

The next chapter discusses how automation and chargeback relate to each other and service management, and discusses them in relation to System Center 2012 Service Manager.

Automation and Chargeback

Automation is about using control systems to minimize or reduce human intervention. Chargeback is a mechanism used by Information Technology (IT) departments to allocate and/or bill costs associated with departmental usage. Both are part of the IT service management life cycle, and are typically introduced after an organization adopts and matures its processes using the Information Technology Infrastructure Library (ITIL) framework or Microsoft Operational Framework (MOF). Service Manager aligns directly with ITIL and MOF; in addition to helping organizations improve their processes, it provides automation and chargeback capabilities.

This chapter explores how automation and chargeback relate to each other and service management, and discusses them in relation to System Center 2012 Service Manager. This functionality is included with Service Manager, removing the need to purchase third-party tools as solutions.

You can accomplish automation in Service Manager in a number of ways, including

▶ Templates

▶ Built-in workflows

▶ PowerShell and SMLets

▶ System Center Orchestrator

Integration with Orchestrator offers the highest level of automation in Service Manager. Orchestrator is System Center 2012's runbook automation component that empowers organizations to automate business and technology processes. Orchestrator interacts with Service Manager's service catalog and request fulfillment functionality, and demonstrates the benefits of automating your service management processes.

REAL WORLD: FORRESTER RESEARCH REPORT SHOWS BENEFITS OF SERVICE MANAGEMENT AUTOMATION

The following are key points from a Forrester Research report titled "Sustain Service Management and Automation Funding Report" (Stephen Mann, June 7, 2012). These highlight that the benefits of service management automation (SMA) have real world impact:

- ▶ **Improvements to your service management or automation capabilities benefit your business:** To varying degrees, commonly adopted and up-and-coming service management processes improve productivity, quality, costs, and perception. At the same time, automation delivers benefits of increased speed and quality while reducing costs.

- ▶ **When combined, service management and automation amplifies benefits to your business:** These capabilities make technology services even faster, better, and cheaper. However, it is important to realize that if the process is good, you speed up the good actions and achieve excellence. If the process is poor, you only speed up the bad actions.

- ▶ **Improved staff productivity allows your business to become more competitive:** An Infrastructure and Operations (I&O) professional's time is too valuable to be spent fighting fires and performing repetitive tasks. Rather, embrace service management that applies standardized processes to simplify execution. When automation tools are applied to good processes, productivity skyrockets to a level unachievable by manual methods, with SMA freeing up staff time that could be allocated to new projects to make your business more innovative and competitive.

- ▶ **Heightened quality of service improves business uptime and customer experience:** In today's age of 24x7x365 global operations and unrelenting customer demand, downtime can erode your competitive edge quickly.

- ▶ **Operational costs are reduced, enabling reinvestment in new and innovative initiatives:** The I&O organization consumes roughly 50% of the overall IT budget, with staff accounting for approximately 33% of this spending. Moreover, firms typically allocate 70% of IT spending to what Forrester calls MOOSE—the costs to maintain ongoing operations, systems, and equipment—rather than to new or innovative projects. While the IT MOOSE ratio has improved to 50% since 2010, I&O leaders can keep the pressure on with SMA because more standard and automated processes improve productivity that over time reduces operational costs.

- ▶ **Improved reputation with the business:** Most self-aware I&O organizations acknowledge that their reputation with business stakeholders isn't sterling. This is a critical problem, but you can't fix it overnight—changing an organization's culture, institutionalized behaviors, and stereotypes takes time and energy. 65% of SMA professionals believe that ITIL has improved their reputation with the business.

The complete report can be found at http://media.cms.bmc.com/documents/1206_Forrester_Sustain_Service_Management.pdf.

System Center 2012 Service Pack (SP) 1, released in December 2012, adds chargeback functionality to Service Manager. As IT processes mature, organizations increasingly look at chargeback as an approach for managing costs. Because chargeback is still a relatively new concept for most IT departments, they may lack a full understanding of its capabilities, but they realize chargeback is a tool that can better help the business understand the cost of the IT resources being consumed. For those organizations implementing a private cloud environment, chargeback helps IT with tracking and charging for the services it provides.

Overview of Service Management and Automation

While traditional IT has struggled to keep up with the rapid pace of a changing infrastructure, incorporating ITIL can be a step in the right direction for mature IT processes. ITIL can also assist with the adoption of cloud computing. Cloud computing and private cloud transform datacenters and increase their complexity; using ITIL can help support a full-blown private cloud as it matures IT processes and standards. These processes should be matured and standardized before being automated. Automation enables improved management of cloud-based datacenters.

The Role of Automation

Many datacenters are moving toward becoming service-based and incorporating private cloud, with automation a part of the realization of private cloud. However, without mature IT processes and a good handle on service management, automation provides minimal benefit. Automating bad processes and routines only equals bad automation.

Service management, introduced in Chapter 1, "Service Management Basics," is about moving to a service-based model, delivering technology as a service, and running on top of service-oriented architectures. Automation is critical to service-focused environments. Service-based environments, including private cloud, consist of multiple technology layers with automation as the integration point automating across these layers, such as compute, processing, storage, networking, servers, and applications. Service management automation improves the following areas:

▶ Quality and control

▶ Standardization and documentation

▶ Speed and agility

▶ Accountability and compliance

There is also a growing need for self-service by end users, with many end users bringing their own devices (BYOD) to use in enterprise networks. End users today expect services to be delivered at a faster pace. Automation helps enforce compliance and standardization, and speeds up the real time delivery of services meeting the needs of BYOD.

Service Manager's Role in Private Cloud

Service management and automation with Service Manager tie into its role in the private cloud architecture. Private cloud is about organizations rethinking traditional infrastructure and transforming their datacenters into cloud-based to make IT components more dynamic, giving IT the ability to expand and contract as demand goes up or down and to meet the growing needs of the organization and its more technically savvy end users. Incorporating private cloud enables IT to be offered as a service. Accomplishing this requires that IT components become more dynamic on multiple layers. These layers include

▶ Service Delivery layer

▶ Software layer

▶ Platform layer

▶ Infrastructure layer

▶ Operations layer

▶ Management layer

A successful private cloud implementation requires that organizations have dependable and reliable fabrics, measurements, monitoring, data protection, service level agreements (SLAs), automation, and processes. System Center 2012, which is positioned as a cloud and datacenter management solution, can help organizations grow in these areas.

Each System Center component plays a role in a private cloud. Figure 12.1 displays the areas of private cloud management into which each System Center component fits. Service Manager is a part of the service delivery, infrastructure, operations, and management layers of the datacenter.

Table 12.1 lists Service Manager capabilities with private cloud layers, incorporating information from http://social.technet.microsoft.com/wiki/contents/articles/13641.system-center-2012-integration-guide-service-manager.aspx#Role_in_the_Microsoft_Private_Cloud, and directly mapping Service Manager's capabilities to the different layers in private cloud and MOF.

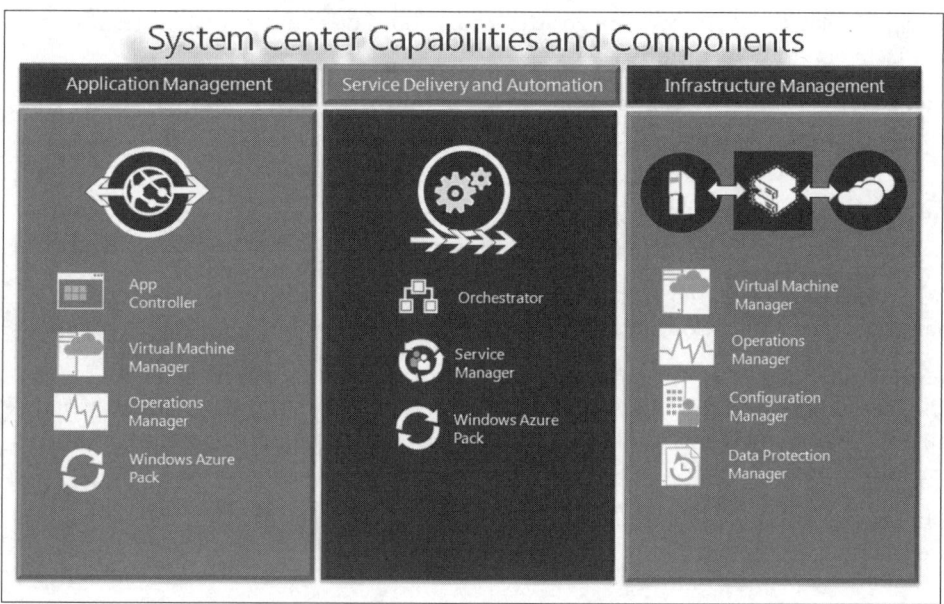

FIGURE 12.1   Private cloud roles.

TABLE 12.1   Service Manager Capabilities with Private Cloud Layers

Layer	Description
Service Delivery	The primary function of Service Manager within the Service Delivery layer is maintaining the service catalog.
Infrastructure	Service Manager maintains the configuration management database (CMDB), which represents artifacts of the Infrastructure layer as configuration items and their relationships to each other.
Service Operations	The Service Operations layer includes all the routine administrative tasks performed on the private cloud infrastructure. Service Manager captures and automates these business processes.
Management	Service Manager provides the means to manage workloads supporting Fabric Management. It also holds the configuration database and service catalog that can be correlated with status information to report on overall health.

To summarize Table 12.1, Service Manager sits under four layers but really shines under the Service Delivery and Operations layers.

▶ **Service Delivery:** Service Manager improves upon the request fulfillment process through its service catalog along with self-service capabilities, automation, and service level management.

This layer is the connection point between IT and the business. It is where technology becomes a service to meet business needs.

▶ **Operations:** Service Manager improves processes through Incident Management, Change Management, Configuration Management, and Knowledge Management.

The Operations layer is geared toward delivery of IT as a service through the operational procedures and processes required to keep IT services running. This is where ITIL and MOF frameworks play a significant part in applying best practices to the datacenter.

Service Manager thus provides the capability for administrators to manage the transforming datacenter and enable self-service for end users.

Workflows in Service Manager

Service Manager workflows can be utilized to automate processes. Areas for automation with workflows include routing incidents, creating incidents when computers are out of compliance, and sending an email when the status changes on an incident. Workflows can be set by a trigger condition. There are two types of trigger conditions:

▶ **Database query:** Also known as a subscription, this kicks off a workflow when the trigger is set by a type of change occurring to a specific class of object. The three types of changes in a class follow:

  ▶ Created

  ▶ Updated

  ▶ Deleted

▶ **Timer:** Also known as a schedule, a timer allows the workflow trigger condition to be a schedule of some interval such as days of a week and time.

Service Manager comes with default workflows, and you can create new workflows in the Service Manager console or more advanced ones using the Service Manager Authoring Tool. Workflows are stored within management packs, making them portable to other Service Manager environments. You could also acquire third-party or community-based add-ons to automate processes in Service Manager that are essentially workflows.

The most common and easiest way to utilize workflows is through the Service Manager console. Workflows are often used in combination with templates to automate processes. They can be accessed by going to **Administration -> Workflows**, as shown in Figure 12.2, where you see folders (containers) for Configuration and Status:

▶ Configuration is where you can edit existing workflows and create new ones.

▶ The Status folder is where you can see whether workflows are enabled or disabled, turn them off or on, and view success and failures of workflows, along with logs to assist in troubleshooting.

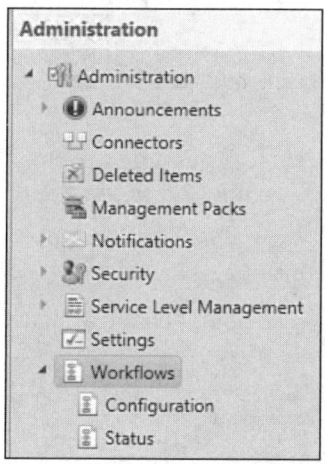

FIGURE 12.2   Workflow area in the Service Manager console.

Selecting **Configuration** shows the workflow configurations listed in groups based on the different processes they pertain to (see Figure 12.3). Double-clicking a workflow configuration opens a window with all the actual workflows.

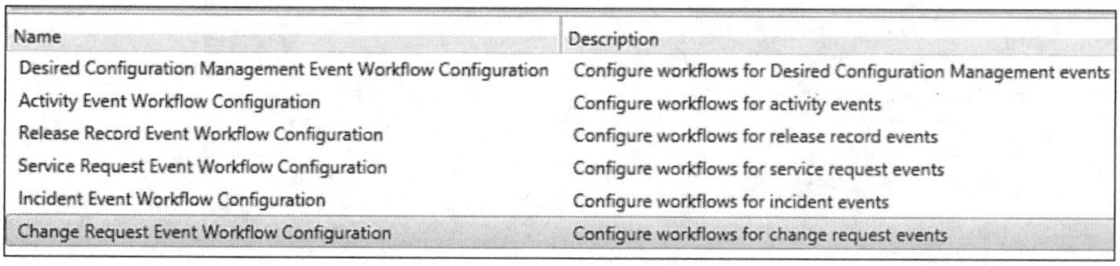

Name	Description
Desired Configuration Management Event Workflow Configuration	Configure workflows for Desired Configuration Management events
Activity Event Workflow Configuration	Configure workflows for activity events
Release Record Event Workflow Configuration	Configure workflows for release record events
Service Request Event Workflow Configuration	Configure workflows for service request events
Incident Event Workflow Configuration	Configure workflows for incident events
Change Request Event Workflow Configuration	Configure workflows for change request events

FIGURE 12.3   Workflow configurations.

In the Configure Workflows window, selecting **Add** opens the Add Incident Event Workflow Wizard, which you can use to build your own workflows. To create a simple incident workflow, follow these steps:

1. Click **Next** on the Before You Begin page.

2. Enter a Name for the workflow and optional description. Select the event to be checked; options are **When an object is created** or **When an object is updated**. Select or create a new management pack in which to store this workflow and check the **Enabled** box. Click **Next** to continue.

3. On the Event Criteria page, set the criteria this workflow looks for to start. This is the trigger for the workflow. Under the Changed to section, select a property of the class and set the criteria as seen in Figure 12.4. Click **Next**.

4. The Select Incident Template page allows you to apply a template. Leave **Do not apply a template** selected and click **Next**.

5. On the Select People to Notify page, you can select people to notify as a part of this workflow. This also lets you select an email template to use. Figure 12.5 shows these options. Click **Next** to continue.

6. Next is a Summary page for the workflow. Click **Next** to continue.

7. On the Completion page, click **Close** and the workflow is created and enabled. You now have a new workflow.

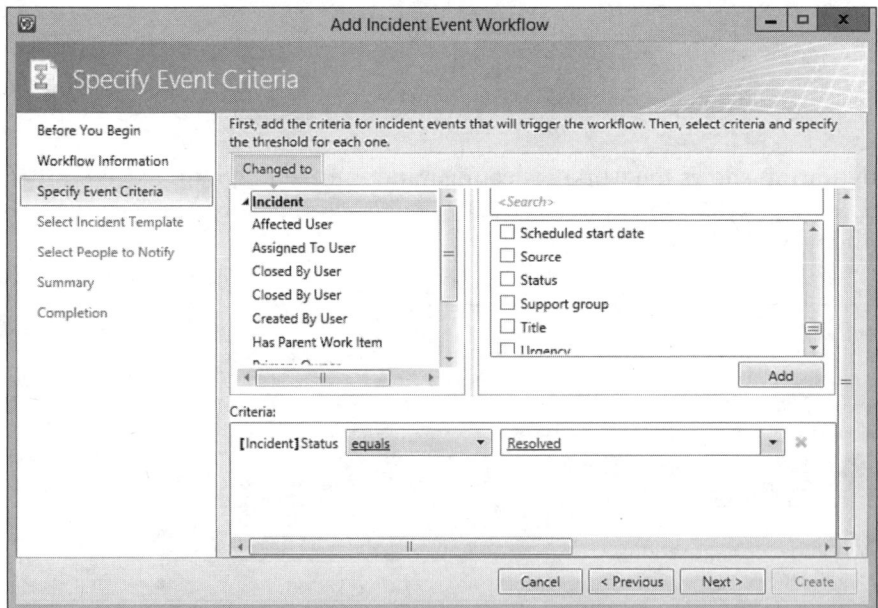

FIGURE 12.4   Specifying workflow criteria.

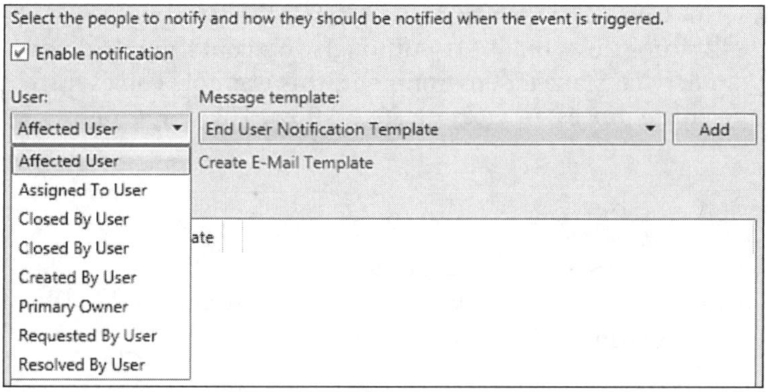

FIGURE 12.5   Workflow notification.

Service Manager SMLets

SMLets are a set of PowerShell cmdlets you can use to automate common tasks in Service Manager and are discussed in Chapter 24, "Using PowerShell." They are a community-based project with no support from Microsoft. SMLets must run on a Service Manager management server or a computer with the Service Manager console installed. The majority of SMLet functions are actions that cannot be performed from the Service Manager console.

This section walks through an example of automation using SMLets, showing how to create a custom workflow in the Service Manager Authoring Tool using an SMLet script to automate the closing of resolved incidents on a schedule. The example covers working with the SMLet script, creating a custom workflow, and importing the workflow into the console.

SMLets are often used to automate closing resolved incidents. Service desks typically resolve incidents rather than close them, as a closed an incident cannot be reopened without using a workaround. Not being able to reopen incidents is by design to align with ITIL processes. Service desk teams resolve incidents and leave them in this status for some time so they can be reopened if necessary.

Marcel Zehner, a System Center MVP, published an SMLet script to close resolved incidents automatically and blogs about it at http://marcelzehner.ch/2011/01/12/auto-close-resolved-incidents/. A revised version of the script by coauthor Samuel Erskine can be downloaded or copied from TechNet Gallery at http://gallery.technet.microsoft.com/SCSM-2012-Auto-Close-1b26911f.

Follow these steps to create, import, and use a workflow to close resolved incidents automatically:

1. Download and install SMLets on your Service Manager server. SMLets can be downloaded from http://smlets.codeplex.com/releases/view/84853. Additional information is in Chapter 24.

2. Copy Samuel Erskine's script from TechNet Gallery at http://gallery.technet.
microsoft.com/SCSM-2012-Auto-Close-1b26911f. Although you could simply download and deploy it to your Service Manager environment, this example copies it so
you can step through the entire process of creating a workflow. The script follows:

```
Import-Module SMLets -Force


$Maxage = (Get-Date).adddays(-14)
$Class = Get-SCSMClass -Name System.Workitem.Incident$
$ResolvedStatusID = (Get-SCSMEnumeration -Name incidentstatusenum.resolved$).id
$resolvedincidents = Get-SCSMObject -Class $Class -filter
  "status -eq $resolvedstatusid"
$IncidentsToClose = $resolvedincidents | where{$_.resolveddate -lt $maxage}
if($incidentstoclose)
 {
 $incidentstoclose | Get-SCSMObject -property status -value closed
 }
Remove-Module SMLets -Force
```

3. Open the Service Manager Authoring Tool, which you can download from
http://www.microsoft.com/en-us/download/details.aspx?id=40896.

NOTE: LEARN TO USE THE SERVICE MANAGER AUTHORING TOOL

As you will find you frequently need to customize Service Manager, the authors recommend you become familiar with the Service Manager Authoring Tool. For information about
the Authoring Tool, see Chapter 20, "Management Packs," Chapter 22, "Customizing
Service Manager," and the information at http://technet.microsoft.com/en-us/library/
hh495563.aspx.

---

4. Click **File** -> **New** to create a new management pack.

5. In the Management Pack Explorer pane, right-click **Workflows**. Select **Create**, as
shown in Figure 12.6.

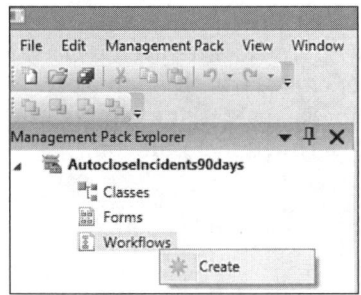

FIGURE 12.6   Create a custom workflow.

6. Give the new workflow a name and description. Click **Advanced** to change the **Interval** and **Maximum time** the workflow will run (see Figure 12.7).

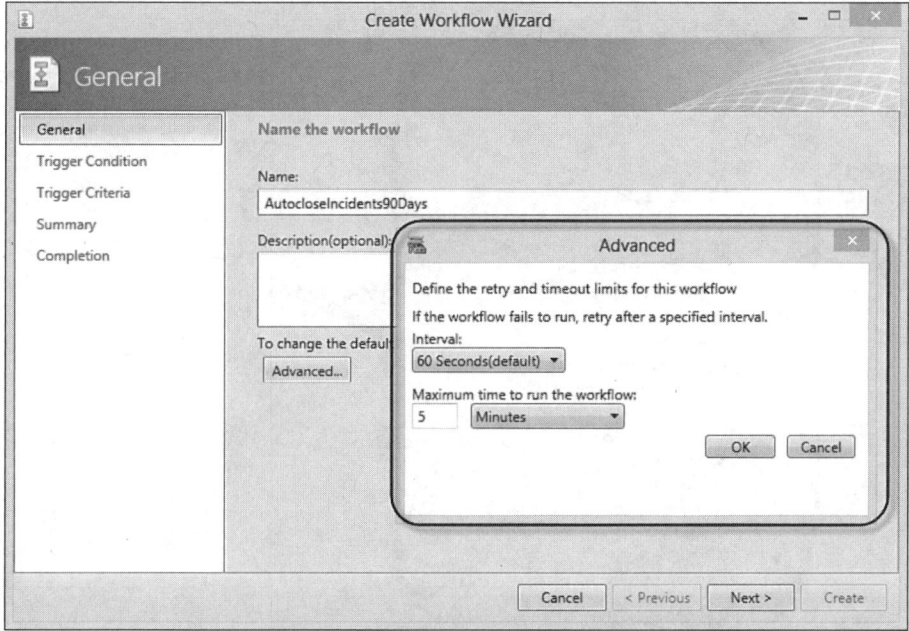

FIGURE 12.7   General page of creating a custom workflow.

7. On the Trigger Condition page, select **Run at a scheduled time or at scheduled intervals** and click **Next**. On the Trigger Criteria page, set the recurring schedule for this workflow. Click **Next**. Review the Summary page and click **Create** to create the workflow.

8. Click **Close** on the Completion page. The workflow in the Management Pack Explorer with the workflow details in the middle pane displays (see Figure 12.8).

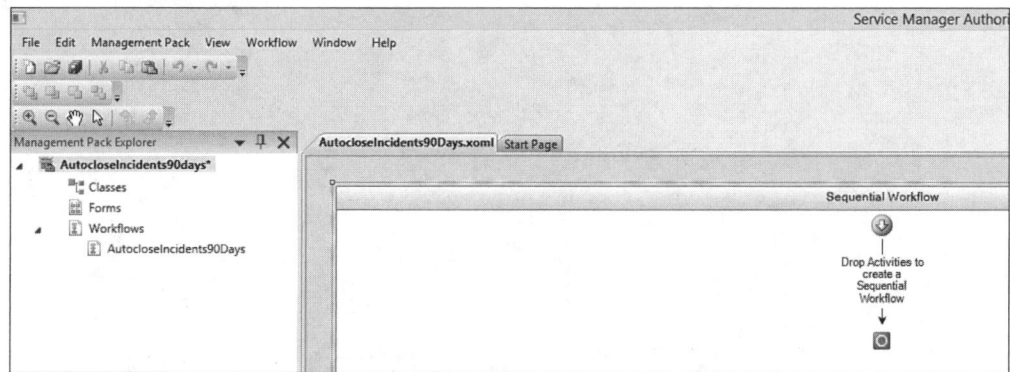

FIGURE 12.8   Custom workflow details.

9. From the right pane, drag Windows PowerShell Script from the Activities Toolbox onto the details of the workflow (see Figure 12.9).

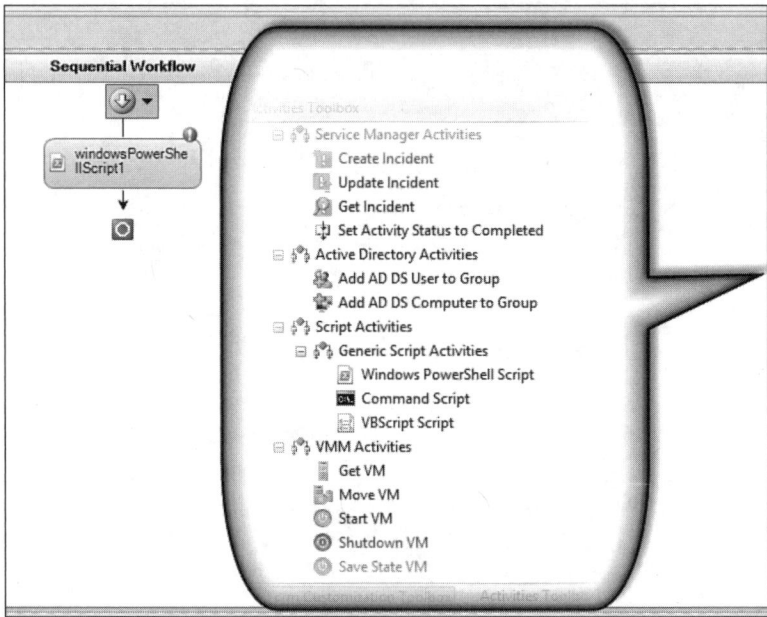

FIGURE 12.9   Script Activities Toolbox.

10. Click **Windows PowerShell Script** in the middle pane to display the Details pane for the script. Locate the Script Body field; click the whitespace of the blank field and an ellipse button appears. Click that button to open the Configure a Script Activity pop-up window.

11. On the Script Body page, click **View** or **Edit Script**. This can be confusing; Figure 12.10 shows an example.

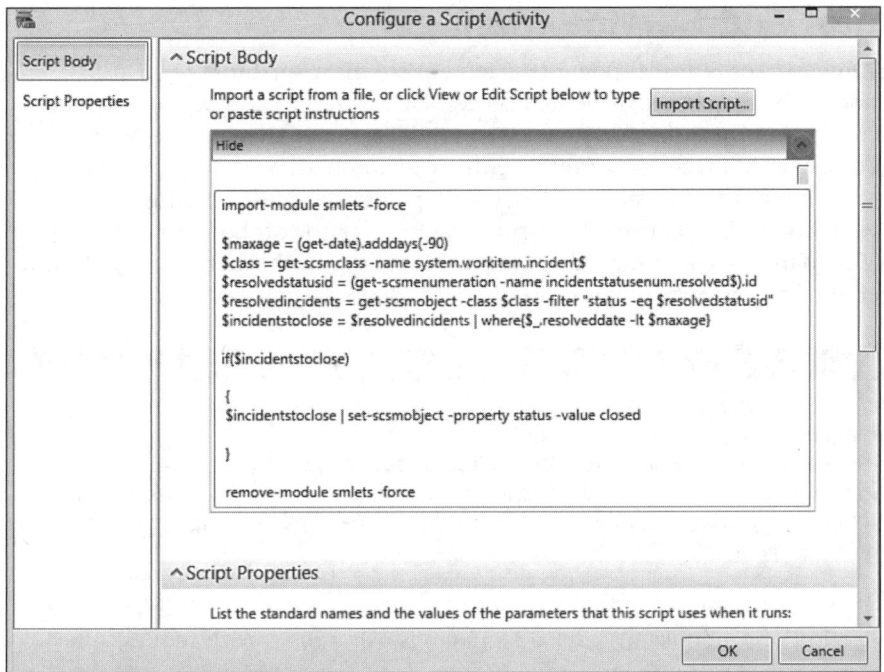

FIGURE 12.10   Editing the script body.

12. In the script body, paste the script that was copied earlier in this section and change **$maxage = (Get-Date).adddays(-14)** to **$maxage = (Get-Date).adddays(-90)**. This automatically closes resolved incidents older than 90 days. Click **OK**. Save your management pack by clicking **File -> Save All**.

13. Navigate to the folder containing your management pack. It contains five files, but you only need the **.XML** and **.DLL** files. Copy the .DLL file to your Service Manager installation folder (by default %*ProgramFiles*%\Microsoft System Center 2012\Service Manager).

14. Open the Service Manager console. In **Administration -> Management Packs**, under the Tasks pane, click **Import** and import the new management pack.

15. Your workflow now runs as scheduled. You can view the workflow by navigating to **Administration -> Workflow -> Status**. Figure 12.11 shows an example.

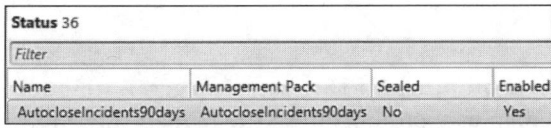

FIGURE 12.11   Workflow Status pane.

Orchestrator and Service Manager

System Center Orchestrator is a workflow management solution, enabling IT to automate business and IT processes across the datacenter. Orchestrator has integration points with many Microsoft and third-party systems, including Service Manager. Integrating Orchestrator and Service Manager can provide enhanced automation to improve self-service delivery. Examples include mapping user prompts on a request offering to runbooks to automate specific processes, or using an Orchestrator runbook to create an incident in Service Manager The integration occurs by syncing Orchestrator runbooks into Service Manager and then triggering the runbooks from Service Manager.

TIP: CONFIGURING SERVICE MANAGER IN ORCHESTRATOR

Service Manager and Orchestrator integration requires configuring settings in Service Manager and implementing the Service Manager integration pack in Orchestrator. For detailed information on how to configure the integration pack for Service Manager in Orchestrator, refer to *System Center 2012 Orchestrator Unleashed* (Sams, 2013), or the links at http://technet.microsoft.com/en-us/library/hh519779.aspx and http://technet.microsoft.com/en-us/library/hh832008.aspx.

A common utilization of runbooks in Service Manager is using them with request offerings. A good automation starting point for Orchestrator and Service Manager is to automate the creation of new users, which is a typical part of the new hire process. Automating this step can save system administrators or service desk staff the time of creating a user account in Active Directory, adding it to the needed groups, and creating an Exchange mailbox for the new user. Let's go through the process of using Service Manager and Orchestrator to automate and create new user accounts, including mailbox creation. The Orchestrator connector is already in place between Service Manager and Orchestrator (see Chapter 8, "Working with Connectors," for details).

You first must create a runbook. Figure 12.12 shows an example of a basic runbook. This runbook prompts for the new user's information, generates a random password, creates the user account and the mailbox at the same time, and then emails the new user's information to a specified person such as a hiring manager.

| Prompt for | Generate | Create | Email user |
| new user info | Password | User/Mailbox | account info |

FIGURE 12.12   Create user and mailbox runbook.

After the runbook is created, it needs to be synchronized into Service Manager. A runbook automated activity template is then used to map user prompts from the request offering to parameters in the runbook. Follow these steps to create a runbook automated activity template:

1. In the Service Manager console, navigate to **Library -> Runbooks**. In the Tasks pane, select **Create Runbook Automation Activity Template**.

2. Give the template a name and optional description, select an existing management pack or create a new one, and then click **OK**.

3. The Runbook Activity Template form opens. Complete the fields you need, such as Title, Description, and so on. Ensure that you select **Is Ready For Automation**, which tells Service Manager it can use this runbook activity. If not checked, this activity must be started manually. Click **OK** when done.

   Select the Runbook tab to see the parameters from the **Prompt for new user info** activity in the runbook (see Figure 12.13). These parameters are mapped to user prompts in the request offering.

4. Click **OK** to create the template.

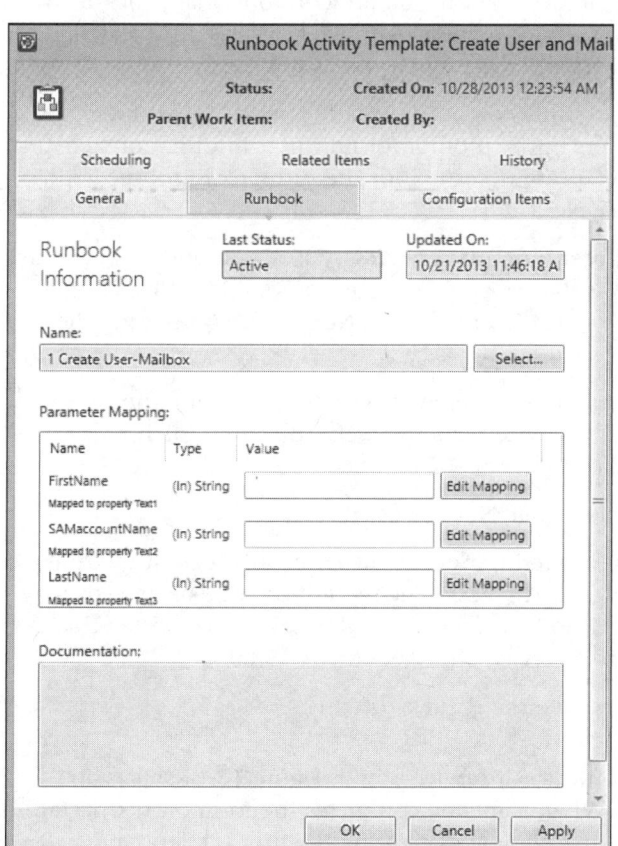

FIGURE 12.13   Runbook activity template.

The final part of Service Manager and Orchestrator integration is creating a request offering and tying it into the runbook activity template. Perform the following steps:

1. In the Service Manager console, go to **Library -> Templates**; in the Tasks pane select **Create Template**.

2. Give the template a name and description, browse to select Service Request class, and create a new or use an existing management pack. Click **OK** to create the template.

3. Complete any needed fields on the General tab.

4. Select the Activities tab. Then click the green + icon to add an activity. A Select Template window opens; select the runbook automation activity and click **OK**.

5. In the console, navigate to **Library -> Service Catalog -> Request Offerings**; in the Tasks pane, select **Create Request Offering**.

6. Give the request offering a title and description, add an icon (optional), click **Browse -> Service Request**, and select the service request template that was just created. Select an existing management pack or create a new one. Click **Next**.

7. On the next page, add the user prompts you need. Be sure to add at least user prompts that match the parameters in the prompt for new user information activity from the runbook. These parameters are necessary for the runbook to proceed and were shown in Figure 12.13. Click **Next**.

8. On the next page, configure the user prompts if necessary. For example, if you added a list as a user prompt, then this is the screen where you can build that list. The parameters from the runbook are in text format. Click **Next** after configuring the user prompts.

9. On the next page, map the information gathered for each user prompt on the request offering form to a field of a service request or related activity such as the runbook automation activity. Click **Next**.

10. Add any needed knowledge articles. Click **Next** to continue.

11. Now choose to publish the request offering. Set the owner of this request offering and add any needed internal notes. Click **Next**. The request offering also needs to be added to a service offering for it to be displayed on the self-service portal; this process is discussed in Chapter 10, "Service Manager Service Catalog."

12. On the last page, click **Create** to create the request offering.

The request offering is now available on the self-service portal. Figure 12.14 shows an example of what this might look like. When someone completes the form on the portal, Service Manager initiates the runbook and completes creating the user account and mailbox.

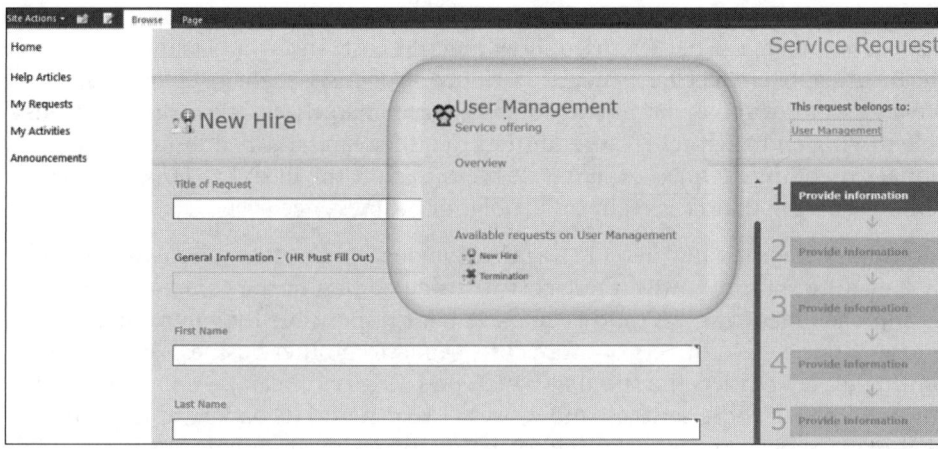

FIGURE 12.14   New user request offering.

Overview of Chargeback

Chargeback is an accounting strategy utilized by IT as a means to apply costs to IT consumption. Chargeback falls within ITIL's financial management process in its ITIL v3 Service Strategy. This process is responsible for managing an IT service provider's budgeting, accounting, and charging requirements. It is also the process that quantifies the value that IT services contribute to the business.

Chargeback is the method of allocating an expense to a unit of measurement. Units of measurement differ by organization. Some units of measurement follow:

- ▶ IT services
- ▶ Hardware
- ▶ Number of servers
- ▶ Processing power
- ▶ Storage capacity
- ▶ Bandwidth usage
- ▶ Software
- ▶ Hardware
- ▶ Number of users
- ▶ Number of applications supported

Chargeback drives efficiency and lowers IT expenses due to economies of scale. Chargeback is used to align what was used, how much it cost, and what business unit incurred it. By utilizing chargeback systems, IT can control costs, manage budgets, and scale resources up or down based on demand and usage. Chargeback assists organizations in better identifying and aligning IT expenditures to either capital expenditure (CapEx) or operational expenditure (OpEx) expenses. It helps to shift the idea that IT is just a cost center to understanding that IT is really an enabler of business needs.

Organizations have traditionally viewed IT as the sole department holding the budget for IT costs of the entire company, with these costs considered part of the company's overhead. This approach made the CIO and IT management responsible for controlling IT costs, even though the main drivers of those costs came from other business units. Using this accounting model hinders the speed at which new IT services can be rolled out to the business unit in need of those services, and causes IT to dip into its budget to fund the newly requested IT service or not roll it out at all due to lack of funding in the current budget cycle.

Slow rollout of new IT services hurts the entire organization. In today's business world, many organizations compete with their competitors on the technology front. A slow rollout of new technology equals a slower move to new technologies and results in an organization's losing competitive advantages.

Chargeback shifts the accounting toward business units, making them responsible for their part of the overall IT expense. The chargeback accounting model provides transparency into the factors and decisions that drive costs. This allows organizations to budget more accurately and allocate funds according to real needs. Another benefit of the chargeback model is the ability to invest more into technology that increases profitability.

Chargeback in IT services breaks the accounting responsibility down even further, all the way to the user level. When an end user consumes a service, it can be tracked to the department and to that user within that department, making the user aware of the cost behind his IT consumption. This empowers end users by making them responsible and accountable for their consumption and cost to the organization.

As an example, consider an end user from a marketing business unit that needs to spin up a web application for the duration of a marketing campaign. The application is not required after the campaign. The end user will be able to see the cost of that web application. Imagine the web application consists of one SQL database, three web servers, and another server with BI analytic tools. That is a significant amount of IT resources consumed for this single marketing campaign. The end user would have insight into all of this and be more responsible in notifying IT to remove the web application after the marketing campaign ends. This demonstrates how chargeback results in saving money and affecting the bottom line.

Chargeback is not only about saving money; it also is a way to help organizations increase revenue by finding and creating new revenue streams. CIOs and IT management can analyze the metrics from chargeback systems to assess whether revenue generated by new business opportunities enabled through technology justifies the associated expenses. This enables CIOs to identify areas of profit and loss.

Overall, the chargeback model shifts IT from a cost center to a service provider for the business. The following sections discuss how to install, configure, and use chargeback in Service Manager.

Installing and Using Chargeback

Chargeback in Service Manager focuses on private cloud pricing and charging around System Center Virtual Machine Manager's fabric to show underutilized or oversubscribed resources, helping to reduce and control virtual machine sprawl. This section shows how to install and configure chargeback in Service Manager. The following components make up the chargeback model in System Center 2012:

▶ System Center 2012 SP1/R2 Virtual Machine Manager

▶ System Center 2012 SP1/R2 Operations Manager

▶ System Center 2012 SP1/R2 Service Manager

▶ Microsoft Excel 2010 or later

▶ PerformancePoint

These components must be deployed before you can deploy chargeback. You must configure each component as part of setting up chargeback. The following is a high-level summary of what must occur to prepare and enable System Center 2012 for chargeback:

1. Deploy Virtual Machine Manager (VMM). The fabric is defined as a part of this process. This is not covered in this chapter.

2. Deploy Operations Manager. This is not covered in this chapter.

3. Install the Operations Manager agent and console on the Virtual Machine Manager server. This is not covered in this chapter.

4. Import the VMM management pack into Operations Manager.

5. Configure Operations Manager to discover VMM fabric for chargeback. This is not covered in this chapter.

6. Deploy Service Manager and the data warehouse. See Chapter 6, "Installing and Upgrading to System Center 2012 Service Manager," for information.

7. Configure Service Manager to obtain fabric data from Operations Manager and Virtual Machine Manager.

8. Install the Service Manager chargeback feature.

9. Create chargeback price sheets in Service Manager.

10. Configure desired chargeback reports in Service Manager data warehouse.

This chapter assumes that Virtual Machine Manager, Operations Manager, Service Manager, and the Service Manager data warehouse are deployed, so the procedures for these are not covered here. You must have clouds configured in Virtual Machine Manager. Configuring clouds in Virtual Machine Manager is outside the scope of this book; the process is described at http://technet.microsoft.com/library/gg696967.aspx.

Operations Manager Management Server Configuration

The first component of System Center 2012 configured is Operations Manager. Operations Manager and Virtual Machine Manager must share information to track resources and usage and to determine when changes occur. This information can then be tracked with Service Manager. This integration is accomplished through a CI connector between Operations Manager and Service Manager, which is used for discovering information about VMM fabric.

The chargeback report files must be installed on the Operations Manager management server. These are management packs imported into Operations Manager. A PowerShell script, ImportToOM.ps1, imports the chargeback management pack files. This script is located on the Service Manager management server at %*ProgramFiles*%\Microsoft System Center 2012\Service Manager\Chargeback\Dependencies. Copy this script file to the Operations Manager management server. The script imports the following management packs from the management pack catalog:

- Microsoft.Windows.InternetInformationServices.CommonLibrary.mp

- Microsoft.Windows.Server.Library.mp

- Microsoft.SQLServer.Library.mp

- System.Virtualization.Library.mp

- Microsoft.Windows.Server.2008.Discovery.mp

- Microsoft.Windows.InternetInformationServices.2003.mp

- Microsoft.Windows.InternetInformationServices.2008.mp

- Microsoft.SystemCenter.VirtualMachineManager.PRO.Library.mp

- Microsoft.SystemCenter.VirtualMachineManager.PRO.V2.Library.mp

- Microsoft.SystemCenter.VirtualMachineManager.Pro.2008.Library.mp

- Microsoft.SystemCenter.VirtualMachineManager.2012.Discovery.mp

- Microsoft.SystemCenter.VirtualMachineManager.Library.mp

If any of these management packs are already installed, they are skipped during the import. Now follow these steps:

1. Log on to the Operations Manager management server.

2. Launch Windows PowerShell as an administrator.

3. Set the execution policy to `remotesigned`, using the following syntax:

   ```
   Set-ExecutionPolicy -force RemoteSigned
   ```

4. Within PowerShell, navigate to the folder where you copied the script.

5. Type .**ImportToOM.ps1** and press Enter. The script takes 2 to 3 minutes to complete.

Check to ensure that Operations Manager has discovered the needed data from VMM. To verify this, perform the following steps:

1. Open the Operations Manager console.

2. Go to the Monitoring workspace.

3. Navigate to **Virtual Machine Manager -> Managed Resources**.

4. Click on the **Cloud Health dashboard** view. This path is shown in Figure 12.15.

Operations Manager shows views similar to the cloud dashboard in Figure 12.16 and the cloud diagram distributed application in Figure 12.17.

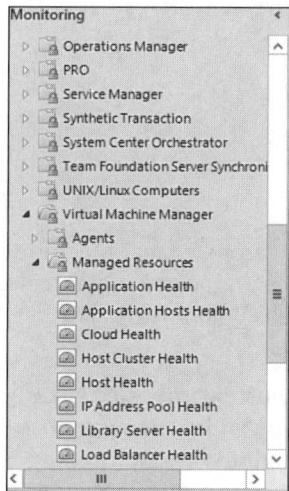

FIGURE 12.15   Cloud dashboard path.

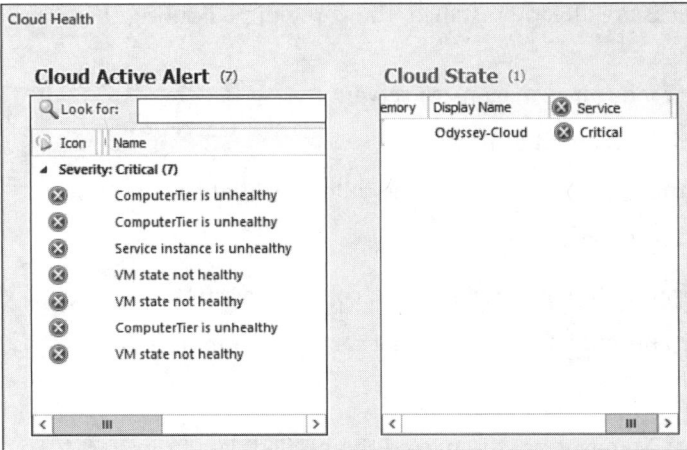

FIGURE 12.16   Cloud dashboard.

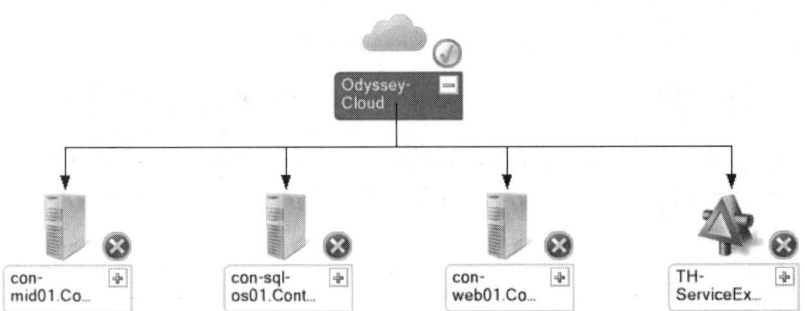

FIGURE 12.17   Cloud diagram distributed application.

Service Manager Management Server Configuration

Service Manager holds all information about resources brought over from Virtual Machine Manager and Operations Manager. The data is imported into Service Manager via connectors, and can be put into price sheets and reported on using chargeback reporting. The reporting takes place in the Service Manager data warehouse.

The chargeback management pack is not installed by default and must be imported manually. This management pack enables the chargeback functionality in Service Manager. Use a PowerShell script to import the needed management pack. This script is also located at *%ProgramFiles%*\Program Files\Microsoft System Center 2012\Service Manager\ Chargeback\ and is named ImportToSM.ps1.

To import the chargeback management pack, follow these steps:

1. Log on to the Service Manager management server.

2. Launch Windows PowerShell as administrator.

3. Set the execution policy to `remotesigned`, using the following syntax:

```
Set-ExecutionPolicy -force RemoteSigned
```

4. Within PowerShell, navigate to the Chargeback folder.

5. Type **.\ImportToSM.ps1** and press **Enter**. The script can take up to 5 minutes to complete.

Running the script imports the chargeback management pack. You must complete several additional steps in the data warehouse to complete the chargeback installation process. Perform the following steps:

1. Open the Service Manager console and navigate to **Data Warehouse -> Data Warehouse Jobs**.

2. Select **MPSyncJob**; then under Tasks on the right side of the console, click **Resume**.

3. Close the Service Manager console and reopen it.

Verify chargeback is installed properly by navigating in the console to **Administration -> Chargeback -> Infrastructure**. There should be folders for Clouds and Price Sheets.

Configuring Chargeback

With the chargeback management pack imported, the next task to set up chargeback in Service Manager is configuring the Operations Manager CI connector. Configuring this connector brings the needed objects from the Virtual Machine Manager fabric into Service Manager via Operations Manager. This data consists of objects such as virtual machines, CPUs, and storage. See Chapter 8 for information on configuring the connector.

Once the Operations Manager CI connector is created, you can create a chargeback price sheet. The price sheet enables you to define prices for cloud objects that are discovered by the Operations Manager CI connector. You associate clouds to a price sheet—one or multiple clouds can be associated to a price sheet. To create a price sheet, follow these steps:

1. In the Service Manager console, navigate to **Administration -> Chargeback -> Infrastructure -> Price Sheets**.

2. Click **All Price Sheets** and in the **Tasks** pane under All Price Sheets, click **Create Price Sheet**.

The price sheet form opens. Perform the following steps:

1. On the General tab, give a title to the price sheet in the Name box, and add a description.

2. Click the **Price** tab, where you need to specify daily base prices for your cloud components. Add prices for the following:

   ▶ VMM Base Price per day

   ▶ Cloud Membership Price per day

   ▶ VM CPU Price per Core/day

   ▶ VM Memory Price per GB/day

   ▶ VM Storage Price per GB/day

   ▶ Highly Available VM Price per day

   ▶ Static IP Price per day

   ▶ Expanding VHD Price per day

3. To publish the price sheet, click **Publish** on the right-hand side under **Tasks ->** **VMM Cloud Price Sheet**. Once the price sheet is published, you can assign clouds to it.

Follow these steps to assign clouds to a price:

1. Click the Assigned Clouds tab.

2. Click **Add** to open the Select objects dialog box.

3. Select one or more private cloud objects from the list of private cloud objects and then click **Add** to add them to the Selected objects list.

4. Click **OK**. The cloud or clouds are assigned to the price sheet.

Using Chargeback Reports

The last activity in configuring chargeback is being able to see the reports, allowing you to measure the cost of used clouds and cloud resources. In Service Manager, chargeback data is sent to the data warehouse. The chargeback data can be viewed from any of the reporting tools in the data warehouse such as SQL Server Reporting Services (SSRS) and Excel PowerPivot. This section discusses how to view chargeback data in Excel PowerPivot. The following is what can be seen in chargeback reporting:

▶ Cost centers

▶ Clouds

▶ VMM user roles

▶ Price sheets

▶ Spending trend

▶ Overall spending

The ChargebackReport.xlsx spreadsheet is an out of the box sample chargeback report, located at %*ProgramFiles*%\Microsoft System Center 2012\Service Manager\Chargeback. You can modify this report to fit your organization's requirements.

The report obtains its data from an OLAP data cube in the Service Manager data warehouse and stays current by pulling data directly from the OLAP cube. The default OLAP cube for chargeback is SystemCenterServiceManagerChargebackCube. You could also publish this report to an Analysis library in the Service Manager data warehouse. For more information about the data warehouse, including how to create an analysis library, see Chapter 21, "Data Warehouse and Reporting."

The Chargeback report has three tabs:

▶ **Dashboard:** This shows an overview of your chargeback in Service Manager including cost centers, clouds, VMM user roles, price sheets, spending trend, and overall spending. You can change the time period by using the date slicer.

▶ **Chargeback Daily Details:** This tab shows a detailed daily cost breakdown of your clouds and their resources.

▶ **Chargeback Monthly Details:** This shows another detailed list of costs assigned to price sheets.

Figure 12.18 shows the Dashboard tab in the Chargeback Excel report.

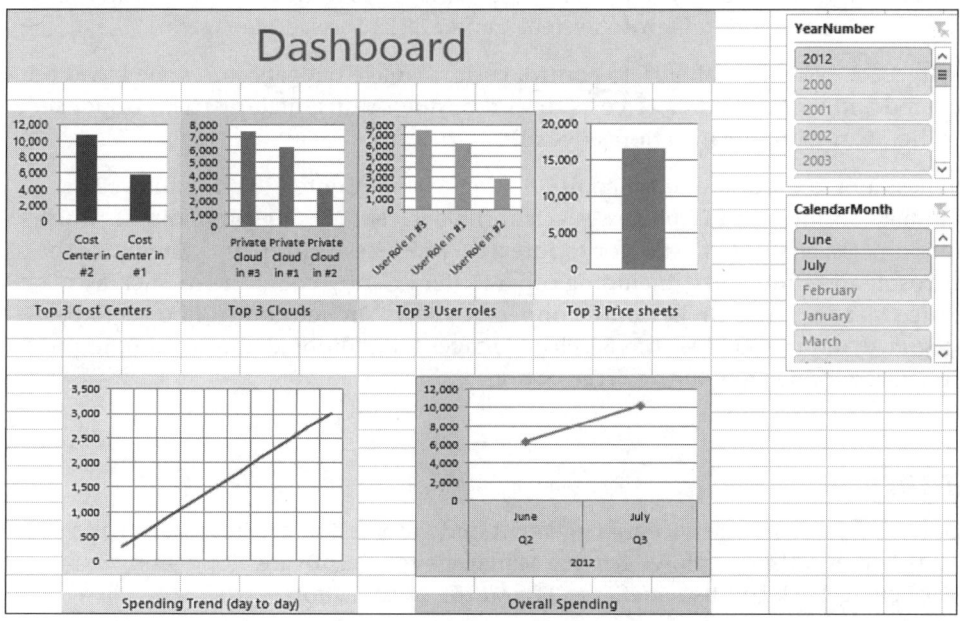

FIGURE 12.18   Chargeback Excel report dashboard.

Make a copy of this report, and modify the copy for it look to like and show the data you want to see. You also need to connect this report to the OLAP data cubes in the Service Manager data warehouse. To connect the report, follow these steps:

1. Open the Chargeback Excel report, click the Data tab, and then select **Connections**.

2. When the Workbook Connections dialog box opens, you should see a connection named .DWASDataBase SystemCenterServiceManagerChargebackCube. Click this and select **Properties**.

3. In the connection Name field, give it a new name if desired. Leave the rest of the settings to default and click **Definition**.

4. In the Definition tab, there already are connection settings to connect to your SystemCenterServiceManagerChargebackCube OLAP cube. In the Connection string field, change **localhost** in **Data Source=localhost** to the name of your Service Manager data warehouse management server.

5. Click **OK** and your chargeback Excel report is ready to pull data directly from the Service Manager data warehouse.

Fast Track

Automation and chargeback have changed significantly in this version of Service Manager. While workflows have not changed from Service Manager 2010 to 2012, chargeback and the Orchestrator connector are new to System Center 2012 Service Manager.

▶ Chargeback systems enable IT to control costs, manage budgets, and scale based on demand and usage. It shifts IT costs toward business units, making them responsible for their part of an organization's overall IT expense.

▶ Orchestrator is the automation component of System Center 2012. It allows IT to automate business and IT processes across the datacenter using runbooks. Its integration packs enable Orchestrator to integrate processes with many systems, both Microsoft and third party, including other System Center components such as Service Manager. The Orchestrator connector allows Orchestrator runbooks to be integrated and triggered within Service Manager for additional automation, improving self-service delivery to the organization.

Summary

This chapter discussed how service management and automation are important parts of IT today. The chapter further explored Service Manager's role in private cloud along with an overview of chargeback and its benefits to IT and the organization.

The chapter also covered how to configure the different areas of functionality that enables automation in Service Manager and how to configure and use chargeback. The next chapter discusses Problem Management.

Problem Management

System Center Service Manager implements and automates the Problem Management process. The primary objectives of Problem Management are to identify the root cause of problems and initiate activity to create workarounds or permanent solutions to those problems. These activities are primarily technical and performed outside the service management tool. Service Manager provides an interface to manage the problem life cycle with interfaces to other management functions such as Incident Management and Change Management.

Chapter 3, "MOF, ITIL, and System Center," discusses the Information Technology (IT) service management concepts and Problem Management process; this chapter discusses configuring Problem Management in Service Manager 2012. It discusses the process and explains the configuration options for Service Manager.

Understanding the Problem Management Process

A problem is defined as *the unknown cause of one or more incidents*. Problem Management is the management function that removes errors from the IT infrastructure that lead to incidents. It is related closely to Incident Management, as one or more incidents may cause a problem. However, an incident and the Incident Management process are distinct from a problem and the Problem Management process, respectively.

Comparing Incident Management with Problem Management

Think of an incident as a single instance where a user is unable to work, or a server or other IT component is unavailable. The goal of Incident Management is to resolve that incident, whatever it takes, using a workaround if necessary. Incident Management is not about determining the root cause of multiple related incidents, and for good reason—that requires ensuring incidents are resolved in a timely manner. However, someone, following some process, needs to determine the root cause of multiple incidents; this is the function of Problem Management.

In Incident Management, analysts search for the root cause of problems or provide workarounds to try to minimize the impact of the problem until it can be resolved. Problems could be defined by analyzing logged incidents or events. Multiple, similar incidents logged in a given period of time could lead to creating a problem work item. Regularly reviewing the top *N* incidents can also help determine patterns for creating problem work items. Tasks could include reviewing resolution information and recurring similar incidents, or analyzing incidents for a specific service.

In contrast, Problem Management can result in one of the following:

▶ Creating an RFC (request for change)

▶ Defining the problem as a known error with a workaround

▶ Updating problem work items if the problem is resolved

The goal is to minimize the negative impact of incidents on business services caused by errors in the IT infrastructure and to prevent incidents from recurring. Problem Management includes those activities necessary to investigate the root cause of incidents and determine their resolution. Any resolution is implemented through appropriate control procedures, in particular Change Management and Release Management.

Problem Management Functionality

Service Manager provides an interface for managing the problem life cycle. You can configure notifications, workflows, and console customizations to enable this process. Other functionality follows:

▶ **Problem class:** The `Problem` class in Service Manager includes properties that define a problem's work items. Although the problem management process management packs do not include Problem Management workflows, you can extend the default class and functionality as needed.

▶ **Problem management process management packs:** These management packs include knowledge to link problem work items with one or more incident or change work items. These related work items could include information to help resolve a problem.

▶ **Operations Manager connector:** You can use the Operations Manager connector to extend Problem Management functionality, similar to Incident Management. Those problem work items based on incidents created by the connector contain information about the alert (the Operations Manager management pack that defines the alert includes information related to the event); this information assists in diagnosing the problem.

▶ **Knowledge:** Service Manager Problem Management maintains problem information with appropriate workarounds and resolutions; this helps reduce the number and impact of incidents over time. As such, Problem Management has a strong interface with Knowledge Management.

This process does not have to be complicated. You could begin by selecting the top 5 to 10 incidents in your business critical services. Analyzing these incidents may result in creating a problem work item and determining the root cause of the error.

Effective Problem Management requires identifying individuals involved in the process and their role in each process activity, and defining an effective Incident Management process. Only the Problem Analyst role exists in Service Manager by default; you can create additional user roles as necessary.

To assist with process definition, the following terms are used with Problem Management. More information is available in Chapter 3:

▶ **Problem:** This is an unknown error, the underlying cause of one or more incidents.

▶ **Error:** An error is a fault, bug, or behavior issue in an IT service or system.

▶ **Root cause:** This is the specific reason contributing most directly to the occurrence of an error.

▶ **Known error:** A known error is a problem for which a root cause and permanent fix or workaround is identified, but the fix is not yet implemented. This is an error that has been observed and documented.

▶ **Workaround:** This is a temporary fix or technique eliminating the end user's reliance on the faulty service component.

You can build a Problem Management process with different activities, resulting in a configuration that enables this process in Service Manager. In general, following is how to split the configuration tasks:

▶ **General Problem Management settings:** These settings enable Problem Management functionality. They include settings in the Problem Management Settings area of the Administration workspace of the console, which contains the basic settings for the process.

▶ **Problem Management user roles:** The Problem Analyst role is the only predefined user role for Problem Management. This role has access to all work items, views, queues, and tasks from the problem management process management packs. You may need to define more granular access rights for your roles.

▶ **Enumeration (drop-down) lists in the Service Manager console:** These consist of a list of properties shown in drop-down lists on forms and dialog boxes. Examples include problem classification, status, and source; these contain a default set of list items you can adjust with specific values for your organization.

▶ **Problem Management customization:** Customization incorporates the Authoring Tool or custom development in Visual Studio; this could include adding or hiding fields and drop-down lists and check boxes, and creating custom workflows in your Problem Management process. Chapter 22, "Customizing Service Manager," provides additional information.

Problem Management in Service Manager

Problem Management is optimized when integrated with processes such as Incident Management, Change Management, and Configuration Management, and when it incorporates Knowledge Management.

Service Manager orchestrates interactions between the involved processes. As an example, Problem Management must gather data from Incident Management and configuration items (CIs) such as business services, computers, or software. Incident information is necessary to detect and diagnosis problems; this is extended with information about configuration items that helps define the problem's priority. Connectors can automatically update CI information in Service Manager; the quality of information in the incident work item depends on support staff including that information at the data source. The Problem Analysts user role can access this information to investigate the root cause of the problem.

Information concerning incidents or problems is important in this process. Following is how Service Manager excels in these areas:

▶ Providing information regarding CIs through the Active Directory, Operations Manager, and Configuration Manager CI connectors

▶ Using event information provided by the Operations Manager alert connector(s)

▶ Utilizing its built-in knowledge management capabilities

▶ Using its built-in capability to cross-reference CIs, knowledge articles, known errors, problems, incidents, and changes

▶ Built-in reporting and analysis functionality that facilitates proactive Problem Management

Service Manager provides extended functionality: While the service desk can log many incidents, the Operations Manager connector generates additional incidents. The connector extends Operations Manager's proactive alerting to Service Manager, such that events detected by Operations Manager become Service Manager incident work items (infrastructure problem work items are also created as necessary). This is known as *auto-ticketing*. The Operations Manager Alert connector synchronizes all knowledge information available from the Operations Manager management pack generating the event/incident related to the problem work item. When a permanent fix or workaround is determined, the analyst can create an RFC to remove the problem; this can lead to fewer recurring incidents against relevant CIs and services.

Service Manager manages the life cycle of all different elements in the Problem Management process:

▶ Problems can be created from the Incident Management view based on information on an incident form.

▶ Problems can result in known error status and have a temporary (or final) workaround defined. These work items are stored in the same database but can be differentiated from other problem work items. A known error in Service Manager is a property of a problem work item.

▶ Service Manager automates populating the configuration management database (CMDB) with information and keeping it current. CMDB information is used as context for problem forms, dialog boxes, and tasks. A service desk analyst can use the console to view problem details and related and affected items; this integration can help resolve problems.

▶ Knowledge articles can assist analysts with understanding and solving problems, and provide a platform to document workaround information for problems when a resolution is unavailable. In this way, the Problem Management process provides knowledge to the Knowledge Management process that helps incident analysts resolve incidents.

▶ Problem Management is linked to other Service Manager management functions such as Change, Incident, Configuration, Release, and Knowledge Management. This means you can look at a problem and see related incidents, services, CIs, and so on.

▶ Problem information is stored in the data warehouse for further reporting.

▶ The Problem Management process can be extended with the Authoring Tool.

Figure 13.1 provides an overview of Problem Management in Service Manager 2012.

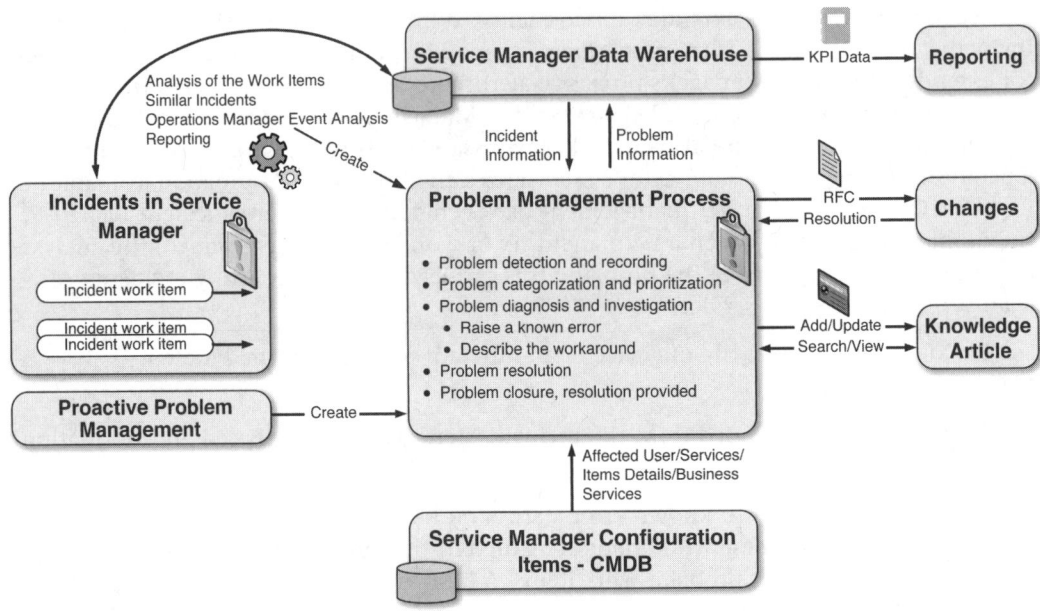

FIGURE 13.1   Problem Management in Service Manager 2012.

Building a Problem Management team is an initial step in defining the management function. Configuration in Service Manager is associated with support team roles and occurs
in different areas of the console, the primary area being the Problem Settings area in the
Administration workspace. Some of those settings follow:

▶ **Problem Work Item Prefix:** In Service Manager, all problem numbers start with the
  letters PR, although you can change the prefix that is used.

▶ **Problem File Attachment Policy:** Your company policy may limit the number of
  files that can be attached to each problem to a maximum of five and a maximum
  file size for each file of 500KB. The maximum number of attached files and
  maximum file size settings also apply to attached files in the Related Items tab for
  CIs. Note that certain tickets may require a number of attachments/screenshots to
  resolve.

To reduce storage requirements, consider establishing a policy and providing training to problem analysts for handling attachments. Consider screenshot resolution
guidelines and storing commonly used documents on a SharePoint site with a link
from Service Manager (this provides an added benefit of version control) to mitigate
the storage impact of attachments in work items.

▶ **Problem Priority Calculation:** This is rated on a scale from 1 to 9, with 1 normally the highest priority. Priority is based on a combination of impact and urgency; these settings are defined as High, Medium, or Low and are determined when the problem is created.

▶ **Problem Notifications:** Notifications can be created for problems, similar to notifications for other management functions. The notifications channel, custom problem notification templates, and subscriptions are components for building a Problem Management notification plan.

Use the Library workspace of the console to configure groups, knowledge, lists, problem queues, and tasks. A definition of these items follows:

▶ **Groups:** Groups are a collection of CIs. These can be used to assign problem work items to a specific support team.

▶ **Knowledge articles:** Knowledge articles can help service desk analysts and end users understand issues and apply workarounds for existing problems as new incidents occur. You can add knowledge to the problem work item as an additional source of information for resolving the problem.

▶ **Problem Management lists:** A problem work item is an object that includes a set of properties. A list represents a property of an object and includes one or more list items. Each list item represents a possible value selectable in the problem work item form. Service Manager includes default problem lists.

▶ **Problem queues:** Queues are used to group similar work items meeting specified criteria.

▶ **Tasks:** Tasks are actions listed to the right side of the problem work item in the console, and they automate the repetitive actions a service desk analyst performs. The Problem Management team typically uses tasks to help manage problems.

The Service Manager Authoring Tool can be used to configure or automate the Problem Management process with your own management packs. See Chapter 20, "Management Packs," and Chapter 22 for a discussion of the Authoring Tool. Chapter 23, "Advanced Customization Scenarios," includes additional information.

The next section maps Problem Management process activities to Service Manager functionality.

Problem Management Process Activities

Associating Problem Management process activities with Service Manager functionality should facilitate defining your company's Problem Management process and configuring the problem management process management packs. This provides cohesion between how you work in your processes and utilize the functionality in the tool. The "Configuring Problem Management" section later in the chapter discusses configuring this functionality in Service Manager.

Start by defining several additional key Problem Management terms. Problem Management processes can be defined as reactive or proactive:

▶ **Reactive:** Reactive Problem Management responds to reports of incident work items that have already occurred:

  ▶ The support analyst consults reports from the Incident Management process.

  ▶ The Problem Management team analyzes this information for similarities in the description of the work items.

  ▶ If a previously identified problem does not explain the symptoms, a new problem work item is created.

▶ **Proactive:** Proactive Problem Management takes preemptive steps to eliminate problems. This could include performing a trend analysis on existing problem and incident work items. Proactive Problem Management is a responsibility of other management functions and not within the scope of this book.

With Service Manager and the Operations Manager connector in place, you can proactively detect problems from the incidents (based on Operations Manager alerts) raised before an event affects a business service. You can utilize Operations Manager's proactive monitoring to obtain a closer look at errors on the back-end infrastructure of your business service.

NOTE: PROBLEM MANAGEMENT ACTIVITIES

Problem Management activities occur outside Service Manager; results are logged in a Service Manager problem work item and utilize information logged in that work item. Service Manager assists by providing a location to store related information.

The essential activities within Problem Management are discussed in Chapter 3. These activities are illustrated in Figure 13.2.

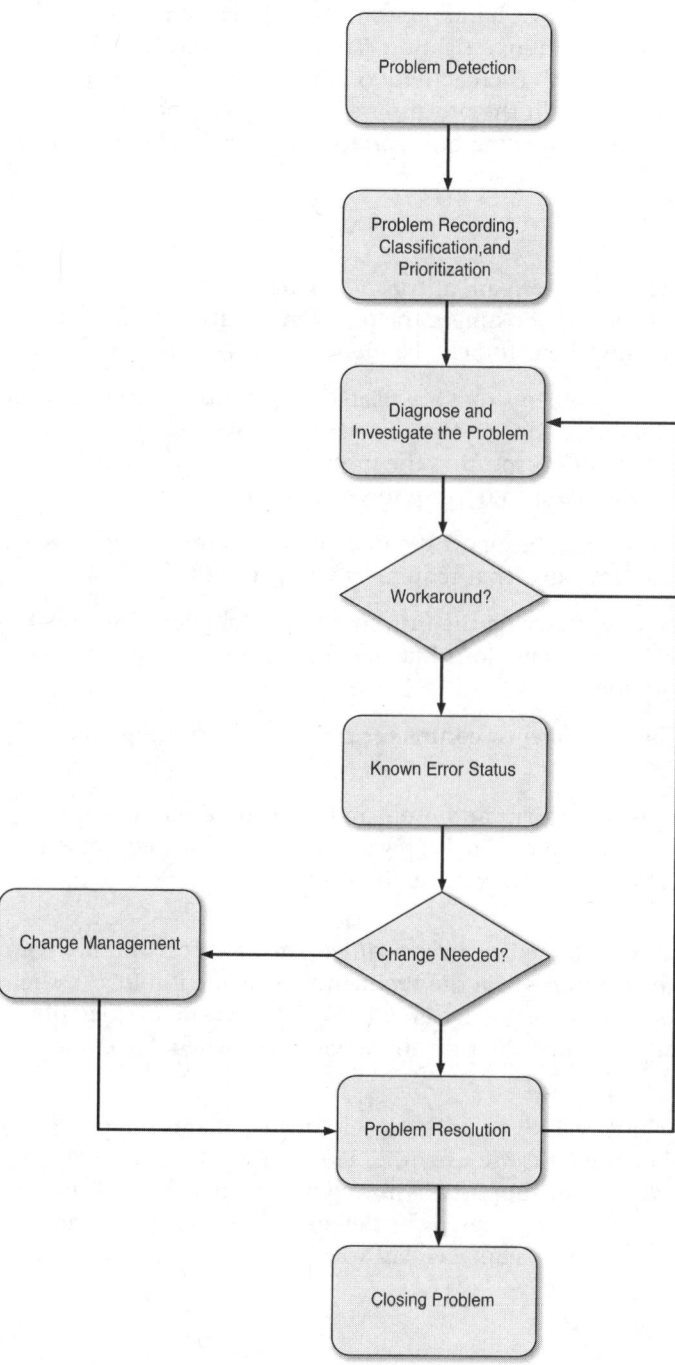

FIGURE 13.2   Activities in Problem Management.

You can recognize the activities discussed in Chapter 3; some additional activities are added to show the outcome of the problem investigation. The next sections further discuss how Service Manager can assist with each activity of the process. The process and why the activities should be included in the process are discussed in Chapter 3; this chapter extends the process information showing how Service Manager can help execute the Problem process activities.

Problem Detection

Detection focuses on incidents without a permanent fix and recurring incidents on business services. Problems can be detected by looking at the top N incidents or analyzing logged incidents; these may occur anywhere and can be identified in various ways:

▶ The service desk could identify problems that are related or the cause of one or more incident work items. For example, a service desk analyst may have resolved an incident without determining its cause. Suspecting the problem is likely to recur, the analyst can raise a problem work item to try to resolve the underlying cause.

▶ Analysis of an incident by a technical support group could reveal there is an underlying problem, or that a problem exists that requires investigation.

▶ A problem could be detected by analyzing the infrastructure or application-related incident work item created by the Operations Manager connector; this may reveal the need for a problem work item.

▶ Notification of a problem by a supplier or contractor could be the starting point for creating a problem work item.

▶ Frequent and regular analysis of incident and problem data is necessary to identify trends. This requires meaningful and detailed categorization of incidents/problems and regular reporting of patterns in areas with high occurrence.

Problems that are detected must be evaluated against recorded known errors and problem work items. The information can be accessed via the Problem Management folder in the Work Items workspace of the console. A knowledge article should be created to describe the workaround. This may already be a first filter for the service desk when detecting and defining problems.

The Service Manager console includes work items, views, and queues that can assist in detecting problems. You should configure those user roles required for the various functions; specifics depend on the size of your support environment. You may have dedicated personnel assigned to Problem Management roles; a smaller-sized support environment may combine these roles with other service management roles.

The Service Manager features involved follow:

▶ **Service Manager reporting:** Reporting provides access to incident information and can be used for trend analysis and to analyze incident recurrence.

▶ **Operations Manager Alert connector:** The connector automatically creates incidents based on alert subscriptions in Operation Manager. Additional information from the Operations Manager alert is included with the incident work item. This information can be useful in root cause analysis.

▶ **Incident Management:** Incident Management information can be analyzed. The incident work item is important when investigating the error. Incident work items can be integrated into the problem work item as related items.

Problem Recording, Classification, and Prioritization

As discussed in the previous section, problems are detected in various ways. After detection, the next activity is recording the problem. This facilitates classifying the problem, prioritizing its resolution, and linking it to work items of existing incidents. After you record a problem, assess its impact on the business services and determine the urgency of resolving it.

TIP: TAKE PROBLEM SEVERITY INTO ACCOUNT FOR PRIORITIZING PROBLEMS

Problem prioritization made during the recording activity should also consider its severity. Severity in this context refers to how serious it is from a business service perspective.

In the Service Manager console, the Create Problem work item task is available in different work item forms and tasks; this assists in integration with other management functions. Figure 13.3 illustrates the default Problem Management form. When you select the Create Problem task from a single incident work item or CI, the problem work item form is prepopulated with information from that incident work item/CI. You can select multiple items to define the related items in the form.

Similar to Incident Management, every problem work item has an impact and urgency that defines its priority. The impact describes the potential to which the business is vulnerable, and urgency illustrates the time available to avert, or at least reduce, that impact. Both define a problem work item's priority.

Information regarding the affected CI or business service is important when defining the problem work item. As with other Service Manager management functions, data source information must be current and valid; otherwise, information on the affected CIs is outdated or invalid and may lead to incorrect decisions.

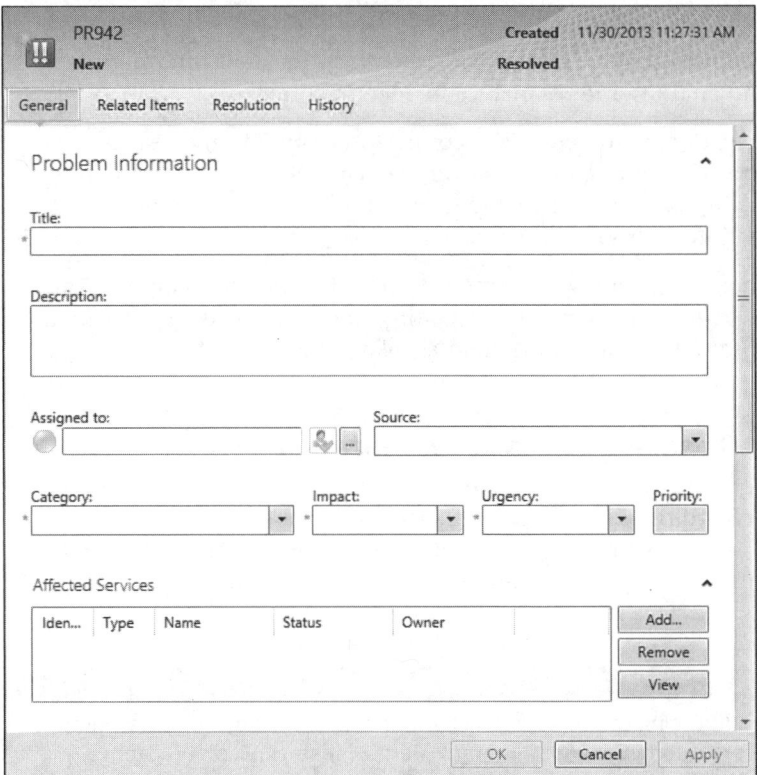

FIGURE 13.3   Default Problem Management form in Service Manager.

NOTE: DEFINING PROBLEM CLASSIFICATION AND PRIORITIZATION

Both Incident Management and Problem Management settings in Service Manager have classification lists and a prioritization matrix. Keeping classification lists consistent between the two functions can provide more effective communication when dealing with related incidents and problems.

Utilizing business services in Service Manager can be important when recording the problem. The ability to look at involved CIs, incident history, and other items related to the business service enables a detailed problem definition.

The Service Manager features involved follow:

▶ **Default problem form:** Service Manager includes a problem form based on problem work item class properties and relationships (refer to Figure 13.3). You can extend this form to include additional problem work items; see Chapter 22 for information.

▶ **Incident Management:** An important input for Problem Management is information gathered by Incident Management. A well-performing Incident Management process is required for effective Problem Management.

▶ **Configuration items:** CIs are a primary source of information and can be imported into Service Manager automatically with connectors. The Problem Management team uses CI information to make decisions, and loses time or makes incorrect decisions if this is outdated or incomplete.

▶ **Business services:** Defining business services assists with Problem Management, as the Problem Management team can easily categorize and prioritize problem work items based on the affected business service.

Problem Investigation and Diagnosis

Investigating problems is similar to investigating incidents (see Chapter 11, "Incident Management"), but the primary objective is significantly different:

▶ The Problem Management process activity deals with investigating the problem and diagnosing the root cause of one or more incidents.

▶ Incident investigation focuses on service recovery, with the root cause of an incident potentially undetermined even when the incident is closed.

As part of your investigation, consider recreating the failure in a lab environment to understand what went wrong and find the most appropriate and cost-effective resolution. You can add these results to the problem work item.

You may determine a workaround for the incidents created by the problem. This could be a temporary approach to overcome service difficulties, or a permanent workaround should the indicated change be cost-prohibitive. Once a workaround is determined, keep the problem record open and document details of the workaround with the problem work item. In Service Manager, you can mark the problem work item with a Known Error status when a workaround is found (more information is in the next section).

Following the Information Technology Infrastructure Library (ITIL) definitions of Problem Management, the Problem Management process includes dealing with high impact and/ or urgent issues that require additional planning, coordination, resources, and communication, and may result in initiating a formal project. You can associate these problems in Service Manager with a priority status on the problem work item.

The Service Manager features involved follow:

▶ **Incident Management:** Information in the related incident work item is important during diagnosis and investigation. Management pack information from incidents created with the Operations Manager connector can provide further information for diagnosis and investigation.

▶ **Service Manager knowledge:** Using the functionality available in the initial support activity and with other management functions, the Problem Management team can search for documented solutions or workarounds using different search providers. Knowledge articles can be created to document workarounds and/or known errors.

▶ **Configuration items:** CIs in Service Manager are an important source of information used by the Problem Management team during this activity.

▶ **Business services:** Defining business services in Service Manager enables the service desk to see the service relationship on a configuration item. When investigating problems, the problem work item includes all related information around the service, such as other open incidents or configuration items that enable the service.

Known Error Control in Service Manager

The known error control process addresses correcting known errors. Think of it as bug tracking for the production environment. Support teams can use this process as such, and should transfer any problems, such as bugs in Microsoft Team Foundation Server (TFS) and known errors in the system, as they release services, applications, or infrastructure solutions. The objective is to change components or procedures to remove known errors affecting the infrastructure and prevent incidents from recurring.

The known error designation is included with the resolution information on a problem work item (see Figure 13.4). A problem work item in Service Manager can be marked as a known error when the root cause of the problem is determined and a workaround identified. The error description and the workaround's description for the known error are specified on the Resolution tab of the problem form. While the process flowchart in Figure 13.2 indicates this is a mandatory step, it is not a mandatory field in the Service Manager problem form. This implies that the property must be defined before closing a problem work item.

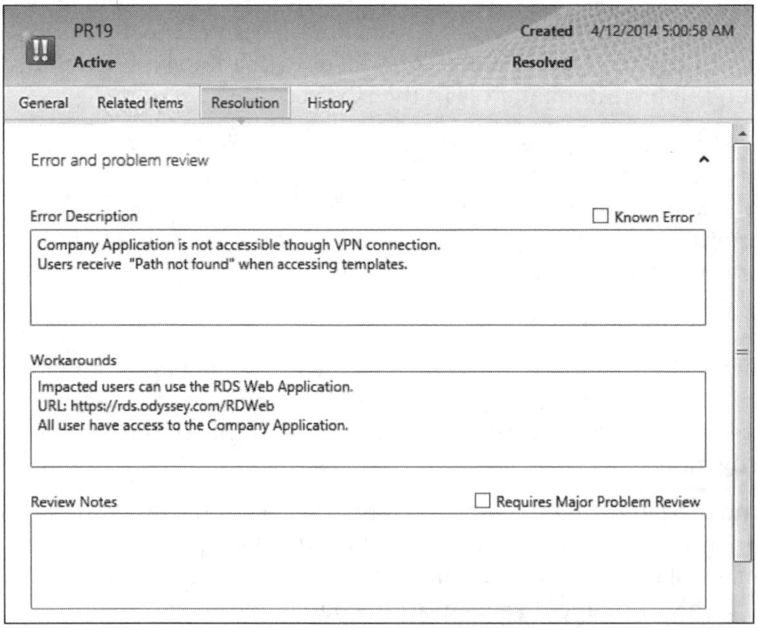

FIGURE 13.4   Known error in default problem form.

You might want to create a known error record, describe the workaround, and create a company knowledge base article even earlier in the Problem Management process. Informing the support team of a workaround means that they can apply it immediately in daily operations. Although the diagnosis may be incomplete or not include a workaround, the authors recommend setting a concrete procedural point in the process to raise the problem work item as a known error. This enables the support team to search in Service Manager and find the knowledge article information, eventually resolving the incident by applying the workaround or associating new incidents with an existing problem.

Service Manager enables marking a problem work item as a known error and initiating a change request to implement the fix or workaround. Steps around this activity are defined in your Problem Management process. For example, notification of known error status is important because it means some progress has occurred toward fixing the problem and the support team can be informed. Service Manager's notification functionality lets you notify a support group when a problem work item is marked as a known error. That team can review the workaround and consider it when handling incident work items.

TIP: NOT ALL KNOWN ERRORS MUST BE RESOLVED

Your organization can decide whether to allow known errors to remain. This may occur when the resolution to fix the error is cost-prohibitive, technically impossible, is resolved in a future version of the application, or requires too much time to resolve.

The following Service Manager features are involved:

► **Default problem form:** Service Manager provides known error information in the Resolution tab of the problem form. The description of the workaround is associated with the known error status of a problem work item.

► **Service Manager knowledge:** You may decide to implement a workaround as a temporary solution for a problem or implement the final solution at a later date. In any case, the support team must be informed; you can do this using information in the problem form or a knowledge article describing the procedure. Company knowledge articles can help manage this information in Service Manager.

► **Service Manager notification:** The Problem Management process should include the required steps/workflows to inform the support team of any progress in resolving the problem. Configuring accurate notifications and subscriptions in Service Manager is necessary to support this requirement.

► **Change Management:** If any change in functionality is required, an RFC must be created and approved before applying the resolution. The RFC should follow the established Change Management process in Service Manager, with the resolution applied only when the change has been approved and scheduled for release.

Problem Resolution

You should record resolution information for each known error in the problem work item. This includes information about the CIs, symptoms, and a description of the resolution. This information is then available for incident matching and provides guidance to resolve and circumvent future incidents.

When setting the problem work item status to Resolved, you can optionally select to automatically resolve all problem work item related incidents. This is a setting on the Resolution tab of the work item; it is not a global workflow applied to all resolution state changes for problems, although this could be included in your template.

The following Service Manager features are involved:

▶ **Default problem form:** Resolution information in the problem work item provides information regarding its category and description. The problem work item form consolidates this information for further handling.

▶ **Service Manager notification:** The Problem Management process should include the required steps/workflows to inform the support team of any progress in resolving the problem. This requires configuring accurate notifications and subscriptions in Service Manager.

Problem Closure

Once a change is completed (and successfully reviewed) and the problem resolved, the problem work item should be formally closed. Any related incident work items still open should be closed as well. The problem closure activity reserves time in the process to review completeness of error and resolution details.

Confirm that the record contains a full historical description of all events and update as necessary. It is vital to save all information related to CIs, symptoms, and resolution or circumvention actions related to the problem. You can create company knowledge articles and make them available to the support team, building organizational knowledge base.

Closing a problem work item can be adjusted later in Service Manager if necessary. If the provided workaround or fix does not actually solve the problem, the work item could be reopened. Service Manager 2012 includes a built-in task to reactivate a closed problem work item. Closing problems differs from procedures in Incident Management. Problem work items can be closed when a technical issue is solved (or workaround is defined); incidents are closed after user acceptance.

Major problem review can be set as a property on the work item. If set, the review can be part of the closure activity, or defined as a dedicated activity in your process. Conduct a review after each major problem to learn lessons for the future. This review could examine those things done right, wrong, and what might be done better. The review could check how to prevent recurrence of the major problem, if there is any third-party responsibility, and whether follow-up actions are needed (such as monitoring for early warnings for the error). In Service Manager, a problem work item can be marked as Review Needed, with information added after the review meeting.

The Service Manager features involved follow:

- ▶ **Default problem form:** Closing a problem provides information about its resolution category and describes the resolution. The Service Manager problem work item form maintains this information for future handling. From here, you can also resolve all incidents associated with the problem.

- ▶ **Service Manager notification:** The Problem Management process should include the required steps/workflows to keep the support team informed of any progress in resolving the problem. This requires configuring accurate notifications and subscriptions in Service Manager.

Configuring Problem Management

The "Problem Management Process Activities" section earlier in the chapter provides a summary of the Problem Management activities from a Service Manager perspective. This section presents an overview of configuration options.

The configuration required is minor and depends on your organization's Problem Management process. Settings such as prefix, priority calculation, user roles, and configuring notification are global settings; these are similar to other management functions in Service Manager. As part of the different activities in the process, the Problem Management team can record appropriate information in the problem work item form and retrieve information from different work items and CIs. Consider providing access to different user roles, configuring the Problem Management settings, and defining problem list items for your particular environment. All other requirements to enable Problem Management are provided by other management functions or outside the tool.

As with other customizations, define what you need to configure before actually starting to implement that functionality. The "Problem Management Process Activities" section of this chapter can help define the necessary functionality to enable the process. The next sections cover Problem Management configuration, including console tasks; user roles, groups, queues, and lists; general settings; and notification.

Problem Management Console Tasks

Problem work items can be created in multiple locations of the console. The Create Problem task can be initiated from the Problem Management or Incident Work item folder to create a new problem. Figure 13.5 is an example of a new problem work item form.

- ▶ On the General tab, specify work item settings such as Title, Urgency/Impact, affected CIs, and services.

- ▶ Use the Related Items tab to specify further information.

- ▶ Specify resolution information under the Resolution tab.

- ▶ The History tab logs all actions taken on the problem work item.

▶ The Tasks pane (to the right) lists tasks you can perform on a problem work item. This includes changing status, closing, resolving, and reactivating the work item. The Create Change Request task creates an RFC for those actions necessary to fix the error.

When a problem work item is created from an incident work item, the title, affected CIs, and related items are automatically included. You can also link the incident directly to an existing problem using a task in the Tasks pane.

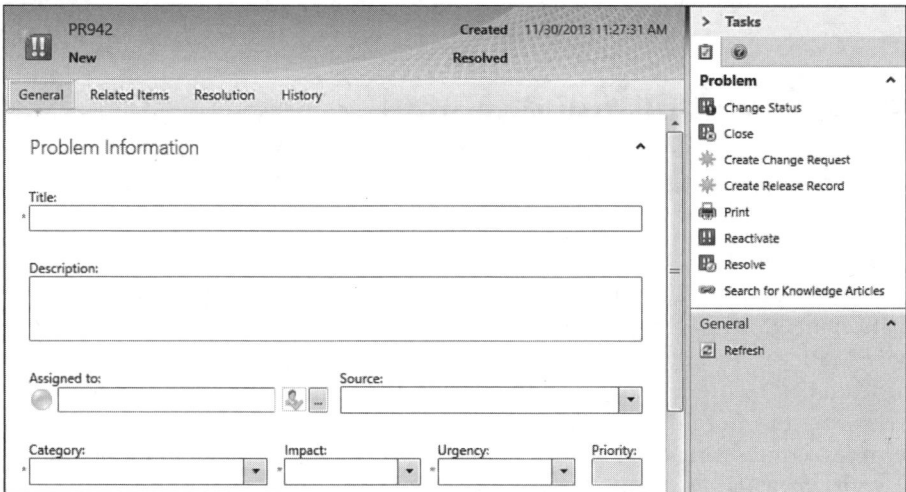

FIGURE 13.5   New problem work item form.

Problem Management User Roles, Groups, Queues, and Lists

Begin by ensuring the Problem Management team can access work items, CIs, views, and tasks. By default, the Problem Analysts user role has access to all incident work items, views, and so on. Configuring user roles for Problem Management can be difficult and depends on your specific team's setup. If there are team members that combine different roles in the overall Service Management, make sure you provide the required access to the different objects in the Service Manager console.

The process for creating Problem Management user roles is similar to that for creating user roles for Incident Management. Refer to Chapter 17, "Service Manager Security," to create user roles in Service Manager.

Several default list items in Service Manager exist for Problem Management and can be adjusted for your environment. Table 13.1 provides an overview of the default problem lists provided by the problem management process management packs.

TABLE 13.1   Problem Management Lists

List Name	Description	Management Pack
Problem Status	Problem Status List	Problem Management Library
Problem Source	Problem Source List	Problem Management Library
Problem Classification	Problem Classification List	Problem Management Library
Incident Resolution	Problem Resolution List	Problem Management Library

The authors recommend aligning the problem classification lists with those for Incident Management, providing a clear classification for both management functions. You can address urgency and impact configuration in a similar manner, described in the next section.

Configuring General Problem Management Settings

General Problem Settings is a globally scoped configuration for Problem Management. Problem ID prefix, attachments, and the priority matrix are configurable settings and are applied to each new problem work item. The configuration is similar to that of Incident Management, discussed in Chapter 11.

Configuring Priority Calculation and Target Resolution Time for Problem Work Items

Before configuring priority, first define the terms *impact* and *urgency* for your organization:

▶ **Impact:** The measure of how business critical the problem is. A best practice for priority settings in Problem Management is to align this setting with that in Incident Management.

▶ **Urgency:** The time required to resolve a problem. Urgency is the extent to which resolution of a problem or error can be delayed. As with defining impact, make this setting consistent with those for Incident Management.

Review how priority settings are defined for Incident Management and align your Problem Management priority settings appropriately. Utilize the priority levels defined for the Incident Management process and currently defined business services in Service Manager. Configuring priority levels for four or five levels is generally recommended. Make sure that you have a priority defined for major problems, as you would treat these differently from more normal operations problems.

By default, impact and urgency settings are defined as High, Medium, or Low, and are mandatory when the problem is created in Service Manager. The default impact and urgency values are adjustable by configuring the Impact List and Urgency List in the Library workspace. You can configure the priority on a problem work item with a priority calculation matrix, similar to Incident Management. Figure 13.6 illustrates the settings you can make in Service Manager 2012 for problem work item priority calculation based on impact and urgency.

Configure the urgency impact settings for Problem Management in the Service Manager console. Perform the following steps:

1. In the Administration workspace, expand **Administration -> Settings -> Problem Settings**.

2. In the Tasks pane, under Problem Settings, click **Properties**.

3. In the Problem Settings dialog, select the **Priority** tab.

4. For each of the High, Medium, and Low settings for impact and urgency, select a priority value from 1 to 9, and then click **OK**. In this example, the priority consists of five levels, similar to the Odyssey Incident Management priority configuration. Figure 13.6 displays these settings.

5. Click **OK** to close the Problem Settings dialog.

NOTE: ADJUSTING THE IMPACT AND URGENCY LIST ITEMS

As specified in this section, impact and urgency settings are defined as High, Medium, or Low. These values can be adjusted or additional levels can be defined using the Urgency and Impact List configuration in the Lists folder of the Library pane. Be careful with adjusting the values of these list items; they are applied in all work items' priority matrixes.

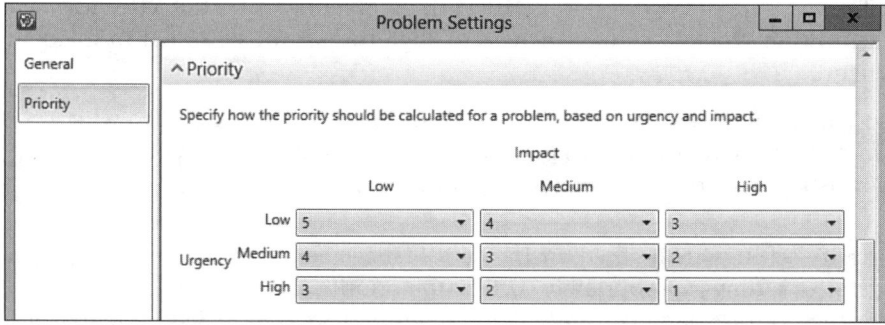

FIGURE 13.6   Sample priority calculation.

Configuring Notification

Notification is an important component of Problem Management. Team members may want to be notified when there are changes in problem status. In other cases, say for major problems, you want to notify the complete support team that a specific business service is affected. Using Service Manager, you can ensure that notifications are generated for almost any type of change. For example, you could configure sending notification subscriptions for a specific change on the problem work item. This can be for a status change of the work item, or when a property of the problem changes. A notification subscription could be created to send an email when a problem is marked as a known error. The service desk can then apply the solution to similar incidents.

NOTE: NOTIFICATION FOR PROBLEM MANAGEMENT

Notifications can be sent through Service Manager when a problem work item is created or updated. Before creating a notification subscription, there are several steps to take in Service Manager to send out notifications:

► Enable email notifications.

► Establish a notification channel with your SMTP mail server.

► Create a notification template for use with your notification messages.

Creating notifications is described in Chapter 16, "Managing Notifications."

Automating Problem Management

The Problem Management process in Service Manager does not include workflows or additional templates. Should you need certain adjustments to the default problem work item template or need to create workflows, use the Service Manager Authoring Tool and create your own management pack.

Although the console does not include an interface for Problem Management workflow configuration, you could use eXtended Markup Language (XML) to create workflows in your management pack. Review the workflow runtime in **Administration** -> **Workflows** -> **Status**. To obtain an example, you could create the workflow for Incident Management, export the management pack that includes this workflow, and review the XML syntax. For a problem workflow, change the class references to the problem class and update the criteria to meet your requirements. This is a high-level overview on how to create Problem Management workflows to apply a template. Additional information about creating management packs is in Chapter 20 and Chapter 22.

Fast Track

Functionality and configuration of the Problem Management process is unchanged from Service Manager 2010. Problem work items can be created from different processes, tasks are available to manage work items, and notifications can be configured to send email messages based on defined criteria. These support the defined process and control the life cycle of the problem work item as in the previous version.

Summary

This chapter discussed Problem Management in Service Manager. The "Understanding the Problem Management Process" and "Problem Management in Service Manager" sections of the chapter discussed the overall process and provided information on how Service Manager can help manage the problem life cycle in your environment. Using the process breakdown described in the "Problem Management Process Activities" section, you should be able to analyze your own process and map that to Service Manager settings. The "Configuring Problem Management" section discussed actual configuration in the Service Manager console, using examples to explain configuring Problem Management.

Your own process may require additional customization to the default problem management process management packs. Information about extending the problem form template and creating custom workflows and notifications is discussed in Chapter 22 and Chapter 16, respectively. Reporting requirements can have an impact on customizing your Problem Management environment; see Chapter 21, "Data Warehouse and Reporting," for additional information on this topic.

The next chapter discusses Change Management in Service Manager 2012.

Change Request and Configuration Management

Service Manager facilitates managing the life cycle of changes through the different interfaces to other management functions such as Incident, Configuration, Release, and Problem Management. Chapter 3, "MOF, ITIL, and System Center," discusses the definitions and activities in the Change Management process; this chapter builds upon that information and discusses the configuration of Change and Configuration Management in Service Manager 2012. It shows how to define your Change Management processes with templates, workflows, and notifications. The chapter describes the functionality of the different components that build a Change Management process. The initial configuration is minimal; the actual process is created using Service Manager activities. The chapter also provides information about change request configuration. It includes examples to provide a complete overview of the Change Management functionality in Service Manager 2012.

Change Management in Service Manager

Your Information Technology (IT) environment must align itself with your organization's strategy to remain competitive. This means that IT should be delivering value and that changes made to the IT environment must not disrupt the business service delivered to your users, as IT must maintain stability even during change. ITIL defines a service change as *the addition, modification, or removal of anything that could affect IT services.*

Service Manager includes an interface for managing the Change Management process. The change management process management packs installed with Service Manager provide templates, activities, and the functionality to create workflows. Change Management integrates with other management functions to provide a complete overview of impact analysis and post review activities:

▶ Change Management request work items derive from the default work item class and include details such as reason, priority, and impact as well as links to configuration items (CIs) affected by the change.

▶ A change request can be initiated directly from the CI or other work items, using predefined templates to ensure accurate and consistent recording.

▶ The change management process management packs provide flexibility to adapt and change review stages in accordance with your organization's guidelines and policies.

▶ Change Management process steps are activities in the change request template. Activity Management provides manual, review, parallel, sequential, dependent, and runbook automation activity templates. Change request templates are created for similar change requests with activities defined in the process.

▶ Communication is important in the Change Management process. Notification functionality is integrated with Change Management and can send out notifications based on a criteria list with predefined email templates.

▶ Change request event workflows can be used to apply templates and send notifications. You could also use workflows to automate evaluating a request. For example, checking required fields for values can quickly verify whether the change request is valid.

The basis of Change Management is the configuration baseline; this is where the current state of the CIs in scope of the change is documented. Defining the scope of the change or reviewing its impact requires current information regarding affected and related CIs. Service Manager connectors can automate this information from different data sources.

The change request in Service Manager begins with creating the change work item in the console. A change template is selected, which ensures the defined path is followed for the change. Six Change Management templates are preinstalled; you can adjust these to your needs. Table 14.1 lists the default change request types.

TABLE 14.1   Change Request Types

Type of Change	Description	Example
Standard Change Request	These are preapproved and used for low-risk, pretested change operations.	Installation of an approved standard software package.
Minor Change Request	Minor change requests can be approved by a change manager. Use these for low-risk and low-impact changes according to the change policies of your organization.	Weekly update of a virus identification file.
Major Change Request	These should be screened by the change manager. The change advisory board (CAB) approves the initial request and change deployment as two separate review activities. This type of request includes a post-implementation review. Use the Major Change Request template for high-risk/high impact changes according to the change policies of your organization.	Implementing/upgrading companywide software.
Emergency Change Request	Emergency change requests are used for urgent changes that should be implemented in less than 24 hours and cannot follow the normal Change Management process. These should be approved by the emergency CAB (ECAB) and contain a mandatory post-implementation review. These are used for urgent changes according to the change policies of your organization.	The replacement of a firewall due to a broken network card.
Security Release	Use this template for security patch scenarios. It includes typical steps for planning, developing, testing, and rolling out security patches in the IT environment.	Monthly patching of the environment with new release security patches.
Publish Offering	This template can be used for change requests on service and request offerings.	New, update, or remove request offerings published on the self-service portal.

You can select change request templates from the Service Manager console or apply them using workflows. Service Manager provides templates for review, manual, parallel, sequential, dependent, and runbook automation activities. You could also extend Service Manager to include your own custom activities.

Change Management workflows can be created to apply a change template or send a notification when a certain criterion on the work item is fulfilled. Activity workflows can be used similarly to other workflows. These workflows can apply an activity template and send notifications. An example of using an activity workflow is to check whether the activity implementer is specified; if not, apply a template to assign this activity to a default group. Having unassigned activities can delay the change's implementation and negatively affect the change.

Service Manager orchestrates the interactions between the processes, and the Service Manager console is used to manage change requests. While actual implementation of the change is outside Service Manager, you can enforce the steps in the process using the activities in change request templates. Change Management reports provide precise information making it easy to evaluate your change processes. These reports include Change Management KPI Trend, Change Request Details, and List of Change Requests.

Figure 14.1 provides an overview of Change Management in Service Manager 2012 and summarizes the process.

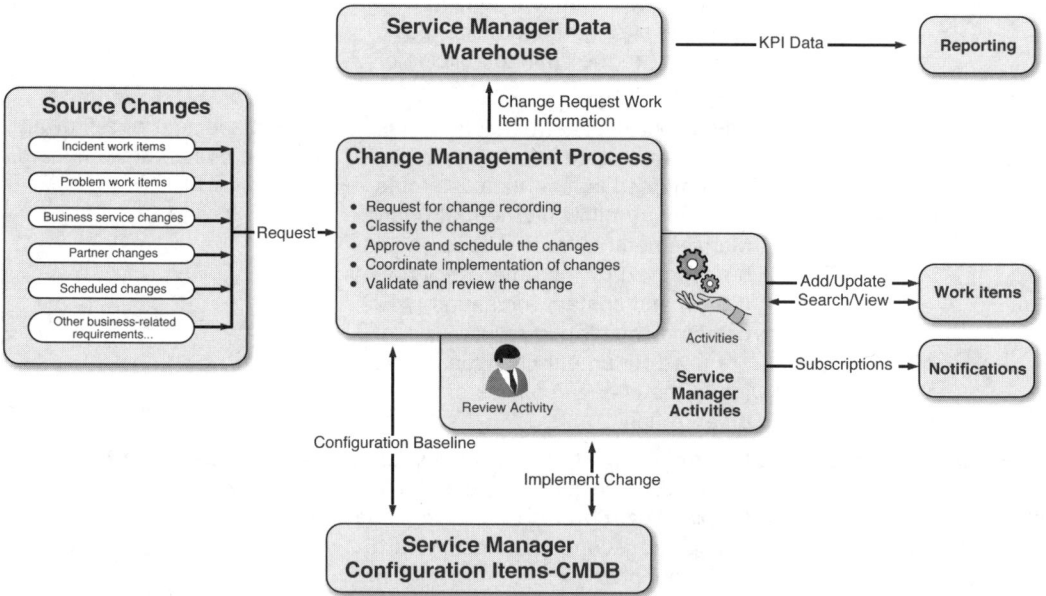

FIGURE 14.1   Change Management in Service Manager 2012.

Configuring Change Management occurs in different areas of the Service Manager console, the primary area being the Change Request Settings area in the Administration workspace. Some of those settings follow:

▶ **Configuring Change Request Work Item Prefix:** Service Manager 2012 prepends all change request work item numbers with CR. Activities in the Change Management process use the AC prefix for Activity, MA for Manual Activity, and RA for Review Activity. This is modifiable.

▶ **Change Request File Attachment Policy:** The maximum number of attached files and maximum file size (64 kilobytes [KB]) policy specified in the Change Management Settings apply to the attached files in the Related Items tab on the change request form.

Note that certain change work items may require a number of attachments or screenshots to document the change. Evaluate this option to store commonly used documents on a Change Management SharePoint site that is accessible with a link from Service Manager. SharePoint adds version control to the change document library and is accessible outside the Service Manager console.

▶ **Change Request Notifications:** Notifications can be created as with other management functions. The notifications channel, change and activity notification templates, and subscriptions are components used to build your notification plan for Change Management. See Chapter 16, "Managing Notifications," for more information.

Use the Library workspace of the console to configure groups, knowledge, queues, change and activity management lists, change request queues, and tasks.

The Service Manager Authoring Tool can be used to extend or automate the Change Management process with your own activities or custom workflows. Chapter 20, "Management Packs," and Chapter 22, "Customizing Service Manager," discuss this tool.

The next section maps change request process activities to Service Manager functionality.

Change Management Process Activities

Change Management process activities define a roadmap for the change requiring implementation. You should create a change request work item for even the smallest change, as any undocumented change could have an impact. For trivial changes or those repeated at intervals, you might establish standard procedures that do not require approval on a case-by-case basis. You could simplify the Change Management process for these types of changes with predefined templates that create the change request work item, event workflows, and appropriate notification subscriptions for the requested change.

The Change Management process activities are illustrated in Figure 14.2, which provides an overview of the process flow to determine the required changes and implement them with minimal adverse impact to the business service. You should evaluate and examine each activity to determine Service Manager technology usage and optimization.

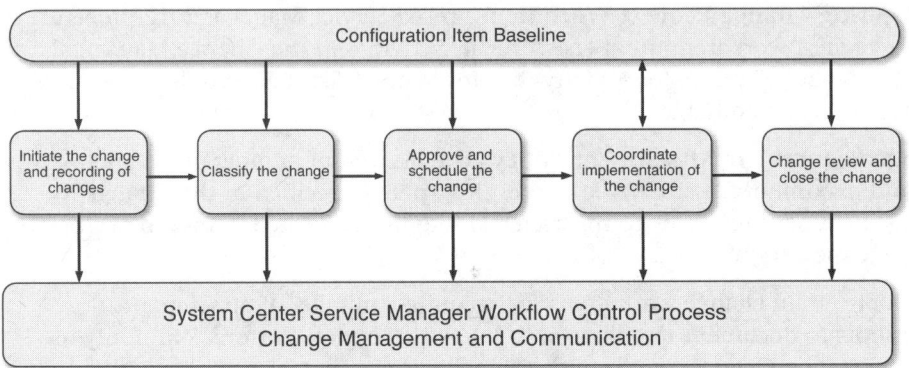

FIGURE 14.2   Activities in Change Request Management.

A description of the process activities follows:

- **Configuration item baseline:** This is the baseline of a configuration that has been formally agreed upon and is managed through Change Management. The baseline is used as a basis for future changes and can be used for restoring to a known configuration if a change fails.

- **Initiate and record the change:** Information provided with the change request work items is used as input for upcoming activities. At a minimum, the following is required: date received, unique identifier of the RFC, and description of the proposed change.

- **Classification of the change:** Once the RFC is recorded, a preliminary assessment should be made of its validity and importance. After it is accepted, it should be assigned a priority and category depending on urgency and impact.

- **Approve and schedule the change:** In this activity, the CAB should analyze and, where appropriate, approve the pending RFCs and prepare the schedule of changes. Effective Change Management requires planning. Information on CIs and other work items can provide input for appropriate change implementation planning.

- **Coordinate implementation of the change:** While Change Management is not responsible for implementing the change (Release Management is), it is responsible for supervising and coordinating the process from beginning to end. Implementation steps are Service Manager activities; these configured activities should reflect the designed implementation roadmap.

- **Change review and closing the change:** Before closing the change request work item, you should evaluate its implementation. This enables assessing the impact of the change to the organization's business service.

Configuration Item Baselines

Creating a configuration item baseline is described in the MOF guidance and is important to mention, as Service Manager can create these baselines.

An up-to-date CMDB allows you to create a configuration baseline and use this in different processes. The baseline is a snapshot taken at a specific point in time. In the case of Change Management, this snapshot could be used for a definition of the original state of an affected CI or service. After the change is implemented, it can be tracked in relation to this baseline.

Service Manager does not include functionality to document configuration baselines. As an alternative, you could gather this information in a document and attach the file as a related item to the CI or service.

TIP: TAKE CONTROL OF DATA SOURCE OF THE CONNECTORS

Service Manager uses connectors to create or update information from a data source such as Active Directory or Configuration Manager into the Service Manager database. You should define your own processes to ensure only valid CIs are imported into Service Manager. As an example of such a process, user and computer objects could be created in a temporary organizational unit (OU) in Active Directory; once they become active, they are moved to an OU being monitored by the Service Manager connector. If you have implemented System Center Configuration Manager, you could use a dedicated collection to import and update configuration items. When the CIs are retired, they are removed from the monitored OU and collection. Using this type of configuration lets only "managed" CIs be present in the CMDB.

Say an update needs to be made to a production application to introduce new functionality. Based on the business service defined for this application, you can determine the type, risk, and impact of the change request. Adding CI information to the relevant fields of the change request form would enable you to submit a complete set of information for approval and scheduling. The implementation then changes CI settings or properties; the CMDB information must be updated either as part of the process or via the connectors. In addition, all activity history in the Change Management process is logged on the change work item.

The Service Manager features involved follow:

▶ **Service Manager connectors:** Importing and updating CI information provides accurate CI information used during different activities of the process.

▶ **Configuration Management:** The Configuration Management process maintains information about the CIs required for delivering an IT service, including their relationships. In addition to configuring the connectors, you must define a process to control CI data in Service Manager.

Initiating and Recording Changes

The initiating and recording activity initiates an RFC by opening a change request form and entering information about the requested change. Initiating the RFC starts with selecting the type of change. For Service Manager, this corresponds to selecting a change request template; Figure 14.3 shows the selection dialog displayed when you create a new change request. Templates created for the `Change Management` class appear in the list of available change request templates; the items shown on this list can be limited through Change Management user roles. The Change Initiators role can be scoped on groups, queues, tasks, and templates; Change Initiators see only those templates to which they have rights. For additional information on scoping, see Chapter 17, "Service Manager Security."

CAUTION: SELECTING CHANGE REQUEST TEMPLATES

Be aware that once you select a template, you can't go back to select another template. For example, should you select a standard change, enter it, and later decide it is a minor change, you must reenter the change as a minor change. This makes it important to train IT analysts as to which types of changes qualify for each type (emergency, major, and so on).

Templates have predefined fields and change work item activities to simplify creating the RFC and to ensure appropriate procedures are followed. Service Manager includes six change request templates you can adjust to your organization's needs, and you could create additional templates for specific recurring changes.

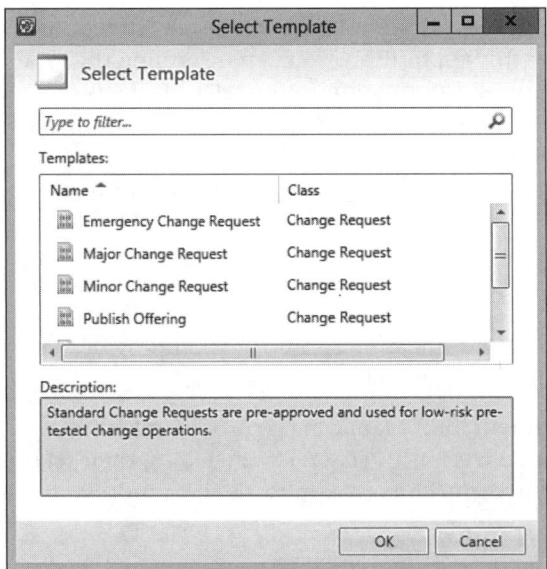

FIGURE 14.3   The change request template selection.

You can initiate change requests in Service Manager from any configuration item or work item in the console. This opens a new change request form and automatically associates the selected item with the new change request (Figure 14.4 shows the default form). Linked CIs such as services, computers, printers, software, knowledge articles, and other custom imported classes can be specified in the Config Items To Change section (see Figure 14.5).

You can use the Planning tab to include all change implementation plans and planning related information. On this page, implementation, risk assessment, test, and backout plan information can be specified. Start and end dates for the change request can be provided as well. Figure 14.6 shows the Planning tab.

The steps to implement the change are in the activity workflow specified on the Activities tab. Each template available in the selection can include a different flow of activities. You can use review, manual, parallel, sequential, dependent, and runbook automation activity templates to create the desired flow. Add activities by using the green plus sign (+) on the upper-right side of the page. Next to this icon are buttons to delete activities, change the size of the activity icons, and change the view of the activity workflow.

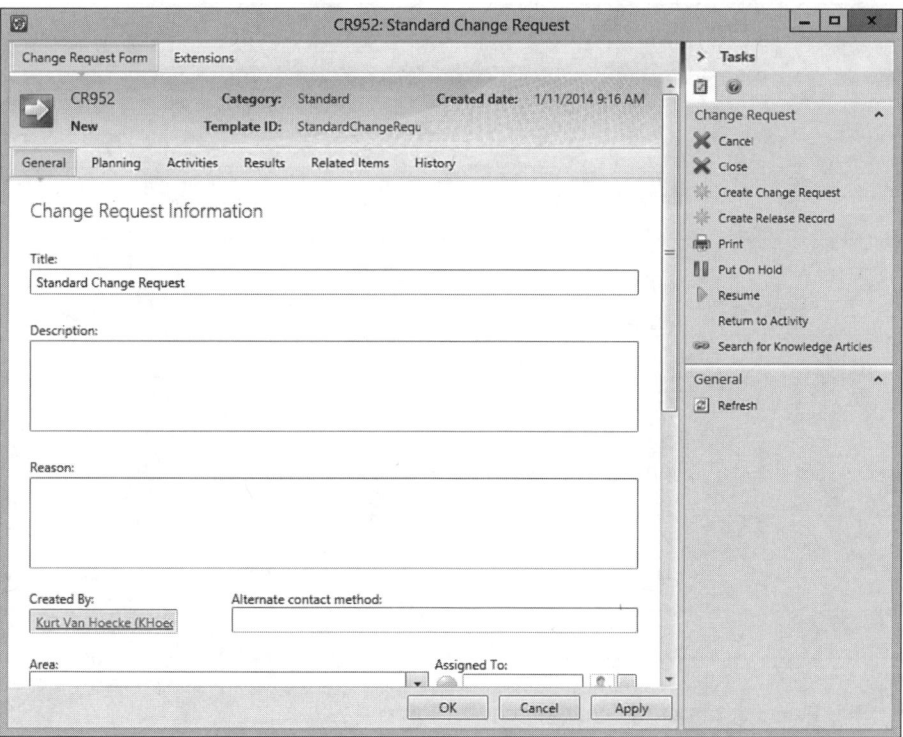

FIGURE 14.4   The default change request form.

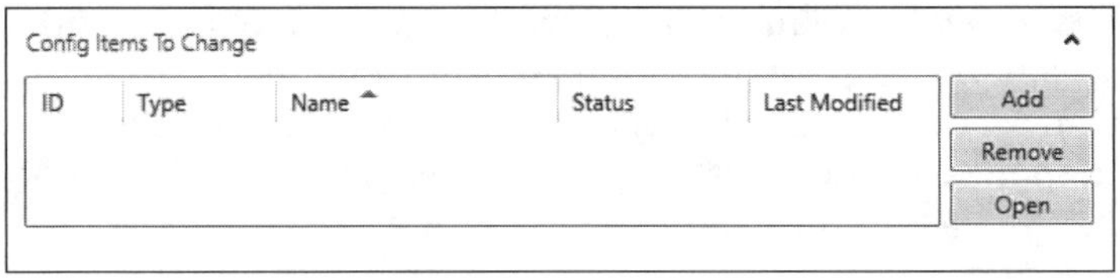

FIGURE 14.5   The Config Items To Change list view of the change request form.

You can adjust the activity workflow defined in the template at any time, and add or remove different types of activities as needed. Figure 14.7 illustrates the activity workflow in the Standard Change Request template. You can edit each activity added to the flow by double-clicking it, or right-clicking the activity and selecting **Open**. Figure 14.8 shows available actions for the activity. You cannot delete an activity in a change request if the change request is in progress; however, you can skip the activity or place the change request on hold and then delete the activity. The different activity types are explained in the "Coordinating Change Implementations" section later in this chapter.

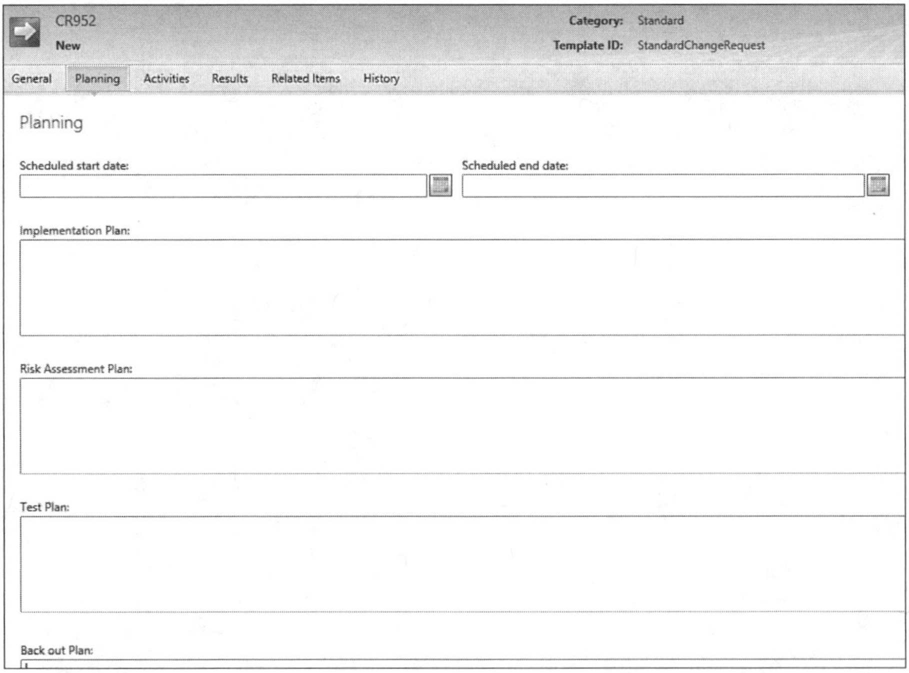

FIGURE 14.6   The Planning tab of the change request form.

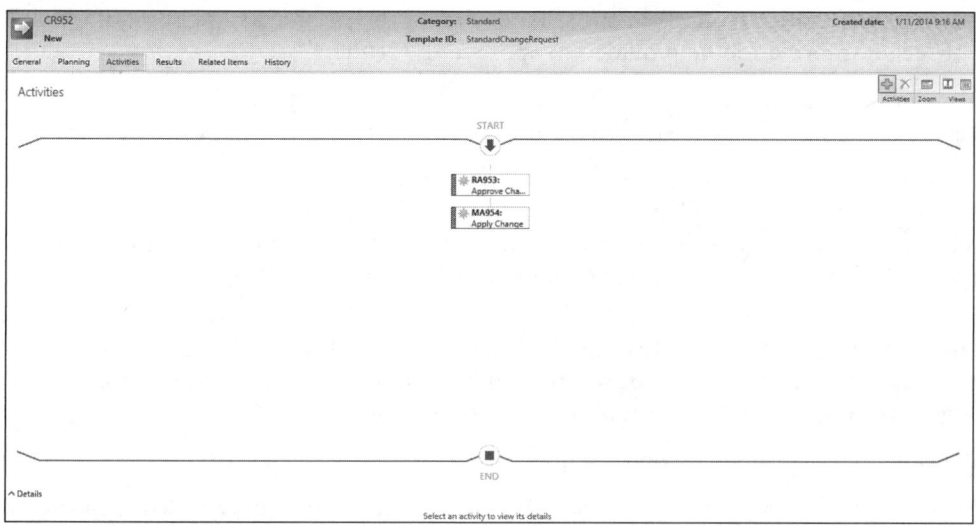

FIGURE 14.7   Activity workflow.

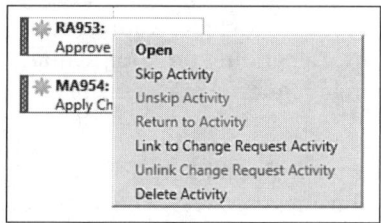

FIGURE 14.8   Configuring the activity.

Work items such as incidents, other change requests, and problems are related to the change request and can be linked to the work item using the Related items tab.

Service Manager Change Management functionality is adjustable to meet the requirements of your organization. You must evaluate whether the change request templates you need are available, whether the default form includes all required fields, and that the Change Management user roles are defined such that change requests can be created and coordinated. There are two user roles by default: Change Initiators and Change Managers. Similar to with other management functions in Service Manager, these roles are globally scoped and cannot be deleted; you can only associate users or groups to these roles. You can create additional user roles as needed with access specified to queues, groups, tasks, views, and templates.

Different types of change requests in the Change Management process might require that different sets of information be provided to approve the request.

▶ For minor changes, you could add a simple indication of what the change involves to the Planning tab of the change request form.

▶ For other types of requests, you might need to create an implementation, risk assessment, test, and backout plan. You could add a URL to your document library system, such as SharePoint, as a related item in the change request form. Figure 14.6 illustrated the location in the form for adding this type of information.

It is important that the appropriate individuals be notified of the request. Use notification subscriptions to trigger a notification when a change request work item is properly created or changed. For information about notifications, see Chapter 16.

The Service Manager features involved follow:

▶ **Default change request form:** A default change request form is provided with the change management management packs. This form provides tabs and fields to include the information necessary for requesting the change.

▶ **Change event templates:** Change request templates are useful for creating a change request for a recurring type of issue; you can set a category and define a standard priority, effect, and risk level in the template. Service Manager includes a number of templates to use for creating change request work items. Depending on your Request process, you might create additional templates for change request work items or to use in change request event workflows.

▶ **Change event notification:** The Change Management team should keep the user informed of any changes that could affect production business services. This requires configuring accurate notifications and subscriptions.

▶ **Configuration items:** CIs in Service Manager are the primary source of information during the Change Management process. The Change Management process and implementation team makes decisions based on this information, and might lose time or make incorrect decisions if the information is outdated or incomplete. Connectors automate importing CI object information into Service Manager.

▶ **Activities:** An activity is a set of actions designed to achieve a particular result. Activities are defined as part of the process and are used to build an activity workflow that implements the desired future state.

▶ **Change request event workflows:** Change request event workflows can evaluate the change request when it is created. Using a set of criteria, a change template could be applied and notifications sent.

Classifying Changes

Requests for changes should be reviewed by a change manager. Some requests may not be practical or feasible; other requests might be a duplication of efforts. Once the RFC is recorded, there should be a preliminary assessment of the request's validity and importance. Classifying the change request involves setting its priority, impact, and risk. This could indicate the change request can go further in the process for approval, or that a different process needs to be followed (a different type of change template). Within ITIL, the "seven R's" of Change Management is a quick checklist that is a good starting point for evaluating a request for change. This list is a practical and common sense way to minimize change rejection at the first point of logging changes:

▶ Who *raised* the change?

▶ What is the *reason* for the change?

▶ What *return* is required from the change?

▶ What *risks* are there if you do or do not carry out the change?

▶ What *resources* are required to perform this change?

▶ Who is *responsible* for building, testing, and implementing the change?

▶ What *relationships* exist between this and other changes?

The classification categories (area, priority, impact, and risk) in the change request are predefined values (list items) selectable in the change request form that can be adjusted to comply with your organization's needs. Change request templates can predefine classification fields and change activities.

Configuration item information in scope of the requested change is important input during the classification phase. Although a requested change may appear to be simple, it could affect an important business service. This type of information can be retrieved on the CI.

The Service Manager features involved follow:

▶ **Default change request form:** A change request form is provided with the change management management packs. You can review the change request information and use a console task to update status.

▶ **Change Management lists:** These are lists of properties that display in drop-down lists on forms and dialog boxes. An example is Change Priority; this list contains a default set of list items that can be adjusted with specific values for your organization.

▶ **Configuration items:** CIs are a major source of information. The change manager uses this information during execution of this activity.

▶ **Change request event workflows:** Based on classification, the appropriate templates can be assigned via workflows to automate the Change Management process.

14

Approving and Scheduling Changes

Approval of a change request is driven by its category. The approval process for a major or emergency change request can begin by presenting the change to the appropriate change reviewers. These key people represent many perspectives and are held accountable for the results of the change. Differing from the "seven R's" in the change classification activity, the CAB evaluates the change request for approval in a somewhat different perspective:

▶ What are the expected benefits of the proposed change?

▶ Do these benefits justify the costs entailed by the Change Management process?

▶ What are the associated risks?

▶ Are there necessary resources available to make the change with certainty of success?

▶ Can the change be postponed?

▶ What is the general impact on the IT infrastructure and quality of service?

▶ Could the change affect established IT security levels?

You can use user and group CIs mapped to Active Directory users and groups to identify change reviewers. Individual reviewers represent and vote for themselves; group reviewers contain multiple users, and any member of the group could vote on behalf of the group. Service Manager review activities can use one of the following voting logic types by default (additional approval conditions can be created using the approval list in the Library workspace):

▶ **Unanimous:** All reviewers must vote at this review activity.

▶ **Percentage:** Defines a minimum percent of reviewers that must vote for approval.

▶ **Automatic:** This can be used for automatically approved review activities.

Figure 14.9 shows the review activity form.

You might also use the Active Directory Manager property on a user object with the Line Manager Should Review check box in Figure 14.9. When the check box is selected, the manager of the user creating the change request is added as one of the reviewers. (Make sure this is set properly before implementing it, as a change can be impacted if the affected users do not have a manager defined in Active Directory.) When adding reviewers to the review activity form, two review modifiers allow enforcement of the review logic:

▶ Must Vote indicates that the reviewer cannot skip the review activity.

▶ The Has veto flag indicates that the identified reviewer can reject the review, regardless of how other reviewers vote.

Figure 14.10 shows the dialog to select a user or group as reviewer and the two check boxes used to enforce your review logic.

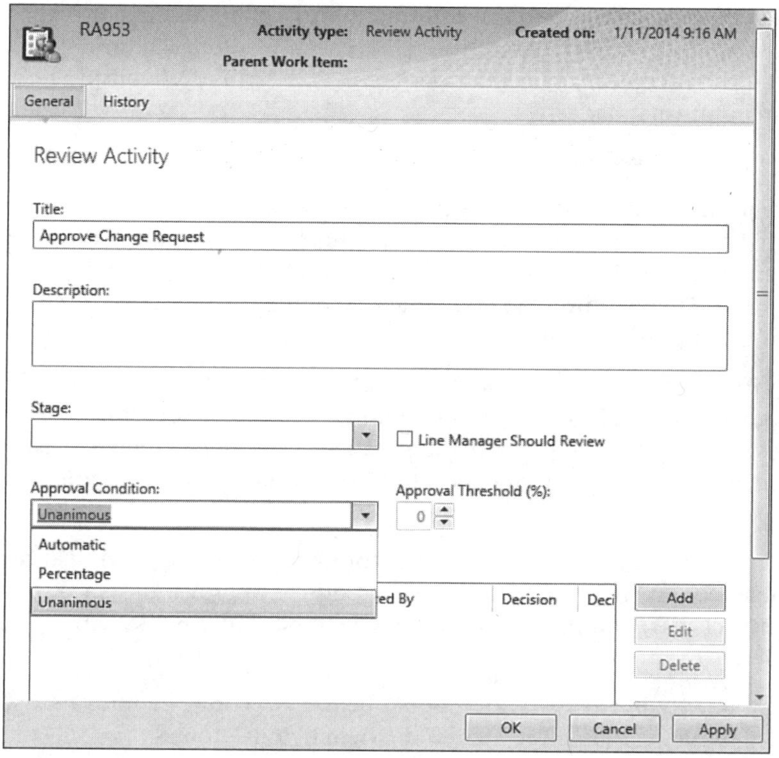

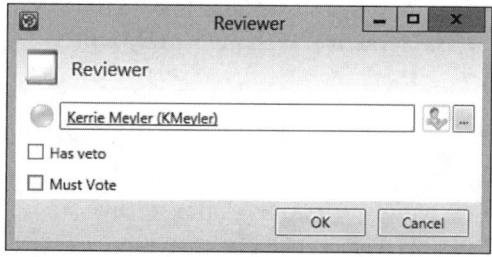

FIGURE 14.9   Approval conditions in the review activity form.

FIGURE 14.10   Specify whether the reviewer is required to review the activity.

Planning change implementation activities is essential. You can review configuration item and work item information in the console to help with planning the change. Planning approved change requests can be affected by the relationships between the involved CIs or changes already planned to CIs. Given that business services in Service Manager define relationships between different CIs, it is important that this information is available in different activities of the Change Management process. You could create a change calendar using a custom task in the console, and create a task that is available in the change work item form for publishing the change request information to a shared calendar, perhaps on a SharePoint portal. For additional information, check Vladimir Bakhmetyev's blog post at http://blogs.technet.com/b/servicemanager/archive/2012/07/02/publishing-work-item-to-part-1-sharepoint-calendar.aspx.

The Service Manager features involved follow:

▶ **Default change request form:** Service Manager includes a change request form based on `Change` and `Activity` class properties and relationships. This form is extensible; Chapter 22 and Chapter 23, "Advanced Customization Scenarios," provide additional information. The Planning tab and review activity provide the required fields to document the process activities.

▶ **Change event notification:** Notification is used to inform required personnel of an approved change request. Configuring accurate notifications and subscriptions in Service Manager is necessary to support this process. You can use change request properties as the trigger for sending notification to different sets of change team members.

▶ **Configuration items:** CIs are a primary source of information when approving and planning the change request. This information is used during approval to reevaluate the request's impact, risk, and priority, and to see whether other work items may influence the request.

▶ **Activities:** A review activity in the workflow should be used to control approvals. Multiple approval activities can be integrated as defined in your process.

▶ **Work items:** Other work items can affect approving and planning a change request. If the request is initiated from another work item, it is a related item. Alternatively, change planning can be affected when a change is requested on a business service, and you then determine that another change request already affects one of the components. In this case, you should plan to implement the change after implementing the previously planned change.

Coordinating Change Implementations

Most change implementation activities equate to activities in Service Manager; this can be similar to a checklist or milestones in the project plan. The following list provides an overview of the available activities for building your activity flow:

▶ **Review activity:** Approvals or validations in the Change Management process can be managed with review activities. Approval criteria and reviewers are examples of properties you can set on a review activity. These activities can be approved or rejected.

▶ **Manual activity:** Steps defined in the Change Management process are manual activities in Service Manager. The actual task to be performed could be anything that the process defines (e.g., plug cable into server). Manual activities can be marked as completed or failed.

▶ **Sequential and parallel activity:** Parallel and sequential activities are used to create new activities containing activities that should be grouped together to form a single process. These types of activities are container activities because their primary function is to contain one or more individual activities.

▶ **Dependent activity:** The primary purpose of a dependent activity is to be a mechanism for associating a change request with a release record. The association is made with a manual activity in a release record that is linked to the dependent activity in a change request. When completed, the dependent activity indicates the Release Management process is complete for the change request.

▶ **Runbook automation activity:** Runbook-automated activities enable automating steps in the process by running Orchestrator runbooks.

Activities defined in the Change template that are not started have a status of Active. As the change is developed and tested, the change coordinator can mark each step in the process by updating its status. To make this clearer, the following example describes an implementation flow for a major change:

1. **Approval of change request:** Approval of the change request is part of a previous activity of the Change Management process and a requirement for implementing the change.

2. **Change development:** This is the actual design of the change. This manual activity requires that all design information gathered be recorded on the Planning tab in the form. This includes the change implementation plan, risk assessment plan, test plan, and backout plan. Information recorded should ensure that any usage scenarios, operational requirements, and design information satisfies the change.

3. **Change testing:** During this manual activity, the change is implemented in a test environment. Change design information created in the change development activity, such as the implementation, risk assessment, test, and backout plan, is input for testing the change in a lab or test environment.

4. **Approval of the change for deployment:** This manual activity of approving the change request after development and testing is a review, or voting, activity. This is the go or no-go decision to implement the change in production.

5. **Change deployment:** This manual activity is the introduction of the change in the production environment. The updated information from testing is used to implement the change in production.

6. **Post-implementation review:** This manual activity reviews the implementation to ensure that the change is implemented as required and delivers the expected result. This activity is described in the next section, "Reviewing and Closing Changes." Similar to other manual activities, the status can be set as complete; if all are successful, the change is ready for closure.

14

Although change reviewers and owners update the change request throughout its life cycle, it is particularly important that the status of each manual and review activity be recorded during development and testing. Different status levels of implementation activities can be configured in the Lists folder of the Library workspace. The Activity Status list has default values that can be adjusted to your organization's needs to follow the different activities during the process. The authors recommend renaming the default list items in the activity status list as a best practice.

TIP: MAINTAINING CONTROL OF CHANGE INFORMATION

Change event workflows can be used to apply templates and send notifications. You could also define workflows with criteria for checking whether the change requester added all required information for the type of change.

For example, when a major change is created and requires an implementation, risk, test, and backout plan be added to this type of request, you could specify a workflow criterion that notifies the requester of a noncompliant request and the approval activity could be set on hold until the request is compliant.

Configuring workflow is described in the "Change Management Workflows" section later in this chapter.

Activities in the Change Management process can be assigned to various individuals. The Work Items pane of the console provides views to follow up the different active manual and review activities. You can create your own views, queues, and groups, similar to other management functions in Service Manager. This lets you personalize the console for users assigned work items.

The Service Manager features involved follow:

▶ **Default change request form:** Activity recording and follow-up is performed in the Activities tab of the change request work item.

▶ **Service Manager Activity Management:** Default review and manual activities are available that define the steps of your Change Management process.

▶ **Service Manager notification:** Status notification flow can be created using Service Manager notification functionality.

▶ **Service Manager activities:** Activities are defined in the change request template. Using review activities and manual activities, you can build a change template to ensure a predefined path is followed to implement the change. You can create automated activities for similar minor changes.

▶ **Configuration items:** CIs are updated, changed, or replaced as part of implementing the change. Log files are reviewed during the technical evaluation of a successful implementation; service failures can be monitored using Operations Manager. The configuration change itself is updated with the Active Directory and Configuration Manager connectors or a custom CSV file import.

Reviewing and Closing Changes

When any change is released into the production environment, its release must be validated and the implementation reviewed. After this change review, you can close the change work item.

Determining whether the released change is effective and achieves the desired results requires that it is monitored in a production environment. By using Operations Manager to monitor the service, the Operations Manager Alert connector can forward any alerts to Service Manager.

Validating a minor change may consist of checking that the component still works as intended. Larger changes might require monitoring network and server information, performance data, event logs, and response times. This can be a complex task that could be fully automated with Operations Manager, with the information reported to Service Manager. Configuration Manager's desired configuration management functionality can also be helpful. If you have defined a desired state for a service component in Configuration Manager for the configuration item, when the change is implemented the state can be reevaluated with compliancy reported to Service Manager. Using connectors to integrate information from Configuration Manager and Operations Manager with Service Manager provides a considerable amount of information for use during change review.

By default, you cannot reopen closed change requests in Service Manager. The Closed status in the change request work item in Service Manager can only be set after the work item is at Completed status. This status occurs automatically when all implementation activities defined in the template are set to Completed.

The Service Manager features involved follow:

▶ **Default change request form:** Closure information in the change request work item finalizes the work item and provides a description of the closure. The work item form holds this information for further handling.

▶ **Service Manager notification:** Those individuals involved in the change request should be notified of the progress of the request and its implementation. When the change request work item is closed, appropriate notifications can be sent.

Configuring Change Management

The changes required for Service Manager to provide a basic platform for Change Management is minor; most of what is required depends on the change process definitions (activities) in your organization. Settings such as prefix, user roles, and notification are global settings. During the various activities in the process, the Change Management team can record the necessary information in the change request work item form and retrieve information from different work items and CIs.

Determine Service Manager access requirements for the different user roles so they can perform their functions in the Change Management process. Configure the change request settings, and define those change list items values appropriate to your environment. Changes include activities; the next sections also discuss configuring Activity Management in Service Manager.

As with any other modification, define what should be configured before actually starting to make those changes. The "Change Management Process Activities" section earlier in this chapter can help identify what is necessary for Service Manager. The next sections guide you through configuring the Change Management settings, specifically:

▶ Change Management console tasks

▶ Change Management user roles, groups, queues, and lists

▶ General Change Management settings

▶ Change Management notification

▶ Change request templates

▶ Change Management workflows

Change Management Console Tasks

The location in the console from where you select the Create Change Request or Create Related Change Request task affects the information automatically populated in the form:

▶ When a request is created from the Change Management template folder, an empty work item form opens, from which the change request management team can input information to describe the change. CIs and related items must be added manually.

▶ If a request is created from the Configuration Item node, the CI is directly added to the Config Items To Change list view of the change request work item form.

▶ If a request is created from a Work Items node, the CI is directly added to the Related Items - Work Items field of the change request work item form.

The Tasks pane, displayed in Figure 14.11, lists tasks to perform on the change request work item. These include a complete set of tasks to change the status, update work item information, and control activities in the Change Management process.

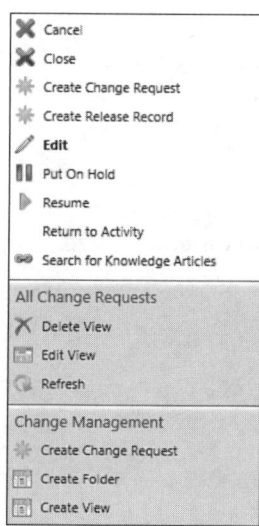

FIGURE 14.11   Change request tasks in the Service Manager console.

Service Manager activities in the change request form have their own status levels and tasks. For Change Management, these include tasks to put the change on hold or resume a change work item. The status change related to these tasks is applied only on the change work item; activities in progress remain In Progress status. Tasks to control activity work items are available in the Activity form and from the Activity Management folder of the console. The activity's status also defines the status of the change request work item, as all activities must be complete before a change request can be closed.

In addition to those tasks provided in the console, you can create your own tasks to automate similar recurring tasks. Chapter 23 discusses creating tasks.

Change Management User Roles, Groups, Queues, and Lists

Configuring Change Management starts with ensuring the Change Management team can access the required work items, configuration items, views, and tasks. By default, two user roles, Change Initiators and Change Managers, are defined with access to all change request work items, views, and so on. The process of creating Change Management user roles is similar to the procedure to create user roles for other management functions. Chapter 17 discusses how to create user roles in Service Manager.

The change request work item form includes fields for categorizing and prioritizing the work items. The selectable values in the form's drop-down lists are Service Manager list item values. Several default list items in Service Manager exist for Change and Activity Management and can be adjusted to your needs.

14

Configuring General Change Request Management Settings

General Change and Activity Settings is a globally scoped configuration in Service Manager. Change Request Settings are configured in the Administration workspace of the Service Manager console and consist of the change request ID prefix and attachments settings. Chapter 11, "Incident Management," discusses how to configure these settings.

The Change request ID prefix setting is shown in Figure 14.12. This figure also shows the attached file policy settings. Configure the number of files and the maximum file size; defaults are a maximum of 10 files and file size of 64KB.

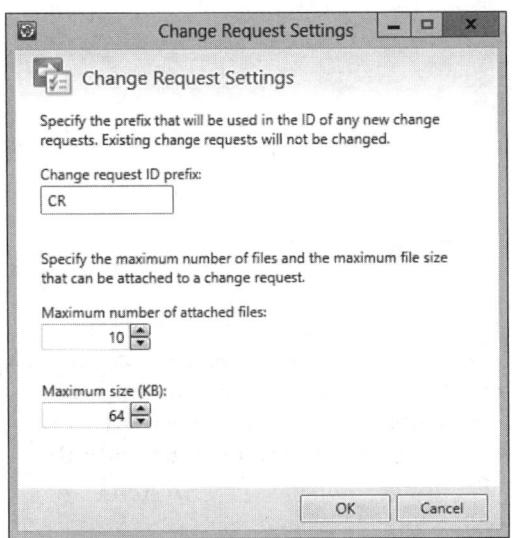

FIGURE 14.12   Change Request Settings.

Activity settings are configured in the same location of the console. The activity prefix specification for the various activities can be specified in the activity settings. The procedure to define the activity settings is similar to the other processes. Figure 14.13 shows the prefixes that can be set.

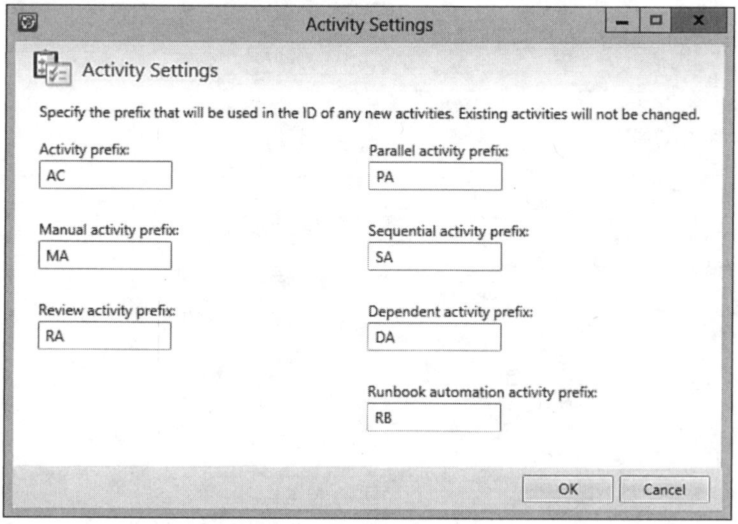

FIGURE 14.13   Defining activity settings.

Configuring Notification

Service Manager can send notifications when a change request work item is created or updated. Before creating notification subscriptions, there are several necessary steps to send out notifications—enabling email notifications, establishing a notification channel with your Simple Mail Transfer Protocol (SMTP) mail server, and creating a notification template to use as the basis for your notification message. This process is described in Chapter 16.

Communication and associated notification to the individuals involved in a change request are important parts of an efficient Change Management process. Team members may want to be notified when a change request is created or when changes occur to change request work item properties. In addition to email notification, you could also use announcements to communicate major changes to a larger group of users.

A subscription for Change Management can be created when a new request is created or an existing one is updated. You need to specify the Change Request class; the criteria are defined based on the change request class properties, as shown in Figure 14.14.

Chapter 16 provides a detailed description of notification functionality. That chapter discusses procedures to create your own email templates to use in change request notification subscriptions.

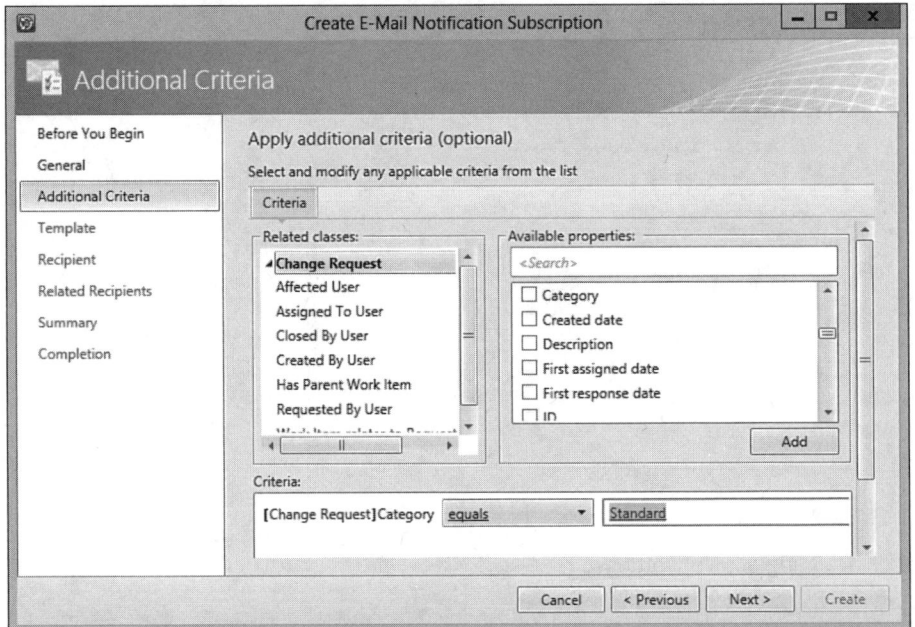

FIGURE 14.14   Specifying notification criteria.

Creating a Change Request Template

Service Manager includes several templates for creating change requests. These templates include activities that may not be applicable for your Change Management process. You can adjust the existing templates or create new templates and start from scratch.

Consider a scenario where a standard change request template is required. The process defines that the following is required to implement the future state:

▶ **Manual activity:** This is for change request work item validation. The change manager should review the requested change before it goes to the CAB.

▶ **Review activity:** Results of the CAB meeting are captured in this activity.

▶ **Dependent activity:** This is required to link the implementation of the request to Release Management.

The following steps describe creating a new change request template.

1. In the Service Manager console, navigate to **Library -> Templates**. In the Tasks pane, click **Create Template**.

2. On the Create Template page of the wizard, specify a name for the template. Click **Browse** to specify the class and select the management pack to save the template. Click **OK**.

3. An empty change request form opens. Provide a title on the General page. Use the Activities tab to configure the processes for standard changes.

   ▶ Select the Activities tab and then click **Add**. In the Select Template dialog box, click **Default Manual Activity**, and then click **OK**. Specify the required information on the activity work item and then click **OK**.

   ▶ Click **Add** to add a review activity in the template. In the Select Template dialog box, click **Default Review Activity**, and then click **OK**. In the empty review activity form, specify the required information and click **OK**.

   ▶ Click **Add** to add a dependent activity to the template. In the Select Template dialog box, click **Default Dependent Activity**, and then click **OK**. On the empty dependent activity form, specify the required information and click **OK**.

4. The activity workflow for this example is now complete (see Figure 14.15). The activity sequence can be changed by dragging and dropping one activity above another.

5. When all information in the template is provided, click **OK** to save the template.

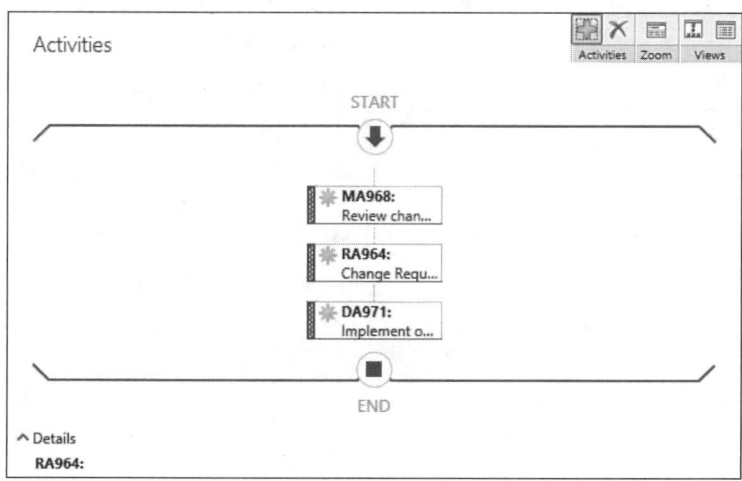

FIGURE 14.15   Activity workflow overview in change request template.

Change Management Workflows

Workflows enable process enforcement and automation. A criterion can be defined as a trigger for the workflow, and the output could be a template that is applied or a notification that is sent. Figure 14.16 presents a graphical overview of the steps in a change request event workflow.

Creating a workflow is similar to the process described in Chapter 11, although the usage of event workflows could be completely different between these two functions. For Incident Management event workflows, criteria are built to apply templates (and automatically complete incident work items or route a work item to the appropriate support group). For Change Management, information about the change request must come from the change request initiator. Work item properties such as priority, impact, and risk are evaluated for each request. Workflows can be of huge benefit in your Change Management process; you can configure change request event workflows to check compliancy of the request, which is provided in the change request work item. For example, you could set criteria in the workflow to check whether the required information is provided for the selected type of change request. If not compliant (a match criteria), the change request initiator is notified and can adjust the request.

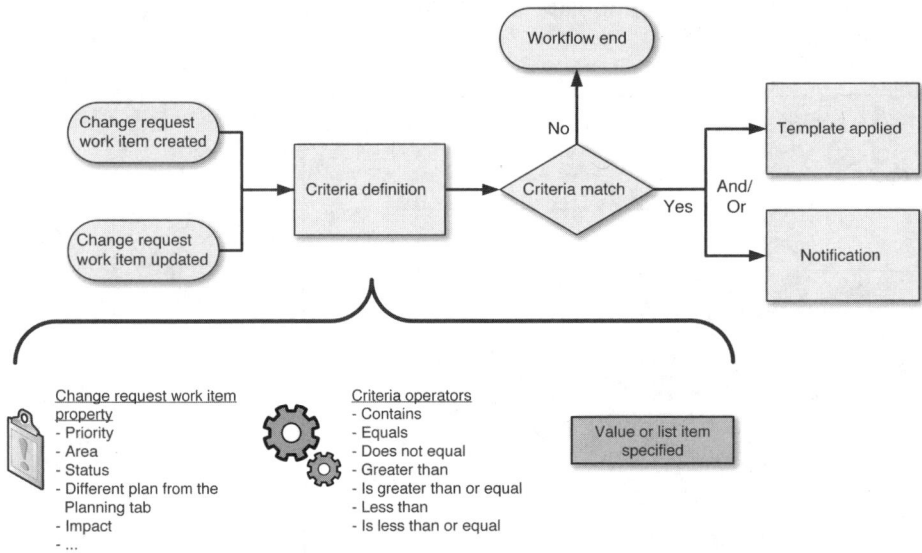

FIGURE 14.16   Overview of workflow automation in Change Management.

Figure 14.16 shows the following:

1. The first trigger in a change request event workflow is an action on the work item. An incident work item is created or updated.

2. The criteria definition checks the change request work item property for a specific value. Different operators can evaluate the change request work item property.

3. Once there is a match, you can apply a template and/or send a notification. You could create workflows only for applying templates or only to send out notification based on the defined criteria, or you could combine the two. The actual process steps of a change request are defined in a change request template.

The next procedure describes creating a new change request event workflow. The workflow applies the Odyssey standard change request template, which sets a title and includes the activity workflow to follow that implements the change. The New Activity Assigned Received template sends notification to Steve and his manager Kerrie. You can perform the following steps to create a template that is applicable for your environment:

1. In the Service Manager console, navigate to **Administration** -> **Workflows** -> **Configuration**.

2. Double-click **Change Request Event Workflow Configuration** and select **Add** to create a new workflow.

3. In the Configure Activity Event Workflows dialog box, click **Add**.

4. Follow these steps in the Configure workflows for objects of class Change Request Wizard:

   ▶ On the Before You Begin page, click **Next**.

   ▶ On the Workflow Information page, in the Name box, type a name for the workflow, such as **Apply Odyssey standard change template workflow**. In the Check for events list, select **When an Object is created**. Verify the Enabled check box is selected, and click **Next**.

   ▶ On the Specify Criteria page, click the Changed to tab. In the Available Properties list, select **Area**, and then click **Add**. In the Criteria box, select **equals**. In the list, select **Software\Patch** as criteria. Select the other properties for the workflow, priority that is required for this example, and select Medium or Low as the criteria value. Figure 14.17 shows these values. Click **Next**.

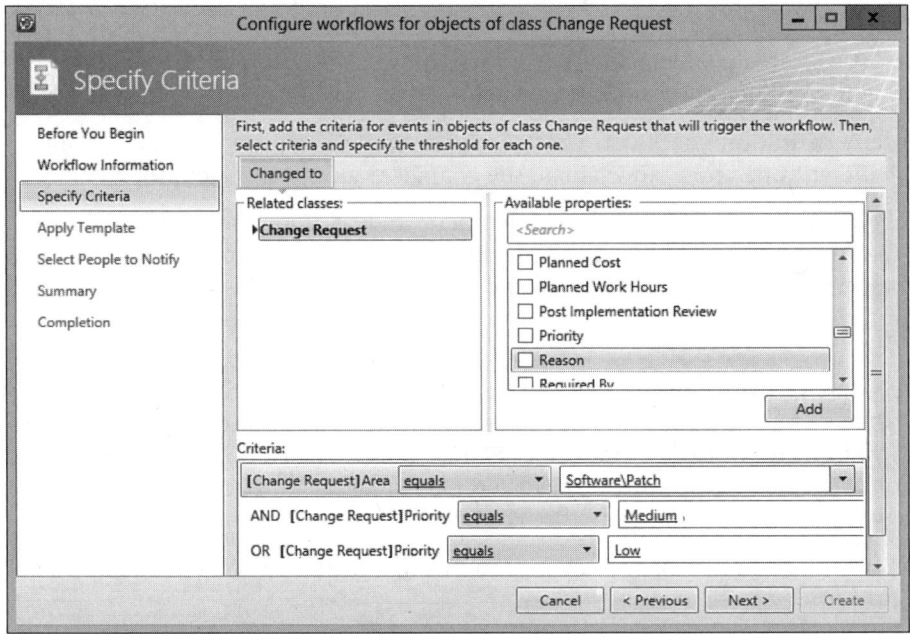

FIGURE 14.17 Specifying criteria.

- ▶ On the Select Incident Template page, check the **Apply the selected template** check box. Select the **Odyssey standard change template**. Click **Next**.

- ▶ On the Select People to Notify page, optionally select the **Enable notification** check box, select the user to notify, and then click **Next**.

5. Review your settings on the Summary page and click **Create**. Click **Close** on the Completion page, and click **OK** in the Configure Incident Event Workflows dialog box.

The workflow is now triggered whenever a change request is created. A template is applied when the criteria defined in the workflow is valid.

Fast Track

Enhancements to Change Management in Service Manager 2012 include additional activities, bug fixes, and performance improvements from the previous version. Service Manager 2012 provides additional functionality for customizing the Change Management process:

- ▶ In addition to manual and review activities, Change Management includes additional activities from Activity Management. These are the review, sequential, parallel, dependent, and runbook automation activities.

- ▶ Activity notification subscriptions can be configured to periodically notify on defined criteria.

- ▶ Orchestrator runbooks can assist with implementing complex process flows. Use the System Center Orchestrator Service Manager integration pack to create, delete, update, or monitor objects in Service Manager. For information on using this integration pack with Service Manager, see *System Center 2012 Orchestrator Unleashed* (Sams, 2013).

- ▶ Service catalog items in scope of the change can be referenced on the change request work item form. A change management template is available for service offering changes.

Summary

This chapter discussed Change Management in Service Manager 2012. It provided an overview of the Change Management process and described Change Management functionality. Process activities are mapped to Service Manager functionality in the "Change Management Process Activities" section. Change request templates, Service Manager activities, and workflows are specific to your Change Management process; this chapter discussed identifying the required functionality and how to configure these for Service Manager. The "Change Management Configuration" section included examples of configuring templates and workflows, and discussed how to use the activities in your change request template to create a change request for a specific change in your environment.

Effective Change Management includes a requirement for reporting changes in your environment; see Chapter 21, "Data Warehouse and Reporting," for additional information on this topic.

Release Management

System Center 2012 Service Manager enables Release Management, implementing and automating this process in compliance with Microsoft Operations Framework (MOF) and Information Technology Infrastructure Library (ITIL). Chapter 3, "MOF, ITIL, and System Center," introduces the Release Management process. This chapter extends that information, showing how to define this process in Service Manager. Release Management implements approved changes, defining a deployment plan for a specific change without impacting the service. This chapter discusses how to use Service Manager to define the Release Management process and provides an overview of the forms, lists, notifications, and workflows used in Service Manager. The chapter also covers deployment plans, along with activity flow and template creation.

Understanding the Release Management Process

Release Management is responsible for implementation and quality control of all hardware and software releases. This encompasses planning, designing, building, configuring, and testing hardware and software releases to create a defined set of release components. Release Management is closely aligned with Change Management and Configuration Management, ensuring that all information relating to configuration items (CIs) and services is available to build a new release.

System Center Service Manager provides an interface to design release packages and manage the release life cycle. Notifications, workflows, release activities, and console customizations can be configured to enable this process. An overview of the Service Manager functionality available to control the Release Management process follows:

▶ **Release work item class and form:** The `Release` class in Service Manager includes properties that define a release work item. While a base set of release work item properties is available, you can extend the default class and functionality as needed. General information, release packages, scheduling, activity flow, release documentation, and results can be set on the release work item form.

▶ **Activity work item templates:** Activities in Service Manager are used to define the steps to be executed in the release work item. Manual, review, sequential, parallel, dependent, and runbook automation activity templates are available in Service Manager to build the release activity flow.

▶ **Notifications:** Subscription and notification templates can be created for email notifications during the Release Management process. Release or activity work item property changes can be monitored and trigger a workflow to send a notification.

▶ **Release record event workflow configuration:** Service Manager workflows can update a release work item and/or send notifications when various changes occur to the release record. You can create a workflow that defines when and under what circumstances it runs.

▶ **Orchestrator connector:** Orchestrator runbooks can be integrated into the Release Management process to automate steps in the implementation. Different activity templates can be created from synchronized runbooks to extend the default list of activity templates.

Configuring release settings in Service Manager is limited to setting the prefix and file attachment policy. You can also set predefined values for release work items by configuring list items in the Lists folder of the Library workspace. You can build release templates for the different types of releases defined in your Release Management process. Each template could include different properties and activities. In general, following is how you could split the configuration tasks:

▶ **General Release Management Service Manager settings:** Release settings in Service Manager are global settings for the Release Management process; similar to other management functions.

▶ **Enumeration (drop-down) lists in the Service Manager console and the "lists" section of the console:** These consist of a list of properties shown in drop-down lists on forms and dialog boxes. Examples include Release Type and Category; these contain a default set of list items you can adjust with specific values for your organization.

▶ **Release Management process templates:** You can create templates for recurring releases that contain a similar set of properties and activity flow. A default template is provided; you can create your own templates to optimize creating release records.

▶ **Parent/child release work items:** Service Manager Release Management maintains release information with appropriate activities and documentation as a single work item. These individual release work items can be related to parent releases to manage different releases as one unit.

▶ **Release Management user roles:** Release Managers is a default user role in Service Manager. Provide scoped access to work items, tasks, views, and CIs by creating your own roles.

▶ **Release Management automation:** Templates and workflows can automate the Release Management process. Service Manager can create automated activities that could be used for minor changes. The process activity design provides input as to how much you can or need to automate in Service Manager.

Release Management in Service Manager

You can use the Service Manager console to manage the Release Management process, defining process components and manageability of the release records. Base functionality, such as notifications or workflows, can enable the process, which could be extended using the Service Manager Authoring Tool or with runbook automation activities. The release and activity management packs installed with Service Manager provide templates, activities, and the functionality to create workflows. Release Management integrates with other management functions, typically Change Management, to deploy approved changes. Other work items, such as incidents, can be related to release work items for quality measurement. The following list provides an overview of ready-to-use Service Manager functionality enabling your Release Management process:

▶ The default release work item form provides an interface to manage release record properties. Impact, urgency, planning information, and results are examples of properties you could configure on a release work item.

▶ A release work item can be created from any management function in the console. Activities in the release should include only approved changes. Dependent activities could be used to link a Change Management activity with the Release Management activity implementing the change.

▶ Updates, configurations, or installations to be executed in the release are activities in the release work item. Activity Management provides manual, review, parallel, sequential, dependent, and runbook automation activity templates. Release templates are created for similar releases and include activities defined in the process.

▶ As with any management function, communication is important. Notification functionality is integrated with Release Management and can send notifications based on criteria rules with predefined email templates.

▶ Release record event workflows can be used to apply templates and send notifications. Based on the defined criteria to trigger the workflow, template information can be added or updated on the work item. You could send a notification when the workflow applies a template.

▶ Lists of release records and release record details are standard reports in Service Manager. Other management function reports can be used to measure the Release Management process. Incidents related to a specific release record can indicate the quality of the release.

Identifying baselines is a task in Configuration and Change Management. Release Management is not directly affected by this; it assists Configuration and Change Management to release a target operational baseline. Release policies may include activities to first test changes in an isolated environment or deploy changes in phases; the initial deployment is targeted to pilot users or to a specific location. Include all activity steps on the work item to minimize the impact on the services in scope for the release.

Release record templates can help enforce implementation steps to deploy changes. For example, you could create templates based on release category (major, minor, or emergency) that include all base steps. The flow to implement changes from development to test and then production could be already configured in the template with review, manual, sequential, or parallel activities. The actual changes to be implemented could be added when you create the release record. This can save time when creating a release record and ensures all changes are deployed in a similar manner, following the selected template. Release record event workflows and activity workflows can be created to apply a template or send a notification when certain criteria on the work item are met.

Service Manager Release Management manages the release record work item life cycle. You can create release work items by selecting a release template and specifying all related release information on the work item. The release work item includes a deployment plan, if one is specified in the selected template. The release deployment plan is defined in the activity flow; again, a template can predefine the activity flow. The purpose of Release Management is to deploy approved changes. The connection with Change Management can be accomplished using dependent activities linked to Release Management activities.

The release record work item can be updated while in editing mode (status of Editing). Once it is in run mode (status In Progress) it can no longer be edited. The activity status indicates the state of deployment while the release record work item is in progress. Deploying regular changes or process steps can be automated using automated runbook activities, which can be directly integrated into the activity flow of the release record. Reporting can measure process quality and release deployments.

Figure 15.1 provides an overview of Release Management in Service Manager 2012 and summarizes the process.

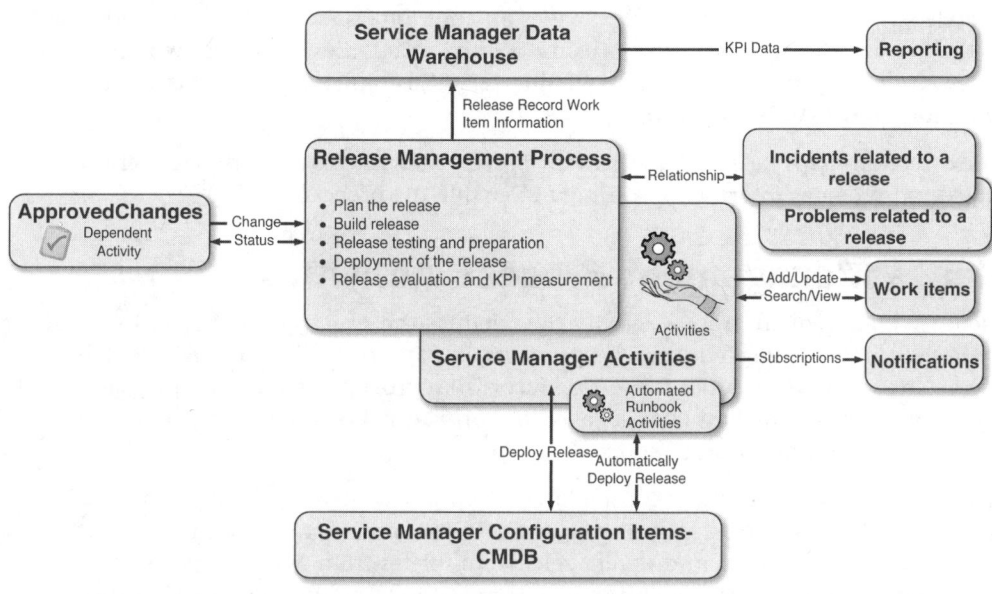

FIGURE 15.1   Release Management in Service Manager 2012.

Configuration occurs in different areas of the console, the primary area being the Release Management Settings area in the Administration workspace. Some of those settings follow:

- ▶ **Configuring Release Record ID Prefix:** Service Manager prepends all release record work item numbers with RR. Activities in the Release Management process use the AC prefix for Activity, MA for Manual Activity, and RA for Review Activity. You can change the prefix that is used.

- ▶ **Release Record File Attachment Policy:** The default file attachment policy is set to 10 files, and the maximum file size to 64 kilobytes (KB). Certain release work items may require a number of attachments or screenshots. The number of attached files and file size directly impact storage requirements. To keep storage reasonable, you might establish a policy and provide training regarding storing commonly used documents. An alternate library, such as a SharePoint site, can be defined to store release information.

Notification administration is performed in the Administration workspace of the console. The notifications channel, release record or activity notification templates, and subscriptions are used to build your notification plan for Release Management. User roles for Release Management and Activity Management are managed in the same workspace under the Security folder. Use the Library workspace to configure groups, knowledge, queues, Release and Activity Management lists, and tasks.

The Service Manager Authoring Tool provides an additional mechanism to extend or automate the Release Management process using your own activities or custom workflows. See Chapter 20, "Management Packs," and Chapter 22, "Customizing Service Manager," for information on the Authoring Tool.

The next section maps Release Management process activities to Service Manager functionality and provides information on how to enable the process.

Release Management Process Activities

The Release Management process activity flow defines those steps necessary to implement an approved change. The change request process and approved changes precede Release Management and provide input for release records. Approved changes should include activities for even the smallest change, avoiding unplanned configuration changes that could have a major impact on a service.

The activity flow in the release record defines an optimized path to deploy changes. The deployment path may vary, depending on the affected service or CIs or change classification. This can be formulated in different release templates from which a specific release record could be created that includes the appropriate activity flow. Service Manager's integration with other System Center components can assist in testing and evaluating the release. During the test and evaluation phases, Operations Manager could be used to monitor the service to see whether any alerts are raised after the deployment.

The Release Management process activities, illustrated in Figure 15.2, provide an overview of the process flow, determining the required changes and implementing them with minimal adverse impact to the business service. Each activity of the process is described in this section of the chapter; a short description follows:

▶ **Configuration item baseline:** This is the baseline of a configuration formally agreed upon and managed through the Change Management process. The Release Management process changes the CI configuration or introduces new CIs.

▶ **Release planning:** Release planning should be defined as guidelines that translate specific service and component releases into production. Creating and managing an overall consolidated release plan must be done in cooperation with Change Management.

▶ **Build and testing the release:** This activity defines, tests, and implements approved changes. This is a task executed during the build activity of a release record. Use procedures, templates, and guidance to enable the release team to build an integrated release record efficiently and effectively. Build and test planning establishes an approach to building, testing, and maintaining your controlled environments prior to production. Release testing occurs after the release is implemented in a test environment.

▶ **Deployment of the release:** This is the execution of the release activity flow in production.

▶ **Release evaluation and process measurement:** Experiences and feedback regarding customer, user, and service provider satisfaction can be captured to measure deployment. Incidents and problems caused by the deployment are another way to evaluate the release. Post implementation review of a deployment is conducted through Change Management.

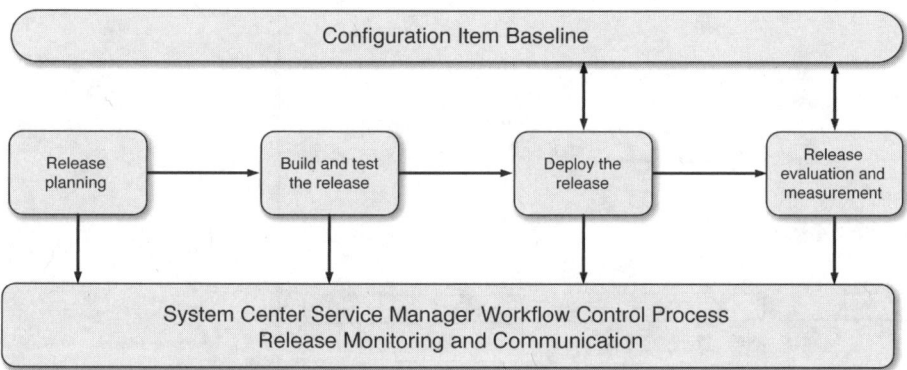

FIGURE 15.2   Activities in Release Management.

Release Planning

The release record is created during your planning activity. A template is selected, and release record information is provided on the release work item. Specific service-related release planning must be defined in cooperation with Change Management. At a minimum, the record should contain the following information:

▶ **Release record description, type, category, and assignment:** This information is defined on the General tab of the release record work item. Types and Category properties are lists; items presented in the drop-down boxes on the work item can be defined in the Library workspace of the console. Figure 15.3 illustrates the default list items for these properties.

FIGURE 15.3   General tab of the release record.

▶ **Impact, risk, and priority assessment:** Results of these assessments can be set on the release record work item. All three properties of a release record are lists and can be adjusted to your needs.

▶ **Configuration items and services affected by the release:** These are defined in the release package. Configuration items modified in the release and affected services can be added to the release record on the Release Package tab of the work item, shown in Figure 15.4. Service Manager release packages normally contain a build and an environment with which the release is tested.

Build and environment are CIs that can be created by the release manager and added to the release package. A build configuration item defines the software, version, documentation, and sources of a build CI. The environment configuration item defines the computers, services, and people of which the environment consists.

▶ **Resources required:** Resources needed for the release, workload, or cost associated with the release can be added on the work item. Cost and workload information on the Scheduling tab and resources can be specified as related items on the work item.

▶ **Criteria for release approval and fallback scenarios:** These can be added to the work item as documentation. Approvals can be enforced in the deployment process by adding review activities in the deployment plan (activity flow).

▶ **Release deployment plan:** This is created on the Activities tab of the release work item. The steps required to implement the changes in the release are defined in the activity flow on the work item. The deployment plan can change for different types of releases. Templates can include the deployment plan for specific releases; based on the selected release template, a predefined deployment is added to the release record.

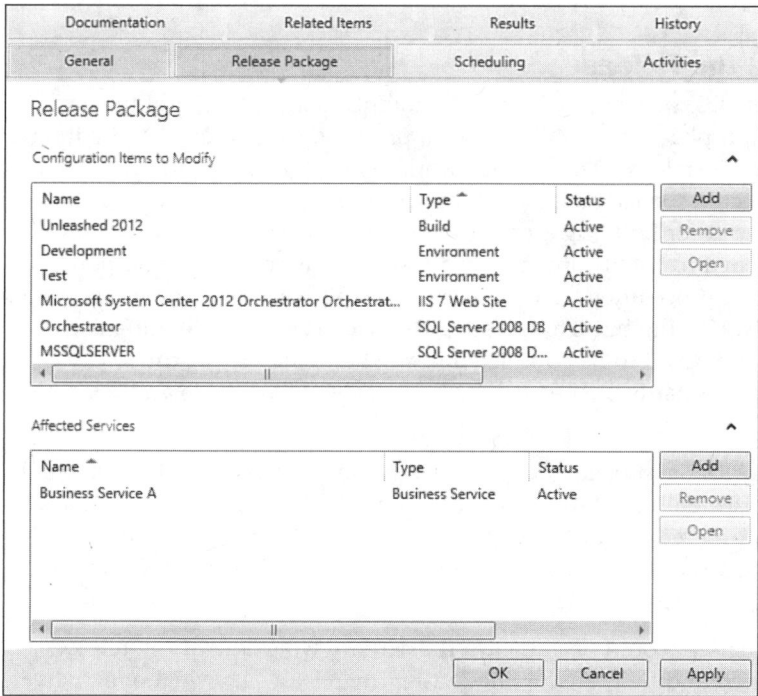

FIGURE 15.4   Release Package tab.

Planning information in the release record can be added to the release work item. Notifications and workflows can be used to update this information or send notifications. Release planning focuses on the actual deployment of the change. Other information, such as a risk assessment, testing, and backout plans, is located on the approved change work item.

The Service Manager features involved follow:

▶ **Release record templates:** These can simplify creating release records with similar properties and deployment plans. A template could be used to prepopulate the release record with release information and a deployment plan.

▶ **Default release record form:** Service Manager includes a problem form based on release work item class properties and relationships (see Figures 15.3, 15.4, 15.5, and 15.6). You could extend this form to include additional information to manage your Release Management process. Chapter 22 provides additional information.

▶ **Change Management:** Planning information to define the release record comes from Change Management. Information regarding the approved change (and approved in the Change Management process) must be added to the record. Any modifications to information coming from the change work item must be communicated with Change Management.

Building and Testing the Release

Change Management provides the primary input for building, scheduling, and testing a release. The implementation plan is available on the approved change request work item, and must be used to build the release. This change work item information and the documentation around the affected service or CIs, such as update procedures or installation documentation, are the input for building an accurate release. Release record activities to implement changes are added to the deployment plan, where environments and policies are already defined. The test procedures are release-specific; this can be a simple functional test or a complete checklist. During build and testing the release, resource requirements must be defined. Examples of tasks to be completed in the build activity of the release include ensuring software and hardware needed for the release are available and assigning support staff to activities.

Scheduling information for the approved change is reevaluated at this time. The release schedule may require adjustment based on release planning, build, and testing. Updates to the schedule must be coordinated with Change Management. If downtime is anticipated, specifying when the affected services are not available could be added on the Scheduling tab of the release record work item (see Figure 15.5).

Activities to implement changes could be added to the activity workflow of the release record. These can be ordered and reordered while testing the release. The goal of activity flow design is to align with the deployment plan previously documented for the approved changes. Changes with similar deployment plans and implementation characteristics could be grouped into one release, which in turn could be related to a parent release record. This lets you create an entire release record that manages different releases on different services.

Any development related to the update can be performed in Change Management or Release Management. Code changes could be required for updates, bug fixes, or new versions for software releases, and can follow its own release process before being released to production.

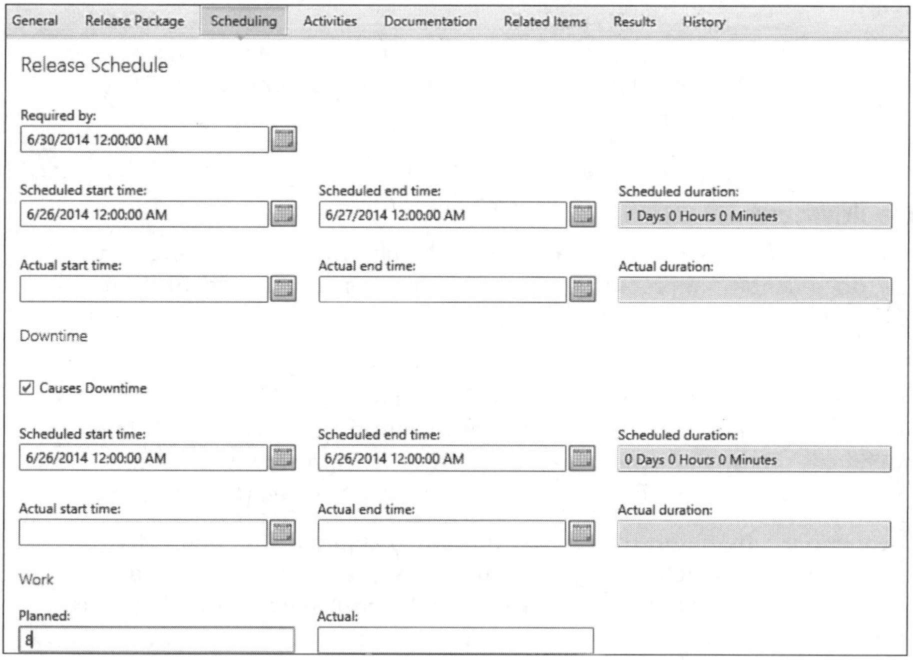

FIGURE 15.5   Release scheduling information.

Automated update release deployment could be integrated in the product used to enable the service, or developed outside Service Manager (say with Orchestrator runbooks). The authors recommend this automated deployment be integrated with the Release Management process, where it can follow those steps defined to test and deploy the update to production. For example, runbook automation activities could be integrated directly into the activity flow of a release record to deploy the update. The runbook automation activity can be triggered from the activity flow of a release record.

The Service Manager features involved follow:

▶ **Default release record form:** Activity description and status follow-up is recorded on the activity work item.

▶ **Release record activities:** Default activity templates define the steps of your deployment plan. This deployment plan can be created on the Activities tab of the release record.

▶ **Configuration items:** CIs are updated, changed, or replaced as part of a release record deployment plan. Log files are reviewed during technical evaluation of a successful implementation; service failures can be monitored using Operations Manager and reported to Service Manager. The configuration change is updated by the Active Directory and Configuration Manager connectors, or using a custom CSV file import.

▶ **Change Management:** Release scheduling information, update plans, and other information are available on the change work item. This information is the base information for building release records.

Release Deployment

Release deployment is the activity responsible for implementing new or changed hardware, software, documentation, processes, and so on to a target environment. It implements the approved changes and executes the activity flow documented on the release record.

Testing the release proves it can be successfully deployed by following the release record activity flow. The release manager assigns activities to administrators of the affected service or individuals on the implementation team. Activity implementers execute the task and update the activity work item on the release record when the work is complete.

Parallel and sequential activities in the activity flow are containers for other activities. These define how constituent activities must be implemented, resulting in the deployment plan for the release record. Parallel activities can be implemented simultaneously, while sequential activities must be executed one after another. The implementation team is responsible for updating the activities to which they are assigned, while another team typically reviews the execution. Review activities can be integrated in the deployment plan to integrate the implementation reviews.

Deploying a release could be a set of tasks that need to be executed in a single release record or part of a complete deployment consisting of multiple release records. It is important to update individual activities to help keep track of the deployment.

The Service Manager console provides an interface for managing release record and activity work items. The release record is a work item you can manage like any other work item. The activity flow defined in the release record can be monitored from the release record work items (see the Activities tab in Figure 15.6), or from the Activity Management folder in the Work Items workspace. The implementation team can update assigned activities via the self-service portal or through the console. Status updates and comments can be added to the activity using the self-service portal without opening the Service Manager console.

Notifications can be used to inform the release manager that the release is progressing or the release record is updated. The implementation team deploys the changes and can be notified when an activity changes from Pending to In Progress status. This should be the trigger to start executing the activity and applying changes.

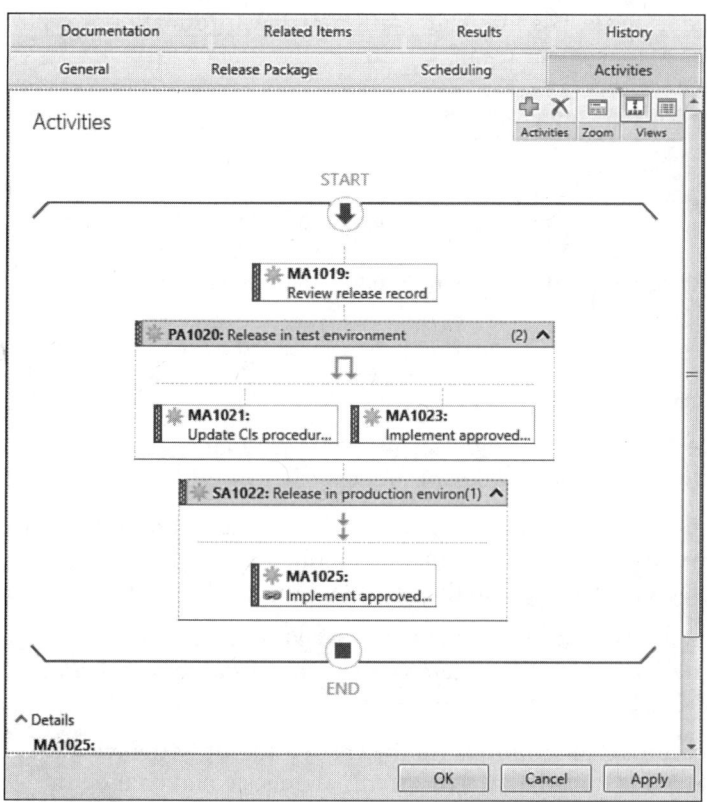

FIGURE 15.6   Release record activity flow example.

TIP: ADDING PROJECTIONS FOR DETAILED VIEWS

Service Manager includes views to manage work items. When using the Activity Management folder, you might miss the combined classes (projections that include process information together with the activity) to add information in the activity view of the release record. You could resolve this by creating your own projections that include the Contains Activity relationship with the related work item. This enables you to create your own views with all required information from the different processes. Chapter 22 discusses creating type projections.

After deployment, you should update deployment schedules, workload, and cost in the release record work item. Each item has a planned and actual value. This information can be used for different measurements against the release record and the Release Management process, and communicated to the Change Management team. Activity execution can be synchronized automatically by dependent activities in Change Management. The implementation result of the release record is a list item selection; like any other list in Service

Manager you can adjust it to your needs. Post-implementation review information is typically discussed with the Change Management team.

TIP: SYNCHRONIZING POST-IMPLEMENTATION REVIEW INFORMATION

Your change and release management processes may state that the post-implementation review is performed in one of these two management functions. The information between the two processes can be synchronized using a Service Manager workflow or Orchestrator runbook. Information about creating workflows can be found in Chapter 11, "Incident Management." Orchestrator runbooks are described in *System Center 2012 Orchestrator Unleashed* (Sams, 2013).

The Service Manager features involved follow:

▶ **Service Manager console:** The console provides an interface to manage release records and activities in the Release Management process.

▶ **Release record activity flow:** The deployment plan for the release record is defined in the activity flow on the work item. Review, manual, sequential, parallel, and dependent activity templates are available to define the release deployment.

▶ **Self-service portal:** The self-service portal enables the logged-on user to access her assigned activities. The implementation team can use the portal to review and update activities without needing to open the console.

▶ **Service Manager notifications:** Subscriptions can be created to notify the release team when the release record is updated. Activity status changes could be used in subscriptions to notify the activity implementer.

▶ **Service Manager workflows:** Service Manager workflows can apply templates and send a notification when the defined criteria is valid.

▶ **Configuration items:** CIs are updated, changed, or replaced during deployment of the release. The service impact can be monitored using Operations Manager and reported to the implementation team. The configuration change on the CI is reported to the configuration management database (CMDB) using the Service Manager connectors or a custom CSV file import.

▶ **Orchestrator connector:** The Orchestrator connector synchronizes runbooks into Service Manager, where you can create runbook automation activity templates. This automation can be integrated in the activity flow of the release record and enables automation during deployment.

▶ **Operations Manager connector:** The CIs and services in the release package are updated or new ones are introduced during release deployment. CI readiness is monitored before and during deployment. Impact of the changes is evaluated shortly after deployment; alerts can become incidents, which could be related to a specific release record.

▶ **Change Management:** Approved changes are implemented during the deployment activity. Activity stages before deployment depend on information from the approved change. Status synchronization between approved changes and related release records can be automated with a dependent activity.

Release Evaluation and KPI Measurement

Release evaluation consists of checking whether any incidents or problems are raised after the release is deployed. The CIs or services in the release package can be monitored by the implementation team shortly after deployment to verify there is no capability, resource, capacity, or performance issues. (Testing should be integrated in the activity flow of the release record.) If no alerts are logged, the release can be considered a success. In addition to monitoring the deployment, user or implementation team experiences and feedback can be evaluated to rate the deployment. Post implementation review of a deployment is conducted as a part of Change Management.

TIP: SATISFACTION SURVEY FOR DEPLOYMENT EVALUATION

SharePoint includes built-in survey functionality. You can create surveys and link them to the self-service portal. For details, see http://office.microsoft.com/en-us/sharepoint-foundation-help/create-a-survey-HA010378260.aspx.

Key performance indicators (KPIs) can be measured using the built-in reporting and OLAP cube functionality provided with the Service Manager data warehouse, and you could create custom reports to report on the KPIs defined for your environment. OLAP cubes can help with analyzing the release record work item information. KPIs in Release Management could be defined on different areas in the process; each one must be mapped to a critical success factor (CSF). Areas that KPI measurements could be defined based on include

▶ Measuring release operations (number of success/failed releases, incidents caused by releases, and so on)

▶ Controlling the release in production (number of releases without an RFC for example)

▶ Measuring on-time releases (proportion of releases finalized within the agreed schedule)

Service Manager reporting and OLAP cubes are discussed in Chapter 21, "Data Warehouse and Reporting."

The Service Manager features involved follow:

▶ **Reporting:** Service Manager reporting is an important part of evaluating the Release Management process. It provides input to other information technology service management (ITSM) processes (Incident Management, Change Management, and so on) that can be related or impacted by the release.

▶ **Incident and Problem Management:** Incidents or problem work items caused by the release can be related to the release record. The number of incidents related to a release could indicate the quality of the deployment.

▶ **Service Manager self-service portal:** SharePoint survey functionality can be integrated with the self-service portal to capture user feedback.

Configuring Release Management

The "Release Management Process Activities" section earlier in the chapter presents an overview of the process from a Service Manager perspective. This section includes an overview of configuration options for Release Management.

Setting configurations are minor. The release record prefix and file attachment policy settings can be defined in the Administration workspace; all other configurations are performed using Service Manager functionality. Workflows and notifications can be used to enforce updates on the release record or send notifications when the properties of a release record change. The activity flow on the release record is a visual representation of the deployment plan and release implementation. Release templates can help define a deployment plan for specific releases. By creating new release records from a template, the deployment plan (and potentially other properties of the release record) is prepopulated on the Activities tab of the work item. Approved changes are input for creating release records. Change Management must be consulted and updated during different activities of the Release Management process; using dependent activities in Change Management and linking release activities to these dependent activities can automate status updates between both processes.

To enable your Release Management process in Service Manager, you should configure the change request settings in Service Manager and define those change list item values appropriate to your environment. Console access for user roles must be defined so they can perform their functions in the Release Management process. The "Release Management Process Activities" section can help identify the necessary templates, workflows, and notifications. The next sections guide you through configuring the Release Management settings, specifically:

▶ Using Release Management console tasks

▶ Creating Release Management user roles, groups, queues, and lists

▶ Configuring general Release Management settings

▶ Creating a release template

▶ Building release records

Using Release Management Console Tasks

To create a release record, select the Create Release Record task in the Tasks pane of the console. Running this task starts with a template selection and adds the work item (incident, problem, and so on) from where it is executed. This creates the release record; additional information can be added to the record as it progresses through the process.

The Tasks pane, displayed in Figure 15.7, lists tasks you can perform on the work item. This includes creating other work items (change or release records) and a task that searches for knowledge. Selecting one of these tasks opens a pop-up window to select implementation results and/or provide comments. Implementation results are added to the release record, and comments are added to the Notes field on the form. An overview of release record-specific tasks follows:

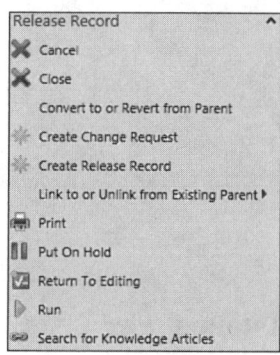

FIGURE 15.7   Release Record tasks in the Service Manager console.

- ▶ **Cancel:** Cancel the release. All incomplete activities and the release record work are updated with a status of Cancelled.

- ▶ **Close:** Records with a status of Completed can be closed.

- ▶ **Convert to or Revert from Parent:** Parent release records have an additional tab with a list view of all child release records (see Figure 15.8). This task enables you to define a parent release record or revert parent release records to normal/child release records.

- ▶ **Link to or Unlink from Existing Parent:** This task links/unlinks the release record to an existing parent release record. It does not create a parent release record.

- ▶ **Put On Hold:** A status of On Hold is set on the release record work item (In Progress status) and activities.

- ▶ **Return to Editing:** Release records having In Progress status can no longer be edited. To change the release record work item, run this task to set the status back to Editing.

▶ **Run:** When the release record is built and ready for deployment, the status of the work item can be updated from Editing to In Progress.

In addition to those tasks provided in the console, you can create others to automate recurring tasks. Creating tasks is discussed in Chapter 23, "Advanced Customization Scenarios."

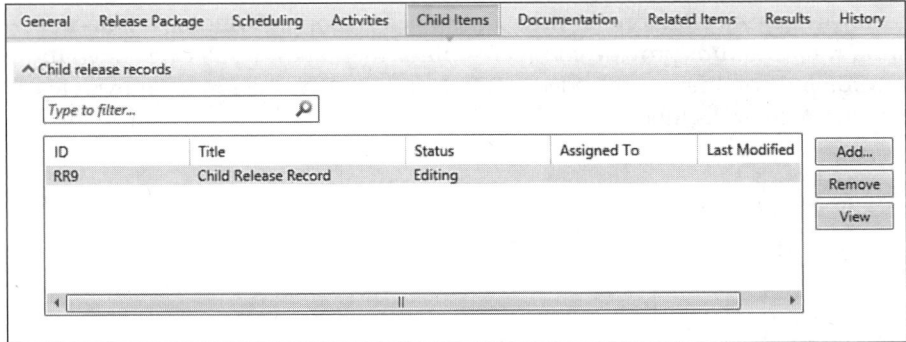

FIGURE 15.8   Parent release record with Child Items tab.

Creating Release Management User Roles, Groups, Queues, and Lists

Individuals involved in the Release Management process and on the implementation team require access to required work items, CIs, views, and console tasks. The Release Managers and Activity Implementers roles provide access to all release record work items, views, and so on. The process of creating Release Management user roles is similar to that of creating user roles for other management functions. Chapter 17, "Service Manager Security," discusses creating user roles.

The release and activity lists to build a Release Management environment compliant with the Release Management process can be adjusted to your needs. The steps to update the process lists are described in Chapter 11.

Configuring General Release Management Settings

General Release and Activity Settings is a globally scoped configuration in Service Manager. This section discusses the customizations available for the Release Management and Activity Management settings.

Release Management and Activity Settings are configured in the Administration workspace; this is the same location where you specify the settings for Incident, Problem, Service Request, and Change Management. In the Service Manager console, navigate to **Administration -> Settings -> Release Management Settings** (or **Activity Settings**) to define settings for the different processes.

The Release record ID prefix shown in Figure 15.9 is the first setting displayed. This figure also shows the attached file policy settings. Configure the number of files and the maximum file size; defaults are a maximum of 10 files and file size of 64KB. When defining your Release Management file attachment policy, consider the information to be available in the release record work item. Make sure you do not block the Release Management team from adding important information yet be able to prevent bulk uploading of files in the work item.

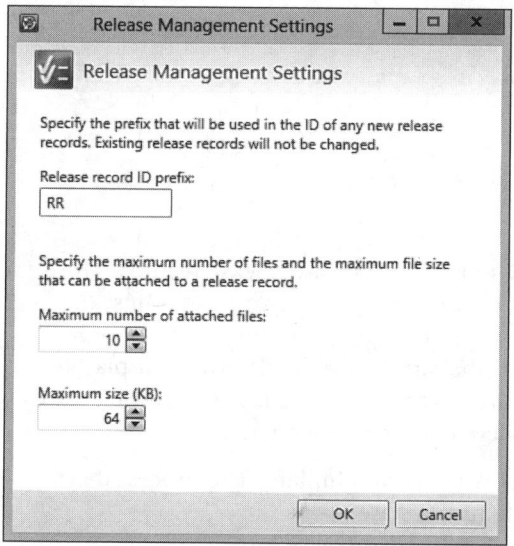

FIGURE 15.9   Release Management Settings.

Use the Activity Settings to define the ID prefix for the different activities in Service Manager. For each activity you can set a specific prefix, shown in Figure 15.10.

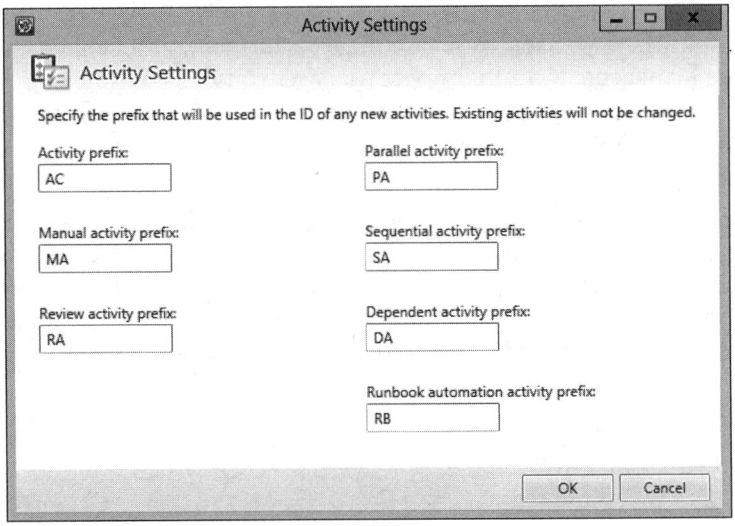

FIGURE 15.10   Defining activity settings.

Configuring Release Templates

By default, Service Manager provides an empty template to create release records. This template includes a title without any activities or other properties. You can adjust the template or create new templates and start from scratch. The primary advantage of using templates in Release Management is that you can define the deployment plan for each type of release record. You can use templates to predefine scenarios to test before the release can be implemented in production, reviews, and for other activities.

Consider a scenario that requires a monthly release record template. The process defines that the following is required to implement the future state:

▶ A manual activity begins the deployment plan for the release record. This task gathers all information, sources, and procedures necessary to implement the release.

▶ A parallel activity must be added for all changes to be deployed in a test environment and to update the documentation around CIs in the release package.

▶ A sequential activity must be added for all changes deployed in production.

The next sections describe creating the release records. Creating templates is discussed in Chapter 11. The assumption made in this chapter is that the template has been created and the general information to add is provided in the template. These procedures focus on creating the deployment plan in the release template, and provide a simplified example for a release where the deployment is traversing from a test to production environment.

Adding a Manual Activity to the Template

Perform the following steps to add a manual activity to the release record activity flow:

1. On the new template, select the Activities tab and click **Add**. In the Select Template dialog box, select **Default Manual Activity**, and then click **OK**.

2. On the empty manual activity form, specify the required information:

   ▶ Title of the activity, such as **Review release record**.

   ▶ Description of the task, area, and other activity properties can be set in the template.

3. Click **OK** when finished.

Adding a Parallel Activity to the Template

Perform the following steps to add a parallel activity to the release record activity flow:

1. Click **Add** to add a parallel activity in the template. In the Select Template dialog box, select **Default Parallel Activity**, and then click **OK**. In the empty parallel activity form, specify the required information:

   ▶ Title of the activity, such as **Release in test environment**.

   ▶ Description of the task, stage, and other properties can be defined in the template.

2. Click **OK** when complete.

Figure 15.11 displays a manual activity added in the parallel activity for updating the documentation of the CIs in the release package. The implementation activities can run parallel to this manual activity.

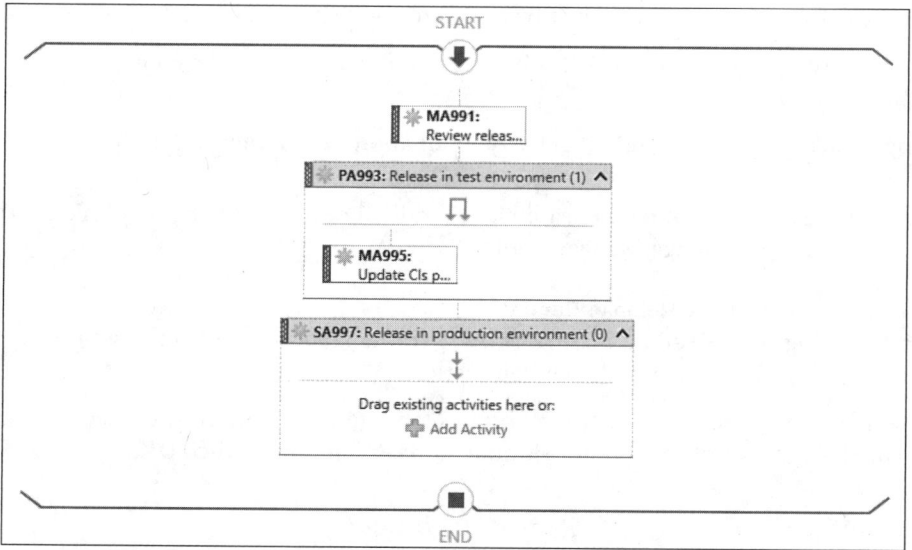

FIGURE 15.11   Release record activity flow.

Adding a Sequential Activity to the Template

Follow these steps to add a sequential activity to the release record activity flow:

1. Click **Add** to add a sequential activity to the template. In the Select Template dialog box, select **Default Sequential Activity**, and then click **OK**. In the empty sequential activity form, specify the required information:

   ▶ Title of the activity, such as **Release in production environment**.

   ▶ Description of the task, stage, and other properties can be defined in the template.

2. Click **OK** after providing this information.

Building Release Records

Another approach for defining release deployment plans is creating a release template for each environment separately and linking them to a parent. In the parallel activity, you could add a sequential activity to group a series of activities in the deployment process. During the build activity, manual or other activities can be added to create a complete activity flow for the release record.

Service Manager release templates can be used to predefine steps in the deployment plan. Building release records includes completing release record information, gathering all required sources for the deployment, and completing the activity flow with approved changes. Completing the form and specifying the required information are straightforward. This section discusses designing the activity flow that defines the deployment.

The procedure in this section uses the release template created previously in the "Configuring Release Templates" section. A release record is created using the Odyssey template, and the following activities must be added to the deployment plan:

1. A manual activity that can be linked with the approved changes (dependent activities)

2. Linking an activity to a dependent activity of an approved change

The next sections describe updating a release record to include activities that are linked to dependent activities from Change Management.

Adding a Manual Activity to the Release Record

Perform the following steps to add a manual activity to the release record activity flow and link it to a Change Management dependent activity:

1. On the new release record, select the Activities tab and click **Add**. In the Select Template dialog box, select **Default Manual Activity**, and then click **OK**.

2. On the empty manual activity form, specify the required information:

  ▶ Title of the activity, such as **Review release record**.

  ▶ Description of the task, area, and other activity properties can be set in the template.

3. Drag and drop the new manual activity to the location in the activity flow where it needs to be executed.

4. In this example, add a manual activity for implementation in the test environment. Perform steps 2 and 3 twice to add two manual activities for the implementation in the test and production environments.

5. Right-click the activity that is a placeholder for the production implementation, and then select **Link to Change Request Activity**. The Select Change Request Activity form opens, shown in Figure 15.12:

  ▶ The form includes a list view with all available change request dependent activities to link to the release activity.

  ▶ By clicking the Change request entry, you can see the list of dependent activities in the request. Selection is made at the activity level.

6. Click **OK** when finished.

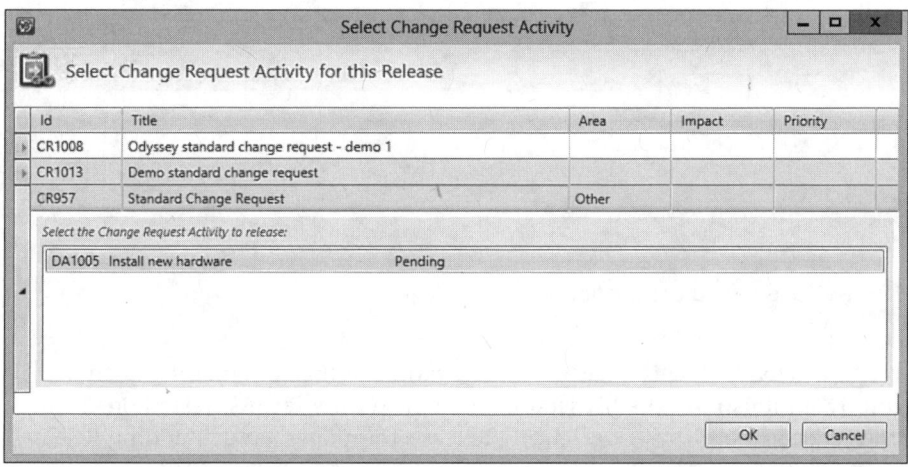

FIGURE 15.12   Change request activity selection.

Reviewing the Activity Flow

Release records can include complex deployment plans with many activities to achieve the desired result. The activity that implements the approved change can be linked to change request dependent activities. The Activities tab of the release record work item includes different views for the activity flow. The diagram view, displayed in Figure 15.13, graphically shows this flow. The diagram view can be adjusted using the Zoom button to show extra small, small, medium, or large activities in the diagram.

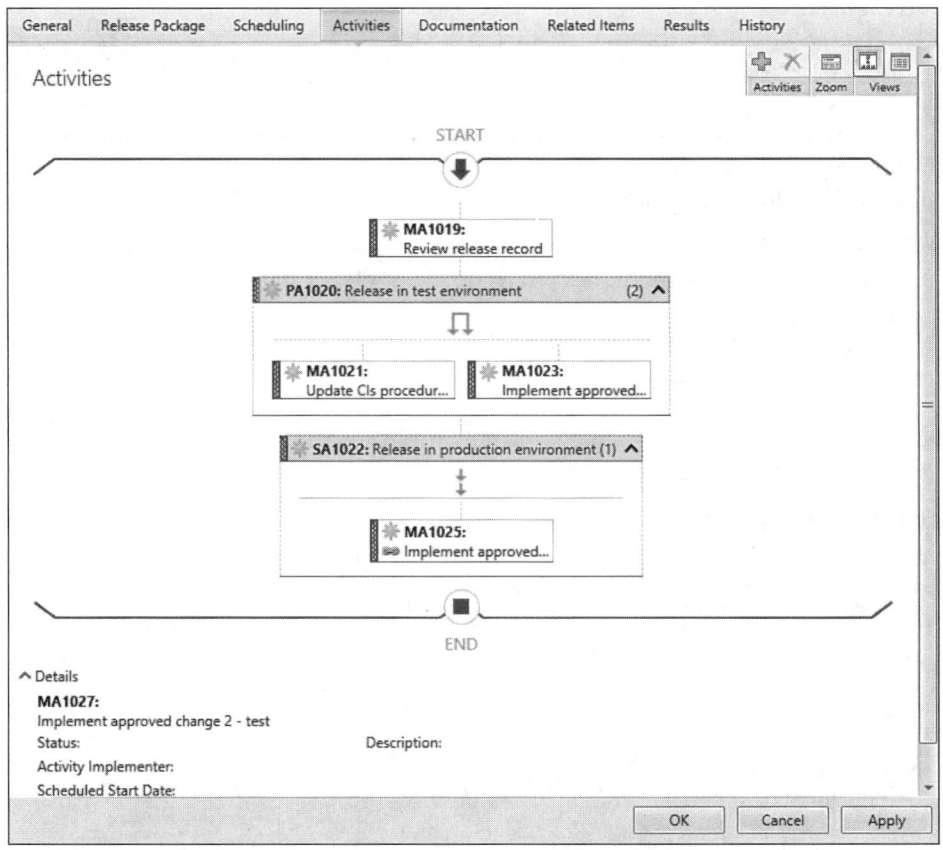

FIGURE 15.13   Release record activity flow – diagram view.

The list view of the activity flow is a flatter representation of the activities included in the flow. Figure 15.14 illustrates the list view of the new release record created previously using the procedures in the "Configuring Release Templates" and "Building Release Records" sections of this chapter.

TIP: LINKED ACTIVITIES IN THE RELEASE RECORD

When you link an activity to a dependent activity for Change Management, the selected activity shows a linking indicator that resembles a chain icon. The tooltip for the selected activity shows IDs for the linked change request dependent activity, illustrated in Figure 15.15.

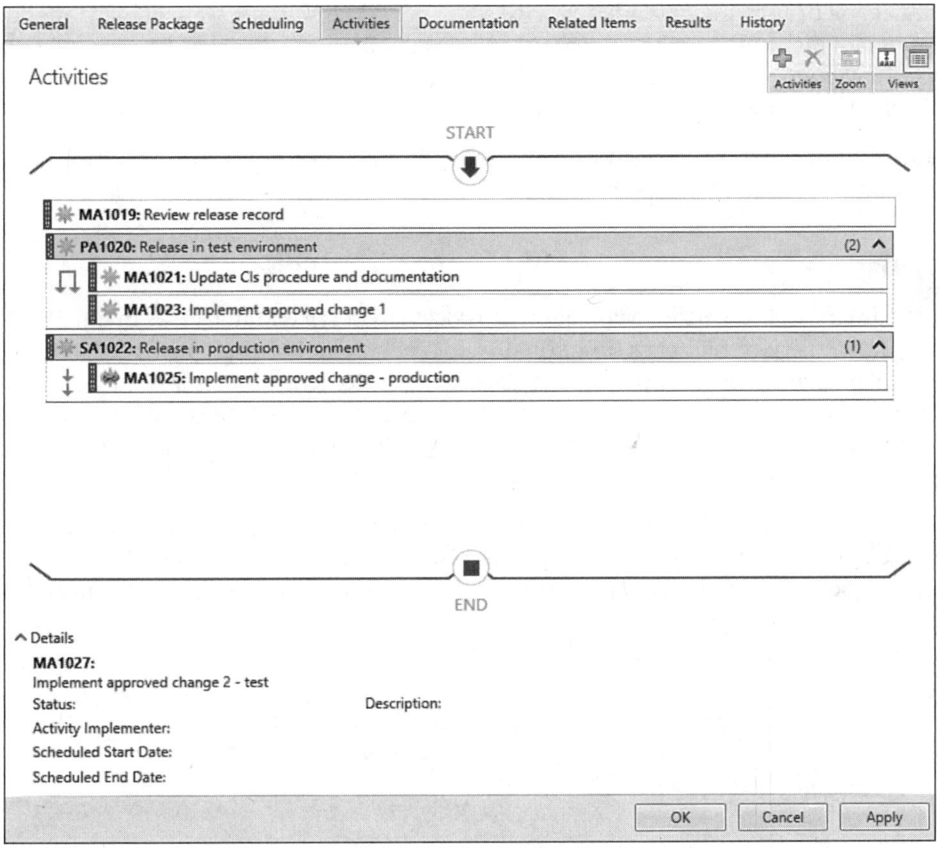

General
Release Package
Scheduling
Activities
Documentation
Related Items
Results
History
Activities
Activities
Zoom
Views
START
MA1019: Review release record
PA1020: Release in test environment
(2)
MA1021: Update CIs procedure and documentation
MA1023: Implement approved change 1
SA1022: Release in production environment
(1)
MA1025: Implement approved change - production
END
Details
MA1027:
Implement approved change 2 - test
Status:
Description:
Activity Implementer:
Scheduled Start Date:
Scheduled End Date:
OK
Cancel
Apply

FIGURE 15.14 Release record activity flow – list view.

MA1025:
Implement approved...
Open Linked Activity (DA1005)

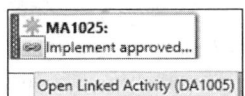

FIGURE 15.15 Linked activity icon and tooltip.

Fast Track

Service Manager 2010 included support for incident, problem, and change requests; Service Manager 2012 introduces Release Management. This is an extension to the default work item class, making it possible to reuse existing Service Manager functionality as you can with other management functions. User roles, templates, workflows, and notifications can be created as with other processes.

Release Management uses the extended Service Manager 2012 Activity Management model to design a deployment plan for the release record. Manual and review activities previously existed in Service Manager 2010. Sequential, parallel, dependent, and runbook automation activities can now be added to the activity flow.

Orchestrator runbooks can assist with implementing approved changes, and you can use runbook automation to implement these changes.

Summary

This chapter discussed the Release Management process in Service Manager. It mapped release activities to Service Manager functionality for each activity in the process. The deployment plan is an important part of the Release Management process and can be defined in the activity flow on the release record. Templates can be used to enforce certain deployment plans for specific releases. The chapter described creating templates and designing the activity flow.

The chapter also described the flow from process definition to configuration in Service Manager, discussing how you can organize, configure, and optimize the Release Management process in Service Manager. The next chapter discusses using notifications.

PART IV

Administering Service Manager

IN THIS PART

Managing Notifications

Core to System Center 2012 Service Manager is its notification workflow feature, which is the engine that underpins all aspects of notification. You may want to utilize this feature when an incident is created or a service request is approved.

The Service Manager notification workflow includes the following capabilities:

▶ Creating and forwarding email messages

▶ Customizing the messaging format at the user level

▶ Adapting the messaging format to the target user's language

▶ Providing redundancy through multiple Simple Mail Transport Protocol (SMTP) server support

▶ Supporting custom classes and all default classes

Using this feature ensures that notifications are generated for almost any type of change or event occurring in Service Manager.

Notification Overview

The high-level steps to configure notification follow:

1. **Establish a notification channel:** In Service Manager, this notification channel is via SMTP, using email.

2. **Create notification subscription(s):** Each subscription defines groups, classes, when to notify, and whom to notify. The subscription also includes information regarding which template to use in the notification email. Subscriptions are established in the Service Manager console under Administration -> Notifications -> Subscriptions.

3. **Verify the notification account:** Service Manager uses the management server's (workflow server's) workflow account. This account requires permissions to send emails using the SMTP server and email address specified in the notification channel. Be sure this account has the appropriate rights for the notification channel it will use.

4. **Verify the notification template:** In the subscription, you must specify a notification template to use. You need to verify its format, message body, and subject. You also want to verify the language used in the template. The template can include a message and subject for each language. This is a useful capability to have when there are end users in different countries and you want each notified in his local language.

TIP: RECIPIENTS IN SERVICE MANAGER

If you are familiar with System Center 2012 Operations Manager, you may notice a step missing with Service Manager—creating recipients. Service Manager does not create recipients, as it synchronizes users and email addresses from Active Directory. If the recipient is not in Active Directory, you can create a user object in Service Manager with the correct email address. Service Manager does not support sending text (SMS) or Lync messages. As an alternative, many organizations are using mobile email.

Notification Setup

Notification contains of a number of objects, recipients, channels, and a subscription. Each of these must be configured correctly before notification emails can be sent. These are discussed in the next sections.

Using Recipients

Service Manager synchronizes user information from Active Directory, including the email address of the user. As Figure 16.1 shows, you can look at a user configuration item (CI) object and see the notification address. If you modify this address in Service Manager, the Active Directory connector overwrites your changes the next time synchronization occurs. Changes to the address should be made in Active Directory or in Exchange. Service Manager uses the user's primary email address. If there are multiple email addresses, only the primary address is synchronized.

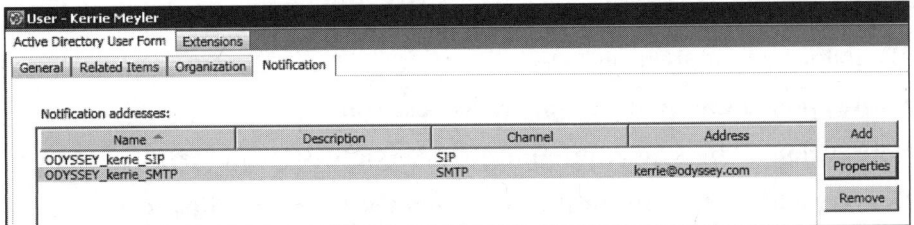

FIGURE 16.1   Notification address of a user CI, in this example only an SMTP address.

If you need to send notifications to a recipient not in your Active Directory, you can create a user object in Service Manager. For example, you might want to notify an external vendor when there is an issue with a product from that vendor. The following procedure creates a user object for an external vendor. Follow these steps:

1. In the Service Manager console, navigate to **Configuration Items -> Users**.

2. In the Tasks pane, click **Create User**.

3. In the User dialog box, input a First Name and a Last Name for the new user, for example, as shown in Figure 16.2:

   ▶ **First Name: Eclipse Servicedesk**

   ▶ **Last Name: (External)**

   ▶ **Company: Eclipse**

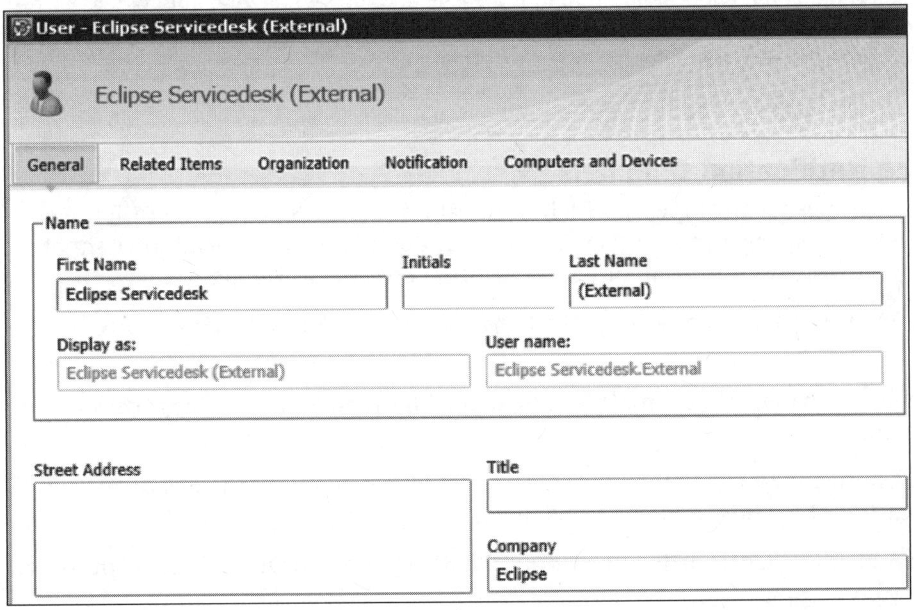

FIGURE 16.2   Configuration of external recipient in the configuration database (CMDB).

4. Switch to the Notification tab and click **Add**.

5. Input the following, and then click **OK**:

    ▶ **Notification address name: support@eclipse.com**

    ▶ **Notification address description: Eclipse Servicedesk (External)**

    ▶ **Delivery address for this notification channel: support@eclipse.com**

6. Click **OK** in the User dialog box.

After the user is created, it can be used for notification, as shown in Figure 16.3.

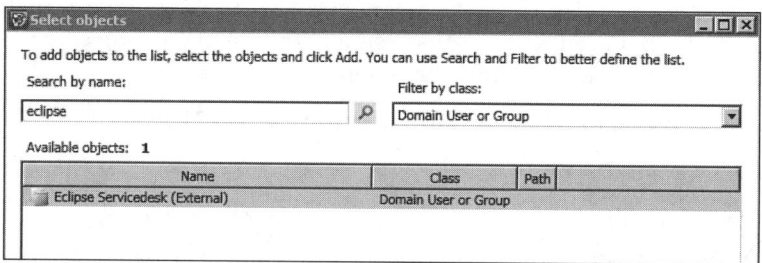

FIGURE 16.3   External recipient as member of a notification subscription.

NOTE: ABOUT THE SMINTERNAL DOMAIN

You may see a domain named SMInternal in the Service Manager console. This is the default domain name used when you create users directly in Service Manager and do not synchronize from an Active Directory or other external source.

Configuring Notification Channels

Notification channels are the pipe by which notification messages are sent to recipients. Before Service Manager can send email, you must configure a notification channel. Perform the following steps to configure a notification channel in Service Manager:

1. In the Service Manager console, navigate to **Administration -> Notifications -> Channels**.

2. In the Results pane, select **E-mail Notification Channel**, and click **Properties** in the Tasks pane.

3. In the Configure E-mail Notification Channel dialog box, check the **Enable e-mail notification checkbox**, and then click **Add**.

4. In the Add SMTP Server dialog box, input the SMTP server (FQDN), such as **pioneer. odyssey.com**.

5. Select the authentication method from the drop-down menu and port number, depending on your mail server configuration. Click **OK**.

6. In the Configure E-mail Notification Channel dialog box, input a return email address, in this example **support@odyssey.com**. This address is used as the From address when Service Manager sends notifications. Ensure the Service Manager work-flow account is permitted to use this email address.

7. Verify your notification channel settings (see Figure 16.4) and click **OK**.

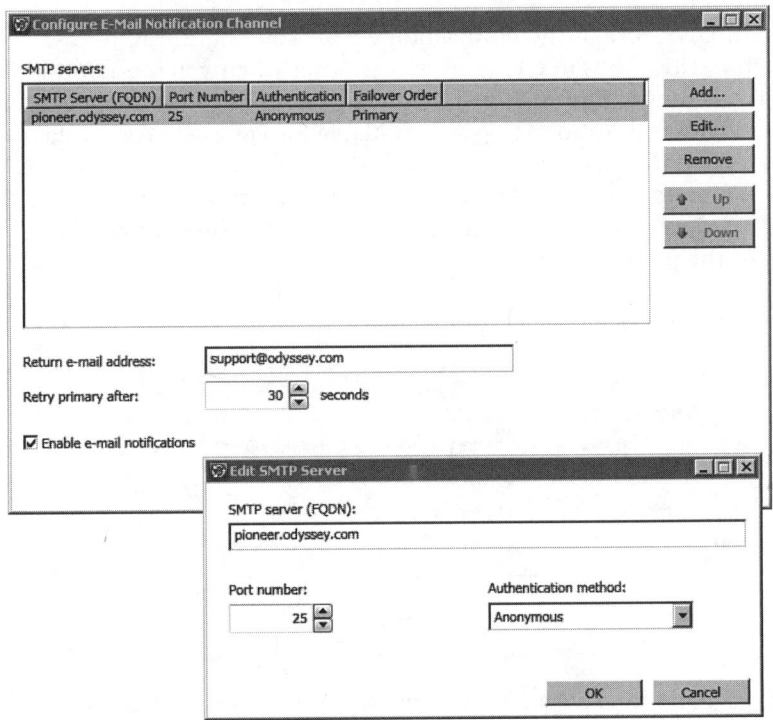

FIGURE 16.4   Configuring SMTP notification channel settings.

Service Manager only supports email notification channels. To receive Short Message Service (SMS) notifications, consider using gateway software that can receive email and convert those messages to SMS. Many mobile service operators provide this functionality as a service. Another alternative is to use System Center 2012 Orchestrator (http://technet.microsoft.com/en-us/library/hh237242.aspx). You can also use Orchestrator to connect Service Manager with other systems.

To provide fault tolerance, the authors recommend you have more than a single SMTP server in your email notification channel.

TIP: MOBILE DEVICE CONNECTIVITY TO SERVICE MANAGER

Gridpro, a Microsoft Certified Partner with a Gold Competency in Application Development and a member of the Microsoft System Center Alliance, has developed the MobileFront for Service Manager app, which connects mobile devices to Service Manager. MobileFront for Service Manager is designed for engineers on the go who need mobile access to Microsoft System Center Service Manager. MobileFront can be used as an alternative for notification for engineers, operators, and administrators.

Creating Templates

Notification templates are used to format the notification email. You might want to use one format when you send notifications to end users and another when you send notifications to support teams within the Information Technology (IT) department. Service Manager includes four standard notification templates available for your use. You could also use these four templates, shown in Figure 16.5, as a foundation for customization. You can also create new templates. The procedure discussed in this section creates a notification template, which is used to send notifications to the Tier 2 support group regarding assigned incidents. Perform the following steps:

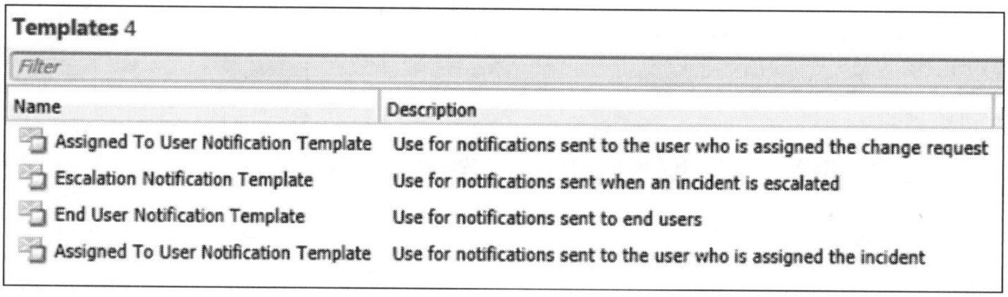

Templates 4	
Filter	
Name	**Description**
Assigned To User Notification Template	Use for notifications sent to the user who is assigned the change request
Escalation Notification Template	Use for notifications sent when an incident is escalated
End User Notification Template	Use for notifications sent to end users
Assigned To User Notification Template	Use for notifications sent to the user who is assigned the incident

FIGURE 16.5   Service Manager default notification templates.

1. In the Service Manager console, navigate to **Administration -> Notifications -> Templates**.

2. In the Tasks pane, click **Create E-mail Template**.

3. In the General page of the Create E-mail Notification Template Wizard, input

   ▶ **Name: Odyssey - Notification to Tier 2 Target class: Incident**

   ▶ **Management pack:** Select a suitable unsealed management pack or leave the default value.

4. Click **Next**.

5. On the Template Design page, input the following:

   ▶ **Message subject: Incident assigned to Tier 2, priority** [Trouble Ticket/ Priority]

▶ **Message body: Incident** [WorkItem/ID] **has been assigned to Tier 2. Title of the incident is** [WorkItem/Title].

Everything between [ ] are parameters that can be populated with the Insert button, which inserts a dynamic value from the incident. Each time this template is used for notification, the parameter value is populated from the current incident. This configuration is shown in Figure 16.6.

6. Click **Next**.

7. At the Summary page, review all settings and click **Create**.

8. On the Completion page, verify that the notification template was created successfully and click **Close**.

CAUTION: AVOID COPY/PASTE WITH SUBSTITUTION STRINGS BETWEEN TEMPLATES

Copying and pasting substitution strings from one notification template to another typically does not work. Avoid copy/paste between templates to prevent unnecessary errors with the text.

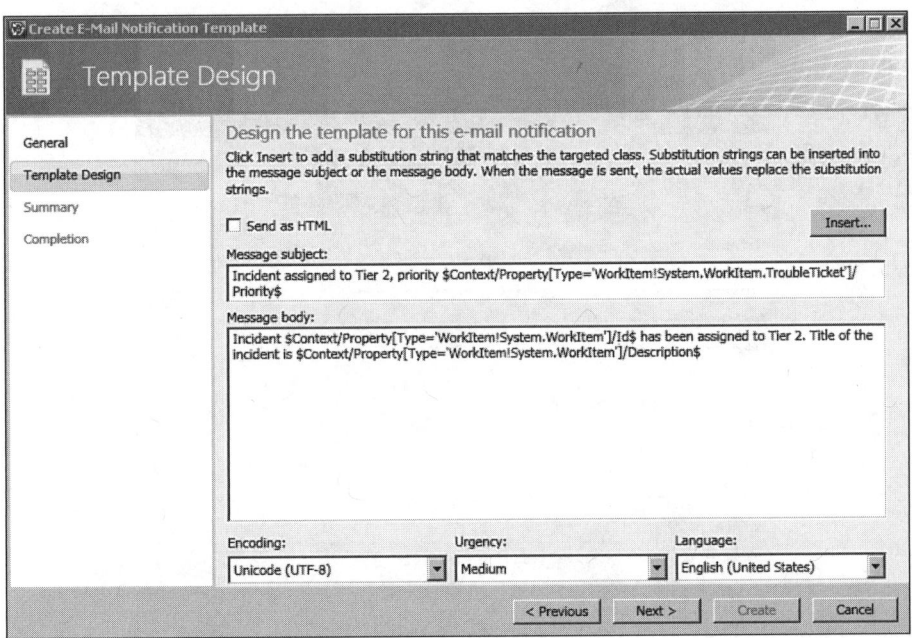

FIGURE 16.6   Configuring an email notification template.

Using Subscriptions

After you synchronize users, create a notification template, and configure a notification channel, you create a subscription for the users to receive email notification. The subscription controls only what is sent to the recipient and its format. The next procedure configures a subscription for all new Tier 2 incidents in Service Manager. This subscription sends a notification when an incident is updated with Support group equals 2. Follow these steps:

1. In the Service Manager console, navigate to **Administration -> Notifications -> Subscriptions**.

2. In the Tasks pane, click **Create Subscription**.

3. Click **Next** on the Before You Begin page of the Create E-Mail Notification Subscription Wizard.

4. On the General page, input the following settings, also shown in Figure 16.7:

   ▶ **Notification subscription name: Odyssey - Notification for Tier 2**

   ▶ **Description (optional): Notification for all incidents updated to Tier 2**

   ▶ **When to notify: When an object of the selected class is updated**

   ▶ **Targeted class: Incident**

   ▶ **Management pack:** Select an appropriate unsealed management pack or use the default.

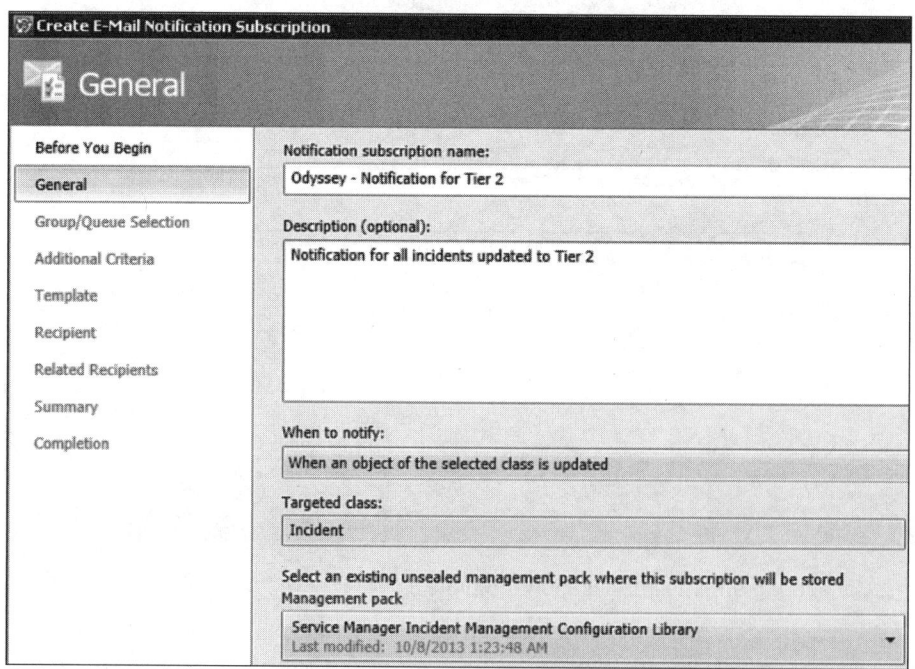

FIGURE 16.7   General properties of an email notification subscription.

Notice the Targeted class drop-down has you choose the class for which you will be sending notifications. Any class can be selected, such as Service Request, Incident, or Manual Activity. The notification subscription feature is not limited to Service Manager default classes.

5. Click **Next** to continue.

6. On the Group/Queue Selection page, select a queue or group to filter those objects to track. Click **Next**.

   You can use both groups and queues in Service Manager. This capability is dependent on whether you select a work item class or a configuration item class as the target class for your subscription.

   ▶ Groups are used to group objects, typically CIs. These can contain objects of the same class or different classes.

   ▶ A queue is used to group work items that meet specified criteria, such as all change requests that are classified as email related change requests.

   Both queue and group memberships can be dynamic and are periodically recalculated to ensure the membership list is current.

7. Click the **Changed To** tab on the Additional Criteria page. This tab is used when you want to send a notification to this support group when an incident is modified. The Changed From tab is used for notification when an incident is changed from Tier 2 to another support group.

> **NOTE: ADDITIONAL CRITERIONS**
>
> In some scenarios, you may need to add criteria directly in eXtended Markup Language (XML); say, when you need to use 2 does not equals criteria. The Microsoft Service Manager team has a blog post discussing this at http://blogs.technet.com/b/servicemanager/archive/2010/11/30/using-and-or-criteria-in-workflow-and-notification-subscriptions.aspx.

8. In the Available properties list, scroll down and select **Support Group**. Click **Add** to add it to the criteria field. In the Criteria field, select **Tier 2** in the drop-down menu, as shown in Figure 16.8. Click **Next** to continue.

16

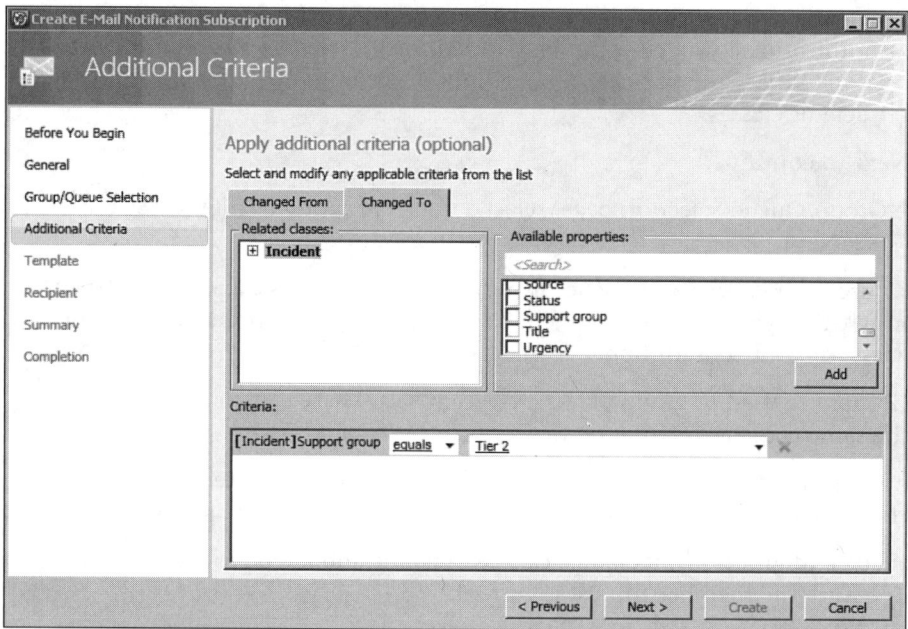

FIGURE 16.8   Specifying additional criteria for email notification subscription.

9. On the Template page, click **Browse** and select the **Odyssey - Notification to Tier 2** template in the Select E-mail notification template dialog box. Click **OK**. Click **Next** to proceed to the next page of the wizard.

10. Click **Add** on the Recipient page. In the Select objects dialog box, select the recipient for the subscription. The authors recommend using shared mailboxes rather than sending notifications individually to everyone in a team. You can also use Active Directory distribution lists as recipients. Distribution lists show as instances of the Active Directory `Group` class. Click **Add** to add recipients and then click **OK**. Click **Next** to continue.

11. On the Related Recipients page, click **Next**. Related Recipients is a new feature in Service Manager 2012. These can be used to notify recipients in context, such as a user that is related to an incident, say the user that is assigned to the incident or primary owner. You can use related recipients from the work item to get the related user for an incident. For an example of how to use related recipients for service level agreements, see the Microsoft Service Manager engineering blog at http://blogs. technet.com/b/servicemanager/archive/2012/02/07/notifying-before-sla-breaches. aspx.

12. On the Summary page, review your settings and click **Create** to create the subscription.

13. On the Completion page, verify the subscription was created successfully (see Figure 16.9). Click **Close**.

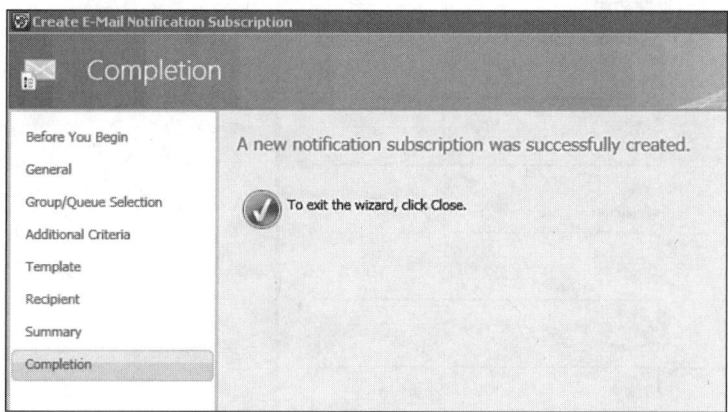

FIGURE 16.9   Subscription created successfully.

Incorporating Different Languages in Subscriptions

Some organizations require that notification messages be in the target user's native language. Should your organization have employees in France and Sweden, you would then configure Service Manager to send notifications in either French or Swedish, depending on the target user. The Locale attribute on the user CI, displayed in Figure 16.10, controls the language in which the user receives the notification.

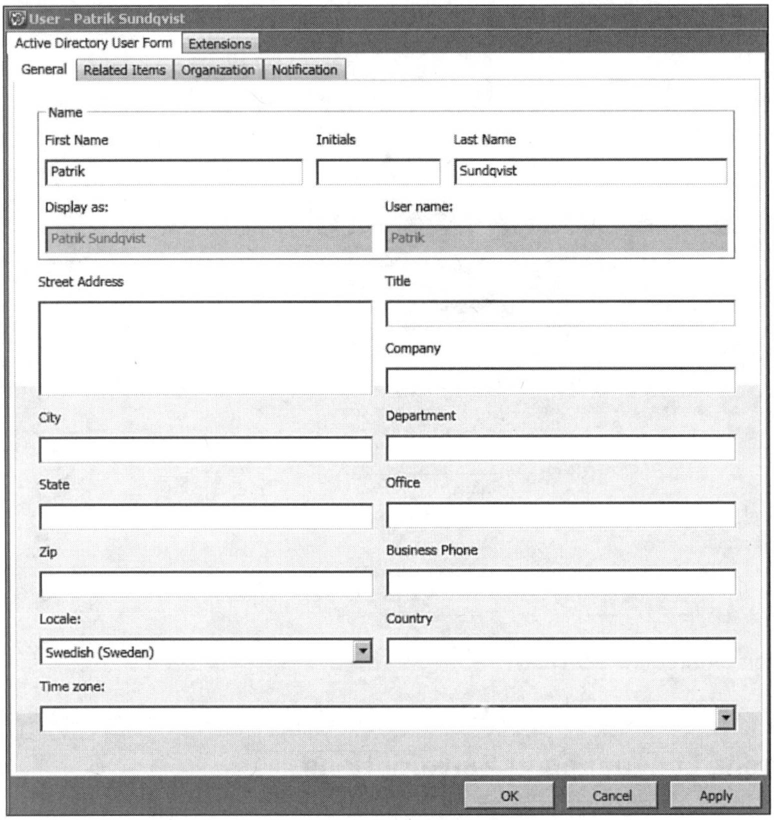

FIGURE 16.10   Viewing the Locale attribute of a user CI.

To configure Service Manager to support different languages in notification emails, you must configure a notification template that includes the message body in each language. The following procedure updates the Odyssey - Notification to Tier 2 template to support multiple languages.

1. In the Service Manager console, navigate to **Administration** -> **Notifications** -> **Templates**.

2. In the Results pane, select the **Odyssey - Notification Tier 2** template previously created in the "Creating Templates" section. From the Tasks pane, select **Properties**.

3. In the Odyssey - Notification to Tier 2 dialog box, select the Template Design page. Use the Language drop-down menu to select other languages. Both the message box and the message subject are blank when you select another language, French in this example. After inputting your text in French (see Figure 16.11), select **Sweden** and input your Swedish subject and message body. Click **OK** when complete.

4. The final step is to verify your users have the Locale attribute configured. Remember that if you change the value of this attribute in Service Manager, the Active Directory connector overwrites it during its next synchronization.

NOTE: CONFIGURING THE ACTIVE DIRECTORY CONNECTOR

Remember to configure your Active Directory connector not to write null values; otherwise, the Active Directory connector overwrites the CMDB—even with a blank value.

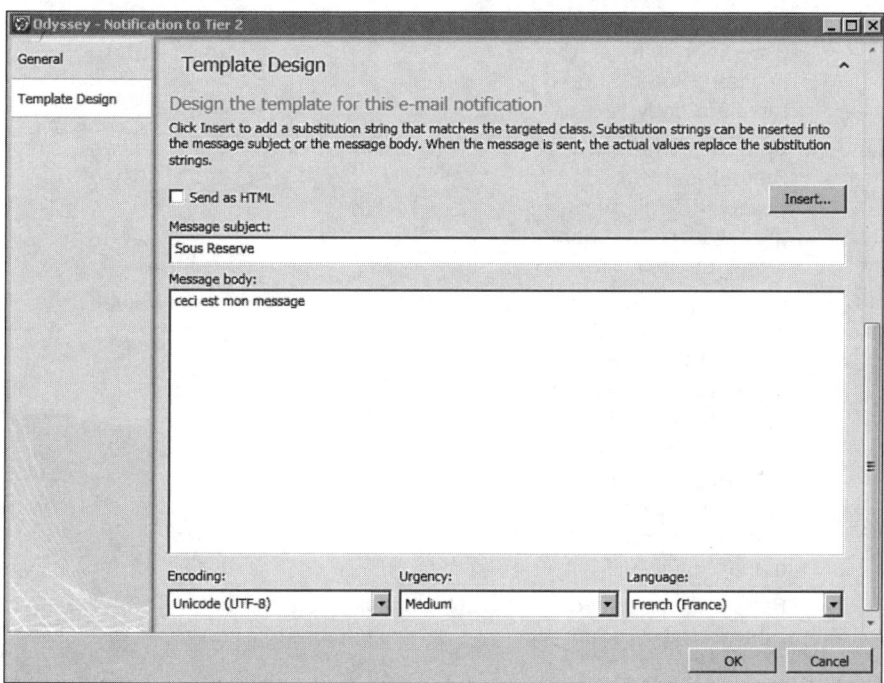

FIGURE 16.11   Configuring the template for multiple languages.

Adding Localization to Notification Emails

There may be scenarios where you see notification emails with a value such as `IncidentClassificationEnum.Hardware`. Here the category parameter was inserted into the notification template. You could expect it to say Hardware problem, but the reason you see `IncidentClassificationEnum.Hardware` is because there is no display string for the category list value in that notification recipient language.

Table 16.1 lists the results you get depending on template language and the user's `Locale` property.

TABLE 16.1   Results Based on Template Language and User's Locale Property

User Locale Property	Notification Template Language	Available Display String	Result in Email Notification
Sweden (Swedish)	Sweden (Swedish) (only language configured).	US-EN (Default)	Incorrect list values
English (United States)	Sweden (Swedish) (only language configured).	US-EN (Default)	Correct list values
English (United States)	Both English (United States) and Sweden (Swedish). Will use the English (United States) template body.	US-EN (Default)	Correct list values
Sweden (Swedish)	Both English (United States) and Sweden (Swedish). Will use the Sweden (Swedish) template body.	US-EN (Default)	Incorrect list values
blank/null	Both English (United States) and Sweden (Swedish). Will use the Sweden (Swedish) template body that was first configured in the template. Swedish is also the local settings on the service manager server.	US-EN (Default)	Incorrect list values
Other language (example) Sweden (Finnish)	Both English (United States) and Sweden (Swedish).	US-EN (Default)	No email

To get the correct notification email message body for, say, Swedish, you must add localization in the Service Manager Incident Management Configuration Library management pack and configure the management pack to support Swedish. Microsoft's Service Manager team discusses this at http://blogs.technet.com/b/servicemanager/archive/2009/07/24/localizing-management-pack-content.aspx.

Here are the general steps to add localization:

1. Export the Incident Management Configuration management pack.

2. Open it with an XML editor, such as XML Notepad, downloadable at http://www.microsoft.com/downloads/en/details.aspx?familyid=72d6aa49-787d-4118-ba5f-4f30fe913628&displaylang=en. (At the Microsoft Download Center at http://www.microsoft.com/downloads, search for **XML Notepad**.)

3. Add languagepack and localization display strings for your language. The following example shows the default English display string and the display string for Swedish.

```
<LanguagePacks>
 <LanguagePack ID="ENU" IsDefault="true">
    <DisplayStrings>
       <DisplayString ElementID="Enum.3d1g9i4v1d41u332l6a5f4a32r4e1">
         <Name>Printer Issue</Name>
         <Description>Use this incident classification for all cases where the
              user has printer related problems. </Description>
       </DisplayString>
    </DisplayStrings>
  </LanguagePack>
</LanguagePacks>
</ManagementPack>
```

Now add a language pack for Russian since it doesn't exist, and then add display strings for this new list item.

```
<LanguagePack ID="SVE" IsDefault="false">
  <DisplayStrings>
     <DisplayString ElementID="Enum. 3d1g9i4v1d41u332l6a5f4a32r4e1">
       <Name>Printer problem</Name>
       <Description>Använd denna incident kategori när användaren har skrivar
            relaterade problem.</Description>
     </DisplayString>
  </DisplayStrings>
</LanguagePack>
```

4. Save the management pack.

5. Import the management pack back into Service Manager.

Culture XX is a Neutral Culture

Should you try to send a notification email to a recipient with a Locale attribute value not supported by the notification template, an event is generated. This event will be on the Service Manager server in the Operations Manager log with Event Id 33880. The following text shows an example of an event ID 33880. To prevent this from occurring, make sure you have the same language support in your management pack and notification template as your user has as his Locale attribute value.

```
A Windows Workflow Foundation workflow failed during execution.
Workflow Type: Microsoft.EnterpriseManagement.ServiceManager.Incident.Workflows.
AutomaticIncidentChangeWorkflow
Workflow Identifier: 742dc6d1-90cf-9834-044f-9906bcf9dbf9
Exception Type: System.NotSupportedException
Exception Message: Culture 'en' is a neutral culture. It cannot be used in
formatting and parsing and
```

therefore cannot be set as the thread's current culture.
Exception Stack: at System.Globalization.CultureInfo.CheckNeutral
(CultureInfo culture)
at System.Globalization.CultureInfo.get_DateTimeFormat()
at System.DateTime.ToString(IFormatProvider provider)
at Microsoft.EnterpriseManagement.Notifications.Workflows.IReplaceableToken.
GetLocalizedPropertyValue(UserSettings settingsIn,
EnterpriseManagementObject instance)
at Microsoft.EnterpriseManagement.Notifications.Workflows.TokenizedMessage.
PopulateTokenValues(UserSettings userSettings,
EnterpriseManagementObject instance,
Dictionary`2 relationshipIdToInstanceToRelatedObjectMapping)
at Microsoft.EnterpriseManagement.Notifications.Workflows.RecipientGroupMessage.
PopulateTokenValues(UserSettings userSettings,
EnterpriseManagementObject instance, Dictionary`2
relationshipIdToInstanceToRelatedObjectMapping)
at Microsoft.EnterpriseManagement.Notifications.Workflows.SendNotificationsActivity.
Execute(ActivityExecutionContext executionContext)
at System.Workflow.ComponentModel.ActivityExecutor`1.Execute(T activity,
ActivityExecutionContext executionContext)
at System.Workflow.ComponentModel.ActivityExecutor`1.Execute(Activity activity,
ActivityExecutionContext executionContext)
at System.Workflow.ComponentModel.ActivityExecutorOperation.Run
(IWorkflowCoreRuntime workflowCoreRuntime)
at System.Workflow.Runtime.Scheduler.Run()

Using Notification Workflows

Service Manager includes functionality to configure a number of default workflows and author your own workflows. A *workflow* is a sequence of activities that automate a process, such as selecting information from a change request and carrying out tasks in Active Directory based on the information in that change request.

A workflow could also update and modify work items within Service Manager, such as changing the priority of an incident work item. Incident workflows can apply a template to an incident and send notification emails. You can use the Service Manager console to build workflows around

▶ Desired Configuration Management event workflow

▶ Release Record event workflow

▶ Service Request event workflow

▶ Activity event workflow

▶ Incident event workflow

▶ Change Request event workflow

The Service Manager Authoring Tool can be used to build custom workflows with other activities, an example of which is shown in Figure 16.12. You can also use the Authoring Tool to author new activities. System Center Orchestrator includes an integration pack to connect to Service Manager, making it also possible to build Service Manager workflows in Orchestrator. (For examples, see *System Center 2012 Orchestrator Unleashed* [Sams, 2013]).

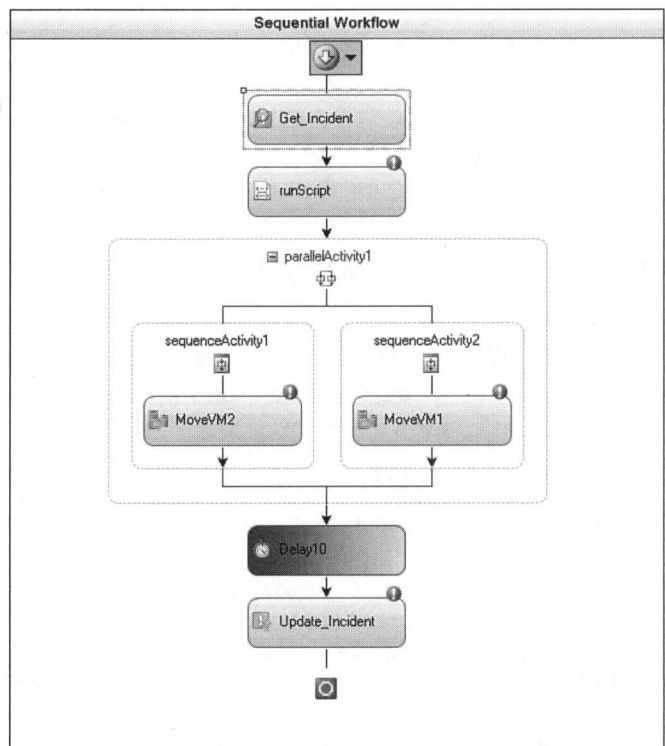

FIGURE 16.12   Workflow built in Service Manager Authoring Tool.

Configuring a Workflow to Change the Impact of an Incident

The following procedure configures a workflow that changes the impact of the incident and sends an email notification to the security team when an incident is created with a description containing the word **virus**. The procedure uses the High Priority Incident template, which is a default incident template in Service Manager. You can modify the template; in this scenario, for example, add the modification of **assigned to**.

The High Priority Incident template changes the following settings of an incident:

▶ **Impact:** Changes to High

▶ **Urgency:** Changes to High

▶ **Assigned to:** Changes to Odyssey Antivirus Team

▶ **Support group:** Changes to Tier 1

Perform the following steps:

1. In the Service Manager console, navigate to **Administration -> Workflows -> Configuration**.

2. In the Results pane, select **Incident Event Workflow Configuration**.

3. In the Tasks pane, click **Properties**.

4. Click **Add** in the Configure Incident Event Workflows dialog box.

5. Click **Next** on the Before You Begin page of the Add Incident Event Workflow Wizard.

6. On the Workflow Information page, input the following settings, also shown in Figure 16.13:

   ▶ **Name: Update virus related incidents**

   ▶ **Description: For incidents that contain virus in the description, priority will be increased and a notification email will be sent.**

   ▶ **Check for events: When an incident is created**

   ▶ **Management pack:** Select a suitable unsealed management pack or leave the default setting.

7. Click **Next** to continue.

8. On the Specify Event Criteria page, select the description property, click **Add**, and configure the criteria as [**Work Item**] **Description contains virus**. This is shown in Figure 16.14.

9. Click **Next** to continue.

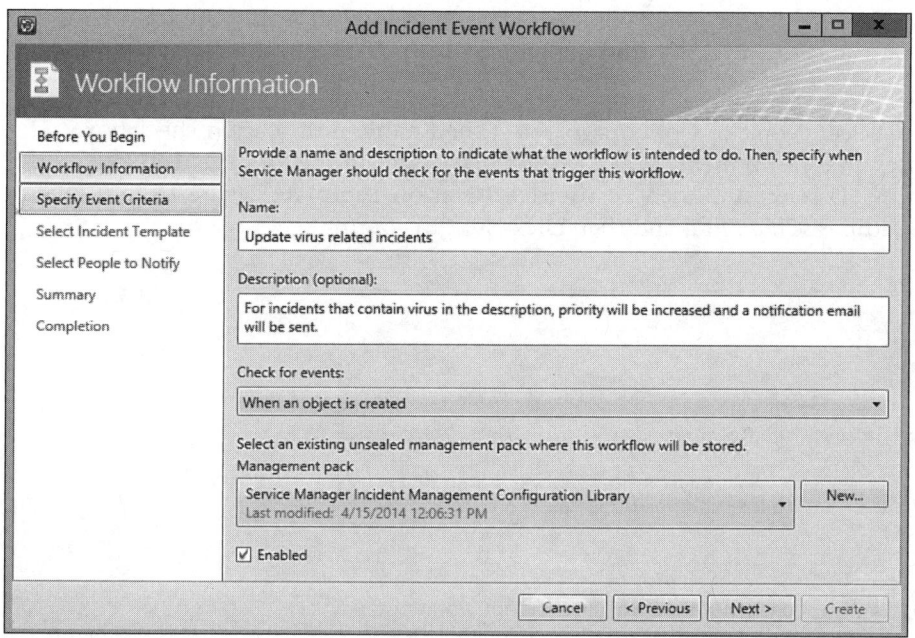

FIGURE 16.13   Workflow information settings of an incident workflow.

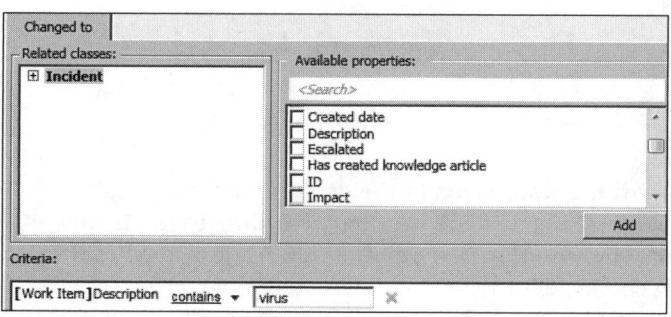

FIGURE 16.14   Event criteria of an incident workflow.

10. On the Select Incident Template page of the wizard, select **Apply the following template**, and select **High Priority Incident Template** from the drop-down menu. Click **Next**.

11. On the Select People to Notify page, select the **Enable notification** check box. In the User drop-down menu, select **Assigned To User**; in the Message template drop-down menu, select **Assigned To User Notification Template**. Figure 16.15 displays these settings. Click **Add**, and then click **Next** to continue.

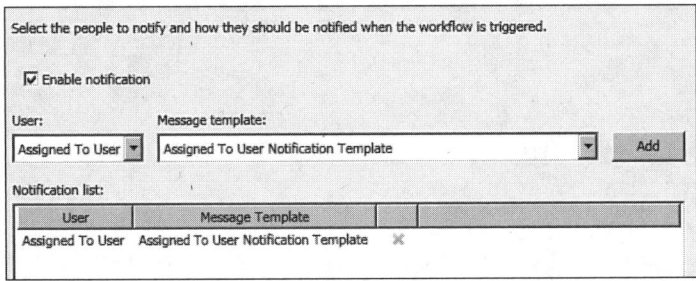

FIGURE 16.15   Notification settings of an incident workflow.

12. Click **Create** on the Summary page.

13. Verify the incident event workflow was created successfully on the Completion page, and click **Close**.

14. Click **OK** in the Configure Incident Event Workflow dialog box.

Using the Workflow

When a new incident is created with the word **virus** in the description, the workflow created in the previous section runs and updates the incident according to the template specified in the Workflow Wizard. The workflow also sends a notification email to the Odyssey antivirus team regarding the incident. The workflows are visible in the Service Manager console, under Administration -> Workflows -> Configuration. This view can help with troubleshooting workflows and seeing when they last ran. Figure 16.16 shows information about the workflow created in this procedure.

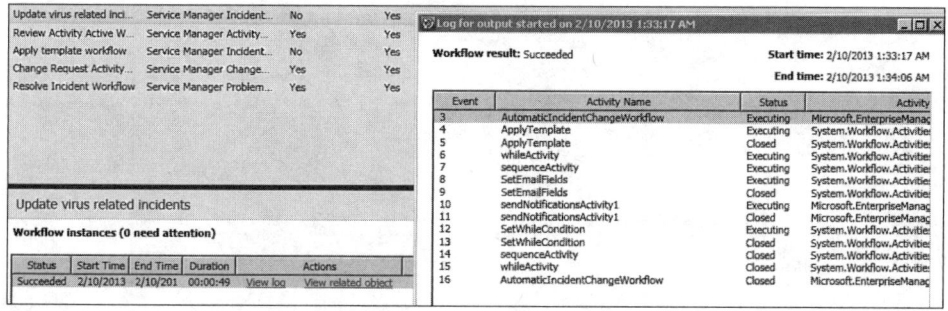

FIGURE 16.16   Displaying workflow status.

Figure 16.17 and Figure 16.18 show the incident before and after the workflow runs.

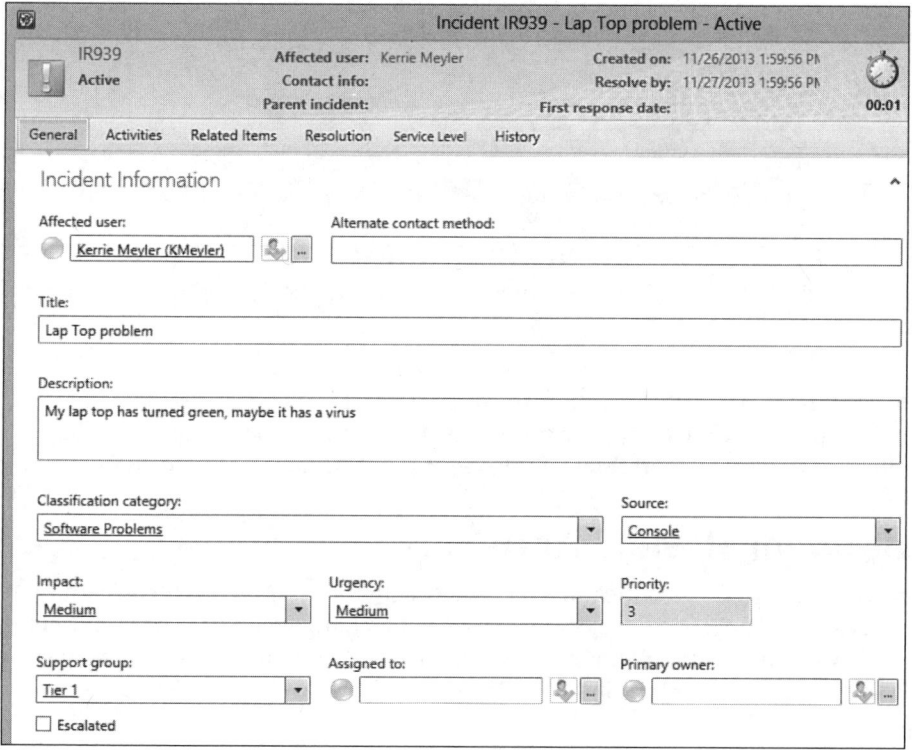

FIGURE 16.17   Incident before workflow has run.

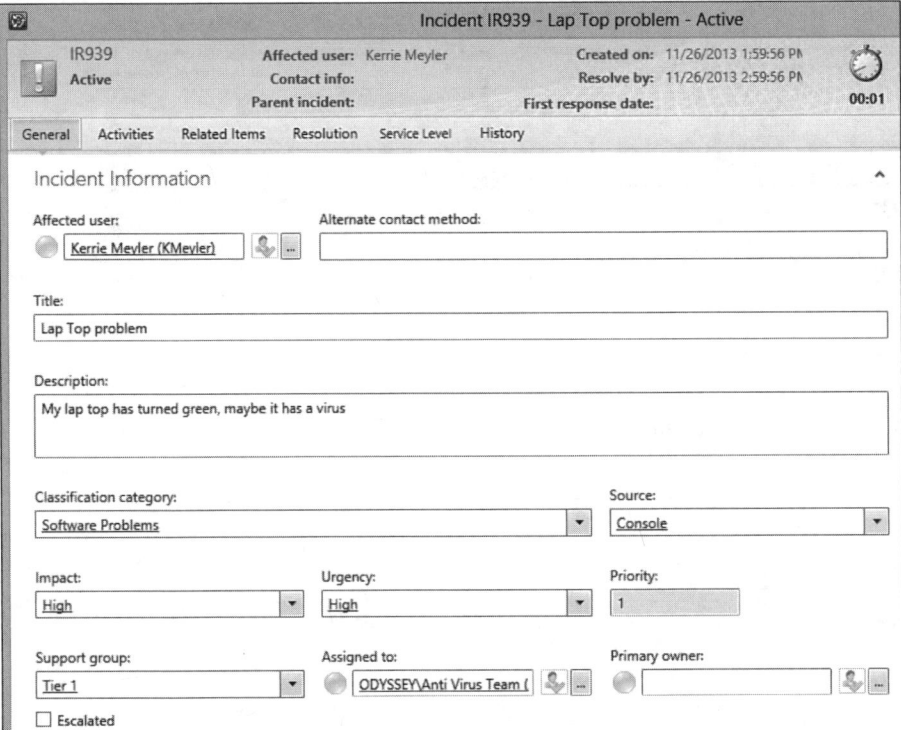

FIGURE 16.18   Incident after workflow has run; Impact, Urgency, Priority, and Assigned to are modified.

In Figure 16.18, the, Impact, Urgency, Priority, and Assigned to fields were updated by the workflow. Support Group was already set to Tier 1; otherwise, that would have been updated by the workflow. The workflow has also sent a notification to the antivirus team.

Notification for Review Activities

The next procedure configures notification for review activities to notify reviewers that they need to review and approve or reject an activity in a change request. The reviewers receive an email with information about the work item and a link to the Service Manager self-service portal. This procedure is divided into two areas, discussed in the following sections:

▶ **Creating a notification template:** Service Manager uses the notification template to define the format of the email it sends to reviewers.

▶ **Configuring notification workflow:** The workflow sends the email to reviewers, formatted according to the notification template.

Creating a Notification Template

To create a notification template for use with a change request, perform the following steps:

1. In the Service Manager console, navigate to **Administration -> Navigation -> Notifications -> Templates**.

2. Click **Create E-mail Template** in the Tasks pane.

3. On the General page of the Create E-mail Notification Template Wizard, add this information:

   ▶ **Name: Odyssey - Template for Reviewers Notification**

   ▶ **Targeted Class:** Review Activity (select class from menu)

   ▶ **Management Pack:** Optionally choose a different management pack

   Click **Next**.

4. On the Template Design page, add the following, also shown in Figure 16.19:

   ▶ **Send as HTML:** Checked

   ▶ **Message subject:** Activity to Review. ID: [WorkItem/ID]

   (Note that the WorkItem ID is a parameter inserted by the Insert button.)

   ▶ **Message Body: Hi,
**

   A review activity has been assigned to you for review. Please click the link to approve or reject the activity. <A HREF=http://server:82/SMPortal>Link to SCSM portal</A>

   **
**

   Thanks

   Notice that the URL in the text needs to be adapted for your environment. It should point to the Service Manager self-service portal. Reviewers can then simply click the link to access the activity to review.

16

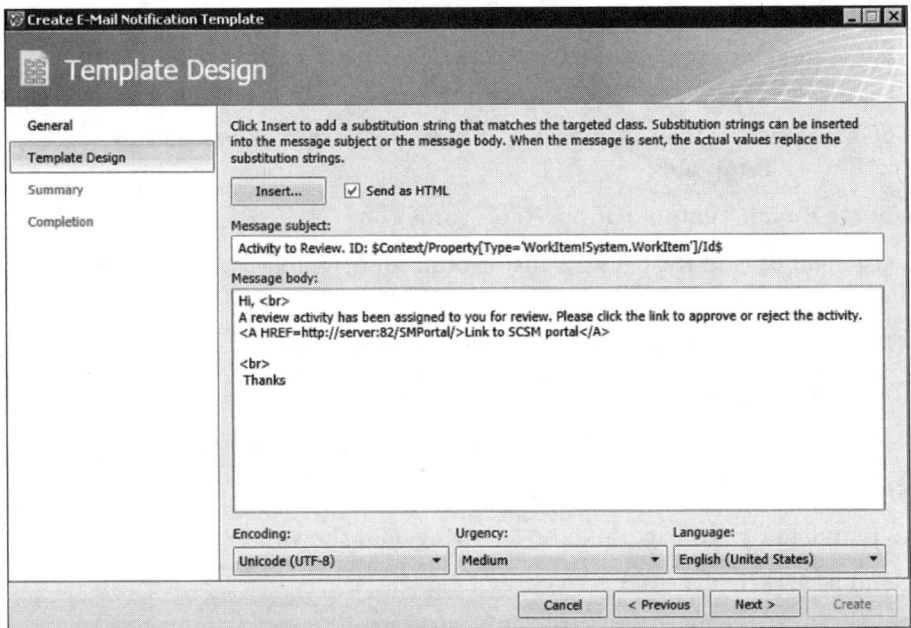

FIGURE 16.19   Message format of reviewer notification template.

5. Click **Next** on the Template Design page.

6. Click **Create** on the Summary page.

7. At the Completion page of the wizard, verify that the new email notification template was created successfully. Click **Close**.

Configuring an Activity Event Workflow

This section discusses configuring a workflow to send a notification. Activity event workflows are used for notifications when a notification needs to be sent based on a specific event. Examples of events include when an incident is reassigned from one support group to another or a change request is created with a specific word in the description field.

The next procedure configures an activity event workflow that sends a notification to reviewers. The notification is sent when the review activity is updated to In Progress. This occurs when previous activities are completed and Service Manager is now waiting for the reviewer to approve or deny the review activity. Follow these steps:

1. In the Service Manager console, navigate to **Administration -> Workflows -> Configuration**.

2. In the Results pane, select **Activity Event Workflow Configuration**.

3. In the Tasks pane, click **Configure Workflow Rules**.

4. In the Select a class dialog box, select **Review Activity** and then click **OK**.

5. In the Configure Workflows dialog box, click **Add**.

6. Click **Next** on the Before You Begin page of the Configure workflows for objects of class Review Activity Wizard.

7. On the Workflow Information page, input the information shown in Figure 16.20 and click **Next**.

   ▶ **Name: Odyssey - Notification to reviewers**

   ▶ **Check for events: When an object is updated**

   ▶ **Management pack:** Optionally choose a different management pack

8. On the Specify Criteria page, select the **Changed To** tab and configure as shown in Figure 16.21.

   `[Activity] Status Equals In Progress`

9. Click the **Changed From** tab and configure as shown in Figure 16.22.

   `Status does not equal In Progress`

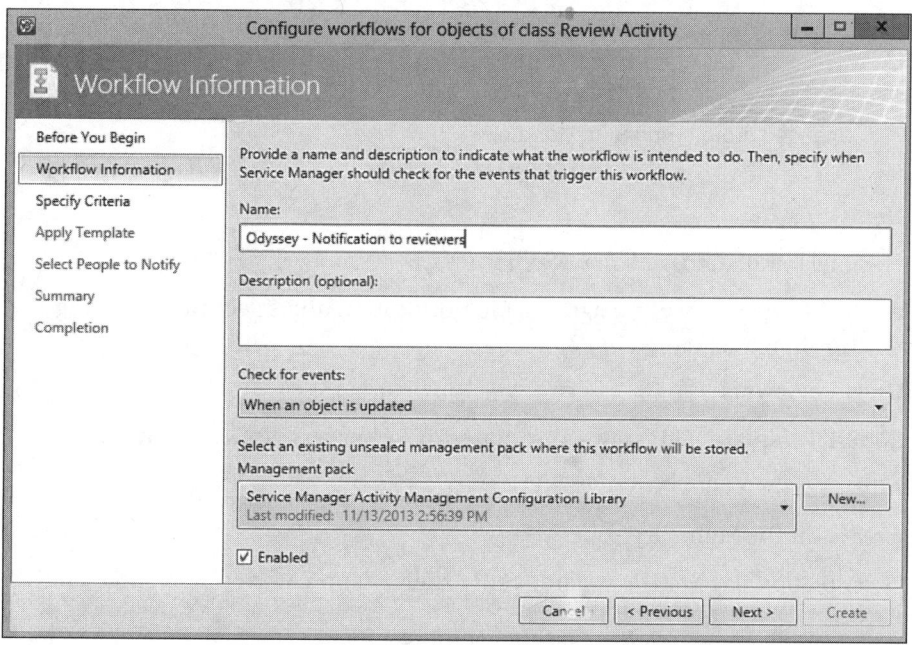

FIGURE 16.20   Workflow information.

16

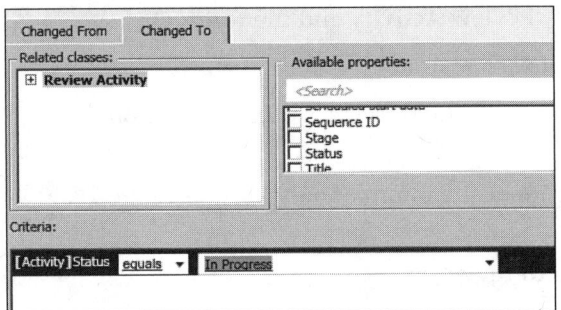

FIGURE 16.21   Changed To settings in workflow.

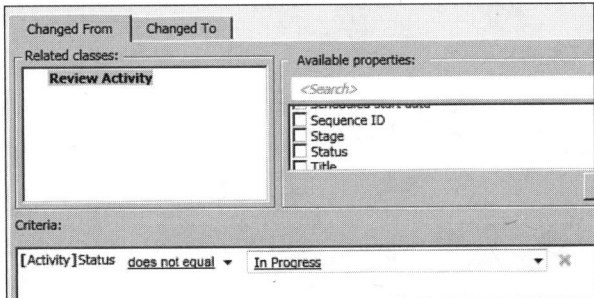

FIGURE 16.22   Changed From settings in workflow.

10. Click **Next**.

11. On the Apply Template page, click **Next**.

12. On the Select People to Notify page, enable notification and select the following settings, also shown in Figure 16.23:

    ▶ **User: Reviewers**

    ▶ **E-mail Template: Odyssey - Template for Reviewers Notification**

13. Click **Add**, and then click **Next**.

14. Click **Create** on the Summary page.

15. At the Completion page of the wizard, verify the workflow was created successfully. Click **Close**.

16. Click **OK** in the Configure Workflows dialog box.

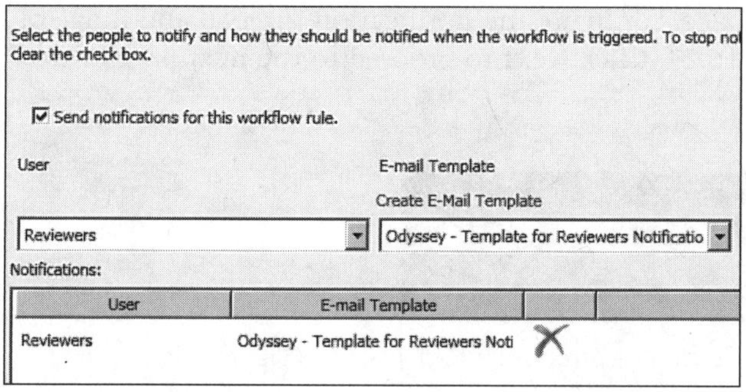

FIGURE 16.23   Notification settings in workflow.

You have configured a workflow that is triggered each time a review activity changes status from Not in progress to In progress. The workflow sends out a notification email to the reviewer specified in the review activity.

Creating Recurring Notifications

Service Manager 2012 introduces the ability to configure recurring notifications. The following procedure configures a notification subscription for all change requests that contain "Exchange" in the description and are scheduled to occur within a week. An email is sent for each work item fulfilling the specified criteria; thus if there are 15 active change requests for Exchange, there will be 15 emails each day. Follow these steps to configure the subscription:

1. In the Service Manager console, navigate to **Administration -> Notifications -> Subscriptions**.

2. In the Results pane, select **Create Subscription**.

3. Click **Next** on the Before You Begin page.

4. On the General page, input the following information and click **Next**:

   ▶ **Notification subscription name: Exchange Change Requests**

   ▶ **When to notify: Periodically notify when objects meet a criteria**

   ▶ **Target Class: Change Request**

   ▶ **Management Pack:** Optionally choose a different management pack

5. On the Additional Criteria page, configure the following criteria and click **Next**.

```
[Work Item] Description contains Exchange
AND [Work Item] Scheduled start date is less than or equals relative [now+7d]
AND [Change Request] Status does not equals Completed
OR [Change Request] Status does not equals Failed
OR [Change Request] Status does not equals Cancelled
```

6. On the Recurring Notification page, configure the notification interval and range of recurrence according to Figure 16.24. Click **Next** to proceed to the next page of the wizard.

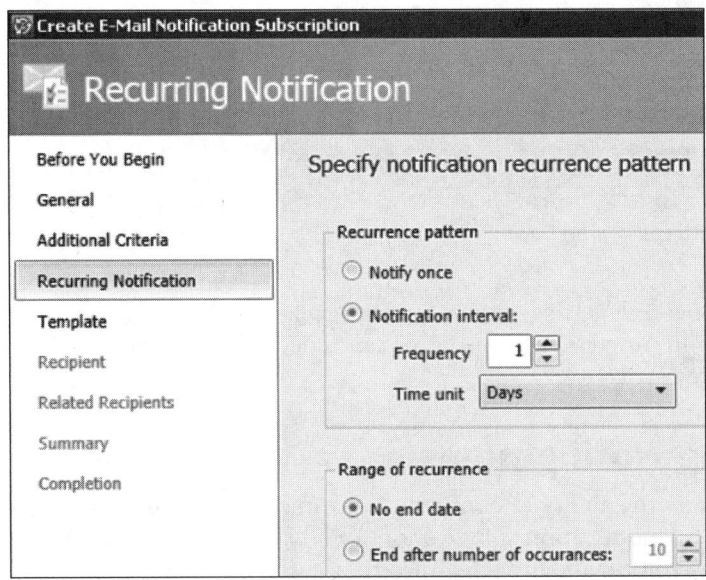

FIGURE 16.24   Notification recurring daily.

7. On the Template page, select a template to use for the notification, and then click **Next**.

8. On the Recipient page, select the recipient for the subscription. Click **Next** to proceed to the next page of the wizard.

9. On the Related Recipients page, select related recipients or click **Next**.

10. On the Summary page, review your settings and click **Create** to create the subscription.

11. On the Completion page, verify the subscription was created successfully. Click **Close**.

You now have configured a notification subscription that is triggered daily. The subscription sends an email for each Exchange-related change request that takes place within a week.

Fast Track

Service Manager 2012 does not introduce many new features for notification out of the box. Changes include updates to some of the wizards and user interface updates. The following are the significant changes in System Center that affect notification:

▶ **Recurring notifications:** When creating a notification subscription, you can configure recurring notifications. This feature sends notification emails based on a configurable interval as long as criteria for the subscription are fulfilled; for example, as long as an incident is unassigned you could have Service Manager send a notification email every 10 minutes or until 20 notifications have been sent.

▶ **System Center Orchestrator:** The System Center 2012 Orchestrator component can be used for notification scenarios. Orchestrator, which is an automation and integration platform, can integrate with Service Manager and many other systems from Microsoft and other vendors.

Summary

This chapter did not cover much clicking and navigation in the console. It focused on notification and the components on which notification is built. The chapter discussed how to configure notification, including the different components. This included recipients, the notification channel used to send the notification email, and configuring a notification template and a subscription. The chapter also discussed configuring different notification formats for different languages. You can use this feature to configure the notification language based on the recipient's Locale setting.

The chapter covered using notification in workflows. It discussed an example of when an antivirus related incident was routed within Service Manager and a notification email was sent. The chapter also discussed how to configure notification for review activity. Notification is useful in the review activity scenario. For change request reviewers that do not use the Service Manager console regularly, notifications are a great way to receive information about new review activities. The notification email could include a direct link to the Service Manager portal where the reviewer can work with the review activity.

The authors recommend you review all notification subscriptions and subscribers before activating them. Sending too many email notifications often leads to a recipient adding an automatic delete rule to his email client. Having too many workflows can also affect the performance of Service Manager.

16

Service Manager Security

Whether implementing Service Manager in a small, medium, large, or enterprise-sized company, security is an important consideration. There are multiple reasons:

▶ Security ensures that only specific individuals have access to specific parts of the system, which is crucial to any information technology service management (ITSM) system.

▶ The user's daily experience using the system can be optimized by showing only those parts to which the user has access, making her daily work more efficient.

Service Manager has a wide range of users that access it using different methods. This varies from end users, who might report an incident via the self-service portal, to administrators with full access. The list of employee types who interact includes

▶ Tier 1 analysts

▶ Tier 2-3 advanced operators

▶ Managers

▶ End users

▶ Administrators

▶ Developers

▶ Change managers

In addition to this list, Service Manager 2012 is a platform for Information Technology (IT) process automation. Not only must Service Manager be secure itself, it needs to interact with other systems in a secure manner. This could include using various user accounts for different purposes, as with workflow connections. Service Manager includes a configuration management database (CMDB); to read or update the database, other systems might need to connect to the Service Manager CMDB. This chapter describes the Service Manager security model and how you can use it to enable appropriate access without compromising security.

Role-Based Security

Service Manager uses a security model founded on the concept of role-based access control (RBAC), where each user in an organization is classified according to his or her job function. By grouping users with similar job functions together and applying a security scope, access can be limited to only what each user needs. Security boundaries can be created to grant or deny access to groups. Service Manager optimizes the user experience by limiting what users can see or use, based on the permissions granted.

You begin by defining a scope. This could be a security boundary to limit access to specific information, or a user experience scope to optimize the experience of the user's daily use of the console or portal. You then create a user role and provide access to the security boundaries. Finally, you add users or user groups to the user role to grant access. A user or group can be a member of multiple roles, providing the access they need.

Security Boundary Scoping

Different types of boundaries define security scopes. Service Manager 2012 includes six types of security scope boundaries:

- ▶ **Management pack:** A management pack can contain many types of classes (see Chapter 20, "Management Packs").

- ▶ **Configuration item groups:** A collection of objects (typically configuration items); as an example, all servers belong to web servers.

- ▶ **Catalog item groups:** A collection of service offering or request offering items for the self-service portal (SSP).

- ▶ **Queues:** A collection of work items, such as web incidents.

- ▶ **Classes:** An item that you manage, an example being `Windows Computer`.

- ▶ **Properties:** A piece of information about an object defined at the class level, such as a computer's fully qualified domain name (FQDN).

Each scope must define the management packs that contain the specific groups, queues, or classes. Examples follow:

- ▶ **Subdividing the configuration items, work items, or other items in the CMDB:** As an example, an administrator might want to group your servers depending on location. By using these groups of servers and creating a security boundary for the specific users, the administrator can ensure that users can only browse and use the configuration items of the servers at their location.

▶ **Limiting access to offerings:** An administrator might want to limit end users by using catalog item groups to only view and use a subset of the available offerings, displaying another set of offerings for database administrators.

▶ **Subdividing work items into several groups through the use of queues:** Users from Location A would not see the incidents related to Location B. This reduces the amount of unnecessary information viewed by the user, improves performance, and reduces load on the server and database.

▶ **Limiting access to specific properties in a class:** For example, some users might need to be able to write the implementation plan for a change request, while others should only have read access. This level of security can only define if a user can write to a property, or if it is read-only; it cannot limit the user's view of the property.

User Experience Optimization Scoping

To optimize the user experience, there are several approaches for limiting user access to areas of Service Manager. This includes using tasks, views, and form templates.

▶ **Tasks:** Also known as console tasks, these are actions the user can execute to perform a specific task on a specific type of object. Different tasks can be displayed to different types of users. As an example, the database administrators might have recovery console tasks to fix problems on their servers, while Tier 1 support staff only has access to a reduced set of tasks, or no tasks at all.

▶ **Views:** A view is a part of the console that shows a type of item. Items can be filtered for use with a specific purpose. The Service Manager console contains many views. Most users do not need access to all these views; by minimizing access, the console automatically hides them. This simplifies the user experience, since there is no visible view to access.

▶ **Form templates:** These are templates for a work item. A template is a partially complete object used to create a new object or applied to an existing object to set property values and add or remove relationships. An administrator might want to limit access to specific templates. For example, the administrator might only want specific users to be able to apply specific service request templates. This could be templates triggering specific runbooks, or a major work item such a change request based on the Major Change Request template.

Operations on the Data Access Service

Introduced in Chapter 4, "Looking Inside System Center 2012 Service Manager," the System Center Data Access Service is a Windows service that runs on each of the management servers deployed in a management group. It is a Windows Communication Foundation (WCF)-based web service through which all data access in Service Manager must pass. As such, it represents a single point of control for security authentication and authorization checks. Also known as the Data Access Service or DAS, this service has a number of different operations that can be called on the application programming interface (API). The four standard operations relevant to role-based security follow:

▶ **View:** This operation has permission to see information about an object.

▶ **Create:** This has permission to create an object.

▶ **Edit:** The Edit operation has permission to edit an object (or some properties of an object).

▶ **Delete:** This operation has permission to delete an object from the database.

Each operation focuses on a specific class of objects. For example, access could be granted to only view incidents, or only delete users. This is particularly important when creating custom code or services to automate specific actions. In this case, you want to limit user permissions to the absolute minimum.

About User Roles

A user role is the combination of the following:

▶ User role profile

▶ Security scopes (group, queue)

▶ User experience optimization scopes (templates, views, console tasks)

▶ Assignment of users and user groups to the user role

User roles define the connection between the different parts of the security model. Service Manager contains a number of predefined, default user roles, which you can assign to users or groups in your Active Directory.

You cannot change these roles, since they are designed to follow the different parts of the Information Technology Infrastructure Library (ITIL) and Microsoft Operations Framework (MOF), and they should be sufficient for the majority of Service Manager environments. If you need more specific user roles, you can create your own custom roles. When creating these roles you need to base the user role on a user role profile, and then you can customize the role to include or exclude different security scopes.

Default User Roles

Service Manager contains a number of user roles by default. These roles are similar to the user role profiles, and there is one user role for each user role profile, except that some of the profiles cannot be used in standard user roles (such as implied user roles). All user roles are globally scoped and cannot be deleted. The Administrators user role differs from the others in that it must contain one or more global groups.

The default user roles in Service Manager 2012 follow:

▶ Change Managers

▶ Incident Resolvers

- ▶ Activity Implementers

- ▶ Workflows

- ▶ Administrators

- ▶ Problem Analysts

- ▶ Advanced Operators

- ▶ Authors

- ▶ Change Initiators

- ▶ Release Managers

- ▶ Service Request Analysts

- ▶ Read-Only Operators

- ▶ End Users

User Role Profiles

Service Manager includes a number of user role profiles. A user role profile is a predefined object that describes and defines security scopes to provide or deny access to different parts of Service Manager. These user role profiles are used as a basis for a set of default user roles, which roles are intended to map to typical job functions in an organization according to MOF and ITIL best practices.

You can also create custom user roles. When creating a custom user role, an administrator must use a built-in user role profile upon which to build the custom role.

Built-in and Implied User Role Profiles

Out of the box, Service Manager provides the user role profiles listed in Table 17.1 and Table 17.2:

- ▶ Table 17.1 lists the user profiles used in built-in user role profiles, most of which could be used to create a custom role (Appendix A, "User Role Profiles Supplement," provides additional information on custom roles). The user role profiles are ordered in rough approximation of the scope of permissions, as End User and Read-Only Operator profiles have the least privileges and the Administrator profile has the most.

- ▶ Table 17.2 lists the user profiles you cannot use in any user role; these user profiles are *implied* user roles and are used whenever a specific permission is needed because of a relationship. As an example, the Implied Incident Affected User permission gives the affected user access to read the related incident.

Appendix A provides a detailed list of those permissions granted to each user role profile.

17

TABLE 17.1   Service Manager 2012 User Role Profiles

User Role Profile Name	User Role Profile Description
Report User	Individuals assigned a user role based on the Report User profile can view the Reporting workspace in the console and connect to the SQL Server Reporting Services (SSRS) server. Security for individual reports or folders of reports is configured in SSRS. Any user added to a user role based on the Report User profile must also be granted the Browser role, Publisher role, or Content Manager role on the SSRS server for the System Center\Service Manager report folder.
End User	Individuals assigned a user role based on the End User profile can use the self-service portal to create incidents, request software installation, view announcements, and search the knowledge base.
Read-Only Operator	Those individuals assigned a user role based on the Read-Only Operator profile have read-only access to work items in their queue scope and to configuration items in their group scope.
Change Initiator	Individuals assigned a user role based on the Change Initiator profile can create new change requests and activities for configuration items in their assigned group scope. These users also have read-only access to other work items such as incidents, change requests, or problems in their assigned queue scope.
Incident Resolver	Individuals assigned a user role based on the Incident Resolver profile can edit and create incidents, problems, and manual activities that are in their queue scope. They also have read-only access to other work items such as change requests in their queue scope and to configuration items in their group scope.
Activity Implementer	Individuals assigned a user role based on the Activity Implementer profile can edit only manual activities that are in their queue scope. They have read-only access to other work items in their queue scope and to configuration items in their group scope.
Operator	User roles based on the Operator profile can create work items and update incidents in their queue scope and can update status and notes of manual activities that are in their group scope. They also have read-only access to other work items in their queue scope and other configuration items in their group scope.
Service Request Analyst	User roles based on the Service Request Analyst profile can create and edit service requests and activity work items (such as review activities and manual activities) in their queue scope. These individuals also have read-only access to other work items in their queue scope and to configuration items in their group scope.
Problem Analyst	Individuals assigned a user role based on the Problem Analyst profile can edit and create problems in their assigned queue scope. They also have read-only access to other work items such as requests or incidents in their queue scope, and to configuration items in their group scope.

User Role Profile Name	User Role Profile Description
Change Manager	User roles based on the Change Manager profile can create and edit change requests and activity work items (such as review activities and manual activities) in their queue scope. Change Manager also has read-only access to other work items in their queue scope and to configuration items in their group scope.
Release Manager	User roles based on the Release Manager profile can create and edit release records and activity work items (such as review activities and manual activities) in their queue scope. These individuals also have read-only access to other work items in their queue scope and to configuration items in their group scope.
Advanced Operator	User roles based on the Advanced Operator profile can create or edit any work items in their queue scope and any configuration items in their group scope.
Workflow	User roles based on the Workflow profile can create and edit any configuration item or work item.
Author	User roles based on the Author profile can create or edit any work items in their queue scope and any configuration items in their group scope. They can also make limited customizations that are stored in management packs. Such customizations can include creating, editing, and deleting list items, tasks, templates, views, and view folders.
Administrator	User roles based on the Administrator profile have full access to all operations. Similarly, their queue scope and their group scope contain all objects in the system. This cannot be limited.

17

TABLE 17.2   Service Manager 2012 Implied User Role Profiles

User Role Profile Name	User Role Profile Description
Implied Incident Affected User	The Implied Incident Affected User profile includes a set of privileges designed to enable the incident's affected user to read and update the incident. Explicit user roles cannot be created based on this profile. User roles are created based on relationship assignments.
Implied Config Item Custodian	This profile includes a set of privileges designed to enable the configuration item's custodian to read the configuration item. Explicit user roles cannot be created based on this profile. User roles are created based on relationship assignments.
Implied Primary Computer User	The Implied Primary Computer User profile includes a set of privileges designed to enable the computer's primary user to read the computer configuration item. Explicit user roles cannot be created based on this profile. User roles are created based on relationship assignments.
Implied Activity Editor	The Implied Activity Editor can edit activities.

User Role Profile Name	User Role Profile Description
Implied Reviewer	The Implied Reviewer profile includes a set of privileges designed to enable the reviewer to vote and comment. Explicit user roles cannot be created based on this profile. User roles are created based on relationship assignments.

Console Workspace Access Permissions

Access to different workspaces of the Service Manager console is controlled by user role profiles as defined in Table 17.3.

TABLE 17.3   Workspace Access by User Role Profile

Profile	Work Items	Configuration Items	Authoring	Admin	Data Warehouse	Reports
Reporting User						X
End User						
Read-Only Operator	X	X				
Change Initiator	X	X				
Incident Resolver	X	X				
Activity Implementer	X	X				
Operator	X	X				
Service Request Analyst	X	X				
Problem Analyst	X	X				
Change Owner	X	X				
Release Manager	X	X				
Advanced Operator	X	X	X			
Workflow						
Author	X	X	X			
Service Manager Administrator	X	X	X	X		
Data Warehouse Administrator					X	

As an example, compare the visibility of different workspaces between an incident resolver user and an administrator, displayed in Figure 17.1.

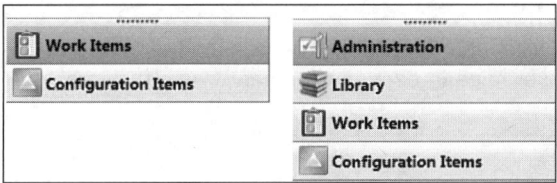

FIGURE 17.1   Workspaces visible to an incident resolver (left), and administrator user (right).

NOTE: WORKSPACES CREATED BY NON-MICROSOFT MANAGEMENT PACKS

Workspaces created by non-Microsoft management packs, such as the SLA Management workspace generated by importing the Cased Dimensions (a Microsoft partner) management pack are visible to users regardless of what user roles they are in.

Management Pack Elements Permissions

User role profiles determine those permissions a user has to create, edit, and delete management pack elements. Only those individuals assigned user roles associated with the Administrator and Author user role profiles can create, edit, and delete the following management pack elements:

▶ Templates

▶ Console tasks

▶ Views

▶ List items (in an existing list)

▶ Service offerings

▶ Request offerings

Administrators have full access to these management pack elements regardless of their target class. You can scope a user role based on the Author user role profile to only create, edit, or delete management pack elements depending on those classes to which they are targeted. As an example, you may want to allow a Tier 1 help desk manager to create only incident templates for his team and not to create change request templates.

Best Practices for Creating Custom User Roles

Often, you have to create your own user roles to supplement the ones provided with Service Manager. Before creating a custom user role, verify you have already created the custom groups, queues, templates, console tasks, and views with which you will be scoping your new user role. As a best practice, group together related queues, groups, views, console tasks, and templates to be assigned to a given user role into a single

17

management pack. This makes it easier to find and select those items when using the User Role Wizard.

TIP: USER ROLES ARE NOT TRANSPORTABLE

User roles are not stored in management packs and thus cannot be transported from one environment to another. You must create user roles in each environment where they are needed.

Using the Service Manager Console to Create Custom User Roles

Creating user roles with the console is straightforward as it is wizard-driven. To create a custom user role using the console, follow these steps:

1. Navigate to the Administration workspace. With the exception of managing announcements, only Administrators can manage configuration settings found in the Administration workspace.

2. In the Administration workspace, navigate to **Security -> User Roles**.

3. Select **Create User Role** in the Tasks pane, and you are asked to choose which user role profile to base the new user role on. You can create custom user roles based on any of the user role profiles indicated in the Able to Create Custom User Role column in Table 17.4.

TABLE 17.4   User Role Profiles

User Role Profile	Able to Create Custom User Role
Activity Implementer	X
Administrator	X
Advanced Operator	X
Author	X
Change Initiator	X
Change Manager	X
End User	X
Implied Activity Editor	
Implied Config Item Custodian	
Implied Incident Affected User	
Implied Primary Computer User	
Implied Reviewer	
Implied User Preference	
Incident Resolver	X
Operator	
Problem Analyst	X

User Role Profile	Able to Create Custom User Role
Read-Only Operator	X
Release Manager	X
Report User	X (in data warehouse)
Service Request Analyst	X
Workflow	

▶ It is not necessary to have multiple user roles based on the Report User user role profile, as that profile only controls access to the information regarding where the SQL Server Reporting Services server is located. SSRS controls all report security.

▶ The Workflow user role profile is a special user role profile designed to give workflows the rights necessary to perform typical workflow functions, thus there is no need for additional user roles based on that user role profile.

▶ As the Administrator user role profile has permissions to everything in the system, there is no need (nor is it possible) to create scoped custom user roles based on the Administrator profile.

▶ The End User user role profile is specifically designed to give users the permissions they need to use the self-service portal and therefore not designed to be used in custom user roles.

4. Select a user role profile to start the User Role Wizard. You see the same series of pages in the wizard for all user role profiles except the Author user role profile. When you create a user role based on the Author user role profile, you may also optionally scope the user role by classes.

You can scope custom user roles based on the Author user role profile using classes. This determines the classes for which the role is allowed to create templates, views, console tasks, and other management pack elements.

REAL WORLD: COMBINING USER ROLES FOR DIFFERENT PROCESSES

Rather than creating all encompassing, multiprocess user roles in Service Manager, create process-related user roles and combine the memberships. This approach requires fewer user roles and provides a better overview of how the roles are configured.

17

Using PowerShell to Create Custom User Roles

To automate the creation of a specific user role, use the New-SCSMUserRole PowerShell cmdlet provided with Service Manager 2012.

The following command creates a new user role using Service Manager management shell, based on the Author user role profile:

```
New-SCSMUserRole -UserRoleType Author -DisplayName "PowerShell Author Role" -View
  $views -Group @() -Queue @() -Task @() -User "Odyssey\testuser"
```

- ▶ Access is being granted to all views contained in the $views array.
- ▶ No access is granted to groups, queues, or tasks.
- ▶ Access to all form templates and classes is granted, because they are not defined.

The example first uses the UserRoleType parameter to define the base user role profile, and then it uses the View, Group, and Task parameters to grant access. There are parameters to define Class, FormTemplate, Group, Queue, Task, and View. If one of them is not defined, access will be granted to all objects of the specific type. The parameters accept an array of the specific type of objects.

To populate the $views array, use the following command:

```
$views = Get-SCSMView -DisplayName "*Service request*"
```

This snippet retrieves all views with a DisplayName containing "Service request". To provide access to none of a specified type, you should provide an empty array by using the syntax @().

Use Cases

To better understand the concepts of user roles, this section steps through a comprehensive example of setting up role-based security. You could use a table similar to Table 17.5 to map out your own business requirements to assist with implementing user roles in Service Manager. Follow these steps:

TABLE 17.5 Mapping Security Requirements to User Roles

User Type	Users	Users' Requirements to Interact with the System	Role & Scope	Group/Queue Scope	Views, Templates, Console Tasks Scope
End Users	HRStaff Employees of HR Department (since this is a pilot deployment only)	Create incidents on the SSP. Access HR request offerings on the SSP from the HR service offering. Search and read the knowledge base. View announcements.	Custom End Users user role	N/A	N/A
Tier 1 Service Desk Staff	T1SDStaff	Create and edit all incidents in main console. Search knowledge base. Create and edit service requests.	Incident Resolvers user role. Service Request Analysts user role	All	All
HR Applications Tier 2 and 3 support staff	HRAppsSupport	Create and edit all HR Apps incident in main console. Search knowledge base. Create and edit service requests. Create problems. Edit HR Apps problems. View only those configuration items related to HRWeb apps.	Custom Incident Resolvers user role. Custom Problem Analysts user role. Service Request Analysts user role	HRApps Incident Queue. HRApps Problem Queue. HRApps Service Request Queue. HRApps Servers & Services Group	HRApps views. HRApps templates

17

User Type	Users	Users' Requirements to Interact with the System	Role & Scope	Group/Queue Scope	Views, Templates, Console Tasks Scope
HR Application & Dev/Test team	HRAppsDevTest	Create and edit all types of work items related to HR Apps. View only those configuration items related to HRWeb apps.	Custom Advanced Operators user role	HRApps Incident Queue HRApps Problem Queue HRApps Change Request Queue HRApps Servers & Services Group	HRApps views HRApps templates
HR Apps Support Group Managers	HRAppsMgmt	Create and edit all types of work items related to HR Apps. View only those configuration items related to HRWeb apps. Create and edit templates, views, console tasks, and list items for incidents, problems, and service requests.	Custom Authors user role (Scoped to HR Apps problem, incident, and service requests)	HRApps Incident Queue HRApps Problem Queue HRApps Service Request Queue HRApps Servers & Services Group	HRApps views HRApps templates

1. Create and populate user groups in Active Directory with user accounts (you may already have these groups):

   ▶ HRStaff

   ▶ T1SDStaff

   ▶ HRAppsSupport

   ▶ HRAppsDevTest

   ▶ HRAppsMgmt

2. Create work item queues for each type of work item for HR Apps:

   ▶ HR Apps incidents

   ▶ HR Apps service requests

   ▶ HR Apps problems

   See Chapter 11, "Incident Management," for information on creating queues.

3. Create a configuration item group that contains all the HRWeb related configuration items such as servers, databases, web sites, services, and so on. Chapter 11 discusses creating groups.

4. Create views for HR application related incidents, problems, service requests, and configuration items. Chapter 11 includes information on creating views.

5. Create templates for HR application related incidents, problems, and service requests. Chapter 11 includes information on creating templates.

6. Create request offerings for the HR application and add them to the HR Apps service offering. Chapter 10, "Service Manager Service Catalog," describes creating a request offering.

7. Create a catalog group for HR request offerings and service offerings. Chapter 10 includes information on creating catalog groups.

After completing these actions, you (as the administrator) can proceed with creating the user roles. In this scenario, you need to assign users to several of the default user roles and create four custom user roles.

Create a Custom End User Role to Enable Access to SSP (HRStaff)

The staff in the HR department needs access to the self-service portal. This requires that you create a new custom user role based on the End User user role profile. Perform the following steps:

1. In the Service Manager console, navigate to **Administration** -> **Security** -> **User Roles**.

2. In the Tasks pane shown in Figure 17.2, click **Create User Role** -> **End User**.

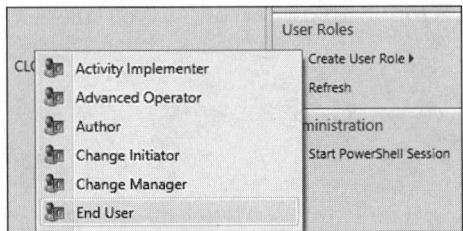

FIGURE 17.2   User role profile list in the console.

3. Click **Next** on the Welcome page.

4. Type in a name for the user role, such as **HR Tier 1 Service Desk Staff**. Click **Next**.

5. Select the management packs needed for the user role (see Figure 17.3). This selection limits the rest of the wizard, making it easier to select the objects in the next steps. Click **Next**.

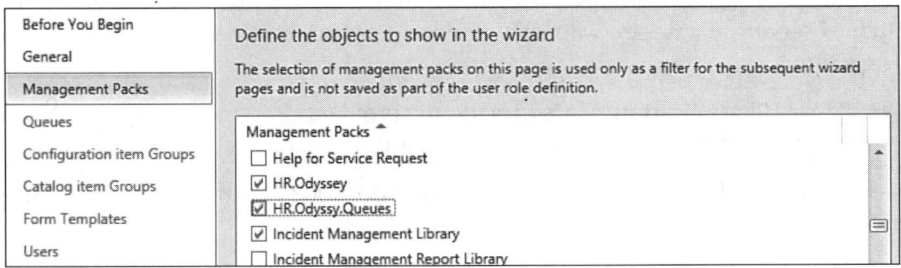

FIGURE 17.3   Management pack selector.

6. On the Queues page, select **Provide access to only the selected queues**. Do not select any queues for this user role. Click **Next** to continue.

7. On the Configuration Item Groups page, select **Provide access to only the selected groups**. Do not select any groups for this user role. Click **Next**.

8. On the Configuration Item Groups page, select **Provide access to only the selected groups** (see Figure 17.4). Select **HR Catalog Group**; this contains all the offerings for HR. Click **Next**.

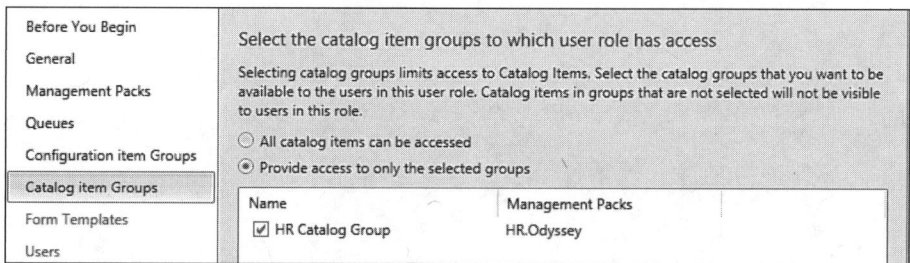

FIGURE 17.4   Catalog item groups selector.

9. On the Form Templates page, select **Provide access to only the selected forms**. Do not select any forms, and click **Next**.

10. On the Users page, add users to the user role. For this user role, add the **HRStaff** Active Directory group (see Figure 17.5). Click **Next**.

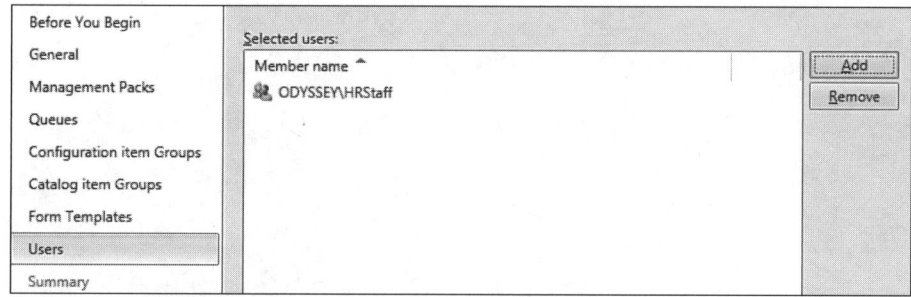

FIGURE 17.5   User selector.

11. Review the information on the Summary page and click **Create**.

The user role is now successfully created.

When a user from the HRStaff group accesses the self-service portal, all other offerings than those contained in the HR Catalog group are hidden, providing a simple view for the users. Figure 17.6 shows the self-service portal for a user in HRStaff.

An administrative user would see all offerings available. Figure 17.7 shows the self-service portal from an administrator point of view.

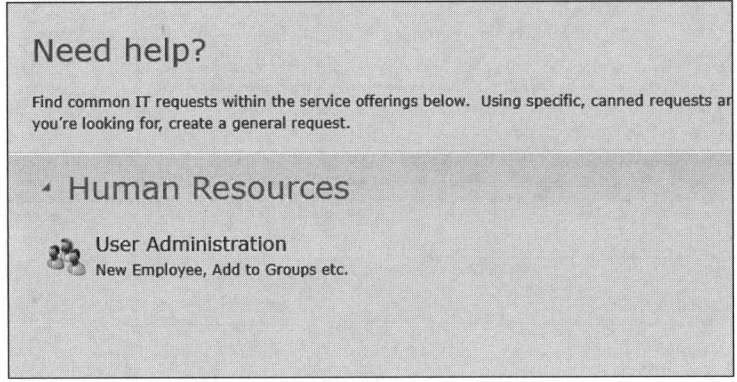

FIGURE 17.6   HRStaff user self-service portal view.

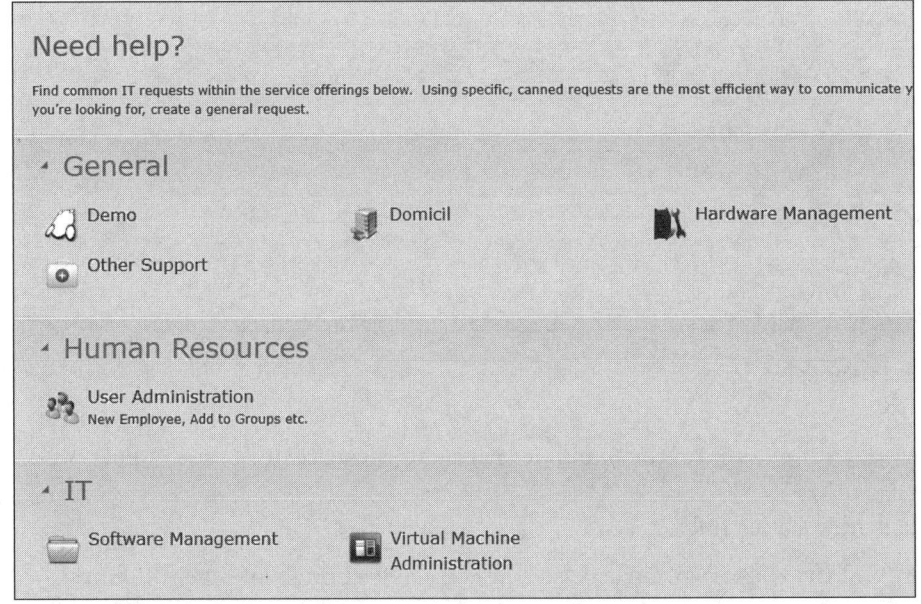

FIGURE 17.7   Administrator user self-service portal view.

As an end user does not have access to the console, a console view is not shown.

Create a Custom Author Role with Access to Only Specific Areas of Service Manager

An example of a more advanced user role is HR Apps Support Group Managers. Table 17.5 described the access that users need, which is provided by this user role. Notice there are more pages in the wizard for a user role based on the Author user role profile than there are for the End User profile. Perform the following steps to create this role:

1. In the Service Manager console, navigate to **Administration -> Security -> User Roles**.

2. In the Tasks Pane, click **Create User Role -> Author**.

3. Click **Next** on the Welcome page.

4. Provide a name for the user role, such as **HR Apps Support Group Managers**. Click **Next**.

5. Select the management packs needed for the user role (see Figure 17.8). This selection limits the rest of the wizard, making it easier to select the objects in the next steps. Click **Next**.

   ▶ **HR.Odyssey:** Contains the HR apps templates, views, queues, and groups already created

   ▶ **Incident Management Library:** Contains the `Incident` class

   ▶ **Service Manager Library Management Pack:** Contains the Templates, Tasks, Queues, Groups, and Lists views

   ▶ **Service Manager Knowledge Management Configuration Library:** Contains the Knowledge views

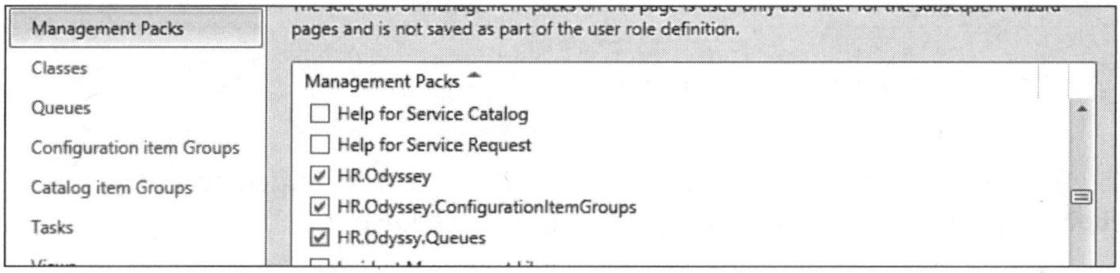

FIGURE 17.8   Filtering access by management packs.

6. On the Classes Page, select **Provide access to only the selected classes**. Select all HR class queues, as shown in Figure 17.9, and click **Next**.

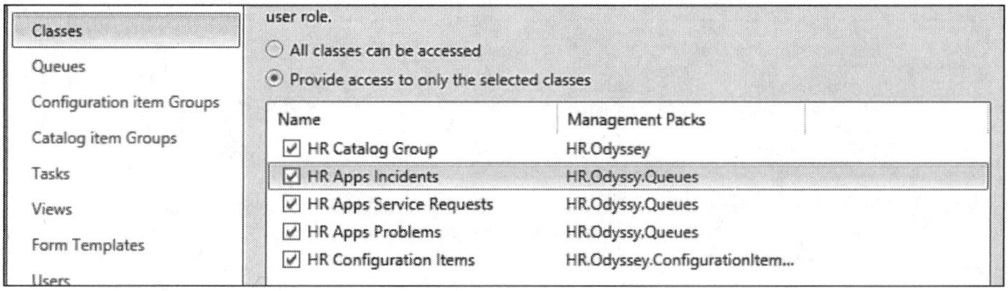

FIGURE 17.9   Using the class selector.

7. On the Queues page, select **Provide access to only the selected queues**. Select all HR queues for this user role as shown in Figure 17.10 and click **Next**.

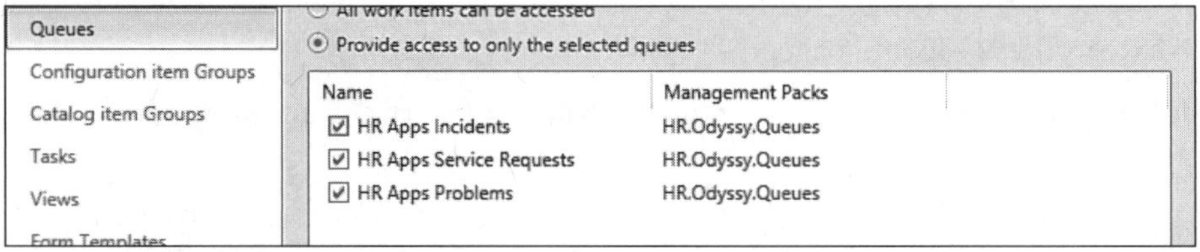

FIGURE 17.10   Using the queue selector.

8. On the Configuration Item Groups page, select **Provide access to only the selected groups**. Select the **HR Configuration Items** group (see Figure 17.11) and click **Next**.

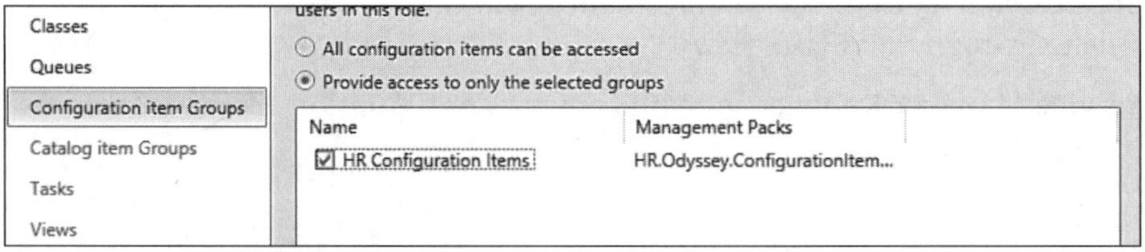

FIGURE 17.11   Configuration item groups selector.

9. On the Catalog Item Groups page (see Figure 17.12), select **Provide access to only the selected groups**. Select **HR Catalog Group** and click **Next**.

10. On the Tasks page, select **All tasks can be accessed** and click **Next** to continue.

11. On the Views page (see Figure 17.13), select **Provide access to only the selected views**. Select all HR views. Click **Next**.

12. On the Form Templates page, shown in Figure 17.14, select **Provide access to only the selected forms**. Select all HR forms and click **Next**.

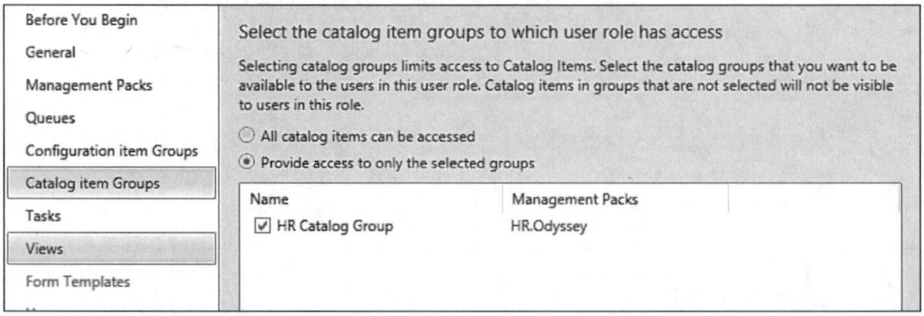

FIGURE 17.12   Catalog item groups selector.

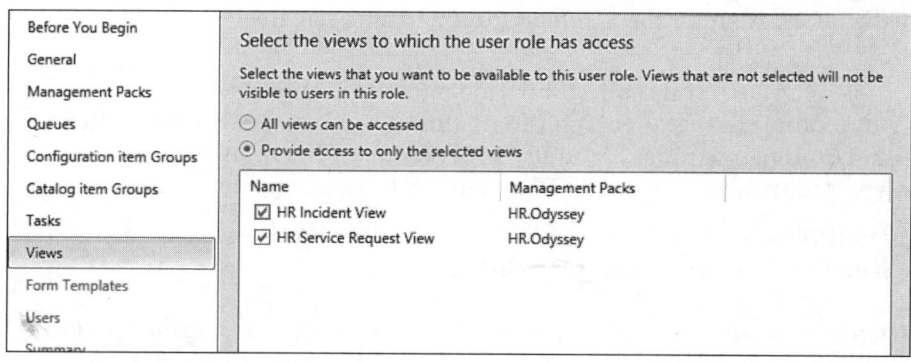

FIGURE 17.13   Views selector.

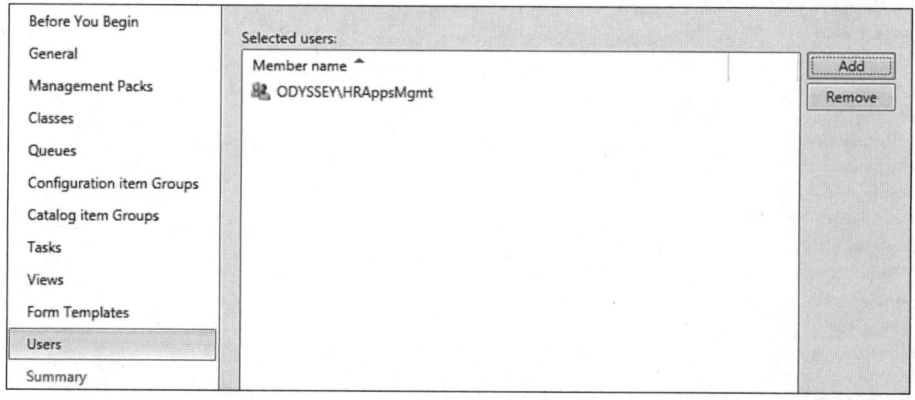

FIGURE 17.14   Form templates selector.

13. On the Users page (see Figure 17.15), add the users to the user role. For this user role, add the **HRAppsMgmt** Active Directory group. Click **Next**.

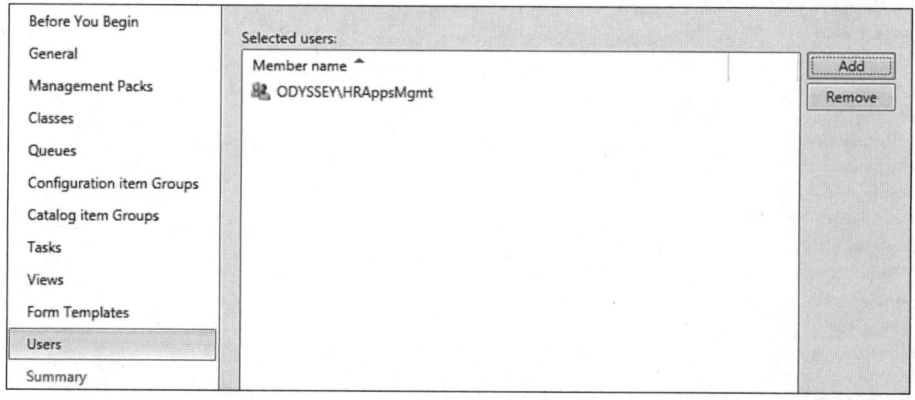

FIGURE 17.15   Users selector.

14. Review the information on the Summary page and click **Create**.

Once the user role is created, you can test it by adding a test user to the user role and then opening the console as that user. You can do this by either logging in to a different Windows session or using the runas.exe utility in Windows to launch the console in a different process. The syntax for the `runas` command to launch the console follows:

```
runas.exe /user:odyssey\testuser
Microsoft.EnterpriseManagement.ServiceManager.UI.Console.exe
```

Make sure that you only run one console process at a time. In addition, ensure you log out of the test user session or close the console after making changes to user roles to ensure the latest permissions are applied.

When you log on as the test user for this user role, you will notice that the user has a different experience than an administrator. As an example, the test user cannot see the Administration, Reports, or Data Warehouse workspaces (see Figure 17.16).

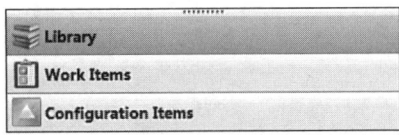

FIGURE 17.16   Workspace tabs seen by a user in the new custom Author user role.

Figure 17.17 shows the visible workspaces for a user in this role.

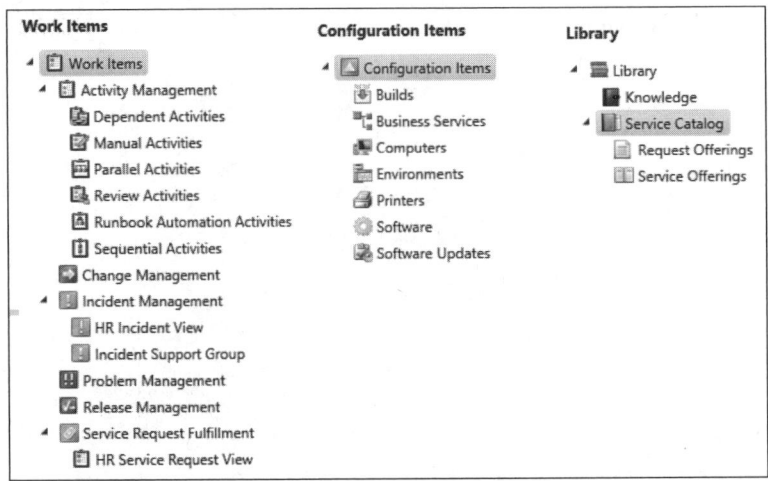

FIGURE 17.17   Workspace views seen by a user in the new custom Authors user role.

REAL WORLD: SERVICE MANAGER 2012 AND VIEW SCOPING

Nodes such as Activity Management, Manual Activities, Review Activities, Incident Support Group, Business Services, Computers, Printers, Software, and Software Updates look like views but are actually folders containing views. Each of these nodes does not have an expander next to it because there are no views contained in those folders that are visible to this test user. This is not the ideal user experience, as there is no action for a user to take on those folder nodes in the tree, and the nodes clutter the user experience. Unfortunately, this is just the way Service Manager currently works, but at least it is better than showing all the folders and all the views.

If you will be creating many views and use user roles to scope the views, consider using a long list of views and few if any folders. An administrator's user experience will be terrible because the views will not be organized, but the other scoped users in the system will have a clutter-free experience without useless folders appearing. There is one case where it is good to show the folders to a given user even if there are no views visible to the user in that folder—this is when the user is a member of Authors or Administrators user roles so the person can create new views in those folders.

The user can see only those views explicitly granted in the user role. Because the user role was not granted any configuration item views, only the folders are displayed. This could become an issue for people in this user role since it would be inconvenient to view the data. This oversight was intentional to illustrate the effect of not granting all the necessary views in all the workspaces. If you forget to add something like this, you can go back to the User Role properties dialog and add it. If you need to go back and edit the user role though, you will need to sift through all the templates, tasks, views, classes, queues, and groups pages of the wizard. It is much more efficient to get it right using the management pack filtering the first time through the wizard!

Data Warehouse and Reporting Security

The data warehouse and reporting platform used by Service Manager is designed as the long-term platform for all of System Center reporting. As such, it stands separate from Service Manager and simply uses Service Manager as a data source. The data warehouse can consume data directly from other sources such as Operations Manager and Configuration Manager (see http://technet.microsoft.com/en-us/library/hh519633.aspx), and even user-defined data sources. Therefore, the data warehouse and reporting has its own security model and infrastructure. Data warehouse security is a combination of role-based security similar to what you find in Service Manager and the role-based security model of SSRS. The data warehouse databases and workflow infrastructure are secured using the System Center common platform capabilities similar to Service Manager. Reports are secured using SSRS. Differing from Operations Manager, Service Manager does not replace rights on SSRS.

Data Warehouse Administrators User Role

During setup of the data warehouse, the account or group specified during installation is placed into the Administrators role in the data warehouse management group. The following is the process used for determining whether a user is a data warehouse administrator and therefore should have visibility to the data warehouse:

1. The console connects to a Service Manager management group management server.

2. The console gets a global setting, which stores the name of the data warehouse management group management server name. Remember that any user can read the global settings.

3. The console attempts to connect to the data warehouse management group management server. The Data Warehouse workspace icon is displayed if the user is in the Administrators user role in the data warehouse management group.

If necessary, you can manage the membership of the data warehouse management group Administrators user role using the User Roles view in the Data Warehouse workspace.

Granting Access to Reports

To access reports in the Service Manager console, a user must be a member of the Report Users user role in the data warehouse management group. A data warehouse administrator can manage the membership of the Report Users user role from the User Roles view in the Data Warehouse workspace. The user also must be granted permissions in SQL Server Reporting Services to at least some of the reports under the System Center -> Service Manager folder. See http://technet.microsoft.com/en-us/library/bb522824.aspx for information on roles and permissions in SSRS.

Following are the conditions Service Manager uses to determine which reports to show to a user:

▶ **Ability to open the Service Manager console:** Is the user in a Service Manager user role other than the End Users user role?

  This determines whether the user can even open the Service Manager console.

▶ **Service Manager data warehouse association:** Is the Service Manager management group the console is connecting to associated with a data warehouse?

  This determines whether the console should even attempt to display the Reports workspace.

▶ **Ability to view the Reports workspace:** Is the user in the Report Users user role in the data warehouse management group?

  This determines whether the console should show the Reports workspace and attempt to retrieve the list of reports visible to the user from SQL Server Reporting Services.

▶ **Report permissions:** Does the user have permission to read any of the reports on the SSRS instance associated with the data warehouse?

This list of reports/folders will be displayed in the Service Manager console's Reports workspace.

Users can always access reports directly through the SQL Server Reporting Services browser interface without going through the Service Manager console, but they can only open those reports to which the SSRS administrator has granted access.

Some best practices for report security follow:

▶ **Remember that security goes through SSRS:** SSRS controls report security, not Service Manager. Just because someone is not in the Report Users user role in Service Manager does not mean she cannot access the reports; she can always get around Service Manager security by using the SSRS browser interface. The Report Users user role simply controls whether the reports are visible in the Service Manager console.

▶ **Utilize Active Directory security groups:** Create a user group for each logical group of report users and grant these user groups access to the reports on SSRS. Create a parent user group containing these user groups and place that in the Report Users user role and some other Service Manager user role so all can access the reports through the Service Manager console. This enables you to manage just the membership of the child groups as people come and go. Ideally, you would use Forefront Identity Manager or similar software to delegate administration of these user groups to area owners.

▶ **Data in the Service Manager data warehouse cannot be scoped:** Just because a user does not have permission to view some data in the Service Manager database doesn't mean he cannot see it in the data warehouse. Do not give users scoped in Service Manager via user roles access to run reports that are not scoped!

▶ **Use linked and scheduled reports:** Create linked reports prescoped to some particular scope such as a queue or group, and then grant users access to those linked reports only. For additional security, schedule prescoped reports and deliver these to the user through email, SharePoint, or a file share—rather than allowing the user to run the reports on SSRS directly.

Advanced User Role Scenarios

Although not entirely obvious, there are ways to utilize user roles to fulfill commonly requested scenarios; these typically involve scoping access to self-service portal content. As an example, it is common to want to display one set of announcements to one group of end users and show a different set of announcements to other users. This could be because there are announcements pertinent only to a certain group of users because of location, the services they use, or their job function. Similarly, organizations often also want to filter the knowledge articles displayed on the portal or the list of software titles that can be requested based on the person's job role.

Scoping Knowledge Articles

Scoping knowledge articles is easy to accomplish using the existing data model for knowledge articles. Before starting, determine how to classify knowledge articles so you can divide them into different groups of knowledge articles. You could use the Keywords field to enter special strings into, although that is somewhat error prone. A better choice is using the Category field. You can modify this list to contain options that make sense in your organization by navigating to Authoring -> Lists-> Knowledge Article in the console, and clicking Properties in the Tasks pane. Another option is to create your own custom field and customize the form to show it using the Service Manager Authoring Tool.

The example in this section uses the Category field. The Category list (see Figure 17.18) has been modified to include just a few options that can be used to subdivide the knowledge base into articles based on the particular organization—Engineering, Finance, or Human Resources.

Next, you create a series of groups that include knowledge articles based on the Category being a certain value using dynamic membership rules. Create one group for each category. For example, you could create a group called Engineering Knowledge Articles, which have criteria like that seen in Figure 17.19.

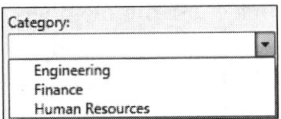

FIGURE 17.18   Knowledge form Category field after modification in the Lists view.

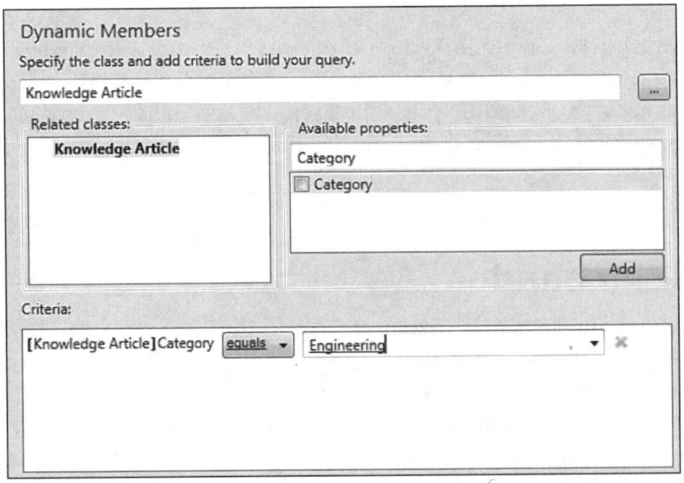

FIGURE 17.19   Setup criteria for the Knowledge Article group.

You also need to create a group of all users in the database by creating a dynamic membership rule with the `Domain User` or `Group` class and no additional criteria. You could call it the All Users and Groups group.

Finally, to modify and create the user roles, follow these steps:

1. Remove the Authenticated Users user group from the End Users user role. This user group is placed in the End Users user role out of the box for convenience, but it also grants any member of that role the ability to view all configuration items including knowledge articles.

2. Create a user group in Active Directory for each group of users in each organization: Engineering, Finance, Human Resources.

3. Create a user role based on the Incident Resolver user role for each of the organizations. Do not grant the user role permission to any queues. Grant permission to the All Users and Groups group you just created and to the corresponding group of knowledge articles for each organization. As an example, if you are creating the Engineering Incident Resolvers user role, grant permission to the Engineering Knowledge Articles group you created in this section. Add the Active Directory user group for the Engineering users.

4. Assuming you want end users to submit change requests from the portal, you need to create a user role based on the Change Initiator user role profile for each of the organizations. In this user role, don't grant any groups or queues.

Scoping Announcements

Scoping announcements is similar to scoping knowledge articles; the only difference is that there is not a good out of the box field to categorize announcements by. You can add a new field based on the List data type to the Announcement class using the Authoring Tool. After importing the management pack, you can add list values in the Lists view in the Authoring workspace. As an example, you could add a new property called Organization with list items of Engineering, Finance, and Human Resources. Use the same pattern for creating groups and users roles to scope announcements as described previously in the "Scoping Knowledge Articles" section.

Scoping Software Packages

You can also scope the list of software packages available for request from the SSP. The approach is essentially the same as for announcements and knowledge articles:

1. Remove the Authenticated Users group from the End Users user role.

2. Create groups of software packages.

3. Follow the same approach as explained previously in the "Scoping Announcements" section by creating a new property on the `Package` class.

4. Create groups with dynamic membership rules. It may be more appropriate to select specific packages on the Included Members page of the wizard. Figure 17.20 shows selecting specific software packages to include in the group.

5. After creating the groups, you can assign them to the appropriate user roles.

When users log in to the self-service portal they can only select from those software packages they have permission to.

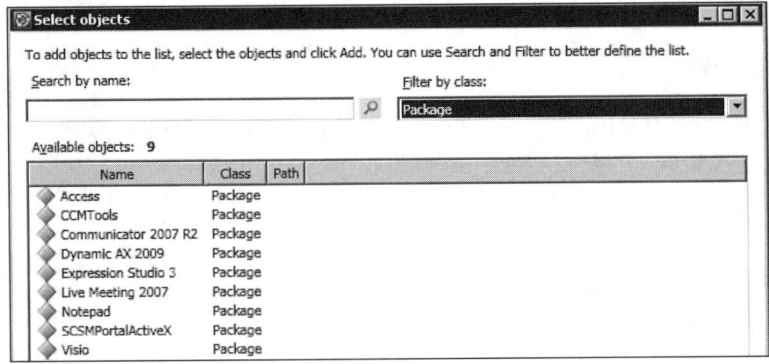

FIGURE 17.20   Selecting packages to include in a group.

Run As Accounts

The concept of Run As accounts has been carried over as part of the System Center common platform from Operations Manager. If you are familiar with Run As accounts in Operations Manager, you have a head start on understanding them in Service Manager. Run As accounts allow different processes to run under the security context of specified user credentials.

All Run As accounts are tested by the system. The system tries to authenticate the accounts by attempting a logon. If the logon fails, event ID 7000 is logged to the event log.

Run As Account Usage Scenarios

Following are some scenarios where you can use Run As accounts:

▶ System Run As accounts are used to allow system processes to access system resources such as the databases and local resources on the management servers. In some cases, system Run As accounts are used to access resources outside Service Manager.

▶ Run As accounts can be specified when creating connectors. This enables the connectors to connect to those other systems as a user account that has the appropriate permissions required in those systems.

► You can create custom Run As accounts to use when running your workflows. When the management packs containing the definition of those Run As accounts are imported into the system, the administrator can specify the user account to use for that Run As account.

► Similar to how organizations can create custom Run As accounts, partners can declare Run As accounts in their management packs. When the organization imports those management packs, the administrator can specify which user account to use for that partner's Run As account.

Out of the Box Run As Accounts

Two user accounts are specified to install Service Manager: the system account and the workflow account.

► The account provided for the system account is used for the System Center Data Access Service and the System Center Management Configuration Windows services on the management server. It is also used for the Operational System Run As account. This account is added to the local Administrators group on the management server, and is effectively an administrator in Service Manager. Any process that can run under this security context on the management server has complete control of Service Manager and the management server.

► The workflow account is used only for the Workflow Run As account. It is added to the Workflows user role so that workflows running under this security context have the permissions necessary to query and update Service Manager.

When new workflows are created using the Authoring Tool, they default to using the Operational System account Run As account for the `DataSourceModule` element, regardless of whether you use a `System.Scheduler` (see http://msdn.microsoft.com/en-us/library/ee692985.aspx for a reference guide) or a subscription data source module.

You can see this in the eXtended Markup Language (XML), where it looks like

```
RunAs="SystemCenter!Microsoft.SystemCenter.DatabaseWriteActionAccount"
```

The management pack alias `SystemCenter!` is for the Microsoft.SystemCenter.Library management pack. Operational System account is the display name for `Microsoft.SystemCenter.DatabaseWriteActionAccount`.

The Operational System Run As account is also used to submit the task that will execute the Windows Workflow Foundation. All of this should be essentially transparent to a workflow author because it just works!

The Windows Workflow Foundation workflow, command line activity, VBScript, or PowerShell script always executes under the security context of the workflow account Run As account. In the XML, it looks like this:

```
RunAs="Core!Microsoft.SystemCenter.ServiceManager.WorkflowAccount"
```

17

The management pack alias `Core!` is for the ServiceManager.Core.Library management pack.

Therefore, if creating workflows in Service Manager using the Authoring Tool, there are three things to take into consideration given that the actual work will be performed in the part of the workflow running as the workflow account Run As account:

▶ Verify the workflow account has the permissions required to perform the actions you need in Service Manager itself. Out of the box, this account is added to the Workflows user role, which is based on the workflows user role profile. Review the permissions granted to the workflows user role profile in Table 17.3 to ensure the objects you want to query and update in Service Manager are allowed to do so. If they are not, add the account used for the workflow Run As account to the Administrators user role that has global access.

▶ If your workflow will be accessing resources locally on the management server (such as the Registry or event log), grant the account used for the workflow account the local permissions required on the management server.

▶ If your workflow will be accessing resources on some other system such as querying another database or running PowerShell against Active Directory, verify the workflow account has the permissions required on those external systems.

Creating and Using Custom Run As Accounts

On occasion, it might not be feasible or appropriate to use the workflow account to access remote resources. Such cases could include domain trust issues or where a given user account is not allowed to access multiple secured resources due to separation of authority policies in an organization. In these cases, you can use a custom Run As account instead of the workflow account.

Run As accounts can be created using several different methods:

▶ In the Service Manager console

▶ Using PowerShell in the Service Manager Shell

▶ In management pack XML

The next sections describe how to create Run As accounts, usage, and the pros and cons of the different creation methods.

Run As accounts can be defined using three different account types:

▶ Local System account

▶ Network Service account

▶ Windows account

The last option listed is the most widely used method, since it allows defining any Windows user local or domain account.

Using the Console to View and Edit Existing Run As Accounts

Current Run As accounts can be viewed using the console. Perform the following steps to view existing Run As accounts in a Service Manager environment:

1. In the Service Manager console, navigate to **Administration -> Run As Accounts** (see Figure 17.21).

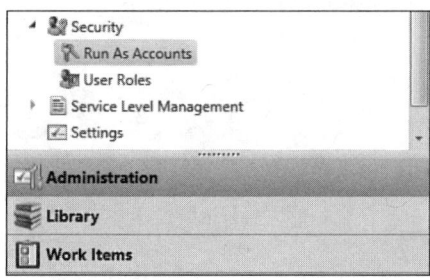

FIGURE 17.21   Run As Accounts view in the Service Manager console.

2. Double-click an account to open the Run As Account page shown in Figure 17.22.

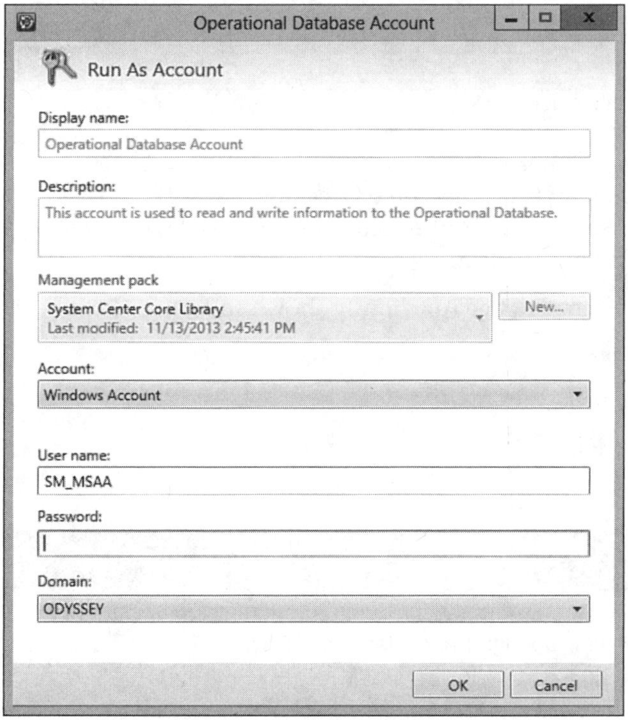

FIGURE 17.22   Run As Account page.

3. Change the account type and/or user account information on the page.

4. Click **OK**.

Using the Console to Select a Run As Account on a Connector

When you need to select a Run As account, you can do so in the Run As account selector. The selector (displayed in Figure 17.23) is shown in several different places:

▶ When creating a connector

▶ Editing a connector

▶ Settings for custom add-ons

FIGURE 17.23   Run As Accounts selector.

Use the drop-down list to select a Run As account.

Using the Console to Create a Run As Account

Run As accounts cannot be created directly from the Run As Account view. To create a Run As account in the console, the Run As Account selector must be available in the console. Follow these steps to create a new account:

1. Click **New** to open the Run As Account page (previously shown in Figure 17.22).

2. Fill in the account type.

3. Fill in the username and password.

4. Click **OK**.

NOTE: CONSOLE RUN AS ACCOUNTS ARE ALWAYS SAVED IN DEFAULT MANAGEMENT PACK

Run As accounts created from the console are always saved in the default management pack Service Manager Linking Framework Configuration. Use PowerShell or XML to save the account in a custom management pack.

Using the Service Manager Shell to List Existing Run As Accounts

Using the Service Manager Shell to manage your Run As accounts provides more flexibility than with the console:

▶ In the Service Manager Shell, the following cmdlet lists all Run As accounts:

```
Get-SCSMRunAsAccount
```

▶ To search for a specific Run As account, you can use the different parameters for this cmdlet such as Id, Name, DisplayName, UserName, and/or Domain.

▶ To retrieve all the Run As accounts that start with the letter W you can use the
   -DisplayName parameter.

```
Get-SCSMRunAsAccount -DisplayName "W*"
```

Using the Service Manager Shell to Create a Run As Account

When you use PowerShell to create your Run As account, you can place the account in any management pack. This gives you an advantage compared to creating it with the console.

To create a Run As account in PowerShell you must first create a new management pack or get an existing management pack reference. To create a new management pack in PowerShell, use the following snippet:

```
$mp = New-SCSMManagementPack -DisplayName "Run As Account ManagementPack" -PassThru
```

This creates a management pack named Run As Account Management Pack and saves a reference to it in the variable called $mp. The -PassThru parameter is used to send the new management pack reference to the variable.

This snippet gets a reference for an existing management pack by name:

```
$mp = Get-SCSMManagementPack -Name "My Management Pack"
```

This example retrieves the management pack reference for the management pack called My Management Pack.

To create a new Run As account, you then use the reference for the management pack together with the New-SCSMManagementPack cmdlet:

```
New-SCSMRunAsAccount -ManagementPack $mp -Domain "odyssey" -UserName "jsvendsen" `
-Password (ConvertTo-SecureString -String "Start123" -AsPlainText -Force) `
-DisplayName "MyRunAsAccount" -PassThru | Format-List *
```

This snippet uses the management pack saved in $mp to create a new Run As account with the name MyRunAsAccount and uses the user jsvendsen from the domain Odyssey with the password Start123. To add the password, you must first convert it into an encrypted text string (secure string) and then pass it to the password parameter in the New-SCSMRunAsAccount cmdlet.

17

Your output will show information regarding the new account (see Figure 17.24). The `SecureReference` property contains the value that is used to reference the Run As account in the management pack XML (see the "Using Management Pack XML to Define a Run As Account" section).

```
Description     :
DisplayName     : MyRunAsAccount
Domain          : odyssey
UserName        : jsvendsen
Password        : System.Security.SecureString
SecureReference : SecureReference.b9c37e6e962447b2832655045542a3dc
```

FIGURE 17.24   Output from `New-SCSMRunAsAccount`.

NOTE: SECURE REFERENCE NAME

Unfortunately, you cannot specify the name of the secure reference when using PowerShell. This can make it slightly more complicated to use it in XML. To define a name, use management pack XML to define your Run As account.

Using Management Pack XML to Define a Run As Account

This section describes authoring management packs in XML; for information about authoring see Chapter 22, "Customizing Service Manager."

When using XML to create custom management packs, a developer can choose to include a Run As account in the management pack. As an example, a Run As account can be used as an alternative account for a workflow, or a custom connector. In XML, a Run As account is called a `SecureReference`.

The following code defines a Run As account in management pack XML:

```
<TypeDefinitions>
    <SecureReferences>
      <SecureReference ID="MyRunAsAccount" Accessibility="Public"
        Context="System!System.Entity"/>
    </SecureReferences>
</TypeDefinitions>
```

`ID` can be defined to a value of your choice. The value is used to reference this Run As account in other parts of this management pack or other management packs.

The `System!` management pack reference points to the `System.Library` management pack, which needs to be referenced in the reference section of the management pack using the alias `System`.

The `<TypeDefinitions>` section needs to appear immediately after the `<Manifest>` section.

▶ If you have an `<EntityTypes>` section inside the `<TypeDefinitions>` element, put the `<SecureReferences>` section immediately after the `<EntityTypes>` section.

▶ If you have a `<ModuleTypes>` section inside `<TypeDefinitions>`, place the `<SecureReferences>` section just before `<ModuleTypes>`.

To define a location for the system to save the credential information, a `SecureReferenceOverride` must be added to the management pack. The following code defines a `SecureReferenceOverride`:

```
<Monitoring>
  <Overrides>
    <SecureReferenceOverride ID="SecureReferenceOverride.MyRunAsAccount"
      Context="System!System.Entity" Enforced="false"
      SecureReference="MyRunAsAccount">
      <Value>0</Value>
    </SecureReferenceOverride>
  </Overrides>
</Monitoring>
```

The `SecureReference` attribute must reference an existing `SecureReference`; this examples references the `MyRunAccount` that was previously defined.

The `<Value>` node needs to have a value set for the management pack to be validated. Therefore add "0" as a default value in this node. This sets the credentials to "local system" when the Run As account is imported; afterward it can be set to the credential of choice.

The `SecureReferenceOverride` has to be placed in the `<Overrides>` section of the `<Monitoring>` section.

In the management pack, the `<Monitoring>` section must appear immediately after the `<Categories>` section.

NOTE: USING VISUAL STUDIO AUTHORING EXTENSIONS TO DEFINE SECUREREFERENCE OVERRIDES

The current version of Visual studio Authoring Extensions (VSAE) does not support adding a `SecureReferenceOverride` to a Service Manager management pack. To develop the management pack in VSAE, create a new Operations Manager 2012 R2 management pack, and reference the Service Manager management pack. See Chapter 23, "Advanced Customization Scenarios," for additional information on VSAE.

A good practice is to add a display string to any management pack element. Users see this name in the console. To add a display string for this secure reference, add the following to the `<DisplayStrings>` section of a `<LanguagePack>` in the `<Languages>` section of the management pack.

```
<DisplayString ElementID="MyRunAsAccount">
    <Name>My Run As Account</Name>
</DisplayString>
```

Multiple language packs can be added to support multiple languages.

Any Run As account defined in the XML is not shown to the user unless it is added to a built-in category called `System.VisibleToUser`. To add the reference to the category, use the following code inside the `<Categories>` section of the management pack:

```
<Category ID="MyRunAsAccountVisibleToUser" Target="MyRunAsAccount"
          Value="System!VisibleToUser"/>
```

The `Target` attribute defines which secure reference to add to the category.

After importing this management pack into Service Manager, you need to set the credentials to use for this Run As account. You can set the credentials using the UI or using PowerShell. To set the credentials using PowerShell, use the `Set-SCSMRunAsAccount` cmdlet provided in the SMLets CodePlex project (http://smlets.codeplex.com). To update the Run As account, run these two commands:

```
$cred = Get-Credential
Get-SCSMRunAsAccount -Name "My Run As Account"  | Set-SCSMRunAsAccount $cred
```

The `Get-Credential` cmdlet opens a dialog box where you can securely enter the credentials; they are stored securely in the `$cred` variable in memory. The display name of the Run As account should be passed to the `-Name` parameter of the `Get-SCSMRunAsAccount`. Remember that if the display name contains spaces you must enclose it in quotes so the command line parser doesn't get confused. The `Set-SCSMRunAsAccount` cmdlet securely stores the credentials in the Service Manager database. From this point on you can manage your custom Run As account like any other Run As account in the system.

Using Management Pack XML to Use a Run As Account

Some of the elements you define in your management packs require a Run As account. Using a Run As account in the XML typically occurs when you want to change the Run As account on a custom workflow.

When you define a workflow in the Authoring Tool, a `WriteActionModuleType` is defined in the XML of the management pack. By default, the workflow uses the Service Manager workflow account.

```
<WriteActionModuleType ID="IR_Send_Email.Script" Accessibility="Public"
RunAs="Core!Microsoft.SystemCenter.ServiceManager.WorkflowAccount" Batching="false">
```

This Run As account is defined by the `RunAs` attribute:

```
RunAs="Core!Microsoft.SystemCenter.ServiceManager.WorkflowAccount"
```

Change this line to point to your newly created secure reference:

```
RunAs="MyRunAsAccount"
```

If your workflow is in a different management pack than your secure reference, you need to reference the management pack in the `<References>` section in the management pack manifest.

Security Best Practices

This part of the chapter describes some security best practices that go beyond what is in the Microsoft documentation. These are intended to help you avoid common configuration mistakes that can leave you open for attack or data loss, or at least help you trace who did something.

Sensitive data such as Run As account passwords are encrypted in the ServiceManager database (or DWStagingAndConfig database for the data warehouse management server) and transmitted between the database server and the management server in encrypted form using a symmetric key encryption scheme. The symmetric encryption key is generated the first time a management group (either Service Manager or data warehouse) is created by installing the first management server and a database. The first management server gets a copy of the symmetric encryption key, which is encrypted using a private encryption key for that management server.

Each time an additional management server or portal server is installed, it gets a copy of the symmetric encryption key for the management group. This copy of the symmetric encryption key is encrypted using a private encryption key generated for each management server or portal server.

Thus, there is a symmetric key for the entire management group, used to actually encrypt all the passwords, and a private key for each management server or portal server to encrypt the symmetric key for that server.

The account passwords provided during setup and any other Run As account passwords later created are all encrypted using this same symmetric encryption key. Using that symmetric encryption key, the Microsoft Monitoring Agent can decrypt the passwords at the appropriate time when running workflows so they can be used to log in to local or remote systems. The System Center Data Access Service can use the symmetric encryption key to encrypt the password when new Run As accounts are created. The passwords are never passed on the wire in clear text, and only an administrator of the management server has access to the private encryption key and thus the symmetric encryption key.

Following are best practices for securing the private encryption key:

▶ Back up the private encryption key immediately after installing each management server and portal server in each management group (including the data warehouse management group). Setup will recommend doing this immediately after setup is complete. Keep in mind that each management server or portal server will have its own private encryption key, which must be backed up.

▶ Store the private encryption key backup file in a secure place with redundancy.

▶ Store the password to the private encryption key file in a secure location with redundancy, ideally in a separate place from the encryption key backup file. As there is no way to recover the password, be very careful how you store it so you can retrieve it if necessary. Multiple people should know the password or have access to the password in the event people leave the organization, forget, and so on.

▶ Any local administrator on a management server or portal server has access to the private encryption key and thus the symmetric encryption. If a person knows what he is doing, that person could retrieve the system and Run As account passwords. Ensure only those individuals who would already have access to those passwords are local administrators on these servers.

▶ Ideally have more than one management server in a management group. Then, should the management server fail and you forget the password or lose the backup of the encryption key, you can install a new management server and get the encryption key from the secondary management server.

▶ If you forget to back up your private encryption keys when you first install the product, forget the password, or misplace the backup file, you can back them up at any time by running the encryption backup tool. Instructions are provided in the disaster recovery guide at http://technet.microsoft.com/en-us/library/hh495602.aspx.

Securing Database Access

All data with the exception of Run As account passwords are stored in plain text in the databases. This makes it important to minimize any direct access to the databases. You should scrutinize all users with the exception of Service Manager administrators to determine whether they need access to the databases.

During setup, the System Center Data Access Service and Management Configuration service accounts are granted appropriate permissions on the databases automatically. All access by non-Service Manager administrators should go through the Data Access Service. Workflows should never directly access the database either and should always go through the Data Access Service, which is secured by role-based security.

As a best practice, configure the Operational System account Run As account to have a different account than the account used for the workflow account Run As account. This ensures that even if a rogue workflow were to be executed in the system, it would not have full permissions over the Service Manager database.

Enabling Auditing

Service Manager out of the box stores a history of every new object created, every property value change, and every relationship add and removal. This history is visible on the forms on the History tab. For most organizations, this provides an adequate trail of activity for auditing purposes. However, there are cases this does not cover:

▶ **Administrative access:** Someone with access to the Service Manager databases such as a Service Manager administrator could delete the history records, thus covering her tracks.

▶ **History only keeps track of data changes for objects:** History is not maintained for other changes in the database including configuration settings such as user roles, Run As accounts, notification settings, or anything that goes into management packs, including templates, views, or enumeration values.

▶ **History is groomed periodically:** Unless the data is configured to be archived in the data warehouse, history changes are removed when they reach their expiration time.

If a more comprehensive and detailed audit trail is required, you can enable auditing on the System Center Data Access Service. When auditing is enabled, the System Center Data Access Service logs an event to the Windows Security event log for each operation called on the System Center Data Access Service. It logs who performed the action and the method called at what time. You can aggregate and analyze these event logs using System Center Operations Manager Audit Collection Services (ACS).

Perform the following steps to enable auditing on the System Center Data Access service on each management server:

1. On the Start menu/screen, navigate to **Local Security Policy**.

2. In the Local Security Policy window, expand **Local Policies** and select **Audit Policy**.

3. Open **Audit Object Access** from the list and select Success and/or Failure depending on what you want to log in the event log. Click **OK**.

Once you enable auditing, the System Center Data Access service starts logging events in the Security event log from the source MOMSDK Service Security. This source name is a residual effect of evolving the System Center Operations Manager infrastructure to be the System Center common infrastructure platform that underlies Service Manager today. (The old name of the System Center Data Access Service was the SDK Service.)

Fast Track

Service Manager 2012 security uses the same model as the 2010 version. Therefore, most of the security best practices and guidelines are similar. Some additions have been made to the available types of objects in Service Manager 2012, including

▶ **Catalog items:** Service offering or request offering items for the SSP.

▶ **Catalog item groups:** A collection of catalog items. Using catalog item groups enables the catalog items to be scoped for each user role, providing a nice and simple listing in the self-service portal.

New user roles and user role profiles have been added. This is primarily because of service request support in Service Manager 2012. The added user roles are

▶ Change Managers

▶ Operators

▶ Release Managers

▶ Service Request Analysts

17

Service Manager 2012 includes an extended PowerShell module, which contains cmdlets that enable the administrator to manage different areas of security, such as Run As accounts. The module contains a number of new security cmdlets:

▶ Get-SCSMRunAsAccount

▶ Get-SCSMUserRole

▶ New-SCSMRunAsAccount

▶ New-SCSMUserRole

▶ Remove-SCSMRunAsAccount

▶ Update-SCSMRunAsAccount

▶ Update-SCSMUserRole

The Server Manager 2010 cmdlet `Set-SCSMRunAsAccount` has been renamed to `Update-SCSMRunAsAccount`.

Summary

The security model for Service Manager is flexible enough to meet the requirements of the most demanding organizations. It is also simple enough for those "configure and go" organizations with more basic requirements. Following the best practices outlined in this chapter enables your organization to securely operate Service Manager and provide a user experience tailored to each person's role. The next chapter discusses maintenance, backup, recovery, and other vital parts of a secure and properly functioning Service Manager environment.

Maintenance, Backup, and Recovery

System Center 2012 Service Manager is a strategic asset to your organization. A Service Manager outage can affect the organization's reputation and significantly affect the services delivered using this System Center component. Information Technology (IT) products do and will eventually suffer outages; the likelihood of any outage usually comes down to how you maintain the product—with its impact determined by the maintenance, backup, and restore processes in place.

"I am prepared for the worst, but hope for the best," is a quote by Benjamin Disraeli that sums up the goal and objectives of this chapter, albeit with a difference. The difference is this chapter prepares you for the worst and discusses some best practices that can turn hope into certainty for how best to recover should the worst happen to your Service Manager deployment. This chapter provides information on how to maintain, back up, and recover System Center 2012 Service Manager.

The chapter discusses recommended maintenance activities, the types of backups you must perform, and available recovery options. The specifics of each area depend on the scenario you will face and vary by environment. The chapter delves into common scenarios you may encounter and is based on official Microsoft supported disaster recovery options.

Chapter 4, "Looking Inside System Center 2012 Service Manager," and Chapter 5, "Planning and Designing System Center 2012 Service Manager," discuss Service Manager features and available deployment types. To recap those chapters, a full production deployment of Service Manager typically consists of the following:

▶ Service Manager management server

▶ Service Manager database server

▶ Service Manager data warehouse management server

▶ Data warehouse database server

▶ Self-service portal server (SharePoint)

A minimum supported production deployment requires the Service Manager management server and Service Manager database server. The data warehouse and self-service portal server(s) are optional. The Service Manager servers and their underlying operating systems form three layers, as shown in Figure 18.1.

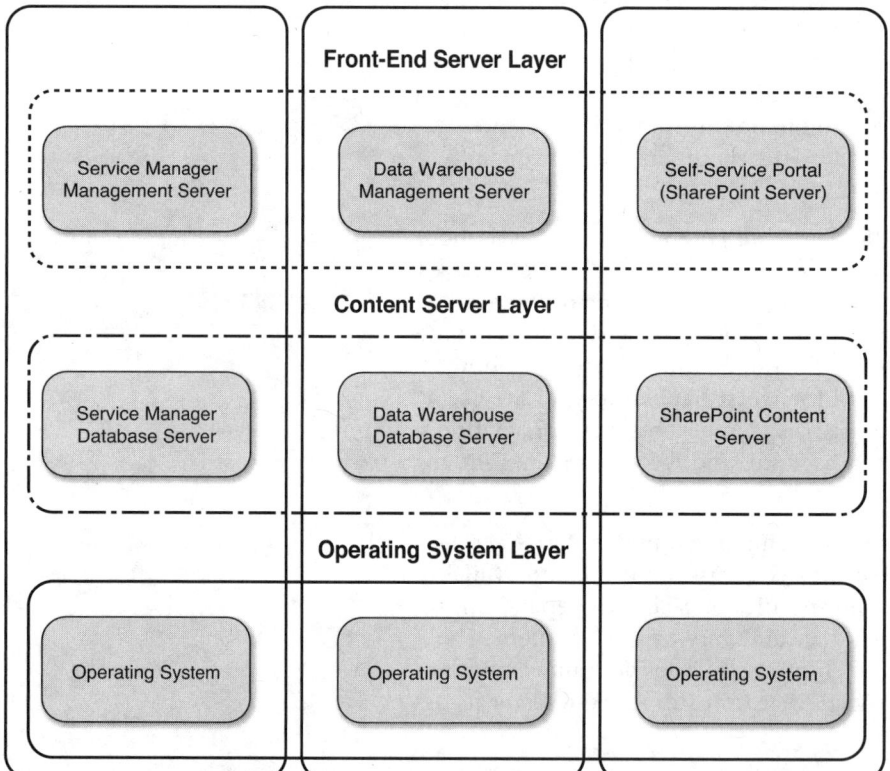

FIGURE 18.1   Service Manager deployment components.

The three tiers listed as layers in the figure are the front-end server, content server, and operating system layers. These three layers and their dependents are the focus of the activities discussed in the "Performing Maintenance," "Planning and Performing Backup," and "Planning and Performing Recovery" sections of this chapter.

Performing Maintenance

Service Manager, much like any software or hardware system, requires maintenance to ensure it is secure, optimally performing, and operating at expected service delivery levels. Table 18.1 lists the maintenance activities to plan for at each layer.

TABLE 18.1   Maintenance Activities Performed at the Service Manager Layers

Service Manager Layer	Recommended Activities
Front-end server layer	Monitor the Operations Manager log for Service Manager warning and error events.
	Review software updates and plan to update the servers with applicable updates.
	Monitor the Service Manager services. You can use System Center Operations Manager to monitor the health of the servers.
	Check the status of configured connectors.
	Check the status of internal and custom workflows.
Content server layer	Monitor the SQL Server logs and performance counters.
	Update the database engine to the Service Manager component supported level.
	Apply tested and approved security updates for SQL Server.
Operating system layer	Monitor the operating system event logs.
	Monitor disk space usage and implement threshold warning processes. An example would be creating an alert if the percentage of disk space available falls below an agreed threshold.

The recommended activities performed at each layer in Table 18.1 are the minimum to plan for in terms of maintenance. These complement the optimization options available to you as discussed in Chapter 19, "Managing Service Manager Performance." Microsoft's official blog site at http://blogs.technet.com/b/servicemanager/ is a great resource for product updates, tips and tricks, and much more.

There are two additional categories of maintenance; the authors recommend you include these as an organization best practice:

▶ **Change management:** The primary cause of outages is unplanned changes. Service Manager changes should be included in your organization's change management process. Evaluate and test all changes in a controlled environment before implementing into production.

▶ **Standards auditing:** Plan to establish standards; and more importantly, monitor for adherence to the standards. Examples include management pack naming and management pack versioning.

Often overlooked is documentation. You should document the architecture, build, and operational procedures for your Service Manager environment. The change management process for the Service Manager infrastructure should include documenting version updates.

TIP: MAINTAINING CONNECTOR SOURCES

The source environments from which the Service Manager connectors import information often have their own maintenance activities. During these maintenance periods, inaccurate data may be generated and imported into Service Manager. The authors recommend disabling connectors such as the Configuration Manager or the Operations Manager Alert connector during periods of testing and maintenance in their respective source environments.

Planning and Performing Backup

Planning and executing appropriate backup procedures requires an understanding of the underlying objects of Service Manager. These underlying objects are one part of backup planning; the second is the recovery scenarios you plan to support with your backup strategy.

Service Manager's flexible framework and architecture make simpler backup and recovery options possible than with other products in this IT service management (ITSM) category. The following are the three Service Manager areas to back up:

▶ **Configuration:** This area includes management packs and data warehouse reports.

  ▶ **Management packs:** Service Manager's initial configuration is defined by the management packs provided with the installation media and imported during the installation process. Additional sealed or unsealed management packs containing new or updated settings are typically imported into Service Manager post installation. These management packs make changes to the underlying databases used by Service Manager.

  ▶ **Data warehouse reporting:** The data warehouse relies on SQL Server Reporting Services (SSRS). The reports you create are typically stored in report definition language (RDL) files.

  The management packs and RDL files are the specific Service Manager files you must plan for in your backup processes.

▶ **SQL Server databases:** Service Manager stores its configuration and instances of objects in Service Manager specific databases, which store their metadata in SQL Server system databases. Additionally, SSRS stores reporting information in the reporting services database. These databases are listed in Table 18.2.

▶ **Operating system:** The final area of Service Manager when planning for backups is the operating system configuration used to install Service Manager. The Registry of the operating system stores Service Manager information. Plan to back up the operating system of each Service Manager server with a solution that supports backing up the Windows system files including the Registry and system state.

TABLE 18.2   Service Manager Databases

Database	Description
ServiceManager	The Service Manager configuration management database (CMDB); this contains the current configuration and process work items.
DWStagingAndConfig	The Service Manager extract job writes to this staging database before the data is transformed into the correct format for the data warehouse.
DWRepository	The transformed ServiceManager database is loaded into the DWRepository database.
DWDataMart	This is the final database location of the extract transform load (ETL) process. Data is loaded from the DWRepository into the DWDataMart. The DWDataMart is used as the reporting source database.
DWASDatabase	This database is used by the Service Manager cubes, which is managed by SQL Server Analysis Services (SSAS).
OMDWDataMart	This database is used when you connect Operations Manager to the Service Manager data warehouse without using the Operations Manager CI and Alert connectors to the CMDB. This optional database is only available if selected during data warehouse installation.
CMDWDataMart	This database is used when you connect Configuration Manager to the Service Manager data warehouse without using the Configuration Manager connector to the CMDB. This optional database is only available if selected during data warehouse installation.
ReportServer	The SSRS database stores the SSRS configuration and custom reports created for Service Manager.
Master	SQL Server system database.
Model	SQL Server system database.
MSDB	SQL Server system database used for scheduling and alerts.

As mentioned earlier in this section, the initial settings for Service Manager are written to the databases using information in sealed and unsealed management packs.

▶ Settings from sealed management packs can only be modified by importing an updated version of the same sealed management pack. Consider settings from sealed management packs as read-only in the database. The original copy of the sealed management pack serves as backup and does not require that you perform any specific backup procedures other than maintaining a copy of the source files.

▶ Settings written to the database with unsealed management packs can be changed using the Service Manager console. These edited changes are stored in the database and only available to you as updated unsealed management packs when you perform a management pack export.

You can back up the editable configuration settings (typically written to unsealed management packs) and the Service Manager databases to local disk storage and/or backup media. This approach can reduce the need for costly enterprise backup products that require agent licenses to back up SQL Server databases. System Center Data Protection Manager (DPM) includes the capability to back up to local disk storage and/or backup media without incurring additional SQL agent costs. The local storage can be a dedicated logical drive on the Service Manager servers.

Performing the backup initially to a local disk drive can reduce the time required to restore Service Manager due to the proximity of the restore files. You must plan for additional disk space for the backup files and implement cleanup maintenance to remove old backup files if you take this approach. You will also want to back up these backup files to tape or offsite storage so they are available in the event of a local server crash.

TIP: USE DEDICATED STORAGE FOR BACKUPS

The authors recommend you back up to a destination other than the servers that host Service Manager or use logical drives that reside on separate physical disk storage like a dedicated Logical Unit Number (LUN) drive of a Storage Area Network (SAN) device.

Scheduling Considerations

Your backup schedule depends on your organizational policies for backups. The authors recommend the following for the three areas of Service Manager that you should back up:

▶ **Configuration information (contained in unsealed management packs and RDL files):** Perform daily backups and plan to include a backup step before implementing high-risk changes. If this information is stored on file system drives, backups should occur prior to file system backup.

▶ **Service Manager databases:** Perform backups on a daily schedule or as specified in your organization's backup policy. The SQL Server system databases can be backed up on a lower frequency (monthly), but due to the small size of these databases, there is minimal impact when using a daily schedule.

▶ **Operating system and file system:** The authors recommend a daily backup, which you should perform after completing any of the other backups that place their files on local server storage.

Appropriate scheduling can significantly reduce the risk of lost work should you experience an unplanned outage. For example, if you perform monthly database backups and have a database failure, you could potentially lose a month's worth of incident records. Schedule your backups to be in line with business expectations and acceptable data loss as a trade-off with the cost of storing those backups. If the business goal is to ensure you can recover to within 15 minutes of data entry, you must adjust the backup schedule to meet this requirement.

> **TIP: DATABASE ENCRYPTION KEYS**
>
> After installing the Service Manager management server and the data warehouse management server, be sure to back up the encryption key, which is used by Service Manager databases to encrypt security sensitive information and is required to perform a management server restore. Chapter 6, "Installing and Upgrading to System Center 2012 Service Manager," discusses the process to back up the encryption key.

Configuration Backup

Service Manager settings and customizations are typically stored in unsealed management packs. Adding a new list item or creating a view modifies information in the database. The modified changes typically are associated with an unsealed management pack.

> **TIP: CONFIGURATIONS NOT STORED IN MANAGEMENT PACKS**
>
> Some configuration information is stored in the Service Manager database rather than in management packs. An example is security roles. This type of information must be documented so it can be reapplied if necessary. Alternatively, you could clone the security role to a test environment using the TechNet Gallery community-developed solution from Dieter Gasser available at http://gallery.technet.microsoft.com/SCSM-Clone-User-Role-Task-8ba8ac58.

Settings Stored in Unsealed Management Packs

Exporting an unsealed management pack saves its contents for later reuse. This provides a fast and efficient means to restore Service Manager settings by using the Import management pack task. You have two options available to back up (export) the management packs: manual and automated. Follow these steps to back up the management packs manually to the local file system:

1. In the Service Manager console, navigate to **Administration -> Management Packs**.

2. Select the unsealed management pack you want to back up and click **Export**. Navigate to the folder the exported management pack will be stored in and click **OK** as shown in Figure 18.2.

This approach of exporting multiple management packs is neither efficient nor practical, as it requires repeating steps 1 and 2 for each management pack you want to back up. You cannot multiselect management packs to export using the Service Manager console as described in this procedure.

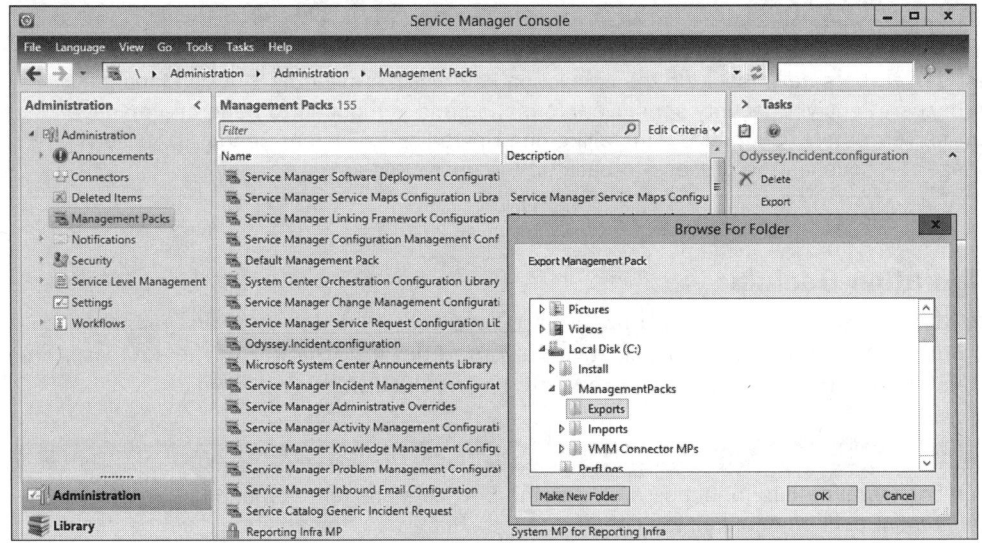

FIGURE 18.2   Manual backup of configuration stored in a management pack.

Alternatively, you could automate this process using a scheduled task that executes a PowerShell script to export all unsealed management packs. The SMLets PowerShell code in Listing 18.1 exports all unsealed management packs to a folder. This example has the script test for the existence of a folder named C:\SCSMBackup\ManagementPacks and then creates a subfolder with a date stamp each time it runs. This listing is also provided online, see Appendix C, "Available Online," for additional information.

LISTING 18.1   Exporting All Management Packs to a Folder

```
#Initializing the SCSM 2012 PowerShell snapin
Set-Executionpolicy unrestricted -force
Import-Module SMLets
#Create TargetDir if it doesn't exist
if (test-path C:\SCSMBackup\ManagementPacks)
{
"Folder Exists"
}
else
{
md "C:\MPBackup"
}
#Remove old backups
$xDays = (Get-Date).addDays(-30)
Get-ChildItem C:\SCSMBackup\ManagementPacks -Recurse | where
    {$_.lastWriteTime -le $xDays} | Remove-Item -recurse -force
#Create new backup dir
```

```
md "C:\SCSMBackup\ManagementPacks\MP_$((Get-Date).toString('yyyyMMddhhmm'))"
#Backup unsealed MP's
Get-SCSMManagementPack|where-object {! $_.Sealed}
 |Export-SCSMManagementPack -TargetDirectory
 "C:\SCSMBackup\ManagementPacks\MP_$((Get-Date).toString('yyyyMMddhhmm'))"
```

To automate the process further, you could perform automatic daily backups to the Windows file system. To provide easy access to previous configurations stored in unsealed management packs you can schedule the backup using a scheduled task. You can use the built-in Windows Task Scheduler (Control Panel -> System and Security -> Administrative Tools) to perform this process. Additional information about the Windows Task Scheduler is at http://windows.microsoft.com/en-us/windows/schedule-task#1TC=windows-7.

TIP: USING SERVICE MANAGER WORKFLOW VERSUS THE TASK SCHEDULER

You can achieve the same automated backup as with the Task Scheduler using a Service Manager workflow and the Authoring Tool. The workflow could be configured to run the PowerShell script on a schedule. The disadvantage of using a workflow is that all changes you make involve copying the Dynamic Link Library (DLL) file to the Service Manager installation folder (the DLL contains the workflow logic including the PowerShell script). This is not the case when you use the Task Scheduler. An added benefit of using the Task Scheduler is you can run the job manually as needed, such as for a first step before implementing any changes.

Documenting Security Role Membership Using PowerShell

Service Manager security role settings are stored in the Service Manager database. Documenting the role assignments enables a console-driven restore of the settings without the need to perform a full database restore. Documenting the information is manual and may be prone to human error. You can use the PowerShell/SMLets script in Listing 18.2 to display the current security settings for the default and custom roles. Save this listing to a .PS1 file. Run the script to display your current settings and document the output as part of your backup for Service Manager settings. This script is available as online content; Appendix C provides additional information.

LISTING 18.2   Displaying Security Role Assignments

```
Import-Module SMLets

$Roles = Get-SCSMUserRole
ForEach ($Role in $Roles)
{
    Write-Output "======================================================="
    Write-Output $Role.DisplayName "(" $Role.ProfileDisplayName ")"
    Write-Output $Role.Description
    Write-Output "======================================================="
    Write-Output "USERS"
```

```
    ForEach ($User in $Role.Users)
    {
        Write-Output "  " $User
    }
    Write-Output " "
    Write-Output "VIEWS"
    ForEach ($View in $Role.Views)
    {
        Write-Output "  " $View.DisplayName
    }

    Write-Output " "
    Write-Output "OBJECT SCOPES"
    ForEach ($Object in $Role.Objects)
    {
        Write-Output "  " $Object.DisplayName
    }

    Write-Output " "
    Write-Output "TEMPLATES"
    ForEach ($Template in $Role.Templates)
    {
        Write-Output "  " $Template.DisplayName
    }

    Write-Output " "
    Write-Output "CLASSES"
    ForEach ($Class in $Role.Classes)
    {
        Write-Output "  " $Class.DisplayName
    }

    Write-Output " "
    Write-Output "CONSOLE TASKS"
    ForEach ($CredentialTask in $Role.CredentialTasks)
    {
        $T = Get-SCSMConsoleTask $CredentialTask.First
        Write-Output " " $T.DisplayName
    }


}
```

Chapter 24, "Using PowerShell," discusses the SMLets module.

SQL Server Database Backup

The next layer to back up is the SQL Server layer. Service Manager stores its data and configuration information in SQL Server databases. You could use an enterprise product such as System Center 2012 Data Protection Manager to back up the Service Manager and data warehouse databases. Alternatively, you could back up the databases using native SQL Server tools. The output of the backup process is a file that can be backed up using any enterprise backup software including DPM. The advantage of this approach is it provides quicker restore options and reduces licensing costs, as some backup products require additional licenses for SQL backups. Perform the following steps to create a backup and cleanup maintenance task in SQL Server:

1. On the Service Manager database server, start Microsoft SQL Server Management Studio using the Run as administrator option.

2. Navigate to **Management -> Maintenance Plans**. Right-click and select **New Maintenance Plan** as illustrated in Figure 18.3.

3. Type a name for the maintenance plan, such as **SM CMDB Backup**. Click **OK**.

4. Using the View menu, select **Toolbox**. Select **Back Up Database Task** and drag it to the middle pane as shown in Figure 18.4.

5. Double-click the task in the middle pane and configure the properties as follows (see Figure 18.5), and click **OK**:

   ▶ **Connection:** Local server connection

   ▶ **Backup type:** Full

   ▶ **Database(s):** All databases

   ▶ **Create a backup file for every database:** Check **Create a sub-directory for each database**, and type a folder path in the Folder field.

   ▶ **Verify backup integrity:** Checked

18

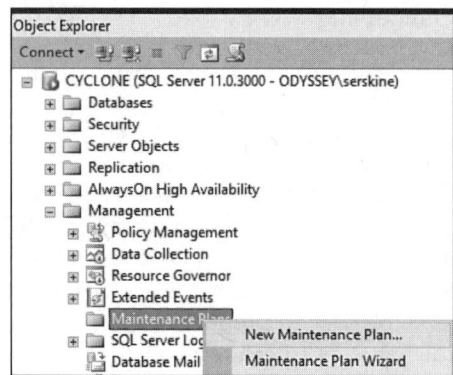

FIGURE 18.3   Create a SQL Server maintenance plan.

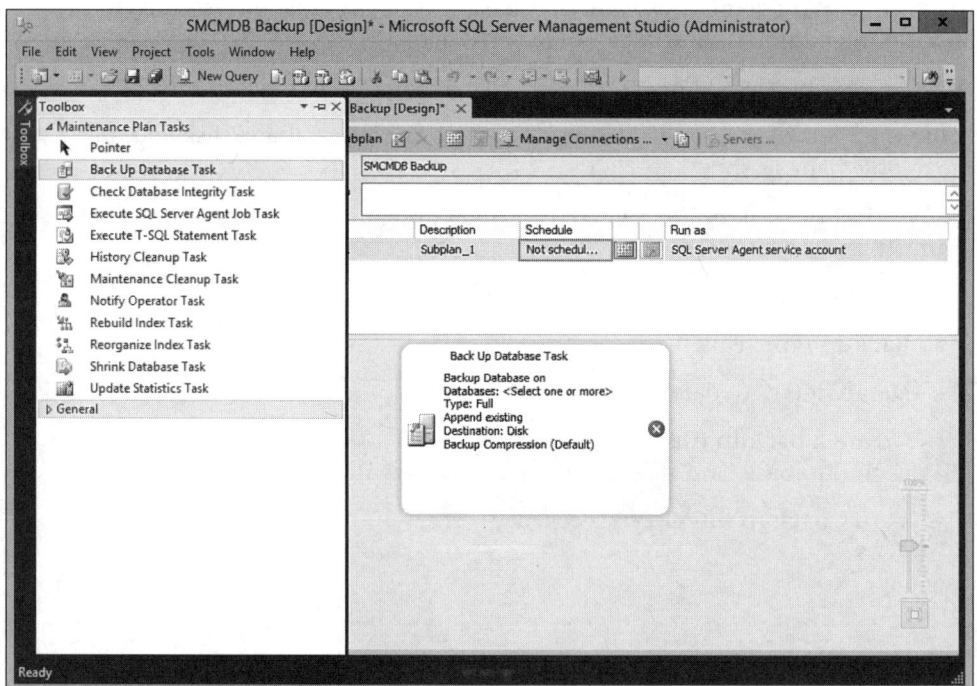

FIGURE 18.4   Back up database toolbox task.

6. Double click **Subplan_1**, change the name and description to meet your standards, and select a schedule for the backup task as indicated in Figure 18.6.

7. Create a cleanup task. In the toolbox, select **Maintenance Cleanup Task**. Drag the task to the middle pane below the Backup task. Link the two tasks by dragging the green arrow from the backup task to the maintenance task.

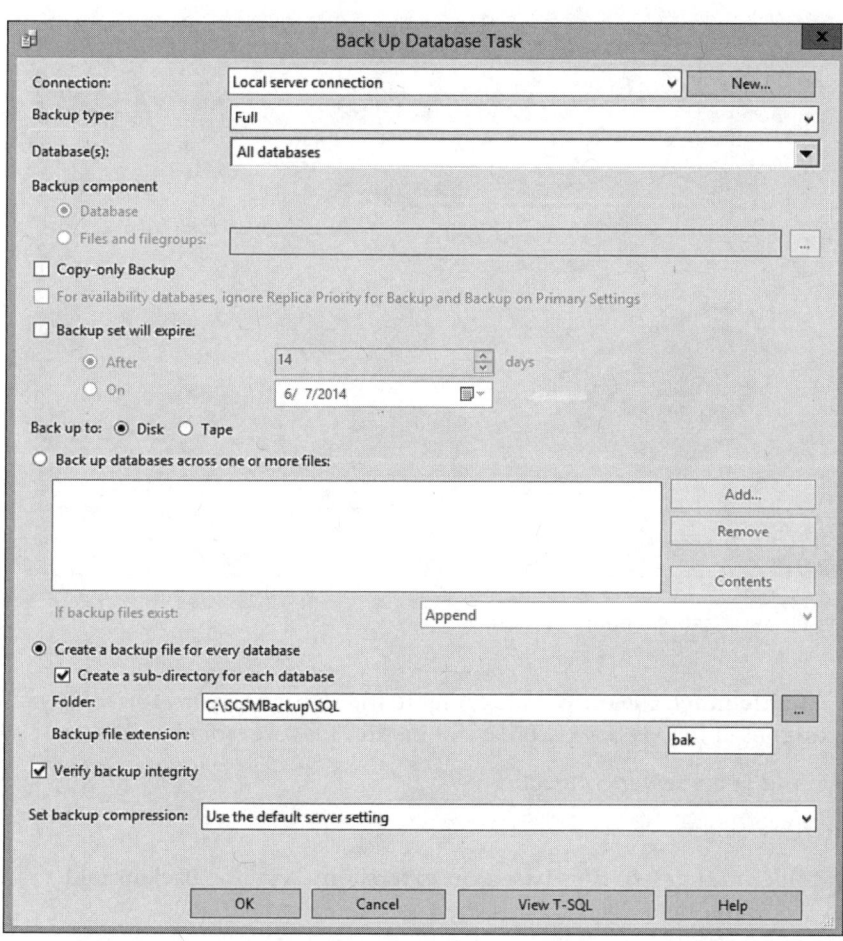

FIGURE 18.5   Back Up Database Task configuration settings.

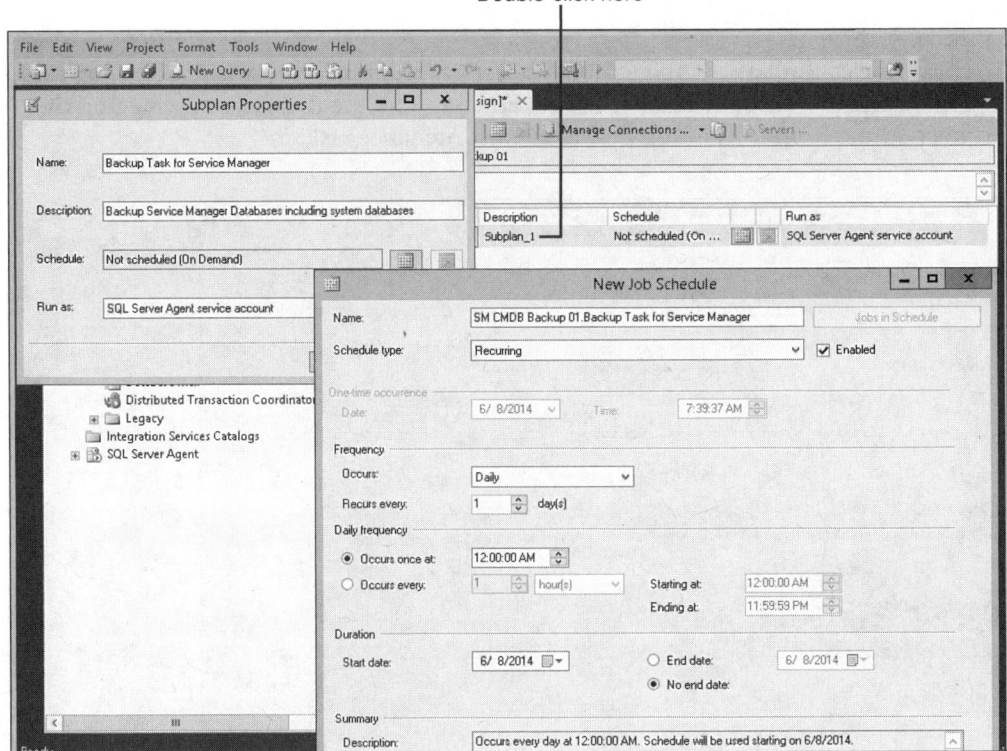

FIGURE 18.6   Back up database schedule properties.

8. Double-click **Maintenance Cleanup** and configure the settings. Figure 18.7 illustrates the settings used in Odyssey (two days of backup files are stored on disk).

> ▶ **Connection:** Local server connection

> ▶ **Backup files:** Select

> ▶ **Search folder and delete files based on extension:** Type the backup folder
> path in the Folder field. Type **bak** in the File extension field.

> ▶ **Delete files based on the age of the file at task run time:** Checked

> ▶ **Delete files older than the following:** Set to your preferred value (in Odyssey
> this is set to 2 days).

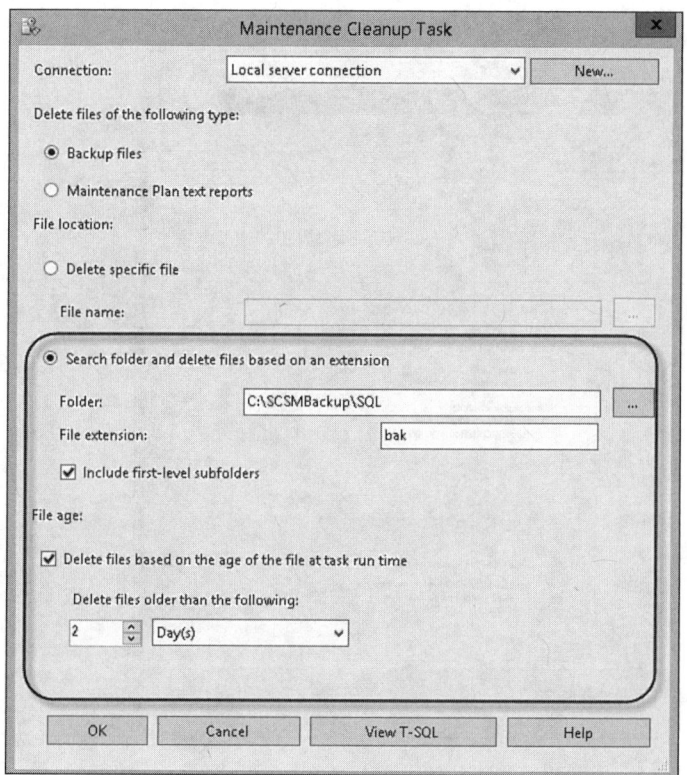

FIGURE 18.7   Configuring the Maintenance Cleanup Task.

9. Save and test the new maintenance task, which is displayed under SQL Server Agent -> Jobs. A successful run of the job creates subfolders matching the database names and a .bak file for each database in its subfolder. Figure 18.8 and Figure 18.9 illustrate the settings and the folders created in Odyssey and the backup file for the Service Manager database.

The backup files created in this procedure include the SQL Server system databases; this is optional and recommended by the authors. You must also configure the SQL Server Agent service startup option as Automatic.

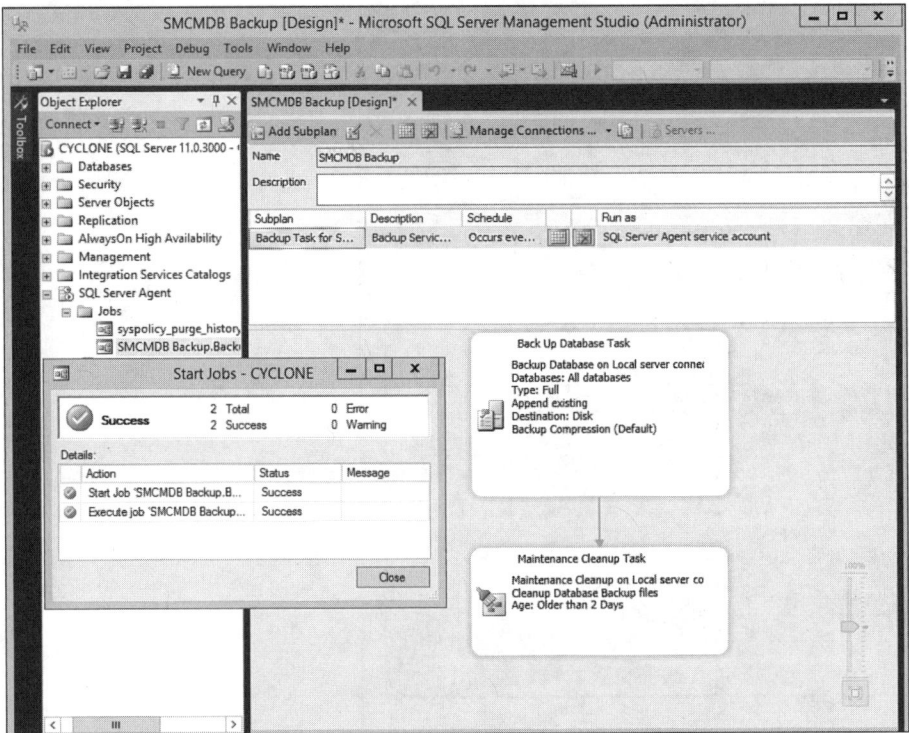

FIGURE 18.8   Backup and cleanup task configuration tasks validation.

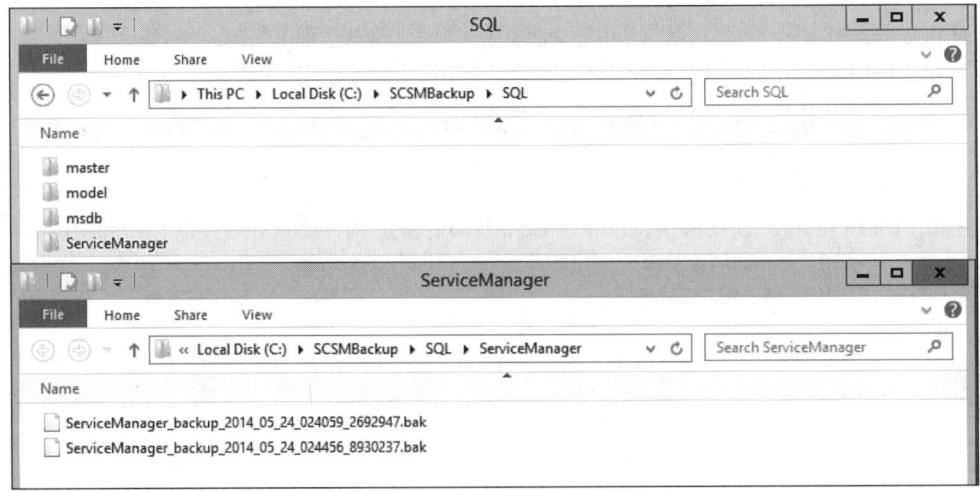

FIGURE 18.9   Database backup folders and file.

Backing Up the SQL Log File

The procedure discussed in the "SQL Server Database Backup" section earlier in the chapter produces a full database backup. Full database backups include the database and database log files. The database log file, also known as the transaction log, tracks all changes until they are committed to the database. You can back up the log without performing a full backup; this option requires at least one successful full database backup prior to backing up the transaction log. Transaction log backups allow you to perform a restore of incremental changes since the last full backup, dependent on the frequency of your backup. If you schedule a full backup daily at 8 p.m. and a transaction log backup every two hours, you can roll back in two-hour increments from the point of failure.

Backing up the transaction log file requires additional space. You must also select Full or Bulk-logged as the Recovery model for this type of backup. Figure 18.10 illustrates the settings available for the SQL database recovery model. The default recovery model is Simple, which does not support transaction log backup. For more information on SQL Server transaction log backups and best practices, see http://technet.microsoft.com/en-us/library/ms191429.aspx.

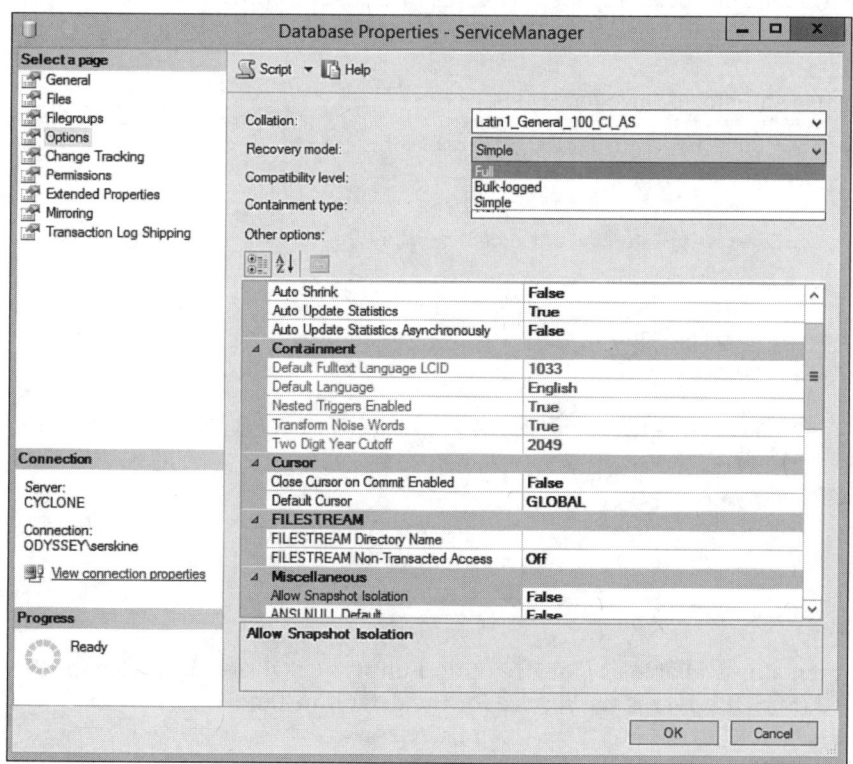

FIGURE 18.10   Setting the database recovery model.

REAL WORLD: SYSTEM CENTER BETTER TOGETHER

The native SQL backup approach requires planning for disk space utilization. The authors recommend creating and assigning a dedicated backup logical drive for SQL backups. This would ensure that a full disk does not affect the SQL services that Service Manager depends on. You could also use the integration of System Center to its maximum potential: Back up with DPM, monitor the disk space utilization with System Center Operations Manager, and create incidents using the Service Manager Operations Manager Alert connector when a predefined free disk space threshold is reached.

Performing SQL Backups with a Mapped Drive

The SQL backup wizard does not list mapped drives when you perform a database or transaction log backup to a local disk. You may want to use a mapped drive as a temporary device if the local drives do not have enough space for the backup file. This might be required if the transaction log file is full and requires a full backup to free up disk space (truncate the log). You can map a drive letter using the SQL XP_CMDSHELL stored procedure. You must enable advanced SQL options to execute the mapped drive command. Listing 18.3 (also available online; see Appendix C for information) provides details of the query syntax you must type and execute in the SQL query window.

LISTING 18.3   Mapping a Remote Drive for SQL Server

```
-- Enable the advanced options (0=disabled, 1=enabled)
sp_configure 'show advanced options', 1
GO
 -- To update the configured value for advanced options.
RECONFIGURE
GO
 -- Enable the command shell in SQL
 EXEC sp_configure 'xp_cmdshell', 1
GO
 -- To update the currently configured value for the command shell.
 RECONFIGURE
GO
-- Map a drive for example T: mapped to \\ComputerName\Share
EXEC xp_cmdshell 'net use <Drive letter> <share path>'
GO
```

The mapped drive remains available as a device option until the SQL Server service for the instance is restarted (MSSQLServer is the service for the default instance).

Rebuilding Database Indexes

There is an additional, optional database maintenance task you could perform to improve the health of the Service Manager databases. This maintenance task reorganizes and rebuilds indexes. SQL Server automatically tracks deletions and insertions using indexes. These indexes become fragmented over time, which may reduce the performance of those applications that depend on the database. This is similar to operating system hard disk drive fragmentation.

The reindexing process can be resource intensive and requires SQL Server database administration skills. The authors recommend you plan this activity by

1. Engaging with those database administrators responsible for managing and maintaining your organization's Service Manager SQL servers.

2. Scheduling this activity outside business operating hours. The authors recommend reindexing on a monthly basis. You can adjust this to meet your needs and align with your business agreed upon maintenance plans.

3. Checking the state of fragmentation manually. For information on detecting fragmentation, see http://technet.microsoft.com/en-us/library/ms189858. aspx#Fragmentation.

Operating System Backup

The final layer in your backup strategy is to perform a full operating system backup. This type of backup is performed using an enterprise backup product such as DPM. You could also use virtualization snapshots if the Service Manager servers are installed on virtual machines. You must ensure this backup includes all the files you store on local disk, including but not limited to management packs, RDL files, and any custom solutions provided by vendors to enhance Service Manager.

TIP: SECONDARY MANAGEMENT SERVERS

Plan to deploy at least one secondary management server as part of your IT continuity strategy. A secondary management server provides you with the simplest restore option for the Service Manager workflow feature that is only assigned to the first (primary) Service Manager management server.

18

Planning and Performing Recovery

Available recovery options vary based on the scenario driving the need. Examples of typical scenarios include

▶ Deleted Service Manager console views

▶ Database server disk drive corruption

▶ Management server failure

▶ Operating system failure

Microsoft's Service Manager documentation includes a detailed guide on how to recover from hardware or software failures. The specific document for recovery is called SC2012_ServiceMgr_DisasterRecovery in PDF or Microsoft Word versions and can be downloaded from http://www.microsoft.com/en-us/download/details.aspx?id=27850.

The following section complements the information in that document. The focus of the section is on the process side of recovery.

Configuration and Settings Recovery

The Service Manager console can be used to restore settings stored in your sealed and unsealed management packs. Using this method successfully requires meeting the prerequisites listed in Table 18.3 for these management packs.

TABLE 18.3   Prerequisites for Management Pack Recovery

Management Pack Type	Prerequisites
Sealed	A copy of the original management pack if it has not been modified (extended).
	The unsealed version of the management pack and the key used to seal the management pack.
	In the case of extensions to the original management pack, you must have a copy of this extended version.
Unsealed	A backup of the management pack with the configuration settings you want to restore.

To restore items such as Service Manager console views that are stored in management packs, follow these steps:

1. In the Service Manager console, navigate to **Administration -> Management Packs**.

2. Under Tasks, select **Import** and browse to the file system location of the management pack. Select the management pack and click **OK**. In the case of sealed (.MP) and bundled (.MPB) management packs, ensure you change the file type option.

   The import process automatically deletes the current version of the management pack and replaces it. A warning message states that this will occur.

3. Close and reopen the console to verify the change.

There are two additional areas of settings:

- ▶ **Custom reports:** Restore these settings using the RDL files or recreate these reports.

- ▶ **Service Manager user roles:** You must reapply the user role settings or restore these settings as part of the Service Manager database restore.

Feature Recovery

The following are the available Service Manager feature restore options:

- ▶ **Service Manager management server:** This is the first installed management server and is assigned the workflow and console features.

- ▶ **Service Manager database server:** This server hosts the SQL Server configuration management database.

▶ **Service Manager data warehouse management server:** This management server is responsible for reporting and may optionally host the SQL Reporting Services feature.

▶ **Service Manager data warehouse database server:** This server hosts the data warehouse databases and the SQL Reporting Services feature.

▶ **Service Manager secondary management servers:** These are additional management servers that host console connections.

▶ **Self-service portal server:** This SharePoint-based server feature is responsible for communicating with the Service Manager management server to present the service catalog to end users.

These six listed features require you to perform specific recovery steps for each feature.

Restoring the Service Manager Management Server

The first management server that is installed becomes the Service Manager workflow server. The server is also the console connection server. You can install additional management servers, but these will only be assigned the console connection feature. You have two options if you lose the workflow management server:

▶ Restore the original management server.

▶ Promote a secondary management server.

The steps to restore the original management server follow:

1. Install the operating system (Windows Server 2012 R2).

2. Restore the encryption key for the management group by running SecureStorageBackup.exe and selecting the restore option. Follow the instructions in the utility, and when requested provide the location of the encryption key backup file created for the management group.

3. Run the setup steps for Service Manager as discussed in Chapter 6 with the following exception; specify **Use an existing database** on the database page of the wizard and provide the details of the Service Manager database management server and instance name.

4. Restore additional file system files required for workflows.

The following are the high-level steps to promote a secondary management server:

1. Close all console connections to the secondary management server.

2. Stop the three Service Manager services (System Center Data Access Service, Microsoft Monitoring Agent, and System Center Management Configuration) using the Windows services applet.

3. Delete the Heath Service State folder and its contents, located in *%ProgramFiles%* Microsoft System Center 2012 R2\Service Manager.

18

4. Run SQL Server Management Studio using a user account with SQL Server administrative rights on the Service Manager database management server and connect to the ServiceManager database.

5. Type and execute the following SQL query in a new query window (ensure you first select the ServiceManager database).

```
EXEC p_PromoteActiveWorkflowServer '<server FQDN>'
```

6. On successful confirmation of the SQL query execution in step 5, restart the three services you stopped in step 2.

Restoring the Service Manager Database Server

To restore the CMDB, perform a database restore of the Service Manager database to the SQL Server instance. This assumes only the database requires a restore. If the operating system or the SQL server installations are also corrupt, you must perform one of these two steps:

▶ **Operating system and SQL Server restore from backup:** Restore the server and all its software from backup to a point in time corresponding to the last successful SQL backup file. Then restore the Service Manager database.

▶ **Reinstallation of operating system and SQL Server:** Reinstall the operating system with the same server name, install SQL Server using the same instance name provided during the original installation, and restore the Service Manager database.

Restoring the Service Manager Data Warehouse Management Server

You must perform a full operating system restore of this feature. The data warehouse management server feature cannot be failed over to another server. Should you need to reinstall this management server to the server where it was installed previously, you must first restore the symmetric encryption key by providing a backup of the private encryption key. This is described in the product documentation in the disaster recovery guide at http://technet.microsoft.com/en-us/library/hh495602.aspx.

The only other option is to install a new data warehouse management server with a different management group name and perform the registration process. Using a new data warehouse and registration process may lead to historical data loss. The information available from the original Service Manager environment depends on the data retention settings that were configured.

> **TIP: USING THE DATA RETENTION SETTINGS AS AN ADDITIONAL OPTION**
>
> The default installation setting for data retention of work items is 90 days for incidents, 365 days for the other work items, and 365 days for history. You could adjust these settings to provide a simplified recovery option for the data warehouse server. As an example, you could change the default settings to 730 days (two years). A two-year setting would provide the option to perform a new data warehouse server registration

with a different server name within the two-year period without needing to restore the old data warehouse in the event of a failure. This option is not a substitute for a full disaster recovery scenario and requires adequate disk space for the Service Manager database to store the work items for a longer period. Data retention settings are located in the Administration workspace of the Service Manager console, and are illustrated in Figure 18.11.

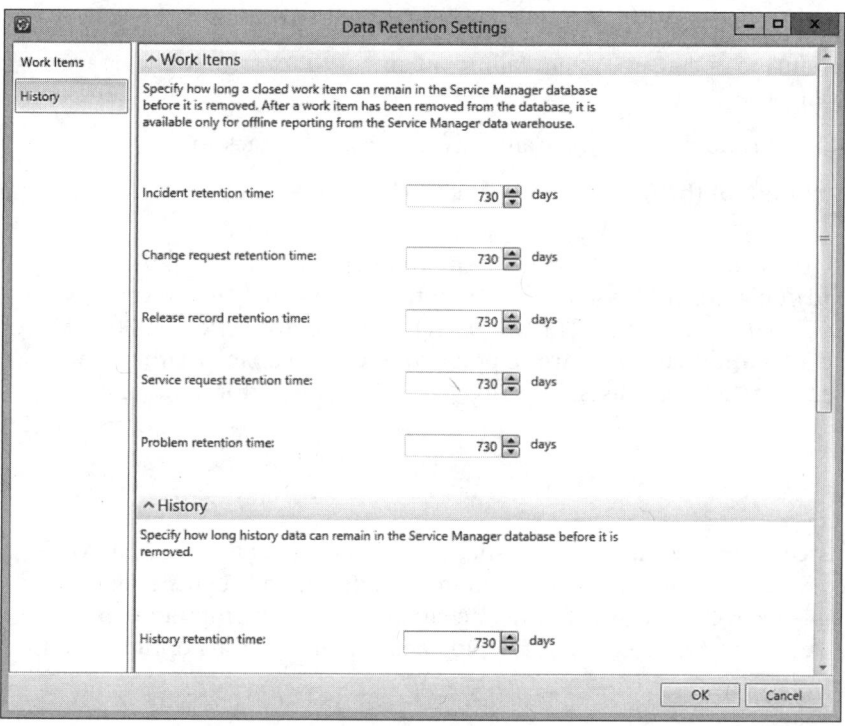

FIGURE 18.11   Custom work item retention settings.

Restoring the Service Manager Data Warehouse Database Server

You must restore all the data warehouse databases to the same point in time to the original fully operational data warehouse database server. You do not need to restore the SSAS database if this is still operational.

Restoring the Service Manager Secondary Management Server

Recovery options for the secondary management server are either a full restore of the server or a reinstallation of both the operating system and this Service Manager feature. If you reinstall, you can use a different server name, but you must update any Service Manager consoles that use the server as a connection point with the new server name.

Restoring the Service Manager Self-Service Portal

Restoring the self-service portal requires performing an operating system restore of the self-service portal management server or installing a new instance of this feature. When asked during reinstallation, select the same management server database used by the original (failed portal). The service catalog information presented in the self-service portal is stored in the database. Any SharePoint web parts customization of the failed portal must be reapplied.

Full Operating System Recovery

In the event of a complete operating system failure on any of the Service Manager roles, two options are available:

▶ Server rebuild and restore of Service Manager features from a backup

▶ Revert to a snapshot of the server if it is virtualized

The option you choose depends on your specific environment and backup policies. The authors recommend you perform disaster recovery testing to validate the integrality of your production backups. The article at http://technet.microsoft.com/en-us/library/dn520899.aspx includes information for using production data in a lab environment. You can use the steps in the article as a disaster recovery test that you perform on an agreed-upon schedule.

Summary

This chapter discussed recommended maintenance activities for your Service Manager environment. It covered the types of backups you must perform, and then stepped through the available recovery options. The next chapter discusses performance and tuning options to keep your Service Manager deployment operating at its optimal levels.

Managing Service Manager Performance

System performance is important for any online, interactive system that is accessible to end users, and this is applicable to System Center Service Manager, an interactive system that promotes self-service. When an interactive system performs poorly, it becomes less likely to be adopted or used. Service Manager's self-service and automation capabilities expose Information Technology (IT) to the rest of the organization and help it better understand how service management is organized.

Service Manager is a three-tiered application, consisting of a database, a data access module, and a console. These three tiers, be they physical or virtual, are included in every Service Manager deployment topology, and should be designed to provide acceptable performance. This is not that different from any other IT-related system you might have. It comes down to how you define your Service Manager environment to achieve maximum results in terms of performance.

This chapter presents some best practices and guidelines for optimal performance from Service Manager. It describes the different tiers of a System Center Service Manager system, providing background from an infrastructure and technical perspective. The chapter does not cover planning and sizing for optimal memory, disk, and file system performance; those are discussed in Chapter 5, "Planning and Designing System Center 2012 Service Manager."

Understanding Service Manager Performance

Service Manager performance has been a pain point since its initial release with Service Manager 2010, particularly when deployed by inexperienced staff lacking consideration or preparation for the people and process side of the tool.

REAL WORLD: THE IMPORTANCE OF PLANNING AND DESIGN

There is no magic switch that turns your Windows Server system into a high performance system, and the same holds for a service management system. A high-performing system must be designed as such, starting with the basics of gathering requirements. Designing Service Manager is described in Chapter 5.

Because System Center 2012 licensing includes licenses for Service Manager, some organizations already using other System Center components install Service Manager simply because it is "no cost." However, running the setup program does not mean you have a ready-to-use product. The following points should be kept in mind:

▶ Service Manager is more than a typical service management system that just logs incidents and changes, and it cannot be compared to any other service management product in terms of self-service and automation. This is the primary mistake made with nearly every Service Manager project—from a people and process perspective and also from a technical and infrastructure perspective.

▶ Service Manager cannot and will not run using the same infrastructure as a previously implemented service management product. Service Manager is designed to deliver automation; it delivers this automation using workflows running on its management servers. It also includes a configuration management database (CMDB) where various configuration items are related to each other; this CMDB, which is part of the Service Manager operational database, is populated automatically by the use of connectors.

▶ Service Manager can provide self-service in combination with automation to deliver a full self-service experience. Automation is provided for common requests, with the goal of minimizing the work performed by IT personnel to where ideally only an approval is required and the request itself is completely handled by the system. This self-service also delivers reporting to the entire organization.

These are just highlights of Service Manager functionality, and are not characteristic of a typical service management system. If you have used another service management system, the authors suggest you forget everything you know about that system and design a new infrastructure specifically for Service Manager.

While this may seem logical, nearly every IT department implementing System Center Service Manager starts with an incorrectly sized Service Manager infrastructure. The primary reason for poor Service Manager performance is that IT organizations start with the minimum recommended hardware, or even less; proper sizing is not performed during system design.

NOTE: SERVICE MANAGER SIZING

Microsoft provides a utility to assist with sizing your Service Manager infrastructure; this is the SM2012_Sizer Excel spreadsheet (in the Job Aids kit for System Center 2012 Service Manager). The information provided by the sizer is based on best practices from the field and covers implementations of all sizes, from small to very large-scale deployments.

You can download the Job Aids kit along with the other Service Manager documentation at http://www.microsoft.com/en-us/download/details.aspx?id=27850.

Performance ultimately comes down to budget and resources. While organizations tend to spend large amounts of money on business-wide applications, service management is typically considered an IT-only application and therefore not high value. This is not the case with Service Manager.

As Service Manager is available to the entire organization, a fast, responsive environment can benefit the entire business. Delivering self-service is another way to promote IT to the organization, as it lets them know that you are in control of delivering full service management.

Performance requirements must be explained, to build awareness of how Service Manager works and the impact of poor performance to the service management process. You must have the necessary technical resources for building your infrastructure. The remainder of the chapter discusses how an adequate infrastructure can deliver optimal performance from a Service Manager deployment.

Typically, there are three areas where performance is most noticeable in Service Manager:

▶ **Console responsiveness:** This can be defined as the length of time it takes from the moment you take some type of action in the console until it completes. Approaches for improving console performance are discussed in the "Service Manager Console Performance" and "Self-Service Portal Performance" sections of this chapter.

▶ **Data insertion time for connectors:** This is how long it takes to import data when a connector synchronizes. Connectors are discussed in the "Data Collection and Connectors" section later in the chapter.

▶ **Workflow completion time:** This is the length of time it takes workflows to apply some type of action automatically (by default around 60 seconds). Workflows are discussed later in the chapter in the "Use of Workflows" section.

When a system such as Service Manager utilizes a SQL Server engine, SQL Server performance can affect each of these areas. SQL performance is discussed in the "Service Manager SQL Server Database Performance" and "Service Manager Data Warehouse SQL Server Database Performance" sections of this chapter.

19

Service Manager Console Performance

The Service Manager console is used by those individuals delivering service management. This is the first area that can affect adoption of System Center Service Manager. (The other area would be the self-service portal experience as described in the "Self-Service Portal Performance" section of this chapter.) Even though Service Manager is basically an IT service management (ITSM) system, it could be opened up to other request-logging departments, with the caveat that it would need to be scaled accordingly, particularly in the area of console connections. This makes tuning console connections of particular importance.

NOTE: SERVICE MANAGER CONSOLE REQUIREMENTS

The Service Manager 2012 console has both hardware and software requirements, which are slightly different for the Service Pack (SP) 1 and R2 versions.

► **Operating System:**

Service Manager 2012 SP1 supports Windows 7, Windows 8, Windows Server 2008 R2 SP1, and Windows Server 2012 on both 32-bit and 64-bit platforms (http://technet.microsoft.com/en-us/library/jj628213.aspx).

Service Manager 2012 R2 supports Windows 7, Windows 8, Windows 8.1, and Windows Server 2008 R2 SP1, Windows Server 2012, Windows Server 2012 R2 on both 32-bit* and 64-bit systems (http://technet.microsoft.com/en-us/library/dn281934.aspx).

► **Hardware (Service Manager 2012 SP1 and Service Manager 2012 R2):**

CPU 2-Core 2.0 GHZ

► **Memory:** 4GB of RAM

► **Disk space:** 10GB

For additional information, see http://technet.microsoft.com/en-us/library/hh524328.aspx.

Software requirements are discussed at http://technet.microsoft.com/library/hh519608.aspx.

The first bits released of Service Manager 2012 R2 did not include the 32-bit installation files on the media; these were included as of 11/5/2013.

Infrastructure Performance

To optimize performance for console connections, you should inventory those client systems that will connect to Service Manager. You need to understand the requirements of using the console (described in the Note in the previous section) and the number of systems requiring use of the console. This information can help to determine whether the client system can deliver the anticipated console performance, and whether the Service Manager environment can deliver the expected connections. These are critical when providing console access. Alternatively, you can decide to not deliver consoles directly to the desktop and provide them by Remote Desktop or use third-party web-based console solutions, as discussed in the "Service Manager Add-ons" section of this chapter.

Client Desktop

The client desktop is often the most overlooked and underestimated part of the system. You must have adequate memory on your desktop systems to run the Service Manager console. While requirements are minimal (see the Note: "Service Manager Console Requirements"), verify that your systems fulfill these requirements, particularly from a memory perspective. As users tend to run multiple applications, test and size accordingly.

Number of Connections

The number of connections can affect console performance. Calculate how many connections you expect, and be aware that all these connections connect to your management server(s). When there are a large number of connections, adding an additional management server can provide load balancing and tremendous improvements to console performance.

A general rule of thumb is to have no more than 30 to 40 console connections for each management server. Although the official documentation states 40 to 50 connections, the authors recommend, based on experiences from the field, a maximum of 30 to 40 connections before adding an extra management server dedicated for console connections. If you have a single management server, realize this server will not only handle all console connections but all workflows as well and should be sized appropriately (see the Note: "Service Manager Console Requirements").

Network Latency

Another infrastructure-related performance bottleneck is the line speed between the console and the management server. The network latency should be less than 100 milliseconds (msec). With higher latency, responsiveness of the console is degraded. The hard limit is generally above 200 msec. Consider using remote desktop connections to deliver a better experience and allocating a dedicated server to handle these connections, as the memory requirements for running multiple consoles is high, with each connection taking up to 4GB of memory.

Configuration Performance

In addition to those performance improvements that you can resolve on an infrastructural level, there are some changes you can make at the configuration level to optimize response time. These are discussed in the next sections.

Accurate Scoping of Reporting

A minor change that can improve performance is to provide reporting only to those users who will actually use this feature from the console. Loading reporting components affects console startup. If the Reporting workspace is not required by the entire organization, you can scope this role to a subset of users. The high-level steps follow:

   1. The Report Users user role is assigned to authenticated users by default. You could scope this role by creating an Active Directory security group such as SCSM_ReportingUsers and adding users that need access to reporting to this group.

19

2. In the Service Manager console, navigate to **Data Warehouse -> Security -> User Roles**. Select the Report Users role, remove the authenticated users group from this role, and add the Active Directory group SCSM_ReportingUsers.

This scopes the Report Users role to the members of the SCSM_ReportingUsers Active Directory security group and not all authenticated users.

Targeting Views and Filtering

Views can have a large impact on the user experience. The reason for slow views, especially custom ones, is often due to incorrect targeting of these views. When you create a new view, you need to specify the class you want to target, as shown in Figure 19.1.

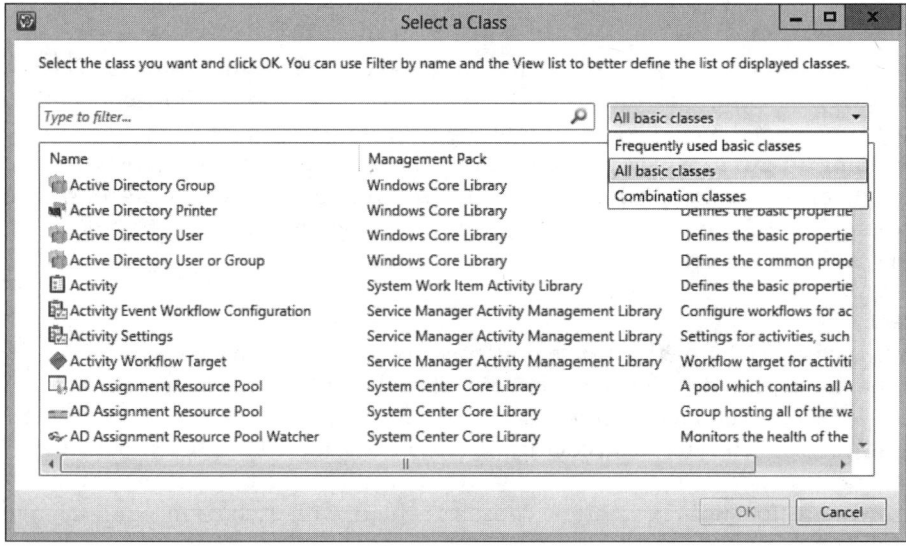

FIGURE 19.1   Targeting views.

Two options are available, a basic class, or a combination class:

▶ **Basic:** This is a single class with its properties. You can only select the properties in of a particular class to show in the columns or criteria, as shown in Figure 19.2.

▶ **Combination:** This is basically a type projection (explained in Chapter 22, "Customizing Service Manager"), which combines one class and its related classes. As shown in Figure 19.3, you can use these in your columns or criteria.

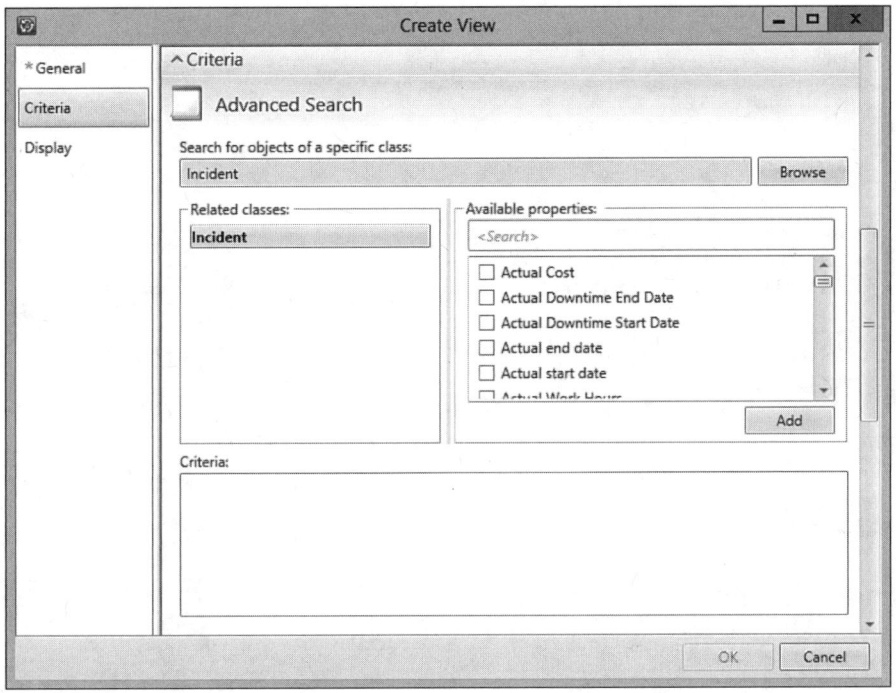

FIGURE 19.2   Viewing a basic class.

When you want a filter on related objects to a particular class or want to show the related class properties in the columns, you should select the nearest combination class or type projection.

In the incident example shown in Figure 19.4, notice that there are multiple combination classes. Incident (advanced) is purely for the incident form and not to be used in views. Incident (typical) can be your selected class.

The reason not to select the Incident (advanced) combination class is it pulls the Incident class and all related classes from the database when you open the view. This negatively affects performance, since it must retrieve a large amount of data, especially when you are viewing all incidents. An example follows:

Assume there are 1,000 incidents. A typical class pulls all 1,000 incidents with all properties and 1,000 related affected users and its properties, and 1,000 assigned-to users and their properties. So just for objects, it pulls 3,000 objects rather than 1,000. This is only the objects; imagine all properties and enumerations accompanying these.

19

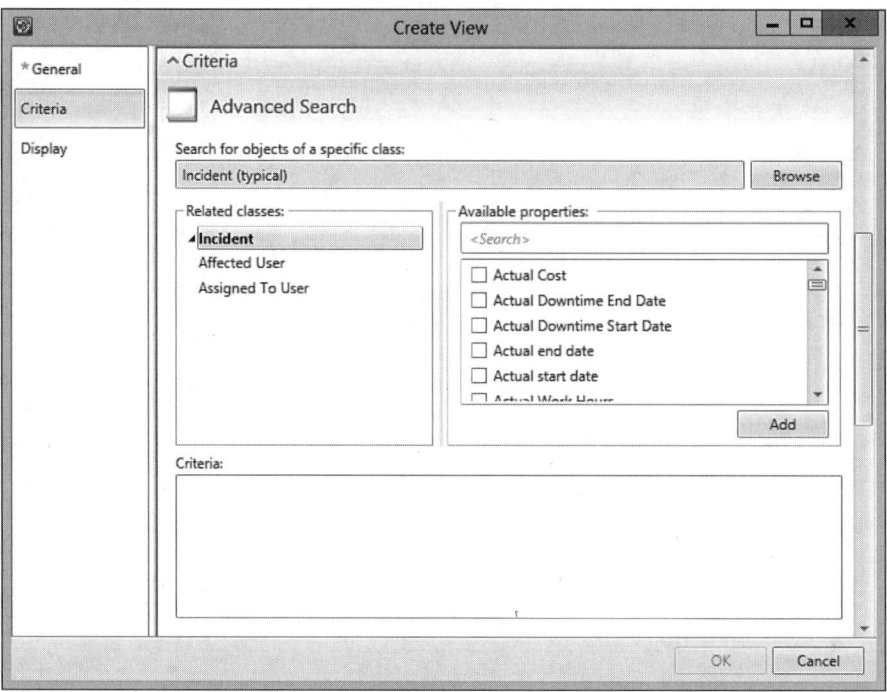

FIGURE 19.3   Viewing a combination class.

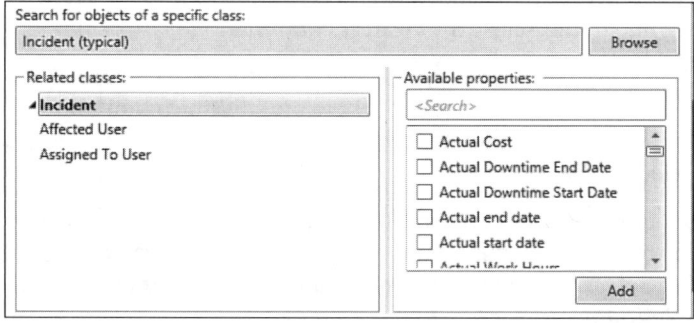

FIGURE 19.4   Typical combination class.

You need to query not only the data of the Incident class but for every related class as well for every incident. Using this view can make the query for incidents increase its data by a factor of 100. Figure 19.5 shows the advanced class and all related classes, which in their turn have relationships.

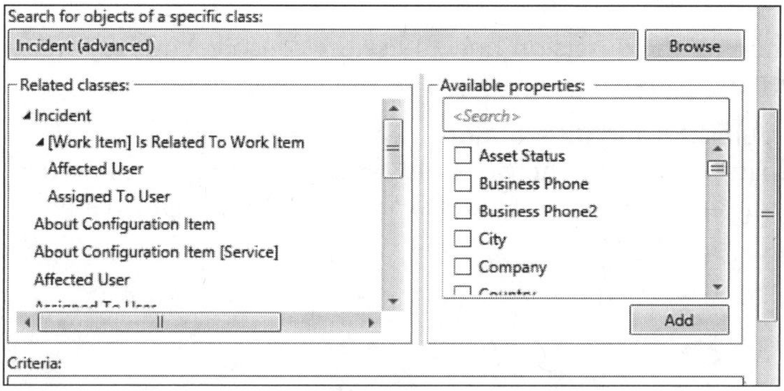

FIGURE 19.5   Advanced combination class.

Should you need a related class not provided in the typical combination class, consider creating a new type projection. For an overview on type projections, see Chapter 22.

When selecting the correct basic class or combination class, you want to filter the data. It is better to create multiple smaller views for a particular purpose than to create one massive view that has everything, but 90% of the properties aren't used.

Also, consider when you have many views but only some of them are used. The authors recommend narrowing the amount of views available to users by utilizing user roles. As every view is cached, this would deliver only the necessary views.

TIP: REFRESH RATE OF VIEWS

You can set views to refresh automatically as discussed at http://social.technet. microsoft.com/Forums/systemcenter/en-US/2d034882-b441-4b10-85a5-eae514a729a9/ views-refresh-time?forum=systemcenterservicemanager. Export the management pack that contains the view and modify the eXtended Markup Language (XML) by adding the following attributes to the View element you want to modify:

```
IsRecurring="True"
RecurrenceFrequency="30000"
FullUpdateFrequency="1"
```

Know that every refresh re-retrieves the data from the Service Manager database. Avoid using this setting unless necessary; set the interval high and beware of the negative impact.

Another option for delivering auto refresh is provided by the Advanced View Editor delivered by Anton Gritsenko; see http://scsmsolutions.com/freetools/3-ave2free#download for information.

19

Training Users

Many organizations neglect training their users on how to use the console. You may want to enhance their console experience by giving them tips on how to search.

Using standard search as in Figure 19.6 and filter options (see Figure 19.7) can result in a much faster user experience than when using the views only. Searching for particular incidents by using the search shown in Figure 19.8 provides an easy way to trace incidents.

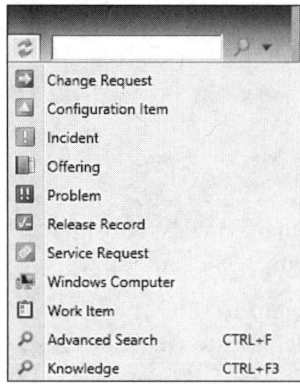

FIGURE 19.6   Search options.

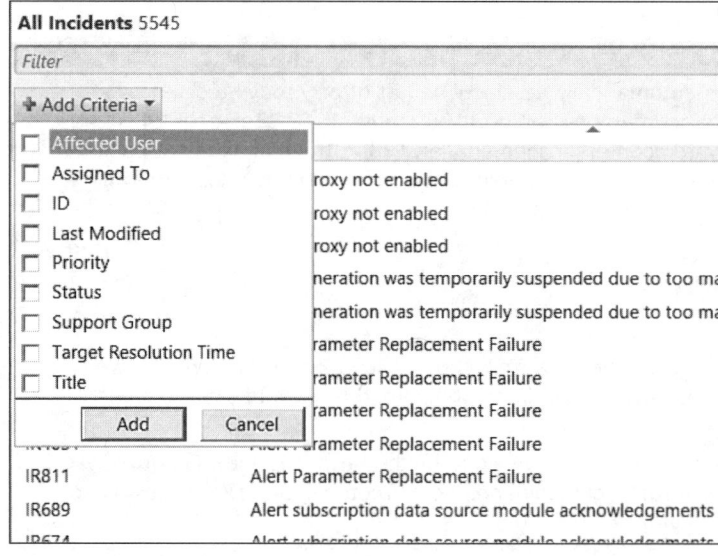

FIGURE 19.7   Filter options.

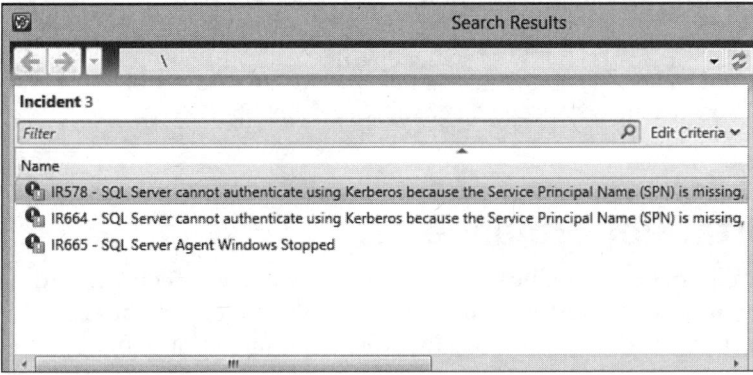

FIGURE 19.8   Search results.

If the standard search functionality is inadequate, you could select advanced search options as shown in Figure 19.9.

Training your users to use these features more frequently and providing guidance on how to effectively search and filter will greatly benefit the overall user experience.

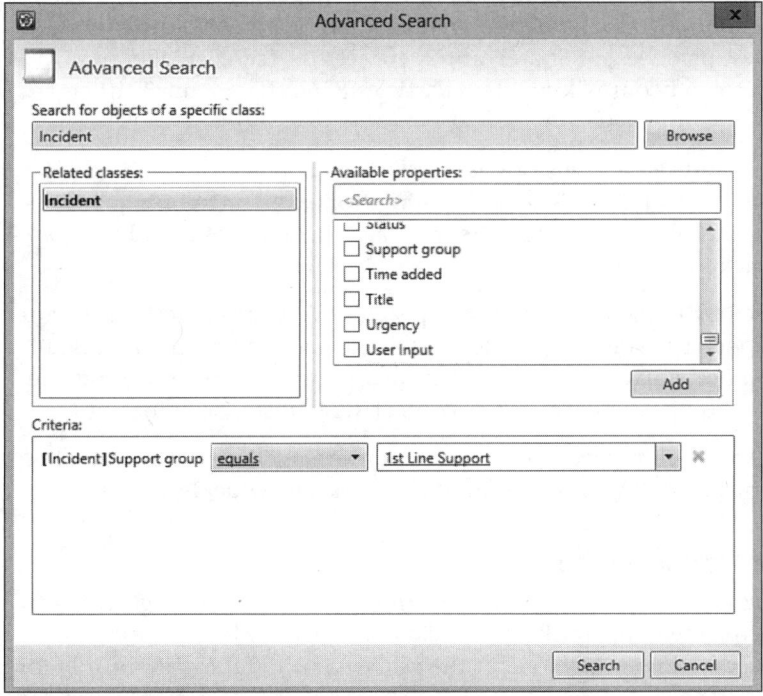

FIGURE 19.9   The Advanced Search dialog.

TIP: SAVE SEARCH QUERIES

Anton Gritsenko has developed an add-on with search functionality where you can save common search strings. You can download the add-on from the TechNet Gallery at http://gallery.technet.microsoft.com/Advanced-Search-with-Saver-fbe5b6af.

Self-Service Portal Performance

Service Manager self-service portal performance is crucial since it directly affects the end user. It is important that you provide a fast way to log and handle requests in the self-service portal. The next sections discuss approaches to improve portal performance.

Self-Service Portal Sizing

As with any other product or component, be sure you understand the sizing of the different features. Separating the web content server from the SharePoint components can improve performance. For heavy usage, consider placing multiple web content servers in a network load-balanced NLB.

SharePoint 2010 Performance

The self-service portal uses a SharePoint engine. Follow best practices concerning SharePoint 2010 when designing your SharePoint environment. For a complete overview on performance-related best practices for SharePoint 2010, see the TechNet Wiki page at http://social.technet.microsoft.com/wiki/contents/articles/8666.sharepoint-2010-best-practices.aspx.

By default, SharePoint 2010 automatically stops and restarts all application pools each night (at a unique time for each). This unloads everything from memory; consequently, the delay you see in the morning is when users first hit pages in SharePoint and the application pool loads them back into memory.

This delay can be addressed by implementing warm-up scripts. A warm-up script runs after the recycle occurs (usually set up using a scheduled task) and loads commonly accessed pages in the site, such as a home page. This way, when people arrive in the morning and fire up SharePoint, there is no loading delay as the content has already been loaded.

Searching for SharePoint warm-up scripts provides many examples. There is also a tool on CodePlex you can use: Download SPWakeUp from http://spwakeup.codeplex.com/.

Web Content Server Performance

Application pool recycling is a feature of IIS and resets the application pool nightly, similar to SharePoint as explained previously in the "SharePoint 2010 Performance" section. The recycling causes a slow initial load of the self-service portal each morning for those users first logging in to the self-service portal. To change these settings, perform the following steps:

1. On the Web Content server, open IIS Manager.

2. Expand **Application pools** and right-click **SCSM application pool (Default:)**.

3. Select **Advanced Settings** to change the recycling behavior as shown in Figure 19.10:

> ▶ **Turn off application pool recycling when idle:** Idle-Time-out (Minutes) to **0**.

> ▶ **Turn off recycling on interval:** Regular Time Interval (minutes) to **0**.

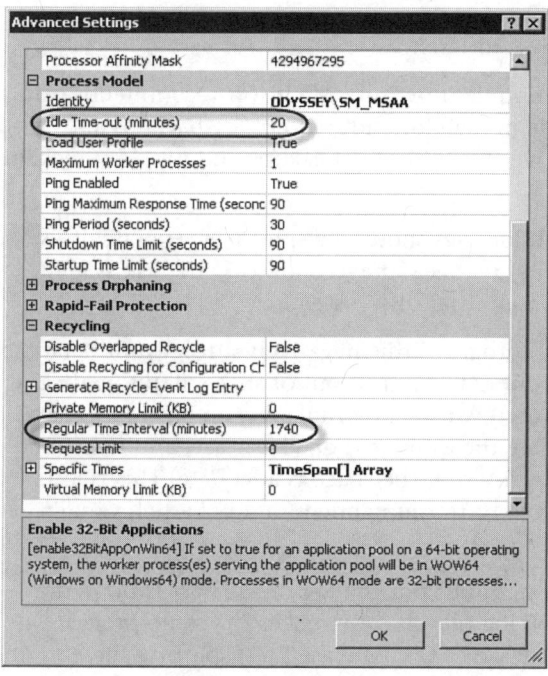

FIGURE 19.10   Application pool recycling.

For additional information, see http://blogs.technet.com/b/servicemanager/archive/2011/ 05/11/faq-why-is-the-self-service-portal-so-slow.aspx. This article discusses changing the setting to recycle the application pool.

Custom Icons

Designing your service offerings and request offerings with numerous custom icons can negatively affect overall performance of the self-service portal. When you open the portal, all icons are downloaded, so limiting custom icons improves performance.

Chris Ross, a System Center Cloud and Datacenter Management (SCCDM) MVP, put together a nice lightweight icon pack to be used with the portal, available at http://www.cireson.com/scsm/scsm-portal-icon-pack-download/.

Service Manager SQL Server Database Performance

Perhaps the largest performance improvements are realized when you deliver a well-performing and well-designed SQL Server. As all the work is performed in the background by SQL Server, it is the core of your Service Manager environment. You can follow all other best practices and guidelines, but if your SQL Server is not correctly designed and using appropriate resources, you will suffer from performance issues.

Database performance is always the most difficult part of any Service Manager project, because the Service Manager operational database isn't just any database. The Service Manager database differs from many other databases in terms of configuration; make sure your database administrators understand these differences:

▶ The database recovery model is set to Simple (not Full); Microsoft recommends using the Simple recovery model. The Simple model does not require log backups and automatically reclaims space. Full recovery requires log backups and does not reclaim space.

▶ The Service Manager database files and log files should be split over separate disks. A best practice is to place the database file, ServiceManager.mdf, on one disk system, and the log file, ServiceManager.ldf, on another disk system.

▶ If database files and log files are set to autogrow, this negatively affects your database performance. This is because should your database run out of space, it automatically grows as it needs additional space. Autogrow uses a considerable amount of I/O and causes database fragmentation. Calculate the estimated database size, and monitor growth using Operations Manager to verify that the space is adequate. This is also true for autoshrink; this is not supported or recommended for any System Center database.

▶ The TempDB database files should be split, but not the log files. There is no performance gain from splitting the TempDB log files; it only makes the setup process more complex. The heavy load is on the TempDB database files; splitting these across multiple drives allows multiple writes at the same time.

The default settings for the Service Manager database are defined to maximize Service Manager performance. Changing these settings to be consistent with other databases will doom your implementation from the beginning.

There are also a number of improvements to enhance your SQL Server performance, discussed in the next sections.

> ### TIP: SYSTEM CENTER AND SQL SERVER
>
> Paul Keely, SCCDM MVP, provides an excellent guide discussing SQL Server and System Center 2012 R2. This 194-page document gives details on how to tune and configure your SQL Server for optimal usage with System Center.

In addition to discussing performance best practices, the guide includes

▶ SQL Server and System Center in Windows Azure (by Pete Zerger, SCCDM MVP)

▶ SQL Server and System Center backup (Robert Hedblom, SCCDM MVP)

▶ SQL Server and System Center monitoring (Matthew Long)

▶ SQL Server and System Center clustering (Craig Taylor and Richard James Green)

Download the guide from the TechNet Gallery at http://gallery.technet.microsoft.com/
SQL-2012-and-System-Center-553b5161.

Input/Output per Second (IOPS)

Always double-check the IOPS of the logical unit number (LUN) where your Service Manager database and log files are placed. Since everything in Service Manager goes through the Service Manager database, be sure it can deliver the performance you need.

Following are some tools to assist you in calculating and measuring SQL Server IOPS:

▶ **SQL I/O Disk Subsystem Benchmark Tool:** http://www.microsoft.com/en-us/download/details.aspx?id=20163.

▶ **SQL Server Best Practices:** http://technet.microsoft.com/en-us/library/cc966412.aspx.

▶ **SM_Job_Aids (includes SMSizer):** http://www.microsoft.com/en-us/download/details.aspx?id=27850.

▶ **SM2012_Sizer.xlsm document:** This is part of the SM_Job_Aids kit (http://www.microsoft.com/en-us/download/details.aspx?id=27850) and provides guidance on estimating and calculating IOPS.

Database and Log Files

Placement of your database and log files can affect performance. Be sure to place the Service Manager database and the Service Manager log file on separate fast (IOPS) LUNs.

Available Memory

Be sure adequate memory is available for SQL Server. Service Manager relies on SQL Server having enough memory. Follow the guidelines in the Sizer document and make sure you leave enough memory (2GB) for the operating system itself to run.

Placement of TempDB

The Service Manager database relies heavily on the TempDB. Place TempDB on a fast LUN (IOPS). Another option is to split the TempDB database file into multiple small database files; a rule of thumb is to have one TempDB per two CPU cores.

19

Service Manager Data Warehouse SQL Server Database Performance

Data warehouse management server performance does not have a large impact on daily jobs in your Service Manager environment but affects the delivery of reporting and cube processing. This might not be a daily requirement but could have a large impact on individuals required to review and run these reports and on the process owners responsible for managing the processes.

Splitting Data Warehouse Databases

To improve performance of the data warehouse you can split the databases. Be aware that you cannot split the DWRepository and DWStaging databases, since they need to be on the same SQL Server instance. The other databases can be split over multiple instances.

Cube Processing

Cube processing by SQL Server Analysis Services can have a large performance penalty. You can offload the performance pressure by installing this component on a separate SQL Server instance.

A more expensive solution is to use SQL Server Enterprise, as there are several benefits concerning Analysis Services and cube processing, which are only available in SQL Server Enterprise edition:

▶ **Incremental cube processing:** SQL Server Enterprise uses incremental processing of cubes, which only runs the changes to the cube, instead of processing the entire cube each time as with SQL Server Standard edition.

▶ **Analysis database:** SQL Server Enterprise supports moving the analysis services database to another drive. You can place the database on a fast drive to ensure enough IOPS during cube processing.

TIP: DATABASE DATA RETENTION

Consider how long data is stored on your databases. By default the Service Manager database stores data up to 90 days, which is a long time considering this setting only applies to closed work items. Only closed work items are groomed.

The data warehouse holds data for three years, which can be adjusted by following the procedure described at http://blogs.technet.com/b/servicemanager/archive/2011/06/07/how-much-data-do-we-retain-in-the-service-manager-data-warehouse.aspx.

Additional information regarding the grooming process is available at http://blogs.technet.com/b/servicemanager/archive/2009/09/18/data-retention-policies-aka-grooming-in-the-servicemanager-database.aspx.

Data Collection and Connectors

Service Manager performance depends heavily on the database and its size. Think about and discuss with those individuals responsible for the CMDB the data you want to store and the level of detail.

Be sure you only collect the information necessary to process a new work item and to resolve work items such as incidents, changes, and service requests. Collecting too much information uses storage, creates overhead, and affects performance.

It comes down to "garbage in, garbage out." If your source data is not accurate, the result is inaccurate information in Service Manager. Make sure that Active Directory, System Center Operations Manager, and System Center Orchestrator are cleaned up and properly configured. Setting up a connector and trying to filter out inaccurate data is a lot of work and does not provide the results you desire. Cleaning up the data before turning on the connectors can save you a lot of pain and grief.

Types of Data

You need to understand the different types of data, and understand why you should care about storing this data in your Service Manager database. The database is built on objects and relationships between those objects. It needs to store the data, not only the objects but also the relationships between these objects.

Contained data is considered bad data because of containment relationships. Contained data is a class that contains another class or containment relationship. An example of what is contained data and why it matters follows:

Operations Manager uses many containment relationships. For example, a computer contains IIS, which contains websites, and websites contain application pools. Table 19.1 provides an example of the relationships between container objects and contained objects.

TABLE 19.1   Computer, Web Server, Websites, and Application Pools

Container Object	Contained Object
Server01	IIS Server 01
IIS Server 01	Website01
IIS Server 01	Website02
Website01	Application Pool01
Website01	Application Pool02
Website02	Application Pool AA
Server01	Website01
Server01	Website02
Server01	Application Pool01
Server01	Application Pool02
Server01	Application Pool AA

Container Object	Contained Object
IIS Server 01	Application Pool01
IIS Server 01	Application Pool02
IIS Server 01	Application Pool AA

Table 19.1 shows one server with IIS installed and two websites with three application pools. Notice the number of relationships added based on this common scenario of a single server.

Be careful with this information; the authors are not saying you should not import the data, but be aware of the extra workload it puts on your databases. Some common pointers concerning bad data follow:

▶ **Users:** In general, these are not desired because of the many relationships they contain.

▶ **Action logs:** Many relationships contain relationships.

▶ **Contained activities:** Activities contain other activities with more relationships.

▶ **Computers from Operations Manager:** As described in Table 19.1, there are many containment relationships.

▶ **CI data from Operations Manager:** Not only do computer objects have may nested objects, the same goes for other objects from Operations Manager.

Following are examples of good data that have little or minimal nested objects:

▶ **Incidents with no activities or action logs:** This is simple flat information; consider keeping activities within incidents to a minimum.

▶ **Service requests without activities or action logs:** Simple flat information, consider keeping service requests as flat as possible.

▶ **Computer objects from Active Directory or Configuration Manager:** These do not have contained objects, which makes them flat data that requires less space to store. This is the opposite of an Operations Manager computer object, where you would relate more and more components to the computer object.

▶ **File attachments:** Despite what one might think, this is flat data with no contained objects.

Once you understand the difference in the collected data for the CMDB, you can plan and design your CMDB accordingly. Only collect that information you really need; understand the performance impact should you need to collect additional information.

Connector Settings

Apart from the amount of data being gathered, you could use the following configuration settings for your connectors to ensure the least amount of performance penalty on your environment.

▶ **Operations Manager connector:** Be selective in the amount of data you want to pull in by identifying requirements and the classes you want to collect as explained previously in the "Types of Data" section.

Be sure your Operations Manager environment is well tuned before turning on the Operations Manager Alert connector. There are no hard numbers regarding this, but you should expect a certain amount of workload added for each alert generated. Not only will the connector create tons of incidents that will need to be actionable, it will also put pressure on performance since the connector must synchronize the incidents with alerts in Operations Manager.

Be sure to scope correctly the alerts that you want to generate incidents. Only alerts that can be actioned upon by an incident should end up in Service Manager.

TIP: USING THE OPERATIONS MANAGER ALERT CONNECTOR

When considering using Operations Manager alerts to automatically create Service Manager incidents, first understand the potential consequences. After configuring the connector, you need to specify which alerts the connector should transfer, as once the connector is configured, it automatically creates incidents from Operations Manager alerts.

▶ Make sure you have your Operations Manager environment tuned before turning on the connector, and that you send only relevant alerts.

▶ Start with only critical alerts or perhaps only certain alerts for a particular monitor.

▶ A poorly tuned Operations Manager environment leads to numerous alerts in Service Manager, which can negatively affect its performance.

For more information on configuring the Operations Manager Alert connector, see Chapter 8, "Working with Connectors."

For information on tuning, see the Operations Manager By Example series on System Center Central, http://www.systemcentercentral.com/search-results/?search=by%20example.

19

▶ **Configuration Manager connector:** Similar to the Operations Manager connector, make sure you are only pulling over those collections you need. Don't pull in everything just for logging!

The desired configuration management (DCM) feature in Configuration Manager is another culprit when it comes to performance. As the DCM rules run every 60 seconds on all incidents in your environment, consider only using this when absolutely required.

If you are not using DCM, consider turning off the DCM rule in Service Manager to prevent the workflow from running. The blog article at http://blogs.technet.com/b/mihai/archive/2012/11/30/configuration-manager-connector-s-dcm-rule-can-cause-massive-performance-issues-in-service-manager.aspx explains why and how to turn off this rule, which is enabled by default.

▶ **Active Directory connector:** Be sure to scope the connector. It is better to have multiple connectors than one that pulls in all information, including information you are not planning to use.

Another option is to schedule the AD connector; you can use PowerShell to run the connector at certain times. See Thomas Ellermann's solution at http://blogs.technet.com/b/thomase/archive/2011/09/27/scheduling-and-disabling-the-ad-connector-via-powershell.aspx.

▶ **Orchestrator connector:** Consider a dedicated management server to be targeted by all runbooks running on the Orchestrator server. If you only have a single management server to run all Service Manager workflows and Orchestrator points to this server when running runbooks, there will be a big performance impact. Choose your management server wisely. Adding an extra server can provide a well performing Orchestrator and Service Manager environment.

Service Manager Management Server Performance

If you have multiple management servers, this only provides the ability to have more console connections, as a single management server runs all workflows.

It is important to understand the impact of workflows and how best to split the workload of these workflows. The next sections discuss some common rules for getting the most you can out of the workflow server.

Using Orchestrator Runbooks

Service Manager has several workflows running by default that cannot be offloaded. As you want to increase automation, consider offloading additional workflows to System Center Orchestrator. Large performance improvements can be gained when you design your notifications from Orchestrator rather than Service Manager.

Another option is to have "controlling" workflows that place the correct incidents in the correct resolving group. This is also a perfect candidate to run in Orchestrator instead of Service Manager.

You can start with configuring these workflows in Service Manager; should you notice a high load on your workflow server, try moving some or all of them to Orchestrator, leaving Service Manager to run only the internal workflows.

Using Groups and Queues

When working with groups and queues, be aware that these will negatively affect performance. Always try to keep these to a minimum.

Groups and queues are often used for scoping. Although this can be a good approach, there might be other ways, such as training users how to search and view objects, explained in the "Training Users" section earlier in this chapter. Is it that bad it if someone sees more than those work items for which he is responsible?

You can add views to get to the same result, focusing only on those work items for which the user is responsible. Even when using many groups and queues, you can ease the workload by tuning the interval group calculation in which rules run; this is every 30 seconds by default. You can change the interval by altering the Registry on the management server:

```
HKEY_LOCAL_MACHINE\SOFTWARE\Microsoft\System Center\2010\Common\
GroupCalcPollingIntervalMilliseconds
```

Use of Workflows

Workflows are the focus of activity for the primary Service Manager management server. This management server runs those internal workflows that you cannot alter and runs any custom workflows you develop. As mentioned in the "Using Orchestrator Runbooks" section, this means you should consider offloading custom workflows to Orchestrator or turning off unwanted workflows. Following are some examples of workflows you might want to turn off if not required:

▶ **First assigned relationship:** If you are not going to report on the first assigned to relationship, you might want to turn this off by setting an override in an override management pack to WorkItem_SetFirstAssignedTo_RelationshipAdd_Rule.

▶ **New priority calculation:** If this is not a requirement, you can choose to turn this off; disable Incident_Adjust_PriorityAndResolutionTime_Custom_Rule. Add a rule using a management pack override if using service level objectives (SLOs).

▶ **DCM workflow:** As described in the "Connector Settings" section, you might want to turn off this workflow since it is enabled by default to run and query every existing incident in Service Manager.

Most workflows in Service Manager 2012 run for 60 seconds, which is a vast improvement compared to Service Manager 2010, where workflows could take up to five minutes to run. This is because Microsoft improved the workflow processing responsiveness in the managementhostkeepalive management pack.

To review duration of the workflows, run the script in Listing 19.1, which is also included as online content for this book. Appendix C, "Available Online," provides further information.

19

LISTING 19.1   Check Duration of Workflows

```
Import-Module -Force
"%ProgramFiles%\Microsoft System Center 2012\Service Manager\Powershell\
System.Center.Service.Manager.psd1"
  # Save all WF into $workflow
  $workflow = Get-SCSMWorkflowStatus

  # Loop $workflow
  ForEach ($wf in $workflow)
{
  $status = Get-SCSMWorkflowStatus -Name $wf.Name
  $status = $status.GetStatus()

  write-host Workflow $wf.name -ForegroundColor Cyan
    ForEach ($st in $status)
       {

                    write-host $st.status  " "  $st.TimeStarted  " "
                      $st.TimeFinished  " "  $st.RelatedObject  " "
                      $st.Duration -ForegroundColor red


       }


}
```

This script is slightly changed from that by Thomas Strömberg (http://www.zgc.se/index.php/2014/01/09/check-for-failed-workflow-jobs-in-scsm-using-powershell/), and queries each workflow for start time, end time, and duration. This lets you easily review any workflow issues.

If you are experiencing workflow issues, consider the article at http://blogs.technet.com/b/servicemanager/archive/2013/01/14/troubleshooting-workflow-performance-and-delays.aspx for assistance with pinpointing the workflow and troubleshooting it.

Testing Performance

A frequently asked question is how to test the performance of your environment. Especially when moving from test to production, you want to make sure you have enough resources to deliver an appropriate self-service experience to your users.

Although you can configure everything, including the connectors to the other System Center products, and fill your CMDB with data, Service Manager does not provide a way to measure the expected workload. Following the best practices and using the Service Manager sizing sheet provides a baseline, although it cannot tell you if your design can cope with the workload. The next sections discuss some approaches.

Stress Testing Service Manager

Until recently there was no alternative to stress testing other than running a pilot phase with some test users, which was not always ideal. As of October 2013, there is a new CodePlex project, SCSM Perf Test Harness—see http://scsmperftestharness.codeplex.com/. This project delivers a complete solution to fully stress test your Service Manager environment. It is designed to measure the workload on large installations but can be used in any other case as well.

When you look at the CodePlex website, notice there is no download available in the Download section. This is because only the source code of this project is provided. You must download the project and compile the solution in Visual Studio. Be sure you copy the solution to a computer with access to Service Manager to be able to load and run the tester. Follow these steps:

1. Download the source project by selecting the Source code tab and clicking **Download**. Once the project is downloaded, you can extract the zip file.

2. Open the solution scsmperftestharness-30218\Loadgen\LoadGen.sln in Visual Studio and compile the solution.

3. Now, navigate to scsmperftestharness-30218\LoadGen\LoadGen\LoadGen\bin\ Release (or debug depending on your compile settings). Start Loadgen.exe to start the load generator (see Figure 19.11).

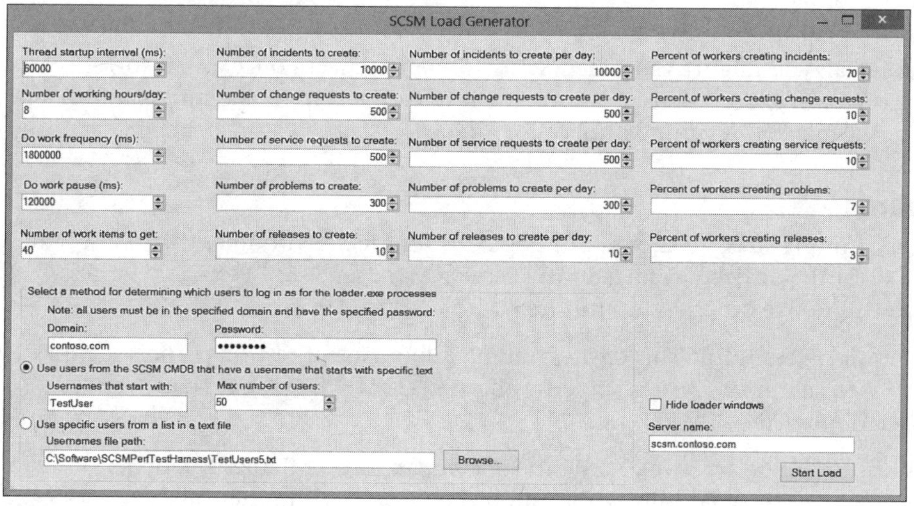

FIGURE 19.11   SCSM Load Generator.

There are several settings to configure for simulating the anticipated workload for your environment. Be sure you have a clear overview of the expected workload, based on historic information from your old service management tool, or gather the necessary information from the help desk and IT support groups. While this may not provide precise numbers, it can give you an idea of the anticipated workload. Also, don't forget to double check this information with the responsible process owners, as the information you collect may vary from actual experience.

NOTE: RUNNING THE SCSM LOAD GENERATOR

Be aware that running the load generator generates work items and mimics user connections to the management server.

To test against production without having hundreds or thousands of test data items in your database, back up your entire environment prior to running the tests. See Chapter 18, "Maintenance, Backup, and Recovery," for details on the backup and restore process.

Alternatively, if running in a virtual environment, you can make snapshots prior to testing so you can revert after testing.

After verifying the settings and amounts of working items, you are ready to run the test. While testing, be sure to monitor your servers carefully; collect the data for analysis afterward.

The tool mimics user console connections and creating work items. The self-service portal is not tested. To test the self-service portal, you must experience the behavior yourself by manually logging requests while the tool is running. You can run the tool as often as you want, and you could adjust settings using the information in this chapter to test those effects.

Although not ideal, you might even schedule performance checks once a year to verify performance is within expectations and compare it to earlier tests. Make sure you back up and restore again to avoid retaining unnecessary data.

Lab Resources

In addition to running stress tests, you can populate your lab environment with test data. When you look at the different folders in the Service Manager SCSM Perf Test Harness solution, you will notice other useful utilities:

▶ **Enumeration generator:** This creates enumeration lists for testing purposes. Find the tool (see Figure 19.12) at scsmperftestharness-30218\LoadGen\LoadGen\LoadGen\EnumGen\Bin\Release.

▶ **CSV Imports:** There are several CSV and accompanying XML files to populate your CMDB automatically with test objects. You can find these at scsmperftestharness-30218\CSV\.

▶ **Notification Rule Editor:** This tool creates notification rules for testing purposes. The tool, shown in Figure 19.13, is located at scsmperftestharness-30218\NotificationRuleEditor\bin\Debug.

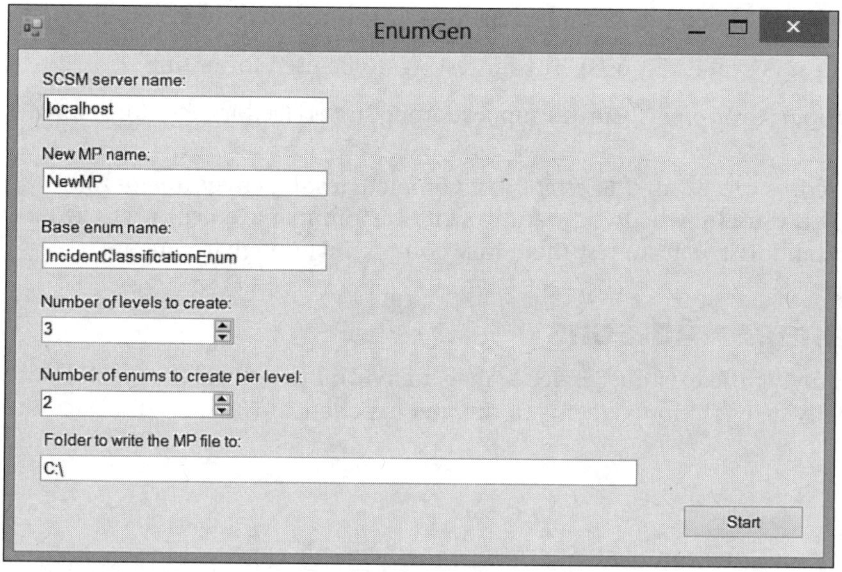

FIGURE 19.12   Enumeration generator.

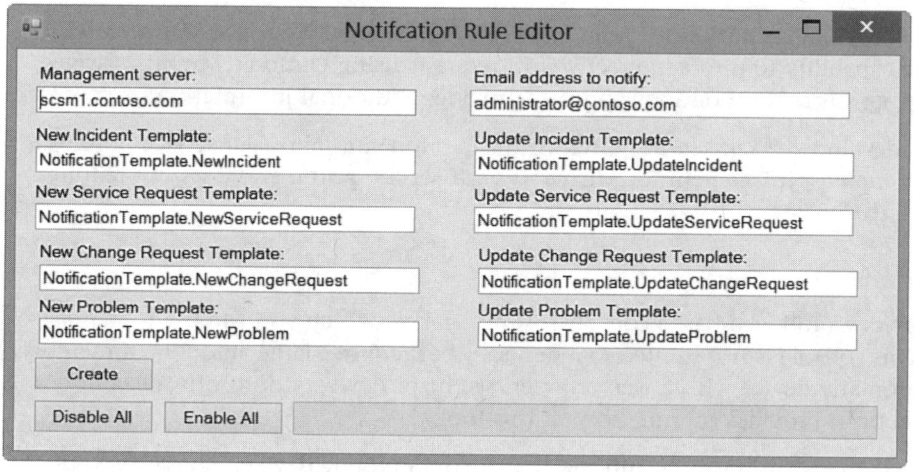

FIGURE 19.13   Notification Rule Editor.

In addition to these tools, several PowerShell scripts are located in the root folder of the project, scsmperftestharness-30218\, to populate your Active Directory quickly with test groups and test users:

▶ **Add-usersTOGroups.ps1:** Requires an input file for support groups and adds users to these groups

▶ **Create-groups.ps1:** Requires a text input file to automatically create AD groups

▶ **Create-Users.ps1:** Creates test users in your test AD to be used for testing

▶ **Generate-SupportGroup.ps1:** Creates support group in Service Manager for testing

These PowerShell scripts can be used to establish a complete testing environment for Service Manager. This is useful when you want to write custom management packs, workflows, or runbooks, and first want to test them in a non-production environment.

Service Manager Add-ons

In addition to improving the existing Service Manager environment, third-party solutions exist that can quickly deliver improvements to the user experience. These are discussed in the next sections.

Cireson

Cireson delivers a standalone console that provides a full console experience using a web interface. This console uses HTML 5, which runs on any device. The speed of this console is vastly improved when compared to the default Service Manager console, providing fast response times. For information, see http://www.cireson.com/app-store/scsm-web-console/.

Cireson also provides a solution for full Outlook integration with Service Manager, which provides the capability to interact directly with requests using Outlook. See http://www.cireson.com/app-store/scsm-outlook-console/ provides additional information.

Cireson has developed a self-service portal (http://cireson.com/apps/self-service-portal/), which is a complete replacement for Microsoft's self-service portal and does not require SharePoint 2010.

Gridpro

Gridpro provides a full web-based console for the analyst, which you can use to manage incidents. This console is not limited to a desktop that requires large amounts of memory, but can run on any device with a web browser. See http://www.gridprosoftware.com/en/products/webfront provides information on this tool.

Gridpro also delivers a solution to run the console on a mobile device. This is based on HTML 5 and runs on nearly every device. See http://www.gridprosoftware.com/en/products/mobilefront provides information on this as well.

Gridpro even delivers a solution to integrate your phone system automatically with Service Manager. To automatically record incidents directly from a phone call to an incident, see http://www.gridprosoftware.com/en/products/cti.

Summary

Performance in Service Manager is different for every deployment and requires thorough knowledge of this System Center component to configure the environment properly for maximum performance.

In Service Manager 2012, performance is vastly improved from the previous version, workflows run considerably quicker, and there are vast performance improvements to the user experience. Nonetheless, there could be situations where you want to get the maximum from your environment, making it necessary to tune the environment accordingly.

There are easy ways to improve performance by just reading and following the recommendations in this chapter and training users how to use Service Manager. The biggest change with Service Manager is transforming how people work, which has the largest impact on the overall performance concerning service management within your organization.

19

PART V

Beyond Service Manager

IN THIS PART

CHAPTER 20

Management Packs

Service Manager provides a unique approach to making customizations and ensuring preservations of those customizations during upgrades through the use of management packs. Similar to the management packs found in other System Center components such as Operations Manager, Service Manager management packs enable Microsoft and its software partners to deliver additional value and allow administrators to store customizations.

Management packs are used to extend or customize Service Manager in multiple ways. They facilitate an easy way to apply customizations and functionality within the system. By storing customizations in management packs, Service Manager provides an easier upgrade path over other service desk products in the market. Management packs also provide a mechanism for third-party vendors to package solutions for Service Manager using a straightforward installation process. The level of working with management packs ranges from easy, such as storing list updates, to complex, such as authoring a management pack from scratch.

This chapter discusses the key concepts of management packs. It defines management packs, explains how to deploy them into Service Manager, provides detail regarding sealed and unsealed management packs, outlines approaches for authoring management packs, and breaks down the management pack schema.

As a Service Manager administrator, you will work with management packs and might even need to author your own. It is important that you have a solid understanding of management packs and how they apply to Service Manager, how to manage them, and how to use them to shape Service Manager to fit your organization's specific needs.

Management Packs Defined

A management pack is an eXtensible Markup Language (XML) file made up of XML code. Management pack files can be opened by development tools such as Visual Studio, notepad editors such as Notepad ++, and XML editors such as XML Notepad. Management packs typically are authored by Microsoft, by third parties, and by IT professionals. Management packs have a standard structure (schema) to which they must adhere. More information on management pack schema is covered later in the "Management Pack Schema" section of this chapter.

Following standards allows management packs to be easily built, distributed between management servers, and upgraded. While management packs are also used in System Center Operations Manager and share a common schema, they are used in somewhat different ways because System Center Operations Manager is used for monitoring while System Center Service Manager is used for service management. Being familiar with System Center Operations Manager management packs can help in working with Service Manager.

Management packs serve as the building blocks for all information and objects, and define the structure and functionality that make up Service Manager. For example, Incident Management, Activity Management, and Knowledge Management consist of groups of management packs. Without management packs, these areas of functionality would not exist within Service Manager.

NOTE: MANAGEMENT PACKS IMPORTED DURING INSTALLATION

Service Manager 2012 is preloaded with 142 default management packs when installed. These default management packs have the information and definitions necessary for core features such as Incident Management, Change Management, Service Request Fulfillment, and the configuration management database (CMDB). These default management packs also provide core components such as templates, workflows, lists, and views. Many of these default management packs are libraries. *Libraries* are MPs that provide a foundation of object types (classes) and settings that other management packs depend on. When adding custom management packs they often require (have dependencies on) one or more of these libraries.

A benefit of using management packs as a part of the core in Service Manager is that it enables Microsoft (and others) to introduce entirely new functionality by deploying new management packs for solutions, one example being to manage chargeback. Chargeback management is functionality that Microsoft developed for Service Manager that is not in the system out of the box. Microsoft includes the management packs for chargeback with Service Manager; it can be implemented at any time by deploying those management packs. More information on chargeback can be found in Chapter 12, "Automation and Chargeback." Figure 20.1 shows the management packs that make up Incident Management, Activity Management, and Knowledge Management.

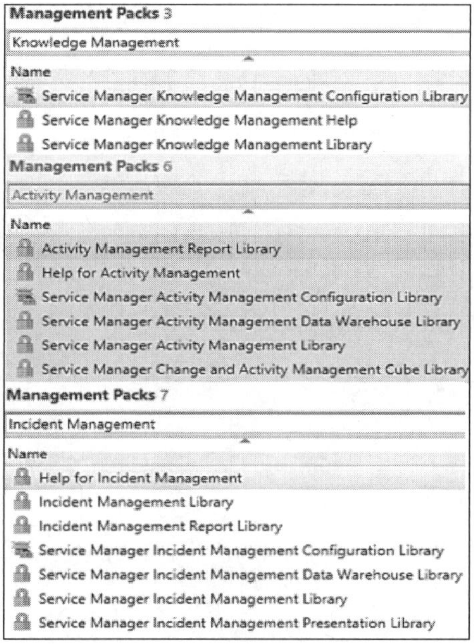

FIGURE 20.1   Groups of management packs for Service Manager functionality.

Management packs could also contain objects such as configuration items found in the CMDB, data found in lists, and information about objects and their relationships to each other. Service Manager uses model-based management packs. A *model* refers to a definition of an object such as a server, user, or service, and the components making up that entity. It describes the relationships between the components; how the server, user, or service relates to other objects within Service Manager, such as incidents, change requests, and installed software. Model-based management requires that objects be modeled in management packs.

Service Manager includes a core model for management packs. This core model is used to declare common types of objects (classes) and provides a starting point for management pack authors to refine the model. The model consists of a collection of classes, relationship types, modules, data types, and other building blocks. Service Manager functionality is defined in an extensible way through management packs. Model-based management packs define the semantics of objects, including

▶ Classes

▶ Combination classes

▶ Relationships

The objects from this list are model extensions and become dependencies for other management packs that contain presentation-type objects. Separate management packs reference those management packs containing model-based objects. Model-based management packs allow for further customizations of Service Manager that are related to presentation, such as

▶ Templates

▶ Views

▶ Forms

▶ Reports

Other types of objects stored and defined through management packs include

▶ Workflows

▶ Lists

▶ Tasks

Management packs are used to extend Service Manager in various ways. Following are some examples of what could be extended through management packs:

▶ New objects such as forms, views, templates, and lists

▶ New functionality such as telephony integration, Outlook integration, billable time, and more

▶ Service Manager's behavior such as controls on forms

Purpose of Management Packs

Management packs serve two primary purposes:

▶ They provide storage of customizations.

▶ They are a packaging mechanism for Microsoft partners to deliver additional solutions on top of the Service Manager platform.

Most customizations made to Service Manager are stored in a management pack. Extensions to the data model, form customizations, workflow rules, notification subscriptions, list items, views, templates, notification templates, groups, queues, console tasks, data warehouse extensions, reports, workflows, and new custom forms are all stored in management packs.

Microsoft software partners can deliver their solutions to customers easily using management packs. An analogy commonly used is that Service Manager is a platform similar to SharePoint. Partners deliver solution management packs for Service Manager much like developers provide solutions that can be deployed to SharePoint to extend functionality. A common extension provided in the form of management packs from third-party vendors is a full asset management solution. Even those solutions by Microsoft out of the box such as change, incident, problem, configuration, and knowledge management are actually just management packs imported during setup.

There are several important advantages to storing customizations in management packs:

▶ Uninstallation

▶ Transportation

▶ Versioning

▶ Componentization

The next sections discuss these topics.

Uninstalling Management Packs

When a management pack is imported into Service Manager, it may extend the database schema and add additional content into the system such as forms, templates, and list items. One of the advantages of a management pack is that it is extremely easy to revert those extensions and customizations by simply deleting the management pack. If the database schema is extended to add new tables and fields when the management pack is imported, those same tables and fields are deleted when the management pack is deleted. It would be as if those schema extensions never happened, and all the data stored in those tables and fields no longer exists. Any new forms, templates, console tasks, and so on defined in that management pack are also removed. This is advantageous to Service Manager installations in several ways:

▶ Management packs make it simple to try out a software partner's solution; should you decide not to move forward or want to start over, you can just delete those management packs.

▶ You can easily remove artifacts used to support a new process that is no longer needed or being used. You simply delete the management pack.

▶ If you suspect that a particular management pack is causing some type of problem with a workflow or form, you can easily remove that offending management pack while you determine the source of the problem.

Transporting Management Packs

Management packs are transportable in the form of an .xml, .mp, or .mpb file. This allows software partners to offer complete solutions that you can easily download from the Internet—similar to any other file—and import these into Service Manager. Administrators can also create and test all of their customizations to Service Manager in a preproduction environment, export those management packs, and then import them into production, alleviating the need to move complicated step-by-step code-based customizations between environments. Management packs do not have a complicated build or deployment process. This transportability also enables Microsoft, partners, and administrators to share

20

solutions easily with each other in the community on sites such as blogs, CodePlex, or forums.

Management Pack Versioning

Management packs can be versioned over time as they are modified. This enables upgrade-ability of both Service Manager itself and the partner and customer management packs created on top of Service Manager. It also enables rollback. Administrators can treat management packs like source code with a source control system. You should preserve each version of the management pack, so that at any point you could roll back to a previous version of the management pack or compare differences between a previous version and the current version.

Management Pack Componentization

Componentization is the concept of grouping together sets of customizations into a management pack (or set of management packs). For example, if you are adding a new automated process to provision new users, you may want to store the data model extensions, forms, form customizations, list items, views, templates, and queues associated with that process in a single management pack. This makes it easy to manage the artifacts of the complete solution in a single package that can be transported, versioned, and easily uninstalled.

Working with Management Packs

There are multiple ways to work with management packs, some ways being easier than others. You can work with management packs directly in the Service Manager console, the Service Manager Authoring Tool, Visual Studio, or through an XML editor. The next sections discuss management pack deployment and working with management packs through the Service Manager console. For more information on other ways of working with management packs see Chapter 22, "Customizing Service Manager," and Chapter 23, "Advanced Customization Scenarios." The most common way of working with management packs is through the Service Manager console. Management packs can be sealed or unsealed, as discussed in the next section.

Sealed and Unsealed Management Packs

Management packs can be sealed (not modifiable) or unsealed (modifiable). Microsoft, software partners, and in some cases, administrators, seal a management pack to prevent modifications to the management pack itself. This ensures upgradeability without concern of breaking any customizations that have been applied, as the customizations are stored in another management pack. Typically, these customizations are stored in unsealed management packs, allowing them to be easily modified at any time.

Several other characteristics are important to understand about sealed and unsealed management packs. Management packs can depend on each other, but only when the management pack depended on is sealed:

▶ A management pack (sealed or unsealed) can depend on a sealed management pack.

▶ A management pack (sealed or unsealed) cannot depend on an unsealed management pack.

This dependency is called a *reference* and is discussed further in the "Management Pack Schema" section of this chapter.

Management packs that are sealed can be upgraded from one version to another without losing any data, because the management pack remains intact at all times. "Upgrading" an unsealed management pack is effectively uninstalling and reinstalling that management pack; in some cases, this could result in data loss, particularly in cases where it contains data model extensions.

Management packs can be sealed using either a command line utility called fastseal.exe or the Service Manager Authoring Tool. Fastseal.exe is appropriate when using an automated management pack build system, where you need to seal many management packs as part of the build of a complete solution including other code. You can download fastseal.exe from the Service Manager Engineering Team's blog at http://blogs.technet.com/servicemanager/archive/2009/12/25/sealing-management-packs.aspx. Run `fastseal.exe /?` to see usage. Some sample syntax follows:

```
fastseal.exe MyManagementPack.xml /Company "My Company"
/Copyright "Copyright 2011 My Company" /KeyFile MyKeyFile.snk
```

NOTE: USING A STRONG NAME FILE

Sealing a management pack requires a strong name key file (.snk). You can create one using the Strong Name Tool (sn.exe), which is a tool in the Windows software development kit (SDK) that you can download from http://www.microsoft.com/downloads/en/details.aspx?FamilyID=e6e1c3df-a74f-4207-8586-711ebe331cdc&displaylang=en, or use the Authoring Tool. See Chapter 23 for information on creating a strong name key.

Alternatively, you can use the Service Manager Authoring Tool. Follow these steps:

1. Start the Seal Management Pack Authoring Tool dialog by right-clicking the management pack name in the Management Pack Explorer (see Figure 20.2).

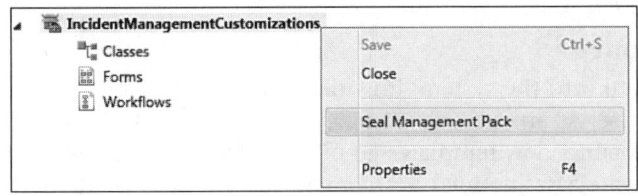

FIGURE 20.2   Launching the seal utility in the Service Manager Authoring Tool.

20

2. When the Seal Management Pack dialog (see Figure 20.3) opens, provide the output directory (folder) for the .mp file, the .snk key file, and company information. A copyright can also optionally be included. Clicking **Seal** saves a sealed .mp file into the folder indicated as the output folder.

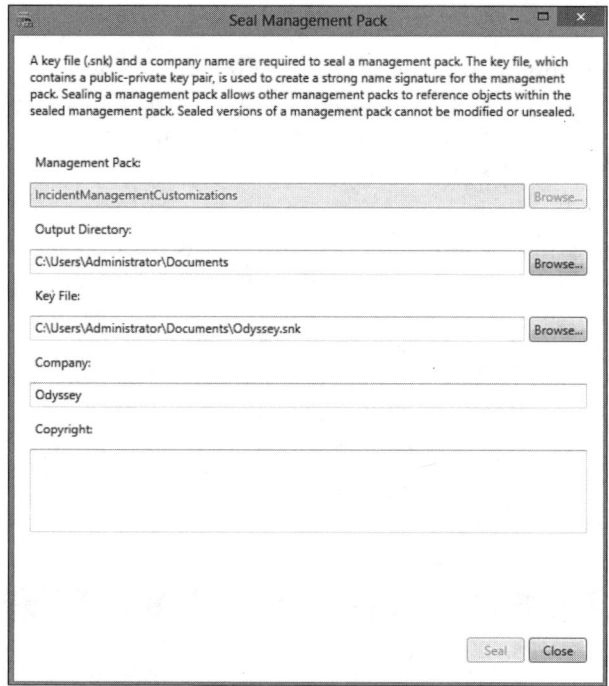

FIGURE 20.3   The Management Pack Sealing Tool in the Service Manager Authoring Tool.

Sealing a management pack turns a management pack from an .xml file to an .mp file, which is a binary representation of the management pack instead of a human readable XML file. This is not for the purpose of protecting intellectual property! It is solely to make it possible to digitally sign the file. Only binary files can be signed. Signing a binary assures the receiver that the file was signed by the provider of the file and that it has not been modified.

Management Pack Deployment

When a management pack is imported into the system, it is sliced into its different components and stored in the database. As an example, any new views declared in the management pack go into the Views table, new templates go into the ObjectTemplate table, and so on. Any new nonabstract classes defined in the management pack create new database tables. Class extensions result in new columns that are added to the nonabstract class tables. Other components of a management pack must be deployed to other places in addition to the Service Manager database. Workflow assemblies must be manually copied to the \%*ProgramFiles*%\Microsoft System Center\Service Manager 2012 folder.

View type assemblies, console task handler assemblies, and form assemblies are stored in the database during management pack import. Later, when a user tries to use a view, console task, or form for which the console does not already have the assembly, the console requests the assembly from the System Center Data Access Service. The Data Access Service retrieves the requested file from the Service Manager database and sends it to the console computer. The console caches that file in the \%*UserProfile*%\AppData\ Local\Microsoft\System Center Service Manager 2010\%*ServerName*% folder. This folder contains a folder for each unique management pack version. Resource assemblies are stored in the version folder corresponding to the version of the management pack with which they are associated. The console verifies that it has the latest version of the required resource assembly. Thus, if a new version of the management pack is imported and contains a new assembly, the next time the console needs to use that assembly it will download and cache the new version of the assembly.

Image files are also stored in the database during management pack import. The console downloads all required images when it starts and caches them for quick access. Should you introduce new images via a management pack import, you must close and reopen the console to see the new images.

Data warehouse and reporting management pack elements have a special deployment process. The management pack must first be imported into the Service Manager management group. A workflow called MPSync is then triggered (every 60 minutes by default or on demand). This workflow takes all sealed management packs from the Service Manager management group and imports them into the data warehouse management group. In addition to synchronizing all sealed management packs, the MPSync workflow synchronizes groups, queues, and enumeration values in unsealed management packs. Similar to when the management packs were imported into the Service Manager management group, importing these management packs extends the database schema of the DWStagingAndConfig database, preparing that database to receive data from the Service Manager management group. The data is extracted from the ServiceManager database and staged in the DWStagingAndConfig database. It remains in that database until transformed and loaded into the DWRepository and DWDataMart databases. The MPSync workflow process is as follows:

1. Once MPSync completes, the workflow begins the deployment.

2. For each data warehouse element in the new management packs that have been imported, the workflow deploys the additional schema changes required to extend the DWRepository and DWDataMart databases to store the additional dimensions and facts.

3. The .sql transform script resource files are deployed and the reports published to the SQL Server Reporting Services web service.

4. The next time the extract, transform, and load jobs run, the data begins to be populated in the new tables and shows up in the new reports.

More information about the data warehouse and reporting can be found in Chapter 21, "Data Warehouse and Reporting."

Creating a Management Pack Using the Service Manager Console

The Service Manager console provides two ways to create a management pack. You could create a management pack using a console task in the Administration -> Management Packs area in the console. Alternatively, a management pack can be created within the Service Manager console when adding new items to a list in Service Manager.

Follow these steps to create a management pack using a console task:

1. In the Service Manager console, navigate to **Administration -> Administration -> Management Packs**.

2. Under **Tasks -> Management Packs**, select **Create Management Pack**.

3. When the Create Management Pack window opens, give the management pack a Name and a Description (see Figure 20.4). Click **OK**.

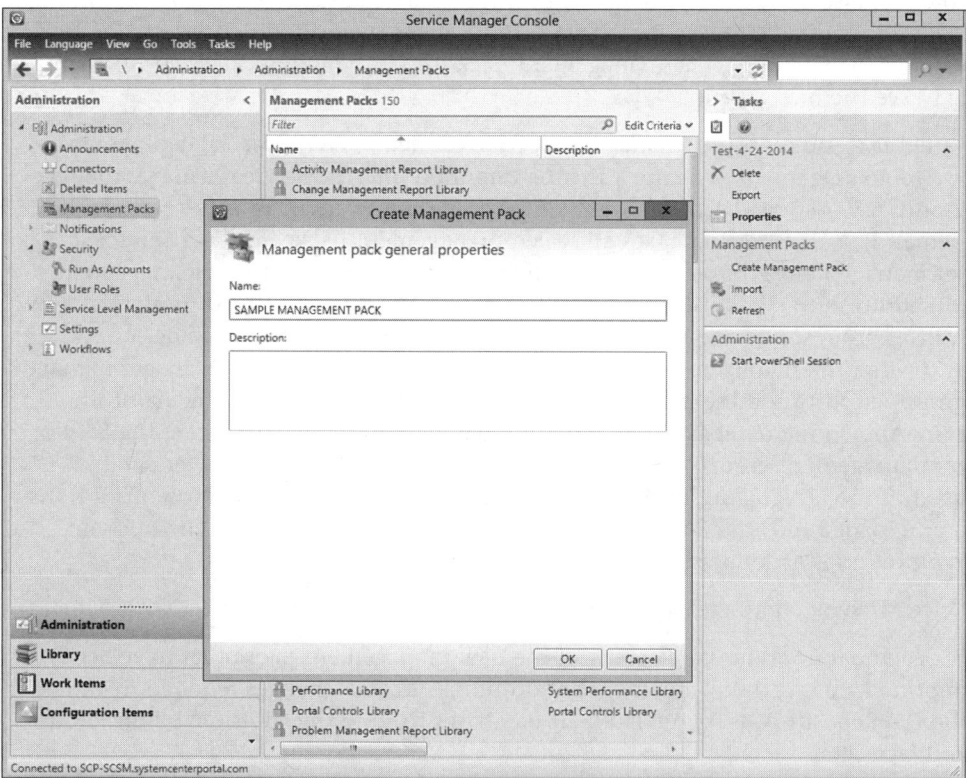

FIGURE 20.4   Creating a management pack.

Alternatively, you could create a management pack when adding an item to a list. Perform the following steps:

1. In the Service Manager console, navigate to **Library -> Lists -> Management Packs**.

2. Right-click a name in the list and select **Properties**.

3. In the List Properties window, click **Add Item**.

4. The Select management pack dialog opens, displayed in Figure 20.5. You can select an existing management pack or create a new management pack by clicking **New**, which opens the same Create Management Pack dialog shown in Figure 20.4.

5. Give the management pack a Name and Description. This new management pack now stores all items you add to the list.

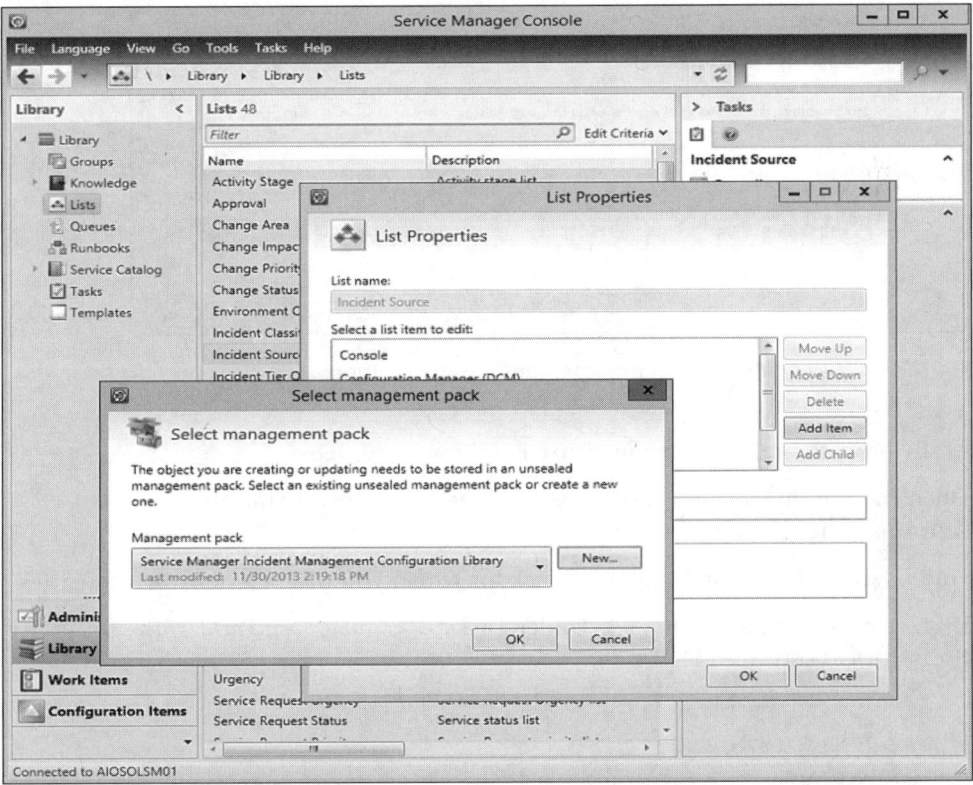

FIGURE 20.5   Creating a management pack from a list item.

Viewing the Properties of a Management Pack

Viewing the properties of a management pack provides detailed information about the name, description, and any dependencies it has. This information is useful to know when working with management packs. Figure 20.6 shows a management pack's properties.

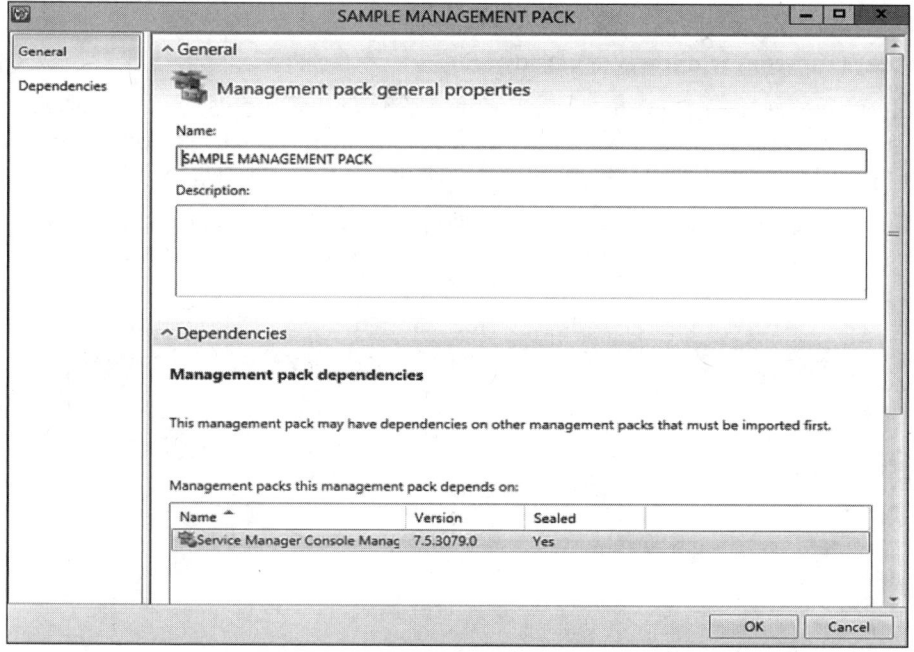

FIGURE 20.6   Viewing or modifying management pack properties.

To view the properties of a management pack, follow these steps:

1. Open the Service Manager console and navigate to **Administration ->
   Administration -> Management Packs.**

2. Find or search for the management pack for which you want to view the properties.

3. Highlight the management pack. Under **Tasks** -> *<ManagementPackName>*, select
   Properties as shown in Figure 20.7.

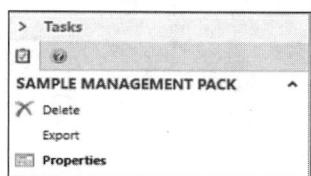

FIGURE 20.7   Selecting management pack properties.

4. The management pack's properties dialog opens. Here you can view or edit the
   settings of the management pack. You see the following properties:

   ▶ Name

   ▶ Description

   ▶ Dependencies

Dependencies show you what management packs this management pack depends on and what other management packs depend on the management pack whose properties you are viewing.

5. Click **OK** to close the dialog box.

Exporting a Management Pack

To move management packs to other Service Manager management groups or back them up, they must be exported. To export a management pack, perform the following steps:

1. Open the Service Manager console and navigate to **Administration -> Administration -> Management Packs**.

2. Locate the management pack you want to export in the list or type the name of the management pack in the search field (**Sample** in this example).

3. Highlight the management pack.

4. Under **Tasks** -> *<ManagementPackName>*, click **Export** (see Figure 20.8).

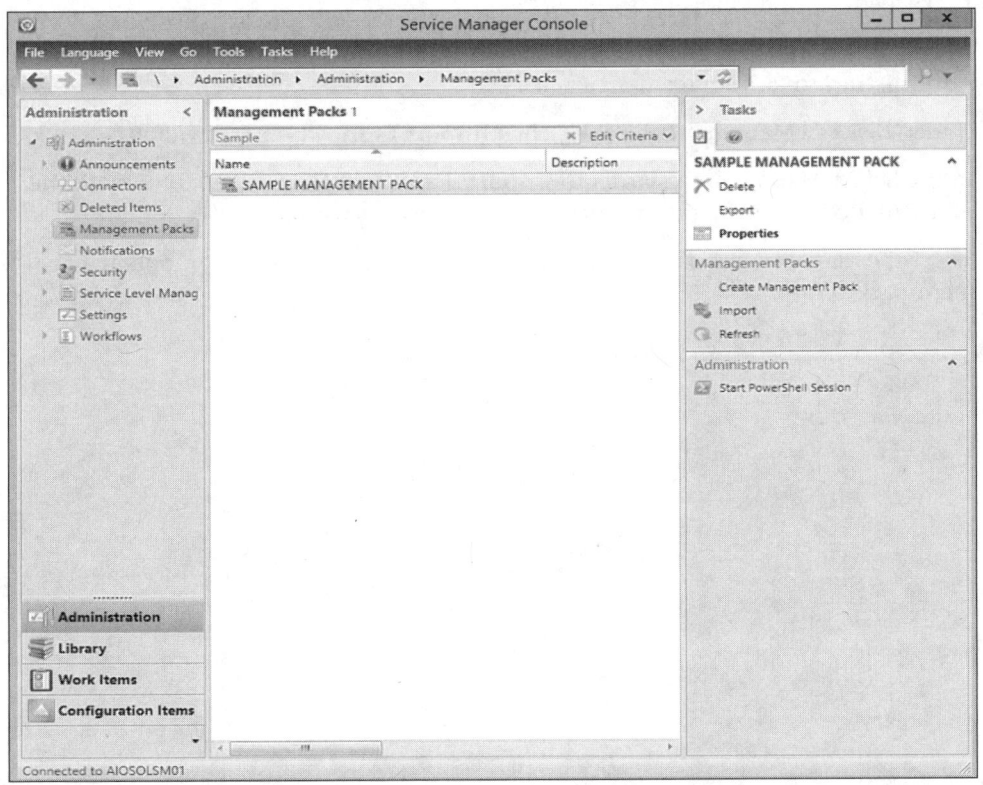

FIGURE 20.8 Exporting a management pack.

5. A dialog box opens. Browse to a folder to save the exported management pack in. Select a folder and click **OK**.

You can navigate to the folder to which you exported the management pack. The management pack will be an XML file with the extension .xml. The name of the management pack will be in a format similar to `Managementpack.66826344e8324a499eff2b46b6795aa2.xml`.

You could perform multiple actions with this management pack:

▶ Import it into another Service Management deployment.

▶ Edit the management pack and reimport into the existing Service Manager to override the existing management pack.

▶ Store it somewhere for backup purposes.

Importing a Management Pack

Moving management packs to other Service Manager management groups or restoring them into Service Manager requires importing them into the system. To import management packs, perform the following steps:

1. Open the Service Manager console and navigate to **Administration** -> **Administration** -> **Management Packs**.

2. Under **Tasks** -> **Management Packs**, click **Import** as shown in Figure 20.9.

3. In the **Select Management Packs to Import** dialog (see Figure 20.9), browse to the folder that contains the management pack you want to import.

4. Select the management pack(s) and **Open**. You can import more than one management pack at a time.

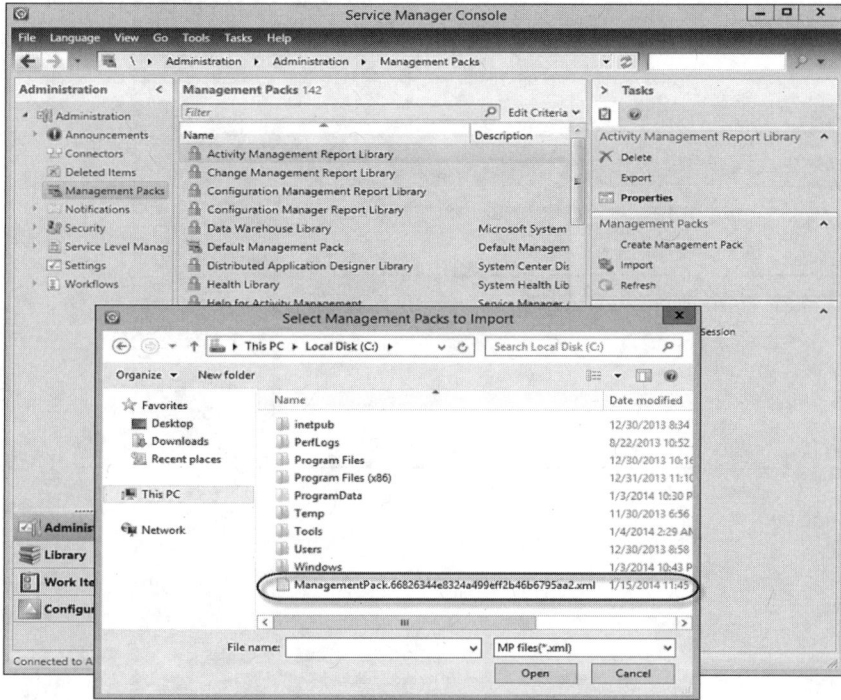

FIGURE 20.9   Importing a management pack.

5. The management pack(s) should now be listed in an Import Management Packs dialog as shown in Figure 20.10. Add additional management packs to this import by clicking **Add** and selecting more management packs.

6. Select **Import** to perform the actual management pack import.

7. After the import successfully completes, you see the management pack(s) in the list of management packs.

20

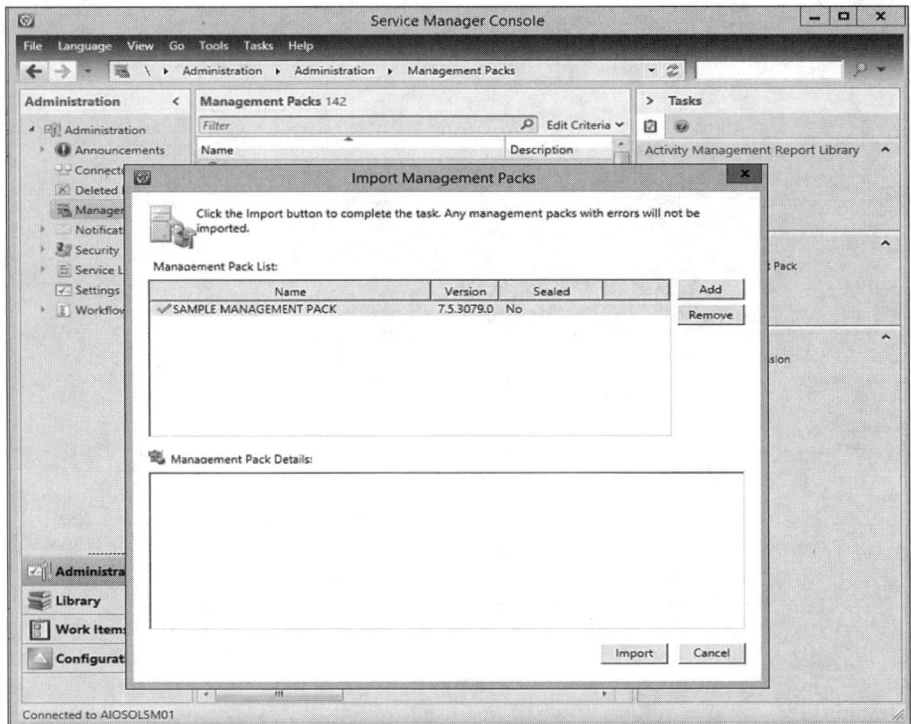

FIGURE 20.10   Import Management Packs dialog.

Management Pack Bundles

Management pack bundles are used to group together a management pack with its associated resources (assemblies, image files, or other files) or to group together multiple related management packs. A management pack bundle is actually just an MSI file with an .mpb file extension. The .mpb file acts as a cabinet to bundle up multiple files—.xml, .mp, .dll, .sql, .png, and so on into a single file for convenience. You can import .mpb files into Service Manager just as you do .mp or .xml files by using the management pack import dialog in the Management Packs view in the Service Manager console, or a PowerShell cmdlet such as Import-SCSMManagementPack.

To create a management pack bundle you must first declare the management pack resources in the management pack XML (see the "Management Pack Schema" section for additional information). You then place each of those resource files in the same folder as the management pack file. Finally, you can use a PowerShell script such as New-MBPFile. ps1 to create the management pack bundle. Here is an example:

```
New-MPBFile.ps1 MyManagementPack.xml MyManagementPack
```

This command creates a file called MyManagementPack.mpb. You can download the New-MPBFile.ps1 script from the Service Manager Engineering Team's blog at http://blogs.technet.com/b/servicemanager/archive/2009/09/04/introducing-management-pack-bundles.aspx.

Once a management pack bundle is imported into Service Manager, the concept of a bundle is no longer present. The management packs imported as part of the bundle are independently managed.

TIP: USING MANAGEMENT PACK BUNDLES FOR RESOURCES AND DEPENDENCIES

When a management pack requires resources (such as forms or images) that are stored separately, these resources and the management pack must be bundled into an .mbp file.

You might also want to bundle management packs together when one depends on another. Say you have a custom template depending on a list defined in another management pack. The management pack containing the definitions must be sealed, and must be imported prior to any management packs that depend on it. Alternatively, you could bundle that management pack along with the required resources and the depending management pack, eliminating the need to first import the management pack with the definitions.

Management Pack Schema

Management packs at their core are XML files that must match a particular schema. The schema can be broken down into the following commonly used areas:

▶ Identity

▶ References

▶ Entity Types

▶ Secure References

▶ Categories

▶ Presentation

▶ Language Packs

▶ Resources

▶ Images

▶ Enumerations

▶ Combination Classes

▶ Console Tasks

▶ Resources

▶ Forms

These areas are discussed in the following sections.

Identity Section

The Identity section uniquely identifies the management pack by name and version.

```
<Identity>
  <ID>System.Library</ID>
  <Version>7.5.8501.0</Version>
</Identity>
```

The GUID ID of all the management pack elements in the management pack when they are imported into the database is a hash of the ID of the management pack and the ID of the management pack element. Therefore, changing the ID of the management pack changes the ID of all the management pack elements contained in that management pack. This also means that management pack elements have the same GUID in all installations of Service Manager.

As an example, the incident class GUID is `A604B942-4C7B-2FB2-28DC-61DC6F465C68` in every installation of Service Manager. That GUID is a hash of the management pack ID `System.WorkItem.Incident.Library` and the class ID `System.WorkItem.Incident`. If Microsoft were to change the management pack ID of the management pack that contains the incident class, change the incident class ID, or move the incident class from one management pack to another, the GUID would change. This would break many different places in the code of the product itself and potentially any code written by partners or other developers against the Service Manager SDK. Therefore, as a best practice, ensure you choose the correct ID for your management pack at the very beginning and don't change it over time.

Versioning

Versions also control upgradeability of management packs. If you try to import a lower version of a sealed management pack on top of a higher version, the system rejects the import attempt. You can only import a sealed management pack on top of an existing version of the same management pack if the version you are importing is the same or higher. You can import any version of an unsealed management pack on top of any version of the same unsealed management pack, because the system treats that as a delete/import instead of an in-place upgrade. If you import a management pack that has the same version as the same management pack that already exists in the database, the System Center Management Configuration service will not be aware that there is new content in the management pack that needs to be downloaded to the workflow engine. To avoid this situation, increment the version number before importing the management pack. The same is true of management pack synchronization to the data warehouse.

About References

Management packs can take a dependency on or "reference" another management pack. An example of this would be a view that is in one management pack that is configured to show objects of a class defined in another management pack. If the management pack containing the class were deleted, the view in the other management pack would be useless. In this case, the management pack containing the view would take a dependency on the management pack containing the class. The system enforces this dependency, and does not allow the management pack containing the class to be removed until all management packs depending on it are removed.

Management pack dependencies are declared as references in the management pack XML. To create a reference, the ID, version, and public key token for the management pack that is being referenced must be provided. Here is an example of a management pack reference:

```
<Reference Alias="System">
  <ID>System.Library</ID>
  <Version> 7.5.8501.0</Version>
  <PublicKeyToken>31bf3856ad364e35</PublicKeyToken>
</Reference>
```

The ID is the same as the ID element in the referenced management pack, which must also be the same as the management pack file name. The version number in the reference is used to make sure that a certain version *or higher* of the referenced management pack exists.

The public key token is determined by the strong name key file (.snk) that is used to seal the management pack. The public key token for all officially released Microsoft sealed management packs is 31bf3856ad364e35. To look up the public key token or version for another management pack that is already in the system, run this query in the ServiceManager database:

```
SELECT MPName, MPFriendlyName, MPVersion, MPKeyToken FROM ManagementPack
WHERE MPIsSealed = 1 ORDER BY MPName
```

The alias of a management pack reference is used as a shorthand way to point to that management pack. As an example, in this RelationshipType declaration, the System management pack alias System! is used.

```
<RelationshipType .... Base="System!System.Reference">
```

This is saying that this RelationshipType is based on the System.Reference RelationshipType contained in the management pack with the alias System. The System alias is defined to point to the System.Library management pack in the Reference XML example shown at the beginning of this section.

A reference can only be made on management pack elements that are configured to be publicly accessible. As an example, the System.Reference RelationshipType in the System.Library management pack looks like this:

```
<RelationshipType ID="System.Reference" Accessibility="Public" Abstract="true">
```

Accessibility being Public allows other management pack elements in other management packs to refer to this RelationshipType. If the Accessibility attribute is set to Internal, other management pack elements within the same management pack can refer to it, but other management pack elements in other management packs cannot. Setting Accessibility to Internal is useful if you want to ensure that no other management packs ever depend on a management pack element. You may want to set Accessibility to Internal if at some point you might want to remove that management pack element.

Entity Types Section

The Entity Types section contains classes, properties on those classes, relationship types, type projections, and enumeration types. Chapter 22 describes these concepts in detail.

Secure References

Secure references are described in detail in Chapter 17, "Service Manager Security."

Using Categories

Categories are used to categorize management pack elements in the management pack. The possibilities for how to use categories are essentially limitless. Categories are used to categorize console tasks, icons, views, search options, and many other things. For example, adding the following category to a management pack and importing it into Service Manager hides the Extensions tab on the incident form:

```
<Category
Value="Admin!Microsoft.EnterpriseManagement.ServiceManager.UI.Administration.
Enumeration.HideExtensionTab" Target="Incident!System.WorkItem.Incident.ConsoleForm"
ID="HideIncidentFormExtensionTab"/>
```

A Category has a Value attribute and a Target attribute. The Target attribute is the management pack element that is being categorized. The Value attribute is the category. Values typically point at an EnumerationValue such as in the example in this section. You could create another Category with the same Value attribute and a Target that pointed at the change request, computer, or other forms.

About Templates

You can think of templates as partially completed objects. Templates serve two purposes.

▶ They are used to create or update objects in a standardized way. For example, each time you create a change request to add more RAM to a server the classification of that kind of change request, who it is assigned to, what the activities are to implement the change request, and so on should be the same. Creating these types of change requests from the same template can help ensure standardized procedures are followed. The data is more standardized and consistent, which improves searching and reporting.

▶ Templates are used to speed up data entry. Rather than filling out the same fields on a form over and over, a user can simply choose to create an object from a template or update an object from a template, which may fill out many of the fields on the form with several clicks.

Templates are also used to store notification templates in management packs. Notification templates are used to format email notifications sent by Service Manager. Administrators can insert properties of the object being notified into the subject or body of the message.

Templates are always targeted at a class or a type projection. When templates are targeted at a type projection, related objects can also be created or updated whenever an object is updated. A type projection always has a "seed" class. You can add components to the type projection by specifying the relationship type to traverse over. An example follows:

```
<TypeProjection Type="System.WorkItem.Incident">
   <Component Path="$Target/Path[Relationship=
    'WorkItem!System.WorkItemAssignedToUser']$"
    Alias="AssignedTo" />
   <Component Path="$Target/Path[Relationship=
    'WorkItem!System.WorkItemAffectedUser']$"
    Alias="AffectedUser" />
   <Component Path="$Target/Path[Relationship=
    'WorkItem!System.WorkItemCreatedByUser']$"
    Alias="CreatedBy" />
   <Component Path="$Target/Path[Relationship=
    'WorkItem!System.WorkItemRelatesToConfigItem']$"
    Alias="RelatesToCI" />
</TypeProjection>
```

The "seed" class is specified in the `Type` attribute on the `TypeProjection` element. Components can then be added that specify which related objects to include. Each `Component` identifies a relationship type path over which to traverse.

When a type projection object is returned by the System Center Data Access Service for this type projection, it includes the incident object as the "seed" object, the user object that is assigned to the incident, the user object that is the affected user, the user object for the user that created the incident, and all configuration item objects related to the incident.

Presentation Section

The Presentation section of a management pack is where forms, views, folders, and console tasks, image references, and string resources are defined. Forms can be either a new form created in Visual Studio or Expression Blend, a customized form, or a simple form created using the Service Manager Authoring Tool. Views and folders are most easily created using the console, since constructing them by hand in XML would be pretty challenging!

It is possible to do things in views in XML that are not possible with the UI. After defining a view, you can export out the management pack containing that view and modify column headings, as an example. Image references are used to specify which icon should be used for views and console tasks. String resources are a layer of indirection used by forms and views to specify a localizable string shown in the user interface such as a label over a control on a form or a column header in a view.

20

Language Packs

Language packs store the localized display strings for all the user interface elements defined in management packs. Class names, property names, view names, template names, and many other things can be localized using language packs. A management pack can contain many different language packs. Each language pack contains a display string and optionally a description for each management pack element. A management pack can also contain localized display strings for management pack elements in other referenced management packs.

When something is created in the console, the name and description provided for that are stored in the language in which the console is running. Users viewing that item in a different language may see the ID of the item instead of the string the first user entered. The logic for determining what to show for each display string is to first look for a display string that is the same as the console (which is the same as the operating system). If a display string doesn't exist for that language, the console looks for a display string defined in a default language pack (typically English). If the display string doesn't exist in the default language pack, the console displays the ID of the management pack element.

An example of a language pack and display string follows:

```
<LanguagePack ID="ENU" IsDefault="true">
  <DisplayStrings>
      <DisplayString ElementID="System.Library">
        <Name>System Library</Name>
        <Description>System Library: Root for all Management Packs. Contains
         platform independent definitions.</Description>
      </DisplayString>
  </DisplayStrings>
```

The ID attribute of a language pack (ENU in the example) is a three-letter code for that language from ISO standard 639. You can see a list of those codes at http://www.sil.org/iso639-3/codes.asp. Each display string has an `ElementID` attribute that points to the management pack element's ID. In this case, `System.Library` points to the ID of the management pack itself. The `Name` element is required, although the `Description` element is optional.

Resources Section

The Resources section of the management pack declares resource files that are external to the management pack XML file itself. These include form assemblies, workflow assemblies, view type assemblies, console task handler assemblies, image files, SQL script files (.sql), report files (.rdl), and other files the management pack author deems must be included with the management pack for the management pack to function correctly. Resources are declared as an `Assembly`, `Resource`, `ReportResource`, or `Image` resource element. When resources are declared in a management pack, the associated files must be included in a management pack bundle. When a management pack bundle is imported into the system, the resource files are stored in the database and then deployed automatically to the appropriate location.

Image Files

Images are not stored directly within management packs. Image files are referenced within management packs. This is done through an image resource shown in the following example.

```
<Resources>
    <Image ID="TestLibrary.Resources.Image1" Accessibility="Public" FileName=
    "image.png"/>
</Resources>
```

About Enumerations

Enumerations are a tree of values that determine the attributes and value of properties. Enumerations have a unique ID attribute and a Parent attribute.

```
<EnumerationTypes>
    <EnumerationValue ID="SampleServerState" Accessibility="Public"/>
    <EnumerationValue ID="SampleServerState.Running" Parent="SampleServerState"
    Accessibility="Public"/>
   <EnumerationValue ID="SampleServerState.Stopped" Parent="SampleServerState"
    Accessibility="Public"/>
    <EnumerationValue ID="SampleServerState.Error" Parent="SampleServerState"
    Accessibility="Public" />
    <EnumerationValue ID="SampleServerState.Error.RROD" Parent="SampleServerState.
    Error" Accessibility="Public" />
</EnumerationTypes>
```

Combination Classes

Combination classes (type projections) combine different components that are related in management packs. They store and retrieve all the aggregated data into a view. Combination classes make it easier to use the data in forms and database operations. An example follows:

```
<TypeProjections>
    <TypeProjection ID="System.WorkItem.Incident.View.ProjectionType"
        Accessibility="Public" Type="Incident!System.WorkItem.Incident">
        <Component Alias="AffectedUser"
         Path=
         "$Target/Path[Relationship='SMCore!System.WorkItemCreatedForUser']$"/>
        <Component Alias="AssignedUser"
        Path=
         "$Target/Path[Relationship='SMCore!System.WorkItemAssignedToUser']$"/>
    </TypeProjection>
    <TypeProjection ID="System.WorkItem.Incident.View.DCMProjectionType"
     Accessibility=
     "Public" Type="Incident!System.WorkItem.Incident.DCMIncident">
```

```
    <Component Alias="AffectedUser" Path=
     "$Target/Path[Relationship='SMCore!System.WorkItemCreatedForUser']$"/>
    <Component Alias="AssignedUser" Path=
     "$Target/Path[Relationship='SMCore!System.WorkItemAssignedToUser']$"/>
    <!--Baseline and Configuration Item Information-->
    <Component Alias="AffectedComputer"
    Path=
     "$Target/Path[Relationship=
     'Incident!System.WorkItem.Incident.DCMIncident.Refers.
     NonComplianceComputer']$"/>
</TypeProjection>
<TypeProjection ID="System.WorkItem.ChangeRequestViewProjection"
 Accessibility="Public" Type="System.WorkItem.ChangeRequest">
    <Component Alias="AssignedTo"
     Path="$Target/Path[Relationship='SMCore!System.WorkItemAssignedToUser']$"/>
</TypeProjection>
<TypeProjection ID="System.WorkItem.ChangeRequestProjection"
 Accessibility="Public" Type="System.WorkItem.ChangeRequest">
    <Component Alias="Activity"
    Path=
     "$Target/Path[Relationship='SMActivity!System.WorkItemContainsActivity']$">
      <Component Alias="ActivityAssignedTo"
       Path=
       "$Target/Path[Relationship='SMCore!System.WorkItemAssignedToUser']$"/>
      <Component Alias="ActivityRelatedWorkItem"
       Path=
       "$Target/Path[Relationship='SMCore!System.WorkItemRelatesToWorkItem']$">
      <Component Alias="ActivityRelatedWorkItemAssignedTo"
       Path=
       "$Target/Path[Relationship='SMCore!System.WorkItemAssignedToUser']$"/>
      </Component>
      <Component Alias="ActivityRelatedConfigItem"
       Path=
       "$Target/Path[Relationship='SMCore!System.WorkItemRelatesToConfigItem']$"/>
      <Component Alias="ActivityAboutConfigItem"
       Path=
       "$Target/Path[Relationship='System!System.WorkItemAboutConfigItem']$"/>
      <Component Alias="ActivityFileAttachment"
       Path=
       "$Target/Path[Relationship='System!System.WorkItemHasFileAttachment']$">
      <Component Alias="ActivityFileAttachmentAddedBy"Path=
       "$Target/Path[Relationship='System!System.FileAttachmentAddedByUser']$"/>
      </Component>
      <Component Alias="Reviewer"
       Path=
       "$Target/Path[Relationship='SMActivity!System.ReviewActivityHasReviewer']$">
```

```
        <Component Alias="User"
         Path=
         "$Target/Path[Relationship='SMActivity!System.ReviewerIsUser']$"/>
        <Component Alias="VotedBy"
         Path=
         "$Target/Path[Relationship='SMActivity!System.ReviewerVotedByUser']$"/>
        </Component>
      </Component>
      <Component Alias="CreatedBy"
       Path="$Target/Path[Relationship='SMCore!System.WorkItemCreatedByUser']$"/>
      <Component Alias="AssignedTo"
       Path="$Target/Path[Relationship='SMCore!System.WorkItemAssignedToUser']$"/>
      <Component Alias="CreatedFor"
       Path="$Target/Path[Relationship='SMCore!System.WorkItemCreatedForUser']$"/>
      <Component Alias="RelatedWorkItem"
       Path="$Target/Path[Relationship='SMCore!System.WorkItemRelatesToWorkItem']$">
      <Component Alias="RelatedWorkItemAssignedTo"
       Path="$Target/Path[Relationship='SMCore!System.WorkItemAssignedToUser']$"/>
      </Component>
      <Component Alias="RelatedConfigItem"
       Path=
       "$Target/Path[Relationship='SMCore!System.WorkItemRelatesToConfigItem']$"/>
      <Component Alias="AboutConfigItem"
       Path='$Target/Path[Relationship='System!System.WorkItemAboutConfigItem']$"/>
      <Component Alias="FileAttachment"
       Path="$Target/Path[Relationship='System!System.WorkItemHasFileAttachment']$">
      <Component Alias="FileAttachmentAddedBy"
       Path=
       "$Target/Path[Relationship='System!System.FileAttachmentAddedByUser']$"/>
      </Component>
    </TypeProjection>
    <TypeProjection ID="System.FileAttachmentProjection"
     Accessibility="Public" Type="System!System.FileAttachment">
      <Component Alias="FileAttachmentAddedBy"
       Path=
       "$Target/Path[Relationship='System!System.FileAttachmentAddedByUser']$"/>
    </TypeProjection>
</TypeProjections>
```

Console Tasks

Console tasks are no longer pointers to executable files and the folder they are stored in. Console tasks are now handler code that references the Microsoft .NET Framework assembly in which the code is housed. An example follows:

```
<ConsoleTask ID="MyLibrary.ConsoleTasks.T1"
   Accessibility="Public"
     Target="System!System.Entity"
     Enabled="true"
     RequireOutput="true">
   <Assembly>MyLibrary.Resources.Assembly1</Assembly>
   <Handler>Some.Handler.Name</Handler>
   <Parameters>
     <Argument Name="Application">cmd.exe</Argument>
     <Argument Name="WorkingDirectory">%TEMP%</Argument>
     <Argument>test1</Argument>
     <Argument>test2</Argument>
   </Parameters>
</ConsoleTask>
```

Resources

Binary data is stored externally in a resource file. Binary data can be generic forms, images, assemblies, or report definitions. Metadata about the binary data is stored in the management pack and references the binary data resource file. An example follows:

```
<Resources>
  <Resource ID="TestLibrary.Resources.Test1" Accessibility="Public"
    FileName="res1.xml"/>
  <Resource ID="TestLibrary.Resources.Test2" Accessibility="Public"
    FileName="res2.xml"/>
  <Assembly ID="TestLibrary.Resources.Assembly1" Accessibility="Public"
    QualifiedName="Baz, Version=1.0.0.0" FileName="baz.dll"/>
  <Assembly ID="TestLibrary.Resources.Assembly2" Accessibility="Public"
    QualifiedName="Yoyo, Version=1.0.0.0" FileName="yoyo.dll">
    <Dependency ID="TestLibrary.Resources.Assembly1"/>
  </Assembly>
  <ReportResource ID="TestLibrary.Resources.Report1" Accessibility="Public"
    MIMEType="text/xml" FileName="res1.xml"/>
  <Image ID="TestLibrary.Resources.Image1" Accessibility="Public"
    FileName="image.png"/>
</Resources>
```

Forms

Forms are based on the Windows Presentation Framework (WPF). Forms are defined in assemblies and in management packs. Forms are located in the Resources section of management packs. Forms, similar to binary data, are not stored in the management pack; the binary data of the form is simply referenced in the resource manifest. An example follows:

```
<Forms>
  <Form ID="LobbyForm" Target="Projection" Assembly="FormAssembly"
   TypeName="MyFormClass">
  <Configuration>
      <ShowServers>yes</ShowServers>
  </Configuration>
  </Form>
</Forms>
```

Management Pack Best Practices

A number of methods and best practices should be followed when working with management packs in Service Manager. These best practices are centered around management pack naming conventions and how you store customizations in management packs. Following these best practices ensures you don't run into avoidable problems with your Service Manager deployment and makes working with and maintaining management packs easier.

It is easy for managing your management packs to get out of control; this could include forgetting where certain customizations are stored when you need to find them, and needing to pull out certain customizations but you can't because they are stored with other customizations you want to keep. Utilizing best practices keeps your management packs organized and makes it easier to move customizations to other management groups and to back up those customizations. Using best practices can also help utilize standards when multiple members of a team are managing management packs.

This section discuses some best practices you can use when working with management packs. Utilize these best practices, and apply them as guidelines for managing management packs in your deployment. Following are key best practices for managing management packs:

- ▶ **Avoid modifying the out of the box Service Manager management packs:** Do not store anything in the management packs delivered with Service Manager. Storing customizations in these management packs could result in losing those customizations during an upgrade.

- ▶ **Use prefixes in management pack names:** Add a prefix such as "Odyssey" to the names of management packs you create. As an example, `Odyssey.sample.managementpack.xml`. Doing this helps you easily identify your own management packs among all the other management packs.

- ▶ **Use meaningful names:** Give management packs meaningful names that relate to what the management pack does. For example, if you are creating a management pack for items on one of the incident lists, call it something like `Odyssey.custom.incidentmanagement.xml`.

- ▶ **Use description fields:** Use the description fields when creating management packs to further document information about the management pack.

20

▶ **Use version control:** Increment the version number before importing a management pack. As discussed earlier in the "Versioning" section, you cannot import a lower version of a sealed management pack on top of a higher version, although any version of an unsealed management pack can be imported on top of another version of that same unsealed management pack.

▶ **Separate list customizations:** List customizations should have a separate management pack even if they are related to a class. Do not store customizations in the management packs delivered with Service Manager. There should be a management pack for each list. For example, when you add items to the list incident tiers or change status, store these in a new management pack created specifically for this use. For this case, the list management packs would be named something similar to `Odyssey.custom.incidenttiers.xml` and `Odyssey.custom.changestatus.xml`.

▶ **Use a separate management pack for each class:** Create a new unsealed management pack for each class for which you will be making customizations. As an example, create a management pack `Odyssey.ChangeViews.Customizations.xml` for all of your customizations related to change management views, `Odyssey.ChangeQueues.Customizations.xml` for all of your customizations related to change management queues, and `Odyssey.ChangeTasks.Customizations.xml` related to change management tasks.

▶ **Group customizations into separate management packs:** Similar to the previous bullet, each type of customization should be in a separate management pack. This includes storing model extensions and presentation extensions in separate management packs. Model management packs could include new classes and class extensions (including properties and corresponding icons), new lists, combination classes, relationships, child enumeration values that should not be modified, and forms for viewing and editing objects of the defined classes and respective assembly resources.

Customizations should be grouped by the solution you are developing. This means incident management-related customizations and settings should be separate from change management-related customizations and settings. Customizations should also be grouped based on usage considerations—customizations you need to test and deploy as a unit should be in the same management pack.

▶ **Seal model management packs:** Management packs containing base classes and other model objects on which other definitions in other management packs depend should be sealed to prevent modification. Sealing a management pack also enables synchronizing its definitions into the data warehouse database.

▶ **Back up regularly:** Export your custom management packs on a regular schedule. This is good practice for backup of your customizations.

Fast Track

Management pack changes from Service Manager 2010 to Service Manager 2012 are minimal. The area that has seen change is in the management pack schema. Service Manager 2012 has the following types added to the schema:

- ▶ Images
- ▶ Enumerations
- ▶ Relationships
- ▶ Console tasks
- ▶ Resources
- ▶ Forms

Using Service Manager 2012 allows you to transfer the majority of your knowledge if you have experience working with the prior version.

Summary

Management packs provide the essential value-added content that runs on the Service Manager platform. They make it easy to store, version, and transfer solutions and customizations. Administrators and partners can leverage content created in one management pack in multiple Service Manager components when those components are built on the common System Center technology platform centered on management packs. Administrators and partners that become familiar with management pack concepts and learn how to customize and extend one System Center component can immediately apply that knowledge to other System Center components.

This chapter contains content critical to have as an administrator of Service Manager, as you will work with management packs almost immediately when you start working with Service Manager. To expand your knowledge about management packs, learn to author them from scratch. Information regarding authoring management packs can be found in Chapter 22 and Chapter 23.

20

CHAPTER 21

Data Warehouse and Reporting

The data warehouse is part of the end game in regards to the Information Technology Information Library (ITIL), service management, and Service Manager in particular. If you are focused on ITIL, you may have already spent a considerable amount time and effort working to improve your Information Technology (IT) department through implementing ITIL processes and deploying Service Manager. Two critical questions are always associated with ITIL and Service Manager projects; these relate to measuring results and showing value:

▶ What is the use of all that effort if you cannot measure the outcome?

▶ How can you show value to your customers and end users?

These questions can be answered by the *data warehouse*. The data warehouse is a measurement tool that enables you to pull data from Service Manager, which can show the value of using the many ITIL processes and service level agreements (SLAs), progress in IT performance, percentages of improvement from self-service, and more. Think of Service Manager's data warehouse as the IT department's very own business intelligence solution.

A data warehouse consists of many components and moving pieces. If the concept of a data warehouse is new to you, it can be an intimidating part of Service Manager. The purpose of this chapter is to help you become more familiar with Service Manager's data warehouse and gain confidence to start working with the data warehouse within your own installation.

The chapter explores the data warehouse and explains its architecture in Service Manager. It shows how to deploy the Service Manager data warehouse and use its many reporting tools.

Data Warehouse Overview

Understanding what comprises a data warehouse is fundamental in learning how to deploy and use the one provided with Service Manager. This background assists with understanding why the data warehouse was built the way it is and functions as it does. There are best practices and standards regarding business intelligence and data warehouses, which Microsoft followed in architecting the Service Manager data warehouse. The following sections present an overview of a data warehouse, including its components.

Data Warehouse Explained

A data warehouse is a central repository of data brought in from disparate data sources. These data sources are other operational databases in live systems. In terms of System Center, operational databases could be from Operations Manager, Configuration Manager, Data Protection Manager, and even Active Directory. Moving data to a data warehouse is a way to organize a company's information consistently in a central location from multiple source systems to be able to utilize this information. The data warehouse is often used for analysis, reporting, dashboards, online analytical processing (OLAP) analysis, and data mining.

Data in a data warehouse is stored as historical snapshots. This data is not updated; it is refreshed on an interval from the disparate data sources. The data is brought into a data warehouse through a process known as extract, transform, and load (ETL). The ETL process can be broken down as follows:

▶ **Extract:** This is the process of identifying the data needed from external systems, reading the data, and migrating it to the data warehouse. The data is typically moved to a staging database for cleansing using a transform process before moving it to a reporting database.

▶ **Transform:** This process converts the data into an OLAP-friendly format that consists of a star schema, facts, and dimensions used by the data warehouse. The data is converted into an OLAP format while cleansing the source data. Cleansing data consists of manipulating the data through a variety of operations; this includes removing inconsistencies in the source, performing joins from multiple data sources, data aggregation, validation, and sorting. It is important to note that while many manipulations are available to clean up data, not all data requires cleanup and not all data warehouses use the same data cleansing techniques. The cleansing techniques performed vary depending on the specific data warehouse vendor.

▶ **Load:** This process moves the transformed data into a final database structure, often referred to as the data mart database, and into OLAP cubes. The data can be reported on after it is loaded into the final data mart and OLAP cubes.

Figure 21.1 shows the ETL process as part of a data warehouse architecture.

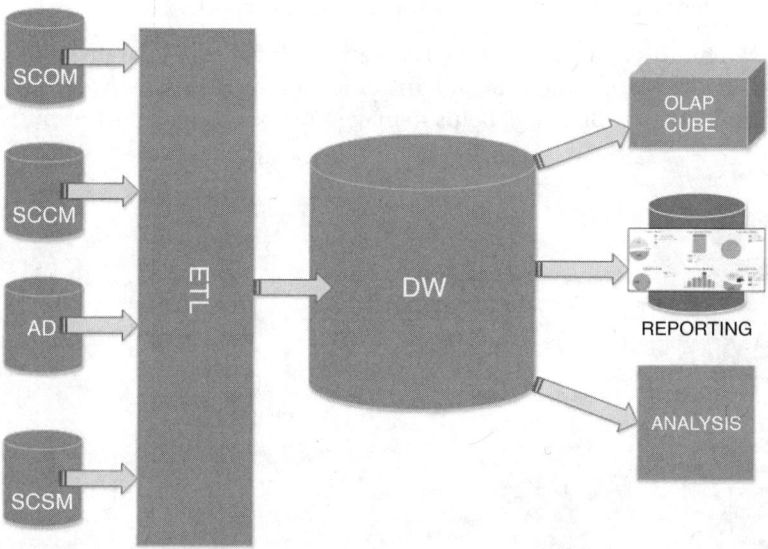

FIGURE 21.1   Diagram of a data warehouse architecture including the ETL process.

Data in a data warehouse is structured such that the most relevant data is grouped together for easy retrieval by end users, with multiple copies of data from varied points in time remaining together in a logical state. The description of the ETL process refers to star schema, facts, and dimensions as the required format for the data in a data warehouse. Knowing what the star schema, facts, and dimensions are is fundamental to understanding how data warehouses work:

▶ A *star schema* is a dimensional model organized into facts and dimensions. Star schemas are structured in an optimal way to query large data sets. At the center of a star schema is a fact table with the associated dimensions surrounding it giving it a visual representation of a star, which is how it received its name. A star schema is the most common and simplest architecture of a data warehouse.

▶ A *fact* is normally a measurement in the form of a numeric value and a foreign key relationship to a dimension. Examples of data contained in a fact are the units sold, month-to-date sales, or account detail on a specific date.

▶ A *dimension* is a hierarchy of attributes describing a piece of data (measurement) in a fact table. An example would be a client (Dimension) for the unit sold (Fact) or product (Dimension) for the month-to-date sales (Fact).

Figure 21.2 shows a visual representation of a star schema to help provide a better understanding of how star schemas are organized. The "Data Warehouse Schema" section later in the chapter discusses facts and dimensions as they apply to the schema.

Data warehouse reporting tools typically are easy to use for end users creating ad hoc reports and scheduling reports. Examples include using Microsoft Excel PowerPivot for ad hoc reports and SQL Server Reporting Services (SSRS) for scheduled reports.

Organizations use data warehouses as a part of their business intelligence (BI) strategy. BI is a set of tools often utilized by management to stay informed about what is happening in the business. Having the data that BI brings helps management teams make better business decisions.

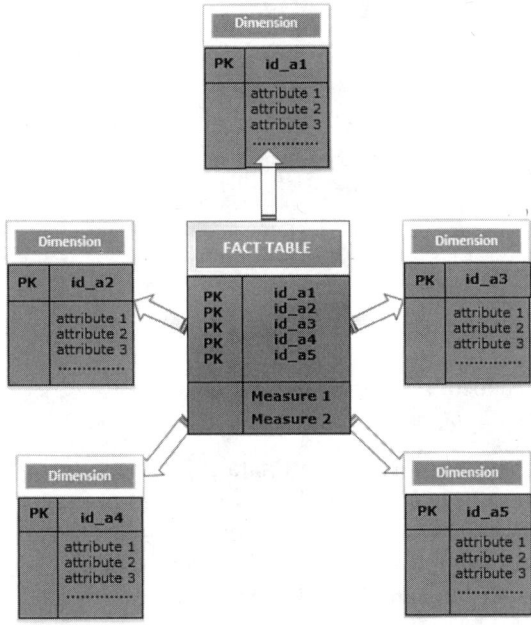

FIGURE 21.2   Representation of a star schema.

Service Manager Data Warehouse Rationale

System Center Service Manager is an IT service management (ITSM) system built on the ITIL framework. Microsoft includes the System Center data warehouse as part of Service Manager. The data warehouse is the tooling that provides IT managers the capability of service reporting.

ITIL includes a continual service improvement (CSI) process. CSI, introduced in Chapter 3, "MOF, ITIL, and System Center," provides IT managers with insight into past successes and failures of an IT department's service management over a period of time. Service management is measured and analyzed through service reporting, which is used to improve the quality of IT processes and service delivery. The ability to measure and analyze enables IT to show value to customers and improve service management by knowing when SLAs are not being met and when changes are occurring. Service reporting involves measuring using metrics and analyzing through reports, charts, key performance indicators (KPIs), dashboards, and more.

Service Manager's implementation of a data warehouse utilizes a separate management group with a management server and is built on top of Microsoft's business intelligence stack of technologies. The business intelligence technologies that can be used in the System Center Service Manager data warehouse include

▶ SQL Server

▶ SQL Server Reporting Services

▶ SQL Server Analysis Services

▶ SharePoint Performance Point (deployed separately)

▶ Excel PowerPivot (deployed separately)

These technologies, with the exception of SQL Server, are discussed in the following sections. These combined technologies make up the many facets of the data warehouse architecture and reporting, such as its databases, cubes, dashboards, KPIs, charts, and reports. The data warehouse also serves additional functions beyond reporting, as it provides a way to offload data from Service Manager's operational database, which improves performance of the operational database and helps keep it to a manageable size. The data warehouse also provides long-term storage for service management data. Long-term storage can be utilized for archiving and compliance needs.

Online Analytical Processing Explained

More commonly known as OLAP, online analytical processing is a business-intelligence technology used to analyze information from multiple database systems. End users can use OLAP technology to analyze data from different points of view.

Because the data is from different dimensions (also known as being multidimensional), it can be analyzed from different points of view. OLAP data, which is often used for data mining, is stored within multidimensional databases known as *cubes* (also referred to as OLAP cubes), which live on an OLAP server. Microsoft's implementation of an OLAP server is SQL Server Analysis Services (SSAS).

Data warehouses typically employ OLAP cubes to help provide ad-hoc reporting for end users. Using OLAP makes it quick and easy to filter data from different perspectives. OLAP is faster than reporting from traditional relational databases because it is optimized for querying and reporting, rather than processing transactions.

OLAP data is analyzed using software that connects to the OLAP cubes. There are many types of OLAP software on the market such as QuickView, Oracle Business Intelligence Foundation Suite, RapidAnalytics, and Excel PowerPivot (covered in this chapter). OLAP software such as Excel PowerPivot allows you to slice and dice the data as needed on the fly, quickly displaying large sets of data in a report format.

An example of using OLAP reporting would be an IT department that wants to compare incidents to the number of service requests opened in the last year, with a breakdown of which branch locations had the highest amounts of each.

Analysis Library Explained

An analysis library is a location on a server used to store OLAP reports for later use. Using OLAP reports and storing them in an analysis library ensures fast and easy retrieval by end users. This library is another way for an organization to centralize reports. Permissions could be granted to other users in that organization to access the OLAP reports.

SQL Server Reporting Services Explained

SSRS is Microsoft's server-based reporting software. It is used to create, deploy, and manage SQL-based reports. It is web-based and hosted on Internet Information Services (IIS). SSRS has many useful features and functionalities, such as the ability to view reports in a web browser, subscribe to reports, schedule and deliver reports via email, and provide permission-based access to reports for end users. SSRS comes with the Report Builder tool, which can be used to create custom reports by IT professionals without a SQL background. Reports stored on SSRS could also be embedded into other software such as SharePoint, Operations Manager reporting, Configuration Manager reporting, and Data Protection Manager reporting. The reports seen in the Service Manager console are physically stored in SSRS, not in Service Manager.

PowerPivot Explained

PowerPivot is an add-on for Excel introduced in Office 2010. That version required a download to install PowerPivot, which is now preloaded with Excel 2013. PowerPivot extends Excel to provide end users with the power of business intelligence and is considered a self-service BI product. PowerPivot connects to external data sources such as cubes and makes it possible to create charts directly from PowerPivot. It enables Excel to handle massive volumes of data for analysis.

Once charts and reports are created in PowerPivot, refreshing the data from the external data source automatically updates what is on the chart. PowerPivot workbooks can also be shared or hosted on SharePoint; this provides easy access for other users. Using PowerPivot enables end users to surface data from Service Manager's data warehouse in PowerPivot charts and share that data with others.

PerformancePoint Explained

PerformancePoint is a separately purchased business intelligence platform hosted on top of SharePoint Enterprise and has existed since SharePoint 2007. Its purpose is to provide a place to create dashboards complete with reports, KPIs, scorecards, analytic charts, and grids.

PerformancePoint comes with a dashboard designer used to build the rich business intelligence experience that exists on SharePoint. Because PerformancePoint lives on SharePoint, it is easy to secure and to share data across the organization. Service Manager data can be surfaced from the data warehouse and presented in many forms on PerformancePoint in SharePoint, such as KPIs, scorecards, charts, and more. Using PerformancePoint with Service Manager enables management to stay informed about service desk metrics in near real time.

Data Warehouse Architecture

It is important to understand the data warehouse architecture before deploying the data warehouse. Understanding the architecture is also useful when troubleshooting any issues with the data warehouse. The data warehouse architecture consists of services, databases, and workflow processes. The following sections break down the architecture by the services and databases and then the workflow processes including management pack synchronization, ETL, data warehouse jobs, and schema.

Data Warehouse Services

Service Manager's data warehouse is installed in its own management group. This means it contains the same services that are on the Service Manager management server. These services are covered in detail in Chapter 4, "Looking Inside System Center 2012 Service Manager," and are

▶ System Center Data Access Service

▶ Microsoft Monitoring Agent

▶ System Center Management Configuration

These services are installed when the data warehouse is deployed on a server, and must be running for the data warehouse to function.

Data Warehouse Databases

The System Center Service Manager data warehouse consists of its own databases that are separate from the Service Manager management server database. As introduced in Chapter 4, these consist of three physical databases, one being a data warehouse database, and the other two data mart databases:

▶ **DWStagingandConfig:** This is the data warehouse database and is used to store management packs. It is a temporary location for the data that comes over from the Service Manager operational database and includes configuration data. Some of the configuration data is generic, such as data warehouse configuration data, and other configuration data is from the ETL process.

▶ **DWRepository:** This database is used to store the data after it is transformed and is optimized for reporting.

▶ **DWDataMart:** This database is the last step in the chain and holds the transformed data that is published to be queried for reports.

Having separate databases allows an administrator to place the databases on separate SQL servers and host systems to provide better performance and scale.

Management Pack Synchronization Process

When the data warehouse is first deployed, a process brings over management packs from Service Manager. These management packs provide the data warehouse's structure, data, and reports. Without these management packs there would be no structure to the data. Two types of management packs are brought over from Service Manager:

▶ **Management packs specific to Service Manager:** These contain information about the configuration management database (CMDB) structure.

▶ **Management packs specific to the data warehouse:** These management packs contain information about the data warehouse structure, processes, and databases.

After this initial synchronization of management packs, the data warehouse continues to synchronize management packs from Service Manager on a regular interval (Table 21.1 lists the scheduled intervals), ensuring that changes in Service Manager are reflected in the data warehouse. Note that only sealed management packs synchronize to the data warehouse. The management pack synchronization process works as follows:

1. A management pack is imported into Service Manager.

2. The management pack synchronization process workflow starts. This runs on a schedule.

3. The management pack synchronization process connects to Service Manager to identify management packs that are new, changed, or deleted. The workflow looks at each management pack's management pack version number to identify changes to classes and relationships.

4. The management pack synchronization process synchronizes data to the DWStagingandConfig database.

5. The management pack synchronization process gets source Service Manager names from DWStagingandConfig using the data warehouse Data Access Service.

6. The management pack list in the data warehouse is compared with the management pack list in Service Manager. The management pack synchronization process makes any needed inserts/updates/deletes.

Extract, Transform, and Load Process

The ETL process populates the data warehouse database and data marts with data for reporting purposes. Each step in the ETL process breaks down as follows:

▶ **Extract:** The extract process workflow gets new delta data (schedules in Table 21.1) from the operational database (the Service Manager CMDB). The extract process workflow writes the data to the DWStagingandConfig database. The data from

Service Manager's CMDB that is moved to the DWStagingandConfig database remains in the format it had in the operational database.

▶ **Transform:** The transform process workflow performs any needed cleansing, reformatting, and aggregation of the delta data in the DWStagingandConfig database. This prepares the delta data for the final format necessary for reporting. The transform process workflow moves the data to the DWRepository database after reformatting the data.

▶ **Load:** The load process workflow moves the data from the DWRepository database into the DWDataMart database, from where reports are run.

Data Warehouse Jobs

The data warehouse contains a number of data warehouse jobs. Each job serves a different purpose to help the data warehouse function. The data warehouse jobs must run in a specific sequential order. To provide a better understanding of what these jobs are, what they do, and the order in which they need to run, a description of each follows:

▶ **DW maintenance job:** This job is not visible in the Service Manager console; it can only be interacted with through PowerShell. This job must run before any other job. It performs maintenance on the data warehouse, including indexing and updating statistics.

▶ **MPSyncJob job:** MPSyncJob collects the source Service Manager name(s) from the DWStagingandConfig database, via the Data Access Service. Its purpose is to synchronize the Service Manager management packs with the data warehouse. This job must run before the ETL jobs; if it fails, the ETL and cube processing jobs will not run.

▶ **ETL jobs:** The ETL jobs were discussed previously in the "Extract, Transform, and Load Process" section and are part of the data warehouse jobs. These are

  ▶ Extract jobs

  ▶ Transform jobs

  ▶ Load jobs

▶ **Cube processing jobs:** Processing of cubes is the final set of jobs after the ETL jobs run. Cube processing loads data from the data mart into the cubes. Once the data is moved into the cubes, it can be browsed.

▶ **Grooming job:** Similar to the DW maintenance job, this job is not viewed with the other data warehouse jobs in the console. Grooming cleans out the data that has exceeded the configurable time period. The data warehouse grooming settings are configured in the Service Manager console at Administration -> Settings -> Data Retention Settings, under History retention time. The default setting for History retention time is 365 (days).

The data warehouse jobs run on a schedule. Each has a start time and an interval the job runs on. All data warehouse jobs are enabled by default. Table 21.1 lists additional information about the data warehouse jobs.

TABLE 21.1   Data Warehouse Job Schedules

DW Job	Start Time	Interval
MPSyncJob	Midnight	Every hour
DW Maintenance	Midnight	Every hour
Extract	Midnight	Every 5 minutes
Transform	Midnight	Every 30 minutes
Load	Midnight	Every hour

To view the data warehouse jobs and their statuses, navigate to **Data Warehouse -> Data Warehouse Jobs** within the Service Manager console. These are shown in Figure 21.3.

To view the data warehouse jobs using PowerShell, launch PowerShell from the console. Select the Data Warehouse workspace and click **Start PowerShell Session** under **Tasks -> Administration** on the right side of the console. Launching PowerShell this way loads the Service Manager cmdlets. Use the Get-SCDWJob cmdlet to show the data warehouse jobs. PowerShell cmdlets and SMLets are discussed in Chapter 24, "Using PowerShell."

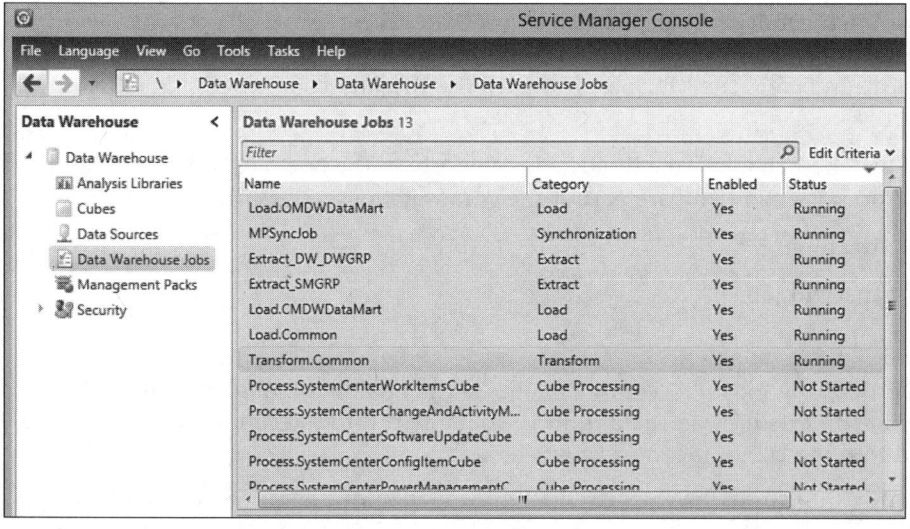

FIGURE 21.3   Data warehouse jobs.

Data Warehouse Schema

All data warehouses are built using a particular schema. Two cofounders of data warehousing, Bill Inmon and Ralph Kimball, shaped the structure behind today's data warehouse technology. Each had a different approach to modeling the data warehouse. The Kimball approach to data warehousing is to build data marts first and pull source data into them, optimize the data for performance, and prepare it for fast and easy reporting. Inmon's approach is to build a data warehouse first; then the data marts, which are populated from the data warehouse. Data is then pulled out of these data marts for reporting. You can learn more about these different data warehouse approaches at http://searchbusinessintelligence.techtarget.in/tip/Inmon-vs-Kimball-Which-approach-is-suitable-for-your-data-warehouse.

All data warehouses today are built using one of these approaches. Service Manager's data warehouse utilizes the Kimball approach and utilizes a star schema. The Service Manager data warehouse schema is dimensional and consists of several types of tables:

▶ Dimensions

▶ Facts

▶ Outriggers

A breakdown of these tables follows:

▶ Dimensions tables contain dimensions that represent the classes. For example, you can have a Computer dimension containing many types of computer classes; one of the classes targeted is the `Microsoft.Windows.Computers` class. There are attributes for each class, such as manufacturer or chassis type.

▶ Facts tables track transactions that occur over time and can be quantified and summarized as metrics. They track relationships between instances of classes. For example, a fact tracks the relationship of incidents related to a computer.

▶ Outriggers tables contain outriggers that describe an instance of a class. Examples of an outrigger are `ProblemResolution`, which describes problems, and `IncidentClassification`, which describes incidents.

Deploying the Data Warehouse

Deploying the Data Warehouse management server role, sometimes referred to as the SCSMDW role in Service Manager 2012, is a straightforward process. The deployment of the data warehouse consists of three steps:

1. Preparing for the data warehouse (discussed in Chapter 6, "Installing and Upgrading to System Center 2012 Service Manager")

2. Installing the data warehouse (discussed in Chapter 6)

3. Registering the data warehouse

Once the data warehouse is installed, it must be registered with the Service Manager management group. (You can also register a data warehouse with multiple Service Manager management groups all using the same data warehouse.) Once the data warehouse is registered, you can access cubes to build reports in PowerPivot, the SSRS reports, and more. Follow these steps:

1. In the Service Manager console, open the Administration workspace. Navigate to **Administration Overview -> Register with Service Manager's Data Warehouse** to select **Register with Service Manager Data Warehouse** (see Figure 21.4).

2. The Data Warehouse Registration Wizard opens. Click **Next** on the Before You Begin page.

3. On the Data Warehouse page, type the FQDN of the data warehouse server in the **Server Name** field and click **Test Connection**. The wizard should return a successful result. Click **Next**.

4. On the Credentials screen, select a Run As account or create a new one as shown in Figure 21.5. You should use an account with administrative access to the Service Manager management server. This account is used for the data warehouse to connect to the Service Manager server. Click **Next** after selecting the account.

5. Check your settings on the Summary page and click **Create** to complete the data warehouse registration as shown in Figure 21.6.

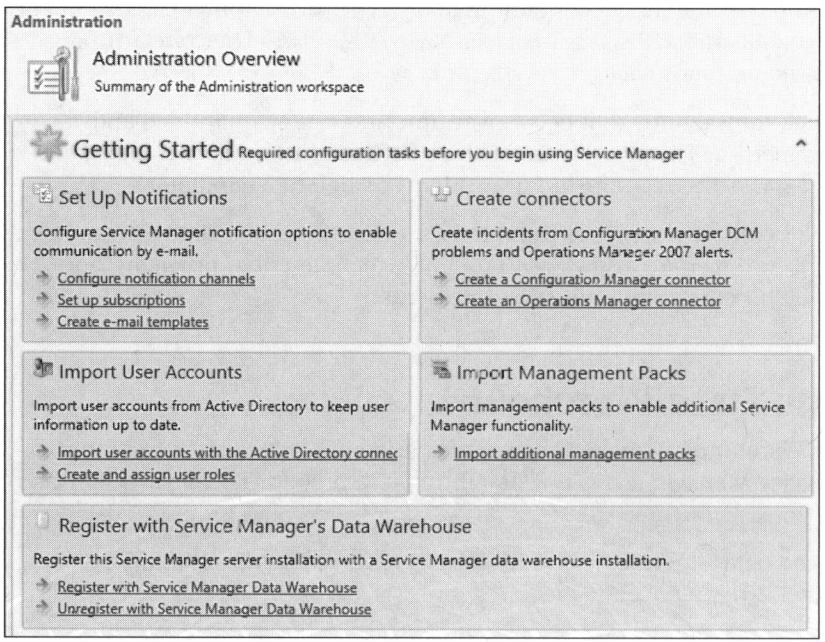

FIGURE 21.4   Register with Service Manager's data warehouse.

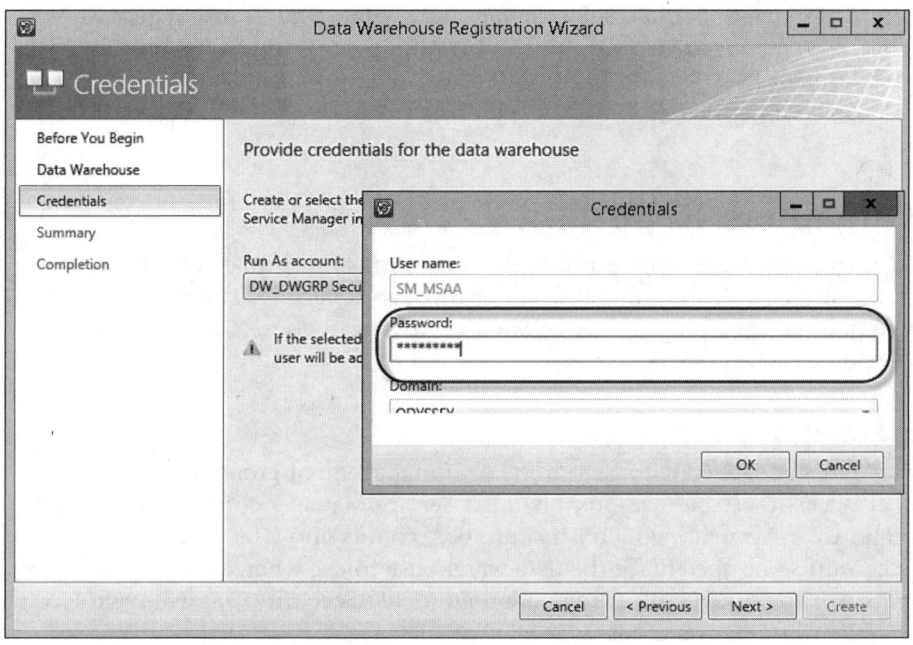

FIGURE 21.5   Credentials for the data warehouse.

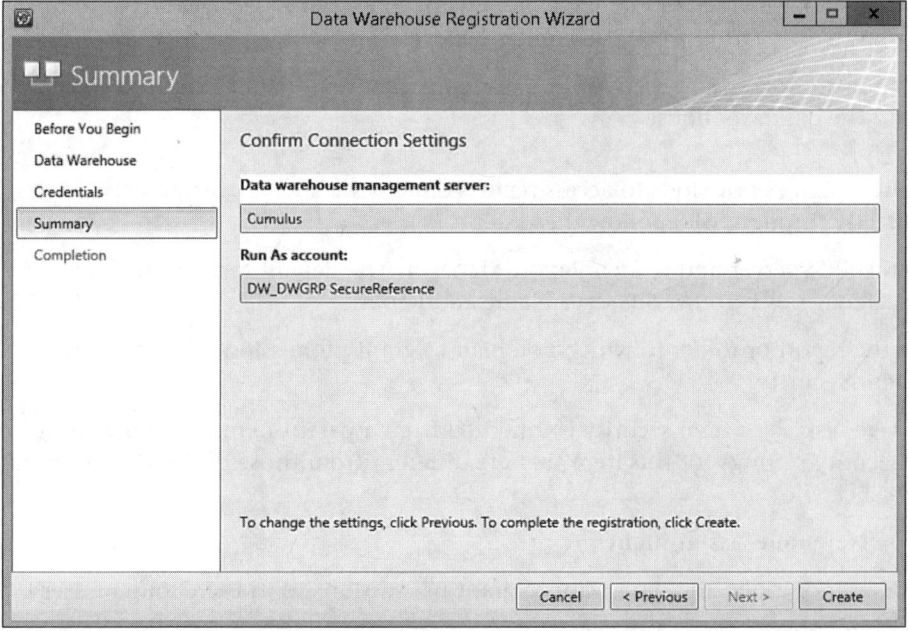

FIGURE 21.6   Data warehouse registration summary.

6. The Completion page should display the result **The data warehouse registration succeeded**. The management pack synchronization process (discussed previously in the "Management Pack Synchronization Process" section) begins immediately. The process takes a while the first time, so be patient.

Data Warehouse Reporting

Bringing data into a data warehouse is only part of meeting an organization's IT reporting needs. You must also be able to pull that data out through reporting. The next sections discuss how to pull reports from the Service Manager data warehouse. There are various ways to pull reports; each is covered.

Reporting Permissions

As the Service Manager data warehouse is in its own management group, it has its own permissions. To access these permissions, open the Service Manager console and navigate to **Data Warehouse -> Security**, which lists Run As Accounts and User Roles. Run As accounts are accounts you specify for the data warehouse to use when accessing source systems from which to pull data. User roles are used to add accounts that will have access to the Service Manager data warehouse.

There are two user roles by default—Report Users and Administrators:

▶ Report Users can view the standard SSRS-based reports in the Reporting workspace in Service Manager. The standard SSRS reports in the Service Manager console are located in the Reporting workspace under Reports.

▶ The Administrators role is used for user accounts that require full administrative access to the data warehouse.

You could also assign permissions to access reports directly in SSRS. To assign users access to reports directly through SSRS, follow these steps:

1. Go to the SRSS server and launch Report Manager. The default location for the Report Manager is http://<SSRSServerName>:80/Reports.

2. Locate the report or folder to which you plan to grant permission. Click **Security -> Edit Item Security**.

3. A message displays: "Item security is inherited from a parent item. Do you want to apply security settings for this item that are different from those of the Home parent item?" Click **OK**.

4. Click on **New Role Assignment**.

5. Add the user or group that you want to grant permissions to in the Group or user name box.

6. Click **OK**.

Viewing Standard Reports

To access the standard SSRS-based reports in the Service Manager Reporting workspace, open the Service Manager console and open the Reporting workspace. Expand **Reports** and select one of the folders. Each folder contains many reports in its respective area that correlate to an area in Service Manager. The default folders are

- ▶ Activity Management
- ▶ Change Management
- ▶ Configuration Management
- ▶ Incident Management
- ▶ Problem Management
- ▶ Favorite Reports

Favorite and Linked Reports

Favorite reports are reports configured to show desired data and saved so they can easily be run later. Adding a report as a favorite adds it to the Favorite Reports folder in the Reporting workspace.

A linked report is a shortcut to a report. Linking a report adds it to the Analysis Library in the Reporting workspace.

To add a report as a favorite report, follow these steps:

1. Open the Service Manager console and navigate to the Reporting workspace. Locate the report you want to make a favorite, and select **Run Report** in the Tasks pane.

2. The report opens. Click **Save as Favorite Report** in the Tasks pane.

3. Give the favorite report a name and click **OK**.

4. Close the report.

5. In the Reporting workspace, click on the **Favorite Reports** folder to see the report you just added as a favorite.

To create linked reports, follow these steps:

1. Open the Service Manager console and navigate to the reporting workspace. Locate the report you want to link, and in the Tasks pane click **Run Report**.

2. The report opens. In the Tasks pane, click **Save as Linked Report**.

3. Give the linked report a name and description. Select a management pack or create a new one and then click **OK**.

4. Choose one of the report folders to save the linked report in and click **OK**.

5. Close the report.

Subscribing to and Publishing Reports in SSRS

A common requirement in service management is for reports to be published on a regular basis, such as daily, weekly, or monthly, and to be distributed automatically to service owners, IT managers, or anyone responsible for service, technology, or assets within the IT department. Publishing updates a report on a regular schedule; subscriptions email a report to a subscriber of a report. Service Manager's data warehouse provides both report publishing and subscriptions through the Service Manager SSRS engine. These are discussed in the next sections.

Publishing Reports

Publishing reports refers to using SSRS to create reports on a schedule and store them in a Windows share for later access by users. Reports published in this manner provide an easy method for service owners/teams to get current information from a central location. You can also use file share security to control who can read reports from specific file shares.

To publish reports, perform the following steps on the Service Manager data warehouse server:

1. Configure the SQL Agent Service on your Service Manager data warehouse server to start automatically and start the service if it is not already running. This is required to run the scheduled publishing and subscription activities.

2. Create a publishing share. Create a file share to which you will publish the report, and where your target users can retrieve it. You need a user account that can write to the share, and your users must have Read rights.

3. Open a browser and navigate to http://localhost/reports (assuming you have not modified the default SSRS URL). The first time you visit this URL it may take a little longer to load.

4. Click **SystemCenter** -> **ServiceManager** -> **ServiceManager.Console. Reporting.ConfigurationManagement** -> **ServiceManager.Report. ConfigurationManagement.ComputerInventory**.

   You should now have the full Computer Inventory report displayed in the browser.

5. Click on **Subscriptions** -> **New Subscription**.

6. Complete the form with your desired settings:

   ▶ **Delivered by:** Select a Windows file share.

   ▶ **File Name:** Enter the file name you want to save the report as.

   ▶ **Path:** Enter the path to the share you previously configured.

   ▶ **Render Format:** Select the format for the report from the list of XML, CSV, PDF, HTML, MHTML, Excel, RPL, TIFF, and Word.

   ▶ **Credentials used to access the file share:** Enter the username and password for an account that can write to the share.

Complete the remaining options as desired. During testing, it is useful to set the schedule to publish frequently (i.e., every 5 minutes) to test whether everything is working as expected.

7. At the bottom of the page, click **OK** to create the subscription.

8. Verify the report is created in the publishing share and you are done.

Subscribing to Reports

Perform the following steps to subscribe to reports on the Service Manager data warehouse server. These instructions assume you have a Simple Mail Transport Protocol (SMTP) server such as Microsoft Exchange in place to send the email. You also need an SMTP notification channel configured to use the SMTP server within Service Manager. For information on notifications, see Chapter 16, "Managing Notifications."

1. If you haven't already, configure the SQL Agent on your Service Manager data warehouse server to start automatically and also start the service if it is not already running. This is required to run the scheduled publishing and subscription activities.

2. Open the Reporting Services Configuration Manager and connect to the report server instance (it likely is already populated with the correct default values).

3. Click **Email Settings** and enter the email address that you want to send the reports from and the SMTP server to use to send the email.

4. Click **Apply**, and then **Exit**.

5. Open a browser and navigate to http://localhost/reports (assuming you have not modified the default SSRS URL). The first time you visit the URL it may take a while to load.

6. Click **SystemCenter** -> **ServiceManager** -> **ServiceManager.Console. Reporting.ConfigurationManagement** -> **ServiceManager.Report. ConfigurationManagement.ComputerInventory**.

You should now have the full Computer Inventory report displayed in the browser.

7. Click **Subscriptions** -> **New Subscription**.

8. Complete the form with your desired settings:

  ▶ **Delivered by:** Select E-Mail.

  ▶ **To, Cc, Bcc, Reply-To, Subject, Priority, Comment:** Enter the email details you want to use.

  ▶ **Render Format:** Select the format for the report from the list of XML, CSV, PDF, MHTML, Excel, RPL, TIFF, and Word.

  ▶ **Include Report:** Enabling this check box attaches the report to the email.

  ▶ **Include Link:** Enabling this check box includes a link to the web-based report in the email message body.

A nice feature of published and subscribed reports is that you can configure them with specific report parameters. For example, if your environment contains multiple domains, you could email reports for specific domains to specific users. Any report parameters available interactively are available to configure for subscriptions. Custom reports also expose their parameters.

Complete the remaining options as you desire. During testing, it is helpful to set the schedule to publish frequently (i.e., every 5 minutes) to verify that everything is working as expected.

9. At the bottom of the page, click **OK** to create the subscription.

10. Check your target Inbox to see your report.

You now can schedule reports to be emailed automatically and on a regular basis directly to those who need the information related to incidents, problems, and configuration items. These report subscriptions can become an important part of your service management processes.

Reports Using Excel PowerPivot

PowerPivot for Microsoft Excel is a data analysis tool that delivers computational power directly within the Excel application, an application with which many users are already familiar.

Using PowerPivot lets you transform enormous quantities of data with incredible speed into meaningful information to get the answers you need. You can easily share your findings with others. PowerPivot can even help IT improve operational efficiencies through SharePoint-based management tools.

PivotTables continue to be indispensible for allowing users to analyze their data flexibly and interactively. However, using a PivotTable that connects to an OLAP data source requires such a data source to exist. In Service Manager 2012, OLAP cubes are automatically generated and displayed within the Service Manager console. These cubes are the data source that Excel PowerPivot connects to for data analysis. Six cubes are generated by default:

▶ Software Update cube

▶ Service Manager WorkItems cube

▶ Service Manager ConfigItem cube

▶ Power Management cube

▶ Change and Activity Management cube

▶ Service Manager Service Catalog Library cube

These cubes must be processed before they can be used to analyze data. Processing the cubes simply means the data is prepared in the OLAP format, making them viewable for use for fast and efficient reporting on the fly.

NOTE: ADDING CHARGEBACK TO SERVICE MANAGER ADDS ADDITIONAL CUBE

Deploying chargeback in Service Manager (available with Service Manager 2012 Service Pack 1 and above) adds the Service Manager Chargeback cube. More information on chargeback is available in Chapter 12, "Automation and Chargeback."

The PowerPivot functionality is delivered by SQL Server's Analysis Services team in collaboration with the Excel team and is based on their experiences delivering the Microsoft Business Intelligence platform. There are two components of PowerPivot:

▶ PowerPivot for Excel 2010/2013

▶ PowerPivot for SharePoint 2010/2013

PowerPivot for Excel is designed for business users and leverages the familiar Excel features. PowerPivot enables users to quickly transform enormous quantities of data from virtually any source into meaningful information to get the answers they need in seconds. PowerPivot for Excel consists of the following components:

▶ The Excel 2010 add-in (not an add-on for Excel 2013; it is there by default in Excel 2013), which delivers the seamless PowerPivot user experience integrated within Excel.

▶ The VertiPaq engine, which compresses and manages millions of rows of data in memory with extremely fast performance.

To unleash the power of PowerPivot in Service Manager, verify you have PowerPivot for Excel 2010 installed or are running Excel 2013. There are two ways to build a PowerPivot report. The first way is a manual process starting from Excel and connecting to the Service Manager data warehouse as the data source. The second approach to generate a PowerPivot report is by analyzing a cube in the Service Manager console, which allows Service Manager to build the data source connection for you. Use the following steps for each process:

Manually build a PowerPivot Report:

1. Open Excel 2010 or Excel 2013.

2. Start the PowerPivot window.

3. Choose the following:

    ▶ **From Database: SQL**

    ▶ **Server name: svcmgrdw.odyssey.com**

    ▶ **Database: DWDataMart**

    ▶ **Next: Query**

Paste this query, replacing the date values:

```
DECLARE @StartDate date
, @EndDate date

SET    @StartDate='1/1/2014'
SET    @EndDate='3/31/2014'

SELECT     Convert(date, i.CreatedDate) as Date
         , COUNT(*) as CreatedIncidents

FROM  IncidentDim i
WHERE i.CreatedDate between @StartDate and @EndDate
GROUP BY Convert(date, i.CreatedDate)
Order By Convert(date, i.CreatedDate)
```

Click **Finish**, and then **Close**.

4. Rename the tab to **Incidents**.

5. In the Home tab, click **PivotTable** and select **Single PivotChart**.

6. Select **Existing Worksheet** and click **OK**.

7. Configure the Tasks pane:

   ▶ Check mark in CreatedIncidents box

   ▶ Check mark in Date box

8. Right-click **Chart** and select **Change Chart Type**.

9. Select **Line**, and then click **OK**.

10. Right-click **Chart Y-axis**, and then select **Format Axis**.

11. Set Maximum to **250** and then click **OK**.

12. Click in the chart, and select the PowerPivot / Layout tab.

13. Click **Trendline**, and then select **Linear Trendline**.

14. Also, create a trendline for incidents.

15. Drag Date under Alerts to Slicers Vertical in the Tasks pane.

16. Show pivoting, for example, date from X to Y.

TIP: HOW TO CREATE AN INCIDENT DASHBOARD WITH POWERPIVOT

The procedure in this section is only one way to create a dashboard. The article at http://blogs.technet.com/b/antoni/archive/2013/05/18/how-to-create-an-incident-dashboard-using-excel-in-system-center-2012-sp1-service-manager-scsm-2012.aspx discusses creating a Service Manager incident dashboard using Excel PowerPivot.

Analyze a cube from Service Manager to build a PowerPivot Report:

1. Open the Service Manager console and navigate to **Data Warehouse -> Cubes**.

2. Click a cube to highlight it, and then under Tasks on the right, click **Analyze Cube in Excel**.

3. Excel opens and the data is loaded from the cube that you selected in Service Manager. Here you can begin to drag and drop fields from the PivotTable Field List and start building your PowerPivot chart. (Chapter 1, "Service Management Basics," shows an example of a PowerPivot report.)

Launching a new PowerPivot chart from the Service Manager console is an easier process than having to create a connection manually from Excel to the Service Manager data warehouse as in Service Manager 2010. Either option starts your PowerPivot charts. Once you have launched a PowerPivot report, you can perform your data analysis from there.

To save a PowerPivot report, simply save the Excel workbook. The authors recommend saving your PowerPivot report to your Analysis Library for easy retrieval later from a centralized location. The next section discusses how to create folders in the Analysis Library.

Using Analysis Library to Store and View PowerPivot Reports

After building reports using PowerPivot for Microsoft Excel, the next step is to save these reports. These PowerPivot reports can be saved into Service Manager's Analysis Library. The Analysis Library is a group of file shares used to store Microsoft Excel data files that are accessible from the Service Manager console. Begin by ensuring you have a folder set up in the Analysis Library and that Excel is installed on the computer where the Service Manager console is running. Follow these steps:

1. Open the Service Manager console and navigate to **Data Warehouse -> Analysis Libraries**.

2. Click on **Add Library Folder** in the Tasks pane.

3. The Add Library Folder dialog box opens. Enter a name for the new analysis library folder in the Name field and a description in the Description field.

   For the Analysis Library you need to create some file shares. You must have a file share for every Analysis Library folder you intend to create. The authors recommend naming the file share the same as the Analysis Library folder to make it easy for organization and tracking. Some examples of UNC file shares would be

   ▶ \\<*ComputerName*>\IncidentManagmentReports\

   ▶ \\<*ComputerName*>\ChangeManagmentReports\

   ▶ \\<*ComputerName*>\ProblemManagmentReports\

4. In the UNC Path field, enter a path for this library folder.

To view a PowerPivot report, follow these steps:

1. Open the Service Manager console and navigate to **Reporting -> Analysis Library**. Select the folder that contains the PowerPivot Excel workbooks you want to open.

2. Click on the PowerPivot Excel workbook you want to open and under the Tasks list in the right pane click **Open Excel File**. This opens your PowerPivot Excel workbook in Excel.

Your PowerPivot report now opens. To refresh the data in the PowerPivot Excel workbook, click the Data tab and select **Refresh All** to update the workbook. Refreshing the data in the workbook ensures the most current data is displayed in the PowerPivot Excel workbook.

Dashboards in SharePoint PerformancePoint

In information systems, a *dashboard* is an executive information system user interface that (similar to an automobile's dashboard) is designed to be easy to understand. As an example, a product might obtain information from the local operating system in a computer, from one or more applications that may be running, and from one or more remote sites on the Internet, and present it as though it all came from the same source. Dashboards should not be confused with scorecards.

Using Service Manager 2012, you have the ability to deploy dashboards using PerformancePoint on SharePoint and data from Service Manager's data warehouse. The dashboard is a view of multiple sets of Service Manager statistics on a single web page. Users can view data in the form of pie charts, graphs, or Dundas gauges.

Service Manager dashboards provide IT managers with a consolidated, near real time view of their IT service management processes (which include incidents, activities, and change management) of their organization infrastructure, even if they do not have access to or knowledge of the Service Manager console application.

The Service Manager dashboards that can be built in PerformancePoint are designed to work with an existing Service Manager infrastructure. The dashboard queries the Service Manager data warehouse and uses the resulting data set to present key infrastructure metrics and KPIs in a graphical format. This section discusses the process to build a dashboard in PerformancePoint. Before you begin building the actual dashboards, you must have SharePoint deployed with PerformancePoint deployed on that SharePoint instance. You can deploy PerformancePoint to SharePoint 2010 or SharePoint 2013.

NOTE: SHAREPOINT 2013 SUPPORT

Service Manager's self-service portal is not supported on SharePoint 2013. However, the use of dashboards in PerformancePoint on SharePoint 2013 is supported.

Reference one of the following URLs for instructions on how to deploy PerformancePoint depending on your version of SharePoint.

▶ **PerformancePoint SharePoint 2010:** http://technet.microsoft.com/en-us/library/ee748643%28v=office.14%29.aspx

▶ **PerformancePoint SharePoint 2013:** http://technet.microsoft.com/en-us/library/ee748644.aspx

After deploying PerformancePoint, you need a site to host your dashboards. You can create a Business Intelligence Center site in SharePoint, which can be deployed on the same web application as your Service Manager self-service portal if desired. To deploy a Business Intelligence Center site, follow the steps on the link for your version of SharePoint:

▶ **SharePoint 2010:** http://technet.microsoft.com/en-us/library/hh223274%28v=office.14%29.aspx

▶ **SharePoint 2013:** http://technet.microsoft.com/en-us/library/jj219656.aspx

Perform the remaining steps to create and publish a dashboard to your new Business Intelligence Center site:

1. In a web browser, navigate to your Business Intelligence Center site.

2. Under the Quick Launch bar on the left side, click on **Data Connections**.

3. On the Data Connections page, click the **Documents** tab in the ribbon.

4. Select **new document** and then **PerformancePoint Data Source**. Dashboard Designer launches.

5. In Dashboard Designer, on the Select Data Source Template page, choose **Analysis Services** (see Figure 21.7)

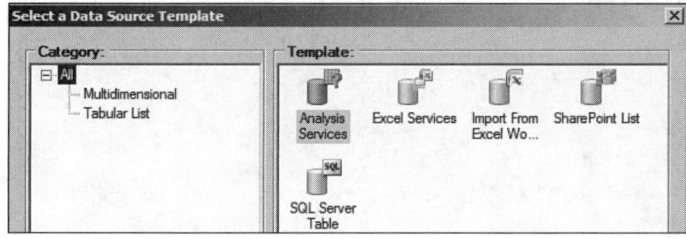

FIGURE 21.7   Select a data source template.

6. Next, enter the information for your data connection.

    ▶ In the server field, select the SQL Server that contains your analysis services databases.

> ▶ In the database field, select **DWASDatabase**.

> ▶ In the cube field, select the cube you want to use depending on the data you want to surface in your dashboard. For example, select the **Chargeback Cube** or the **Service Manager WorkItems Cube**.

7. After entering all your information, click **Test data source**. If everything is correct, you should get a successful connection in a Test connection dialog box.

8. In the Test connection dialog box, click **Close**. You should still be in the Dashboard Designer. Click the Windows logo in the upper left and select **Save**.

9. To set the list where you will be storing the reports, click **Home** in the ribbon bar and click **Add Lists**. The Add List dialog box opens and you see your Business Intelligence Center site listed. Expand **Business Intelligence Center** and select **PerformancePoint Content**. Once PerformancePoint Content is selected, click **OK**.

10. PerformancePoint Content should now be listed in the Dashboard Designer Workspace Browser. Right-click the PerformancePoint Content list in the Dashboard Designer Workspace Browser. Select **New** and then click on **Report**.

11. On the following page, you need to select a template for the new report. Select **Analytic Grid**.

12. You now see the new report in the Workspace Browser. Rename the report to something meaningful by right-clicking the report and selecting **Rename**.

13. Double-click the report to open it. When the report opens, it is in a grid format so it is easy to work with.

14. Start populating the grid with data by dragging the measures and dimensions into the rows and columns. For example, you could drag **IncidentDimCount** and **IncidentClassificationValue** into the report.

15. After you have the data you want in the reports grid, you can change it to be more visually appealing. Change the report to a pie chart by right-clicking anywhere in the grid; then click on **Report Type** and select **Pie Chart** (see Figure 21.8).

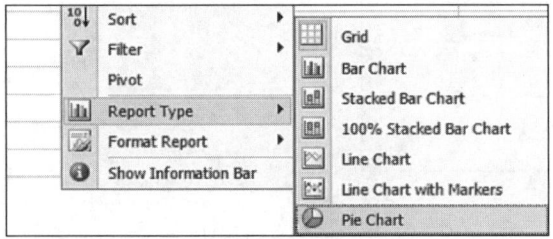

FIGURE 21.8   Selecting a report type.

16. Save the report by clicking the Windows logo in the upper-left corner of the Dashboard Designer and selecting **Save**.

Now you can go back to your Business Intelligence Center site and display the pie chart report you just created. Follow these steps:

1. Open your Business Intelligence Center site and go to a page on the site or create a new page.

2. You need to add a PerformancePoint web part to the page. Click **Site Actions** and then click **Edit Page**.

3. Under Editing Tools, click on **Insert** and then click on **Web Part** (see Figure 21.9).

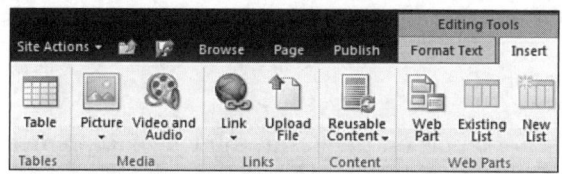

FIGURE 21.9   Inserting a web part.

4. In the Categories window, scroll down and select the **PerformancePoint** folder. In the Web Parts window, select **PerformancePoint Report** and click **Add**.

5. The PerformancePoint Report web part is added to the page. You should see a **Click here to open the tool pane** link. Click this link to open the tool pane for the web part on the right side of the screen.

6. Click the button to the right of the **Location:** field (see Figure 21.10) in the web part tool pane.

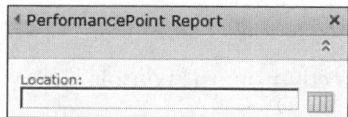

FIGURE 21.10   PerformancePoint Report tool pane.

7. Navigate to **Business Intelligence Center -> Content Type -> PerformancePoint Report**.

8. As shown in Figure 21.11, you see the report you created using the Dashboard Designer. Double-click the report to add it to the **Location:** field on the web part tool pane.

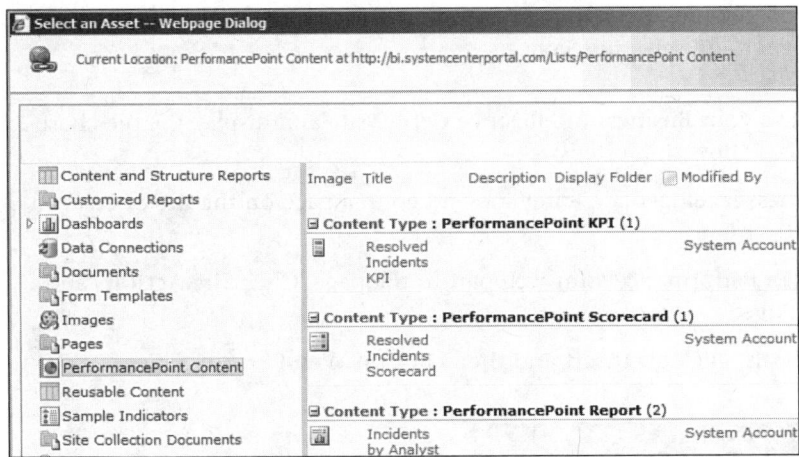

FIGURE 21.11   PerformancePoint Report Webpage Dialog.

9. Save your page and you see the dashboard report on the Business Intelligence Center sites page.

Additional information on creating PerformancePoint dashboards is available at http://office.microsoft.com/en-us/dashboard-designer-help/create-a-basic-performance-point-dashboard-HA010369176.aspx.

Fast Track

There have been no changes in the Service Manager 2012 data warehouse in regard to the architecture of the data warehouse, the way the data is processed, the way the data warehouse is deployed, or the SSRS reports.

New to the Service Manager 2012 data warehouse is the following:

▶ Pre-built OLAP cubes that are displayed within the Service Manager console

▶ The ability to analyze the cubes in Excel PowerPivot directly from the console

▶ The Analysis Library

▶ The ability to use the PerformancePoint Service in SharePoint to create reporting dashboards

Summary

This chapter contained information regarding the Service Manager data warehouse. It should help you become more familiar with data warehouses in general and their architecture, specifically the Service Manager data warehouse architecture; how to deploy and register the data warehouse; how to report out of the data warehouse; and how to build dashboards using PerformancePoint. This chapter also introduced you to reporting and how it applies to service management as a part of the ITIL framework.

Customizing Service Manager

By now you should be familiar with the functionality provided by System Center 2012 Service Manager. However, Service Manager consists of far more than its built-in functionality, as Microsoft designed this System Center component to be infinitely customizable. This chapter discusses opportunities and strategies for customizing Service Manager, enabling you to provide increased value to your organization. It also discusses the specifics of performing and implementing these customizations, from customizing the console with new views and console tasks to creating classes, workflows, and forms.

There are several areas of consideration when customizing Service Manager. This chapter

▶ Describes areas that are customizable

▶ Highlights important questions to address before starting

▶ Increases your understanding of the knowledge required to customize Service Manager in different ways

▶ Provides a basic understanding of some of the technologies that are core components in Service Manager

▶ Shows how to perform common customizations

Planning Your Customization

Microsoft has invested considerable resources to make Service Manager easy to customize, providing tools for performing typical customizations. For advanced customizations that require development resources, Service

Manager offers an accessible platform built upon known frameworks and technologies, making it easy for a wide range of developers to build upon the functionality delivered out of the box.

Using the modular platform introduced by System Center Operations Manager, Service Manager expands that platform and is customizable in every area—from the data layer through workflows to the presentation layer. Customizing Service Manager can require varying types of knowledge, depending on the area under consideration. For example, when customizing the presentation layer in the Service Manager console, it is useful to know the basic concepts of Windows Presentation Foundation (WPF) and its data binding feature, while familiarity with PowerShell scripting makes it easy to provide console users with useful tools in the form of tasks.

What You Can Customize

Similar to Operations Manager, Service Manager utilizes management packs as an operational roadmap. The modular architecture of management packs provides the flexibility for adapting Service Manager to meet your specific needs. This section introduces potential areas of customization and provides some examples.

Following are things you can customize from the console:

▶ The navigation structure, by creating folders or workspaces

▶ Views, by adding or removing columns and changing criteria

▶ Groups

▶ Queues

▶ Console tasks

▶ Templates

▶ Notification templates

▶ Subscriptions

▶ Event workflows

▶ Lists

▶ User roles

▶ Run as accounts

▶ Service level agreements

Figure 22.1 demonstrates the flexibility of the console presentation layer. The figure shows a custom view created using a WPF browser control. The view is placed in a custom folder in the Navigation pane, and the folder is located in a custom workspace in the console.

FIGURE 22.1   Service Manager console custom view containing a web browser control.

You can also customize the self-service portal (SSP). For example, you could customize the SharePoint site hosting the SSP web parts to company brand the portal or configure the web parts to show and hide certain elements and change font styles.

The Service Manager Authoring Tool enables further customization of Service Manager using data models, forms, and workflows. This tool is discussed in the "Using the Service Manager Authoring Tool" section later in this chapter.

The software development kit (SDK) facilitates developing custom components. Following are examples of what you can customize:

▶ Advanced custom forms

▶ Custom connectors

▶ View types

▶ Workflow activities (extending the library provided out of the box)

▶ Advanced workflows

Deploying new reports is also straightforward, as the Service Manager reporting infrastructure utilizes SQL Server Reporting Services (SSRS), which includes tools that simplify creating new reports.

Planning for Management Packs Customization

Management packs consist of eXtensible Markup Language (XML) files that define data models as well as objects such as views for the Service Manager console, workflows, groups, queues, tasks, connectors, and so on. This section provides general information regarding management packs to consider before customizing.

Management pack structure consists of the relationships between and organization of management packs and resources within them; consider this structure as part of your planning. You must identify the resources to place in each management pack and determine whether to seal your management packs. Sealing a management pack enables resources such as class types in the sealed management packs to be referenced in other management packs (sealed or unsealed). Examples of referencing scenarios follow:

▶ Extending an existing class type; this refers to using the existing class type as the base class for the new class type.

▶ Customizing an existing form.

▶ Defining a new relationship between an existing and a new class type.

Each of these scenarios involves referencing resources in an existing management pack. To reference a resource in a different management pack, the management pack holding the referenced resource must be sealed. A management pack is sealed using a strong name key; this guarantees the integrity of the management pack as only the owner of the key can change future versions of that management pack without breaking its identity. Sealing a management pack provides the author with control of the management pack content, guarantees consistency of the management pack, and prevents others than the key holders from customizing the management pack.

> **NOTE: MORE INFORMATION ON MANAGEMENT PACKS**
>
> Chapter 20, "Management Packs," discusses management pack schema details, referencing resources, strong name keys, and the process of sealing a management pack. It describes strategies and considerations regarding deploying customizations in the form of management packs and related resources. The chapter also discusses how management packs are used, what they can contain, and important considerations when working with management packs.

Determine which resources to store in sealed management packs; following are some considerations when planning where to place resources:

▶ The extent to which you want to allow other parties to customize the resource

▶ Whether you need to reference this resource in other management packs

▶ How you plan to group functionality from the perspectives of test and release management

Consider the following approach for organizing resources when a vendor creates a boxed solution for multiple customers:

▶ Sealed management packs store resources that are important for core functionality of the delivered solution.

▶ Unsealed management packs deliver resources the customer should be able to modify (for example, notification templates).

Some general recommendations and best practices follow:

▶ Group related/similar customizations into a single management pack.

▶ Group related management packs using a naming standard. For example, when related customizations are in both sealed and unsealed management packs, you should name those management packs using common naming conventions and elements to make them easy to identify. Figure 22.2 shows how Microsoft utilizes naming conventions to group functionality.

Name	Sealed	Version	Created
Service Manager Release Management Library	Yes	7.5.3079.0	2/23/2014 6:13:37 AM
Service Manager Release Management Data Warehouse Library	Yes	7.5.3079.0	2/23/2014 6:16:48 AM
Service Manager Release Management Configuration Library	Yes	7.5.3079.0	2/23/2014 6:13:57 AM
Service Manager Problem Management Library	Yes	7.5.3079.0	2/23/2014 6:15:54 AM
Service Manager Problem Management Data Warehouse Library	Yes	7.5.3079.0	2/23/2014 6:17:31 AM
Service Manager Problem Management Configuration Library	No	7.5.3079.0	2/23/2014 6:16:04 AM
Service Manager Power Management Cube Library	Yes	7.5.3079.0	2/23/2014 6:21:10 AM
Service Manager Operations Manager Connector Library	Yes	7.5.3079.0	2/23/2014 6:09:28 AM
Service Manager Linking Framework Library	Yes	7.5.3079.0	2/23/2014 6:09:00 AM
Service Manager Linking Framework Configuration	No	7.5.3079.0	2/23/2014 6:16:15 AM
Service Manager Library Management Pack	Yes	7.5.3079.0	2/23/2014 6:10:25 AM
Service Manager Library Help Management Pack	Yes	7.5.3079.0	2/23/2014 6:10:33 AM
Service Manager Knowledge Management Library	Yes	7.5.3079.0	2/23/2014 6:10:53 AM
Service Manager Knowledge Management Help	Yes	7.5.3079.0	2/23/2014 6:11:00 AM
Service Manager Knowledge Management Configuration Library	No	7.5.3079.0	2/23/2014 6:11:03 AM
Service Manager Incident Management Presentation Library	Yes	7.5.3079.0	2/23/2014 6:15:39 AM
Service Manager Incident Management Library	Yes	7.5.3079.0	2/23/2014 6:14:34 AM
Service Manager Incident Management Data Warehouse Library	Yes	7.5.3079.0	2/23/2014 6:17:12 AM
Service Manager Incident Management Configuration Library	No	7.5.3079.0	2/23/2014 6:15:08 AM
Service Manager Inbound E-Mail Library	Yes	7.5.3079.0	2/23/2014 6:10:47 AM
Service Manager Inbound Email Configuration	No	7.5.3079.0	2/23/2014 6:10:50 AM
Service Manager Grooming Library	Yes	7.5.3079.0	2/23/2014 6:16:19 AM
Service Manager Grooming Configuration	Yes	7.5.3079.0	2/23/2014 6:16:22 AM
Service Manager Data Warehouse Library	Yes	7.5.3079.0	2/23/2014 6:16:56 AM

FIGURE 22.2   Example of grouping management pack functionality by name.

To separate management packs from each other (and as shown in Figure 22.2), Microsoft often uses the following conventions:

▶ **Library:** As a suffix for sealed management packs

▶ **Configuration Library:** For unsealed management packs

▶ **Data Warehouse Library:** For data warehouse resources

▶ Store all model-related customizations in sealed management packs.

About Data Modeling

The Service Manager configuration management database (CMDB) is customizable by extending existing data models or creating new ones. This section highlights some important areas of the Service Manager modular database (the CMDB) and discusses how it can be customized, what is possible, and required resources.

For an object to be tracked in the CMDB, it must be described in a data model. A Service Manager data model consists of class types and relationships between these class types. The core part of the model and its properties are described using one or more class types that together describe the characteristics of the object.

About Class Types

A *class type* in Service Manager is the description of an object type containing definitions of the different properties necessary to describe objects of such type, excluding how such an object type relates to objects of other types. Table 22.1 lists examples of properties and their values.

TABLE 22.1   Class Type Properties—Examples

Name	Value
ID	IR1011
Title	Website Problem
Description	Company Website is Down
Classification	Website Problems - External
CreatedDate	2014-02-04 20:00:00

Each property is defined using a set of parameters, such as `Type`, `MinLength`, `MaxLength`, and so on, ensuring the quality of the data stored in that property. You can use these parameters to mark a property as `Required`, meaning an object based on the class type containing the property cannot be saved to the CMDB without providing a value for that property. You can also give the property other constraints, such as maximum length, to control the length and attributes of a string value stored in that property.

When defining the class type(s) for a data model, all properties common to other types of objects are consolidated; this separates those class types that are reusable by other class types and uses the concept of deriving classes.

A *derived class type* inherits all properties and relationships defined for its parent class type. Since almost all class types have properties or other definitions common to other class types, the first consideration when creating a new class type in Service Manager is which class type should be the new class type's *base class*. Figure 22.3 shows a simplified class type hierarchy example from Service Manager. (Additional class types are involved besides those illustrated in the figure.)

The diagram shows how the most common properties are defined by the class type `System.Entity`. Deriving from that class type is the `System.ConfigItem` and `System.WorkItem`, which inherit all properties and relationships defined by the `System.Entity`. At the bottom of the diagram is the class type `System.WorkItem.Incident`, which inherits all properties from `System.Entity` and `System.WorkItem`. Therefore, it is often said that the further down the hierarchy a class type is described, the more specialized the type. This makes `System.WorkItem.Incident` a specialized version of `System.WorkItem`.

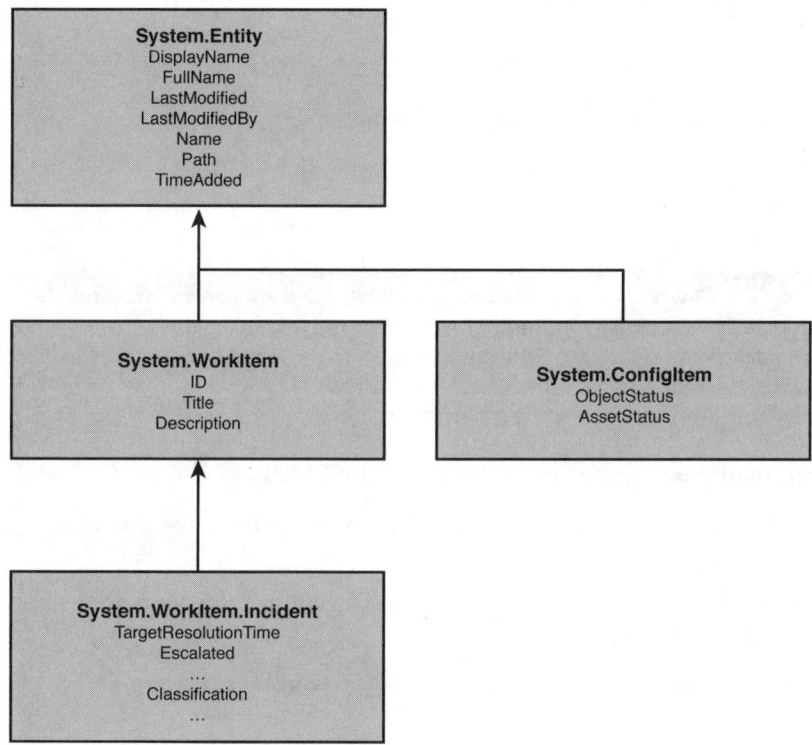

FIGURE 22.3   Class type hierarchy from Service Manager (simplified).

Defining Relationships

After you define the required class types to describe the core part of the data model, define how the data model relates to other objects. A data model is seldom complete without defining these relationships, which could, for example, document the owner of the object.

When defining a *relationship*, you must specify a source and a target class type. You must also specify the cardinality of the source and target, as this restricts how instances of the two different class types can relate to each other. Cardinality is described using a minimum and maximum value for both the source and target. By combining these in different ways, the relationship restricts how instances of the class types can relate to each other.

Cardinality Example

Listing 22.1 contains the definition of the relationship called `Affected User`, which has the source class type `Work Item` (e.g., an incident) and target class type `User`. This is the relationship used to show the affected user in the incident form in the Service Manager console, as displayed in Figure 22.4.

LISTING 22.1   Definition of Affected User Relationship

```
<RelationshipType ID="System.WorkItemAffectedUser" Accessibility="Public"
  Abstract="false" Base="System!System.Reference">
    <Source ID="IsCreatedForUser" MinCardinality="0" MaxCardinality="2147483647"
      Type="System.WorkItem" />
    <Target ID="RequestedWorkItem" MinCardinality="0" MaxCardinality="1"
      Type="System!System.User" />
</RelationshipType>
```

NOTE: MEANING OF NUMBERS GREATER THAN 1

Numbers larger than one in a cardinality statement are evaluated as "unlimited" when a management pack is imported into Service Manager. This means that `MaxCardinality="2"` is the same as `MaxCardinality="2147483647"`.

In Listing 22.1, the cardinality establishes several rules for the CMDB:

▶ `<Source ID="IsCreatedForUser" MinCardinality="0" MaxCardinality="2147483647" Type="System.WorkItem" />`

From a user perspective, for a specific user, there can be zero or more work items where the user is the affected user.

▶ `<Target ID="RequestedWorkItem" MinCardinality="0" MaxCardinality"=1" Type="System!System.User" />`

From a work item perspective, for a specific work item, there can exist zero or one affected users.

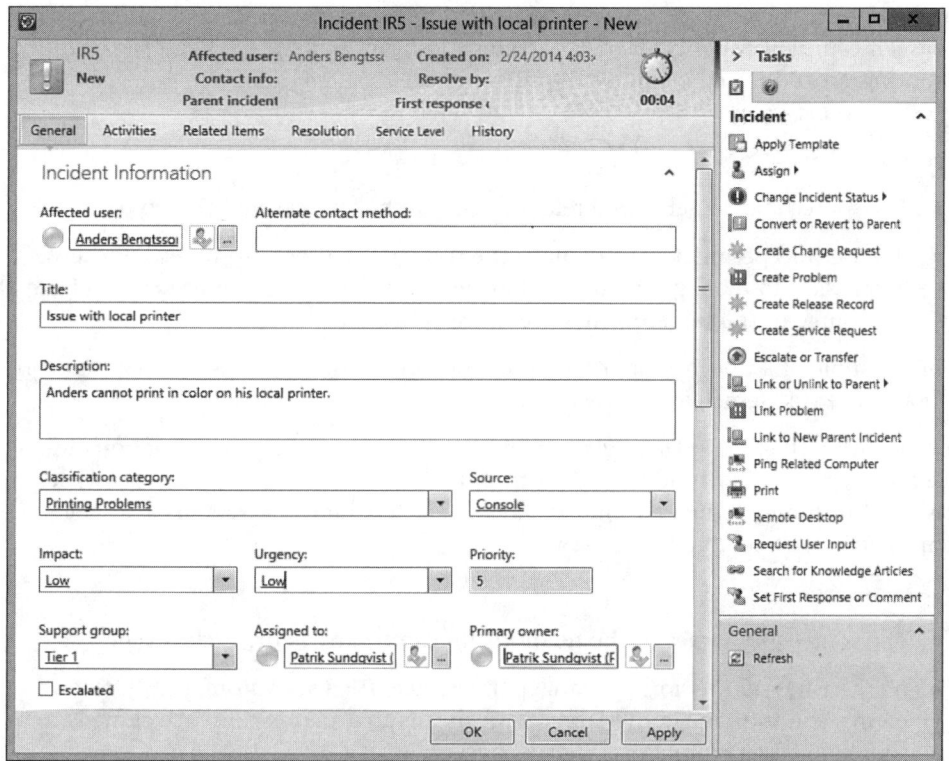

FIGURE 22.4   An affected user in the incident form.

Relationship Types

Service Manager has four core definitions of relationship types, which can be utilized to define new relationships by using one of the four as a base. Each type has its own characteristics; these affect its functionality and behavior inside the tool. It is important to know the differences of each type when designing a new data model, as the different types could affect things such as how permissions are inherited between objects. The four relationship types follow:

▶ **Reference:** The simplest type of relationship is the `Reference` relationship type, which is as simple as a pointer between two objects in the CMDB. The source and target receive no special dependency between each other by being part of this type of relationship. Deleting one of the objects (source or target) removes the association/reference between these two objects, nothing more and nothing less.

Type behavior: The source and target of the relationship can be any defined class type.

For example, an affected user in an incident is related to the incident using the relationship `System.WorkItemAffectedUser` (a.k.a. `Affected User`), which is based on the `System.Reference` (a.k.a. `Reference`) membership type.

▶ **Containment:** The Containment relationship type has the Reference relationship as base, meaning it inherits all the characteristics from that type. This relationship introduces an additional behavior that distinguishes the Containment type from the Reference type.

Type behavior:

  ▶ The source and target of the relationship can be any defined class type.

  ▶ If a user has permission to manage the source, the user automatically receives permission to manage the target. In other words, permissions are cloned from the source to the target from a user perspective.

As an example, if a user has permission to work with a queue, he is also able to work with all the work items within the queue.

▶ **Membership:** The Membership relationship type has the Containment relationship as base and thereby inherits all behaviors from the Containment and Reference type. This relationship introduces a third behavior that separates the Membership type from the Containment type.

Type behavior:

  ▶ The source and target of the relationship can be any defined class type.

  ▶ If a user has permission to manage the source, the user automatically receives permission to manage the target. This means that permissions are cloned from source to target from a user perspective.

  ▶ The target in the relationship has a dependency to the source of the relationship; if the source is deleted, the target is automatically deleted as well.

Consider a file attachment that is related to a configuration item or work item by means of relationships that use System.Membership (a.k.a. Membership) as the base and thereby inherits the characteristics of the Membership relationship type.

▶ **Hosting:** The Hosting relationship type has the Membership relationship as its base and thereby inherits all behaviors from the Containment, Reference, and Membership types. This relationship introduces three additional behaviors that separate the Hosting type from the Membership type.

Type behavior:

  ▶ The source and target of the relationship can be any defined class type.

  ▶ If a user has permission to manage the source, the user automatically receives permission to manage the target. In other words, permissions are cloned from source to target from a user perspective.

  ▶ The target in the relationship has a dependency to the source of the relationship; if the source is deleted, the target is automatically deleted as well.

  ▶ The target class type must be defined as Hosted. This means that the target cannot exist without a host.

▶ Hosted instances share identity with the host, meaning there can be two hosted instances with the same key as long as they aren't hosted by the same host. In other words, uniqueness is only required within the host.

▶ The target in the relationship can only be related to one hosted relationship.

For example, a `Microsoft.Windows.Computer` (represents a logical computer) is hosted by a `Microsoft.SystemCenter.ConfigurationManager.DeployedComputer` (represents the physical computer) through the relationship `LogicalComputerOnPhysicalComputer`. The `LogicalComputerOnPhysicalComputer` uses the `Hosting` base class, which means it inherits all the characteristics from the `Hosting` relationship type.

Planning Type Projections

Type projections, also known as *combination classes*, are commonly compared to database views because they can summarize data from several related objects and display this information to the viewer as one object. While type projections thus have similarities to views, they are different in that they are hierarchy-aware.

A type projection object is defined using a `Type` (a class type) and components (relationships where the `Type` is either source or target). Within each included component, there can be other components; this lets the type projection expose data coming from objects related to related objects (nested objects). Listing 22.2 shows parts of the type projection `System.WorkItem.ChangeRequestProjection` defined in the ServiceManager. ChangeManagement.Library management pack. The definition contains an example of nested components where it first includes the relationship `Activity`, and within that component, includes components such as `AssignedTo`.

LISTING 22.2   Extract of `System.WorkItem.ChangeRequestProjection`

```
<TypeProjection ID="System.WorkItem.ChangeRequestProjection" Accessibility="Public"
  Type="CoreChange!System.WorkItem.ChangeRequest">
  <Component Path=
    "$Target/Path[Relationship='CoreActivity!System.WorkItemContainsActivity']$"
    Alias="Activity">
  <Component Path="$Target/Path
    [Relationship='CoreActivity!System.WorkItemContainsActivity'
      SeedRole='Target']$"
    Alias="ParentWorkItem" />
  <Component Path="$Target/Path
    [Relationship='WorkItem!System.WorkItemCreatedByUser']$"
    Alias="ActivityCreatedBy" />
  <Component Path="Target/Path
    [Relationship='WorkItem!System.WorkItemAssignedToUser']$" Alias="AssignedTo" />
      ...
  </Component>
...
</TypeProjection>
```

One purpose of type projections is to provide a mechanism for the user interface (the Service Manager console) to display data from related objects using a form. As an example, the incident form (targeted at a type projection) shows both data from the incident and the affected user. Type projections are also used when performing complex queries against the CMDB, which involve search criteria on related objects (such as all incidents with an affected user in department X).

Type projections are used in several places in Service Manager, views being an example. When defining a new view in the Service Manager console, type projections are commonly utilized to enable showing data from related objects directly in the view and/ or be able to define a search criteria based on a related item. For example, when creating a view for all incidents with an affected user in the HR Department, the view needs to target a type projection, which in its turn has the `Type` of `System.WorkItem.Incidents`. The type projection needs to include the `Affected User` relationship, as a component.

The My Incidents view in Figure 22.5 provides an example of a view that targets a type projection to use a criterion based on a relationship, in this case showing all incidents where the current user is set as "assigned to." This would not be possible if the view were not targeting a type projection. Most views utilize targeting a type projection.

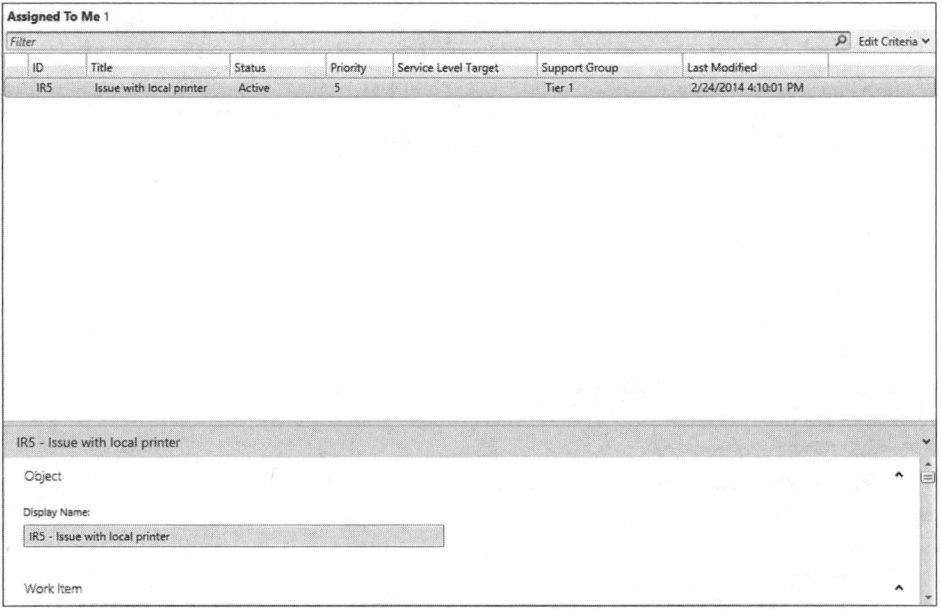

FIGURE 22.5   Type projections used in views.

Presenting Data in Service Manager

Service Manager provides several channels for presenting data from the CMDB, listed in Table 22.2. You should consider whether there is a requirement for custom implementations (such as a new view) to present model customizations. This can help in allocating the correct resources. The next sections describe some underlying techniques used for the different channels and the knowledge required to create custom implementations. They include additional examples of using type projections and discuss why a view must target a type projection and not a simple class.

TABLE 22.2   Presentation Channels

Channel	Description
Views	Shows data in table form where each row is supported by a type projection or a single configuration item or work item
Forms	Shows data based on a type projection or a single configuration item or work item
Reports	Shows data based on SQL queries
Web	Shows data based on custom queries and presentation based on ASP.NET

About Data Binding

To understand the underlying requirements for presenting data in Service Manager, first understand the concept of *data binding*. The Service Manager console is built using WPF, which uses data binding to display data in controls (text boxes, labels, data grids, and so on). Following are two terms that explain data binding:

▶ **Data context:** An object that contains a data object to be presented in a user interface (UI) or part of a UI. Example in Service Manager: An incident.

▶ **Binding Path:** The name of a property, the value of which one wants to present in a UI control such as a text box. Example in Service Manager: Title of incident (path=Title).

Service Manager typically uses a data binding technique for displaying content. This is generally used to present data in forms and views. Consider looking at a change request using the change request form: When a user double-clicks a change request in a view, this tells Service Manager to display a form showing data from the change request. Service Manager then retrieves the object representing the change request from the CMDB and sets the data context of the form to the retrieved object.

Controls such as labels are bound together with a property such as a change request description through a binding path. The binding path is what tells the UI the property of the data context (such as change request) to bind to the control. Each control in the presentation layer can have a configured binding path. Following is an example of defining a data binding in a WPF application:

```
<TextBox Name="bodyText"
         Text="{Binding Path=Description}" />
```

This example could come from the change request form in the Service Manager console. The text box in the example would then show the description of the change request to which the form is currently bound.

Planning Views

Views use the data binding technique described in the previous section. When selecting a view in the Service Manager console, the query configured for the specific view is executed against the CMDB. When the result is presented in the view, each row in the table has a data context of the target type (type projection or class type). This means that if the view is configured to target type projections, each row represents an object of the projection targeted type wrapped in the given type projection. An example of this could be the change request view displayed in Figure 22.6. The view targets a type projection that has the seed class `System.WorkItem.ChangeRequest`. This means that each row has a data context of a change request wrapped in a type projection that includes other objects such as `Assigned User`, and so on, making it possible to display data not only for the change request but also data such as the `Display Name` of the assigned user.

To show data of a related object, the binding path of the control (in this case the column of the view) must contain the full path to the property containing the value to be shown. The path to a related object is built using the component alias from the targeted type projection. In the example just described, the column binding path is included in the `DisplayMemberBinding` attribute in Listing 22.3.

LISTING 22.3   All Change Requests Assigned to User Display Name

```
<mux:Column Name="aDisplayName" DisplayMemberBinding=
  "{Binding Path=AssignedTo.DisplayName}" Width="200"
  DisplayName="Header_Owner" Property="AssignedTo.DisplayName"
  DataType="s:String" />
```

Note that the binding path syntax in the listing is `<Alias>.<PropertyName>`. This means the type projection the view is targeting must have the `Assigned to User` component (see Figure 22.6); otherwise, the data would not be available for presentation in the view.

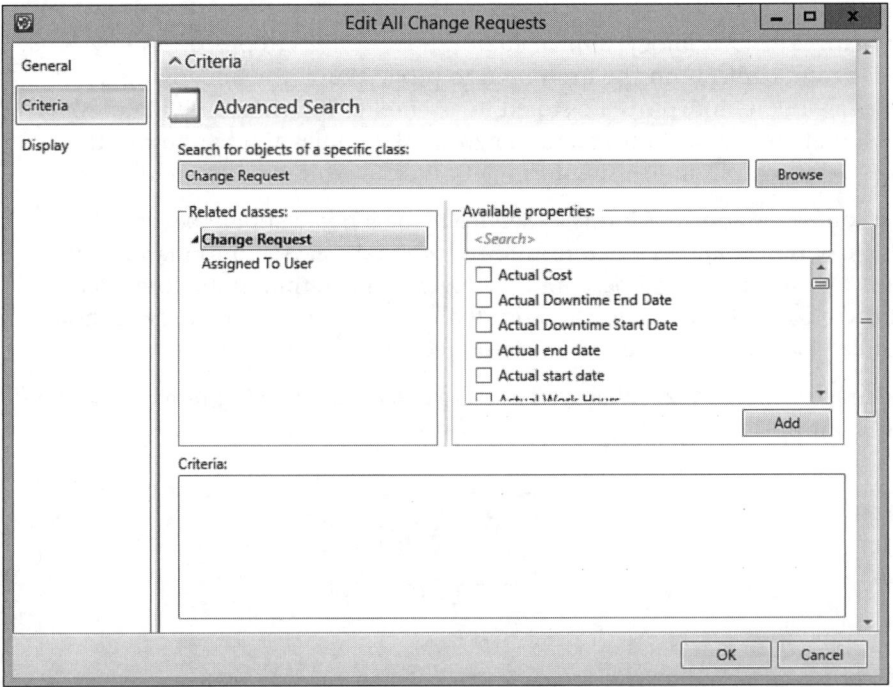

FIGURE 22.6   Criteria tab in configuration of a change request view.

Creating new views to display data from the CMDB is straightforward and can be performed using the Service Manager console by almost anyone with permission to do so. Should the wizard not be adequate, such as when wanting to change the column header text, you could utilize someone having a basic knowledge of management packs and WPF binding paths. You can first create the view in the Service Manager console, export the management pack where the view is stored, and then modify it manually to display the correct text.

You could use a more advanced approach to display data in forms without using a standard view in the console. The individual tasked for this would need to be comfortable in WPF and have in-depth knowledge of defining management pack elements.

TIP: MORE ABOUT VIEW DEFINITIONS

Chapter 23, "Advanced Customization Scenarios," discusses the view definition in a management pack and how to modify it. It also discusses custom view types and displaying data in forms without using a standard view in the console.

Planning Forms

Forms use standard WPF technology. Similar to how a view binds to properties in columns, the different controls on the form bind to properties of the underlying data context (such as a work item). Forms are stored in assemblies (dynamic link libraries, known as DLLs) that are bundled into management pack bundles and bound together with class types or type projections using form definitions within management packs.

To understand some limitations of forms in Service Manager, you should become familiar with the logic of how it knows what form to use when displaying information about an object in the CMDB. Figure 22.7 describes the logic that determines the form to use, showing that there can only be one form associated with a given class type, even though it can be an indirect association through a type projection.

Consider the scenario of creating a change request; expect the following to happen when using the flow chart in Figure 22.7:

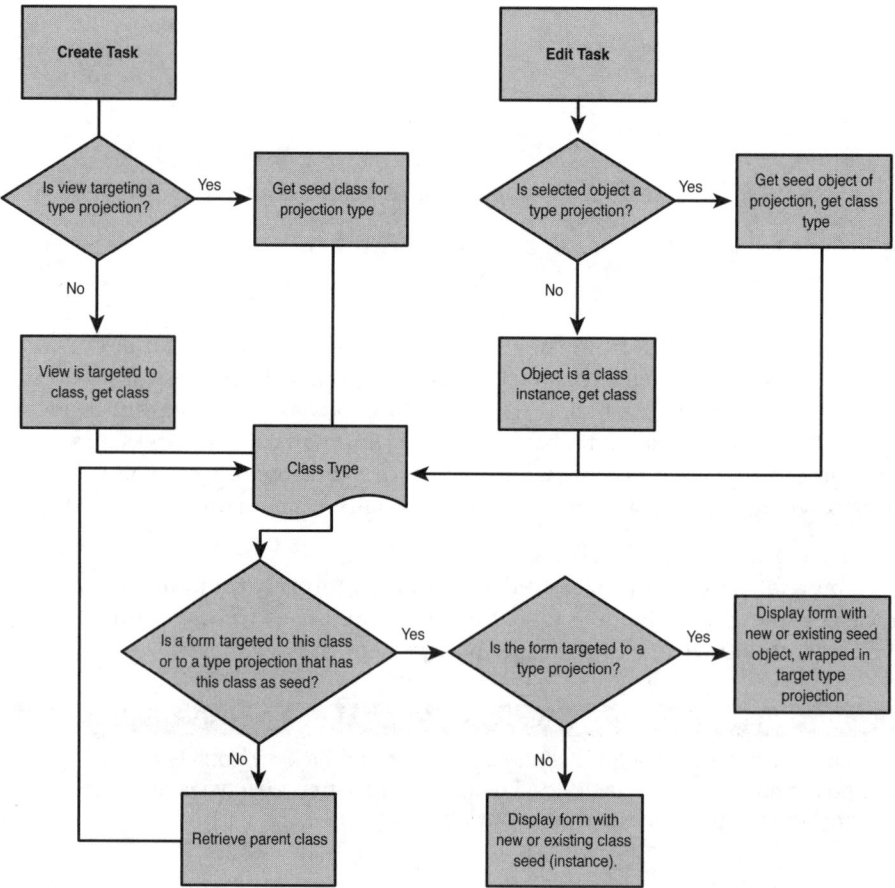

FIGURE 22.7   Determining the form to use.

1. Service Manager checks whether the currently selected view in the console is targeting a type projection or a class type.

2. If the current view targets a type projection, Service Manager locates the class type used as seed for the type projection. If not, Service Manager already has the class type.

3. Using the class type, Service Manager finds a form that is targeted to the class type or a form that targets a type projection that has the class type as seed. If no form is found, Service Manager retrieves the parent class type (the class type used as base for the current class type) and tries to find a form using that class type. Service Manager continues to retrieve a parent class until a form is found or no parent class is found.

4. If a form is located, Service Manager either wraps a new seed (instance) of the class type in the given type projection and uses the type projection as a data context for the form, or just uses the new class type seed as data context for the form. The decision is based on whether the form was targeting a class type or a type projection.

Given that the choice of form is always based on the class type, this means there can be only one form associated with a class type within Service Manager.

> **CAUTION: ONLY ONE FORM CAN BE ASSOCIATED WITH AN OBJECT**
>
> Service Manager allows only one form at a time to be associated with objects of a given class type. Trying to associate multiple forms with different type projections based on a given class does not work, as the logic used to locate a form for a new or existing object is always based on a class type and not the type projection.

Generic Form

Service Manager can always locate a form, since the top class, `System.Entity` (also known as `Object`), is associated with a fallback form known as the generic form. This form, displayed in Figure 22.8, shows the properties of the `Build` class, which uses the `Configuration Item` class as base. The generic form is used since no other form is associated with the class.

The generic form is designed at runtime, where each class type in the class type hierarchy of the given object results in a separate panel in the form. The class type at the top of the hierarchy, known as the *most derived class type*, is represented in the first panel of the form where all the properties are listed. In Figure 22.8, the most derived class type is `System.Entity` (`Object`), the second most derived class type is `System.ConfigItem` (a.k.a. `Configuration Item`), which is therefore placed just below `Object`. As shown in the figure, the properties of the class types (definitions in Listing 22.4) are shown in each of the rendered panels of the generic form.

LISTING 22.4   Definition of `System.Entity` and `System.ConfigItem`

```
<ClassType ID="System.Entity" Accessibility="Public" Abstract="true" Hosted="false"
  Singleton="false" Extension="false"
  <Property ID="DisplayName" Type="string" AutoIncrement="false" Key="false"
CaseSensitive="false" MaxLength="4000" MinLength="0" Required="false" />
</ClassType>
<ClassType ID="System.ConfigItem" Accessibility="Public" Abstract="true"
  Base="System.Entity" Hosted="false" Singleton="false" Extension="false">
  <Property ID="ObjectStatus" Type="enum" AutoIncrement="false" Key="false"
    CaseSensitive="false" MaxLength="256" MinLength="0" Required="false"
    EnumType="System.ConfigItem.ObjectStatusEnum"
    DefaultValue="System.ConfigItem.ObjectStatusEnum.Active" />
    <Property ID="AssetStatus" Type="enum" AutoIncrement="false" Key="false"
    CaseSensitive="false" MaxLength="256" MinLength="0" Required="false"
    EnumType="System.ConfigItem.AssetStatusEnum" />
    <Property ID="Notes" Type="richtext" AutoIncrement="false" Key="false"
    CaseSensitive="false" MaxLength="4000" MinLength="0" Required="false" />
</ClassType>
```

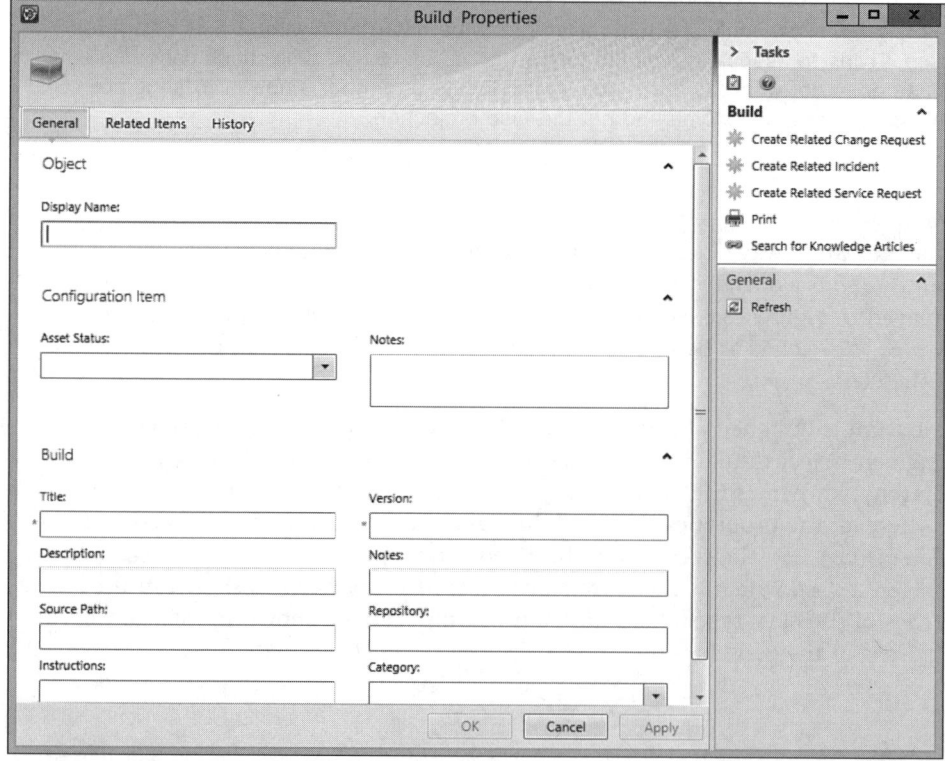

FIGURE 22.8   Example of generic form.

History

All objects within the CMDB are tracked when they change. The following data is stored in the CMDB for each change performed:

▶ Who performed the change

▶ When was the change performed

▶ What was changed (from value, to value)

Figure 22.9 shows an example of how history is presented for a given object in the CMDB.

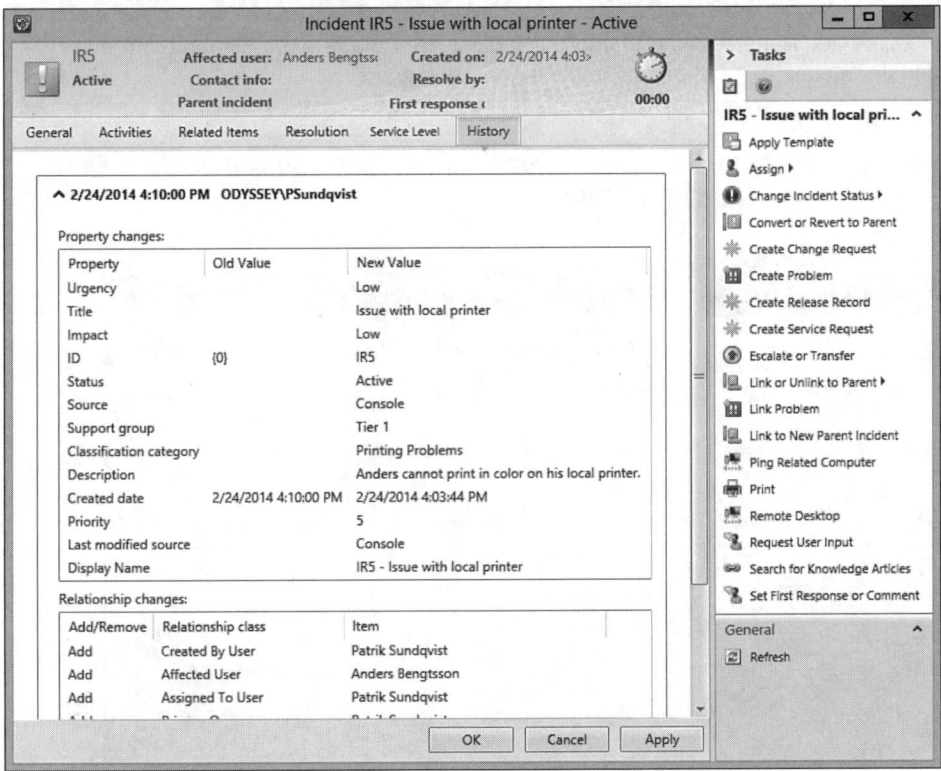

FIGURE 22.9   Viewing the History tab in the incident form.

The History tab is not visible when creating custom forms for Service Manager, although history data remains available for all CMDB objects (including custom objects). While the Authoring Tool does not provide the capability to add the control that is used to show the history data of an object, there are ways to reuse the control to show history data in a custom form.

Planning Reports

Service Manager uses a reporting solution that exposes reports based on data from the data warehouse. A number of reports are available out of the box. Figure 22.10 lists some of these reports.

When planning for customization, know that when you implement custom data models or extend existing models, the new data introduced to Service Manager is not automatically available in the data warehouse for custom reports. One needs to "tell" the infrastructure this information should be available for reporting and how it should be available, which requires defining fact tables, dimensions, and outriggers.

TIP: UNDERSTAND REPORTING CAPABILITIES

Chapter 21, "Data Warehouse and Reporting," discusses the reporting infrastructure in detail and introduces fact tables, dimensions, and outriggers.

As the reporting infrastructure is based on SSRS, you can easily add custom reports and publish them in the Service Manager console.

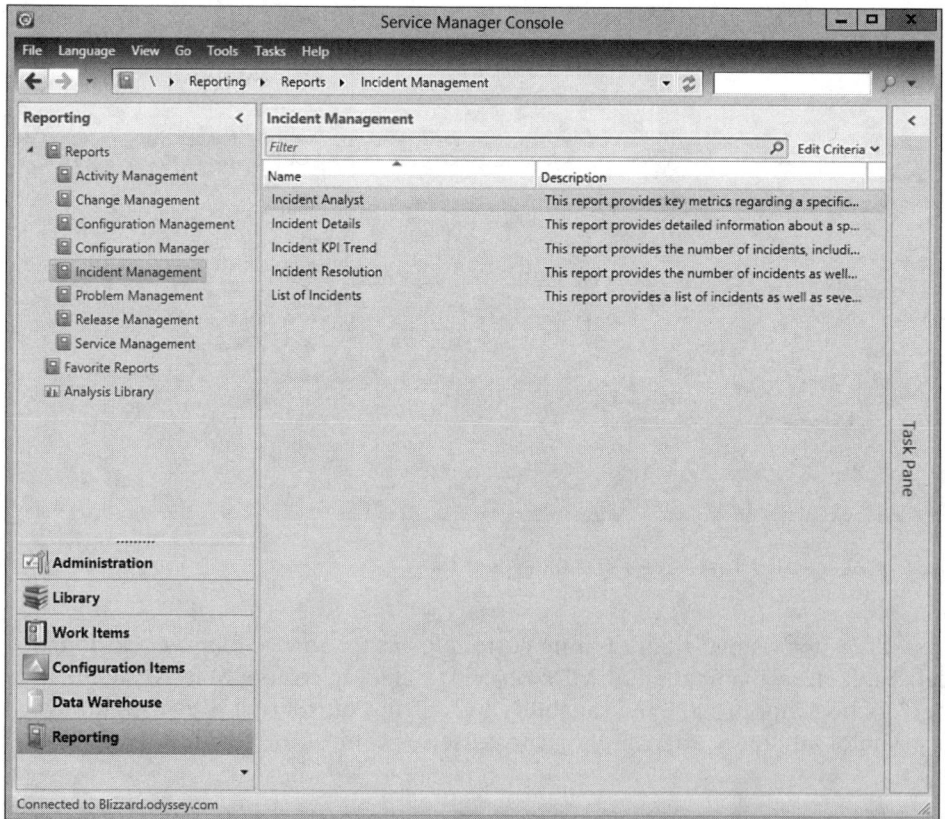

FIGURE 22.10   Some of the out-of-the-box reports in Service Manager.

Planning Web Portal

The self-service portal uses Silverlight to present data. Since the portal is the least customizable part of Service Manager, there are no special considerations regarding these portals when planning your customization.

Automating Processes with Workflows

Service Manager can provide large time savings by automating IT processes and increasing quality of service; these are areas to consider when planning your implementation and approaches to customization that could provide the most value. By using the workflow engine to automate the most common IT processes, IT can move its focus from repetitive tasks such as resetting passwords to providing business value by developing processes and services that better align it with existing and future business needs.

The workflow engine is accessible to Service Manager implementers as a platform for automation. The engine is built to support different types of workflows, with Windows Workflow Foundation (WF) the most accessible of the supported technologies. Using WF workflows is appropriate for automating common IT tasks with Service Manager.

Following are the different ways to trigger workflows in Service Manager:

▶ **Subscription based:** Example: Activity status goes from Pending to Active.

▶ **Scheduled:** Example: Every 24 hours.

▶ **Task initiated:** Example: Synchronize now (as seen when selecting a configured connector).

You can implement user-defined workflows in different ways in Service Manager; the console wizards can manage the simpler workflow implementation scenarios. Some predefined workflows include

▶ Incident event workflows

▶ Service request event workflows

▶ Change request event workflows

▶ Activity event workflows

▶ Desired configuration management (DCM) event workflows

Incident, change request, and activity event workflows can trigger predefined workflows that apply templates and notify the related individuals (as the affected user of an incident) to an object of one of the five class types (incidents, service requests, change requests, release records, or activities) being created or updated.

DCM event workflows can control how noncompliance reports from System Center Configuration Manager should transform to incidents by specifying incident templates. You can also use these workflows to configure notifications for noncompliance reports.

TIP: MORE ABOUT INCIDENT AND CHANGE REQUEST MANAGEMENT

Read more about incident and desired configuration management event workflows in Chapter 11, "Incident Management." To learn about change request event workflows, see Chapter 14, "Change Request and Configuration Management."

Service Manager also includes predefined workflows for generic notifications.

Service Manager can assist with automating IT tasks. These can be virtually any task executed in or using a computerized system, including internal maintenance jobs such as escalating all active incidents with a priority of 5 and over four days old, and automating requests for new user accounts.

As shown in Figure 22.11, you can use the Service Manager Authoring Tool to build workflows. You could also write managed code to create a workflow, or create re-usable workflow activities you can import with the Authoring Tool and then use to build a complete workflow. As Service Manager comes with an activity library containing some useful activities, you can begin automating without writing code, although to create the most useful workflows you would at a minimum need an individual capable of writing PowerShell scripts when using the built-in workflow engine.

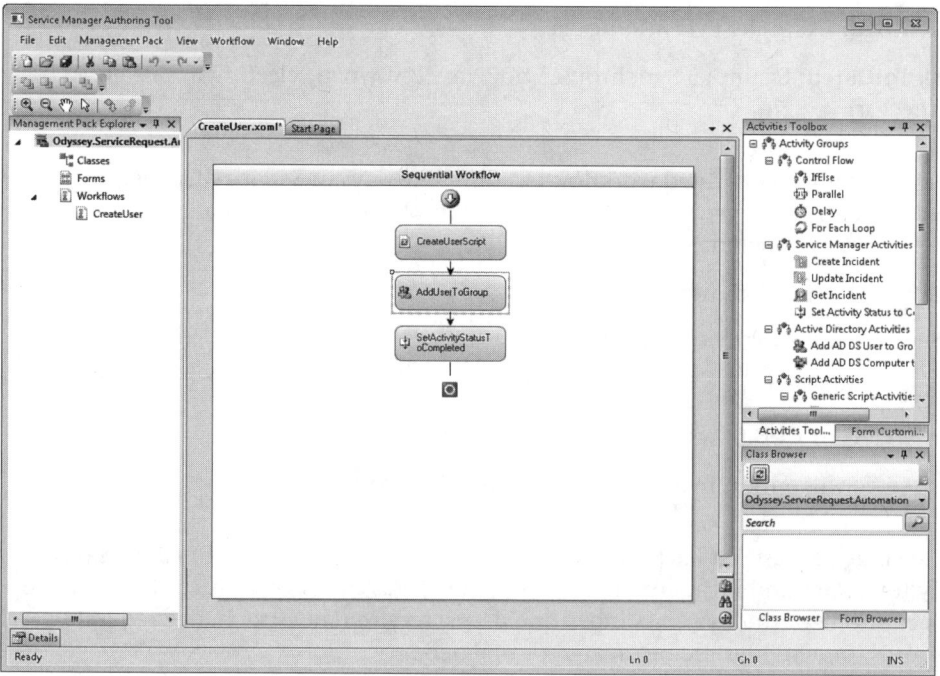

FIGURE 22.11   The work design surface in the Service Manager Authoring Tool.

> **TIP: USE SYSTEM CENTER ORCHESTRATOR FOR SERVICE MANAGER AUTOMATION AND INTEGRATION WORKFLOWS**
>
> Consider exploring System Center Orchestrator's capabilities in combination with Service Manager. Its large number of integration packs provides you with the capability to automate an almost infinite number of tasks. For example, while you can use Service Manager to trigger and track change requests, you could also automate the process with Orchestrator using its built-in drag-and-drop automation. For additional information about Orchestrator, see *System Center 2012 Orchestrator Unleashed* (Sams, 2013).

The skills required to create workflows that automate IT tasks can vary, depending on the task to be automated. One can get far with having basic knowledge in PowerShell, although it doesn't hurt to have access to a .NET developer.

Determine those tasks to automate and the human resources needed to implement the customization. You should also consider areas such as account permissions and firewall ports.

Permissions in Target Systems

All workflows in Service Manager are executed in the context of a service account. By default, this is the account specified as the workflow account during installation. Keep this in mind when planning to automate IT tasks, as the workflow account must be delegated the required access and permissions in each target system. For example, if you are automating the creation of user accounts, the workflow account must have the necessary rights in Active Directory to create the account. If the new user account should be given an Exchange mailbox, the workflow account needs to have the required rights in Exchange to create the mailbox.

Firewall Configurations

Depending on the actions the custom workflows perform and the technology you are using, you must configure the infrastructure to support the required access between the Service Manager management server (the first management server installed, which runs the workflows) and the target system. For instance, if a PowerShell script used in a workflow to automate a task in Configuration Manager is using Windows Management Instrumentation (WMI), you must configure firewalls in-between the systems and on the target server to allow the WMI traffic to pass through.

Utilizing Groups and Queues

The primary purpose of groups is to limit the access to configuration items (computers, printers, and so on). When you create a user role in Service Manager, you can limit its access to objects in the groups you specify. This is also true for queues, although their main purpose is to limit access to work items (such as incidents and change requests). If no group or queue is associated with a user role, the role has access to all objects.

In addition to limiting access, following are some ways you can use groups and queues:

▶ As criteria when creating a custom report

▶ As target in a notification scenario

As part of the planning process, you should understand scoping capabilities and limits, as these can help to achieve the desired access control on existing and new object types. Consider those scenarios you need to support, the user roles these include, and then the groups and queues necessary to build those roles.

General Considerations for Customization

There are some general considerations during the planning process so you do not under-estimate the necessary resources. These include globalization as well as validation and constraints, discussed in the next sections.

Globalization Considerations

Since Service Manager supports multiple languages, an organization might decide (or require) to use multiple languages. Supporting multiple languages affects several signifi-cant areas:

▶ Any notification templates you create must be translated to the supported languages.

▶ It becomes important to set the `Locale` property of the user configuration items in the CMDB appropriately, as this is the language used when Service Manager sends notifications to a user. If a template exists in the specified language, that template is used when sending the message.

▶ Creating custom list items requires exporting management packs so localized display strings can be added to the custom list items in the supported languages.

Validation and Constraints Considerations

Data models support constraints such as properties with maximum lengths or are required fields. This ensures the data in the CMDB is guaranteed to have a particular level of quality. When using the generic form, the UI gives visual feedback of any data errors entered, such as showing a red star next to a text box bound to a required field. If you implement a custom form that includes visual feedback, plan for the feedback to be imple-mented by the individual creating the custom form. This could include the same type of feedback as the generic form, but a custom form requires that it is handled explicitly.

Defining constraints can ensure a property value exists when used by a custom workflow. The flip side is that you should not add constraints that are not absolutely necessary and valid in all scenarios. Generally, a better way to utilize constraints is by adding validation in custom forms (when possible). Should you later decide to override the constraints, you could change the custom form or use other methods to update the data.

Required Knowledge

The following sections describe the knowledge required to perform customizations in Service Manager. The knowledge required depends on the level of customization planned.

Console Customizations

Many customizations can be performed in the console, such as creating new user roles, list items, templates, and so on. In addition to the knowledge available in this book and through reading the documentation, the authors suggest you know some basic hypertext markup language (HTML), as this can be useful for formatting notification templates.

Data Modeling

Learning the concepts of data modeling and the Authoring Tool can get you far. However, some scenarios require manual editing of the XML in management packs; consider using Visual Studio Authoring Extensions, discussed in Chapter 23.

Customizing Forms

The "Performing Customizations in Service Manager" sections of this chapter describe how to customize existing forms and create simple new ones. By knowing WPF, you could use tools such as Microsoft Visual Studio (with or without the Authoring Extensions) and Expression Blend to create custom forms from scratch, making use of the full power in WPF.

Customizing Workflows

The Authoring Tool is often sufficient for creating basic workflows. However, the authors recommend you know some basic PowerShell scripting. In addition, using Windows WF and knowing how to write managed code present endless possibilities.

Using the Service Manager Authoring Tool

The Authoring Tool is designed for use by IT professionals and does not require knowing PowerShell or how to write code; although if you are creating advanced workflows it is best if you have capabilities in one of these areas.

Creating Custom Reports

When writing custom reports for Service Manager, you could use either the Report Builder or Business Intelligence Development Studio, included with SQL Server. These tools provide drag and drop functionality and wizards to aid in building reports. It is also useful to have some basic knowledge of Transact SQL (T-SQL) and SSRS. For information on the Business Intelligence Development Studio, see http://msdn.microsoft.com/en-us/library/ms173767(v=sql.105).aspx.

Performing Customizations in Service Manager

The first part of this chapter discussed how to plan for customizations. This next part takes you through the actual steps to implement those customizations. These include customizing the console, creating data modules, creating workflows, customizing forms, sealing your management packs, and using web portals.

Customizing the Console

Most everything in the Service Manager console can be customized. The next sections describe the most common customizations you can perform directly in the console, although some scenarios may require a bit of XML editing.

Customizing the Navigation Pane

You can customize the Navigation pane in the Service Manager console (displayed in Figure 22.12) in several ways. The most common scenarios are creating new views and modifying existing ones. New views are placed in folders. You can place new folders and views in any of the out-of-the-box workspaces (Administration, Library, Work Items, Configuration Items, and so on). You can also create custom workspaces; Figure 22.12 includes Odyssey Workspace as an example.

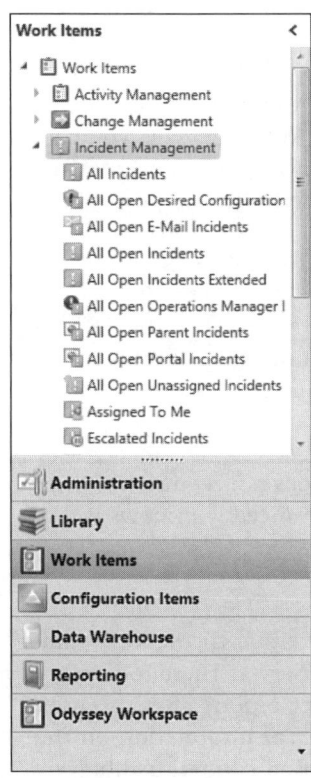

FIGURE 22.12   Navigation pane in the Service Manager console.

Customizing Folders

You can create a folder in one of the following ways:

▶ Within the console

▶ Editing the XML that defines a management pack

Where available, the Create Folder task (shown in Figure 22.13) creates a new folder below the currently selected folder. This task is only available in certain parts of the navigation tree and is based on the folders associated with the Create Folder task. If this task is unavailable where you want to create a folder, you could create the folder manually by editing a management pack.

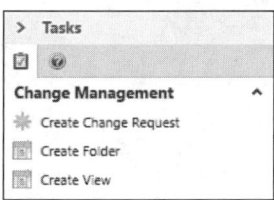

FIGURE 22.13   The Create Folder console task.

Folders created from the console can only be saved to unsealed management packs.

▶ Any views created beneath that folder must be saved to the same management pack, as long as the management pack defining the folder is left unsealed.

▶ If a folder is declared in a sealed management pack (which enables external referencing), views stored in any management pack can be placed beneath the folder.

Folders are declared in the `Presentation` element of a management pack. The placement of the folder in the navigation tree is based on the `ParentFolder` attribute. Listing 22.5 shows the declaration of a folder just below the Incident Management folder in the Work Items workspace.

LISTING 22.5   Management Pack Folder Declaration

```
<Presentation>
  <Folders>
    <Folder ID="Odyssey.Folders.MyCustomViews" Accessibility="Public"
    ParentFolder=
      "IncidentManagement!ServiceManager.Console.IncidentManagement" />
  </Folders>
<Presentation>
```

NOTE: ABOUT MANAGEMENT PACK REFERERENCES

`IncidentManagement!` in Listing 22.5 points to a reference `Alias`. For additional information about management pack references, see Chapter 20.

For a folder to appear in the Service Manager console, use a declaration similar to Listing 22.5. If you want a friendlier name to appear in the console or are enabling localization, you should also declare a display string element folder. Chapter 20 discusses display strings.

Listing 22.6 builds on Listing 22.5, showing a more complete declaration of the custom folder. The listing includes an image reference to improve the appearance of the folder navigation pane and two `FolderItems` to cause the Create View and Create Folder tasks to appear in the Folder Tasks section for the custom folder, shown in Figure 22.13.

LISTING 22.6 Folder Declaration Including Tasks

```
<Presentation>
  <Folders>
    <Folder ID="Odyssey.Folders.MyCustomViews" Accessibility="Public"
    ParentFolder="IncidentManagement!ServiceManager.Console.IncidentManagement" />
  </Folders>
  <FolderItems>
    <FolderItem ElementID=
  "EnterpriseManagement!Microsoft.EnterpriseManagement.
  ➥ServiceManager.UI.Console.Task.CreateGridView"
      ID="Odyssey.FolderItem.CreateView" Folder="Odyssey.Folders.MyCustomViews" />
    <FolderItem ElementID=
  "EnterpriseManagement!Microsoft.EnterpriseManagement.
  ➥ServiceManager.UI.Console.Task.CreateFolder"
      ID="Odyssey.FolderItem.CreateFolder"
      Folder="Odyssey.Folders.MyCustomViews " />
  </FolderItems>
  <ImageReferences>
    <ImageReference ElementID="Odyssey.Folders.MyCustomViews"
      ImageID=
  "EnterpriseManagement!Microsoft.EnterpriseManagement.
  ➥ServiceManager.UI.Console.Image.Folder" />
  </ImageReferences>
</Presentation>
```

Customizing Workspaces

The lower portion of Figure 22.12 displayed some of the built-in workspaces in Service Manager. The workspaces area in this figure was extended with a custom workspace.

A workspace is defined as a folder in a management pack. Using the built-in folder named `ServiceManager.Console.RootFolder` as the parent folder causes the custom folder to appear as a workspace.

Listing 22.7 declares the custom folder with the ID `Odyssey.Console.WorkSpace` as a workspace, shown in Figure 22.14 as Odyssey Workspace.

LISTING 22.7   Workspace Declaration

```
<Presentation>
  <Folders>
    <Folder ID="Odyssey.Console.WorkSpace" Accessibility="Public"
      ParentFolder="EnterpriseManagement!ServiceManager.Console.RootFolder" />
    <Folder ID="Odyssey.Console.WorkSpace.Root" Accessibility="Public"
      ParentFolder="Odyssey.Console.WorkSpace" />
    <Folder ID="Odyssey.Folders.lvl1" Accessibility="Public"
      ParentFolder="Odyssey.Console.WorkSpace.Root" />
    <Folder ID="Odyssey.Folders.lvl2" Accessibility="Public"
       ParentFolder="Odyssey.Folders.lvl1" />
  </Folders>
  <FolderItems>
    <FolderItem ElementID=
      "EnterpriseManagement!Microsoft.EnterpriseManagement.
➡ServiceManager.UI.Console.Task.CreateGridView"
      ID="Odyssey.FolderItem.CreateView" Folder="Odyssey.Folders.lvl1" />
  </FolderItems>
  <ImageReferences>
    <ImageReference ElementID="Odyssey.Console.WorkSpace"
      ImageID="SMWorkItem!WorkItemImage32x32" />
    <ImageReference ElementID="Odyssey.Console.WorkSpace"
      ImageID="SMWorkItem!WorkItemImage16x16" />
    <ImageReference ElementID="Odyssey.Console.WorkSpace.Root"
      ImageID="SMWorkItem!WorkItemImage16x16" />
    <ImageReference ElementID="Odyssey.Folders.lvl1"
      ImageID="EnterpriseManagement!Microsoft.EnterpriseManagement.
➡ServiceManager.UI.Console.Image.Folder" />
    <ImageReference ElementID="Odyssey.Folders.lvl2"
      ImageID="EnterpriseManagement!Microsoft.
➡EnterpriseManagement.ServiceManager.UI.Console.Image.Folder" />
  </ImageReferences>
</Presentation>
```

The parent of the custom folder points at the built-in root folder (defined using a referenced management pack alias in Listing 22.8), making the custom folder appear as a workspace. The folder called `Odyssey.Console.WorkSpace.Root` uses the Odyssey Workspace folder as its parent folder. This results in it being the root node in the Odyssey Workspace navigation tree, displayed in Figure 22.14 as Workspace Root. The listing also includes several image references to make the nodes look more attractive and a folder item to enable creating views in the folder named Folder in the figure. The names displayed in Figure 22.14 are controlled by display strings, which enable localization.

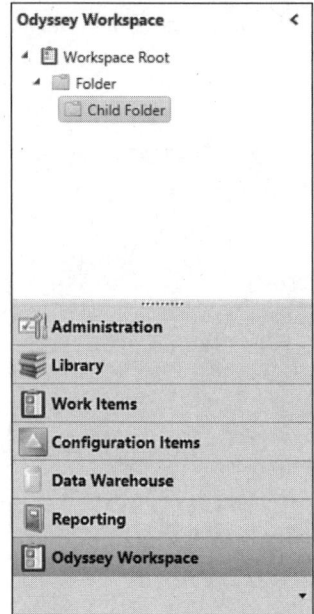

FIGURE 22.14   Custom Workspace.

LISTING 22.8   Required Reference

```
<Reference Alias="EnterpriseManagement">
    <ID>Microsoft.EnterpriseManagement.ServiceManager.UI.Console</ID>
    <Version>7.5.2905.0</Version>
    <PublicKeyToken>31bf3856ad364e35</PublicKeyToken>
</Reference>
```

After defining a workspace and a root folder for the workspace, you can add folders and views from the console using console tasks (if these were enabled using `Categories` and `FolderItems`) as described in the previous section.

Customizing Views

Folders have a single purpose in the Service Manager console: to act as a container for views. Using the Create View console task lets you easily create a view below the selected folder. Follow these steps:

   1. Start the Create View console task to launch the Create View Wizard; Figure 22.15 shows the General tab.

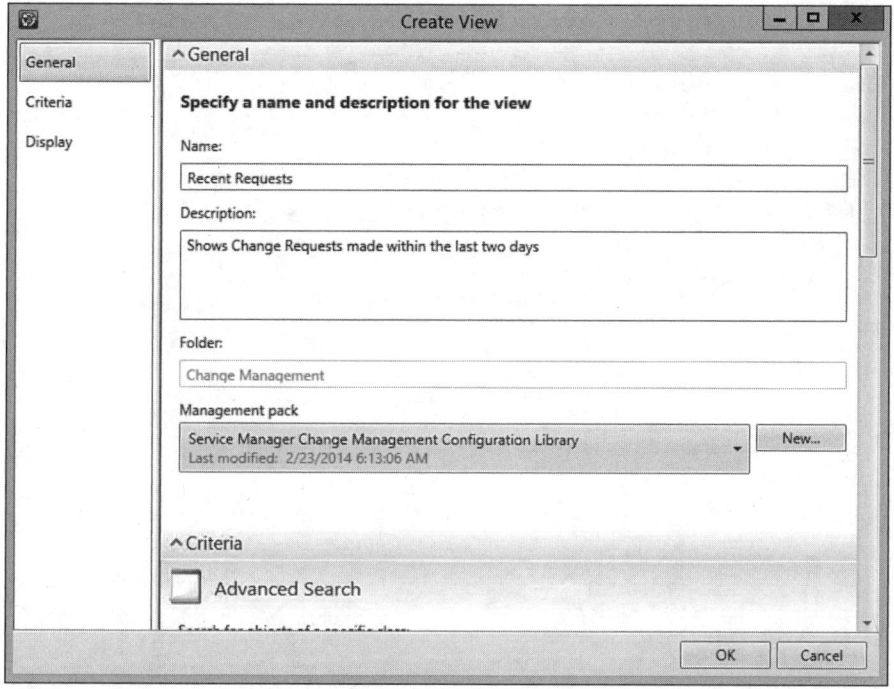

FIGURE 22.15   General tab of the Create View Wizard.

2. In the General page of the wizard, enter a name for the view and choose the management pack in which to store the view.

3. Specify criteria for the view on the Criteria tab, shown in Figure 22.16. The criteria are basically a query definition used to query the CMDB when the view is selected in the Navigation pane.

When specifying the view criteria, start by choosing a class to base the search on. The class specifies those objects the search result should contain.

4. Click **Browse** to open the Select a Class dialog. This initially presents you with a list of frequently used basic classes, shown in the drop-down in Figure 22.17. Notice you can choose a combination class (such as `Type Projection`) as the target for the view instead of a basic class. You would do this by selecting **Combination classes** in the View list, also shown in Figure 22.17. If the view criteria or the data presented contain information regarding related objects, you would have to build the criteria on a combination class rather than a basic class.

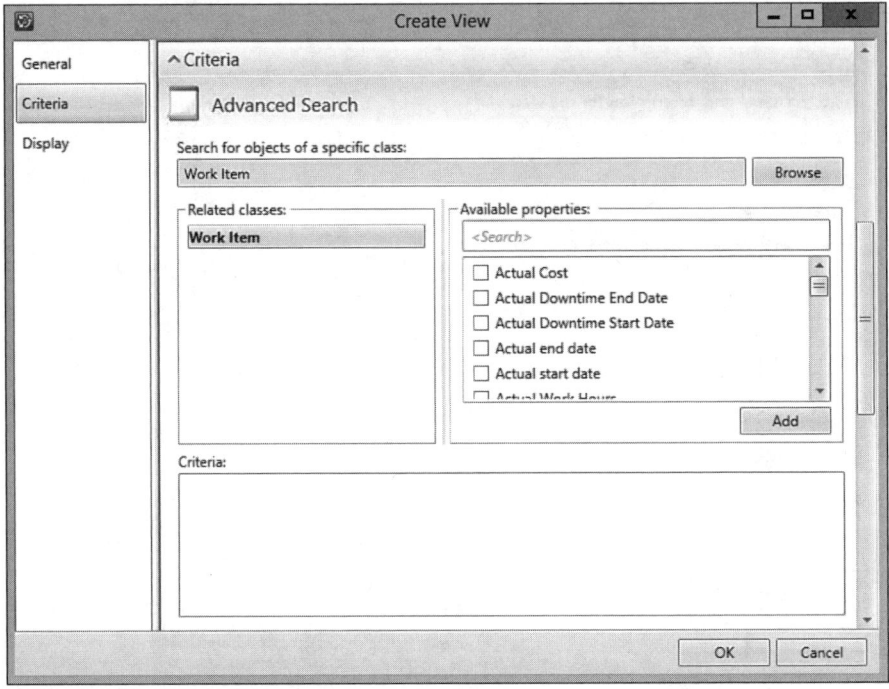

FIGURE 22.16   The Criteria tab of the Create View Wizard.

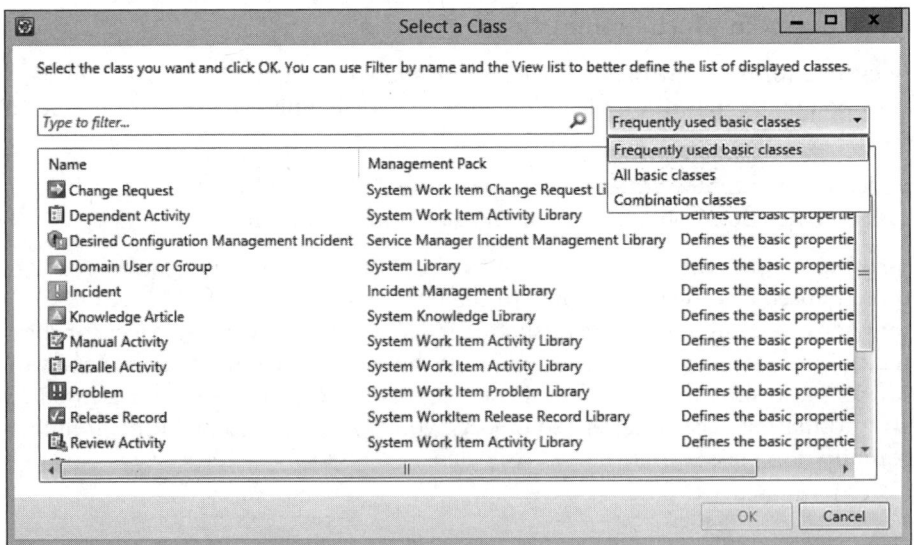

FIGURE 22.17   Selecting a class in the Create View Wizard.

5. Based on the class chosen, the properties associated with that class type are listed as available properties on the Criteria tab. Selecting a property and clicking **Add** adds the property to the search criteria, and enables you to specify a condition for that property that should be fulfilled by objects included in the view. This is shown in Figure 22.18.

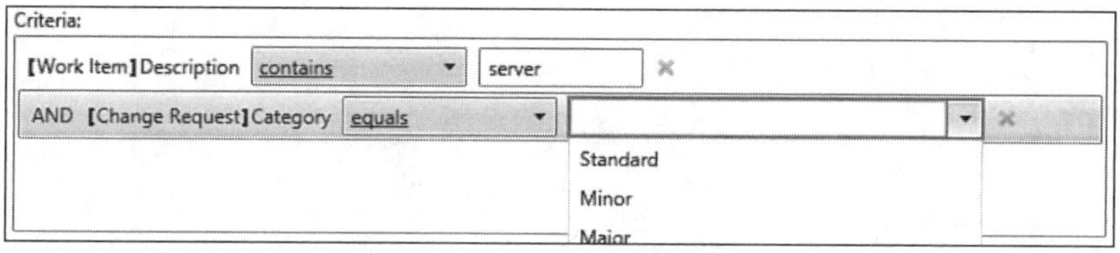

FIGURE 22.18   Criteria builder dialog in the Create View Wizard.

Building the criteria is generally self-explanatory. Based on the data type of a property, the criteria builder shows a suitable list of operators (equals, like, contains, and so on) that can be used. Functionality is also available to create a dynamic criterion, which requires some explanation:

When specifying conditions in a criterion, there is a concept known as *tokens*; these are placeholders and replaced with values at runtime. Tokens enable having a criterion evaluated dynamically based on factors such as time [Now] and who is using the view [me] (which user is running the console). Chapter 23 discusses how to use tokens in a view criterion.

6. The final step in creating a view is specifying those properties to display in the view, shown in Figure 22.19. Each property selected is represented by a column in the finalized view. As mentioned in step 4, if you want a column showing a property value of a related object (such as the assigned user of an incident), you must use a combination class as the base for the criteria.

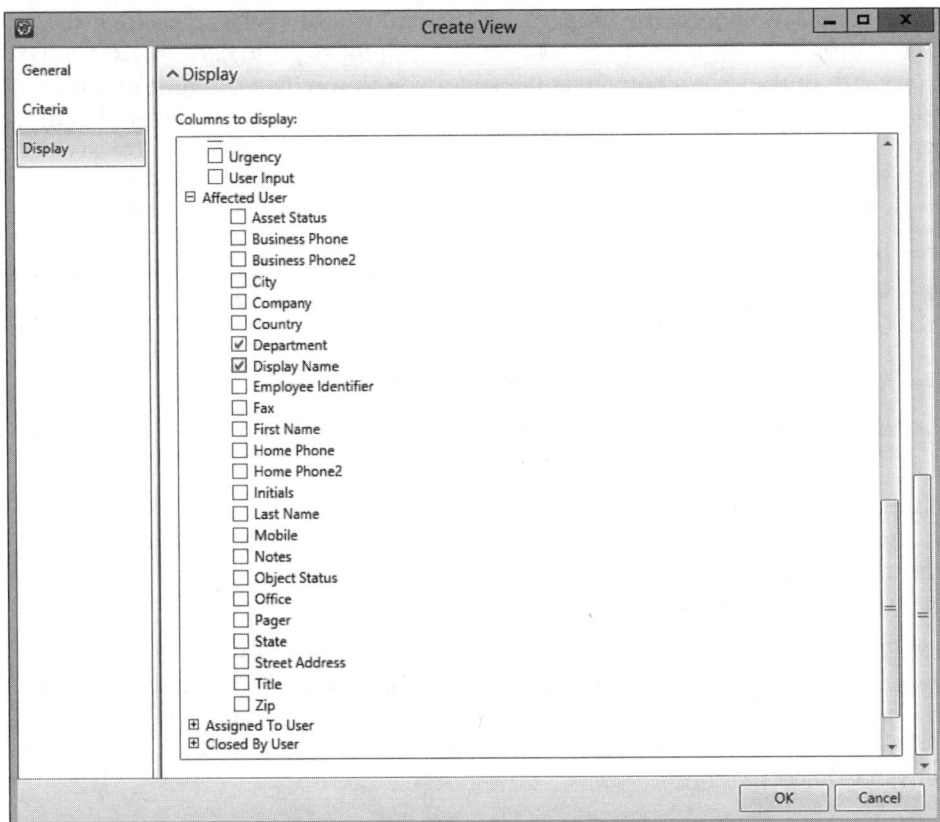

FIGURE 22.19   Display tab of the Create View Wizard.

Customizing Console Tasks

You can use console tasks in Service Manager to execute commands such as Ping Related Computer (shown in Figure 22.20) to simplify troubleshooting or automate repetitive tasks. While a number of useful tasks are provided out of the box, you can also extend Service Manager with custom console tasks.

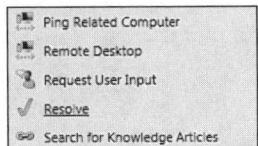

FIGURE 22.20   Example of console tasks.

Console tasks can execute virtually anything that can be provided in a .NET assembly (.NET 3.5 is currently supported) or executed from a command line. This means you can write managed code, compile it into an assembly, and declare the use of that assembly in a management pack, presenting vast possibilities for adding useful console tasks. Implementing custom console tasks does not require writing code; you can use the Create a Task Wizard to create console tasks that execute any type of useful command line, such as executing a custom script or executable.

The next procedure provides an example of creating a custom console task using the Create a Task Wizard. It creates a custom console task that executes a Trace Route command against an affected computer in an incident. Perform the following steps:

1. Go to **Library** - > **Tasks** and launch the Create a Task Wizard by clicking the **Create Task** console task.

2. On the General tab (see Figure 22.21), provide a name and description for the console task. You also must specify a target class; this has several purposes:

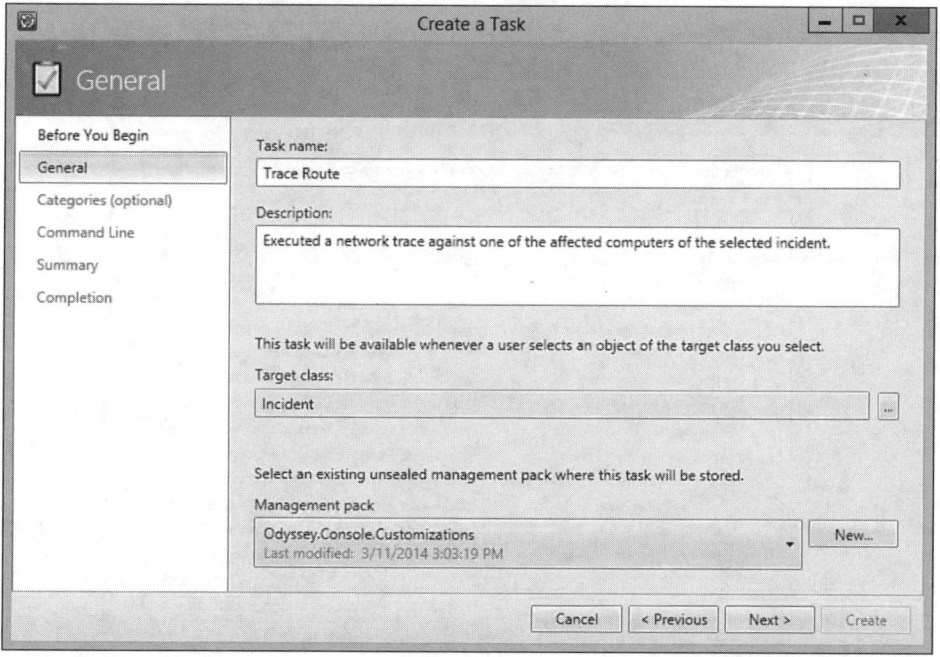

FIGURE 22.21   General tab of the Create a Task Wizard.

▶ It associates the console task in the Service Manager with objects of the target class(es) deriving from the target class. This means the console task is available in the console whenever an object of specified class type is selected.

▶ This enables use of target class properties or properties of classes related to the target's class, as arguments in a command line executed by the console task.

As this example intends to execute a Trace Route against an affected computer of an incident, the `Incident` class is used as the target class.

3. Select a management pack in which to store the console task. Click **Next** to continue.

4. The Categories (optional) tab (see Figure 22.22) enables the task to be added to categories that associate it with folders. This makes the console task visible whenever a specified folder or child folder of the specified folder is selected in the Navigation pane. For example, selecting the Incident Management Folder Tasks category makes the task visible as a task for the Incident Management folder.

   The Trace Route task requires that arguments be passed from a selected incident. As this makes the console task useless in those scenarios when an incident is not selected, this particular example does not choose a category.

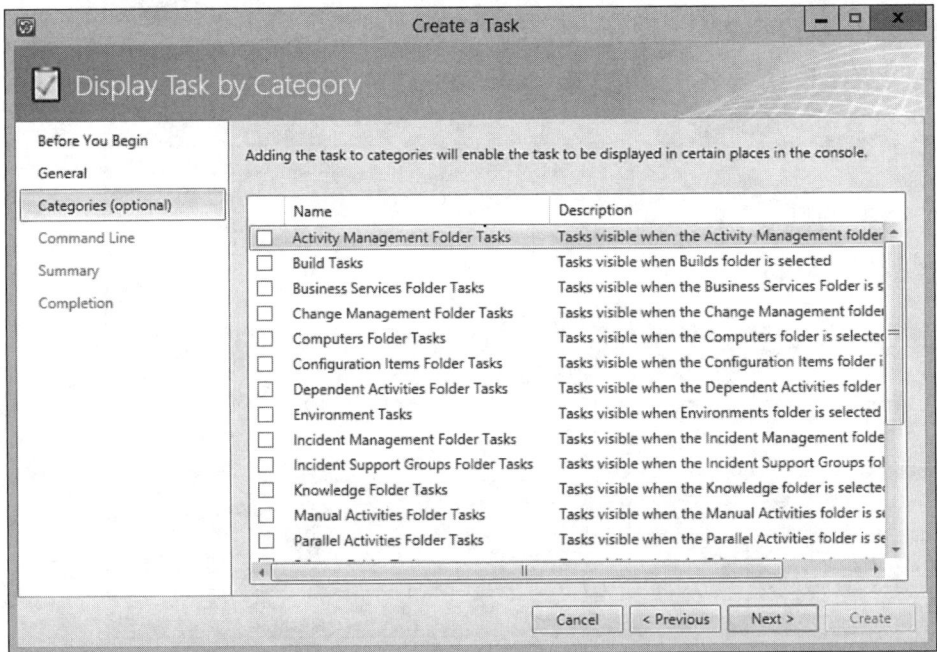

FIGURE 22.22   Selecting categories in the Create a Task Wizard.

5. The Command Line tab shown in Figure 22.23 is where you specify the command to be executed and the arguments that should be passed to the command.

   ▶ **Full path to command:** Specify an executable to execute. This is used in combination with the Working directory option on this page. The Trace Route example executes the command **tracert.exe**.

▶ **Parameters (optional):** This section is used to pass arguments to the specified command. The arguments can be static arguments in the form of text as passed in a command in a console, or an expression pointing to a class property evaluated at runtime.

Selecting **Insert Property** opens the Select Property dialog displayed in Figure 22.24. Use this to select a property from the target class or classes related to the target class and add that as an argument to the command.

The Trace Route example passes the NetBIOS computer name of computers related by the About Configuration Item relationship.

▶ **Working directory (optional):** Specify the folder to use. The Trace Route example executes the command tracert.exe. The working directory can therefore be left at its default value **%windir%\system32**, as this is where tracert.exe is located.

▶ **Log in action log when this task is run:** Specify whether the output should be logged in the action log (such as the incident action log visible in the incident form).

▶ **Show output when this task is run:** Specify whether output should be shown in a pop-up window when the task is executed.

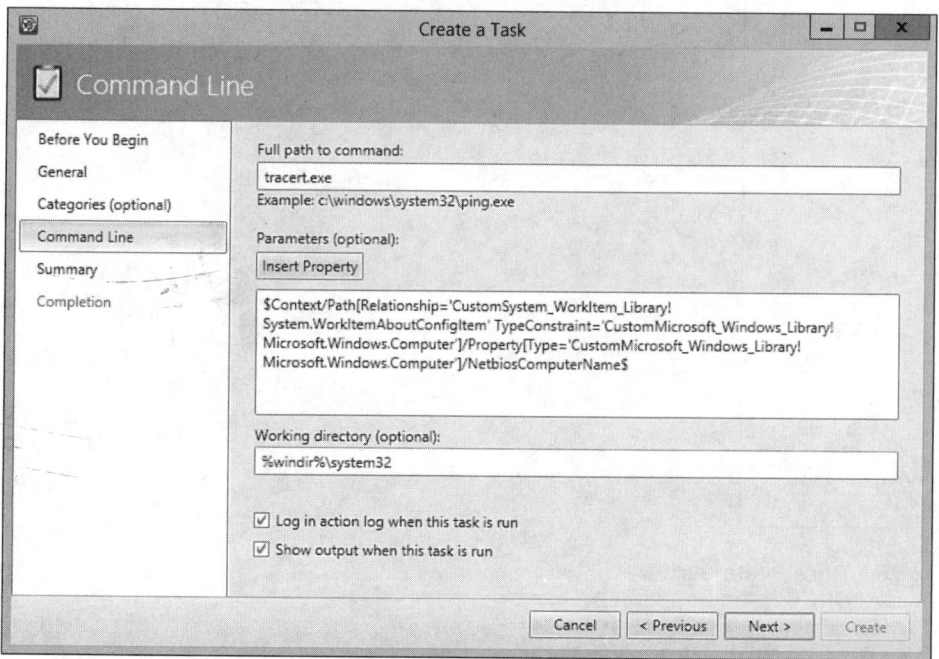

FIGURE 22.23 Command Line tab in the Create a Task Wizard.

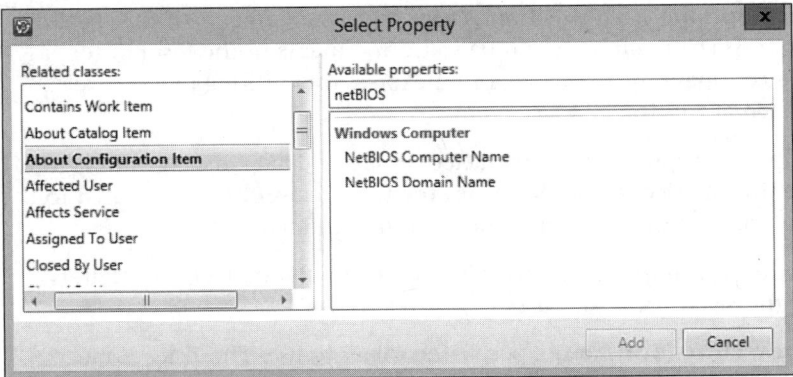

FIGURE 22.24   Selecting a property in the Create a Task Wizard.

Figures 22.25, 22.26, and 22.27 show the result of implementing the console task described in this example.

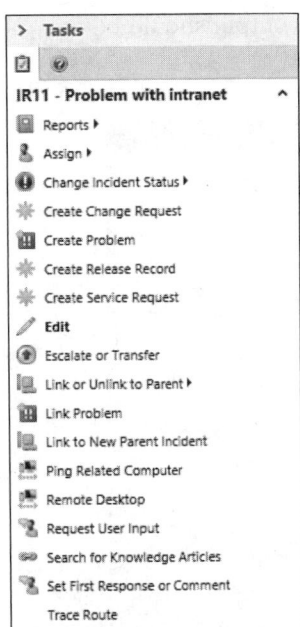

FIGURE 22.25   Trace Route task.

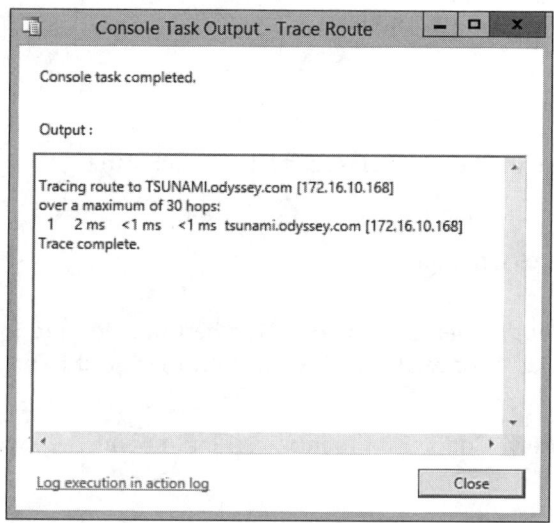

FIGURE 22.26   Trace Route output.

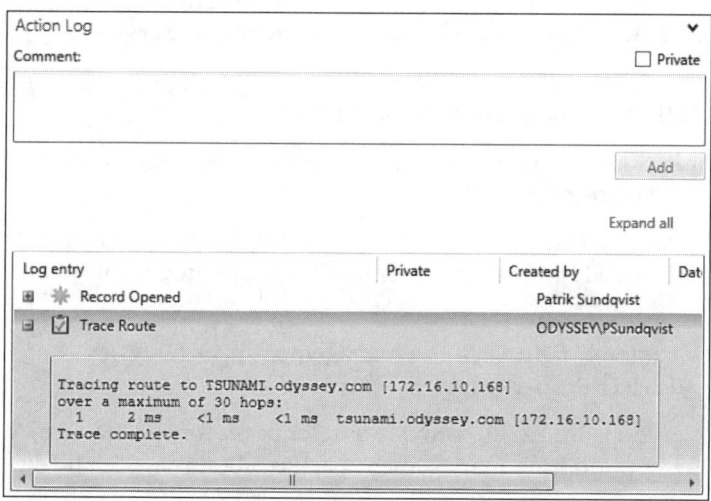

FIGURE 22.27   Trace route action log.

Creating Data Models

Service Manager stores objects as instances of classes. The classes define those properties and relationships you can use to describe an object. At a high level, following are the steps required to create a new data model for Service Manager:

1. Create a management pack in which to store the model.

2. Create classes for the model.

3. Add properties to the classes.

4. Add relationships to the classes to describe how the classes relate to each other.

5. Seal the management pack containing the data model.

6. Import the management pack into Service Manager.

Sealing a management pack containing a data model, or parts of it, is a best practice and is required when there are resources such as classes or relationships within it that need to be referenced.

The next sections describe each step separately; Chapter 23 includes an end-to-end scenario creating a new data model.

Creating a Management Pack

To create a new management pack using the Service Manager Authoring Tool, perform the following steps:

1. To start the Service Manager Authoring Tool, click **Start -> All Programs -> Microsoft System Center 2012 R2 -> Service Manager Authoring -> Service Manager Authoring Tool**.

2. In the Service Manager Authoring Tool, Select **File -> New**.

3. In the New Management Pack dialog, enter a File name for the management pack (an example is displayed in Figure 22.28).

4. In the New Management Pack dialog, click **Save**. The management pack is created by the Authoring Tool and loaded into the Management Pack Explorer, displayed in Figure 22.29.

5. In the Management Pack Explorer, right-click the management pack (Odyssey. Buildings.Library.xml) and select **Properties**.

6. In the Details pane (shown in Figure 22.30), provide a description for the management pack. Providing a description for a management pack is a best practice and recommended by the authors.

7. Now, save the new management pack by selecting **File -> Save All**.

You have now created an unsealed management pack, which you can use for storing customizations.

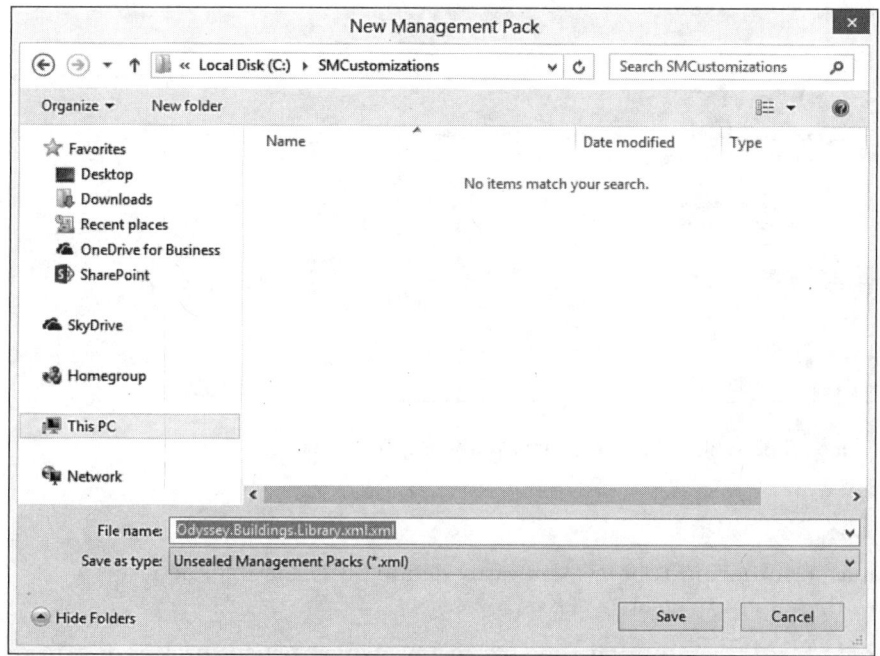

FIGURE 22.28   New Management Pack dialog in Service Manager Authoring Tool.

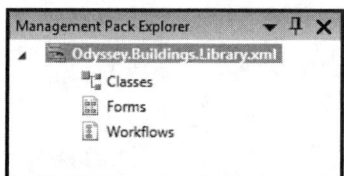

FIGURE 22.29   Management Pack Explorer in Service Manager Authoring Tool.

TIP: DETAILS OF SELECTED ITEM

The Details pane provides the capability to view and change the properties of the currently selected item, whether it is a selected node in the Management Pack Explorer, or a workflow activity in the Workflow Designer.

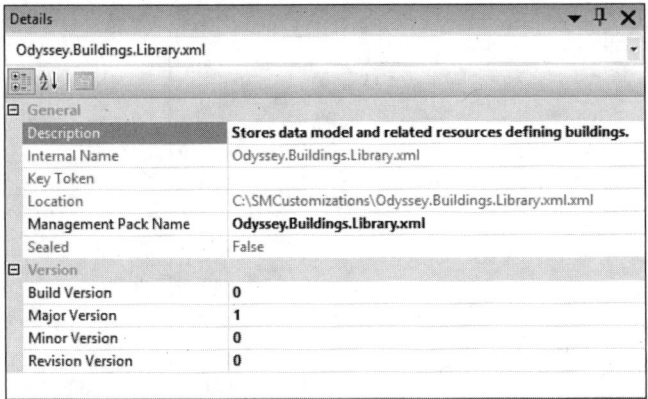

FIGURE 22.30   Details pane in Service Manager Authoring Tool.

Creating a New Class

The Service Manager Authoring Tool lets you easily define new classes for Service
Manager. Follow these steps to create a class:

1. In the Service Manager Authoring Tool, create a new management pack as described
   in the previous section, or open an existing unsealed management pack using **File ->
   Open**.

2. In the Management Pack Explorer, right-click **Classes** and select a base class by
   choosing one of the alternatives.

   ▶ Create Configuration Item Class

   ▶ Create Work Item Class

   ▶ Create Other Class

   Choose the most suitable option for the type of class you are creating. For advice on
   choosing the base class, see the "Choosing a Base Class" section later in this chapter.

3. In the Create class dialog, enter an Internal Name for the class type and click **OK**.
   After adding a new class, all derived properties and relationships are visible in the
   Authoring pane, as shown in Figure 22.31.

4. In the Management Pack Explorer, right-click the new class below the Classes node. Select **Properties**.

5. In the Details pane showing the class type properties (see Figure 22.32), enter a Name and Description for the class type (the Name is the Display Name shown in the Service Manager console).

6. In the Service Manager Authoring Tool, select **File -> Save All** to save the management pack. You can now define the class by adding properties and relationships.

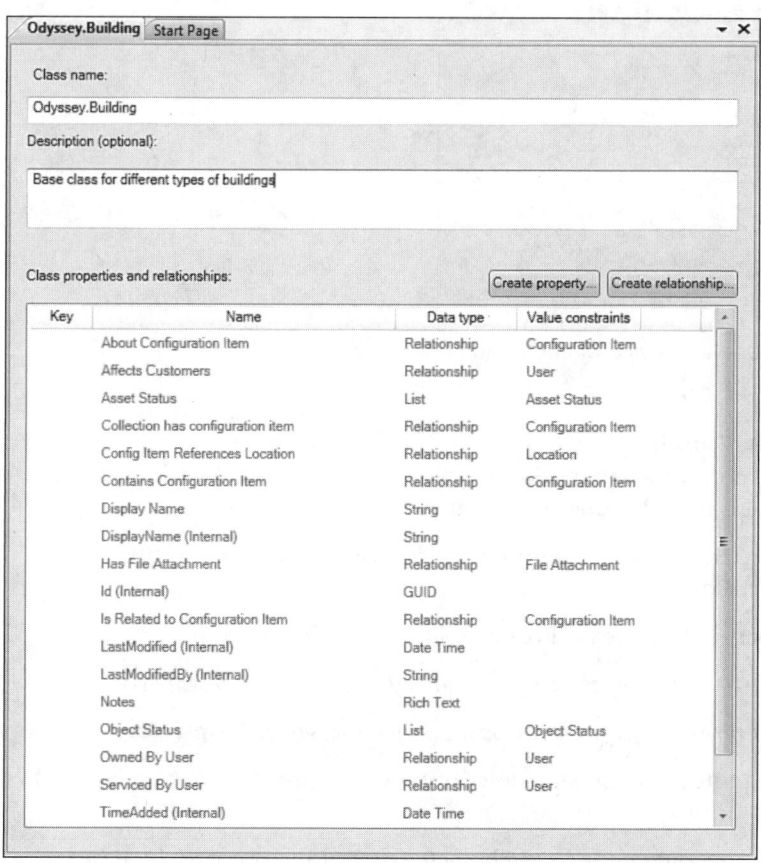

FIGURE 22.31   Authoring pane in Service Manager Authoring Tool.

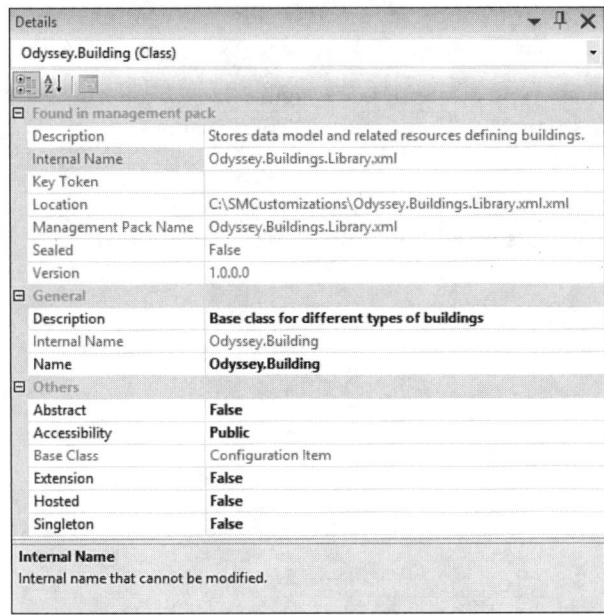

FIGURE 22.32   Details pane in Service Manager Authoring Tool.

Adding Properties and Relationships

After preparing a new class or a class extension in the Service Manager Authoring Tool, follow these following steps to add properties to the class:

1. In the Management Pack Explorer, right-click the class to which you want to add properties and select **Edit**.

2. In the Authoring pane, click **Create Property**.

3. In the Create Property dialog, enter an Internal Name for the new property.

4. Right-click the new property in the Authoring pane, and select **Properties**.

5. In the Details pane, enter a Name and Description of the property. See Figure 22.33 for an example.

   This is also where you would define the characteristics of the property by defining the data type (string, integer, bool, and so on) and suitable constraints. This is discussed in the next section of this chapter.

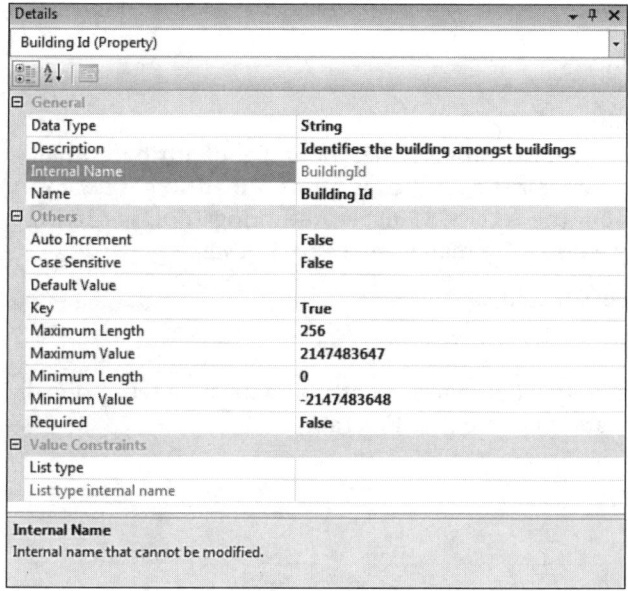

FIGURE 22.33   Property details in the Service Manager Authoring Tool.

Perform the following steps to add relationships:

1. In the Management Pack Explorer, right-click the new class to which you want to add a relationship and select **Edit**.

2. In the Authoring pane, click **Create Relationship**.

3. In the Create Relationship dialog, enter an Internal Name for the relationship and click **OK**.

4. Right-click the newly added relationship in the Authoring pane, and select **Properties**.

5. In the Details pane, enter a Name and Description for the relationship. You can also define the characteristics of the relationship by adding the following relationship attributes:

    ▶ Relationship Type

    ▶ Abstract

    ▶ Source Class

    ▶ Source Class Min Cardinality

    ▶ Source Class Max Cardinality

    ▶ Target Class

▶ Target Class Min Cardinality

▶ Target Class Max Cardinality

Property Characteristics and Constraints

When a new property for a class is defined, the property has a number of attributes that can be specified to provide different characteristics and constraints. All attributes except the RegEx attribute can be specified from the Service Manager Authoring Tool; specifying the RegEx attribute requires manually editing the management pack XML.

The next sections describe the different attributes.

Data Type

To determine the data type of the property value, the Type attribute must be set to one of the supported data types. Supported data types are listed in Table 22.3.

TABLE 22.3   Supported Data Types

Type	Example
Integer	1
Decimal	2.2
Double	2.2
String	Printing Issue
Date Time	3/9/2014
GUID	26b70304-135f-4c77-af26-6bf952cd7caf
Bool	True/False
List	Low/Medium/High (Available values are determined by the value of the List Type attribute, see the "List Type" section for a description.)
Rich Text (formatted text)	The user is having *problem*...
Binary	1011 1001...

Auto Increment   Setting Auto Increment to True causes the property to increase its value by one automatically for each new instance created in the CMDB. Setting Auto Increment is only applicable for data types String and Integer.

Case Sensitive   Marking a property as Case Sensitive makes the property value sensitive for case. This is only applicable for properties of data type String.

Default Value   All properties with a Default Value use the Default Value as their value if another value is not provided.

Key   Setting Key to True makes the property part of the class identity, used to identify an instance uniquely among others; mark a property as Key to make the property required.

Maximum Length   Setting Maximum Length is only applicable for properties of data type String. By specifying a number for Maximum Length, you prevent strings longer than the given value from being stored as property values in the CMDB.

Minimum Length   Setting Minimum Length is only applicable for properties with data type String. Specifying a number for Minimum Length prevents strings shorter than the given value from being stored as property values in the CMDB.

Maximum Value   Setting Maximum Value is only applicable for properties with data type Integer. Specifying a number for Maximum Value prevents values higher than the given value from being stored as property values in the CMDB.

Minimum Value   Setting Minimum Value is only applicable for properties with data type Integer. By specifying a number for Minimum Value, you prevent values lower than the given value from being stored as property values in the CMDB.

Required   Setting the Required attribute to True prevents instances without a given property value from being stored in the CMDB.

List Type   Use of the List Type attribute is only valid for data type List and used to specify which list to tie to the property value. Setting the List Type attribute ensures that only values from the given list are accepted as property values.

RegEx   The RegEx attribute is only valid for data type String and used to enforce that a string stored as a property value follows a given pattern.
In Listing 22.9, the RegEx attribute is given a value of Room [0-9]+. This means that a string stored as a property value in the property RoomName must start with the text Room followed by a whitespace and a number. The + means there can be any number of occurrences of the preceding character (which in this example is a digit between 0 and 9).

LISTING 22.9   Regular Expression Example

```
<Property ID="RoomName" Type="string" RegEx="Room [0-9]+" />
```

TIP: LEARNING MORE ABOUT REGULAR EXPRESSIONS

To learn how to master the regular expression language, see the article at http://msdn. microsoft.com/en-us/library/28hw3sce.aspx, which introduces regular expressions.

List Types

Enumeration, also known as lists in Service Manager, is a special data type available for class type properties. Lists are frequently used as a data type, as it limits the possible values of a property to the list entries. Use this data type if planning to present a user with a list to choose a value from, as seen in the incident form in Figure 22.34.

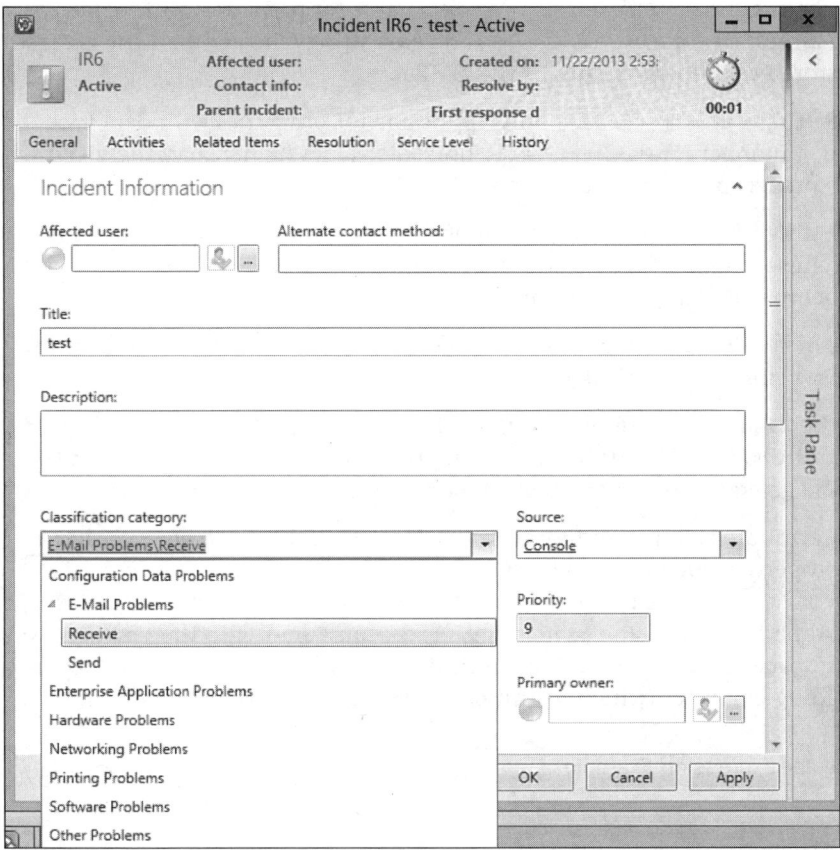

FIGURE 22.34   Example of using List type.

As displayed in the figure, lists in Service Manager have hierarchy (parent-child) support, which makes them even more useful. For example, say you want to describe the location of a server rack. You could either create a list that looks like Listing 22.10 or use a list picker on the computer form for the user to pick a location. Alternatively, you could create new classes for `Buildings`, `Floors`, `Rooms`, and `Racks`, add hosting relationships between these, and use an object picker from the computer form to have the user pick an instance of the rack class to describe the location. The first alternative is easy to implement compared to the second and could probably fulfill the requirements of most scenarios. However, the second and more complex alternative might be a better solution in some scenarios since it provides some advantages, such as

▶ The ability to view all computers in a building, floor, room, or rack

▶ Creating a change request related to a room through derived or added relationships

▶ The ability to create reports based on the different classes

LISTING 22.10   Example of List Hierarchy

```
Building 1
-- Floor 1
---- Room 1
------ Rack 1
-- Floor 2
---- Room 1
------ Rack 1
------ Rack 2
Building 2
```

Perform the following steps to add a property of data type `List` to a class:

1. While adding properties to a new class or extending an existing class, click **Create Property**.

2. In the Create Property dialog, enter an internal name for the property and click **OK**.

3. In the Authoring pane, right-click the new property and click **Details**.

4. In the Details pane, give the property a description and change the data type to **List**.

5. In the Select a list dialog that opens (see Figure 22.35), select the list you want the property to be bound to and click **OK**. If there isn't a suitable list, click **Create List**:

    ▶ In the Create List dialog, enter an internal name, a display name, a description for the new list, and click **Create**.

    ▶ Back in the Select a List dialog, select the new list and click **OK**.

6. Click **File -> Save All** to save the changes to the management pack.

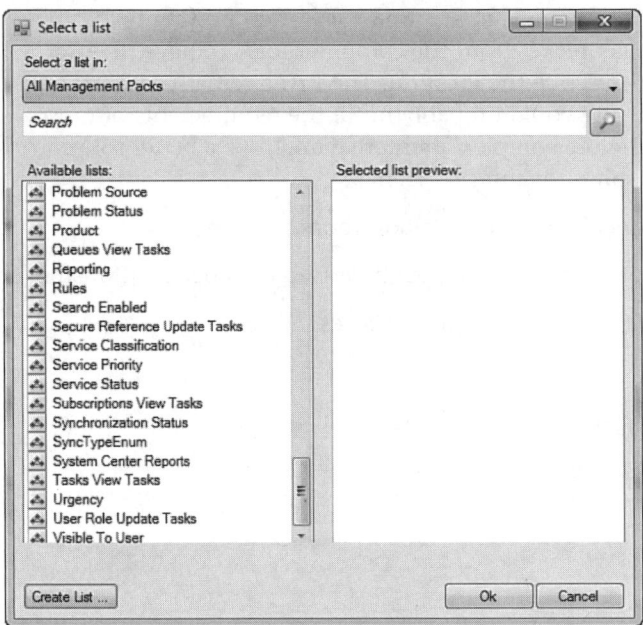

FIGURE 22.35 Select a list dialog in the Service Manager Authoring Tool.

> **NOTE: SEAL MANAGEMENT PACKS WITH DATA MODEL RESOURCES**
>
> Store all data model resources such as class definitions, including relationships and list type definitions (definition of the `List` root element), in sealed management packs.

When the management pack containing the `List` definition is imported into Service Manager, you can add list values using the console. To manage the values of a list, open the Service Manager console and go to **Library -> Lists**. If these are stored in an unsealed management pack, list items you create from the console (in the Library workspace) are automatically stored in the same unsealed management pack. If you seal the management pack where the list definition is stored, creating new list items for the list using the console lets you choose an unsealed management pack in which to store the list items.

Extending an Existing Class

To extend an existing class, perform the following steps:

1. In the Service Manager Authoring Tool, open an existing unsealed management pack or create a new one.

2. In the Management Pack Explorer, right-click the Classes node of the management pack where you want to store the class extension, and select **Create Other Class**.

3. In the Base class dialog shown in Figure 22.36, locate and select the class you want to extend. Select the class, such as `Incident`, and click **OK**.

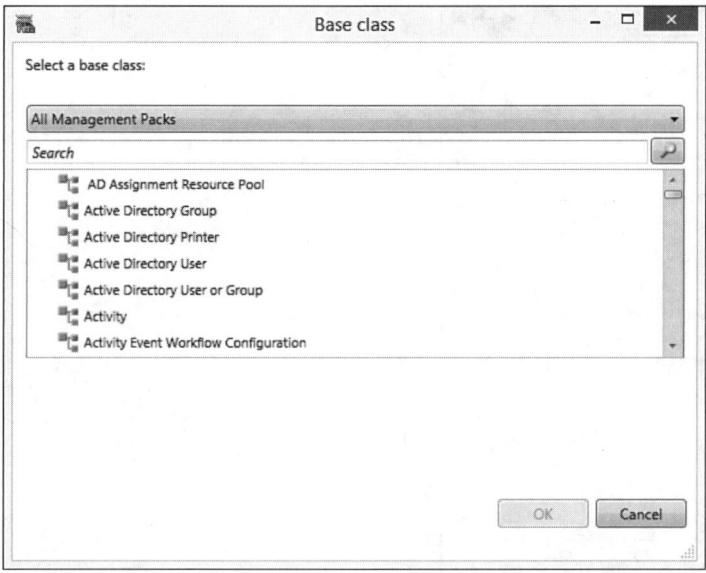

FIGURE 22.36 Selecting a base class in the Service Manager Authoring Tool.

4. In the Create Class dialog, enter an Internal Name for the new class extension.

5. In the Management Pack Explorer, right-click the class node named in step 4 and select **Properties**.

6. In the Details pane, change the value of Extension to **True**, and enter a Name and a Description for the class extension. Figure 22.37 displays an example.

7. In the Service Manager Authoring Tool, select **File -> Save All** to save all changes. The class is now ready to be extended by adding properties and relationships, previously described in the "Adding Properties and Relationships" section of the chapter.

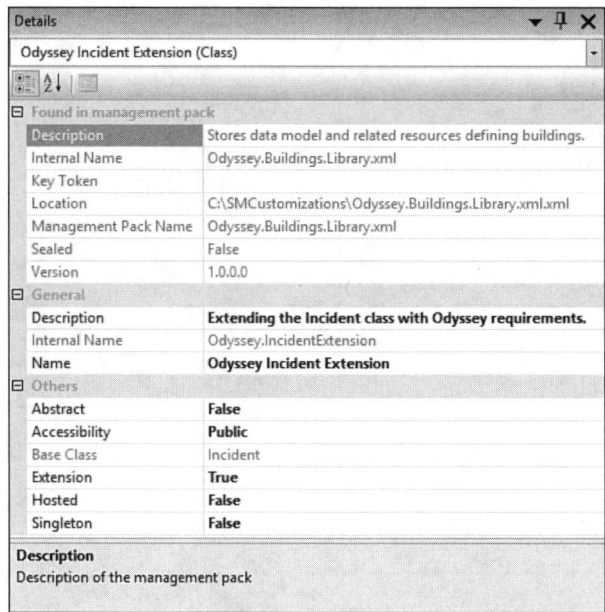

FIGURE 22.37   Details pane showing extension class.

Choosing a Base Class

When choosing a base class, base your decision on the characteristics you want the new class to inherit. All properties and relationships are derived from the base class; the type of object the class describes should be the foundation for selecting a base class with suitable characteristics. Service Manager comes with classes that fulfill the needs of most types, whether describing a physical or logical configuration item (such as a computer or an operating system) or describing a work item (such as a change request).

By reusing existing classes within Service Manager as base classes, your custom classes can gain useful characteristics other than derived data model characteristics such as properties and relationships. Following are some examples:

▶ Reusing existing relationship types enables instances of the new class to be incorporated and managed from a related object's form.

▶ Instances of the new class are included in views targeting derived classes.

The next sections describe the most commonly used base classes.

Work Item

When defining a new work item for the Service Manager CMDB, use the class common for `Incident`, `Problem`, `Change Request`, `Service Request`, `Release Record`, and `Activity`, which is the `Work Item` class (internal name `System.WorkItem`). This provides a good start for defining a new type of work item.

Choosing `Work Item` as base or using a class deriving from the `Work Item` class for a new class enables the use of existing lists of related work items to associate instances of the class with objects such as CIs or existing work items.

Configuration Item

When defining a new configuration item, say a mobile phone, use the common class for all out-of-the-box configuration items called `Configuration Item`. This class has the internal name `System.ConfigItem`.

By deriving from the `Configuration Item` class, you automatically gain the functionality to add instances of the class as related configuration items in the change request form.

Settings

In special cases, you might want to create a class to contain settings used by a workflow, an advanced console task, and so on. In these cases, you can use the `Solution Settings` class (internal name `System.SolutionSettings`) as base. This scenario is also a perfect example of when a class should be marked as singleton, as you commonly only want one instance to exist of such a class. Read about singleton classes in the "Singleton Classes" section, later in this chapter.

Using the `Solution Settings` class, a base class causes instances of the class to appear in the Settings view found in the Administration workspace. This lets you manage all Service Manager-related settings in one place. Figure 22.38 shows how Odyssey Solution Settings displays in the view by just using the `Solution Settings` class as base class.

TIP: PROVIDING A GOOD USER EXPERIENCE FOR CUSTOM SETTINGS

As the Settings view differs from the normal views in the Service Manager console, you must register a task handler to be able to open up custom singleton instances in forms from the Settings view. For more information, see http://blogs.technet.com/b/service-manager/archive/2010/01/04/creating-a-custom-administration-setting.aspx.

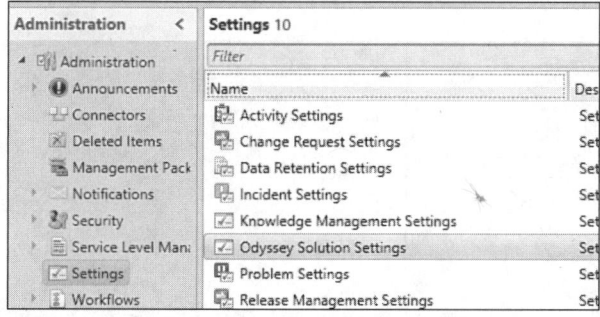

FIGURE 22.38   Settings view in Administration workspace.

Activities

When creating a new type of activity to hold process instructions, such as a manual activity or a review activity, use the `Activity` class (internal name `System.WorkItem.Activity`), which is the base class for both these out-of-the-box activities. Creating a class that derives from the `Activity` class, and adding an object template for that class, makes the template accessible (see Figure 22.39) from the Activity tab in the change request form when using the Add button.

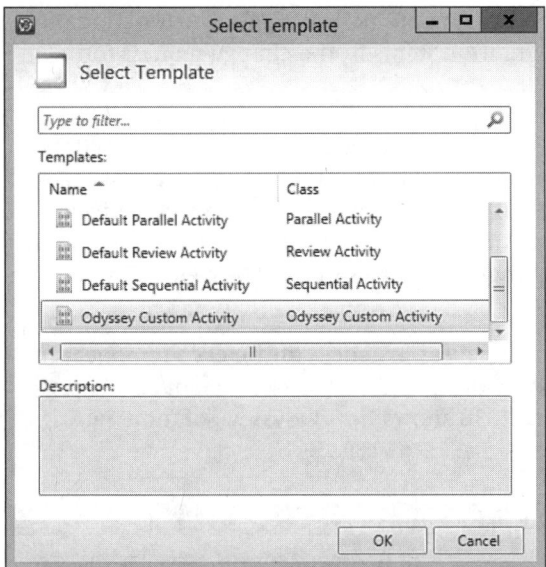

FIGURE 22.39   Template picker showing Odyssey Custom Activity template.

When deriving from the `Activity` class, you can use the Activity Event workflows for automation triggered by events from instances of your custom class (see Figure 22.40).

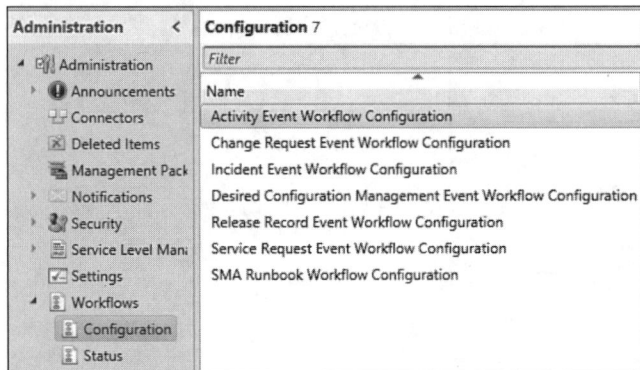

FIGURE 22.40   Activity Event Workflow for custom activities.

22

Singleton Classes

The singleton class type is unique as there is always one, and no more than one, instance of a singleton class. When you import a management pack containing a singleton class, an instance is immediately accessible in the CMDB, where the class GUID (generated on import) and the instance ID are the same. Therefore, you can say "the single instance is the class." A common use for singleton classes is to store settings inside the CMDB, as seen in the Administration -> Settings section in the console.

To create a singleton class, follow the steps in the "Creating a New Class" section earlier in the chapter and mark the class as `Singleton = True` using the Details pane in the Service Manager Authoring Tool.

NOTE: KEY NOT REQUIRED FOR A SINGLETON

A singleton does not require a `Key` property, as there can be only one instance of the class.

Abstract Classes

An abstract class is a class for which no instances can exist. Its primary purpose is to consolidate common characteristics and act as a base class for deriving classes. The common characteristics (properties and relationships) do not always make sense in a standalone way, making it helpful to be able to mark a class as abstract to ensure no instances are created using the class.

Even though an instance cannot be created of an abstract class, abstract classes can be used as targets for views and workflows to make the views and workflows "hit" all instances of classes deriving from the abstract class. For example, this could occur when designing a data model for a car of a specific brand. Create a base class for a car, which contains all properties of a car. Mark it as `Abstract` to make sure a generic car cannot be created. The class would need a new class based on the generic car, such as a `Ford car` class or a `BMW car` class.

To create an abstract class, follow the steps in the "Creating a New Class" section earlier in the chapter and mark the class as `Abstract = True` using the Details pane in the Service Manager Authoring Tool. The two most frequently used abstract classes in the CMDB are `System.WorkItem` (`Work Item`) and `System.ConfigItem` (`Configuration Item`).

Creating Workflows

As you may have noticed throughout this book, there are many types of workflows in Service Manager. Chapter 16, "Managing Notifications," discussed how to use the event workflows configurable within the Service Manager console to notify users and apply object templates. This section discusses how to add custom workflows to Service Manager using the Service Manager Authoring Tool.

Given the number of formations a workflow can have in Service Manager, you can create and add them in a number of ways. At a high level, to implement a custom workflow into Service Manager you must

1. Create a management pack or open an existing (unsealed) management pack to store the workflow.

2. Define the workflow schedule or trigger.

3. Design the workflow using workflow activities.

4. Save the management pack.

5. Deploy the workflow to Service Manager.

Use the Service Manager Authoring Tool to create two types of workflows:

▶ Run at a scheduled time or at scheduled intervals.

▶ Run only when a database object meets specified conditions.

Creating a Scheduled Workflow

Scheduled workflows are useful for performing maintenance jobs within the CMDB. For example, scheduling a workflow to run on an interval lets you check for incidents breaching a specific service level agreement (SLA) and take appropriate action.

To create a scheduled workflow, follow these steps:

1. Open the Service Manager Authoring Tool.

2. Open an existing or create a new management pack.

3. In the Management Pack Explorer, right-click the Workflows node; then select **Create**, as displayed in Figure 22.41.

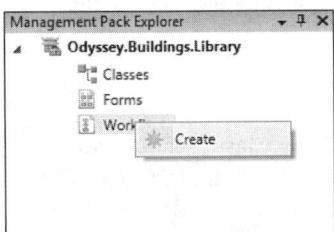

FIGURE 22.41   Creating a workflow in the Service Manager Authoring Tool.

4. In the General tab of the Create Workflow Wizard shown in Figure 22.42, enter a Name and Description (optional), and click **Next**.

    Optionally, click **Advanced** to adjust the retry and timeout limits of the workflow.

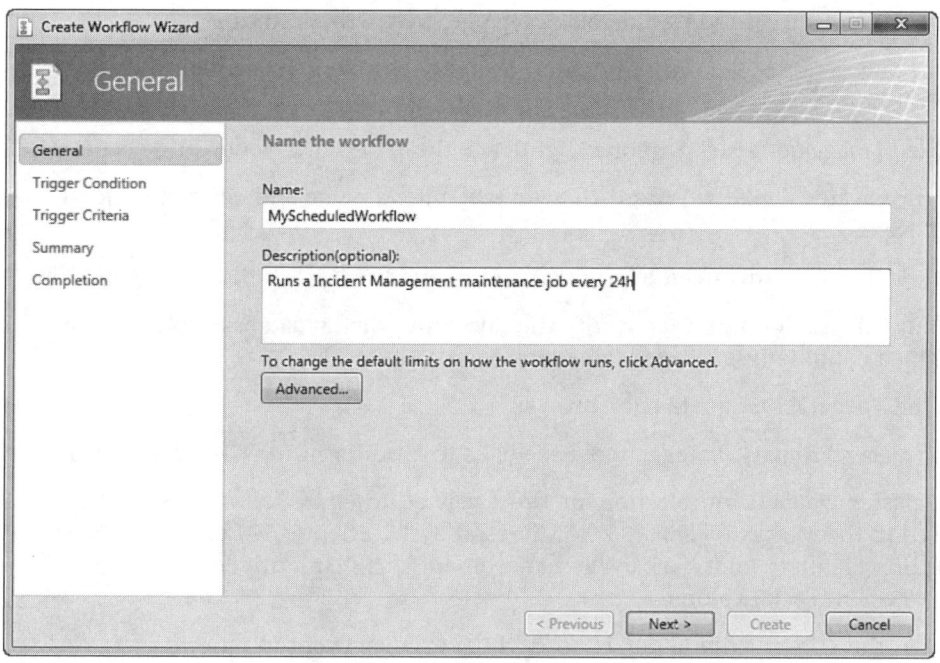

FIGURE 22.42   General tab of the Service Manager Authoring Tool.

5. On the Trigger Condition tab, leave the selection at Run at a scheduled time or at scheduled intervals, and click **Next**.

6. On the Trigger Criteria tab, choose the schedule or interval on which you want to execute the workflow. Click **Next**.

7. On the Summary tab, review the details and click **Create** and then click **Close** on the Completion tab to create the new scheduled workflow.

The Authoring pane now shows the workflow design surface and is ready for you to add workflow activities to the design surface. The "Adding Workflow Activities and Setting Up the Required Properties" section later in the chapter discusses this process.

Creating a Workflow Triggered By a Database Change
Workflows triggered by a database change respond to a given state occurring in the CMDB. As an example, you could use this functionality to automate IT processes based on registration and approval of a standard change. When a manager requests a user account for a new employee, this is normally registered in a service request in the CMDB. When a review activity portion of the service request is approved, the status update can trigger a workflow to create the user account.

To create a workflow triggered by a database change, follow these steps:

1. In the Service Manager Authoring Tool, open an existing management pack or create a new one.

2. In the Management Pack Explorer, right-click the Workflows node and select **Create**.

3. On the Create Workflow Wizard General tab, enter a name and description, and click **Next**.

   Optionally, click **Advanced** to adjust the retry and time out limits of the workflow.

4. On the Trigger Condition tab, verify the Run only when a database object meets specified conditions is selected, and click **Next**.

5. On the Trigger Criteria tab, click **Browse**.

6. In the Class Property dialog, choose the class to monitor in the CMDB and click **OK**.

   The classes available for selection are those classes stored in the management packs placed in the *%ProgramFiles (x86)%*\Microsoft System Center 2012\Service Manager Authoring\Library folder, or in the management packs currently loaded in the Management Pack Explorer.

7. Back at the Trigger Criteria tab, choose which Change Event to monitor:

   ▶ When an object of the selected class is created

   ▶ When an object of the selected class is updated

   ▶ When an object of the selected class is deleted

8. Optionally, you can specify additional criteria by selecting **Additional Criteria** and specifying property values. The following restrictions apply:

   ▶ Additional criteria cannot be specified for Delete Change events.

   ▶ For Create Change events, the additional criteria must be fulfilled by the new object you are creating.

   ▶ For Updated Change events, the criteria can be specified covering both the prechange state (Changed From) and postchange state (Changed To) as seen in Figure 22.43.

   When the criteria have been set, click **Next**.

9. On the Summary tab, review your changes and click **Create** and then click **Close** on the Completion tab to create the workflow.

After the workflow is created, the Authoring pane shows the workflow design surface, and you can add workflow activities to the design surface. This is discussed in the "Adding Workflow Activities and Setting Up the Required Properties" section later in the chapter.

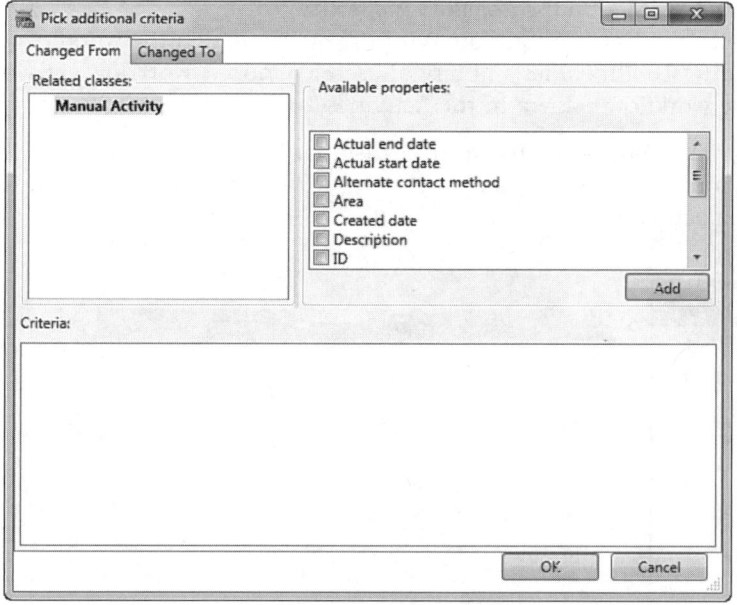

FIGURE 22.43   Specifying additional workflow criteria.

Editing Workflow Details after Creation

To edit workflow details such as the workflow description after creating the workflow, perform the following steps:

1. In the Management Pack Explorer, right-click the workflow you want to edit and select **Details**.

2. In the Details pane, select a property such as Description and click the [...] button shown in Figure 22.44. This opens the Workflow Properties dialog, where you can edit the workflow details.

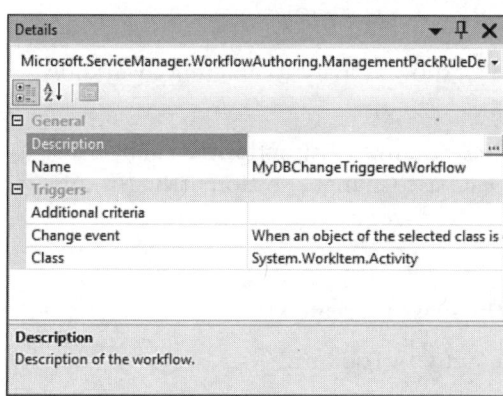

FIGURE 22.44   Workflow Details - Service Manager Authoring Tool.

Adding Workflow Activities and Setting Up the Required Properties

After creating a workflow with the Create Workflow Wizard, you can design the workflow. The Service Manager Authoring Tool includes a library of useful Windows workflow activities you can use to build the workflow, shown in the Activities Toolbox in Figure 22.45.

The Service Manager Authoring Guide, available at http://technet.microsoft.com/en-us/ library/hh542404.aspx, describes the different activities along with instructions for extending the toolbox with custom activities.

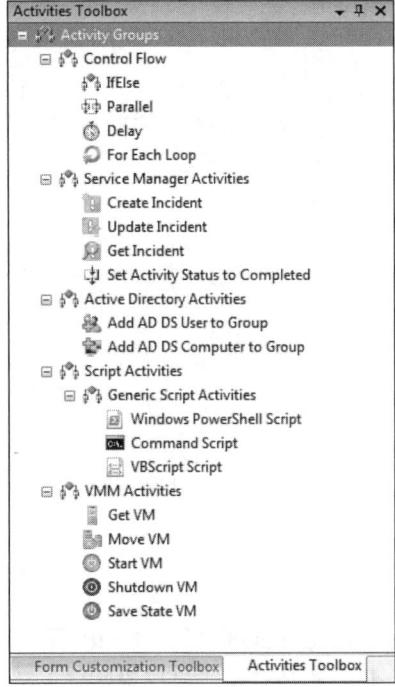

FIGURE 22.45   Activities Toolbox in the Service Manager Authoring Tool.

Following is an example showing how to add a workflow activity to an empty workflow. Perform the following steps:

1. Create a new workflow triggered by a database change (instructions available in the "Creating a Workflow Triggered By a Database Change" section earlier in this chapter) using these trigger criteria:

   ▶ **Class name: Incident**

   ▶ **Change event: When an object of the class is created**

2. Select the **Command Script** activity in the Activity Toolbox.

3. Drag the activity onto the workflow design surface and drop the activity between the start (green arrow) and end point (red circle).

4. In the Authoring pane on the workflow design surface, right-click the newly dropped Command Script activity and select **Details**.

5. In the Details pane, enter the following:

   ▶ **Name: CreateEvent**

   ▶ **Description: Writes Incident ID to the Application Event Log**

6. Still in the Details pane, click the ellipses [...] on the Script Body row.

7. In the Configure a Script Activity, click the down arrow shown in Figure 22.46.

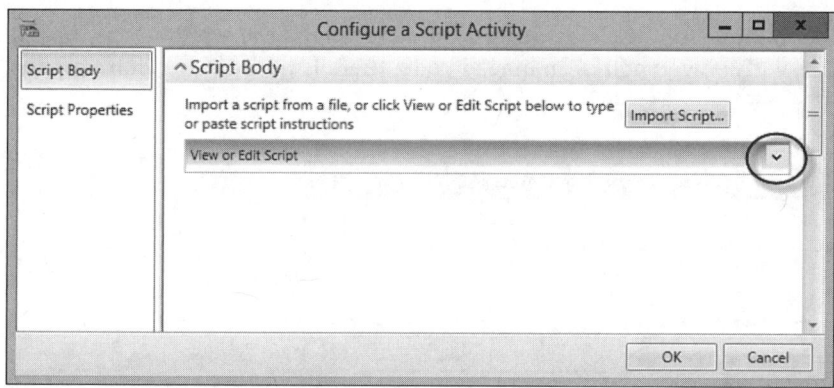

FIGURE 22.46   The Configure a Script Activity dialog.

8. In the Configure a Script Activity dialog, in the area expanded by clicking the down arrow, type

   EventCreate /L Application /T Success /ID 1 /D "The Incident that triggered this workflow has the id: %1"

9. In the Configure a Script Activity dialog, click the **Script Properties** tab.

10. On the Properties tab, click **New**, and then click the ellipses [...] on the new argument row.

11. In the Define input for the Activity dialog, select **Use a class property**.

12. In the Define input for the Activity dialog, select the ID property as shown in Figure 22.47, and click **OK**.

13. In the Configure a Script Activity dialog, click **OK**.

14. In the Service Manager Authoring Tool, click **File -> Save All** to save the management pack and compile the workflow into an assembly.

15. Deploy the workflow using the instructions in the next section of this chapter.

After the workflow is successfully deployed, follow these steps to test the workflow:

1. In the Service Manager console, navigate to **Work Items -> Incident Management** and select the **Create Incident** task.

2. Enter required details and click **OK**.

3. On the Service Manager management server responsible for workflows, click **Start -> All Programs -> Administrative Tools -> Event Viewer**.

4. In the Event Viewer, open the Application log and look for an event with source `EventCreate`.

This example used properties from the class instance that triggered the workflow as input. You can combine this with PowerShell or managed code; there is no limit to what you can automate.

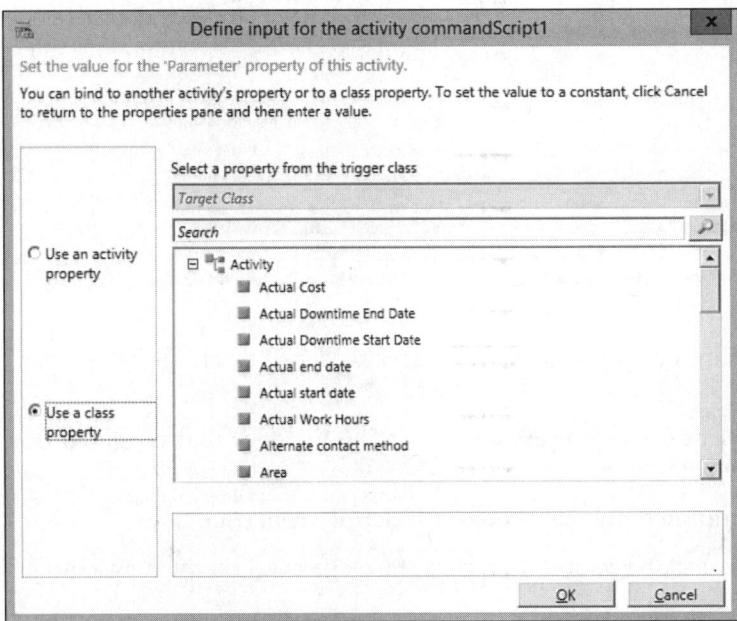

FIGURE 22.47   Define input for the activity dialog.

Deploying Custom Workflows

With the custom workflow built, it can be deployed to the Service Manager management server. Perform the following steps to deploy a custom workflow built using the Service Manager Authoring Tool:

1. While still in the Service Manager Authoring Tool, click **File -> Save All** to save the management pack and compile all workflows to assemblies.

2. Go to the folder where the management pack is saved, and copy the assembly with the same name as the workflow created in the Service Manager Authoring Tool.

3. Paste the assembly into the Service Manager 2012 installation folder, typically *%ProgramFiles%*\Microsoft System Center 2012 R2\Service Manager on the Service Manager management server responsible for workflows.

4. Open the Service Manager console and navigate to **Administration -> Management Packs**.

5. Click **Import**.

6. In the Select Management Packs to Import dialog, select the management pack to import and click **Open**.

7. In the Import Management Packs dialog, click **Import** followed by **Close**.

TIP: IF THINGS GO BAD WHEN COMPILING THE WORKFLOW

If there are problems compiling the workflow in the Service Manager Authoring Tool, click **View** and select **Output** to see the compiler output. This is the best place to look for errors caused when compiling workflows.

Customizing Service Manager Forms

After creating new classes, you can create forms to manage instances of the classes in the Service Manager console. Since Service Manager includes the generic form, you do not always need to create a form after creating a class. The "Generic Form" section earlier in the chapter describes how the generic form is used when Service Manager is not aware of the existence of a specific form for a class. As the form automatically generates fields for all simple properties, you may decide to use it to create and manage instances of a custom class if the presentation demands are not too high. However, if there are higher demands for presentation or the generic form cannot deliver the functional requirements, you can create new forms using the Service Manager Authoring Tool, Visual Studio 2013, or Expression Blend.

In addition to being able to use the Service Manager Authoring Tool to create new forms for new classes, you can use it to customize existing out-of-the-box forms. Using the Authoring Tool, you can "record" changes of a form into a management pack and import those into Service Manager. When the form is opened, Service Manager checks for customizations and applies these on top of the form by replaying all customizations before the form is visible to the user.

Forms must target a type projection instead of a simple class to be able to show data on related objects. When using the Service Manager Authoring Tool to create a new form, the tool creates a type projection automatically if a control such as a User Picker is bound to a related object using the tool. This means that when you use the Authoring Tool to create the new form, you generally need not be concerned with type projections.

The following sections discuss how to create a new form for a custom class and customize an existing form.

Creating New Forms

As mentioned in the previous section, you can create new forms using the Service Manager Authoring Tool, Visual Studio 2013, or Expression Blend. There are some differences in what you can accomplish with the Service Manager Authoring Tool versus the two other tools.

The Service Manager Authoring Tool supports drag-and-drop to add controls. The tool provides a way to bind the values between the control and the underlying data model, consisting of the targeted class or type projection, through a user-friendly binding dialog (see Figure 22.48). The binding dialog makes it easy to bind a control such as a text box to a property in your data model.

However, the Authoring Tool limits you from doing much more than that. You can control visibility and binding mode (more on this in the example in this section that creates a new form), but performing more advanced customization requires Visual Studio.

Using Visual Studio or Expression Blend you can add validation data and visual feedback of that validation result directly in the presentation layer. These also enable use of "code behind" to do things such as validating data against custom logic before submitting the data to the CMDB. Both tools enable use of the full range of controls available for WPF, including custom controls. Using Visual Studio to create new forms lets you do virtually anything with the form, only limited by the capabilities of those resources performing the development. Visual Studio has the added advantage of being able to create all parts of the management pack, while Expression Blend only supports developing the form itself. While the Authoring Tool enables someone unfamiliar with development or Visual Studio to easily create new forms, Visual Studio 2013 and Expression Blend development necessitate using a developer who is familiar with WPF development. Chapter 23 contains information about creating a custom form using Visual Studio 2013.

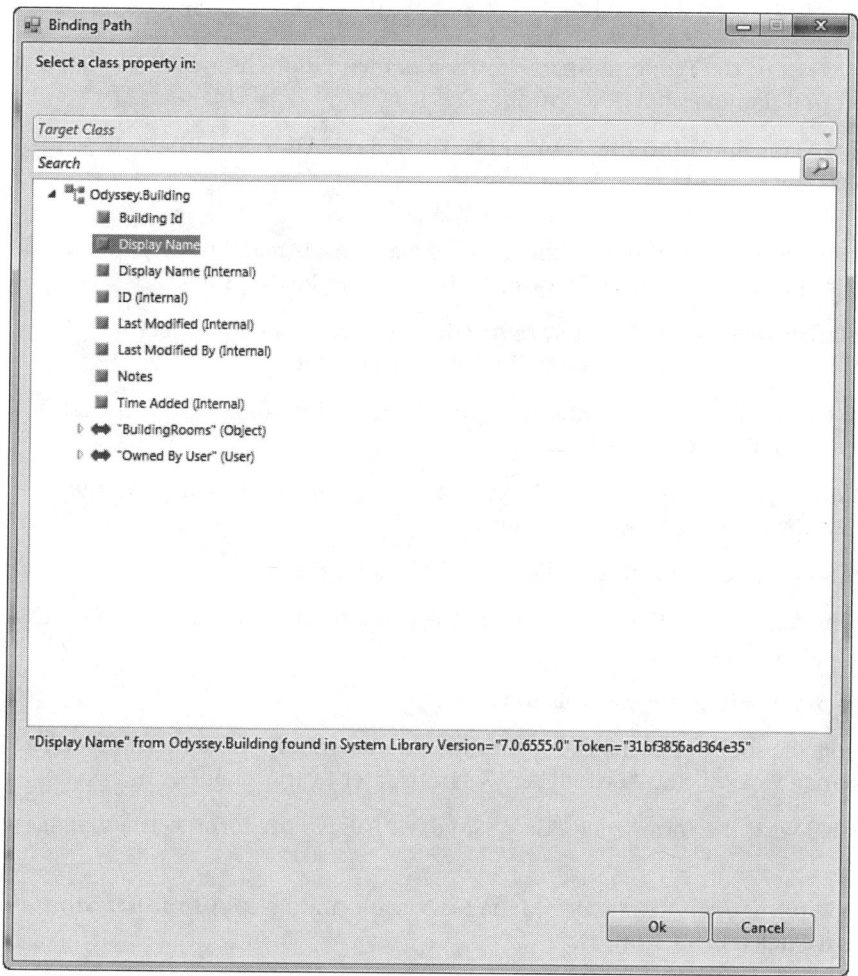

FIGURE 22.48   Binding dialog in the Service Manager Authoring Tool.

To create a new form with the Service Manager Authoring Tool, follow these steps:

1. In the Service Manager Authoring Tool, open an existing management pack or create a new one in which to store the new form.

2. In the Management Pack Explorer, right-click the **Forms** node in the management pack where you want to store the form and select **Create**.

3. In the Choose Base Class dialog, select the base class for the form and click **OK**. Choosing the base class associates the form to the chosen class and tells the Service Manager console to use this form to display data from instances of that class.

4. In the Create Form dialog, enter an internal name for the form and click **Create**. The Authoring pane opens a form design surface for the new form.

5. In the Management Pack Explorer, right-click the new form and select **Properties**.

   As a best practice, in the Properties pane, enter a name (a more user-friendly name than the internal name) and a description.

6. In the Service Manager Authoring Tool, click **File -> Save All** to save the new form to the management pack.

A new form has now been created for the chosen base class and is ready to be populated with controls. To add controls to the new form, perform the following steps:

1. Using the Management Pack Explorer, right-click the new form and select **Customize**. The Authoring pane opens the form design surface.

2. In the Form Customization Toolbox, select and drag the Text Box control onto the Authoring pane, showing the new form.

3. In the Authoring pane, select the new Text Box control and verify you have the Details pane showing the properties of the selected control.

4. In the Details pane, click the ellipses [...] on the Binding Path row.

5. In the Binding path dialog that opens, select the property that you want to bind the text box to and click **OK**.

6. Repeat steps 3-5 to add more controls to the form.

   Some controls require special instructions; these are described in the "User Picker," "Single Instance Picker," and "List Picker" sections later in this chapter.

7. When satisfied with the form, click **File -> Save All** to save the form to the management pack.

8. To deploy the form, open the Service Manager console and go to **Administration -> Management Packs**. Click **Import**.

9. In the Select Management Packs to Import dialog box, select the management pack to import and click **Open**.

10. In the Import Management Packs dialog, click **Import** and then click **Close**.

Customizing Built-in Forms

You can use the Authoring Tool to customize out-of-the-box forms. To customize a form, perform the following steps:

1. Open the Service Manager Authoring Tool. Verify the Form Browser is visible. If not, click **View -> Form Browser**.

2. In the Form Browser, search for and select the form you want to customize.

3. Right-click the form in the Form Browser, and then select **View**. This adds the management pack hosting the form to the Management Pack Explorer.

4. In the Management Pack Explorer, right-click the form you want to customize and select **Customize**.

5. In the Target Management Pack dialog, select a management pack into which to store the form customizations and click **OK**. (You can create a new management pack or browse for an existing one.)

6. In the Management Pack Explorer, right-click the form you want to customize and select **Customize**. The name of the management pack ends with (Customized).

7. In the Authoring pane showing the form to be customized, add new controls as described in the "Creating New Forms" section earlier in this chapter.

8. In the Authoring pane, select the existing controls and make required modifications using the Details pane.

9. After customizing the form, click **File** -> **Save All** to save your changes to the management pack.

10. Import the management pack containing the form customizations to Service Manager to begin using the customized forms.

TIP: ACTIVE TAB ON A CUSTOMIZED FORM

When customizing forms that contain tabs, the tab where the last recorded modification took place is the one that is selected when opening the customized form in the console.

User Picker

A user picker binds user objects to the class instance currently being managed by the form. It lets you search for a user and updates the targeted relationship with the selected user object.

Perform the following steps to add a user picker to a form:

1. In the Form Customization Toolbox, select and drag the User Picker control onto the Authoring pane, showing the new form.

2. In the Authoring pane, select the new User Picker control and confirm the Details pane shows the properties of the selected control.

3. In the Details pane, click the ellipses [...] on the Binding Path row.

4. In the Binding path dialog box that appears, select the relationship you want to manage using the User Picker control and click **OK**.

The User Picker control only lets you choose relationships that have a source object class user and source max cardinality of 1 or target object class of User and a target max cardinality of 1.

Single Instance Picker

A single instance picker is used to bind objects to each other using relationships. The control lets you choose an instance of a given class and adds that as the related object.

Perform the following steps to add a single instance picker to a form:

1. In the Form Customization Toolbox, select and drag the Single Instance Picker control onto the Authoring pane, showing the new form.

2. In the Authoring pane, select the new Single Instance Picker control and confirm the Details pane shows the properties of the selected control.

3. In the Details pane, click the ellipses [...] on the Instance Type row.

4. In the Select a class dialog, choose the class you want to use as a constraint for the Single Instance Picker and click **OK**. The control only shows instances of a given type when used to select an instance.

5. In the Details pane, click the ellipses button [...] on the Binding Path.

6. In the Binding path dialog box that appears, select the relationship you want to bind the control to, and click **OK**.

The Single Instance Picker control only lets you choose relationships that have a source object class of specified type (or derives from that type) and source max cardinality of 1 or target object class of specified type (or derives from that type) and a target max cardinality of 1.

List Picker

A list picker is used to manage properties of data type `List`. To add a list picker to a form, follow these steps:

1. In the Form Customization Toolbox, select and drag the List Picker control onto the Authoring pane, showing the new form.

2. In the Authoring pane, select the new List Picker control and verify the Details pane shows the properties of the selected control.

3. In the Details pane, click the ellipses [...] on the Binding Path row.

4. In the Binding path dialog that pops up, select the list property you want to bind the control to and click **OK**.

The Single Instance Picker control only lets you choose properties of data type `List`, for obvious reasons.

For a description of other controls such as the Tab Control available in the Form Customization Toolbox, see the Service Manager Authoring Guide at http://technet.microsoft.com/en-us/library/hh542404.aspx.

Alternative Way to Add Controls to a Form

The Service Manager Authoring Tool provides an alternative approach for adding controls to a form, rather than dragging controls from the Form Customization Toolbox. When a form design surface is visible in the Authoring pane, select the form by clicking the design surface. Ensure the Class browser is visible (if not, click **View -> Class Browser**). When a form is selected in the Authoring pane, the Class Browser automatically shows the form's base class and related classes. By selecting a property from the base class or a related class and dragging that onto the form design surface in the Authoring pane, the Authoring Tool automatically chooses an appropriate control and sets the binding path of the control to the dragged property. Dragging a node representing a related object (seen in Figure 22.49) causes the Authoring Tool to create a user picker on the form design surface and automatically sets the binding path of the control.

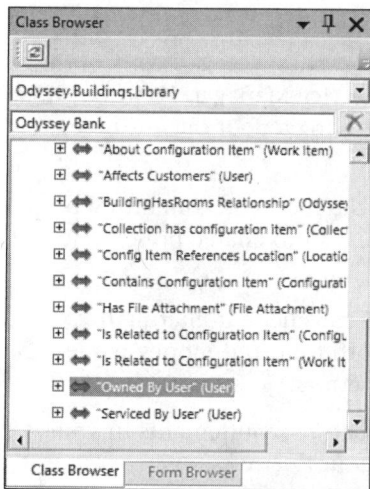

FIGURE 22.49   Class Browser in Service Manager Authoring Tool.

Fast Track

Basic customization and authoring are similar in Service Manager 2012 to Service Manager 2010. This eases the job of converting old customizations to be compatible with Service Manager 2012.

The primary improvement in authoring is the new Visual Studio extension known as Authoring Extensions, used to develop more advanced management packs and described in detail in Chapter 23.

Summary

There are a number of items to consider when planning for customization. Following are key areas to remember:

▶ Different types of relationships can affect how permissions are cloned from object to object. A user given permission on one object type can end up having permissions on a related object.

▶ Having resources in a sealed management pack enables referencing those resources in other management packs. For example, this enables adding new properties through the concept of class extensions in a third-party management pack.

▶ Sealing a management pack protects the content of the management pack, as it cannot be changed by anyone except the key owners without changing the identity of the management pack.

▶ By using constraints when defining class types and properties, you can control the characteristics and thus the quality of data stored in Service Manager. However, it may be a better approach to validate data in the UI, leaving a door open for scenarios where the constraints end up being a problem.

▶ Type projections must be defined to enable creating search criteria containing properties of related objects. Type projections are also necessary to enable presentation of properties of related objects in views and forms.

▶ Locate the real cost drivers regarding IT processes and consider automating these using the Service Manager workflow engine to save both time and money while increasing quality by removing the chance of human errors.

▶ When planning to automate IT tasks, include infrastructure requirements in your plan in terms of firewall configuration and service account permissions.

This chapter also discussed the specifics of less advanced customizations for Service Manager. It went through the steps required for implementing the different customizations, from customizing the console with new views and console tasks to creating classes, workflows, and forms. Chapter 23 takes this discussion to a deeper level.

Advanced Customization Scenarios

The complexity of customizing Service Manager varies based on the type of project under consideration. Chapter 22, "Customizing Service Manager," describes the fundamental concepts necessary for basic customization scenarios. This chapter utilizes the concepts discussed in that chapter, provides a data modeling example, and describes several techniques for custom views. It describes how to create console tasks using PowerShell, and discusses how to create a complete management pack using Visual Studio Authoring Extensions (VSAE), including custom views and a custom form.

The online content available for this book includes a management pack containing the custom classes, relationship, view, and form built using the detailed instructions in this chapter. Appendix C, "Available Online," provides details.

TIP: ABOUT VISUAL STUDIO AUTHORING EXTENSIONS

VSAE, an extension to Visual Studio 2012 and 2013, lets you develop management packs in Visual Studio. VSAE is available for download at http://www.microsoft.com/en-us/download/details.aspx?id=30169.

VSAE works directly with management pack content and allows you to create any management pack element. It provides eXtended Markup Language (XML) templates and includes IntelliSense for different management pack elements, so you do not need to have detailed knowledge of the management pack schema. You can create XML fragments containing different management pack elements, which can be copied within the management pack project or to another management pack project. The fragments are merged into a management pack when you build the solution.

This chapter uses Visual Studio 2013, although both versions of Visual Studio provide the same options for using VSAE.

Creating Console Tasks Using PowerShell

There are many ways to use PowerShell in Service Manager. You can create workflows, query for information, or launch PowerShell scripts through console tasks. This section describes creating PowerShell console tasks.

Service Manager console tasks are created using a wizard started from the Tasks folder in the Library workspace. Following are items to consider when integrating PowerShell scripts into your console tasks:

▶ **Task being executed:** This is the desired action executed by the task and could be an interaction with the work item or a PowerShell script that reads information from the work item and uses that information to interact with other services.

▶ **PowerShell script:** The console script executes a PowerShell script.

  ▶ Make sure that the PowerShell modules used in the script are available on the system where the task is launched.

  ▶ Consider a similar folder structure for storing the scripts on all your management servers. Console tasks use a working directory (folder); for the task to execute successfully, this must be similar for all management servers from where the task is launched.

▶ **Console task creation:** The Create Task task starts a wizard to create a console task.

  ▶ The console task executes the Powershell.exe command.

  ▶ The Parameters section specifies the script to execute and its parameters. Work item properties can be added similar to when you create notification templates or workflows.

  ▶ The working directory is the folder on the management server where the script is saved.

  ▶ Specify logging in the action log of the work item, or show the output of the command.

The example discussed in this section creates a console task that executes a script prompting the user for a reason to force the status of the currently selected incident to a status of Active. As the full .NET Framework can be used from a PowerShell script, you can render your own forms from the script and interact with the user running the task. The PowerShell script used in this example, shown in Listing 23.1, includes the commands to create the form and update the selected incident status. For your convenience, this script, ForceActivate.ps1, is available as online content for the book. See Appendix C for details.

The PowerShell script requires that the community-developed Service Manager PowerShell cmdlets (SMLets) are installed on the machines where the console task is used. For information on SMLets, see http://smlets.codeplex.com/.

LISTING 23.1 PowerShell Script to Force Incident Status to Active

```powershell
param($ID)
Import-Module SMLets -Force

[void] [System.Reflection.Assembly]::LoadWithPartialName("System.Drawing")
[void] [System.Reflection.Assembly]::LoadWithPartialName("System.Windows.Forms")

$objForm = New-Object System.Windows.Forms.Form
$objForm.Text = "Force Incident Status"
$objForm.Size = New-Object System.Drawing.Size(400,200)
$objForm.StartPosition = "CenterScreen"

$objForm.KeyPreview = $True
$objForm.Add_KeyDown({if ($_.KeyCode -eq "Enter")
    {$x=$objTextBox.Text;$objForm.Close()}})
$objForm.Add_KeyDown({if ($_.KeyCode -eq "Escape")
    {$objForm.Close()}})

$OKButton = New-Object System.Windows.Forms.Button
$OKButton.Location = New-Object System.Drawing.Size(125,120)
$OKButton.Size = New-Object System.Drawing.Size(75,23)
$OKButton.Text = "OK"
$OKButton.Add_Click({$x=$objTextBox.Text;$objForm.Close();$result="OK"})
$objForm.Controls.Add($OKButton)

$CancelButton = New-Object System.Windows.Forms.Button
$CancelButton.Location = New-Object System.Drawing.Size(200,120)
$CancelButton.Size = New-Object System.Drawing.Size(75,23)
$CancelButton.Text = "Cancel"
$CancelButton.Add_Click({$objForm.Close()})
$objForm.Controls.Add($CancelButton)

$objLabel = New-Object System.Windows.Forms.Label
$objLabel.Location = New-Object System.Drawing.Size(10,20)
$objLabel.Size = New-Object System.Drawing.Size(360,20)
$objLabel.Text = "Please enter a reason for forcing the incident status to Active:"
$objForm.Controls.Add($objLabel)

$objTextBox = New-Object System.Windows.Forms.TextBox
$objTextBox.Location = New-Object System.Drawing.Size(10,40)
$objTextBox.Size = New-Object System.Drawing.Size(360,60)
$objTextBox.Multiline = "True"
$objForm.Controls.Add($objTextBox)
```

```
$objForm.Topmost = $True

$objForm.Add_Shown({$objForm.Activate()})
[void] $objForm.ShowDialog()

if($result -eq "OK")
{
    Set-SCSMIncident -ID $ID -Status Active
    Write-Host "Incident status forced to Active"
    if($x -gt 0)
    {
        Write-Host "Reason for action: $x"
    }
    else
    {
        Write-Host "No reason provided"
    }
}
else
{
    Write-Host "Force to active status aborted"
}
```

Follow these steps to prepare the script:

1. Create a folder named C:\Customizations if one does not already exist.

2. Create a file named ForceActivate.ps1 in the folder created in step 1.

3. Open the file, and then copy and paste the PowerShell script from Listing 23.1 (or download from the online content for this book, see Appendix C for details). Save and close the file.

Perform the following steps to create the console task:

1. In the Service Manager console, navigate to **Library** -> **Tasks**.

2. In the Tasks pane, select **Create Task**.

3. In the Create a Task Wizard, click **Next** to begin creating the console task.

4. Perform the following actions on the General tab of the wizard:

   ▶ Enter the name **Force Activate**.

   ▶ Browse and select **Incident** as the Target class.

▶ Select **New** to create a new management pack. (Alternatively, if you already have a suitable management pack for storing the console task you can use that management pack.) In the Create Management Pack dialog, enter the name **Odyssey.Customization.Configuration** and click **OK**.

Click **Next**.

5. On the Categories (optional) tab, select **Incident Management Folder Tasks** and click **Next**.

6. On the Command Line tab:

   ▶ Enter **powershell.exe** in the field for Full path to command.

   ▶ Enter **&'.\ForceActivate.ps1'** in the Parameters text box. (There should be a space after the ps1'.)

   ▶ Select **Insert Property**.

In the Select Property dialog, enter **ID** in the search box as displayed in Figure 23.1.

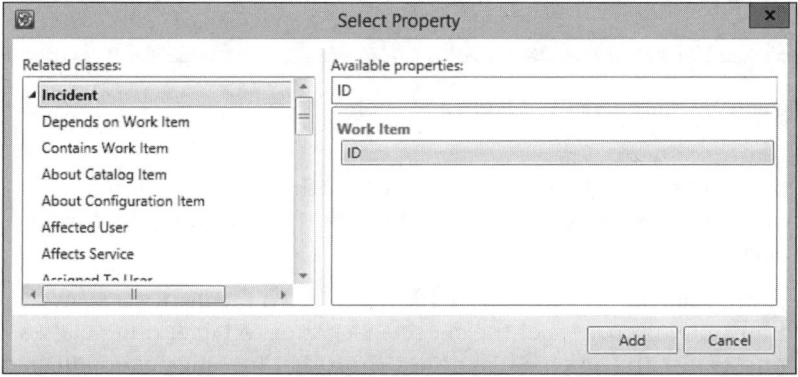

FIGURE 23.1   Inserting a property value as an argument in a console task.

Select **ID** and click **Add**.

   ▶ Set the Working directory to **C:\Customizations**.

   ▶ Check both **Log in action log when this task is run** and **Show output when this task is run**.

Verify that the Command Line tab looks like Figure 23.2 and click **Next**.

7. On the Summary tab, click **Create** followed by **Close** to complete creating the console task.

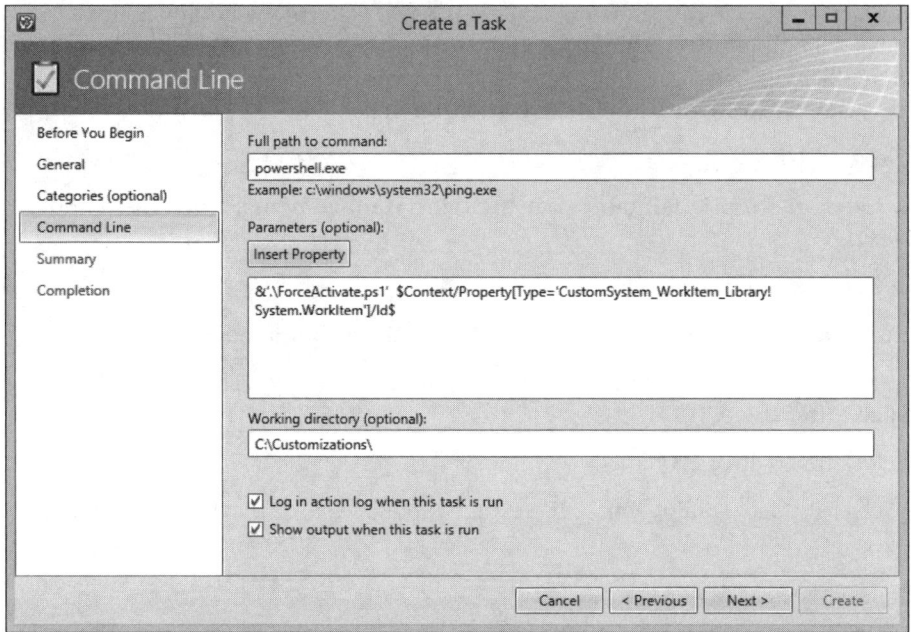

FIGURE 23.2   Inserting console task command and parameters.

To verify the console task works properly, select an incident with a status of Closed. Run the Force Activate console task and confirm that the status changes with the reason recorded in the action log.

This is an example of a task that changes a property for the selected incident. You can use the same approach for other properties of the `Incident` class or to target other classes. You could also use a console task to launch a diagnostic script that investigates an affected configuration item (CI) when an incident is created. There are many scenarios where PowerShell console tasks are useful. Creating these console tasks brings the power of PowerShell to the Service Manager console.

Using Custom Data Models

You can create or customize data models in Service Manager. Data models were introduced in Chapter 4, "Looking Inside System Center 2012 Service Manager."

To explain the concept of data modeling, this section discusses how to create a data model that describes different types of buildings in the Service Manager database. The example is a simplified version of how a real model would look; its purpose is to show what you can do in Service Manager, rather than to show how to define a perfect model for buildings.

Before creating a new model, you should identify its requirements. This example identifies several common properties between different types of buildings that the model should describe. All buildings should have these common properties, regardless of type, location, and so on. The common properties follow:

▶ ID

▶ Description

▶ Address

▶ City

▶ State

▶ ZIP Code

In addition to these common properties, several relationships are identified as common for all types of buildings:

▶ The building should define an owner that can be contacted if necessary. Using this relationship, the user owning the building can easily be looked up in the configuration management database (CMDB), with contact information for that user displayed.

▶ A class type is added to the model that describes the different rooms in a building and the characteristics of a room. A relationship is also added, tying the rooms together to a building. The relationship type used for the rooms is of type `Containment`, ensuring that a user who has access to edit the building can also edit the room.

The room class type should have several basic properties:

▶ RoomNumber

▶ Availability

▶ SquareFeet

Each type of building described using this model is represented by its own class type, deriving from a class containing the common properties for buildings and adding the unique properties for that type of building. Some of these class types have properties added that are specific for that type of building.

The model described to this point is visualized in Figure 23.3, where the `Odyssey.Building.Base` class type contains the common properties for buildings. The `System.User` class, which is an existing class type in Service Manager, is related to the building (`Odyssey.Building.Base`) through the `BuildingHasOwner` relationship, which identifies the owner of the building. A class representing a room, `Odyssey.Building.Room` is related to the building through the `BuildingHasRooms` relationship, which describes the rooms of a building. Different types of buildings use the `Building` class type as base to derive all the properties and relationships from the `Building` class type. To make sure that any user who has access to an instance of a building is able to create, modify, or delete an instance of a room, the authors use the `System.Containment` relationship type.

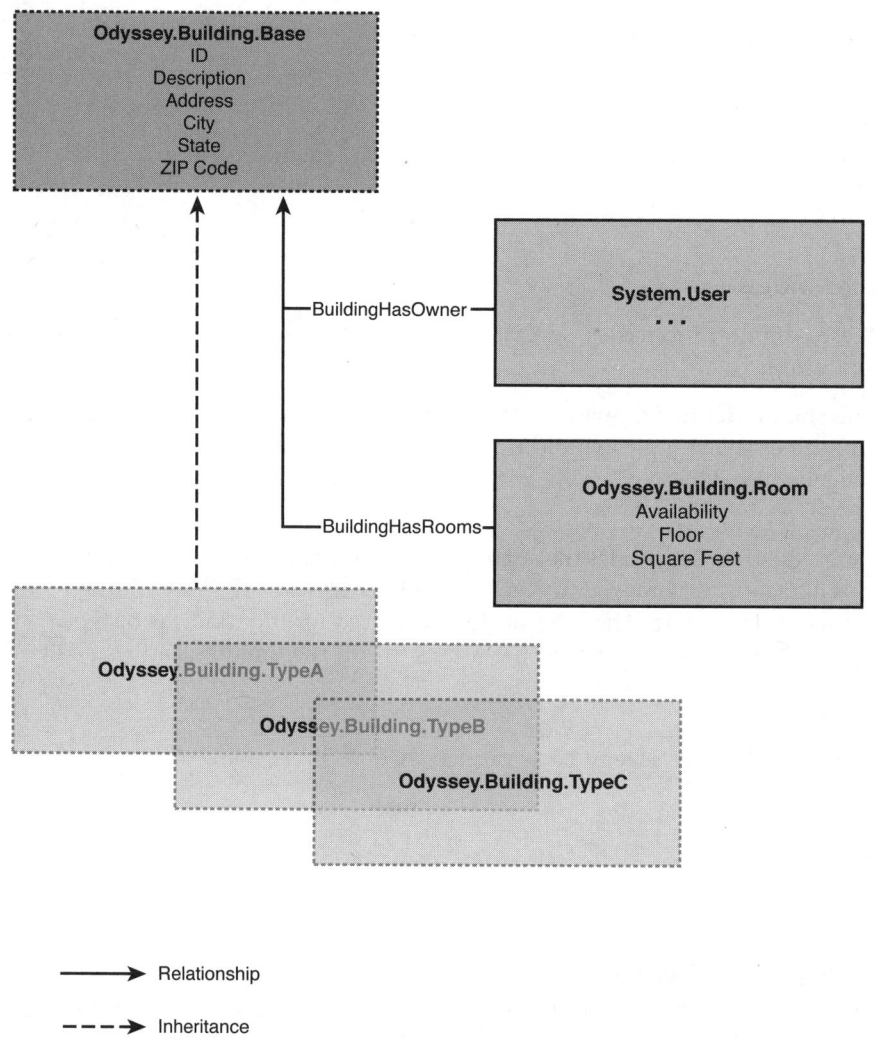

FIGURE 23.3   Data model sketch for Building.

To begin working with the data model, you must create a management pack in which to store the model. This is discussed in the next sections, which define a complete management pack based on parts of this model.

The management pack defined in this chapter contains a class to represent a bank, called Odyssey.Building.Bank. This is seen in the model as Odyssey.Building.TypeX. The bank class has one property added, VaultType, to describe the type of vault used in the bank.

Creating a Management Pack Using Visual Studio Authoring Extensions

The next sections describe how to create a custom management pack using VSAE and add different parts of the management pack to that solution, ultimately creating a production-ready management pack. One of your goals when developing a management pack in VSAE should be to organize it in a structured manner, which makes it easier to modify later.

Creating the Management Pack

Begin by creating a new management pack. VSAE 1.1 supports management pack projects for System Center 2012 Service Manager and Operations Manager. To create a new management pack in VSAE, follow these steps:

1. In Visual Studio 2013, click **New Project**.

2. Expand **Installed -> Templates -> Management Pack -> Service Manager**.

3. Select **Service Manager 2012 R2 Management Pack** (see Figure 23.4).

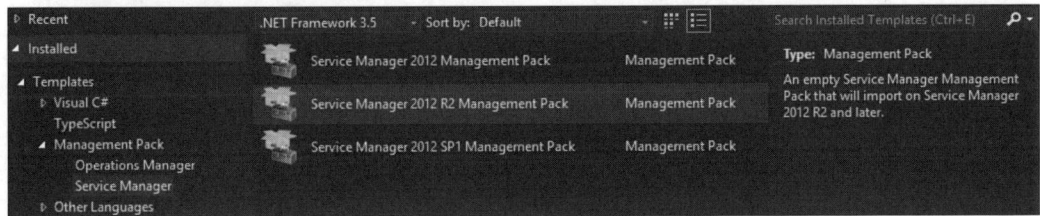

FIGURE 23.4   Selecting the management pack type.

4. Name the management pack **Odyssey.Buildings.Library**, and select a location to save the files (see Figure 23.5). You can specify that Visual Studio automatically create a folder for the solution based on the solution name. You could also add the solution to source control software such as Team Foundation Server or Git (see http://git-scm.com/ for information on Git).

FIGURE 23.5   Specifying the management pack name and creating a directory (folder) for the solution.

5. Click **OK**.

Defining the Management Pack Display Name

To make sure that the management pack appears correctly in the list of management packs in the console, provide a friendly name for the management pack and, optionally, a description. This is defined in the management pack properties.

To define the properties of the management pack, follow these steps:

1. In the Solution Explorer, right-click the management pack (see Figure 23.6) and select **Properties**.

FIGURE 23.6   Selecting the management pack in the Solution Explorer.

2. In the management pack properties dialog, select the Management Pack tab on the left.

3. Click the **Find or Create the Management Pack Display Name and Description** link, shown in Figure 23.7.

4. Change the value of the `<Name>` node inside the `<DisplayString>` node to `Odyssey Buildings Library`.

Listing 23.2 shows the XML for the management pack properties.

LISTING 23.2   Management Pack Display Strings

```
<DisplayStrings>
  <DisplayString ElementID="Odyssey.Buildings.Library">
    <Name>Odyssey Buildings Library</Name>
    <Description>Odyssey.Buildings.Library</Description>
  </DisplayString>
</DisplayStrings>
```

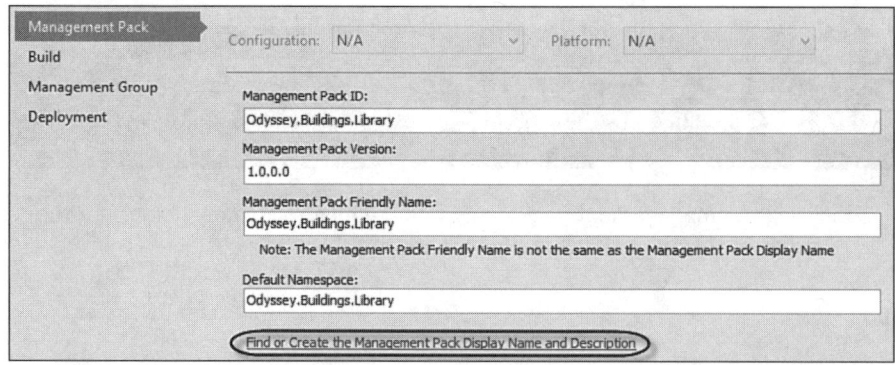

FIGURE 23.7   Management pack name and description link.

Adding References to the Management Pack

A new VSAE project references several management packs by default. These often are not sufficient, and the example in this chapter requires adding additional management pack references to the project. Consider defining aliases for your management packs; setting aliases for references makes them easier to use in the management pack. Table 23.1 specifies the management packs and aliases used by the authors.

TABLE 23.1   Management Pack Names and Aliases

Management Pack	Alias
ServiceManager.ConfigurationManagement.Library	ConfigurationManagement
Microsoft.EnterpriseManagement.ServiceManager.UI.Console	Console
Microsoft.EnterpriseManagement.ServiceManager.UI.Authoring	Authoring

To add a reference, follow these steps:

1. In the Solution Explorer, right-click **References** and select **Add Reference**.

2. Select **Browse**.

3. Navigate to the location of the management pack .mp file.

TIP: MANAGEMENT PACK LIBRARY LOCATIONS

Management pack references may be challenging to set up. When you install VSAE, a number of management packs are installed in *%ProgramFiles(x86)%*\System Center 2012 Visual Studio Authoring Extensions\References\SM2012R2. Since these management packs are insufficient for Service Manager authoring, the authors recommend installing the Service Manager Authoring Tool, which installs a number of management packs at *%ProgramFiles(x86)%*\Microsoft System Center 2012\Service Manager Authoring\ Library. If you cannot find the management pack you need, you could export it manually from your Service Manager management server, or export all management packs using PowerShell and create a new library. If you place the exported management packs in *%ProgramFiles(x86)%*\System Center 2012 Visual Studio Authoring Extensions\ References\SM2012R2, Visual Studio finds them automatically when you import or open a project.

---

4. Select the management pack and click **OK**.

5. In the Solution Explorer, select the management pack.

6. In the Properties dialog, set the Alias to the alias listed in Table 23.1. This is shown in Figure 23.8.

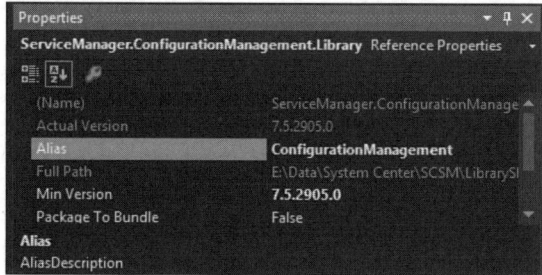

FIGURE 23.8   Management pack reference alias.

7. Repeat steps 1 to 6 for each management pack in Table 23.1.

Creating the Building Base Class

If you are creating a management pack that contains a data model, the first component added is usually classes. If multiple types of classes need to use the same properties, the authors recommend you create a base class to base these on. As described in Chapter 22, a class can be marked as abstract if you do not plan to create any instances of that class. Since the `Odyssey.Building.Base` should be used only as base for other classes (such as the bank class in the "Creating the Odyssey Building Bank Class" section later in this chapter) rather than directly, this example uses the abstract class type.

To create your first base class, follow these steps:

1. In the Solution Explorer, right-click the management pack (previously shown in Figure 23.6).

2. Click **Add -> New Folder** (see Figure 23.9).

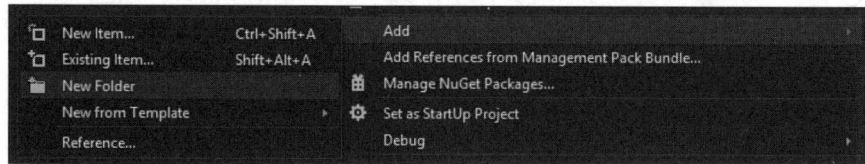

FIGURE 23.9   Creating a new folder.

3. Name the folder **Base Class**.

NOTE: MANAGEMENT PACK SOLUTION STRUCTURE

The management pack components can be sorted in any way you like. This example utilizes different folders for the different components.

---

4. Right-click the Base Class folder and select **Add -> New Item**.

5. Select **Class** and name the file **Odyssey.Building.Base.mpx** (see Figure 23.10).

6. Click **Add**. You have added a class to the management pack; now you need to configure that class:

> ▶ In the `<ClassType>` node, select the ID and search for and replace it with `Odyssey.Building.Base` (see Figure 23.11).

> ▶ Change Type to `System!System.ConfigItem` and change Accessibility to `Public`. The public accessibility setting enables other management packs to reference and use this class.

7. Now you are ready to add properties to the class. Create each property by adding a `<Property>` node. Begin by editing the example of a property, which is in the file you are working on. Change this property and then copy and paste it to resemble the XML in Listing 23.3. Make sure you set all property options such as `Type` and `Key`.

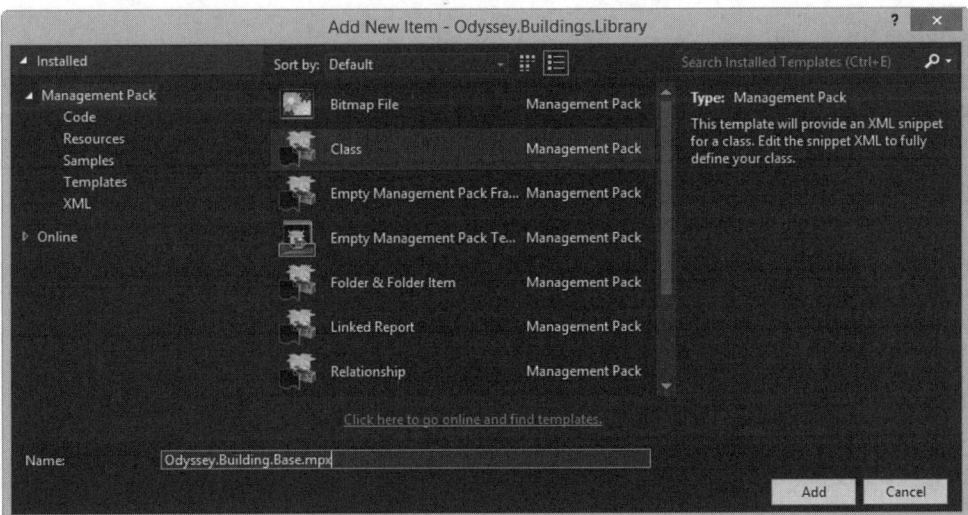

FIGURE 23.10   Adding a new class.

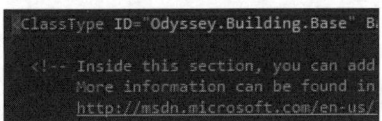

FIGURE 23.11   Changing the class ID.

LISTING 23.3   Base Class Properties for `Odyssey.Building.Base`

```
<ClassType ID="Odyssey.Building.Base" Base="System!System.ConfigItem"
  Accessibility="Public" Abstract="true" Hosted="false" Singleton="false">
    <Property ID="ID" Key="true" Type="string" AutoIncrement="true"
            DefaultValue="OB {0}" />
    <Property ID="Description" Key="false" Type="string" />
    <Property ID="Address" Key="false" Type="string" />
    <Property ID="City" Key="false" Type="string" />
    <Property ID="State" Key="false" Type="string" />
    <Property ID="ZIPCode" Key="false" Type="string" />
    <Property ID="Built" Key="false" Type="int" />
</ClassType>
```

8. For the management pack to function properly in the console, each property needs a friendly name. Friendly names are added to the `<LanguagePacks>` section of the XML. An example of a display string for a property already exists in the XML comments; uncomment this section to use as a base for your definition.

9. Change the `SubElementID` attribute value to `ID`.

10. Change the `<Name>` node value to `ID`. Optionally add a description. Your result should resemble Listing 23.4.

LISTING 23.4   Class Property Display String

```
<DisplayString ElementID="Odyssey.Building.Base" SubElementID="ID">
  <Name>ID</Name>
  <Description></Description>
</DisplayString>
```

11. Repeat steps 7 to 10 for all properties, creating a display string for each property.

NOTE: DISPLAY STRINGS AND LANGUAGE PACKS

Language packs make it possible to localize the names of the types in your management pack, such as classes or properties. Read more about language packs in Chapter 20, "Management Packs."

The base class is now complete.

Creating the Odyssey Building Room Class

As described earlier in "Using Custom Data Models," an `Odyssey.Building.Room` class is needed for use with the `Odyssey.Building.Base` class. A custom relationship between the two classes is also necessary, discussed in the upcoming "Adding the BuildingHasRoom Custom Relationship Type" section of the chapter.

With your base class defined, you can create the room class and basic properties. Perform the following steps:

1. Right-click the **Base Class** folder and select **Add -> New Item** (refer to Figure 23.9).

2. Select **Class** (refer to Figure 23.10) and name the file **Odyssey.Building.Room.mpx**.

3. Click **Add**. This adds a class to the management pack, but it needs to be configured. In the `<ClassType>` node, select the ID and search (refer to Figure 23.11) and replace it with `Odyssey.Building.Room`, and change the Type to `System!System.ConfigItem`.

4. Now change the settings of the `Odyssey.Building.Room` class:

   ▶ Set the Hosted attribute to `False`.

   ▶ Change the Accessibility to `Public`.

5. Create properties for this class by adding a `<Property>` node. Initially there is a single property. Change this property and then copy and paste it to resemble Listing 23.5.

LISTING 23.5   Room Class Basic Properties

```
<ClassType ID="Odyssey.Building.Room" Base="System!System.ConfigItem"
  Accessibility="Public" Abstract="false" Hosted="false" Singleton="false">
   <Property ID="RoomNumber" Key="true" Type="string" AutoIncrement="true" />
   <Property ID="SquareFeets" Key="false" Type="int" MinValue="0"/>
</ClassType>
```

6. Add a display string for each property. (See the earlier "Creating the Building Base Class" section for a detailed description.)

Adding the Room Availability Enumeration to the Room Class

The `Odyssey.Building.Room` class is missing a property. This is the `Availability` property, which is a custom enumeration type property. Before you can add the property to the class, you must add the enumeration. Enumerations were introduced in Chapter 20.

To add the availability property and enumeration, perform the following steps:

1. In the Odyssey.Building.Room.mpx file, navigate to the line below the `</ClassTypes>` node.

2. Insert a start node for `<EnumerationTypes>`, and on the line below insert a closing node `</EnumerationTypes>`. Between these two nodes you can define your enumerations.

3. Type in the enumeration from Listing 23.6. This is the first enumeration and does not have a parent defined. When the enumeration is without a parent, it is the root of a new enumeration.

LISTING 23.6   Root Enumeration

```
<EnumerationValue ID="Odyssey.Building.Room.Availability" Accessibility="Public" />
```

4. Define each enumeration value for the newly created enumeration by defining the ID Odyssey.Building.Room.Availability as its parent. Add two values with ID as Odyssey.Building.Room.Avalability.Free and Odyssey.Building.Room.Avalability.Occupied. Your complete enumeration XML should resemble Listing 23.7.

LISTING 23.7   Complete Enumeration

```
<EnumerationTypes>
  <EnumerationValue ID="Odyssey.Building.Room.Availability"
    Accessibility="Public" />
  <EnumerationValue Parent="Odyssey.Building.Room.Availability"
    ID="Odyssey.Building.Room.Availability.Free" Accessibility="Public" />
  <EnumerationValue Parent="Odyssey.Building.Room.Availability"
    ID="Odyssey.Building.Room.Availability.Occupied" Accessibility="Public" />
</EnumerationTypes>
```

5. Enumerations need display strings to be easily readable. Add a display string for each of the enumeration values by referencing the ElementID as its ID, similar to Listing 23.8.

LISTING 23.8   Enumeration Display String

```
<DisplayString ElementID="Odyssey.Building.Room.Availability">
  <Name>Availability List</Name>
  <Description></Description>
</DisplayString>
```

6. Add the EnumType property to the Odyssey.Building.Room class by using the definition in Listing 23.9.

LISTING 23.9   Enumeration Property

```
<Property ID="Availability" Key="false" Type="enum"
  EnumType="Odyssey.Building.Room.Availability"/>
```

The enumeration and values are now ready to be used in any form, but for this example you want the user to be able to add more values to the list. This requires adding the enumeration to two built-in categories, which makes them appear in the console.

To add the enumeration to the categories, follow these steps:

1. In the Odyssey.Building.Room.mpx file, navigate to the line below the `</TypeDefinitions>` node.

2. Insert a start node for `<Categories>`, and on the line below insert a closing node `</Categories>`. Between these two nodes you can define the categories.

3. Insert the categories in Listing 23.10. The ID must be unique. The `Target` points at the root enumeration, and the categories selected are two built-in categories. The `VisibletoUser` category makes sure the enumeration is displayed in the list in the Library -> Lists section of the console. The `Microsoft.EnterpriseManagement.ServiceManager.UI.Authoring.EnumerationViewTasks` category enables the user to get the default list functions, such as Edit.

LISTING 23.10   Enumeration Categories

```
<Category ID="Odyssey.Buildings.Library.BuildingHasRoom.Category1"
  Target="Odyssey.Building.Room.Availability"
  Value="Authoring!
➡Microsoft.EnterpriseManagement.ServiceManager.UI.Authoring.EnumerationViewTasks" />
<Category ID="Odyssey.Buildings.Library.BuildingHasRoom.Category2"
  Target="Odyssey.Building.Room.Availability" Value="System!VisibleToUser" />
```

The `Room` class is now complete and ready to have the `BuildingHasRoom` relationship added. This occurs in the next section.

Adding the BuildingHasRoom Custom Relationship Type

To be able to connect a room to a building, you need a custom relationship called `BuildingHasRoom`. This relationship can then be added and removed by the custom form, as discussed in the "Creating Console Forms" section later in this chapter. Custom relationships enable you to save any type of relationship between data in the CMDB. Relationships are discussed in Chapter 4 and Chapter 22. To add this custom relationship type, follow these steps:

1. In the Solution Explorer, right-click the management pack (previously shown in Figure 23.6).

2. Click **Add -> New Folder** (refer to Figure 23.9).

3. Name the folder **Relationship**.

4. Right-click this folder and select **Add -> New Item**.

5. Select **Relationship** (refer to Figure 23.10) and name the file **Odyssey.Building. BuildingHasRoom.mpx**.

6. Click **Add**. This adds a relationship example to the management pack, but it must be configured.

7. Uncomment the existing relationship example, and using Listing 23.11 as a guide, change ID, Base, Source and Target. Add MaxCardinality.

LISTING 23.11   BuildingHasRoom Relationship

```
<RelationshipType ID="Odyssey.Buildings.Library.BuildingHasRoom"
Base="System!System.Containment" Abstract="false" Accessibility="Internal">
  <Source ID="Source" Type="Odyssey.Building.Base" MaxCardinality="1" />
  <Target ID="Target" Type="Odyssey.Building.Room" MaxCardinality="2147483647"/>
</RelationshipType>
```

8. Uncomment the display string example and change it to resemble Listing 23.12.

LISTING 23.12   BuildingHasRoom Relationship Display String

```
<DisplayString ElementID="Odyssey.Buildings.Library.BuildingHasRooms">
  <Name>BuildingHasRooms Relationship</Name>
  <Description></Description>
</DisplayString>
```

The relationship type is complete and ready for use in forms, views, or other parts of the management pack.

Creating the Odyssey Building Bank Class

As described in the "Using Custom Data Models" section earlier in this chapter, the model needs an Odyssey.Building.Bank class. This class uses Odyssey.Building.Base as a base for the class. The bank has an extra property added to save information about the vault type in the bank but is otherwise identical to Odyssey.Building.Base including the relationship to rooms.

To create the bank class, follow these steps:

1. In the Solution Explorer, right-click the management pack (previously shown in Figure 23.6).

2. Click **Add** -> **New Folder** (refer to Figure 23.9).

3. Name the folder **Class**.

4. Right-click this folder and select **Add** -> **New Item**.

5. Select **Class** and name the file **Odyssey.Building.Bank.mpx**.

6. Click **Add** to add a class to the management pack. Now configure the class:

▶ In the `<ClassType>` node, select the ID and search for and replace it with `Odyssey.Building.Bank`.

▶ Change the Base to `Odyssey.Building.Base`.

▶ Change the Accessibility to `Public`.

7. The newly created file contains a property example. Change this property to resemble Listing 23.13. Make sure to set all property options like `Type` and `Key`.

LISTING 23.13   Bank Class Properties

```
<ClassType ID="Odyssey.Building.Bank" Base="Odyssey.Building.Base"
  Accessibility="Public" Abstract="false" Hosted="false" Singleton="false">
  <Property ID="VaultType" Key="false" Type="string" />
</ClassType>
```

8. To function correctly in the console, each property requires a friendly name. This is added to the `<LanguagePacks>` section of the XML. An example of a display string for a property already exists in the XML comments. Uncomment this section and make the following modifications:

▶ Change the `SubElementID` attribute value to `VaultType`.

▶ Change the `<Name>` node value to `Vault Type`. Optionally add a description.

Your result should resemble Listing 23.14.

LISTING 23.14   Class Property Display String

```
<DisplayString ElementID="Odyssey.Building.Bank" SubElementID="VaultType">
  <Name>Vault Type</Name>
  <Description></Description>
</DisplayString>
```

Adding a Type Projection to the Bank Class

The "Adding Views to the Management Pack" and "Creating Custom Views" sections later in this chapter use the `Bank` class for views and a form. To be able to show all data, you must create a type projection that contains the `Bank` class and the `BuildingHasRoom` relationship. Read more about type projections in Chapter 22.

To add a type projection to the management pack, follow these steps:

1. In the Solution Explorer, open the file Odyssey.Building.Bank.mpx.

2. Insert a start node for `<TypeProjections>`, and on the line below insert a closing node `</TypeProjections>`. You can define a type projection between these two nodes.

3. To define a type projection that contains the relationship and defines an alias for the relationship `BuildingHasRoom`, type in the XML shown in Listing 23.15.

LISTING 23.15   Class Property Display String

```
<TypeProjection ID="Odyssey.Building.Bank.TypeProjection"
  Accessibility="Public" Type="Odyssey.Building.Bank">
    <Component Path=
      "$Context/Path[Relationship='Odyssey.Buildings.Library.BuildingHasRoom']$"
      Alias="BuildingHasRoom" />
</TypeProjection>
```

4. Add a display name to make the name more user friendly in the console, inserting the XML from Listing 23.16.

LISTING 23.16   Type Projection Display String

```
<DisplayString ElementID="Odyssey.Building.Bank.TypeProjection">
  <Name>Odyssey Bank (advanced)</Name>
</DisplayString>
```

The data model for the management pack is now complete. It includes base class, class, relationships, and a type projection. It is ready to build and to add the presentation elements such as views and forms.

Creating a Strong Name Key

As you are planning to seal your management pack, a strong name key is required. You can reuse this strong name key for as many management packs as needed. Keep the key in a safe place; it is required should the management pack later need to be extended or updated. If you seal a new version of an existing management pack using a new key, you cannot upgrade the management pack in Service Manager; you must delete the management pack and reimport it. Additionally, all references to the management pack are lost, since they use the strong name key token as part of the reference.

You can get a key file from any certificate authority, or you can generate one using the Microsoft software development kit (SDK) tools, which come with the Service Manager Authoring Tool, Visual Studio, or can be installed separately. This section describes how to create a new strong name key.

To create a strong name key, perform the following steps:

1. Open a new command prompt.

2. Type the following:

```
cd "C:\Program Files (x86)\Microsoft SDKs\Windows\v6.0A\Bin\"
```

and press Enter (on 32-bit systems, use "C:\Program Files\" rather than "C:\Program Files (x86)\").

3. To generate a key, type the following and then press Enter:

```
sn.exe /k C:\Customizations\mykey.snk
```

The management pack is ready to be compiled and sealed.

Building and Sealing the Management Pack

An advantage of using VSAE is its capability to have the management pack built, verified, sealed, and even bundled automatically. Whenever a management pack is built, the following occurs:

▶ **Build:** All management pack fragments are merged into a single management pack. Any references are checked and added.

▶ **Verify:** All parts, such as references or display names of the management pack are verified.

▶ **Seal:** Optionally the management pack is automatically sealed by using FastSeal.exe.

▶ **Bundle:** Optionally any selected references to class library projects, such as a custom form, are bundled into an .mpb file.

By default, VSAE builds an unsealed management pack. By adding a strong name key, the management pack is built as an .mp (sealed management pack) and .mpb (sealed management pack bundle). Only sealed management packs can be bundled with other files.

To seal and bundle the management pack, follow these steps:

1. In the Solution Explorer, right-click the management pack and select **Properties**.

2. Switch to the Build tab shown in Figure 23.12.

3. In the Build tab, check the **Generate sealed and signed management pack** check box.

4. Type in the company name and copyright information.

5. Click **Browse** and navigate to a strong name key.

6. Save the solution.

Management Pack		
Build*		
Management Group		
Deployment		

Configuration: Active (Debug) ▾   Platform: Active (x86) ▾

☑ Generate sealed and signed management pack

☐ Delay signing

Company Name:

Odyssey

Copyright:

Copyright (c) Odyssey. All rights reserved.

Key File:

E:\Data\System Center\OdysseyMP.snk   Browse...

FIGURE 23.12   Build tab of management pack properties.

The management pack is ready to be built. To build the management pack, follow these steps:

1. In the Solution Explorer, right-click the management pack and select **Properties**.

2. Click **Build** (see Figure 23.13). (Choosing Rebuild rebuilds all parts of the management pack, even the parts that have not changed, ensuring that all parts are updated.)

Solution 'Odyssey.Buildings.Library' (1 project)
...sey.Buildings.Library
Build   eferences
Rebuild   ase Class
Clean   ⚡ Odyssey.Building.Base.mpx

FIGURE 23.13   Build in the context menu of the management pack.

3. Check the Output window to see the results. Notice that the status bar says **successfully build** before the process is complete. The result should show 0 failed, as seen in Figure 23.14.

Output

Show output from: Build

```
------ Rebuild All started: Project: Odyssey.Buildings.Library, Conf
    Starting MP Build Clean for Odyssey.Buildings.Library.
    Starting MP Build for Odyssey.Buildings.Library.
    Starting Fragment Verification
    Resolving Project References
    Starting Merge Management Pack Fragments
    C:\Program Files (x86)\System Center 2012 Visual Studio Authorin
    Starting MP Verify
    Resolving resources
========== Rebuild All: 1 succeeded, 0 failed, 0 skipped ==========
```

FIGURE 23.14   Build result in Output window.

4. If there are any errors, the Error List lists those errors. Use the identification IDs and names to find the errors (see Figure 23.15). Note that the errors do not disappear in the Error List until they are fixed and the management pack is rebuilt.

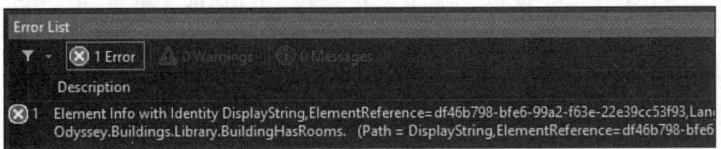

FIGURE 23.15   Error List of the management pack.

> **NOTE: LINE NUMBERS DO NOT MATCH**
>
> Some errors describe a line and character number. These numbers do not fit with any of the fragment files contained in the project. They describe a line number in the build management pack itself. Luckily, the management pack is always available after any build. Navigate to <Solution Folder>\<Project Folder>\obj\Debug\ to find the .xml file. If you have selected a Release type configuration when building, the Debug folder has the name Release.

The management pack is now ready to be imported. Import the management pack into Service Manager and verify that the import does not produce any errors.

There currently are no views or folders added to the management pack. The next section describes how to add a view to your management pack, which contains columns with customized column display names.

Adding Views to the Management Pack

The base structure and data model of the management pack is complete. Now you can add one or more views to be able to create instances of the class types. The view type is used to show instances of a class, known as a GridView.

The XML for a view is fairly advanced; one of the easiest methods requires several high-level steps, used in this section to create and modify a view for the Odyssey bank classes:

1. Create a new management pack for use in the next steps.

2. Create a folder for the view in the console.

3. Create a view in the console.

4. Export the management pack.

5. Copy and paste the XML for the view and folder from the management pack to the Visual Studio solution.

6. Replace reference names to match the references in the solution.

The next procedure discusses how to create a view for the `Odyssey.Bulding.Bank` class. The same technique can be used to create the view for the `Odyssey.Bulding.Room` class, used to create and edit rooms for use with the bank.

Before you begin, make sure that the management pack that includes the classes has been imported into Service Manager. Create the folder in a new management pack by following these steps:

1. In the Service Manager console, navigate to the Configuration Items workspace and right-click the **Configuration Items** root node.

2. Select **Create Folder**.

3. In the Create new folder dialog, type a name. This example uses the name **Odyssey**. Optionally add a description.

4. Click **New** to create a new management pack.

5. Choose a name for the management pack, for example, **Odyssey Temp Dev**. Click **OK**.

6. The result should resemble Figure 23.16. If so, click **OK**.

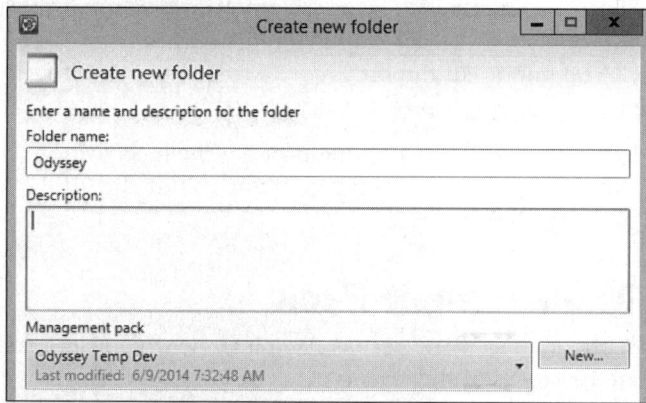

FIGURE 23.16   The Create new folder dialog.

Following are the high level steps to create the view in the console:

1. In the Service Manager console, in the Configuration Items workspace, right-click the newly created Odyssey folder.

2. Select **Create View** (see Figure 23.17).

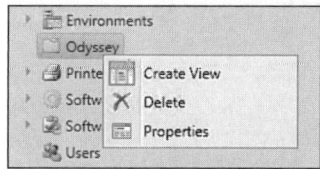

FIGURE 23.17   Create View menu item.

3. In the General tab of the Create View dialog, type a name for the view, such as **Odyssey Banks**.

4. Switch to the Criteria tab and click **Browse** to open the Select a Class dialog.

5. As shown in Figure 23.18, select **Combination classes** from the drop-down and on the left (Type to filter) search box, type in the search term **Odyssey**.

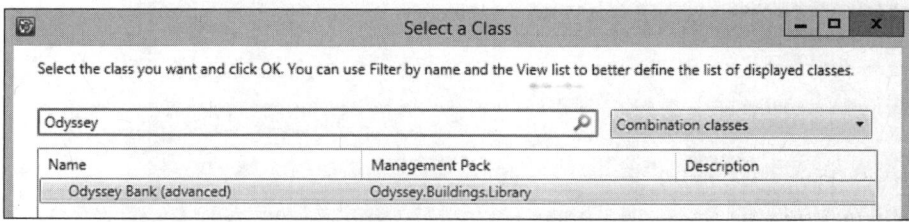

FIGURE 23.18   Select a Class dialog.

6. Select the **Odyssey Bank (advanced)** class as shown in Figure 23.18. Click **OK**.

7. Optionally select a criterion, or leave the default to show all instances of the Odyssey Bank class.

8. Switch to the Display tab and select the columns to show. Choose any you like or use the selections in Figure 23.19. Click **OK**.

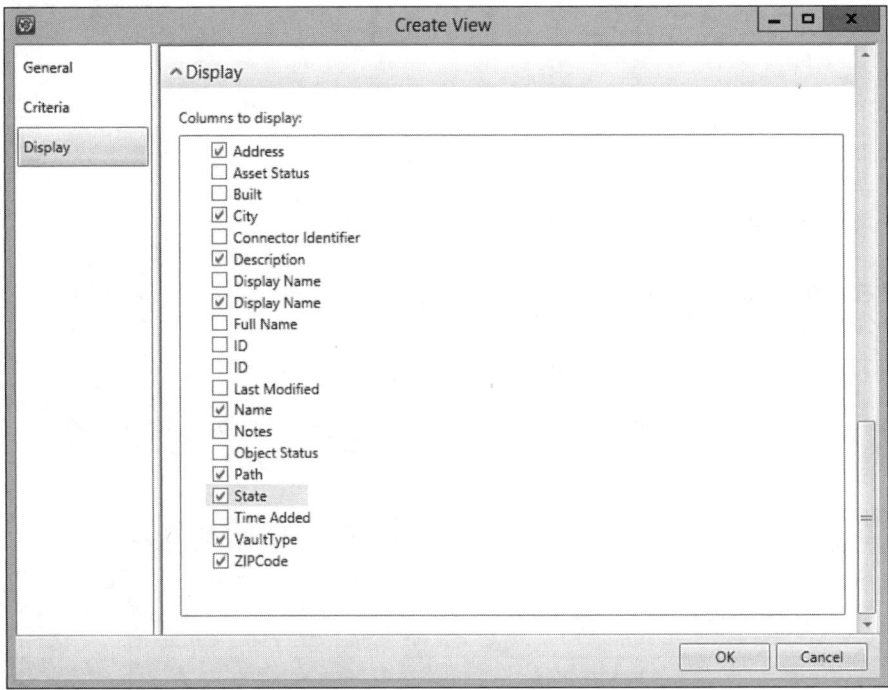

FIGURE 23.19   Display tab of the Create View dialog.

The new view displays in the Odyssey folder. The next high-level step is to export the management pack. To export the management pack, follow these steps:

1. In the Service Manager console, navigate to **Administration -> Management Packs**.

2. Select the **Odyssey Temp Dev** management pack.

3. Click **Export** and select a folder to save the management pack.

The view is exported into an .xml file at the path selected in the previous procedure. Next, copy and paste this view from Odyssey Temp Dev into your Visual Studio solution. Follow these steps:

1. Open the exported management pack using a text editor.

TIP: USE POWERSHELL ISE TO EDIT XML

Numerous text editors supporting XML are available for download or purchase. These editors make your work easier by highlighting the different parts of the XML text by using colors, which provides a better overview of the files. You can use your favorite editor, or use the built-in PowerShell ISE in Windows Server 2012 R2 (also available in other Windows versions). This editor has great support for XML highlighting.

---

2. Before performing the copy and paste, the management pack solution must have an empty file added to the VSAE solution. Switch to Visual Studio and create a folder called **Views** in the root of the solution.

3. Right-click the newly created Views folder and select **Add** -> **New Item** as highlighted in Figure 23.20.

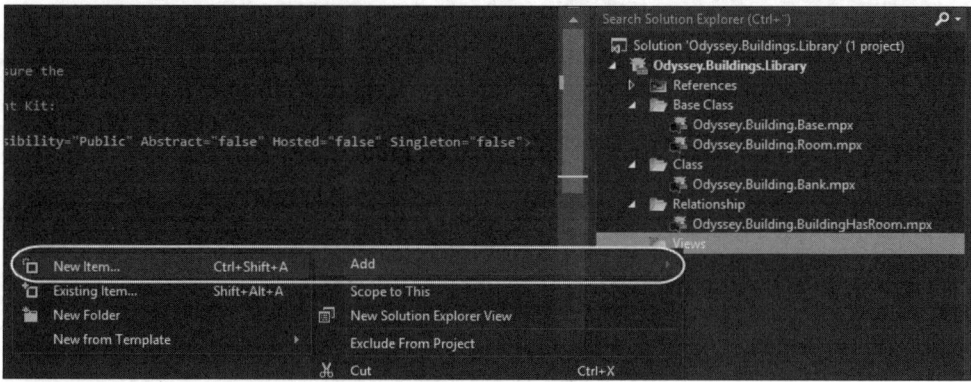

FIGURE 23.20   New item in context menu.

4. Select **Empty Management Pack Fragment**.

5. Name the file **Odyssey.Building.Bank.Views.mpx** and click **Add**. The new file opens in the editor.

6. Switch back to the Odyssey Temp Dev management pack in the text editor.

7. Copy all text between `</Manifest>` and `</ManagementPack>`.

8. Paste the text into the newly created file in the VSAE solution.

The view and folder are now part of the solution, but the solution is not ready to build. You should remove some text, and there are reference names to other management packs that require editing. Perform the following steps:

1. Remove the management pack category, which is generated when you build the management pack solution. Remove the text shown in Listing 23.17. Note that your text might be slightly different since some IDs are automatically generated.

LISTING 23.17   Management Pack Category

```
<Category ID="Category.f5f2c02ead49466c847933950f40251e" Value=
"EnterpriseManagement!Microsoft.EnterpriseManagement.ServiceManager.ManagementPack">
  <ManagementPackName>ManagementPack.a64270e970e6483698fc1bc893eee940
  </ManagementPackName>
  <ManagementPackVersion>7.5.3079.0</ManagementPackVersion>
</Category>
```

2. In the `<DisplayStrings>` section, remove the display string that references the category. This is usually the first display string in the section, and the ID includes the name `ManagementPack`.

3. Next, rename the references to all management packs. This is because names for the references are automatically generated in the console, while the reference in your solution might have different names. In the Odyssey Temp Dev management pack, locate the `<References>` section.

4. Locate the first reference and note the alias. The alias in Listing 23.18 is `EnterpriseManagement`.

LISTING 23.18   Reference Alias

```
<Reference Alias="EnterpriseManagement">
  <ID>Microsoft.EnterpriseManagement.ServiceManager.UI.Console</ID>
  <Version>7.5.3079.0</Version>
  <PublicKeyToken>31bf3856ad364e35</PublicKeyToken>
</Reference>
```

5. Switch to Visual Studio and find the reference to the same management pack. Figure 23.21 shows that the alias for the management pack in Listing 23.18 is `Console`.

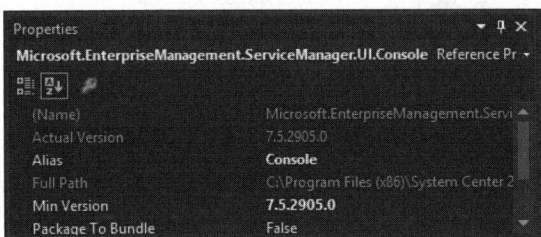

FIGURE 23.21   Management pack reference alias.

6. Open the Odyssey.Building.Bank.Views.mpx file in the editor and use search and replace to replace `EnterpriseManagement!` with `Console!`. Notice the exclamation mark after the alias.

7. Repeat steps 4 to 6 for all management pack references with exception of the reference to the `Odyssey.Buildings.Library`:

   ▶ In the Odyssey Temp Dev management pack, note the alias of the reference to the `Odyssey.Buildings.Library`.

   ▶ Replace this reference adding an exclamation mark, for example, `CustomOdyssey_Buildings_Library!` with an empty string, since there is no need for a reference as the view is part of the management pack solution.

8. Before making more changes, build the management pack to verify that all references are resolved and that the view works in the management pack.

If the management pack builds successfully, you are ready to edit the column display names, discussed in the next section.

Customizing View Columns

As described in Chapter 22, while it is simple to create a view in the console, you cannot change the display name of the column or perform other advanced functionalities, such as changing the predefined order, sorting, or grouping; these require manual editing of the view XML, described in the following sections.

Changing the Display Name of a Column

To set a custom display name in the added view, follow these steps:

1. Locate the `<DisplayStrings>` section in the view XML.

2. Locate the display string for the column. Listing 23.19 shows an example of a column display string.

LISTING 23.19   Column Display String

```
<DisplayString ElementID="Address.236f5deef1b44023bb0c6f6f3c249d04">
  <Name>Address</Name>
</DisplayString>
```

3. Change the name value in the display string.

4. Build and test the management pack.

Adding Predefined Sorting, Grouping, Width, or Other Advanced Attributes to a Column

Service Manager grid views support predefining a number of properties by adding an attribute to the column in the XML.

All attributes are added the same way; however, some are easier to use than others. Following is information about the available attributes in the management pack:

▶ **Name:** Defines a name for the column. The name can be used to reference the column in advanced scenarios, such as when using converters.

▶ **CellTemplate (DataTemplate):** Use this property to reference a Windows Presentation Foundation (WPF) DataTemplate, which is used to show the data. To read more about this attribute, refer to the WPF documentation at http://msdn.microsoft.com/en-us/library/system.windows.datatemplate.aspx.

▶ **CellTemplateSelector (DataTemplateSelector):** Use this property to reference a WPF DataTemplateSelector, which can be used to dynamically select a DataTemplate for the `CellTemplate` property, depending on the values provided. For additional information, refer to http://msdn.microsoft.com/en-us/library/system.windows.controls.datatemplateselector(v=vs.110).aspx.

▶ **Converter (IValueConverter):** A converter can be used to dynamically decide which data to show, depending on the value. For information on how to use this attribute, refer to the IValueConverter documentation at http://msdn.microsoft.com/en-us/library/system.windows.data.ivalueconverter.aspx.

▶ **DataType (Type):** A converter can be used to dynamically decide the data to show depending on the original value.

▶ **DisplayMemberBinding (BindingBase):** This optional property is used as content of the cell for this column in each row. If this property along with the CellTemplate property is not defined, a default binding is created using the value of Property.

▶ **DisplayName (String):** Use this property to set the display name of the column. This usually is defined as a reference to a display string, as described previously in the "Changing the Display Name of a Column" section in this chapter.

▶ **Header (String):** Defines the header for the column. If this optional property is not set, the value of Display Name is set to this property.

▶ **HeaderTemplate (DataTemplate):** Similar to CellTemplate, this property can be used to define a DataTemplate for the content of the header of the column.

▶ **HeaderTemplateSelector (DataTemplateSelector):** Similar to CellTemplateSelector, this property can be used to define a DataTemplateSelector for the content of the header of the column.

▶ **IsRequired (Boolean):** Defines whether the user can hide the column.

▶ **IsVisible (Boolean):** Defines whether the column is initially visible. The console user can show hidden columns by using the column selector. Default value is True.

▶ **Property (String):** Defines which property of the data is associated with the column. The property is used for sorting, filtering and grouping. If no CellTemplate or DisplayMemberbinding is defined, this is also used for displaying.

▶ **Width (Double):** Defines the initial width of the column, The default value is Auto, in which the columns share the available spare equally. The WPF documentation includes additional information regarding possible widths in WPF; see http://msdn.microsoft.com/en-us/library/system.windows.frameworkelement.width.aspx.

▶ **SortDirection (String):** Used to define the initial sort order if the view is sorted by this column. The default value is Ascending. Accepted values are Ascending and Descending.

► **GroupDirection (String):** Used to define the initial group order if the view is grouped by this column. The default value is Ascending. Accepted values are Ascending and Descending.

► **SortIndex (Integer):** Defines the index of the column in the sorted columns list. The default value is -1, which mean that the column is not in the sorted columns list and the view is not sorted by the column.

► **GroupIndex (Integer):** Defines the index of the column in the grouped columns list. The default value is -1, which mean that the column is not in the grouped columns list and the view is not grouped by the column.

Additional information on management pack attributes is available at http://blogs.technet.com/b/servicemanager/archive/2010/03/03/grid-view-configuration-and-what-it-means.aspx.

To define a property for a column in the management pack solution, follow these steps:

1. Locate the `<Columns>` section in the view XML.

2. Locate the column in the column definitions. Listing 23.20 shows an example of a column definition.

LISTING 23.20   Column Definition

```
<mux:Column Name="Address" DisplayMemberBinding="{Binding Path=Address,
Mode=OneWay}" Width="100" DisplayName="Address.236f5deef1b44023bb0c6f6f3c249d04"
Property="Address" DataType="s:String" />
```

3. Add any of the properties and define a value for each.

4. Build and test the management pack.

Creating Custom Views

As discussed in Chapter 22, you can create custom views that can be implemented in the Service Manager console. Figure 22.1 showed a view based on the overview view type named Overview Type, also used in the Administration Overview built-in screen, shown in Figure 23.22. This section covers how to create custom views, which requires some basic knowledge of eXtensible Application Markup Language (XAML).

Although you can create custom view types, using the predefined Overview view type is a powerful and easy way to implement custom views in the Service Manager console. This view type can be used in several different ways to implement custom views:

► Designed directly in the management pack using XAML, which is the design language used by the Service Manager console.

▶ Defined in a WPF UserControl and compiled into an assembly referenced in a view definition in a management pack. This gives you the ability to add code that interacts with Service Manager through the SDK.

As the second approach requires a full development environment and developer skills, this chapter discusses only the first alternative.

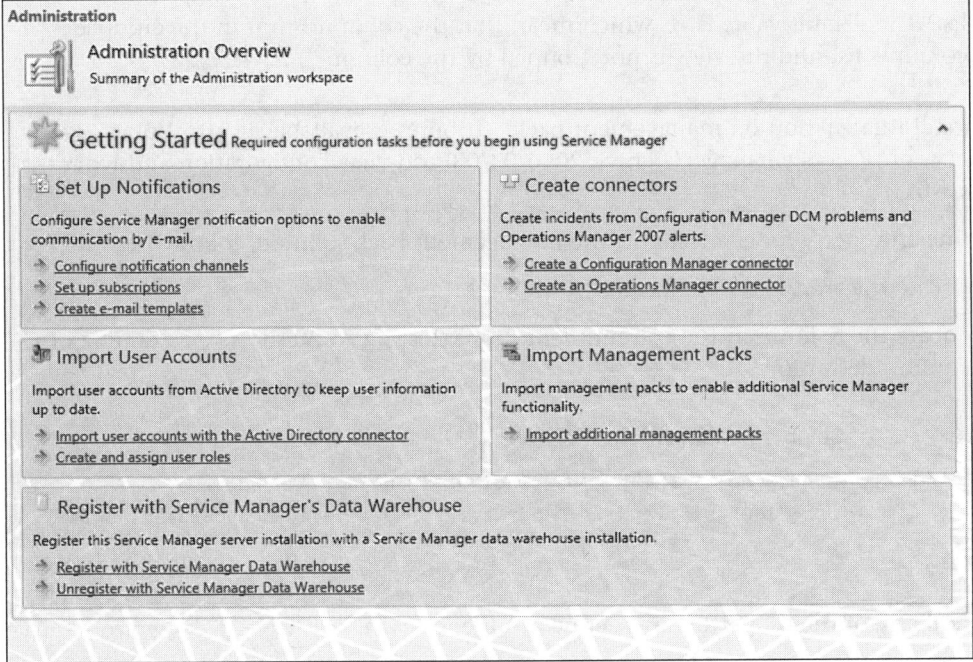

FIGURE 23.22   Administration Overview in the Service Manager console.

To declare a custom view in a management pack using the Overview view type, follow these steps:

1. In the Visual Studio solution, declare a reference to the `Microsoft.EnterpriseManagement.ServiceManager.UI.Console` management pack, and set the alias to `EnterpriseManagement`.

2. Add an empty management fragment to the solution.

3. Define a view type similar to the one shown in Listing 23.19, which uses a view type defined in an assembly referenced in the management pack referenced in step 1.

4. Once the view type is defined, you can proceed to define the custom view as in the example in Listing 23.20. It is important that the `TypeID` is pointing at the ID given when you declared the overview type (as in Listing 23.21).

5. With the view defined, you can adjust the elements within the header and content tag to suit your needs. It helps to define the XAML code using a tool such as Visual Studio.

TIP: LIGHTWEIGHT ALTERNATIVE TO VISUAL STUDIO

If you do not have access to Visual Studio, you could use Kaxaml to design the XAML code. Kaxaml is a lightweight XAML editor that can render the result as you type the XAML code. Kaxaml is available at http://www.kaxaml.com/.

---

6. After defining the view, it must be placed in a folder. This is accomplished using a <FolderItem> declaration as in the example in Listing 23.22. The FolderItem ID must be a unique value, the ElementID should be set to the ID of the folder (in this example Odyssey.Views.CustomOverview), and the Folder property should be set to the ID of a declared folder item.

Figure 23.23 shows the result of the management pack XML in this section. Listing 23.21 and Listing 23.22 show the resulting XML. Notice how the XAML elements from Listing 23.22 are rendered inside the Service Manager console.

LISTING 23.21   Overview Type Declaration

```
<PresentationTypes>
 <ViewTypes>
  <ViewType ID="OverviewType" Accessibility="Public">
    <Configuration>
      <xsd:any minOccurs="0" maxOccurs="unbounded"
       processContents="skip" xmlns:xsd="http://www.w3.org/2001/XMLSchema" />
    </Configuration>
    <ViewImplementation>
      <Assembly>EnterpriseManagement!WpfViewsAssembly</Assembly>
      <Type>Microsoft.EnterpriseManagement.UI.WpfViews.Overview</Type>
    </ViewImplementation>
   </ViewType>
 </ViewTypes>
</PresentationTypes>
```

LISTING 23.22   Custom View

```
<Views>
  <View ID="Odyssey.Views.CustomOverview" Accessibility="Public" Enabled="true"
    Target="System!System.Entity" TypeID="OverviewType" Visible="true">
   <Category>Overview</Category>
   <Configuration>
     <Presentation>
     <Header >
```

```xml
    <UserControl Margin="10"
      xmlns="http://schemas.microsoft.com/winfx/2006/xaml/presentation"
      xmlns:x="http://schemas.microsoft.com/winfx/2006/xaml">
    <Grid>
    <Grid.RowDefinitions>
    <RowDefinition Height="Auto" />
    <RowDefinition Height="Auto" />
    </Grid.RowDefinitions>
    <Grid.ColumnDefinitions>
    <ColumnDefinition Width="*" />
    <ColumnDefinition Width="Auto" />
    </Grid.ColumnDefinitions>
    <TextBlock Text="Bing Browser" FontSize="18" FontWeight="DemiBold" />
    <TextBlock Grid.Row="1"
    Text="The bing browser is a custom implementation of the Overview ViewType"
    FontWeight="DemiBold" />
    </Grid>
    </UserControl>
    </Header>
    <Content>
    <UserControl Margin="10"
      xmlns="http://schemas.microsoft.com/winfx/2006/xaml/presentation"
      xmlns:x="http://schemas.microsoft.com/winfx/2006/xaml">
  <Grid>
      <WebBrowser Name="wb1" Source="http://www.bing.com" />
    </Grid>
    </UserControl>
    </Content>
    </Presentation>
    </Configuration>
  </View>
  </Views>
<Folders>
  ...
  <Folder ID="Odyssey.Folders.lvl2" Accessibility="Public"
  ParentFolder="Odyssey.Folders.lvl1" />
</Folders>
<FolderItems>
  ...
  <FolderItem ElementID="Odyssey.Views.CustomOverview"
  ID="FolderItem.ab59125f-452d-4212-9d38-40a32d367c27"
  Folder="Odyssey.Folders.lvl2" />
</FolderItems>
```

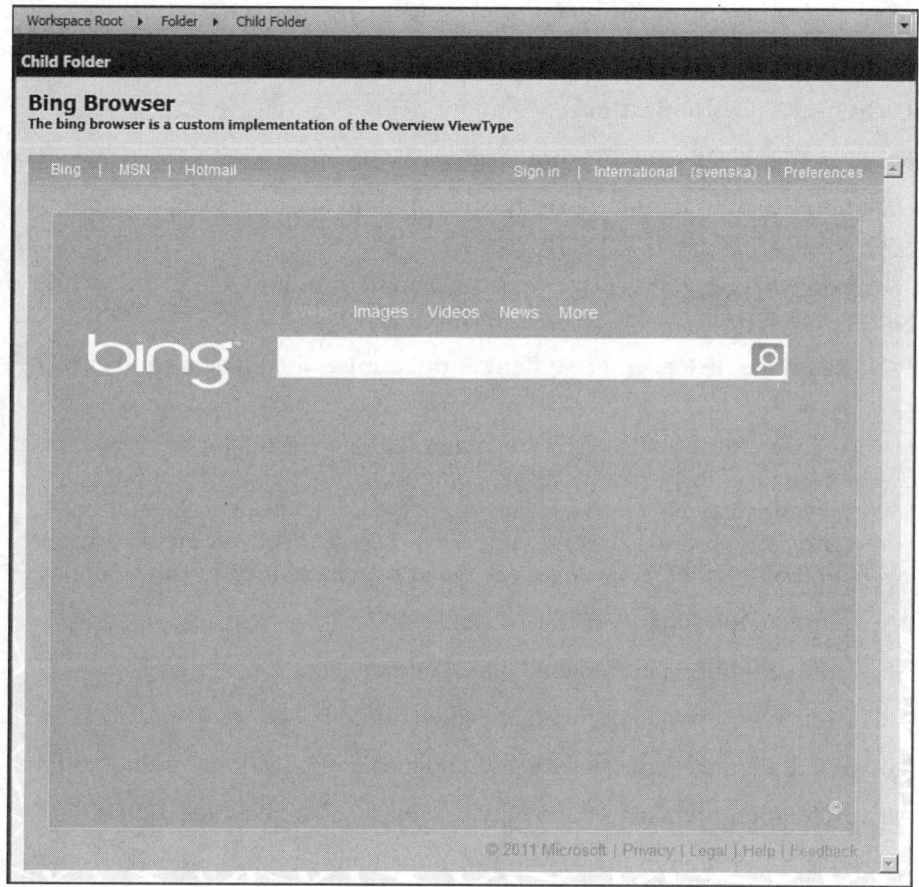

FIGURE 23.23   Custom view based on `OverviewType`.

Creating Console Forms

Sometimes you want to go further than the Authoring Tool can deliver in the sense of a user interface (UI) experience. With Visual Studio or Expression Blend, your custom form can be as customized as you want. Using one of these tools to create a form for Service Manager enables you to add code to perform custom validations as well as have total control over the XAML code used to generate the UI.

To create a custom form for Service Manager based on C# using Visual Studio, follow these steps:

1. In the Visual Studio solution, select **File -> New -> Project**.

2. In the New Project dialog, select the WPF User Control Library template from the Visual C# - Windows folder.

3. In the New Project dialog, enter the following details and then click **OK**:

> ▶ **Name: Odyssey.CustomForms**
>
> ▶ **Location: C:\Customizations**
>
> ▶ **Solution name: Odyssey.CustomForms**

4. In the Solution Explorer, right-click **UserControl1.xaml** and select **Delete**. Confirm that you want to delete the user control.

5. In the Solution Explorer, right-click **Odyssey.CustomForms** and select **Add -> User Control**.

6. In the Add New Item dialog, enter **MyBankForm.xaml** as the filename and click **Add**.

7. In Visual Studio, confirm that the required references are created for the form project. The references in your projects depend on the functionality you want to integrate into your custom form. To create the reference, navigate to References folder of your project in the Solution Explorer and select **Add Reference -> Browse** to navigate to the DLL file. Following is the list of references used in this example:

> ▶ Microsoft.EnterpriseManagement.UI.Control.dll
>
> ▶ Microsoft.EnterpriseManagement.UI.SMControls.dll
>
> ▶ Microsoft.EnterpriseManagement.UI.Foundation.dll
>
> ▶ Microsoft.EnterpriseManagement.ServiceManager.Application.Common.dll
>
> ▶ Microsoft.EnterpriseManagement.ServiceManager.SharedResources.dll

8. The form project is created in the solution with the library project. Add a reference in the library management pack to the form project; this bundles the assembly with the management pack when building the management pack bundle.

To create the project reference, navigate to References folder of your project and click **Add Reference**. Click the Projects tab, select **Odyssey.CustomForms** as the project, and click **OK**. The project reference is visible in the References folder. Navigate to the referenced project properties and set Package To Bundle to **true**.

9. In Visual Studio, make sure the Toolbox is visible. If not, select **View -> Toolbox**.

TIP: USE SERVICE MANAGER CONTROLS IN YOUR FORM

You can use Service Manager controls in your custom form project. Add a new tab in the Toolbox pane of the Visual Studio project (provide a name for the tab) and follow these steps:

1. Right-click in the empty space of the tab and select **Choose Items**.

2. On the WPF Components tab, browse to the DLL file and click **OK**. The smcontrol.dll file is located in the PackageToLoad folder under the Authoring program folder. The DLLs listed in this TIP contain the source code for the controls. They are available for use in your project and provide a similar look and feel to the controls used in the Authoring Tool. The following DLL files include form controls:

▶ Microsoft.EnterpriseManagement.UI.Controls.dll

▶ Microsoft.EnterpriseManagement.UI.ExtendedControls.dll

▶ Microsoft.EnterpriseManagement.UI.SMControls.dll

3. Select the files you want to use in your project and click **Open**. The controls included in the selected DLL files are highlighted. Click **OK**.

4. The list of controls that are added can be reviewed in the Overview page.

5. Click **OK** to add the controls in the Toolbox tab.

You can now use the Service Manager controls in your custom form.

---

10. Start creating the custom form by dragging and dropping labels from the Toolbox onto the design surface of MyBankForm.xaml as shown in Figure 23.24.

11. On the design surface of MyBankForm.xaml, select a label and press F4 to display the Details pane. In the Details pane, set content to **Display name**. Repeat this step for every label existing in your form.

12. Drag and drop other controls from the Toolbox onto the design surface of MyBankForm.xaml as in Figure 23.24. For the example in this section, text boxes are required to specify the class properties.

13. On the design surface of MyBankForm.xaml, right-click the TextBox, and then select **View XAML**.

14. In the XAML window, verify that the TextBox XAML has the following text attribute defined: `Text="{Binding Path=DisplayName}"`. Repeat this step for every TextBox in your form to bind the TextBox to a property of the class.

15. Adding the view to display the rooms of the bank is a multistep process. The controls can be added using the Toolbox or directly in the XAML code. Following is how the view and buttons are defined in the expander control of the example:

   ▶ The form binding, grid, and two columns are defined in the expander definition of the form (see Listing 23.23). One column in the expander is for the SortableListView, and the other is for the buttons. The code behind the Loaded event in the form is included in Listing 23.26.

   ▶ The SortableListView control is added to the first column in the expander. Different properties are set to control the behavior of the SortableListView and the binding to the `BuildingHasRoom` alias (defined in the `Bank` class TypeProjection definition). Listing 23.24 shows an example of the XAML code, with the code behind in Listing 23.27.

   ▶ A StackPanel control is added in the second column of the expander with the code in Listing 23.25, which also defines the button and events. The code behind the example is explained in step 16.

23

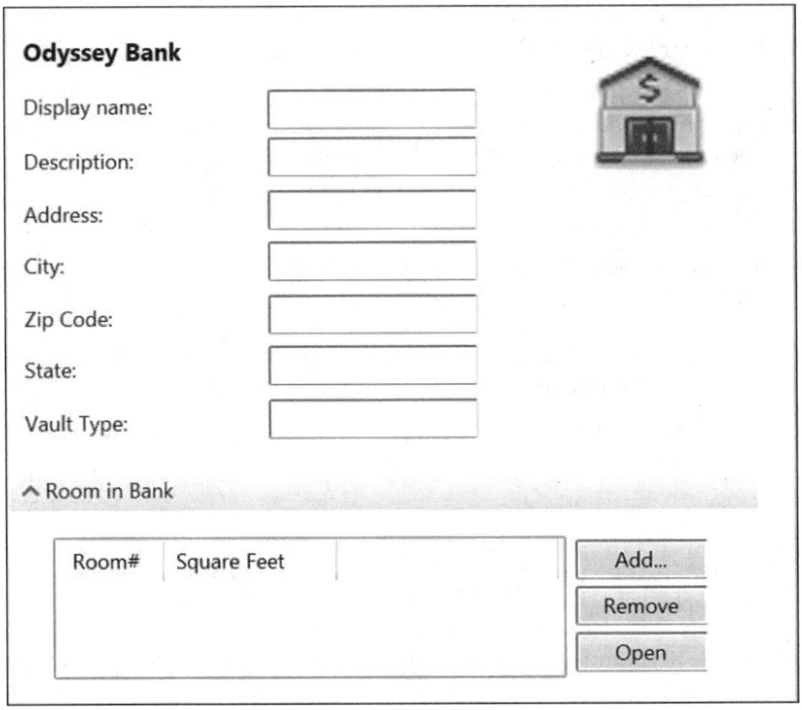

FIGURE 23.24   User Control form design with labels added.

LISTING 23.23   Expander Definition

```
<Expander Name="ExpandRooms"  IsExpanded="True" Margin="0,265,20,10"
  Header="Room in Bank" Loaded="ExpandRooms_OnLoaded" >
  <Grid  Background="{Binding ElementName=MyBankForm,Path=Background}"
    Margin="25,0,25,0">
                <Grid.ColumnDefinitions>
                    <ColumnDefinition Width="*" />
                    <ColumnDefinition Width="Auto" />
                </Grid.ColumnDefinitions>
                <Grid.RowDefinitions>
                    <RowDefinition Height="Auto" />
                    <RowDefinition Height="Auto" />
                </Grid.RowDefinitions>
  </Grid>
</Expander>
```

LISTING 23.24   SortableListView Definition

```
<scwpf:SortableListView x:Name="ListViewRooms" Grid.Column="0"
  ListBox.SelectionMode="Extended" Control.VerticalContentAlignment="Stretch"
  FrameworkElement.VerticalAlignment="Stretch" FrameworkElement.MinHeight="80"
  FrameworkElement.MinWidth="110" FrameworkElement.Height="Auto"
  FrameworkElement.Width="Auto" FrameworkElement.HorizontalAlignment="Stretch"
    Control.HorizontalContentAlignment="Stretch" FrameworkElement.Margin="0,15,0,0"
  FrameworkElement.MaxHeight="200" ItemsControl.ItemsSource=
    "{Binding Path=BuildingHasRoom, Mode=TwoWay}">
    <ListView.View>
      <GridView>
        <scwpf:SortableGridViewColumn SortPropertyName="RoomNumber"
          GridViewColumn.Width="60" GridViewColumn.DisplayMemberBinding=
          "{Binding Path=RoomNumber, Mode=TwoWay}" GridViewColumn.Header=
          "{Binding Path=Strings[stringName].Value, FallbackValue=Room#,
          RelativeSource={RelativeSource FindAncestor,
          AncestorType={x:Type views:FormView}}}" />
<scwpf:SortableGridViewColumn SortPropertyName="SquareFeets"
  GridViewColumn.Width="100" GridViewColumn.DisplayMemberBinding=
  "{Binding Path=SquareFeets, Mode=TwoWay}" GridViewColumn.Header=
  "{Binding Path=Strings[stringName].Value, FallbackValue='Square Feet',
  RelativeSource={RelativeSource FindAncestor, AncestorType=
{x:Type views:FormView}}}" />
      </GridView>
    </ListView.View>
</scwpf:SortableListView>
```

LISTING 23.25   Buttons Definition

```
<StackPanel Margin="0,15,0,0" Width="Auto" HorizontalAlignment="Left"
    VerticalAlignment="Top" Grid.Column="1">
      <Button Name="ButtonAddRooms" Height="23" VerticalAlignment="Top" Width="60"
        Content="{Binding Path=Strings[buttonAdd].Value, FallbackValue=Add...,
        RelativeSource={RelativeSource FindAncestor, AncestorType={x:Type
          views:FormView}}}" Click="ButtonAddRooms_OnClick"  />
      <Button Name="ButtonRemoveRooms" Height="23" VerticalAlignment="Top"
        Width="60"
        IsEnabled="{Binding ElementName=ListViewApprovers,Path=SelectedItems.Count}"
        Content="{Binding Path=Strings[buttonRemove].Value, FallbackValue=Remove,
        RelativeSource={RelativeSource FindAncestor, AncestorType={x:Type
          views:FormView}}}" Click="ButtonRemoveRooms_Click"  />
        <Button Name="ButtonOpenRoom" Height="23" VerticalAlignment="Top" Width="60"
        IsEnabled="{Binding ElementName=ListViewApprovers,Path=SelectedItems.Count}"
        Content="{Binding Path=Strings[buttonOpen].Value, FallbackValue=Open,
```

23

```
    RelativeSource={RelativeSource FindAncestor, AncestorType={x:Type
        views:FormView}}}" Click="ButtonOpenRoom_Click" />
</StackPanel>>
```

LISTING 23.26   Expander Loaded Code Behind

```
private void ExpandRooms_OnLoaded(object sender, RoutedEventArgs e)
{
    var headeredContentControl = new HeaderedContentControl
    {
        OverridesDefaultStyle = true,
        Foreground = Brushes.Black,
        Header = "Room in Bank"
    };
    this.ExpandRooms.Header = headeredContentControl;
}
```

LISTING 23.27   SortableListView Definition Code Behind

```
public SortableListView ListViewAllRooms { get; set; }
private SortableListView GetListView(string Name)
{
    switch (Name)
    {
        case "ButtonAddRooms":
        case "ButtonRemoveRooms":
        case "ButtonOpenRoom":
            {
                return this.ListViewAllRooms;
            }
        default:
            {
                throw new Exception(String.Format
                  ("ListView for control: {0}- not found", Name));
            }
    }
}
```

TIP: REUSE RELATED ITEMS AND HISTORY TAB CONTROLS

In addition to using single Service Manager controls in your custom form project, you can reuse complete tab controls such as the Related Items and History tab items from the default incident form. Patrik Sundqvist explains the procedure for reusing these tab items at http://blogs.litware.se/?p=1434.

16. The buttons are defined in the XAML code but do not include any functionality without adding code behind the form. The following events are examples used in the form in this procedure:

▶ **Add button:** This calls the function to launch an Instance Picker control to add Rooms. Listing 23.28 shows an overview of the code.

▶ **Remove button:** This gets the content of the items in the view and removes the selected items (see Listing 23.29).

▶ **Open button:** This has the same functionality as the double-click event. The selected item is captured and the form utility PopoutForm is used to display the details. Listing 23.30 shows the code behind the form.

LISTING 23.28   Add Button Click: Event Code Behind

```
private void ButtonAddRooms_OnClick(object sender, RoutedEventArgs e)
    {
        ButtonAdd_Click(new Guid("1629f73c-edaa-a729-5b99-74b2ce224ce5"),
          ListViewRooms); // Odyssey.Bulding.Room
    }

    private void ButtonAdd_Click(Guid mpClassGuid, ItemsControl listView)
    {
        FormUtilities.Instance.LaunchAddInstancePickerDialog
          (listView.ItemsSource as Collection<IDataItem>, mpClassGuid);
    }
```

LISTING 23.29   Remove Button Click Event: Code Behind

```
private void ButtonRemoveRooms_Click(object sender, RoutedEventArgs e)
    {
        var button = (Button)sender;
        var sortableListView = GetListView(button.Name);
        if (sortableListView == null) return;
        var list = (IList<IDataItem>)sortableListView.ItemsSource;
        if (list == null) return;
        foreach (IDataItem item in new
            ArrayList(sortableListView.SelectedItems))
        {
            list.Remove(item);
        }
    }
```

23

LISTING 23.30   Open Button Click Event: Code Behind

```
private void ButtonOpenRoom_Click(object sender, RoutedEventArgs e)
        {
            var button = (Button)sender;
            var sortableListView = GetListView(button.Name);
            if (sortableListView == null) return;
            OpenInstance(sortableListView);
        }


    public void OpenInstance(SortableListView sortableListView)
        {
            if (sortableListView == null) return;
            foreach (IDataItem dataItem in sortableListView.SelectedItems)
            {
                FormUtilities.Instance.PopoutForm(dataItem);
            }


        }
```

17. In Visual Studio, navigate to your form project and click **Build -> Build Solution**.

The DLL file to integrate into your custom management pack is created in Visual Studio. The layout and bindings are set in the file, but the link to the class is configured using XML in your management pack. The next procedure adds the reference to the form and resource DLL (UserControl) to your management pack. Follow these steps:

1. Navigate to your management pack project in Visual Studio; the example used for this chapter is **Odyssey.Buildings.Library**. Right-click the project and select **Add -> New Folder**. Provide a name for the new folder.

2. Right-click the new folder and select **Add -> New Item**.

3. Select **Empty Management Pack Fragment**, provide a name for the file, and click **Add**.

4. In the XML file editor, navigate to `</ManagementPackFragment>`. Above this tag insert the XML in Listing 23.31.

LISTING 23.31   Add Custom Form Reference in Management Pack

```
<Presentation>
  <Forms>
    <Form ID="Odyssey.Building.Bank.Form" Accessibility="Public"
    Target="Odyssey.Building.Bank.TypeProjection" Assembly="Forms"
    TypeName="Odyssey.CustomForms.MyBankForm" >
      <Category>Form</Category>
      <FormStrings>
```

```
    <FormString ID="labelTitle">
      $MPElement[Name="Form.label_Title"]$
    </FormString>
  </FormStrings>
</Form>
</Forms>
</Presentation>
<LanguagePacks>
  <LanguagePack ID="ENU" IsDefault="true">
    <DisplayStrings>
      <DisplayString ElementID="Form.label_Title">
        <Name>Odyssey Bank</Name>
      </DisplayString>
    </DisplayStrings>
  </LanguagePack>
</LanguagePacks>
```

5. Below the `</LanguagePacks>` tag, insert the XML from Listing 23.32 to add the form DLL resource in the management pack.

LISTING 23.32   Add Resource Reference in Management Pack

```
<Resources>
  <Assembly ID="Forms" QualifiedName="Odyssey.CustomForms"
   FileName="Odyssey.CustomForms.dll" Accessibility="Public" />
</Resources>
```

The management pack is now complete and you can create the management pack bundle. The procedure to build a management pack bundle was previously described in the "Building and Sealing the Management Pack" section of this chapter.

Additional Resources

The customization scenarios around Service Manager are many; most are covered in this book. To further assist in customizing Service Manager, define processes, or add functionality, the next sections discuss several additional valuable resources.

Viewing Criteria Based on Tokens

Views in Service Manager can be based on *tokens*. A token is a placeholder that is replaced by a value at runtime when a view criterion is used to query the Service Manager database. The following tokens are available in Service Manager:

▶ [me]: This token is replaced by the user identifier of the logged on user running the console. Example: Change Request - Created By User

▶ **[mygroups]:** This token is replaced by a list of groups that the logged on user running the console is a member of.

▶ **[Now]:** This token is replaced by the current date and time at the time of the view querying the CMDB.

Read how to use these tokens in a view criterion at http://blogs.technet.com/b/service-manager/archive/2010/04/30/how-to-update-views-to-change-the-criteria-from-assigned-to-me-to-assigned-to-me-or-a-group-that-i-belong-to.aspx.

Building a Custom UserControl to Integrate into Forms

Service Manager comes with an extensive SDK, enabling different actions that can be coded to interact with forms. See http://blog.scsmsolutions.com/2011/08/create-custom-user-control-for-scsm-2010/ for information on how to utilize the SDK and build a UserControl that interacts with Service Manager.

Additional Custom Console Tasks

The "Creating Console Tasks Using PowerShell" section earlier in the chapter discussed a procedure to use PowerShell scripts and create console tasks. Console tasks can also be created using the SDK. The complete procedure to create console tasks with the SDK is explained at http://blogs.technet.com/b/servicemanager/archive/2010/12/22/tasks-part-2-custom-console-tasks-for-create-edit-delete.aspx.

Additional Form Customizations

When a class is extended in Service Manager, the forms are equipped with a new tab that shows the values of all extension properties. See http://blogs.technet.com/b/servicemanager/archive/2010/02/08/overview-of-the-forms-infrastructure-and-the-generic-form.aspx for information on how to hide this tab, hide the properties in the generic form, and more.

Using the TechNet Gallery for Service Manager

The TechNet Gallery is a library of resources that includes solutions for Service Manager. Before diving into customizations, first search in this library to determine whether any ready-to-use solutions are available that meet your needs. To access the Service Manager library, go to http://gallery.technet.microsoft.com. Select **System Center** as the category from the list on the left side of this page to display the System Center subcategories. You then can select **Service Manager** to access the gallery items.

Fast Track

The techniques behind creating custom objects, such as views or folders, have not changed since Service Manager 2010. Most custom views should work without changes or with little editing.

VSAE is a new addition for your Service Manager 2012 toolbox. This tool makes it easier to develop and maintain custom management packs than using several separate tools.

Summary

This chapter discussed how to use the Visual Studio Authoring Extensions to create a management pack, which contains several different types of customizations, such as custom classes, views, and a form. You can use the information available for creating custom forms for Service Manager in Visual Studio to do anything possible in Windows Presentation Foundation while integrating it into the Service Manager console.

The examples in Chapter 22 and Chapter 23 can help prepare you for most customization scenarios in Service Manager. Chapter 24, "Using PowerShell," discusses using PowerShell with Service Manager.

23

CHAPTER 24

Using PowerShell

PowerShell, the scripting and automation language of choice for Microsoft software, is a necessity in the toolbox of a more effective and efficient administrator. Knowing this language can save time and effort with System Center Service Manager as well as numerous other Microsoft products.

Using PowerShell is also important because of System Center Service Manager's focus on automation and integration with other systems, making it different from typical service management products that focus only on manual procedures.

PowerShell first debuted as Monad in 2005. Each version continues to improve its capabilities and functionality; this release of Service Manager includes improved PowerShell support and integration. While you can continue to leverage the Service Manager console on a daily basis, PowerShell provides the opportunity to fully automate Service Manager processes and make administration as easy as clicking a button.

This chapter focuses on PowerShell, native to Service Manager, and the additional functionality delivered by the CodePlex project SMLets. It includes a short primer on the PowerShell language and some practical examples on how to leverage PowerShell for your Service Manager environment, presenting a basic approach and more advanced scenarios that can deliver self-service.

Windows PowerShell Cmdlet Primer

Before looking at PowerShell in Service Manager, it is useful to understand some PowerShell basics. PowerShell consists of *cmdlets*. These are .NET programs designed to interact with PowerShell. Each cmdlet consists of a certain format that is a verb-noun construct, such as Get-*<noun>*, Set-*<noun>*, and Format-*<noun>*. PowerShell cmdlets use these three common verbs, placed before the nouns:

- ▶ **Get:** Cmdlets that fetch data.

- ▶ **Set:** Cmdlets that set or change data.

- ▶ **Format:** Cmdlets that format data for output.

It is important to note that while the output to the PowerShell console may look and act like text when you copy it to the clipboard, it is just a text representation of the underlying .NET objects exposed from the code that is run.

TIP: POWERSHELL IS NOT CASE SENSITIVE

Although this chapter uses mixed-case in cmdlet syntax for readability, PowerShell is not case sensitive.

Frequently Used and Useful Cmdlets

The next sections discuss some of the more frequently used cmdlets; use these to familiarize yourself with them if you are not familiar with PowerShell.

Get-Help Cmdlet

Get-Help can be used with any cmdlet in PowerShell to provide help for the exact usage of the cmdlet.

You can use Get-Help with the following parameters to retrieve additional information:

- ▶ **-full:** This shows all the help information on a cmdlet or topic.

- ▶ **-detailed:** This shows the majority of the help file.

- ▶ **-examples:** This shows only the synopsis and the examples given in the help file.

Examples follow using Get-SCSMClassInstance, which retrieves all Service Manager instances of a class:

```
Get-Help Get-SCSMClassInstance -full
Get-Help Get-SCSMClassInstance -detailed
Get-Help Get-SCSMClassInstance -examples
```

TIP: GET-HELP CMDLET ENHANCEMENT

While you can use Get-Help with the -full, -detailed, and -examples parameters, not every cmdlet is well documented. There might be situations where using -examples does not retrieve any examples!

However, updates to Get-Help only occur with new releases of the PowerShell module. To provide faster access to cmdlet documentation, Microsoft has implemented the -online parameter. Using this parameter points you directly to a TechNet article that discusses the cmdlet with associated help information.

For example, Get-Help Get-SCSMClassInstance -online opens the TechNet article describing this cmdlet at http://technet.microsoft.com/library/hh316279.aspx.

Alternatively, you could update the help files on your system by running the Update-Help cmdlet. Update-Help -module * -Force -Verbose updates help for all PowerShell modules.

After running the Update-Help cmdlet, you can also obtain help on a certain subject. Get-Help about_* displays all subjects.

Using Get-Command

This cmdlet gets basic information about cmdlets and other elements in PowerShell.

▶ Running Get-Command by itself gets all the cmdlets, functions, and aliases in the current PowerShell session.

▶ Running Get-Command with the -Module parameter retrieves all the cmdlets, functions, and aliases in that particular module.

```
Get-Command -Module System.Center.Service.Manager
```

By specifying System.Center.Service.Manager as the module in this example, using the Get-Command cmdlet retrieves just those cmdlets from the Service Manager module, as shown in Figure 24.1.

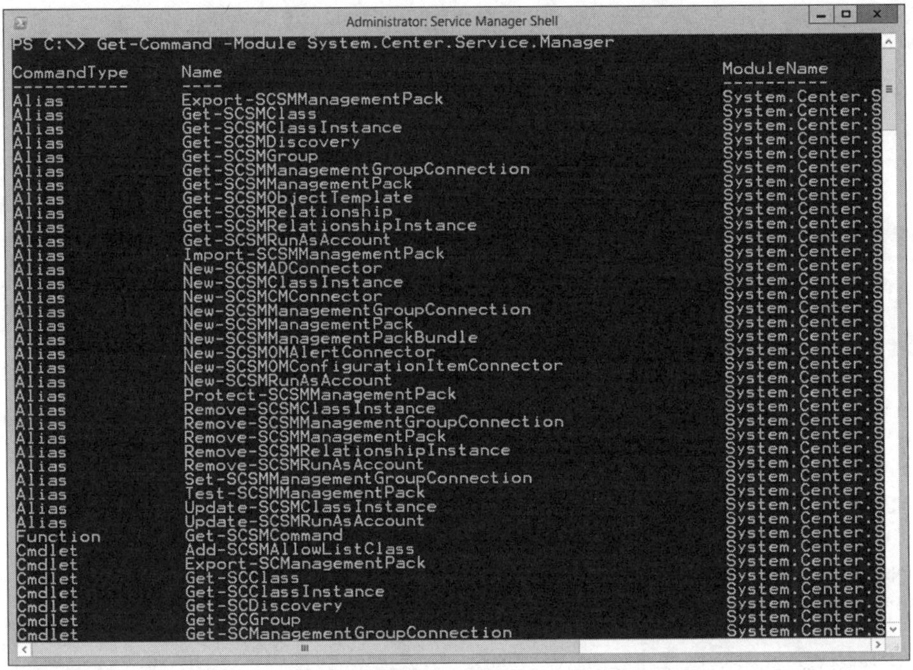

FIGURE 24.1 `Get-Command -Module System.Center.Service.Manager`.

About the Get-Member Cmdlet

A basic rule to know when using PowerShell cmdlets is they retrieve objects and not just results. This is far superior to previously used scripting languages.

`Get-Member` lets you retrieve all properties and methods available for a particular cmdlet.

▶ Properties contain information about the object type or instance, such as `Name`, `DisplayName`, and `ID`. To determine which properties you can retrieve for a particular cmdlet, use the `-MemberType` parameter:

```
Get-SCSMClass |Get-Member -MemberType Properties
```

Looking at the properties of the object retrieved using `Get-SCSMClass` shows all properties that could be retrieved using that cmdlet.

Now you can retrieve the properties of interest; the next command retrieves the `DisplayName` and whether the class is abstract:

```
Get-SCSMClass |Select-Object DisplayName, abstract
```

The following command retrieves only classes where the `abstract` property is set to True:

```
Get-SCSMClass -abstract $True
```

▶ Methods can act on the property of an object. Methods must be called using trailing brackets () and may require additional input, which you can determine using the `Get-Help` cmdlet previously demonstrated in the "Get-Help Cmdlet" section.

The next example retrieves all classes and uses the method `GetManagementPack` to retrieve the management pack `DisplayName` of the classes.

```
Get-SCSMClass |Select-Object Name, {$_.GetManagementPack().DisplayName}
```

`Get-Member` often reveals more information about a type or instance than you would see simply by running a cmdlet. `Get-Member` is displayed in Figure 24.2. `Get-Member` is helpful when trying to determine what information is available from the cmdlet you are working with, and indispensable when trying to write PowerShell scripts where native Service Manager cmdlets do not provide parameters to accomplish the task at hand.

Pipe Function

Use the `pipe` function "`|`" to retrieve the properties and methods of a particular cmdlet. As an example, `Get-SCSMClass |Get-Member` retrieves all methods and properties for the `Get-SCSMClass` cmdlet. This is shown in Figure 24.2.

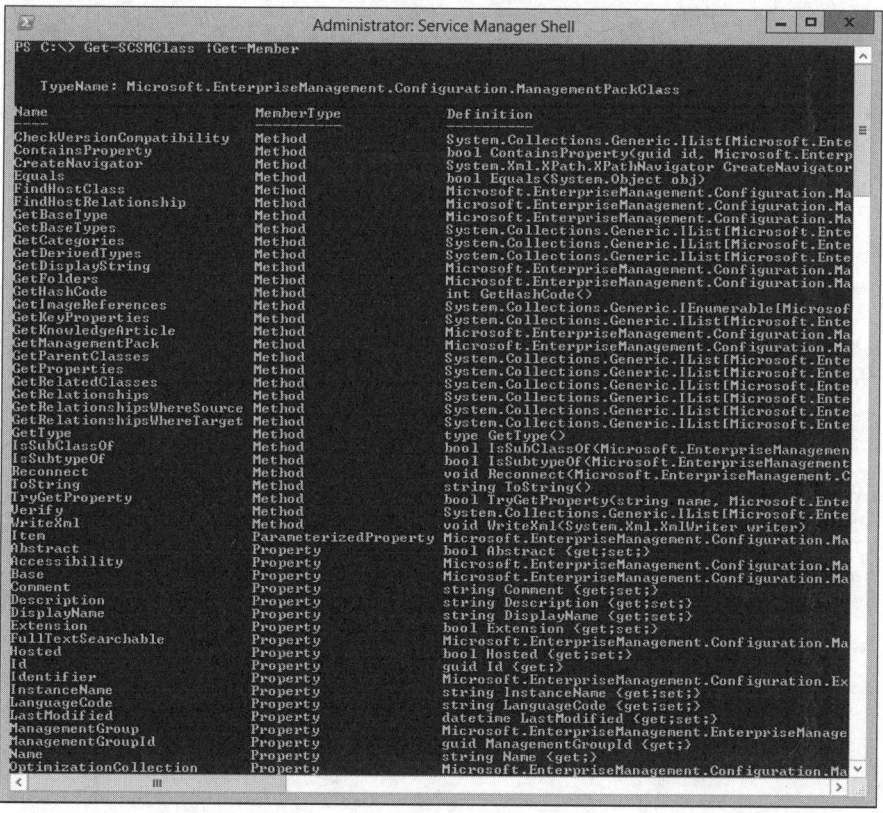

FIGURE 24.2   Using the `Get-Member` cmdlet.

The `pipe` function lets you pass output from one cmdlet, such as `Get-SCSMClass`, to the next cmdlet, `Get-Member`. Using these properties, you can then retrieve classes with a particular property. An example follows:

```
Get-SCSMClass -DisplayName "Incident"
```

This retrieves the `Incident` class. Extending this with `|Select-Object ID` retrieves the guid of the class:

```
Get-SCSMClass -DisplayName "Incident" |Select-Object ID
```

TIP: USING SELECT-OBJECT ID

`Select-Object ID` can be used to retrieve any guid. This is an easy way to retrieve the guid of an object in Service Manager; more advanced scenarios with Service Manager and PowerShell often require the guid of an object.

This small PowerShell cmdlet can be particularly useful when you want to combine usage of Orchestrator and PowerShell.

Combining Commands Using Pipe

The `pipe` function also lets you combine commands. You can retrieve an object in the first cmdlet and use this result in the next cmdlet by incorporating the `pipe` function; this provides additional opportunities to query and retrieve data results with PowerShell. An example follows:

```
Get-SCSMClass -DisplayName "Incident" |Get-SCSMClassInstance
```

This snippet retrieves all incidents from Service Manager. It first pulls the `Incident` class and then provides this information as input to the `Get-SCSMClassInstance` cmdlet.

Formatting and Grouping Results in PowerShell

You can easily format the results of your PowerShell command by using the `Format-List` or `Format-Table` cmdlets. Numerous options are available to format the results, and you can check all of them using `Get-Help`:

▶ **Format-List:** Results are shown in a list output; use `Get-Help Format-List -full` for a full explanation on this topic.

▶ **Format-Table:** Results are shown in a table; use `Get-Help Format-Table -full` for a complete explanation on this topic.

```
Get-SCSMClass -DisplayName "Incident" |Get-SCSMClassInstance |Format-Table ID,
    Title
```

This snippet displays all incidents in a table with the headers ID and Title, as shown in Figure 24.3.

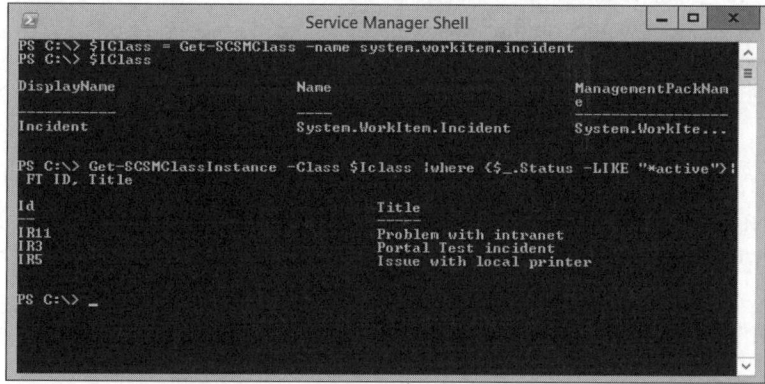

FIGURE 24.3   `Format-Table` cmdlet.

You can easily pull all incidents from your Service Manager environment using a single PowerShell command. You can use the `Format-List` or `Format-Table` cmdlets to format the result. You can also group the results based on a property on the object, such as grouping all incidents on status:

```
Get-SCSMClass -DisplayName "Incident" |Get-SCSMClassInstance |Format-Table ID, Title
   -groupby Status
```

This snippet provides the results grouped by status. If you look closely, it groups the results by status but not all of them are grouped correctly. This is shown in Figure 24.4.

The reason the `-groupby` function doesn't deliver the desired results is because `Format-Table` is stream-oriented. This means it processes the object and moves on to the next object. If you really want to use `-groupby`, all results should first be collected and then grouped.

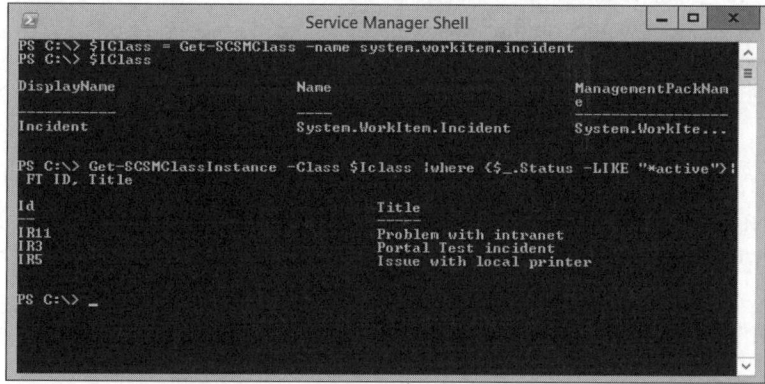

FIGURE 24.4   Using the `-groupby` function.

Sort-Object

To have `Format-Table` deliver the correct result, use the `Sort-Object` cmdlet to sort the results prior to placing them in the formatted table:

```
Get-SCSMClass -DisplayName "Incident" |Get-SCSMClassInstance |Sort-Object
  Status|Format-Table ID, Title -groupby Status
```

You can sort your results with the `Sort-Object` cmdlet. Notice how you can use the pipe symbol to create a pipeline of piping one result into the other one. Let's break down the snippet to understand exactly what occurs:

1. `Get-SCSMClass -DisplayName "Incident"` gets the `Incident` class from Service Manager and puts it into the pipeline.

2. Once in the pipeline, the object is sent to the next cmdlet, `Get-SCSMClassInstance`, which retrieves all instances from the earlier retrieved `Incident` class and puts the results in the pipeline.

3. You now have all incident objects in the pipeline, and they can be sorted by the property `Status`.

4. In the last step, the sorted incident objects are taken from the pipeline; only the `ID` of the incident object and the `Title` are retrieved. They are then grouped by `Status`.

Using this example, you should be able to understand how you can pipe `"|"` results from one cmdlet to the other resulting in a pipeline.

TIP: MORE INFORMATION ON THE PIPELINE

A full discussion regarding the PowerShell pipeline is beyond the scope of this chapter. For additional information about the pipeline, PowerShell MVP Don Jones provides several resources:

▶ Http://technet.microsoft.com/en-us/magazine/2007.07.powershell.aspx provides a nice discussion of the pipeline and what it can do for you.

▶ Don created a pipeline input workbook that walks through how the pipeline works, available on the morelunches.com website. See http://morelunches.files.wordpress.com/2013/12/psh3-pipelineinput.pdf for information.

Filtering Results

When running PowerShell cmdlets, you want to be able to filter your results to retrieve only the information in which you are interested.

When you take the example provided in the previous "Sort-Object" section to retrieve incidents, you might want to modify it to retrieve only certain incidents, such as those that are opened or closed. Examples follow:

```
Get-SCSMClass -DisplayName "Incident" |Get-SCSMClassInstance |Where-Object
  {$_.Status -LIKE "*active"}| Format-Table ID, Title
```

```
Get-SCSMClass -DisplayName "Incident" |Get-SCSMClassInstance |Where-Object
  {$_.Status -LIKE "*closed"}| Format-Table ID, Title
```

Notice the `Where-Object {$_.Status -LIKE "*closed"}`:

1. `Where-Object` is the cmdlet to filter your results.

2. `$_` is the variable for the object, in this example the Service Manager class instance object, and `.Status` is the property of the retrieved object. Remember to use the `Get-Member` cmdlet to retrieve all possible properties and methods.

3. `-LIKE` is the comparison operator and `"*closed"` the value to compare to the property `Status` of the retrieved object. The `*` character is used as a wild card, meaning that any value ending with `*closed` is used.

The entire filter must be in curly brackets `{}`.

Table 24.1 lists the possible comparison operators used within PowerShell.

TABLE 24.1   Comparison Operators in PowerShell

Operator	Description
-LT	Less than
-LE	Less than or equal to
-GT	Greater than
-GE	Greater than or equal to
-EQ	Equal to
-NE	Not equal to
-LIKE	Use wild cards for pattern matching
-MATCH	A match using regular expressions
-CONTAINS	Used to see if a collection or group of items contain a given item

Aliases and Variables in PowerShell

PowerShell supports aliases for cmdlets; these assign another (generally shorter) name to a cmdlet. As an example, if you use `Where-Object`, the predefined alias for this cmdlet is `Where`. Another example is `FT` for `Format-Table` or `FL` for `Format-List`.

Using aliases can help you write shorter (and quicker) PowerShell scripts or commands. Use the `Get-Alias` cmdlet to retrieve aliases:

```
Get-Alias | Where-Object {$_.Name -like "*SCSM*"}
```

This command retrieves all aliases with a name containing *SCSM*.

For additional information on aliases within PowerShell, see http://technet.microsoft.com/en-us/library/ee692685.aspx.

Using Variables

Another great feature of PowerShell is its use of variables. You can use variables to "store" data or cmdlets to be used later in PowerShell. These could come in handy particularly when you are going to write PowerShell scripts.

Variables are denoted by a dollar sign $, you can test this with the examples. If you write `$Result` = in front of your command, you can store data in the variable.

Test this by running `$InClass = Get-SCSMClass -DisplayName "Incident"`. This snippet stores the result on the variable `$InClass`. You can test this by running `$InClass`; it should show the result of `Get-SCSMClass -DisplayName "Incident"`.

Because you are still in the same PowerShell session, you can now reuse the variable throughout that session.

```
$InClass|Get-SCSMClassInstance |Format-Table ID, Title
$InClass|Get-SCSMClassInstance |where {$_.Status -LIKE "*active"}| FT ID, Title
```

This is actually the same command used previously in the "Filtering Results" section. See Figure 24.5 for the results.

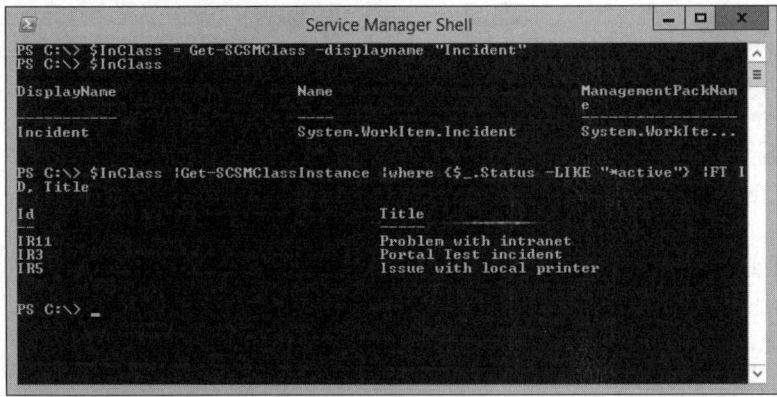

FIGURE 24.5   Using variables, aliases, and filters.

TIP: ().COUNT

A well-known .NET method you can also use in PowerShell is the `()`.Count method.

You can use this to calculate the objects collected. In the following example, using this method gives you the current total open number of incidents:

```
($InClass |Get-SCSMClassInstance |where {$_.Status -LIKE "*active"}| FT
    ID, Title).count
```

Using the PowerShell Integrated Scripting Environment

You can use any editor to write PowerShell scripts, although the authors recommend the PowerShell Integrated Scripting Environment (ISE). Accessing the ISE varies depending on the version of Windows you are running:

▶ The PowerShell ISE is installed by default beginning with Windows Server 2012. Windows 2012 loads all modules by default, including the Service Manager modules if the Service Manager console is installed on the server or desktop.

▶ For Windows 2008 Release 2 (R2), you need to add the feature Windows PowerShell Integrated Scripting Environment (ISE). You must add the module before you can start using it in ISE; use the Import-Module cmdlet to load the module in Windows 2008 R2 ISE.

Figure 24.6 shows the PowerShell Integrated Scripting Environment.

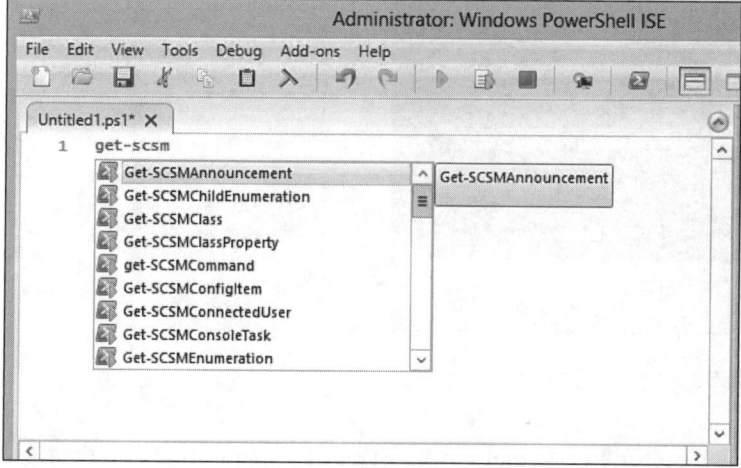

FIGURE 24.6   PowerShell Integrated Scripting Environment.

When using ISE, you can also use IntelliSense by pressing Ctrl and the spacebar. For instance, when you start typing Get-SCSM and press Ctrl and spacebar, you are automatically shown all cmdlets starting with Get-SCSM as displayed in Figure 24.7.

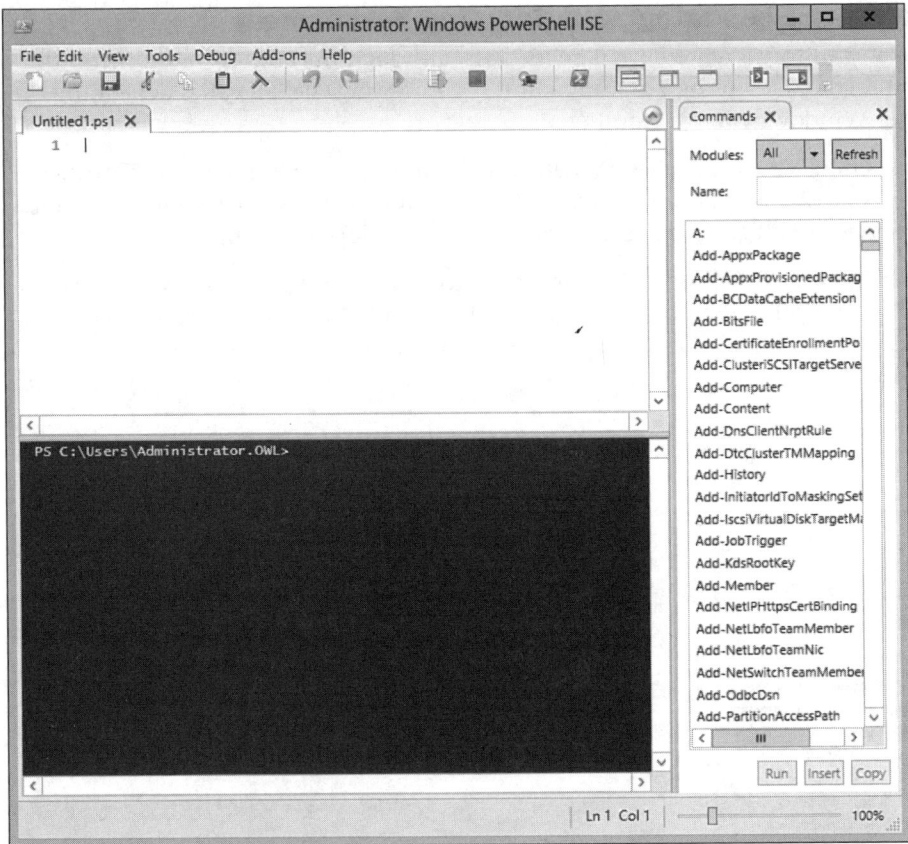

FIGURE 24.7   ISE and IntelliSense.

You can also easily view the help for a particular cmdlet. The right pane shows all cmdlets and the parameters these cmdlets accept.

Although the scripting environment loads the modules, you still must add the `Import-Module` line in your script since the script runs in a default PowerShell shell without any loaded modules.

Service Manager and PowerShell

You can use PowerShell in Service Manager by writing a PowerShell script or using the PowerShell cmdlets in the Service Manager Shell.

The Service Manager Shell, which can be accessed from the Windows Start menu, starts PowerShell and loads the Service Manager PowerShell module. Figure 24.8 shows the Service Manager Shell.

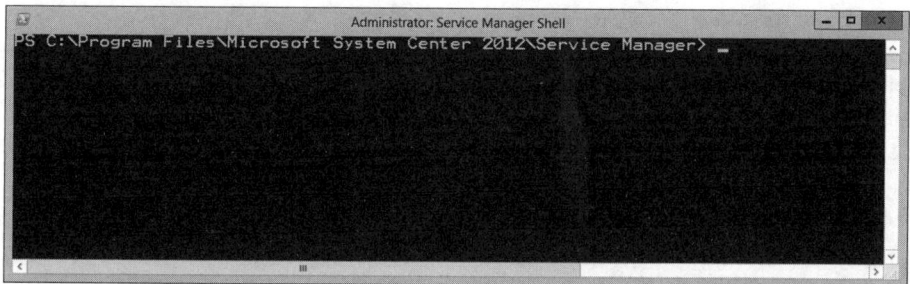

FIGURE 24.8   Service Manager Shell.

Connecting to Service Manager Management Server from PowerShell

When running PowerShell from the Service Manager console, you need to specify the Service Manager management server to which you want to connect.

Using the parameter -ComputerName behind a cmdlet runs the cmdlet on the specified management server:

```
Get-SCSMClass -ComputerName Blizzard
```

This connects to the Service Manager management server Blizzard and runs the cmdlet Get-SCSMClass.

Alternatively, you could connect the PowerShell session itself to your management group by using the cmdlet New-SCSMManagementGroupConnection:

```
New-SCSMManagementGroupConnection -ComputerName Blizzard
```

This establishes a management group connection to the Service Manager management server Blizzard. After setting up the management group connection, using any cmdlet without specifying a Service Manager management server causes the cmdlet to run against the connected management group.

TIP: SERVICE MANAGER AND OPERATIONS MANAGER POWERSHELL

Service Manager is built on the same framework as Operations Manager. Under the hood, Service Manager is Operations Manager without a monitoring function or agents. As the framework is the same, the cmdlets in Operations Manager and Service Manager often are the same.

When you look at the cmdlets in Service Manager, you notice most of them are aliases of cmdlets starting with sc instead of scsm.

For example, `Get-SCSMCLass` is an alias for `Get-SCClass`.

`Get-SCClass` works with both Operations Manager and Service Manager, and the code for this cmdlet is exactly the same.

Most cmdlets used in System Center 2012 Operations Manager are now renamed to `Get-SC...`, instead of `Get-SCOM....`

Once you know how to use the PowerShell cmdlets in either System Center component, you can reuse these cmdlets and even scripts.

Service Manager Cmdlet Use Cases

There are currently 90 cmdlets in the Service Manager native module. The next sections provide some examples on how to use these cmdlets.

Retrieving Information on Open Incidents, Changes, and Service Requests

To get information quickly regarding currently open incidents, changes, or service requests, use a combination of `Get-SCSMClass` and `Get-SCSMClassInstance`.

Using `Get-SCSMClass`, you retrieve the actual class and can put these results in a variable, shown in Figure 24.9.

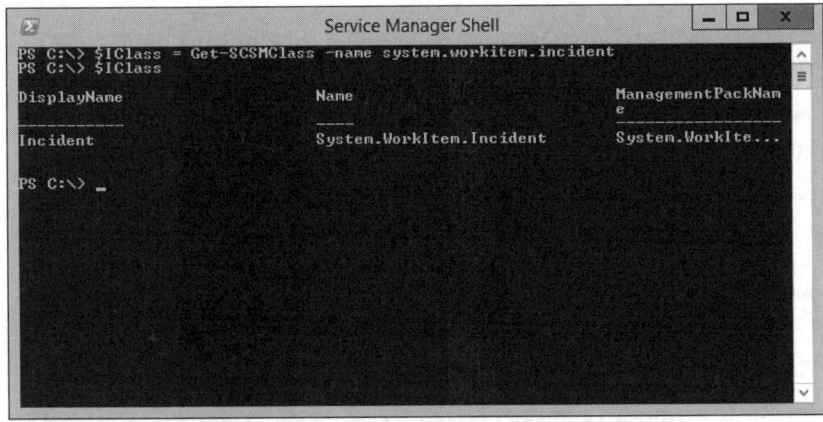

FIGURE 24.9   Putting the results in a variable.

```
$IClass = Get-SCSMClass -Name system.workitem.incident
$CClass = Get-SCSMClass -Name system.workitem.changerequest
$SClass = Get-SCSMClass -Name system.workitem.servicerequest
$PClass = Get-SCSMClass -Name system.workitem.problem
```

Retrieving an Instance of a Work Item

With `Get-SCSMClassInstance`, you can retrieve an actual instance of a work item (see Figure 24.10).

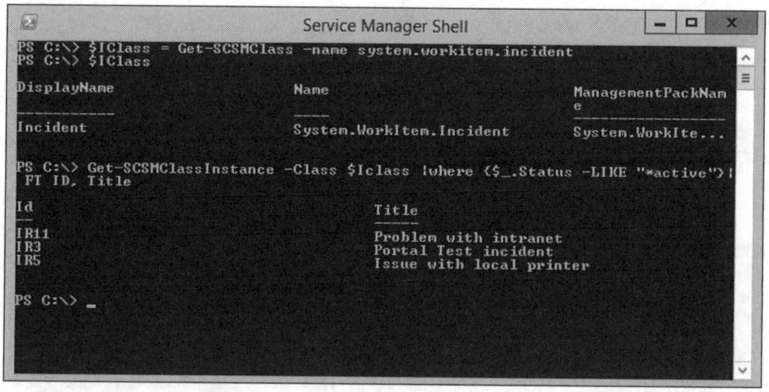

FIGURE 24.10   Instance of a work item.

The following examples also use the variables created in the previous section to specify the type of class:

```
Get-SCSMClassInstance -Class $Iclass |where {$_.Status -LIKE "*active"}| FT ID,
   Title
Get-SCSMClassInstance -Class $CClass |where {$_.Status -LIKE "*active"}| FT ID,
   Title
Get-SCSMClassInstance -Class $SClass |where {$_.Status -LIKE "*active"}| FT ID,
   Title
Get-SCSMClassInstance -Class $PClass |where {$_.Status -LIKE "*active"}| FT ID,
   Title
```

Retrieving Open Incidents with Their Assigned User

Use `Get-SCSMIncident` to retrieve open incidents and their assigned user:

```
Get-SCSMIncident -status Active |FT ID, Title, affecteduser,assigned to
```

This displays all open incidents with the affected user that are assigned to user relationships.

Reopening Incidents

You can use a simple one-liner to reopen a closed incident:

```
Get-SCSMIncident -id IR116 | Set-SCSMIncident -status Active
```

This retrieves an incident with ID IR116 and sets the status to Active.

Retrieving the Allowed List

Use the next cmdlet to retrieve the Allowed List for the Operations Manager connector; these are the classes allowed to be imported from Operations Manager to Service Manager:

```
Get-SCSMAllowList
```

This command retrieves all classes that are "allowed" to be synchronized with the Operations Manager connector.

Retrieving Run As Accounts

Retrieve Run As accounts to see all Run As accounts configured in Service Manager:

```
Get-SCSMRunAsAccount
```

This retrieves all Run As user accounts from Service Manager.

Connection Settings

To retrieve connection settings for the current connection to Service Manager, use this next cmdlet:

```
Get-SCSMManagementGroupConnection
```

This example gets the current connection settings from your PowerShell session to Service Manager.

By using `New-SCSMManagementGroupConnection`, you can create a new management group connection; you can use this to connect to any Service Manager management group:

```
New-SCSMManagementgroupconnection -ComputerName Cumulus
```

This connects to the data warehouse management group (Cumulus in the Odyssey lab). To remove the connection to the management group:

```
Get-SCSMManagementGroupConnection -ManagementGroupName dw_DWGRP|
  Remove-SCSMManagementGroupConnection
```

This removes the connection to the data warehouse management group dw_DWGRP.

Retrieving Classes in a Management Pack

The next snippet retrieves all classes from a particular management pack:

```
Get-SCSMClass |where {$_.GetManagementPack().DisplayName -eq " Windows Server
  Operating System Library
"}
```

This uses the method approach to retrieve all classes within the management pack.

Writing Service Manager PowerShell Scripts

When you write a PowerShell script and run the script, it runs from the default PowerShell shell. You need to be aware that when you want to use other modules (such as the Service Manager module), you must first load these modules in your script.

The previous examples are all run from the Service Manager Shell, which is basically a shortcut to start the PowerShell shell and load the Service Manager module.

When you start writing a script, you first need to add the Service Manager module:

```
Import-Module 'C:\Program Files\Microsoft System Center\Service Manager 2012\
PowerShell\System.Center.Service.Manager.psd1'
```

This line imports the Service Manager PowerShell module. You then can start writing your PowerShell script.

TIP: IMPORT MODULES

To use a module in your PowerShell script, you can use the `Import-Module` cmdlet. Examples follow:

▶ **Service Manager module:**

```
Import-Module 'C:\Program Files\Microsoft System Center 2012\Service
Manager\PowerShell\System.Center.Service.Manager.psd1'
```

▶ **Service Manager data warehouse module:**

```
Import-Module 'C:\Program Files\Microsoft System Center 2012\Service
Manager\ Microsoft.EnterpriseManagement.Warehouse.Cmdlets.psd1'
SMLets module -Import-Module SMLets
```

To load the modules by default, check Rob Ford's walkthrough on how to add the modules to your PowerShell profile, available at
http://scsmnz.net/setting-up-your-powershell-profile-to-run-service-manager-commandlets/.

After adding `Import-Module` to your PowerShell script, you can start writing the rest of the script.

An example of how the PowerShell script should appear follows, showing a simple script to export unsealed management packs. This script is based on the unsealed MPbackup management pack, originally written by Steve Beaumont for Service Manager 2010 and available at http://gallery.technet.microsoft.com/Service-Manager-2010-9fd2ea90.

At that time, the script required using SMLets; with Service Manager 2012, these cmdlets are native in the Service Manager module. This change is reflected in the `Import-Module` statement:

```
$TargetFilePath = 'C:\ExportUnsealedMP'
#Initializing the SCSM 2012 Service Manager Module
Import-Module 'C:\Program Files\Microsoft System Center 2012\Service Manager\
PowerShell\System.Center.Service.Manager.psd1'

#Create TargetDir if it doesn't exist
if (test-path $TargetFilePath)
{
"Folder Exists"
}
else
{
md "$TargetFilePath"
}
```

```
#Create new backup dir
md "$TargetFilePath\MP_$((get-date).toString('yyyyMMdd'))"

#Backup unsealed MPs
Get-SCSMManagementPack|Where-Object {! $_.Sealed}|Export-SCSMManagementPack
  -TargetDirectory "$TargetFilePath\MP_$((get-date).toString('yyyyMMdd'))"
```

An explanation of the script follows:

1. Declare the target folder to a variable $TargetFilePath.

2. Import the Service Manager PowerShell module.

3. Check whether the target folder exists; if not, create a new one.

4. Check whether date-specific folder exists; if not, create a new one.

5. The last line retrieves all unsealed management packs and exports them to the target folder.

Service Manager PowerShell Script Use Cases

The next sections include commonly used examples of PowerShell in combination with Service Manager. You can use these scripts for automation within Service Manager or in combination with Orchestrator.

Retrieving All Manual Activities Related to a Service Request

The script in this section can be used to automate or change manual activities in bulk. An example is a runbook, which copies the title of a service request to all manual activities for a particular service request.

The following code snippet gets all manual activities related to a service request.

1. The snippet starts by importing the Service Manager module to use the Service Manager cmdlets:

   ```
   # Importing Service Manager Module
   Import-Module "%Program Files%\Microsoft System Center 2012\Service Manager\
   PowerShell\System.Center.Service.Manager.psd1"
   ```

2. It then creates a variable $SRQ to store the ID of the service request.

   ```
   $SRQ="SR207"
   ```

3. Next, it creates a variable ParentRequestRelationshipID to store the GUID. For information on how to retrieve the GUID, see the earlier tip "Using Select-Object ID."

   ```
   $ParentRequestRelationshipID = "2da498be-0485-b2b2-d520-6ebd1698e61b"
   ```

4. It retrieves the service request class using `Get-SCSMClass` and stores it in a variable called `$SRQclass`.

```
$SRQclass = Get-SCSMClass -Name System.WorkItem.ServiceRequest
```

5. Next, it gets the relationship class `WorkItem` and stores it in the `$SRQAObjectRelClass` variable.

```
# Get object relationship
$SRQMAObjectRelClass =
    Get-SCSMRelationshipClass -Name System.WorkItemContainsActivity
```

6. It retrieves the Incident object by class = variable `$SRQClass` and ID equals variable `$SRQ`.

```
# Get SRQ Object
$SRQobject = Get-SCSMObject -Class $SRQclass -Filter "ID -eq $SRQ"
```

7. It then gets the related child activity objects filtered on ID starting with MA and stores these in variable `$RelatedChildActivity`.

```
#Get All Manual activities related to the SRQ
$RelatedChildActivity = (Get-SCSMRelationshipObject -BySource $SRQobject |
    ?{$_.RelationshipID -eq $ParentRequestRelationshipID -and $_.IsDeleted -eq
    $False -and $_.TargetObject.Name -like "MA*"})
```

8. Last, it creates a variable result and stores the name of the related child activity object.

```
$Result=$RelatedChildActivity.Targetobject.Name
Return $Result
```

The script pulls all manual activities from a service request. You can use the script to retrieve all manual activities from a service request and change the title of the activities to the same as the service request.

You could also use this script to change or update any property on the activities at once. This script would be extremely powerful if you use it with System Center Orchestrator to automatically populate the service request ID.

Changing this script in step 7 as in the following example has it pull all review activities:

```
$RelatedChildActivity = (Get-SCSMRelationshipObject -BySource $SRQobject |
  ?{$_.RelationshipID -eq $ParentRequestRelationshipID -and $_.IsDeleted -eq $False
  -and $_.TargetObject.Name -like "RA*")
```

Service Manager Console Extensions—Impacted Business Services

This next script shows impacted business services for a particular change. You could use it to easily identify which business services are impacted by a change.

```
#Note:  Replace the value in $svr to your Service Manager management server
$svr = "SM01"

#Import-Module SMLets;
$Args = ([string]$CRid);

#$CRid = "CR3710";
#$CRid = "CR2473";
$CRid = "CR2485";

#Line below not used; can be used to pass the CR from the command line.  scriptname
#<Crid>
#$CRid = $Args ;

#Defines the empty array for Impacted Services
$ImpactedServices = @();

#Step 1 get the CR;
$CRProj = Get-SCSMTypeProjection System.WorkItem.ChangeRequestProjection
  -ComputerName SM01;
$GetCR = Get-SCSMObjectProjection $CRProj -Filter "ID -eq $CRID" -ComputerName SM01

#Un-Comment the following 2 lines to see the 'Change Request' Projection from the CR.;
#Write-Host "The Current Change Request:";
#$GetCR;

#Step 2 Identify Items to Change from CR form;
$ItemsToChangeInCR = @();
$ItemsToChangeInCR = $GetCR|%{$_.HasRelatedWorkItems};
$ItemsToChangeInCR = $ItemsToChangeInCR.DisplayName;
$ItemsToChangeInCR = @($ItemsToChangeInCR);
$NumOfItemsToChangeInCR=$ItemsToChangeInCR.count;

#Un-Comment the following 2 lines to see the 'Items to Change' items from the CR.;
#Write-Host "List Items that will be changed in the change request:";
#$ItemsToChangeInCR;

#Step 3 Initialize Business Services;
$GetBSVS = Get-SCSMTypeProjection Microsoft.System.Service.FormProjectionType
  -ComputerName $svr;
$index=0;$mycmd="";$myfullcmd="";ForEach ($myargs in $ItemsToChangeInCR){$mycmd =
  $mycmd + '$_.TargetConfigItem -match $itemsTOchangeInCR['+$index+'] -or ' ;$index++}

#Step 4  Remove the trailing text and execute the command;
#To Strip the Trailing "-or"
```

```
$mycmd = $mycmd.substring(0,$mycmd.Length -5)

#build the command to execute
$Myfullcmd = '$GetBSVSProj = Get-SCSMObjectProjection $GetBSVS -ComputerName $svr |
  where {'+ $mycmd + '}'

#Execute the string as a PowerShell command
iex -command $Myfullcmd

#Step 6 (optional) retrieve the Business Services projection
#Un-Comment the following 2 lines to see the 'Business Services' projection Note:All
#Business Services.;
#Write-Host "List to Business Services Projection:";
#$GetBSVSProj;

Write-Host "Impacted Business Services" for $GetCR.ID;
Write-Host "=======================================";

#If we don't have items to change then there's no impacted business services.
if (!($ItemsToChangeInCR)) {"<none>";
exit};

$ImpactedServices = $GetBSVSProj.DisplayName
$ImpactedServices|Sort-Object|Get-Unique
```

The complete solution, written by John Wilson and including how to add this script to a Service Manager task, can be found at the TechNet Gallery; see http://gallery.technet.microsoft.com/SCSM-Console-Extensions-ff8a1026.

Retrieve Email Address of Service Manager User

A common task is to use PowerShell to retrieve a user's email address.

```
#Comment: Change User Displayname to retrieve the email of a different user or you
#can use this script in Orchestrator to use published data from a Get-User activity
#to populate the user DisplayName.

$userdisplayname = "Oskar.Landman"
param($userdisplayname)
Import-Module SMLets
#Comment: The User class has a relation called "User has Preference" which
#we are storing in a variable.
$userpreferenceclass = Get-SCSMRelationshipclass -Name System.Userhaspreference$
#Comment: Now we will select the User that we got from the previous object.
#But first we have to select the object class for it.
$class = Get-SCSMClass -Name System.User$
$user = Get-SCSMObject -Class $class -filter "displayname -eq $userdisplayname"
```

```
#Comment: Now we access the SMTP address by using the relationship. The
#output will be the SMTP address.
$mail = (Get-SCSMRelatedObject -smobject $user -relationship $userpreferenceclass |
  where{$_.displayname -match "smtp"}).targetaddress
return $mail
```

Using PowerShell for Data Warehouse Administration

You can administer your data warehouse with PowerShell; all configuration settings and more can be set with PowerShell. These cmdlets are located in the module `Microsoft.EnterpriseManagement.Warehouse.Cmdlets`.

To load the module:

```
Import-Module
  'C:\Program Files\Microsoft System Center 2012\Service Manager\
Microsoft.EnterpriseManagement.Warehouse.Cmdlets.psd1'
```

Once the module is loaded, you can also execute `Get-Command -Module Microsoft.EnterpriseManagement.Warehouse.Cmdlets` to retrieve all the cmdlets in this module.

NOTE: DATA WAREHOUSE CONNECTION

When using the cmdlets to administer your data warehouse management server, you must always specify the data warehouse management server.

You can do this by adding the parameter `-ComputerName` and the name of the data warehouse server. An example follows, where the data warehouse management server is Cumulus:

```
Get-SCDWJob -ComputerName Cumulus
```

This connects to the data warehouse management server and retrieves all jobs on the data warehouse management server.

Data Warehouse Cmdlet Use Cases

The data warehouse cmdlets are discussed in the following sections. For online information regarding these cmdlets and full descriptions and examples, see http://technet.microsoft.com/en-us/library/hh541724(v=sc.20).aspx.

Working with Data Warehouse Jobs

A number of cmdlets are associated with data warehouse jobs:

▶ **Enable-SCDWJob:** This cmdlet allows data warehouse administrators to enable jobs so that they can run according to their specified schedule or run manually. To disable the jobs, use the `Disable-SCDWJob` cmdlet.

```
Enable-SCDWJob -ComputerName Cumulus -JobName MPSyncJob
```

This enables MPSyncJob on the data warehouse management server.

▶ **Disable-SCDWJob:** This cmdlet allows data warehouse administrators to disable jobs to prevent the jobs from running. This means that the jobs cannot be run according to their defined schedule, and they cannot be run manually. To re-enable the jobs, use the `Enable-SCDWJob` cmdlet.

```
Disable-SCDWJob -ComputerName Cumulus -JobName MPSyncJob
```

This disables MPSyncJob on the data warehouse server.

▶ **Get-SCDWJob:** Gets the list of all data warehouse jobs, displaying information such as the status of these jobs.

```
Get-SCDWJob -ComputerName Cumulus
```

This example retrieves all jobs from the data warehouse management server Cumulus.

▶ **Start-SCDWJob:** Starts a data warehouse job.

```
Start-SCDWJob -ComputerName Cumulus -JobName MPSyncJob
```

This starts MPSyncJob on the data warehouse management server.

▶ **Stop-SCDWJob:** Stops a data warehouse job.

```
Stop-SCDWJob -ComputerName Cumulus -JobName MPSyncJob
```

This stops MPSyncJob on the data warehouse management server.

▶ **Get-SCDWJobModule:** Returns detailed status information about the modules of the specified job.

```
Get-SCDWJobModule -ComputerName scsmdw01 -JobName MPSyncJob
```

This retrieves all modules from MPSyncJob on the data warehouse management server.

Working with Job Categories

All data warehouse jobs are categorized in categories; using the category lets you manage all data warehouse jobs for that category.

▶ **Enable-SCDWJobCategory:** This cmdlet allows data warehouse administrators to enable jobs in a Job category so that the jobs can run according to their specified schedule or run manually. To re-enable the jobs, use the `Enable-SCDWJobCategory` cmdlet. Example:

```
Enable-SCDWJobCategory -ComputerName Cumulus -JobCategoryName synchronization
```

This enables all jobs with category "Synchronization" (MPSyncJob).

▶ **Disable-SCDWJobCategory:** This cmdlet allows data warehouse administrators to disable jobs affiliated with the specified data source, preventing the jobs from running.

```
Disable-SCDWJobCategory -ComputerName Cumulus -JobCategoryName synchronization
```

This disables all jobs with category "Synchronization" (MPSyncJob).

Working with Job Schedules

All data warehouse jobs are scheduled to run at certain intervals. By using the job schedule cmdlets you can manage, add to, or edit these schedules.

▶ **Enable-SCDWJobSchedule:** The cmdlet allows data warehouse administrators to enable job schedules so that jobs run according to their specified schedule. If the job schedule was previously disabled, enabling the job schedule retains the job schedule's settings. To disable the job schedule, use the `Disable-SCDWJobSchedule` cmdlet. To modify the job's schedule, use the `Set-SCDWJobSchedule` cmdlet.

```
Enable-SCDWJobSchedule -ComputerName Cumulus -JobName MPSyncJob
```

This enables the schedule for job MPSyncJob on the data warehouse management server.

▶ **Disable-SCDWJobSchedule:** The cmdlet disables a data warehouse job schedule.

```
Disable-SCDWJobSchedule -ComputerName Cumulus -JobName MPSyncJob
```

This disables the schedule for job MPSyncJob on the data warehouse management server.

▶ **Get-SCDWJobSchedule:** The `Get-SCDWJobSchedule` cmdlet displays scheduling information for data warehouse jobs.

```
Get-SCDWJobSchedule -ComputerName Cumulus
```

This retrieves all job schedules from the data warehouse management server Cumulus.

▶ **Set-SCDWJobSchedule:** Sets the schedule for a data warehouse job.

```
Set-SCDWJobSchedule -ComputerName Cumulus -JobName Transform.Common
  -DailyFrequency 00:30 -DailyStart 00:00
```

This sets the schedule of the Transform.Common job on the data warehouse management server.

Using Data Sources

Data sources in Service Manager are the connections from other databases to the data warehouse database. You can manage these data sources by using the data source cmdlets in the data warehouse module.

▶ **Enable-SCDWSource:** This cmdlet allows data warehouse administrators to enable jobs affiliated with the specified data source to prevent the jobs from running, so that jobs run according to their specified schedule.

```
Enable-SCDWSource -ComputerName Cumulus -DataSourceName SMGRP
```

This enables the data source SMGRP on the data warehouse management server.

▶ **Disable-SCDWSource:** This cmdlet allows data warehouse administrators to disable jobs affiliated with the specified data source to prevent the jobs from running.

```
Disable-SCDWSource -ComputerName Cumulus -DataSourceName SMGRP
```

This disables the data source SMGRP on the data warehouse management server.

▶ **Get-SCDWSource:** Gets specific instances of data sources that are registered to the data warehouse.

```
Get-SCDWSource -ComputerName Cumulus
```

This retrieves all data sources from data warehouse management server Cumulus.

▶ **Register-SCDWSource:** Registers instances of data source types, such as Service Manager, Operations Manager, and Configuration Manager, to the data warehouse.

```
Register-SCDWSource -ComputerName Cumulus -DataSourceTypeName OperationsManager
  -SourceComputerName Helios -DataSourceDbName OperationsManager
  -DataSourceDbServerName Thundercloud\sql_om
  -FullPathToSourceManagementPackBundle "%ProgramFiles%\Microsoft System
Center\Service Manager 2012\OperationsManagerMP.mpb"
```

This registers an Operations Manager data source.

▶ **Get-SCDWSourceType:** Gets the types of data sources that can be registered to the data warehouse.

```
Get-SCSMDWSourceType -ComputerName Cumulus
```

This retrieves all data source types from the data warehouse management server (Cumulus)

▶ **New-SCDWSourceType:** Creates a new type of data source that can be registered to the data warehouse. This cmdlet is used to create a custom data source type, based on a management bundle where you define the data source, classes, and relationships.

```
New-SCDWSourceType -ComputerName Cumulus -SourceConfigFile
  "%ProgramFiles%\Microsoft System Center\Management Packs\
CustomHumanRelationsDataSource.mpb"
```

This creates a new data source type, in this case for a human resources database.

▶ **Set-SCDWSource:** Updates the definition of classes and relationships that can be populated for an instance of a data source.

```
Set-SCDWSource -DataSourceType ConfigurationManager.DataSource
  -DataSourceName MSITData -Properties @{ Version=
  "D0925349-F1FC-1084-0761-EE60D21B1141}"
  -FullPathToSourceManagementPackBundle "C:\DataSource\CMSourceTest.mpb"
  -ComputerName Cumulus
```

This updates the version of the Configuration Manager data source.

▶ **UnRegister-SCDWSource:** Unregisters a data source from the data warehouse.

```
UnRegister-SCDWSource -ComputerName Cumulus
  -DataSourceTypeName "ServiceManager" -DataSourceName "DW_DWGRP"
```

This unregisters a data source from the data warehouse management server.

Data Warehouse Entities

A data warehouse entity is basically a view or table within the DWDatamart database. The Get-SCDWEntity cmdlet lets you retrieve all fact, tables, dimensions, and outriggers; this is a quick way to identify the entities for reporting purposes.

▶ **Get-SCDWEntity:** This cmdlet retrieves a list of fact tables, dimensions, tables, and outriggers that exist in a data warehouse. An example of Get-SCDWEntity follows, with output displayed in Figure 24.11.

```
Get-SCDWEntity -ComputerName Cumulus
```

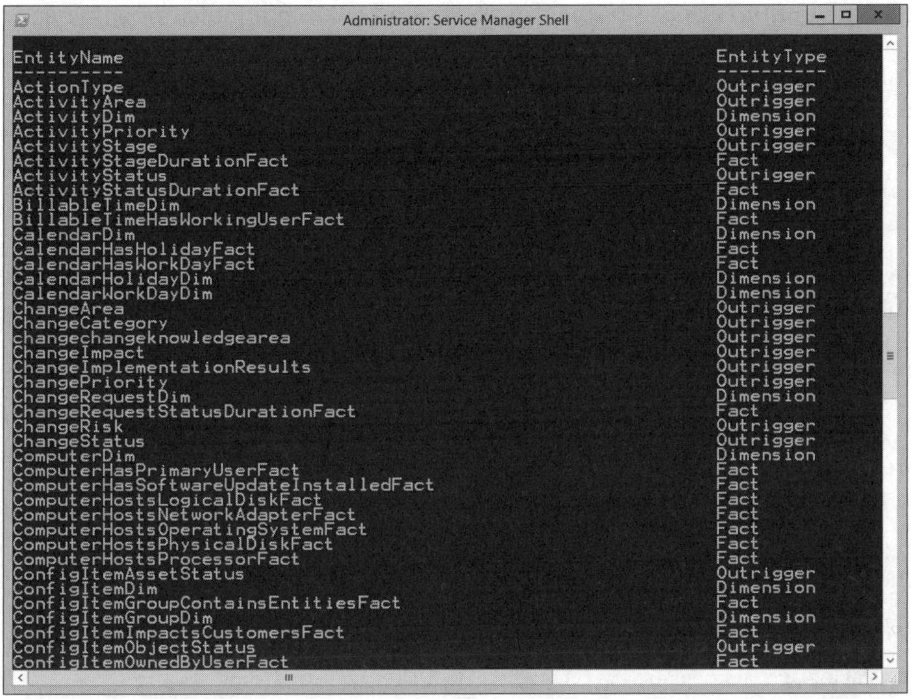

FIGURE 24.11 `Get-SCDWEntity`.

Working with Retention Periods

The retention period on various tables within the DWDatamart database can be changed by using the retention period cmdlets. These cmdlets allow you to manage how long the data is stored in these tables.

▶ **Get-SCDWRetentionPeriod:** Gets the data retention period in minutes for either a specific fact table within a specific data warehouse database or the default for fact tables within the database.

```
Get-SCDWRetentionPeriod -ComputerName Cumulus -DatamartComputerName Monsoon
    -DatabaseName OMDWDatamart
```

This retrieves the retention period of the OMDWDatamart source running on the SQL Server Monsoon.

▶ **Set-SCDWRetentionPeriod:** Sets the data retention period in minutes for either a specific fact table within a specific data warehouse database, or sets the default for fact tables within the database. Data that is eligible for grooming and older than the retention period is groomed out of the database.

```
Set-SCDWRetentionPeriod -ComputerName Cumulus -DatamartComputerName Monsoon
  -DatamartDatabaseName CMDWDatamart -EntityName
  ComputerHasSoftwareUpdateInstalledFact -DurationInMinutes 1576800
```

This updates the retention period on the ComputerHasSoftwareUpdateInstalledFact fact table.

Working with Watermarks

A watermark in the data warehouse is the last time the data was transferred to the data warehouse. You can use this information to check when the last data was transferred, or when you are experiencing issues with synchronization. Retrieving the watermark shows the last time the synchronization ran for a particular job on a dimension table.

By modifying this watermark, you can manipulate the synchronization process when you are troubleshooting data synchronization issues.

▶ **Get-SCDWWaterMark:** Gets the latest watermark for the specified job module.

```
Get-SCDWWaterMark -ComputerName Cumulus -ModuleType transform
  -ModuleName TransformSoftwareUpdateDim
```

This retrieves the last watermark of the transform job module TransformSoftwareUpdateDim.

▶ **Set-SCDWWaterMark:** Sets the watermark from which subsequent data processing should continue.

```
Set-SCDWWaterMark -ComputerName Cumulus -EntityName SoftwareUpdateDim
  -WaterMarkValue 1/1/2013
```

This sets set the watermark to 1/1/2013; this is the point in time from which the next update of this dimension should continue.

Working with Management Packs and the Data Warehouse

MPSyncJob is responsible for installing management packs on the data warehouse management server. When you install a sealed management pack on the Service Manager management server, MPSyncJob synchronizes this management pack to the data warehouse. Uninstalling management packs from the data warehouse uses the same approach; if you uninstall a management pack from Service Manager, MPSyncJob uninstalls the management pack from the data warehouse as well.

There may be situations where the synchronization of management packs stalls or generates error messages. When this occurs, you can troubleshoot MPSyncJob issues by uninstalling management packs directly from the data warehouse.

▶ **UnRegister-SCDWManagementPack:** Removes a management pack bundle directly from the data warehouse.

```
UnRegister-SCDWManagementPack -ComputerName Cumulus
  -DataSourceType ConfigurationManager.DataSource
  -DataSourceName Test
  -ManagementPackBundle "C:\MPB\TestDataWarehouse.Library.mpb" -UninstallMP
```

This example uninstalls the TestDataWarehouse library bundle from the data warehouse management server. This command enables you to only uninstall management pack bundles from the data warehouse management server.

▶ **Remove_SCSMManagementPack:** Uninstalls a management pack.

The `UnRegister-SCDWManagementPack` cmdlet only uninstalls management pack bundles; it cannot be used to remove a single management pack. To uninstall a single management pack from the data warehouse, use the `Remove_SCSMManagementPack` cmdlet.

The data warehouse management server is another management group. You can connect to this management group and use the `Remove_SCSMManagementPack` cmdlet from the native Service Manager module.

1. To connect to the data warehouse management group:

```
New-SCSMManagementGroupConnection -ComputerName Cumulus
```

This establishes a new connection to the data warehouse management server Cumulus.

2. After establishing the connection, you can query for the installed management packs:

```
Get-SCSMManagementPack
```

This cmdlet retrieves a list of all installed management packs on the data warehouse management server.

3. You can now use the `Remove-SCSMManagementPack` cmdlet to uninstall a management pack from the data warehouse management server:

```
Get-SCSMManagementPack | where{ $_.name -match "Unleashed" }
  |Remove-SCSMManagementPack
```

This example retrieves all management packs with Unleashed as part of their name, and removes them from the data warehouse management server.

Because removing a management pack using PowerShell or the Service Manager console automatically deletes it from the data warehouse the next time MPSyncJob runs, this cmdlet should only be used to troubleshoot custom management pack issues.

Although you can uninstall any management pack this way, it should only be used when there is no bundle to uninstall, as you would uninstall the management pack but fail to uninstall the other objects within the bundle. When you need to uninstall a management pack bundle, use the UnRegister-SCDWManagementPack cmdlet.

Using PowerShell to Manage the Data Warehouse

When managing the Service Manager data warehouse, the console should be adequate for configuring data sources and reports. PowerShell provides a more advanced way to administer and configure the data warehouse. This includes more advanced settings, such as scheduling data warehouse jobs to spread the workload.

While PowerShell is optional for changing general settings, it is a must-have when troubleshooting data warehouse issues and synchronization issues. PowerShell lets you check the exact error messages to determine why a job is failing and allows you to start and stop jobs manually.

There are several articles about how to troubleshoot these issues and resolve them:

▶ **Service Manager Product Team blog:** http://blogs.technet.com/b/servicemanager/archive/2010/06/07/troubleshooting-the-data-warehouse-an-overview.aspx

▶ **Travis Wright wrote a great script that uses these cmdlets to start all DW jobs in sequence to quickly check if everything is working:** http://gallery.technet.microsoft.com/PowerShell-Script-to-Run-a4a2081c/view/Discussions

SMLets PowerShell Module

Any discussion of PowerShell in Service Manager should include SMLets. SMLets is a project providing cmdlets for System Center Service Manager 2010-2012 that can be used to automate common tasks. It was initiated to provide additional automation capabilities beyond what was available in Service Manager 2010. With Service Manager 2012, most SMLets are implemented natively in the Service Manager 2012 PowerShell module.

NOTE: SMLETS CODEPLEX PROJECT AND SERVICE MANAGER

The SMLets project shows how the community can affect a product's adoption and usage. The project was initiated by Travis Wright, then a senior program manager on the Microsoft Service Manager team. It is because of the community's contributions that PowerShell in Service Manager is now a mature part of this System Center component.

SMLets are located at http://smlets.codeplex.com/. Resources available to effectively use these cmdlets include

▶ **SMLets examples of New-SCSMObjectProjection:** http://gallery.technet.microsoft.com/SMLets-Examples-of-New-77c2f411

▶ **Service Manager 2012 auto close resolved incidents workflow:** http://gallery.technet.microsoft.com/SCSM-2012-Auto-Close-1b26911f

▶ **Service Manager user role PowerShell scripts:** http://gallery.technet.microsoft.com/Service-Manager-SCSM-User-ebcdfcd6

Although many SMLets are now natively included with the Service Manager PowerShell module, there are still some SMLets cmdlets not provided out of the box. This is particularly the case for more advanced automation.

Currently 98 cmdlets are included in the SMLets module, although there is some overlap with the native PowerShell module. For a complete overview of the relation and comparison between the SMLets module and the native module, see Anton Gritsenko's blog article at http://blog.scsmsolutions.com/2012/02/reference-between-smlets-and-scsm-2012-native-cmdlets/.

Installing SMLets

You must download and install the SMLets before using them. The installation files are available at http://smlets.codeplex.com/releases/view/84853.

Install the SMLets.msi file and you can use the SMLets module in your PowerShell session; run `Import-Module SMLets` to load the module. Running `Get-Command -Module SMLets` displays all the cmdlets. Use the `Get-Help` cmdlet to check each of the SMLets.

SMLets provide advanced ways to create, update, and query objects from Service Manager. The next section includes a subset of cmdlets and discusses how you could use them, based on a sample script to relate objects back to business services.

Using SMLets

A commonly asked question is how to view a particular configuration item and see to the business service to which it is related. The example in this section reads all objects from the Service Components tab (see Figure 24.12) in the Business Service form and relates these objects back to the business service as related objects.

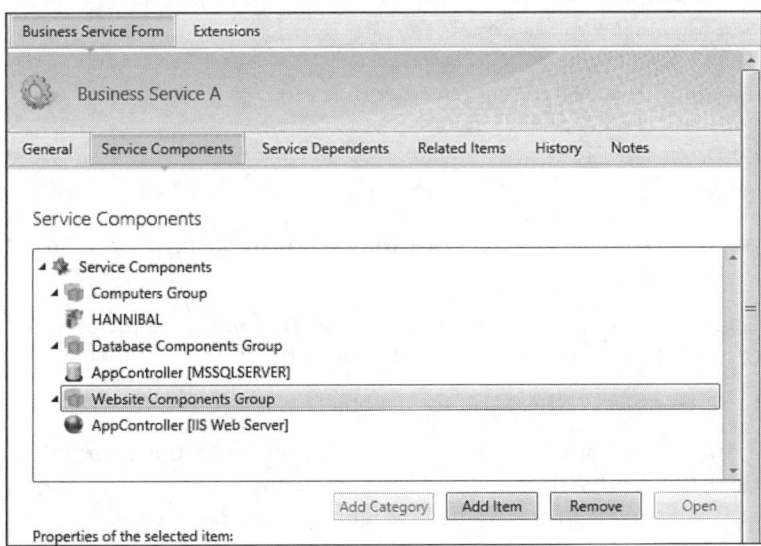

FIGURE 24.12   Service components.

The cmdlets used follow:

▶ **Get-SCSMObject:** Gets the list of all objects in Service Manager. You can use the parameters for filtering the objects. Requires the `-Class` parameter to specify which class to query:

```
Get-SCSMObject -Class (Get-SCSMClass -Name System.Service$)
```

This command retrieves all business service objects from Service Manager.

In this example, the cmdlet between the parentheses `()` is used to retrieve the service class; note the `$` sign that tells the query to only retrieve `System.Service` and not `System.ServiceOffering`. Leaving out the `$` sign would retrieve all classes starting with `System.Service`.

When you look at the results, you notice it retrieved all business service objects.

You can use `| Select-Object DisplayName` to only select the `DisplayName`.

Replacing the class `System.Service$` with any other class allows you to query any object in Service Manager.

▶ **Get-SCSMRelationshipObject:** Gets the related objects of an object in Service Manager.

This example reuses the query from `Get-SCSMObject` and gives it a variable:

```
$BusinessServices = Get-SCSMObject -Class (Get-SCSMClass -Name System.Service$)
```

The variable `$BusinessServices` now holds multiple business service objects.

To retrieve the relationships for each object, use a `ForEach` loop.

```
$BusinessServices = Get-SCSMObject -Class (Get-SCSMClass -Name System.Service$)
ForEach ($BusinessService in $BusinessServices)
{
Get-SCSMRelationshipObject -BySource $BusinessService   | ?{$_.IsDeleted -eq
  $False} |Select-Object TargetObject

}
```

Running this script retrieves each business service and each relationship to the business service.

The line `?{$_.IsDeleted -eq $False}` translates to where the `IsDeleted` property is False. This line is necessary to avoid gathering deleted objects.

The result shows all related objects where the source object is a business service.

Next is to filter the results; you want only the objects and not the groups containing the objects. To filter the results, first look at the relationship you want to have. Notice the `RelationshipId` shown in the results in Figure 24.13 (to get the full results, just remove `|Select-Object TargetObject` from the script).

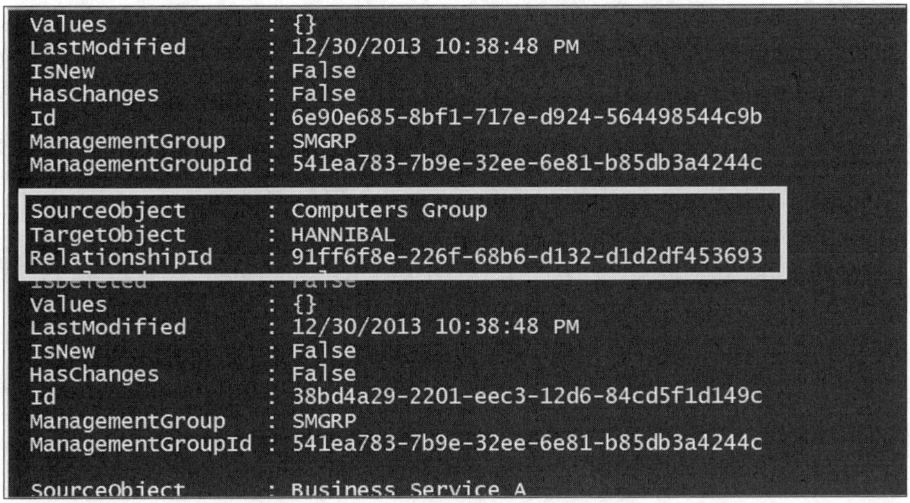

```
Values            : {}
LastModified      : 12/30/2013 10:38:48 PM
IsNew             : False
HasChanges        : False
Id                : 6e90e685-8bf1-717e-d924-564498544c9b
ManagementGroup   : SMGRP
ManagementGroupId : 541ea783-7b9e-32ee-6e81-b85db3a4244c

SourceObject      : Computers Group
TargetObject      : HANNIBAL
RelationshipId    : 91ff6f8e-226f-68b6-d132-d1d2df453693
IsDeleted         : False
Values            : {}
LastModified      : 12/30/2013 10:38:48 PM
IsNew             : False
HasChanges        : False
Id                : 38bd4a29-2201-eec3-12d6-84cd5f1d149c
ManagementGroup   : SMGRP
ManagementGroupId : 541ea783-7b9e-32ee-6e81-b85db3a4244c

SourceObject      : Business Service A
```

FIGURE 24.13   Viewing the `RelationshipId`.

▶ **Get-SCSMRelationshipClass:** Gets the relationship class in Service Manager.

To verify this is the correct relationship, use the following line:

```
Get-SCSMRelationshipClass -ID  91ff6f8e-226f-68b6-d132-d1d2df453693
```

This should give you the relationship you want:

```
System.ConfigItemContainsConfigItem
```

Now add the filter to the script:

```
Get-SCSMRelationshipObject -BySource $BusinessService -Filter "RELATIONSHIPID
  -eq '91ff6f8e-226f-68b6-d132-d1d2df453693'"| ?{$_.IsDeleted -eq $False}
```

You want to assign a variable so the data can be stored and reused. You also need to retrieve the new relationship you are going to add; this is the relationship shown in the Related Items tab of a configuration item. This relationship is the `System.ConfigItemRelatesToConfigItem` relationship. This relationship object is also stored in a variable.

The script now looks like this:

```
Import-Module SMLets
$BusinessServices = Get-SCSMObject -Class (Get-SCSMClass -Name System.Service$)
ForEach ($BusinessService in $BusinessServices)
{

$Groups = (Get-SCSMRelationshipObject -BySource $BusinessService -Filter
  "RELATIONSHIPID -eq '91ff6f8e-226f-68b6-d132-d1d2df453693'")| ?{$_.IsDeleted
  -eq $False} |Select-Object TargetObject
```

24

```
$ConfRelConf = Get-SCSMRelationshipClass -Name
  System.ConfigItemRelatesToConfigItem$
```

```
}
```

Your objects are stored in the variable $Groups. You want to add a new relationship for every object to the business service. To accomplish this requires a ForEach loop again to relate every object.

```
ForEach ($Group in $Groups)
{
```

Next, retrieve the target object itself. This line must be in between to retrieve the object itself and not only the DisplayName. You also need to add |Where-Object to filter only the active objects; you don't want to add relationships to deleted objects.

```
$Target = Get-SCSMObject -Id $Group.TargetObject.Id |Where-Object ObjectStatus
  -like "*Active"
```

This command retrieves the object; notice the use of the Id of the $Group.TargetObject.Id to be sure you are retrieving the correct object.

▶ **New-SCSMRelationshipObject:** Creates a new relationship object in Service Manager; it requires a source and target object.

To create a relationship $ConRelConf between two components, target $Target and source $Businessservice. The cmdlet New-SCSMRelationshipObject is used.

To create the relationship for every target object:

```
$CreatedRel = New-SCSMRelationshipObject -Relationship $ConfRelConf -Source
  $BusinessService -Target $Target -Bulk
```

Listing 24.1 shows the full script. For your convenience, the script is available as online content for the book; see Appendix C, "Available Online," for information.

LISTING 24.1   Add Service Components as Related Items to Business Service

```
Import-Module SMLets
$BusinessServices = Get-SCSMObject -Class (Get-SCSMClass -Name System.Service$)
ForEach ($BusinessService in $BusinessServices)
{
$Groups = (Get-SCSMRelationshipObject -BySource $BusinessService -Filter
  "RELATIONSHIPID -eq '91ff6f8e-226f-68b6-d132-d1d2df453693'")| ?{$_.IsDeleted
-eq $False} |Select-Object TargetObject
$ConfRelConf = Get-SCSMRelationshipClass -Name System.ConfigItemRelatesToConfigItem$
ForEach ($Group in $Groups)
{
$Target = Get-SCSMObject -Id $Group.TargetObject.Id |Where-Object ObjectStatus
  -like "*Active"
```

```
$CreatedRel = New-SCSMRelationshipObject -Relationship $ConfRelConf -Source
  $BusinessService -Target $Target -Bulk
}
}
```

Running this script creates relationships for every business service in your environment. For testing, you may want to filter down the business service to just one by its DisplayName:

```
$BusinessServices = Get-SCSMObject -Class (Get-SCSMClass -Name System.Service$)
  -Filter 'DisplayName -eq Business Service A'
```

After running the script, the results should be similar to Figure 24.14, shown from the business service.

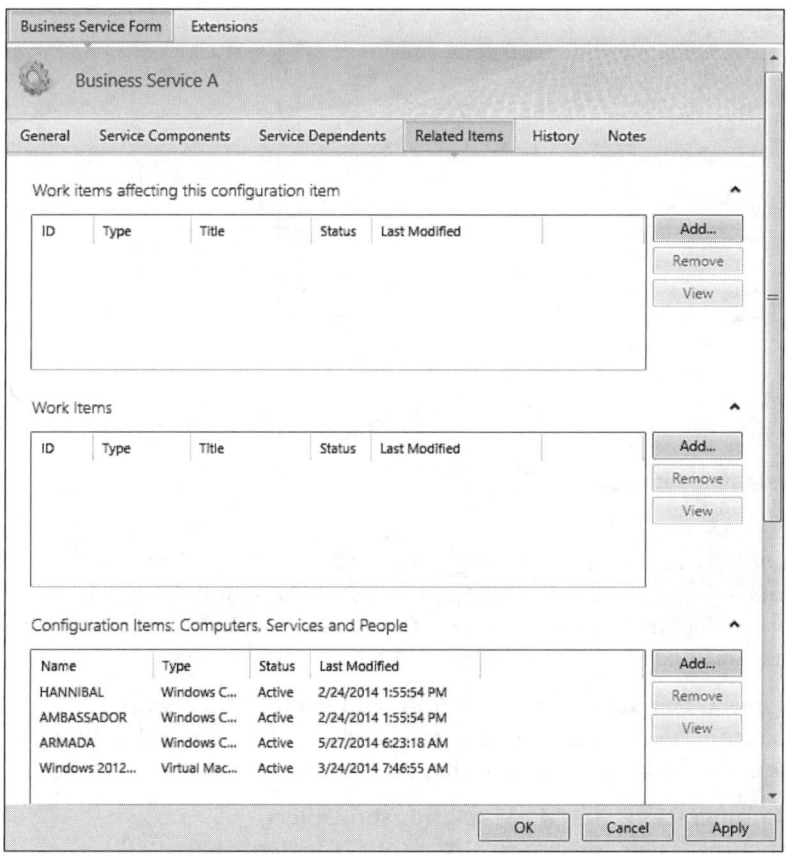

FIGURE 24.14   Business service-related items.

Figure 24.15 shows the related items from the Computer CI. Now you can easily identify a computer belonging to a particular business service with a single mouse click!

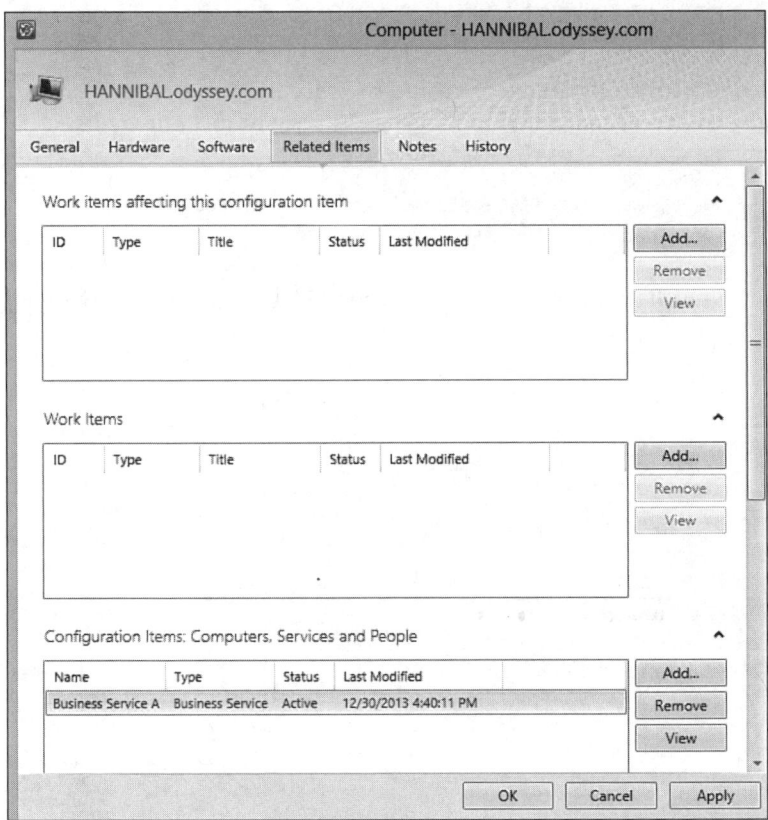

FIGURE 24.15   Computer-related items.

This is just an example of how to use the SMLets in a more advanced way. For more examples of using SMLets, refer to the Service Manager Engineering Team's blog, which includes 12 posts on this subject including examples of how to use SMLets (these links are also available as live links in Appendix B, "Reference URLs"):

▶ **Using Get-SCSMObject, Get-SCSMClass to dump data from Service Manager:** http://blogs.technet.com/b/servicemanager/archive/2011/04/21/using-smlets-beta-3-post-1-using-get-scsmobject-get-scsmclass-to-dump-data-from-scsm.aspx

▶ **Using Get-SCSMEnumeration, Get-SCSMRelationshipObject, Get-SCSMRelationshipClass to automatically resolve incidents when all child activities are completed:** http://blogs.technet.com/b/servicemanager/archive/2011/04/21/using-smlets-beta-3-post-2-using-get-scsmenumeration-get-scsmrelationshipobject-get-scsmrelationshipclass-to-automatically-resolve-incidents-when-all-child-activities-are-completed.aspx

▶ **Using Set-SCSMObject to bulk update properties on objects:** http://blogs.technet. com/b/servicemanager/archive/2011/04/22/using-smlets-beta-3-post-3-using-set-scsmobject-to-bulk-update-properties-on-objects.aspx

▶ **Using New-SCSMObject to create objects:** http://blogs.technet.com/b/ servicemanager/archive/2011/05/03/using-smlets-beta-3-post-4-using-new-scsmobject-to-create-objects.aspx

▶ **Getting the GUID ID of an object:** http://blogs.technet.com/b/servicemanager/ archive/2011/05/12/using-smlets-beta-3-post-5-getting-the-guid-id-of-an-object.aspx

▶ **Getting the owner of a service:** http://blogs.technet.com/b/servicemanager/ archive/2011/05/24/using-smlets-beta-3-post-6-getting-the-owner-of-a-service.aspx

▶ **Deleting any object in the UI:** http://blogs.technet.com/b/servicemanager/ archive/2011/05/25/using-smlets-beta-3-post-7-deleting-any-object-in-the-ui.aspx

▶ **Getting the GUID of an enumeration:** http://blogs.technet.com/b/servicemanager/ archive/2011/06/24/using-smlets-beta-3-post-8-getting-the-guid-of-an-enumeration. aspx

▶ **Deleting objects:** http://blogs.technet.com/b/servicemanager/ archive/2012/07/10/3441338.aspx

▶ **Getting a user's manager and a manager's reports:** http://blogs.technet.com/b/ servicemanager/archive/2011/12/03/using-smlets-beta-3-post-10-getting-a-user-s-manager-and-a-manager-s-reports.aspx

▶ **Getting a list of all the classes in a management pack:** http://blogs.technet. com/b/servicemanager/archive/2012/01/04/using-smlets-beta-3-post-11-getting-a-list-of-all-the-classes-in-a-management-pack.aspx

▶ **Getting a GUID ID of an object (especially for work items):** http://blogs.technet. com/b/servicemanager/archive/2012/01/05/using-smlets-beta-3-post-12-getting-a-guid-id-of-an-object-especially-for-work-items.aspx

Other well known SMLets script examples include

▶ **Create incident from service request and copy various attributes by Thomas Ellermann:**
http://gallery.technet.microsoft.com/Create-Incident-from-f19aaea0#content

▶ **Service Manager user role PowerShell scripts by Travis Wright:** http://gallery. technet.microsoft.com/Service-Manager-SCSM-User-ebcdfcd6

Fast Track

PowerShell in Service Manager has made large strides from version 2010 to 2012. There are improvements in PowerShell cmdlets for Service Manager from both an administration perspective and an automation perspective.

The native cmdlets from Service Manager 2012 are now based on the previous version of the SMLets, combined with existing cmdlets from Operations Manager as well as Service Manager. In Service Manager 2010, the PowerShell snapin contained 22 cmdlets. The 2012 module now contains 122 cmdlets. Using PowerShell enables you to manage Run As accounts, workflows, connectors, and subscriptions.

The SMLets for Service Manager (BETA 4) were updated in March 2012 and contain 98 cmdlets to manage and administer Service Manager 2012.

Summary

Using PowerShell enables you to fully automate service management and provide a full self-service experience to the end user. PowerShell today is a necessary read and learn for any IT professional Service Manager and System Center are all about automation and self-service, where PowerShell is a minimal requirement to get an IT department to become a fully automated business enabler.

PART VI

Appendixes

IN THIS PART

User Role Profiles Supplement

This appendix provides information about permissions granted to user role profiles in Service Manager. It also discusses the mappings of user role profiles with roles in the Information Technology Infrastructure Library (ITIL) and the Microsoft Operations Framework (MOF).

User Role Profile Classes and Relationship Permissions

Table A.1 provides a detailed list of those permissions granted to each user role profile. You can use this table to understand exactly which security scopes (classes, properties, and relationships) a user role profile has permission to perform each operation on. It describes the object names used, enhancing the TechNet documentation (see http://technet.microsoft.com/en-us/library/hh495625.aspx), which at the time of writing this chapter does not include this information.

TABLE A.1   User Role Profile Classes and Relationship Permissions

Role	Operation	Class/Relationship Permissions
Report User	Read	`MS.SC.RAL.SrsResourceStore`
	Update	None
	Create	None
	Delete	None
End User	Read	All
	Update	`System.WorkItem.Log`
		`System.FileAttachment`
		Relationships:
		`System.Knowledge.DocumentHasAverageRating`
		`System.UserHasPreference`
		`System.WorkItemAffectedUser`
		`System.WorkItemAssignedToUser`
		`System.WorkItemCreatedByUser`
		`System.FileAttachmentAddedByUser`
		`System.WorkItem.BillableTimeHasWorkingUser`
		`System.WorkItem.IncidentPrimaryOwner`
		`System.WorkItem.TroubleTicketResolvedByUser`
		`System.WorkItem.TroubleTicketClosedByUser`
		`System.ReviewerIsUser`
		`System.ReviewerVotedByUser`
		`System.WorkItemRelatesToWorkItem`
		`System.WorkItemRelatesToRequestOffering`
		`System.WorkItemRelatesToConfigItem`
		`System.WorkItemAboutConfigItem`
	Create	`System.WorkItem`
		`System.Reviewer`
		`System.WorkItem.Log`
		`System.FileAttachment`
		All relationships for the specified types
	Delete	None

Role	Operation	Class/Relationship Permissions
Read-Only Operator	Read	All
	Update	System.WorkItemAboutConfigItem
		System.WorkItemRelatesToConfigItem
		System.EntityLinksToKnowledgeDocument
		System.UserHasPreference
		System.WorkItemAffectedUser
		System.WorkItemAssignedToUser
		System.WorkItemCreatedByUser
		System.FileAttachmentAddedByUser
		System.WorkItem.BillableTimeHasWorkingUser
		System.WorkItem.IncidentPrimaryOwner
		System.WorkItem.TroubleTicketResolvedByUser
		System.WorkItem.TroubleTicketClosedByUser
		System.ReviewerIsUser
		System.ReviewerVotedByUser
		System.WorkItemRelatesToRequestOffering
		System.WorkItemRelatesToWorkItem
	Create	System.UserPreference
	Delete	None

A

Role	Operation	Class/Relationship Permissions
Incident Resolver	Read	All
	Update	`System.WorkItem.Log`
		`System.FileAttachment`
		`System.WorkItem.Activity.ManualActivity`
		Relationships:
		`System.WorkItemAboutConfigItem`
		`System.WorkItemRelatesToConfigItem`
		`System.EntityLinksToKnowledgeDocument`
		`System.WorkItemRelatesToWorkItem`
		`System.Knowledge.DocumentHasAverageRating`
		`System.UserHasPreference`
		`System.WorkItemAffectedUser`
		`System.WorkItemAssignedToUser`
		`System.WorkItemCreatedByUser`
		`System.FileAttachmentAddedByUser`
		`System.WorkItem.BillableTimeHasWorkingUser`
		`System.WorkItem.IncidentPrimaryOwner`
		`System.WorkItem.TroubleTicketResolvedByUser`
		`System.WorkItem.TroubleTicketClosedByUser`
		`System.ReviewerIsUser`
		`System.ReviewerVotedByUser`
	Create	`System.WorkItem.Incident`
		`System.WorkItem.Activity.ManualActivity`
		`System.FileAttachment`
		`System.WorkItem.Log`
		`System.UserPreference`
		Relationships:
		All for the specified types
	Delete	`System.WorkItem.Activity.ManualActivity`
		`System.FileAttachment`
		Relationships:
		All for the specified types

Role	Operation	Class/Relationship Permissions
Change Initiator	Read	All
	Update	System.StarRating
		Relationships:
		System.WorkItemAboutConfigItem
		System.WorkItemRelatesToConfigItem
		System.EntityLinksToKnowledgeDocument
		System.WorkItemRelatesToWorkItem
		System.Knowledge.DocumentHasAverageRating
		System.UserHasPreference
		System.WorkItemAffectedUser
		System.WorkItemAssignedToUser
		System.WorkItemCreatedByUser
		System.FileAttachmentAddedByUser
		System.WorkItem.BillableTimeHasWorkingUser
		System.WorkItem.IncidentPrimaryOwner
		System.WorkItem.TroubleTicketResolvedByUser
		System.WorkItem.TroubleTicketClosedByUser
		System.ReviewerIsUser
		System.ReviewerVotedByUser
		System.WorkItemAboutCatalogItem
	Create	System.WorkItem.ChangeRequest
		System.WorkItem.Activity
		System.FileAttachment
		System.WorkItem.Log
		System.Reviewer
		System.UserPreference
		Relationships:
		All for the specified types
	Delete	None

A

Role	Operation	Class/Relationship Permissions
Activity Implementer	Read	All
	Update	System.WorkItem.ManualActivity (only the .Status and .Notes properties).
		System.WorkItemAboutConfigItem
		System.WorkItemRelatesToConfigItem
		System.EntityLinksToKnowledgeDocument
		System.WorkItemRelatesToWorkItem
		System.Knowledge.DocumentHasAverageRating
		System.UserHasPreference
		System.WorkItemAffectedUser
		System.WorkItemAssignedToUser
		System.WorkItemCreatedByUser
		System.FileAttachmentAddedByUser
		System.WorkItem.BillableTimeHasWorkingUser
		System.WorkItem.IncidentPrimaryOwner
		System.WorkItem.TroubleTicketResolvedByUser
		System.WorkItem.TroubleTicketClosedByUser
		System.ReviewerIsUser
		System.ReviewerVotedByUser
	Create	System.UserPreference Relationships: All for the specified types
	Delete	None

Role	Operation	Class/Relationship Permissions
Problem Analyst	Read	All
	Update	`System.WorkItem.Problem`
		`System.FileAttachment`
		`System.WorkItem.Log`
		`System.StarRating`
		Relationships:
		`System.WorkItemAboutConfigItem`
		`System.WorkItemRelatesToConfigItem`
		`System.EntityLinksToKnowledgeDocument`
		`System.WorkItemRelatesToWorkItem`
		`System.Knowledge.DocumentHasAverageRating`
		`System.UserHasPreference`
		`System.WorkItemAffectedUser`
		`System.WorkItemAssignedToUser`
		`System.WorkItemCreatedByUser`
		`System.FileAttachmentAddedByUser`
		`System.WorkItem.BillableTimeHasWorkingUser`
		`System.WorkItem.IncidentPrimaryOwner`
		`System.WorkItem.TroubleTicketResolvedByUser`
		`System.WorkItem.TroubleTicketClosedByUser`
		`System.ReviewerIsUser`
		`System.ReviewerVotedByUser`
	Create	`System.WorkItem.Problem`
		`System.FileAttachment`
		`System.WorkItem.Log`
		`System.UserPreference`
		Relationships:
		All for the specified types
	Delete	`System.FileAttachment`
		Relationships:
		All for the specified types

Role	Operation	Class/Relationship Permissions
Service Request Analyst	Read	All
	Update	`System.WorkItem.ServiceRequest`
		`System.WorkItem.Activity`
		`System.Reviewer`
		`System.FileAttachment`
		`System.WorkItem.Log`
		Relationships:
		`System.WorkItemAboutConfigItem`
		`System.WorkItemRelatesToConfigItem`
		`System.EntityLinksToKnowledgeDocument`
		`System.WorkItemRelatesToWorkItem`
		`System.Knowledge.DocumentHasAverageRating`
		`System.WorkItemAffectedUser`
		`System.UserHasPreference`
		`System.WorkItemAssignedToUser`
		`System.WorkItemCreatedByUser`
		`System.FileAttachmentAddedByUser`
		`System.ReviewerIsUser`
		`System.ReviewerVotedByUser`
		`System.WorkItemRelatesToRequestOffering`
	Create	`System.WorkItem.ServiceRequest`
		`System.WorkItem.Activity`
		`System.Reviewer`
		`System.FileAttachment`
		`System.WorkItem.Log`
		`System.StarRating`
		Relationships:
		All for the specified types
	Delete	`System.WorkItem.Activity`
		`System.Reviewer`
		`System.FileAttachment`
		Relationships:
		All for the specified types

Role	Operation	Class/Relationship Permissions
Release Manager	Read	All
	Update	`System.WorkItem.ReleaseRecord`
		`System.WorkItem.Activity`
		`System.Reviewer`
		`System.FileAttachment`
		`System.WorkItem.Log`
		`System.StarRating`
		Relationships:
		`System.WorkItemAboutConfigItem`
		`System.WorkItemRelatesToConfigItem`
		`System.EntityLinksToKnowledgeDocument`
		`System.WorkItemRelatesToWorkItem`
		`System.Knowledge.DocumentHasAverageRating`
		`System.WorkItemAffectedUser`
		`System.UserHasPreference`
		`System.WorkItemAssignedToUser`
		`System.WorkItemCreatedByUser`
		`System.FileAttachmentAddedByUser`
		`System.ReviewerIsUser`
		`System.ReviewerVotedByUser`
	Create	`System.WorkItem.ReleaseRecord`
		`System.WorkItem.Activity`
		`System.Reviewer`
		`System.FileAttachment`
		`System.WorkItem.Log`
		`System.StarRating`
		Relationships:
		All for the specified types
	Delete	`System.WorkItem.Activity`
		`System.Reviewer`
		`System.FileAttachment`
		Relationships:
		All for the specified types

Role	Operation	Class/Relationship Permissions
Change Manager	Read	All
	Update	`System.WorkItem.ChangeRequest`
		`System.WorkItem.Activity`
		`System.Reviewer`
		`System.FileAttachment`
		`System.WorkItem.Log`
		`System.StarRating`
		Relationships:
		`System.WorkItemAboutConfigItem`
		`System.WorkItemRelatesToConfigItem`
		`System.EntityLinksToKnowledgeDocument`
		`System.WorkItemRelatesToWorkItem`
		`System.Knowledge.DocumentHasAverageRating`
		`System.WorkItemAffectedUser`
		`System.UserHasPreference`
		`System.WorkItemAssignedToUser`
		`System.WorkItemCreatedByUser`
		`System.FileAttachmentAddedByUser`
		`System.WorkItem.BillableTimeHasWorkingUser`
		`System.WorkItem.IncidentPrimaryOwner`
		`System.WorkItem.TroubleTicketResolvedByUser`
		`System.WorkItem.TroubleTicketClosedByUser`
		`System.ReviewerIsUser`
		`System.ReviewerVotedByUser`
	Create	`System.WorkItem.ChangeRequest`
		`System.WorkItem.Activity`
		`System.Reviewer`
		`System.FileAttachment`
		`System.WorkItem.Log`
		`System.UserPreference`
		Relationships:
		All for the specified types
	Delete	`System.Announcement.Item`
		`System.Reviewer`
		`System.FileAttachment`
		Relationships:
		All for the specified types

Role	Operation	Class/Relationship Permissions
Advanced Operator	Read	All
	Update	`System.WorkItem`
		`System.ConfigItem`
		`System.Announcement.Item`
		`System.Reviewer`
		`System.WorkItem.Log`
		`System.FileAttachment`
		`System.UserPreference`
		Relationships:
		`System.Knowledge.DocumentHasAverageRating`
		`System.UserHasPreference`
		`System.WorkItemAffectedUser`
		`System.WorkItemAssignedToUser`
		`System.WorkItemCreatedByUser`
		`System.FileAttachmentAddedByUser`
		`System.WorkItem.BillableTimeHasWorkingUser`
		`System.WorkItem.IncidentPrimaryOwner`
		`System.WorkItem.TroubleTicketResolvedByUser`
		`System.WorkItem.TroubleTicketClosedByUser`
		`System.ReviewerIsUser`
		`System.ReviewerVotedByUser`
		`System.WorkItemRelatesToRequestOffering`
	Create	`System.WorkItem`
		`System.ConfigItem`
		`System.Announcement.Item`
		`System.Reviewer`
		`System.WorkItem.Log`
		`System.FileAttachment`
		`System.UserPreference`
		Relationships:
		All for the specified types
	Delete	`System.WorkItem.Activity`
		`System.Announcement.Item`
		`System.Reviewer`
		`System.FileAttachment`
		Relationships:
		All for the specified types

Role	Operation	Class/Relationship Permissions
Author	Read	All
	Update	`System.WorkItem`
		`System.ConfigItem`
		`System.Announcement.Item`
		`System.Reviewer`
		`System.WorkItem.Log`
		`System.FileAttachment`
		Relationships:
		`System.WorkItemCreatedByUser`
		`System.WorkItemAssignedToUser`
		`System.WorkItemCreatedForUser`
		`System.WorkItemResolvedByUser`
		`System.FileAttachmentAddedByUser`
		`System.WorkItemRelatesToWorkItem`
		`System.WorkItemAboutConfigItem`
		`System.WorkItem.IncidentCallingUser`
	Create	`System.WorkItem`
		`System.ConfigItem`
		`System.CatalogItem`
		`System.Announcement.Item`
		`System.Reviewer`
		`System.WorkItem.Log`
		`System.FileAttachment`
		`System.UserPreference`
		Relationships:
		All for the specified types
	Delete	`System.Announcement.Item`
		`System.Reviewer`
		`System.FileAttachment`

Role	Operation	Class/Relationship Permissions
Workflow	Read	All
	Update	`System.WorkItem`
		`System.ConfigItem`
		`System.Announcement.Item`
		`System.Reviewer`
		`System.WorkItem.Log`
		`System.FileAttachment`
		`System.SLA`
		`System.StarRating`
		Relationships:
		`System.Knowledge.DocumentHasAverageRating`
		`System.UserHasPreference`
		`System.WorkItemAffectedUser`
		`System.WorkItemAssignedToUser`
		`System.WorkItemCreatedByUser`
		`System.FileAttachmentAddedByUser`
		`System.WorkItem.BillableTimeHasWorkingUser`
		`System.WorkItem.IncidentPrimaryOwner`
		`System.WorkItem.TroubleTicketResolvedByUser`
		`System.WorkItem.TroubleTicketClosedByUser`
		`System.ReviewerIsUser`
		`System.ReviewerVotedByUser`
	Create	`System.WorkItem`
		`System.ConfigItem`
		`System.Announcement.Item`
		`System.Reviewer`
		`System.WorkItem.Log`
		`System.FileAttachment`
		`System.SLA`
		`System.UserPreference`
		Relationships:
		All for the specified types
	Delete	`MS.SC.CM.DCM_NonCompliance_CI`
		Relationships:
		All for the specified types
Administrator	Read	All
(Service	Update	All
Manager or Data	Create	All
Warehouse)	Delete	All

In addition to the permissions listed in Table A.1, all user role profiles have permission to

▶ View global settings (System.GlobalSetting).

▶ Create/Update/Read personal notifications, which are notifications whose target is the user itself (Microsoft.EnterpriseManagement.Subscriptions. InstanceTypeSubscription).

Mapping User Role Profiles with ITIL/MOF Roles

ITIL and MOF, introduced in Chapter 3, "MOF, ITIL, and System Center," are two of the most commonly used information technology service management (ITSM) process frameworks today. Both frameworks define user roles in the Information Technology (IT) organization and specify responsibilities of users in those organizational user roles. You can map these roles to user roles in Service Manager to grant users in those roles the appropriate permissions required to perform their jobs.

ITIL Role Types

ITIL defines several different user roles related to ITSM in the Service Operation phase. Several of these roles can be directly mapped to Service Manager user roles, shown in Table A.2. Other roles are not as specific to a particular user role in a service desk tool and thus not included in this table. Specific information on what each role is responsible for is found in the ITIL documentation at http://www.best-management-practice.com. (Viewing this documentation requires an ITIL license.)

TABLE A.2   ITIL Role Types

Phase	Area	Role in ITIL	User Role Profile in Service Manager
Operation	Service Desk	Service Desk Manager	Advanced Operator
Operation	Service Desk	Service Desk Supervisor	Advanced Operator
Operation	Service Desk	Service Desk Analyst	Incident Resolver and/or Service Request Analyst
Operation	Service Desk	Super Users	End User
Operation	Technical Management	Technical Managers/ Team Leaders	Advanced Operator
Operation	Technical Management	Technical Analysts/ Architects	Author
Operation	Technical Management	Technical Operator	Advanced Operator
Operation	IT Operations Management	IT Operations Manager	Advanced Operator

Phase	Area	Role in ITIL	User Role Profile in Service Manager
Operation	IT Operations Management	Shift Leader	Advanced Operator
Operation	IT Operations Management	IT Operations Analyst	Advanced Operator
Operation	Application Management	Application Manager/ Team Leader	Advanced Operator (scoped to application)
Operation	Application Management	Application Analyst/ Architect	Author (scoped to application)
Operation	Incident Management	Incident Manager	Advanced Operator
Operation	Incident Management	1st, 2nd, 3rd, Line Support Group	Incident Resolver
Operation	Problem Management	Problem Manager	Advanced Operator
Operation	Problem Management	Problem Solving Group	Problem Analyst
Operation	Request Fulfillment	Service Request Fulfillment Group	Service Request Analyst
Operation	Request Fulfillment	Service Request Manager	Advanced Operator
Service Improvement	Service Management	Service Manager	Advanced Operator (scoped to service)
Service Improvement	Service Management	Service Owner	Advanced Operator (scoped to service)
Service Improvement	Service Management	Reporting Analyst	Reporting User
Service Transition	Service Transition Management	Service Transition Manager	Change Manager
Service Transition	Asset & Configuration Management	Service Asset Manager	Advanced Operator (scoped to assets related to the service)
Service Transition	Asset & Configuration Management	Configuration Manager	Advanced Operator
Service Transition	Asset & Configuration Management	Configuration Analyst	Advanced Operator
Service Transition	Asset & Configuration Management	Configuration Administrator	Advanced Operator
Service Transition	Configuration Control Board	Change Authority	Uses implied permissions
Service Transition	Configuration Control Board	Change Manager	Change Manager

A

Microsoft Operations Framework Role Types

Microsoft Operations Framework version 4.0 was first published in April 2008 and updated in July 2010. MOF is an integrated set of best practices, principles, and guidelines for achieving high levels of service in an IT organization. It defines multiple phases of an IT service life cycle:

▶ Plan

▶ Deliver

▶ Operate

▶ (Continuously) Manage

Each phase contains service management functions (SMFs). Within each SMF, MOF defines the role types of people working in various job functions. Service Manager is primarily concerned with the Operate phase, which has four SMFs:

▶ Operations

▶ Service Monitoring and Control

▶ Customer Service

▶ Problem Management

Service Manager also provides support for the Change and Configuration Management SMF in the Manage layer. Tables A.3, A.4, and A.5 in the next sections define the mapping of these MOF user role types to Service Manager user role profiles.

Operations and Service Monitoring and Control SMF Role Types

The primary team accountability that applies to the Build SMF is Operations Accountability. Table A.3 lists the role types within that accountability and their primary activities within this SMF and their mapping to a Service Manager user role profile.

TABLE A.3   Operations and Service Monitoring and Control SMF Role Types

Role Type	Responsibilities	Role in This SMF	User Role Profile in Service Manager
Operator	Executes tasks with predictable results based on instructions	Conducts planned operations tasks	Advanced Operator
Administrator	Executes tasks that are not well defined, requiring a deeper level of knowledge	Conducts unplanned or undefined operations tasks	Advanced Operator

Role Type	Responsibilities	Role in This SMF	User Role Profile in Service Manager
Technology area manager	Owns short-term performance of components in a technology area Owns the work instructions Ensures operational requirements are met for the technology area	Ensures work instructions are carried out as intended	Advanced Operator
Monitoring manager	Responsible for Service Monitoring and Control SMF tasks Ensures that the right systems are monitored Facilitates effective monitoring mechanisms Is the expert on how to monitor, not what to monitor	Ensures needed monitoring information is generated	Author
Scheduling manager	Plans schedule of individual activities within operations Owns timing decisions Plans operational work, including maintenance	Schedules operational work	Advanced Operator
Operations manager	Accountable for Operations and Service Monitoring and Control SMFs	Management oversight	Author

Customer Service SMF Role Types

The primary team accountability that applies to the Customer Service SMF is Support Accountability. Table A.4 displays the role types within that accountability, primary activities within this SMF, and the mapping to a Service Manager user role profile.

TABLE A.4   Customer Service SMF Role Types

Role Type	Responsibilities	Role in This SMF	User Role Profile in Service Manager
Customer Service Representative	Handles calls as the first contact with the user Registers and categorizes calls Determines supportability and dispatches calls	Interacts with customers, including recording, categorizing, classifying, resolving, and closing customer requests	Incident Resolver and Service Request Analyst
Incident Resolver	Diagnoses, investigates, and resolves	Resolves incident requests, including troubleshooting, escalating if necessary, and applying a fix or workaround	Incident Resolver
Incident Coordinator	Responsible for incident from beginning to end Owns quality control	Oversees all incident requests	Incident Resolver
Problem Analyst	Investigates and diagnoses	Investigates and resolves an underlying problem	Problem Analyst
Problem Manager	Identifies problems from the incident list	Determines whether an underlying problem exists	Problem Analyst
Customer Service Manager	Accountable for goals of Support Desk Covers incidents and problems	Oversees customer service	Author

Change and Configuration SMF Role Types

The primary team SMF accountability that applies to the Change and Configuration SMF is Management Accountability. Table A.5 lists the role types associated with Management Accountability, as well as the responsibilities and roles and mapping to Service Manager user role profile for each role type.

TABLE A.5   Change and Configuration SMF Role Types

Role Type	Responsibilities	Role in This SMF	User Role Profile in Service Manager
Change Manager	Manages the activities of the change management process for the IT organization	Ensures changes are made with the least amount of risk and impact to the organization	Change Manager
Configuration Administrator	Tracks what is changing and its impact Tracks configuration items (CIs), updates configuration management system (CMS)	Ensures a known state at all times	Advanced Operator

A

APPENDIX B
Reference URLs

This appendix includes a number of reference URLs associated with System Center 2012 Service Manager. URLs do change—although the authors have made every effort to verify the references here as working links, there is no guarantee they will remain current. It is possible some will change or be "dead" by the time you read this book. Sometimes the Wayback Machine (http://www.archive.org/) can rescue you from dead or broken links. This site is an Internet archive, and it will take you back to an archived version of a site...sometimes.

General Resources

A number of websites provide excellent resources for Service Manager.

▶ A great source of information for all things System Center related including Service Manager is System Center Central (http://www.systemcentercentral.com).

▶ myITforum (http://www.myITforum.com) is a community of worldwide Information Technology (IT) professionals and a website established in 1999 by Rod Trent. myITforum includes topics on System Center and IT.

▶ myITforum.com/forums now hosts the *Windows IT Pro* forums.

▶ If you are not already receiving email notifications of new articles in the Microsoft Knowledge Base from kbalertz, sign up at http://kbalertz.com/. You just need to create an account and select those technologies you want to be alerted about.

▶ If you are interested in understanding the Customer Improvement Program, read Marnix Wolf's blog post series at http://thoughtsonopsmgr.blogspot.com/2010/02/ceip-odr-and-lot-what-are-they-and-why.html.

▶ The System Center Virtual User Group provides educational resources and collaboration between users of System Center technologies worldwide. Meetings include topics presented by industry experts, including Microsoft engineers. These Live Meeting sessions are recorded for your convenience. To join the user group, go to http://www.linkedin.com/groupRegistration?gid=101906. You can also visit the System Center User Group website at http://www.systemcenterusergroup.net/.

▶ The Windows Server technical library is located at http://technet.microsoft.com/en-us/library/bb625087.aspx.

▶ The TechNet Manageability Center at http://go.microsoft.com/?linkid=7280963 contains links to resources and TechNet Magazine articles.

▶ Microsoft's Sysinternals website is at http://technet.microsoft.com/en-us/sysinternals/default.aspx.

▶ *Windows IT Pro* publishes online articles about System Center and other topics. See http://www.windowsitpro.com/ for information.

▶ Information on the IO (Infrastructure Optimization) model is available at http://technet.microsoft.com/en-us/library/bb944804.aspx.

▶ *Biztech* discusses Microsoft's IO model at http://www.biztechmagazine.com/article.asp?item_id=569.

▶ Read about Service Modeling Language (SML) at http://www.w3.org/TR/sml/. Visit http://technet.microsoft.com/en-us/library/bb725986.aspx for additional technical information on SML from Microsoft.

▶ To learn more about the Microsoft Operations Framework (MOF), and version 4.0, see http://technet.microsoft.com/library/cc506049.aspx.

▶ Information on the MOF Deliver Phase is at http://technet.microsoft.com/en-us/library/cc506047.aspx.

▶ You can read about the MOF Envision SMF at http://technet.microsoft.com/en-us/library/cc531013.aspx.

▶ See http://technet.microsoft.com/en-us/library/cc506048.aspx for information on MOF 4.0 and the Manage layer.

▶ Details about the Microsoft Solutions Framework (MSF) are located at http://www.microsoft.com/downloads/details.aspx?familyid=50DBFFFE-3A65-434A-A1DD-29652AB4600F&displaylang=en and http://www.microsoft.com/downloads/details.aspx?familyid=a71ac896-1d28-45a4-880c-8b0cc8265c63&displaylang=en.

▶ Microsoft's white paper on performance tuning guidelines for Windows Server 2012 R2 is at http://msdn.microsoft.com/en-us/library/windows/hardware/dn529133.aspx.

▶ Following are links to previous versions of performance tuning guidelines:

  ▶ For Windows Server 2012, see http://download.microsoft.com/download/0/0/
    B/00BE76AF-D340-4759-8ECD-C80BC53B6231/performance-tuning-guidelines-
    windows-server-2012.docx.

  ▶ You can view the Windows Server 2008 R2 version at http://download.
    microsoft.com/download/6/B/2/6B2EBD3A-302E-4553-AC00-9885BBF31E21/
    Perf-tun-srv-R2.docx.

  ▶ The Windows Server 2008 version is at http://download.microsoft.com/
    download/9/c/5/9c5b2167-8017-4bae-9fde-d599bac8184a/Perf-tun-srv.docx.

▶ For an overview of performance-related best practices for SharePoint 2010, see
  the TechNet Wiki page at http://social.technet.microsoft.com/wiki/contents/
  articles/8666.sharepoint-2010-best-practices.aspx.

▶ "Wake up" your SharePoint sites using the script at http://spwakeup.codeplex.com/.

▶ http://technet.microsoft.com/en-us/library/cc732906(WS.10).aspx provides information on requesting an Internet Server certificate.

▶ See http://msdn.microsoft.com/en-us/library/bb897401.aspx for information on
  Authorization Manager (AzMan).

▶ The article at http://support.microsoft.com/kb/269181 discusses querying Active
  Directory using a bitwise filter.

▶ Information about the Windows Task Scheduler is at http://windows.microsoft.com/
  en-us/windows/schedule-task#1TC=windows-7.

▶ Information regarding Windows network load balancing (NLB) is available in the
  Network Load Balancing Deployment Guide at http://technet.microsoft.com/en-us/
  library/cc754833(WS.10).aspx.

▶ Microsoft provides solution accelerators, which are guidelines and tools to leverage the full functionality of Microsoft usage within your organization. These
  are available for download at no cost at http://technet.microsoft.com/en-us/
  solutionaccelerators/dd229342.

▶ Trying to understand licensing?

  ▶ General licensing information is at http://www.microsoft.com/licensing/
    default.mspx.

  ▶ http://www.microsoft.com/calsuites/en/us/products/default.aspx discusses
    Server client access licenses (CALs) and the suites they may be included on.
    Find the most current list of Microsoft CAL suite technologies at http://www.
    microsoft.com/licensing/about-licensing/client-access-license.aspx#tab=3.

▶ System Center volume licensing is discussed at http://www.microsoft.com/licensing/about-licensing/SystemCenter2012.aspx.

▶ Software Assurance is discussed at http://www.microsoft.com/licensing/software-assurance/by-product.aspx.

Microsoft's Service Manager Resources

The following list includes some general Microsoft resources available for System Center 2012 Service Manager:

▶ http://technet.microsoft.com/en-us/library/hh305220.aspx is the location of the Service Manager 2012 TechCenter.

▶ The documentation library for Service Manager 2012 R2 is available online at the Service Manager 2012 TechCenter (http://technet.microsoft.com/en-us/library/hh305220.aspx). This includes the planning guide, deployment guide, administrators guide, operations guide, authoring guide, upgrade guide, disaster recovery guide, what's new, a glossary, and release notes. You can also download the documentation at http://www.microsoft.com/en-us/download/details.aspx?id=27850.

▶ Microsoft discusses updates in the R2 release at http://technet.microsoft.com/en-us/library/dn299380.aspx, and what's new in System Center 2012 SP 1 Service Manager is documented at http://technet.microsoft.com/en-us/library/jj614408.aspx.

▶ To find the latest update release (UR) for System Center, http://social.technet.microsoft.com/wiki/contents/articles/4226.list-of-build-numbers-for-system-center-service-manager.aspx provides a complete overview of build numbers and update releases.

▶ Watch Anders Ravnholt's presentations at TechEd 2014 on Channel 9 at https://channel9.msdn.com/Events/Speakers/anders-ravnholt. Anders is the technical editor for this book.

▶ View Service Manager presentations at TechEd 2014 on Channel 9 at http://channel9.msdn.com/Events/TechEd/NorthAmerica/2014?sort=sequential&direction=desc&term=service+manager#fbid=.

▶ Service Manager presentations at Microsoft Management Summit (MMS) 2013 are available at http://channel9.msdn.com/Events/MMS/2013/?sort=sequential&direction=desc&term=service+manager.

▶ Service Manager 2012 presentations at MMS 2012 are at http://channel9.msdn.com/Events/MMS/2012/?sort=sequential&direction=desc&term=service+manager.

▶ Find system requirements for System Center 2012 R2 at http://technet.microsoft.com/en-us/library/dn281925.aspx. Software requirements are discussed at http://technet.microsoft.com/library/hh519608.aspx.

▶ Microsoft provides a sizing helper for Service Manager. This utility can assist you in determining the hardware required based on certain scenarios. Download SM_job_aids.zip from http://go.microsoft.com/fwlink/p/?LinkID=232378.

▶ Deployment scenarios for Service Manager are discussed at http://technet.microsoft.com/en-us/library/hh519675.aspx.

▶ Read how to plan for performance and scalability in Service Manager 2012 at http://technet.microsoft.com/en-us/library/hh495684.aspx and http://technet.microsoft.com/en-us/library/hh519624.aspx.

▶ Speed up the self-service portal by changing the Internet Information Services (IIS) setting to recycle the application pool, discussed at http://blogs.technet.com/b/servicemanager/archive/2011/05/11/faq-why-is-the-self-service-portal-so-slow.aspx.

▶ The Microsoft Service Manager Engineering Team blog is located at http://blogs.technet.com/b/servicemanager/. An MSDN blog is at http://blogs.msdn.com/b/scplat/.

▶ Following are some individual blogs by members of the engineering team:

  ▶ **Marc Umeno:** http://blogs.technet.com/b/umeno/.

  ▶ **Jakub Olesky:** http://blogs.msdn.com/b/jakuboleksy/.

  ▶ **Jim Truher:** http://jtruher3.wordpress.com/.

▶ Ready to set up a Service Manager lab environment with production data? The article at http://technet.microsoft.com/en-us/library/dn520899.aspx discusses the process.

▶ Ports used by Service Manager are documented at http://technet.microsoft.com/en-US/library/hh495567.aspx.

▶ To monitor Service Manager using Operations Manager, download the Service Manager monitoring management pack from http://www.microsoft.com/en-us/download/details.aspx?id=29980.

▶ If you heard rumors that Service Manager was going into maintenance mode, read how Microsoft plans to continue to update and develop Service Manager, reiterated in the February 18, 2014, posting at http://blogs.technet.com/b/servicemanager/archive/2014/02/18/system-center-service-manager-a-phoenix-in-its-own-right.aspx.

▶ At TechEd 2011, Sean Christensen and Travis Wright gave a deep dive into automating the Information Technology Infrastructure Library (ITIL) and MOF with Service Manager. View the presentation at http://channel9.msdn.com/events/TechEd/NorthAmerica/2011/SIM209.

▶ For an example of how to use related recipients for service level agreements, see http://blogs.technet.com/b/servicemanager/archive/2012/02/07/notifying-before-sla-breaches.aspx.

▶ Read about using AND/OR criteria in workflow and notification subscriptions at http://blogs.technet.com/b/servicemanager/archive/2010/11/30/using-and-or-criteria-in-workflow-and-notification-subscriptions.aspx.

B

▶ http://technet.microsoft.com/en-us/library/hh495651.aspx discusses user roles in Service Manager.

▶ The Security Manager security matrix (discussed in Appendix A, "User Role Profiles Supplement") states that Administrators, Advanced Operators, and Authors can create announcements. However, the Announcement view is only available in the Administration workspace by default, limiting access to Service Manager administrators. Travis Wright describes a solution for this at http://blogs.technet.com/b/servicemanager/archive/2010/12/01/faq-how-can-i-enable-non-admins-to-create-edit-delete-announcements.aspx.

▶ Sean Christensen discusses how Service Manager offers easy customization of processes and decisions at http://technet.microsoft.com/en-us/video/sean-christensen-discusses-how-service-manager-2012-offers-easy-customization-of-processes-and-decisions.aspx.

▶ Read how System Center and Service Manager capabilities map to private cloud layers at http://social.technet.microsoft.com/wiki/contents/articles/13641.system-center-2012-integration-guide-service-manager.aspx#Role_in_the_Microsoft_Private_Cloud. You must sign in to the wiki to access this page.

▶ Travis Wright discusses the Allowed List at http://blogs.technet.com/b/servicemanager/archive/2010/02/26/managing-the-allowed-list-for-the-operations-manager-ci-connector-with-powershell.aspx.

▶ To automatically delete objects in Pending Delete status, see http://technet.microsoft.com/en-us/library/hh519650.aspx/.

▶ Read about Service Manager activities at http://technet.microsoft.com/en-us/library/hh832016.aspx.

▶ See http://technet.microsoft.com/en-us/library/hh914195.aspx for a discussion of self-service portal deployment scenarios.

▶ Map Service Manager properties to Configuration Manager database views at http://technet.microsoft.com/en-us/library/hh519741.aspx.

▶ Take a work item from Service Manager and publish it to a SharePoint calendar through a console task; read Vladimir Bakhmetyev's blog post at http://blogs.technet.com/b/servicemanager/archive/2012/07/02/publishing-work-item-to-part-1-sharepoint-calendar.aspx.

▶ Information about configuring the Orchestrator integration pack for Service Manager is at http://technet.microsoft.com/en-us/library/hh519779.aspx and http://technet.microsoft.com/en-us/library/hh832008.aspx.

▶ Read about the incoming mail processing feature at http://technet.microsoft.com/en-us/library/hh519602.aspx.

▶ http://blogs.technet.com/b/servicemanager/archive/2009/01/27/the-system-center-platform-in-service-manager-part-2-the-model-based-database.aspx introduces Service Manager's model-based database.

▶ System Center schema updates are discussed at http://technet.microsoft.com/en-us/library/hh524231.aspx.

▶ If you are experiencing workflow issues, consider the article at http://blogs.technet.com/b/servicemanager/archive/2013/01/14/troubleshooting-workflow-performance-and-delays.aspx for assistance with pinpointing the workflow and troubleshooting it.

▶ Read how to create a custom administration setting at http://blogs.technet.com/b/servicemanager/archive/2010/01/04/creating-a-custom-administration-setting.aspx.

▶ Service Manager 2010 functionality is documented at http://blogs.technet.com/b/systemcenter/archive/2010/04/23/system-center-service-manager-2010-an-integrated-platform-for-it-service-management.aspx and http://windowsitpro.com/system-center/getting-started-system-center-service-manager-2010.

▶ Microsoft's announcement on Service Manager's delayed release until 2010 is at http://blogs.technet.com/b/systemcenter/archive/2008/02/07/system-center-service-manager-update.aspx.

Other Service Manager Resources

Microsoft of course is not the only organization to discuss Service Manager. A number of websites provide excellent resources for Service Manager.

▶ An early look at the product that eventually became Service Manager is available at http://itservicemngmt.blogspot.com/2007/05/microsoft-system-center-service-manager.html.

▶ Computer World reviews Service Manager 2012 at http://www.computerworld.com/s/article/9227022/Microsoft_System_Center_2012_review_Streamlined_cloud_service_management_. A Network World review of Service Manager 2010 is at http://www.networkworld.com/reviews/2011/012411-microsoft-system-center-test.html?source=NWWNLE_nlt_daily_pm_2011-01-25. Thoughts on the product in early 2010 prior to its first release are at http://plannetplc.wordpress.com/2010/02/17/microsoft-system-center-service-manager-2010-a-credible-challenger-in-the-service-management-software-market/.

▶ For an overview of Service Manager 2012, see the video by coauthor Kurt Van Hoecke at http://technet.microsoft.com/en-us/video/system-center-service-manager-2012-overview.aspx.

▶ A list of links to Service Manager demos is at http://blogs.technet.com/b/servicemanager/archive/2010/01/13/system-center-service-manager-demos.aspx (scroll down to see demos for Service Manager 2012).

▶ At MMS 2013, Nate Lasnoski discussed configuring Service Manager for performance and scale. See his presentation at http://channel9.msdn.com/Events/MMS/2013/SD-B312. Pete Zerger also discusses improving Service Manager 2012 performance at http://www.systemcentercentral.com/faq-a-collection-of-tips-to-improve-service-manager-performance/.

▶ To learn how to target announcements, read the blog posting by contributing author Anders Bengtsson at http://contoso.se/blog/?p=1243.

▶ Cireson provides several utilities that can help your Service Manager performance:

  ▶ A standalone console that provides a full console experience using a web interface, with vast improvements in response times when compared to the default Service Manager console—for information, see http://www.cireson.com/app-store/scsm-web-console/.

  ▶ A solution for full Outlook integration with Service Manager, providing the capability to interact directly with requests using Outlook—http://www.cireson.com/app-store/scsm-outlook-console/ provides additional information.

  ▶ The Cireson Portal is a complete replacement of Microsoft's self-service portal for Service Manager—see http://cireson.com/apps/self-service-portal/.

▶ Gridpro provides a number of Service Manager tools:

  ▶ A full web-based console for the analyst, which you can use to manage incidents—this console is not limited to a desktop that requires large amounts of memory but can run on any device with a web browser. http://www.gridprosoftware.com/en/products/webfront provides information on this tool.

  ▶ A solution to run the console on a mobile device—this is based on HTML 5 and runs on nearly every device. http://www.gridprosoftware.com/en/products/mobilefront provides information on this as well.

  ▶ The capability to integrate your phone system automatically with Service Manager—to automatically record incidents directly from a phone call to an incident, see http://www.gridprosoftware.com/en/products/cti.

▶ Dieter Gasser created a task to clone a Service Manager user role; download the management pack from the TechNet Gallery at http://gallery.technet.microsoft.com/SCSM-Clone-User-Role-Task-8ba8ac58.

▶ MVP Marcel Zehner published an SMLet script to close resolved incidents automatically. Read about the script at http://marcelzehner.ch/2011/01/12/auto-close-resolved-incidents/. A revised version of the script by coauthor Samuel Erskine can be downloaded or copied from TechNet Gallery at http://gallery.technet.microsoft.com/SCSM-2012-Auto-Close-1b26911f.

▶ Set views to refresh automatically; see http://social.technet.microsoft.com/Forums/systemcenter/en-US/2d034882-b441-4b10-85a5-eae514a729a9/views-refresh-time?forum=systemcenterservicemanager.

▶ Another option for delivering auto refresh is provided by the Advanced View Editor delivered by Anton Gritsenko; see http://scsmsolutions.com/freetools/3-ave2free#download and http://gallery.technet.microsoft.com/Advanced-View-Editor-20-377353f5 for information. This can be used to configure views in the console.

▶ Anton also developed an add-on with search functionality where you can save common search strings. You can download the add-on from the TechNet Gallery at http://gallery.technet.microsoft.com/Advanced-Search-with-Saver-fbe5b6af.

▶ The SCSM Perf Test Harness Codeplex project lets you fully stress test your Service Manager environment. It is designed to measure the workload on large installations but can be used in any other case as well. Http://scsmperftestharness.codeplex.com/ provides information.

▶ Read about how to forward knowledge articles to specific users at a blog post by Anders Bengtsson at http://contoso.se/blog/?p=1262.

▶ Anders Bengtsson describes how to target software packages to specific users at http://contoso.se/blog/?p=1269.

▶ Anders Bengtsson also describes how to create a notification for an unassigned incident, see http://contoso.se/blog/?p=1875.

▶ http://scug.be/blogs/scsm/archive/2010/03/21/service-manager-role-based-security-scoping.aspx by coauthor Kurt Van Hoecke discusses role-based security scoping.

▶ MVP Chris Ross put together a nice lightweight icon pack to be used with the self-service portal, available at http://www.cireson.com/scsm/scsm-portal-icon-pack-download/.

▶ A Forrester research report shows the benefits of service management automation; see http://media.cms.bmc.com/documents/1206_Forrester_Sustain_Service_Managemen.pdf.

▶ Need to reset a user's password but haven't implemented Microsoft Forefront Identity Manager (FIM)? Anders Bengtsson describes one approach, which sends the user a new password in an email and creates a closed incident for the Service Desk to track the number of password reset incidents. Read his post at http://contoso.se/blog/?p=1605.

Service Manager Authoring

The following references contain information on authoring:

▶ Download the Service Manager 2012 R2 Authoring Tool at http://www.microsoft.com/en-us/download/details.aspx?id=40896. An overview of the tool is available at http://technet.microsoft.com/en-us/library/hh495563.aspx.

▶ Visual Studio Authoring Extensions (VSAE) is available at http://www.microsoft.com/en-us/download/details.aspx?id=30169.

▶ Service Manager 2012 SDK documentation is available at http://msdn.microsoft.com/en-us/library/hh965050.aspx. Download the SDK at http://www.microsoft.com/en-us/download/details.aspx?id=29559.

▶ Use XML Notepad 2007 to brows and edit XML documents. Read about it at http://msdn2.microsoft.com/en-us/library/aa905339.aspx, and download the tool from http://www.microsoft.com/downloads/details.aspx?familyid= 72d6aa49-787d-4118-ba5f-4f30fe913628&displaylang=en.

▶ If you do not have access to Visual Studio, you could use Kaxaml to design eXtensible Application Markup Language (XAML) code. Kaxaml, a lightweight XAML editor that can render the result as you type the XAML code, is available at http://www.kaxaml.com/.

▶ http://blogs.technet.com/b/servicemanager/archive/2009/07/24/localizing-management-pack-content.aspx provides information on localizing Service Manager management packs.

▶ Management pack bundles are described at http://blogs.technet.com/b/ servicemanager/archive/2009/09/04/introducing-management-pack-bundles.aspx.

▶ Use fastseal.exe to seal your management packs. You can download the utility from the Service Manager Engineering Team's blog at http://blogs.technet.com/ servicemanager/archive/2009/12/25/sealing-management-packs.aspx.

▶ The Strong Name Tool can be used to create a strong name key file (.snk) used to seal a management pack. The tool is available in the Windows software development kit (SDK) at http://www.microsoft.com/downloads/en/details. aspx?FamilyID=e6e1c3df-a74f-4207-8586-711ebe331cdc&displaylang=en.

▶ http://msdn.microsoft.com/en-us/library/28hw3sce.aspx introduces regular expressions.

▶ Management pack attribute information is available at http://blogs.technet.com/b/ servicemanager/archive/2010/03/03/grid-view-configuration-and-what-it-means.aspx.

▶ Articles on Windows Presentation Foundation (WPF) data binding are at http:// msdn.microsoft.com/en-us/library/aa480224.aspx and http://msdn.microsoft.com/ en-us/library/aa480226.aspx.

▶ Read how to use tokens in a view criterion in the blog post at http://blogs.technet. com/b/servicemanager/archive/2010/04/30/how-to-update-views-to-change-the-criteria-from-assigned-to-me-to-assigned-to-me-or-a-group-that-i-belong-to.aspx.

▶ http://blog.scsmsolutions.com/2011/08/create-custom-user-control-for-scsm-2010/ discusses how to utilize the SDK and build a UserControl that interacts with Service Manager.

▶ To create console tasks with the SDK, read the blog post at http://blogs.technet. com/b/servicemanager/archive/2010/12/22/tasks-part-2-custom-console-tasks-for-create-edit-delete.aspx.

▶ When a class is extended in Service Manager, the forms are equipped with a new tab that shows the values of all extension properties. http://blogs.technet.com/b/service-manager/archive/2010/02/08/overview-of-the-forms-infrastructure-and-the-generic-form.aspx discusses how to hide this tab, hide the properties in the generic form, and more.

PowerShell and SMLets

You can find information on PowerShell at the following sites:

▶ The official PowerShell site is at http://www.microsoft.com/powershell.

▶ The Microsoft TechNet social forum covering general PowerShell discussions is at http://social.technet.microsoft.com/Forums/en-US/winserverpowershell/threads.

▶ You may want to check all the PowerShell webcasts by the Scripting Guys at http://www.microsoft.com/technet/scriptcenter/webcasts/ps.mspx.

▶ The PowerShell guy's blog (Marc van Orsouw, PowerShell MVP) is located at http://thepowershellguy.com/.

▶ The Windows PowerShell team blogs at http://blogs.msdn.com/b/powershell/.

▶ Find PowerShell script examples at http://www.microsoft.com/technet/scriptcenter/hubs/msh.mspx.

▶ PowerShell+ is a free PowerShell editing and debugging environment. You can get a free personal copy at http://www.powershell.com/downloads/psp1.zip.

▶ For information on aliases within PowerShell, see http://technet.microsoft.com/en-us/library/ee692685.aspx.

▶ Read about the PowerShell pipeline at http://technet.microsoft.com/en-us/magazine/2007.07.powershell.aspx and http://morelunches.files.wordpress.com/2013/12/psh3-pipelineinput.pdf.

▶ Read how to view the Service Manager data model using PowerShell at http://blogs.technet.com/b/servicemanager/archive/2011/11/09/viewing-the-data-model-using-powershell.aspx.

▶ See a walkthrough by Rob Ford on how to add the Service Manager modules to your PowerShell profile at http://scsmnz.net/setting-up-your-powershell-profile-to-run-service-manager-commandlets/.

▶ http://technet.microsoft.com/en-us/library/hh519688.aspx lists the Service Manager cmdlets. Read about using the cmdlets at http://technet.microsoft.com/en-us/library/hh305229.aspx.

▶ Information regarding Service Manager data warehouse cmdlets, including full descriptions and examples, is at http://technet.microsoft.com/en-us/library/hh541724(v=sc.20).aspx.

▶ Use PowerShell to troubleshoot data warehouse issues and synchronization issues. Articles include http://blogs.technet.com/b/servicemanager/archive/2010/06/07/troubleshooting-the-data-warehouse-an-overview.aspx and http://gallery.technet.microsoft.com/PowerShell-Script-to-Run-a4a2081c/view/Discussions.

▶ Read about using Service Manager cmdlets in Orchestrator runbooks at http://systemcentertech.com/2013/06/12/using-service-manager-powershell-cmdlets-from-orchestrator-runbooks/.

B

▶ You must download and install the SMLets before using them. The installation files are available at http://smlets.codeplex.com/releases/view/84853.

▶ Chris Jones of Microsoft discusses useful cmdlets for Service Manager 2012 using SMLets at http://blogs.technet.com/b/letsdothis/archive/2013/11/05/useful-smlets-cmdlets-for-system-center-2012-service-manager.aspx.

▶ http://blog.scsmsolutions.com/2012/02/reference-between-smlets-and-scsm-2012-native-cmdlets/ is a reference between SMLets and the Service Manager 2012 native cmdlets.

▶ http://smlets.codeplex.com is your starting point for information on SMLets. Resources to use these cmdlets include

> **SMLets examples of New-SCSMObjectProjection:** http://gallery.technet.microsoft.com/SMLets-Examples-of-New-77c2f411.

> **Service Manager 2012 auto close resolved incidents workflow:** http://gallery.technet.microsoft.com/SCSM-2012-Auto-Close-1b26911f.

> **Service Manager user role PowerShell scripts:** http://gallery.technet.microsoft.com/Service-Manager-SCSM-User-ebcdfcd6.

> **Using Get-SCSMObject, Get-SCSMClass to dump data from Service Manager:** http://blogs.technet.com/b/servicemanager/archive/2011/04/21/using-smlets-beta-3-post-1-using-get-scsmobject-get-scsmclass-to-dump-data-from-scsm.aspx.

> **Using Get-SCSMEnumeration, Get-SCSMRelationshipObject, Get-SCSMRelationshipClass to automatically resolve incidents when all child activities are completed:** http://blogs.technet.com/b/servicemanager/archive/2011/04/21/using-smlets-beta-3-post-2-using-get-scsmenumeration-get-scsmrelationshipobject-get-scsmrelationshipclass-to-automatically-resolve-incidents-when-all-child-activities-are-completed.aspx.

> **Using Set-SCSMObject to bulk update properties on objects:** http://blogs.technet.com/b/servicemanager/archive/2011/04/22/using-smlets-beta-3-post-3-using-set-scsmobject-to-bulk-update-properties-on-objects.aspx.

> **Using New-SCSMObject to create objects:** http://blogs.technet.com/b/service-manager/archive/2011/05/03/using-smlets-beta-3-post-4-using-new-scsmobject-to-create-objects.aspx.

> **Getting the GUID ID of an object:** http://blogs.technet.com/b/servicemanager/archive/2011/05/12/using-smlets-beta-3-post-5-getting-the-guid-id-of-an-object.aspx.

> **Getting the owner of a service:** http://blogs.technet.com/b/servicemanager/archive/2011/05/24/using-smlets-beta-3-post-6-getting-the-owner-of-a-service.aspx.

▶ **Deleting any object in the UI:** http://blogs.technet.com/b/servicemanager/
archive/2011/05/25/using-smlets-beta-3-post-7-deleting-any-object-in-the-ui.
aspx.

▶ **Getting the GUID of an enumeration:** http://blogs.technet.com/b/service-
manager/archive/2011/06/24/using-smlets-beta-3-post-8-getting-the-guid-of-an-
enumeration.aspx.

▶ **Deleting objects:** http://blogs.technet.com/b/servicemanager/
archive/2012/07/10/3441338.aspx.

▶ **Getting a user's manager and a manager's reports:** http://blogs.technet.
com/b/servicemanager/archive/2011/12/03/using-smlets-beta-3-post-10-getting-
a-user-s-manager-and-a-manager-s-reports.aspx.

▶ **Getting a list of all the classes in a management pack:** http://blogs.technet.
com/b/servicemanager/archive/2012/01/04/using-smlets-beta-3-post-11-getting-
a-list-of-all-the-classes-in-a-management-pack.aspx.

▶ **Getting a GUID ID of an object (especially for work items):** http://blogs.
technet.com/b/servicemanager/archive/2012/01/05/using-smlets-beta-3-post-
12-getting-a-guid-id-of-an-object-especially-for-work-items.aspx.

▶ **Create incident from service request and copy various attributes by Thomas Ellermann:** http://gallery.technet.microsoft.com/
Create-Incident-from-f19aaea0#content.

▶ **Service Manager user role PowerShell scripts by Travis Wright:** http://
gallery.technet.microsoft.com/Service-Manager-SCSM-User-ebcdfcd6.

▶ Add a console task to display impacted business services for a given change request
using the solution found at the TechNet Gallery by John Wilson at http://gallery.
technet.microsoft.com/SCSM-Console-Extensions-ff8a1026.

▶ Morten Meisler discusses a bug in the `Set-SCSMTemplate` in SMLets at http://blog.
coretech.dk/mme/set-scsmtemplatewithactivities-powershell-script/.

▶ Patrik Sundqvist gives performance tips on using SMLets with type projections at
http://blogs.litware.se/?p=1230.

▶ Matthew Dowst talks about installing SMLets on Windows Server 2012 without
the Service Manager console at http://blogs.catapultsystems.com/mdowst/archive/
2013/10/29/install-smlets-on-windows-server-2012-without-scsm-console.aspx/.

Service Manager Connectors

Connectors bring information from Active Directory, Exchange, and other System
Center components into Service Manager. Following are some useful references regarding
connectors:

▶ Using connectors to import data into Service Manager is documented at http://technet.microsoft.com/en-us/library/hh524326.aspx.

▶ Service Manager 2012 connectors are discussed at http://4sysops.com/archives/system-center-service-manager-2012-part-3-connectors/.

▶ MVPs Brad Bird and Anders Asp discuss using connectors in architecting and planning a deployment in a Microsoft Virtual Academy module at http://channel9.msdn.com/posts/MVA-System-Center-Service-Manager-2012-Connectors.

▶ Change the Service Manager connector schedule using the information at http://www.code4ward.net/main/Blog/tabid/70/EntryId/144/Change-Service-Manager-Connector-Schedule.aspx.

▶ http://myitforum.com/myitforumwp/2014/03/17/remove-orphaned-connectors-in-service-manager/ discusses removing orphaned connectors.

▶ You can download the Codeplex Service Manager CSV connector from http://scsmcsvconnector.codeplex.com/. For a discussion by Travis Wright, see http://blogs.technet.com/b/servicemanager/archive/2009/12/30/how-to-write-a-custom-connector-csv-connector-example.aspx.

▶ Download the Exchange connector at http://www.microsoft.com/en-us/download/details.aspx?id=38791. http://www.msexchange.org/articles-tutorials/exchange-server-2010/monitoring-operations/configuring-exchange-connector-service-manager-2012.html discusses configuring this connector for Service Manager.

▶ Discussing how to configure a Configuration Manager connector for an extended SMS_def.mof file is at http://technet.microsoft.com/en-us/library/hh495523.aspx.

▶ The Configuration Manager connector's DCM rule can cause massive performance issues in Service Manager. If not using DCM, consider turning off the DCM rule in Service Manager to prevent the workflow from running. The blog article at http://blogs.technet.com/b/mihai/archive/2012/11/30/configuration-manager-connector-s-dcm-rule-can-cause-massive-performance-issues-in-service-manager.aspx explains why and how to turn off this rule, which is enabled by default.

▶ Use PowerShell to schedule the Active Directory connector to run at certain times. See Thomas Ellermann's article at http://blogs.technet.com/b/thomase/archive/2011/09/27/scheduling-and-disabling-the-ad-connector-via-powershell.aspx.

▶ VMM connector information is available at http://blogs.technet.com/b/servicemanager/archive/2012/02/09/faq-installing-all-the-prerequisite-mps-for-the-cloud-services-management-pack.aspx.

▶ Use the PowerShell `Remove-SCSMConnector` cmdlet to delete a connector from Service Manager, documented at http://technet.microsoft.com/library/hh316239.aspx.

▶ http://windowsitpro.com/service-manager/delete-orphaned-connector-service-manager-2012 discusses deleting an orphaned Exchange connector.

▶ http://technet.microsoft.com/en-us/library/hh524309.aspx documents what occurs to configuration items when you delete the connector that created them.

System Center 2012

Following are some references and articles regarding other components of System Center 2012:

▶ With the release of System Center 2012, Microsoft bundles the previously different products as components in the System Center product. http://www.microsoft.com/en-us/server-cloud/system-center/datacenter-management-capabilities.aspx provides an overview of the System Center components and capabilities.

▶ The Microsoft System Center website is http://www.microsoft.com/en-us/server-cloud/products/system-center-2012-r2/.

▶ Operations Manager is Microsoft's end-to-end service management product and is the cornerstone of the common system architecture used by other System Center products including Service Manager. A product overview is available at http://technet.microsoft.com/library/hh205987.aspx. Kerrie Meyler discusses the common system architecture at http://www.networkworld.com/article/2228309/microsoft-subnet/a-common-system-center-architecture.html.

▶ For an overview of Configuration Manager, see http://www.microsoft.com/system-center/en/us/configuration-manager/cm-overview.aspx and http://technet.microsoft.com/library/gg682129.aspx.

▶ Data Protection Manager (DPM) delivers data protection for SQL Server, Exchange, SharePoint, virtual servers, file servers, Windows desktops and laptops, as well as managing system state and bare metal recovery. For an overview of this System Center component, visit http://technet.microsoft.com/library/hh758173.aspx.

▶ Information on Virtual Machine Manager is available at http://technet.microsoft.com/library/gg610610.aspx.

▶ Read about Orchestrator at http://technet.microsoft.com/en-us/library/hh237242.aspx.

▶ InfoWorld provides a tour of the System Center 2012 components (as of RTM) at http://www.infoworld.com/d/microsoft-windows/tour-of-microsoft-system-center-2012-185442. John Joyner of ClearPointe provides an overview of 10 new things in the R2 release at http://www.techrepublic.com/blog/10-things/10-new-things-you-should-know-about-in-system-center-2012-r2/.

▶ Microsoft's System Center Pack Catalog contains multiple pages for Service Manager, Virtual Machine Manager, Operations Manager, Configuration Manager, Data Protection Manager, and Essentials. You can access the catalog at http://pinpoint.microsoft.com/en-US/systemcenter/managementpackcatalog.

▶ Microsoft's System Center 2012 R2 whitepaper can be downloaded from http://download.microsoft.com/download/7/7/2/7721670F-DEF0-40D3-9771-43146DED5132/System_Center_2012%20R2_Overview_White_Paper.pdf. The datasheet is available at http://download.microsoft.com/download/A/A/D/AADE864E-F61A-42F8-9AEF-DE2E1D1F988D/System_Center_2012_R2_Datasheet.pdf.

SQL Server Resources

Microsoft SQL Server is the heart of each System Center component. If it performs poorly, so does System Center. Following are some references regarding SQL Server:

▶ If you are considering virtualizing SQL Server, see Keith Mayer's posting at http://blogs.technet.com/b/keithmayer/archive/2012/08/30/virtualizing-microsoft-sql-server-on-windows-server-2012-winserv-mssql-itpro-sqlpass.aspx. You may also want to download the best practices document at http://download.microsoft.com/download/6/1/D/61DDE9B6-AB46-48CA-8380-D7714C9CB1AB/Best_Practices_for_Virtualizing_and_Managing_SQL_Server_2012.pdf.

▶ Following are some tools to assist with calculating and measuring SQL Server input/output per second (IOPS):

   ▶ **SQL I/O disk subsystem benchmark tool:** http://www.microsoft.com/en-us/download/details.aspx?id=20163.

   ▶ **SQL Server I/O best practices:** http://technet.microsoft.com/en-us/library/cc966412.aspx.

   ▶ **SM_Job_Aids (includes SMSizer):** Available at the technical documentation download page for Service Manager 2012 at http://www.microsoft.com/en-us/download/details.aspx?id=27850.

   ▶ **SM2012_Sizer.xlsm document:** Part of the SM_Job_Aids kit (available at the technical documentation download page for Service Manager 2012 at http://www.microsoft.com/en-us/download/details.aspx?id=27850), this provides guidance on estimating and calculating IOPS.

▶ MVP Paul Keely provides an excellent guide discussing SQL Server and System Center 2012 R2. This 194-page document gives details on how to tune and configure your SQL Server for optimal usage with System Center. Download the guide from the TechNet Gallery at http://gallery.technet.microsoft.com/SQL-2012-and-System-Center-553b5161.

▶ Read about monitoring and tuning SQL Server 2012 for performance at http://technet.microsoft.com/en-us/library/ms189081.aspx.

▶ http://blogs.msdn.com/b/sqlserverfaq/archive/2014/02/06/how-to-move-databases-configured-for-sql-server-alwayson.aspx discusses moving databases configured for SQL Server AlwaysOn.

▶ For information on SQL Server best practices, see http://technet.microsoft.com/en-us/sqlserver/bb671430.aspx.

▶ Read about the SQL Server 2012 Best Practice Analyzer at http://blogs.msdn.com/b/sqlsecurity/archive/2012/04/19/sql-server-2012-best-practices-analyzer.aspx, and download it from http://www.microsoft.com/download/en/details.aspx?id=29302.

▶ Read about SQL Server transaction logs and best practices at http://technet.microsoft.com/en-us/library/ms191429.aspx.

► Reorganizing and rebuilding SQL indexes is discussed at http://technet.microsoft. com/en-us/library/ms189858.aspx#Fragmentation.

► Use the SQL Server Profiler to view SQL requests sent to a SQL Server database. See http://msdn.microsoft.com/en-us/library/ms187929.aspx for information.

Reporting and Data Warehouse Resources

Service Manager's data warehouse offloads data from the main Service Manager database to improve Service Manager performance, provide long term data storage, and provide data for reports. It is a business intelligence (BI) platform built on the Microsoft BI stack (SSRS, SharePoint, and Excel). Following are references regarding the data warehouse:

► Microsoft was in the top spot for Gartner Group's Magic Quadrant for Business Intelligence in 2013 (http://www.zdnet.com/ gartner-releases-2013-bi-magic-quadrant-7000011264/).

► Learn about the Inmon and Kimball approaches to data warehouses at http://searchbusinessintelligence.techtarget.in/tip/ Inmon-vs-Kimball-Which-approach-is-suitable-for-your-data-warehouse.

► http://technet.microsoft.com/en-us/library/hh519643.aspx provides an overview of key concepts and procedures for managing the data warehouse.

► Travis Wright discusses the data warehouse at http://blogs.technet.com/b/service-manager/archive/2009/10/23/the-system-center-platform-in-service-manager-part-6-the-data-warehouse.aspx.

► Read how to extend the data warehouse to store additional data at http://blogs. technet.com/b/servicemanager/archive/2009/10/23/the-system-center-platform-in-service-manager-part-6-the-data-warehouse-try-it.aspx.

► http://technet.microsoft.com/en-us/ff657833.aspx provides information on SQL Server Reporting Services (SSRS).

► See http://technet.microsoft.com/en-us/library/bb522824.aspx for information on roles and permissions in SSRS.

► Michael Pearson has an excellent article discussing SSRS recovery planning, available from the SQL Server Central community (SQLServerCentral.com) at http://www. sqlservercentral.com/columnists/mpearson/recoveryplanningforsqlreportingservices. asp. You must register with SQL Server Central to view the full article.

► http://msdn.microsoft.com/en-us/library/ms157403.aspx provides a complete listing of SSRS log files.

► http://technet.microsoft.com/en-us/library/ms156421.aspx discusses moving the SSRS databases to another computer.

▶ You can script report backups using RS.exe. Documentation is available at http://msdn.microsoft.com/en-us/library/ms162839.aspx and http://msdn.microsoft.com/en-us/library/ms159720.aspx.

▶ Want to create drilldown SSRS reports? See http://technet.microsoft.com/en-us/library/dd207042.aspx.

▶ The Business Intelligence Development Studio, included with SQL Server, provides drag and drop functionality and wizards to aid in building reports. See http://msdn.microsoft.com/en-us/library/ms173767(v=sql.105).aspx for information on this tool.

▶ Learn about using the Visual Studio Report Designer at http://msdn.microsoft.com/en-us/library/bb558708.aspx.

▶ Want to know how grooming works? Travis Wright provides details at http://blogs.technet.com/b/servicemanager/archive/2009/09/18/data-retention-policies-aka-grooming-in-the-servicemanager-database.aspx.

▶ The data warehouse holds data for three years; you can adjust this by following the procedure described at http://blogs.technet.com/b/servicemanager/archive/2011/06/07/how-much-data-do-we-retain-in-the-service-manager-data-warehouse.aspx.

▶ http://blogs.technet.com/b/antoni/archive/2013/05/18/how-to-create-an-incident-dashboard-using-excel-in-system-center-2012-sp1-service-manager-scsm-2012.aspx discusses creating a Service Manager incident dashboard using Excel PowerPivot.

▶ Information on creating PerformancePoint dashboards is available at http://office.microsoft.com/en-us/dashboard-designer-help/create-a-basic-performancepoint-dashboard-HA010369176.aspx.

▶ If you are interested in customizing the data warehouse and reporting capabilities in Service Manager, check out these postings (while written for Service Manager 2010, they are still current):

  ▶ http://blogs.msdn.com/b/scplat/archive/2010/03/29/a-deep-dive-on-creating-relationship-facts-in-the-data-warehouse.aspx is a deep dive on creating relationship facts in the data warehouse.

  ▶ http://blogs.msdn.com/b/scplat/archive/2010/03/29/a-deep-dive-on-creating-outriggers-and-dimensions-in-the-data-warehouse.aspx discusses creating outriggers and dimensions.

  ▶ http://blogs.msdn.com/b/scplat/archive/2010/03/29/a-deep-dive-on-creating-relationship-facts-in-the-data-warehouse.aspx discusses creating relationship facts.

  ▶ You may also want to watch Sean Christensen's presentation at http://vimeo.com/21656681.

▶ Read about registering source systems to the System Center data warehouse at http://technet.microsoft.com/en-us/library/hh519633.aspx.

▶ Troubleshoot data warehouse errors at http://technet.microsoft.com/en-us/library/hh542403.aspx.

▶ View the complete data warehouse schema in Visio format at http://blogs.technet.com/cfs-file.ashx/__key/CommunityServer-Blogs-Components-WeblogFiles/00-00-00-62-41-DW/2425.DWDataMart.zip. A description is available at http://blogs.technet.com/b/servicemanager/archive/2011/03/14/service-manager-data-warehouse-schema-now-available.aspx.

Blogs

Following are some blogs the authors have used. Some are more active than others, and new blogs seem to spring up overnight!

▶ A great source of information is System Center Central (http://www.systemcenter-central.com), managed by MVP Pete Zerger.

▶ If you're interested in keeping up with VMM, the VMM team has a blog at http://blogs.technet.com/scvmm/.

▶ See a blog by Stefan Stranger (former MVP and now at Microsoft) at http://blogs.technet.com/stefan_stranger/.

▶ http://systemscentre.blogspot.com/ is a blog by MVP Steve Beaumont.

▶ http://bink.nu is managed by Steven Bink, former MVP for Windows Server Technologies. According to the blog, it "watches Microsoft like a hawk." You can also watch Steven on Twitter at http://twitter.com/sbink.

▶ You may want to look at the Acceleres Service Manager blog, http://blog.acceleres.com/. Acceleres provides Service Manager implementation and training.

▶ http://scsm.us/ is by MVP Chris Ross.

▶ Frederik Baert blogs at http://frederikbaert.wordpress.com/.

▶ http://itservicemngmt.blogspot.com/ is a blog discussing basic ITSM knowledge points for new people in ITIL. For additional information on ITIL, visit http://www.itil-officialsite.com.

▶ Everything System Center Service Manager—http://marcelzehner.ch/—is a Service Manager blog run by Marcel Zehner and itnetx, a consulting and engineering company located in Switzerland.

▶ Walter Chomak's blog on System Center is at http://www.systemcentercentral.com/author/wchomak/.

▶ Find MVP Alexandre Verkinderen's blog at http://www.savision.com/resources?f[0]=type%3Ablog.

▶ Ian Blyth, previously a Lead Technical Specialist at Microsoft UK, blogs at http://ianblythmanagement.wordpress.com/ on System Center technologies.

▶ The Service Manager Engineering Team blog is at http://blogs.technet.com/b/servicemanager/.

▶ A good blog on Service Manager administration and development by MVP Anton Gritsenko is at http://blog.scsmsolutions.com/.

▶ Dieter Gasser blogs about Service Manager at http://blog.dietergasser.com/.

Following are our own blogs:

▶ http://www.networkworld.com/author/kerrie-meyler/ is a blog by Kerrie Meyler with general discussion topics, but concentrating on Microsoft management.

▶ Coauthor and MVP Kurt Van Hoecke blogs at http://scug.be/scsm/.

▶ Coauthor and MVP Steve Buchanan blogs at http://www.buchatech.com/.

▶ http://itprocessed.com/articles/ is coauthor Samuel Erskine's blog.

▶ Contributing author and MVP Jakob Gottlieb Svendsen blogs at http://blog.coretech.dk/author/jgs/.

▶ http://www.contoso.se/blog/ is the System Center blog by Anders Bengtsson, former MVP, now a PFE at Microsoft and contributing author to this book. For a list of Anders' postings on Service Manager, see http://contoso.se/blog/?cat=25.

▶ Contributing author and former MVP Kenneth van Surksum blogs at http://www.vansurksum.com/.

▶ Peter Quagliariello, a contributing author to this book, blogs at http://blog.acceleres.com/.

▶ Contributing author Kathleen Wilson blogs at http://blogs.technet.com/b/kathleen_wilson/.

▶ Contributing author and former MVP Oskar Landman blogs at http://www.systemcentercentral.com/author/oskarl/ and http://www.authoringfriday.com/.

▶ Contributing author and former MVP Patrik Sundqvist blogs at http://blogs.litware.se/.

Public Forums

If you need an answer to a question, the first place to check is the Microsoft public forums. A list of the current Service Manager forums follows:

▶ http://social.technet.microsoft.com/Forums/systemcenter/en-US/home?category=servicemanager takes you to the Service Manager forums. Links to specific forums follow:

  ▶ **General:** http://social.technet.microsoft.com/Forums/systemcenter/en-US/home?forum=systemcenterservicemanager.

▶ **Setup:** http://social.technet.microsoft.com/Forums/systemcenter/en-US/
home?forum=setup.

▶ **Customization using the SDK and Authoring Tool:** http://social.technet.
microsoft.com/Forums/systemcenter/en-US/home?forum=customization.

▶ **Data Warehouse, Reporting, and Dashboards:** http://social.technet.microsoft.
com/Forums/systemcenter/en-US/home?forum=dwreportingdashboards.

▶ **ITIL and MOF Processes – Incident, Problem, Change, Release, Service
Request Management:** http://social.technet.microsoft.com/Forums/
systemcenter/en-US/home?forum=itilmofprocesses.

▶ **Administration (User Roles, Notifications, Workflows, etc.):**
http://social.technet.microsoft.com/Forums/systemcenter/en-US/
home?forum=administration.

▶ **System Center Integration and Connectors:** http://social.technet.microsoft.
com/Forums/systemcenter/en-US/home?forum=connectors.

▶ **Portals:** http://social.technet.microsoft.com/Forums/systemcenter/en-US/
home?forum=portals.

▶ **Documentation:** http://social.technet.microsoft.com/Forums/systemcenter/
en-US/home?forum=documentation.

APPENDIX C

Available Online

Online content is available to provide add-on value to readers of *System Center 2012 Service Manager Unleashed*. This material, organized by chapter, can be downloaded from. http://www.informit.com/store/system-center-2012-service-manager-unleashed-9780133744194. This content is not available elsewhere. Note that the authors and publisher do not guarantee or provide technical support for the material.

Backup and Recovery

Chapter 18, "Maintenance, Backup, and Recovery," includes three scripts as online content:

▶ **Export all management packs to a folder.ps1:** The SMLets PowerShell code exports all unsealed management packs to a folder. The script tests for the existence of a specific folder (C:\SCSMBackup\ ManagementPacks), creates it if it does not exist, and creates a subfolder with a date stamp each time it runs.

▶ **Map remote drive.sql:** This script maps a drive letter using the SQL XP_CMDSHELL stored procedure. This can be useful for performing SQL backups to a remote drive.

▶ **Display security role assignments.ps1:** This PowerShell/SMLets script displays the current security settings for the default and custom roles, which can be used to document your Service Manager settings as part of your backup and recovery procedures.

Managing Workflows

Chapter 19, "Managing Service Manager Performance," includes a script to check the duration of your Service Manager workflows. This script, Check duration of workflows.ps1, is available as online content.

Building a Management Pack

Chapter 23, "Advanced Customization Scenarios," includes a PowerShell script (ForceActivate.ps1) as online content that forces the status of an incident to Active. The chapter also steps through how to build a custom management pack; online content consists of a management pack containing the custom classes, relationship, view, and form built using the detailed instructions provided in that chapter. The ZIP file includes the compiled management pack, source code, and the odysseyMP.snk key file used to seal the management pack.

Adding Service Components to a Business Service

Chapter 24, "Using PowerShell," steps through an example of using PowerShell/SMLets to add service components as related items to a business service. This script, Add Service Components As Related Items to Business Service.ps1, is provided as online content.

Live Links

Reference URLs (see Appendix B, "Reference URLs") are provided as live links. These include nearly 300 (clickable) hypertext links and references to materials and sites related to Service Manager and System Center.

A disclaimer and unpleasant fact about live links: URLs change! Companies are subject to mergers and acquisitions, pages move and change on websites, and so on. Although these links were accurate in mid 2014, it is possible some will change or be "dead" by the time you read this book. Sometimes the Wayback Machine (http://www.archive.org/index.php) can rescue you from dead or broken links. This site is an Internet archive, and it takes you back to an archived version of a site...sometimes.

Index

Symbols

A

default user roles, 538-539

Default Value attribute, 730

defining

   display name for management packs, 764

   relationships, 691

      Containment relationships, 694

      Hosting relationships, 694-695

      Membership relationships, 694

      Reference relationships, 693

   ticket prefix, 363

Deleted Items node (Administration workspace), 205

deleting

   connectors, 104

   management packs, 106

Deliver phase (MOF), 55

dependencies, 646

dependent activities, 51

deploying Service Manager

   availability, 141-144

   build and configuration phase, 125

   capacity planning

      minimum recommended requirements, 136

      workload assessment, 136-137

   design scenarios

      five-server design, 134-135

      three-server design, 133-134

   establishing business requirements, 120

   licensing, 128-130

      CML, 129-130

      SML, 129

   network considerations, 140-141

   pilot phase, 125-126

   planning and design phase, 124

   planning stages

      capturing current environment, 122-124

      scoping deployment objectives, 120-122

   reviewing plans, 127

   security and authentication planning, 137-140

      administrative users, 138-140

      end users, 138-140

      infrastructure management server security, 137

      service accounts, 137-138

      system groups, 137-138

      test environment, 144-145

deployment plans, Release Management, 81

deployment team members, 121-122

derived class types, 690

design phase of Service Manager deployment, 124

design scenarios, 131-135

   five-server design, 134-135

   test environment, incorporating, 144-145

   three-server design, 133-134

designing releases, 80

desired configuration management workflows, creating, 385-387

Desired Configuration Manager event workflow, 231

detecting

   incidents, 61-62, 346-347

   problems, 434-435

development environment, 125

diagnosing

   incidents, 350-351

   problems, 437-438

dimensions, 661

disaster recovery

   configuration and settings recovery, 594

   full operating system recovery, 598

   SC2012_ServiceMgr_DisasterRecovery.pdf, 593

display name, defining for management packs, 764

E

H

I

S

U

X-Y-Z

UNLEASHED

Unleashed takes you beyond the basics, providing an exhaustive, technically sophisticated reference for professionals who need to exploit a technology to its fullest potential. It's the best resource for practical advice from the experts and the most in-depth coverage of the latest technologies.

informit.com/unleashed

Unleashed titles are available in print and eBook formats. InformIT provides eBooks in PDF, MOBI, and EPUB formats.

System Center 2012 Orchestrator Unleashed
ISBN-13: 9780672336102

OTHER UNLEASHED TITLES

Microsoft System Center 2012 Unleashed
ISBN-13: 9780672336126

Microsoft Lync Server 2013 Unleashed
ISBN-13: 9780672336157

Windows Server 2012 Unleashed
ISBN-13: 9780672336225

Microsoft Dynamics CRM 2013 Unleashed
ISBN-13: 9780672337031

Microsoft Exchange Server 2013 Unleashed
ISBN-13: 9780672336119

SharePoint 2013 Unleashed
ISBN-13: 9780672337338

Microsoft SQL Server 2012 Unleashed
ISBN-13: 9780672336928

Windows 8.1 Apps with XAML and C# Unleashed
ISBN-13: 9780672337086

Windows 8.1 Apps with HTML5 and JavaScript Unleashed
ISBN-13: 9780672337116

WPF 4.5 Unleashed
ISBN-13: 9780672336973

Windows Phone 8 Unleashed
ISBN-13: 9780672336898

ASP.NET Dynamic Data Unleashed
ISBN-13: 9780672335655

Microsoft Visual Studio 2012 Unleashed
ISBN-13: 9780672336256

C# 5.0 Unleashed
ISBN-13: 9780672336904

Visual Basic 2012 Unleashed
ISBN-13: 9780672336317

HTML5 Unleashed
ISBN-13: 9780672336270

System Center 2012 Operations Manager Unleashed
ISBN-13: 9780672335914

System Center 2012 R2 Configuration Manager Unleashed
ISBN-13: 9780672337154

informit.com/sams